RPG II AND RPG III PROGRAMMING

RPG II AND RPG III PROGRAMMING

Nancy Stern
Hofstra University

Alden Sager
Nassau Community College

Robert A. Stern
Nassau Community College

John Wiley & Sons
New York Chichester Brisbane Toronto Singapore

Library of Congress Cataloging in Publication Data:

Stern, Nancy B.
RPG II and RPG III programming.

Includes index.
1. RPG (Computer program language) 2. Electronic
digital computers—Programming. I. Sager, Alden.
II. Stern, Robert A. III. Title. IV. Title: R.P.G. 2
and R.P.G. 3 programming.
QA76.73.R25S7 1984 001.64'24 83-12536
ISBN 0-471-87625-9

Printed in the United States of America

10 9 8

To

Lori Anne Stern and Melanie Mara Stern
N. S. and R. A. S.

Alden and Myrtle Sager,
and in memory of Joseph Perlman
A. S.

Preface

To the Instructor

The following items are of particular interest to people teaching a course in RPG II or III.

Market
This book will provide computing majors at colleges, users in the field, and professional programmers with the tools necessary to program efficiently and effectively in RPG.

Content
This is a stand-alone text that not only focuses on the fundamentals of the RPG language but also provides an in-depth analysis of programming tools and techniques. Students who use this book and then become RPG programmers will not only learn the code but will also understand how the specifications are actually interpreted by their computer system. This will make them better RPG programmers and will also make it far easier to learn other programming languages and systems design techniques as well. The text also considers the advantages and limitations of RPG programming. Students will thus be able to understand when it is best to program in RPG and when other languages might prove more useful.

This text focuses primarily on RPG II. It also provides an in-depth analysis of RPG III and the unique features that make it particularly useful for data base manipulation and structured programming environments. In addition to the RPG III language specifications, we explain the concepts inherent to data bases and to structured programming.

In summary, the uniqueness of this text is characterized by the following topics that are covered in depth.

1. Current state-of-the-art applications of RPG II.
2. Proper programming form that focuses on overall logical design and flowcharts.
3. Practical programming procedures for file maintenance, file reporting, and inquiring about particular records within files.
4. On-line, real-time applications.
5. RPG III concepts emphasizing data base technology.
6. Structured programming and subroutines.
7. Debugging RPG II programs.
8. Job control specifications.

Pedagogic Approach

The Stern–Sager–Stern pedagogic approach that has proved so effective in *370/360 Assembler Language Programming* is used in this text as well. Unlike most books, we focus on programming concepts that are traditionally used by all programmers, regardless of the language employed.

The text combines the format of a traditional text with that of a workbook. That is, each topic is followed by numerous self-evaluating questions, applications, practice problems, and a summary to both reinforce the material presented and to relate it to previous chapters. In addition, the organization of the text and of each chapter serves to enhance the student's understanding of overall program design as well as RPG II and RPG III fundamentals. Each chapter begins with a detailed outline that indicates content, organization, and specific approach. Key terms listed at the end of each chapter are defined in the Glossary at the end of the book.

There are two supplements available with this text. An Instructor's Manual is provided that includes not only solutions to text questions but also detailed chapter outlines and summaries, test questions, additional applications, and hints for classroom discussion. There is also a package of Transparency Masters with RPG solutions to text problems and illustrations of text material.

The pedagogic approach, then, includes

1. Reinforcement of concepts with self-evaluating quizzes, review questions, practice problems, and applications.
2. Presentation of chapter objectives, at the beginning of each chapter, to familiarize the student with the topics to be emphasized.
3. Lists of key terms to familiarize the student with the most important terms to be covered.
4. Summaries throughout each chapter that reinforce material and serve as future reference.
5. Complete sample programs illustrating each concept as it is presented.
6. Programming techniques emphasizing logic rather than disjointed instructions.
7. Combination text-workbook approach requiring active student participation.
8. Extensive debugging and analysis of programming problems.
9. Job control for the computers on which RPG is generally used.

In addition to a primary focus on RPG II and RPG III language fundamentals, this text emphasizes proper programming techniques. The following elements are designed for this purpose.

1. Debugging by Desk Checking Most chapters provide numerous illustrations that require the reader to study a program or program excerpt and determine errors. The goal of these exercises is to demonstrate the importance of desk checking and to familiarize the student with techniques used in desk checking a program.

2. Flowcharting as an Integral Programming Tool Many logic problems are illustrated with the use of a flowchart. Moreover, each segment of the RPG II cycle is explained by using flowcharts for illustrative purposes. The ultimate goal is to familiarize students with flowcharts and to assist them in using the flowchart as a planning tool.

3. *Problem Definitions* Every illustrative program is explained with the use of a problem definition. We familiarize students with input layout sheets and Printer Spacing Charts in an effort to provide a "real world" environment and to help establish a standard format for problem definitions.

4. *Data Set for Practice Problem 2* Practice Problem 2 in each chapter uses the same input. Appendix E has a complete data set that you may use when assigning this problem. Some instructors prefer to use a standard data set that is provided in the text when making programming assignments.

5. *The Unit Approach* The text is divided into four units. It is recommended that an instructor give an exam at the end of each unit. Sample exams are provided in the Instructor's Manual.

This text closely follows the RPG curriculum developed by the DPMA in organization and in content. The following is a listing of topics prepared by DPMA and their corresponding chapters in the book.

REPORT PROGRAM GENERATOR (RPG) PROGRAMMING (CIS-18)
(Lower Division Course)

Topics	*Chapters in Text*	*Percentage of Time*
1. Elements of RPG Programming and Program Execution	1,2	1Ø
File Description		
Input		
Calculation		
Output		
Basic RPG Program Logic		
Coding RPG Programs		
Executing RPG Programs		
2. Calculations	3,4	15
Arithmetic Operations		
Move Operations		
Logical Operations		
Indicator Control Operations		
The Calculation Specifications Sheet		
3. Files, File Organization, and File Processing	5,6	25
Records and Files		
File Organization		
RPG and File Organization		
File Processing		
Special Purpose Files		
File Extension Specifications		
4. Programming Tape File Applications	7,8	15
File Description Entries		
Tape Updating Applications		
Building Tape Files		
5. Programming Disk File Applications	7,9	2Ø
Record Storage		
Record Access		
Summary of RPG Disk File Processing		
Summary of RPG Disk File Description Entries		
6. Tables, Arrays, and Subroutines	1Ø–12	15

We would like to take this opportunity to thank James R. Moyles, Data Processing Consultant, for his technical assistance, Carol Eisen for her herculean effort in the preparation of the manuscript, and Nancy Johnke for her invaluable help in the preparation of the artwork.

We would also like to express our appreciation to the following people at John Wiley & Sons who were enormously helpful in bringing this manuscript to fruition: Carol Beasley, editor; Gene Davenport, executive editor; Elaine Rauschal, production manager; Alej Longarini, production supervisor; Madelyn Lesure, designer.

Finally, we express our gratitude to IBM for their permission to use forms and other material.

We revise our programming language textbooks with some frequency and welcome your comments, suggestions, and even criticisms. We can be reached at

Dr. Nancy Stern
Department of Computer Information Systems
Hofstra University
Hempstead, New York 11550
(516) 560-5717

Dr. Alden Sager
Department of Computer Science
Nassau Community College
Garden City, New York 11530
(516) 222-7392

Dr. Robert A. Stern
Department of Computer Science
Nassau Community College
Garden City, New York 11530
(516) 222-7383

To the Student or Reader

RPG is a programming language taught with increasing frequency at many schools. The growth of minicomputer systems and mainframes has made RPG an extremely effective programming tool for both large and small systems. Moreover, as increasing numbers of users gain familiarity with computing and become interested in generating their own programs, RPG has become even more popular and useful.

This text is designed to provide you with a step-by-step approach to writing programs in RPG. It has been tested in numerous classes and for individual instruction and has been found to be highly readable and serviceable as a stand-alone text.

The book is written primarily for the university, junior college, or technical school market but can be used by others as well. Although it would be helpful if you had some prior information processing experience (know what a computer is and how it operates), this background is not required. The book presumes no knowledge on the part of the student; all information processing terms used are defined.

At the beginning of each chapter is a list of objectives defining what you should be looking for when studying the chapter. After reading the chapter, you should make certain that you understand each program that is illustrated. Summaries are included that provide a review of key items.

The self-evaluating quizzes that are always at the end of each chapter and sometimes at the end of key sections within each chapter are designed to enable you to test yourself. Try to answer the question and then check your answer with the solutions provided.

Each chapter has a list of key terms that are defined within the chapter. Be sure you understand the meaning of each. A glossary is provided at the end of the text to help you with definitions.

Understanding how to debug programs is a critical part of programming. Most chapters have a debugging unit that provides a sample program with both errors in following RPG rules and errors in logic. You are assigned the task of finding these errors. For part of these exercises, the solutions are provided, in order to help you test yourself and to help you better understand the process of debugging.

There are also review questions and practice problems at the end of each chapter that do not have solutions provided. These may be assigned by your instructor for homework.

N. Stern
A. Sager
R. A. Stern

Contents

All chapters begin with

- Chapter Outline
- Chapter Objectives

All chapters end with

- Key Terms
- Self-Evaluating Quiz
- Review Questions
- Debugging Exercises (where appropriate)
- Practice Problems (where appropriate)

UNIT 1

RPG II PROGRAM FUNDAMENTALS

CHAPTER 1

Introduction to Programming in RPG

Objectives

- To review basic programming concepts and terms.
- To provide an overview of the RPG language and the coding forms used.
- To introduce the concept of the RPG II Logic Cycle.
- To illustrate how a problem definition is provided and how an RPG program is coded from it.

I. Programming Concepts

A. Introduction to Computer Programming

No matter how complex a computer may be, its actions are directed by individual computer instructions written and tested by a computer **programmer**. A **program** consists of a set of instructions that will operate on input data and convert it to output. A computer, then, can operate only as efficiently and effectively as it is programmed.

All instructions to be operated on must be in **machine language**. It is very tedious and cumbersome for the programmer to code instructions in this form. Memory addresses must be remembered, and complex numeric computer codes must be used.

Since programming in a machine language is so difficult, advances in programming technology were developed to enable the programmer to write in an English-like or **symbolic programming language**. The instructions in a symbolic language, however, must be translated or **compiled** into machine language before they can be executed. The computer itself performs this translation into machine language with the use of a program called a **compiler.**

Among the numerous symbolic programming languages that can be translated into machine form is RPG, which is used most often for commercial applications.

The programmer, then, writes a set of instructions, called the **source program**, in one of the symbolic programming languages. This source program cannot be executed or operated on by the computer until it has been translated into machine language.

The source program is generally punched into cards by a keypunch machine or keyed into the computer from a terminal. The source program is read by the computer and must then be translated into a machine language program called the **object program** before execution can occur. The **compiler** is the special program that translates source programs in a particular language into object programs.

A program specifies the logical sequence of computer instructions. When the logic of a program becomes complex, pictorial representations called **program flowcharts** are drawn *prior to* the coding of the program. These pictorial representations clearly illustrate program logic, thus facilitating the writing of the program.

Such flowcharts will be used throughout this text to illustrate the logic used in a program. They are also useful as a documentation tool, which will be discussed later in this chapter. **Documentation** describes how the program operates and what it is intended to accomplish. For the beginner in information processing with no previous exposure to flowcharting, Appendix C provides an introduction to the basic concepts.

B. Types of Program Errors

There are two major types of programming errors that may be encountered by a programmer: syntax errors and logic errors.

1. Syntax Errors

In RPG, programmers usually key in their own programs, although organizations sometimes have key operators to do this. Typographical errors may be made by the person keying in the program. Incorrectly keyed entries could be diagnosed by the computer during translation or they might not be detected until the program is tested.

While the computer is performing the translation of the source program to the object program, any rule violations or typographical errors detected by the compiler will be listed. That is, any violation of a programming rule is denoted as an error. This type of error is referred to as a **syntax error**. For example, if the instruction to add two numbers is spelled AD instead of ADD, the computer will print an error message. If errors are of considerable magnitude, it will not be possible to execute the program until after the errors are corrected.

2. Logic Errors

Errors detected during a compilation are *not* of a logical nature. A **logic error** is one in which the *sequence* of programming steps is not executed properly. The machine generally has no way of judging the logic in a program; thus the program must be *tested* by executing it with **test data.**

Logic errors are caused by incorrect sequencing of program instructions or a misunderstanding of the required logic. **Debugging** is the procedure used to eliminate all program errors.

If syntax errors are not present in the source program or only minor violations of rules occur, the program can then be executed, or tested, at this point. If, however, execution is not desirable at this time, the object program may be saved by storing it on some medium such as tape or disk for future processing. Figure 1.1 illustrates the steps involved in programming a computer.

C. The Nature of RPG

RPG is an abbreviation for Report Program Generator. It is a **high-level language** in which the programmer codes specifications for a problem and the computer generates a program. Since RPG consists of a series of specifications, it is considered very easy to code and is regarded as one of the highest level—or least machinelike—languages available.

RPG was developed by IBM in the 1960s. As originally conceived, and as the name implies, RPG was intended for applications that required report generation. Early RPG programs were written almost exclusively to read input data, perform a series of simple calculations, and print the results.

As the popularity of the language increased, its uses grew as well. In 1974, RPG II was introduced. It has far greater applicability than the original version and is well suited for handling high-level and complex input and output. This text focuses on RPG II.

In 1980, RPG III was introduced. RPG III is designed for use in more sophisticated information processing environments where some of the more recent programming concepts and techniques have been implemented. RPG III is specifically designed to be used with two such techniques: **structured programming** and **data bases**. Currently, RPG III is only available on a limited number of IBM models such as the s/38. Although this text focuses on RPG II, Chapters 11 and 12 discuss the major features of RPG III.

Structured programming is a technique that results in more efficient and more standardized programs. By avoiding the use of branch instructions, each

Figure 1.1
Steps involved in programming a computer.

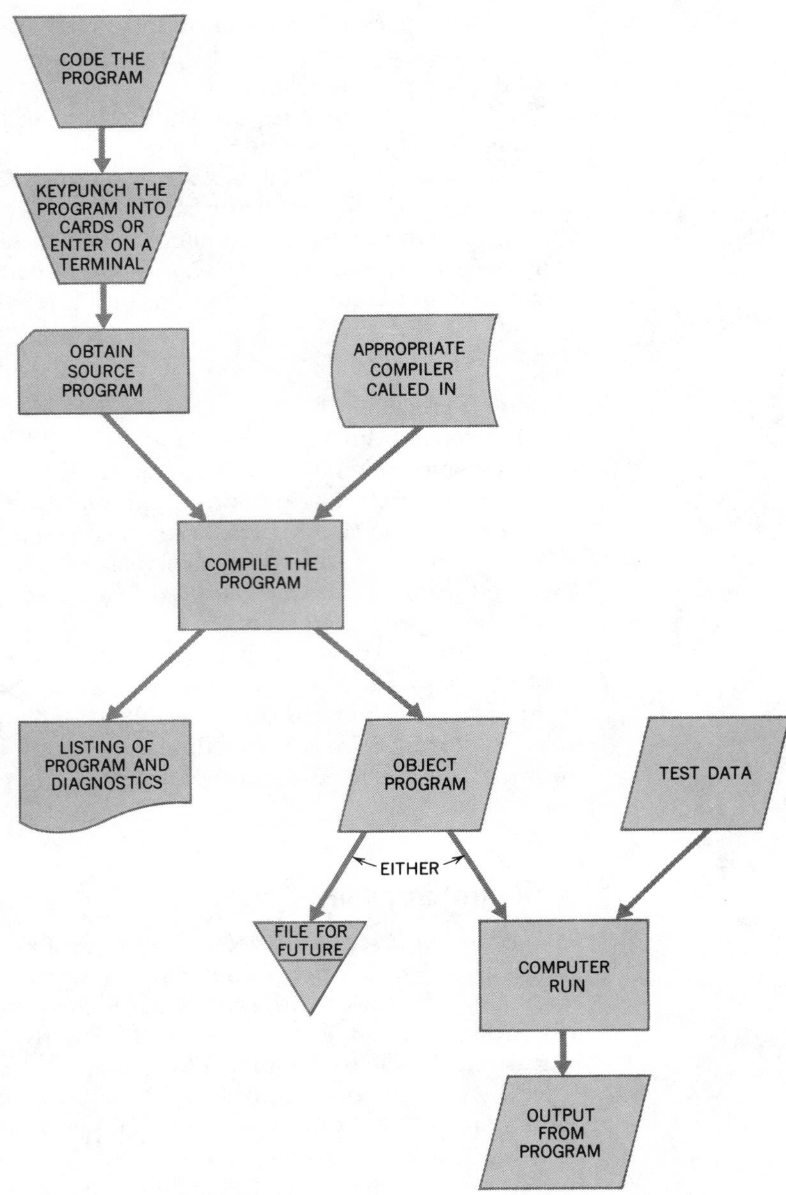

program can be modularized into a series of segments that can be evaluated and debugged separately. This concept, and how it is implemented in RPG II and RPG III, is discussed in Chapter 11.

Data base technology enables all users to access one central store of data for all applications. The manner in which a data base is manipulated, retrieved, and updated depends in large part on the programming languages used. RPG III has specific instructions and techniques designed to be used with data bases (see Chapter 12).

Both RPG II and RPG III are used on large, medium, and small computers, as well as on minicomputers. In addition to IBM, many other computer manufacturers and vendors have made RPG II available.

Self-Evaluating Quiz

The questions in these exercises are followed by solutions. They are included to help you evaluate your own understanding of the material presented.

1. The major task of a computer programmer is to ________ .
2. A set of instructions that will operate on input data and convert it to output is called a(n) ________ .
3. To be executed by the computer, all instructions must be in ________ language.
4. Programs are written in ________ language. Why?
5. Programs written in a language other than machine language must be ________ before execution can occur.
6. ________ is an example of a high-level programming language.
7. ________ is the process of converting a source program into machine language.
8. The program written in a language such as RPG is called the ________ program.
9. The source program is the ________ .
10. The object program is the ________ .
11. A ________ converts a(n) ________ program into a(n) ________ program.
12. The errors that are detected during compilation denote ________ and are usually referred to as ________ errors.
13. The logic of a program can be checked by ________ .
14. After a program has been compiled, it may be ________ or ________ .
15. The two types of errors likely to be made by a programmer are ________ and ________ .

Solutions

1. write and test computer instructions
2. program
3. machine
4. symbolic programming
   Machine language coding is tedious and cumbersome.
5. translated or compiled
6. RPG
7. Compilation
8. source
9. set of instructions in a symbolic language such as RPG
10. set of instructions that have been converted into machine language
11. compiler
    source
    object
12. any violations of programming rules
    syntax
13. testing it or executing it in a "test run" with sample data
14. executed
    saved in translated form for future processing
15. syntax errors
    logic errors

II. RPG Coding Requirements

A. The Four Basic Specifications Forms

Figure 1.2 shows the four basic RPG specifications forms, which consist of the following.

RPG Coding Forms

Name	*Description*
1. Control and File Description Specifications	Lists the files to be used, the devices they will employ, and special features to be included.
2. Input Specifications	Describes the format of input files.
3. Calculation Specifications	Describes arithmetic and logic operations to be performed.
4. Output Format Specifications	Describes the format of output files.

Typically, the Control and File Description Specifications form includes a single control-specifications line at the beginning of the program to provide information on the nature of the computer equipment.

The control specification would be the *first* entry of an RPG program followed in sequence by the other entries: file description, input, calculations, and output. The entries must be included in the sequence specified.

Other RPG forms are available. If included, they too must be in a specified sequence. Some of these additional forms are for informational or documentation purposes only; others are required for more advanced applications. The first few chapters of this text will focus exclusively on the four basic forms since they are usually sufficient for most applications.

B. Basic Structure of an RPG Program

The four basic specifications forms are referred to as **RPG coding** or **program sheets.** All these forms have space for *80 columns* of information. Each line of a program sheet will be either keypunched into a single punched card or entered on one line of a terminal. Some computer systems that allow RPG program entry from a terminal will display the coding sheet format on a screen for ease of data entry (see Figure 1.3). Thus, for each line written on a coding sheet, either one punched card or one line of program entry on a terminal is obtained. The entire program keyed from coding sheets is called the **RPG source program**. See Figure 1.4 for a listing of an RPG source program.

Let us examine the RPG forms more closely. Note that the top of each form contains the same data (see Figure 1.5).

Entries on Top of Each RPG Form

1. Date.	4. Keying Instructions.
2. Program name.	5. Page.
3. Programmer name.	6. Program Identification.

Figure 1.2
The four basic RPG specifications forms.

(Continued on next page.)

RPG CONTROL AND FILE DESCRIPTION SPECIFICATIONS

Program | Keying Instruction | Graphic | Key | Card Electro Number | Page 1 2 of | Program Identification 75 76 77 78 79 80

Programmer | Date

Control Specifications

For the valid entries for a system, refer to the RPG reference manual for that system.

H

Line | Form Type | Size to Compile | Object Output | Listing Options | Size to Execute | Debug | Reserved | Currency Symbol | Date Format | Date Edit | Inverted Print | Reserved | Number of Print Positions | Alternate Collating Sequence | Reserved | Inquiry | Reserved | Sign Handling | 1 P Forms Position | Indicator Setting | File Translation | Punch MFCU Zeros | Nonprint Characters | Reserved | Table Load Halt | Shared I/O | Field Print | Formatted Dump | RPG to RPG II Conversion | Number of Formats | S/3 Conversion | Subprogram | CICS/DL/I | Transparent Literal

0 1 H

File Description Specifications

For the valid entries for a system, refer to the RPG reference manual for that system.

F

Line | Form Type | Filename | File Type I/O/U/C/D | File Designation P/S/C/R/T/D/F | End of File E | Sequence A/D | File Format F/V/S/M/D/E | Block Length | Record Length | Mode of Processing L/R | Length of Key Field or of Record Address Field | Record Address Type A/P/I/K | Type of File Organization or Additional Area I/X/D/T/R/ or 2 | Overflow Indicator | Key Field Starting Location | External Record Name | Extension Code E/L | Device | Symbolic Device | Labels S/N/E/M | Name of Label Exit | Extent Exit for DAM | Storage Index | Continuation Lines: K, Option, Entry | A/U | File Addition/Unordered | Number of Tracks for Cylinder Overflow | Number of Extents | Tape Rewind R/U/N | File Condition U1–U8, UC

0 2 F
0 3 F
0 4 F
0 5 F
0 6 F
0 7 F
0 8 F
0 9 F
1 0 F
F
F

(a)

RPG INPUT SPECIFICATIONS

Program | Keying Instruction | Graphic | Key | Card Electro Number | Page 1 2 of | Program Identification 75 76 77 78 79 80

Programmer | Date

I

Line | Form Type | Filename or Record Name | Data Structure Name | O R / A N D | Sequence | Number (1/N), E | Option (O), U, S | Record Identifying Indicator, **, or DS | External Field Name | Record Identification Codes 1, 2, 3: Position, Not (N), C/Z/D, Character | Stacker Select | P/B/L/R | Field Location: From, To | Data Structure: Occurs n Times, Length | Decimal Positions | RPG Field Name | Control Level (L1–L9) | Matching Fields or Chaining Fields | Field Record Relation | Field Indicators: Plus, Minus, Zero or Blank

0 1 I
0 2 I
0 3 I
0 4 I
0 5 I
0 6 I
0 7 I
0 8 I
0 9 I
1 0 I
1 1 I
1 2 I
1 3 I
1 4 I
1 5 I
1 6 I
1 7 I
1 8 I
1 9 I
2 0 I
I
I
I
I
I

(b)

Figure 1.2
(continued)

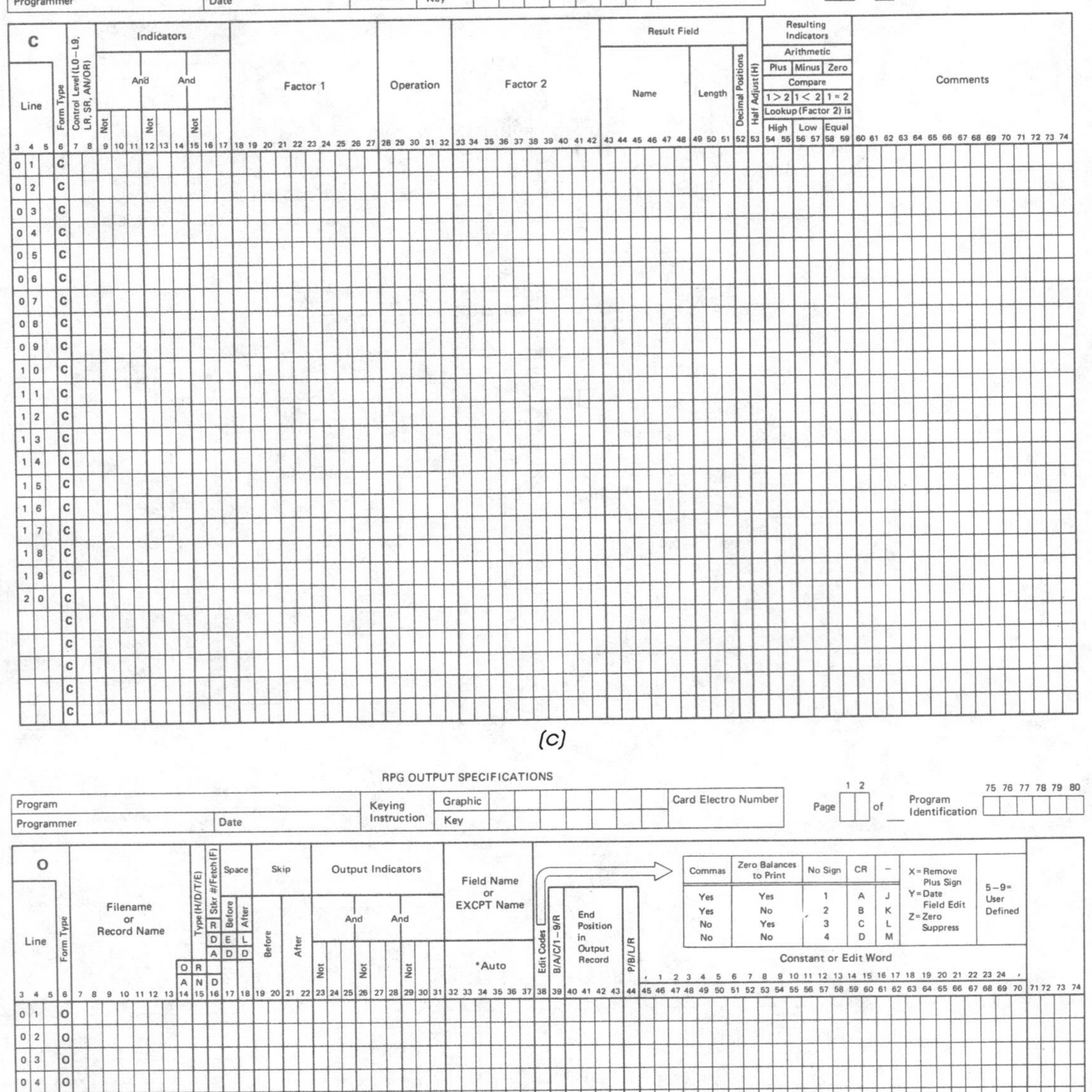

RPG CALCULATION SPECIFICATIONS

Program | Programmer | Date | Keying Instruction | Graphic | Key | Card Electro Number | Page 1 2 of | Program Identification 75 76 77 78 79 80

Line	Form Type	Control Level (L0–L9, LR, SR, AN/OR)	Indicators (Not, And, Not, And, Not)	Factor 1	Operation	Factor 2	Result Field: Name	Length	Decimal Positions	Half Adjust (H)	Resulting Indicators: Arithmetic Plus, Minus, Zero; Compare 1 > 2, 1 < 2, 1 = 2; Lookup (Factor 2) is High, Low, Equal	Comments
3 4 5	6	7 8	9 10 11 12 13 14 15 16 17	18 19 20 21 22 23 24 25 26 27	28 29 30 31 32	33 34 35 36 37 38 39 40 41 42	43 44 45 46 47 48	49 50 51	52	53	54 55 56 57 58 59	60 61 62 63 64 65 66 67 68 69 70 71 72 73 74
0 1	C											
0 2	C											
0 3	C											
0 4	C											
0 5	C											
0 6	C											
0 7	C											
0 8	C											
0 9	C											
1 0	C											
1 1	C											
1 2	C											
1 3	C											
1 4	C											
1 5	C											
1 6	C											
1 7	C											
1 8	C											
1 9	C											
2 0	C											
	C											
	C											
	C											
	C											
	C											

(c)

RPG OUTPUT SPECIFICATIONS

Program | Programmer | Date | Keying Instruction | Graphic | Key | Card Electro Number | Page 1 2 of | Program Identification 75 76 77 78 79 80

Commas	Zero Balances to Print	No Sign	CR	–	
Yes	Yes	1	A	J	X = Remove Plus Sign
Yes	No	2	B	K	Y = Date Field Edit
No	Yes	3	C	L	Z = Zero Suppress
No	No	4	D	M	5–9 = User Defined

Line	Form Type	Filename or Record Name	Type (H/D/T/E) (OR, AND)	Stkr #/Fetch (F) (DEL, ADD)	Space: Before, After	Skip: Before, After	Output Indicators (Not, And, Not, And, Not)	Field Name or EXCPT Name (*Auto)	Edit Codes	B/A/C/1–9/R	End Position in Output Record	P/B/L/R	Constant or Edit Word	
3 4 5	6	7 8 9 10 11 12 13	14 15	16	17 18	19 20 21 22	23 24 25 26 27 28 29 30 31	32 33 34 35 36 37	38	39	40 41 42 43	44	45 46 47 48 49 50 51 52 53 54 55 56 57 58 59 60 61 62 63 64 65 66 67 68 69 70 (1 2 3 4 5 6 7 8 9 10 11 12 13 14 15 16 17 18 19 20 21 22 23 24)	71 72 73 74
0 1	O													
0 2	O													
0 3	O													
0 4	O													
0 5	O													
0 6	O													
0 7	O													
0 8	O													
0 9	O													
1 0	O													
1 1	O													
1 2	O													
1 3	O													
1 4	O													
1 5	O													
1 6	O													
1 7	O													
1 8	O													
1 9	O													
2 0	O													
	O													
	O													
	O													
	O													
	O													

(d)

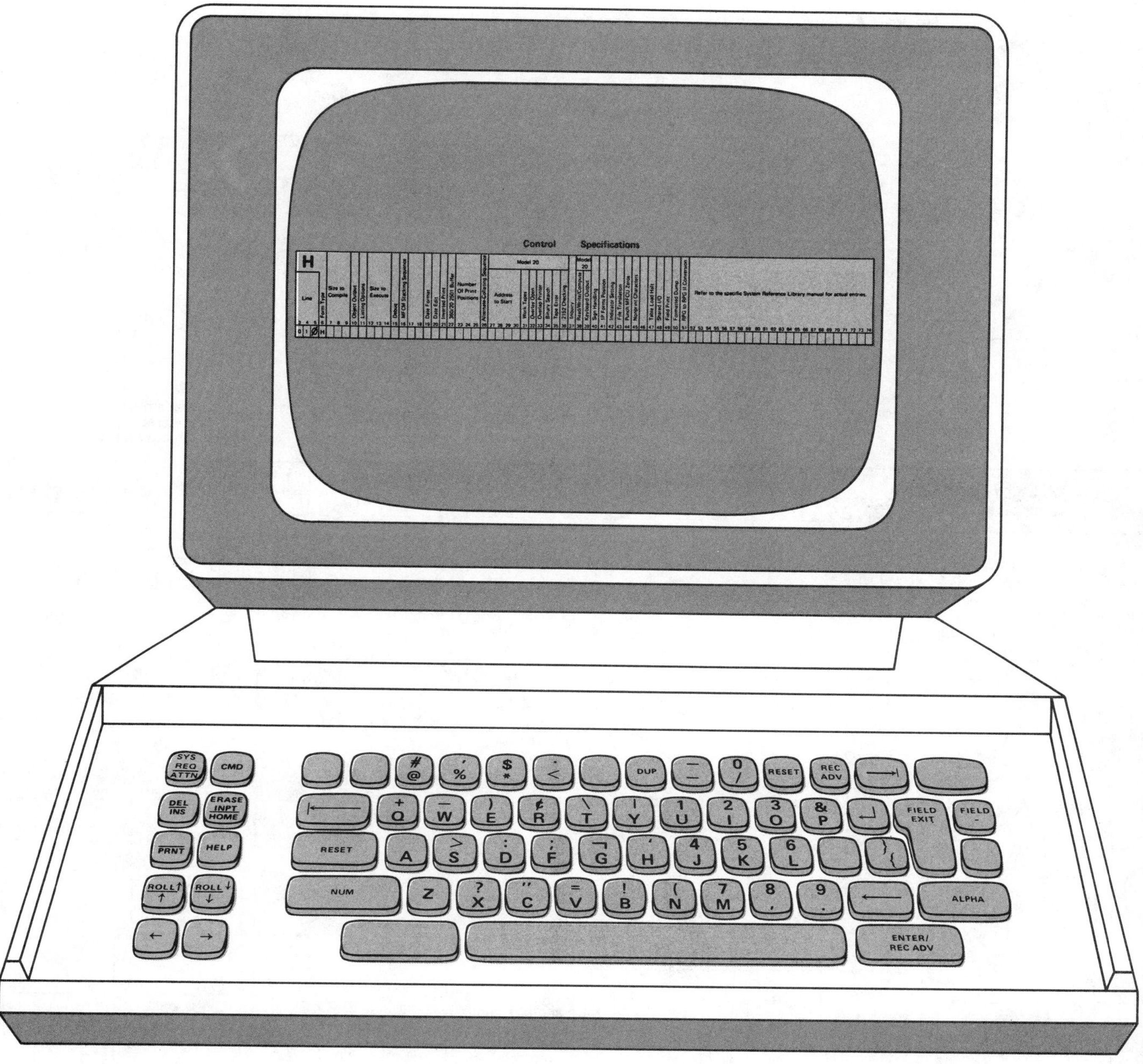

Figure 1.3
RPG coding form displayed on a terminal screen.

The first four entries—date, program, programmer, and keying instructions—are not actually part of the program. The date, program name, and programmer name are used for identification purposes only—just in case the forms are misplaced. If a data entry operator will be keying in the program for the programmer, keying instructions are used to explain which characters to enter, thereby eliminating any possible confusion. Since the letter O, for example, might be misinterpreted by a data entry operator as a zero, the programmer would probably use the convention of slashing zeros (Ø) to distinguish

Figure 1.4
Listing of an RPG source program.

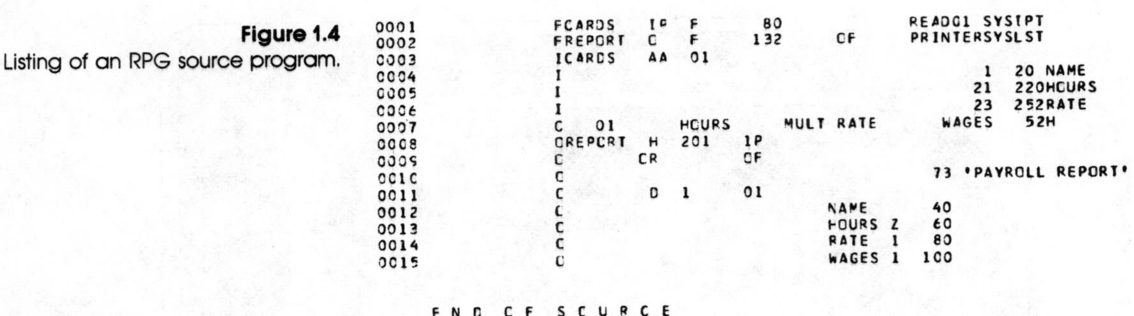

```
FCARDS   IP  F       80            READ01 SYSIPT
FREPORT  O   F      132    OF      PRINTERSYSLST
ICARDS   AA  01
I                                            1  20 NAME
I                                           21  220HOURS
I                                           23  252RATE
C   01       HOURS     MULT RATE       WAGES   52H
OREPORT  H  201    1P
O          OR        OF
O                                       73 'PAYROLL REPORT'
O          D 1       01
O                            NAME       40
O                            HOURS Z    60
O                            RATE  1    80
O                            WAGES 1   100

END OF SOURCE
```

Identification entries—not keyed into source program

Instructions to key operator

Program ID—entered on source program

RPG CONTROL AND FILE DESCRIPTION SPECIFICATIONS

Program WEEKLY WAGES
Programmer N STERN Date 5/27/84

Keying Instruction: Graphic Ø, Key ZERO

Card Electro Number

Page Ø2 of

Program Identification WAGES1 (75 76 77 78 79 80)

Control Specifications

For the valid entries for a system, refer to the RPG reference manual for that system.

H: Line (3–5), Form Type (6), Size to Compile (7–9), Object Output (10), Listing Options (11), Size to Execute (12–14), Debug (15), Reserved (16–17), Currency Symbol (18), Date Format (19), Date Edit (20), Inverted Print (21), Reserved (22), Number of Print Positions (23–25), Alternate Collating Sequence (26), Reserved (27–36), Inquiry (37), Reserved (38–39), Sign Handling (40), 1 P Forms Position (41), Indicator Setting (42), File Translation (43), Punch MFCU Zeros (44), Nonprint Characters (45), Reserved (46), Table Load Halt (47), Shared I/O (48), Field Print (49), Formatted Dump (50), RPG to RPG II Conversion (51), Number of Formats (52–53), S/3 Conversion (54), Subprogram (55), CICS/DL/I (56), Transparent Literal (57), 58–74

Line 01 H

File Description Specifications

For the valid entries for a system, refer to the RPG reference manual for that system.

F: Line (3–5), Form Type (6), Filename (7–14), File Type (15), File Designation (16), End of File (17), Sequence (18), File Format (19), Block Length (20–23), Record Length (24–27), Mode of Processing (28), Length of Key Field or of Record Address Field (29–30), Record Address Type (31), Type of File Organization or Additional Area (32), Overflow Indicator (33–34), Key Field Starting Location (35–38), Extension Code E/L (39), Device (40–46), Symbolic Device (47–52), Labels S/N/E/M (53), Name of Label Exit (54–59), Continuation Lines: K, Option (54–59), Entry (60–65), Extent Exit for DAM, Storage Index, A/U (66), File Addition/Unordered, Number of Tracks for Cylinder Overflow (68–69), Number of Extents, Tape Rewind (70), File Condition U1–U8, UC (71–72), External Record Name

I/O/U/C/D; P/S/C/R/T/D/F; E; A/D; F/V/S/M/D/E; L/R; A/P/I/K; I/X/D/T/R/ or 2; R/U/N

Lines 02, 03, 04, 05, 06, 07, 08, 09, 10 F

Page and line number used for sequencing program lines

Refers to card columns to be punched or positions on a screen to be keyed

Figure 1.5
Common entries on the top of each RPG form.

them from the letter O. The programmer might remind the operator of this convention by entering the following under Keying Instructions.

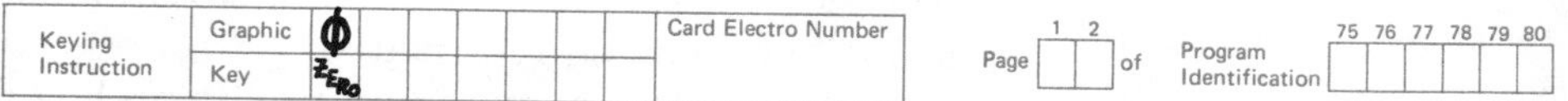

This book uses the convention of slashing zeros (Ø) to distinguish them from the letter O.

Other characters that are sometimes confused by data entry operators are

The letter I and the digit 1.
The letter Z and the digit 2.
The letter S and the digit 5.

These might also be clearly specified under Keying Instructions.

The Page specification on the top of each RPG form is accompanied by the numbers 1 and 2. These refer to the column numbers into which this field is keyed. That is, if the RPG program is keypunched, card columns 1 and 2 are used for page number; if the RPG program is entered using a terminal, page number may be automatically entered in the first two columns depending on the system.

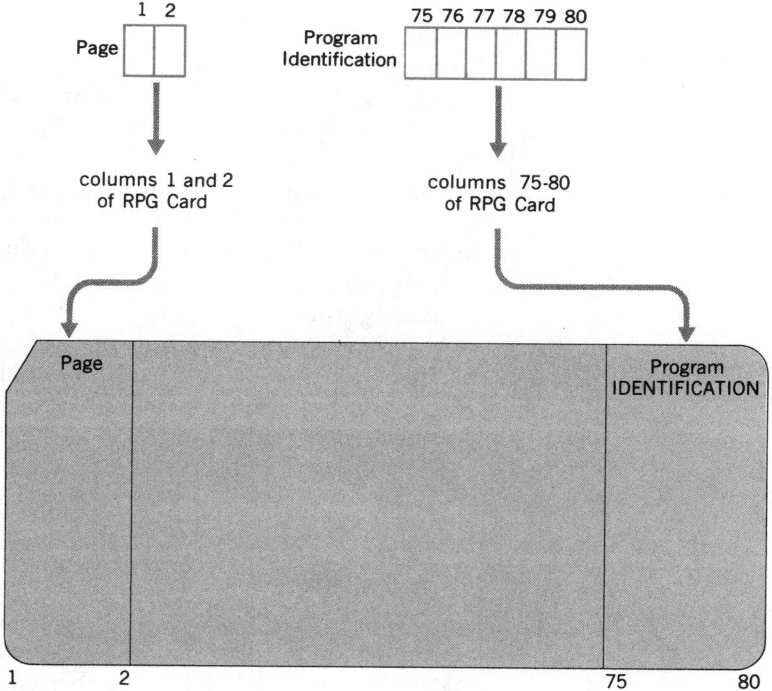

Thus if Page Ø2 were entered on the Input Specifications form, all entries on that page would have Ø2 in the first two columns. The use of this field will minimize the risk of program entries being sequenced improperly. The page number field does not, however, have any effect on the compilation.

Program Identification, also on the top of the form, is used to identify the program and is coded in columns 75-8Ø of each line. It may be assigned by a programming manager or it may simply be defined by the programmer. If an RPG card is lost or misplaced and it has the identification, there is a good chance it will be found and returned.

Both the page number and program identification entries are *automatically* entered by many computers when the program is keyed from a terminal. If the program is entered on cards, then the programmer must specify what should be included and the data will then be keyed in. These entries are for informational and documentation purposes only and thus can be omitted entirely.

The body of each form begins with a Line number field, columns 3-5. Columns 3-4 are precoded on the form. The first entry would generally contain a line number Ø1Ø, the next Ø2Ø, and so on. The entries are numbered by tens, so that insertions can easily be made. That is, if a line was inadvertently omitted after line Ø1Ø, it could be numbered as Ø15.

Thus columns 1-5 of a form might contain Ø1Ø1Ø, which denotes page 1, line Ø1Ø. These five columns, then, can be used to indicate the sequence of the program. Line numbers, like page numbers, are, however, optional.

Column 6 indicates the Form Type.

F for File description.

I for Input.

C for Calculation.

O for Output.

Line numbers and Form Type are automatically entered by many computers when the program is keyed from a terminal. When the program is entered on cards, these fields must be keyed in.

Column 7 of all coding forms can be used to designate any line as a comment by coding an asterisk (*) in that column. Comments are very useful for providing documentary information about the coding. Because these comments are printed on the program, they can also help the programmer recall particular aspects of the coding during debugging.

All other coding requirements of the RPG specifications forms depend on the specific forms being used. This chapter provides coding rules for the File Description and Input forms in detail and indicates how the Calculation and Output forms are used as well.

The following will serve as a review of RPG coding rules.

RPG Coding Rules

Item	*Meaning*	*Columns into Which Data is Keyed*
Page number (upper right corner).	Used to number coding sheets—optional, with no effect on the compiler.	1-2 (of each line)
Line number.	Prenumbered except for the low-order or right-most digit.	3-5

Form Type.	Indicates specifications sheet: F-File description. I-Input specifications. C-Calculation specifications. O-Output specifications.	6
RPG statements.	These columns are coded according to established specifications.	7-74
Program Identification (upper right corner of form).	Identifies the program to the computer—an optional entry.	75-8Ø (of each line)

III. Illustrative RPG Program

A. Problem Definition

A computer center of a large company is assigned the task of calculating weekly wages for all nonsalaried personnel. To process data, the input must be in a form that is acceptable or understandable to the computer. Magnetic disk, punched cards, magnetic tape, and terminal data are common forms of input to a computer system.

1. The Input

In this illustrative problem, the employee data will be received from the payroll department in the form of time cards. These time cards will contain three fields, as indicated in Figure 1.6. In our RPG program, these fields will be specified as follows:

Field	*Length*
NAME	2Ø
HOURS	2
RATE	3 (1 integer, 2 decimal positions)

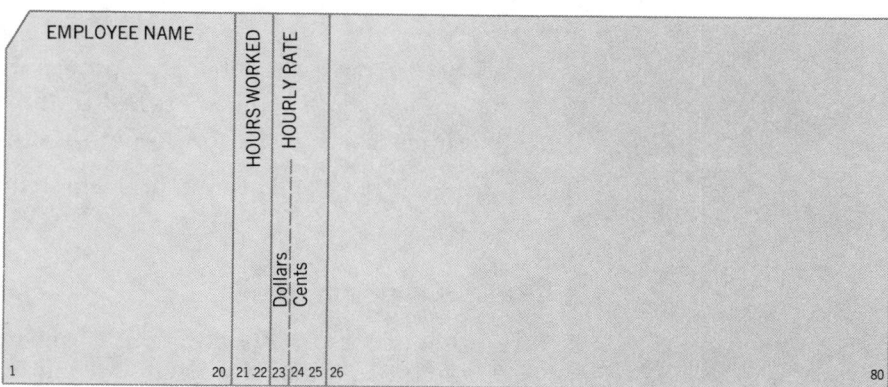

Figure 1.6
Input card format for sample program.

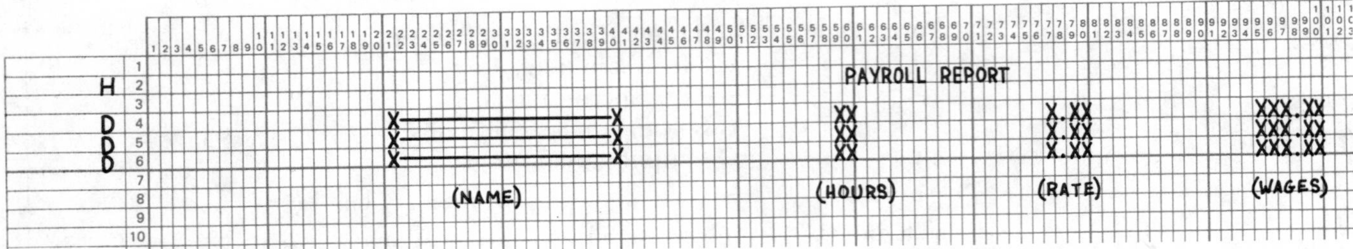

Figure 1.7
Printer Spacing Chart for sample program.

For each employee, the three fields of data will be transcribed or keypunched onto a punched card that will be accepted as input to the information processing system.

Card columns 1 to 2Ø of input records are reserved for each NAME. If any name contains less than 2Ø characters, the low-order, or right-most, positions are left blank. Similarly, HOURS will be placed in columns 21 and 22, and RATE in columns 23 to 25. The RATE figure, as a dollars-and-cents amount, is to be interpreted as if it had two decimal positions. That is, 125 in columns 23 to 25 is to be interpreted by the computer as 1.25. The decimal point is not generally entered for commercial applications since it would waste a card column and a storage position in memory. As will be seen, this method of *implying* or assuming decimal points is easily handled in RPG.

A deck of employee cards, with the format just described, will be keypunched and then read as input to the computer. WAGES will be calculated by the computer as

WAGES = HOURS × RATE

2. The Output

The output will be a printed report with the format illustrated in the Printer Spacing Chart in Figure 1.7. The three input fields will be printed in addition to the WAGES field, which is calculated as HOURS times RATE.

The Printer Spacing Chart indicates that a Heading (denoted by H) will appear on line 2 of each page. The Detail or D lines will consist of four fields: the first is a 2Ø-character name field, followed by a two-character hours worked field, followed by a three-digit dollars-and-cents rate field, and, finally, a five-digit dollars-and-cents wages field. The names in parentheses on the chart are *not* printed; they simply indicate what the output fields are.

Each problem definition in the text which describes the program to be written will consist of

1. A brief narrative describing the problem.
2. An input layout form or punched card image describing the input.
3. A Printer Spacing Chart or layout form describing the output.

These are standard elements in a problem definition.

B. The RPG Forms in Detail

Figure 1.8 illustrates the specifications forms required to code the program in RPG. These forms will be discussed in detail.

RPG programs are generally written on the four specifications forms illustrated in Figure 1.8 in the order indicated. Additional forms, which are dis-

RPG CONTROL AND FILE DESCRIPTION SPECIFICATIONS

Program PAYROLL
Programmer N.STERN Date 4/2Ø/--
Keying Instruction: Graphic Ø 2; Key ZERO TWO
Card Electro Number
Page Ø1 of 4 Program Identification (75–80) SSSØ1A

Control Specifications

For the valid entries for a system, refer to the RPG reference manual for that system.

Line (3–5)	Form Type (6)
01Ø	H

File Description Specifications

For the valid entries for a system, refer to the RPG reference manual for that system.

Line (3–5)	Form Type (6)	Filename (7–14)	File Type (15)	File Designation (16)	File Format (19)	Record Length (24–27)	Overflow Indicator (33–34)	Device (40–46)	Symbolic Device (47–52)
02Ø	F	CARDS	I	P	F	8Ø		READØ1	SYSIPT
03Ø	F	REPORT	O		F	132	OF	PRINTER	SYSLST
04	F								
05	F								

(a)

RPG INPUT SPECIFICATIONS

Program PAYROLL
Programmer N.STERN Date 4/2Ø/--
Keying Instruction: Graphic Ø 2; Key ZERO TWO
Card Electro Number
Page Ø2 of 4 Program Identification (75–80) SSSØ1A

Line (3–5)	Form Type (6)	Filename or Record Name (7–14)	Sequence (15–16)	Record Identifying Indicator (19–20)	Field Location From (44–47)	Field Location To (48–51)	Decimal Positions (52)	RPG Field Name (53–58)
01Ø	I	CARDS	NS	Ø1				
02Ø	I				1	2Ø		NAME
03Ø	I				21	22	Ø	HOURS
04Ø	I				23	25	2	RATE
05	I							
06	I							

(b)

Figure 1.8
Specifications forms for the sample RPG program: (a) Control and File Description Specifications form; (b) Input Specifications form;
(Continued on next page.)

cussed in the text, are required for specialized processing. Usually, however, the basic four forms are sufficient.

Each specifications form has space for 8Ø columns of information. Each *line* of a form is keypunched into one punched card or entered on one line on a terminal.

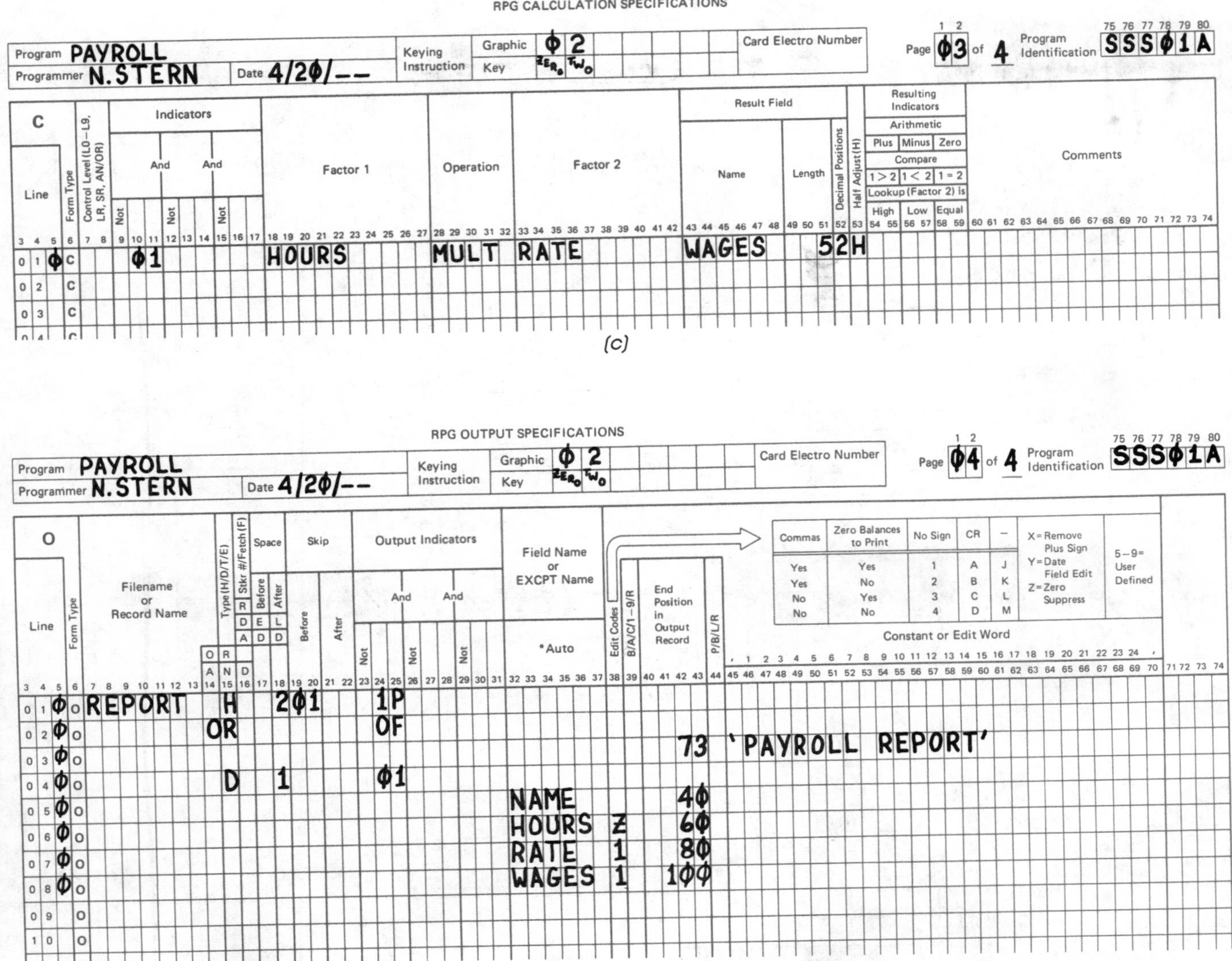

RPG CALCULATION SPECIFICATIONS

Program PAYROLL — Programmer N.STERN — Date 4/2Ø/-- — Keying Instruction: Graphic Ø 2, Key ZERO TWO — Page Ø3 of 4 — Program Identification SSSØ1A

Line	Form Type	Indicators	Factor 1	Operation	Factor 2	Result Field Name	Length	Decimal Positions	Half Adjust (H)
01Ø	C	Ø1	HOURS	MULT	RATE	WAGES	5	2	H
02	C								
03	C								
04	C								

(c)

RPG OUTPUT SPECIFICATIONS

Program PAYROLL — Programmer N.STERN — Date 4/2Ø/-- — Keying Instruction: Graphic Ø 2, Key ZERO TWO — Page Ø4 of 4 — Program Identification SSSØ1A

Line	Form Type	Filename or Record Name	Type (H/D/T/E)	Space Before	Space After	Skip Before	Output Indicators	Field Name or EXCPT Name	Edit Codes	End Position in Output Record	Constant or Edit Word
01Ø	O	REPORT	H	2		Ø1	1P				
02Ø	O		OR				OF				
03Ø	O									73	'PAYROLL REPORT'
04Ø	O		D		1		Ø1				
05Ø	O							NAME		4Ø	
06Ø	O							HOURS	Z	6Ø	
07Ø	O							RATE	1	8Ø	
08Ø	O							WAGES	1	10Ø	
09	O										
10	O										

(d)

Figure 1.8 *(continued)*
(c) Calculation Specifications form;
(d) Output Specifications form.

1. The Control and File Description Specifications Form

a. The Control Specifications Consider the sample form in Figure 1.8*a*. In addition to the File Description Specifications, it includes the RPG Control Specifications (some older forms say RPG Control Card Specifications). These specifications consist of a single line that provides information on the computer being used. Generally, the computer center will provide the RPG programmer with the information to be coded on this line. The one line of control specifications is always the *first* entry in the program, and it contains an H in column 6. The RPG specifications manual provided by your computer manufacturer will indicate if any additional information on control specifications is required.

The remainder of this section focuses on the File Description Specifications.

b. The Purpose of the File Description Specifications Form The File Description Specifications form performs several functions.

> ***Functions of the File Description Specifications Form***
> 1. Defines the input and output files.
> 2. Briefly describes these files.
> 3. Assigns the files to their respective devices.

You will recall that columns 1-2 of *all* RPG source programs are keyed with the page number indicated at the top of the form. For this form, PAGE usually contains an Ø1, since the File Description typically represents the first sheet in a program.

Columns 3-5 contain LINE number, the first two positions of which have been precoded for ease of programming. Column 5 may be left blank or a number (usually Ø) may be used, with 1-9 reserved for insertion lines. Keep in mind that the two fields of PAGE and LINE number are used exclusively for purposes of sequence-checking lines in a program. They do not affect the compilation.

Column 6 of the File Description Specifications form will always contain an F to denote its Form type.

The most important fields on this form will now be considered in depth. These are the fields used in the sample program in Figure 1.8. Other fields will be discussed throughout the text as the need arises.

FILENAME (Columns 7-14)

A **file** is a major grouping or collection of information. For example, there are inventory files, accounts receivable files, and payroll files. Generally, one file is assigned to a specific device; that is, there may be inventory tape files, accounts receivable card files, payroll disk files, and so on. The FILENAME field of the File Description Specifications form defines each file to be used in the program and then associates it with a device.

Each file to be used in the program is identified by assigning a name in columns 7-14. One file is assigned on each line of this form.

> ***Rules for Forming File Names***
> 1. Must begin in column 7 (left-justified).
> 2. Must begin with an alphabetic character.
> 3. May include letters and digits but no embedded blanks or special characters except #, $, and @. (An embedded blank is a blank within the field.)
> 4. Must be eight characters or less.
> 5. Should be a meaningful name.

The input filenames are used again when describing the input on the Input Specifications form. The output filenames are used again when describing output on the Output Specifications form.

In the sample program, CARDS is the name assigned to the input file of time cards and REPORT is the name assigned to the output print file.

Self-Evaluating Quiz

1. A file is a ________ .
2. The three main purposes of the File Description Specifications form are ________ , ________ , and ________ .

Indicate what, if anything, is wrong with the following filenames (3-7):

3. FILE-4
4. FILE1233
5. FILE A
6. PAYROLLFILE
7. DISCT%
8. If FILE12 were a designated filename, it would appear in columns ______ through ______ in the FILENAME field.

Solutions

1. major group or collection of data
2. to define the files
   to describe the files
   to assign the files to specified devices
3. The hyphen is a special character that is not permitted in a filename.
4. OK
5. There is an embedded blank between FILE and A, which is not permitted in a filename.
6. A maximum of eight positions is permitted in a filename.
7. The percent sign, %, is a special character that is not permitted in a filename.
8. 7
   12

The main portion of the File Description Specifications form describes the file to the system. The entries necessary for disk, card, tape, or print programs are relatively straightforward and standard. Specific tape and disk concepts will be considered in Chapters 7 through 9.

FILE TYPE (Column 15)

A disk, card, tape, or print file is usually designated in column 15, as

I for Input.
O for Output.

Although other entries may be used, the discussion will be confined for now to I and O, the most frequently coded entries. In the sample program, the input file called CARDS is designated with an I and the output file called REPORT is designated with an O.

FILE DESIGNATION (Column 16)

The specification for column 16 is used for input files only. Column 16 must be blank for output files. Input files may be designated in column 16 as

P for Primary.
S for Secondary.

One and only one primary file must be defined in a program. If there is more than one input file in a program, then one is defined as primary and the other(s) as secondary.

Since there is only one input file in the sample problem, it is designated with a P for primary. This position is left blank for the output file called REPORT.

FILE FORMAT (Column 19)

A file can have a format of

F for Fixed-length records.

V for Variable-length records.

Fixed-length records are records that are all the same size within a file; **variable-length records** are records of different lengths within a given file.

Card and print files always contain an F in column 19 because they are fixed in length; that is, they always contain a fixed number of positions in a record. Tape and disk files can contain *either* fixed-length records, when all are the same size, or variable-length records.

BLOCK LENGTH (Columns 2Ø-23) and RECORD LENGTH (Columns 24-27)

BLOCK LENGTH and RECORD LENGTH are used to specify the size of input and output records. Tape and disk records are often blocked to conserve space. This will be discussed in Chapter 7. All other file types (card and print files, specifically) will usually contain the *same entry* for BLOCK LENGTH and RECORD LENGTH. If BLOCK LENGTH is omitted, it is assumed to be the same as RECORD LENGTH.

The two entries require *numeric* quantities to denote the number of characters in a record and in a block. Numeric fields in RPG are right-justified. That is, the numeric quantities are placed in the right-most positions, with nonfilled left-most positions remaining blank.

Thus 8Ø in the RECORD LENGTH field would be placed in columns 26-27 for the input card file in this illustrative problem. Columns 24-25 would remain blank or contain zeros. The record length of 132 is placed in columns 25-27 for the sample output print file.

RECORD LENGTH for *standard* card files is always 8Ø, since card records are typically 8Ø positions long. There are, however, 96-column cards used with some IBM systems. (These are discussed in Appendix D.) The RECORD LENGTH for print files will usually be 8Ø, 1ØØ, 12Ø, or 132, depending on the printer. Most of the illustrations in this book will use 132.

For tape and disk files, the RECORD LENGTH and BLOCK LENGTH will vary according to the size of the records. In general, RPG programmers are supplied with the record and block sizes for files by the systems programmer. If a record size and a blocking factor (the number of records per block) are given, then BLOCK LENGTH is determined by multiplying the blocking factor by the record size.

OVERFLOW INDICATOR (Columns 33-34)

The OVERFLOW INDICATOR, designated as OF, may be coded in this field for print files. Use OF if you want the computer to test if the end of a page has been reached during processing.

DEVICE (Columns 4Ø-46) and SYMBOLIC DEVICE (Columns 47-52)

DEVICE and SYMBOLIC DEVICE are machine-dependent entries that are provided to the programmer by the computer center. This book will use the following entries for DEVICE.

DEVICE *(Columns 4Ø-46)*
TAPE
DISK

PRINTER

READER or READ Ø1 (for card reader)

CONSOLE (for terminal)

PUNCH (for card punch)

SYMBOLIC DEVICE may be SYSIPT for the system input device (usually the card reader) or SYSLST for the system's list device (usually the printer). For other files, SYS*nnn* is used, where *nnn* is a number.

In this sample program, then, there are two files: an input file of 8Ø-character records assigned to the card reader and an output file of 132-character records assigned to the printer.

The remainder of the File Description Specifications is not required for elementary-level programs. See Figure 1.9 for a review.

Figure 1.9
Review of Control and File Description Specifications form.

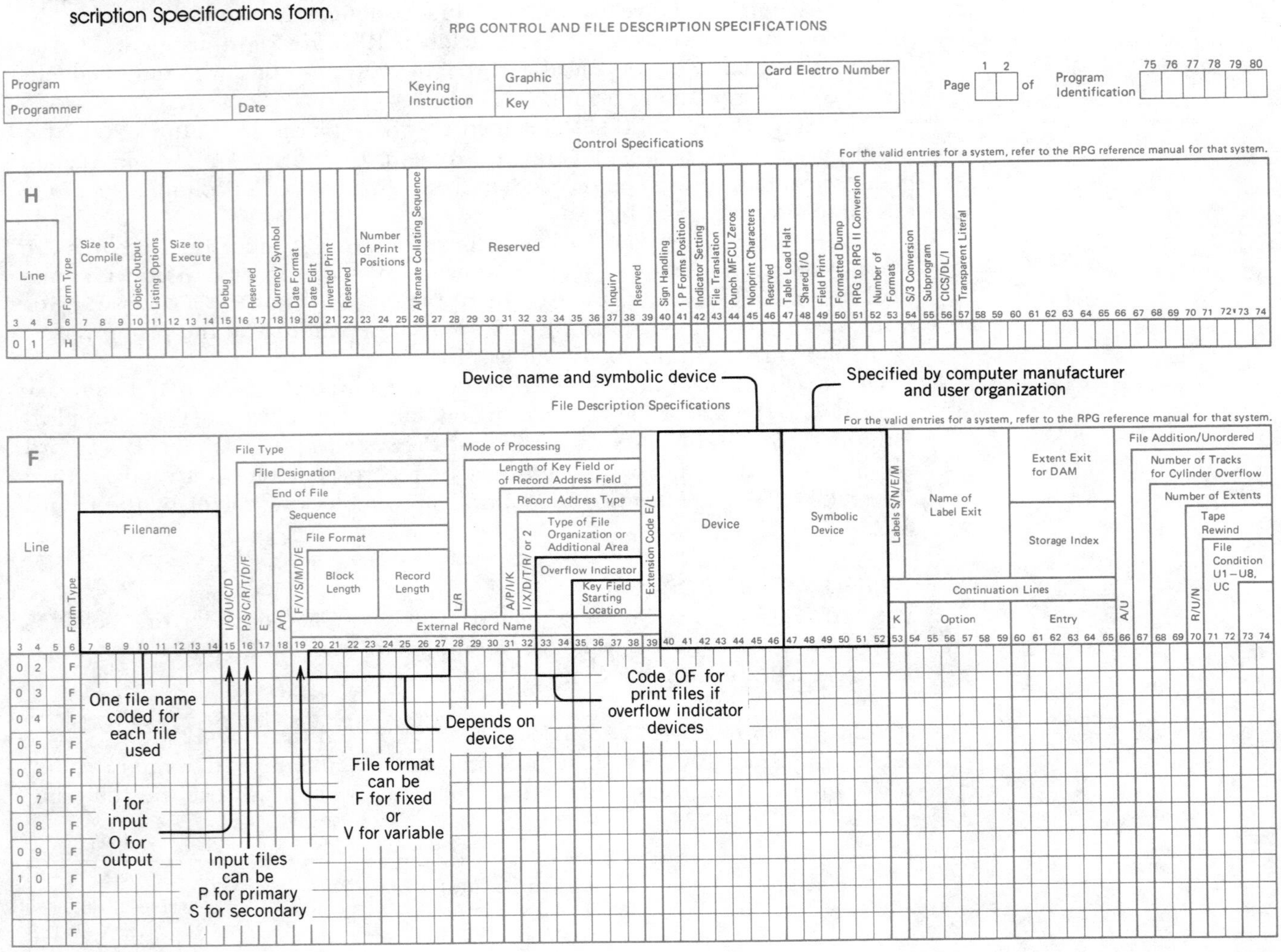

RPG CONTROL AND FILE DESCRIPTION SPECIFICATIONS

Self-Evaluating Quiz

We have arbitrarily selected tape or sequential disk files for input. Both these file types, as well as cards, would be processed in exactly the same way.

1. Code the File Description Specifications form for a program that reads a payroll disk (8Ø-character records) and produces a salary report.

File Description Specifications

For the valid entries for a system, refer to the RPG reference manual for that system.

Line (3–5)	Form Type (6)	Filename (7–14)	File Type I/O/U/C/D (15)	File Designation P/S/C/R/T/D/F (16)	End of File E (17)	Sequence A/D (18)	File Format F/V/S/M/D/E (19)	Block Length (20–23)	Record Length (24–27)	L/R (28)	Length of Key Field or of Record Address Field (29–30)	Record Address Type A/P/I/K (31)	Type of File Organization or Additional Area I/X/D/T/R/ or 2 (32)	Overflow Indicator (33–34)	Key Field Starting Location (35–38)	Extension Code E/L (39)	Device (40–46)	Symbolic Device (47–52)	Labels S/N/E/M (53)	Name of Label Exit (54–59)	Extent Exit for DAM / Storage Index (60–65)	File Addition/Unordered A/U (66)	Number of Tracks for Cylinder Overflow (67)	Number of Extents (68–69)	Tape Rewind R/U/N (70)	File Condition U1–U8, UC (71–72)	(73–74)
0 2	F																										
0 3	F																										
0 4	F																										
0 5	F																										

Continuation lines: External Record Name (19–28); K (53); Option (54–59); Entry (60–65).

2. Code the File Description entries for a program that reads data from a master inventory tape file (1ØØ-character records) and produces a summary report and an error file on tape.

File Description Specifications

For the valid entries for a system, refer to the RPG reference manual for that system.

Line (3–5)	Form Type (6)	Filename (7–14)	File Type I/O/U/C/D (15)	File Designation P/S/C/R/T/D/F (16)	End of File E (17)	Sequence A/D (18)	File Format F/V/S/M/D/E (19)	Block Length (20–23)	Record Length (24–27)	L/R (28)	Length of Key Field or of Record Address Field (29–30)	Record Address Type A/P/I/K (31)	Type of File Organization or Additional Area I/X/D/T/R/ or 2 (32)	Overflow Indicator (33–34)	Key Field Starting Location (35–38)	Extension Code E/L (39)	Device (40–46)	Symbolic Device (47–52)	Labels S/N/E/M (53)	Name of Label Exit (54–59)	Extent Exit for DAM / Storage Index (60–65)	File Addition/Unordered A/U (66)	Number of Tracks for Cylinder Overflow (67)	Number of Extents (68–69)	Tape Rewind R/U/N (70)	File Condition U1–U8, UC (71–72)	(73–74)
0 2	F																										
0 3	F																										
0 4	F																										
0 5	F																										

Continuation lines: External Record Name (19–28); K (53); Option (54–59); Entry (60–65).

3. Code the File Description entries for an *update* program that reads a master payroll tape file (1ØØ-character records) and salary change cards, and produces a new, updated master payroll tape file.

File Description Specifications

For the valid entries for a system, refer to the RPG reference manual for that system.

Line (3–5)	Form Type (6)	Filename (7–14)	File Type I/O/U/C/D (15)	File Designation P/S/C/R/T/D/F (16)	End of File E (17)	Sequence A/D (18)	File Format F/V/S/M/D/E (19)	Block Length (20–23)	Record Length (24–27)	L/R (28)	Length of Key Field or of Record Address Field (29–30)	Record Address Type A/P/I/K (31)	Type of File Organization or Additional Area I/X/D/T/R/ or 2 (32)	Overflow Indicator (33–34)	Key Field Starting Location (35–38)	Extension Code E/L (39)	Device (40–46)	Symbolic Device (47–52)	Labels S/N/E/M (53)	Name of Label Exit (54–59)	Extent Exit for DAM / Storage Index (60–65)	File Addition/Unordered A/U (66)	Number of Tracks for Cylinder Overflow (67)	Number of Extents (68–69)	Tape Rewind R/U/N (70)	File Condition U1–U8, UC (71–72)	(73–74)
0 2	F																										
0 3	F																										
0 4	F																										
0 5	F																										

Continuation lines: External Record Name (19–28); K (53); Option (54–59); Entry (60–65).

4. In question 3, the salary-change card file would be considered a secondary file because ______ .
5. Code the File Description Specifications form for a program that reads disk input (1ØØ-character records) and produces a printed report (132-character records).

File Description Specifications

For the valid entries for a system, refer to the RPG reference manual for that system.

F | Line | Form Type | Filename | File Type (I/O/U/C/D) | File Designation (P/S/C/R/T/D/F) | End of File (E) | Sequence (A/D) | File Format (F/V/S/M/D/E) | Block Length | Record Length | Mode of Processing (L/R) | Length of Key Field or of Record Address Field | Record Address Type (A/P/I/K) | Type of File Organization or Additional Area (I/X/D/T/R/ or 2) | Overflow Indicator | Key Field Starting Location | Extension Code E/L | External Record Name | Device | Symbolic Device | Labels S/N/E/M | Name of Label Exit | Extent Exit for DAM | Storage Index | Continuation Lines: K, Option, Entry | A/U | File Addition/Unordered | Number of Tracks for Cylinder Overflow | Number of Extents | Tape Rewind (R/U/N) | File Condition U1–U8, UC

3 4 5 6 7 8 9 10 11 12 13 14 15 16 17 18 19 20 21 22 23 24 25 26 27 28 29 30 31 32 33 34 35 36 37 38 39 40 41 42 43 44 45 46 47 48 49 50 51 52 53 54 55 56 57 58 59 60 61 62 63 64 65 66 67 68 69 70 71 72 73 74

0 2 F
0 3 F
0 4 F
0 5 F

6. A standard card file always has a format of ______ because ______ .
7. The P in column 16 is used to indicate ______ .
8. (T or F) Output files must be coded with a P or S in column 16.
9. Code the File Description Specifications form for a card input program that produces a tape, which duplicates the input card format, and produces an error list.

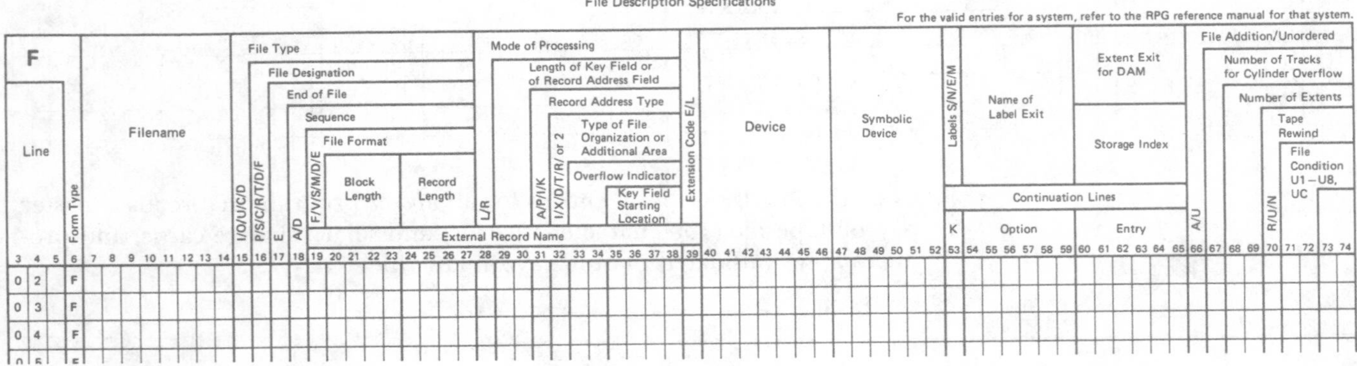
File Description Specifications

For the valid entries for a system, refer to the RPG reference manual for that system.

F | Line | Form Type | Filename | File Type (I/O/U/C/D) | File Designation (P/S/C/R/T/D/F) | End of File (E) | Sequence (A/D) | File Format (F/V/S/M/D/E) | Block Length | Record Length | Mode of Processing (L/R) | Length of Key Field or of Record Address Field | Record Address Type (A/P/I/K) | Type of File Organization or Additional Area (I/X/D/T/R/ or 2) | Overflow Indicator | Key Field Starting Location | Extension Code E/L | External Record Name | Device | Symbolic Device | Labels S/N/E/M | Name of Label Exit | Extent Exit for DAM | Storage Index | Continuation Lines: K, Option, Entry | A/U | File Addition/Unordered | Number of Tracks for Cylinder Overflow | Number of Extents | Tape Rewind (R/U/N) | File Condition U1–U8, UC

3 4 5 6 7 8 9 10 11 12 13 14 15 16 17 18 19 20 21 22 23 24 25 26 27 28 29 30 31 32 33 34 35 36 37 38 39 40 41 42 43 44 45 46 47 48 49 50 51 52 53 54 55 56 57 58 59 60 61 62 63 64 65 66 67 68 69 70 71 72 73 74

0 2 F
0 3 F
0 4 F
0 5 F

10. Code the File Description Specifications form for a program that reads an input inventory tape and produces an output PARTS LIST report. The input consists of 1ØØ-position records, blocked 1Ø.

File Description Specifications

For the valid entries for a system, refer to the RPG reference manual for that system.

Line	Form Type	Filename	File Type	File Designation	End of File	Sequence	File Format	Block Length	Record Length	Device	Symbolic Device
02	F										
03	F										
04	F										

11. The BLOCK LENGTH and the RECORD LENGTH often contain different entries for tape and disk files because ________ .
12. Code the File Description Specifications form for a payroll program that produces output time cards and a weekly journal from an input tape.

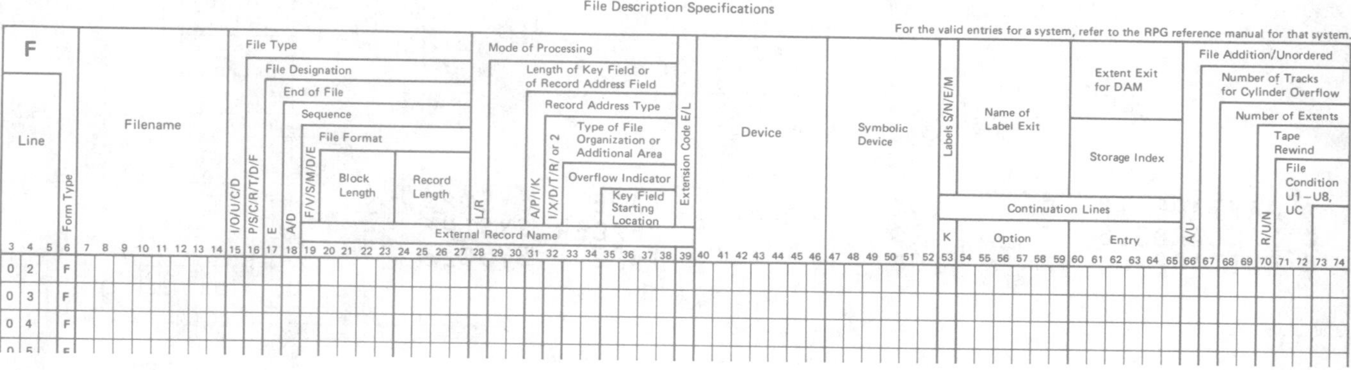

Solutions 1.

File Description Specifications

For the valid entries for a system, refer to the RPG reference manual for that system.

Line	Form Type	Filename	File Type	File Designation	File Format	Record Length	Device	Symbolic Device
02Φ	F	PAY	I	P	F	8Φ	DISK	SYSΦ15
03Φ	F	SALRPT	O		F	132	PRINTER	SYSLST
04	F							
05	F							

2.

File Description Specifications

For the valid entries for a system, refer to the RPG reference manual for that system.

Line	Form Type	Filename	File Type	File Designation	File Format	Record Length	Device	Symbolic Device
02Ø	F	INVTAPE	I	P	F	1ØØ	TAPE	SYSØ16
03Ø	F	SUMRPT	O		F	132	PRINTER	SYSLST
04Ø	F	ERRTAPE	O		F	1ØØ	TAPE	SYSØ17
05	F							
06	F							

3.

File Description Specifications

For the valid entries for a system, refer to the RPG reference manual for that system.

Line	Form Type	Filename	File Type	File Designation	File Format	Record Length	Device	Symbolic Device
02Ø	F	PAYTAPE	I	P	F	1ØØ	TAPE	SYSØ2Ø
03Ø	F	SALCARDS	I	S	F	8Ø	READER	SYSIPT
04Ø	F	OUTTAPE	O		F	1ØØ	TAPE	SYSØ22
05	F							
06	F							

Note: There must be two *tape files, an old master and a new master, since information cannot be added to an existing tape file (see Chapter 7).*

4. its purpose is to alter the contents of the primary or most significant file, the master payroll tape file.

5.

File Description Specifications

For the valid entries for a system, refer to the RPG reference manual for that system.

Line	Form Type	Filename	File Type	File Designation	File Format	Record Length	Device	Symbolic Device
02Ø	F	DISKIN	I	P	F	1ØØ	DISK	SYSØ25
03Ø	F	PRINTOUT	O		F	132	PRINTER	SYSLST
04	F							
05	F							

6. F for Fixed
   card records always contain 8Ø characters
7. that the specific input file is the primary form of input
8. F—This field may only be used for input.
9.

File Description Specifications

For the valid entries for a system, refer to the RPG reference manual for that system.

Line	Form Type	Filename	File Type	File Designation	End of File	Sequence	File Format	Block Length	Record Length	Device	Symbolic Device
02Ø	F	CARDS	I	P			F		8Ø	READER	SYSIPT
03Ø	F	TAPE	O				F		8Ø	TAPE	SYSØ3Ø
04Ø	F	ERRLIST	O				F		132	PRINTER	SYSLST
05	F										
06	F										

10.

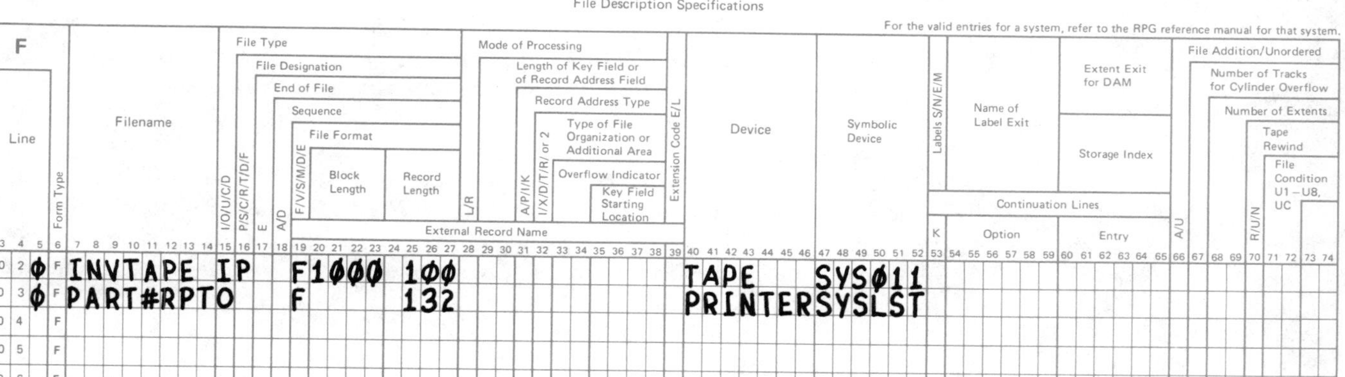

File Description Specifications

For the valid entries for a system, refer to the RPG reference manual for that system.

Line	Form Type	Filename	File Type	File Designation	End of File	Sequence	File Format	Block Length	Record Length	Device	Symbolic Device
02Ø	F	INVTAPE	I	P			F	1ØØØ	1ØØ	TAPE	SYSØ11
03Ø	F	PART#RPT	O				F		132	PRINTER	SYSLST
04	F										
05	F										

11. tape records are usually blocked
12.

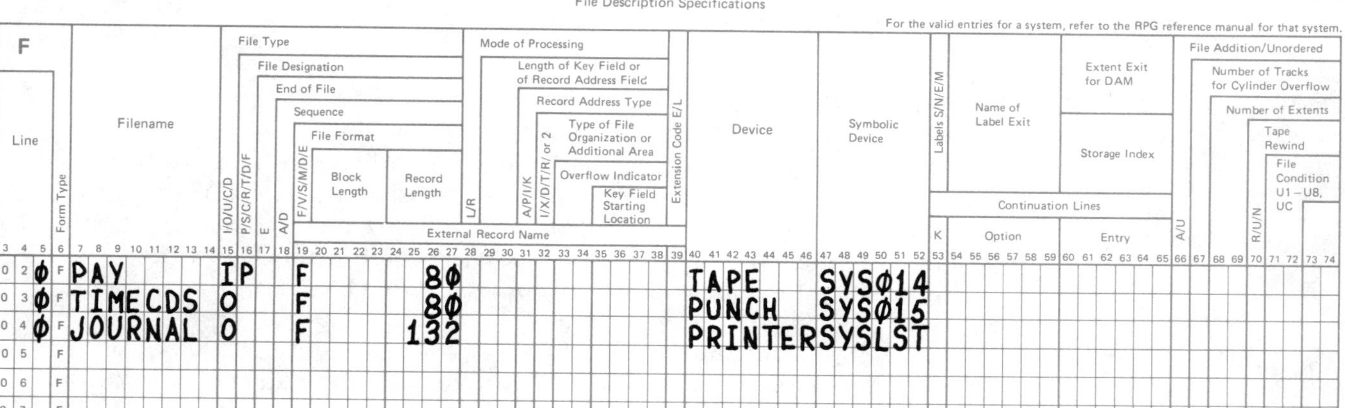

File Description Specifications

For the valid entries for a system, refer to the RPG reference manual for that system.

Line	Form Type	Filename	File Type	File Designation	End of File	Sequence	File Format	Block Length	Record Length	Device	Symbolic Device
02Ø	F	PAY	I	P			F		8Ø	TAPE	SYSØ14
03Ø	F	TIMECDS	O				F		8Ø	PUNCH	SYSØ15
04Ø	F	JOURNAL	O				F		132	PRINTER	SYSLST
05	F										
06	F										

2. Input Specifications Form
Input and output files consist of records that contain fields of data.

Field:	Consecutive positions that represent a unit of data (i.e., AMT, CUSTNO, etc.).
Record:	A set of related fields representing a unit of information (transaction record, employee record, etc.).
File:	A set of related records stored on a single medium (accounts receivable tape file, payroll disk file, etc.).

Section VII of this chapter provides an in-depth review of data elements and data file organization.

Each input file defined on the File Description Specifications form must be described, in detail, on the Input Specifications form. This form is illustrated in Figure 1.8*b*. A record within the input file is defined on the first line followed by each field within that record. Each field is placed on an independent line. If there is more than one record for a file, then each additional record must follow with specific field identifiers. It is considered better programming form to code the most frequently occurring records first, followed by those that occur less frequently.

Once again, this chapter will consider only those fields on the Input Specifications form that are necessary for coding elementary level programs. The other fields will be considered in subsequent chapters as needed.

PAGE and LINE (Columns 1-5)
The entry for PAGE appears on the top of the form. The LINE field is usually precoded beginning with Ø1 and ending with 2Ø. The last position of the LINE field may be left blank or the programmer may supply additional line entries. The five lines on the bottom of each form may be used by the programmer for insertions.

FORM TYPE (Column 6)
The FORM TYPE field always contains a precoded I for Input Specifications. The Input Specifications form consists of entries that describe the overall record, called record description entries. A record is described on a single line of an Input Specifications form. Following the description of the record are field description entries on subsequent lines, with each field specified on a single line.

a. Record Identification Entries
FILENAME (Columns 7-14)
For each input file specified in the File Description Specifications form, an entry is required on the Input Specifications form. The FILENAME for this input file must appear exactly the same on both forms. This name appears only *once* on the Input Specifications form, on the *first* line defining the first record for that file. Consider the sample Input Specifications form in Figure 1.8*b*. Note that the name of the file appears only once in the FILENAME field.

SEQUENCE (Columns 15-16)
The SEQUENCE field can be used for checking the sequence of records. This will be discussed in Chapter 8. For now, our programs will include NS in the

sequence field for No Sequence to indicate that a sequence check is not required. Any two letters, however, would be permissible to indicate that no sequence checking is to be performed. In Figure 1.10, where there are numerous records and no sequence checking is required, AA, AB, and AC are coded in the SEQUENCE field for each record. Where there is just one record, NS for No Sequence, as indicated, is frequently coded.

RECORD IDENTIFYING INDICATOR **(Columns 19-2Ø)**

The purpose of the RECORD IDENTIFYING INDICATOR field is to identify the record uniquely. RPG uses indicators that serve as record identifiers. In the sample problem, the record identifying indicator Ø1 is turned on for all input records.

Each record in a file can be identified by RECORD IDENTIFICATION CODES in columns 21-41. Since all records have the same format in the example, it is not necessary to provide for individual codes; thus the RECORD IDENTIFICATION CODES are not used.

Following the line that identifies a record, the fields are listed in sequence. Figure 1.1Ø describes an input file with three different types of records. The first input record is defined by RECORD IDENTIFYING INDICATOR Ø1. This record is identified by the character X in position 8Ø. The second record is defined by the letter Z in column 8Ø and the digit 5 in column 79. If 5Z appears in columns 79-8Ø, then indicator Ø2 is turned on. Finally, a third record is described that turns on indicator Ø3 if column 8Ø has a character of a T.

A RECORD IDENTIFYING INDICATOR then can be used in conjunction with RECORD IDENTIFICATION CODES to identify a record uniquely. In both the Calculation and Output forms, the record to be processed is specified by its RECORD INDICATOR. Any number from Ø1-99 may be used as a RECORD INDICATOR, and the number may appear in any sequence.

Figure 1.10
Input Specifications form that describes an input file with three different types of records.

RPG INPUT SPECIFICATIONS

Program | Programmer | Date | Keying Instruction: Graphic, Key | Card Electro Number | Page of | Program Identification

Line	Form Type	Filename or Record Name	Sequence	Record Identifying Indicator	Position (1)	C/Z/D (1)	Character (1)	Position (2)	C/Z/D (2)	Character (2)	From	To	Decimal Positions	RPG Field Name
01Ø	I	TRANSACT	AA	Ø1	8Ø	C	X							
02Ø	I										1	5		ACCTNO
03Ø	I										6	2Ø		NAME
04Ø	I										21	4Ø		ITEM
05Ø	I										41	45	Ø	UNPRIC
06Ø	I										46	48	Ø	QTY
07Ø	I										49	52	Ø	TAX
08Ø	I		AB	Ø2	8Ø	C	Z	79	D	5				
09Ø	I										1	6		DATE
10Ø	I		AC	Ø3	8Ø	C	T							
11Ø	I										1	5		ACCTNO
12Ø	I										6	1Ø	Ø	CRAMT
13	I													
14	I													
15	I													

RECORD IDENTIFICATION CODES (Columns 21-41)

As indicated, RECORD IDENTIFICATION CODES provide a method for identifying each type of record. Using a single line, a record can be uniquely identified by a maximum of *three* codes. This is indicated by a 1, 2, or 3 as a subheading under RECORD IDENTIFICATION CODES on the sheet. If more than three identifying codes are required for a single record, then *two* lines are required. Let us discuss the subfields for the RECORD IDENTIFICATION CODES.

POSITION (Columns 21-24)

This field refers to the single position on the input record that contains the code. This field, as all numeric fields, is right-justified.

NOT (Column 25)

If the *absence* of a specific character in a position is used to specify the code, then an N is placed here.

C/Z/D (Column 26)

C/Z/D stands for Character, Zone or Digit test, respectively, for the field. If a full character is to be tested, use C. If only the zone portion is to be tested, use Z. If the digit portion only is to be tested, use D.

CHARACTER (Column 27)

Any alphabetic, numeric, or special character may be used in column 27 to specify a record identification code.

Columns 28-34 and columns 35-41 are repetitions of the previous fields. Thus, when two or more characters in specified positions are required for record identification, these fields are used.

Columns 21-24 may be left blank if all records within a file are to be processed in the same way. If the following is the only entry for the record fields on the Input Specifications form, then all input records automatically turn on indicator 15.

RPG INPUT SPECIFICATIONS

Line (3-5)	Form Type (6)	Filename or Record Name (7-14)	Sequence (15-16)	Record Identifying Indicator (19-20)	Field Location From (44-47)	Field Location To (48-51)	Decimal Positions (52)	RPG Field Name (53-58)
01ϕ	I	FILE1	NS	15				
02ϕ	I				1	5		ACCTNO
03ϕ	I				6	1ϕ	ϕ	AMT1
04	I							
05	I							

If an input form describes a record with a 1 in position 8Ø, we would have

RPG INPUT SPECIFICATIONS

```
01ØISAMPLE  NS  Ø1  8Ø C1
02ØI
03ØI                                                  .
04ØI                                                  .   } Field descriptions
05 I                                                  .
06 I
07 I
```

Processing will be performed correctly if position 8Ø contains a 1. Since there is no indicator turned on if position 8Ø does not have a 1, the computer will automatically turn on a halt indicator and, unless otherwise instructed, it will abort the job. To prevent this occurrence, add the following coding.

RPG INPUT SPECIFICATIONS

```
01ØISAMPLE  NS  Ø1  8Ø C1
02ØI                                                  .
03ØI                                                  .
04ØI                                                  .
05ØI        NT  Ø2  8ØNC1
06 I
07 I
```

Recall that any two letters are permissible in the sequence field where no sequence checking is to be performed. In this way, indicator Ø2 will be turned on if the required code of 1 in column 8Ø is not present. Then the program can perform whatever error routines are appropriate if indicator Ø2 is on. It is recommended that this additional coding be included to avoid the possibility of the job aborting prematurely.

RPG INPUT SPECIFICATIONS

Line	Form Type	Filename or Record Name	AND/OR (14-16)	Sequence (15-16)	Record Identifying Indicator (19-20)	Position 1	C/Z/D	Character	Position 2	C/Z/D	Character	Position 3	C/Z/D	Character	From	To	Decimal Positions	RPG Field Name
01Ø	I	CARDIN		AA	Ø1	8Ø	C	6	79	C	5	78	C	4				
02Ø	I		AND			77	C	3	76	C	2	75	C	1				
03Ø	I														1	5		ACCTNO
04Ø	I														6	1Ø		NAME
05	I																	
06	I																	
07	I																	

Figure 1.11
Identifying a record with more than three identification codes.

AND or OR Relationships

If more than three conditions are required to identify a given record, then *two* coded lines are necessary. The first line would contain all the aforementioned data with record identification fields coded to include three conditions. The second line would contain the letters AND in columns 14-16 and the additional record identification codes required to identify the given record. If more than six conditions are required to identify a given record, then subsequent lines may be used with AND in columns 14-16. See Figure 1.11 for an illustration.

If the existence of *any one* of a series of possibilities is used to identify a record, these rules can be used with the OR qualifier. The condition or conditions are coded on individual lines with the word OR in columns 14-15 of all but the first line. See Figure 1.12 for an illustration. If positions 79-8Ø contain 56 *or* positions 77-78 contain 34, the Ø1 record identifying indicator is turned on.

Figure 1.12
Identifying a record when any one of a series of possibilities exists.

RPG INPUT SPECIFICATIONS

Line	Form Type	Filename or Record Name	AND/OR (14-16)	Sequence (15-16)	Record Identifying Indicator (19-20)	Position 1	C/Z/D	Character	Position 2	C/Z/D	Character	From	To	Decimal Positions	RPG Field Name
01Ø	I	TAPEIN		AA	Ø1	8Ø	C	6	79	C	5				
02Ø	I		OR			77	C	3	78	C	4				
03Ø	I											1	5		ACCTNO
04Ø	I											6	1Ø	Ø	AMT
05Ø	I											11	3Ø		NAME
06	I														
07	I														
08	I														

b. Field Identification Entries (Columns 43-74) So far, the Input Specifications form has been used to define records within a file. Records are identified with identification codes and accessed by record indicators. One or more lines can be used to define a record.

Once a record has been defined and identified, subsequent lines are required to describe the *fields* within the record, in sequence. The remainder of this chapter will illustrate how we identify fields within given records. The sample program in Figure 1.8 will be used for an example. Note that the field identifications appear on the lines *following* the record description. Note also that only those fields required for processing need be described. Unused input fields need not be identified.

FIELD LOCATION **(Columns 44-51)**

The FIELD LOCATION entry is used to indicate the *boundaries* of the field defined. In the FROM subfield (columns 44-47), enter the left-most or high-order position of the field. In the TO subfield (columns 48-51), enter the right-most or low-order position of the field. As with all numeric items, these entries are *right-justified.*

DECIMAL POSITIONS **(Column 52)**

The DECIMAL POSITIONS entry is coded for all numeric fields to be used in arithmetic operations and remains blank for all other fields. It indicates the number of decimal positions in the numeric field. That is, the number of digits to the right of the decimal point is entered. If the field denoted contains integers only, then Ø is entered here.

FIELD NAME **(Columns 53-58)**

Each field indicated for the record must contain a name.

Rules for Forming RPG Field Names

1. From 1 to 6 characters.
2. Must begin with an alphabetic character.
3. Can contain letters, @, #, and $ only.
4. No embedded blanks.

The name is *left-justified,* beginning in column 53. The name should be meaningful, such as AMT, or DEPT, so that it indicates something about the nature of the field. Each field name should be unique. Only those fields that are required for processing need to be defined. In the sample program, three fields—NAME, HOURS, and RATE—are defined. Since HOURS and RATE are used in a calculation, they are defined as having zero and two decimal places, respectively.

See Figure 1.13 for a review of the Input Specifications form.

Self-Evaluating Quiz

1. Code the Input Specifications form for a program that reads in tape records with a 4 in column 21 and a 5 in column 22. Account for all error conditions by turning on a second indicator if the conditions do not exist. This will be used to print an error.

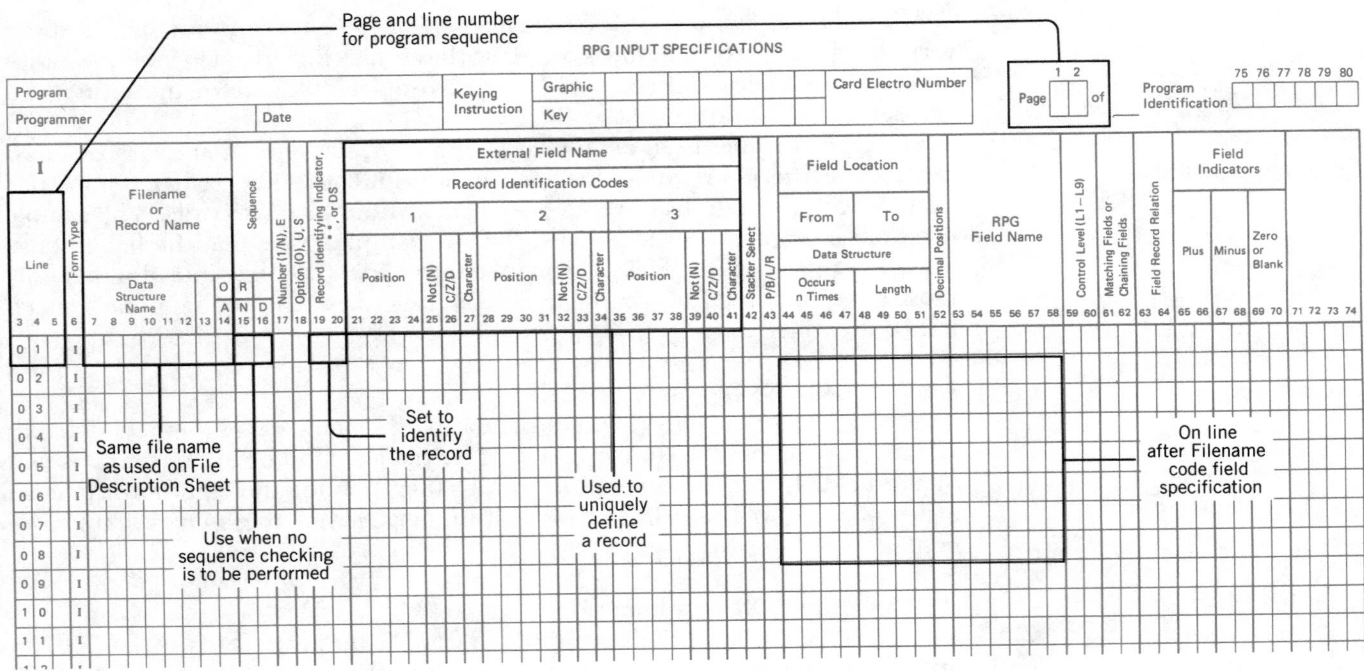

Figure 1.13
Overview of Input Specifications form.

2. Code the Input Specifications form for a record, within the TAPEIN file, with the following identifiers.

Column	*Code*
71	B
72	A
73	L
74	D
75	U
76	E

3. Code the Input Specifications form, insofar as you are able, for a file called TRANS that contains tape records. Credit records contain a C in column 1; debit records contain an S in column 1. No sequence checking is required.
4. The input file, INFILE, has two record formats. The first record, RECORD1, should have a 1 in column 8Ø and a minus sign in column 79. The second record, RECORD2, should have a 2 in column 78, a 6 in column 79, and an A in column 8Ø. Write the Input Specifications for this problem.
5. (T or F) The RECORD IDENTIFYING INDICATORS used must be in numeric sequence.
6. (T or F) When three RECORD IDENTIFICATION CODES are used, any one of the three conditions will turn on the RECORD IDENTIFYING INDICATOR.
7. The NOT subfield of the RECORD IDENTIFICATION CODES is used to denote ________ . If column 8Ø is to be tested for a blank, then ________ is coded in the POSITION field, ________ is coded in the NOT field, ________ is coded in the C/Z/D field, and ________ is coded in the CHARACTER field.

8. Code the Input Specifications form for a program that reads records from a file called TAPEIN. The records are to be processed only if they contain a 7 in column 79 and a 4 in column 8Ø.
9. If all records are to be processed regardless of any format, then the ________ indicator must be coded but the ________ may be left blank.
10. Indicate if the following coding is correct:

RPG INPUT SPECIFICATIONS

Line	Form Type	Filename or Record Name	Sequence	Record Identifying Indicator	Position (1)	Not (N)	C/Z/D	Character	From	To	Decimal Positions	RPG Field Name
01Ø	I	CARDIN	NS	Ø1	8Ø		C	X				
02Ø	I								1	6		CODE
03Ø	I								7	2Ø		NAME
04Ø	I								21	3Ø	Ø	BALANC
05Ø	I								31	35		CUSTNO
06Ø	I								36	5Ø		ADDRES
07Ø	I								51	6Ø		CITY
08Ø	I								61	65		STATE
09Ø	I								66	8Ø		SHIPPR
10	I											
11	I											

Solutions 1.

RPG INPUT SPECIFICATIONS

Line	Form Type	Filename or Record Name	AND/OR	Sequence	Record Identifying Indicator	Position (1)	Not (N)	C/Z/D	Character	Position (2)	Not (N)	C/Z/D	Character
01Ø	I	TAPEIN		AA	Ø1	21		C	4	22		C	5
02Ø	I												
03Ø	I												
04Ø	I												
05Ø	I			AB	Ø2	21	N	C	4				
06Ø	I		OR			22	N	C	5				
07	I												
08	I												

2.

RPG INPUT SPECIFICATIONS

Program | Programmer | Date | Keying Instruction: Graphic, Key | Card Electro Number | Page 1 2 of | Program Identification 75 76 77 78 79 80

Line (3-5)	Form Type (6)	Filename or Record Name (7-14)	Sequence (15-16)	Record Identifying Indicator (19-20)	Record Identification Codes 1: Position (21-24)	Not (N) (25)	C/Z/D (26)	Character (27)	2: Position (28-31)	Not (N) (32)	C/Z/D (33)	Character (34)	3: Position (35-38)	Not (N) (39)	C/Z/D (40)	Character (41)
01Ø	I	TAPEIN	NS	Ø1	71		C	B	72		C	A	73		C	L
02Ø	I	AND			74		C	D	75		C	U	76		C	E
03	I															
04	I															

3.

RPG INPUT SPECIFICATIONS

Line (3-5)	Form Type (6)	Filename or Record Name (7-14)	Sequence (15-16)	Record Identifying Indicator (19-20)	Record Identification Codes 1: Position (21-24)	Not (N) (25)	C/Z/D (26)	Character (27)
01Ø	I	TRANS	AA	Ø1	1		C	C
02Ø	I							
03Ø	I							
04Ø	I							
05Ø	I							
06Ø	I							
07Ø	I							
08Ø	I		AB	Ø2	1		C	S
09	I							
10	I							

Line 01Ø: → When position 1 has a 'C' indicator 01 is turned on

Line 08Ø: → When position 1 has an 'S' indicator 02 is turned on

4.

RPG INPUT SPECIFICATIONS

Line (3-5)	Form Type (6)	Filename or Record Name (7-14)	Sequence (15-16)	Record Identifying Indicator (19-20)	Record Identification Codes 1: Position (21-24)	Not (N) (25)	C/Z/D (26)	Character (27)	2: Position (28-31)	Not (N) (32)	C/Z/D (33)	Character (34)	3: Position (35-38)	Not (N) (39)	C/Z/D (40)	Character (41)
01Ø	I	INFILE	NS	Ø1	79		Z	-	8Ø		D	1				
02Ø	I	OR		Ø2	78		D	2	79		D	6	8Ø		C	A
03	I															
04	I															

5. F
6. F—All three conditions must exist for the indicator to be turned on.
7. that a record identifying indicator should be turned on if a code does not exist
   8Ø; blank; C; blank
8.

RPG INPUT SPECIFICATIONS

Line	Form Type	Filename or Record Name	Sequence	Record Identifying Indicator	Position (1)	Not (N)	C/Z/D	Character	Position (2)	Not (N)	C/Z/D	Character
0 1 Ø	I	TAPEIN	AA	Ø1	79		D	7	8Ø		D	4
0 2 Ø	I		BB	99								
0 3	I											
0 4	I											

9. RECORD IDENTIFYING
   RECORD IDENTIFICATION CODES
10. Yes

3. Calculation Specifications Form

Figure 1.8*c* shows a Calculation Specifications form. Any arithmetic or logic operation is defined on the Calculation Specifications form.

CONTROL LEVELS **(Columns 7-8)**

Since no control fields are used in the sample program, columns 7 and 8 are blank.

INDICATORS **(Columns 9-17)**

Since a multiplication operation (HOURS × RATE) is to be performed for *all* input cards, we use indicator Ø1, which is "turned on" for all input cards. This is the only indicator required in the sample program. In general, the indicator fields are used to specify when calculations are to be performed.

OPERATION **and** RESULT FIELD **(Columns 18-48)**

In the sample program, Factor 1, HOURS, is multiplied (MULT) by Factor 2, RATE, to produce a resultant field called WAGES.

For other operations we may use

- ADD
- SUB
- DIV
- COMP (compare), etc.

The precise format for all calculations is provided in Chapter 3.

FIELD LENGTH **and** DECIMAL POSITIONS **(Columns 49-52)**

In the sample program in Figure 1.8, the field length for the resultant numeric field, WAGES, is 5 (column 51) including two decimal positions (2 in column 52).

HALF ADJUST **(Column 53)**
Column 53, HALF ADJUST, is used for rounding. That is, when the computer is to round the results to the nearest position, an H is coded in this field.

RESULTING INDICATORS **(Columns 54-59)**
The RESULTING INDICATORS in columns 54-59 are turned on only for compare (COMP) operations. This will be discussed in Chapter 3.

COMMENTS **(Columns 6Ø-74)**
Any comments may be included in columns 6Ø to 74. These are printed on the listing but do not affect processing. Entire lines may also be included as comments by using an asterisk (*) in column 7 of any line of any form.

4. Output Specifications Form
Figure 1.8*d* shows an Output Specifications form.

FILENAME **(Columns 7-14)**
For the sample program in Figure 1.8, the output file REPORT would be described using this form. The next chapter will discuss the output form in more detail. This chapter, however, simply illustrates its use.

TYPE **(Column 15)**
Three types of records may be included.

- Heading (H)
- Detail (D)
- Total (T)

Since we only have Heading and Detail records, only H and D types (column 15) have been included.

STACKER SELECT **(Column 16)**
The STACKER SELECT field is appropriate only for punched output, where output data cards can fall into several pockets or stackers.

SPACE **and** SKIP **(Columns 17-22)**
These options are appropriate only for printed output. All printers can be made to space 1, 2, or 3 (and sometimes more) lines either *before* or *after* writing a line. The 2 in SPACE AFTER of the illustration indicates that *after* the Heading line is printed, we wish to space the form two lines. Note, however, that *either* column 17 or 18 must include a 1, 2, or 3 to designate the type of spacing required. A Ø may be used in either one or the other column to suppress spacing entirely. A blank may also be used to indicate one line of spacing after printing. Some systems allow a number greater than three for spacing more than three lines; check your specifications manual.

The SKIP option for printed output is used to position the form at a specific line. An Ø1 in the SKIP field is a code for skipping to the beginning of a new page. In our illustration, we skip to a new page before printing the heading.

Thus the output file REPORT has a heading record (H), which requires the skipping to a new page *before* printing, and two lines of spacing *after* printing.

OUTPUT INDICATORS **(Columns 23-31)**
The OUTPUT INDICATOR 1P (columns 24 and 25) implies that we wish to print the H record (Heading) on the first page (1P). If any other conditions also

require the printing of this heading record, then we code OR on the next line in columns 14 and 15 along with the corresponding condition. The notation OF in columns 24 and 25 indicates that we also wish to print a heading on an overflow, or end-of-page, condition.

In short, we are indicating that we wish the H or heading type record to print on the first page *or* when the end of a page is reached. In either case, we skip the paper to a new page, print the heading, and then advance the paper two lines.

In most print applications, we want headings to print on the first printed page. Also, when we have reached the end of a page, we want the program to skip to a new page and print new headings. In this way, each individual page of the continuous form has a heading so that when the report is separated into individual sheets, each can be identified.

FIELD NAME, EDIT CODES, END POSITION and CONSTANT (Columns 32-7Ø)

The heading PAYROLL REPORT is to print with the last character in print position 73 (see the Printer Spacing Chart in Figure 1.7).

The detail line, D, prints when indicator Ø1 is on, that is, for all input cards. Each time a detail line prints, the form is spaced one line (after printing). Since each input card turns on indicator Ø1, a detail line will print for each input card.

There are four output fields to be printed.

Printing of Output

Field Name	*Print Positions*
NAME	21-4Ø
HOURS	59-6Ø
RATE	77-8Ø (A decimal point prints on output and therefore counts as a position)
WAGES	95-1ØØ (Here, too, a decimal point appears on output)

Note: *On the Output form, indicate the low-order or right-most position for each field (e.g., 4Ø, 6Ø, 8Ø, 1ØØ for the above).*

The first three fields are directly transmitted from the card record. Note that these input and output fields have the same names. NAME requires no editing. HOURS requires zero suppression (Z in column 38) to eliminate leading zeros. RATE requires a decimal point to print after the first integer position. You will recall that to save space on a card, decimal points are often omitted. They are *implied* or *assumed* in input records. The output document, however, must have these decimal points for readability. A 1 in column 38 will print a decimal point in the correct place. We will see later that the Edit Word, columns 45 to 7Ø, may be used in place of column 38.

The four specification forms in Figure 1.8 comprise a complete RPG program that performs the required operations outlined in our problem definition. Although there is no visible step-by-step logic displayed in the specifications, when the forms are coded so that they conform to the RPG rules, a program is compiled that contains the step-by-step logic.

IV.

RPG II Logic Cycle

As we have seen, RPG II is coded using four specification forms that specify

1. Files to be used.
2. Input format.
3. Calculations to be performed.
4. Output format.

The sequence in which RPG performs the required operations is relatively clear in simple programs such as the one discussed in this chapter. But this sequence becomes somewhat less obvious with more complex programming. The **RPG II Logic Cycle** describes in detail the precise sequence in which RPG performs all operations.

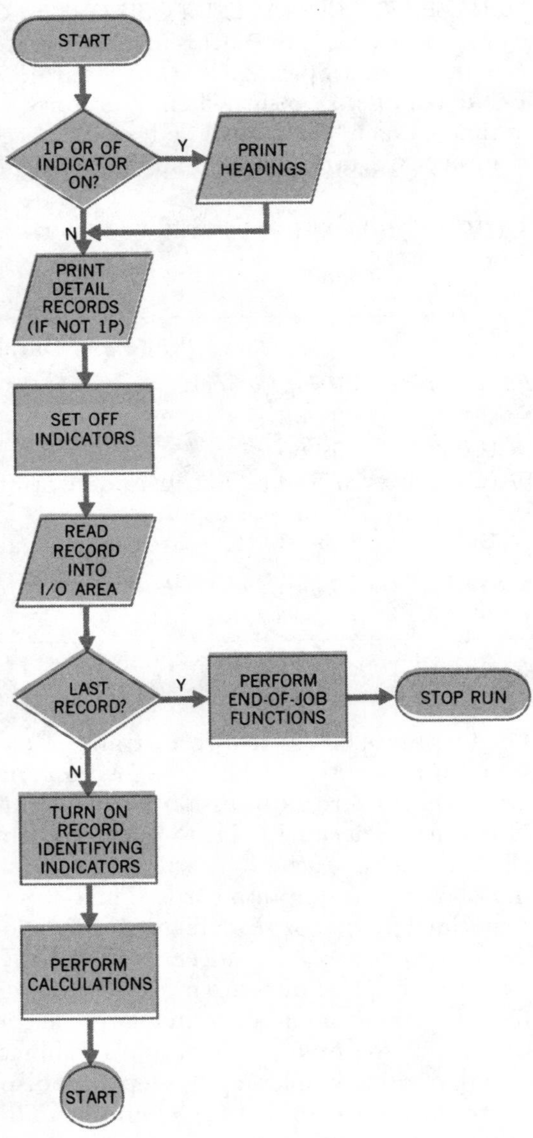

Figure 1.14
RPG II Logic Cycle in flowchart form.

In other programming languages, the programmer is in full control of the sequence in which instructions are executed. With the use of GO TO statements in most languages, FOR . . . NEXT statements in BASIC, PERFORM statements in COBOL, etc., the programmer can precisely specify logical control.

In RPG this logical control can be handled by the compiler, although there are methods to override the established structure. The programmer, then, must fully understand the logical control sequence provided by RPG in order to code programs accurately.

This RPG II Logic Cycle is usually illustrated in pictorial form in one of two ways. Figure 1.14 illustrates the RPG II Logic Cycle in flowchart or top-down form. Figure 1.15 illustrates the same RPG II Logic Cycle in a circular form. Both figures depict the same sequence of operations. All programs in RPG follow this fixed logic sequence.

1. Headings or H records are printed on the first page or if a page overflow occurs.
2. Detail or D records are printed if any record indicators are on.
3. All record identifying indicators are turned off.
4. A record is read.
5. The computer tests for the last record. If the last record has been processed, the LR indicator is turned on and may be used for performing end-of-job calculations or printing end-of-job summaries. If the last record has been processed and the LR indicator is not tested, the program is terminated. (The LR indicator was not used in the sample program.)
6. Record identifying indicators are turned on according to the specifications on the input form.
7. Calculations are performed using the record identifying indicators to specify which calculations are required.
8. The process is repeated by going to Step 1.

Figures 1.14 and 1.15 provide a brief overview of the RPG II Logic Cycle. As our programs get more sophisticated, we will specify the sequence of execution by providing more detail in the RPG II Logic Cycle illustrations. We will use both versions to illustrate the cycle so that you will become familiar with these two types of illustrations.

V. Documentation

The beginning programmer should be aware of some of the reasons why computer systems have failed in the past, and sometimes continue to fail, in providing needed services to users. One main reason for dissatisfied users is the lack of adequate documentation of programs. **Documentation** refers to the set of records that is used to explain in detail how the program operates and what it is intended to accomplish.

All too frequently, programmers view their job as consisting *solely* of writing and debugging a program; they pay little or no attention to providing the user with a documentation package that adequately describes the program. Without required documentation, the following problems are apt to occur:

1. Minor "bugs" in a program, which frequently occur only after it has been running, would be difficult to locate and correct.

Figure 1.15
Alternative illustration of RPG II Logic Cycle.

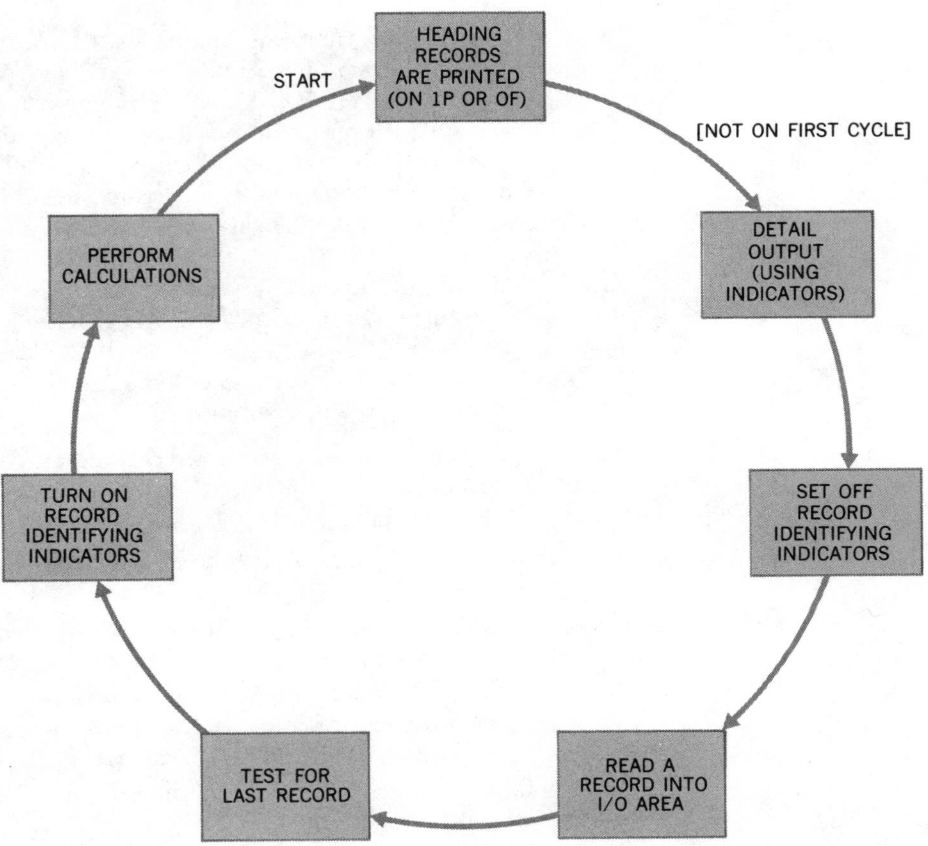

2. If programming modifications are required at a later date, they would be extremely difficult to make.
3. Users, provided only with a working program, will have no sense of exactly how the program functions.

Many computer centers have begun to implement standards that require information processing professionals to supply specific documentation.

Typically, a programmer receives a program assignment from a systems analyst who is responsible for the overall design of the system (i.e., accounting system, inventory system, payroll system, etc.). The systems analyst should provide the programmer with a problem definition including standard specifications used for coding the problem:

1. A brief systems flowchart outlining the input, output, and processing required.
2. Record Layout forms describing all disk, tape, and card input or output.
3. Printer Spacing Charts describing all print output.

See Figure 1.16 for an illustration of a systems flowchart and an input layout for the program described in this chapter (Figure 1.8). Figure 1.7 illustrates the

Systems Flowchart

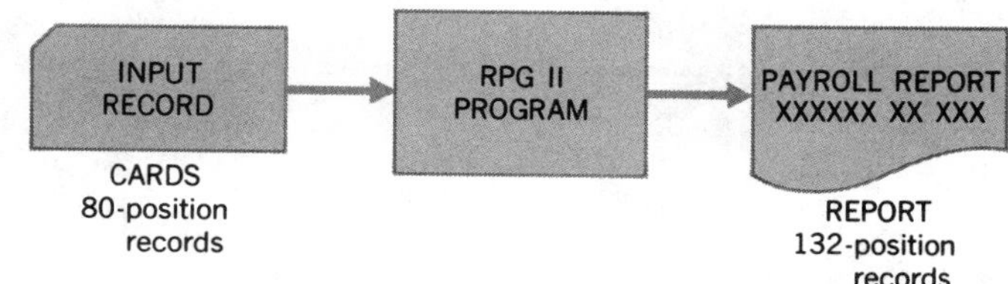

CARDS Record Layout

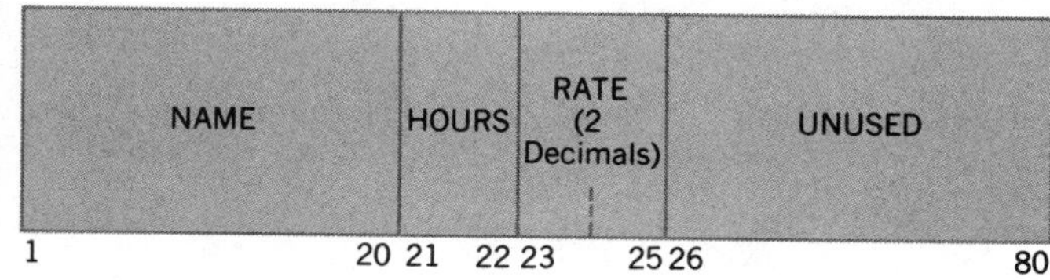

Figure 1.16 Tools used for documenting the program in Figure 1.8.

Printer Spacing Chart. The programmer uses these forms in coding: they then become part of the documentation package.

These forms are standard within the information processing industry. Thus, every program discussed in this text will include the three documentation specifications: systems flowchart, input layout, and Printer Spacing Chart, or output layout. They are essential in providing the programmer with the problem definition, and they can also be examined by users to ensure that all data is processed properly. At the end of the job, they become part of the documentation package.

The programmer also includes a source listing as part of documentation. Since users may wish to examine the listing or other programmers may use it if later modifications are desired, the following two points should be noted:

1. Field and file names should be as meaningful as possible. That is, AMT1 is a better description of the first amount field on a record, than T1, for example.
2. Comments should be included on the listing as often as possible to help describe the processing. See Figure 1.17 for a listing of our sample program, with comments. Note that such comments are also useful as reminders to the programmer during the debugging phase.

For programs with complex logic, it is often useful to draw a *program flowchart* prior to coding to:

1. Ensure that the program logic is clear.
2. Verify with the user or systems analyst that the programmer's understanding of the job requirements is correct.

Program flowcharting is reviewed in Appendix C. If drawn, a program flowchart then becomes part of documentation. In those chapters that consider complex logic control procedures, flowcharts are used extensively.

A program flowchart is not the only tool used for depicting program logic. Programs that use *structured* techniques are more apt to include *pseudocode* as a documentation tool. We will consider pseudocode and structured programming in RPG III in Chapter 11.

```
        01-020  F*********************************************************************SSS01A
        01-030  F* THIS PROGRAM PRODUCES A PAYROLL REPORT, CALCULATING WAGES EARNED *SSS01A
        01-040  F* BY MULTIPLYING TOTAL NUMBER OF HOURS WORKED BY THE RATE OF PAY    *SSS01A
        01-050  F* FOR EACH EMPLOYEE.                                                *SSS01A
        01-060  F*********************************************************************SSS01A
        01-070  F*                                                                    SSS01A
0001    01-080  FCARDS   IP  F      80           READ01 SYSIPT                       SSS01A
0002    01-090  FREPORT  O   F     132     OF    PRINTERSYSLST                       SSS01A
        01-100  F*                                                                    SSS01A
        02-010  I**************************** INPUT RECORD ***************************SSS01A
        02-020  I*                                                                    SSS01A
0003    02-030  ICARDS   AA  01                                                       SSS01A
0004    02-040  I                                         1  20 NAME                  SSS01A
0005    02-050  I                                        21  22 0HOURS                SSS01A
0006    02-060  I                                        23  252RATE                  SSS01A
        02-070  I*                                                                    SSS01A
        03-010  C**************************** CALCULATIONS ***************************SSS01A
        03-020  C*                                                                    SSS01A
0007    03-030  C   01        HOURS     MULT RATE      WAGES    52H                   SSS01A
        03-040  C*                                                                    SSS01A
        04-010  C**************************** HEADING LINE ***************************SSS01A
        04-020  C*                                                                    SSS01A
0008    04-030  CREPORT  H  201     1P                                                SSS01A
0009    04-040  O         OR        CF                                                SSS01A
0010    04-050  O                                   73 'PAYROLL REPORT'               SSS01A
        04-060  C*                                                                    SSS01A
        04-070  O****************************-DETAIL LINE ****************************SSS01A
        04-080  C*                                                                    SSS01A
0011    04-090  O          D 1      01                                                SSS01A
0012    04-100  O                        NAME      40                                 SSS01A
0013    04-110  O                        HOURS Z   60                                 SSS01A
0014    04-120  O                        RATE  1   80                                 SSS01A
0015    04-130  O                        WAGES 1  100                                 SSS01A
        04-140  C*                                                                    SSS01A
        04-150  O*********************************************************************SSS01A


      E N D  O F  S O U R C E
```

Figure 1.17
Listing of sample program with comments.

VI. Debugging a Program

Several levels of debugging should be performed by the programmer.

1. Desk Checking

Programmers should carefully review their programs *before* they have them keyed in. This will minimize computer time and reduce the overall time it takes to debug a program. Frequently, programmers fail to see the need for this phase on the assumption that it is better to let the computer find errors. Note, however, that omitting the desk-checking phase can result in undetected logic errors that could take hours—or even days—to debug. Efficient programmers carefully review their programs before keying and compiling them.

2. Compilation and Syntax Errors

After a program has been translated or compiled, the computer will print a source listing along with any rule violations or syntax errors. The programmer must then correct the errors and recompile the program before it can actually be run with test data.

3. Walkthroughs

After a program has been listed by the computer in a source listing, programmers must test the logic by executing the program with test data. It is best to **walk through** the program manually first to see if it will produce the desired results. This is done prior to machine execution. Such walkthroughs can help the programmer find logic errors without wasting machine time.

Frequently, programming teams work together to test the logic in their programs using the walkthrough approach. This method of debugging could save considerable computer time and make the entire debugging phase more efficient as well.

4. Detecting Logic Errors After Program Execution

In many ways, detecting logic errors after program execution is the most difficult and time-consuming aspect of debugging. If desk checking and program walkthroughs are performed, this will minimize the number of logic errors apt to be encountered during program execution. The DEBUG option may also be used in RPG to facilitate debugging (more on this later).

The preparation of test data is an extremely critical aspect of this phase. It is imperative that the programmer prepare data that will test every possible condition that the program is likely to encounter under normal operating conditions. It is not uncommon for a program that has been supposedly fully tested and running for some time to suddenly experience problems. Most often, these problems arise because a specific condition not previously encountered has occurred and the program has not adequately provided for the situation. If test data includes every conceivable condition, then the risk of undetected errors is minimized.

VII. A Review of Data Organization

Data is processed by the computer in an organized way. Areas are set aside in memory for **files**, **records**, and **fields**. Each of these terms has special significance in RPG and must be fully understood by the programmer. If you are already familiar with these terms, you may skip this section.

A. Files

A **file** is the major classification of data pertaining to a specific application. An organization may have an *inventory file* containing all inventory information. A payroll file, accounts receivable file, and sales file are examples of commonly used business files. Each file is contained on a storage medium such as magnetic disk, magnetic tape, or, perhaps, punched cards.

Most RPG programs use at least one input and one output file. Disk files are unique in that they can be both input and output during a single run. Changes can be made directly to a disk; thus it is possible to read from a disk and write back onto it. All other files are either input or output.

In general, then, for each form of input and output used in a computer application, one file is designated. If weekly transaction data from week 1 were entered from a tape and used to make changes to a master accounting tape, then *three* files would be designated: an input transaction tape, the input master tape, and the newly created output master tape incorporating the change data. Thus *three* tapes would be used.

Each file to be used in a program is defined and described on the File Description Specifications form along with the device to which it will be assigned.

B. Records

A **record** is a collection of data within a file that contains a unit of information. A transaction tape file, for example, may consist of two types of records: credit records and sales records.

In RPG, each record would be designated with the use of a *coded field* that uniquely defines the record. For example, a "C" in position 1 might designate transaction records as credit records and an "S" in position 1 might designate transaction records as sales records. On the Input form, record identifying indicators would be used to specify each record type.

C. Fields

A **field** is a group of consecutive storage positions reserved for a specific data item. A sales record, for example, may consist of the following fields: Account Number, Customer Name, Amount of Purchase, Date of Purchase. Input fields are specified in RPG on the Input form, and output fields are specified on the Output form. In both cases, the relative positions of the field on either the input or the output record must be designated.

Field names are specified as follows.

Rules for Forming Field Names

1. 1 to 6 characters.
2. Must begin with alphabetic character.
3. Can contain letters, digits or @, #, $.
4. No other special characters or embedded blanks.
5. Name is *left-justified* in Field Name columns.

In the case of field names and file names, the name should be meaningful, such as AMT, DEPT, or SALREC.

a. Types of Fields: Group and Elementary There are two major categories of fields: **group items** and **elementary items**. A **group item** is a data field that is further subdivided; that is, it is a major field consisting of minor fields. A DATE field, for example, may be a group item consisting of MO, DAY, and YR. The data fields that are not further subdivided are called **elementary items**. In the example cited, MO, DAY, and YR would be elementary items within the group item DATE. They would be coded on the Input form as follows.

RPG INPUT SPECIFICATIONS

Program		Keying Instruction	Graphic		Card Electro Number	Page (1 2) of	Program Identification (75 76 77 78 79 80)
Programmer	Date		Key				

Line (3 4 5)	Form Type (6)	Filename or Record Name (7–14) / Data Structure Name	Sequence (15 16) / OR, AND	Number (1/N), E (17)	Option (O), U, S (18)	Record Identifying Indicator, **, or DS (19 20)	Record Identification Codes 1: Position, Not (N), C/Z/D, Character (21–27)	2: Position, Not (N), C/Z/D, Character (28–34)	3: Position, Not (N), C/Z/D, Character (35–41)	Stacker Select (42)	P/B/L/R (43)	Field Location From / Data Structure Occurs n Times (44–47)	To / Length (48–51)	Decimal Positions (52)	RPG Field Name (53–58)	Control Level (L1–L9) (59 60)	Matching Fields or Chaining Fields (61 62)	Field Record Relation (63 64)	Field Indicators Plus (65 66)	Minus (67 68)	Zero or Blank (69 70)	71 72 73 74
0 1 φ	I	INFILE	NS			φ1																
0 2 φ	I											1	6		DATE							
0 3 φ	I											1	2		MO							
0 4 φ	I											3	4		DAY							
0 5 φ	I											5	6		YR							
0 6	I																					
0 7	I																					
0 8	I																					

The field called DATE can be used to access the first six positions of the record. Similarly, MO can be used to access the first two positions, DAY can be used to access positions 3-4, and YR can be used to access positions 5-6.

b. Alphanumeric, Alphabetic and Numeric Fields Fields can also be classified as

- Alphanumeric (or alphameric).
- Alphabetic.
- Numeric.

An **alphanumeric** or alphameric **field** is one that can have any combination of letters, digits, and special symbols such as $, ., or %. An **alphabetic field** can contain letters or blanks only. By leaving the DECIMAL POSITIONS field of the Input form (column 52) blank, the computer will assume that the field is alphanumeric or alphabetic.

RPG INPUT SPECIFICATIONS

Program		Keying Instruction	Graphic		Card Electro Number	Page (1 2) of	Program Identification (75 76 77 78 79 80)
Programmer	Date		Key				

Line (3 4 5)	Form Type (6)	Filename or Record Name (7–14) / Data Structure Name	Sequence (15 16) / OR, AND	Number (1/N), E (17)	Option (O), U, S (18)	Record Identifying Indicator, **, or DS (19 20)	Record Identification Codes 1: Position, Not (N), C/Z/D, Character (21–27)	2: Position, Not (N), C/Z/D, Character (28–34)	3: Position, Not (N), C/Z/D, Character (35–41)	Stacker Select (42)	P/B/L/R (43)	Field Location From / Data Structure Occurs n Times (44–47)	To / Length (48–51)	Decimal Positions (52)	RPG Field Name (53–58)	Control Level (L1–L9) (59 60)	Matching Fields or Chaining Fields (61 62)	Field Record Relation (63 64)	Field Indicators Plus (65 66)	Minus (67 68)	Zero or Blank (69 70)	71 72 73 74
0 1 φ	I	MASTER	NS			φ1																
0 2 φ	I											1	2φ	(blank)	NAME							
0 3	I																					
0 4	I																					
0 5	I																					

Leave blank for alphanumeric or alphabetic fields

If a field is to be used in an arithmetic operation, then it is defined as a **numeric field**. The computer assumes a field is numeric if it is defined with an integer in the DECIMAL POSITIONS field.

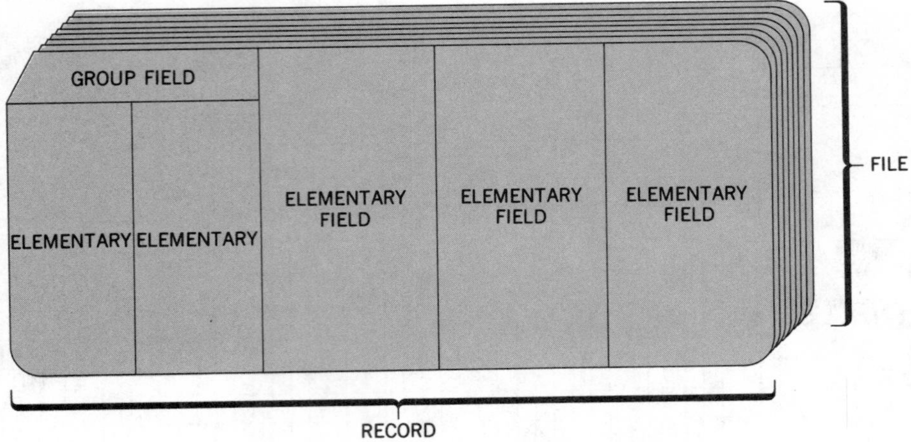

Figure 1.18 Relationships of fields, records, and files.

All numeric fields that are to be used in arithmetic operations must be defined with an integer in the DECIMAL POSITIONS field. A 'Ø' in column 52 (DECIMAL POSITIONS) means that the field consists of all integers; that is, it is a whole number field.

Although input fields will not contain decimal points or other symbols such as a dollar sign or comma, it is a relatively simple matter to have the output print these edit symbols for ease of reading.

Summary of Data Organization

1. **File**—An overall classification of data pertaining to a specific category.
2. **Record**—A unit of data within a file that contains information of a specific nature.
3. **Field**—A group of consecutive columns or positions reserved for a specific kind of data.
   a. **Group item**—A field that is subdivided.
   b. **Elementary item**—A field that is not subdivided.

Note: *Files, records, and fields are all defined in an RPG program by data names. See Figure 1.18 for a review.*

VIII. Chapter Summary

A. Program considerations
   1. Programs are written in a symbolic language that is relatively easy to learn. This program is called the **source program**.
   2. Source programs must be translated into machine language programs before they can be run or executed. These are called **object programs**.
   3. **Debugging** a program is the process of finding and correcting any errors.
      a. **Syntax errors**—violations in the rules of the language; usually found when a program is compiled.
      b. **Logic errors**—mistakes in the structure or logic; usually found when testing the program during execution.

4. Methods of Debugging
   a. **Desk checking**—checking a program before running it on a computer.
   b. Fixing syntax errors after compilation.
   c. Creating test data that will test all possible conditions.
   d. Program **walkthroughs**—manual checks of the logic by following the program through with some sample test data.
   e. Executing the program with test data.

B. RPG II language
1. RPG is an abbreviation for Report Program Generator.
2. RPG II is a more current version of RPG and easier to code.
3. RPG III is a recent advance available on some computers for data base manipulation and structured programming.
4. RPG is useful for a wide variety of business functions including report writing and disk processing.
5. All RPG programs use the following forms in the sequence indicated:
   a. Control and File Description Specifications.
   b. Input Specifications.
   c. Calculation Specifications.
   d. Output Specifications.

   Other forms are also available, but these four are always used for most programs.

C. RPG II Logic Cycle
1. RPG II has a specific sequence in which program statements are executed.
2. Unlike other languages, this sequence is not directly under the programmer's control.
3. Programmers must be familiar with this logic cycle to avoid program errors.

D. Documentation
1. Before coding, all programmers should be provided with the following problem definition:
   a. A systems flowchart describing the input, output, and processing required.
   b. A formal description of the files on Record Layout forms.
   c. A formal description of printed output on a Printer Spacing Chart.
2. These specifications help the programmer to better understand what is required and also provide end-users with needed information about the program.
3. All programs should contain meaningful field and file names.
4. Comments (* in column 7 of any form) should be included in an RPG II program to help explain the processing.

Key Terms

Alphabetic field	Elementary item
Alphanumeric field	Field
Compiler	File
Data base	Fixed-length record
Debugging	Group item
Desk checking	High-level language
Documentation	Logic error

Machine language
Numeric field
Object program
Program
Program sheet
Programmer
Program flowchart
Record
RPG
RPG coding sheet
RPG II Logic Cycle
Source program
Structured programming
Symbolic programming language
Syntax error
Test data
Variable-length record
Walkthrough

Self-Evaluating Quiz

1. RPG is a (high/low)-level language.
2. (T or F) RPG can only be used on small computers.
3. (T or F) RPG II is well suited for handling high-level and complex input and output.
4. (T or F) RPG III can be used for writing structured programs.
5. (T or F) The Control and File Description Specifications form describes the format of input and output fields to be used.
6. The ________ specification is the first entry of an RPG program.
7. RPG coding sheets have space for ________ columns of information.
8. Column ________ on an RPG coding form is used to indicate the Form type.
9. Column 7 of all RPG coding forms can be used to designate any line as a comment by coding a(n) ________ in that column.
10. Excluding sequence numbers, RPG statements are coded in columns ________ to ________ .
11. (T or F) On every RPG coding form, the Identification columns must be filled in.
12. (T or F) A decimal point is not generally entered in an input dollars-and-cents field.
13. The File Description Specifications form always has a(n) ________ in column 6 to denote its Form type.
14. (T or F) On the File Description Specifications form, column 16 (Primary/Secondary) must be blank for output files.
15. (T or F) It is possible to define more than one primary file in an RPG program.
16. If there is more than one input file in a program, then one is defined as Primary and the other(s) as ________ .
17. (T or F) A print file can contain variable-length records.
18. (T or F) If BLOCK LENGTH is omitted for a file, it is assumed to be the same as RECORD LENGTH.
19. An OVERFLOW INDICATOR of ________ can be coded for a print file to test for the end of a page.
20. (T or F) The SEQUENCE field on the Input Specifications form can contain any two letters to indicate that no sequence check is required.
21. (T or F) If all input records have the same format, then RECORD IDENTIFICATION CODES may be omitted.

22. (T or F) The DECIMAL POSITIONS field must be coded for all numeric fields that are to be used in arithmetic operations.
23. Field names are (left/right)-justified.
24. (T or F) All fields in an input record must be defined, even if they are not required for processing.
25. When we want the computer to round the result of a calculation to the nearest position, a(n) ________ is coded in the HALF ADJUST field.

Solutions

1. high
2. F
3. T
4. T
5. F—It lists the files to be used, the devices they will employ, and special features to be included.
6. control or H
7. 8Ø
8. 6
9. asterisk (*)
10. 6
    74
11. F — It is an optional entry. However, it is recommended.
12. T
13. F
14. T
15. F
16. Secondary
17. F
18. T
19. OF
20. T
21. T
22. T
23. left
24. F
25. H

Review Questions

1. Code the Input Specifications form, for a record, within the MASTAPE file with the following identifier.

Column	*Code*
71	B
or 71	D
or 71	W

2. Modify the solution to question 1 so that the test for B, D, or W records also includes a test for 73 in columns 79-8Ø. That is, all B, D, and W records must contain a 73 in columns 79-8Ø.
3. Code the Input Specifications form for a tape file with the record format denoted in Figure 1.19. Assume that no sequence-checking is required.
4. (T or F) A field identifier should always appear on a line with a record identifier.
5. Data fields that are further subdivided are called ________ items.
6. (T or F) Only numeric fields can contain an entry in column 52 of the Input Specifications form.

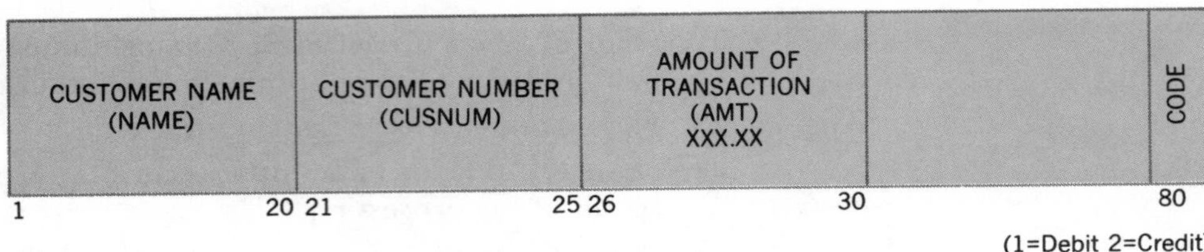

Figure 1.19
TAPEIN record format for Review Question 3.

7. Indicate what, if anything, is wrong with the following RPG names.
   a. 1RPG
   b. NAME 1
   c. NAMEFIELD
   d. NAME-A

Practice Problems

A Note About the Structure of Practice Problems

The problems at the end of each chapter begin with the most elementary and become more complex, with problem 4 being the most difficult. Problem 1 in all chapters is very similar to the practice problem discussed in the text. Problem 2 of every chapter has a common data set provided in Appendix E. Thus, if problem 2 is executed, the user may employ a single data set. Problems 3 and 4 are representative of the type of problems typically coded in RPG.

Note: For the following problems, refer to figure 1.17 on page 44 and Figure 2.8 on page 65 for coding the Output Specifications form. Only the end position of each field to be printed is specified.

1. Consider the following and write an RPG program to produce the results indicated.

Systems Flowchart

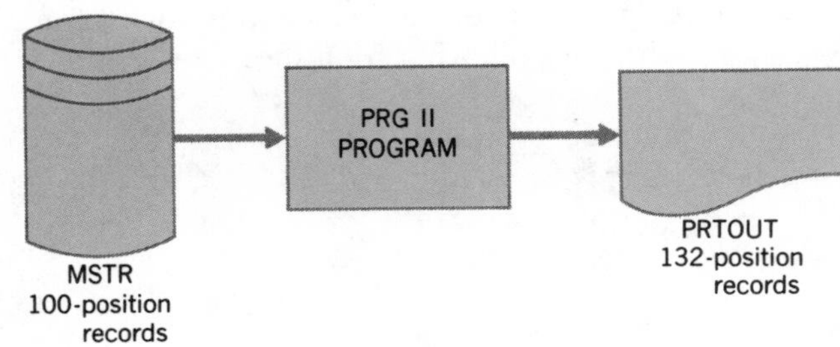

MSTR Record Layout

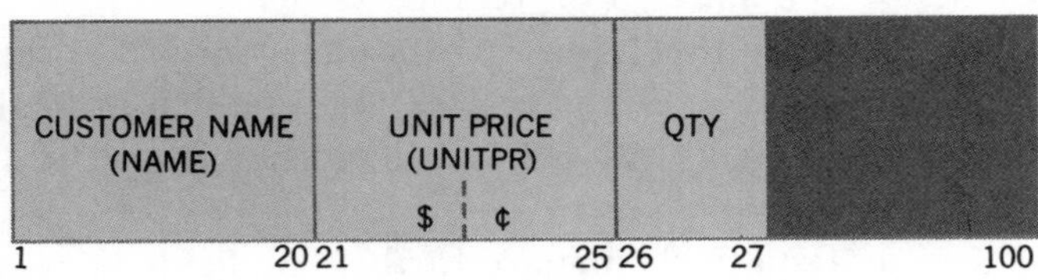

PRTOUT Printer Spacing Chart

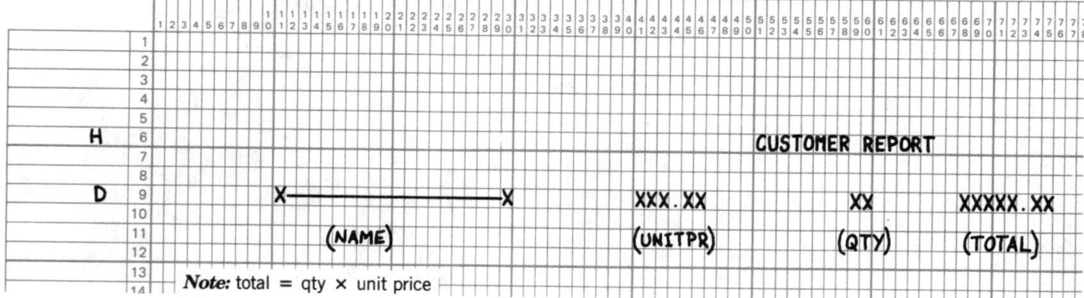

2. Consider the following and write an RPG program to produce the results indicated.

Systems Flowchart

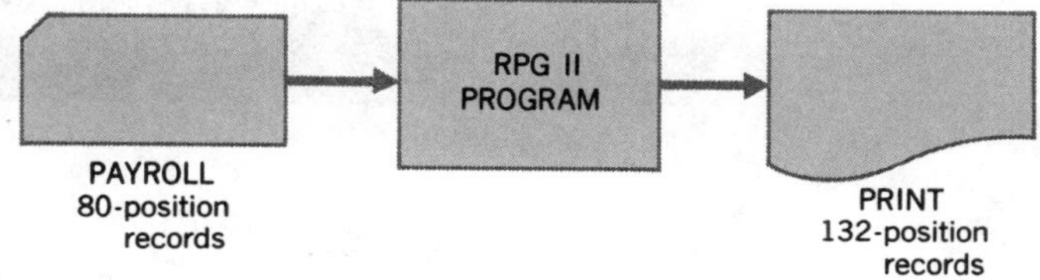

PAYROLL Record Layout

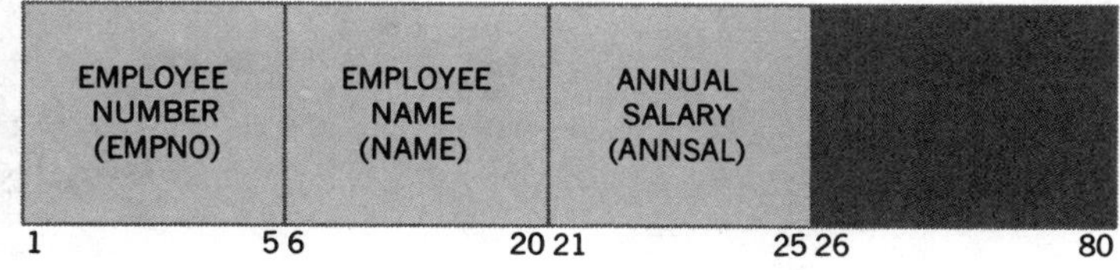

PRINT Printer Spacing Chart

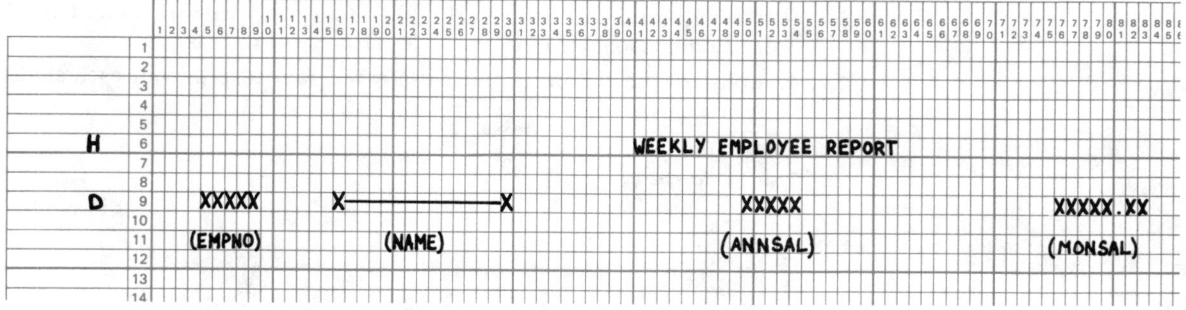

Notes

a. Columns 26-8Ø are not used in this program.
b. MONSAL = ANNSAL / 12.

3. Consider the following and write an RPG program to create a master sales file from input sales disk records.

Systems Flowchart

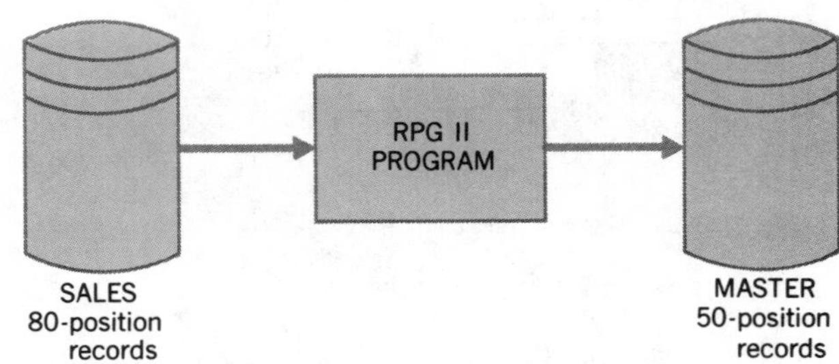

SALES Record Layout

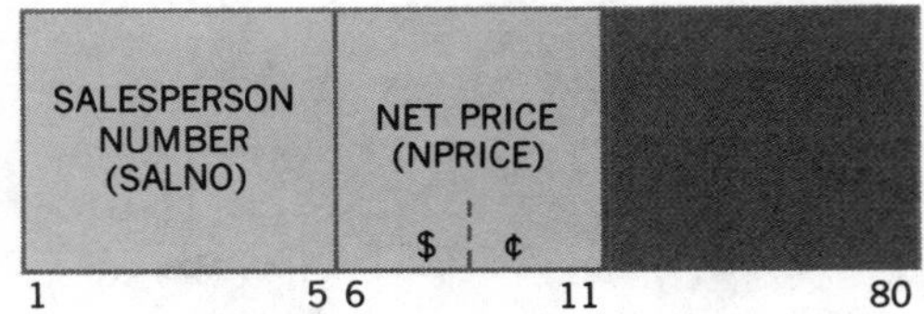

The output file is created on magnetic disk with the following data fields.

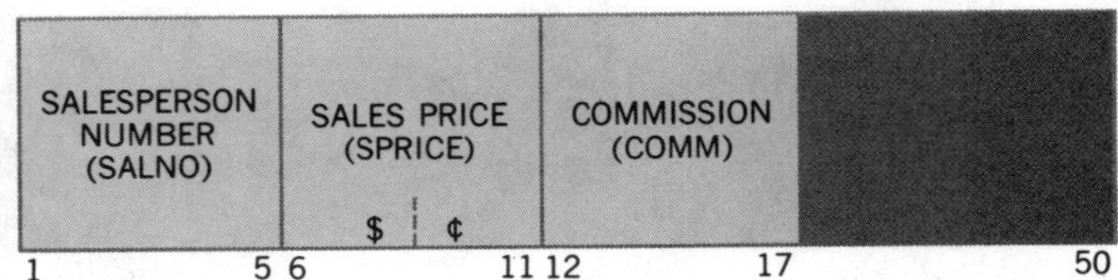

Notes

a. The output disk records are unblocked.
b. Output sales price is equal to the input net price with an added 5% sales tax.
c. Commission is 2Ø% of the price *exclusive* of the tax.

4. Consider the following and write a program to print out each student's name and four exam scores.

Systems Flowchart

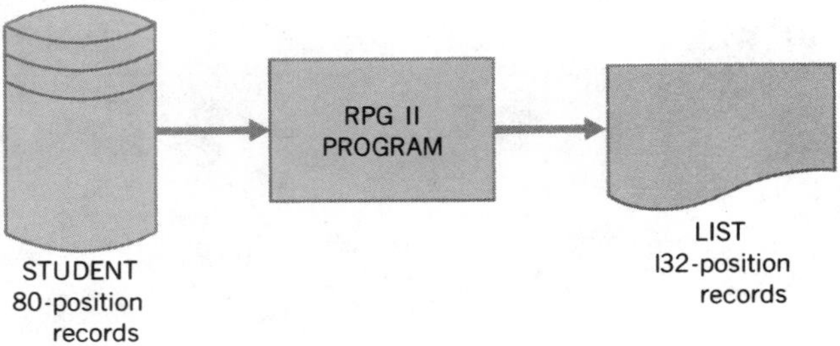

The input is student class records with the following format.

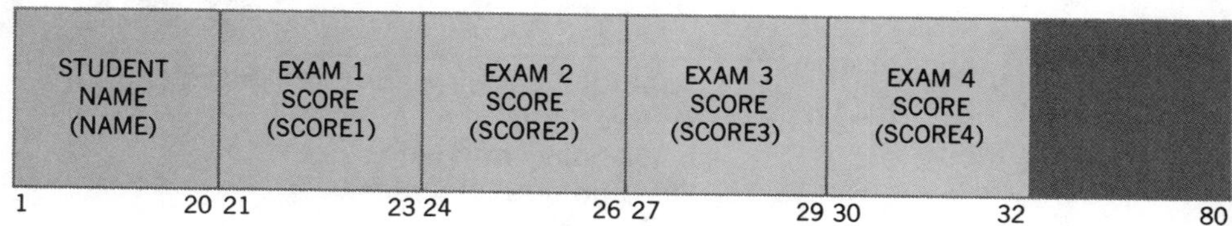

Each output line should contain Student name and the four scores, spaced anywhere on the line. As an added assignment, in this problem you are asked to prepare your own Printer Spacing Chart first. (There is one at the back of this text.)

Notes

a. Class average should be rounded to the nearest integer (i.e., 89.5 = 9Ø).
b. The first line should include the heading CLASS GRADES.

CHAPTER 2

The Printing of Reports

Objectives

- To provide an in-depth understanding of the characteristics of printed output.
- To reinforce the RPG II coding rules.
- To indicate the RPG II coding specifications for printing reports.
- To indicate the major types of editing performed with printed output and to specify how RPG II is used for editing.
- To provide an understanding of the different types of reports typically generated in business organizations and how RPG II is used to produce them.

I. Special Considerations for Printed Output

The printed report is the primary form of output for many computer runs. It is the output form that will be used by management for decision-making purposes and by the operating staff to assist them in their day-to-day activities.

Tape and disk output, created as intermediate products to be used for future reference or processing, are created with efficiency in mind. Fields within tape and disk records are produced as concisely as possible to conserve space and decrease processing time.

The printed report, however, is written with the user in mind. It is designed to be **user-friendly**, that is, clear and easy to interpret. Several characteristics, not applicable to other forms of output, must be considered when printing reports.

A. Headings

Every printed report generated by the computer should have headings that describe the report. The initial **report heading** should contain

Items in a Report Heading

1. A clear and concise title of the report.
2. The date of the run.
3. Page numbers for multiple-page reports.

In addition to the main heading that describes the overall report, there are usually other headings that describe the fields to be printed. In Figure 2.1, for example, two lines were used for the field description heading; *both* lines must be described in the program.

Figure 2.1
Illustration of printed output with more than one heading line.

		CUSTOMER REPORT	JULY, 19xx	→ Report Heading
NAME	AMOUNT OF PURCHASE	AMOUNT OF CREDIT	TOTAL DUE	} Field Description Headings
L B JONES	$1,325.22	$21.10	$1,304.12	} Output Data

B. Spacing and Skipping

Printed output is printed on **continuous forms** (see Figure 2.2) that will be separated into individual sheets after printing. Programs must indicate the alignment of output so that the spacing of lines is appropriate. Moreover, the heading should begin on a specific line of each page of the continuous form so that each individual sheet will have the same identifying data.

Advancing the paper a fixed number of lines is called **spacing**. In RPG, the programmer can space the form one, two, or three lines before or after a line is printed. In addition, the RPG programmer can advance the paper to a specific line. Advancing the paper to a specific line is called **skipping**.

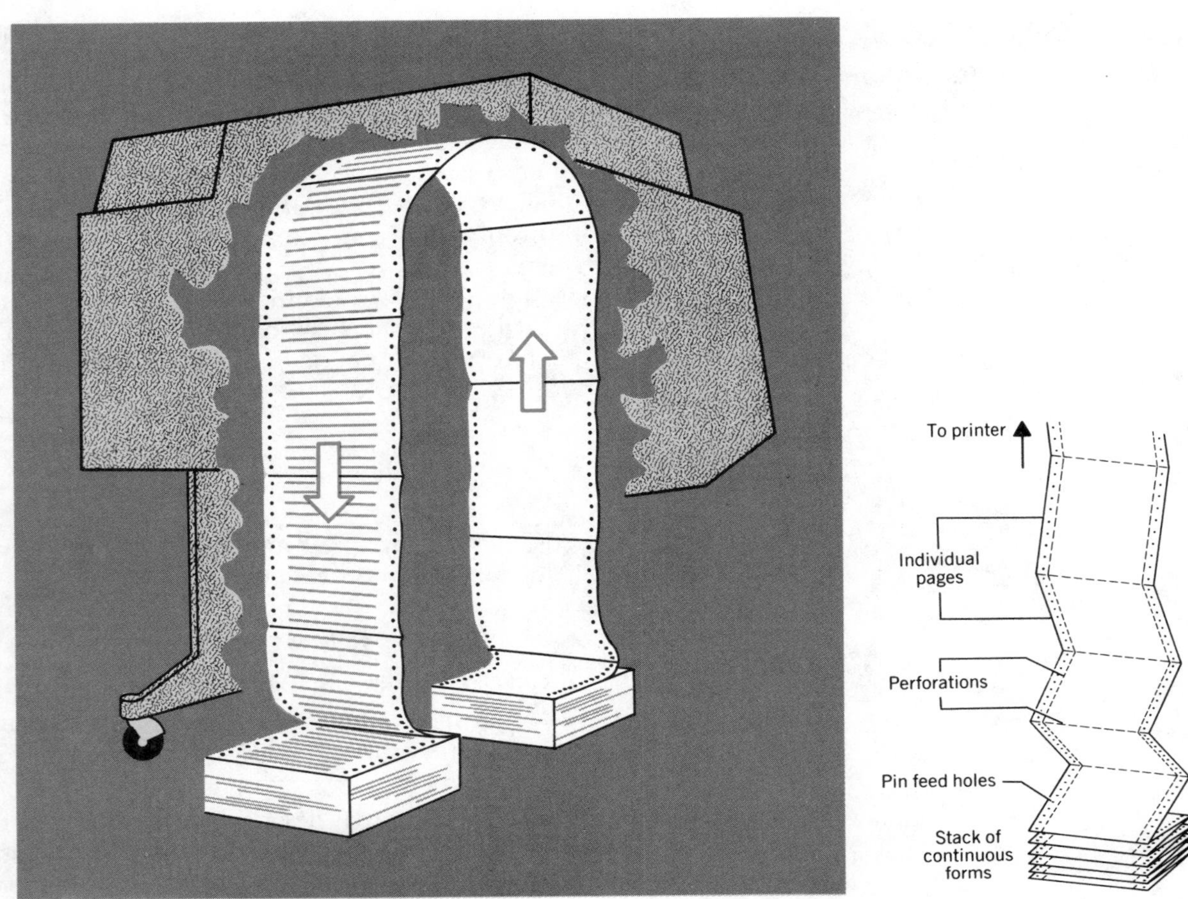

Figure 2.2
Continuous forms. (Courtesy IBM.)

Consider the following excerpt from an RPG Output Specifications form.

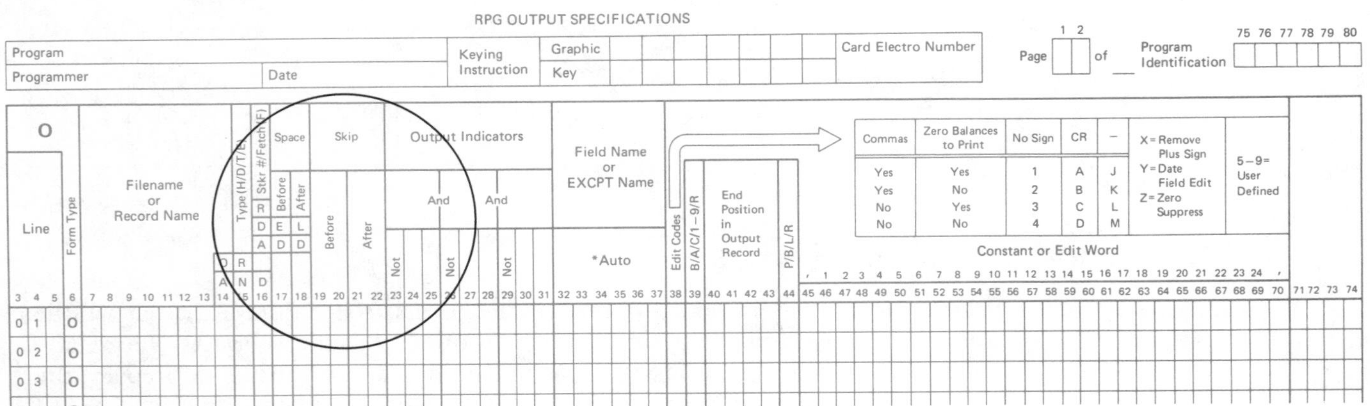
RPG OUTPUT SPECIFICATIONS

Program | Keying Instruction | Graphic | Key | Card Electro Number | Page of | Program Identification
Programmer | Date

O
Line | Form Type | Filename or Record Name | Type (H/D/T/E) | Stkr #/Fetch (F) | OR / AND / ADD / DEL | Space: Before, After | Skip: Before, After | Output Indicators: Not, And, Not, And, Not | Field Name or EXCPT Name | *Auto | Edit Codes | B/A/C/1–9/R | End Position in Output Record | P/B/L/R | Constant or Edit Word

Commas	Zero Balances to Print	No Sign	CR	–
Yes	Yes	1	A	J
Yes	No	2	B	K
No	Yes	3	C	L
No	No	4	D	M

X = Remove Plus Sign
Y = Date Field Edit
Z = Zero Suppress
5–9 = User Defined

01 O
02 O
03 O
04 O

The SPACE fields, columns 17 and 18, can be coded with 1, 2, or 3 to denote single, double, or triple spacing. The numbers 1, 2, or 3 are the only acceptable entries on many systems. You can space *before* a line is printed by using column 17 or *after* a line is printed by using column 18. To advance the paper both before and after printing, use both columns 17 and 18.

The SKIP fields enable the output to print on a specific line. You usually skip to the beginning of a page to print the first heading or to the end of a page to print totals by coding the line number in the BEFORE or AFTER columns of the SKIP field.

Many standard continuous forms have 72 lines, although there are numerous form sizes available. Typically, headings are printed on line 6 and the last output line is printed on line 66 to allow for top and bottom margins, but other conventions can be used.

SKIP options are essential for proper spacing of preprinted forms. **Preprinted forms** are specially designed documents such as bills, checks, and invoices that are sent to clients or customers. Since they require precise printing on specific lines, the SKIP option is frequently used. See Figure 2.3 for an illustration of a preprinted form.

If the programmer does not code the SPACE or SKIP fields on the Output Specifications, the computer will assume single spacing. An assumption of this type made by the system in the absence of specific coding is referred to as a system **default**.

C. Alignment of Data

As previously illustrated, printed output is designed to be as easy to read as possible. Use of top and bottom margins and proper spacing between lines is one method to facilitate the reading of a document. Another is to space data evenly across the page.

The Printer Spacing Chart is used to map out where data will be placed to ensure proper alignment. It is prepared by the systems analyst or the programmer prior to any coding.

D. Editing

As noted, to maximize efficiency, card, tape, and disk data are designed to be as concise as possible. For example, decimal points, dollar signs, and commas are always omitted from input records.

Printed output, on the other hand, should contain all special symbols that

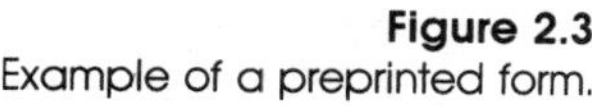

Figure 2.3
Example of a preprinted form.

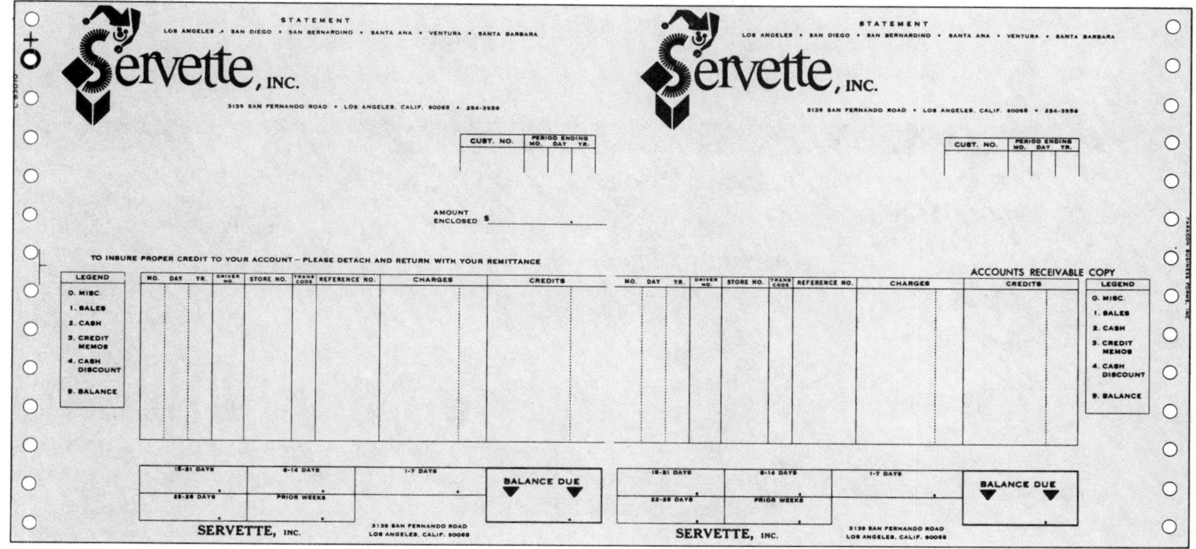

STATEMENT

LOS ANGELES • SAN DIEGO • SAN BERNARDINO • SANTA ANA • VENTURA • SANTA BARBARA

Servette, INC.

3139 SAN FERNANDO ROAD • LOS ANGELES, CALIF. 90065 • 254-3936

CUST. NO.	PERIOD ENDING MO.	DAY	YR.

AMOUNT ENCLOSED $ ________ .

TO INSURE PROPER CREDIT TO YOUR ACCOUNT – PLEASE DETACH AND RETURN WITH YOUR REMITTANCE

LEGEND
0. MISC.
1. SALES
2. CASH
3. CREDIT MEMOS
4. CASH DISCOUNT
9. BALANCE

NO.	DAY	YR.	DRIVER NO.	STORE NO.	TRANS CODE	REFERENCE NO.	CHARGES	CREDITS

15-21 DAYS	8-14 DAYS	1-7 DAYS	BALANCE DUE
22-28 DAYS	PRIOR WEEKS		

SERVETTE, INC. 3139 SAN FERNANDO ROAD LOS ANGELES, CALIF. 90065

STATEMENT

LOS ANGELES • SAN DIEGO • SAN BERNARDINO • SANTA ANA • VENTURA • SANTA BARBARA

Servette, INC.

3139 SAN FERNANDO ROAD • LOS ANGELES, CALIF. 90065 • 254-3936

CUST. NO.	PERIOD ENDING MO.	DAY	YR.

ACCOUNTS RECEIVABLE COPY

NO.	DAY	YR.	DRIVER NO.	STORE NO.	TRANS CODE	REFERENCE NO.	CHARGES	CREDITS

LEGEND
0. MISC.
1. SALES
2. CASH
3. CREDIT MEMOS
4. CASH DISCOUNT
9. BALANCE

15-21 DAYS	8-14 DAYS	1-7 DAYS	BALANCE DUE
22-28 DAYS	PRIOR WEEKS		

SERVETTE, INC. 3139 SAN FERNANDO ROAD LOS ANGELES, CALIF. 90065

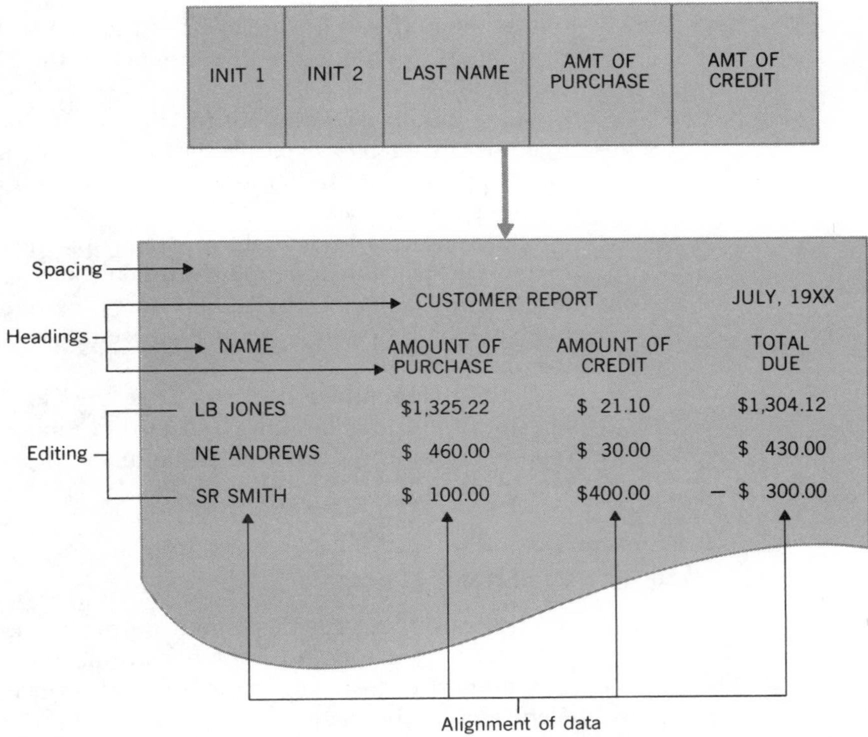

Figure 2.4
Summary of most common items to be considered for printed output.

will improve the readability of the data. The use of such symbols is called **editing**. Typically, editing consists of

> ***Editing Features***
>
> 1. Insertion of dollar signs, commas, and decimal points.
> 2. Printing of a minus sign or CR for negative quantities.
> 3. Suppression of leading zeros.
> 4. Use of a floating dollar sign: i.e., \$57.25 rather than \$ 57.25.

Figure 2.4 provides a summary of the most common items to be considered when preparing printed output.

II. RPG Coding for Printed Output

A. Initial Coding Line on Output Specifications Form

Figure 2.5 lists the fields on the Output Specifications form that must be coded for the first line of the form.

These fields are discussed below.

1. Filename

The filename is the same name as defined on the File Description form. It is only necessary to code the filename once on the Output form. This name, as all names in RPG, is coded beginning in the left-most position of the field. Unfilled right-most positions are left blank. A maximum of eight characters is permitted as a filename, and the name should be meaningful.

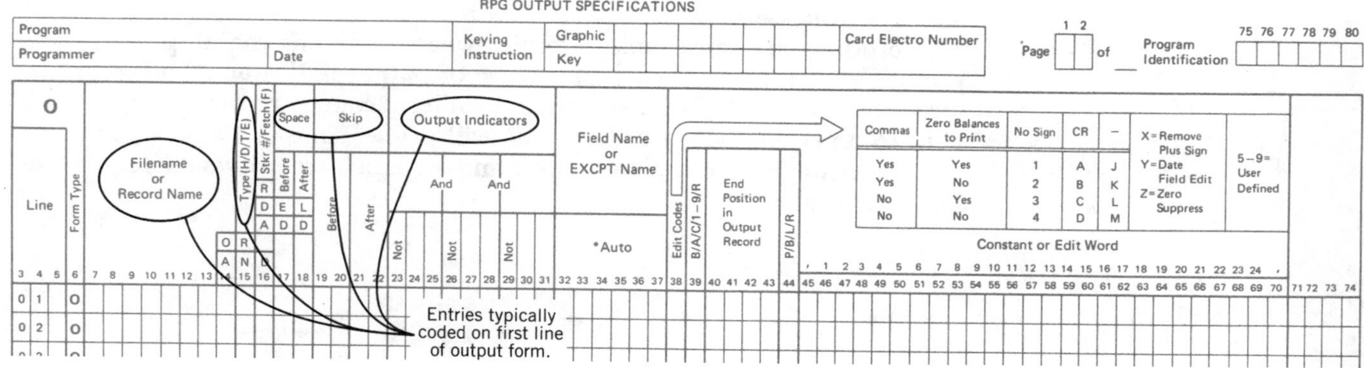

Figure 2.5
Entries coded on the first line of the Output Specifications form.

2. Type

The initial coding line must indicate whether the lines directly following the first will be describing a

Heading (H).
Detail line (D).
Total line (T).

Usually, the first group of lines will describe a heading, followed by descriptions for detail lines and then total lines.

3. Space or Skip

The programmer should indicate what paper-advancing options are desired. You may

1. Space one, two, or three lines before or after printing by coding 1, 2, 3 in columns 17-18.
2. Skip to a specific line before or after printing by coding the line number in columns 19-22. Note that to skip to line 3, for example, you must code Ø3, not 3 itself.

It is possible to use more than one of these Space and Skip options together. For example, you can skip to line 6 before printing and double space after printing by coding

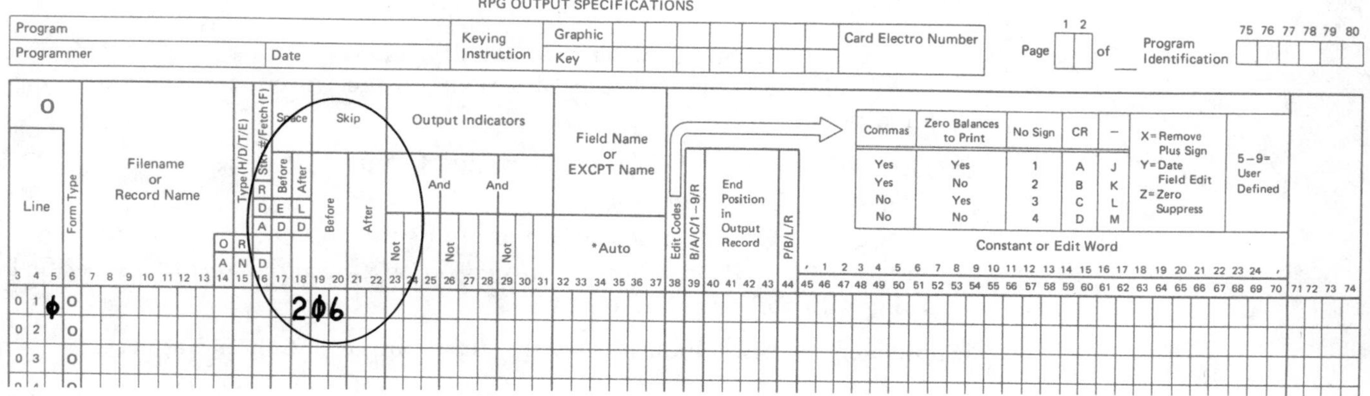

4. Output Indicators
The programmer must indicate under what conditions the output line is to print. This is accomplished with the use of **output indicators**. The record indicators set up on the File Description form for incoming records are frequently used to determine when a detail line will print. Thus, if the Ø1 indicator is turned on for all input records, printing an input record would require the following coding.

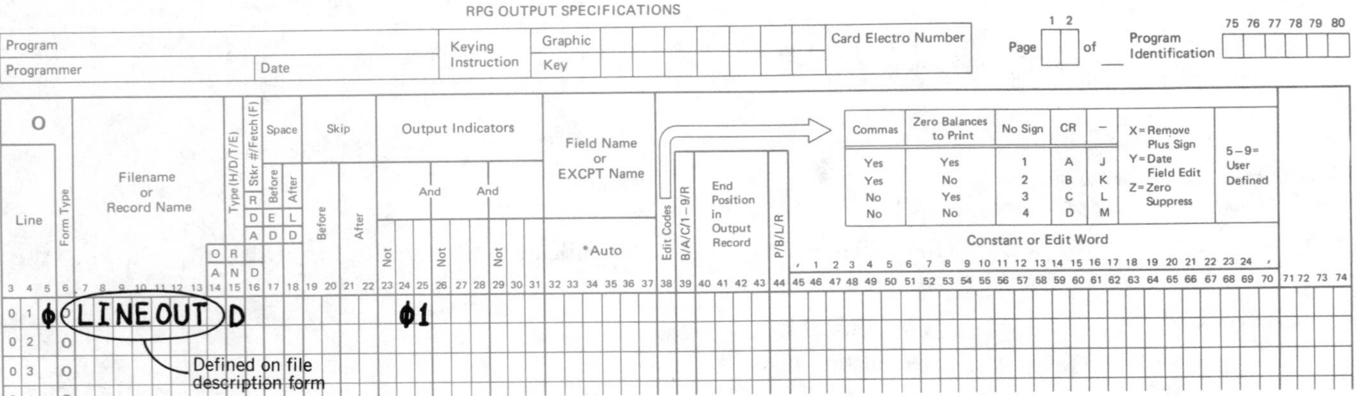

Sometimes, indicators turned on during processing will also be used to control detail printing. You may, for example, wish to print a detail line only if the result of a specific computation is zero. Or you might wish to print a line only if the result is not zero. You can program for printing by specifying that certain indicators should be on or off. A NOT condition in the indicator fields may be used to test for the absence of an indicator. That is, by coding N in an indicator field, printing will occur only if the indicator is off. Indicators are specified with two digits, that is, Ø1, Ø2, ... up to 99.

B. Listing Detail Data in RPG: An Overview

Consider the specification in Figure 2.6. The RPG File and Input Specifications forms for the program that will list input data are given in Figure 2.7. When each record is printed on one or more lines of output, this is referred to as **detail printing**. An in-depth view of the Output Specifications form will be provided since this controls detail printing (see Figure 2.8 for an illustration).

1. Coding Output Specifications for Detail Lines
If the detail line is the first to be described on the Output form, the first line will indicate

FILENAME — Same as on File Description form.
TYPE — D (for Detail).
SPACE — 1, 2, or 3, either before or after printing.
INDICATORS — The indicator "turned on" by the input record is specified along with any others necessary.

Subsequent lines will indicate how the detail output line should appear.

Figure 2.6
Problem definition for sample problem.

Systems Flowchart.

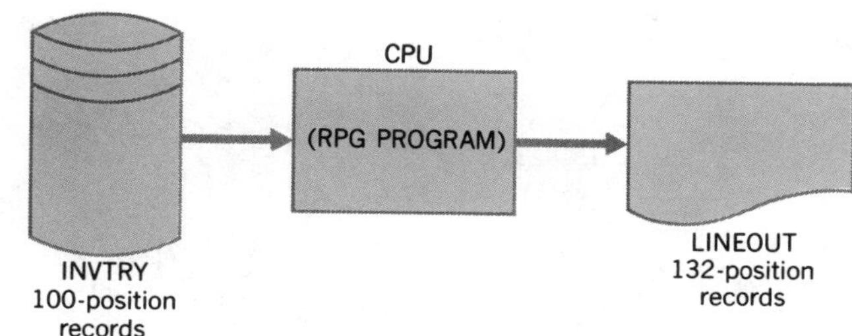

INVTRY Record Layout

NAME OF SUPPLIER (NAME)	ADDRESS OF SUPPLIER (ADDRES)	ITEM SUPPLIED (ITEM)	WAREHOUSE STORED (WAREHS)	UNUSED	CODE
1 20	21 40	41 60	61 62	63 99	100

Code = S

LINEOUT Printer Spacing Chart

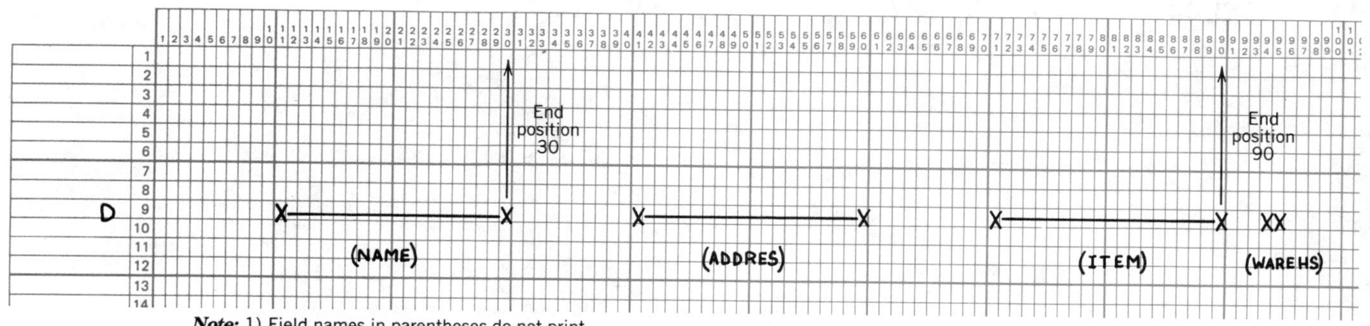

Note: 1) Field names in parentheses do not print
2) Field names are the same as those used in the RPG Program

2. Printing Fields and Constants

a. Fields to be Printed Typically, detail lines print some of, or all, the data that has been read in from input records. The field names defined on the Input form are left-justified; that is, the field name is coded beginning in column 32. Result fields defined on the Calculation form may also be printed.

The END POSITION IN OUTPUT RECORD, columns 4Ø-43 of the Output form, is always coded on the same line as the field name, to indicate the right-most print position in which the field should print. A Printer Spacing Chart is used to determine the actual end position in the output record. This end position will have a numeric value, and, like all numeric entries, it must be right-justified.

RPG CONTROL AND FILE DESCRIPTION SPECIFICATIONS

Program | Programmer | Date | Keying Instruction: Graphic, Key | Card Electro Number | Page 1 2 of | Program Identification 75 76 77 78 79 80

Control Specifications

For the valid entries for a system, refer to the RPG reference manual for that system.

H — Line (3–5); Form Type (6); Size to Compile (7–9); Object Output (10); Listing Options (11); Size to Execute (12–14); Debug (15); Reserved (16–17); Currency Symbol (18); Date Format (19); Date Edit (20); Inverted Print (21); Reserved (22); Number of Print Positions (23–25); Alternate Collating Sequence (26); Reserved (27–36); Inquiry (37); Reserved (38–39); Sign Handling (40); 1 P Forms Position (41); Indicator Setting (42); File Translation (43); Punch MFCU Zeros (44); Nonprint Characters (45); Reserved (46); Table Load Halt (47); Shared I/O (48); Field Print (49); Formatted Dump (50); RPG to RPG II Conversion (51); Number of Formats (52–53); S/3 Conversion (54); Subprogram (55); CICS/DL/I (56); Transparent Literal (57); 58–74

Line	Form Type
01	H

File Description Specifications

For the valid entries for a system, refer to the RPG reference manual for that system.

F — Line (3–5); Form Type (6); Filename (7–14); File Type: I/O/U/C/D (15); File Designation: P/S/C/R/T/D/F (16); End of File: E (17); Sequence: A/D (18); File Format: F/V/S/M/D/E (19); Block Length (20–23); Record Length (24–27); Mode of Processing: L/R (28); Length of Key Field or of Record Address Field (29–30); Record Address Type: A/P/I/K (31); Type of File Organization or Additional Area: I/X/D/T/R/ or 2 (32); Overflow Indicator (33–34); Key Field Starting Location (35–38); Extension Code E/L (39); External Record Name (19–28); Device (40–46); Symbolic Device (47–52); Labels S/N/E/M (53); Name of Label Exit (54–59); Extent Exit for DAM / Storage Index (60–65); Continuation Lines: K (53), Option (54–59), Entry (60–65); A/U (66); File Addition/Unordered; Number of Tracks for Cylinder Overflow (67–68); Number of Extents (69); Tape Rewind: R/U/N (70); File Condition U1–U8, UC (71–72); 73–74

Line	Form Type	Filename	File Type	File Designation	File Format	Block Length	Record Length	Device
02	F	INVTRY	I	P	F	1ϕϕ	1ϕϕ	DISK
03	F	LINEOUT	O		F		132	PRINTER
04	F							
05	F							
06	F							

RPG INPUT SPECIFICATIONS

Program | Programmer | Date | Keying Instruction: Graphic, Key | Card Electro Number | Page 1 2 of | Program Identification 75 76 77 78 79 80

I — Line (3–5); Form Type (6); Filename or Record Name (7–14); Data Structure Name; OR / AND (14–16); Sequence (15–16); Number (1/N), E (17); Option (O), U, S (18); Record Identifying Indicator, **, or DS (19–20); External Field Name; Record Identification Codes 1 (Position 21–24, Not (N) 25, C/Z/D 26, Character 27), 2 (Position 28–31, Not (N) 32, C/Z/D 33, Character 34), 3 (Position 35–38, Not (N) 39, C/Z/D 40, Character 41); Stacker Select (42); P/B/L/R (43); Field Location: From (44–47), To (48–51); Data Structure: Occurs n Times, Length; Decimal Positions (52); RPG Field Name (53–58); Control Level (L1–L9) (59–60); Matching Fields or Chaining Fields (61–62); Field Record Relation (63–64); Field Indicators: Plus (65–66), Minus (67–68), Zero or Blank (69–70); 71–74

Line	Form Type	Filename or Record Name	Sequence	Record Identifying Indicator	Position	Not (N)	C/Z/D	Character	From	To	RPG Field Name
01	I	INVTRY	NS	ϕ1	1ϕϕ		C	S			
02	I								1	2ϕ	NAME
03	I								21	4ϕ	ADDRES
04	I								41	6ϕ	ITEM
05	I								61	62	WAREHS
06	I			ϕ2	1ϕϕ	N	C	S			
07	I										
08	I										
09	I										

Note: 1) NS is used for no sequence; any alphabetic characters could be used
2) Any number 01-99 could be used as a record identifying indicator
3) The 02 indicator is turned on when a record without an S in position 100 is read. If we failed to set an indicator when this happens, the computer will halt the run.

Figure 2.7
File and Input Specifications forms for sample problem.

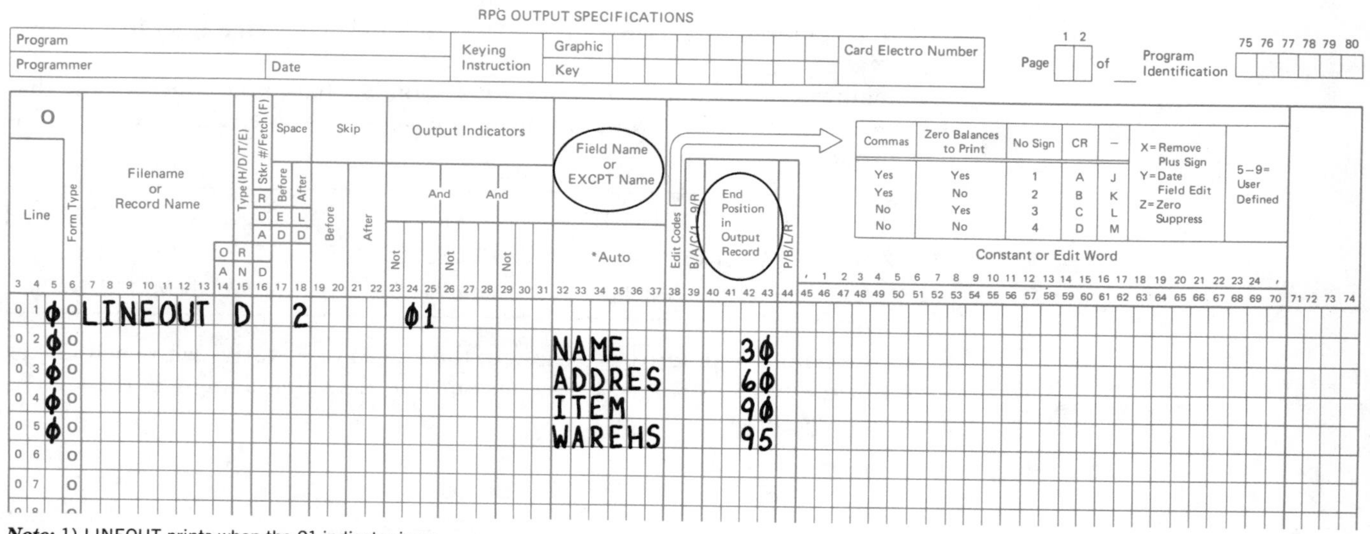
RPG OUTPUT SPECIFICATIONS

Line	Form Type	Filename or Record Name	Type (H/D/T/E)	Space Before	Output Indicators	Field Name or EXCPT Name	End Position in Output Record
01ϕ	O	LINEOUT	D	2	ϕ1		
02ϕ	O					NAME	3ϕ
03ϕ	O					ADDRES	6ϕ
04ϕ	O					ITEM	9ϕ
05ϕ	O					WAREHS	95

Note: 1) LINEOUT prints when the 01 indicator is on.
2) LINEOUT is defined on the File Description form.

Figure 2.8
Output Specifications form for sample problem.

That is, if the Name field is to be printed ending in print position 127, the coding would be as follows.

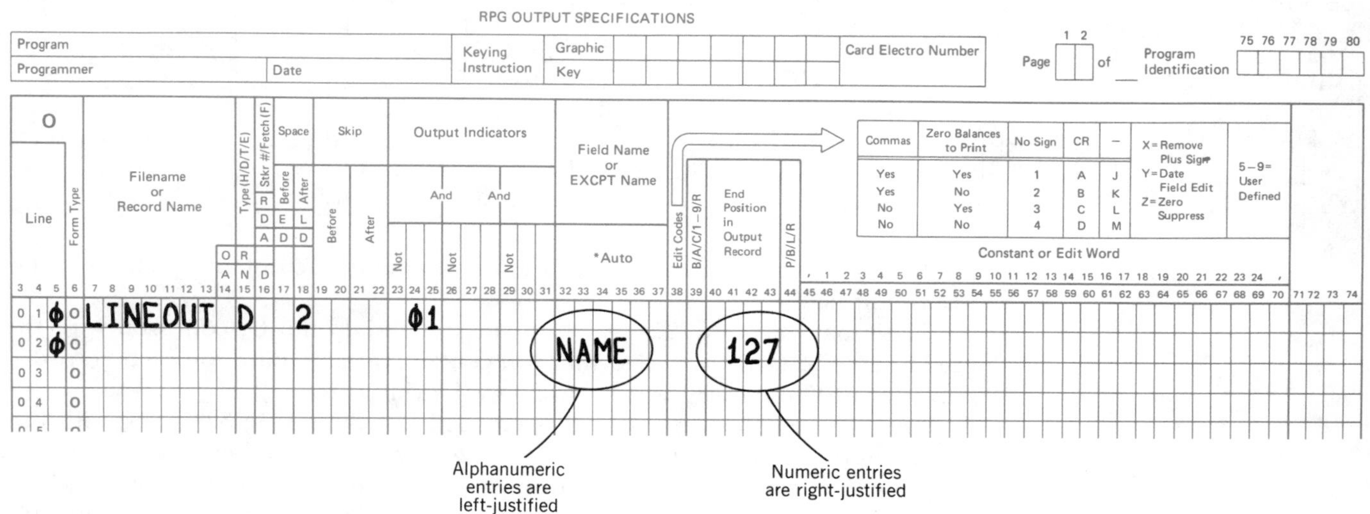
RPG OUTPUT SPECIFICATIONS

Line	Form Type	Filename or Record Name	Type (H/D/T/E)	Space Before	Output Indicators	Field Name or EXCPT Name	End Position in Output Record
01ϕ	O	LINEOUT	D	2	ϕ1		
02ϕ	O					NAME	127

Alphanumeric entries are left-justified
Numeric entries are right-justified

Line Ø1Ø describes information about the *line* to be printed. Subsequent entries describe the fields within the line. Hence, the first line of each record description does *not* contain field description specifications. The description of each field begins on the line following the initial one. Keep in mind that the field names used must be identical to the ones defined on the Input form and the Calculations form. The end positions must be identical to those specified on the Printer Spacing Chart.

b. Constants Input fields contain data that changes from record to record. Hence, we define an area of each record with a field name and we treat the data to be entered as **variable**, that is, it is unknown and changes during every run.

Sometimes the data to be printed is **constant**, such as a message or note that is known initially and will always remain the same. Consider the following sample output.

SEX = M	ROBERT REDFORD	111 SEXY ST.	GARY, MONT 11782
SEX = M	PAUL NEWMAN	782 BLUEEYES AVE.	ST. PAUL, KAN 11825
SEX = F	BROOKE SHIELDS	997 CALVIN ST.	NOME, N.M. 11828

All the names and addresses change; the sex, M or F, varies with each line as well. But the phrase "SEX = " is a constant that does not change. It is coded as a constant as follows.

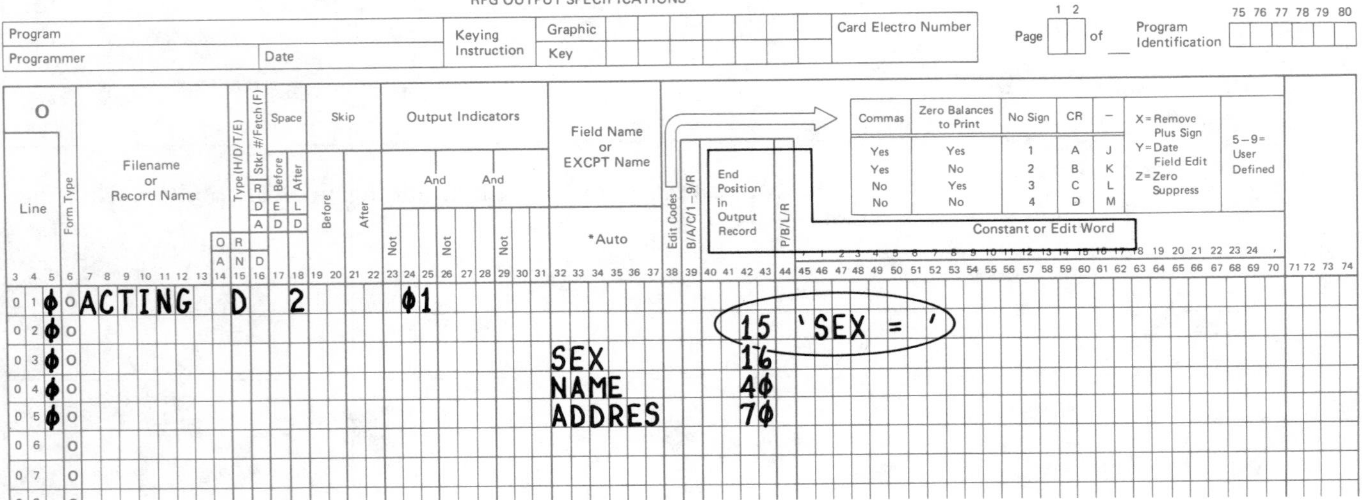
RPG OUTPUT SPECIFICATIONS

Line	Form Type	Filename or Record Name	Type (H/D/T/E)	Space After	Output Indicators	Field Name or EXCPT Name	End Position in Output Record	Constant or Edit Word
01Ø	O	ACTING	D	2	Ø1			
02Ø	O						15	'SEX = '
03Ø	O					SEX	16	
04Ø	O					NAME	4Ø	
05Ø	O					ADDRES	7Ø	

Single quotes (or apostrophes) are used to define a constant or **literal** in the Constant field.

Note that the word 'SEX = ' as a constant should not be confused with the field name SEX. SEX is a field that will contain variable data for each record—an M or F. The phrase 'SEX = ' will always print as is.

Variable fields that are to print are coded in columns 32-37, along with the End Position in Output Record. *Constants* to print are coded in single quotes beginning in column 45 along with the End Position in Output Record. Including the quote marks, constants begin in column 45 and cannot go beyond column 7Ø.

C. Printing Headings

As previously noted, all output reports should contain headings to identify the report.

1. Denoting a Heading Line

Headings are denoted on the Output Specifications form with the use of H in the TYPE field. Typically, headings are printed on the first print line of a page.

The first print line may, for example, be specified as line 6, thereby creating a margin with five blank lines at the top of the page. The following coding instructs the computer to skip to line 6 before printing.

RPG OUTPUT SPECIFICATIONS

```
01ΦO LINEOUT H    Φ6
02 O
03 O
```

Since headings are usually to print first, they are typically coded on the same line as the Filename. The Filename need only be specified once, at the beginning; then the Filename field remains blank unless there is another Output file.

You will recall that the SKIP option is used when you wish to print on a specific line and the SPACE option is used to obtain single, double, or triple spacing. If you wish to skip to a specific line after printing the heading or to space the form one, two, or three lines after printing, you would code the appropriate entry in the columns indicated.

2. Indicators Used for Headings

The printing of output is produced in RPG under the control of output indicators. For detail printing, a detail record indicator or some other indicator must be on if printing is to occur.

To print headings, use two special indicators: 1P and OF. The 1P or **first page indicator** is automatically turned on at the beginning of the RPG II Logic Cycle and then turned off after the heading lines print. Thus the following will cause a heading to print at the very beginning of the run, that is, at the top of the first page.

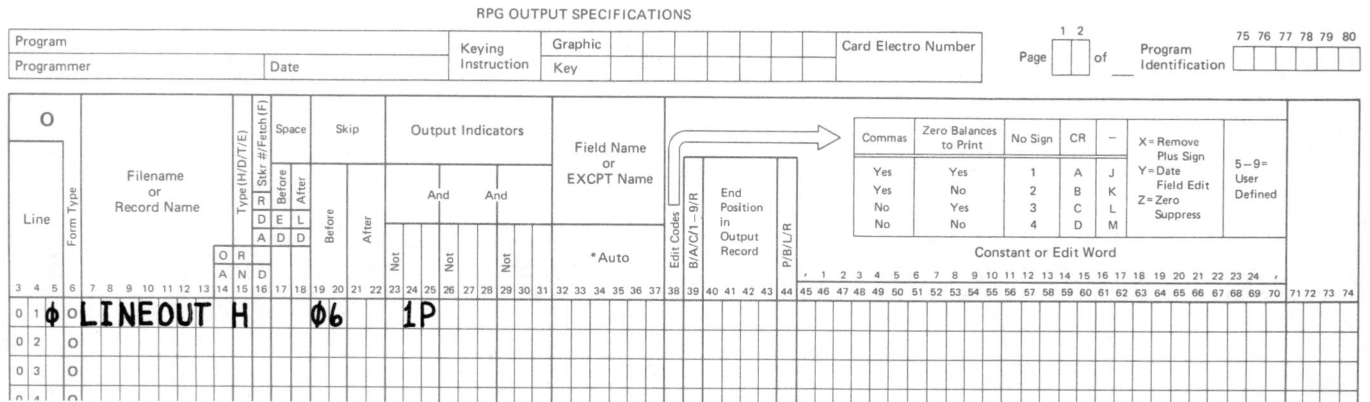

RPG OUTPUT SPECIFICATIONS

```
01ΦO LINEOUT H    Φ6     1P
02 O
03 O
```

The Filename LINEOUT would be coded only once, on the first line of the Output Specifications form. Thus, it would usually be included with the heading description instead of with the detail description since the heading will print first.

Recall that printed output prints on continuous forms. If you have a very long report, and you specify the printing of headings on the first page only, you would have

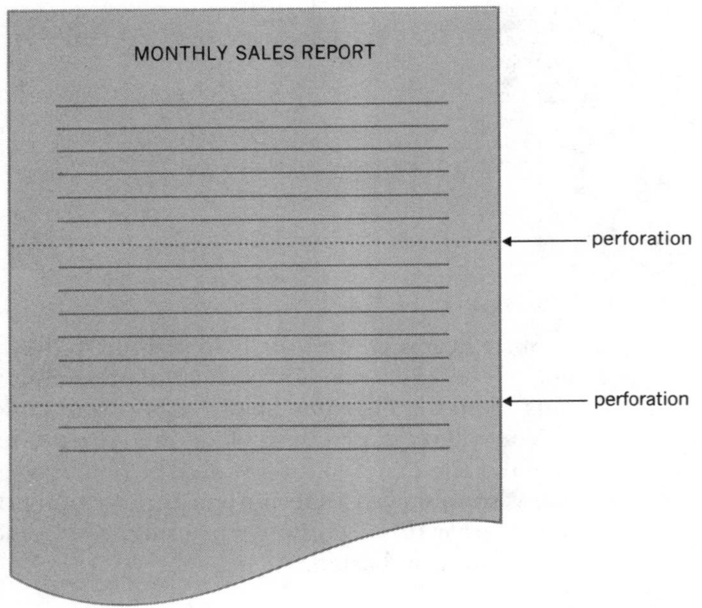

Most frequently, the report is split at the perforation into individual pages. By specifying the 1P indicator only, the first page would contain a heading; all subsequent pages would not be identified.

It would, of course, be better to print a heading on the top of each page. To obtain headings on the top of each page, use the Overflow indicator, **OF**, as well as 1P. On the Output Specifications form, then, you must specify that the heading should print if *either* the 1P indicator or the OF indicator is on.

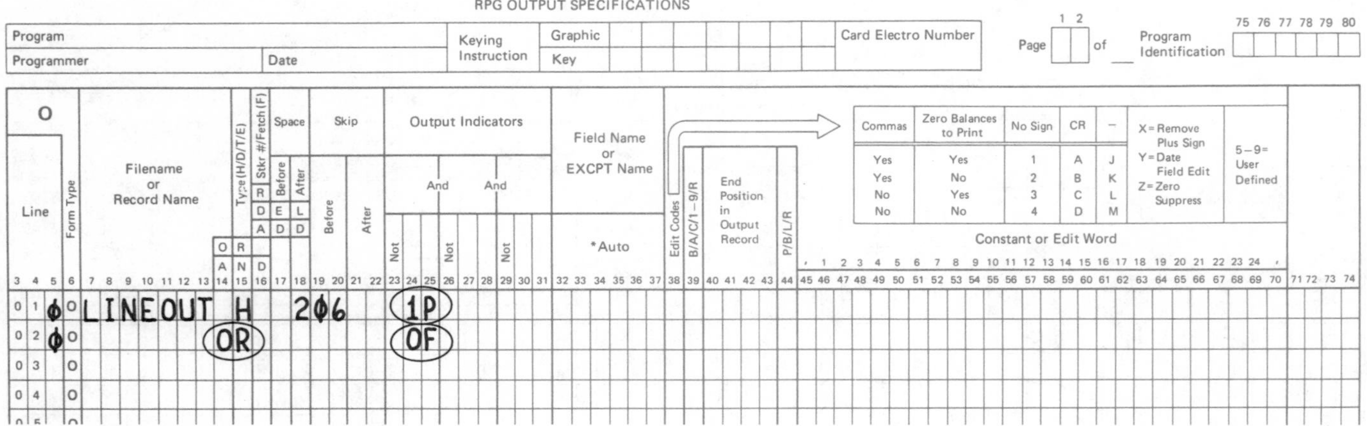
RPG OUTPUT SPECIFICATIONS

Line	Form Type	Filename or Record Name	Type (H/D/T/E)	Space Before	Space After	Skip Before	Skip After	Output Indicators
01ɸ	O	LINEOUT	H	2		ɸ6		1P
02ɸ	O		OR					OF
03	O							
04	O							
05	O							

This means you will print a heading at the beginning of the run and every time an end-of-page condition occurs.

The OF indicator is based on a hardware feature that keeps track of page overflow. You must indicate that your program will use this indicator by including it on the File Description Specifications form.

RPG CONTROL AND FILE DESCRIPTION SPECIFICATIONS

Control Specifications

Line	Form Type
01	H

File Description Specifications

Line	Form Type	Filename	File Type	File Designation	File Format	Record Length	Overflow Indicator	Device
02ϕ	F	INVTRY	I	P	F	1ϕϕ		DISK
03ϕ	F	LINEOUT	O		F	132	OF	PRINTER
04	F							
05	F							
06	F							

3. Printing the Constants

The first line of an output report, then, would typically include: (1) Filename, (2) H in Type, (3) Space and/or Skip option, (4) the 1P indicator. The second line would specify 'OR OF', meaning that if the 1P or OF indicator is on, a heading should print.

On subsequent lines, you specify the exact format for your output. Typically, headings consist of a constant that describes the report. You indicate the rightmost or last position in which you want each field to print, as in the following illustration.

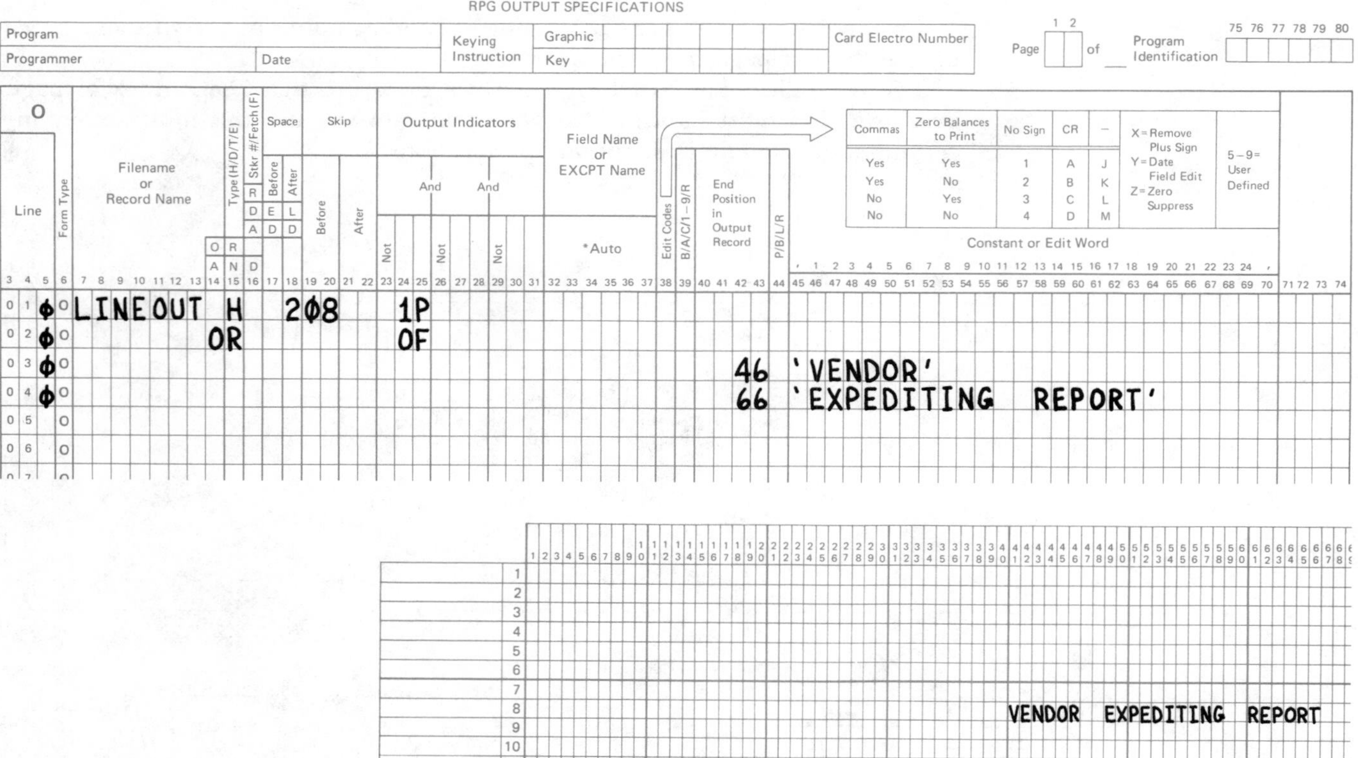
RPG OUTPUT SPECIFICATIONS

```
01 O LINEOUT H   2 08   1P
02 O        OR          OF
03 O                                    46 'VENDOR'
04 O                                    66 'EXPEDITING   REPORT'
```

VENDOR EXPEDITING REPORT

As with detail records, the specifications for each output line begin on the line following the indicator specification, in this instance, line 3.

4. Printing a Date with the Heading

It is usually desirable to include the date of the run as part of the heading. Accomplishing this in RPG is a simple matter: Use the reserved word UDATE in the Field Name columns. UDATE is an abbreviation for user date and is an internally stored entry. Coding UDATE will cause a date consisting of month, day, and year to print. To edit the date so that it prints with slashes as month/day/year, code a Y in the Edit Code column of the line.

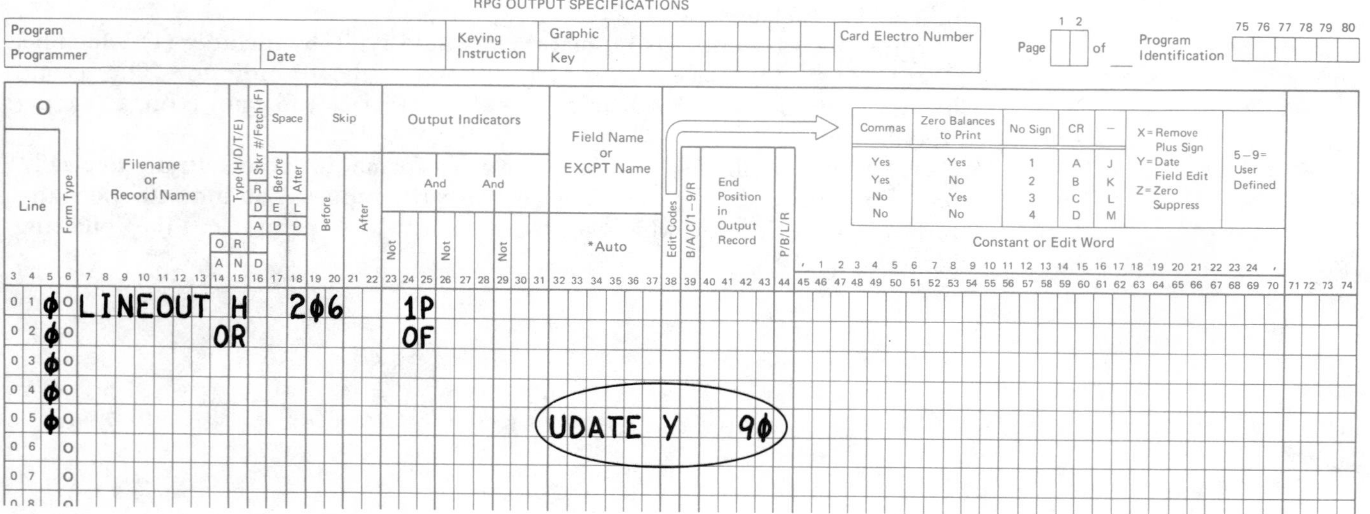
RPG OUTPUT SPECIFICATIONS

```
01 O LINEOUT H   2 06   1P
02 O        OR          OF
03 O
04 O
05 O                         UDATE Y    90
```

Note that the filename LINEOUT is specified only once.

5. Printing a Page Number With the Heading

To instruct the computer to print page numbers, include the reserved word PAGE with the heading. The reserved word PAGE will print 1 on the first page, 2 on the second, and so on. To print the word or constant 'PAGE' along with the number, code

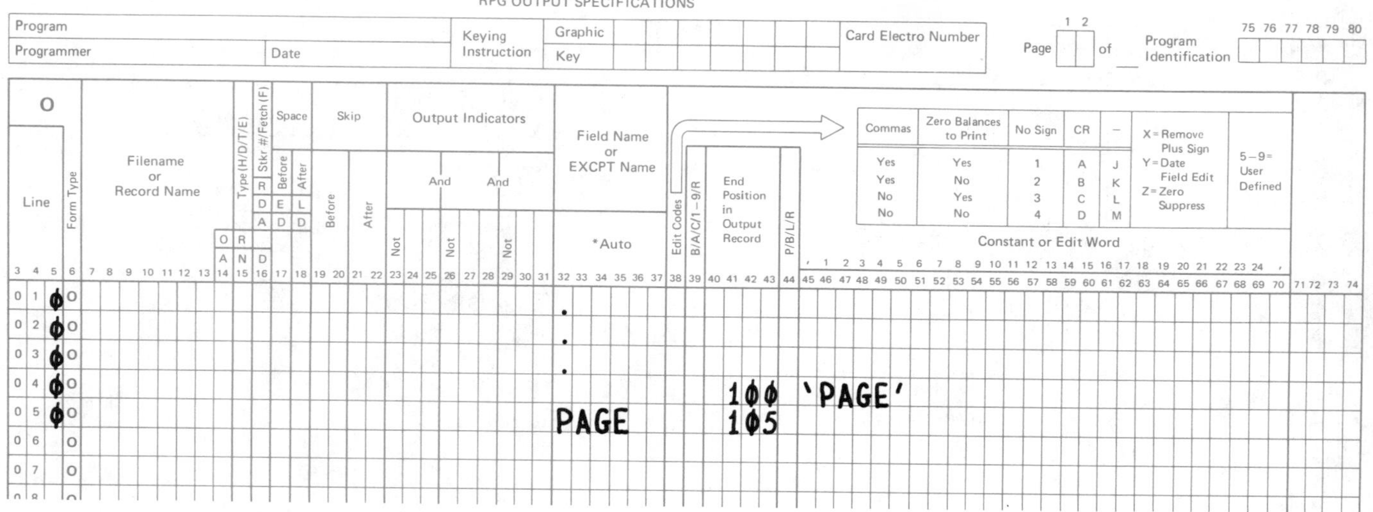

When the constant PAGE prints it will appear in print positions 97-1ØØ. The actual page number will always be located in a four-position field, in this case positions 1Ø2-1Ø5. Leading zeros will be replaced with blanks. For example, ØØØ1 will print as 1.

6. Printing a Heading That Specifies Field Names

Frequently one heading line is not sufficient to describe the report adequately. A second heading line that indicates field names is often desirable. The Output Specifications form on the top of the next page illustrates the RPG coding for the Printer Spacing Chart specified in Figure 2.9.

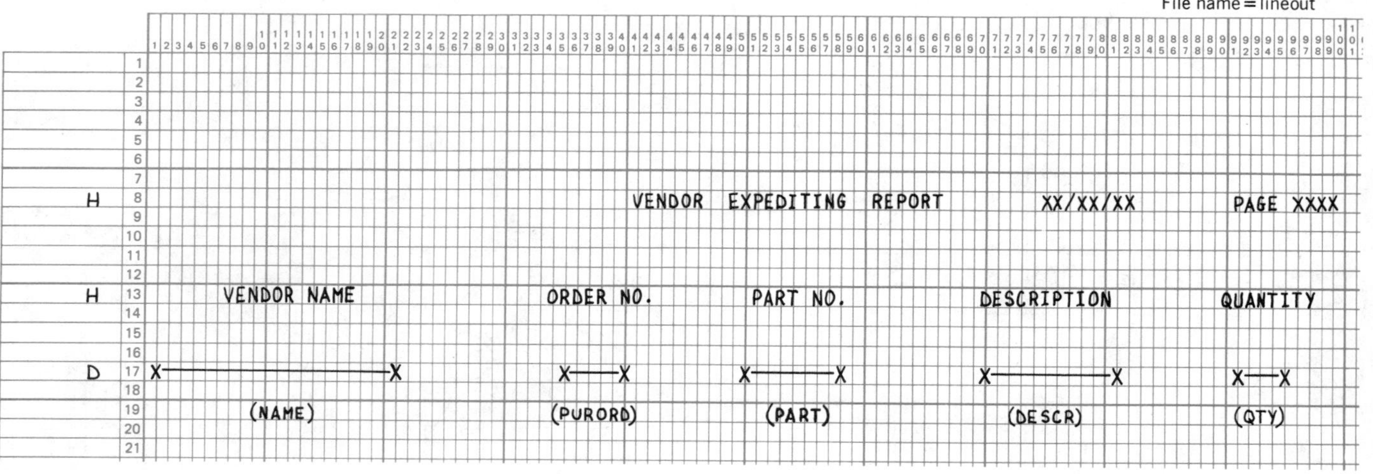

Figure 2.9
Sample Printer Spacing Chart.

RPG OUTPUT SPECIFICATIONS

Program | Keying Instruction | Graphic | Card Electro Number | Page of | Program Identification
Programmer | Date | Key

```
0 1 ØOLINEOUT H  2Ø8   1P
0 2 ØO        OR       OF
0 3 ØO                                    46 'VENDOR'
0 4 ØO                                    66 'EXPEDITING  REPORT'
0 5 ØO                         UDATE Y    82
0 6 ØO                                    94 'PAGE'
0 7 ØO                         PAGE       99
0 8 ØO           H  33     1P
0 9 ØO        OR       OF
1 0 ØO                                    17 'VENDOR NAME'
1 1 ØO                                    42 'ORDER NO.'
1 2 ØO                                    58 'PART NO.'
1 3 ØO                                    8Ø 'DESCRIPTION'
1 4 ØO                                    97 'QUANTITY'
1 5 ØO           D  11     Ø1
1 6 ØO                         NAME       21
1 7 ØO                         PURORD     4Ø
1 8 ØO                         PART       58
1 9 ØO                         DESCR      81
2 0 ØO                         QTY        95
```

Note that headings print on 1P or OF indicators in sequence. That is, the first heading coded is the first one printed.

Constants can be specified any way that is convenient for the programmer. Thus, the first heading could have specified VENDOR EXPEDITING REPORT as

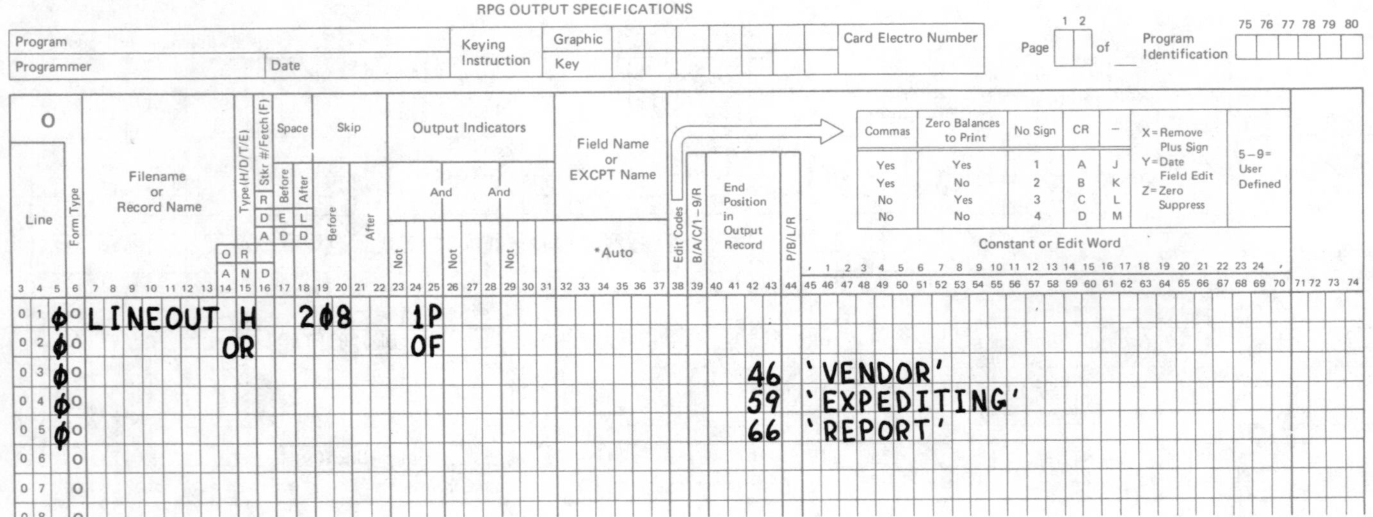

RPG OUTPUT SPECIFICATIONS

Program | Keying Instruction | Graphic | Card Electro Number | Page of | Program Identification
Programmer | Date | Key

```
0 1 ØOLINEOUT H  2Ø8   1P
0 2 ØO        OR       OF
0 3 ØO                                    46 'VENDOR'
0 4 ØO                                    59 'EXPEDITING'
0 5 ØO                                    66 'REPORT'
```

D. Printing Total Lines

Totals can print under numerous conditions.

Types of Totals
1. End of each page.
2. End of each group of records.
3. End of the report.

A T coded in TYPE on the Output Specifications form is used for specifying a total line. Testing for the end of a group of records is specified with level indicators that will be considered in Chapter 6. Page totals can be printed using the OF indicator to indicate when an end-of-page condition has been reached. Reports totals can be printed using the **Last Record** (LR) **indicator** to signal when the last record has been processed. Recall that the LR indicator will be turned on only after the last record has been read and processed.

1. Printing an End-of-Job Message

Suppose you wish to print a total line at the end of a report that states

```
***    END OF OUTPUT REPORT    ***
```

You would add the following to your description for the output file:

RPG OUTPUT SPECIFICATIONS

Line	Form Type	Filename or Record Name	Type (H/D/T/E)	Space Before	Space After	Skip Before	Skip After	Output Indicators	Field Name or EXCPT Name	Edit Codes	B/A/C/1-9/R	End Position in Output Record	P/B/L/R	Constant or Edit Word
01Ø	O		T	2				LR						
02Ø	O											75		'*** END OF OUTPUT'
03Ø	O											88		'REPORT ***'
04	O													
05	O													

2. Printing a Final Total

Most often we use total lines to print accumulated totals. As noted in Chapter 1, the Calculation Specifications form must be coded if you wish to add to totals. Suppose, for example, that indicator Ø1 is turned on for all input records and that you wish to compute the sum of all input AMT fields. The next chapter will discuss options that may be used for performing calculations, but, for now, assume the following coding for this example.

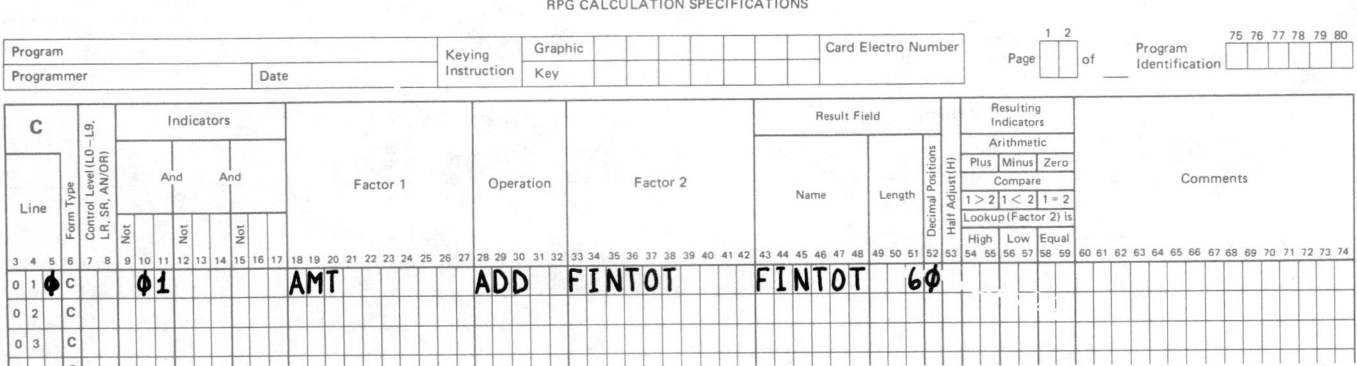

RPG CALCULATION SPECIFICATIONS

```
01ØC      Ø1      AMT       ADD  FINTOT    FINTOT  6Ø
02 C
03 C
```

The field called AMT will be added to FINTOT, which accumulates all AMTs. FINTOT is six positions long. To print FINTOT at the end of the report, code the following on the Output Specifications form:

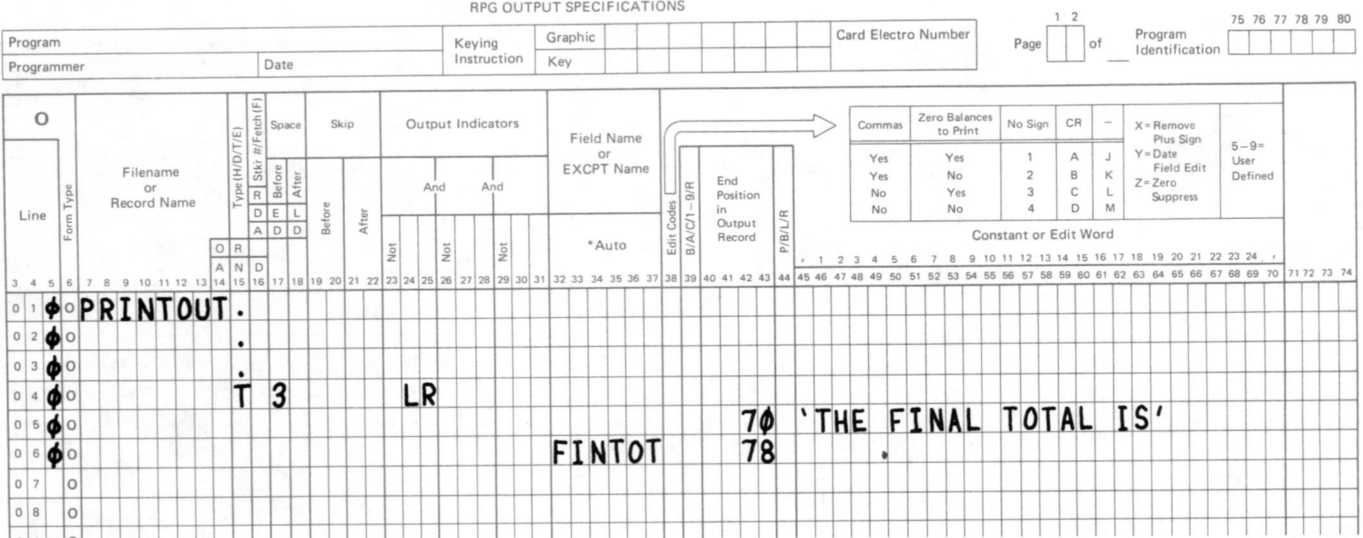

RPG OUTPUT SPECIFICATIONS

```
01ØOPRINTOUT.
02ØO        .
03ØO        .
04ØO        T 3      LR
05ØO                                7Ø 'THE FINAL TOTAL IS'
06ØO                 FINTOT         78
07 O
08 O
```

The total line prints only when the last record indicator is on, which occurs when there are no more records to process.

3. Printing a Count of the Number of Records Processed

Suppose you wish to print the total number of records processed on each page. You would accumulate this total in a field called COUNT, which increments by one each time an input record is processed. Assume indicator Ø1 is turned on for all input. The coding of the Calculation form is as follows (calculations will be covered in more detail in the next chapter).

RPG CALCULATION SPECIFICATIONS

Line	Form Type	Control Level	Indicators	Factor 1	Operation	Factor 2	Result Field Name	Length	Decimal Positions
01Ø	C		Ø1	1	ADD	COUNT	COUNT	3	Ø
02	C								
03	C								
04	C								

For each record, add one to COUNT. Hence, COUNT will contain the total number of records processed. At the end of each page, you must reset COUNT so that it begins at zero again, counting records on the next page. To clear COUNT, code B in the BLANK AFTER field (column or position 39) on the Output form. This indicates that after COUNT prints it should start at Ø again. The total lines, then, are as follows.

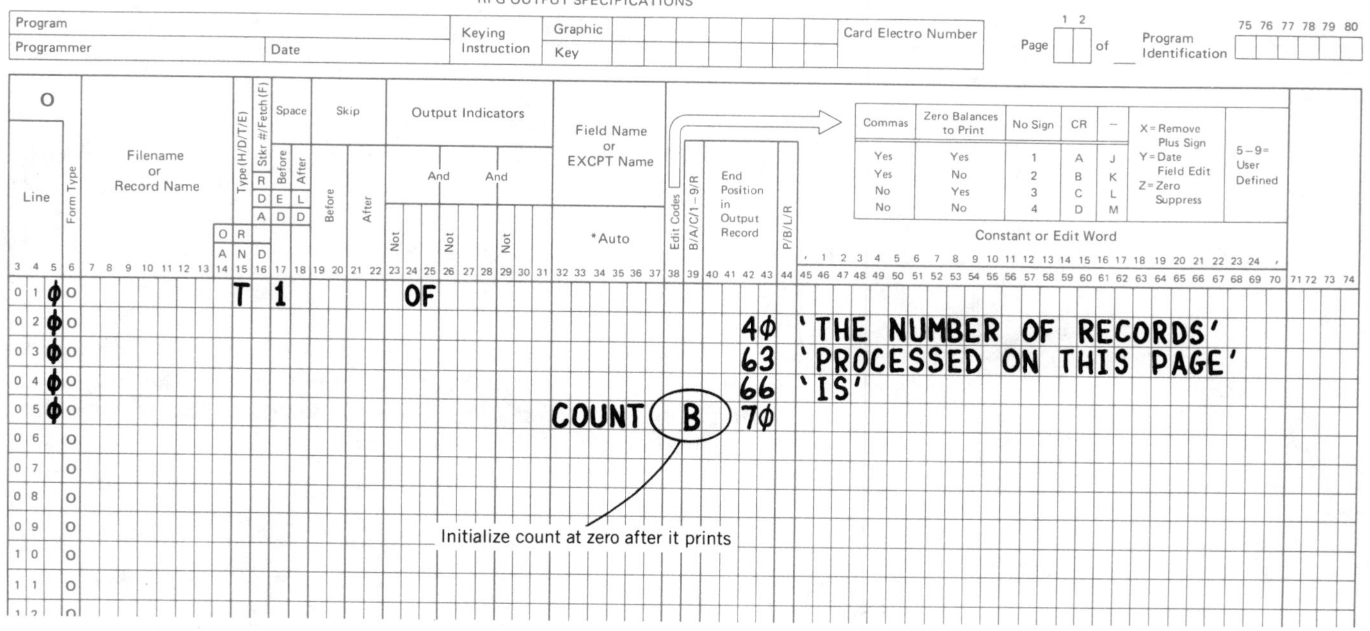

RPG OUTPUT SPECIFICATIONS

Line	Form Type	Type (H/D/T/E)	Space After	Output Indicators	Field Name	Blank After	End Position in Output Record	Constant or Edit Word
01Ø	O	T	1	OF				
02Ø	O						4Ø	'THE NUMBER OF RECORDS'
03Ø	O						63	'PROCESSED ON THIS PAGE'
04Ø	O						66	'IS'
05Ø	O				COUNT	B	7Ø	

Initialize count at zero after it prints

The constant 'THE NUMBER OF RECORDS PROCESSED ON THIS PAGE IS' and the value of COUNT will print at the end of each page. The T line will print each time there is a page overflow condition. But you must also instruct the computer to print a T line after the last record has been processed, even if there is no overflow condition. To accomplish this last page printing, code the following.

RPG OUTPUT SPECIFICATIONS

Line	Form Type	Filename or Record Name	Type (H/D/T/E)	Space Before	Space After	Skip	Output Indicators	Field Name or EXCPT Name	Edit Codes	B/A/C/1–9/R	End Position in Output Record	P/B/L/R	Constant or Edit Word
01	O		T		1		OF						
02	O	OR					LR						
03	O										40		'THE NUMBER OF RECORDS'
04	O										63		'PROCESSED ON THIS PAGE'
05	O										66		'IS'
06	O							COUNT		B	70		
07	O												
08	O												

Total line printing will be considered in more detail in the next chapter.

E. Basic Editing Considerations

As previously noted, printed output must be edited so that it is as easy to read as is possible. Numeric data fields are edited to include, for example,

Basic Editing

1. Decimal points.
2. Commas.
3. Dollar signs.
4. Suppression of leading zeros so that ØØØ8, for example, prints as 8.
5. Printing of a minus sign or the letters CR for a negative amount.

Decimal points, commas, dollar signs, and CR take up space on the output form and must be counted when determining the number of positions in a field.

Most of the editing specified in the above box can be accomplished with the use of the EDIT CODE field on the Output Specifications form.

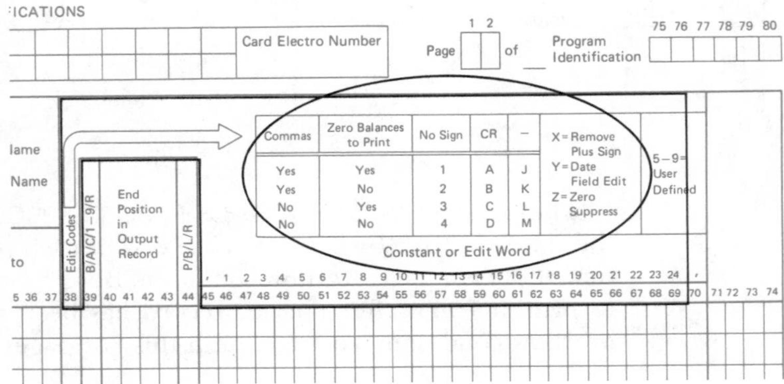

Suppose, for example, you wish to print an amount field so that

1. Commas are included.
2. Zero balances do not print.
3. CR prints for negative amounts.

Code B in column 38 to achieve this editing, as indicated by the instructions on the Output form.

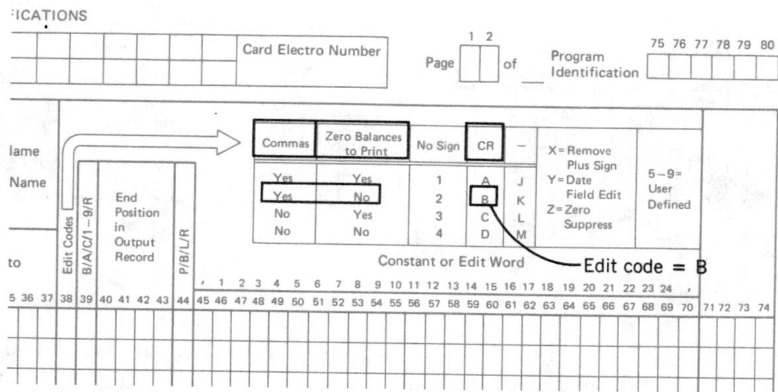
ICATIONS
Card Electro Number
Page 1 2 of
Program Identification 75 76 77 78 79 80
Commas | Zero Balances to Print | No Sign | CR | –
Yes | Yes | 1 | A | J
Yes | No | 2 | B | K
No | Yes | 3 | C | L
No | No | 4 | D | M
X = Remove Plus Sign
Y = Date Field Edit
Z = Zero Suppress
5–9 = User Defined
Edit Codes
B/A/C/1–9/R
End Position in Output Record
P/B/L/R
Constant or Edit Word
Edit code = B

Similarly, suppose you wish to omit commas, print a zero balance, and not include any sign; you would use a 3 in column 38:

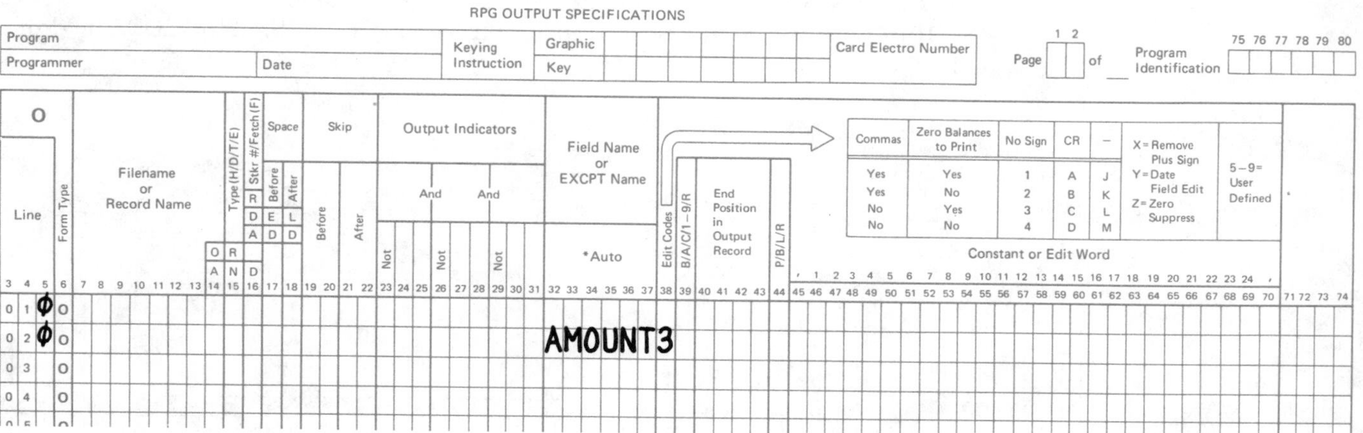
RPG OUTPUT SPECIFICATIONS
Program
Programmer
Date
Keying Instruction
Graphic
Key
Card Electro Number
Page 1 2 of
Program Identification 75 76 77 78 79 80
O
Line
Form Type
Filename or Record Name
Type (H/D/T/E)
Stkr #/Fetch (F)
Space Before After
Skip Before After
Output Indicators And And Not Not Not
Field Name or EXCPT Name
*Auto
Edit Codes
B/A/C/1–9/R
End Position in Output Record
P/B/L/R
Commas | Zero Balances to Print | No Sign | CR | –
Yes | Yes | 1 | A | J
Yes | No | 2 | B | K
No | Yes | 3 | C | L
No | No | 4 | D | M
X = Remove Plus Sign
Y = Date Field Edit
Z = Zero Suppress
5–9 = User Defined
Constant or Edit Word
0 1 Ø O
0 2 Ø O AMOUNT3
0 3 O
0 4 O

Editing of this type can be performed on *numeric* fields only. The RPG programmer indicates numeric input fields by coding column 52, DECIMAL POSITIONS, of the Input Specifications form for incoming fields or the corresponding position on the Calculation form for fields defined during arithmetic operations.

Note, too, that the use of any EDIT CODE automatically

1. Suppresses leading zeros (so that ØØ7 prints as 7). **Zero suppression** means that nonsignificant zeros are replaced with blanks.
2. Places a decimal point in the appropriate position on the output line as indicated in the DECIMAL POSITIONS field of the Input Calculations form.

Consider the following.

RPG INPUT SPECIFICATIONS

Line	Form Type	Filename or Record Name	Sequence	Record Identifying Indicator	Field Location From	Field Location To	Decimal Positions	RPG Field Name
01Ø	I	PAY	NS	Ø1				
02Ø	I				1	5		EMPNO
03Ø	I				6	1Ø	2	AMT
04Ø	I				11	12	Ø	HRS
05	I							
06	I							

Since EMPNO has a blank in column 52 of the Input form, it is treated as an alphanumeric field and cannot be edited. AMT and HRS, however, are numeric fields. AMT is five positions long. The 2 in DECIMAL POSITIONS instructs the computer to treat AMT as a dollars-and-cents field, even though the actual decimal point does not appear within the input field; that is, it has an **implied decimal point**. Using any one of the EDIT CODES specified in the Output form will cause a decimal point to print in the appropriate place. Thus AMT will print as XXX.XX, where the Xs indicate the digits of the amount field.

If HRS is to have just zero suppression, we put a Z in the EDIT CODE field of the Output form:

RPG OUTPUT SPECIFICATIONS

Line	Form Type	Field Name or EXCPT Name	Edit Codes
01Ø	O	AMT	3
02Ø	O	HRS	Z
03	O		
04	O		

Edit code key printed on the Output form:

Commas	Zero Balances to Print	No Sign	CR	–
Yes	Yes	1	A	J
Yes	No	2	B	K
No	Yes	3	C	L
No	No	4	D	M

X = Remove Plus Sign; Y = Date Field Edit; Z = Zero Suppress; 5–9 = User Defined

1. Using Edit Codes

We will now review the various Edit Codes that can be used and illustrate how they affect printed output.

If any Edit Code is specified in column 38,

1. Leading zeros will be suppressed. For example, ØØ8 will print as 8.

2. Decimal points will print where required. For example, AMT is defined in columns 21-25 with two decimal points and is stored as XXX$_\wedge$XX, where $_\wedge$ is an implied decimal point. AMT will print as XXX.XX with the actual decimal point.

We will now examine actual Edit Codes.

a. Edit Code = 1 An Edit Code of 1 results in the following.

1. Commas will print where appropriate.
2. Zeros, not blanks, will print for fields with contents of zero.

Example

RPG OUTPUT SPECIFICATIONS

Line	Form Type	Field Name or EXCPT Name	Edit Codes	End Position in Output Record
0 1 Ø	O	AMOUNT	1	25
0 2	O			
0 3	O			

Value of Amount as Input	*Edited Result*
1234$_\wedge$56	1,234.56
ØØ23$_\wedge$45	23.45
387$_\wedge$24	387.24
ØØØØ$_\wedge$ØØ	.ØØ

b. Edit Code = 2 An Edit Code of 2 results in the following.

1. Commas print where appropriate.
2. Blanks print if the field is zero.

Example

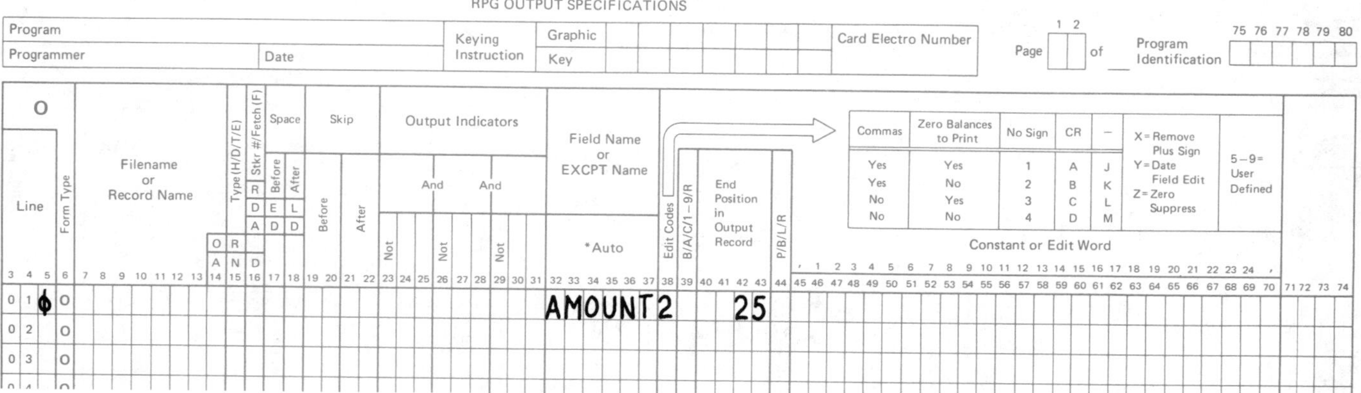

RPG OUTPUT SPECIFICATIONS

Line	Form Type	Field Name or EXCPT Name	Edit Codes	End Position in Output Record
0 1 Ø	O	AMOUNT	2	25
0 2	O			
0 3	O			

Value of Amount as Input	*Edited Result*
1234^56	1,234.56
ØØ23^45	23.45
387^24	387.24
ØØØØ^ØØ	(Blank)

The only difference between an Edit Code of 1 or 2 occurs when the field is zero.

c. *Edit Code = 3* An Edit Code of 3 results in the following.

1. Commas will not print.
2. Zero balances will print.

Example

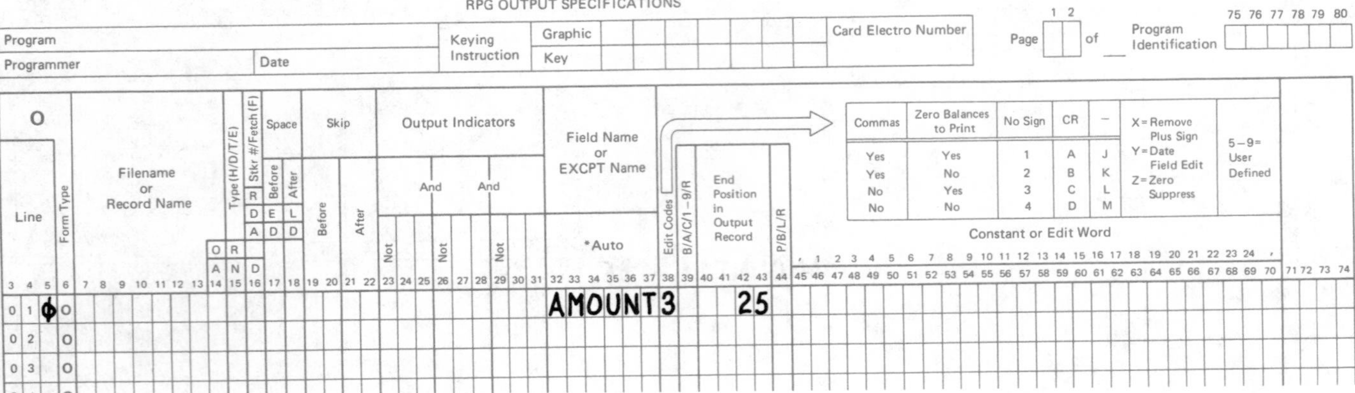

Value of Amount as Input	*Edited Result*
1234^56	1234.56
ØØ23^45	23.45
387^24	387.24
ØØØØ^ØØ	.ØØ

d. *Edit Code = 4*

1. No commas are printed.
2. Blanks print if the field is zero.

Example

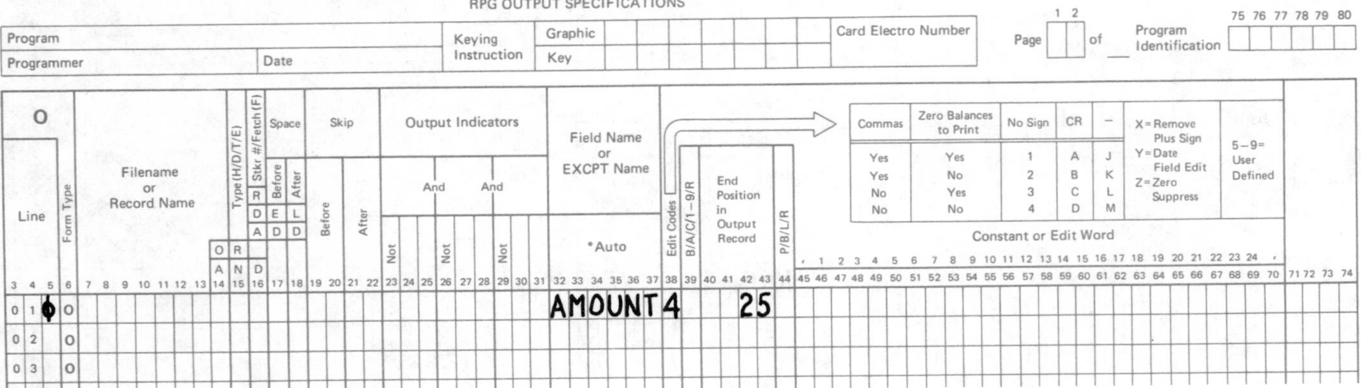

Value of Amount as Input	*Edited Result*
1234‸56	1234.56
ØØ23‸45	23.45
387‸24	387.24
ØØØØ‸ØØ	(blank)

e. Other Edit Codes Codes A-D and J-M are used if a field can contain a negative amount. For conciseness, signed fields are designated in input records with a sign over the right-most position of a field. Hence $38\overline{7}$ entered as input denotes -387. Only 3 positions are used to represent this signed field.

Unless otherwise specified, a sign will not print on the output. To print a minus sign for negative quantities, use codes J-M in the EDIT CODE field. The sign will print to the right of the number. J will cause the same editing as Edit Code 1, but it will also print a minus sign for negative values; similarly, K, L, and M edit the same as edit codes 2, 3, and 4, respectively, but minus signs are also printed for negative amounts. An Edit Code of A-D is used just like 1-4 or J-M except that CR will print for negative amounts. CR stands for Credit. Minus signs and the letters CR use storage positions in the output.

RPG OUTPUT SPECIFICATIONS

Program | Programmer | Date | Keying Instruction | Graphic | Key | Card Electro Number | Page of | Program Identification

Line | Form Type | Filename or Record Name | Type (H/D/T/E) | Stkr #/Fetch (F) | Space: Before, After | Skip: Before, After | Output Indicators: Not, And, Not, And, Not | Field Name or EXCPT Name | *Auto | Edit Codes | B/A/C/1–9/R | End Position in Output Record | P/B/L/R | Constant or Edit Word

Commas	Zero Balances to Print	No Sign	CR	–
Yes	Yes	1	A	J
Yes	No	2	B	K
No	Yes	3	C	L
No	No	4	D	M

X = Remove Plus Sign
Y = Date Field Edit
Z = Zero Suppress
5–9 = User Defined

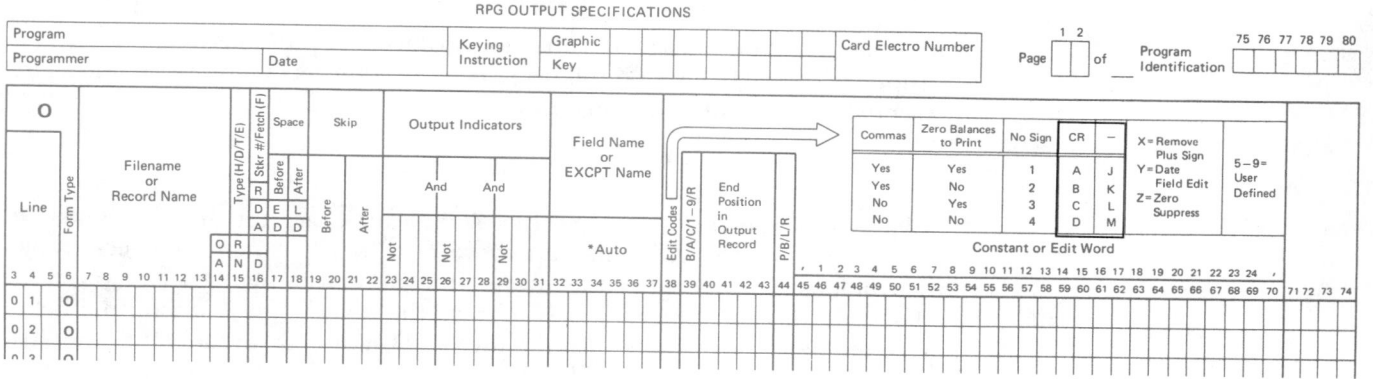

All Edit Codes perform zero suppression up to the decimal point in addition to the specified editing.

The following are samples of the type of editing that will be performed depending on the contents of the field and the Edit Code specified.

Unedited Contents of Field / ***Edit Code***	***1***	***2***	***3***	***4***	***A***	***B***	***C***	***D***	***J***	***K***	***L***	***M***
ØØØØØØ	Ø	(Blank)	Ø	(Blank)	Ø	(Blank)	Ø	(Blank)	Ø	(Blank)	Ø	(Blank)
ØØØØ‸ØØ[a]	.ØØ	(Blank)	.ØØ	(Blank)	.ØØ	(Blank)	.ØØ	(Blank)	.ØØ	(Blank)	.ØØ	(Blank)
ØØØ89$\overline{Ø}$[b]	89Ø	89Ø	89Ø	89Ø	89ØCR	89ØCR	89ØCR	89ØCR	89Ø–	89Ø–	89Ø–	89Ø–
ØØØ‸89Ø	.89Ø	.89Ø	.89Ø	.89Ø	.89ØCR	.89ØCR	.89ØCR	.89ØCR	.89Ø–	.89Ø–	.89Ø–	.89Ø–
54321‸54	54,321.54	54,321.54	54 321.54	54 321.54	54,321.54CR	54,321.54CR	54 321.54CR	54 321.54CR	54,321.54–	54,321.54–	54 321.54–	54,321.54–

[a] ‸ is the implied decimal point. In this instance, the Decimal Position for the field was specified as 2.

[b] –ØØØ89Ø is represented in a six-position field as ØØØ89$\overline{Ø}$.

2. Printing Dollar Signs

If a dollar sign is desired in the left-most position of an edited field, it could be coded as

RPG OUTPUT SPECIFICATIONS

Line	Form Type	Filename or Record Name	Field Name or EXCPT Name	Edit Codes	End Position in Output Record	Constant or Edit Word
01ϕ	O				54	'$'
02ϕ	O		AMT	2	6ϕ	
03	O					
04	O					

where AMT would be specified as having two decimal positions.

Suppose that AMT had the following content: ØØØ$_\wedge$84. Using the editing just presented, the output would print as

$				.	8	4

Blanks between the $ and the first significant character are usually to be avoided. For one thing, if this output were to be a payment or check, some unscrupulous person could easily change the amount to $<u>999</u>.84.

To avoid this situation, it is best to have the dollar sign *float* with the field; that is, the dollar sign should print in the position directly to the left of the first significant digit. Thus ØØØ$_\wedge$84 should print as $.84; ØØØ72$_\wedge$64 should print as $72.64, and so forth, with no spaces between the dollar sign and the first significant digit.

To float a dollar sign in RPG, include the '$' constant on the *same* line as the edited field.

RPG OUTPUT SPECIFICATIONS

Line	Form Type	Filename or Record Name	Field Name or EXCPT Name	Edit Codes	End Position in Output Record	Constant or Edit Word
01ϕ	O		AMT	2	6ϕ	'$' ← Dollar sign floats with field
02	O					
03	O					
04	O					

Where editing is to be performed and a **floating $** is to print:

1. Specify the edit characteristics.
2. Enter the '$' constant on the same line as the field to be edited.

The editing just described is considered basic editing. More advanced editing options can be specified with the use of the EDIT WORD field. Check your specifications manual for a complete description of the edit features available to the RPG II programmer.

The Printer Spacing Chart should indicate the type of editing desired. We will use the following conventions:

Notation	*Meaning*
XXX.XX	Print a five-digit field with a decimal point.
XXØ.XX	Same as the preceding, but zero suppress all integers.
XØX.XX	Zero suppress only the left-most two digits (ØØØ.26 will print as Ø.26).
XX.XX	The dollar sign floats with the field.

F. Summary

H, D, and T type records can be processed using the Output Specifications form. They are usually coded in the sequence shown. The filename need be specified only once, at the beginning. If there are two or more records of the same type that are to be printed when specific indicators are on, then these records will print in sequence as indicated on the Output form. Thus, if there are two headings that are to print if the 1P or OF indicator is on, the first one coded will print first.

See Figure 2.1Ø for an illustration of the RPG II Logic Cycle, expanded to include the features mentioned in this chapter.

III. Advanced Topic: Reporting Concepts Used in Business Systems

A. Categories of Reports

In general, output reports are categorized as follows.

Categories of Reports
1. Detail.
2. Exception.
3. Group.

1. Detail Reports

Detail reports are those that generate lines of output for each input record read. A payroll program, for example, that produces a paycheck for each employee record is an example of a detail report.

The RPG programmer should be aware that producing detail records requires more computer time than other reports and tends to be the most costly as well. Moreover, detail reports are sometimes wasteful. That is, users some-

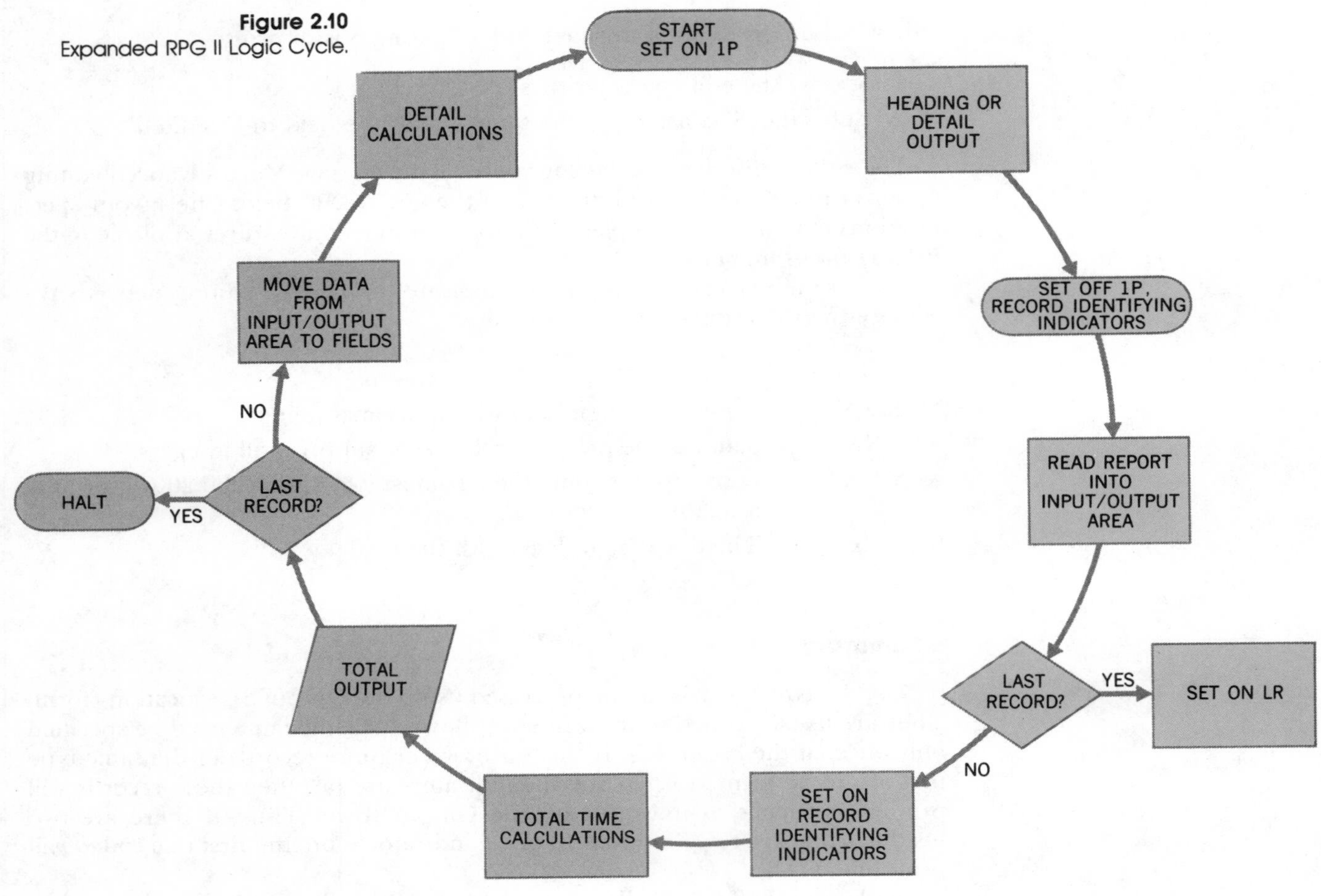

Figure 2.10
Expanded RPG II Logic Cycle.

times request detail reports when other types would serve just as well, or even better.

2. Exception Reports

One alternative to detail reporting is **exception reporting**, which is the printing of only that output that does not fall within established guidelines. Thus, we would be printing output that represents exceptions to some specified rule. For example, suppose a user requests a detail report that prints the names of all employees and the amount they have earned. After careful investigation, the programmer might discover that the purpose of this report is to identify all employees who have a zero or blank field for amount earned. An exception report, then, which lists only these individuals would be a more efficient and effective alternative to the detail listing. Figure 2.11 provides the specifications for such a program, and Figure 2.12 illustrates the RPG program that performs the required operations.

3. Group or Summary Reports

Another alternative to detail reports is summary or **group reports**. These print totals that can sometimes provide the user with enough information so that detail reports are not necessary at all.

Figure 2.11 Problem definition for a program that produces an exception report.

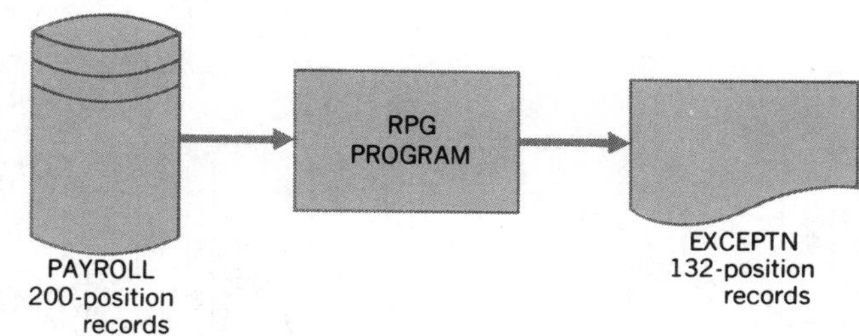

PAYROLL Record Layout

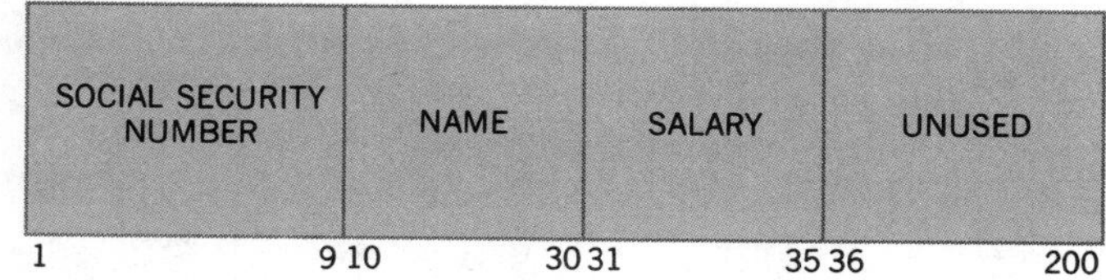

EXCEPTN Printer Spacing Chart

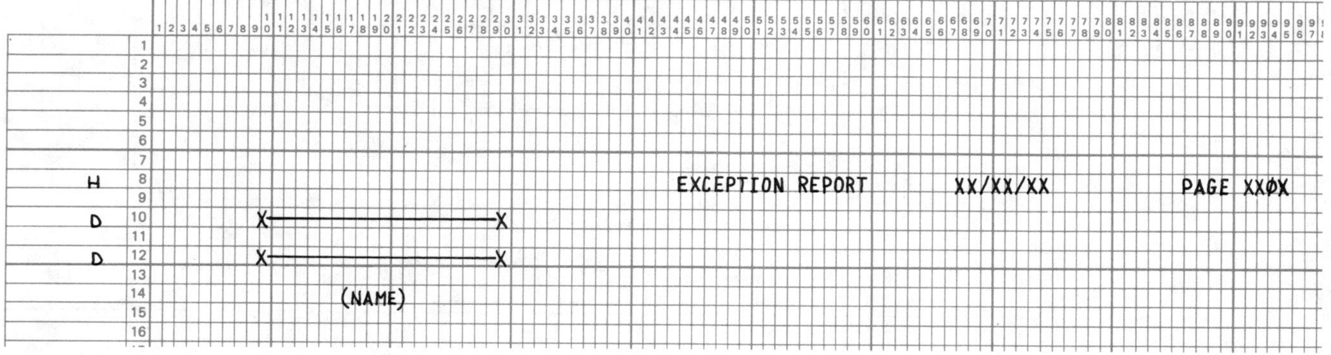

Suppose a user asks for a list of all salespeople and the amount of sales they have brought in during a given period. If each input record contained the amount of sales for each salesperson, then this would be a detail report. Suppose, further, that the programmer discovers that the purpose of this report is to determine the total amount of sales for the company during the given period. It would be far more efficient to provide the user with a **summary listing** that indicates the total amount of sales, rather than providing a detail report. See Figure 2.13 for the specifications and RPG program to produce this group report.

Frequently, summary data requires groups of totals to print; for example, we may wish to print the total sales for each department. This would require the input to be sorted into a specific sequence such as department number. A **control break procedure** would be used to accumulate totals for each department; when a change in the department number occurs, this would cause the total for the previous department to print. Control break procedures will be discussed in Chapter 5.

RPG CONTROL AND FILE DESCRIPTION SPECIFICATIONS

Program | Keying Instruction | Graphic | Key | Card Electro Number | Page 1 2 of | Program Identification 75 76 77 78 79 80

Programmer | Date

Control Specifications

For the valid entries for a system, refer to the RPG reference manual for that system.

```
01 H
```

File Description Specifications

For the valid entries for a system, refer to the RPG reference manual for that system.

```
02ΦFPAYROLL IP  F 2ΦΦ 2ΦΦ              DISK
03ΦFEXCEPTN O   F      132       OF    PRINTER
04 F
05 F
06 F
```

(a)

RPG INPUT SPECIFICATIONS

Program | Keying Instruction | Graphic | Key | Card Electro Number | Page 1 2 of | Program Identification 75 76 77 78 79 80

Programmer | Date

```
01ΦIPAYROLL NS  Φ1
02ΦI                                         1Φ  3Φ NAME
03ΦI                                         31  35 AMOUNT         Φ2
04 I
05 I
06 I
```

(b)

Figure 2.12
RPG program that produces an exception report.

(continued on next page.)

B. Other Types of Output

Output produced by the computer need not always be in printed form. Frequently, output will be a tape or disk file that will need to be stored and processed at some later date.

Figure 2.12 *(continued)*

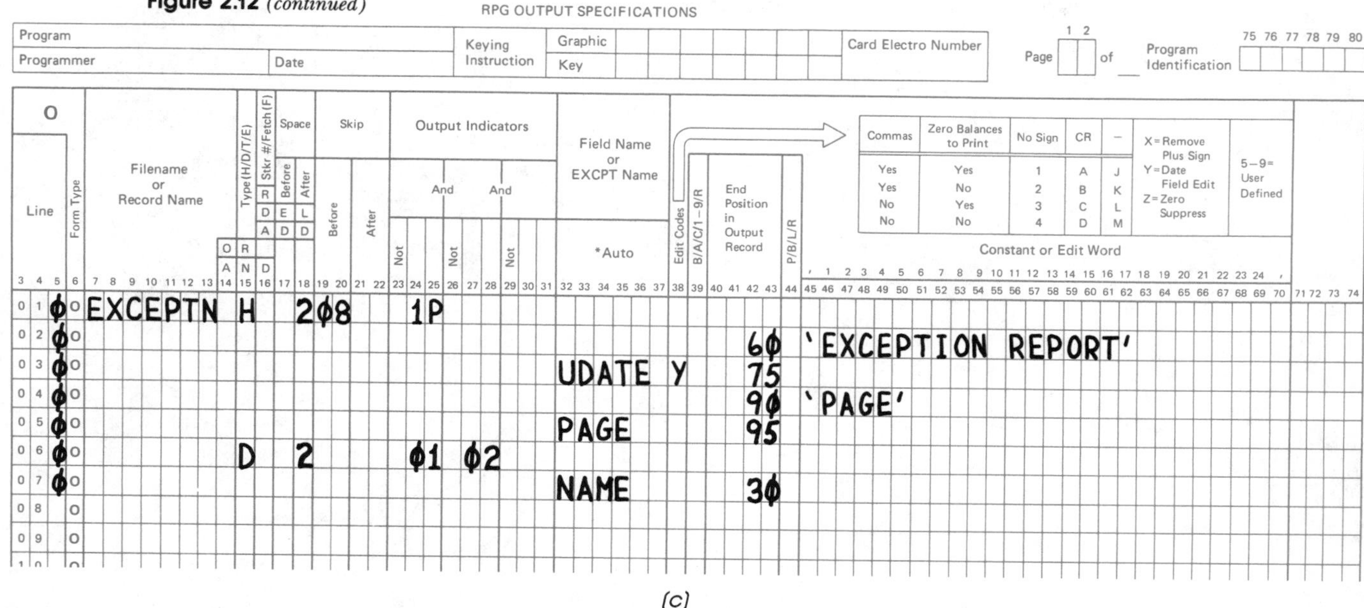
RPG OUTPUT SPECIFICATIONS

Line	Form Type	Filename or Record Name	Type (H/D/T/E)	Space Before	Skip Before	Output Indicators	Field Name or EXCPT Name	Edit Codes	End Position in Output Record	Constant or Edit Word
Ø1	O	EXCEPTN	H	2	Ø8	1P				
Ø2	O								6Ø	'EXCEPTION REPORT'
Ø3	O						UDATE	Y	75	
Ø4	O								9Ø	'PAGE'
Ø5	O						PAGE		95	
Ø6	O		D	2		Ø1 Ø2				
Ø7	O						NAME		3Ø	
08	O									
09	O									

(c)

In RPG, all output, including tape and disk output, must be described using the Output Specifications form. Recall that a Printer Spacing Chart defines the output format for printed reports; for tape and disk output, a record layout form is used for defining the output format.

Most frequently, tape and disk output is designed to be as concise as possible. Thus editing symbols are omitted as on input. A tape or disk output record can contain detail data, that is, one output record for each input record. Or it can contain total or summary information, where one output record summarizes the data from several input records. Since up to eight files can be merged on the System 34 and the System 38, these totals could be used to produce monthly or annual reports.

Systems Flowchart

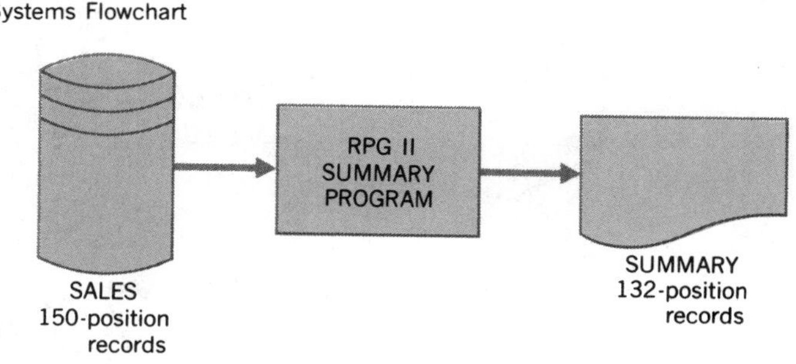

SALES Record Layout

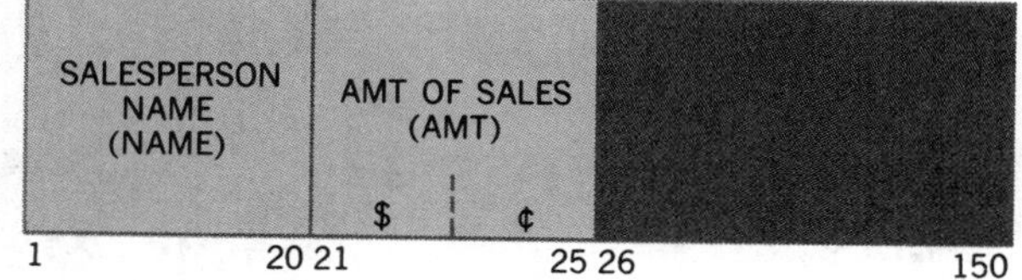

Figure 2.13
Problem definition and RPG program to produce a group report.
(Continued on pages 88 and 89.)

Figure 2.13 *(continued)* SUMMARY Printer Spacing Chart

	Line	Content
	1	
	2	
	3	
	4	
	5	
H	6	SUMMARY SALES LISTING XX/XX/XX
	7	
	8	
	9	
T	10	*** TOTAL SALES FOR PREVIOUS MONTH XX,XX.XX ***
	11	
	12	

RPG CONTROL AND FILE DESCRIPTION SPECIFICATIONS

Program | Keying Instruction | Graphic | Card Electro Number | Page 1 2 of | Program Identification 75 76 77 78 79 80
Programmer | Date | Key

Control Specifications

For the valid entries for a system, refer to the RPG reference manual for that system.

Line (3-5)	Form Type (6)	Size to Compile (7-9)	Object Output (10)	Listing Options (11)	Size to Execute (12-14)	Debug (15)	Reserved (16-17)	Currency Symbol (18)	Date Format (19)	Date Edit (20)	Inverted Print (21)	Reserved (22)	Number of Print Positions (23-25)	Alternate Collating Sequence (26)	Reserved (27-36)	Inquiry (37)	Reserved (38-39)	Sign Handling (40)	1 P Forms Position (41)	Indicator Setting (42)	File Translation (43)	Punch MFCU Zeros (44)	Nonprint Characters (45)	Reserved (46)	Table Load Halt (47)	Shared I/O (48)	Field Print (49)	Formatted Dump (50)	RPG to RPG II Conversion (51)	Number of Formats (52-53)	S/3 Conversion (54)	Subprogram (55)	CICS/DL/I (56)	Transparent Literal (57)	(58-74)
01	H																																		

File Description Specifications

For the valid entries for a system, refer to the RPG reference manual for that system.

Line (3-5)	Form Type (6)	Filename (7-14)	File Type (15)	File Designation (16)	End of File (17)	Sequence (18)	File Format (19)	Block Length (20-23)	Record Length (24-27)	Mode of Processing (28)	Length of Key Field or of Record Address Field (29-30)	Record Address Type (31)	Type of File Organization or Additional Area (32)	Overflow Indicator (33-34)	Key Field Starting Location (35-38)	Extension Code E/L (39)	Device (40-46)	Symbolic Device (47-52)	Labels S/N/E/M (53)	Name of Label Exit (54-59)	Storage Index (60-65)	A/U (66)	Number of Tracks for Cylinder Overflow (67-68)	Number of Extents (69)	Tape Rewind (70)	File Condition U1–U8, UC (71-72)	(73-74)
02Ø	F	SALES	I	P			F		15Ø								DISK	SYSØ2Ø									
03Ø	F	SUMMARY	O				F		132								PRINTER	SYSLST									
04	F																										
05	F																										

RPG INPUT SPECIFICATIONS

Program | Keying Instruction | Graphic | Card Electro Number | Page 1 2 of | Program Identification 75 76 77 78 79 80
Programmer | Date | Key

Line (3-5)	Form Type (6)	Filename or Record Name (7-14)	Sequence (15-16)	Number (1/N), E (17)	Option (O), U, S (18)	Record Identifying Indicator, **, or DS (19-20)	Position 1 (21-24)	Not (N) (25)	C/Z/D (26)	Character (27)	Position 2 (28-31)	Not (N) (32)	C/Z/D (33)	Character (34)	Position 3 (35-38)	Not (N) (39)	C/Z/D (40)	Character (41)	Stacker Select (42)	P/B/L/R (43)	Field Location From (44-47)	Field Location To (48-51)	Decimal Positions (52)	RPG Field Name (53-58)	Control Level (L1–L9) (59-60)	Matching Fields or Chaining Fields (61-62)	Field Record Relation (63-64)	Field Indicators Plus (65-66)	Minus (67-68)	Zero or Blank (69-70)	(71-74)
01Ø	I	SALES	NS			Ø1																									
02	I																				21	25	2	AMT							
03	I																														
04	I																														

RPG CALCULATION SPECIFICATIONS

Line	Form Type	Control Level (L0–L9, LR, SR, AN/OR)	Indicators	Factor 1	Operation	Factor 2	Result Field Name	Length	Decimal Positions	Half Adjust (H)	Resulting Indicators	Comments
01Φ	C		Φ1	AMT	ADD	TOTAL	TOTAL	7	2			
02	C											
03	C											
04	C											

RPG OUTPUT SPECIFICATIONS

Line	Form Type	Filename or Record Name	Type (H/D/T/E)	Space Before	Space After	Skip Before	Skip After	Output Indicators	Field Name or EXCPT Name	Edit Codes	End Position in Output Record	Constant or Edit Word
01Φ	O	SUMMARY	H		2	Φ1		1P				
02Φ	O										33	'SUMMARY SALES'
03Φ	O										41	'LISTING'
04Φ	O								UDATE	Y	51	
05Φ	O		T	2				LR				
06Φ	O										7	'***'
07Φ	O										25	'TOTAL SALES FOR'
08Φ	O										41	'PREVIOUS MONTH'
09Φ	O								TOTAL	1	53	'$'
10Φ	O										59	'***'
11	O											
12	O											
13	O											

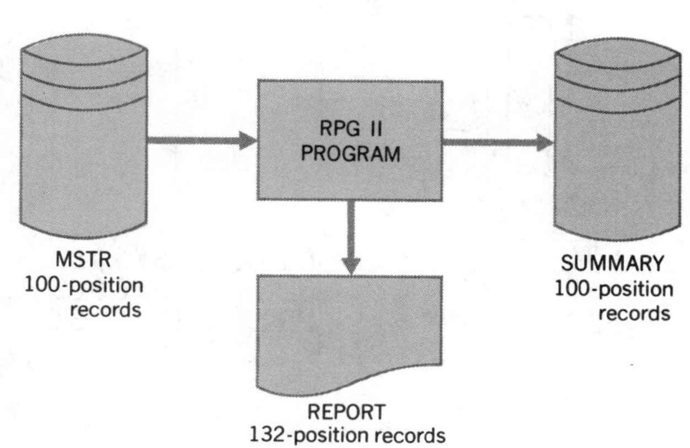

Figure 2.14
Systems flowchart for a program that creates detail print output and disk output.

Example The specifications for a problem that creates detail print output and disk output are indicated in Figure 2.14. The RPG File, Input, and Calculation Specifications forms are described in Figure 2.15. The output files would be described on an Output Specifications Form as follows.

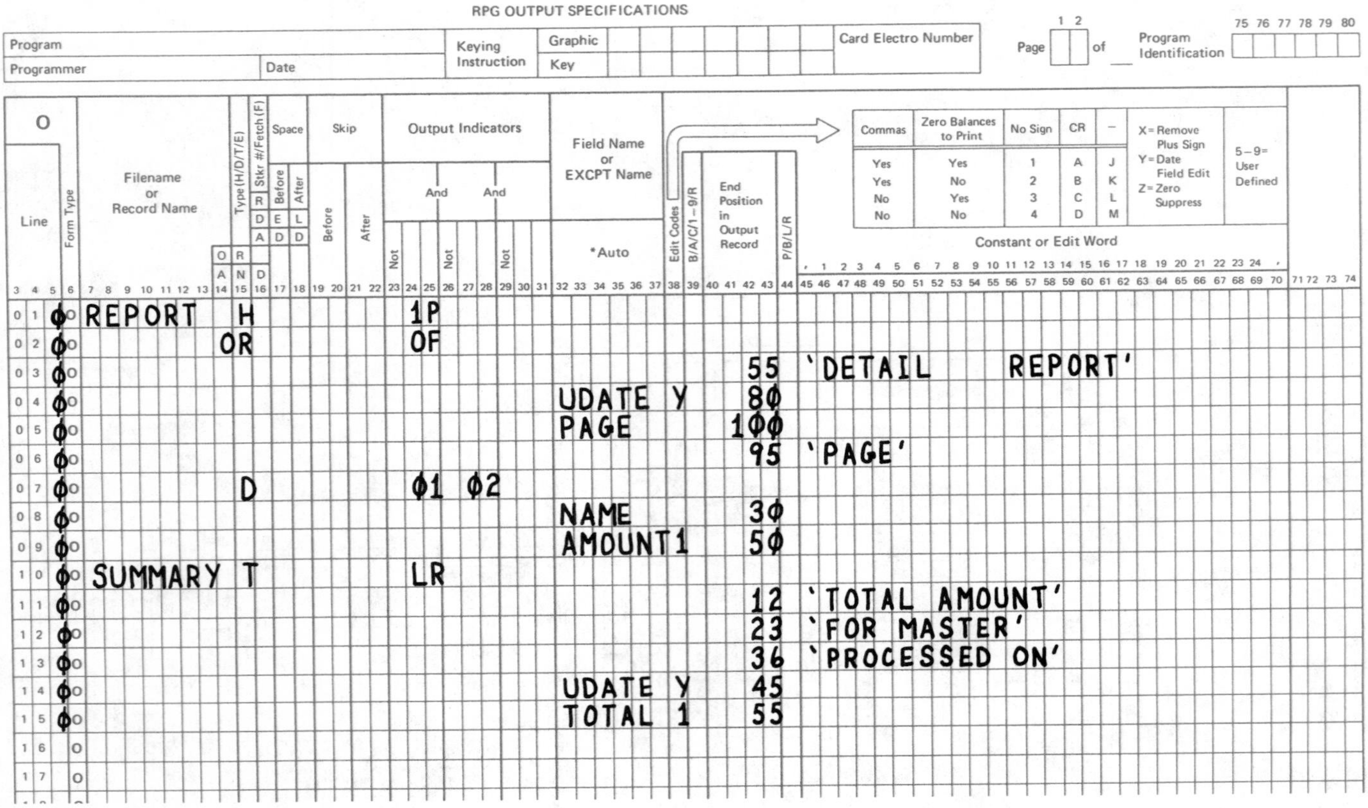

RPG OUTPUT SPECIFICATIONS

Line	Form Type	Filename or Record Name	Type (H/D/T/E) / AND/OR	Output Indicators	Field Name or EXCPT Name	Edit Codes	End Position in Output Record	Constant or Edit Word
01Ø	O	REPORT	H	1P				
02Ø	O		OR	OF				
03Ø	O						55	'DETAIL REPORT'
04Ø	O				UDATE	Y	8Ø	
05Ø	O				PAGE		1ØØ	
06Ø	O						95	'PAGE'
07Ø	O		D	Ø1 Ø2				
08Ø	O				NAME		3Ø	
09Ø	O				AMOUNT1		5Ø	
10Ø	O	SUMMARY	T	LR				
11Ø	O						12	'TOTAL AMOUNT'
12Ø	O						23	'FOR MASTER'
13Ø	O						36	'PROCESSED ON'
14Ø	O				UDATE	Y	45	
15Ø	O				TOTAL	1	55	
16	O							
17	O							

Figure 2.15
Coding to create detail print output and disk output.

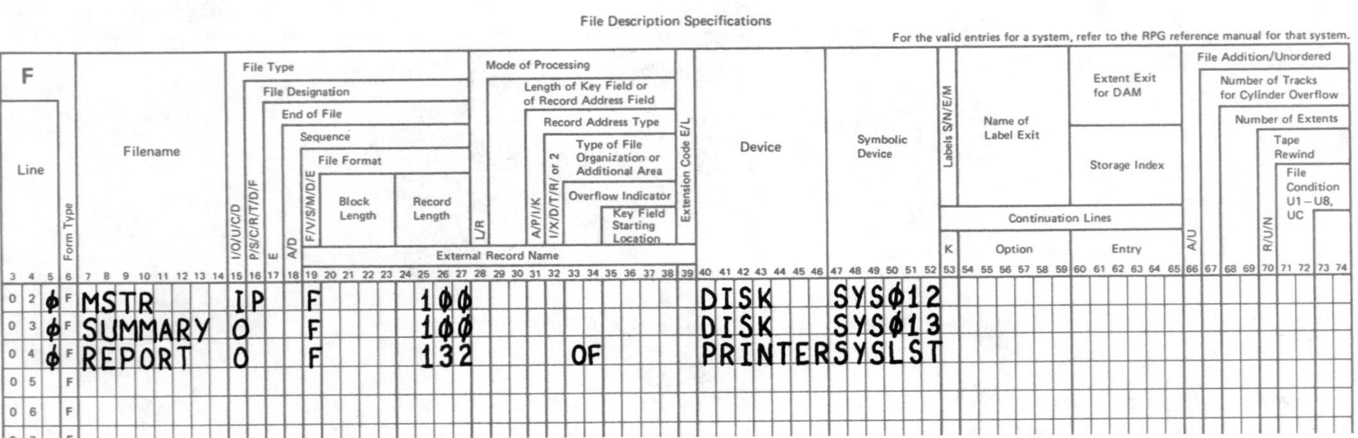

File Description Specifications

Line	Form Type	Filename	File Type	File Designation	File Format	Record Length	Overflow Indicator	Device	Symbolic Device
02Ø	F	MSTR	I	P	F	1ØØ		DISK	SYSØ12
03Ø	F	SUMMARY	O		F	1ØØ		DISK	SYSØ13
04Ø	F	REPORT	O		F	132	OF	PRINTER	SYSLST
05	F								
06	F								

(a)

RPG INPUT SPECIFICATIONS

Program		Keying Instruction	Graphic	Card Electro Number	Page 1 2 of	Program Identification 75 76 77 78 79 80
Programmer	Date		Key			

Line	Form Type	Filename or Record Name	Sequence	Number (1/N), E	Option (O), U, S	Record Identifying Indicator, ** or DS	Record Identification Codes 1: Position	Not (N)	C/Z/D	Character	Field Location From	To	Decimal Positions	RPG Field Name	Control Level (L1–L9)	Matching Fields or Chaining Fields	Field Record Relation	Field Indicators Plus	Minus	Zero or Blank
01Ø	I	MSTR	NS			Ø1	1		C	M										
02Ø	I										2	5		ACCTNO						
03Ø	I										6	25		NAME						
04Ø	I										26	3Ø	2	AMOUNT						
05	I																			
06	I																			
07	I																			

(b)

RPG CALCULATION SPECIFICATIONS

Program		Keying Instruction	Graphic	Card Electro Number	Page 1 2 of	Program Identification 75 76 77 78 79 80
Programmer	Date		Key			

Line	Form Type	Control Level (L0–L9, LR, SR, AN/OR)	Indicators	Factor 1	Operation	Factor 2	Result Field Name	Length	Decimal Positions	Half Adjust (H)	Resulting Indicators Plus / Minus / Zero	Comments
01Ø	C		Ø1	AMOUNT	ADD	TOTAL	TOTAL	6	2			
02	C											
03	C											
04	C											

(c)

Review of RPG Coding Rules

1. Field names and Filenames
   a. Field names have 1 to 6 characters.
      Filenames have 1 to 8 characters.
   b. Names must begin with a letter.
   c. When specified on a form, they are left-justified in the field—i.e., |A|B|C| | | *not* | | |A|B|C|.
   d. No embedded blanks.
   e. Letters, digits, and @, #, $ are permitted.
   f. Names must be unique and should be meaningful.
2. Numeric fields
   a. 1 to 15 digits in the field.
   b. The DECIMAL POSITIONS field must be coded for all numeric fields being defined, either on the Input form or on the Calculation form.
   c. Only numeric fields can be edited.

3. Alphabetic or alphanumeric fields
   a. 1 to 256 characters in the field.
   b. The DECIMAL POSITIONS columns must be blank for alphanumeric fields defined on the Input form.
4. Comments
   To designate any line in RPG as a comment, code an * in column 7.

Review of Output Specifications

1. How the Output Specifications are used
   a. Files coded with 'O' for output in the File Description Specifications must be described on the Output Specifications form.
   b. For printed output, a Printer Spacing Chart is generally used to describe the output format.
   c. For tape or disk output, a Record Layout form describes the output format.
2. Coding the First Line of the Output Specifications
   a. O in column 6 (precoded on the form).
   b. FILENAME begins in column 7.
      (1) Previously defined on the File Description form.
      (2) Coded only once at the beginning of the Output form.
   c. Record TYPE: H, D, or T
      (1) Heading, detail, and total records are used for printed output.
      (2) Detail and total records are used for tape and disk output.
   d. SPACE and SKIP
      (1) Can space the paper 1, 2, or 3 lines before or after printing.
      (2) Can skip to any specific print line.
   e. OUTPUT INDICATORS
      Include indicators that, when on, should result in printing or writing tape or disk output. See Figure 2.16 for a review of indicators.
3. Coding Subsequent Lines of the Output Specifications
   a. Printing Fields
   b. Printing Constants
      (1) Begin on the line following the entries mentioned above (a-e).
      (2) Each field to be printed must be defined on either the Input or Calculation forms.
      (3) The END POSITION refers to the right-most print position for the field, as specified on the Printer Spacing Chart.
      (4) Field names are left-justified in Columns 32-37 of the form.
      Any fixed data or constant to print is specified with single quote marks.

Key Terms

Constant
Continuous form
Control break procedure
Default
Detail printing
Detail report
Edit Code
Editing
Exception report
First page (1P) indicator

Floating dollar sign
Group report
Implied decimal point
Last record (LR) indicator
Literal
Output indicator
Overflow (OF) indicator
PAGE
Preprinted form
Report heading
Skipping
Spacing
Summary listing
UDATE
User-friendly
Variable data
Zero suppression

Figure 2.16
Indicator summary. (Courtesy IBM.)

Indicator	*How Assigned*	*Turned on by*	*Turned off by*	*Usage*
Record Identifying Indicator (can use 01-99)	Input Specifications	Conditions in records	RPG II at end of cycle	For detail processing; for printing detail output
IP	Automatically, at beginning of cycle	RPG II	RPG II after Heading and Detail output	1st-page heading at beginning of run
LR	Automatically in the cycle	After the last record has been processed	RPG II	For obtaining total output and end-of-job processing
OF	Automatic end-of-page or overflow indicator	RPG II	RPG II	To print headings at the beginning of each page

Self-Evaluating Quiz *Consider the following Output Specifications for questions 1 through 5.*

RPG OUTPUT SPECIFICATIONS

Line	Form Type	Filename or Record Name	Type (H/D/T/E)	Space After	Output Indicators	Field Name or EXCPT Name	End Position in Output Record
01	O	HOURLY	D	2	19		
02	O					OVTHRS	47
03	O					REGHRS	34
04	O					EMPNUM	19
05	O						
06	O						

1. The filename HOURLY also appears on the ________ Specifications form.
2. Type D means that the record described is a(n) ________ record.
3. The line described in question 2 will print when ________ .
4. The fields specified must be defined on either the ________ Specifications form or the ________ Specifications form.
5. If REGHRS is a three-digit field, it will print in print positions ________ .
6. Using the Printer Spacing Chart and Input Specifications in Figure 2.17, code the Output Specifications.
7. Only ________ fields can contain Edit Codes for editing.
8. If an input field is specified as having two decimal positions, then a decimal point (is, is not) part of the input record.
9. The use of any edit code will automatically cause ________ and ________ where appropriate.

Indicate the results in each of the following cases (questions 1Ø through 15).

	Input Field	*Edit Code*	*Result*
10.	ØØØ‸ØØ	2	
11.	Ø234‸56	1	
12.	1234‸56	1	
13.	ØØØ‸ØØ	1	
14.	1234‸56	4	
15.	Ø234‸56	2	

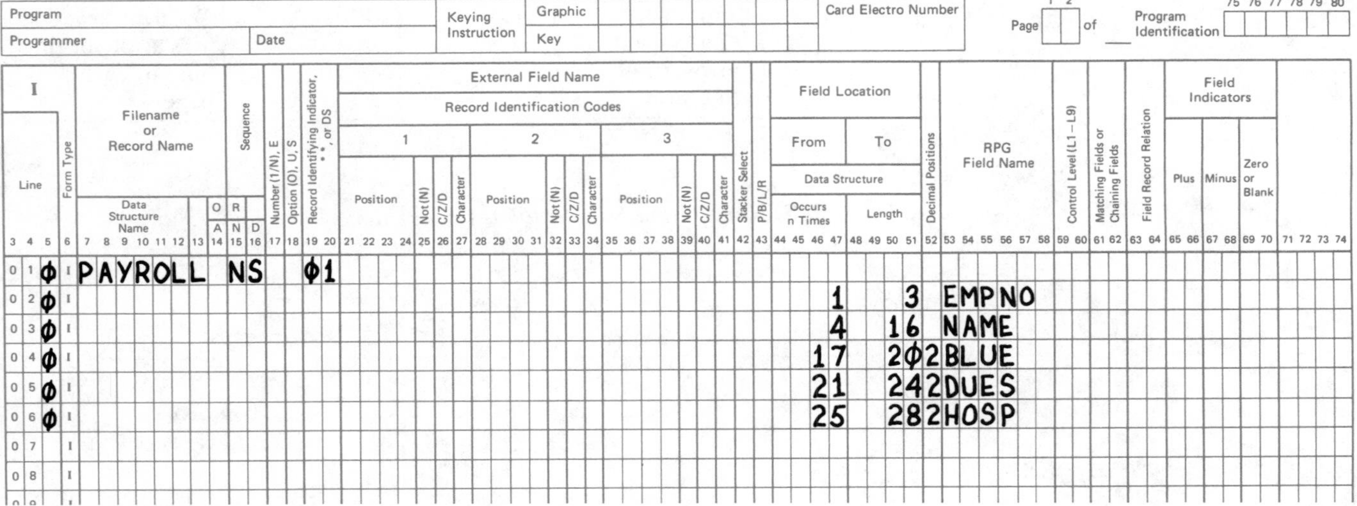
RPG INPUT SPECIFICATIONS

Line	Form Type	Filename or Record Name	Sequence	Record Identifying Indicator	From	To	Decimal Positions	RPG Field Name
01Ø	I	PAYROLL	NS	Ø1				
02Ø	I				1	3		EMPNO
03Ø	I				4	16		NAME
04Ø	I				17	2Ø	2	BLUE
05Ø	I				21	24	2	DUES
06Ø	I				25	28	2	HOSP
07	I							
08	I							

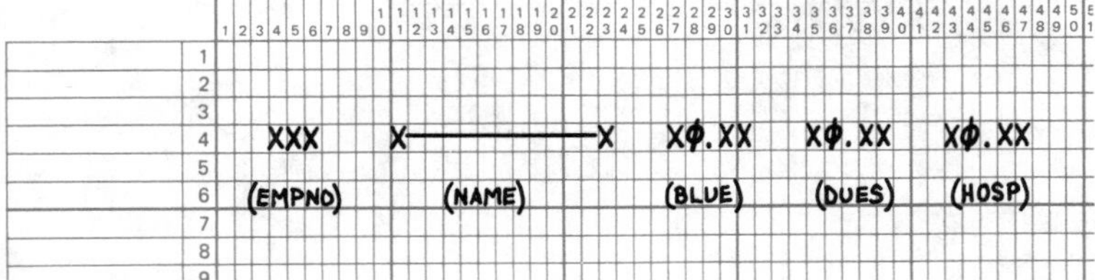

Figure 2.17
Input Specifications and Printer Spacing Chart for question 6.

16. Using the following Output Specifications, how would ØØØØ57 print, assuming the field is defined with two decimal positions?

RPG OUTPUT SPECIFICATIONS

Program | Keying Instruction | Graphic | Key | Card Electro Number | Page [ ][ ] of | Program Identification
Programmer | Date

Line (3–5)	Form Type (6)	Filename or Record Name (7–14)	Type (H/D/T/E) (15)	Stkr #/Fetch (F) (16)	Space Before (17)	Space After (18)	Skip Before (19–20)	Skip After (21–22)	Output Indicators (23–31)	Field Name or EXCPT Name (32–37)	Edit Codes (38)	B/A/C/1–9/R (39)	End Position in Output Record (40–43)	P/B/L/R (44)	Constant or Edit Word (45–70)
01Ø	O									EDIT1	4		25		'$'
02	O														
03	O														

Edit code key: Commas / Zero Balances to Print / No Sign / CR / –: Yes, Yes: 1, A, J; Yes, No: 2, B, K; No, Yes: 3, C, L; No, No: 4, D, M. X = Remove Plus Sign; Y = Date Field Edit; Z = Zero Suppress; 5–9 = User Defined.

17. Using the following Output Specifications, how would ØØØØ57 print, assuming the field is defined with two decimal positions?

RPG OUTPUT SPECIFICATIONS

Line (3–5)	Form Type (6)	Filename or Record Name (7–14)	Type (H/D/T/E) (15)	Stkr #/Fetch (F) (16)	Space Before (17)	Space After (18)	Skip Before (19–20)	Skip After (21–22)	Output Indicators (23–31)	Field Name or EXCPT Name (32–37)	Edit Codes (38)	B/A/C/1–9/R (39)	End Position in Output Record (40–43)	P/B/L/R (44)	Constant or Edit Word (45–70)
01Ø	O												19		'$'
02Ø	O									EDIT2	4		25		
03	O														
04	O														

18. In question 16, the $ is said to ________ with the field.

19. In specifying a Field Name or a Filename in RPG, the name is coded in the <u>(right-, left-)</u> most position of columns 32-37 of the Output form.

2Ø. In specifying an End Position in RPG, the number is <u>(right-, left-)</u> justified in columns 4Ø-43, which means that <u>(left, right)</u> unfilled positions are left blank.

21. (T or F) Negative quantities are represented on input with a minus sign over the right-most position.

22. (T or F) If Edit Codes 1-4 are used for a field that contains a minus sign, the field will print as if it did not have a sign.

23. To print CR along with any negative quantities, use Edit Codes ________.

24. To simply cause zero suppression, use the ________ in the Edit Code field.

25. A numeric field is denoted when the ________ field of either the Input Specifications or the Calculation Specifications is coded.

Solutions

1. File Description
2. detail
3. indicator 19 is on
4. Input
   Calculation
5. 32-34
6.

RPG OUTPUT SPECIFICATIONS

Line	Form Type	Filename or Record Name	Type (H/D/T/E)	Space Before	Space After	Output Indicators	Field Name or EXCPT Name	Edit Codes	End Position in Output Record
01ϕ	O	DEDUCT	D	2	2	ϕ1			
02ϕ	O						EMPNO		6
03ϕ	O						NAME		23
04ϕ	O						BLUE	1	31
05ϕ	O						DUES	1	39
06ϕ	O						HOSP	1	47
07	O								
08	O								

7. numeric
8. is not
9. zero suppression
   printing of decimal points
1ϕ. blank
11. 234.56
12. 1,234.56
13. .ϕϕ
14. 1234.56
15. 234.56
16. $.57
17. $ .57
18. float
19. left
2ϕ. right-
    left
21. T
22. T
23. A-D
24. Z
25. Decimal Positions (column 52)

Review Questions

1. What, if anything, is wrong with the following field names?
   a. 5OUT
   b. AMT-OUT
   c. DESCRIPT
   d. QTY12
   e. AMTIN$
2. What is the purpose of the record identifying indicator and how is it used?
3. What is the purpose of headings? Indicate the items that are coded as part of a heading.
4. What is the meaning of editing? Indicate what symbols are used for editing.

5. State the meaning of the following.
   a. Detail reports
   b. Summary reports
   c. Exception reports
6. When is the Decimal Positions field used on the Input Specifications form?
7. Assume the field EDITFD is defined on the Output form with an Edit Code of 3. Indicate the edited result in each case.

Value in EDITFD	*Edited Result*
1234$_\wedge$56	________
ØØ34$_\wedge$56	________
ØØØØ$_\wedge$25	________
ØØØØ$_\wedge$Ø6	________
ØØØØ$_\wedge$ØØ	________

8. Indicate how the SEQUENCE field is used on the Input Specifications form.
9. How are the following entries used in RPG?
   a. UDATE c. 1P
   b. PAGE d. OF
1Ø. Indicate how numeric entries are coded on the RPG forms.
11. Indicate how nonnumeric entries are coded on the RPG forms.

Debugging Exercises

As noted in Chapter 1, there are several types of errors that may occur in a program and there are several places where errors are likely to occur or to become evident.

1. Coding the program. The programmer may make *syntax errors,* which means that the rules of the language have been violated.
2. Keying the program. The programmer may make *keying or typographical errors* in entering the program.
3. Compiling the program. The computer will list any *syntax errors* or rule violations.
4. Executing the program. The computer will run the program and produce output that may indicate if *logic errors* have occurred.

Recall that **debugging a program** means eliminating all types of errors.

The first two types of errors — coding and keying errors — can be minimized by *desk checking* a program *before* it is compiled. Programmers, then, should review programs carefully at their desks to ensure their accuracy. In the end, it will save them a good deal of time if they make certain that the coding and keying of a program are as accurate as possible before compiling the program. There are likely to be programming errors that are not detected until a program is compiled or executed, but eliminating all obvious errors by desk checking will save computer time as well as overall programming time.

Debugging exercises at the end of each chapter will help identify common programming errors. Three types of exercises will be included.

1. *Debugging by Desk Checking*
   These will include programs on coding sheets that contain errors that you must identify.
2. *Debugging Using a Source Listing*
   These will include programs that have been compiled and that include compiler-generated error messages that you must identify.

3. *Debugging Using an Executed Program and the Output Generated*
These will include programs with logic errors that have been compiled and run. You must identify the logic errors by checking the computer-produced output against the program requirements.

Debugging Exercise

The problem definition for this exercise is shown in Figure 2.18. The coding sheets in Figure 2.19 contain syntax errors. Identify them and illustrate the corrections you would make to the program. The listing in Figure 2.2Ø includes the error diagnostics produced by running the program as coded. The syntax corrections are circled on the computer listing shown in Figure 2.21. There are, however, logic errors in the program. Your assignment is to desk check the program carefully, find the logic errors, and make the necessary corrections.

Figure 2.18
Problem definition for the debugging exercise.

Systems Flowchart

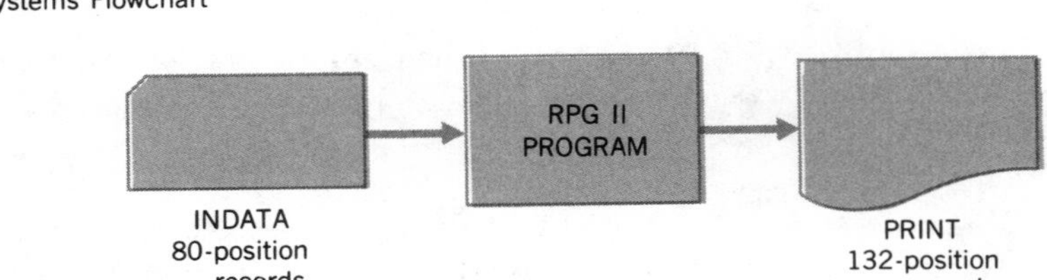

INDATA Record Layout

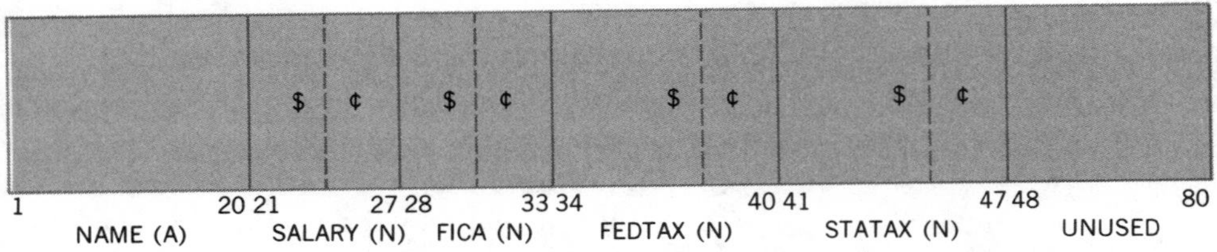

"A" denotes alphameric data; "N" denotes a numeric field containing two decimal positions.

PRINT Printer Spacing Chart

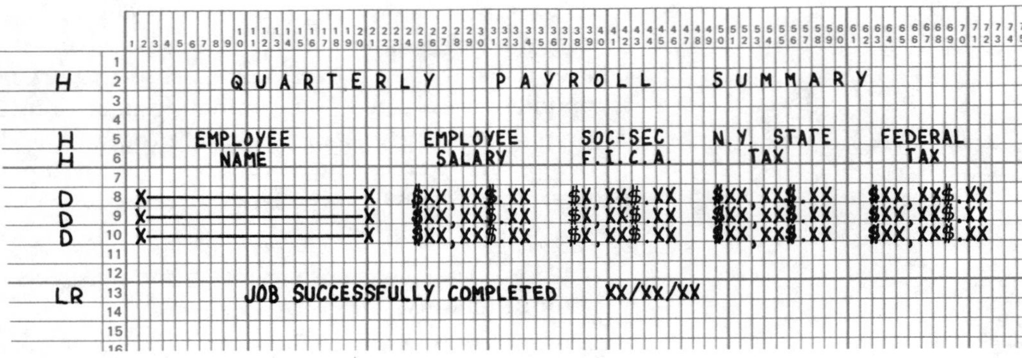

RPG CONTROL AND FILE DESCRIPTION SPECIFICATIONS

Program: QUARTERLY PAYROLL SUMMARY | Keying Instruction: Graphic Ø 1 2, Key ZERO ONE TWO | Card Electro Number | Page Ø1 of 4 | Program Identification SSSØ2

Programmer: A. SAGER | Date: 4/17/--

Control Specifications

For the valid entries for a system, refer to the RPG reference manual for that system.

```
01ØH
```

File Description Specifications

For the valid entries for a system, refer to the RPG reference manual for that system.

```
02ØF********************************************************************
03ØF*     THIS PROGRAM PRODUCES A QUARTERLY PAYROLL SUMMARY, LISTING     *
04ØF*    EMPLOYEE NAME, SALARY, FICA, STATE AND FEDERAL TAX DEDUCTIONS.  *
05ØF********************************************************************
06ØF*
07ØFINDATA  IP  F     8Ø            READØ1 SYSIPT
08ØFPRINT   O   F    132            PRINTERSYSLST
09ØF*
10 F
   F
   F
```

(a)

RPG INPUT SPECIFICATIONS

Program: QUARTERLY PAYROLL SUMMARY | Keying Instruction: Graphic Ø 1 2, Key ZERO ONE TWO | Card Electro Number | Page Ø2 of 4 | Program Identification SSSØ2

Programmer: A. SAGER | Date: 4/17/--

```
01ØI**************************** INPUT RECORD ***************************
02ØI*
03ØIINDATA  NS  Ø1
04ØI                                        1  2Ø NAME
05ØI                                       21  272SALARY
06ØI                                       28  332FICA
07ØI                                       34  4Ø2FEDTAX
08ØI                                       41  472STATAX
09ØI*
10 I
11 I
```

(b)

Figure 2.19 Coding sheets for the debugging exercise. *(Continued on pages 100 and 101.)*

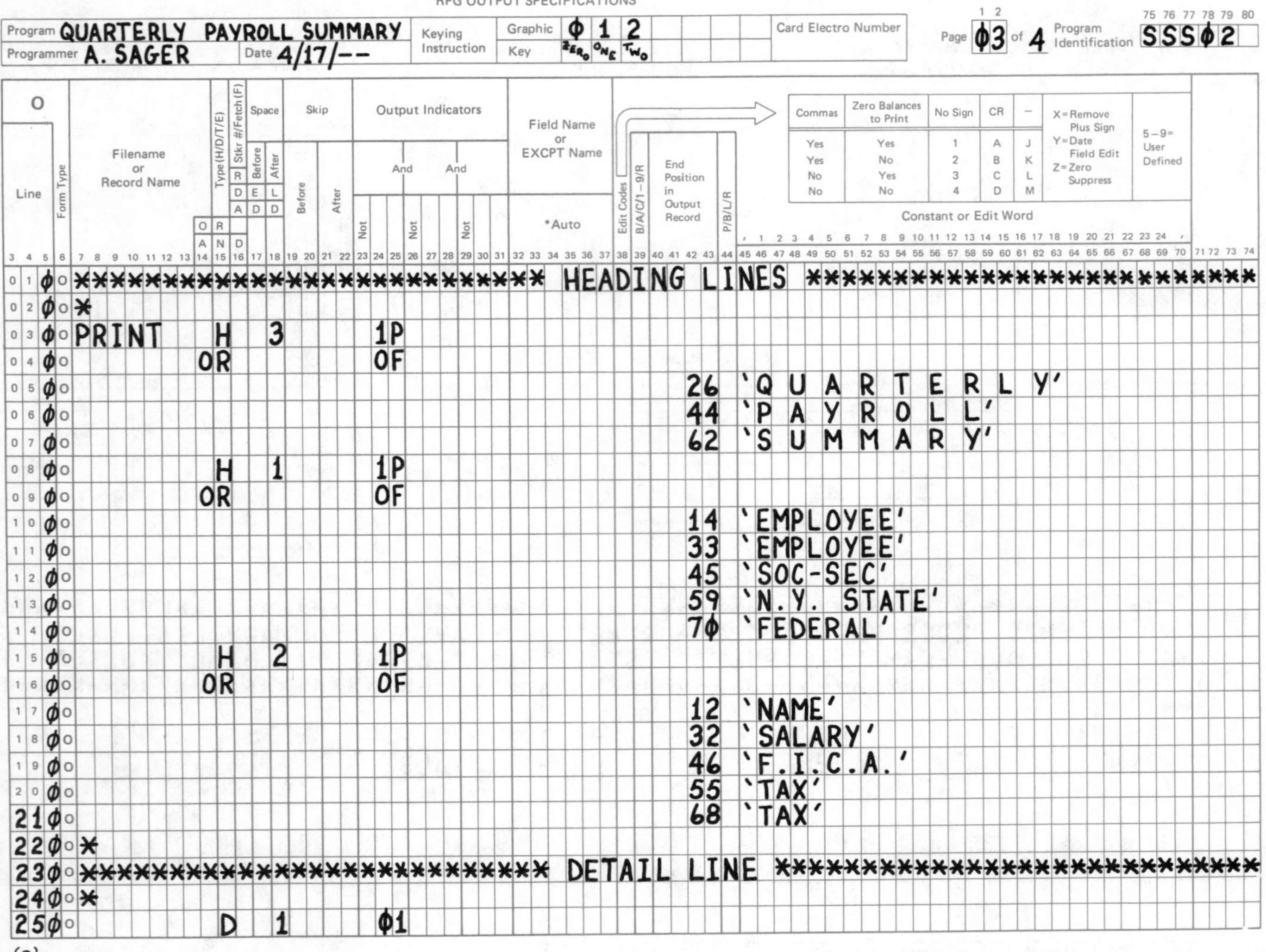

RPG OUTPUT SPECIFICATIONS

Program QUARTERLY PAYROLL SUMMARY | Keying Instruction | Graphic Ø 1 2 | Key ZERO ONE TWO | Card Electro Number | Page Ø3 of 4 | Program Identification SSSØ2

Programmer A. SAGER | Date 4/17/--

Line	Form Type	Filename or Record Name	Type (H/D/T/E)	Space After	Output Indicators	End Position in Output Record	Constant or Edit Word
01Ø	O	************************* HEADING LINES *******************************					
02Ø	O	*					
03Ø	O	PRINT	H	3	1P		
04Ø	O		OR		OF		
05Ø	O					26	'Q U A R T E R L Y'
06Ø	O					44	'P A Y R O L L'
07Ø	O					62	'S U M M A R Y'
08Ø	O		H	1	1P		
09Ø	O		OR		OF		
10Ø	O					14	'EMPLOYEE'
11Ø	O					33	'EMPLOYEE'
12Ø	O					45	'SOC-SEC'
13Ø	O					59	'N.Y. STATE'
14Ø	O					7Ø	'FEDERAL'
15Ø	O		H	2	1P		
16Ø	O		OR		OF		
17Ø	O					12	'NAME'
18Ø	O					32	'SALARY'
19Ø	O					46	'F.I.C.A.'
20Ø	O					55	'TAX'
21Ø	O					68	'TAX'
22Ø	O	*					
23Ø	O	************************* DETAIL LINE ******************************					
24Ø	O	*					
25Ø	O		D	1	Ø1		

(c)

RPG OUTPUT SPECIFICATIONS

Program	QUARTERLY PAYROLL SUMMARY	Keying Instruction	Graphic	ϕ	1	2	Card Electro Number	Page	ϕ4 of 4	Program Identification	SSSϕ2
Programmer	A. SAGER	Date 4/17/--	Key	ZERO	ONE	TWO					

Line (3-5)	Form Type (6)	Filename or Record Name (7-14)	Type (H/D/T/E) (15)	Stkr #/Fetch (F) (16)	Space Before (17)	Space After (18)	Skip Before (19-20)	Skip After (21-22)	Output Indicators (23-31)	Field Name or EXCPT Name (32-37)	Edit Codes (38)	B/A/C/1-9/R (39)	End Position in Output Record (40-43)	P/B/L/R (44)	Constant or Edit Word (45-70)
01ϕ	O									NAME			2		
02ϕ	O									SALARY			25		'$'
03ϕ	O									FICA			38		'$'
04ϕ	O									FEDTAX			5ϕ		'$'
05ϕ	O									STATAX			63		'$'
06ϕ	O	*													
07ϕ	O	************************* TOTAL LINE ******************************													
08ϕ	O	*													
09ϕ	O		T		2				LR						
10ϕ	O												26		'JOB SUCCESSFULLY'
11ϕ	O												26		'COMPLETED'
12ϕ	O									UDATE	Y		48		
13ϕ	O	*													
14ϕ	O	**													
15	O														
16	O														

(d)

```
          01-020  F**************************************************************************SSS02
          01-030  F*      THIS PRCGRAM PRODUCES A QUARTERLY PAYROLL SUMMARY,LISTING      *SSS02
          01-04C  F*    EMPLCYEE NAME,SALARY,FICA,STATE ANC FECERAL TAX DEDUCTIONS.     *SSS02
          01-050  F**************************************************************************SSS02
          01-06C  F*                                                                         SSS02
0001      01-070  FINDATA  IP  F      80             READ01 SYSIPT                          SSS02
0002      01-08C  FPRINT   C   F     132             PRINTERSYSLST                          SSS02
          01-090  F*                                                                         SSS02
          02-010  I*************************** INPUT RECORD ****************************SSS02
          02-02C  I*                                                                         SSS02
0003      02-030  IINDATA  NS  01                                                            SSS02
0004      02-04C  I                                          1  20 NAME                      SSS02
0005      02-05C  I                                         21  272SALARY                    SSS02
0006      02-060  I                                         28  332FICA                      SSS02
0007      02-07C  I                                         34  402FEDTAX                    SSS02
0008      02-08C  I                                         41  472STATAX                    SSS02
          02-09C  I*                                                                         SSS02
          03-010  C*************************** HEADING LINES ***************************SSS02
          C3-02C  C*                                                                         SSS02
0009      03-03C  CPRINT    H  3      1P                                                     SSS02
0010      03-04C  C       CR          CF                                                     SSS02
                                      $                                                              MSG  202
0011      03-050  C                                    26 'C U A R T E R L Y'              SSS02
0012      03-060  C                                    44 'P A Y R O L L'                  SSS02
0013      03-07C  O                                    62 'S U M M A R Y'                  SSS02
0014      03-080  C         H  1      1P                                                     SSS02
0015      03-09C  C       CR          CF                                                     SSS02
                                      $                                                              MSG  202
0016      03-100  C                                    14 'EMPLCYEE'                       SSS02
0017      03-110  C                                    33 'EMPLCYEE'                       SSS02
CC18      03-12C  C                                    45 'SCC-SEC'                        SSS02
0019      03-130  C                                    59 'N.Y. STATE'                     SSS02
0020      03-140  C                                    70 'FEDERAL'                        SSS02
0021      03-15C  C         H  2      1P                                                     SSS02
0022      03-160  O       CR          CF                                                     SSS02
                                      $                                                              MSG  202
0023      03-170  C                                    12 'NAME'                           SSS02
0024      C3-18C  C                                    32 'SALARY'                         SSS02
0025      03-19C  C                                    46 'F.I.C.A.'                       SSS02
0026      03-2CC  C                                    55 'TAX'                            SSS02
0027      03-21C  C                                    68 'TAX'                            SSS02
          03-22C  C*                                                                         SSS02
          03-230  C*************************** DETAIL LINE *****************************SSS02
          03-24C  C*                                                                         SSS02
0028      03-250  C         D  1      01                                                     SSS02
0029      04-010  C                          NAME       2                                    SSS02
0030      04-02C  C                          SALARY    25 '$'                                SSS02
                                                          $                                          MSG  234
0031      04-030  C                          FICA      38 '$'                                SSS02
                                                          $                                          MSG  234
0032      04-04C  O                          FEDTAX    50 '$'                                SSS02
                                                          $                                          MSG  234
0033      C4-05C  C                          STATAX    63 '$'                                SSS02
                                                          $                                          MSG  234
          04-06C  C*                                                                         SSS02
          04-070  O*************************** TOTAL LINE ******************************SSS02
          04-08C  C*                                                                         SSS02
0034      04-09C  C         T 2       LR                                                     SSS02
0035      04-100  C                                    26 'JOB SUCCESSFULLY'               SSS02
0036      04-11C  C                                    26 'CCMPLETED'                      SSS02
0037      04-120  C                          UDATE Y   48                                    SSS02
          04-13C  C*                                                                         SSS02
          04-140  O**************************************************************************SSS02

      E N D  C F  S C U R C E


      C O M P I L E R   D I A G N O S T I C S   S U M M A R Y


ILN202   INDICATOR IS INVALID OR UNDEFINED. DROP ENTRY.

         C0010     C3-04C
         00015     C3-09C
         00022     03-160

ILN234   INVALID NUMBER OF DIGIT PCSITICNS IN EDIT WORD. DRCP EDITING.

         00030     C4-C2C     SALARY
         00031     C4-030     FICA
         00032     C4-040     FEDTAX
         00033     C4-C5C     STATAX

ILN432   FIELD LENGTH GREATER THAN END PCSITICN. LENGTH CF FIELD CR CORRECT END POSITION IS GIVEN. SPEC IS

         DRCPPED.

       D 00029     C4-C10
```

Figure 2.20 Program listing with error diagnostics for the debugging exercise.

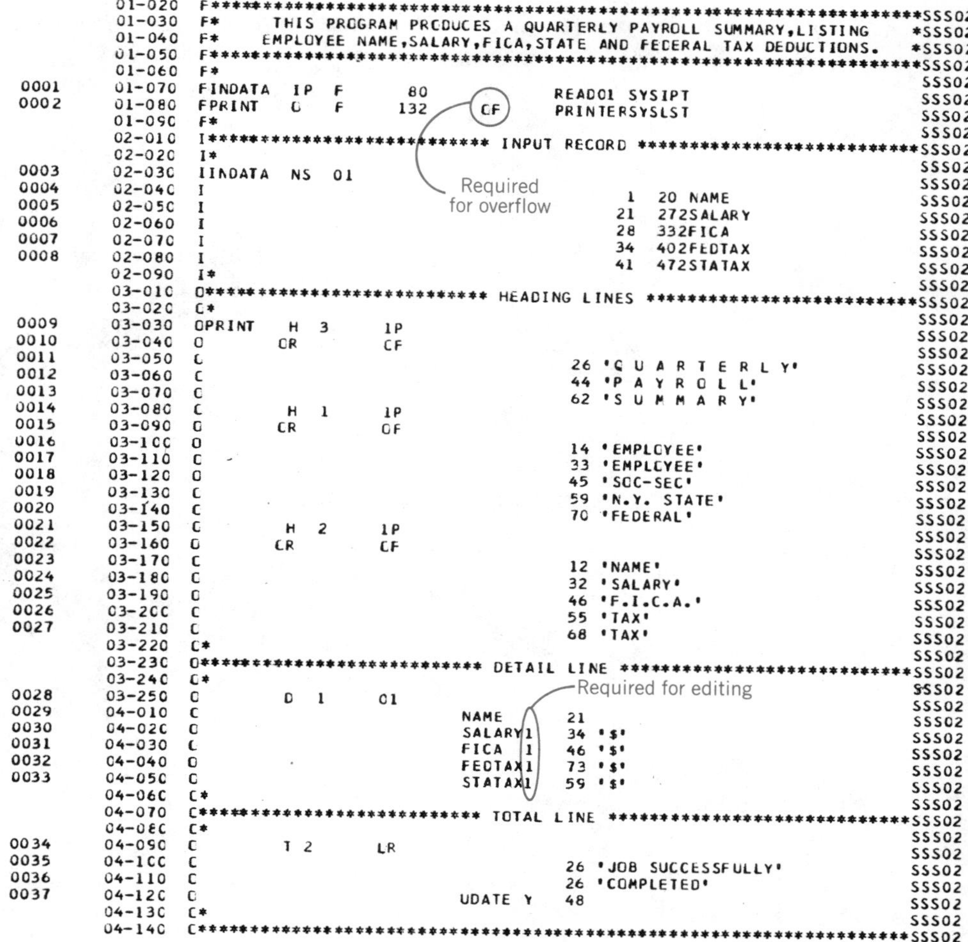


```
01-020 F*****************************************************************SSS02
01-030 F*     THIS PROGRAM PRCDUCES A QUARTERLY PAYROLL SUMMARY,LISTING     *SSS02
01-040 F*    EMPLOYEE NAME,SALARY,FICA,STATE AND FECERAL TAX DEDUCTIONS.    *SSS02
01-050 F*****************************************************************SSS02
01-060 F*                                                                  SSS02
01-070 FINDATA  IP  F     80              READ01 SYSIPT                    SSS02
01-080 FPRINT   C   F    132     CF       PRINTERSYSLST                    SSS02
01-09C F*                                                                  SSS02
02-010 I************************** INPUT RECORD **************************SSS02
02-020 I*                                                                  SSS02
02-03C IINDATA  NS  01                                                     SSS02
02-04C I                                         1  20 NAME                SSS02
02-05C I                                        21  272SALARY              SSS02
02-060 I                                        28  332FICA                SSS02
02-070 I                                        34  402FEDTAX              SSS02
02-080 I                                        41  472STATAX              SSS02
02-090 I*                                                                  SSS02
03-010 O************************** HEADING LINES *************************SSS02
03-020 C*                                                                  SSS02
03-030 OPRINT    H  3     1P                                               SSS02
03-040 O        OR        CF                                               SSS02
03-050 C                                                                   SSS02
03-060 C                                 26 'Q U A R T E R L Y'            SSS02
03-070 C                                 44 'P A Y R O L L'                SSS02
03-080 C                                 62 'S U M M A R Y'                SSS02
03-090 C         H  1     1P                                               SSS02
03-1CC O        CR        OF                                               SSS02
03-110 C                                 14 'EMPLCYEE'                     SSS02
03-120 O                                 33 'EMPLCYEE'                     SSS02
03-130 C                                 45 'SOC-SEC'                      SSS02
03-140 C                                 59 'N.Y. STATE'                   SSS02
03-150 C         H  2     1P             70 'FEDERAL'                      SSS02
03-160 O        CR        CF                                               SSS02
03-170 C                                                                   SSS02
03-180 C                                 12 'NAME'                         SSS02
03-190 O                                 32 'SALARY'                       SSS02
03-20C C                                 46 'F.I.C.A.'                     SSS02
03-210 C                                 55 'TAX'                          SSS02
03-220 C*                                68 'TAX'                          SSS02
03-23C O************************** DETAIL LINE ***************************SSS02
03-240 C*                                                                  SSS02
03-250 O         D  1     01                                               SSS02
04-010 C                       NAME      21                                SSS02
04-02C O                       SALARY1   34 '$'                            SSS02
04-030 C                       FICA  1   46 '$'                            SSS02
04-040 O                       FEDTAX1   73 '$'                            SSS02
04-05C O                       STATAX1   59 '$'                            SSS02
04-06C C*                                                                  SSS02
04-070 C************************** TOTAL LINE ****************************SSS02
04-08C C*                                                                  SSS02
04-090 C         T 2      LR                                               SSS02
04-1CC C                                 26 'JOB SUCCESSFULLY'             SSS02
04-110 C                                 26 'COMPLETED'                    SSS02
04-12C O                       UDATE Y   48                                SSS02
04-13C C*                                                                  SSS02
04-140 C*****************************************************************SSS02
```

END OF COMPULATICK E-R PROGRAM PEAGTHR BEK E COOD84U M BEG R 003492

EMPLOYEE NAME		EMPLCYEE SALARY	SOC-SEC F.I.C.A.	N.Y. STATE TAX	FECERAL TAX
BRONSCN	DANIEL	$5,608.00	$441.91	$377.77	$1,055.73
CALHOUN	RCBERT A.	$7,896.00	$622.20	$531.89	$1,486.45
DIERCKS	GECRGE M.	$10,100.80	$795.94	$680.36	$1,901.51
FOO	LECN A.	$9,765.00	$769.48	$657.80	$1,838.29
FORTGANG	HANS	$13,450.88	$1,059.93	$906.10	$2,532.17
OEST	GILBERT U.	$12,917.17	$1,017.87	$870.12	$2,431.70
SAGER	WESLEY	$9,910.00	$780.91	$667.56	$1,865.60
STERN	MARILYN M.	$12,888.20	$1,015.59	$868.16	$2,462.47
VICTCR	VICTORIA	$11,917.00	$939.06	$802.76	$2,243.42

JCB SUCCCMPLETED 7/29/82

Figure 2.21 Program listing that contains logic errors for the debugging exercise.

Practice Problems

For these problems, your instructor will provide you with the necessary coding for the Calculation forms.

1. Consider the following and write the RPG II program to produce the desired results.

Systems Flowchart

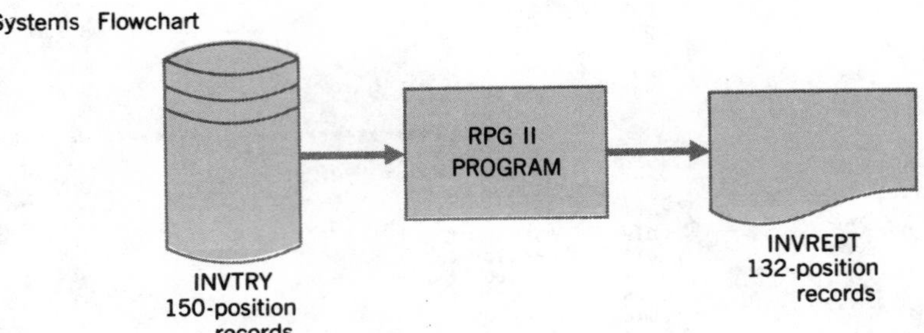

INVTRY Record Layout

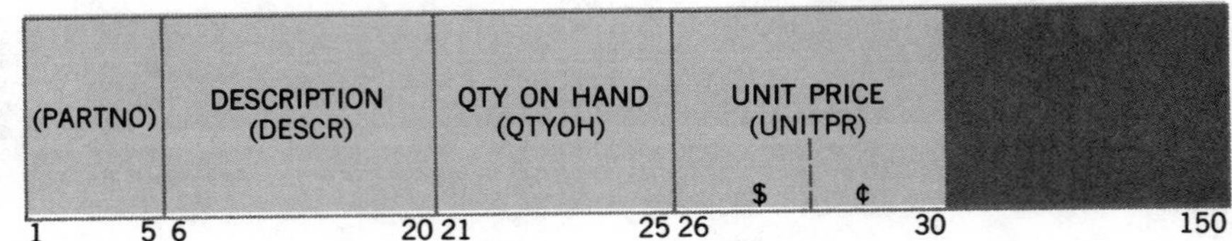

INVREPT Printer Spacing Chart

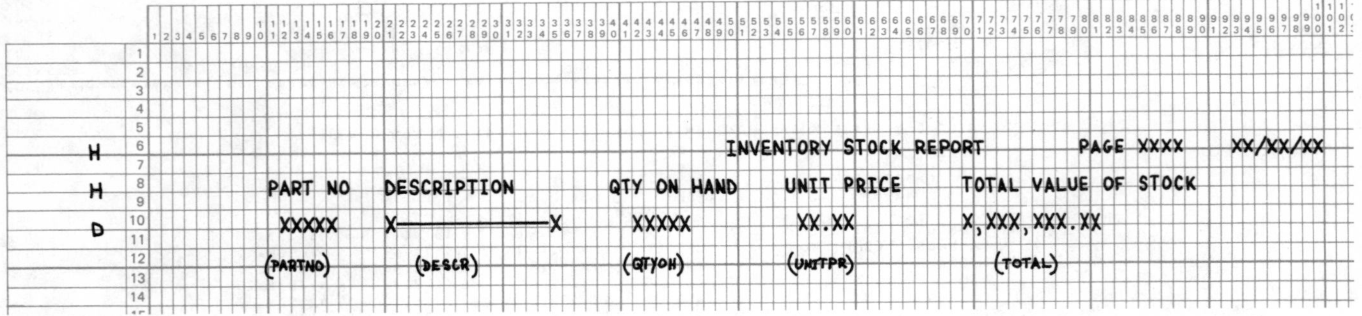

Notes

a. Total value of stock = Qty on hand X unit price.
b. All numeric fields are to be edited.

2. Consider the following and write the RPG II program to produce the desired results.

Systems Flowchart

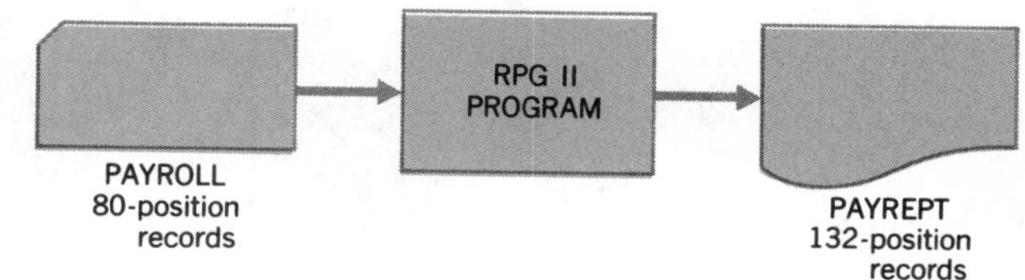

PAYROLL Record Layout

EMPLOYEE NUMBER (EMPNO)	NAME	ANNUAL SALARY (ANNSAL)		YEARLY DUES (DUES) $ ¢	INSURANCE (INSUR) $ ¢	
1–5	6–20	21–25	26–38	39–43	44–48	49–80

PAYREPT Printer Spacing Chart

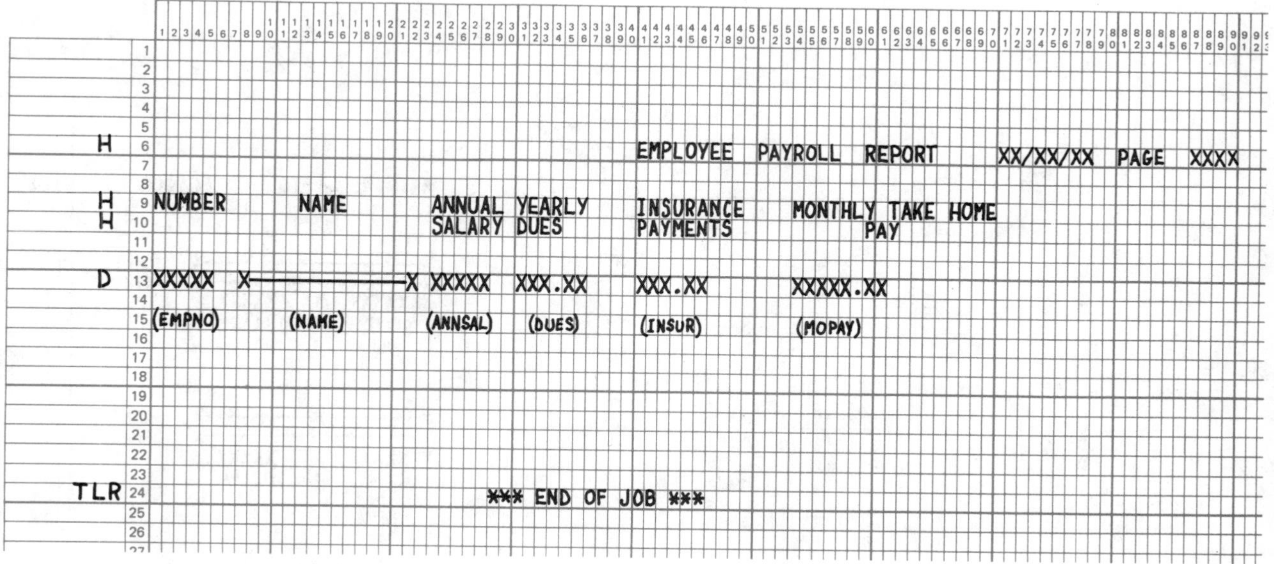

Notes

a. Monthly take-home pay = (Annual salary − yearly dues − insurance) / 12
b. Print *** END OF JOB *** after all records have been processed.

3. Consider the following and write the RPG II program to produce the desired output.

Systems Flowchart

MAILORD
100-position records

RPG II PROGRAM

MAILST
132-position records

MAILORD Record Layout

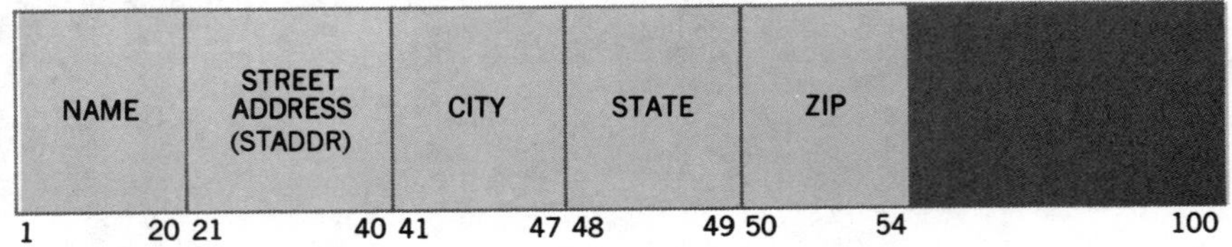

MAILST Printer Spacing Chart

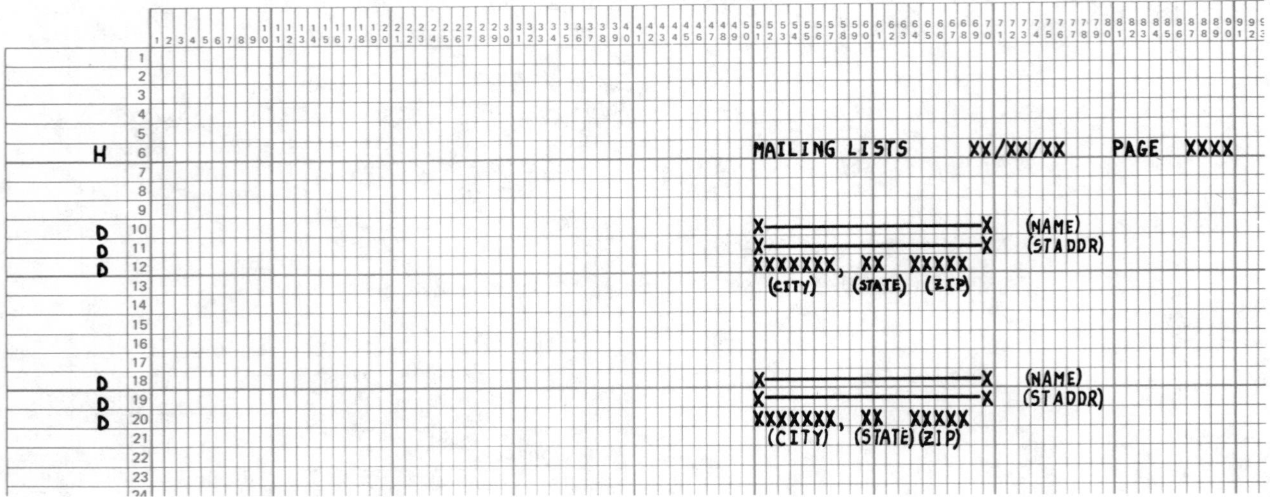

Note For every input record read, *three* lines of output will be generated.

4. Consider the following and write the RPG II program to produce the desired results.

Systems Flowchart

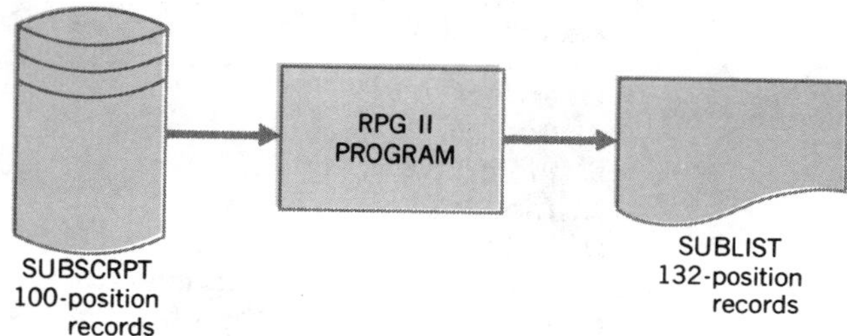

SUBSCRPT Record Layouts

Name record

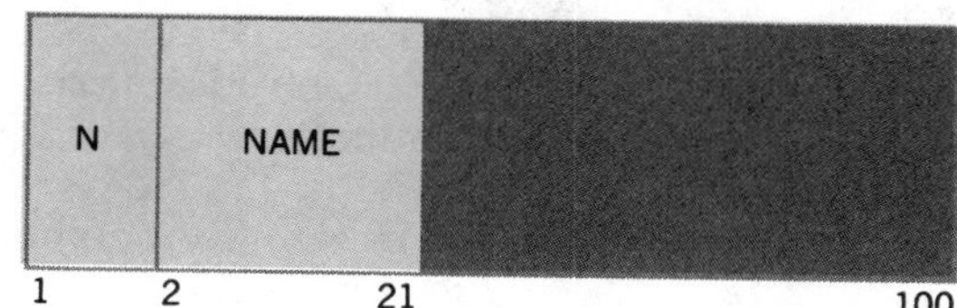

Street record

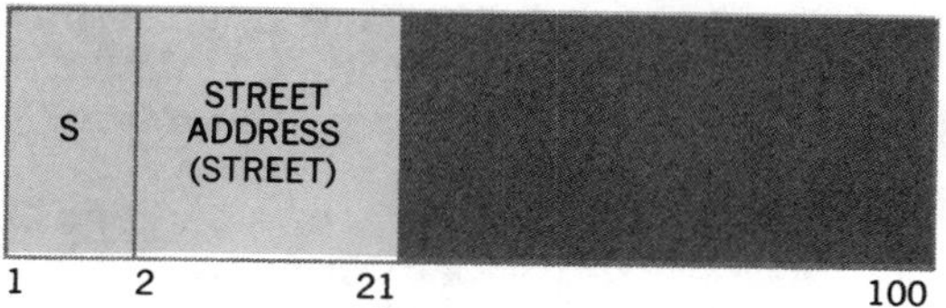

City, State, Zip record

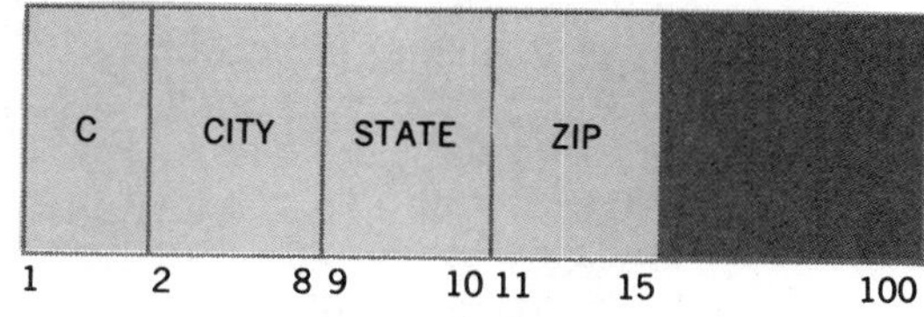

SUBLIST Printer Spacing Chart

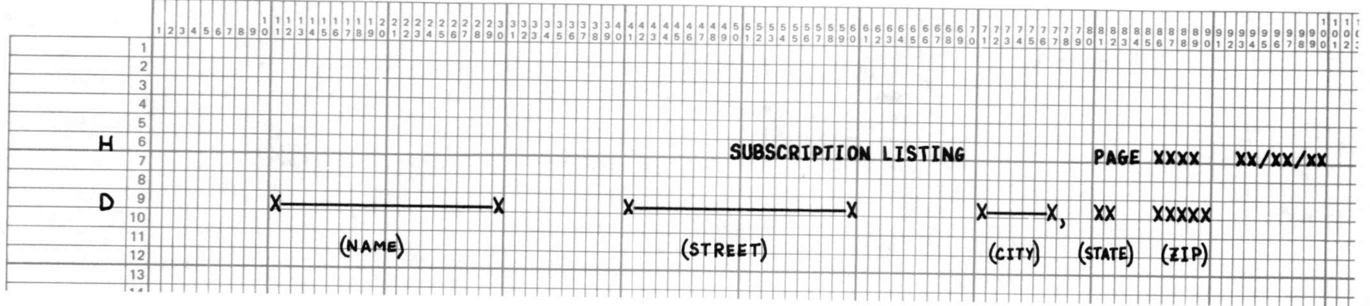

Notes

a. The Name record should precede the Street record, which precedes the City, State, and Zip record.
b. For every three input records read, one output line will print.

CHAPTER 3

Calculations and Arithmetic Operations

Objectives

- To develop an understanding of the programming concepts related to arithmetic operations, counting, and accumulating totals.
- To provide an understanding of how numeric fields are established in RPG for calculations and editing operations when totals are printed.
- To develop a working knowledge of the ADD, SUBtract, MULTiply, and DIVide operations and their basic features.
- To enable the student to enter calculations correctly on the coding sheets for complex arithmetic operations.
- To indicate how the correct size of result fields is determined for various arithmetic operations.
- To provide an understanding of the differences between rounding and truncation.

I. Overview

A. Sample Program 1

The following sample program introduces many of the concepts taught in this chapter. The purpose of the program is to print from a payroll file the regular and overtime hours worked by each employee. The program consists of the File Description form, Input Specifications form, Calculation Specifications form, and Output Specifications form. When coded, these forms must be entered into the computer system in the order indicated if a program is to function properly.

Moreover, an understanding of the RPG logic cycle is necessary in order for the programmer to arrange instructions in the proper sequence. The execution of the program occurs in time frames that correspond to the form being used. For instance, the traditional Input-Process-Output cycle may be thought of as being replaced by the Input form, Calculation form, and Output form. Indicators are used during these different time frames to control the operations to be performed in RPG. The problem definition for the sample program is specified in Figure 3.1. The program itself is illustrated in Figure 3.2. Study this program before continuing.

Systems Flowchart

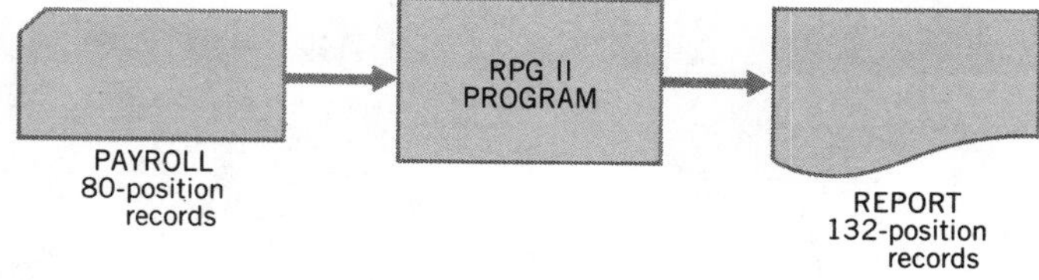

PAYROLL Record Layout

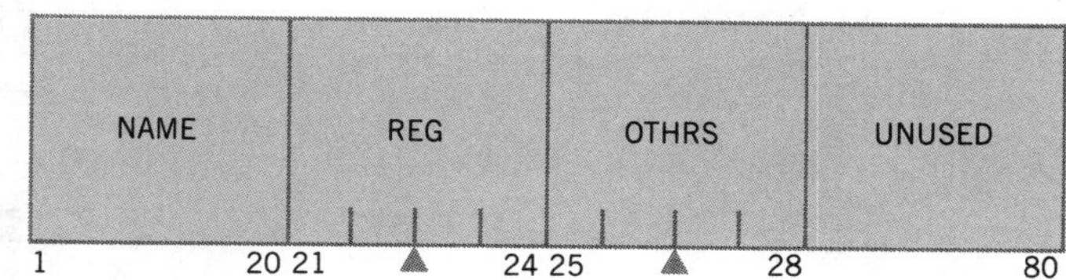

REPORT Printer Spacing Chart

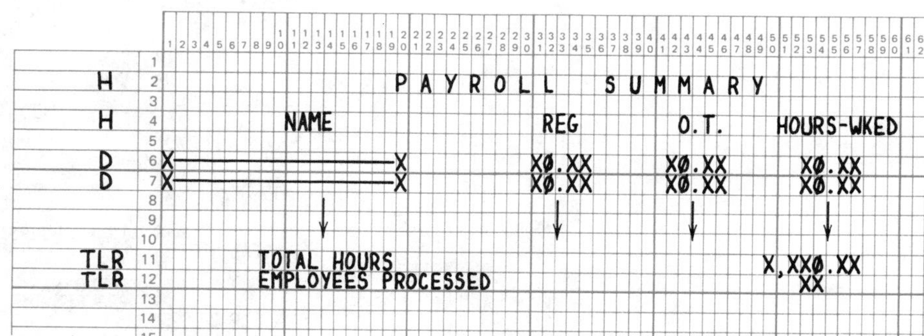

Figure 3.1
Problem definition for Sample Program 1.

Figure 3.2
Coding sheets for Sample Program 1.

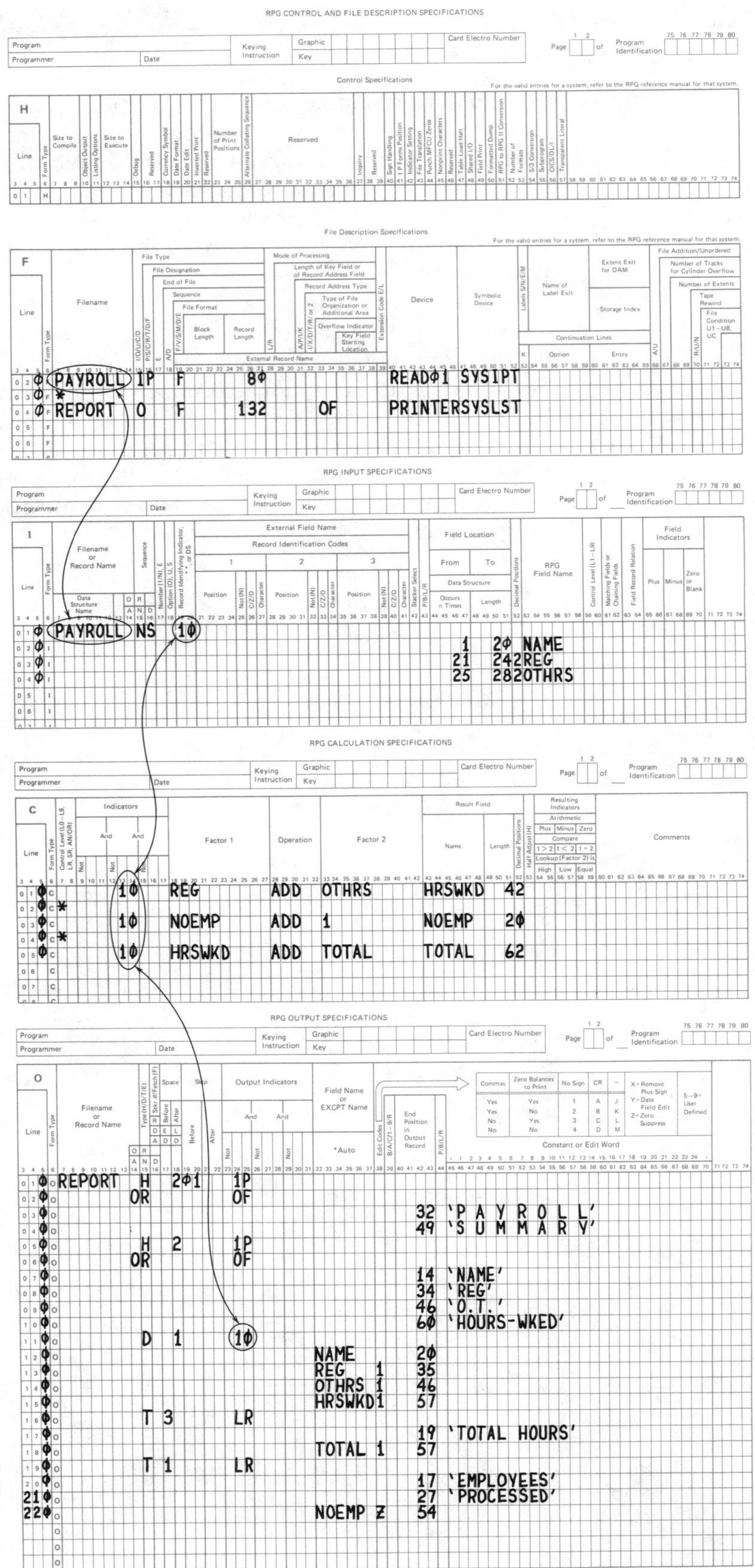

RPG CONTROL AND FILE DESCRIPTION SPECIFICATIONS

```
01 H
02ØF PAYROLL IP  F    8Ø        READØ1 SYSIPT
03ØF*
04ØF REPORT  O   F   132   OF   PRINTERSYSLST
```

RPG INPUT SPECIFICATIONS

```
01ØI PAYROLL NS  1Ø
02ØI                              1   2Ø NAME
03ØI                             21   242REG
04ØI                             25   282OTHRS
```

RPG CALCULATION SPECIFICATIONS

```
01ØC     1Ø  REG      ADD  OTHRS    HRSWKD  42
02ØC*
03ØC     1Ø  NOEMP    ADD  1        NOEMP   2Ø
04ØC*
05ØC     1Ø  HRSWKD   ADD  TOTAL    TOTAL   62
```

RPG OUTPUT SPECIFICATIONS

```
01ØO REPORT  H  2Ø1   1P
02ØO         OR       OF
03ØO                                  32 'P A Y R O L L'
04ØO                                  49 'S U M M A R Y'
05ØO         H  2     1P
06ØO         OR       OF
07ØO                                  14 'NAME'
08ØO                                  34 'REG'
09ØO                                  46 'O.T.'
10ØO                                  6Ø 'HOURS-WKED'
11ØO         D  1     1Ø
12ØO                         NAME     2Ø
13ØO                         REG    1 35
14ØO                         OTHRS  1 46
15ØO                         HRSWKD1  57
16ØO         T  3     LR
17ØO                                  19 'TOTAL HOURS'
18ØO                         TOTAL  1 57
19ØO         T  1     LR
20ØO                                  17 'EMPLOYEES'
21ØO                                  27 'PROCESSED'
22ØO                         NOEMP  Z 54
```

B. Indicators

Indicators may be turned "on" or "off" to check for (1) the presence of a particular condition such as a blank field on an input record, (2) the condition resulting from a comparison (high, low, or equal), or (3) different record types. Referring to the Input form in Figure 3.2, note that indicator 1Ø is turned on or set each time an input record is read. The Calculation form and Output form will specify indicator 1Ø when operations on each input record are to be performed by the program. At the end of the logic cycle for each input record, indicator 1Ø is automatically turned off by RPG. Hence, whenever a new record is read, indicator 1Ø is turned on and the subsequent operations referencing this indicator will be executed as the program steps through the different time frames. Let us now turn our attention to the RPG Logic Cycle.

C. The RPG Logic Cycle

Figure 3.1 includes the Printer Spacing Chart as part of the problem definition. The flowchart in Figure 3.3 depicts the steps necessary to produce the output specified by the Printer Spacing Chart.

Examining the logic diagram in Figure 3.3, we find that calculations are performed on each record being processed. Remember RPG uses indicators to determine if the calculation should be made. If a calculation was required only on records with a "B" in column 1, we would use an indicator to identify these records. The indicator would then be used to specify a calculation (see Figure 3.4).

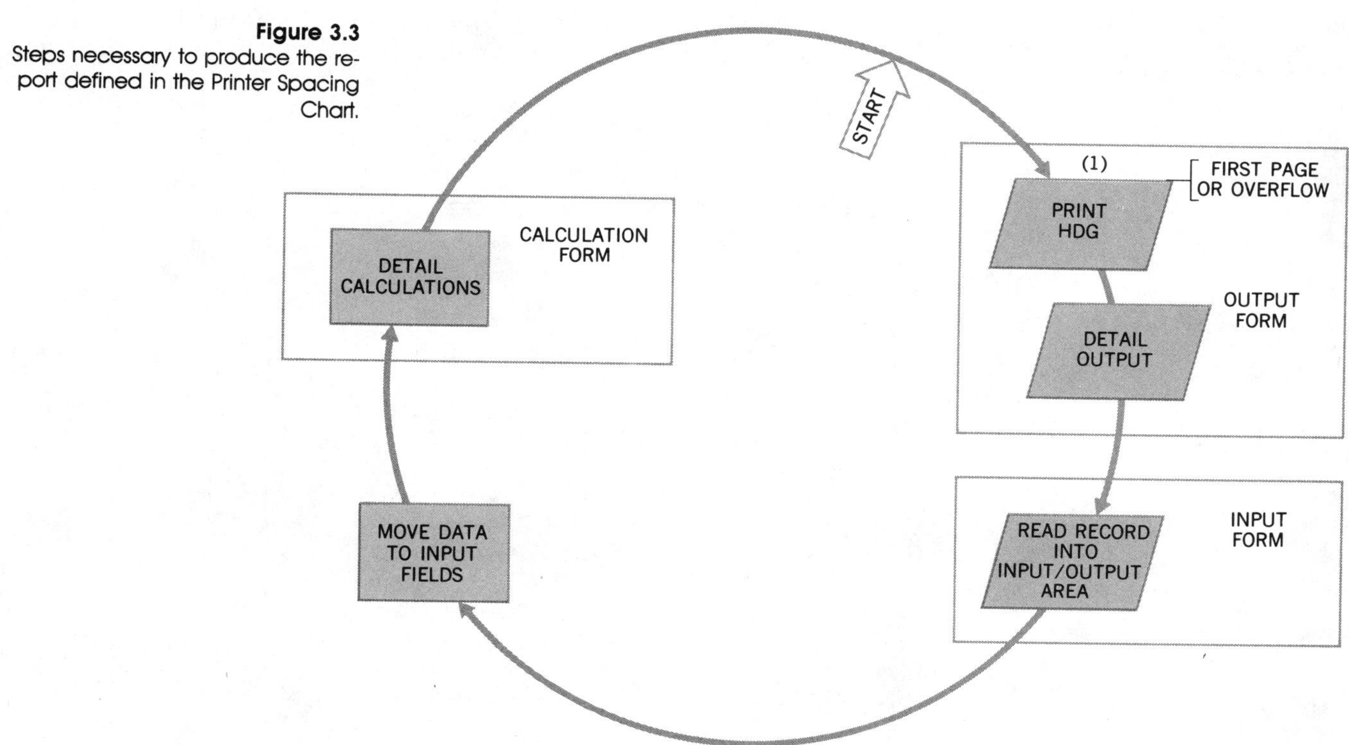

Figure 3.3
Steps necessary to produce the report defined in the Printer Spacing Chart.

The sequence in which the instructions are executed in RPG is again dependent on the logic cycle. The correspondence between the operations to be performed, the indicators, and the coding forms used is illustrated here.

Indicators	*Operation*	*Form*
1. 1P or OF	Headings are printed on the first pass or when a form overflow condition exists.	Output form
2. Record Indicator (Ø1-99)	A data record is read into the computer.	Input form
3. (None)	Input data is moved to the respective input fields.	(Automatic)
4. Record Indicator (Ø1-99)	Detail calculations are performed if the corresponding indicator is on.	Calculation form
5. Record Indicator (Ø1-99)	Detail output is produced if the corresponding indicator is on.	Output form
6. (Repeat cycle)	Repeat, using the next record, step 2.	(Repeat cycle)

Referring to the detail lines of the Printer Spacing Chart in Figure 3.1, note that the regular hours are added to the overtime hours to produce a third or result field containing total hours worked. It is important to realize that this calculation is performed *as each record is processed,* since an indicator (indicator 1Ø) is set each time an input record is read. The total hours field prints on the same line as the input fields. Reviewing the RPG logic diagram in Figure 3.3, note that detail calculations and detail output will result for each record entered as input. As we have already learned, indicators such as LR are also used to

Figure 3.4
The relationship between the Input and Calculation Specifications with respect to Record Indicators.
(Continued on next page.)

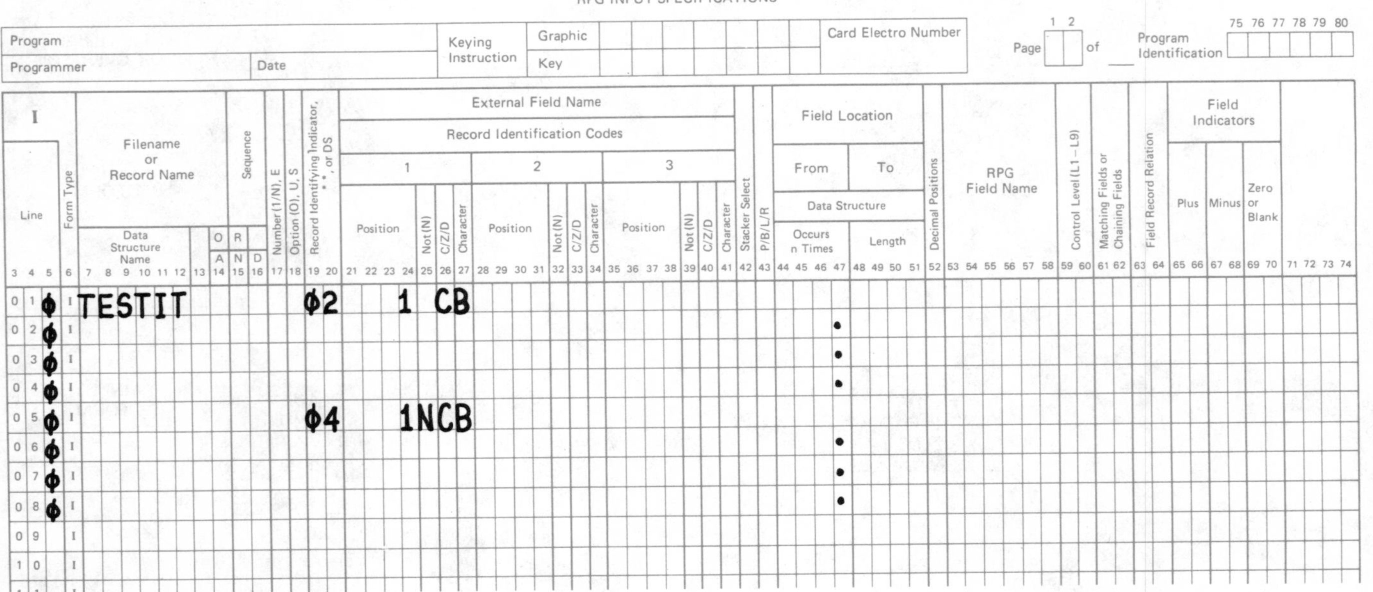
RPG INPUT SPECIFICATIONS

Program | Keying Instruction | Graphic | Key | Card Electro Number | Page of | Program Identification
Programmer | Date

Columns: Line (3–5) | Form Type (6) | Filename or Record Name (7–14); Data Structure Name | Sequence (15–16) | Number (1/N), E (17) | Option (O), U, S (18) | Record Identifying Indicator, **, or DS (19–20) | Record Identification Codes 1, 2, 3: Position, Not (N), C/Z/D, Character | Stacker Select | P/B/L/R | Field Location From, To; Data Structure Occurs n Times, Length | Decimal Positions | RPG Field Name | Control Level (L1–L9) | Matching Fields or Chaining Fields | Field Record Relation | Field Indicators Plus, Minus, Zero or Blank

01 I TESTIT Ø2 1 CB
02 I •
03 I •
04 I •
05 I Ø4 1NCB
06 I •
07 I •
08 I •
09 I
10 I

Record indicators

RPG CALCULATION SPECIFICATIONS

Line	Form Type	Indicators	Factor 1	Operation	Factor 2
01	C	ϕ2	.	ADD	.
02	C		.		.
03	C		.		.
04	C				
05	C				

Indicates that the calculation is to be performed only for records with a B in column 1

Figure 3.4
(continued)

control end-of-job routines and total line output, which are covered in detail later in the chapter. For the present, however, we will focus on detail calculations.

D. Defining Numeric Fields

Calculations can only be performed on fields containing numeric data. That is, arithmetic operations require that data be specified as numeric. Specifying an input field as numeric requires the programmer to enter a digit in column 52, Decimal Positions, on the Input form. If column 52 is left blank, the computer assumes the corresponding field to be alphameric, not numeric. As a consequence, calculations and editing will *not* be permitted on incoming fields that have a blank in Column 52.

The Input form for the sample program is illustrated here.

RPG INPUT SPECIFICATIONS

Line	Form Type	Filename or Record Name	Sequence	Record Identifying Indicator	From	To	Decimal Positions	RPG Field Name
01	I	PAYROLL	NS	1ϕ				
02	I				1	2ϕ		NAME
03	I				21	24	2	REG
04	I				25	28	2	OTHRS
05	I							
06	I							

Numeric field—length four positions including two decimal positions

In the sample program, the input records are contained in the PAYROLL file. In addition to the standard entries, column 52 contains a numeric entry for the number of decimal positions in those fields to be used in arithmetic operations.

The fields named REG and OTHRS both contain a "2" in column 52, indicating that these fields are numeric and that two decimal positions are implied.

It is important to remember that the input record does not contain *actual* decimal points; rather, decimal points are implied. To include the decimal point would waste storage space. Recall that 12345 entered as input will be interpreted by the computer as 123‸45 if a 2 is specified in column 52.

The implied decimal point *must* be specified for numeric fields since it is used by RPG to ensure proper alignment in calculations and editing. Again, numeric fields that are to be used in calculations *must* have an entry in column 52 indicating the number of implied decimal positions, even if it is Ø (zero). Zero denotes that the field contains all integers with no decimal places.

E. Calculation Specifications Form

The Calculation form, the heart of the logic of the program, performs the necessary arithmetic operations of adding, subtracting, multiplying, and dividing. The Calculation form specifies

1. The sequence in which the calculation operations are to be performed.
2. The specific arithmetic operation to be performed on the data.
3. The indicators to be used for determining if subsequent operations should or should not be executed.
4. If there is a need to check the results of an arithmetic operation, and if so, resulting indicators are then set.
5. Each calculation on a separate line of the form, in the sequence in which it is to be processed.

Consider the following calculations.

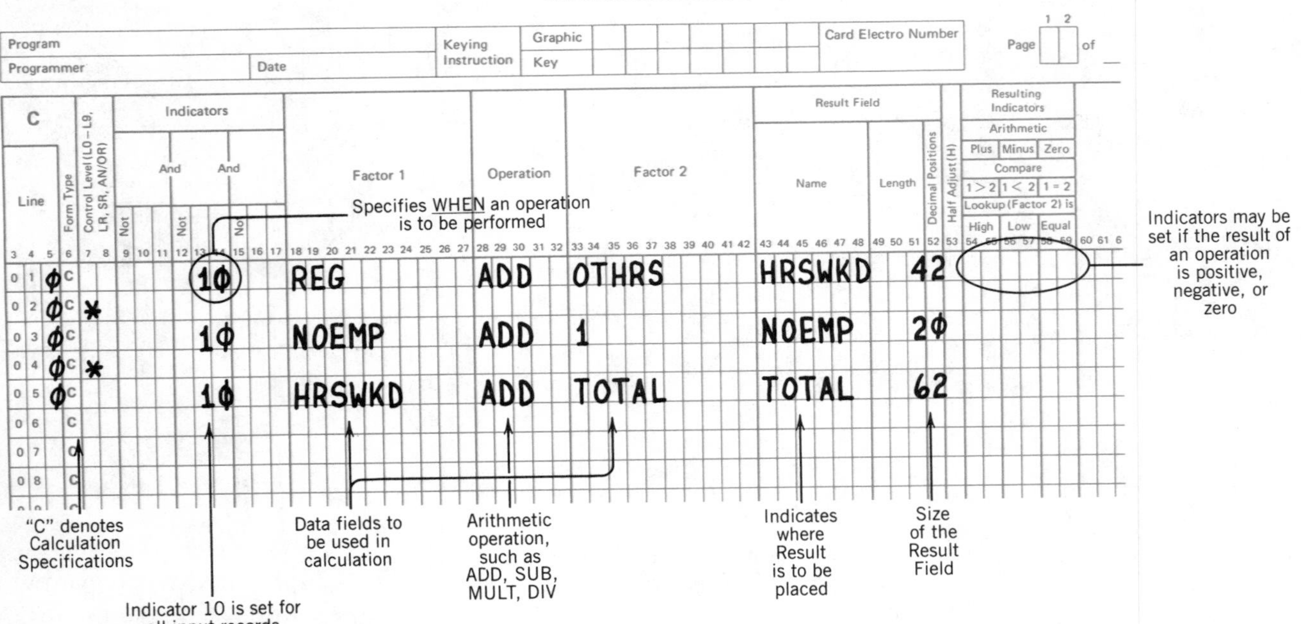

The Calculation form contains entries for

1. The operations to be performed.
2. The fields or constants to be used in the calculations.
3. The result field names.
4. The indicators used to control the operations.

Factor 1 and **Factor 2** may be interchanged for addition and multiplication operations, but you will need to be careful which fields you enter into Factor 1 and Factor 2 when performing subtraction and division operations since the results will be affected. An easy way to remember where to enter the fields is to think of the operation code as if it included the arithmetic symbol. Therefore, subtraction is thought of as Factor 1 *minus* (−) Factor 2; similarly, division is thought of as Factor 1 *divided by* (/) Factor 2. As indicated, with addition and multiplication, the fields assigned to Factor 1 and Factor 2 may be interchanged without affecting the results. We will next analyze the different types of addition operations found in the sample program.

F. Typical Addition Operations in Business Programs

Before considering the use of arithmetic operations in RPG, we will examine three general types of **ADDition operations** that are typically included in business programs.

1. Finding the sum of two fields.
2. Counting the number of records processed.
3. Maintaining a running total.

1. Finding the Sum of Two Fields

Recall that detail calculations are performed on each record being processed. Again, indicators are used to determine if the calculation should be performed. Indicator 1Ø is set each time an input record is read. (Refer to the Input form of the sample program in Figure 3.2.) In the example that follows, which is an excerpt from the sample program, note that the regular hours (REG) are added to the overtime hours (OTHRS) to produce a result field called hours worked (HRSWKD). Any prior contents of HRSWKD will be destroyed. Recall that a **result field** contains the outcome or result of an arithmetic operation.

RPG CALCULATION SPECIFICATIONS

Line	Form Type	Control Level	Indicators	Factor 1	Operation	Factor 2	Result Field Name	Length	Decimal Positions
01Ø	C		1Ø	REG	ADD	OTHRS	HRSWKD	4	2
02	C								
03	C								

Indicator set for each record read.

Result Field

Size of Result Field

In effect, the result field (HRSWKD) is being defined by the programmer on the Calculation form. Factor 1 and Factor 2 could be reversed in this and all ADD operations. The Result Field name, like all field names, must be 6 characters or less, begin with a letter, and contain letters and digits only. It is left-justified on the coding form.

In addition, the length of the field and the number of decimal positions it is to contain must also be specified. If the Result Field specifications for length and decimal position have been previously defined on the Calculation or Input form, then it must *not* be repeated. To illustrate this point, the following Calculation form will compute a value for HRSWKD using a two-step process.

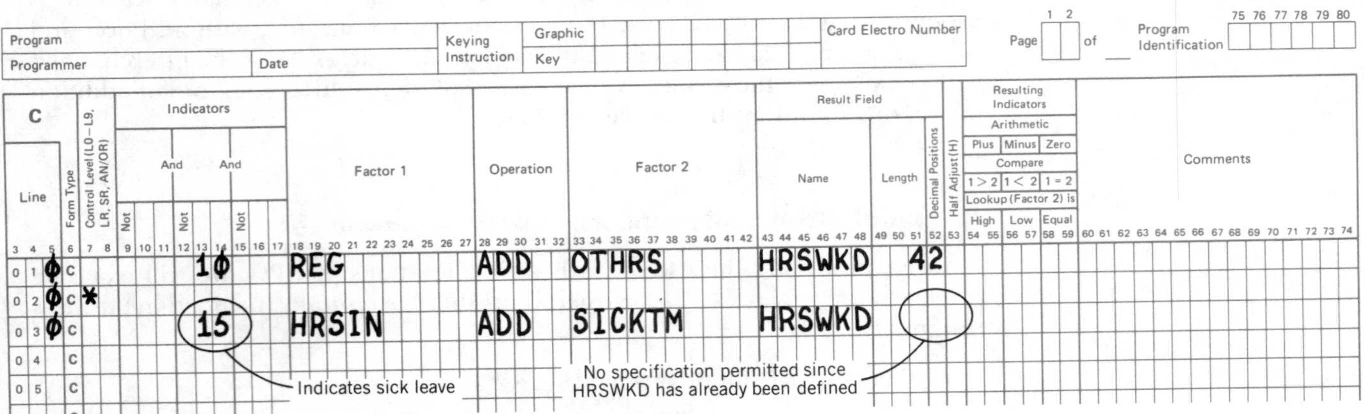

If indicator 15 is on, HRSWKD = SICKTM + HRSIN for this set of conditions. When indicator 1Ø is on, HRSWKD is calculated in the usual way by adding REGHRS and OTHRS. Note that HRSWKD contains length and decimal specifications only *once*, the first time the field is referenced. You can assume that the field called HRSWKD is initialized at zero, since RPG initially sets all fields to zero at the beginning of the program. Different indicators are being used by the different formulas; therefore, the calculation to be performed depends on whether indicator 1Ø or 15 is on. Remember:

> **Rule** Fields may only be defined *once* in an RPG program. That is, the field length and the number of decimal positions are coded once for a result field.

2. Counting the Number of Records Processed

a. Counter Concept A **counter** is used to record how many times an event occurs in a program. Typically, counters are used to count input records, count output lines, and record the number of errors that may occur during the execution of a program. In the sample program in Figure 3.2, the number of employees is counted as each input record is processed. Since the counter starts out with an initial value of zero, and one is added each time a record is processed, the counter will always reflect the number of employee records processed so far. In the following illustrations, the number 1 is a numeric literal or constant.

b. Counter Summary

RPG CALCULATION SPECIFICATIONS

Line	Form Type	Control Level	Indicators	Factor 1	Operation	Factor 2	Result Field Name	Length	Decimal Positions	Half Adjust	Resulting Indicators	Comments
01	C			NOEMP	ADD	1	NOEMP	Add 1 to NOEMP				
02	C											
03	C			NOLINE	ADD	1	NOLINE	Add 1 to NOLINE				
04	C											
05	C			COUNT	ADD	1	COUNT	Add 1 to COUNT				
06	C											
07	C							Meaning				
08	C											

Concept: A literal or numerical value is added to a field each time an event occurs.

Output: Final total counters are usually printed at the end of the run after the last record has been processed and the LR indicator is "on."

Remember, counters are developed by adding a numeric value such as one (1) each time an event occurs.

c. Numeric Literals In discussing the counter concept, it was noted that a constant value of one would be added to the counter field each time an input record is processed if we want to determine the total number of records processed. When actual numeric values are specified as one of the factors to be used in a calculation, they are referred to as **numeric literals** or **constants**. A numeric literal entered on the Calculation Specifications form may be 1 to 1Ø characters long and may contain a decimal point as well as a plus or minus sign. If the field is negative, the minus sign must be the left-most character in the field. The decimal point if used must be included in the constant. Another application of the numeric literal would be the calculation of the circumference of a circle, which is defined as the product of the circle's diameter times pi, or 3.141592. To calculate the circumference as pi times the diameter, pi should therefore be defined as follows on the Calculation Specifications form.

RPG CALCULATION SPECIFICATIONS

Line	Form Type	Control Level	Indicators	Factor 1	Operation	Factor 2	Result Field Name	Length	Decimal Positions	Half Adjust	Resulting Indicators	Comments
01ϕ	C		1ϕ	DIA	MULT	3.141592	CIRCUM	9	4			
02	C											
03	C			Numeric literal or constant								

> ***Summary for Numeric Literals***
>
> 1. The maximum length of a numeric literal is 1Ø digits. This permits a maximum amount of 9,999,999.99 if dollars and cents were to be represented or 9,999,999,999 for integers.
> 2. Numeric literals, as numeric field names, are left justified in either Factor field. The first character of the constant must be placed in the left-most position of the Factor field. If the field is negative, the minus sign must be the first character.
> 3. Numeric literals may not contain embedded blanks, commas, or dollar signs.
> 4. Numeric literals may include a sign and decimal point.

3. Maintaining a Running Total

A **running total** is used to sum or add up the value of a specific field defined in the program. Again, referring to the sample report, note that TOTAL represents the sum or accumulation of all the hours worked (HRSWKD). This running total is accumulated by adding HRSWKD to total hours (TOTAL) as each employee record is processed. Once HRSWKD is determined by adding REG and OTHRS, it is then added to the total field. The final result reflects the total accumulation of the hours worked. This field, TOTAL, would be printed when the LR indicator is set, that is, after the last record has been processed.

Total line output will be discussed in detail at the end of this chapter.

Summary for Running Total

RPG CALCULATION SPECIFICATIONS

Line	Form Type	Factor 1	Operation	Factor 2	Result Field Name	Comments
01	C	HRSWKD	ADD	THRS	THRS	Add HRSWKD to THRS
02	C					
03	C	PAY	ADD	TPAY	TPAY	Add PAY to TPAY
04	C					
05	C	DEDUCT	ADD	TDEDT	TDEDT	Add DEDUCT to TDEDT
06	C					
07	C					Meaning

Concept: A field is added to the total field as each record is processed.

Output: Totals may be printed at the end of the run after the last record has been processed and the LR indicator is "on," or whenever totals are desired.

Self-Evaluating Quiz: Counters and Totals

1. Add a field called HRS into a running total called THRS when indicator 1Ø is on. Assume HRS is defined on the input and THRS should be a seven-position field with two decimal places.

RPG CALCULATION SPECIFICATIONS

Program | Programmer | Date | Keying Instruction | Graphic | Key | Card Electro Number | Page 1 2 of | Program Identification 75 76 77 78 79 80

C | Line (3 4 5) | Form Type (6) | Control Level (L0–L9, LR, SR, AN/OR) (7 8) | Indicators: Not, And, Not, And, Not (9–17) | Factor 1 (18–27) | Operation (28–32) | Factor 2 (33–42) | Result Field: Name (43–48), Length (49–51) | Decimal Positions (52) | Half Adjust (H) (53) | Resulting Indicators: Arithmetic Plus Minus Zero; Compare 1 > 2, 1 < 2, 1 = 2; Lookup (Factor 2) is High Low Equal (54–59) | Comments (60–74)

0 1 C
0 2 C
0 3 C

2. Accumulate a field called GROSS into a field called TOTAL when indicator 15 is on. Assume GROSS has been defined on input and TOTAL is a seven-position field with two decimal places.

RPG CALCULATION SPECIFICATIONS

Program | Programmer | Date | Keying Instruction | Graphic | Key | Card Electro Number | Page 1 2 of | Program Identification 75 76 77 78 79 80

C | Line (3 4 5) | Form Type (6) | Control Level (L0–L9, LR, SR, AN/OR) (7 8) | Indicators: Not, And, Not, And, Not (9–17) | Factor 1 (18–27) | Operation (28–32) | Factor 2 (33–42) | Result Field: Name (43–48), Length (49–51) | Decimal Positions (52) | Half Adjust (H) (53) | Resulting Indicators: Arithmetic Plus Minus Zero; Compare 1 > 2, 1 < 2, 1 = 2; Lookup (Factor 2) is High Low Equal (54–59) | Comments (60–74)

0 1 C
0 2 C
0 3 C
0 4 C

3. Add a field called GRADE into a running total called AVG when indicator 2Ø is on. Assume GRADE and AVG have been defined previously.

RPG CALCULATION SPECIFICATIONS

Program | Programmer | Date | Keying Instruction | Graphic | Key | Card Electro Number | Page 1 2 of | Program Identification 75 76 77 78 79 80

C | Line (3 4 5) | Form Type (6) | Control Level (L0–L9, LR, SR, AN/OR) (7 8) | Indicators: Not, And, Not, And, Not (9–17) | Factor 1 (18–27) | Operation (28–32) | Factor 2 (33–42) | Result Field: Name (43–48), Length (49–51) | Decimal Positions (52) | Half Adjust (H) (53) | Resulting Indicators: Arithmetic Plus Minus Zero; Compare 1 > 2, 1 < 2, 1 = 2; Lookup (Factor 2) is High Low Equal (54–59) | Comments (60–74)

0 1 C
0 2 C
0 3 C
0 4 C

4. Add one to a three-position counter called CTR when indicator 25 is on.

RPG CALCULATION SPECIFICATIONS

Program | Keying Instruction: Graphic / Key | Card Electro Number | Page (1 2) of | Program Identification (75 76 77 78 79 80)
Programmer | Date

Line (3-5)	Form Type (6)	Control Level (L0–L9, LR, SR, AN/OR) (7-8)	Indicators: Not (9-11)	And: Not (12-14)	And: Not (15-17)	Factor 1 (18-27)	Operation (28-32)	Factor 2 (33-42)	Result Field: Name (43-48)	Length (49-51)	Decimal Positions (52)	Half Adjust (H) (53)	Resulting Indicators: Arithmetic Plus / Compare 1>2 / Lookup (Factor 2) is High (54-55)	Minus / 1<2 / Low (56-57)	Zero / 1=2 / Equal (58-59)	Comments (60-74)
01	C															
02	C															
03	C															
04	C															
05	C															
06	C															
07	C															

5. Increment a four-position counter named ODD by two each time indicators 1Ø and 15 are both on.

RPG CALCULATION SPECIFICATIONS

Program | Keying Instruction: Graphic / Key | Card Electro Number | Page (1 2) of | Program Identification (75 76 77 78 79 80)
Programmer | Date

Line (3-5)	Form Type (6)	Control Level (L0–L9, LR, SR, AN/OR) (7-8)	Indicators: Not (9-11)	And: Not (12-14)	And: Not (15-17)	Factor 1 (18-27)	Operation (28-32)	Factor 2 (33-42)	Result Field: Name (43-48)	Length (49-51)	Decimal Positions (52)	Half Adjust (H) (53)	Resulting Indicators: Arithmetic Plus / Compare 1>2 / Lookup (Factor 2) is High (54-55)	Minus / 1<2 / Low (56-57)	Zero / 1=2 / Equal (58-59)	Comments (60-74)
01	C															
02	C															
03	C															
04	C															

6. Accumulate a previously defined field called CREDIT into a total field named TCRED (8 positions, two decimal places) when indicator 35 or 45 is on.

RPG CALCULATION SPECIFICATIONS

Program | Keying Instruction: Graphic / Key | Card Electro Number | Page (1 2) of | Program Identification (75 76 77 78 79 80)
Programmer | Date

Line (3-5)	Form Type (6)	Control Level (L0–L9, LR, SR, AN/OR) (7-8)	Indicators: Not (9-11)	And: Not (12-14)	And: Not (15-17)	Factor 1 (18-27)	Operation (28-32)	Factor 2 (33-42)	Result Field: Name (43-48)	Length (49-51)	Decimal Positions (52)	Half Adjust (H) (53)	Resulting Indicators: Arithmetic Plus / Compare 1>2 / Lookup (Factor 2) is High (54-55)	Minus / 1<2 / Low (56-57)	Zero / 1=2 / Equal (58-59)	Comments (60-74)
01	C															
02	C															
03	C															
04	C															

Solutions 1.

RPG CALCULATION SPECIFICATIONS

Line	Form Type	Indicators	Factor 1	Operation	Factor 2	Result Field Name	Length	Decimal Positions
01	C	1Ø	HRS	ADD	THRS	THRS	7	2
02	C			OR				
03	C	1Ø	THRS	ADD	HRS	THRS	7	2
04	C							
05	C							

2.

RPG CALCULATION SPECIFICATIONS

Line	Form Type	Indicators	Factor 1	Operation	Factor 2	Result Field Name	Length	Decimal Positions
01	C	15	GROSS	ADD	TOTAL	TOTAL	7	2
02	C			OR				
03	C	15	TOTAL	ADD	GROSS	TOTAL	7	2
04	C							
05	C							

3.

RPG CALCULATION SPECIFICATIONS

Line	Form Type	Indicators	Factor 1	Operation	Factor 2	Result Field Name	Length	Decimal Positions
01	C	2Ø	GRADE	ADD	AVG	AVG		
02	C			OR				
03	C	2Ø	AVG	ADD	GRADE	AVG		
04	C							
05	C							

4.

RPG CALCULATION SPECIFICATIONS

Program		Keying Instruction	Graphic	Card Electro Number	Page 1 2 of	Program Identification 75 76 77 78 79 80
Programmer	Date		Key			

Line (3–5)	Form Type (6)	Control Level (L0–L9, LR, SR, AN/OR) (7–8)	Indicators: Not (9)	(10–11)	And: Not (12)	(13–14)	And: Not (15)	(16–17)	Factor 1 (18–27)	Operation (28–32)	Factor 2 (33–42)	Result Field Name (43–48)	Length (49–51)	Decimal Positions (52)	Half Adjust (H) (53)	Resulting Indicators: Arithmetic Plus / Compare 1>2 / Lookup (Factor 2) is High (54–55)	Minus / 1<2 / Low (56–57)	Zero / 1=2 / Equal (58–59)	Comments (60–74)
01	C			25					CTR	ADD	1	CTR	3	Φ					
02	C									—OR—									
03	C			25					1	ADD	CTR	CTR	3	Φ					
04	C																		
05	C																		

5.

RPG CALCULATION SPECIFICATIONS

Program		Keying Instruction	Graphic	Card Electro Number	Page 1 2 of	Program Identification 75 76 77 78 79 80
Programmer	Date		Key			

Line (3–5)	Form Type (6)	Control Level (L0–L9, LR, SR, AN/OR) (7–8)	Indicators: Not (9)	(10–11)	And: Not (12)	(13–14)	And: Not (15)	(16–17)	Factor 1 (18–27)	Operation (28–32)	Factor 2 (33–42)	Result Field Name (43–48)	Length (49–51)	Decimal Positions (52)	Half Adjust (H) (53)	Resulting Indicators: Arithmetic Plus / Compare 1>2 / Lookup (Factor 2) is High (54–55)	Minus / 1<2 / Low (56–57)	Zero / 1=2 / Equal (58–59)	Comments (60–74)
01	C			1Φ		15			ODD	ADD	2	ODD	4	Φ					
02	C									—OR—									
03	C			1Φ		15			2	ADD	ODD	ODD	4	Φ					
04	C																		
05	C																		

6.

RPG CALCULATION SPECIFICATIONS

Program		Keying Instruction	Graphic	Card Electro Number	Page 1 2 of	Program Identification 75 76 77 78 79 80
Programmer	Date		Key			

Line (3–5)	Form Type (6)	Control Level (L0–L9, LR, SR, AN/OR) (7–8)	Indicators: Not (9)	(10–11)	And: Not (12)	(13–14)	And: Not (15)	(16–17)	Factor 1 (18–27)	Operation (28–32)	Factor 2 (33–42)	Result Field Name (43–48)	Length (49–51)	Decimal Positions (52)	Half Adjust (H) (53)	Resulting Indicators: Arithmetic Plus / Compare 1>2 / Lookup (Factor 2) is High (54–55)	Minus / 1<2 / Low (56–57)	Zero / 1=2 / Equal (58–59)	Comments (60–74)
01	C			35															
02	C	OR		45					CREDIT	ADD	TCRED	TCRED	8	2					
03	C									—OR—									
04	C			35															
05	C	OR		45					TCRED	ADD	CREDIT	TCRED	8	2					
06	C																		
07	C																		

Note: Only the last line of an OR condition contains the calculations.

II. RPG Coding Considerations

A. ADD Instruction

Instruction:	ADD
Meaning:	Add two fields together to produce a sum.
Factors:	Factor 1 and Factor 2 are added. The contents of these fields do not change unless one of the factors is also used in the Result field.
Result:	The sum is stored in the Result field (may be the same as Factor 1 or Factor 2).
Limitation:	Make certain the Result field is large enough for the answer (usually at least one position larger than largest field used in ADD). Factor 1, Factor 2, and Result field must be numeric. Factor 1 or 2 may be a numeric literal.

The first instruction in the illustration in Figure 3.2 causes the regular hours (REG) of the input record to be added to the overtime hours (OTHRS) to produce a third field named HRSWKD. The addition only takes place when indicator 1Ø is "on." The field names entered in Factor 1, Factor 2, and the Result field are all left-justified. Decimal points are automatically aligned by RPG II and III. The example that follows illustrates how the ADD operation takes place in storage.

RPG CALCULATION SPECIFICATIONS

Program | Keying Instruction | Graphic | Key | Card Electro Number | Page 1 2 of | Program Identification 75 76 77 78 79 80
Programmer | Date

Line (3–5)	Form Type (6)	Control Level (LO–L9, LR, SR, AN/OR) (7–8)	Indicators (9–17)	Factor 1 (18–27)	Operation (28–32)	Factor 2 (33–42)	Result Field Name (43–48)	Length (49–51)	Decimal Positions (52)	Half Adjust (H) (53)	Resulting Indicators Plus/Minus/Zero (54–59)	Comments (60–74)
01Ø	C		1Ø	REG	ADD	OTHRS	HRSWKD	4	2			
02	C											
03	C											
04	C											

REG		OTHRS		HRSWKD—
4 0 0 0	+	1 0 0 0	=	5 0 0 0

You must specify where the result of a calculation is to be stored by naming that field in positions 43 through 48 on the Calculation form. The field that is entered can be a new field or one already defined on the Input or Calculation form. Only when a new field is named for the first time is the field length specified (columns 49 through 51). The Printer Spacing Chart, which is usually provided by the systems analyst, should indicate the size of all fields. The number of decimal positions for the result field is entered in column 52. In the sample problem, the field length was specified as 4 positions in length with 2 decimal places, because we are assuming that no employee has worked more than 99.99 hours.

B. Result Fields: The Problem of Truncation

The Result field must be of sufficient size to store the maximum value that can be obtained as a result of the calculation. When in doubt about how long to make a field, it is suggested that the programmer lengthen the field by one position. This will ensure that **truncation**, or loss of significant digits, does not occur. Truncation may occur in two different ways.

1. High-Order Truncation

High-order truncation occurs when an insufficient number of integer positions are assigned to the left of the decimal point. If an attempt is made to store the number $123_{\wedge}45$ in a field consisting of 4 positions with 2 decimal positions, high-order truncation will occur. That is, the left-most digit (1) would be lost.

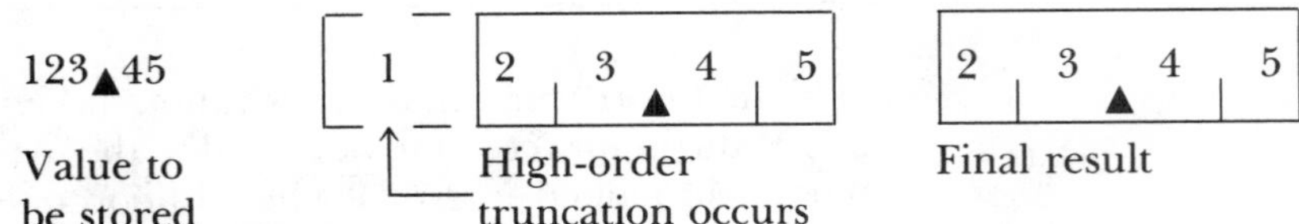

To determine the size of a Result field, perform the arithmetic operations required using the largest conceivable values for the factors. For example, if you assume that regular hours are 4Ø or less and that overtime hours may be as high as 99, you find that the largest result in HRSWKD would be 139, which is a 3-digit integer field.

To determine the size of THRS, or any running total field, you must know the approximate number of records to be processed for each run. If 139 is the maximum HRSWKD and you typically process 8Ø records or less, then the largest possible value for THRS would be 139 × 8Ø or 1112Ø, which is a 5-digit integer field.

2. Low-Order Truncation

Low-order truncation occurs when low-order digits, usually to the right of the decimal point, are truncated. This is not as serious a problem as high-order truncation. For example, if the value $123_{\wedge}45$ were stored in a four-digit field containing one decimal position, then the following would result.

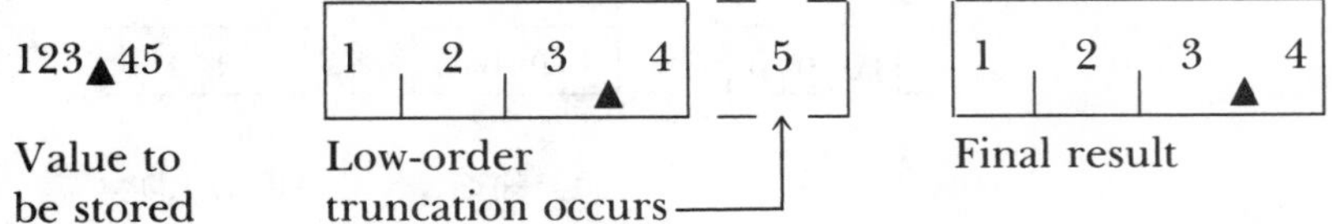

This type of truncation still retains the most significant digits of the original field.

Both these truncation problems can be avoided if the programmer takes the time to determine the maximum size of the field needed for the particular application. Usually the programmer knows in advance the number of decimal positions required for a resultant field. The Printer Spacing Chart is a helpful aid in establishing the size of printed fields, since the location, and thus length, of each field is specified.

Adding Several Fields in RPG

The Calculation form permits coding only two factors at a time for addition. Therefore, if the programmer was required to add FLDA, FLDB, and FLDC in order to produce a total, two steps would be required as illustrated here.

RPG CALCULATION SPECIFICATIONS

Line	Form Type	Control Level	Indicators	Factor 1	Operation	Factor 2	Result Field Name	Length	Decimal Positions
01Φ	C		1Φ	FLDA	ADD	FLDB	TOTAL	6	2
02Φ	C*								
03Φ	C		1Φ	TOTAL	ADD	FLDC	TOTAL		
04	C								
05	C								
06	C								

You will recall that a field is specified only once in the program; therefore, the length of the total field is omitted in the second instruction.

C. Using the ADD to Accumulate Totals

We have seen how the Calculation Specifications form is used to accumulate totals in an RPG program. When running totals are accumulated, the Result field is always one of the factors of the addition (see Figure 3.5 for an illustration).

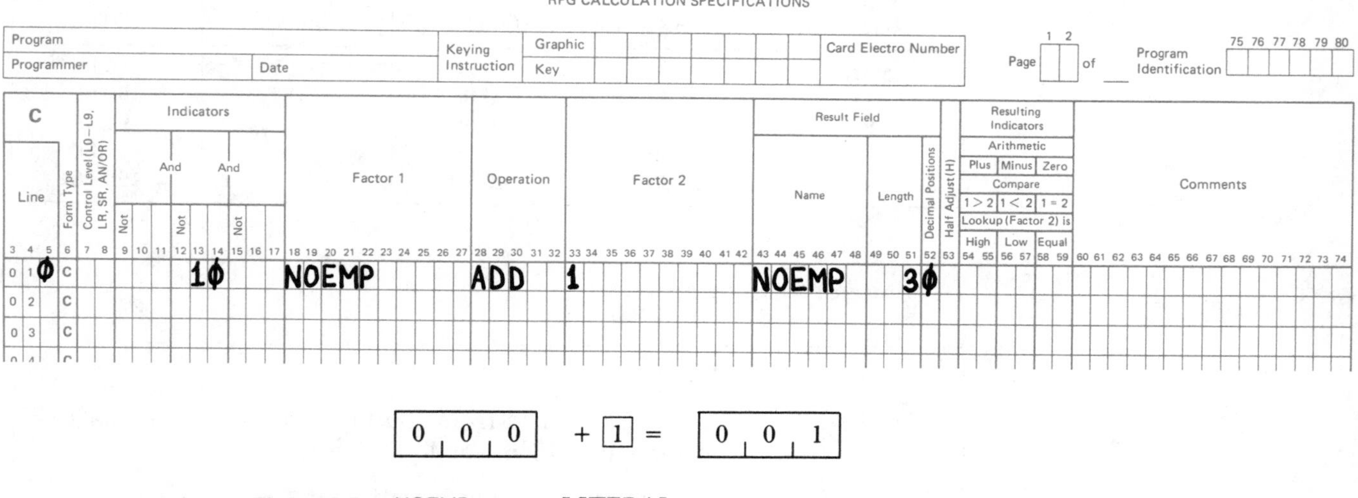

RPG CALCULATION SPECIFICATIONS

Line	Form Type	Control Level	Indicators	Factor 1	Operation	Factor 2	Result Field Name	Length	Decimal Positions
01Φ	C		1Φ	NOEMP	ADD	1	NOEMP	3	Φ
02	C								
03	C								
04	C								

Figure 3.5
Accumulating a running total.

RPG CALCULATION SPECIFICATIONS

Line	Form Type	Control Level	Indicators	Factor 1	Operation	Factor 2	Result Field Name	Length	Decimal Positions	Half Adjust (H)	Resulting Indicators	Comments
01Ø	C		1Ø	HRSWKD	ADD	TOTAL	TOTAL	6	2			
02	C											
03	C											
04	C											

Figure 3.6
Sample ADD instruction.

In Figure 3.5, the field called NOEMP (number of employees) will have the literal 1 added to it each time indicator 1Ø is "on." The results will be accumulated in NOEMP. After all the records have been processed, NOEMP will reflect the number of employees processed by the program. This technique can be used to count records, count lines, count errors, or to count any special conditions occurring in the program.

The field NOEMP was initialized or assigned a starting value of zero at the beginning of the program by the RPG II compiler. Unless it is cleared by the programmer, NOEMP will continue to increase by 1 each time indicator 1Ø is on.

Using Figure 3.2 again, TOTAL is similarly initialized to zero by the computer system at the beginning of the program. TOTAL will contain the sum of all the HRSWKD calculated by the program. Again, the Result field is also one of the factors. The size of the TOTAL field is designated in the Length field, columns 49-51 of the Calculation form. As a numeric entry, the size is right-justified in the field. The number of decimal positions must be specified in column 52 when a Result field is being defined. Consider the instruction in Figure 3.6.

This would cause the following calculations to occur as each record is processed.

Input Record	HRSWKD +	TOTAL	Giving	TOTAL
Start	0.00	0.00		0.00
1	50.00	0.00		50.00
2	44.50	50.00	⟶	94.50
3	46.30	94.50		140.80
4	52.00	140.80		192.80

D. SUBtract Instruction

Instruction:	SUB
Meaning:	Subtract one field from another algebraically. Decimal alignment is maintained.
Factors:	Factor 2 is subtracted from Factor 1 to produce a re-

	sult. The contents of these factors *do not change* (unless either field is used as a result).
Result:	The difference is placed in the Result field.
Limitations:	Make certain the Result field is large enough to accommodate the answer. The order of the factors is important and affects the results obtained. Result = Factor 1 − Factor 2

The SUBtract instruction subtracts the contents of the field referenced in Factor 2 from the contents of the field referenced in Factor 1. The result of the subtraction is placed in the Result field specified in columns 43-48 of the Calculation form. Figure 3.7 illustrates the SUBtraction operation.

RPG CALCULATION SPECIFICATIONS

Line (3-5)	Form Type (6)	Control Level (7-8)	Indicators (9-17)	Factor 1 (18-27)	Operation (28-32)	Factor 2 (33-42)	Result Field Name (43-48)	Length (49-51)	Decimal Positions (52)	Half Adjust (H) (53)	Resulting Indicators (54-59)	Comments (60-74)
01Φ	C		2Φ	PRICE	SUB	DISCT	COST	5	2			
02	C											
03	C											

Figure 3.7
Sample SUBtraction instruction.

PRICE 2 3 4 0 0 − DISCT 2 3 4 0 = COST 2 1 0 6 0

In the example shown in Figure 3.7, indicator 2Ø must be "on" if the subtraction is to take place. The PRICE field identified as Factor 1 is entered in columns 18-27 and, as an alphanumeric name, is left-justified. The DISCT field identified as Factor 2 is coded in columns 33-42, also left-justified. Factor 1 minus Factor 2 will produce a difference or answer to the SUBtraction operation in the Result field. This resulting difference is stored in the Result field named COST. Since COST is a new field, the length and number of decimal positions must be specified in columns 49-51 and column 52, respectively. The operation is entered in columns 28-32 and is again left-justified: names are left-justified, while numeric values are right-justified.

The format for the SUBtraction operation is easy to remember if you think of the calculation as Factor 1 minus Factor 2, which produces a Result field containing the difference.

When subtracting negative numbers, the results may sometimes be confusing unless you are familiar with the rules. Essentially, there is one basic rule to follow.

Rule. Change the sign of the number to be subtracted (Factor 2) and proceed as in addition.

Figure 3.8 illustrates the subtraction of a negative quantity.

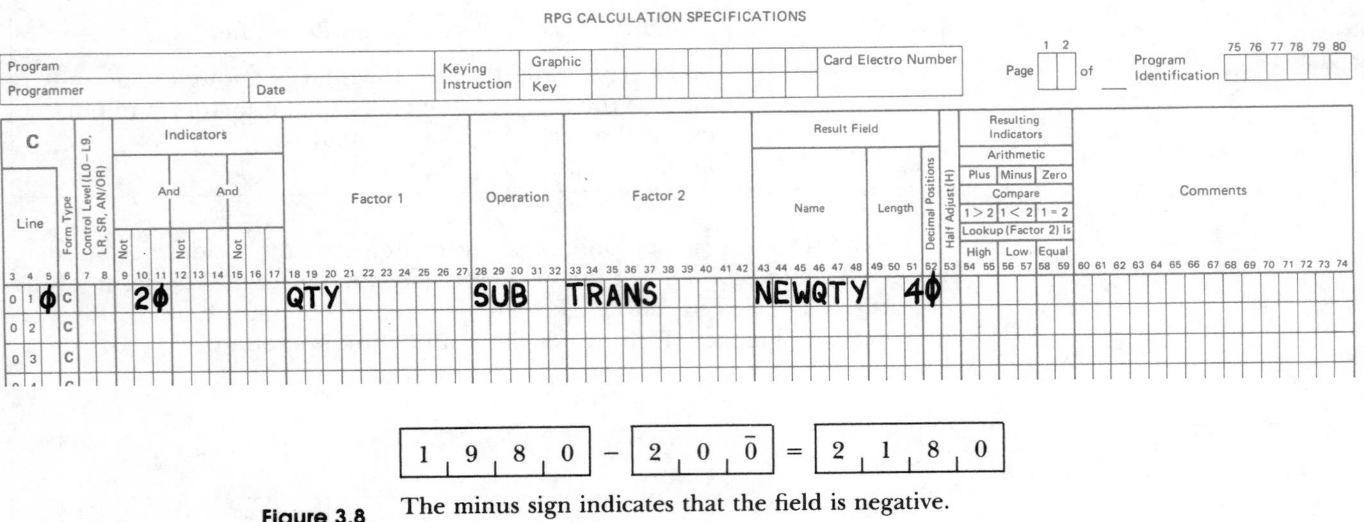

Figure 3.8
Subtraction of a negative quantity.

The minus sign indicates that the field is negative.
1980 − (−200) = 1980 + (+200) = 2180

> ***Subtracting a Negative Quantity***
>
> By changing the sign of Factor 2 and adding, the results of this operation are easy to determine.

Numeric literals can be used as either Factor 1 or Factor 2 in a SUBtraction operation. Additional examples of the SUBtraction operation are as follows.

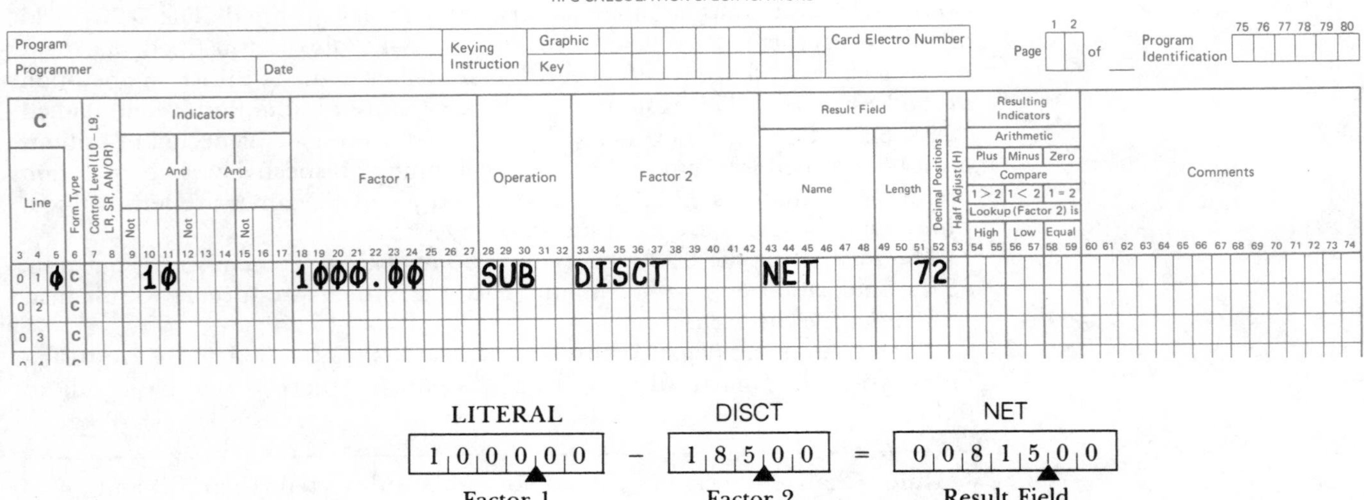

RPG CALCULATION SPECIFICATIONS

Line	Form Type	Control Level	Indicators	Factor 1	Operation	Factor 2	Result Field Name	Length	Decimal Positions	Half Adjust (H)	Resulting Indicators	Comments
01ϕ	C		1ϕ	GROSS	SUB	15ϕ	BONUS	5	2			
02	C											
03	C											

GROSS		LITERAL		BONUS
480.00	−	150.00	=	330.00
Factor 1		Factor 2		Result Field

E. Clearing Fields in Storage

1. Using the SUB Instruction

The need to reinitialize a field to zero often arises in a program; frequently, this reinitialization is required when a particular indicator is "on." The example in Figure 3.9 illustrates how the SUB operation could set the DEPHRS field to zero when indicator 15 is "on."

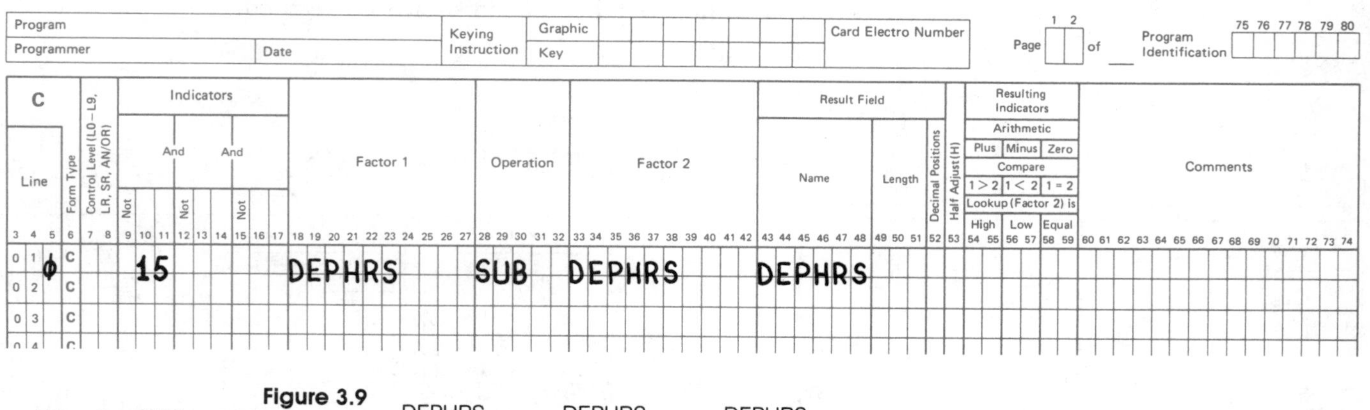
RPG CALCULATION SPECIFICATIONS

Line	Form Type	Control Level	Indicators	Factor 1	Operation	Factor 2	Result Field Name	Length	Decimal Positions	Half Adjust (H)	Resulting Indicators	Comments
01ϕ	C		15	DEPHRS	SUB	DEPHRS	DEPHRS					
02	C											
03	C											

Figure 3.9 Using the SUB operation to set a field to zero when a designated indicator is on.

DEPHRS		DEPHRS		DEPHRS
335	−	335	=	000

2. Using the Z-ADD Instruction

Other methods can be used to "clear" or "initialize" a field to zero. The **zero-and-add** (Z-ADD) **instruction** may be used to initialize or set a field to zero or to save the contents of a numeric field that would be lost as a result of the looping procedure used by the RPG II cycle. The net effect of this operation is to move or copy data from one storage location to another after clearing the result area. Typically, the Z-ADD instruction appears as follows.

RPG CALCULATION SPECIFICATIONS

Line	Form Type	Control Level	Factor 1	Operation	Factor 2	Result Field Name	Length	Decimal Positions	Contents *after* Z-ADD
01	C			Z-ADD	Ø	COUNT	3	Ø	0 in COUNT
02	C	*							
03	C			Z-ADD	NUMBR	SAVE	5	2	contents of NUMBR in SAVE
04	C	*							
05	C			Z-ADD	5	INDEX	3	Ø	5 in INDEX
06	C								
07	C								

Factor 1 is not used in the Z-ADD operation. The Z-ADD instruction causes the field specified as the Result field to be initialized at zero first. The data referenced in Factor 2 is then copied and moved to the Result field. The first example, in which Ø is Z-ADDed to COUNT, is another method for initializing a field. The following examples illustrate this concept and display the contents of storage before and after each instruction shown is executed.

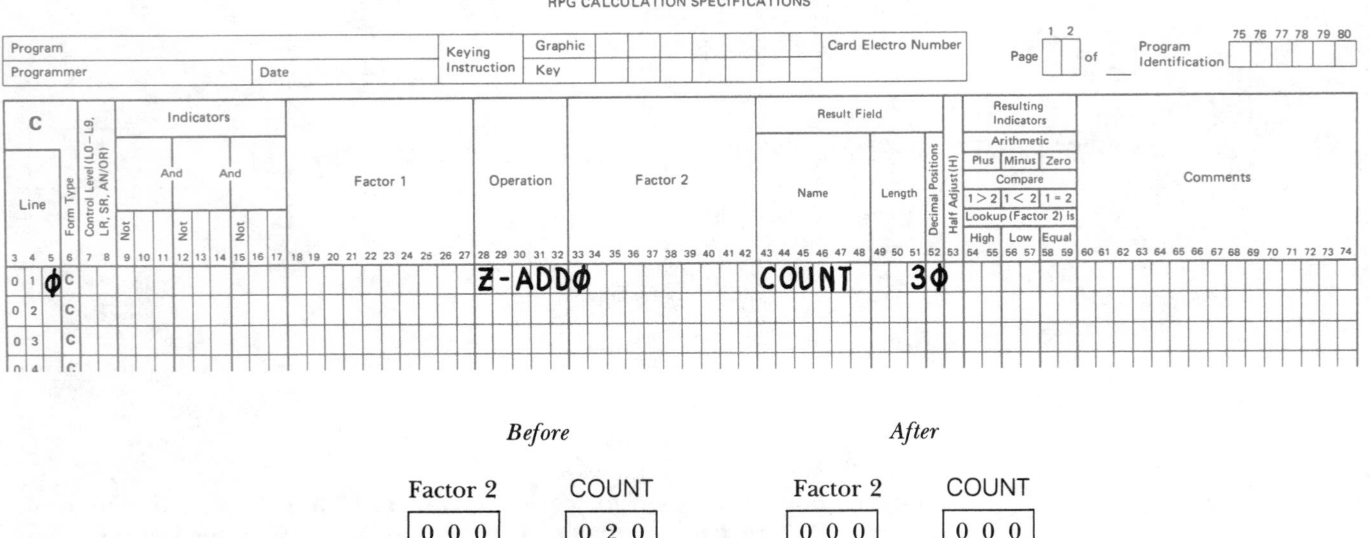

RPG CALCULATION SPECIFICATIONS

Line	Form Type	Factor 1	Operation	Factor 2	Result Field Name	Length	Decimal Positions
01	C		Z-ADD	Ø	COUNT	3	Ø
02	C						
03	C						

Before		*After*	
Factor 2	COUNT	Factor 2	COUNT
0 0 0	0 2 0	0 0 0	0 0 0

RPG CALCULATION SPECIFICATIONS

Line	Form Type	Control Level	Indicators	Factor 1	Operation	Factor 2	Result Field Name	Length	Decimal Positions	Half Adjust	Resulting Indicators	Comments
01	C											
02	C											
03Ø	C				Z-ADD	NUMBR	SAVE	5	2			
04	C											
05	C											

Before — Factor 2: 678 90; SAVE: 123 45

After — Factor 2: 678 90; SAVE: 678 90

RPG CALCULATION SPECIFICATIONS

Line	Form Type	Control Level	Indicators	Factor 1	Operation	Factor 2	Result Field Name	Length	Decimal Positions	Half Adjust	Resulting Indicators	Comments
01	C											
02	C											
03	C											
04	C											
05Ø	C				Z-ADD	5	INDEX	3	Ø			
06	C											
07	C											

Before — Factor 2: 0 0 5; INDEX: 6 9 0

After — Factor 2: 0 0 5; INDEX: 0 0 5

The Z-ADD instruction can be summarized as follows.

Instruction:	Z-ADD
Meaning:	Zero the Result field, and then move the contents of Factor 2 to the Result field. Decimal alignment is maintained
Factors:	Factor 1 is not used. Factor 2 contains the numeric data to be copied and moved to the Result field.
Result:	Factor 2 is copied at the Result field.
Limitations:	The Result field must be large enough to store the answer. Factor 2 may be a numeric literal.

F. MULTiplication Instruction

Instruction:	MULT
Meaning:	Multiply Factor 1 (the multiplicand) by Factor 2 (the multiplier). Decimal alignment is maintained.
Factors:	Factor 1 is multiplied by Factor 2 to produce a product. The contents of these fields do not change unless either is specified as the result.
Result:	The resulting product is stored in the Result field.
Length:	The length of the Result field must be large enough to hold the product, or truncation may occur.
Comments:	Factor 1 and Factor 2 may be interchanged without affecting the results.

Figure 3.10
Input layout to be used in multiplication example.

The input described in Figure 3.1Ø will be used to demonstrate how multiplication is performed.

RPG INPUT SPECIFICATIONS

Program | Programmer | Date | Keying Instruction: Graphic, Key | Card Electro Number | Page 1 2 of | Program Identification 75 76 77 78 79 80

Line (3-5)	Form Type (6)	Filename or Record Name (7-14)	Sequence (15-16)	Record Identifying Indicator (19-20)	Field Location From (44-47)	Field Location To (48-51)	Decimal Positions (52)	RPG Field Name (53-58)
01Ø	I	INVTRY	NS	1Ø				
02Ø	I				1	20	Ø	DESC
03Ø	I				21	25	2	PRICE
04Ø	I				26	27	Ø	QTY
05	I							
06	I							
07	I							

Operation to be Performed	*Terms*	*Sample Contents*	
PRICE	Multiplicand	999.99	Maximum contents
× QTY	Multiplier	99	
= COST	Product	98,999.Ø1	Maximum result

Determining the Size of the Result Field

Multiplication operations produce resulting fields that usually require more storage than either Factor 1 or Factor 2. The number of digits in the product field of a multiplication can be determined by *adding* the number of digits contained in the multiplicand to the number of digits contained in the multiplier.

		Left of decimal	*Right of decimal*	*Total no. of digits*
Number of digits in multiplicand	=	3	2	5
Number of digits in multiplier	=	2	Ø	2
Number of digits in product	=	5	2	7

It is essential that the programmer establish a large enough field for the product of a multiplication. If the product field is too small, *truncation* may result. Recall that truncation results in the loss of the most significant digits. In this example, if the programmer had provided a product field six digits in length with two decimal positions, then the Result field might be too small to store the answer. Hence, the left-most digit could be lost and the results would clearly be incorrect.

If PRICE = 999.99 and QTY = 99 and the product was designated as fewer than five integers, Figure 3.11 would indicate the incorrect results.

Field containing six digits
with two decimal positions

On most computers, the digit is lost due to truncation.

9	8	9	9	9	0	1

Figure 3.11 Truncation.

Again, if the multiply operation is to be successfully executed, the programmer must establish the size of the product field very carefully. If you are certain that COST, for example, never exceeds 9,999.99, then a six-digit Result field would be large enough.

> ***Rules for Determining the Field Size of the Product***
> 1. Calculate the number of integers (digits to the left of the decimal point) required to hold the product.
> 2. Decide the number of decimal places (digits to the right of the decimal point) that you would like.
> 3. Add the two together to determine Result field length.

To multiply PRICE by QTY and to make certain that the result, called COST, is large enough, code the calculation as shown in Figure 3.12.

For the multiplication to be performed, the arithmetic operation MULT must be entered in the Operation field in columns 28-32. As with previous illustrations, the variable entries for Factor 1, Factor 2, and the name of the Result field are left-justified in their respective fields on the Calculation form.

RPG CALCULATION SPECIFICATIONS

Line	Form Type	Control Level	Indicators	Factor 1	Operation	Factor 2	Result Field Name	Length	Decimal Positions	Half Adjust	Resulting Indicators	Comments
010	C		10	PRICE	MULT	QTY	COST	7	2			
02	C											
03	C											

Example

PRICE		QTY		COST
1 1 9 9 9	×	8 8	=	1 0 5 5 9 1 2

Field Size: 5 (2 decimal places) + 2 = 7 (2 decimal places)

Figure 3.12
Example of MULTiplication.

A factor to be used in a MULT instruction can be a numeric literal such as: GROSS MULT .Ø5 TAX.

Multiplying* 3 *Numbers Together

The following 2 operations would be required to compute

$$D = A \times B \times C$$

Note that the field specifications for D are defined only once, the first time D is used. Note that D can be a factor as in the second operation, as well as a result.

RPG CALCULATION SPECIFICATIONS

Line	Form Type	Control Level	Indicators	Factor 1	Operation	Factor 2	Result Field Name	Length	Decimal Positions	Half Adjust	Resulting Indicators	Comments
010	C			A	MULT	B	D	6	2			A × B = RESULT
020	C*											
030	C			C	MULT	D	D					C × RESULT = D
04	C											
05	C											

This technique can be used for multiplying any number of variables.

G. Rounding Concepts

When programming for business applications, results are often expressed as dollars and cents; that is, with two decimal positions. The multiply and divide instructions frequently create situations where **rounding** to two decimal places is necessary. For example, the discount (DISCT) calculated in the following example will result in a product field containing four digits to the right of the implied decimal point.

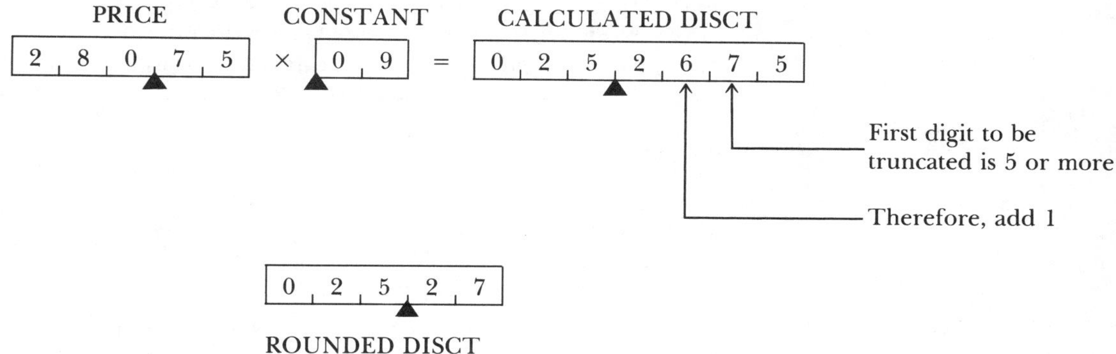

The result of the calculation illustrated is 25.2675. If DISCT were specified as four positions in length with two decimal positions, 25.2675 would be truncated and the result would be 25.26. Thus the last two digits would be lost. In business, however, this result would be more properly rounded to 25.27.

Use H in the **Half-adjust** field (column 53) to obtain rounding (see Figure 3.13).

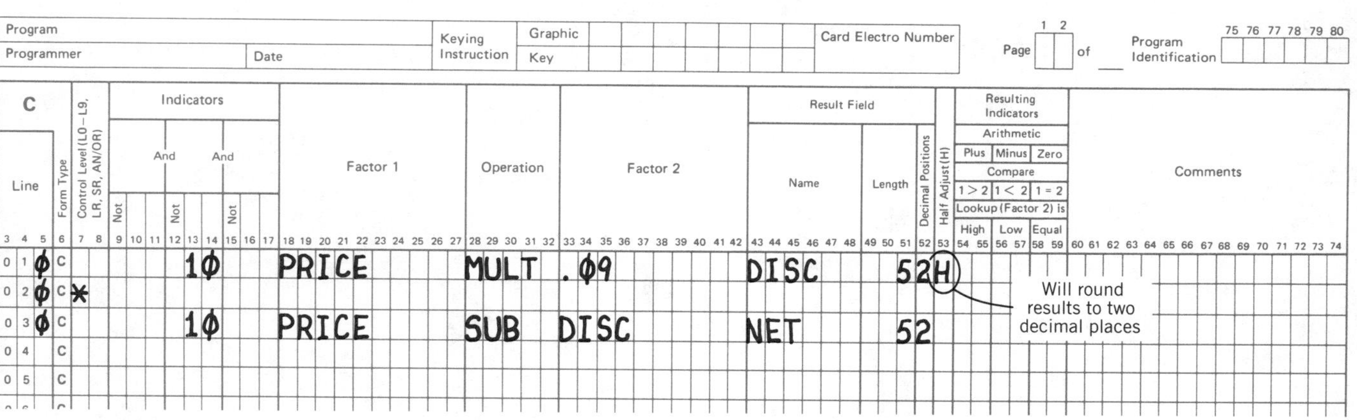

Figure 3.13
Use of the Half-adjust field to obtain rounding.

To further illustrate the concept of rounding, review the following examples.

Round to the Nearest Cent

Field Contents	*Field Rounded*
123.4567	123.46
7.9999	8.ØØ
−73.6578	−73.66
9.345	9.35
13.3333	13.33

Round to the Nearest Integer (Whole Number)

Field Contents	*Field Rounded*
123.4567	123
7.9999	8
−73.6578	−74
9.345	9
13.3333	13

The rounding calculations are performed as illustrated in Examples 1 and 2 below. Notice that a value of five is added to the digit immediately *to the right of the digit to be rounded.* Once the addition is completed, all digits to the right of the rounded digit are truncated.

Example 1 *Round to the Nearest Cent*

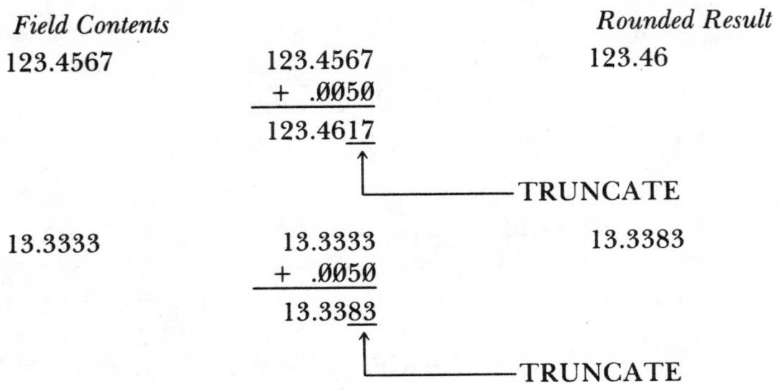

Example 2 *Round to the Nearest Integer*

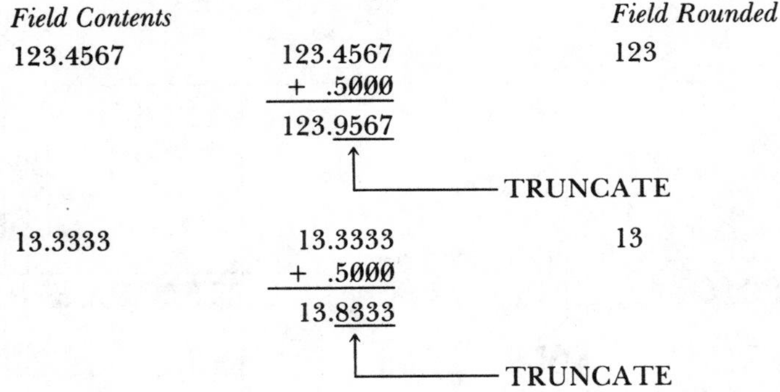

A general rule for rounding is that the final result contains the value that is the nearest approximation to the given number. For example, the rounded result in Example 1, 123.46, is closer to 123.4567 than is 123.45. This can be demonstrated as follows.

```
  123.4567       123.46ØØ
− 123.45ØØ     − 123.4567
    .ØØ67          .ØØ33
```

The error introduced by rounding up and using a value of 123.46 is only .ØØ33, as compared to an error of .ØØ67 that occurs when the result is truncated to 123.45. Therefore, to ensure accuracy and minimize errors resulting from approximation, numbers are rounded by entering an H (half-adjust) in column 53 of the field to be rounded.

Rounding may also introduce errors when running totals are used in a program. For example, if a bank was to pay 12.4% straight interest on a $1,ØØØ deposit, the investor would expect to receive 124.ØØ in interest for 1 year (annual interest = .124 × 1,ØØØ.ØØ = $124.ØØ). If the interest were to be paid monthly, the investor would receive the following.

Monthly interest = Annual interest/12 = 124.ØØ/12 = 1Ø.3333

After rounding, the amount of the monthly interest would be 1Ø.33. Twelve payments of 1Ø.33, however, would introduce an error of 4 cents, since 12 times 1Ø.33 = $123.96. Hence, it is critical that the programmer be aware of the errors that may be introduced by rounding and the overall effect on the results produced by the program. In order to compensate for the error just illustrated, an adjustment in the last interest payment would be required. This type of problem is solved in the Debugging Exercise in Chapter 6.

H. DIVide Instruction

Instruction:	DIV
Meaning:	Factor 1 is divided by Factor 2. Decimal alignment is maintained.
Results:	Factor 1 and Factor 2 remain unchanged. The quotient is referenced by the name entered in the Result field.
Length:	When dividing by a field that is greater than 1, the maximum number of digits in the quotient is equal to the number of digits in the dividend. Additional positions to the right of the decimal may also be specified and rounded.
Limitations:	An attempt to divide by zero will cause an error. Factor 2, therefore, cannot have a zero value. It is useful to test Factor 2 for zero before dividing to make certain that errors do not occur.
Schematic:	$\text{Divisor}\ \overline{)\text{Dividend}}$ with Quotient above

The divide instruction requires the entry of DIV in the operation field specified as columns 28-32. The dividend, contained in Factor 1, is divided by the divisor (Factor 2), resulting in the quotient. The quotient is stored in the Result field. The quotient will be algebraically signed depending on the dividend and the divisor. If their signs are the same, that is, both positive or both negative, then the quotient will be positive. If they contain opposite signs, then the quotient will be negative. Remember, to print a result with a sign, you must use the appropriate Edit Code on the Output form.

Assume, for example, that an input record is defined as in Figure 3.14. Figure 3.15 illustrates how division instructions can be coded.

In the example shown, compute the class average AVG by dividing the total

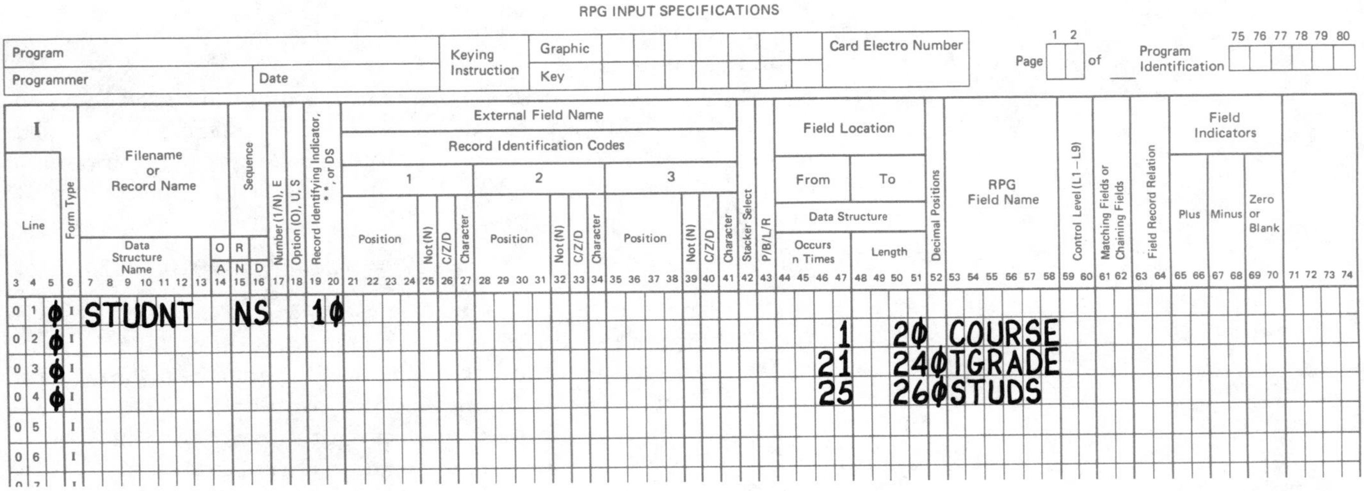

RPG INPUT SPECIFICATIONS

Line	Form Type	Filename or Record Name	Sequence	Record Identifying Indicator	Field Location From	Field Location To	Decimal Positions	RPG Field Name
01	I	STUDNT	NS	1ϕ				
02	I				1	2ϕ		COURSE
03	I				21	24	ϕ	TGRADE
04	I				25	26	ϕ	STUDS
05	I							
06	I							

Figure 3.14 Input Specifications for DIVision example.

Operation	*Terms*	*Calculation*	*Formula*
AVG ←	Quotient	0078	
STUDS)TGRADE ←	Dividend	32)2496	TGRADE / STUDS = AVG
(STUDS) ←	Divisor	224	
		256	
		256	
		00	

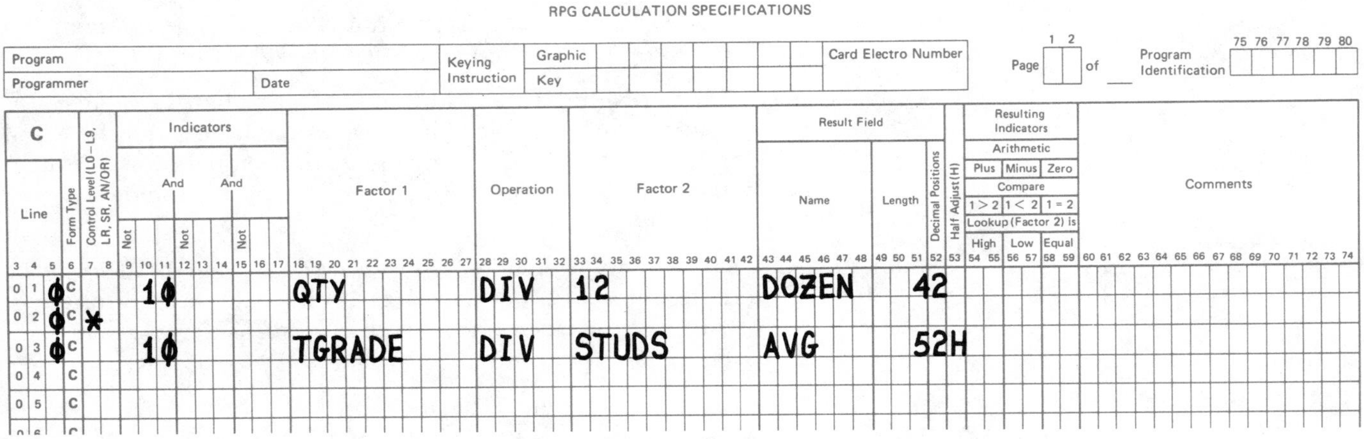

RPG CALCULATION SPECIFICATIONS

Line	Form Type	Control Level	Indicators	Factor 1	Operation	Factor 2	Result Field Name	Length	Decimal Positions	Half Adjust (H)
01	C		1ϕ	QTY	DIV	12	DOZEN	4	2	
02	C	*								
03	C		1ϕ	TGRADE	DIV	STUDS	AVG	5	2	H
04	C									
05	C									

Figure 3.15 Examples of DIVision.

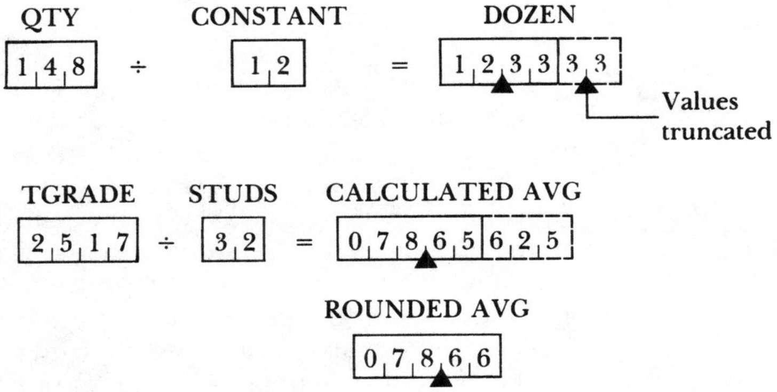

QTY: 148 ÷ CONSTANT: 12 = DOZEN: 12.33 | 33 (Values truncated)

TGRADE: 2517 ÷ STUDS: 32 = CALCULATED AVG: 078.65 | 625

ROUNDED AVG: 078.66

grades (TGRADE) by the number of students (STUDS) in the class. The programmer is again responsible for establishing fields of the proper length to store results. In Figure 3.14, the remainder was zero. However, additional positions to the right of the decimal point could have been specified to provide more accurate results if a decimal component was desired. In the example that follows, the results of the division operation could be extended to include two decimal positions.

```
     0078.50
  32)2512.00
     224
      272
      256
       160
       160
```

The results of the division may also be rounded in a manner similar to that used in multiplication.

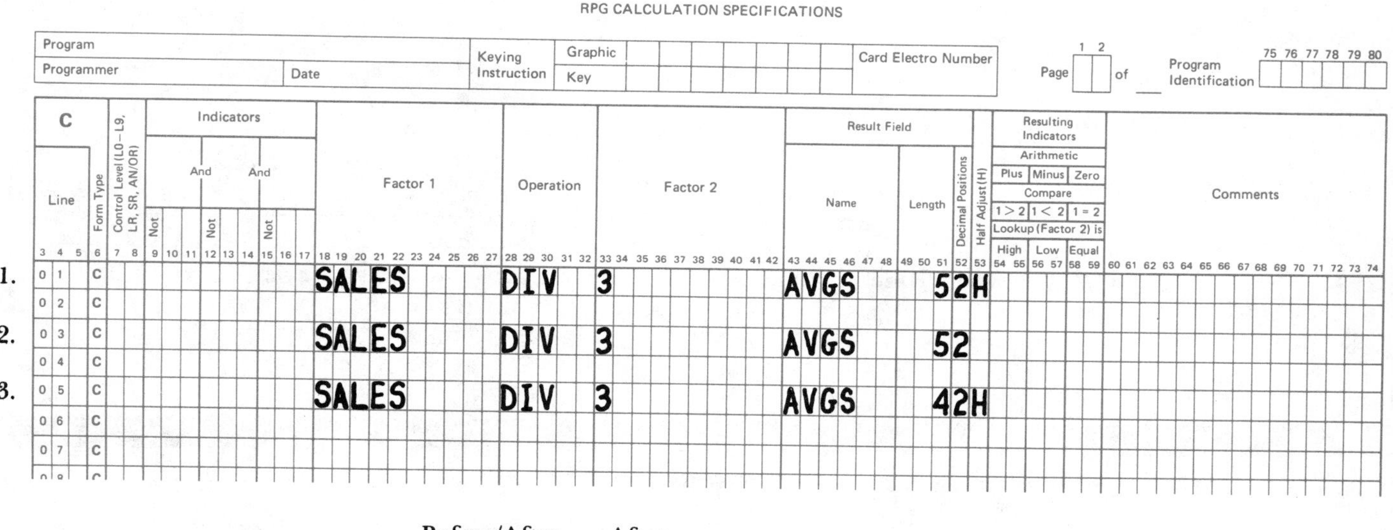

RPG CALCULATION SPECIFICATIONS

	Line	Form Type	Factor 1	Operation	Factor 2	Result Field Name	Length	Decimal Positions	Half Adjust (H)
1.	01	C	SALES	DIV	3	AVGS	5	2	H
	02	C							
2.	03	C	SALES	DIV	3	AVGS	5	2	
	04	C							
3.	05	C	SALES	DIV	3	AVGS	4	2	H
	06	C							
	07	C							

	Before/After calculation SALES	After calculation AVGS	
1.	2000 00	6 6 6 6 7	Rounding
2.	2000 00	6 6 6 6 6	Low-order truncation
3.	2000 00	6 6 6 7	High-order truncation

The field in example 1 is of sufficient size and yields correctly rounded results. Example 2 would result in low-order truncation; that is, the right-most position would not be rounded. In many business applications, rounding of the second decimal position is the usual and accepted practice. There are, however, numerous instances where other types of rounding are required.

In example 3 a more serious error occurs. High-order truncation, as illustrated, is caused when a Result field is sized too small. The importance of **sizing fields** correctly cannot be overemphasized.

To determine the size of a Result field used as a quotient, you must know the range of both the dividend and the divisor. Performing the divisions using these ranges yourself will help you determine the size to be allocated for the result. When in doubt, always make the Result field larger, since it will not adversely affect the processing to do so.

I. Summary of Arithmetic Operations

SUMMARY OF ARITHMETIC OPERATIONS

Factor 1	*Operation*	*Factor 2*	*Result*	*Value After Execution* A	B	C
A	ADD	B	C	A	B	*A + B*
A	ADD	B	B	A	*A + B*	
A	SUB	A	A	*Zero*		
A	SUB	B	C	A	B	*A − B*
A	SUB	B	A	*A − B*	B	
A	MULT	B	C	A	B	*A × B*
A	MULT	B	B	A	*A × B*	
A	DIV	B	C	A	B	*A/B*

Rule. The Result field is *always* assigned new values as shown in italics in each example of the summary chart.

III. Additional Considerations

A. Expanding the RPG Logic Cycle

Thus far, we have focused on accumulator additions that are necessary for the development of running totals and counters. The RPG programming necessary for producing the output was explained in the previous chapter. Recall that the Last Record indicator is turned on or set after all the input records have been processed. When the **LR indicator** is turned on, total calculations and total output operations are to be performed. Figure 3.16 provides an illustration of the RPG II Logic Cycle as it relates to detail and LR processing.

Note that the last record indicator is "on" only after all the input records have been processed. Turning on the last record indicator causes

1. Total Calculations to be performed
2. Total Output to print.

B. Total Calculations

When it is necessary to perform *calculations* after the last input record has been processed, the characters LR are coded in columns 7-8 of the Calculation form as follows.

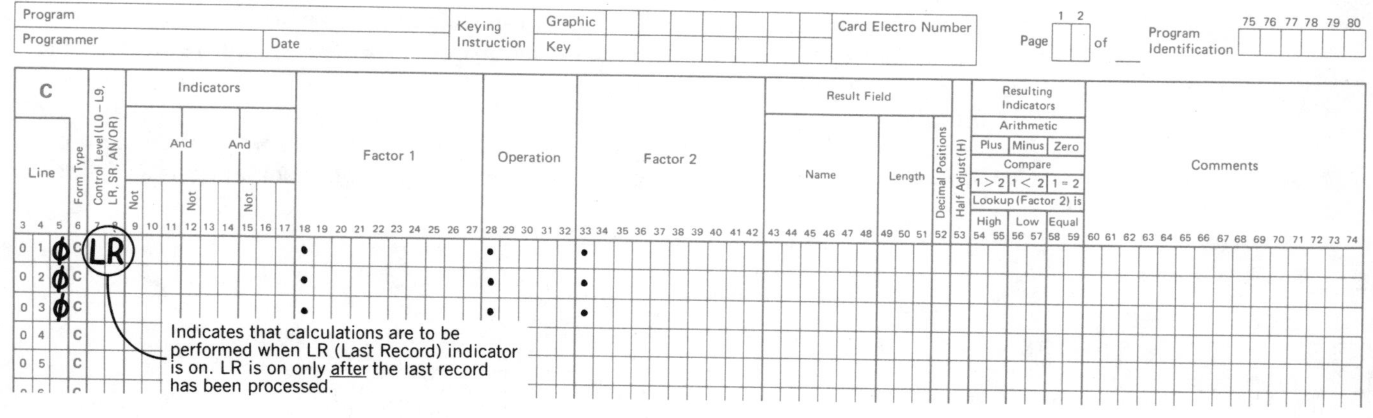

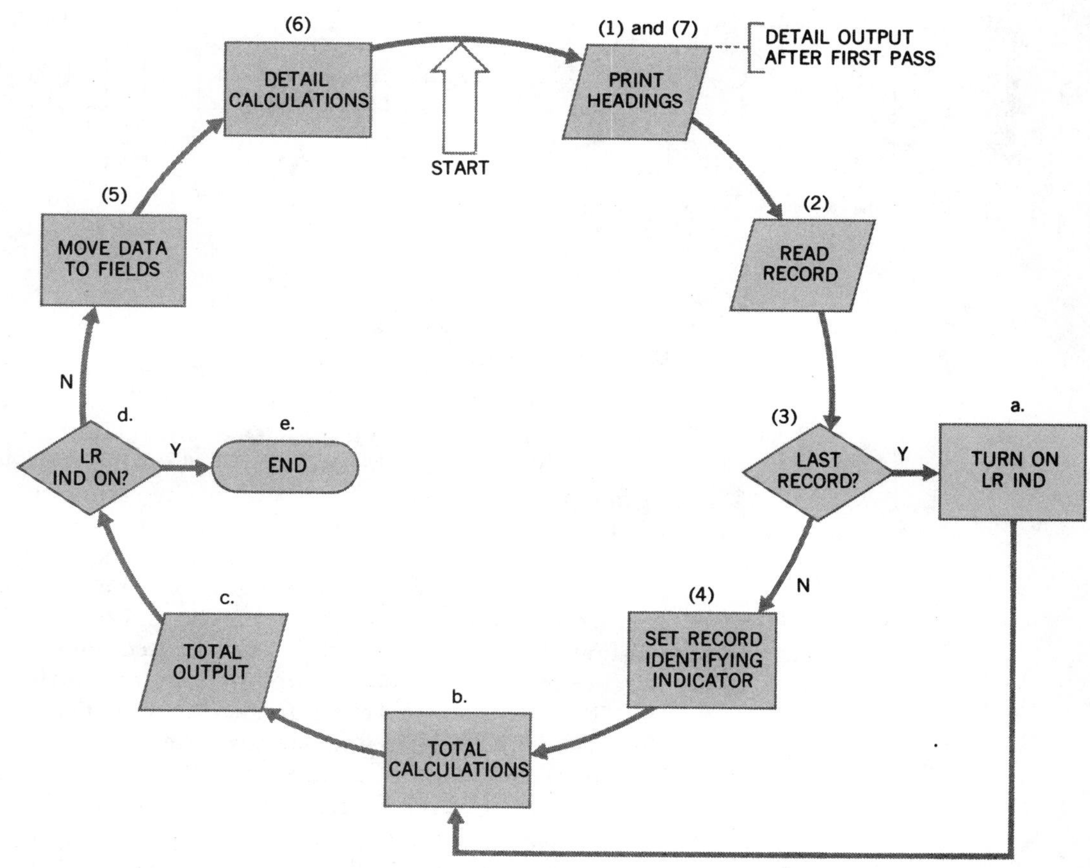

Detail Cycle

1. Print heading on first pass if 1P used
2. Read input record
3. If Last Record perform Last Record cycle
4. Set record identifying indicator
5. Move data to fields
6. Perform detail calculations
7. Perform detail output

Last Record Cycle

a. Turn on LR indicator
b. Perform total calculations
c. Perform total output
d. Test LR indicator
e. Terminate program

Figure 3.16
Illustration of the RPG II Logic Cycle as it relates to detail and LR processing.

Since LR calculations are the last to be performed by the program, they would similarly be the last entries coded on the Calculation form. If the sample program had required you to calculate the average number of hours worked per person (AVGHRS), you could have divided the TOTAL (hours worked) by the number of employees (NOEMP) once all the data had been read and processed by the program. Again, this calculation would be performed when the last record indicator is turned "on." The coding to accomplish this calculation is as follows.

RPG CALCULATION SPECIFICATIONS

Line (3–5)	Form Type (6)	Control Level (7–8)	Indicators (9–17)	Factor 1 (18–27)	Operation (28–32)	Factor 2 (33–42)	Result Field Name (43–48)	Length (49–51)	Decimal Positions (52)
01	C			•					
02	C			•					
03	C			•					
04	C			•					
05	C	LR		TOTAL	DIV	NOEMP	AVGHRS	5	2
06	C								
07	C								
08	C								

Other calculation entries (lines 01–04).

Last entry on the Calculation Form.
Note: The LR indicator can only be coded in columns 7-8, not in 10-11, 13-14 or 16-17.

C. Total Output

In summary, all the records in the input file are processed using the record identifying indicator to control calculations and output. The RPG II Logic Cycle automatically checks if the last record has been processed. Recall that, if the end of file has been reached, the LR indicator is turned on. This process is again illustrated in the flowchart in Figure 3.17.

The Last Record indicator is turned on immediately after the last record has been processed during detail output time. This indicator may then be used to print counters and totals required at the end of the report. The Output Specifications form is used for this purpose. Recalling the example introduced at the beginning of this chapter, we will again review the output requirements for the program. See Figure 3.1 for a review of the Printer Spacing Chart. As previously noted, detail lines (D) are printed for each input record by coding the letter D in column 15 of the Output Specifications form and using the record indicator specified on the Input form. In order to print a total line at the end of the report when the last record has been read, the letter T must be entered in column 15 of the Output form. Total lines follow the detail output specifications and use the last record (LR) indicator to control this last record or end-of-file processing. Figure 3.18 illustrates the Output specifications for the sample problem.

Total lines are not printed for each record but are accumulated and printed at a specified "total" time. In the example just presented the last record indicator is being used to control the printing of these totals. The field specifications for

Figure 3.17
Use of the LR indicator.

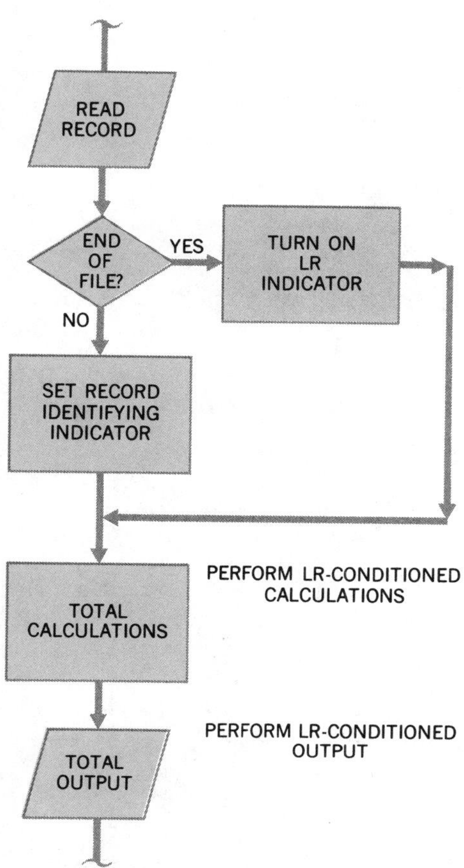

total lines follow the same basic format as that used on detail lines. The total lines specifications contain

First Line	T in column 15 denoting Total line.
	1 in column 17 controlling the spacing of the continuous form.
	LR indicator in columns 24-31 specifying when output is to be printed.
Subsequent Lines	End position of fields and/or constants to be printed, including editing.

D. Resulting Indicators

Resulting indicators are used on the Calculation form to test

1. The results of arithmetic calculations to determine whether the resulting field is plus (positive), minus (negative), or zero.
2. The results of compare operations, which are discussed in detail in the following chapter.

Columns 54-59 may be used to test and record the value of a Result field after the arithmetic operation has been completed. The test determines whether

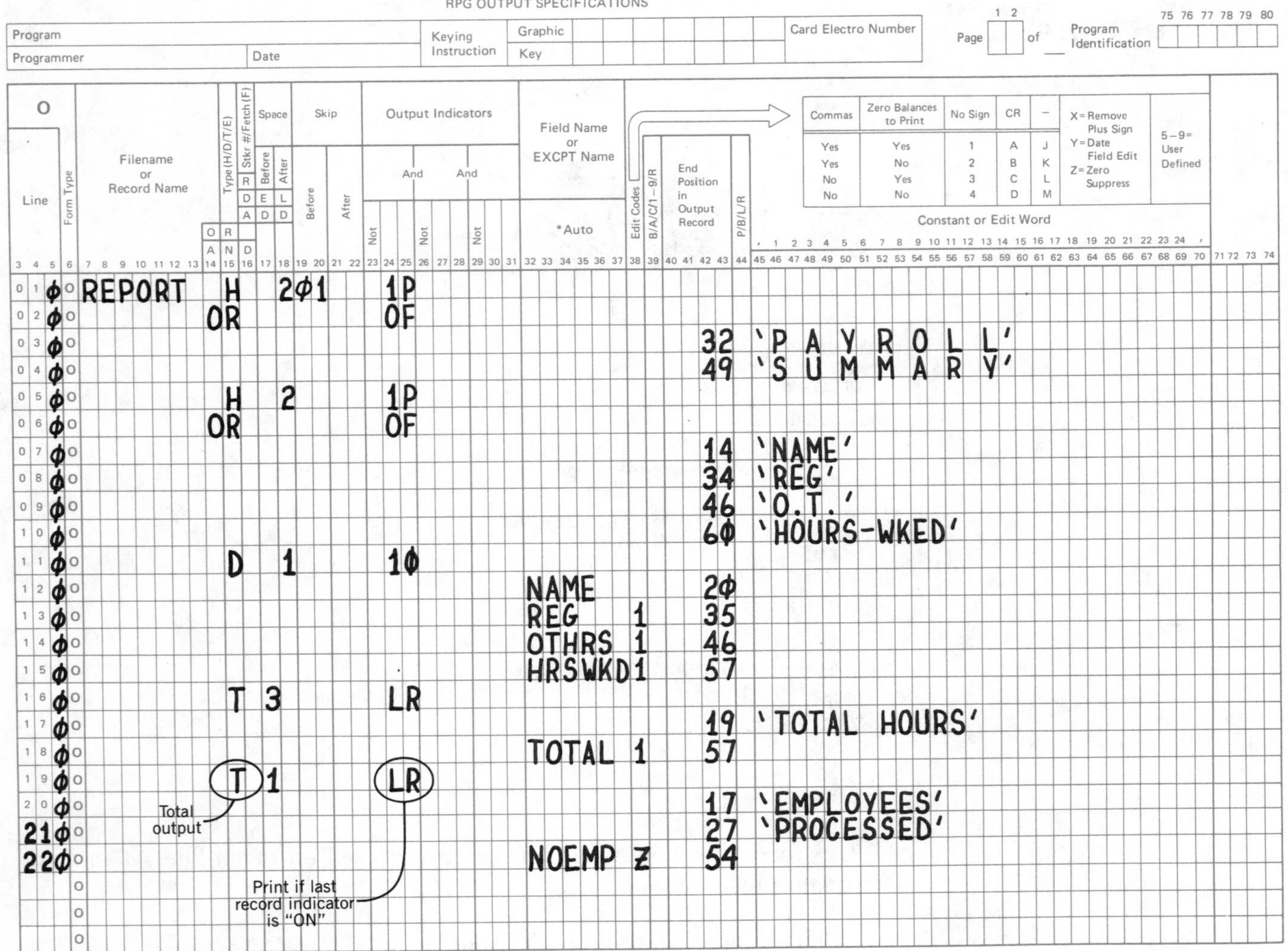

RPG OUTPUT SPECIFICATIONS

Line	Form Type	Filename or Record Name	Type (H/D/T/E)	Space Before	Space After	Skip Before	Skip After	Output Indicators	Field Name or EXCPT Name	Edit Codes	End Position in Output Record	Constant or Edit Word
01Ø	O	REPORT	H	2		Ø1		1P				
02Ø	O		OR					OF				
03Ø	O										32	'P A Y R O L L'
04Ø	O										49	'S U M M A R Y'
05Ø	O		H	2				1P				
06Ø	O		OR					OF				
07Ø	O										14	'NAME'
08Ø	O										34	'REG'
09Ø	O										46	'O.T.'
10Ø	O										6Ø	'HOURS-WKED'
11Ø	O		D	1				1Ø				
12Ø	O								NAME		2Ø	
13Ø	O								REG	1	35	
14Ø	O								OTHRS	1	46	
15Ø	O								HRSWKD	1	57	
16Ø	O		T	3				LR				
17Ø	O										19	'TOTAL HOURS'
18Ø	O								TOTAL	1	57	
19Ø	O		T	1				LR				
20Ø	O										17	'EMPLOYEES'
21Ø	O										27	'PROCESSED'
22Ø	O								NOEMP	Z	54	

Figure 3.18
Output Specifications form for sample problem.

the results are positive, negative, or zero by turning on specific indicators. These indicators are then used to control subsequent calculations or output operations. Figure 3.19 provides an illustration of the use of resulting indicators.

An arithmetic operation can also be used to turn on indicators that will specify whether the result is a positive, negative, or zero balance.

In Figure 3.19, note that the resulting field NBAL will always turn "on" one of the resulting indicators, namely 2Ø, 3Ø, or 4Ø. If an account is overdrawn, a negative balance will result and indicator 3Ø will be turned on. Indicator 3Ø may be used to print a message that designates the account as overdrawn. Similarly, indicator 4Ø may be used on the output form to produce a message denoting a zero balance. A positive balance will turn on indicator 2Ø. Since a positive balance is acceptable, no warning messages would be printed. Indicator 2Ø was included in this example for completeness and may be eliminated without changing the logic of the program. Since indicator 2Ø is not used for other calculations or for printing output, it is not necessary in the program. Some RPG compilers will print a warning level error if an indicator is specified but not used.

Keep in mind that these indicators will remain on until reset. The setting of

RPG CALCULATION SPECIFICATIONS

Line	Form Type	Indicators	Factor 1	Operation	Factor 2	Result Field Name	Length	Decimal Positions	Resulting Indicators Plus (High)	Minus (Low)	Zero (Equal)
01Ø	C	1Ø	OBAL	SUB	DEBIT	NBAL	7	2	2Ø	3Ø	4Ø
02	C										
03	C										

Specifies result

Result field

If NBAL is positive, then indicator 20 is turned ON.

If NBAL is negative, then indicator 30 is turned ON.

If NBAL is zero, then indicator 40 is turned ON.

RPG OUTPUT SPECIFICATIONS

Line	Form Type	Filename or Record Name	Type (H/D/T/E)	Space Before	Skip Before	Output Indicators	Field Name or EXCPT Name	Edit Codes	End Position in Output Record	Constant or Edit Word
01Ø	O	LINEOUT	H		Ø6	1P				
02Ø	O		OR			OF				
03Ø	O								3Ø	'CUSTOMER NAME'
04Ø	O								5Ø	'BALANCE'
05Ø	O								7Ø	'MESSAGES'
06Ø	O		D	1	1	1Ø				
07Ø	O						CNAME		35	
08Ø	O						NBAL	3	5Ø	
09Ø	O					3Ø			73	'**OVER-DRAWN**'
10Ø	O					4Ø			73	'*ZERO BALANCE*'
11	O									
12	O									

Activate printing

Messages

Printer spacing chart:

Line				
H 5		CUSTOMER NAME	BALANCE	MESSAGES
D 7		X——————X	XXXXX.XX	X——————X
9		(CNAME)	(NBAL)	(**OVER-DRAWN** OR *ZERO BALANCE*)

Figure 3.19
Use of resulting indicators.

indicators with a SETON and SETOF command will be considered in later chapters.

In the example the resulting indicators are used in the Output form to produce messages appropriately describing the status of the customer's account. Remember, when indicator 3Ø is on, the message "OVERDRAWN" will print; similarly, indicator 4Ø will condition the message, "ZERO BALANCE", to print. The Printer Spacing Chart reflects the desired output needed to produce an exception report. Again, note that no output will be produced when a positive balance sets indicator 2Ø on, since indicator 2Ø is not used on the Output form.

Also recall that field indicators can be used on the Input form. In the previous chapter, you learned that field indicators can be set if the contents of numeric input fields are positive, negative, or zero; similarly, alphanumeric fields may be tested for spaces or blanks. As with resulting indicators, if the assigned condition is met, the field indicator is turned "on"; if not, it is turned "off."

E. Sample Program 2

Consider the problem definition in Figure 3.2Ø. The program is illustrated in Figure 3.21.

Figure 3.20 Problem definition for Sample Program 2.

Systems Flowchart

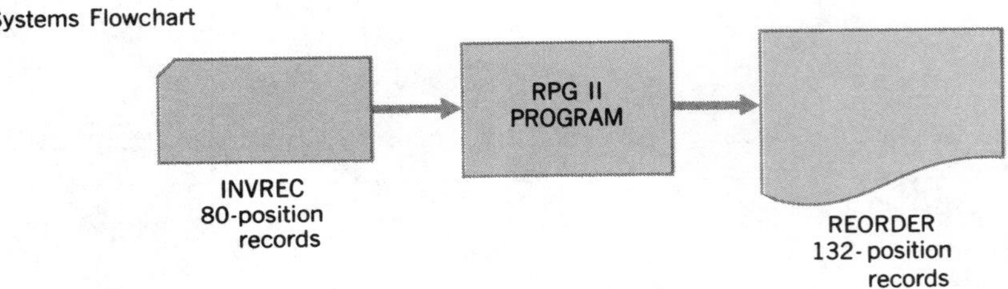

INVREC Record Layout

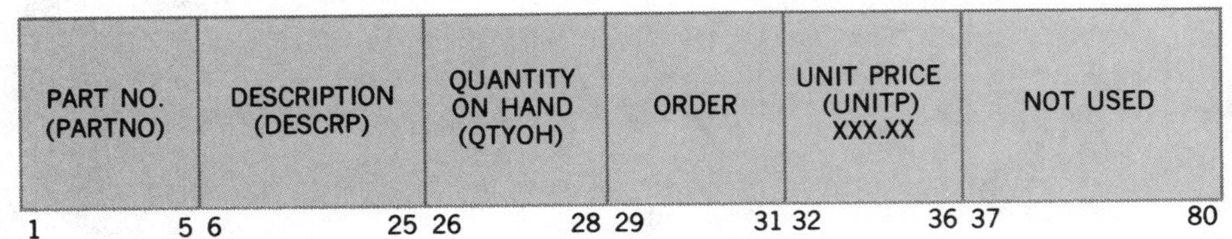

REORDER Printer Spacing Chart

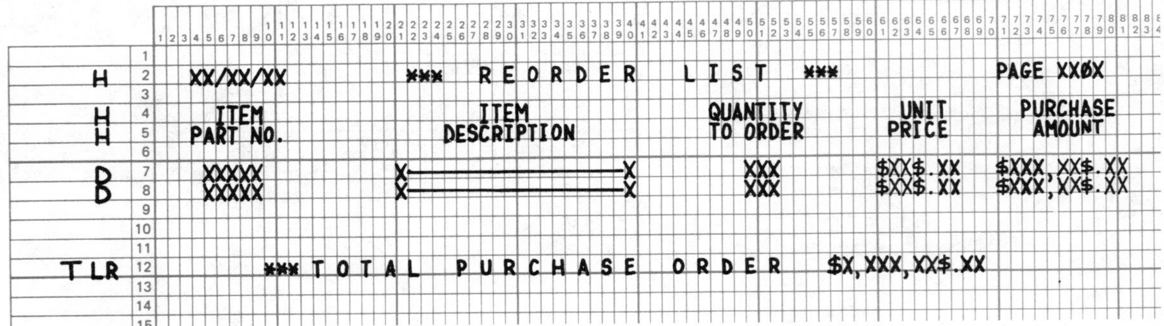

RPG CONTROL AND FILE DESCRIPTION SPECIFICATIONS

Program: REORDER LIST — Programmer: A. SAGER — Date: 5/4/__ — Keying Instruction: Graphic Φ 1 2, Key ZERO ONE TWO — Card Electro Number — Page Φ1 of 5 — Program Identification (75–80): SSSΦ3B

Control Specifications

For the valid entries for a system, refer to the RPG reference manual for that system.

H — Line (3–5), Form Type (6), Size to Compile (7–9), Object Output (10), Listing Options (11), Size to Execute (12–14), Debug (15), Reserved (16–17), Currency Symbol (18), Date Format (19), Date Edit (20), Inverted Print (21), Reserved (22), Number of Print Positions (23–25), Alternate Collating Sequence (26), Reserved (27–36), Inquiry (37), Reserved (38–39), Sign Handling (40), 1 P Forms Position (41), Indicator Setting (42), File Translation (43), Punch MFCU Zeros (44), Nonprint Characters (45), Reserved (46), Table Load Halt (47), Shared I/O (48), Field Print (49), Formatted Dump (50), RPG to RPG II Conversion (51), Number of Formats (52–53), S/3 Conversion (54), Subprogram (55), CICS/DL/I (56), Transparent Literal (57), 58–74

```
01Φ H
```

File Description Specifications

For the valid entries for a system, refer to the RPG reference manual for that system.

F — Line (3–5), Form Type (6), Filename (7–14), File Type: I/O/U/C/D (15), File Designation: P/S/C/R/T/D/F (16), End of File: E (17), Sequence: A/D (18), File Format: F/V/S/M/D/E (19), Block Length (20–23), Record Length (24–27), L/R (28), Mode of Processing, Length of Key Field or of Record Address Field (29–30), Record Address Type: A/P/I/K (31), Type of File Organization or Additional Area: I/X/D/T/R/ or 2 (32), Overflow Indicator (33–34), Key Field Starting Location (35–38), External Record Name, Extension Code E/L (39), Device (40–46), Symbolic Device (47–52), Labels S/N/E/M (53), Name of Label Exit (54–59), Extent Exit for DAM, Storage Index, Continuation Lines: K, Option (54–59), Entry (60–65), A/U (66), File Addition/Unordered, Number of Tracks for Cylinder Overflow, Number of Extents (68–69), Tape Rewind (70), File Condition U1–U8, UC (71–72), R/U/N (70), 73–74

```
02Φ F**********************************************************************
03Φ F*   THIS PROGRAM PRODUCES A REORDER LIST INDICATING ITEM,QUANTITY       *
04Φ F*  TO BE ORDERED,PRICE PER UNIT,AND TOTAL PURCHASE AMOUNT FOR EACH     *
05Φ F*  ITEM WITH NO STOCK ON HAND. ALSO COMPUTED IS THE TOTAL PRICE OF    *
06Φ F*  ALL ITEMS TO BE ORDERED.                                            *
07Φ F**********************************************************************
08Φ F*
09Φ FINVREC  IP  F      8Φ             READΦ1 SYSIPT
10Φ FREORDER O   F     132      OF     PRINTERSYSLST
11Φ F*
    F
```

RPG INPUT SPECIFICATIONS

Program: REORDER LIST — Programmer: A. SAGER — Date: 5/4/__ — Keying Instruction: Graphic Φ 1 2, Key ZERO ONE TWO — Card Electro Number — Page Φ2 of 5 — Program Identification (75–80): SSSΦ3B

I — Line (3–5), Form Type (6), Filename or Record Name (7–14) / Data Structure Name, O R / A N D (14–16), Sequence (15–16), Number (1/N), E (17), Option (O), U, S (18), Record Identifying Indicator, **, or DS (19–20), External Field Name, Record Identification Codes 1: Position (21–24), Not (N) (25), C/Z/D (26), Character (27); 2: Position (28–31), Not (N) (32), C/Z/D (33), Character (34); 3: Position (35–38), Not (N) (39), C/Z/D (40), Character (41), Stacker Select (42), P/B/L/R (43), Field Location From (44–47) To (48–51) / Data Structure Occurs n Times, Length, Decimal Positions (52), RPG Field Name (53–58), Control Level (L1–L9) (59–60), Matching Fields or Chaining Fields (61–62), Field Record Relation (63–64), Field Indicators: Plus (65–66), Minus (67–68), Zero or Blank (69–70), 71–74

```
01Φ I************************************** INPUT RECORD *******************
02Φ I*
03Φ IINVREC  NS  Φ1
04Φ I                                              1    5 PARTNO
05Φ I                                              6   25 DESCRP
06Φ I                                             26   28ΦQTYOH          Φ5
07Φ I                                             29   31ΦORDER
08Φ I                                             32   362UNITP
09Φ I*
10  I
11  I
```

Figure 3.21 Coding sheets for Sample Program 2. *(Continued on next page.)*

RPG CALCULATION SPECIFICATIONS

Program: REORDER LIST — Programmer: A. SAGER — Date: 5/4/__ — Keying Instruction: Graphic Ø 1 2, Key ZERO ONE TWO — Page Ø3 of 5 — Program Identification: SSSØ3B

```
Line  C  Indicators   Factor 1     Operation  Factor 2     Result Field  Len Dec/H
01Ø   C ********************************** CALCULATIONS ******************************
02Ø   C *
03Ø   C ***
04Ø   C ***** IF QYTOH FIELD CONTAINS ZEROS
05Ø   C ***** INDICATOR Ø5 IS TURNED ON AND
06Ø   C ***** CALCULATIONS ARE PERFORMED
07Ø   C ***
08Ø   C    Ø1 Ø5      ORDER        MULT       UNITP        AMOUNT         8  2H
09Ø   C    Ø1 Ø5      AMOUNT       ADD        TOTAMT       TOTAMT         9  2
10Ø   C *
```

RPG OUTPUT SPECIFICATIONS

Program: REORDER LIST — Programmer: A. SAGER — Date: 5/4/__ — Keying Instruction: Graphic Ø 1 2, Key ZERO ONE TWO — Page Ø4 of 5 — Program Identification: SSSØ3B

```
Line  O  Filename  Type Space Skip  Output Ind.  Field Name  Edit  End Pos.  Constant or Edit Word
01Ø   O ********************************** HEADING LINES ******************************
02Ø   O *
03Ø   O REORDER    H     2    Ø1    1P
04Ø   O          OR             OF
05Ø   O                                          UDATE        Y     11
06Ø   O                                                             4Ø    '***    R E O R D E R'
07Ø   O                                                             57    'L I S T    ***'
08Ø   O                                                             74    'PAGE'
09Ø   O                                          PAGE               79
10Ø   O            H     1          1P
11Ø   O          OR                 OF
12Ø   O                                                              9    'ITEM'
13Ø   O                                                             31    'ITEM'
14Ø   O                                                             54    'QUANTITY'
15Ø   O                                                             66    'UNIT'
16Ø   O                                                             8Ø    'PURCHASE'
17Ø   O            H     2          1P
18Ø   O          OR                 OF
19Ø   O                                                             11    'PART NO.'
20Ø   O                                                             35    'DESCRIPTION'
21Ø   O                                                             54    'TO ORDER'
22Ø   O                                                             66    'PRICE'
23Ø   O                                                             79    'AMOUNT'
24Ø   O *
25Ø   O ********************************** DETAIL LINE ******************************
```

Figure 3.21 *(continued)*

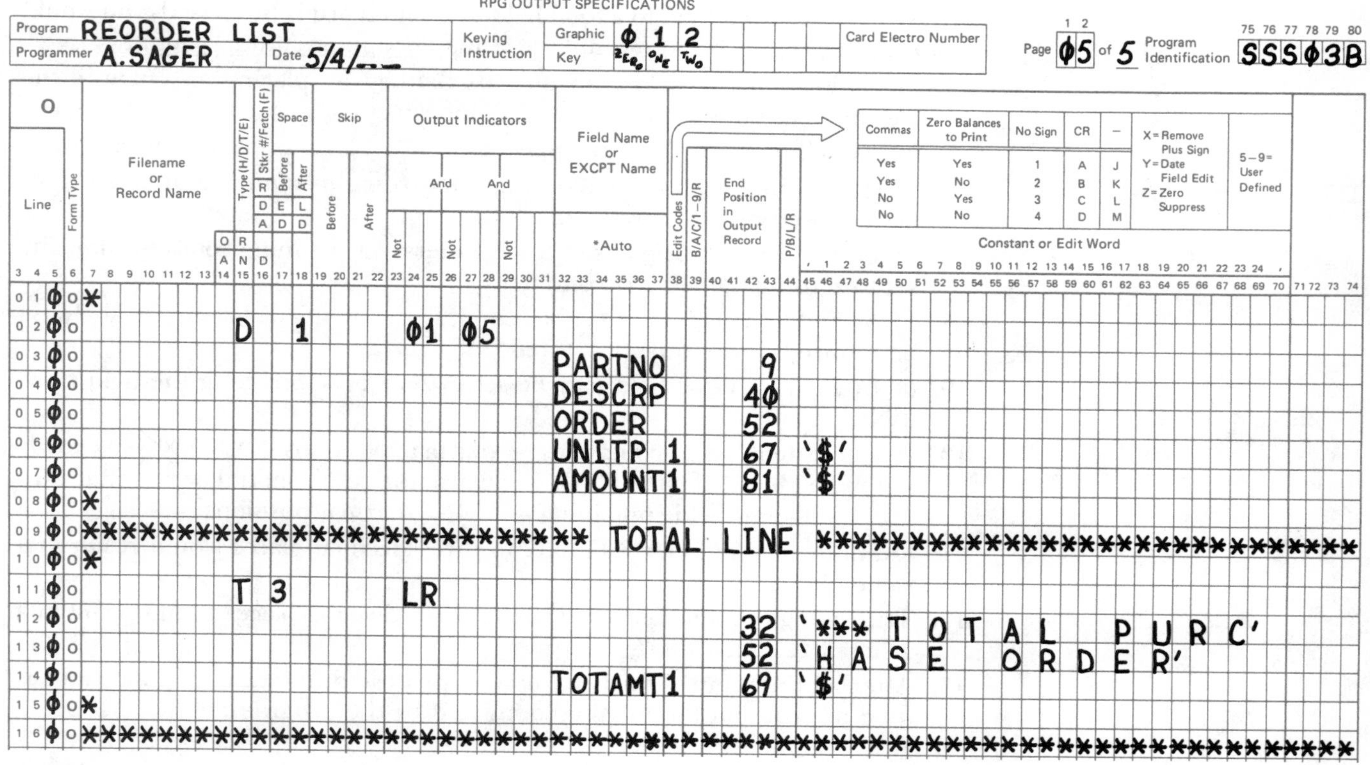

RPG OUTPUT SPECIFICATIONS

Program: REORDER LIST
Programmer: A.SAGER
Date: 5/4/--
Graphic: Ø 1 2 — Key: ZERO ONE TWO
Page Ø5 of 5
Program Identification: SSSØ3B

Line	Form Type	Filename or Record Name	Type (H/D/T/E)	Space Before	Space After	Output Indicators	Field Name or EXCPT Name	Edit Codes	End Position in Output Record	Constant or Edit Word
Ø1	O	*								
Ø2	O		D		1	Ø1 Ø5				
Ø3	O						PARTNO		9	
Ø4	O						DESCRP		4Ø	
Ø5	O						ORDER		52	
Ø6	O						UNITP	1	67	'$'
Ø7	O						AMOUNT	1	81	'$'
Ø8	O	*								
Ø9	O	************************** TOTAL LINE ******************************								
1Ø	O	*								
11	O		T	3		LR				
12	O								32	'*** T O T A L P U R C'
13	O								52	'H A S E O R D E R'
14	O						TOTAMT	1	69	'$'
15	O	*								
16	O	**								

Figure 3.21 *(continued)*

Key Terms

ADDition instruction
Constant
Counter
DIVide instruction
Factor 1
Factor 2
Half-adjust
High-order truncation
Low-order truncation
LR indicator
MULTiply instruction
Numeric literal
Record indicator
Result field
Resulting indicator
Rounding
Running total
Sizing fields
SUBtract instruction
Truncation
Z-ADD instruction

Self-Evaluating Quiz

1. Arrange the following steps in the order in which they occur during the RPG II and RPG III cycle.
   a. PERFORM DETAIL CALCULATIONS
   b. READ A RECORD
   c. PERFORM DETAIL OUTPUT
   d. MOVE DATA TO FIELDS
   e. PRINT HEADINGS
2. If you added 1 to a field each time an event occurred, this would be an example of using a <u>(counter/running total)</u>.

3. When a field is added to a total field as each record is processed, you would consider this to be an example of using a (counter/running total).
4. (T or F) Numeric fields can only be defined by placing an entry in the Decimal Positions field of the Calculation form.
5. Numeric literals or constants may be up to ________ positions in length.
6. (T or F) Numeric literals or constants may contain commas and dollar signs if so desired by the programmer.
7. (T or F) Numeric fields used for counters and running totals are initially set to zero by the RPG II compiler.
8. (T or F) After performing subtraction, the contents of Factor 1 will always be reduced by the quantity stored in Factor 2.
9. (T or F) A numeric field may be set to zero by subtracting the field from itself.
10. If a five-digit field (containing 2 decimal positions XXX.XX) was to be multiplied by a 3-digit field (no decimals), the result should be stored in a(n) ________ -digit field containing ________ decimal positions.
11. Rounding the number 3.141592 to three decimal places would result in a value of ________ .
12. Truncating the number 3.141592 to three decimal places would result in a value of ________ .
13. After all the input records have been processed, the ________ indicator is used to print out the totals accumulated by the program.

In questions 14 through 17, determine the contents of the various fields after the instruction shown has been executed.

14.

RPG CALCULATION SPECIFICATIONS

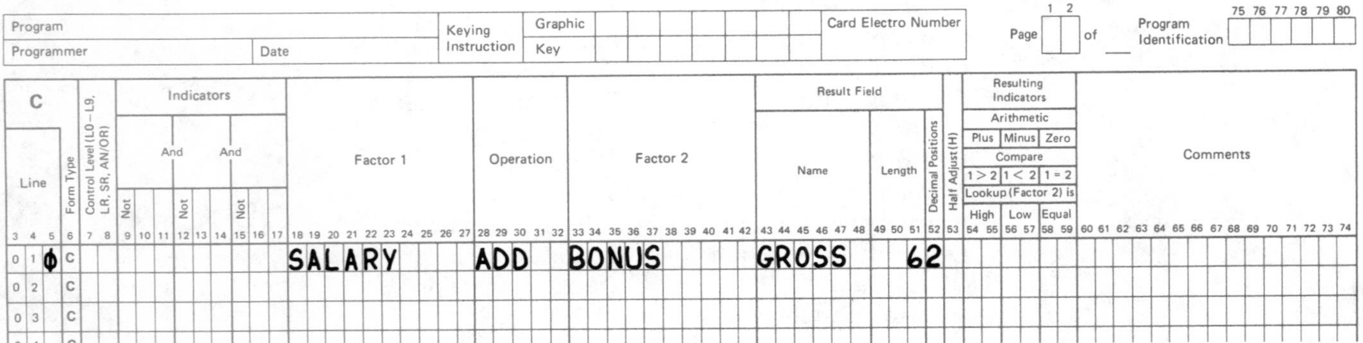

Line	Form Type	Control Level	Indicators	Factor 1	Operation	Factor 2	Result Field Name	Length	Decimal Positions	Half Adjust (H)	Resulting Indicators	Comments
01Ø	C			SALARY	ADD	BONUS	GROSS	6	2			
02	C											
03	C											

BEFORE

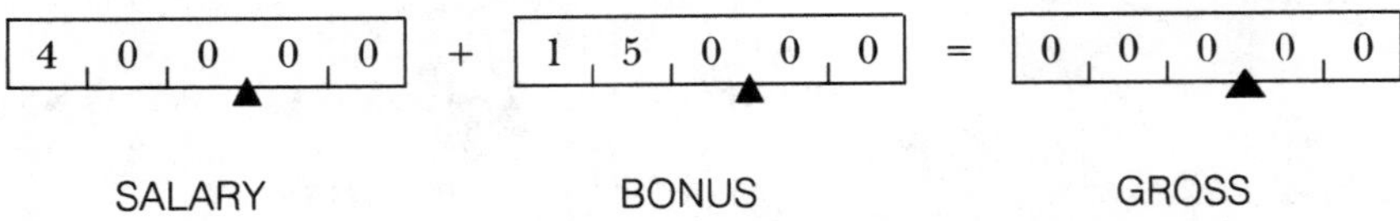

15.

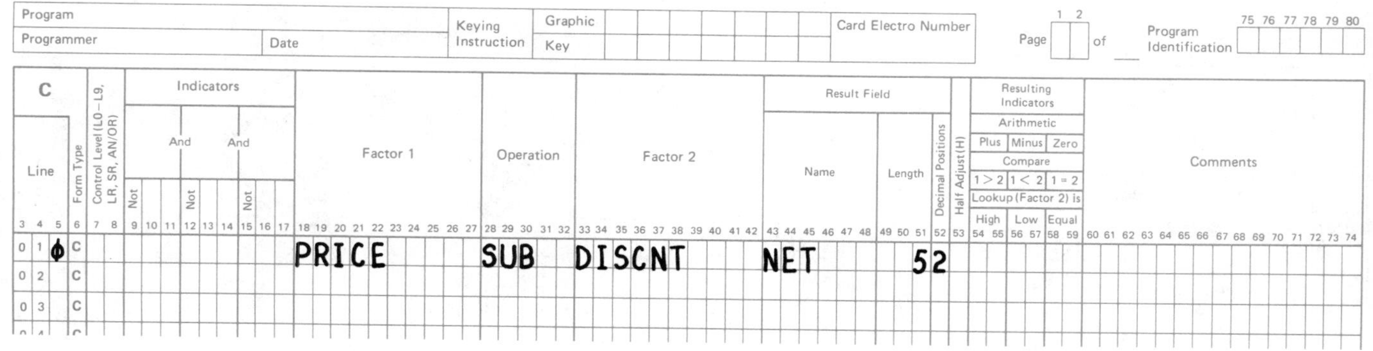
RPG CALCULATION SPECIFICATIONS

Line	Form Type	Factor 1	Operation	Factor 2	Result Field Name	Length	Decimal Positions	Half Adjust (H)
01ϕ	C	PRICE	SUB	DISCNT	NET	5	2	
02	C							
03	C							

BEFORE

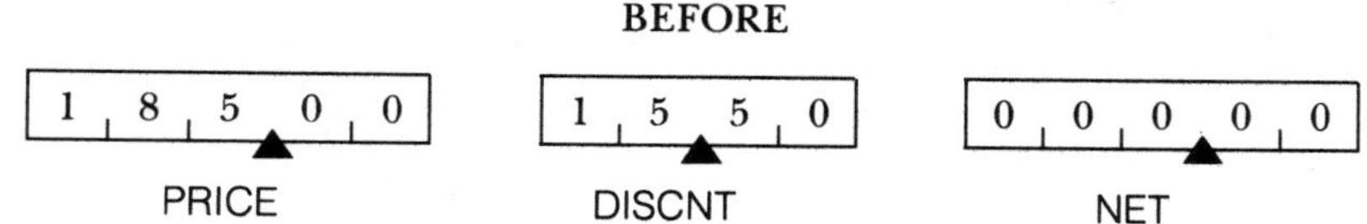

16.

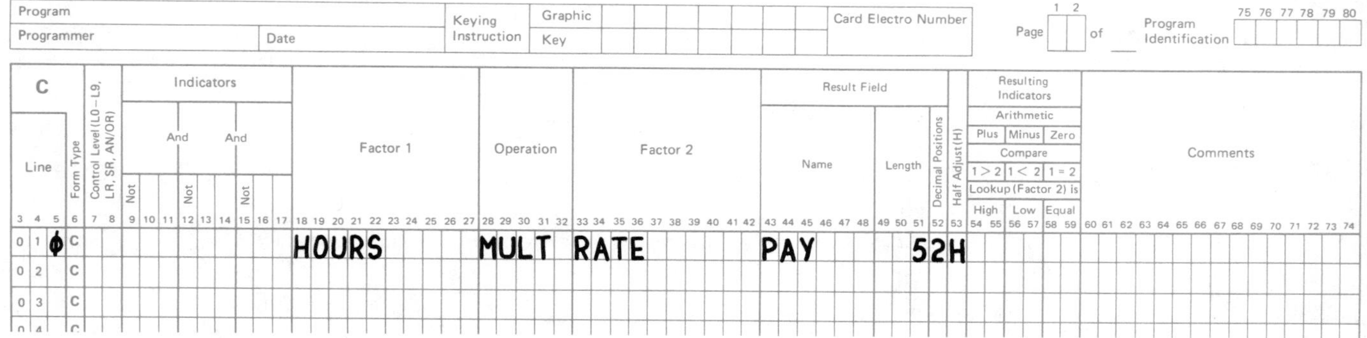
RPG CALCULATION SPECIFICATIONS

Line	Form Type	Factor 1	Operation	Factor 2	Result Field Name	Length	Decimal Positions	Half Adjust (H)
01ϕ	C	HOURS	MULT	RATE	PAY	5	2	H
02	C							
03	C							

BEFORE

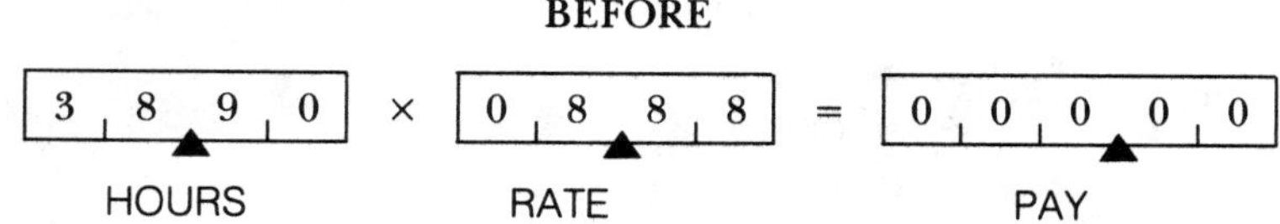

17.

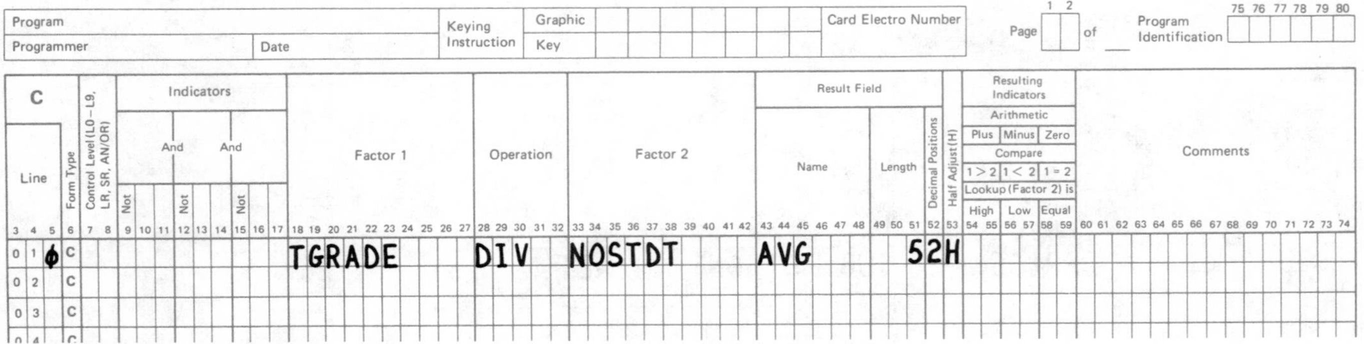

BEFORE

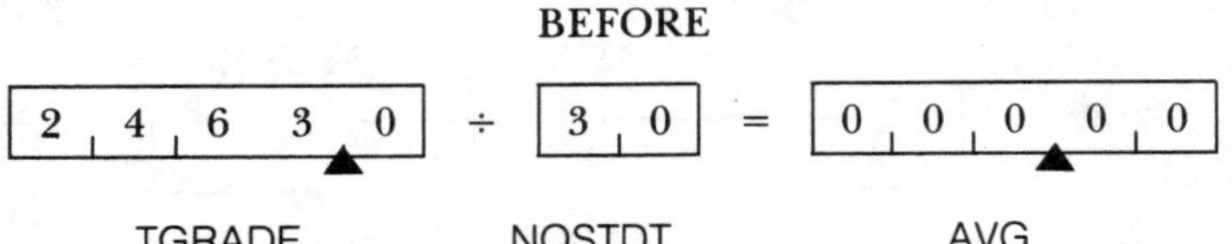

Solutions

1. e
   b
   d
   a
   c
2. counter
3. running total
4. F—Numeric fields may also be defined on the Input form.
5. 1Ø
6. F—Only decimal points and minus signs are permitted.
7. T
8. F—Only the Result Field changes.
9. T
1Ø. eight
    two
11. 3.142
12. 3.141
13. LR (denoting last record)
14.

AFTER

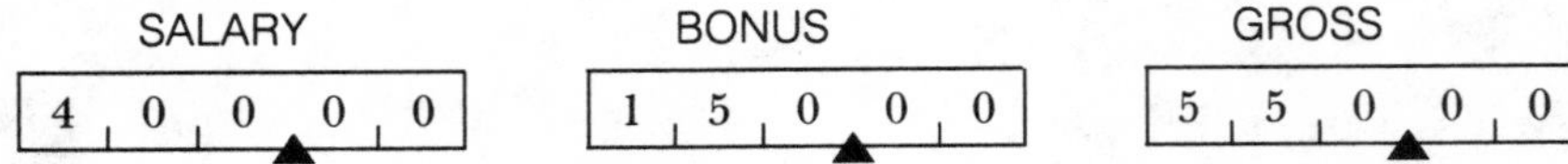

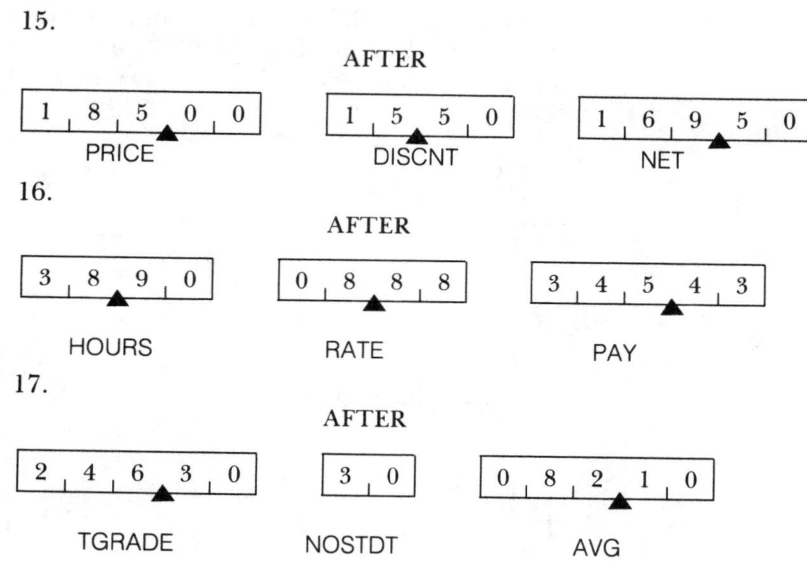

Review Questions

1. Student registration records contain the student's name, number of credits (CRED) for this semester, and the rate per credit (RATE). Each student's tuition is to be calculated using the following formula.

TUITN = CRED × RATE

CRED is 2 positions long (no decimals). RATE is 5 positions long, including 2 decimal positions. Approximately 2ØØ students are enrolled in courses. You are required to count the number of students processed and accumulate a sum of all the students' tuition (SUM). Indicator 1Ø is to be turned on for all input records and is used for these calculations.

RPG CALCULATION SPECIFICATIONS

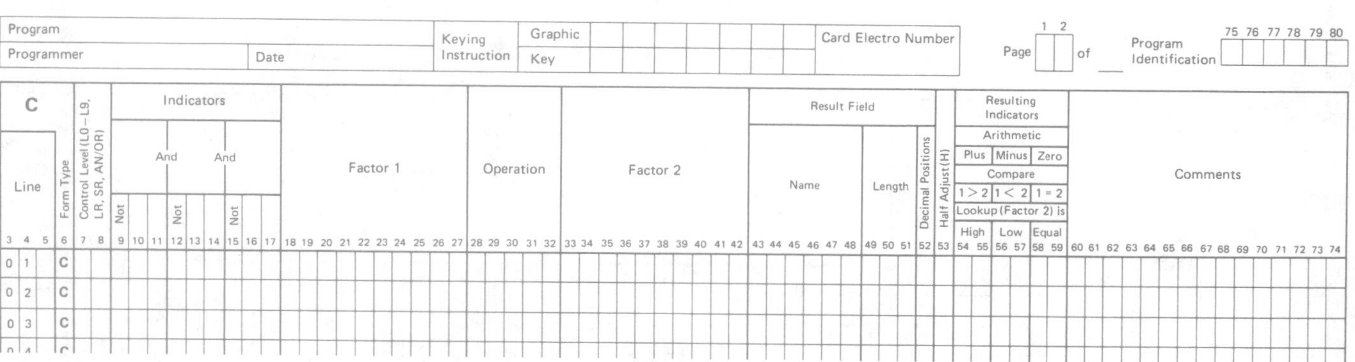

2. An input record contains a customer name, old balance (OBAL), deposits (DEP), and withdrawals (WITH). Write the entries necessary to calculate a new balance (NBAL) using the formula

NBAL = OBAL + DEP − WITH

when indicator 19 is on. Also, count the input records (COUNT) and develop running totals of the deposits (TDEP) and withdrawals (TWITH). All fields should be seven positions long including two decimal positions.

RPG CALCULATION SPECIFICATIONS

Program | Programmer | Date | Keying Instruction: Graphic, Key | Card Electro Number | Page 1 2 of | Program Identification 75 76 77 78 79 80

C | Line (3 4 5) | Form Type (6) | Control Level (L0–L9, LR, SR, AN/OR) (7 8) | Indicators: Not, And Not, And Not (9–17) | Factor 1 (18–27) | Operation (28–32) | Factor 2 (33–42) | Result Field: Name (43–48), Length (49–51) | Decimal Positions (52) | Half Adjust (H) (53) | Resulting Indicators: Arithmetic Plus Minus Zero; Compare 1>2 1<2 1=2; Lookup (Factor 2) is High Low Equal (54–59) | Comments (60–74)

01 C
02 C
03 C
04 C
05 C
06 C

3. S & S Department Store bills customers via an accounts receivable billing system. A service charge of 1.5% of the old balance (OBAL) is assessed each month. The amount due (AMT) each month is calculated as follows.

Credits = Payments + Returns
New Balance = Old Balance + Purchases + Service Charge − Credits

All balance fields are six positions in length including 2 decimal positions. Code the RPG II entries for these calculations using indicator 2Ø.

RPG CALCULATION SPECIFICATIONS

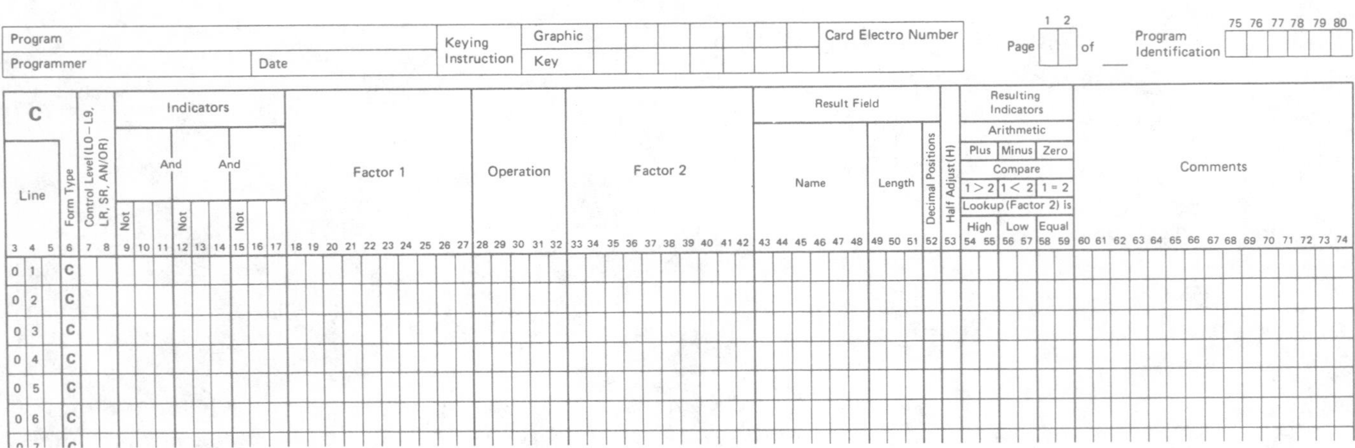

Program | Programmer | Date | Keying Instruction: Graphic, Key | Card Electro Number | Page 1 2 of | Program Identification 75 76 77 78 79 80

C | Line (3 4 5) | Form Type (6) | Control Level (L0–L9, LR, SR, AN/OR) (7 8) | Indicators: Not, And Not, And Not (9–17) | Factor 1 (18–27) | Operation (28–32) | Factor 2 (33–42) | Result Field: Name (43–48), Length (49–51) | Decimal Positions (52) | Half Adjust (H) (53) | Resulting Indicators: Arithmetic Plus Minus Zero; Compare 1>2 1<2 1=2; Lookup (Factor 2) is High Low Equal (54–59) | Comments (60–74)

01 C
02 C
03 C
04 C
05 C
06 C

Using the Calculation form, write the steps necessary to perform the following arithmetic operations.

4. Compute F = (9/5)×C + 32. Round F to 2 decimal positions.

5. Calculate net sales = total sales less a (rounded) discount of 2%. Allow for a result field of six positions, containing 2 decimal places.
6. Convert N (number of feet) to I (number of inches). N will never exceed 99.99 feet.
7. Convert quarts to liters. Recall that 1 quart = Ø.946 liters.
   The maximum entry for quarts is 9.9 for this problem. Do not truncate any digits.
8. Calculate quantity on hand (QOH) = QTYIN − QTYOUT.
   If QOH is zero or negative, do not perform the succeeding step, which is

AVG = TCOST/QOH

Note. All quantity fields are 4-position integers, whereas TCOST has a 6.2 specification.

9. Assume FLDA = 1ØØ.ØØ, FLDB = −75, and FLDC = Ø. Using the instructions depicted here, determine (1) the indicator set on by the instruction, and (2) the contents of the Result fields ANS1 through ANS6.

RPG CALCULATION SPECIFICATIONS

Program		Keying Instruction	Graphic	Card Electro Number	Page 1 2 of
Programmer	Date		Key		

Line	Form Type	Control Level (L0–L9, LR, SR, AN/OR)	Indicators (Not, And Not, And Not)	Factor 1	Operation	Factor 2	Result Field Name	Length	Decimal Positions	Half Adjust (H)	Resulting Indicators Plus / High / 1>2 (54–55)	Minus / Low / 1<2 (56–57)	Zero / Equal / 1=2 (58–59)		(A) Indicator ON	(B) Contents of Result Field
Ø1	C			FLDA	SUB	FLDB	ANS1	3	Ø		Ø1	Ø2	Ø3	(a)		
Ø2	C*															
Ø3	C				Z-ADD	FLDC	ANS2	3	Ø		Ø4	Ø5	Ø6	(b)		
Ø4	C*															
Ø5	C			FLDA	MULT	FLDB	ANS3	4	Ø		Ø7	Ø8	Ø9	(c)		
Ø6	C*															
Ø7	C				Z-ADD	FLDB	ANS4	2	Ø		1Ø	11	12	(d)		
Ø8	C*															
Ø9	C			FLDB	ADD	FLDB	ANS5	2	Ø		13	14	15	(e)		
1Ø	C*															
11	C			FLDB	SUB	FLDB	ANS6	2	Ø		16	17	18	(f)		
12	C															
13	C															
14	C															

Debugging Exercises

Debugging Exercise 1

Misgiven Realty: A Walkthrough Exercise

The following is an exercise requiring you to predict the results of calculations. Programmers use this technique to verify that the program will accomplish its desired goals. The program is checked manually, and the results obtained are compared to those produced by the actual program.

The objective of this program is to compute the monthly payment (MNPYMT) for each parcel of real estate. The monthly payment is the sum of the monthly tax (MNTAX) and the monthly payment of the mortgage (MNMORG). These calculations (MNTAX and MNMORG) are based on the selling price (SELLPR), the amount of down payment (DNPAY), the annual cost of the mortgage (YRMORG), and the annual tax charges (YRTAX).

Figure 3.22 is the problem definition for this exercise. Figure 3.23 shows the coding sheets used for the program. The program listing and output are shown in Figure 3.24.

For this example, assume a selling price (SELLPR) of \$5ØØØØ with a down payment (DNPAY) of \$14,5ØØ. Perform each instruction in the Calculation section, one at a time, and note your results. Compare your results with the program output. Also answer the questions that follow the program.

Figure 3.22 Problem definition for Debugging Exercise 1.

Systems Flowchart

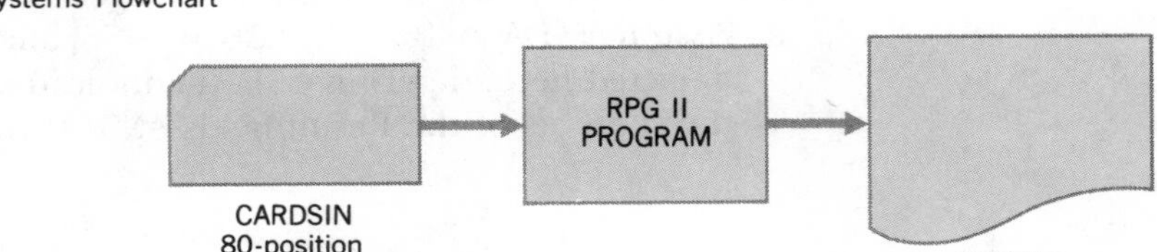

CARDSIN Record Layout

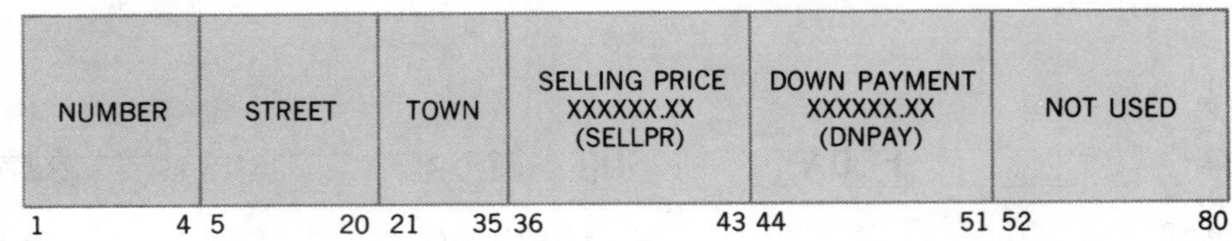

REPORT Printer Spacing Chart

```
   1
H  2  XX/XX/XX                      M I S G I V E N   R E A L T O R S                             PAGE XXØX
   3
H  4                                          SALES REPORT
   5
H  6              LOCATION                  SELLING       DOWN      MONTHLY    MONTHLY    MONTHLY
H  7   NUMBER      STREET         TOWN       PRICE      PAYMENT    MORTGAGE      TAX      PAYMENT
   8
D  9    XXØX  X-------------X  X----------X  XXX,XXØ.XX  XXX,XXØ.XX  X,XXØ.XX  X,XXØ.XX  $X,XX$.XX
D 10    XXØX  X-------------X  X----------X  XXX,XXØ.XX  XXX,XXØ.XX  X,XXØ.XX  X,XXØ.XX  $X,XX$.XX
  11
  12
```

RPG CONTROL AND FILE DESCRIPTION SPECIFICATIONS

Program: REALTY SALES REPORT
Programmer: N. JOHNKE   Date: 5/6/ ...
Keying Instruction — Graphic: Ø 1 2; Key: ZERO ONE TWO
Card Electro Number
Page Ø1 of 5   Program Identification: SSSØ3C

Control Specifications

For the valid entries for a system, refer to the RPG reference manual for that system.

```
01Ø H
```

File Description Specifications

For the valid entries for a system, refer to the RPG reference manual for that system.

```
02Ø F**********************************************************************
03Ø F* THIS PROGRAM PRODUCES A REAL ESTATE SALES REPORT CALCULATING       *
04Ø F* MONTHLY MORTGAGE, MONTHLY TAX AND TOTAL MONTHLY PAYMENT FOR EACH   *
05Ø F* PROPERTY SOLD.                                                      *
06Ø F**********************************************************************
07Ø F*
08Ø FCARDSIN IP  F      8Ø             READØ1 SYSIPT
09Ø FREPORT  O   F     132      OF     PRINTERSYSLST
10Ø F*
```

RPG INPUT SPECIFICATIONS

Program: REALTY SALES REPORT
Programmer: N. JOHNKE   Date: 5/6/___
Keying Instruction — Graphic: Ø 1 2; Key: ZERO ONE TWO
Card Electro Number
Page Ø2 of 5   Program Identification: SSSØ3C

```
01Ø I*********************** INPUT RECORD ************************
02Ø I*
03Ø ICARDSIN NS   Ø1
04Ø I                                         1   4ØNUMBER
05Ø I                                         5  2Ø STREET
06Ø I                                        21  35 TOWN
07Ø I                                        36  432SELLPR
08Ø I                                        44  512DNPAY
09Ø I*
```

Figure 3.23 Coding sheets for Debugging Exercise 1. *(Continued on next page.)*

RPG CALCULATION SPECIFICATIONS

Program: REALTY SALES REPORT | Programmer: N. JOHNKE | Date: 5/6/__ | Keying Instruction: Graphic Ø 1 2, Key ZERO ONE TWO | Card Electro Number | Page Ø3 of 5 | Program Identification: SSSØ3C

Line	Form Type	Control Level	Indicators	Factor 1	Operation	Factor 2	Result Field Name	Length	Decimal Positions	Half Adjust (H)	Resulting Indicators	Comments
01Ø	C	***************************** CALCULATIONS ******************************										
02Ø	C	*										
03Ø	C			SELLPR	SUB	DNPAY	MRGAMT	8	2			MONTHLY
04Ø	C			MRGAMT	MULT	.137	YRMORG	7	2	H		MORTGAGE
05Ø	C			YRMORG	DIV	12	MNMORG	6	2	H		
06Ø	C	*										
07Ø	C			SELLPR	MULT	.Ø45	YRTAX	7	2	H		MONTHLY
08Ø	C			YRTAX	DIV	12	MNTAX	6	2	H		TAX
09Ø	C	*										
10Ø	C			MNMORG	ADD	MNTAX	MNPYMT	7	2			MONTHLY PAYMENT
11Ø	C	*										

RPG OUTPUT SPECIFICATIONS

Program: REALTY SALES REPORT | Programmer: N. JOHNKE | Date: 5/6/__ | Keying Instruction: Graphic Ø 1 2, Key ZERO ONE TWO | Card Electro Number | Page Ø4 of 5 | Program Identification: SSSØ3C

Line	Form Type	Filename or Record Name	Type (H/D/T/E)	Space Before	Space After	Skip Before	Skip After	Output Indicators	Field Name or EXCPT Name	Edit Codes	End Position in Output Record	Constant or Edit Word
01Ø	O	***************************** HEADING LINES ******************************										
02Ø	O	*										
03Ø	O	REPORT	H	2	Ø	1		1P				
04Ø	O		OR					OF				
05Ø	O								UDATE	Y	11	
06Ø	O										48	'M I S G I V E N'
07Ø	O										66	'R E A L T O R S'
08Ø	O										93	'PAGE'
09Ø	O								PAGE		98	
10Ø	O		H	2				1P				
11Ø	O		OR					OF				
12Ø	O										55	'SALES REPORT'
13Ø	O		H	1				1P				
14Ø	O		OR					OF				
15Ø	O										2Ø	'LOCATION'
16Ø	O										64	'SELLING DOWN'
17Ø	O										87	'MONTHLY MONTHLY'
18Ø	O										97	'MONTHLY'
19Ø	O		H	2				1P				
20Ø	O		OR					OF				
21Ø	O										19	'NUMBER STREET'
22Ø	O										53	'TOWN PRICE'
23Ø	O										77	'PAYMENT MORTGAGE'
24Ø	O										97	'TAX PAYMENT'
25Ø	O	*										

Figure 3.23 *(continued)*

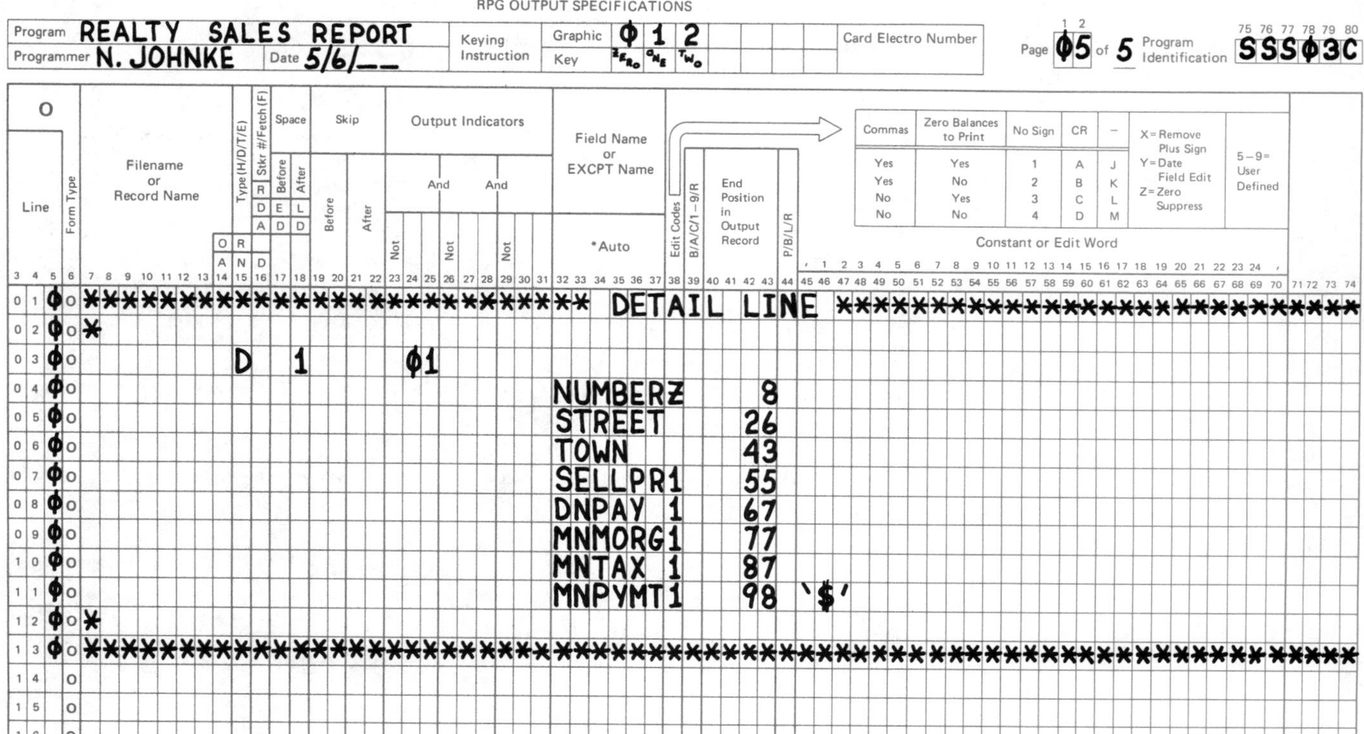

RPG OUTPUT SPECIFICATIONS

Program: REALTY SALES REPORT
Programmer: N. JOHNKE Date: 5/6/__
Keying Instruction — Graphic: Ø 1 2 — Key: ZERO ONE TWO
Card Electro Number
Page Ø5 of 5 Program Identification SSSØ3C

Line	Form Type	Filename or Record Name	Type (H/D/T/E)	Space After	Output Indicators	Field Name or EXCPT Name	Edit Codes	End Position in Output Record	Constant or Edit Word
Ø1	O	************************** DETAIL LINE **************************							
Ø2	O	*							
Ø3	O		D	1	Ø1				
Ø4	O					NUMBER	Z	8	
Ø5	O					STREET		26	
Ø6	O					TOWN		43	
Ø7	O					SELLPR	1	55	
Ø8	O					DNPAY	1	67	
Ø9	O					MNMORG	1	77	
1Ø	O					MNTAX	1	87	
11	O					MNPYMT	1	98	'$'
12	O	*							
13	O	***							
14	O								
15	O								

Figure 3.23 *(continued)*

Figure 3.24
Program listing and output for Debugging Exercise 1.

```
        01-020  F*****************************************************************SSS03C
        01-030  F* THIS PRCGRAM PRCDUCES A REAL ESTATE SALES REPORT CALCULATING    *SSS03C
        01-040  F* MCNTHLY MCRTGAGE, MONTHLY TAX ANC TOTAL MONTHLY PAYMENT FOR EACH *SSS03C
        C1-C5C  F* PRCPERTY SCLD.                                                  *SSS03C
        C1-060  F*****************************************************************SSS03C
        01-C70  F*                                                                 SSS03C
0001    C1-C8C  FCARDSIN IP  F      80              READ01 SYSIPT                  SSS03C
0002    01-C90  FREPCRT  O   F     132      CF      PRINTERSYSLST                  SSS03C
        01-10C  F*                                                                 SSS03C
        02-010  I*************************** INPUT RECORD ************************SSS03C
        02-C2C  I*                                                                 SSS03C
C003    C2-030  ICARCSIN NS  01                                                    SSS03C
C004    02-C40  I                                          1   40NUMBER            SSS03C
OCC5    C2-C5C  I                                          5  20 STREET            SSS03C
0006    02-C6C  I                                         21  35 TOWN              SSS03C
C007    C2-C70  I                                         36  432SELLPR            SSS03C
COC8    C2-C80  I                                         44  512DNPAY             SSS03C
        C2-C9C  I*                                                                 SSS03C
        03-010  C*************************** CALCULATIONS ************************SSS03C
        C3-C2C  C*                                                                 SSS03C
0009    C3-030  C           SELLPR    SUB  DNPAY      MRGAMT  82        MONTHLY    SSS03C
0010    C3-040  C           MRGAMT    MULT .137       YRMCRG  72H       MORTGAGE   SSS03C
0011    C3-050  C           YRMORG    DIV  12         MNMCRG  62H                  SSS03C
        03-060  C*                                                                 SSS03C
0012    03-070  C           SELLPR    MULT .045       YRTAX   72H       MONTHLY    SSS03C
0013    C3-080  C           YRTAX     DIV  12         MNTAX   62H         TAX      SSS03C
        03-090  C*                                                                 SSS03C
0014    C3-100  C           MNMORG    ADD  MNTAX      MNPYMT  72   MONTHLY PAYMENTSSS03C
        C3-11C  C*                                                                 SSS03C
        04-010  O*************************** HEADING LINES ***********************SSS03C
        C4-020  C*                                                                 SSS03C
0015    04-03C  CREPCRT  H  201    1P                                              SSS03C
C016    C4-040  O        CR        CF                                              SSS03C
0017    C4-C5C  C                          UDATE Y   11                            SSS03C
0018    C4-C60  C                                    48 'M I S G I V E N'          SSS03C
0019    04-C70  C                                    66 'R E A L T O R S'          SSS03C
0020    C4-C80  C                                    93 'PAGE'                     SSS03C
0021    C4-C9C  O                          PAGE      98                            SSS03C
0022    C4-10C  C        H  2      1P                                              SSS03C
0023    C4-110  C        CR        CF                                              SSS03C
0024    C4-120  O                                    55 'SALES REPORT'             SSS03C
0025    04-130  C        H  1      1P                                              SSS03C
0026    C4-14C  O        CR        CF                                              SSS03C
0027    C4-150  O                                    20 'LCCATION'                 SSS03C
0028    C4-160  C                                    64 'SELLING        DOWN'      SSS03C
0029    C4-17C  C                                    87 'MONTHLY     MONTHLY'      SSS03C
003C    C4-18C  C                                    97 'MONTHLY'                  SSS03C
0031    C4-190  C        H  2      1P                                              SSS03C
0C32    C4-2CC  O        OR        CF                                              SSS03C
0033    C4-210  C                                    19 'NUMBER     STREET'        SSS03C
0034    C4-220  O                                    53 'TOWN               PRICE' SSS03C
0035    C4-230  C                                    77 'PAYMENT    MORTGAGE'      SSS03C
C036    04-240  C                                    97 'TAX      PAYMENT'         SSS03C
        C4-25C  C*                                                                 SSS03C
        05-C10  C*************************** DETAIL LINE *************************SSS03C
        C5-C2C  C*                                                                 SSS03C
0037    C5-C3C  O        D  1      01                                              SSS03C
0038    05-C40  C                          NUMBERZ    8                            SSS03C
0039    C5-C50  C                          STREET    26                            SSS03C
004C    C5-C6C  C                          TCWN      43                            SSS03C
0041    05-C70  O                          SELLPR1   55                            SSS03C
0042    C5-C80  C                          CNPAY 1   67                            SSS03C
0043    C5-C90  C                          MNMCRG1   77                            SSS03C
0044    C5-10C  C                          MNTAX 1   87                            SSS03C
0C45    C5-110  C                          MNPYMT1   98 '$'                        SSS03C
        C5-12C  C*                                                                 SSS03C
        05-130  O*****************************************************************SSS03C

     E N C  C F  S C U R C E
```

```
12/17/82                      M I S G I V E N   R E A L T C R S

                                       SALES REPORT

          LCCATICN                                 SELLING       DCWN       MONTHLY    MONTHLY    MONTHLY
NUMBER     STREET             TCWN                  PRICE       PAYMENT    MORTGAGE      TAX      PAYMENT

  1932  HAMILTCN DRIVE     CCEANSIDE             50,000.00   14,500.00     405.29     187.50     $592.79
   362  WASHINGTCN AVE     LEVITTCWN             61,900.CO   18,500.00     495.48     232.13     $727.61
   721  LAFAYETTE ST       UNICNDALE             45,C00.00   11,250.C0     385.31     168.75     $554.06
  1045  LANCASTER RC       NCRTHPCRT            105,900.00   37,C65.00     785.87     397.13   $1,183.00
    57  DOGWCCD RD         GARCEN CITY           95,500.00   30,560.00     741.40     358.13   $1,099.53
   566  PUMPKIN LANE       HICKSVILLE            59,950.00   15,C00.00     513.18     224.81     $737.99
     7  SEAVIEW COURT      CYSTER BAY            87,500.00   21,900.00     748.93     328.13   $1,077.06
```

Questions

1. Identify the fields contained in the input record that are numeric.
2. Referring to instructions on the Calculation form, what does the H signify?

3. How is the monthly mortgage calculated?
4. How are new values assigned for each customer in calculating the monthly mortgage?
5. How is the monthly tax calculated?
6. How many dollars are paid for the $35,5ØØ mortgage over a 25-year period?
7. How many total dollars in taxes will be spent over a 25-year period?
8. Indicate the instruction that causes the current date to be printed on the output.
9. Are any of the output fields zero-suppressed?
10. Referring to instruction ØØØ9, does the selling price (SELLPR) change because the down payment (DNPAY) is subtracted?
11. Identify the instruction that numbers each page of the output.
12. Name the primary file used by the program.
13. Do any output fields contain dollar signs?
14. Identify the edited fields in the detail printing of the report.
15. With the editing specified, how will fields containing zeros be printed?

Debugging Exercise 2

The problem definition for this exercise is shown in Figure 3.25. The coding sheets in Figure 3.26 contain 3 syntax errors. Identify them and illustrate the corrections you would make to the program.

The listing in Figure 3.27 includes the error diagnostics produced by running the program as coded. The syntax corrections are circled on the computer listing shown in Figure 3.28. There are, however, logic errors in the program. Your assignment is to desk check the program carefully, find the logic errors, and make the necessary corrections.

Systems Flowchart

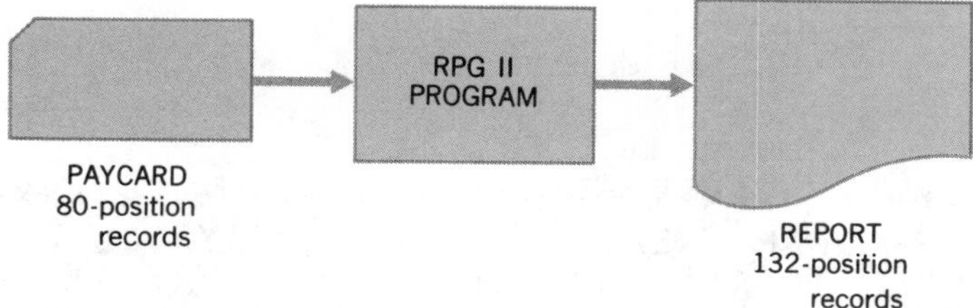

PAYCARD Record Layout

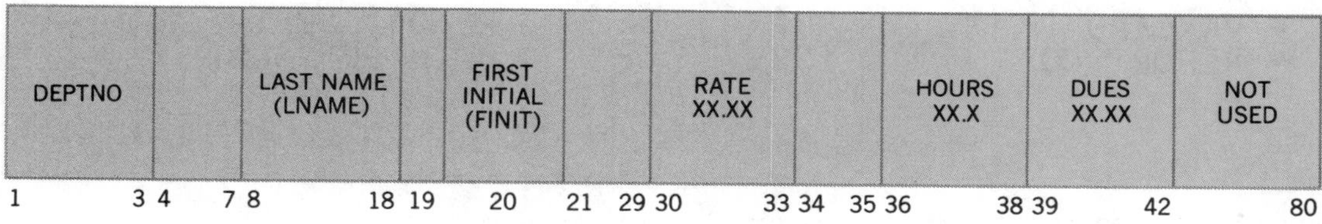

Figure 3.25 Problem definition for Debugging Exercise 2. *(Continued on next page.)*

Figure 3.25 REPORT Printer Spacing Chart
(continued)

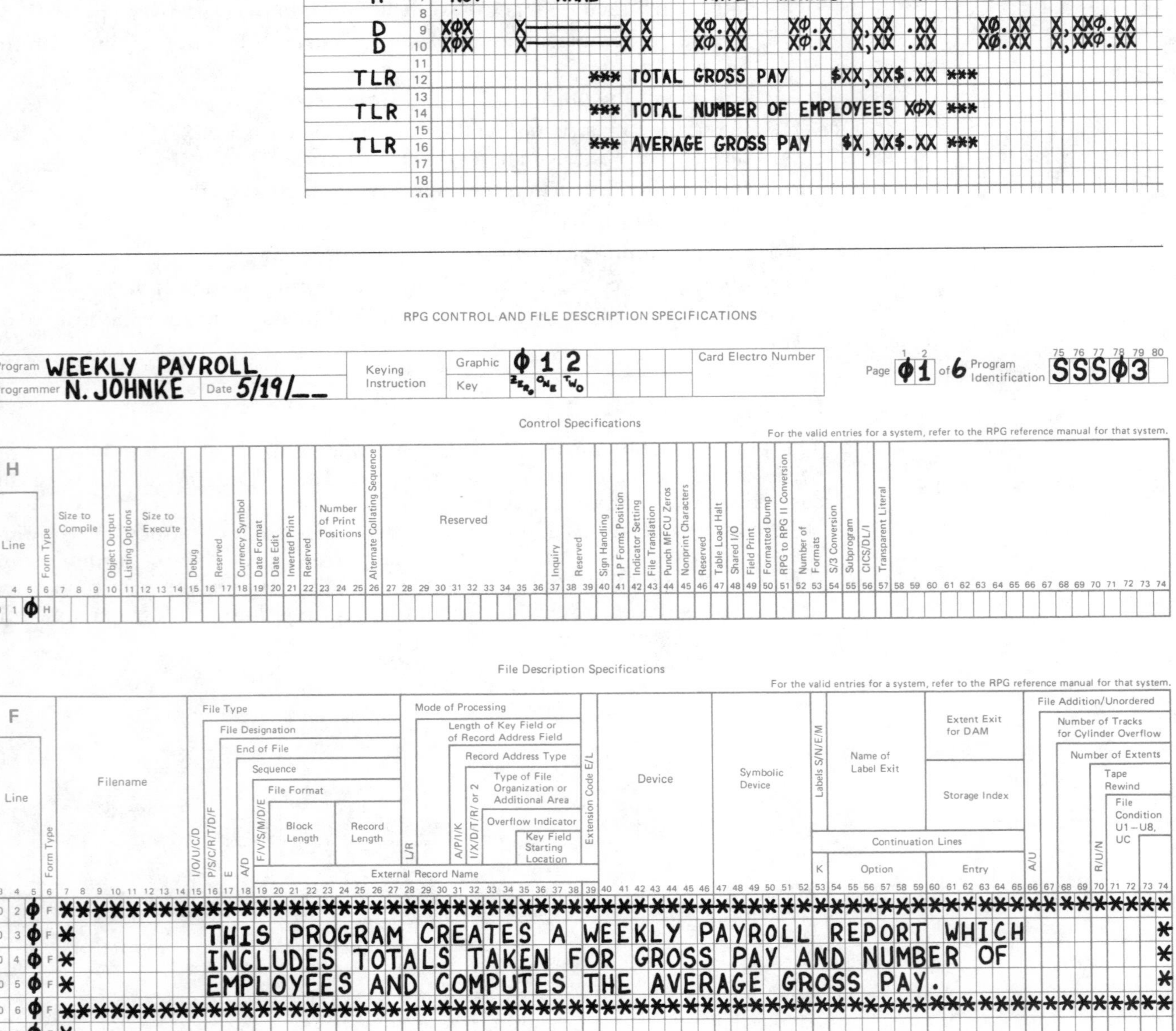

```
H    2                       W I D G E T   P R O D U C T S            PAGE XXØX
H    4                        ** WEEKLY PAYROLL REPORT **             XX/XX/XX
H    6  DEPT      EMPLOYEE          HOURLY   HOURS    GROSS                 NET
H    7  NO.         NAME             RATE    WORKED    PAY       DUES       PAY
D    9  XØX     X—————————X X       XØ.XX    XØ.X   X,XX .XX    XØ.XX   X,XXØ.XX
D   10  XØX     X—————————X X       XØ.XX    XØ.X   X,XX .XX    XØ.XX   X,XXØ.XX
TLR 12                 *** TOTAL GROSS PAY       $XX,XX$.XX ***
TLR 14                 *** TOTAL NUMBER OF EMPLOYEES XØX ***
TLR 16                 *** AVERAGE GROSS PAY      $X,XX$.XX ***
```

RPG CONTROL AND FILE DESCRIPTION SPECIFICATIONS

Program: WEEKLY PAYROLL | Programmer: N. JOHNKE | Date: 5/19/__ | Keying Instruction: Graphic Ø 1 2, Key ZERO ONE TWO | Card Electro Number | Page Ø1 of 6 | Program Identification: SSSØ3

Control Specifications

For the valid entries for a system, refer to the RPG reference manual for that system.

```
01Ø H
```

File Description Specifications

For the valid entries for a system, refer to the RPG reference manual for that system.

```
02Ø F*************************************************************************
03Ø F*                 THIS PROGRAM CREATES A WEEKLY PAYROLL REPORT WHICH     *
04Ø F*                 INCLUDES TOTALS TAKEN FOR GROSS PAY AND NUMBER OF      *
05Ø F*                 EMPLOYEES AND COMPUTES THE AVERAGE GROSS PAY.          *
06Ø F*************************************************************************
07Ø F*
08Ø FPAYCARD IP   F      8Ø                     READØ1 SYSIPT
09Ø FREPORT  O    F     132        OF           PRINTERSYSLST
10Ø F*
    F
    F
```

Figure 3.26 Coding sheets for Debugging Exercise 2. *(Continued on next page.)*

RPG INPUT SPECIFICATIONS

Program WEEKLY PAYROLL
Programmer N. JOHNKE Date 5/19/__
Keying Instruction: Graphic Ø 1 2; Key ZERO ONE TWO
Card Electro Number
Page Ø2 of 6 Program Identification SSSØ3

Line	Form Type	Filename or Record Name	Sequence	Record Identifying Indicator	From	To	Decimal Positions	RPG Field Name
01Ø	I	****************************** INPUT RECORD ******************************						
02Ø	I	*						
03Ø	I	PAYCARD	NS	19				
04Ø	I				1	3	Ø	DEPTNO
05Ø	I				8	18		LNAME
06Ø	I				2Ø	2Ø		FINIT
07Ø	I				3Ø	33		RATE
08Ø	I				36	38	1	HOURS
09Ø	I				39	42	2	DUES
10Ø	I	*						
11	I							
12	I							

RPG CALCULATION SPECIFICATIONS

Program WEEKLY PAYROLL
Programmer N. JOHNKE Date 5/19/__
Keying Instruction: Graphic Ø 1 2; Key ZERO ONE TWO
Card Electro Number
Page Ø3 of 6 Program Identification SSSØ3

Line	Form Type	Factor 1	Operation	Factor 2	Result Field Name	Length	Decimal Positions	Half Adjust (H)
01Ø	C	************************ CALCULATION ROUTINE ************************						
02Ø	C	*						
03Ø	C	TGRPAY	ADD	GRPAY	TGRPAY	7	2	
04Ø	C	RATE	MULT	HRS	GRPAY	6	2	H
05Ø	C	GRPAY	SUB	DUES	NETPAY	6	2	
06Ø	C	*						
07Ø	C	EMPS	ADD	1	EMPS	3	Ø	
08Ø	C	TGRPAY	DIV	EMPS	AVGPAY	6	2	H
09Ø	C	*						
10	C							
11	C							

Figure 3.26
(continued)

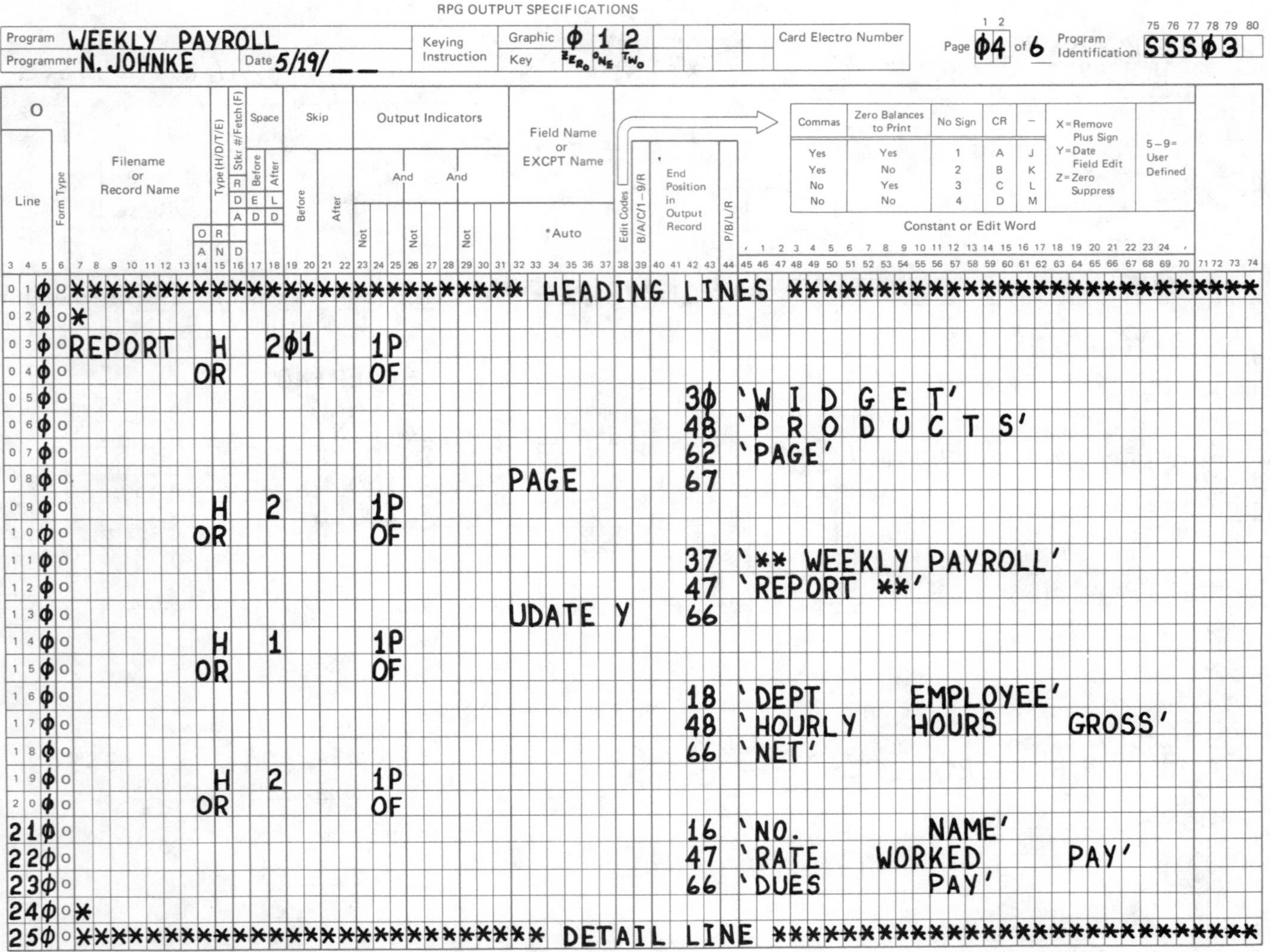

RPG OUTPUT SPECIFICATIONS

Program: WEEKLY PAYROLL | Programmer: N. JOHNKE | Date: 5/19/__ | Graphic: Ø 1 2 | Key: ZERO ONE TWO | Page: Ø4 of 6 | Program Identification: SSSØ3

```
01Ø O******************************** HEADING LINES ****************************
02Ø O*
03Ø OREPORT   H  2Ø1   1P
04Ø O        OR        OF
05Ø O                                    3Ø 'W I D G E T'
06Ø O                                    48 'P R O D U C T S'
07Ø O                                    62 'PAGE'
08Ø O                         PAGE       67
09Ø O         H  2     1P
10Ø O        OR        OF
11Ø O                                    37 '** WEEKLY PAYROLL'
12Ø O                                    47 'REPORT **'
13Ø O                         UDATE Y    66
14Ø O         H  1     1P
15Ø O        OR        OF
16Ø O                                    18 'DEPT      EMPLOYEE'
17Ø O                                    48 'HOURLY    HOURS      GROSS'
18Ø O                                    66 'NET'
19Ø O         H  2     1P
20Ø O        OR        OF
21Ø O                                    16 'NO.       NAME'
22Ø O                                    47 'RATE   WORKED      PAY'
23Ø O                                    66 'DUES      PAY'
24Ø O*
25Ø O****************************** DETAIL LINE *********************************
```

Figure 3.26
(continued)

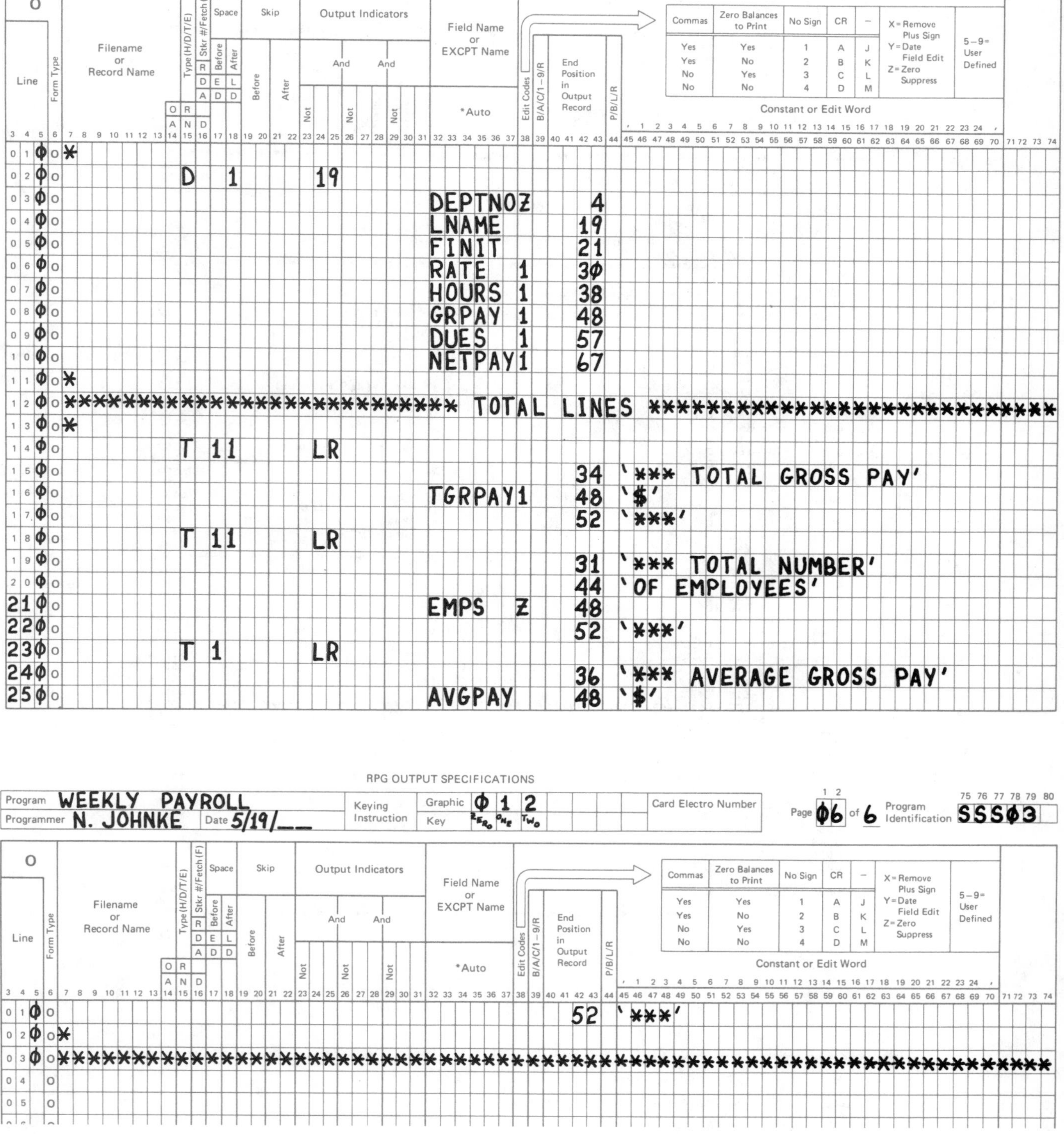

RPG OUTPUT SPECIFICATIONS

Program: WEEKLY PAYROLL — Programmer: N.JOHNKE — Date: 5/19/__ — Keying Instruction: Graphic Ø 1 2, Key ZERO ONE TWO — Page Ø5 of 6 — Program Identification: SSSØ3

```
01ØO*
02ØO         D  1      19
03ØO                           DEPTNOZ    4
04ØO                           LNAME     19
05ØO                           FINIT     21
06ØO                           RATE  1   3Ø
07ØO                           HOURS 1   38
08ØO                           GRPAY 1   48
09ØO                           DUES  1   57
10ØO                           NETPAY1   67
11ØO*
12ØO************************** TOTAL LINES ****************************
13ØO*
14ØO         T 11      LR
15ØO                                     34 '*** TOTAL GROSS PAY'
16ØO                           TGRPAY1   48 '$'
17ØO                                     52 '***'
18ØO         T 11      LR
19ØO                                     31 '*** TOTAL NUMBER'
20ØO                                     44 'OF EMPLOYEES'
21ØO                           EMPS  Z   48
22ØO                                     52 '***'
23ØO         T 1       LR
24ØO                                     36 '*** AVERAGE GROSS PAY'
25ØO                           AVGPAY    48 '$'
```

RPG OUTPUT SPECIFICATIONS

Program: WEEKLY PAYROLL — Programmer: N. JOHNKE — Date: 5/19/__ — Keying Instruction: Graphic Ø 1 2, Key ZERO ONE TWO — Page Ø6 of 6 — Program Identification: SSSØ3

```
01ØO                                     52 '***'
02ØO*
03ØO*****************************************************************
04 O
05 O
```

Figure 3.26 *(continued)*

Figure 3.27 Program listing with error diagnostics for Debugging Exercise 2.

```
           01-020  F*****************************************************************************SSS03
           01-030  F*          THIS PROGRAM CREATES A WEEKLY PAYRCLL REPORT WHICH                 *SSS03
           01-040  F*          INCLUDES TOTALS TAKEN FCR GRCSS PAY AND NUMBER OF                  *SSS03
           01-050  F*          EMPLCYEES AND COMPUTES THE AVERAGE GRCSS PAY.                      *SSS03
           01-060  F*****************************************************************************SSS03
           01-070  F*                                                                             SSS03
0001       01-080  FPAYCARD IP  F      80                 READ01 SYSIPT                           SSS03
0002       01-090  FREPORT  C   F      132      CF        PRINTERSYSLST                           SSS03
           01-100  F*                                                                             SSS03
           02-010  I*************************** INPUT RECORD ******************************SSS03
           02-020  I*                                                                             SSS03
0003       02-030  IPAYCARC NS  19                                                                SSS03
0004       02-040  I                                            1   30DEPTNO                      SSS03
0005       02-050  I                                            8  18 LNAME                       SSS03
0006       02-060  I                                           20  20 FINIT                       SSS03
0007       02-070  I                                           30  33 RATE                        SSS03
0008       02-080  I                                           36  381HCURS                       SSS03
0009       02-090  I                                           39  422DUES                        SSS03
           02-100  I*                                                                             SSS03
           03-010  C*********************** CALCULATION ROUTINE **************************SSS03
           03-020  C*                                                                             SSS03
0010       03-030  C             TGRPAY     ADD  GRPAY      TGRPAY  72                           SSS03
0011       03-040  C             RATE       MULT HRS        GRPAY   62H                          SSS03
0012       03-050  C             GRPAY      SUB  DUES       NETPAY  62                           SSS03
           03-060  C*                                                                             SSS03
0013       03-070  C             EMPS       ADC  1          EMPS    30                           SSS03
0014       03-080  C             TGRPAY     DIV  EMPS       AVGPAY  62H                          SSS03
           03-090  C*                                                                             SSS03
           04-010  O*************************** HEADING LINES *****************************SSS03
           04-020  C*                                                                             SSS03
0015       04-030  CREPORT  H  201    1P                                                         SSS03
0016       04-040  C        CR        CF                                                         SSS03
0017       04-050  O                                      30 'W I C G E T'                       SSS03
0018       04-060  C                                      48 'P R C D U C T S'                   SSS03
0019       04-070  C                                      62 'PAGE'                              SSS03
0020       04-080  O                            PAGE      67                                     SSS03
0021       04-090  O         H  2     1P                                                         SSS03
0022       04-100  O        CR        CF                                                         SSS03
0023       04-110  O                                      37 '** WEEKLY PAYROLL'                 SSS03
0024       04-120  O                                      47 'REPCRT **'                         SSS03
0025       04-130  C                            UDATE Y   66                                     SSS03
0026       04-140  C         H  1     1P                                                         SSS03
0027       04-150  O        OR        OF                                                         SSS03
0028       04-160  C                                      18 'DEPT     EMPLOYEE'                 SSS03
0029       04-170  C                                      48 'HOURLY   HOURS     GROSS'          SSS03
0030       04-180  C                                      66 'NET'                               SSS03
0031       04-190  C         H  2     1P                                                         SSS03
0032       04-200  O        OR        CF                                                         SSS03
0033       04-210  C                                      16 'NC.        NAME'                   SSS03
0034       04-220  O                                      47 'RATE   WCRKED     PAY'             SSS03
0035       04-230  C                                      66 'DUES       PAY'                    SSS03
           04-240  C*                                                                             SSS03
           04-250  O*************************** DETAIL LINE *******************************SSS03
           05-010  C*                                                                             SSS03
0036       05-020  C         D  1     19                                                         SSS03
0037       05-030  C                            DEPTNOZ    4                                     SSS03
0038       05-040  C                            LNAME     19                                     SSS03
0039       05-050  O                            FINIT     21                                     SSS03
0040       05-060  O                            RATE  1   30                                     SSS03
0041       05-070  C                            HOURS 1   38                                     SSS03
0042       05-080  O                            GRPAY 1   48                                     SSS03
0043       05-090  C                            DUES  1   57                                     SSS03
0044       05-100  C                            NETPAY1   67                                     SSS03
           05-110  C*                                                                             SSS03
           05-120  O*************************** TCTAL LINES *******************************SSS03
           05-130  C*                                                                             SSS03
0045       05-140  C         T 11     LR                                                         SSS03
0046       05-150  O                                      34 '*** TCTAL GRCSS PAY'               SSS03
0047       05-160  O                            TGRPAY1   48 '$'                                 SSS03
0048       05-170  O                                      52 '***'                               SSS03
0049       05-180  O         T 11     LR                                                         SSS03
0050       05-190  C                                      31 '*** TOTAL NUMBER'                  SSS03
0051       05-200  C                                      44 'OF EMPLOYEES'                      SSS03
0052       05-210  O                            EMPS  Z   48                                     SSS03
0053       05-220  O                                      52 '***'                               SSS03
0054       05-230  C         T 1      LR                                                         SSS03
0055       05-240  O                                      36 '*** AVERAGE GROSS PAY'             SSS03
0056       05-250  O                            AVGPAY    48 '$'                                 SSS03
                                                             $                                              MSG  234
0057       06-010  O                                      52 '***'                               SSS03
           06-020  C*                                                                             SSS03
           06-030  O*****************************************************************************SSS03
```

```
       E N D   C F   S C U R C E


       C O M P I L E R   D I A G N C S T I C S   S U M M A R Y


ILN234    INVALIC NUMBER OF DIGIT POSITIONS IN EDIT WORD. DROP EDITING.

          00056     C5-25C      AVGPAY

ILN398    FIELD NAME UNDEFINED. SPEC IS DRCPPED.

        D 00011     03-040      HRS

ILN413    EDIT SPECIFIED WITH ALPHAMERIC FIELD. DRCP EDITING.

          00040     C5-06C
```

Figure 3.28
Program listing that contains logic errors for Debugging Exercise 2.
(Continued on next page.)

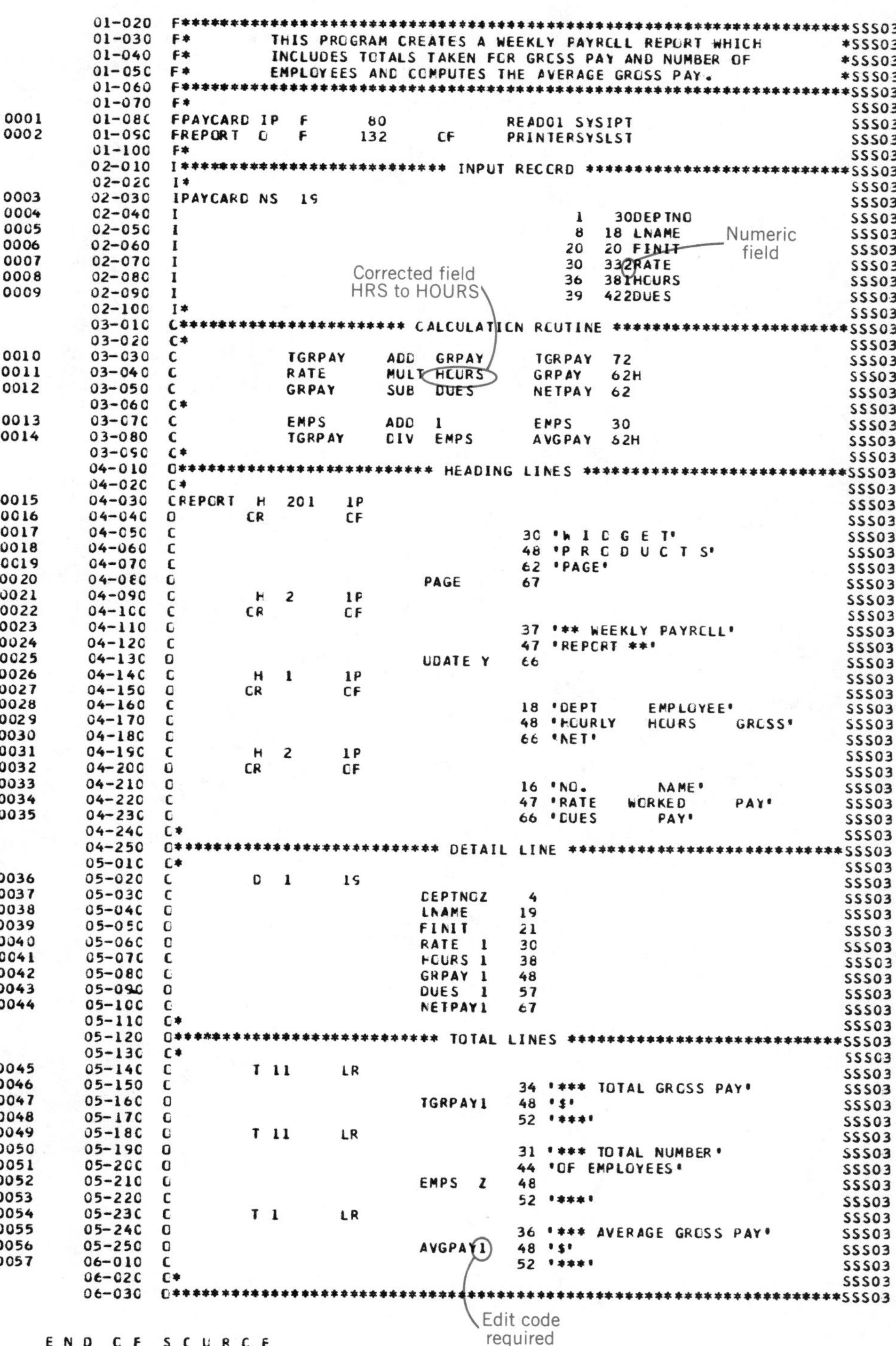


```
01-020 F**********************************************************************SSS03
01-030 F*          THIS PROGRAM CREATES A WEEKLY PAYRCLL REPORT WHICH          *SSS03
01-040 F*          INCLUDES TOTALS TAKEN FCR GRCSS PAY AND NUMBER OF           *SSS03
01-05C F*          EMPLOYEES ANC COMPUTES THE AVERAGE GROSS PAY.               *SSS03
01-060 F**********************************************************************SSS03
01-070 F*                                                                      SSS03
01-08C FPAYCARD IP  F      80            READ01 SYSIPT                         SSS03
01-09C FREPORT  O   F     132     CF     PRINTERSYSLST                         SSS03
01-100 F*                                                                      SSS03
02-010 I************************* INPUT RECCRD ******************************SSS03
02-02C I*                                                                      SSS03
02-030 IPAYCARD NS  15                                                         SSS03
02-040 I                                              1   30DEPTNO             SSS03
02-050 I                                              8  18 LNAME              SSS03
02-060 I                                             20  20 FINIT              SSS03
02-070 I                                             30  332RATE               SSS03
02-080 I                                             36  381HCURS              SSS03
02-090 I                                             39  422DUES               SSS03
02-100 I*                                                                      SSS03
03-01C C*********************** CALCULATICN RCUTINE *************************SSS03
03-020 C*                                                                      SSS03
03-030 C          TGRPAY    ADD  GRPAY     TGRPAY  72                          SSS03
03-040 C          RATE      MULT HCURS     GRPAY   62H                         SSS03
03-050 C          GRPAY     SUB  DUES      NETPAY  62                          SSS03
03-060 C*                                                                      SSS03
03-07C C          EMPS      ADD  1         EMPS    30                          SSS03
03-080 C          TGRPAY    DIV  EMPS      AVGPAY  62H                         SSS03
03-09C C*                                                                      SSS03
04-010 O************************** HEADING LINES ****************************SSS03
04-02C C*                                                                      SSS03
04-030 CREPCRT  H  201   1P                                                    SSS03
04-04C O        CR       CF                                                    SSS03
04-05C C                              30 'W I D G E T'                         SSS03
04-060 C                              48 'P R C D U C T S'                     SSS03
04-070 C                              62 'PAGE'                                SSS03
04-0E0 O                   PAGE       67                                       SSS03
04-090 C        H  2     1P                                                    SSS03
04-1CC C        CR       CF                                                    SSS03
04-110 O                              37 '** WEEKLY PAYRCLL'                   SSS03
04-120 C                              47 'REPCRT **'                           SSS03
04-13C O                   UDATE Y    66                                       SSS03
04-14C C        H  1     1P                                                    SSS03
04-150 O        CR       CF                                                    SSS03
04-160 C                              18 'DEPT      EMPLOYEE'                  SSS03
04-170 C                              48 'HCURLY    HCURS     GRCSS'           SSS03
04-18C C                              66 'NET'                                 SSS03
04-19C C        H  2     1P                                                    SSS03
04-200 O        CR       CF                                                    SSS03
04-210 O                              16 'NO.        NAME'                     SSS03
04-220 C                              47 'RATE   WORKED     PAY'               SSS03
04-23C C                              66 'CUES        PAY'                     SSS03
04-24C C*                                                                      SSS03
04-250 O************************** DETAIL LINE ******************************SSS03
05-01C C*                                                                      SSS03
05-020 C        D  1     15                                                    SSS03
05-03C C                   CEPTNOZ     4                                       SSS03
05-04C O                   LNAME      19                                       SSS03
05-05C O                   FINIT      21                                       SSS03
05-06C O                   RATE  1    30                                       SSS03
05-07C C                   HCURS 1    38                                       SSS03
05-08C C                   GRPAY 1    48                                       SSS03
05-09C O                   DUES  1    57                                       SSS03
05-10C C                   NETPAY1    67                                       SSS03
05-110 C*                                                                      SSS03
05-120 O************************** TOTAL LINES ******************************SSS03
05-13C C*                                                                      SSS03
05-14C C        T 11     LR                                                    SSS03
05-150 C                              34 '*** TOTAL GRCSS PAY'                 SSS03
05-16C O                   TGRPAY1    48 '$'                                   SSS03
05-17C O                              52 '***'                                 SSS03
05-18C O        T 11     LR                                                    SSS03
05-190 O                              31 '*** TOTAL NUMBER'                    SSS03
05-20C O                              44 'OF EMPLOYEES'                        SSS03
05-210 O                   EMPS  Z    48                                       SSS03
05-220 C                              52 '***'                                 SSS03
05-23C C        T 1      LR                                                    SSS03
05-24C O                              36 '*** AVERAGE GRCSS PAY'               SSS03
05-250 O                   AVGPAY1    48 '$'                                   SSS03
06-010 C                              52 '***'                                 SSS03
06-02C C*                                                                      SSS03
06-030 O**********************************************************************SSS03

E N D  C F  S C U R C E
```

Figure 3.28
(continued)

```
                       W I D G E T   P R O D U C T S              PAGE    1
                        ** WEEKLY PAYROLL REPORT **               7/29/82

DEPT     EMPLOYEE          HOURLY    HOURS     GROSS               NET
 NO.       NAME             RATE    WORKED      PAY       DUES     PAY

 10    ADAMS         M      5.00     40.0     200.00      6.75    193.25
 10    BROWN         B      7.00     30.5     213.50      3.50    210.00
 10    DAVIS         C      6.50     39.5     256.75      4.65    252.10
 10    WOLFGANG      N      9.10     40.0     364.00      3.00    361.00
 20    BOSCO         V      8.20     36.0     295.20      5.00    290.20
 20    CARTER        B      4.40     25.5     112.20      4.85    107.35
 20    DONOVAN       D      6.75     33.0     222.75      4.50    218.25
 20    JOHNKE        N      7.10     39.2     278.32      9.50    268.82
 30    EDWARDS       E      3.90     40.0     156.00       .00    156.00
 30    SAGER         A      7.80     36.0     280.80     10.00    270.80
 30    STERN         B      8.00     34.0     272.00      8.00    264.00
 30    WHITE         F      9.90     40.0     396.00     15.00    381.00

              *** TOTAL GROSS PAY            $2,651.52 ***  <-- Incorrect total—should be 3,047.52

              *** TOTAL NUMBER OF EMPLOYEES     12 ***

              *** AVERAGE GROSS PAY            $220.96 ***  <-- Incorrect total—should be 253.96
```

Practice Problems

1. Consider the problem definition shown in Figure 3.29. Write a program to produce the sales report from the disk records. The profit for each item is determined by subtracting the cost of the item from its sales amount. Final totals are to be printed for the sales amount, cost amount, and profit fields.

Figure 3.29
Problem definition for Practice Problem 1.

Systems Flowchart

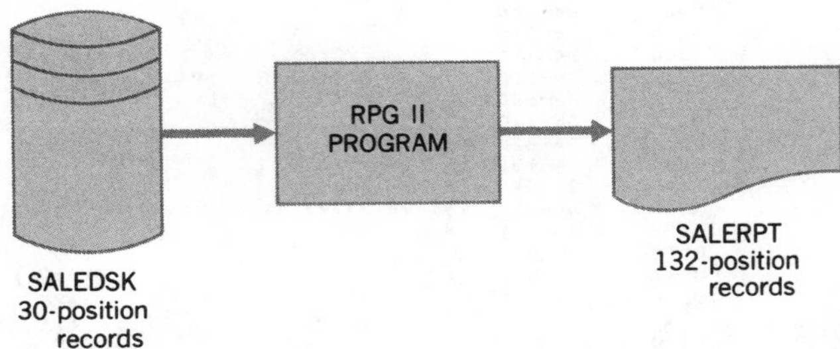

SALEDSK Record Layout

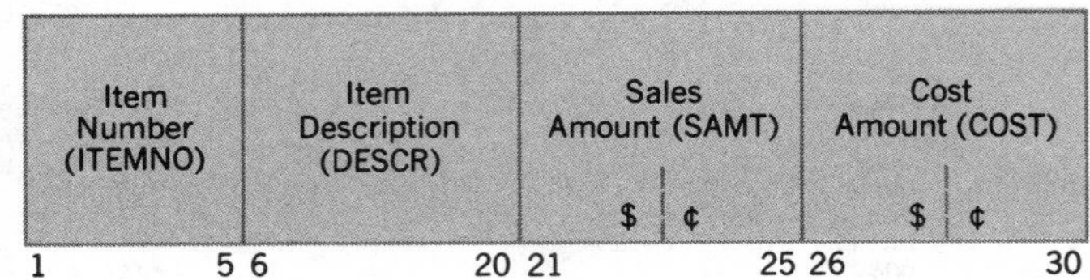

SALERPT Printer Spacing Chart

```
      1
H     2  XX/XX/XX                                SALES   REPORT                         PAGE XX0X
      3
H     4   ITEM        DESCRIPTION                   SALES               COST              PROFIT
      5
D     6  XXXXX       X---------------X             XX0.XX              XX0.XX             XX0.XX
D     7  XXXXX       X---------------X             XX0.XX              XX0.XX             XX0.XX
      8
TLR   9                           TOTALS $XX,XX$.XX           $XX,XX$.XX          $XX,XX$.XX
     10
     11
```

2. Consider the following problem definition.

Systems Flowchart

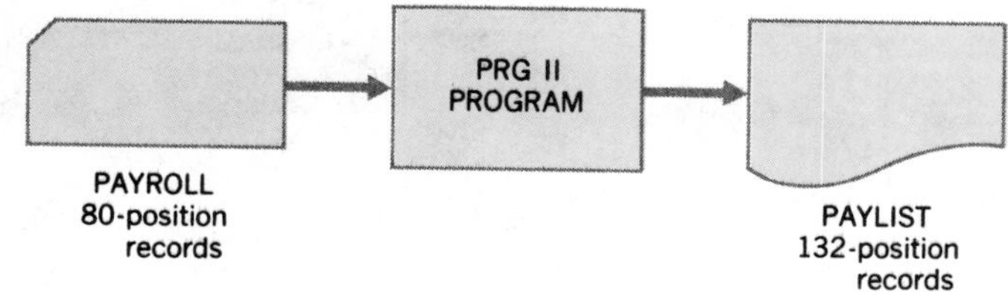

PAYROLL Record Layout

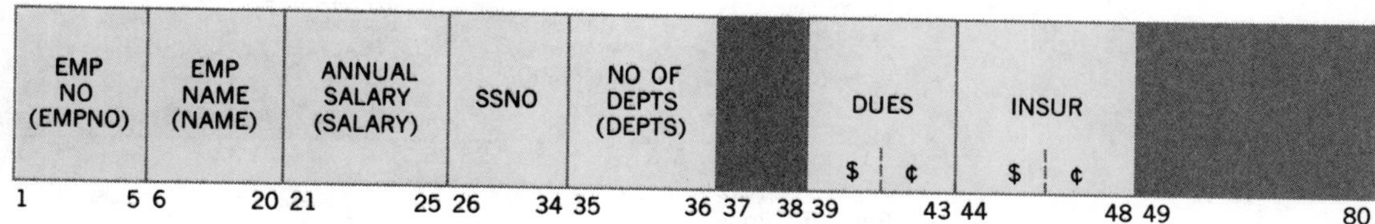

PAYLIST Printer Spacing Chart

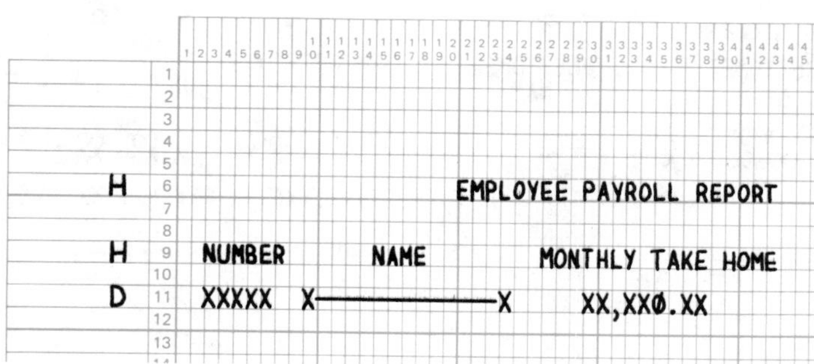

Write a program to produce the desired output. The detail lines on the report should be double-spaced. Calculate take-home pay using the following formulas.

Deduction (DEDUCT) = (.25 X gross salary (SALARY)) – (1ØØØ X number of dependents (DEPTS))
Net salary (NET) = Gross salary (SALARY) – DEDUCT – INSUR – DUES
Take-home pay = NET/12

Note: If DEDUCT is negative, set it to zero.

3. Write an RPG program that will produce a bank balance report. The problem definition is shown in Figure 3.3Ø.

   If the current balance is negative, indicate this by including the word "OVERDRAWN" on the detail line. The formula for calculating current balance is as follows.

   Current balance = BAL + DEP – WDRAW

Figure 3.30 Problem definition for Practice Problem 3.

Systems Flowchart

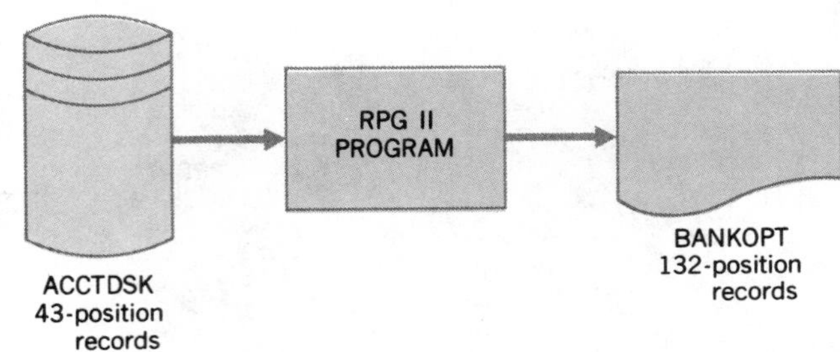

ACCTDSK Record Layout

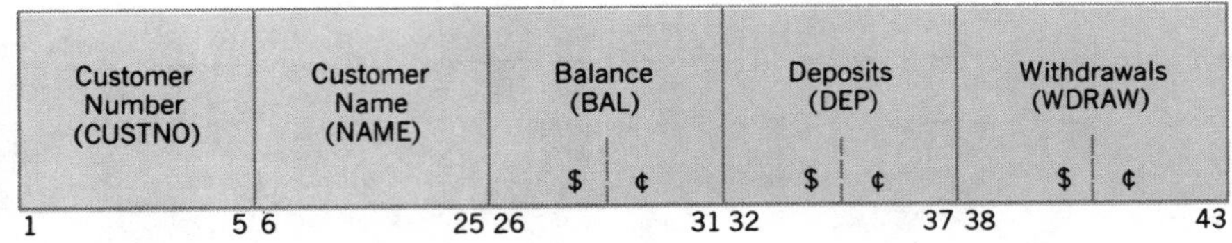

BANKOPT Printer Spacing Chart

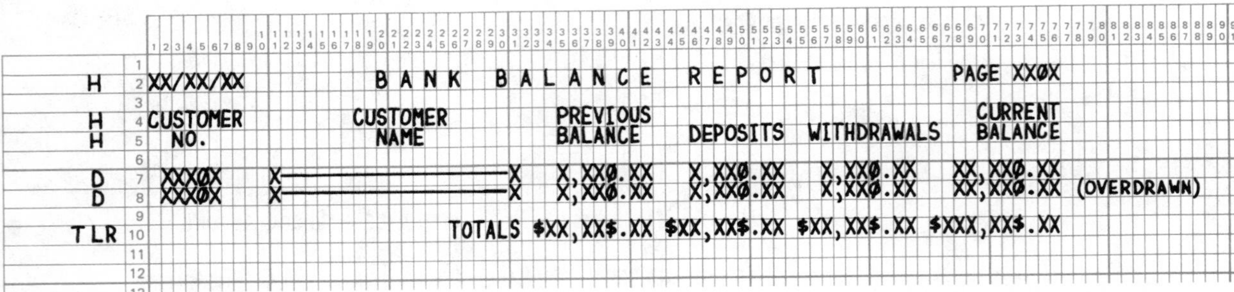

4. Write an RPG program to produce a payroll register. The problem definition is shown in Figure 3.31. The following formulas are to be used.

   FICA = 6.7% of gross pay (assume all employees earn less than the maximum amount subject to FICA tax, which is the Social Security tax).

   Voluntary deductions = Union dues + credit union + health insurance
   Statutory deductions = FICA + federal tax + state tax
   Total deductions = Voluntary deductions + statutory deductions
   Net Pay = Gross pay − total deductions

Figure 3.31 Problem definition for Practice Problem 4.

Systems Flowchart

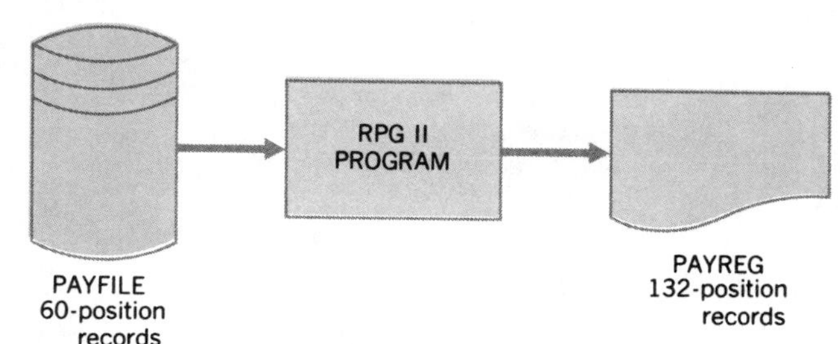

PAYFILE Record Layout

SOC SEC	EMPLOYEE NAME	GROSS PAY	FEDERAL TAX	STATE TAX	UNION DUES	CREDIT UNION	HEALTH INSURANCE	
1–9	10–30	31–35	36–40	41–44	45–48	49–52	53–55	60

PAYREG Printer Spacing Chart

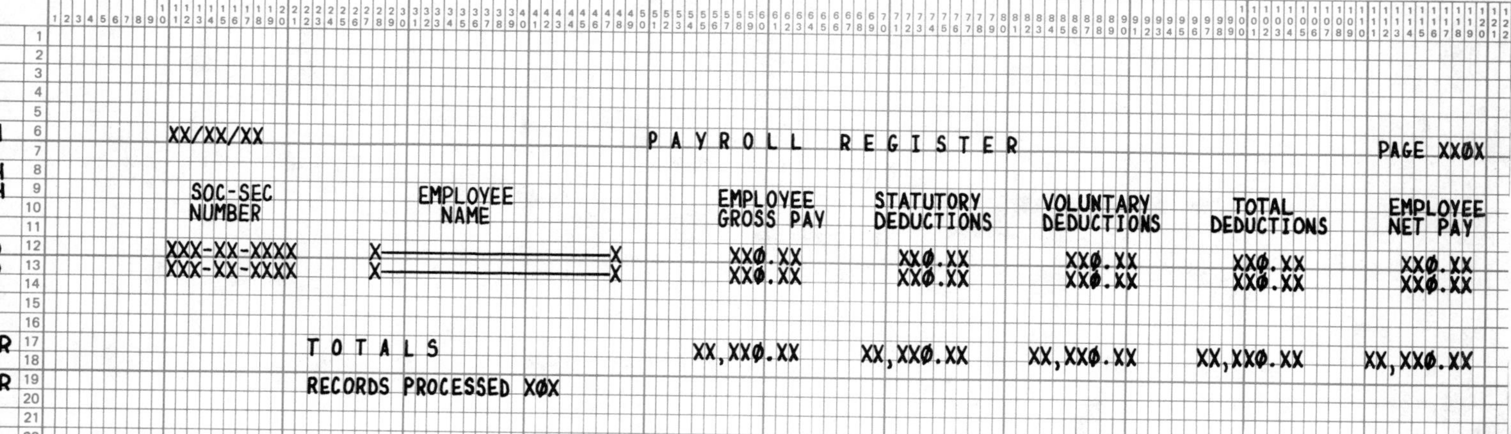

H XX/XX/XX PAYROLL REGISTER
PAGE XXØX
H SOC-SEC NUMBER
EMPLOYEE NAME
H EMPLOYEE GROSS PAY
STATUTORY DEDUCTIONS
VOLUNTARY DEDUCTIONS
TOTAL DEDUCTIONS
EMPLOYEE NET PAY
D XXX-XX-XXXX X———X XXØ.XX XXØ.XX XXØ.XX XXØ.XX XXØ.XX
D XXX-XX-XXXX X———X XXØ.XX XXØ.XX XXØ.XX XXØ.XX XXØ.XX
LR TOTALS XX,XXØ.XX XX,XXØ.XX XX,XXØ.XX XX,XXØ.XX XX,XXØ.XX
LR RECORDS PROCESSED XØX

UNIT II

BRANCHING, LOOPING, AND HANDLING CONTROL BREAKS

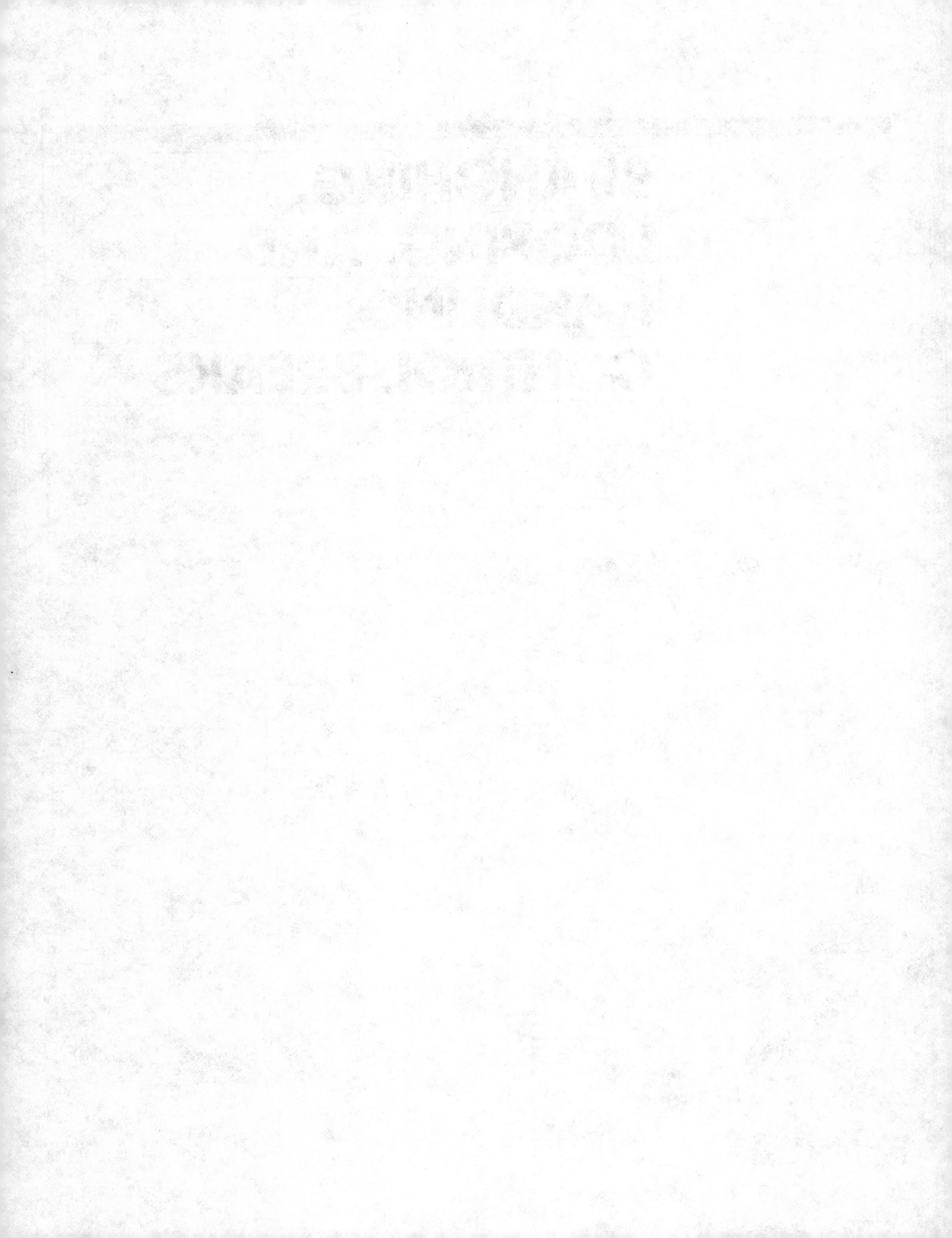

CHAPTER 4

Program Logic and Comparisons

Objectives

- To focus on the ways in which RPG can be used for comparing fields.
- To provide insight into the logical control procedures used in RPG.
- To focus on comparison operations commonly used in business applications.

I. Introduction

A. An Overview of Program Logic and Comparisons

In prior chapters, we found that instructions on the Calculation form were executed in sequence, one step at a time in the order written. In the business world, however, many problems cannot be solved by this direct sequential approach. Programming problems usually impose a variety of conditions requiring the program to make decisions so that alternative actions can be taken. Frequently it is necessary to alter the normal flow and execute a different set of instructions in order to accomplish the objectives of the program.

For example, if an individual works more than 4Ø hours in a week, gross pay must be calculated using a premium rate of time and a half applied against the overtime hours. That is, for all hours worked in excess of 4Ø, the employee will be paid at a rate of 1.5 times the regular rate.

To process input data correctly, the RPG program must have the ability to compare the actual hours worked to the number forty (4Ø) and then decide whether overtime calculations should be included or not. When different sets of instructions are used depending on specific conditions, these sets are referred to as **routines**. In this example there are two routines: a regular pay routine used for employees who worked 4Ø hours or less and an overtime routine used for employees who worked more than 4Ø hours. For any given input data, the routine that will be used depends on the number of hours worked. This may be flowcharted in the following manner.

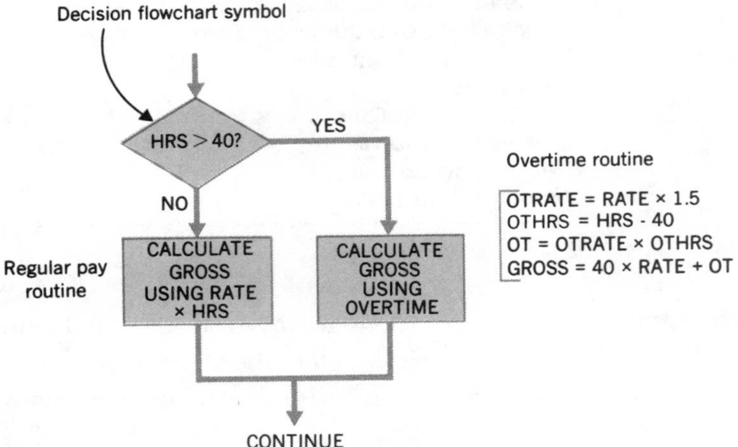

The flowchart illustrates that if the hours worked are greater than 4Ø, then the program should execute the routine that uses overtime hours to calculate the gross pay. Otherwise, the program should calculate the gross pay in the usual manner by simply multiplying RATE times HRS in the regular pay routine.

A decision-making procedure uses a **conditional branch,** which causes the computer to branch or "GO TO" some other sequence if a specific condition exists. This technique is frequently an integral part of the logic of a program. The use of GO TO instructions in RPG will be considered in depth in Chapter 6; this chapter focuses on the use of indicators to test for the existence of certain conditions. If the conditions exist, the indicators will be used to execute specific instructions.

Resulting indicators will be used on the Calculation form to determine if an operation should be performed. The resulting indicators in RPG can be set as a result of a compare instruction coded on the Calculation form. A compare instruction *always* produces one of three results: HIGH, LOW, or EQUAL.

Compare instructions can be used to set on indicators if the result of the comparison is a "high," "equal," or "low" condition; subsequent instructions can then be executed depending on whether the indicator coded was "turned on" during the comparison operation.

Condition	*Result*
First quantity (Factor 1) is greater than second quantity (Factor 2).	HIGH
First quantity (Factor 1) is less than second quantity (Factor 2).	LOW
First quantity (Factor 1) is equal to second quantity (Factor 2).	EQUAL

The following illustration depicts how decisions are made by the computer when an HRS field contains different values ranging from 2Ø to 6Ø.

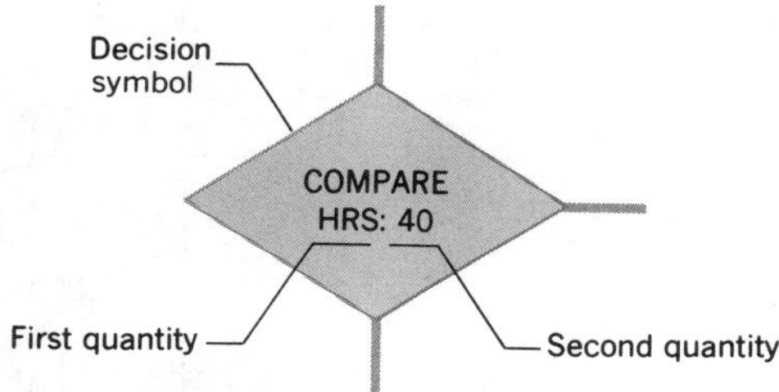

Factor 1	Factor 2	
First Qty (HRS)	Second Qty (4Ø)	Result
20	40	Low
30	40	Low
40	40	Equal
50	40	High
60	40	High

Summary

Factor 1	*Factor 2*	*Result*
First quantity $<$ (less than)	Second quantity	Low
First quantity $=$ (equal to)	Second quantity	Equal
First quantity $>$ (greater than)	Second quantity	High

In RPG, the value of specific fields using the COMP or compare instruction is tested. Depending on whether the result of the comparison is high, low, or equal, we will set on indicators and subsequently perform different operations.

B. The Compare (COMP) Instruction

The compare instruction is an important tool used for decision-making purposes in the RPG language. It is used to compare the contents of a data field to the contents of a second data field or to a literal. The data to be compared may be numeric or alphanumeric, but both factors used in the comparison must have the same format. That is, the fields or literals being compared must both be numeric or both be alphanumeric. Another term for an alphanumeric field is an **alphameric field.**

Simply stated, numeric data cannot be compared with alphameric data because the results are unpredictable and may produce syntax errors.

Compare instructions are coded on the Calculation form as noted in Figure 4.1. Only Factor 1 and Factor 2 are used; the Result field is not used with a COMP instruction.

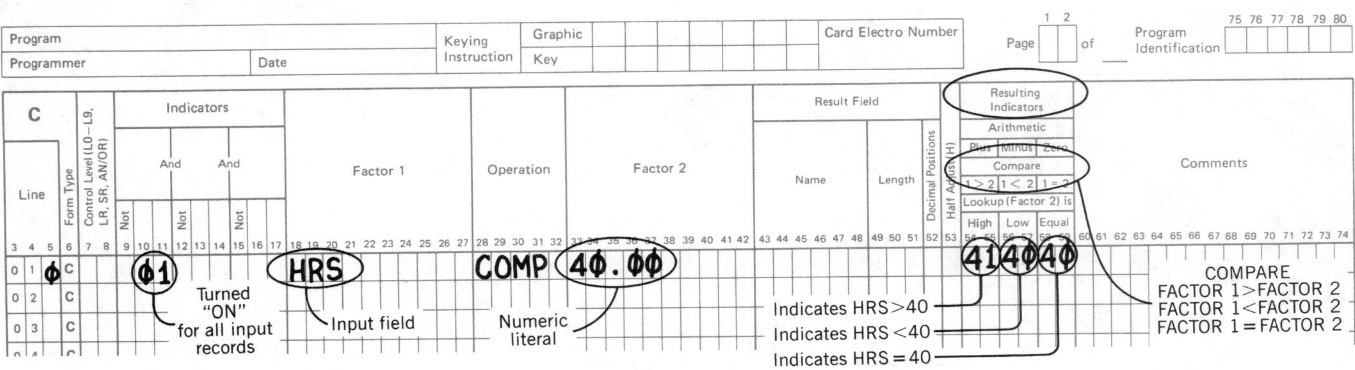

Figure 4.1
Coding COMPare instructions on the Calculation Specifications form.

The COMP instruction automatically triggers an internal **condition code** that is used to set the resulting indicators. Referring to the instruction in Figure 4.1, consider the following.

Compare Factor 1	Factor 2	*Condition* Code	*Indicator* On
2Ø	4Ø	LOW	4Ø
3Ø	4Ø	LOW	4Ø
4Ø	4Ø	EQUAL	4Ø
5Ø	4Ø	HIGH	41
6Ø	4Ø	HIGH	41

Factor 1 contains the contents of the hours-worked field. This field is being compared to the numeric literal 4Ø. Note that when Factor 1 (hours worked) is equal to 4Ø, indicator 4Ø is "turned on." If the hours worked were less than 4Ø, then Factor 1 would be less than Factor 2 and a "low" condition would result. The low condition will also "turn on" indicator 4Ø. Thus indicator 4Ø is turned on when HRS is less than or equal to (≤) 4Ø. However, when the hours exceed 4Ø, then indicator 41 is set "on" because we have a HIGH condition. That is, Factor 1 is greater than Factor 2.

Thus, when indicator 4Ø is "on," the employee did not work more than 4Ø hours; in this case you would calculate the gross as simply the product of rate times the hours worked. This is accomplished at step Ø2Ø of Figure 4.2, which represents the regular pay routine.

RPG CALCULATION SPECIFICATIONS

Line	Form Type	Control Level	Indicators			Factor 1	Operation	Factor 2	Result Field Name	Length	Decimal Positions	Half Adjust (H)	Resulting Indicators High (1>2)	Low (1<2)	Equal (1=2)	Comments
Ø1Ø	C		Ø1			HRS	COMP	4Ø					41	4Ø	4Ø	
Ø2Ø	C		Ø1	4Ø		HRS	MULT	RATE	GROSS	5	2	H				
Ø3Ø	C		Ø1	41		HRS	SUB	4Ø	OTHRS	3	1					
Ø4Ø	C		Ø1	41		RATE	MULT	1.5	OTRATE	4	2	H				
Ø5Ø	C		Ø1	41		OTHRS	MULT	OTRATE	OTPAY	5	2	H				
Ø6Ø	C		Ø1	41		RATE	MULT	4Ø.Ø	REG	5	2	H				
Ø7Ø	C		Ø1	41		REG	ADD	OTPAY	GROSS							
Ø8	C															
Ø9	C															

Figure 4.2
Illustration of the COMPare instruction.

However, when the hours exceed 4Ø, then indicator 41 would be turned "on" and lines Ø3Ø-Ø7Ø, the overtime routine, would be executed. Hence, the entries in columns 54-59 of line Ø1Ø are used to turn on resulting indicators in order that specific instructions may be executed. In effect, the indicators are used to record the relationship of Factor 1 to Factor 2. A sample program that uses these calculations and indicators is included at the end of this chapter. In summary, to compare data in RPG enter COMP in the operation field of the Calculation form. When executed, the instruction performs the following.

> ***Compare Operation***
>
> 1. Compare two fields. The result sets a condition code to HIGH, LOW, or EQUAL.
> 2. Turn on **resulting indicators** depending on the condition code. The resulting indicators are used to retain the results of the comparison made.
> 3. The COMP instruction could be used for turning on 1, 2, or 3 indicators; that is, any one or all the HIGH, LOW, and EQUAL indicators can be used in a program.

Resulting indicators are *not* turned off automatically by RPG, but *rather remain on until the next record is processed* and the compare instruction is again executed. This topic will be discussed in detail later in the chapter.

As previously noted, compare operations are either numeric or alphanumeric (nonnumeric); the two types cannot be mixed. Numeric compare instructions will be considered first.

II. Comparing Numeric Fields

A. Summary

Comparing Numeric Data Fields

Instruction:	COMP
Meaning:	Compare two data fields algebraically.
Operation:	Condition code is set to high, low, or equal as follows: HIGH: Factor 1 is greater than Factor 2. LOW: Factor 1 is less than Factor 2. EQUAL: Factor 1 is equal to Factor 2.
Resulting Indicators:	When results are high, the indicator specified in columns 54-55 is turned "on." When results are low, the indicator specified in columns 56-57 is turned "on." When results are equal, the indicator in columns 58-59 is turned "on."
Limitation:	(1) For numeric compares, both fields being compared must be numeric. Either Factor 1 or Factor 2 may be a numeric literal, but not both. (2) The maximum number of digits for numeric fields is 15.
Special note:	All indicators are initially off. Resulting indicators that are turned on in the calculation phase *are not turned off* by RPG as is the record indicator. Instead, the indicators remain set until the next time the COMP operation is performed whereupon they are reset according to the results obtained.

B. Numeric Specification

First, it is important that the programmer be sure that the fields being compared are specified as numeric in the program. A **numeric field** requires the coding of an integer in column 52 (Decimal Positions) of the form on which it is defined. This would be either the Input or the Calculation form. Numeric fields *must* have a numeric entry in the Decimal Positions field of one of these forms as illustrated in Figure 4.3. If a numeric field consists entirely of integers and has no decimal positions, then enter Ø in column 52 of the Input form, if the field is defined there, or on the Calculation form if the field is defined during a calculation.

In the example in Figure 4.3, RATE and HRS on the Input form contain entries in column 52 (Decimal Positions), thereby defining these fields as numeric. Similarly, GROSS is established on the Calculation form, also with an entry in column

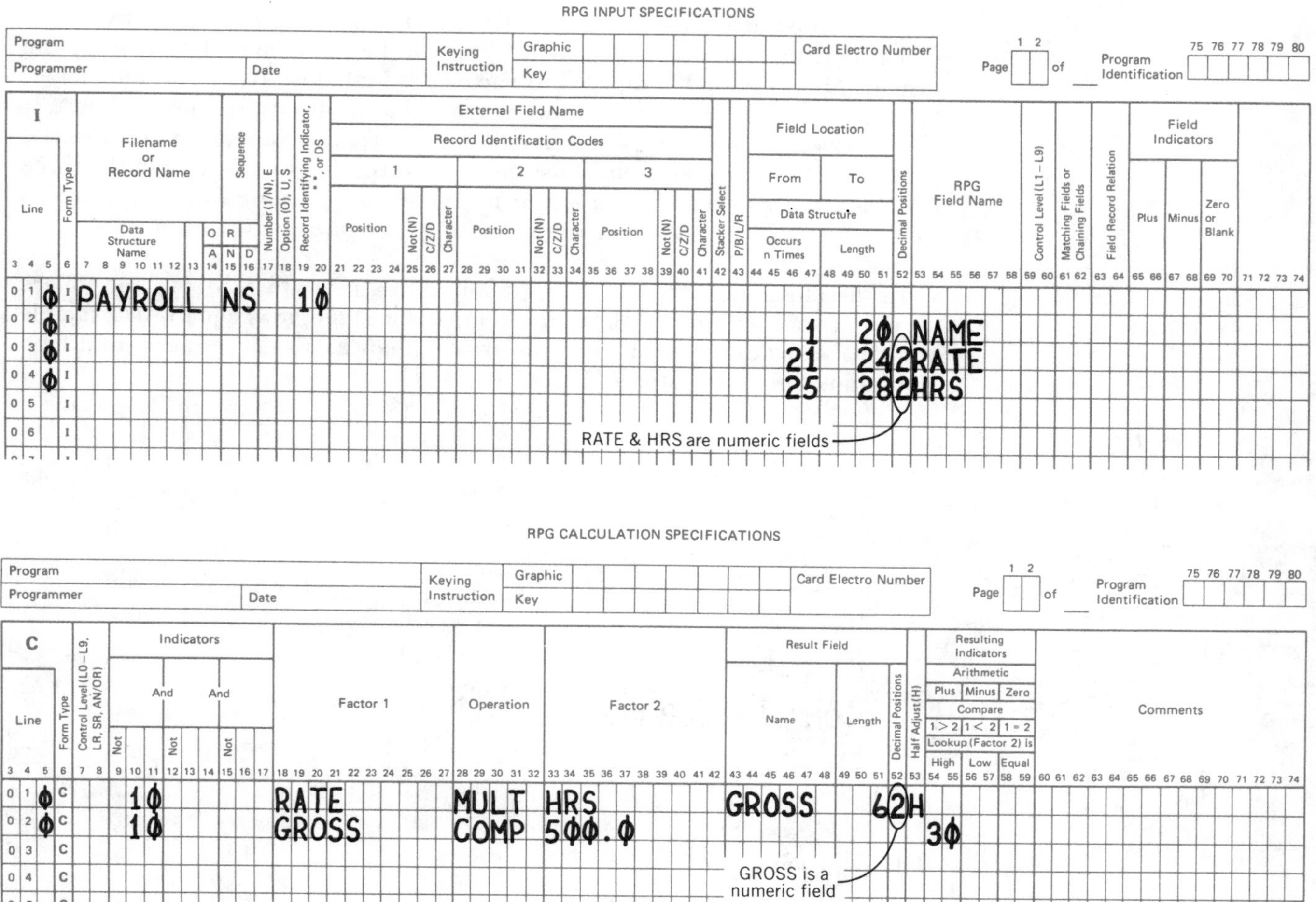

Figure 4.3
Specifying numeric fields.

52 (Decimal Positions). Therefore, GROSS is defined as a numeric field. Only when the fields are properly defined as numeric will numeric comparisons take place. Should the programmer attempt to compare a numeric field with a nonnumeric field (alphameric or alphabetic), an error message may result stating "*Factor 1 and Factor 2 of compare or look up must either be numeric or alphanumeric. Specification is dropped.*" The precise wording of this diagnostic message may vary from one system to another, yet the overall intent will be the same. Do not compare numeric fields with fields that are not numeric since the computer stores the information for each type of field differently. Clearly, arithmetic operations cannot be performed with data that is not numeric and, as a result, the two different types of data (numeric, nonnumeric) cannot be combined. When error messages occur as a result of a COMP operation, check the fields that are intended to be numeric to be sure they have an entry in the Decimal Positions column.

C. Comparing Numeric Fields of Equal Length

Numeric comparisons are **algebraic comparisons**, meaning that the sign is included in the test. Negative quantities will always compare LOW when compared to positive quantities.

A condition code is set (HIGH, LOW, EQUAL) depending on the relative value of Factor 1 as compared to Factor 2. This can be remembered by reading the instruction as Factor 1 compared to Factor 2 is high, low, or equal. Remember, both factors must contain the same type of data (in this case, numeric data).

The examples in Figure 4.4 illustrate the concepts of comparing two numeric fields. All the examples in the illustration show resulting indicators in the three possible entries of the Calculation form. We need only code for the conditions we are trying to check. It may require the use of one entry, two entries, or all three.

In the illustrations in Figure 4.4, observe that indicators 7Ø, 8Ø, and 9Ø are set on according to the results of the comparison (high, low, equal). In Example 1, as would be expected, Factor 1 is greater than Factor 2, resulting in a high condition. Thus, indicator 7Ø is set "on."

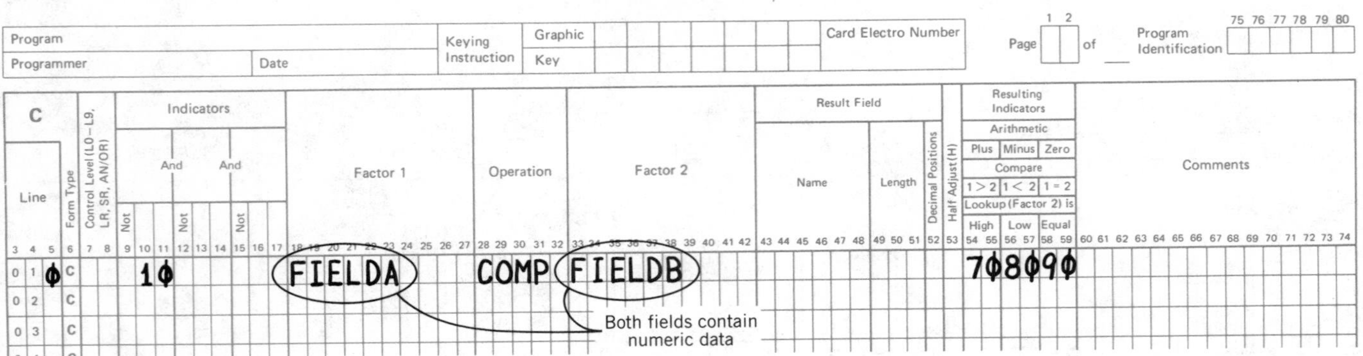

FIELDA is compared to FIELDB

FIELDA FIELDB

Example Number	Factor 1	Factor 2	Condition Result	Indicators "on"	Indicators "off"
1	150▲00	100▲00	High	70	80 90
2	−050▲00	−100▲00	High	70	80 90
3	000▲00	−100▲00	High	70	80 90
4	100▲00	100▲00	Equal	90	70 80
5	050▲00	100▲00	Low	80	70 90
6	−050▲00	100▲00	Low	80	70 90

Figure 4.4
Examples of comparisons.

Example 2 illustrates and reinforces the fact that −5Ø is greater than −1ØØ. Remember that the comparison is *algebraic*. Consider the illustration in Figure 4.5.

Referring to the scale of values shown, −5Ø is higher on this scale or greater than −1ØØ. Also note in Example 3 of Figure 4.4 that zero has a greater value than −1ØØ. When Factor 1 is greater than Factor 2, the result is high and indicator 7Ø is "turned on." Example 4 compares two fields that are equal. As a consequence, indicator 9Ø is set "on." Examples 5 and 6 both contain numeric data in Factor 1 that is less than the numeric contents of Factor 2. The condition or result of each comparison is low, setting "on" indicator 8Ø referenced in columns 56-57 of the Calculation form (Figure 4.4).

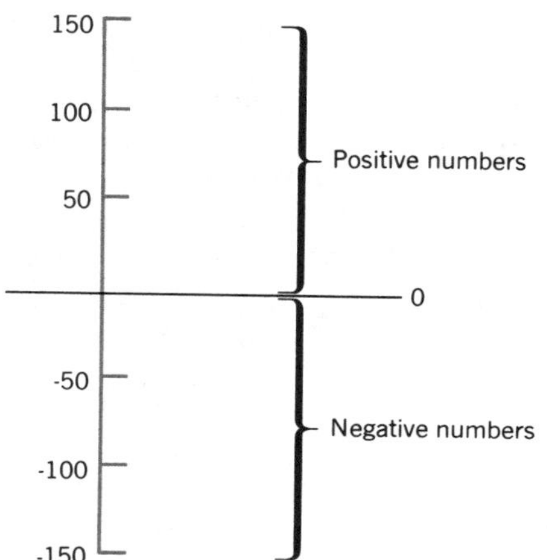

Figure 4.5
Scale of values for algebraic comparisons.

D. Comparing Numeric Fields of Unequal Length

Recall that numeric fields are compared algebraically. However, before any compare operations can take place, RPG aligns the fields according to their decimal points. Any missing digits are filled in with zeros. (The maximum field length for numeric fields that are to be compared is 15 digits.) For example, suppose the following fields are to be compared.

Field 1	1 2 3‸4 5
Field 2	6‸7 8 9

RPG would first extend the decimal positions of Field 1 to match the number of decimal positions in Field 2. This is done by adding a zero to the low-order position of Field 1.

Field 1	1 2 3‸4 5 Ø
Field 2	6‸7 8 9

Then the high-order or left-most positions of Field 2 would be zero-filled, thereby equalizing the number of positions both to the right and to the left of the decimal. Thus the effect would be the same as comparing the following two fields.

FIELD1 | 1 | 2 | 3 ▲ 4 | 5 | 0 |

FIELD2 | 0 | 0 | 6 ▲ 7 | 8 | 9 |

RPG fills high-order zeros

Once the fields are decimally aligned and have the same number of positions as provided by the computer, they can be compared. Remember, the decimal points of the two fields are first aligned. If the decimal positions to the right of the decimal points are unequal, the shorter field is padded (on the right) with zeros. If the positions to the left of the decimal points are *unequal*, then high-order zeros are added to the shorter field. Let us apply these concepts of field alignment to a few practical examples.

Referring to Figure 4.6, note that SALES contains two decimal positions whereas QUOTA contains none. The first step in aligning these fields is to extend QUOTA by padding **low-order** or right-most zeros. The shorter decimal field is always extended by padding zeros in the right-most positions. Next, we find that QUOTA has fewer positions to the left of the decimal point and is the shorter field in this regard. Again, the shorter field is zero-filled. Following alignment, both fields are six digits in length, containing two decimal positions. The result of the comparison is high since the contents of Factor 1 (9ØØØ) is greater than the contents of Factor 2 (9ØØ). Indicator 6Ø, identified in columns 54-55 of the Calculation form, is set "on."

RPG CALCULATION SPECIFICATIONS

Line	Form Type	Control Level	Indicators	Factor 1	Operation	Factor 2	Result Field Name	Length	Decimal Positions	Half Adjust (H)	High (54-55)	Low (56-57)	Equal (58-59)	Comments
01	C		1Ø	SALES	COMP	QUOTA					6Ø	5Ø	7Ø	
02	C													
03	C													

Before alignment		After alignment
9,0,0,0,0,0 SALES	Factor 1	9,0,0,0,0,0 SALES
9,0,0 QUOTA	Factor 2	0,9,0,0,0,0 QUOTA

Decimal alignment

high-order zero fill

Low-order padding of zeros

Before alignment *After alignment*

Result
Condition .... HIGH
Reason .... 9000 > 900
Indicator set on 60

Figure 4.6
Alignment of fields for a comparison, Example 1.

In Figure 4.7, we again find fields of different lengths. In this example, both fields do not contain any decimal positions. A decimal point is, however, *implied* for each field. Once the fields are aligned around the implied decimal points, we find that Factor 1 has fewer positions to the left of the decimal point. The left-most positions of Factor 1 are zero-filled and the algebraic comparison is performed. In this instance, a low condition occurs and indicator 35, specified in columns 56-57 of the Calculation form, is turned on.

Note, then, that in RPG comparisons are performed *logically*. The fact that one field contains fewer characters than another will not adversely affect the logic of the comparison. This is not always the case in other languages.

RPG CALCULATION SPECIFICATIONS

Line	Form Type	Control Level	Indicators	Factor 1	Operation	Factor 2	Result Field Name	Length	Decimal Positions	Half Adjust	Resulting Indicators High	Low	Equal	Comments
01Ø	C		1Ø	QTY	COMP	QTYOH					5Ø	35	35	
02	C													
03	C													

	Before Alignment		After alignment	
Factor 1	1,5,0 QTY	zero fill →	(0,0),1,5,0 QTY	Decimal alignment
Factor 2	0,0,2,0,0 QTYOH		0,0,2,0,0 QTYOH	

Figure 4.7 Alignment of fields for a comparison, Example 2.

Result	
Condition	LOW
Reason	150 < 200
Indicator set on	35

E. Numeric Literals

Thus far, numeric comparisons have focused on comparing one numeric data field with another. Compare instructions may also make use of literals that have numeric values. The comparison is again algebraic, and either Factor 1 or Factor 2 may contain a literal. When using numeric literals, review the following rules.

Numeric Literal Rule Summary

1. A numeric literal may only contain the digits Ø-9, a decimal point, and a sign (+ or −).
2. The maximum length of a numeric literal is 1Ø characters, including a sign and a decimal point.
3. Unsigned literals are assumed positive. If the literal is negative, the minus sign must be the left-most character.
4. Numeric literals must never contain dollar signs, commas, blanks, or any other alphameric character.
5. Numeric literals are left-justified when entered in Factor 1 or Factor 2 of the Calculation form.

Typical examples of numeric literals are illustrated in Figure 4.8. Again, the same rules apply when using numeric literals as with other numeric fields. Alignment is achieved in the same manner.

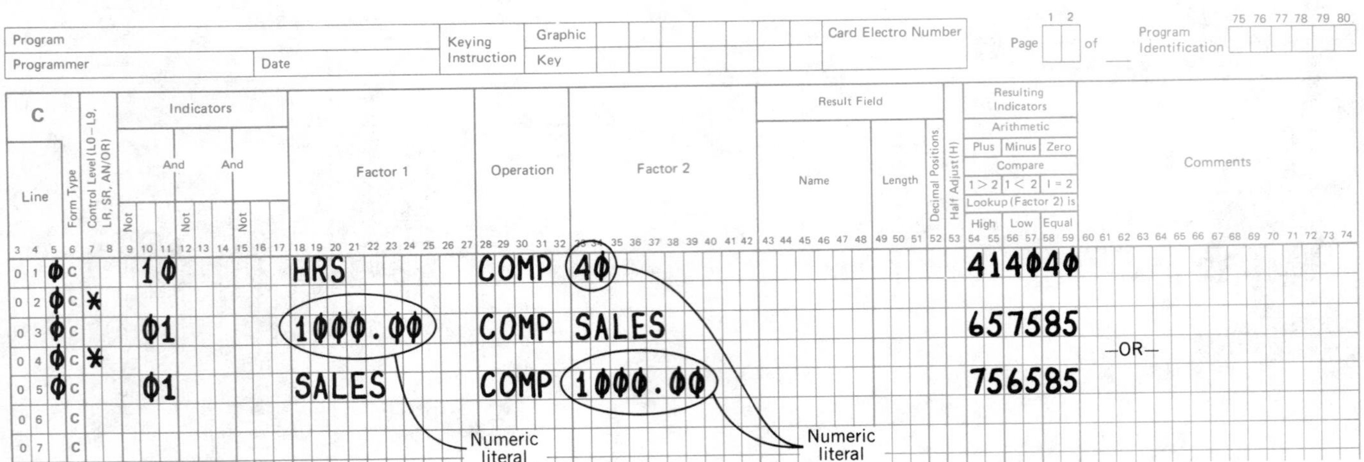

Figure 4.8
Using numeric literals with COMPare instructions.

F. Negating Compares (NOT Entry)

By entering an N in column 9, 12, or 15 of the Calculation form, a test may be made to determine if an indicator is "off" rather than "on." Referring to Figure 4.9, the need for indicator 4Ø has been eliminated by using the NOT entry. The overtime routine will be executed when indicator 41 is on. However, when indicator 41 is "off," then the regular pay instruction would be used to calculate the gross. The NOT operation therefore extends the use of indicators to include NOT HIGH, NOT LOW, and NOT EQUAL conditions. In many instances, the programmer may find these additional commands more direct and useful in refining a program by eliminating unnecessary indicators.

If Factor 1 compared NOT HIGH to Factor 2, this would mean that Factor 1 was less than or equal to Factor 2. Similarly, if Factor 1 compared NOT LOW to Factor 2, this would mean that Factor 1 was greater than or equal to Factor 2.

Figure 4.9
Using the NOT entry in a COMPare.

RPG CALCULATION SPECIFICATIONS

Line	Form Type	Indicators	Factor 1	Operation	Factor 2	Result Field Name	Length	Decimal Positions	Half Adjust (H)	Resulting Indicators (High)	Comments
01Ø	C	1Ø	HRS	COMP	4Ø					41	
02Ø	C	1Ø N41	HRS	MULT	RATE	GROSS	5	2	H		Regular pay
03Ø	C	1Ø 41	HRS	SUB	4Ø	OTHRS	3	1			Overtime routine
04Ø	C		•	•	•	•					
05Ø	C		•	•	•	•					
06Ø	C		•	•	•	•					
07Ø	C		•	•	•	•					
08	C										
09	C										

If indicator 41 is not ON, then perform this instruction

G. Comparing Date Fields

In business, it is often necessary to determine if payments are late in order to bill the customer for late charges. This requires the comparison of date fields, which usually are stored in the typical month, day, year format. Let us examine a problem in which we are to determine if late charges are to be imposed to charge customers of an accounts receivable system. The Input and Calculation Specifications are illustrated in Figure 4.1Ø.

Figure 4.10
Comparing date fields.

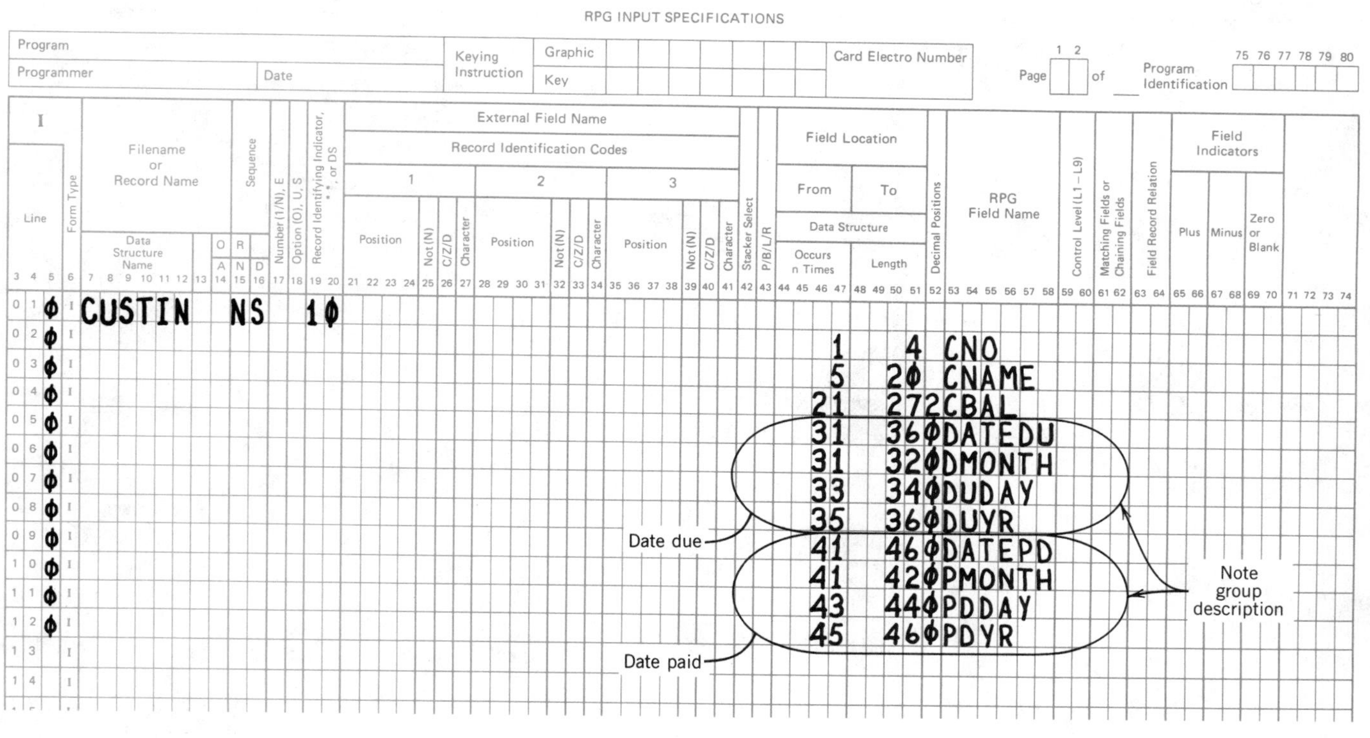
RPG INPUT SPECIFICATIONS

```
01Ø I CUSTIN   NS  1Ø
02Ø I                                        1   4 CNO
03Ø I                                        5  2Ø CNAME
04Ø I                                       21  272CBAL
05Ø I                                       31  36ØDATEDU
06Ø I                                       31  32ØDMONTH
07Ø I                                       33  34ØDUDAY
08Ø I                                       35  36ØDUYR
09Ø I                                       41  46ØDATEPD
10Ø I                                       41  42ØPMONTH
11Ø I                                       43  44ØPDDAY
12Ø I                                       45  46ØPDYR
```


RPG CALCULATION SPECIFICATIONS

```
01Ø C   1Ø       PDYR      COMP DUYR                 2Ø  15
02Ø C*
03Ø C   1Ø 15    PMONTH    COMP DMONTH               2Ø  18
04Ø C*
05Ø C   1Ø 18    PDDAY     COMP DUDAY                2Ø
```

The DATEDU (for date due) field description contains the subordinate fields, DMONTH, DUDAY, and DUYR. The advantage of using this group specification is that the programmer may reference fields as a group or individually by the subordinate field names assigned.

DATEDU (031284)			Group name
DMONTH (03)	DUDAY (12)	DUYR (84)	
Subordinate names			

DATE PD (021484)			Group name
PMONTH (02)	PDDAY (14)	PDYR (84)	
Subordinate names			

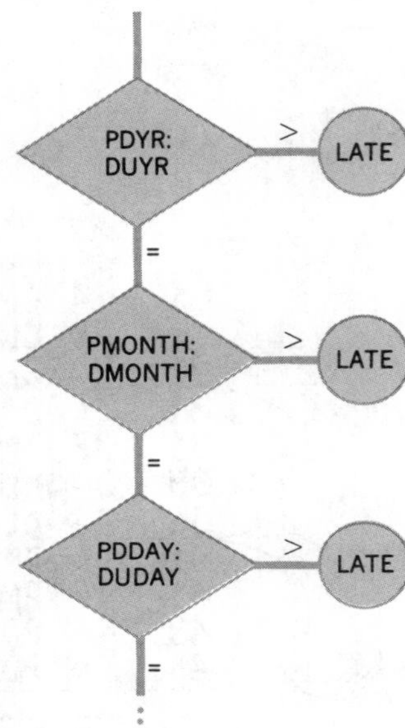

If DATEDU was to be referenced, a six-character numeric field such as Ø31284 for March 12, 1984 would be used. The DATEDU field could be edited in the usual manner by coding the letter 'Y' in column 38 of the Output form. Moreover, the subordinate fields, DMONTH (Ø3), DUDAY (12), and DUYR (84), may also be referenced *individually*. Again, the primary reason for referencing data either as a group or by individual field names is that the programmer has the option of using the field definition that best suits his or her needs. For the checking of date fields, however, it will be necessary to reference the individual fields—DMONTH, DUDAY, and DUYR.

To determine if late charges are to be assessed, the date paid must be compared to the date due in three steps in the sequence shown: first the year, then the month, and, finally, the day. The year is the most critical field, followed by the month, and then the day.

In Figure 4.1Ø, a late payment is noted by setting "on" indicator 2Ø in the program sequence shown. Again, the year field is compared first. If the year in which the bill was paid (PDYR) is greater than the year due, a high condition occurs turning "on" indicator 2Ø. That is, if payment was made in a year greater than the year it was due, then a late charge should be incurred. When, however, the year in which the bill was paid is equal to the year due, you must next check the month.

If the payment was early, that is, if the PDYR is less than the DUYR, a low condition results; in this case no indicator would be turned "on." No further checking is required; clearly, there would not be any late charges incurred. Steps Ø3Ø and Ø5Ø would not be executed because indicator 15 has not been conditioned or "turned on."

If the PDYR was equal to DUYR, check the month of payment (PMONTH) against the month due (DMONTH) and, as before, a HIGH condition would only be caused by a late payment; in this instance, indicator 2Ø would again be turned "on."

If the month paid and the month due are found equal, it will be necessary to check the least-significant field, the day. When indicator 18 is "on," then both steps Ø1Ø and Ø3Ø resulted in equal comparisons, thereby requiring the day fields to be checked. When the year and month are equal, the last comparison to be made will compare the PDDAY with the DUDAY. If the PDDAY is greater than the DUDAY, the payment is late and, as before, indicator 2Ø is set "on." Again, indicator 2Ø denotes a late payment. This last comparison will not be made, however, if the month paid is less than the month due; if PMONTH < DMONTH, this would mean that the customer's payment was early, and indicator 18 would be "off" as a result. This general approach to comparing dates is useful to the programmer; there are, however, advanced techniques that will later prove more efficient.

At this point, you should again review the logic used by the program excerpt. It is a good idea to substitute values for the dates and walk through the problem validating that the logic is indeed correct. For example, use the following data and determine if indicator 2Ø will be set "on" by the program.

Date Paid	*Date Due*
Ø1/15/85	12/Ø1/84
11/29/84	12/Ø1/84
12/Ø2/84	12/Ø1/84

By substituting values and performing each step, one at a time, the logic can be verified. This **program walkthrough** procedure is the basis for establishing logically correct programs in RPG as well as other programming languages. Desk checking a program with walkthroughs is more efficient than using the computer to test the logic.

The programmer may also find instances when dates are to be compared to the current date. The reserved word UDATE may be divided into its three component parts (month, day, year) if you need to access any part of the date. Each part has its own reserved name: UMONTH, UDAY, and UYEAR. UDATE is stored by the computer and need not be read in as input.

<table>
<tr><td colspan="3">UDATE</td><td>} Group name
Current date</td></tr>
<tr><td>MONTH
UMONTH</td><td>DAY
UDAY</td><td>YEAR
UYEAR</td><td></td></tr>
</table>

Subordinate names
Current date

UDATE can be coded as follows.

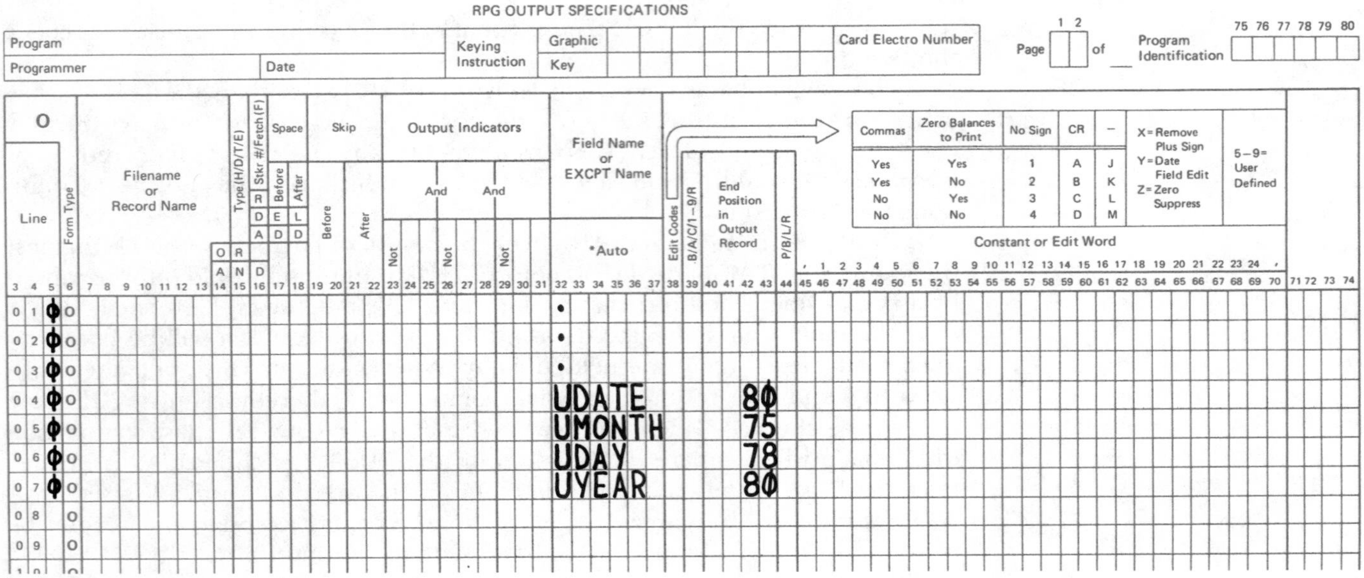

RPG OUTPUT SPECIFICATIONS

Program		Keying Instruction	Graphic	Card Electro Number	Page 1 2 of ___	Program Identification 75 76 77 78 79 80
Programmer	Date		Key			

Line	Form Type	Field Name or EXCPT Name	End Position in Output Record
01	O	•	
02	O	•	
03	O	•	
04	O	UDATE	80
05	O	UMONTH	75
06	O	UDAY	78
07	O	UYEAR	80
08	O		
09	O		
10	O		

The entire UDATE field is subdivided into component fields. Referencing an area by a group name, or a subdivision of the group, is an important feature in RPG. The date due and date paid fields are subdivided in the same manner as the UDATE field. Remember, you can thus access this data in two ways—on a group basis and also on an individual subordinate basis. Later in the text other advantages in using these procedures will be covered.

Self-Evaluating Quiz

1. The contents of both Factor 1 and Factor 2 must be ________ if an algebraic comparison is to take place.
2. Resulting indicators are set according to the relative value of Factor _____ compared to Factor ________ .
3. When the contents of Factor 1 is greater than the contents of Factor 2, the resulting condition is ________ .
4. If Factor 1 contains a numeric literal, then Factor 2 (may/may not) contain a numeric literal.
5. (T or F) Resulting indicators are automatically turned off by RPG at the end of the cycle.
6. The three conditions of the resulting indicators in the order found on the coding form are from left to right, ________ , ________ , and ________ .
7. Since numeric compares are algebraic, negative quantities are (greater than/less than) positive quantities.
8. When numeric fields are of different lengths, the shorter field is extended by adding ________ once the ________ is aligned.
9. Assume a comparison is made and an equal condition results in turning on indicator 3Ø. How can we execute an instruction requiring an unequal condition?
10. Review the illustration in Figure 4.11 and indicate whether the instructions are valid or invalid. If invalid, state the reason. (Assume that all fields are numeric.)

RPG CALCULATION SPECIFICATIONS

Program | Programmer | Date | Keying Instruction: Graphic, Key | Card Electro Number | Page 1 2 of | Program Identification 75 76 77 78 79 80

	Line (3–5)	Form Type (6)	Control Level (L0–L9, LR, SR, AN/OR) (7–8)	Indicators (9–11)	And (12–14)	And (15–17)	Factor 1 (18–27)	Operation (28–32)	Factor 2 (33–42)	Result Field Name (43–48)	Length (49–51)	Decimal Positions (52)	Half Adjust (H) (53)	Resulting Indicators High (54–55)	Low (56–57)	Equal (58–59)	Comments (60–74)
(a)	01Ø	C		1Ø			CTAX	COMP	LIMIT								
	02Ø	C	*														
(b)	03Ø	C		1Ø			YTDGRS	COMP	6785.ØØ					4Ø	5Ø	6Ø	
	04Ø	C	*														
(c)	05Ø	C		1Ø			WAGES	COMP	1Ø,ØØØ.ØØ					7Ø	8Ø	9Ø	
	06Ø	C	*														
(d)	07Ø	C		1Ø			45Ø	COMP	MIN					75	85	95	
	08Ø	C	*														
(e)	09Ø	C		1Ø			SLRY	COMP	$5ØØ.ØØ					45	55	65	
	10Ø	C	*														
(f)	11Ø	C		1Ø			SALES	COMP	SLS8Ø					3Ø	3Ø	3Ø	
	12Ø	C	*														
(g)	13Ø	C		1Ø			YTDFCA	COMP	MAX					1Ø	2Ø	3Ø	
	14	C															
	15	C															

Figure 4.11
Illustration for question 10.

11. State the meaning of the two routines illustrated in Figure 4.12.

RPG CALCULATION SPECIFICATIONS

Program | Programmer | Date | Keying Instruction: Graphic, Key | Card Electro Number | Page 1 2 of | Program Identification 75 76 77 78 79 80

Line (3–5)	Form Type (6)	Control Level (L0–L9, LR, SR, AN/OR) (7–8)	Indicators (9–11)	And (12–14)	And (15–17)	Factor 1 (18–27)	Operation (28–32)	Factor 2 (33–42)	Result Field Name (43–48)	Length (49–51)	Decimal Positions (52)	Half Adjust (H) (53)	Resulting Indicators High (54–55)	Low (56–57)	Equal (58–59)	Comments (60–74)
01Ø	C		1Ø			AGE	COMP	3Ø					66			
02Ø	C		1Ø	66		OVER3Ø	ADD	1	OVER3Ø	3	Ø					
03Ø	C	*														
04Ø	C	*														
05Ø	C		2Ø			HRS	COMP	4Ø.ØØ						3Ø	3Ø	
06Ø	C		2Ø	N3Ø		OVER4Ø	ADD	1	OVER4Ø	3	Ø					
07Ø	C		2Ø	N3Ø		HRS	SUB	4Ø.ØØ	OTHRS	5	2					
08Ø	C		2Ø	N3Ø		OTHRS	ADD	TOTAL	TOTAL	7	2					
09	C															
10	C															

Figure 4.12
Illustration for question 11.

Solutions

1. numeric
2. 1, 2
3. high
4. may not—Only one factor may contain a numeric literal.
5. F—Resulting indicators are set the next time the COMP instruction is executed.
6. high, low, equal
7. less than
8. zeros, decimal point
9. By coding N3Ø in columns 9-17 of the Calculation form.
10. a. Invalid—no resulting indicators.
    b. Invalid—Factor 2 must be left-justified.
    c. Invalid—literal may not contain a comma.
    d. Valid.
    e. Invalid—dollar sign not permitted in a numeric literal.
    f. Invalid—will always turn on indicator 3Ø.
    g. Valid—but it would be poor practice to use the conditioning indicator as a resulting indicator.
11. The first routine counts all records when the field AGE is greater than 3Ø. The counter, OVER3Ø, is updated each time a record is found where the age is greater than 3Ø. The second routine counts the number of records where HRS exceeds 4Ø. In addition the TOTAL overtime hours, that is, the hours in excess of 4Ø, are accumulated in a running total.

III. Comparing Alphanumeric Fields

A. Collating Sequence

For comparison purposes, the computer treats alphabetic fields in exactly the same manner as alphanumeric fields. Let us consider the comparison of two alphabetic fields contained in main storage areas called NAME1 and NAME2. In the illustration that follows, once the values in the two areas are compared, the result would indicate that NAME1 is less than NAME2.

R O B E R T S	<	S A M U E L S
NAME1	Less than	NAME2

S A M U E L S	<	T H O M A S
NAME1	Less than	NAME2

When comparing alphabetic data, the weight or value of each letter of the alphabet increases as we proceed from A-Z. Thus, in the example just presented, the sequence is ROBERT < SAMUELS < THOMAS since the letter "R" is less than the letter "S," and similarly the letter "S" is less than the letter "T." The comparison begins with the first letter of each name. Thus, the entire contents of the field referenced as NAME1 is less than the contents of NAME2 in the two examples shown.

The computer, then, will compare alphabetic characters logically. If the first character of the two factors were equal, the computer would then compare the subsequent characters. Consider the following example.

Z O R R O	>	X E R O X
NAME1	Greater than	NAME2
X E R O X	>	E X X O N
NAME1	Greater than	NAME2

Again, the *first* letter of each name is compared; it can be seen that the letter "Z" is greater than the letter "X," and the letter "X" in turn is greater than the letter "E." As a consequence, the contents of NAME1 is greater than NAME2. That is, ZORRO > XEROX > EXXON.

Alphameric comparisons may not, however, be as simple as those illustrated. Sometimes, the comparison of alphameric data includes fields containing letters, blanks, numbers, and special characters as typically found in street addresses such as "112-Ø5 FIFTY FIRST AVENUE." In order for the programmer to understand alphameric comparisons, he or she must first be aware of the **collating sequence** used by the computer.

Every computer system has a collating sequence. This is the order by which it sorts characters according to their relative weights. The purpose of having these relative weights is to establish whether one character is higher or lower than another. The collating sequence is therefore instrumental in determining the results of alphameric comparisons (see Figure 4.13).

The blank or space has the lowest value in the collating sequence. Thus a blank field will always compare "low" when compared to any nonblank field. For most computers, special characters are followed by the 26 letters of the alphabet (A-Z), which in turn are followed by digits (Ø-9). As a consequence, the letter "B" has a higher value than the letter "A." Zero has a higher value than the letter "Z" and, as we would expect, numbers increase in ascending sequence.

Note that there are some computers with a collating sequence in which numbers are considered less than letters. Most computers that have RPG compilers, however, use the collating sequence described above.

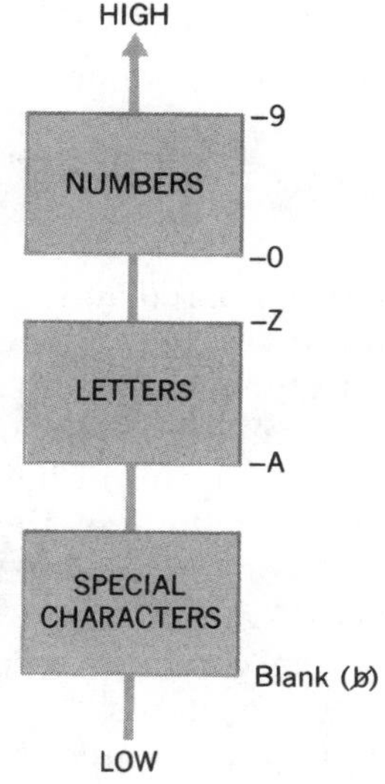

Figure 4.13 Collating sequence for most computers.

B. Rules for Alphanumeric Comparisons

1. The data in Factor 1 and Factor 2 must both be alphameric.
2. Factor 1 is compared to Factor 2.
3. Fields are aligned on the left; if one field is shorter, blanks are added to the low-order position(s) of the shorter field. Thus, a field containing ABC is equal to a field containing ABCbb.
4. The comparison begins in the left-most position and proceeds from left to right, one character at a time, until an inequality occurs or until all the characters are found equal.
5. Alphameric literals are enclosed in single quotes or apostrophes.
6. Up to 256 characters may be compared with an alphameric compare.

C. Comparing Alphanumeric Fields of Equal Length

When fields are defined on the Input form and/or Calculation form, and the Decimal Position (column 52) is left blank, the fields are considered alphanumeric. RPG compares alphameric fields quite differently from numeric fields; a different set of rules apply.

As with numeric fields, Factor 1 is compared to Factor 2 and resulting indicators are used to record the result of the comparison. Consider the following as a review.

Factor 1 is greater than Factor 2	HIGH
Factor 1 is less than Factor 2	LOW
Factor 1 is equal to Factor 2	EQUAL

Alphameric fields are compared by aligning their left-most characters. If one field is shorter than the other, the shorter field is extended by padding blanks or spaces on the right in the **low-order positions.** The comparison begins in the **high-order position** (left-most) and thereafter proceeds from left to right, one character at a time. As soon as an unequal condition occurs, the comparison is terminated. When an inequality is found, one of the following results.

1. If the character in Factor 1 is greater than the character in Factor 2, a HIGH result occurs.
2. If the character in Factor 1 is less than the character in Factor 2, a LOW result occurs.

However, if each position is compared and the end of both factors is reached without an unequal condition occurring, then the result of the comparison is equal. Now that the basis for alphameric comparisons has been established, a few examples will serve to illustrate the points made (see Figure 4.14).

The example in Figure 4.14 illustrates in detail precisely how the COMPare instruction operates. Beginning on the left, the high-order positions of both fields are compared. Since both contain the letter "B" they are equal; therefore the next position is compared. Again, we find the characters (R) equal. This process continues until an unequal condition occurs or the right-most characters of the factors are reached. In the example, the computer compared four characters before an unequal condition was found. Note that each character is com-

RPG CALCULATION SPECIFICATIONS

Line	Form Type	Control Level	Indicators	Factor 1	Operation	Factor 2	Result Field Name	Length	Decimal Positions	Half Adjust (H)	High (1>2)	Low (1<2)	Equal (1=2)	Comments
01Φ	C		Φ1	NAME1	COMP	NAME2					1Φ	2Φ	3Φ	
02	C													
03	C													

	Cycle 1	Cycle 2	Cycle 3	Cycle 4
Factor 2	B R O W N	B R O W N	B R O W N	B R O W N
	↑ (B)	↑ (R)	↑ (O)	↑* (W)
Factor 1	B R O D Y	B R O D Y	B R O D Y	B R O D Y
	EQUAL	EQUAL	EQUAL	NOT EQUAL

*Indicates that an unequal condition occurs in cycle 4 and the compare terminates. Since the "D" in Factor 1 is less than the "W" in Factor 2, the result is LOW. Resulting indicator 20 is set on.

Figure 4.14
Alphameric comparison.

pared, one at a time, from left to right. The collating sequence will determine the relative weight of each character being compared.

D. Comparing Alphanumeric Fields of Unequal Length

Again referring to the instruction in Figure 4.14, note that the conditions HIGH, LOW, and EQUAL will set on indicators 1Ø, 2Ø, and 3Ø, respectively. Let us evaluate a variety of conditions using NAME1 as Factor 1 and NAME2 as Factor 2 in Figure 4.15.

In Example 1 of Figure 4.15, Factor 2 contains fewer characters than Factor 1. Hence, Factor 2 is extended by padding blanks in the right-most positions. After alignment, both factors contain seven characters. We find the result of this comparison to be high since the weighted value of the "S" in Factor 1 is greater than the blank in Factor 2. Thus we see that Factor 1 compared to Factor 2 is high and results in turning on indicator 1Ø.

In Example 2, Factor 1 contains fewer characters th Factor 2. Therefore, during alignment, blanks are padded in the right-most positions of Factor 1. After alignment, both fields are eight characters in length. A low condition results from this comparison since the blank in Factor 1 has a lower weight than the letter "O" in Factor 2. Recall that the low condition turns on indicator 2Ø.

Example 1 of Figure 4.16 illustrates an equal comparison of Factors 1 and 2. Again, alignment causes Factor 1 to be extended by padding blanks in the low-order position(s). However, each character is compared and found equal. Since

Figure 4.15 Alphameric comparisons.

Example 1

J O H N S O N	J O H N	Before alignment
J O H N S O N	J O H N ƀ ƀ ƀ	After alignment

Result

Number of characters compared	5
Condition	HIGH
Reason	S > ƀ
Indicator set on	10

Example 2

Factor 1	Factor 2	
P E T E R S	P E T E R S O N	Before alignment
P E T E R S ƀ ƀ	P E T E R S O N	After alignment

Result

Number of characters compared	7
Condition	LOW
Reason	ƀ < O
Indicator set on	20

Figure 4.16 Alphameric comparisons.

Example 1

Factor 1	Factor 2	
J O N E S R	J O N E S R	Before alignment
J O N E S R ƀ ƀ	J O N E S R	After alignment

Result

Number of characters compared	9
Condition	EQUAL
Reason	All characters equal
Indicator set on	30

Example 2

Factor 1	Factor 2
F O U R T H S T R E E T	4 T H S T R E E T

No alignment necessary. Both factors contain 13 characters.

Result

Number of characters compared	1
Condition	LOW
Reason	F < 4
Indicator set on	20

all nine of the characters compare equal, including the last character of both factors, the compare instruction terminates with the resulting condition code set to equal.

The collating sequence must again be recalled to predict the results of the comparison illustrated in Example 2. Remember, letters have a lesser value in the collating sequence than do numbers for most computers; hence the letter "F" has a lower value than the number 4. This results in the low condition indicated in the example.

E. Alphanumeric Literals

When comparing alphanumeric fields, literals may be used instead of a field name in either Factor 1 or Factor 2. The mechanics of the compare operation are essentially the same as when comparing two alphanumeric fields; however, the literal must be properly defined. The following rules will serve as a review of alphanumeric literals.

Rules for Forming Alphanumeric Literals

1. Any combination of characters may be used.
2. Alphanumeric literals must be enclosed in single quotes.
3. The apostrophes are not part of the literal, but rather serve to indicate its beginning and end points.
4. The maximum length is eight characters, excluding the enclosing apostrophes.
5. When an apostrophe is to be included as part of the literal, as for example in O'CLOCK, then the literal would be written 'O''CLOCK'. Note the two apostrophes preceding the C would ensure that an actual apostrophe is part of the literal.

Figure 4.17 contains an alphabetic literal in Factor 2. Alphabetic literals represent actual information and must be enclosed in quotes to distinguish them from field names. Note that alphabetic literals are treated by the computer in exactly the same manner as alphanumeric literals. In Figure 4.17, if the quotes had been omitted, RPG would interpret ALABAMA to be a field name, thereby causing an error in the program. Remember, alphabetic literals must always be enclosed in apostrophes or single quotes when entered in Factor 1 or Factor 2. The quotes, however, are not included in the comparison. Also observe that Factor 2 is longer than Factor 1. You will recall that the shorter field is extended by padding blanks in the low-order position. Once aligned, the comparison again proceeds from left to right, one character at a time until an unequal condition is found. According to the collating sequence, the S in ALASKA has a higher value than the B in ALABAMA. Therefore, the result is high, setting indicator 1Ø on.

Figure 4.18 illustrates the use of an alphabetic literal as Factor 1. Since the letter "O" is less than "S" in the collating sequence, a low condition will result. Indicator 2Ø will therefore be set on.

Figure 4.17
Using an alphanumeric literal, Example 1.

RPG CALCULATION SPECIFICATIONS

Line	Form Type	Indicators	Factor 1	Operation	Factor 2	Result Field Name	Length	Decimal Positions	Half Adjust (H)	Resulting Indicators High	Low	Equal	Comments
01Φ	C	Φ1	STATE	COMP	'ALABAMA'					1Φ	2Φ	3Φ	
02	C												
03	C												

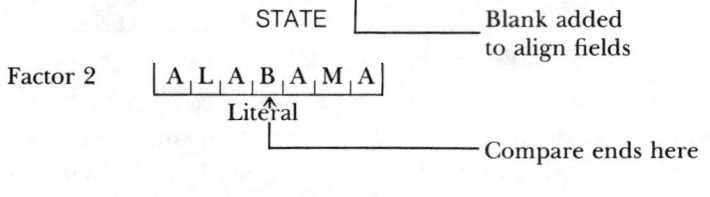

Factor 1 | A L A S K A b̸ |
STATE — Blank added to align fields

Factor 2 | A L A B A M A |
Literal — Compare ends here

Result
Number of characters compared—4
Condition HIGH
Reason (S > B)
Indicator set on: 10

Figure 4.18
Using an alphanumeric literal, Example 2.

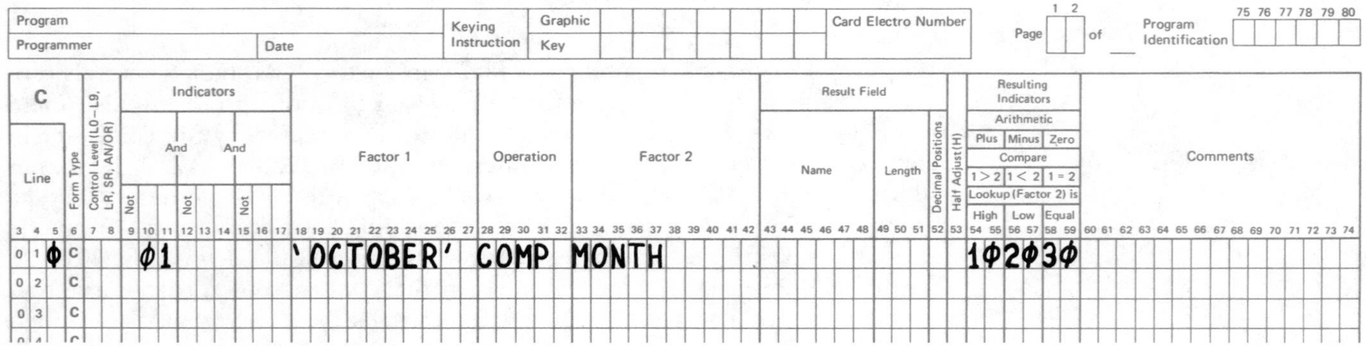

RPG CALCULATION SPECIFICATIONS

Line	Form Type	Indicators	Factor 1	Operation	Factor 2	Result Field Name	Length	Decimal Positions	Half Adjust (H)	Resulting Indicators High	Low	Equal	Comments
01Φ	C	Φ1	'OCTOBER'	COMP	MONTH					1Φ	2Φ	3Φ	
02	C												
03	C												

Factor 1 | O C T O B E R b̸ b̸ |
Literal

Factor 2 | S E P T E M B E R |
MONTH

Result
Number of characters compared—1
Condition LOW
Reason (O < S)
Indicator set on: 20

IV.

Applications of the Compare Instruction

Thus far, we have established the need for program logic using the compare statement. A tool the programmer may use in depicting the logic necessary for coding a series of comparisons is the **flowchart**. Flowcharting standards may be referenced in Appendix C. If you are unfamiliar with drawing flowcharts, review the material in the appendix. Recall the payroll problem coded in the beginning of the chapter in Figure 4.2.

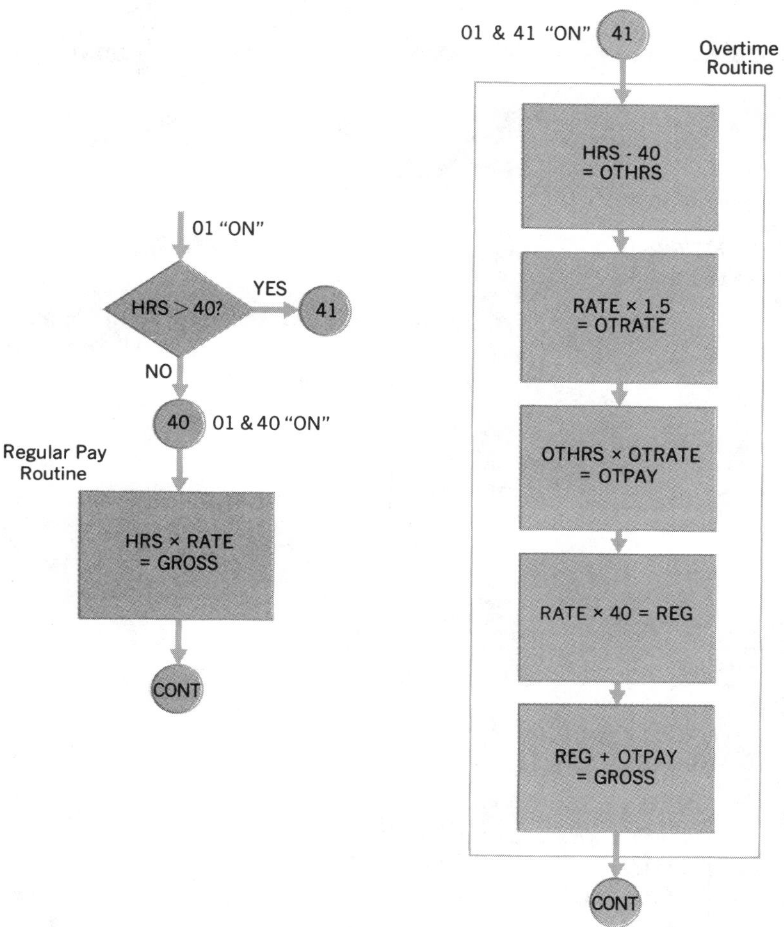

Referring to the flowchart, we find two different sets of calculations can be executed depending on the number of HRS worked. If the hours worked exceed 4Ø, then indicator 41 is set "on" and the instructions representing the overtime routine are executed. Recall that the instructions were conditioned by two indicators, Ø1 and 41, in Figure 4.2. Clearly, indicator 41 could not be set "on" unless indicator Ø1 were already in the "on" state; thus it would still be correct to use only indicator 41 as a condition for executing the instruction. However, the inclusion of both indicators provides better documentation of the program. We will continue this policy in the following practice problems, again including the record identifying indicator Ø1 to condition the execution of instructions in the Calculation and Output specifications.

When resulting indicators are turned on, they remain on until the next time the COMP instruction is executed. To avoid possible incorrect processing, it is useful to issue a SETOF command to reinitialize the resulting indicators after processing data. More on this later. The following problems will further illustrate how the COMP instruction is used.

Example 1 Code the instructions necessary to count the number of records containing an AMT field that is between 5Ø and 1ØØ. The flowchart in Figure 4.19 depicts the steps necessary to code this program excerpt correctly.

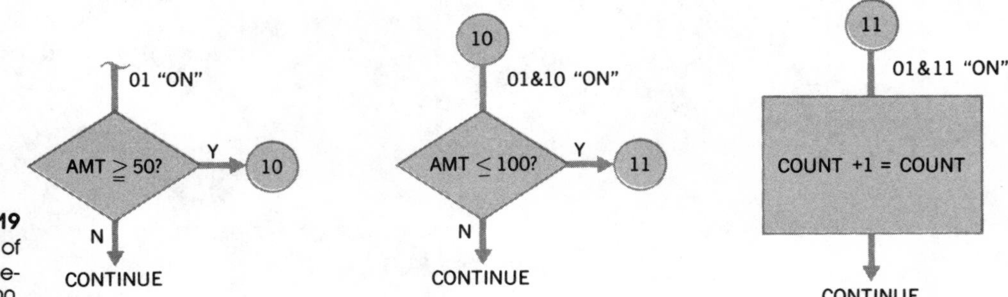

Figure 4.19
The logic to count the number of records with an AMT field between 50 and 100.

First, the AMT field is compared with the numeric value 5Ø, and if AMT is equal to or greater than 5Ø, indicator 1Ø is set "on." Only when indicator 1Ø is "on" can the next test be performed. If indicator 1Ø is "off," the AMT field will not be compared to 1ØØ. When the second COMP instruction is executed, the AMT field is compared with the number, 1ØØ. If the AMT field is less than or equal to 1ØØ, then indicator 11 is set "on." Indicator 11, in effect signals the program that the AMT field is between 5Ø and 1ØØ. Indicator 11 is thus used to condition the instruction: ADD 1 to COUNT. The coding necessary for this problem is shown here.

RPG CALCULATION SPECIFICATIONS

Line	Form Type	Control Level	Indicators	Factor 1	Operation	Factor 2	Result Field Name	Length	Decimal Positions	Half Adjust	Resulting Indicators High (1>2)	Low (1<2)	Equal (1=2)	Comments
01Ø	C		Ø1	AMT	COMP	5Ø					1Ø		1Ø	
02Ø	C		Ø1 1Ø	AMT	COMP	1ØØ						11	11	
03Ø	C		Ø1 11	COUNT	ADD	1	COUNT	3	Ø					
04	C													
05	C													
06	C													
07	C													

Example 2 The pay rate for employees varies depending on the shift worked. Flowchart and code the steps necessary to provide an adjustment in the pay rate depending on the SHIFT. Then calculate the GROSS as RATE × HRS. The RATE adjustment is as follows.

Shift	*Adjustment*
1	Ø (simply use the RATE)
2	1Ø% premium or 1.1Ø × RATE
3	15% premium or 1.15 × RATE

See Figure 4.2Ø for the flowchart and coding of this problem.

Note in the flowchart that we did not test for a SHIFT = 1. The reason for this is that the rate is not supposed to change when the SHIFT is equal to 1. Hence, if the condition was found to be true, that is, if the SHIFT was equal to 1, we would not modify the value

Figure 4.20
Flowchart and coding for Example 2.

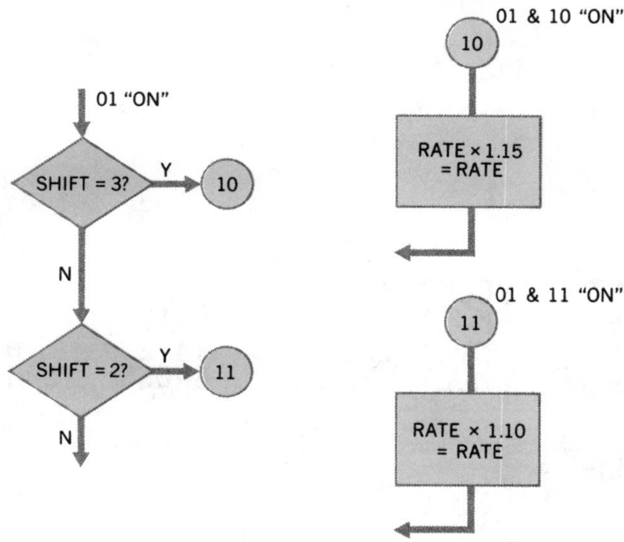

RPG CALCULATION SPECIFICATIONS

Program		Keying Instruction	Graphic	Card Electro Number	Page 1 2 of	Program Identification 75–80
Programmer	Date		Key			

Line (3–5)	Form Type (6)	Control Level (7–8)	Indicators (9–17)	Factor 1 (18–27)	Operation (28–32)	Factor 2 (33–42)	Result Field Name (43–48)	Length (49–51)	Decimal Positions (52)	Half Adjust (H) (53)	Resulting Indicators High (54–55)	Low (56–57)	Equal (58–59)	Comments (60–74)
01Ø	C		Ø1	SHIFT	COMP	3							1Ø	
02Ø	C		Ø1 1Ø	RATE	MULT	1.15	RATE			H				
03Ø	C		Ø1	SHIFT	COMP	2							11	
04Ø	C		Ø1 11	RATE	MULT	1.1Ø	RATE			H				
05Ø	C		Ø1	RATE	MULT	HRS	GROSS	6	2	H				
06	C													

of RATE. We would be wasting time with an instruction that is unnecessary. An alternative to the solution in Figure 4.2Ø is as follows.

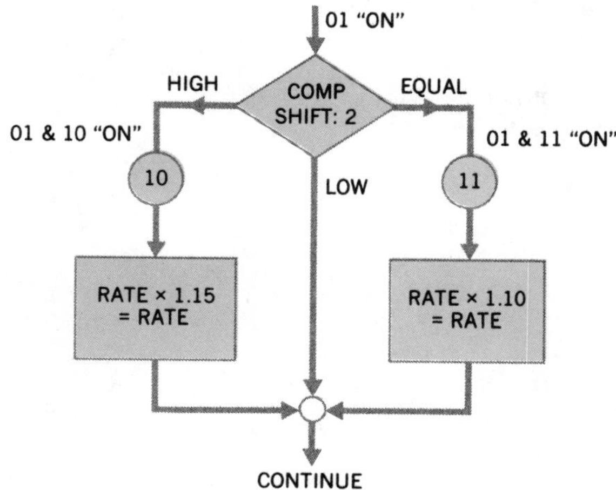

RPG CALCULATION SPECIFICATIONS

Line	Form Type	Control Level	Indicators			Factor 1	Operation	Factor 2	Result Field Name	Length	Decimal Positions	Half Adjust (H)	High	Low	Equal	Comments
010	C		01			SHIFT	COMP	2					10		11	
020	C		01	10		RATE	MULT	1.15	RATE			H				
030	C		01	11		RATE	MULT	1.10	RATE			H				
040	C		01			RATE	MULT	HRS	GROSS	6	2	H				
05	C															
06	C															
07	C															

Example 3 Provide a flowchart and the RPG coding to find the largest of three numbers, identified as N1, N2, and N3. No duplicate values within the set of the three numbers is permitted. The flowchart and coding to solve this problem are as follows.

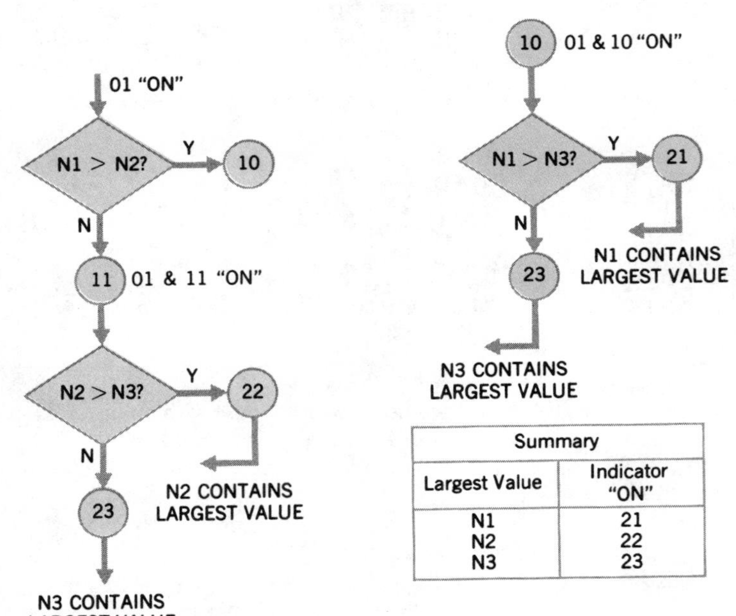

RPG CALCULATION SPECIFICATIONS

Line	Form Type	Indicators	Factor 1	Operation	Factor 2	Result Field	High	Low	Equal	Comments
01Φ	C	Φ1	N1	COMP	N2		1Φ	11		
02Φ	C	Φ1 1Φ	N1	COMP	N3		21	23		
03Φ	C	Φ1 11	N2	COMP	N3		22	23		
04	C									
05	C									

This solution can also be refined as shown in Figure 4.21. Observe that one less indicator is needed for this solution. In addition, since duplicate values are not permitted, indicator 77 will be used to signal an error condition, that is, the presence of duplicate values. It is important that the programmer learn to divide a problem into segments and then refine these segments for efficiency. The simple use of flowcharts as illustrated in the preceding examples will assist you in accomplishing this task. The combination of indicators to be used under different conditions is more apparent when the flowcharting approach is used.

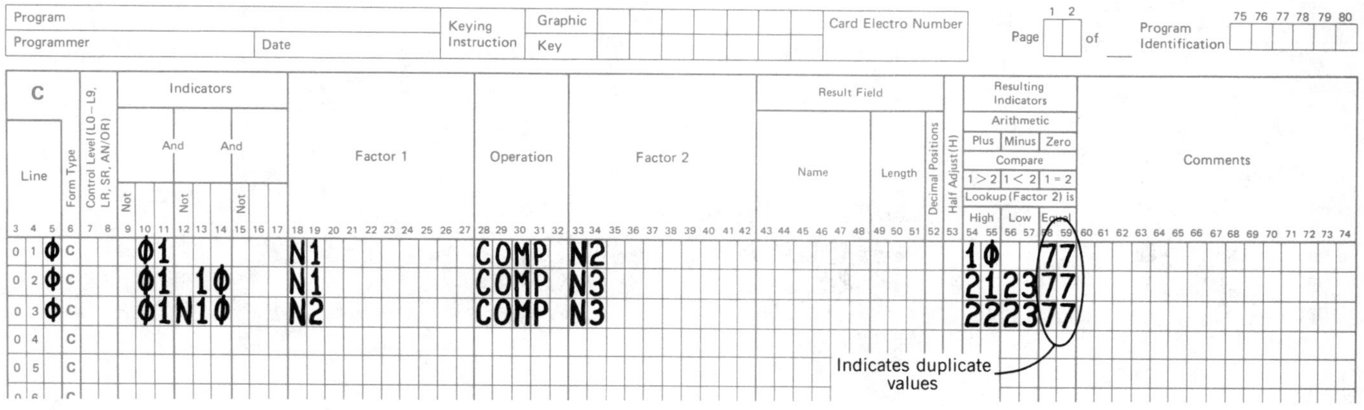
RPG CALCULATION SPECIFICATIONS

Line	Form Type	Indicators	Factor 1	Operation	Factor 2	Result Field	High	Low	Equal	Comments
01Φ	C	Φ1	N1	COMP	N2		1Φ		77	
02Φ	C	Φ1 1Φ	N1	COMP	N3		21	23	77	
03Φ	C	Φ1N1Φ	N2	COMP	N3		22	23	77	
04	C									
05	C									

Figure 4.21
Alternative solution for Example 3.

Example 4 Develop a flowchart and program excerpt to calculate FICA where SALARY is read from an input record. FICA is calculated as 6.7% of the first $35,7ØØ.ØØ earned. FICA is the Social Security tax paid by employees.

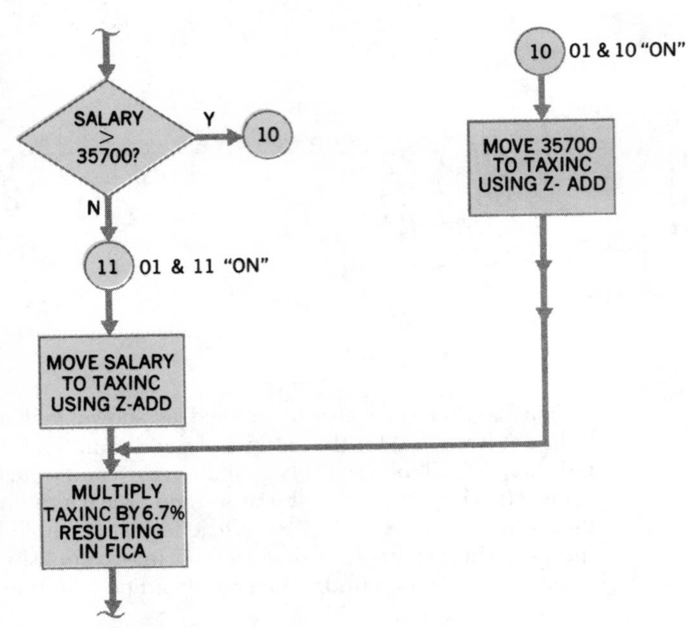

RPG CALCULATION SPECIFICATIONS

Line	Form Type	Control Level	Indicators	Factor 1	Operation	Factor 2	Result Field Name	Length	Decimal Positions	Half Adjust (H)	Resulting Indicators High	Low	Equal	Comments
Ø1	C		Ø1	SALARY	COMP	357ØØ					1Ø	11	11	
Ø2	C		Ø1 1Ø		Z-ADD	357ØØ	TAXINC	8	2					
Ø3	C		Ø1 11		Z-ADD	SALARY	TAXINC							
Ø4	C		Ø1	TAXINC	MULT	.Ø67	FICA	6	2	H				
Ø5	C													
Ø6	C													
Ø7	C													

The need for indicator 11 could be eliminated by conditioning line Ø3Ø with an N1Ø entry, meaning that indicator 1Ø is in the "off" state. The effect of line Ø3Ø would be to initialize the field, TAXINC, with whatever value is stored in SALARY. Recall that *none* of these statements change the contents of the SALARY field in any way because SALARY is *not* a result field. A field must be used as a result field in order for its contents to change. The exception to this rule is the reading of data from an input medium. Once data has been read in and *moved* to the respective fields, new values would be assigned to these fields and the previous input values would no longer be available for processing unless they had been stored elsewhere. Sometimes students have difficulty in differentiating between the use of a field as a factor and using the field to store a result. Remember, result fields are *always* assigned new values each time an arithmetic instruction is executed. Result fields are not used, however, with COMP instructions.

Example 5 Develop a flowchart and code the RPG Calculation form to calculate SALES discounts for customers based on the amount of the sale. Use the following table and set on the indicators as noted.

Sales Amount	*Discount*	*Set "ON"*
Ø–99.99	Ø%	2Ø
1ØØ–199.99	2%	22
2ØØ–299.99	3%	23
3ØØ and over	6%	26

Subtract the discount (DISCT) from the SALES, giving the NET sales. When SALES are less than 1ØØ, no discount is offered.

Note that we began by comparing SALES to 2ØØ.ØØ, the middle point in the table. In this way, if SALES exceeded 2ØØ.ØØ, there would be no need to test the first two conditions (SALES < 1ØØ.ØØ and SALES < 2ØØ.ØØ). This practice of beginning our test with the middle condition, as opposed to the first, is a common programming technique. It is designed specifically to save computer time. When a field compares "greater than" the middle entry, there is no need to compare it to the first half of the table. In general, then, this technique reduces the number of comparisons that will be required to find the appropriate course of action.

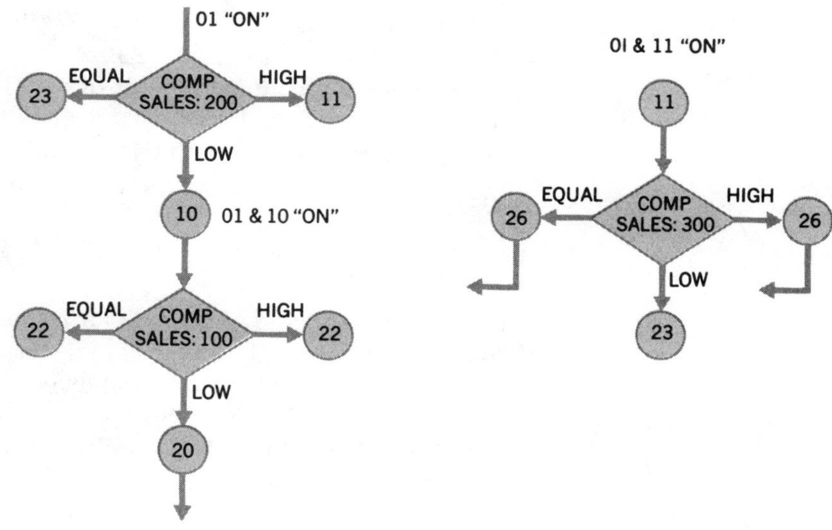

Summary

Greater or Equal	Less Than	Discount %	Indicator "on"
	100.00	0	20
100.00	200.00	2	22
200.00	300.00	3	23
300.00		6	26

RPG CALCULATION SPECIFICATIONS

Program		Keying Instruction	Graphic	Card Electro Number	Page of
Programmer	Date		Key		

Line	Form Type	Control Level (L0–L9, LR, SR, AN/OR)	Indicators: Not	Indicators	And: Not	And	And: Not	And	Factor 1	Operation	Factor 2	Result Field Name	Length	Decimal Positions	Half Adjust (H)	Resulting Indicators High (1>2) Plus	Low (1<2) Minus	Equal (1=2) Zero
01	C			Ø1					SALES	COMP	2ØØ.ØØ					11	1Ø	23
02	C			Ø1		11			SALES	COMP	3ØØ.ØØ					26	23	26
03	C			Ø1		1Ø			SALES	COMP	1ØØ.ØØ					22	2Ø	22
04	C			Ø1		2Ø				Z-ADDØ		DISCT	5	2	H			
05	C			Ø1		22			SALES	MULT	.Ø2	DISCT			H			
06	C			Ø1		23			SALES	MULT	.Ø3	DISCT			H			
07	C			Ø1		26			SALES	MULT	.Ø6	DISCT			H			
08	C			Ø1					SALES	SUB	DISCT	NET	5	2				
09	C																	
10	C																	

Must be specified for rounding each calculation

Self-Evaluating Quiz

1. The character with the lowest value in the collating sequence is the ________ .
2. The letter "A" is (greater than, less than) the letter "B."
3. The digit zero is (higher in, lower in) value relative to the letter "Z."
4. (T or F) When alphanumeric fields of different length are compared, the comparison ends when the last character of the shorter field is tested.
5. If we compared the name "JOHNS" with "JOHNSON", we would find (number) characters were compared, with the name ________ having the higher value.
6. When alphanumeric literals are entered in Factor 1 or Factor 2, they are enclosed in ________ .
7. Suppose a month field in Factor 1 can take on values JAN, FEB, . . . DEC. If we compare Factor 1 to the literal 'APRIL' in Factor 2, we would have (number) of equal comparisons, (number) of high comparisons, and (number) of low conditions after comparing the 12 months of the year.
8. Could we use 'SEPTEMBER' as an alphabetic literal?
9. If in an alphanumeric compare, we compared a field containing 'NEWARK' with 'NEW YORK', how many characters would be compared and which field would have the higher value?
10. A field named SOCSEC contains an entry in column 52 of the Input form. We are required to perform an alphanumeric compare using SOCSEC. Is this acceptable in RPG?

Solutions

1. blank or space
2. less than
3. higher in (for most computers)

4. F—Blanks or spaces are padded on the right of the shorter field.
5. 6
   JOHNSON
6. apostrophes or single quote marks
7. 1,
   11,
   Ø
8. No. It has more than 1Ø characters, including the apostrophes, and therefore will not fit in either Factor 1 or Factor 2.
9. four
   NEWARK (assuming that NEW YORK has a blank in the fourth position)
10. No. The data in both fields must be numeric.

V. RPG Indicator Summary Form

The RPG Indicator Summary form is used to assist the programmer in keeping track of all indicators established in a program. Unlike the other RPG forms considered thus far, the Indicator Summary form has no effect on the translation or execution of the program; it is used primarily for documentation and commentary purposes. Note that all entries on this form have an asterisk (*) in column 7 designating the entry as a comment.

When a programmer sets on numerous indicators in a program, it is quite possible that he or she may inadvertently use the same indicator number for two different purposes. Unless the programmer finds this error before execution, debugging could be a timely and difficult task. The Indicator Summary form is useful in helping the programmer avoid such errors. See Figure 4.22 for an illustration of an RPG Indicator Summary form.

Figure 4.22
Illustration of an RPG Indicator Summary form.

RPG INDICATOR SUMMARY

Program		Punching Instruction	Graphic	Card Electro Number	Page 1 2 of __	Program Identification 75 76 77 78 79 80
Programmer	Date		Punch			

F*

Circle Indicators Used:

General Indicators

	01	02	03	04	05	06	07	08	09
10	11	12	13	14	15	16	17	18	19
20	21	22	23	24	25	26	27	28	29
30	31	32	33	34	35	36	37	38	39
40	41	42	43	44	45	46	47	48	49
50	51	52	53	54	55	56	57	58	59
60	61	62	63	64	65	66	67	68	69
70	71	72	73	74	75	76	77	78	79
80	81	82	83	84	85	86	87	88	89
90	91	92	93	94	95	96	97	98	99

Note: All indicators are not valid with all systems.

Control Level Indicators
L1 L2 L3 L4 L5 L6 L7 L8 L9

Halt Indicators
H1 H2 H3 H4 H5 H6 H7 H8 H9

External Indicators
U1 U2 U3 U4 U5 U6 U7 U8 U9

Command Key Indicators
KA KB KC KD KE KF KG KH KI
KJ KK KL KM KN KP KQ KR KS
KT KU KV KW KX KY

Overflow Indicators
OA OB OC OD OE OF OG OV

Special Purpose Indicators
1P LO HO MR LR

Line (3–5)	Form Type (6)	(7)	Record Identifying (8–10)	Input Field (11–13)	Calculation Result and Command Key (14–16)	Halt and User (17–19)	Control Level and Overflow (20–22)	(23–74)
01Ø	F	*	ID	F	C	H	L	FUNCTION OF INDICATORS
02Ø	F	*						
03Ø	F	*	Ø1					MASTER ACCOUNTS RECEIVABLE RECORD
04Ø	F	*	Ø2					CREDIT TRANSACTION RECORD
05Ø	F	*	Ø3					DEBIT TRANSACTION RECORD
06	F	*						
07	F	*						
08	F	*						

VI.

The TESTN Instruction

Frequently the programmer is called on to write edit programs, the purpose of which is to prevent inaccurate data from being entered into the system thereby creating undesirable results. The TESTN **instruction** is used to validate that the contents of input fields designated as numeric are in fact numeric. This is accomplished by setting a resulting indicator (high) when the contents of a field is numeric. Hence, the TESTN instruction is primarily used to test a field for the presence of numbers. The field to be tested must be defined as alphameric, meaning that the decimal positions entry used to define the field is blank. The field to be tested cannot therefore be used in calculations; however, once it is established that the contents is numeric, the data can be moved to a field defined as numeric. Once the move is completed, the resulting numeric field may then be used in calculations.

The resulting indicator set by the TESTN instruction uses the HIGH entry in columns 54 and 55. When the field tested contains only numbers, then the high indicator is set on. If, however, letters, special characters, or blanks are present, the resulting indicator will be off. Each character in the field must be numeric except the low-order right-most position, which may contain a minus sign. Figure 4.23 illustrates the testing of an AMT field. If AMT is numeric, it is then moved to NUMFD for calculations.

RPG CALCULATION SPECIFICATIONS

Line	Form Type	Control Level	Indicators	Factor 1	Operation	Factor 2	Result Field Name	Length	Decimal Positions	Half Adjust	Resulting Indicators High	Low	Equal	Comments
010	C		01		TESTN		AMT				25			
020	C		01 25		MOVE	AMT	NUMFD	5	2					
030	C		01N25		Z-ADD	0	NUMFD							
040	C				.									
050	C				.									
06	C													
07	C													
08	C													

Figure 4.23
Example of the TESTN instruction.

Key Terms

- Algebraic comparison
- Alphameric field
- Alphanumeric field
- Collating sequence
- Compare (COMP) instruction
- Condition code
- Conditional branch
- Flowchart
- High-order position
- Literal
- Low-order position
- Numeric field
- Program walkthrough
- Resulting indicator
- Routine
- TESTN instruction

Self-Evaluating Quiz

1. A compare instruction always produces one of three results: ________, ________, or ________.
2. (T or F) It is permissible in RPG to compare a numeric field to an alphanumeric field.
3. The COMP instruction automatically triggers an internal ________ that is used to set the resulting indicators.
4. (T or F) The COMP instruction can be used for turning on up to three indicators in a program.
5. (T or F) Resulting indicators are turned off automatically in a RPG program unless they are used immediately.
6. (T or F) In a numeric compare, both Factor 1 and Factor 2 may be numeric literals.
7. To accomplish a numeric comparison of two fields, each field must have a numeric entry in the ________ Positions column of the form on which it is defined.
8. Numeric comparisons are algebraic comparisons, which means that the ________ is included in the test.
9. Before numeric fields of unequal length are compared, they are automatically aligned according to their ________ and missing digits are ________.
10. (T or F) An example of a valid numeric literal is $1,ØØØ.
11. A ________ is a technique used to manually follow the logic of a program before actually running the program.
12. (T or F) When comparing alphanumeric fields, the comparison begins with the low-order or right-most positions.
13. When comparing alphameric fields of different lengths, the shorter field is padded with ________ in the ________ -order positions.
14. (T or F) 'REGISTRATION' is an example of a valid alphanumeric literal.
15. The purpose of the TESTN instruction is to ________.

Solutions

1. high
   low
   equal
2. F
3. condition code
4. T—Any one or all the high, low, and equal indicators can be used.
5. F—They remain on until the next record is processed and the compare instruction is again executed.
6. F—Either Factor 1 or Factor 2 may be a numeric literal, but not both.
7. Decimal
8. sign
9. decimal points
   filled with zeros
10. F—Numeric literals cannot contain dollar signs, commas, blanks, or any other alphanumeric character except a sign and a decimal point.

11. program walkthrough
12. F—It begins with the left-most position.
13. blanks
    low
14. F—The maximum length is 8 characters, excluding the apostrophes.
15. validate that the contents of input fields designated as numeric are actually numeric.

Review Questions

1. Indicate the results of the following comparisons:

Factor 1	*Factor 2*
Ø12	12
12+	12
AEF	AED
12A	B2A
12-	12
AEFG	AEF
4Ø.ØØ	4Ø

2. If Factor 1 is less than Factor 2, a COMP instruction will turn on the ____ indicator.
3. (T or F) Resulting indicators that are turned on as a result of a COMP operation remain on until the next record is processed.
4. Indicate how an RPG programmer defines a field as numeric.
5. (T or F) Alphanumeric fields may be used in arithmetic operations.
6. (T or F) All fields must be the same length if they are to be compared.
7. (T or F) A numeric literal may contain a dollar sign.
8. (T or F) Numeric literals are right-justified when entered in Factor 1 or Factor 2 of the Calculation form.
9. (T or F) By entering an N in column 9, 12, or 15, a test may be made to determine if an indicator is off rather than on.
10. A field that is further subdivided into subordinate fields is referred to as a(n) ____ item.
11. A(n) ____ is a desk-checking procedure that enables the programmer to manually step through the set of procedures used in the program to ensure that the logic is correct.
12. The reserved word ____ contains the current month, day, and year.
13. Alphameric literals are enclosed in ____ to distinguish them from numeric literals.
14. (T or F) An alphanumeric field should only be compared to an alphanumeric literal.
15. (T or F) A blank or space has the lowest value in the collating sequence.

Debugging Exercises

Debugging Exercise 1

The purpose of this program is to produce a weekly payroll register (PAYREG) from employee input records contained in the PAYMAST file. Employees working more than 4Ø hours in a week are paid time and a half for the overtime hours.

Figure 4.24
Problem definition for Debugging Exercise 1.

Systems Flowchart

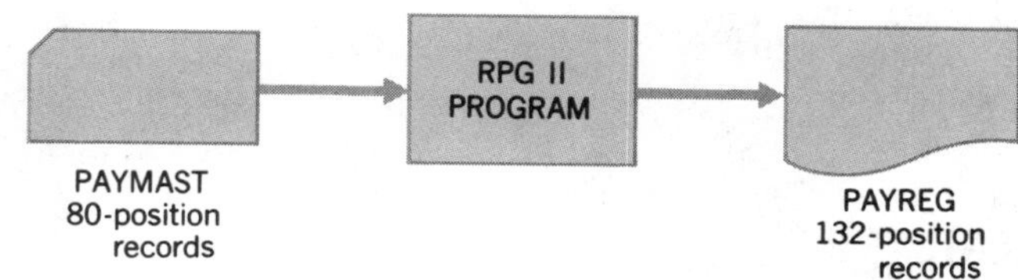

PAYMAST Record Layout

EMPNO	LNAME	FNAME	HRS (2 DECIMALS)	RATE ($ ¢)	UNUSED
1–3	4–23	24–33	34–37	38–41	42–80

PAYREG Printer Spacing Chart

```
     1
H    2  XX/XX/XX                                   P A Y R O L L   R E G I S T E R                                  PAGE XXØX
     3
H    4  EMPLOYEE                                           REG        O/T       PAY      REGULAR    OVERTIME       TOTAL
H    5   NUMBER            EMPLOYEE NAME                   HRS        HRS       RATE     EARNINGS   EARNINGS     GROSS PAY
     6
D    7    XXX      X-------------------X X--------X  XØ.XX      XØ.XX     XØ.XX      XXØ.XX      XXØ.XX         XXØ.XX
D    8    XXX      X-------------------X X--------X  XØ.XX      XØ.XX     XØ.XX      XXØ.XX      XXØ.XX         XXØ.XX
     9
TLR 10                       *** FINAL TOTALS XXØ.XX     XXØ.XX              $X,XX$.XX $X,XX$.XX    $X,XX$.XX
    11
    12
```

Note that if the hours field is blank, the record will not be processed. The problem definition is shown in Figure 4.24.

The program coding sheets in Figure 4.25 contain syntax errors. Identify the errors and indicate the corrections you would make to the program.

The program listing in Figure 4.26 includes the error messages produced by running the program. The syntax corrections are circled on the computer listing shown in Figure 4.27. There are, however, logic errors. (Remember, indicators remain "on" unless set off by the programmer.) Your assignment is to carefully desk check the program, find the logic errors, and make the necessary corrections.

Figure 4.25
Coding sheets for Debugging Exercise 1.
(Continued on next page.)

RPG CONTROL AND FILE DESCRIPTION SPECIFICATIONS

Program PAYROLL REGISTER
Programmer N. JOHNKE Date 5/27/--
Keying Instruction: Graphic Ø 1 2 / Key ZERO ONE TWO
Card Electro Number
Page Ø1 of 5 Program Identification SSSØ4A

Control Specifications

For the valid entries for a system, refer to the RPG reference manual for that system.

```
01Ø H
```

File Description Specifications

For the valid entries for a system, refer to the RPG reference manual for that system.

```
02Ø F*********************************************************************
03Ø F* THIS PROGRAM PRODUCES A WEEKLY PAYROLL REGISTER. EMPLOYEES WORK-  *
04Ø F* ING OVER 4Ø HOURS A WEEK ARE PAID TIME AND A HALF FOR OVERTIME    *
05Ø F* HOURS. FINAL TOTALS ARE CALCULATED FOR REGULAR HOURS,OVERTIME     *
06Ø F* HOURS,REGULAR PAY,OVERTIME PAY AND TOTAL GROSS PAY.               *
07Ø F*********************************************************************
08Ø F*
09Ø FPAYMAST IP  F      8Ø            READØ1 SYSIPT
10Ø FPAYREG  O   F     132     FO     PRINTERSYSLST
11Ø F*
    F
```

RPG INPUT SPECIFICATIONS

Program: PAYROLL REGISTER | Programmer: N. JOHNKE | Date: 5/27/__ | Keying Instruction — Graphic: Ø 1 2; Key: ZERO ONE TWO | Card Electro Number | Page Ø2 of 5 | Program Identification SSSØ4A

Line	Form Type	Filename or Record Name	Sequence	Record Identifying Indicator	Field Location From	Field Location To	Decimal Positions	RPG Field Name
Ø1	I	****************************** INPUT RECORD ******************************						
Ø2	I	*						
Ø3	I	PAYMAST	NS	1Ø				
Ø4	I				1	3	Ø	EMPNO
Ø5	I				4	23		LNAME
Ø6	I				24	33		FNAME
Ø7	I				34	37	2	HRS
Ø8	I				38	41	2	RATE
Ø9	I	*						
10	I							
11	I							

RPG CALCULATION SPECIFICATIONS

Program: PAYROLL REGISTER | Programmer: N. JOHNKE | Date: 5/27/__ | Keying Instruction — Graphic: Ø 1 2; Key: ZERO ONE TWO | Card Electro Number | Page Ø3 of 5 | Program Identification SSSØ4A

Line	Form Type	Indicators	Factor 1	Operation	Factor 2	Result Field Name	Length	Decimal Positions	Half Adjust (H)	Resulting Indicators High	Low	Equal	Comments
Ø1	C	****************************** CALCULATIONS ******************************											
Ø2	C*												
Ø3	C	Ø1	HRS	COMP	4Ø					1Ø	11	11	
Ø4	C*												
Ø5	C	1Ø	HRS	MULT	RATE	REG	5	2	H				REGULAR PAY
Ø6	C*												
Ø7	C	11	HRS	SUB	4Ø.ØØ	OTHRS	4	2					O T
Ø8	C	11	RATE	MULT	1.5	OTRATE	4	2	H				V I P
Ø9	C	11	OTHRS	MULT	OTRATE	OTPAY	5	2	H				E M A
1Ø	C	11	RATE	MULT	4Ø.ØØ	REG			H				R E Y
11	C*												
12	C		REG	ADD	OTPAY	GROSS	5	2					TOTAL GROSS PAY
13	C*												
14	C		THRS	ADD	HRS	THRS	5	2					F T
15	C	11	TOTHRS	ADD	OTHRS	TOTHRS	5	2					I O
16	C		TREG	ADD	REG	TREG	6	2					N T
17	C	11	TOTPAY	ADD	OTPAY	TOTPAY	6	2					A A
18	C		TGROSS	ADD	GROSS	TGROSS	6	2					L L
19	C*												S

Figure 4.25 *(continued)*

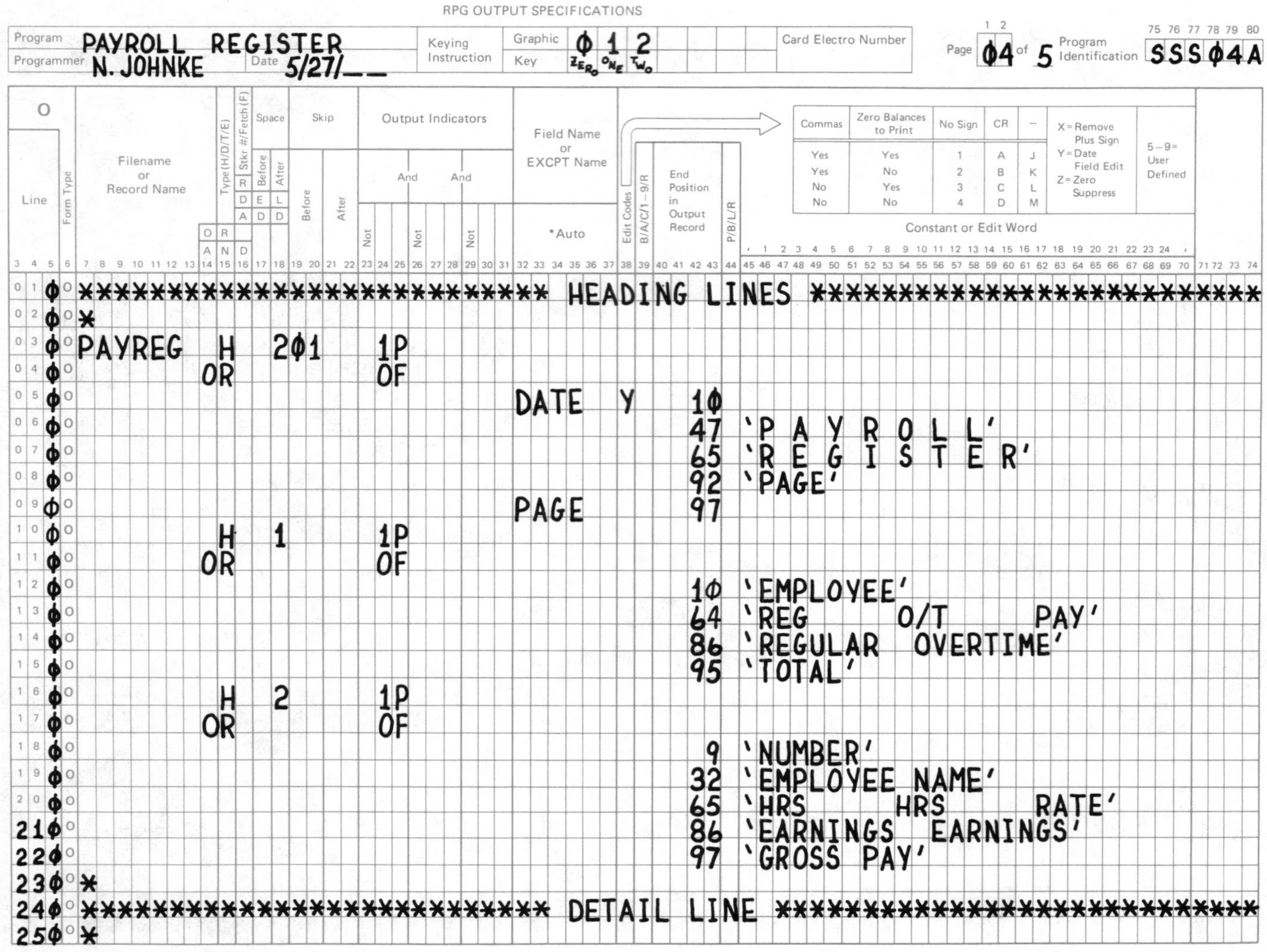

RPG OUTPUT SPECIFICATIONS

Program: PAYROLL REGISTER
Programmer: N. JOHNKE Date: 5/27/__
Keying Instruction: Graphic ϕ 1 2 / Key ZERO ONE TWO
Card Electro Number
Page ϕ4 of 5 Program Identification SSSϕ4A

Line	Form Type	Filename or Record Name	Type (H/D/T/E)	Space After	Skip Before	Output Indicators	Field Name or EXCPT Name	Edit Codes	End Position in Output Record	Constant or Edit Word
01ϕ	O	************************** HEADING LINES **************************								
02ϕ	O	*								
03ϕ	O	PAYREG	H	2	ϕ1	1P				
04ϕ	O	OR				OF				
05ϕ	O						DATE	Y	1ϕ	
06ϕ	O								47	'P A Y R O L L'
07ϕ	O								65	'R E G I S T E R'
08ϕ	O								92	'PAGE'
09ϕ	O						PAGE		97	
10ϕ	O		H	1		1P				
11ϕ	O	OR				OF				
12ϕ	O								1ϕ	'EMPLOYEE'
13ϕ	O								64	'REG O/T PAY'
14ϕ	O								86	'REGULAR OVERTIME'
15ϕ	O								95	'TOTAL'
16ϕ	O		H	2		1P				
17ϕ	O	OR				OF				
18ϕ	O								9	'NUMBER'
19ϕ	O								32	'EMPLOYEE NAME'
20ϕ	O								65	'HRS HRS RATE'
21ϕ	O								86	'EARNINGS EARNINGS'
22ϕ	O								97	'GROSS PAY'
23ϕ	O	*								
24ϕ	O	************************** DETAIL LINE **************************								
25ϕ	O	*								

Figure 4.25 *(continued)*

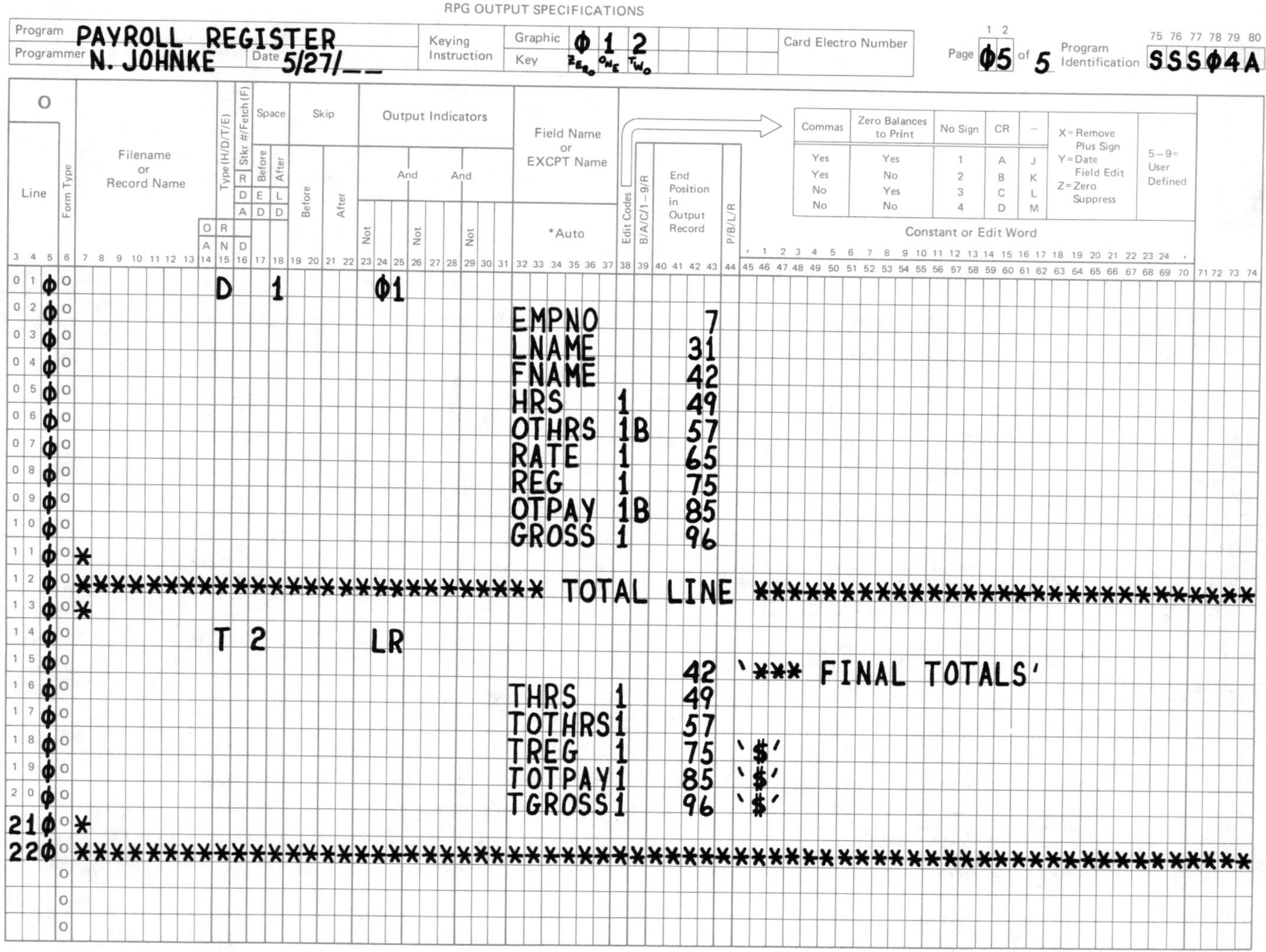

RPG OUTPUT SPECIFICATIONS

Program: PAYROLL REGISTER | Programmer: N. JOHNKE | Date: 5/27/__ | Keying Instruction: Graphic Ø 1 2 / Key Zero One Two | Card Electro Number | Page Ø5 of 5 | Program Identification: SSSØ4A

Line	Form Type	Filename or Record Name	Type (H/D/T/E)	Space Before	Space After	Output Indicators	Field Name or EXCPT Name	Edit Codes	B/A/C/1–9/R	End Position in Output Record	Constant or Edit Word
01Ø	O		D		1	Ø1					
02Ø	O						EMPNO			7	
03Ø	O						LNAME			31	
04Ø	O						FNAME			42	
05Ø	O						HRS	1		49	
06Ø	O						OTHRS	1	B	57	
07Ø	O						RATE	1		65	
08Ø	O						REG	1		75	
09Ø	O						OTPAY	1	B	85	
10Ø	O						GROSS	1		96	
11Ø	O	*									
12Ø	O	*************************** TOTAL LINE *****************************									
13Ø	O	*									
14Ø	O		T	2		LR					
15Ø	O									42	'*** FINAL TOTALS'
16Ø	O						THRS	1		49	
17Ø	O						TOTHRS	1		57	
18Ø	O						TREG	1		75	'$'
19Ø	O						TOTPAY	1		85	'$'
20Ø	O						TGROSS	1		96	'$'
21Ø	O	*									
22Ø	O	**									

Figure 4.25 *(continued)*

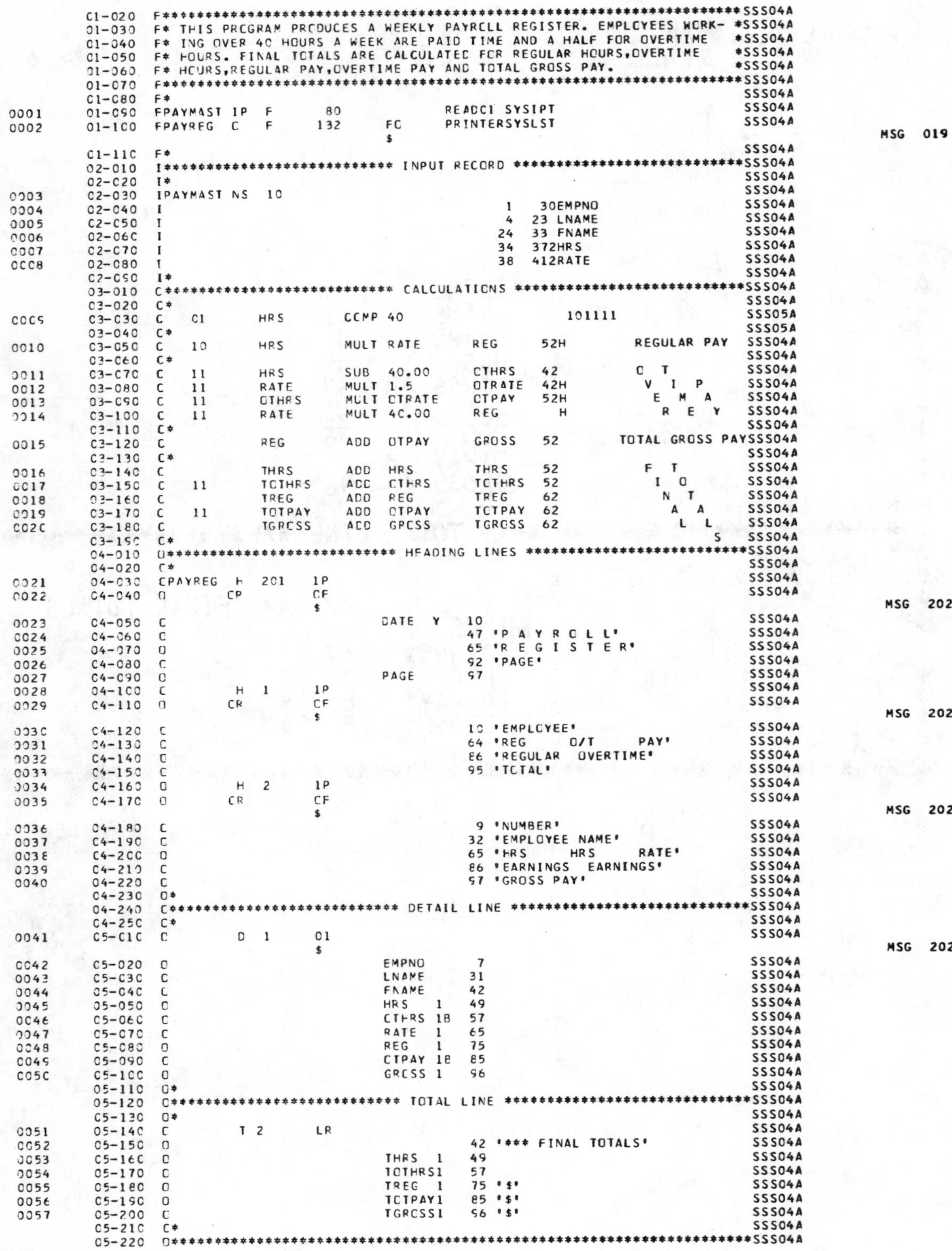

```
          01-020  F*****************************************************************SSS04A
          01-030  F* THIS PROGRAM PRODUCES A WEEKLY PAYROLL REGISTER. EMPLOYEES WORK- *SSS04A
          01-040  F* ING OVER 40 HOURS A WEEK ARE PAID TIME AND A HALF FOR OVERTIME   *SSS04A
          01-050  F* HOURS. FINAL TOTALS ARE CALCULATED FOR REGULAR HOURS,OVERTIME    *SSS04A
          01-060  F* HOURS,REGULAR PAY,OVERTIME PAY AND TOTAL GROSS PAY.             *SSS04A
          01-070  F*****************************************************************SSS04A
          01-080  F*                                                                  SSS04A
0001      01-090  FPAYMAST IP  F       80            READ01 SYSIPT                    SSS04A
0002      01-100  FPAYREG  O   F      132      FC    PRINTERSYSLST                    SSS04A
                                               $                                            MSG  019
          01-110  F*                                                                  SSS04A
          02-010  I************************** INPUT RECORD **************************SSS04A
          02-020  I*                                                                  SSS04A
0003      02-030  IPAYMAST NS  10                                                     SSS04A
0004      02-040  I                                           1   30EMPNO             SSS04A
0005      02-050  I                                           4  23 LNAME             SSS04A
0006      02-060  I                                          24  33 FNAME             SSS04A
0007      02-070  I                                          34  372HRS               SSS04A
0008      02-080  I                                          38  412RATE              SSS04A
          02-090  I*                                                                  SSS04A
          03-010  C************************** CALCULATIONS **************************SSS04A
          03-020  C*                                                                  SSS04A
0009      03-030  C   01       HRS       COMP 40                  101111              SSS05A
          03-040  C*                                                                  SSS05A
0010      03-050  C   10       HRS       MULT RATE      REG     52H       REGULAR PAY SSS04A
          03-060  C*                                                                  SSS04A
0011      03-070  C   11       HRS       SUB  40.00     OTHRS   42         O T        SSS04A
0012      03-080  C   11       RATE      MULT 1.5       OTRATE  42H         V I P     SSS04A
0013      03-090  C   11       OTHRS     MULT OTRATE    OTPAY   52H          E M A    SSS04A
0014      03-100  C   11       RATE      MULT 40.00     REG       H           R E Y   SSS04A
          03-110  C*                                                                  SSS04A
0015      03-120  C            REG       ADD  OTPAY     GROSS   52      TOTAL GROSS PAYSSS04A
          03-130  C*                                                                  SSS04A
0016      03-140  C            THRS      ADD  HRS       THRS    52         F T        SSS04A
0017      03-150  C   11       TOTHRS    ADD  OTHRS     TOTHRS  52          I O       SSS04A
0018      03-160  C            TREG      ADD  REG       TREG    62           N T      SSS04A
0019      03-170  C   11       TOTPAY    ADD  OTPAY     TOTPAY  62            A A     SSS04A
0020      03-180  C            TGROSS    ADD  GROSS     TGROSS  62             L L    SSS04A
          03-190  C*                                                        S         SSS04A
          04-010  O************************** HEADING LINES *************************SSS04A
          04-020  O*                                                                  SSS04A
0021      04-030  OPAYREG  H  201    1P                                               SSS04A
0022      04-040  O        OP        OF                                               SSS04A
                                     $                                                      MSG  202
0023      04-050  O                              DATE  Y  10                          SSS04A
0024      04-060  O                                       47 'P A Y R O L L'          SSS04A
0025      04-070  O                                       65 'R E G I S T E R'        SSS04A
0026      04-080  O                                       92 'PAGE'                   SSS04A
0027      04-090  O                              PAGE     97                          SSS04A
0028      04-100  O          H  1    1P                                               SSS04A
0029      04-110  O        OR        OF                                               SSS04A
                                     $                                                      MSG  202
0030      04-120  O                                       10 'EMPLOYEE'               SSS04A
0031      04-130  O                                       64 'REG     O/T     PAY'    SSS04A
0032      04-140  O                                       86 'REGULAR  OVERTIME'      SSS04A
0033      04-150  O                                       95 'TOTAL'                  SSS04A
0034      04-160  O          H  2    1P                                               SSS04A
0035      04-170  O        OR        OF                                               SSS04A
                                     $                                                      MSG  202
0036      04-180  O                                        9 'NUMBER'                 SSS04A
0037      04-190  O                                       32 'EMPLOYEE NAME'          SSS04A
0038      04-200  O                                       65 'HRS      HRS      RATE' SSS04A
0039      04-210  O                                       86 'EARNINGS  EARNINGS'     SSS04A
0040      04-220  O                                       97 'GROSS PAY'              SSS04A
          04-230  O*                                                                  SSS04A
          04-240  O************************** DETAIL LINE ***************************SSS04A
          04-250  O*                                                                  SSS04A
0041      05-010  O          D  1    01                                               SSS04A
                                     $                                                      MSG  202
0042      05-020  O                              EMPNO     7                          SSS04A
0043      05-030  O                              LNAME    31                          SSS04A
0044      05-040  O                              FNAME    42                          SSS04A
0045      05-050  O                              HRS   1  49                          SSS04A
0046      05-060  O                              OTHRS 1B 57                          SSS04A
0047      05-070  O                              RATE  1  65                          SSS04A
0048      05-080  O                              REG   1  75                          SSS04A
0049      05-090  O                              OTPAY 1B 85                          SSS04A
0050      05-100  O                              GROSS 1  96                          SSS04A
          05-110  O*                                                                  SSS04A
          05-120  O************************** TOTAL LINE ****************************SSS04A
          05-130  O*                                                                  SSS04A
0051      05-140  O          T 2     LR                                               SSS04A
0052      05-150  O                                       42 '*** FINAL TOTALS'       SSS04A
0053      05-160  O                              THRS  1  49                          SSS04A
0054      05-170  O                              TOTHRS1  57                          SSS04A
0055      05-180  O                              TREG  1  75 '$'                      SSS04A
0056      05-190  O                              TOTPAY1  85 '$'                      SSS04A
0057      05-200  O                              TGROSS1  96 '$'                      SSS04A
          05-210  O*                                                                  SSS04A
          05-220  O*****************************************************************SSS04A


     E N D  O F  S O U R C E
```

Figure 4.26
Program listing with error diagnostics for Debugging Exercise 1.
(Continued on next page.)

```
            C O M P I L E R   C I A G N O S T I C S   S U M M A R Y


ILN019   OVERFLOW INCICATOR (PCSITICNS 33-34) IS INVALID. ASSUME BLANK.

          CCC2     C1-1CC      PAYREG

ILN202   INDICATOR IS INVALID CR UNDEFINEC. DRCP ENTRY.

          CC22     04-04C
          CC29     04-11C
          0035     C4-170
          0C41     05-01C

ILN387   INCICATOR REFERENCEC BUT NCT CEFINED. CRCP INDICATCR.

          COC9     03-03C      C1

ILN398   FIELC NAME UNDEFINEC. SPEC IS CRCPPED.

        C CC23     04-C5C      CATE
```

Figure 4.26 *(continued)*

Figure 4.27
Program listing that contains logic errors for Debugging Exercise 1.
(Continued on next page.)

```
01-020  F***************************************************************************SSS04A
01-030  F* THIS PRCGRAM PRCDUCES A WEEKLY PAYRCLL REGISTER. EMPLOYEES WCRK-  *SSS04A
C1-040  F* ING CVEF 40 HCURS A WEEK ARE PAID TIME AND A HALF FCR OVERTIME   *SSS04A
01-050  F* HOURS. FINAL TCTALS ARE CALCULATEC FOR PEGULAR HOURS,OVERTIME    *SSS04A
C1-060  F* HCURS,REGULAR PAY,CVERTIME PAY ANC TCTAL GRCSS PAY.              *SSS04A
01-070  F***************************************************************************SSS04A
01-080  F*                                   Correction 1                    SSS04A
C1-090  FPAYMAST IP   F      80                   READC1 SYSIPT              SSS04A
C1-100  FPAYREG  C    F     132          (CF)     PRINTERSYSLST              SSS04A
C1-110  F*                                                                   SSS04A
02-010  I*************************** INPUT RECORD *****************************SSS04A
C2-C20  I*                                                                   SSS04A
C2-030  IPAYMAST NS (01)—Correction 2                                        SSS04A
C2-040  I                                          1   30EMPNO               SSS04A
C2-C50  I                                          4   23 LNAME              SSS04A
02-060  I                                         24   33 FNAME              SSS04A
02-C70  I                                         34   372HRS                SSS04A
02-080  I                                         38   412RATE               SSS04A
02-090  1*                                                                   SSS04A
03-010  C*************************** CALCULATICNS *****************************SSS04A
C3-C2C  C*                                                                   SSS04A
C3-C30  C    01        HPS       CCMP 40                   101111            SSS05A
03-C40  C*                                                                   SSS05A
03-C50  C    10        HRS       MULT RATE      REG      52H      REGULAR PAY SSS04A
C3-C6C  C*                                                                   SSS04A
03-C70  C    11        HRS       SUB  40.00     OTHRS    42         O  T     SSS04A
C3-C80  C    11        PATE      MULT 1.5       OTRATE   42H         V  I  P SSS04A
03-090  C    11        CTHRS     MULT CTRATE    LTPAY    52H          E  M  A SSS04A
C3-100  C    11        RATE      MULT 40.00     REG        H           R  E  Y SSS04A
03-110  C*                                                                   SSS04A
C3-120  C              REG       ADD  CTPAY     GROSS    52    TOTAL GROSS PAYSSS04A
C3-130  C*                                                                   SSS04A
03-140  C              THRS      ACD  HRS       THRS     52         F  T     SSS04A
03-150  C    11        TCTHRS    ADD  CTHRS     TCTHRS   52          I  O    SSS04A
C3-160  C              TREG      ADD  REG       TREG     62           N  T   SSS04A
03-170  C    11        TOTPAY    ADC  OTPAY     TOTPAY   62            A  A  SSS04A
C3-180  C              TGROSS    ADD  GRCSS     TGRCSS   62             L  L SSS04A
C3-190  C*                                                           S       SSS04A
04-010  U*************************** HEADING LINES ****************************SSS04A
C4-C20  C*                                                                   SSS04A
C4-030  CPAYREG  H  201     1P                                               SSS04A
C4-C40  C          OR       CF                 Correction 3                  SSS04A
C4-C50  C                            (UDATE)Y   10                           SSS04A
C4-C6C  O                                       47 'P A Y R O L L'           SSS04A
04-070  O                                       65 'R E G I S T E R'         SSS04A
04-080  C                                       92 'PAGE'                    SSS04A
04-090  O                            PAGE       97                           SSS04A
04-100  C          H  1     1P                                               SSS04A
04-110  O          CR       CF                                               SSS04A
C4-120  O                                       10 'EMPLOYEE'                SSS04A
C4-130  C                                       64 'REG      O/T      PAY'   SSS04A
C4-140  O                                       86 'REGULAR  OVERTIME'       SSS04A
C4-150  O                                       95 'TCTAL'                   SSS04A
C4-160  C          H  2     1P                                               SSS04A
C4-170  O          CR       CF                                               SSS04A
C4-180  C                                        9 'NUMBER'                  SSS04A
C4-190  C                                       32 'EMPLOYEE NAME'           SSS04A
C4-200  O                                       65 'HRS     HRS      RATE'   SSS04A
04-210  C                                       86 'EARNINGS  EARNINGS'      SSS04A
04-220  C                                       97 'GROSS PAY'               SSS04A
C4-230  C*                                                                   SSS04A
04-240  C*************************** DETAIL LINE ******************************SSS04A
C4-250  O*                                                                   SSS04A
C5-C10  C          D  1     01                                               SSS04A
C5-020  O                            EMPNC       7                           SSS04A
C5-030  C                            LNAME      31                           SSS04A
C5-C40  C                            FNAME      42                           SSS04A
C5-C50  C                            HRS   1    49                           SSS04A
05-060  O                            CTHRS 1B   57                           SSS04A
C5-070  C                            FATE  1    65                           SSS04A
05-C80  O                            PEG   1    75                           SSS04A
C5-C90  O                            CTPAY 1B   85                           SSS04A
05-100  O                            GRCSS 1    96                           SSS04A
C5-110  C*                                                                   SSS04A
05-120  C*************************** TOTAL LINE *******************************SSS04A
C5-130  C*                                                                   SSS04A
05-14C  C          T 2      LR                                               SSS04A
C5-150  O                                       42 '*** FINAL TOTALS'        SSS04A
C5-16C  C                            THRS  1    49                           SSS04A
05-170  C                            TCTHRS1    57                           SSS04A
C5-180  O                            TREG  1    75 '$'                       SSS04A
05-190  O                            TCTPAY1    85 '$'                       SSS04A
05-200  C                            TGROSS1    96 '$'                       SSS04A
C5-210  O*                                                                   SSS04A
05-220  C***************************************************************************SSS04A

E N D  C F  S C L R C E
```

12/17/82 P A Y R O L L R E G I S T E R PAGE 1

EMPLOYEE NUMBER	EMPLOYEE NAME		REG HRS	O/T HRS	PAY RATE	REGULAR EARNINGS	OVERTIME EARNINGS	TOTAL GROSS PAY
010	BEASELY	CAROLE	60.00	.00 (.20)	10.00	600.00	.00	600.00 (Straight time)
485	ALBERTSON	JAMES	37.00	3.00	5.75	230.00	25.89	204.11
172	DOBERMAN	HANS	42.25	.00	6.25	264.06	.00	264.06
501	KAVANAGH	EILEEN	15.00	25.00	5.00	200.00	187.50	12.50
224	LOMBARDO	ANTHONY	45.00	.00	9.50	427.50	.00	427.50
654	LYNCH	ALICE	43.50	.00	8.75	380.63	.00	380.63
345	MACFARLAND	SUSAN	40.00	.00	9.25	370.00	.00	370.00
293	PHILLIPS	DAVID	35.50	4.50	10.00	400.00	67.50	332.50
481	ROSENKRANZ	SAUL	46.25	.00	8.25	381.56	.00	381.56
799	SCHAEFFER	MARION	21.75	18.25	5.75	230.00	157.50	72.50
888	SMITH	ROBERT	40.00	.00	6.25	250.00	.00	250.00
910	TAYLOR	EDWARD	21.75	18.25	5.50	220.00	150.56	69.44
577	ZIMMERMAN	KAREN	45.00	.00	7.50	337.50	.00	337.50
	*** FINAL TOTALS		493.00	69.00		$4,291.25	$588.95	$3,702.30

Figure 4.27 *(continued)*

Debugging Exercise 2

The problem definition for this exercise is shown in Figure 4.28. The program coding sheets in Figure 4.29 contain syntax errors. Identify them and indicate the corrections you would make to the program.

The listing in Figure 4.3Ø includes the error diagnostics produced by running the program as shown. The syntax corrections are circled on the computer listing shown in Figure 4.31. There are, however, logic errors. Your assignment is to desk check this program carefully, find the logic errors, and make the necessary corrections.

Figure 4.28 Problem definition for Debugging Exercise 2.
(Continued on next page.)

Systems Flowchart

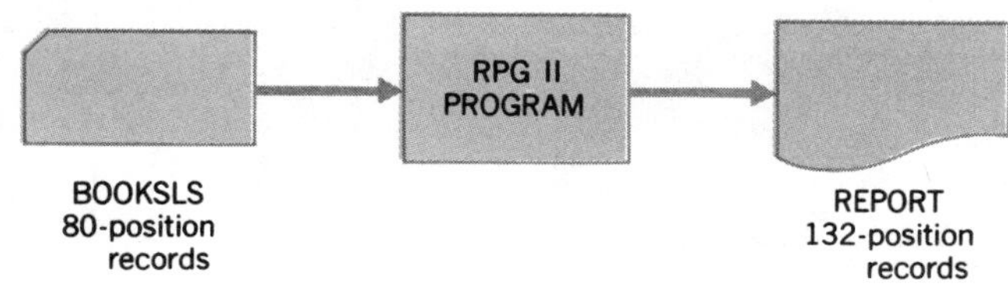

BOOKSLS Record Layout

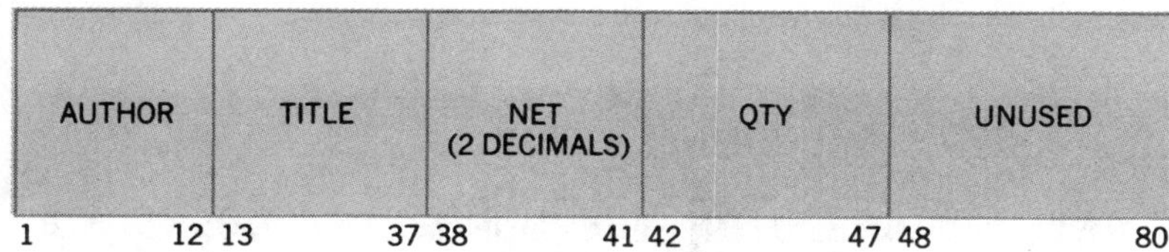

Figure 4.28 *(continued)*

REPORT Printer Spacing Chart

```
H    1  XX/XX/XX                                 ABC PUBLISHING COMPANY                                 PAGE XXØX
     2
H    3                                               ROYALTY REPORT
     4
H    5    AUTHOR            TITLE                        NET    QUANTITY         NET       ROYALTY        ROYALTY
H    6                                                  COST      SOLD          SALES        RATE           PAID
     7
D    8  X----------X  X-----------------------------X  XØ.XX   XXX,XØX       XXX,XXØ.XX     ØX%        $XXX,XX$.XX
D    9  X----------X  X-----------------------------X  XØ.XX   XXX,XØX       XXX,XXØ.XX     ØX%        $XXX,XX$.XX
    10
    11
TLR 12  *** TOTAL ROYALTIES PAID        $X,XXX,XX$.XX
    13
    14
    15
```

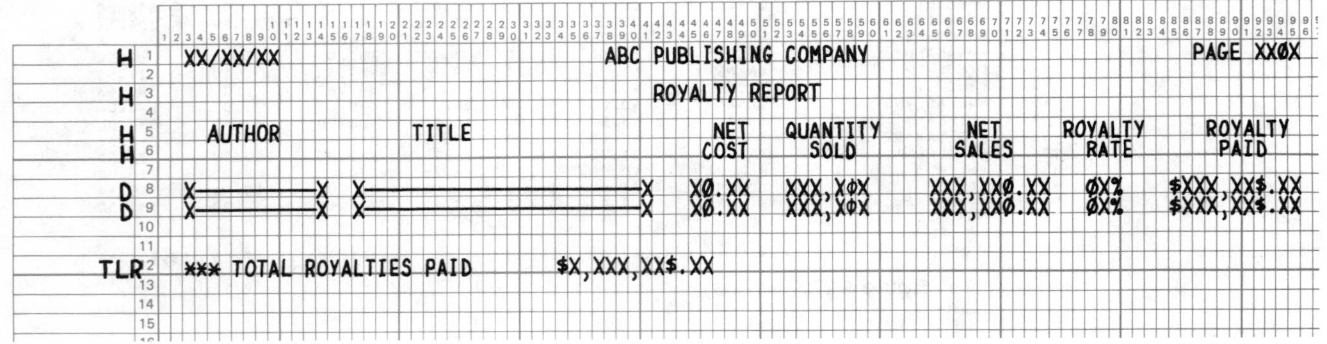

Figure 4.29
Coding sheets for Debugging Exercise 2.
(Continued on next page.)

RPG CONTROL AND FILE DESCRIPTION SPECIFICATIONS

Program	ROYALTY REPORT	Keying Instruction	Graphic	Ø 1 2	Card Electro Number	Page	Ø1 of 5	Program Identification	SSSØ4
Programmer	N. JOHNKE Date 4/17/__		Key	ZERO ONE TWO					

Control Specifications

For the valid entries for a system, refer to the RPG reference manual for that system.

```
01ØH
```

File Description Specifications

For the valid entries for a system, refer to the RPG reference manual for that system.

```
02ØF*******************************************************************
03ØF* THIS PROGRAM CALCULATES ROYALTIES TO BE PAID AN AUTHOR AS A PER-  *
04ØF* CENTAGE OF THE AMOUNT OF THE NET SALES FOR HIS BOOK.THE PERCENT-  *
05ØF* AGE RATE IS BASED ON THE NUMBER OF BOOKS SOLD:5,ØØØ OR LESS,7%;   *
06ØF* 5,ØØ1-1Ø,ØØØ,9%;1Ø,ØØ1-2Ø,ØØØ,17%;OVER 2Ø,ØØØ,25%. IN ADDITION,  *
07ØF* A FINAL TOTAL OF ALL ROYALTIES PAID IS CALCULATED.                *
08ØF*******************************************************************
09ØF*
10ØFBOOKSLS IP  F      8Ø            READØ1 SYSIPT
11ØFREPORT  O   F     132            PRINTERSYSLST
12ØF*
```

RPG INPUT SPECIFICATIONS

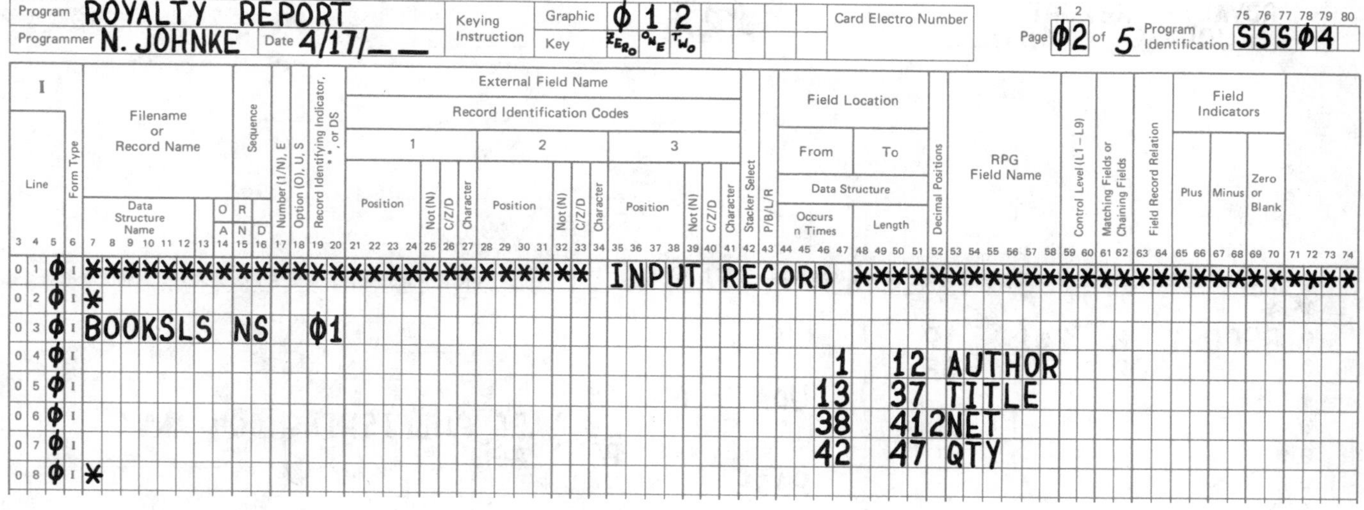

Program: ROYALTY REPORT
Programmer: N. JOHNKE Date: 4/17/__
Graphic: Ø 1 2 Key: ZERO ONE TWO
Page: Ø2 of 5 Program Identification: SSSØ4

Line	Form Type	Filename or Record Name	Sequence	Record Identifying Indicator	Field Location From	Field Location To	Decimal Positions	RPG Field Name
Ø1Ø	I	************************ INPUT RECORD ************************						
Ø2Ø	I	*						
Ø3Ø	I	BOOKSLS	NS	Ø1				
Ø4Ø	I				1	12		AUTHOR
Ø5Ø	I				13	37		TITLE
Ø6Ø	I				38	41	2	NET
Ø7Ø	I				42	47		QTY
Ø8Ø	I	*						

RPG CALCULATION SPECIFICATIONS

Program: ROYALTY REPORT
Programmer: N. JOHNKE Date: 4/17/__
Graphic: Ø 1 2 Key: ZERO ONE TWO
Page: Ø3 of 5 Program Identification: SSSØ4

Line	Form Type	Indicators	Factor 1	Operation	Factor 2	Result Field Name	Length	Decimal Positions	Half Adjust (H)	High (1>2)	Low (1<2)	Equal (1=2)	Comments
Ø1Ø	C	************************ CALCULATIONS ************************											
Ø2Ø	C	*											
Ø3Ø	C	Ø1	QTY	MULT	NET	NETSLS	8	2	H				NET SALES
Ø4Ø	C	***											
Ø5Ø	C	****** DETERMINE ROYALTY RATE BY QUANTITY SOLD:											
Ø6Ø	C	****** IF QTY < OR = 5ØØØ TURN ON INDICATOR Ø7											
Ø7Ø	C	****** IF QTY > 5ØØØ AND < OR = 1ØØØØ TURN ON INDICATOR Ø9											
Ø8Ø	C	****** IF QTY > 1ØØØØ AND < OR = 2ØØØØ TURN ON INDICATOR 17											
Ø9Ø	C	****** IF QTY > 2ØØØØ TURN ON INDICATOR 25											
1ØØ	C	***											
11Ø	C		QTY	COMP	5ØØØ						Ø7	Ø7	
12Ø	C	NØ7	QTY	COMP	1ØØØØ						Ø9	Ø9	
13Ø	C	NØ7NØ9	QTY	COMP	2ØØØØ					25	17	17	
14Ø	C	***											
15Ø	C	****** COMPUTE ROYALTY											
16Ø	C	***											
17Ø	C	Ø7	NETSLS	MULT	.Ø7	ROYLTY	8	2	H				
18Ø	C	Ø9	NETSLS	MULT	.Ø9	ROYLTY			H				
19Ø	C	17	NETSLS	MULT	.17	ROYLTY			H				
2ØØ	C	25	NETSLS	MULT	.25	ROYLTY			H				
21Ø	C	*											
22Ø	C		ROYTLY	ADD	TOTROY	TOTROY	9	2					TOTAL ROYALTIES
23Ø	C	*											

Figure 4.29 *(continued)*

RPG OUTPUT SPECIFICATIONS

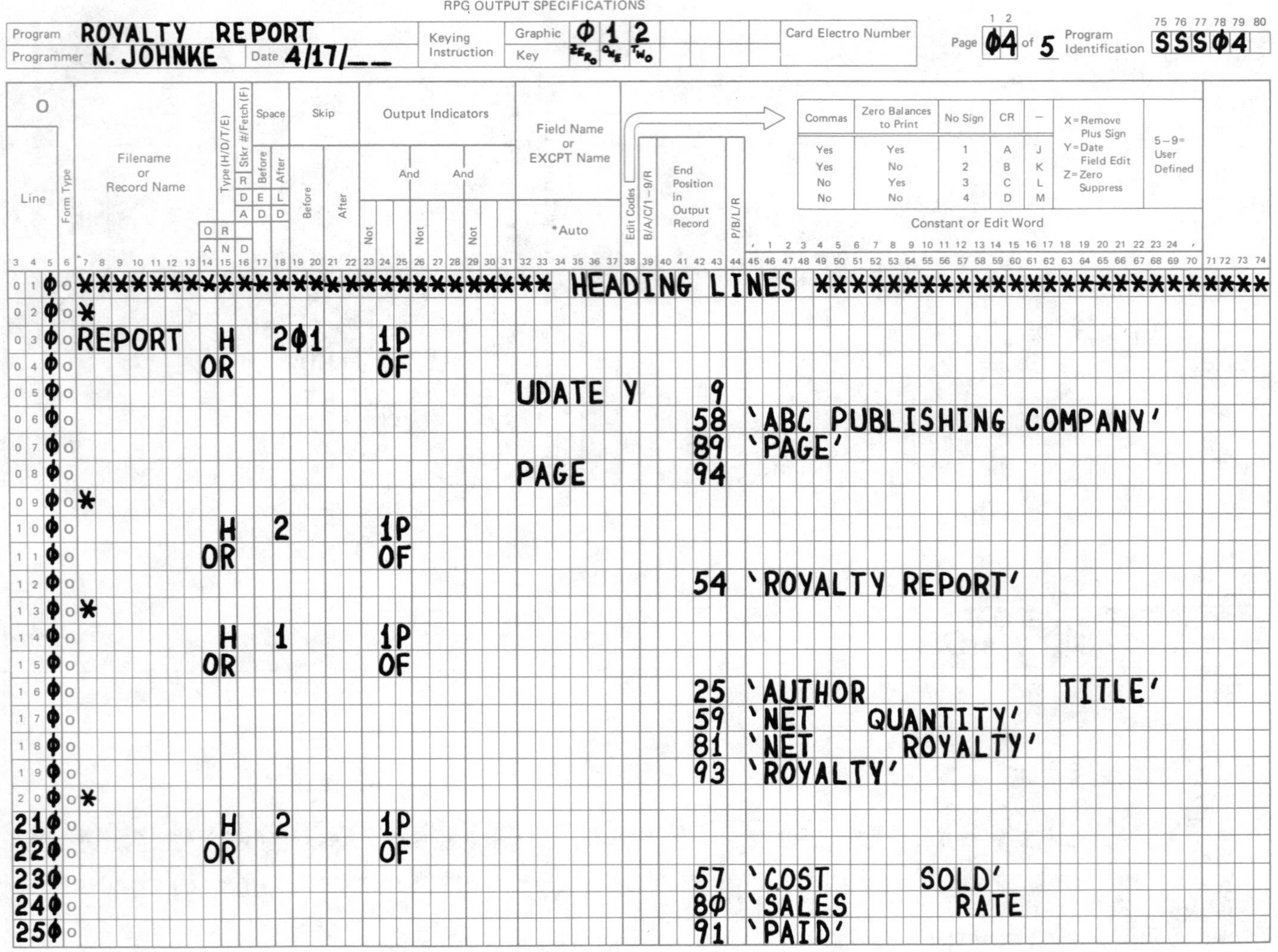

Program: ROYALTY REPORT — Programmer: N. JOHNKE — Date: 4/17/__ — Graphic: Φ 1 2 — Key: ZERO ONE TWO — Page Φ4 of 5 — Program Identification: SSSΦ4

Line	Form Type	Filename or Record Name	Type (H/D/T/E)	Space Before	Space After	Skip Before	Skip After	Output Indicators	Field Name or EXCPT Name	Edit Codes	End Position in Output Record	Constant or Edit Word
01Φ	O	************************** HEADING LINES **************************										
02Φ	O	*										
03Φ	O	REPORT	H		2	Φ1		1P				
04Φ	O		OR					OF				
05Φ	O								UDATE	Y	9	
06Φ	O										58	'ABC PUBLISHING COMPANY'
07Φ	O										89	'PAGE'
08Φ	O								PAGE		94	
09Φ	O	*										
10Φ	O		H		2			1P				
11Φ	O		OR					OF				
12Φ	O										54	'ROYALTY REPORT'
13Φ	O	*										
14Φ	O		H		1			1P				
15Φ	O		OR					OF				
16Φ	O										25	'AUTHOR TITLE'
17Φ	O										59	'NET QUANTITY'
18Φ	O										81	'NET ROYALTY'
19Φ	O										93	'ROYALTY'
20Φ	O	*										
21Φ	O		H		2			1P				
22Φ	O		OR					OF				
23Φ	O										57	'COST SOLD'
24Φ	O										8Φ	'SALES RATE
25Φ	O										91	'PAID'

Figure 4.29 *(continued)*

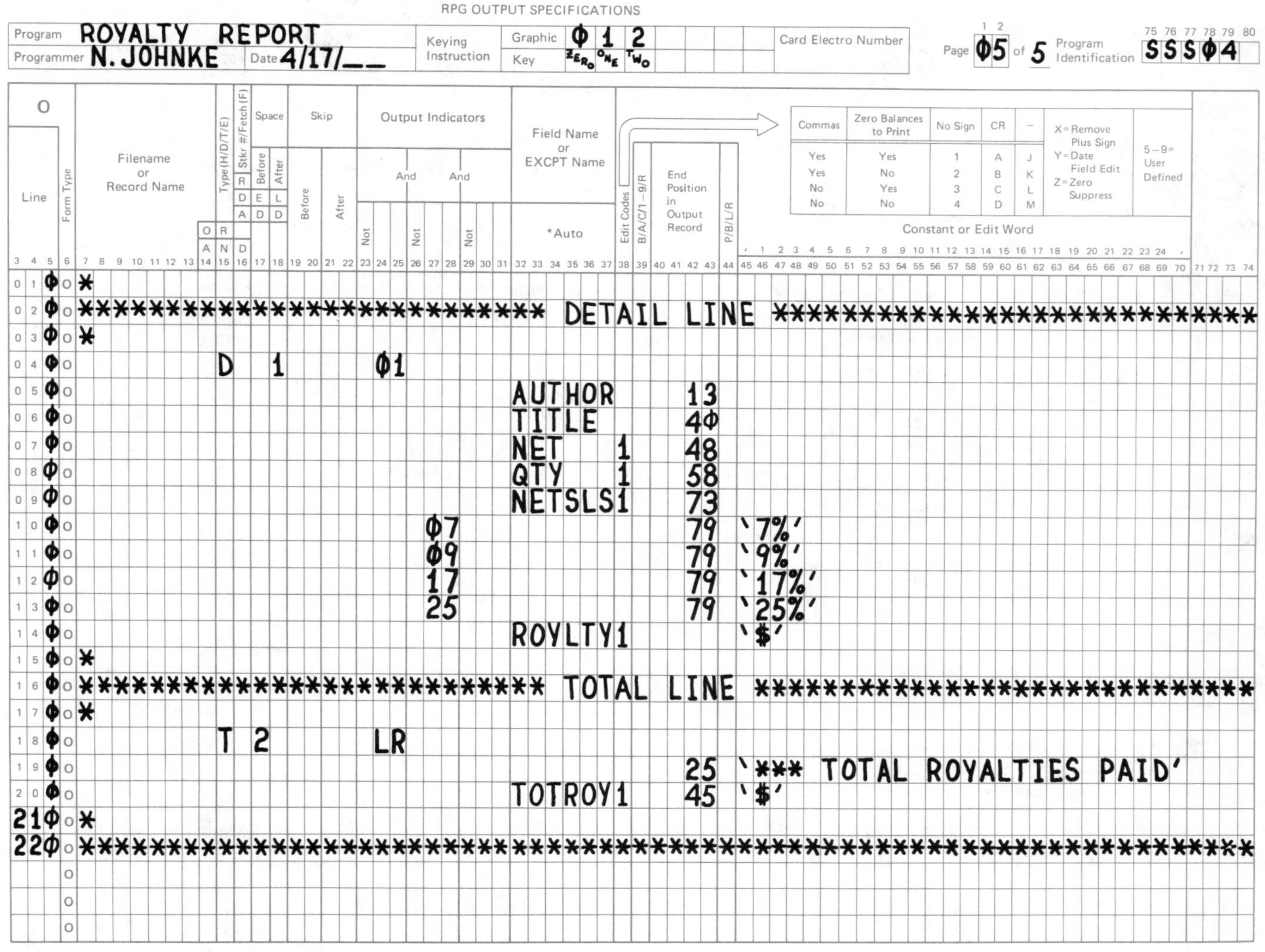

RPG OUTPUT SPECIFICATIONS

Program: ROYALTY REPORT — Programmer: N. JOHNKE — Date: 4/17/__ — Graphic: Φ 1 2 — Key: ZERO ONE TWO — Page Φ5 of 5 — Program Identification: SSSΦ4

Line	Form Type	Filename or Record Name	Type (H/D/T/E)	Space Before	Output Indicators	Field Name or EXCPT Name	Edit Codes	End Position in Output Record	Constant or Edit Word
01Φ	O	*							
02Φ	O	****************************** DETAIL LINE ******************************							
03Φ	O	*							
04Φ	O		D	1	Φ1				
05Φ	O					AUTHOR		13	
06Φ	O					TITLE		4Φ	
07Φ	O					NET	1	48	
08Φ	O					QTY	1	58	
09Φ	O					NETSLS	1	73	
10Φ	O				Φ7			79	'7%'
11Φ	O				Φ9			79	'9%'
12Φ	O				17			79	'17%'
13Φ	O				25			79	'25%'
14Φ	O					ROYLTY	1		'$'
15Φ	O	*							
16Φ	O	****************************** TOTAL LINE ******************************							
17Φ	O	*							
18Φ	O		T	2	LR				
19Φ	O							25	'*** TOTAL ROYALTIES PAID'
20Φ	O					TOTROY	1	45	'$'
21Φ	O	*							
22Φ	O	**							

Figure 4.29 *(continued)*

```
         01-020  F***************************************************************************SSS04
         01-030  F* THIS PROGRAM CALCULATES ROYALTIES TO BE PAID AN AUTHOR AS A PER- *SSS04
         01-040  F* CENTAGE OF THE AMOUNT OF THE NET SALES FOR HIS BOOK.THE PERCENT- *SSS04
         01-050  F* AGE RATE IS BASED ON THE NUMBER OF BOOKS SOLD:5,000 OR LESS,7%;  *SSS04
         01-060  F* 5,001-10,000,9%;10,001-20,000,17%;OVER 20,000,25%. IN ADDITION,  *SSS04
         01-070  F* A FINAL TOTAL OF ALL ROYALTIES PAID IS CALCULATED.                *SSS04
         01-080  F***************************************************************************SSS04
         01-090  F*                                                                   SSS04
0001     01-100  FBOOKSLS IP  F      80            READ01 SYSIPT                      SSS04
0002     01-110  FREPORT  O   F     132      OF    PRINTERSYSLST                      SSS04
         01-120  F*                                                                   SSS04
         02-010  I************************** INPUT RECORD ***************************SSS04
         02-020  I*                                                                   SSS04
0003     02-030  IBOOKSLS NS  01                                                      SSS04
0004     02-040  I                                         1  12 AUTHOR               SSS04
0005     02-050  I                                        13  37 TITLE                SSS04
0006     02-060  I                                        38  412NET                  SSS04
0007     02-070  I                                        42  47 QTY                  SSS04
         02-080  I*                                                                   SSS04
         03-010  C************************** CALCULATIONS ***************************SSS04
         03-020  C*                                                                   SSS04
0008     03-030  C   01      QTY        MULT NET       NETSLS  82H       NET SALES    SSS04
         03-040  C***                                                                 SSS04
         03-050  C****** DETERMINE ROYALTY RATE BY QUANTITY SOLD:                     SSS04
         03-060  C******       IF QTY < OR = 5000 TURN ON INDICATOR 07                SSS04
         03-070  C******       IF QTY > 5000 AND < OR = 10000 TURN ON INDICATOR 09    SSS04
         03-080  C******       IF QTY > 10000 AND < OR = 20000 TURN ON INDICATOR 17   SSS04
         03-090  C******       IF QTY > 20000 TURN ON INDICATOR 25                    SSS04
         03-100  C***                                                                 SSS04
0009     03-110  C           QTY        COMP 5000                  0707               SSS04
0010     03-120  C      N07  QTY        COMP 10000                 0909               SSS04
0011     03-130  C      N07N09QTY       COMP 20000               251717               SSS04
         03-140  C***                                                                 SSS04
         03-150  C****** COMPUTE ROYALTY                                              SSS04
         03-160  C***                                                                 SSS04
0012     03-170  C       07  NETSLS     MULT .07       ROYLTY  82H                    SSS04
                                             $                                                  MSG  178
0013     03-180  C       09  NETSLS     MULT .09       ROYLTY    H                    SSS04
0014     03-190  C       17  NETSLS     MULT .17       ROYLTY    H                    SSS04
0015     03-200  C       25  NETSLS     MULT .25       ROYLTY    H                    SSS04
         03-210  C*                                                                   SSS04
0016     03-210  C           ROYLTY     ADD  TOTROY    TOTROY  92        TOTAL ROYALTIESSSS04
         03-230  C*                                                                   SSS04
         04-010  O************************** HEADING LINES **************************SSS04
         04-020  O*                                                                   SSS04
0017     04-030  OREPORT  H  201     1P                                               SSS04
0018     04-040  O        OR         OF                                               SSS04
0019     04-050  O                            UDATE Y    9                            SSS04
0020     04-060  O                                      58 'ABC PUBLISHING COMPANY'   SSS04
0021     04-070  O                                      89 'PAGE'                     SSS04
0022     04-080  O                            PAGE      94                            SSS04
         04-090  O*                                                                   SSS04
0023     04-100  O        H  2       1P                                               SSS04
0024     04-110  O        OR         OF                                               SSS04
0025     04-120  O                                      54 'ROYALTY REPORT'           SSS04
         04-130  O*                                                                   SSS04
0026     04-140  O        H  1       1P                                               SSS04
0027     04-150  O        OR         OF                                               SSS04
0028     04-160  O                                      25 'AUTHOR          TITLE'    SSS04
0029     04-170  O                                      59 'NET    QUANTITY'          SSS04
0030     04-180  O                                      81 'NET     ROYALTY'          SSS04
0031     04-190  O                                      93 'ROYALTY'                  SSS04
         04-200  O*                                                                   SSS04
0032     04-210  O        H  2       1P                                               SSS04
0033     04-220  O        OR         OF                                               SSS04
0034     04-230  O                                      57 'COST       SOLD'          SSS04
0035     04-240  O                                      80 'SALES       RATE          SSS04
                                                        $                                       MSG  214
0036     04-250  O                                      91 'PAID'                     SSS04
         05-010  O*                                                                   SSS04
         05-020  O************************** DETAIL LINE ****************************SSS04
         05-030  O*                                                                   SSS04
0037     05-040  O        D  1       01                                               SSS04
0038     05-050  O                            AUTHOR    13                            SSS04
0039     05-060  O                            TITLE     40                            SSS04
0040     05-070  O                            NET    1  48                            SSS04
0041     05-080  O                            QTY    1  58                            SSS04
0042     05-090  O                            NETSLS1   73                            SSS04
0043     05-100  O                    07                79 '7%'                       SSS04
0044     05-110  O                    09                79 '9%'                       SSS04
0045     05-120  O                    17                79 '17%'                      SSS04
0046     05-130  O                    25                79 '25%'                      SSS04
0047     05-140  O                            ROYLTY1   94 '$'                        SSS04
         05-150  O*                                                                   SSS04
         05-160  O************************** TOTAL LINE *****************************SSS04
         05-170  O*                                                                   SSS04
0048     05-180  O        T  2       LR                                               SSS04
0049     05-190  O                                      25 '*** TOTAL ROYALTIES PAID' SSS04
0050     05-200  O                            TOTROY1   45 '$'                        SSS04
         05-210  O*                                                                   SSS04
         05-220  O***************************************************************************SSS04

     E N D   O F   S O U R C E
```

Figure 4.30 Program listing with error diagnostics for Debugging Exercise 2. *(Continued on next page.)*

```
                    C O M P I L E R   D I A G N O S T I C S   S U M M A R Y

ILN178   FACTOR 2 IS INVALID. SPEC IS DROPPED IF AN ENTRY IS REQUIRED.
       D 00012     C3-170     MULT
ILN214   LEADING/CLOSING APOSTROPHE IS MISSING ON CONSTANT. SPEC IS DROPPED.
       D 00035     C4-240
ILN413   EDIT SPECIFIED WITH ALPHAMERIC FIELD. DROP EDITING.
         00041     C5-080
ILN442   OPERAND MUST BE NUMERIC. SPEC IS DROPPED.
       D 00008     C3-030     FACTOR 1 ENTRY
ILN485   FACTOR 1 AND FACTOR 2 OF COMP OR LOKUP MUST BOTH BE EITHER NUMERIC OR ALPHAMERIC. SPEC IS DROPPED.
       D 00009     C3-110
       D 00010     C3-120
       D 00011     C3-130
```

Figure 4.30 *(continued)*

Figure 4.31
Program listing that contains logic errors for Debugging Exercise 2.
(Continued on next page.)

```
      01-020  F*************************************************************************SSS04
      01-030  F* THIS PROGRAM CALCULATES ROYALTIES TO BE PAID AN AUTHOR AS A PER-  *SSS04
      01-040  F* CENTAGE OF THE AMOUNT OF THE NET SALES FOR HIS BOOK.THE PERCENT-  *SSS04
      01-050  F* AGE RATE IS BASED ON THE NUMBER OF BOOKS SOLD:5,000 OR LESS,7%;   *SSS04
      01-060  F* 5,001-10,000,9%;10,001-20,000,17%;OVER 20,000,25%. IN ADDITION,   *SSS04
      01-070  F* A FINAL TOTAL OF ALL ROYALTIES PAID IS CALCULATED.                *SSS04
      01-080  F*************************************************************************SSS04
      01-090  F*                                                                        SSS04
0001  01-100  FBOOKSLS IP  F       80              READ01 SYSIPT                        SSS04
0002  01-110  FREPORT  O   F      132      OF      PRINTERSYSLST                        SSS04
      01-120  F*                                                                        SSS04
      02-010  I**************************** INPUT RECORD ******************************SSS04
      02-020  I*                                                                        SSS04
0003  02-030  IBOOKSLS NS  01                                                           SSS04
0004  02-040  I                                             1  12 AUTHOR                SSS04
0005  02-050  I                                            13  37 TITLE                 SSS04
0006  02-060  I                                            38  412NET                   SSS04
0007  02-070  I                                            42  470QTY                   SSS04
      02-080  I*                                                                        SSS04
      03-010  C**************************** CALCULATIONS *****************************SSS04
      03-020  C*                                                                        SSS04
0008  03-030  C   01       QTY       MULT NET       NETSLS  82H       NET SALES         SSS04
      03-040  C***                                                                      SSS04
      03-050  C****** DETERMINE ROYALTY RATE BY QUANTITY SOLD:                          SSS04
      03-060  C******        IF QTY < OR = 5000 TURN ON INDICATOR 07                    SSS04
      03-070  C******        IF QTY > 5000 AND < OR = 10000 TURN ON INDICATOR 09        SSS04
      03-080  C******        IF QTY > 10000 AND < OR = 20000 TURN ON INDICATOR 17       SSS04
      03-090  C******        IF QTY > 20000 TURN ON INDICATOR 25                        SSS04
      03-100  C***                                                                      SSS04
0009  03-110  C            QTY       COMP 5000                   0707                   SSS04
0010  03-120  C      N07   QTY       COMP 10000                  0909                   SSS04
0011  03-130  C      N07N09QTY       COMP 20000                251717                   SSS04
      03-140  C***                                                                      SSS04
      03-150  C****** COMPUTE ROYALTY                                                   SSS04
      03-160  C***                                                                      SSS04
0012  03-170  C      07    NETSLS    MULT .07       ROYLTY  82H                         SSS04
0013  03-180  C      09    NETSLS    MULT .09       ROYLTY    H                         SSS04
0014  03-190  C      17    NETSLS    MULT .17       ROYLTY    H                         SSS04
0015  03-200  C      25    NETSLS    MULT .25       ROYLTY    H                         SSS04
      03-210  C*                                                                        SSS04
0016  03-220  C            ROYLTY    ADD  TOTROY    TOTROY  92        TOTAL ROYALTIESSSS04
      03-230  C*                                                                        SSS04
      04-010  O**************************** HEADING LINES ****************************SSS04
      04-020  O*                                                                        SSS04
0017  04-030  OREPORT  H  201    1P                                                     SSS04
0018  04-040  O        OR        OF                                                     SSS04
0019  04-050  O                           UDATE Y    9                                  SSS04
0020  04-060  O                                     58 'ABC PUBLISHING COMPANY'         SSS04
0021  04-070  O                                     89 'PAGE'                           SSS04
0022  04-080  O                           PAGE      94                                  SSS04
      04-090  O*                                                                        SSS04
0023  04-100  O        H  2      1P                                                     SSS04
0024  04-110  O        OR        OF                                                     SSS04
0025  04-120  O                                     54 'ROYALTY REPORT'                 SSS04
      04-130  O*                                                                        SSS04
0026  04-140  O        H  1      1P                                                     SSS04
0027  04-150  O        OR        OF                                                     SSS04
0028  04-160  O                                     25 'AUTHOR              TITLE'      SSS04
0029  04-170  O                                     59 'NET    QUANTITY'                SSS04
0030  04-180  O                                     81 'NET      ROYALTY'               SSS04
0031  04-190  O                                     93 'ROYALTY'                        SSS04
      04-200  O*                                                                        SSS04
0032  04-210  O        H  2      1P                                                     SSS04
0033  04-220  O        OR        OF                                                     SSS04
0034  04-230  O                                     57 'COST        SOLD'               SSS04
0035  04-240  O                                     80 'SALES          RATE'            SSS04
0036  04-250  O                                     91 'PAID'                           SSS04
      05-010  O*                                                                        SSS04
      05-020  O**************************** DETAIL LINE ******************************SSS04
      05-030  O*                                                                        SSS04
0037  05-040  O        D  1      01                                                     SSS04
0038  05-050  O                           AUTHOR    13                                  SSS04
0039  05-060  O                           TITLE     40                                  SSS04
0040  05-070  O                           NET   1   48                                  SSS04
0041  05-080  O                           QTY   1   58                                  SSS04
0042  05-090  O                           NETSLS1   73                                  SSS04
0043  05-100  O                  07                 79 '7%'                             SSS04
0044  05-110  O                  09                 79 '9%'                             SSS04
0045  05-120  O                  17                 79 '17%'                            SSS04
0046  05-130  O                  25                 79 '25%'                            SSS04
0047  05-140  O                           ROYLTY1   94 '$'                              SSS04
      05-150  O*                                                                        SSS04
      05-160  O**************************** TOTAL LINE *******************************SSS04
      05-170  O*                                                                        SSS04
0048  05-180  O        T  2      LR                                                     SSS04
0049  05-190  O                                     25 '*** TOTAL ROYALTIES PAID'       SSS04
0050  05-200  O                           TOTROY1   45 '$'                              SSS04
      05-210  O*                                                                        SSS04
      05-220  O*************************************************************************SSS04

                E N D  O F  S O U R C E
```

Numeric field

Zero—not a letter

Missing quote

```
7/29/82                    ABC PUBLISHING COMPANY                                   PAGE   1

                               ROYALTY REPORT

  AUTHOR         TITLE                        NET    QUANTITY       NET       ROYALTY     ROYALTY
                                              COST     SOLD        SALES       RATE        PAID

GREEN,A.C.    NEVER SAY NEVER                 7.95     7,890     62,725.50     9%       $5,645.30
JONES,S.S.    GUIDE TO DOWNTOWN HOBOKEN      11.95     5,000     59,750.00     9% 7%    $5,377.50 <— Incorrect royalty
SMITH,H.A.    RPG II FOR FUN AND PROFIT      14.95    25,050    374,497.50    25%      $93,624.38
BROWN,J.B.    THE SENSUOUS COMPUTER           9.95    15,100    150,245.00    17%      $25,541.65
TAYLOR,P.J.   PLUMBING MADE EASY              4.95    10,000     49,500.00    17% 9%    $8,415.00 <— Incorrect royalty
WHITE,R.D.    DIARY OF A MAC PROGRAMMER       9.95     4,999     49,740.05    17% 7%    $8,455.81 <— Incorrect royalty
JENSEN,N.E.   WILL FRIDAY EVER COME          10.95    19,999    218,989.05    17%      $37,228.14
                                                                               ↑
*** TOTAL ROYALTIES PAID          $184,287.78 —— Incorrect          Incorrect logic
                                                  total              to determine
                                                                     royalty % rate
```

Figure 4.31 *(continued)*

Practice Problems

Note: The use of the SETOF instruction may simplify the solutions to the following problems. Refer to the DEBUG instruction on page 353 to check the status of the indicators if necessary.

1. A real estate salesperson is paid a commission based on the amount of the sale. If the sale is over $50,000, then a 6% commission is received. For sales of $50,000 or less, only a 4.5% commission is issued. Using the following problem definition, write an RPG program to produce the required results.

Systems Flowchart

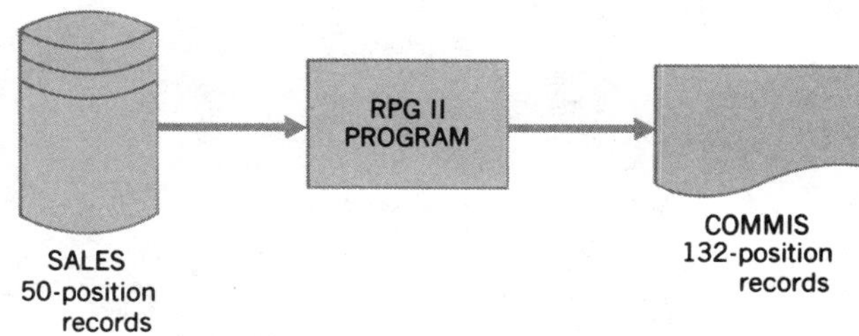

SALES Record Layout

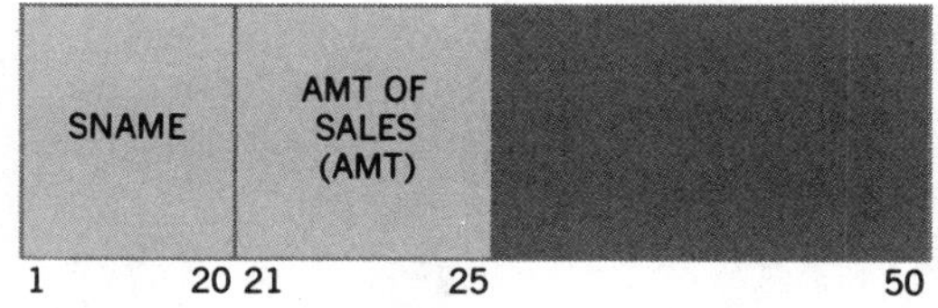

COMMIS Printer Spacing Chart

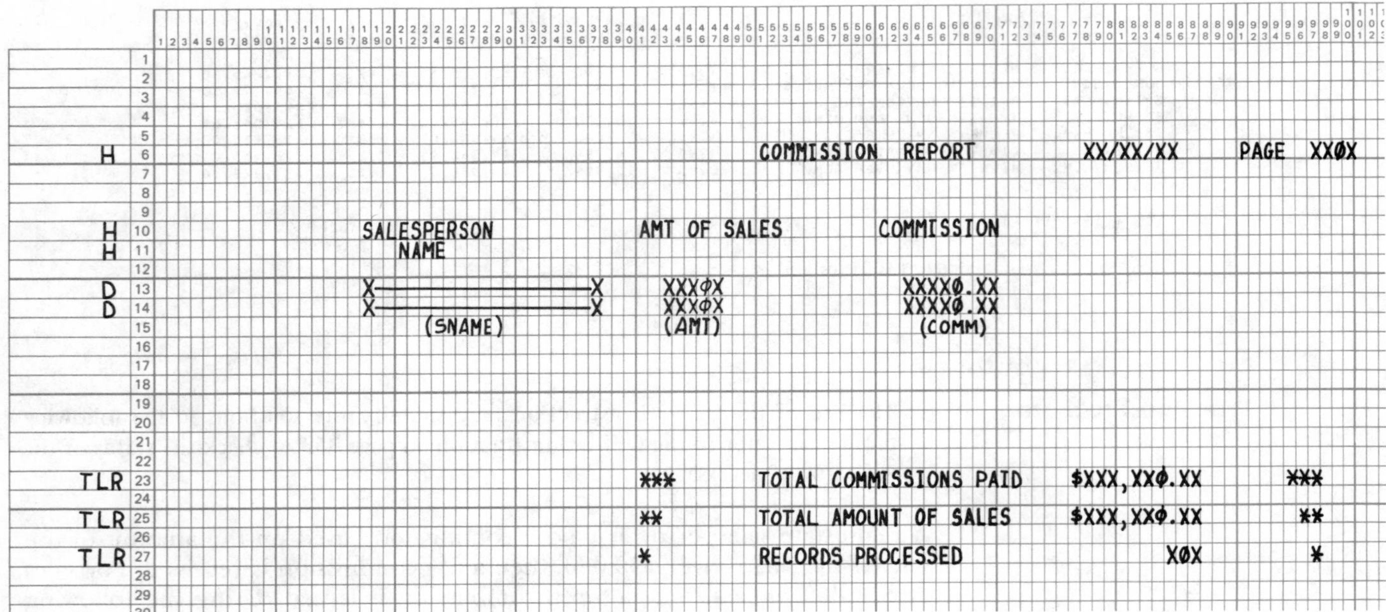

2. Using the following problem definition, code an RPG program to produce the required results.

Systems Flowchart

PAYROLL Record Layout

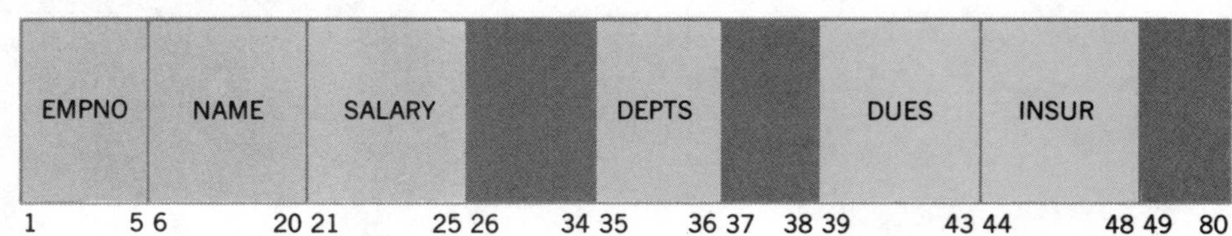

SUMMARY Printer Spacing Chart

```
H    6                          PAYROLL SUMMARY REPORT

TLR  9   % OF EMPLOYEES WHO PAY UNION DUES                       XØ.X

TLR 12   % OF EMPLOYEES WHO EARN < 25000 AND HAVE > 2
TLR 13                                         DEPENDENTS        XØ.X

TLR 16   % OF EMPLOYEES WHO PAY INSURANCE > 3% OF SALARY         XØ.X
```

3. Code an RPG program to calculate the royalty to be paid to an author by a publishing house. The input record contains fields describing the quantity of books sold (QTY) and the (NET) cost of each. The royalty rate is a sliding scale based on the quantity of books sold.

No. of Books Sold	*Royalty Rate %*
5ØØØ or less	7
5ØØ1–1Ø,ØØØ	9
1Ø,ØØ1–2Ø,ØØØ	17
over 2Ø,ØØØ	25

The royalty paid is computed by multiplying the royalty rate by the net sales. In order to determine the net sales, multiply the quantity sold by the net cost. The problem definition is shown here.

Systems Flowchart

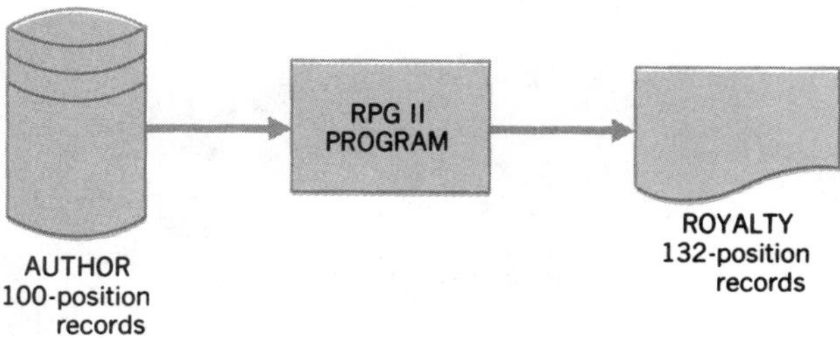

AUTHOR Record Layout

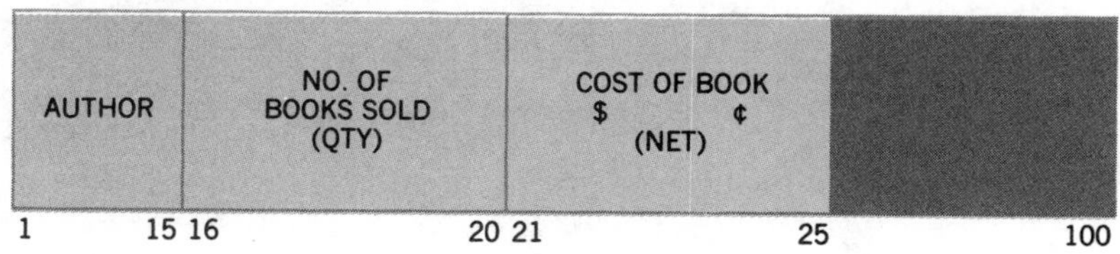

ROYALTY Printer Spacing Chart

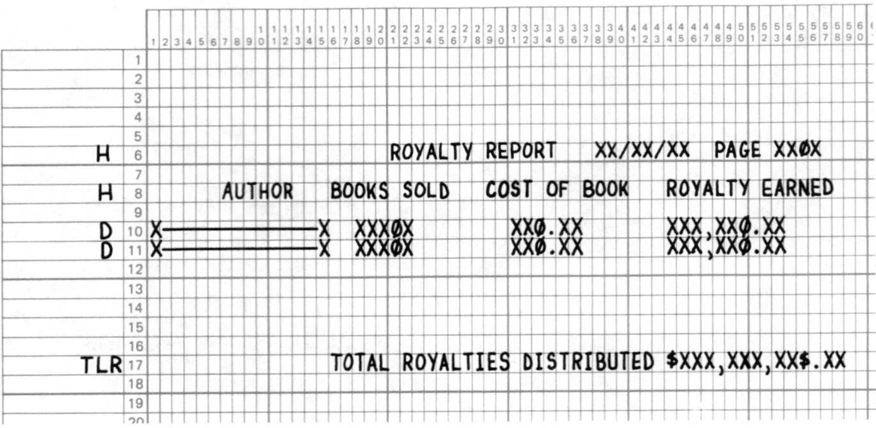

4. Using the following problem definition, code an RPG program to produce the required results.

Systems Flowchart

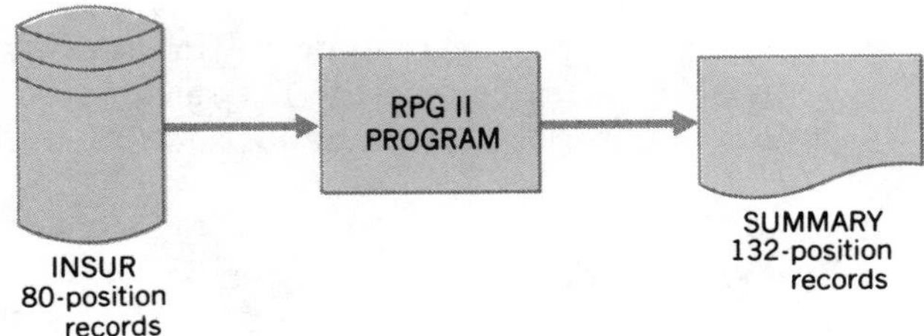

INSUR Record Layout

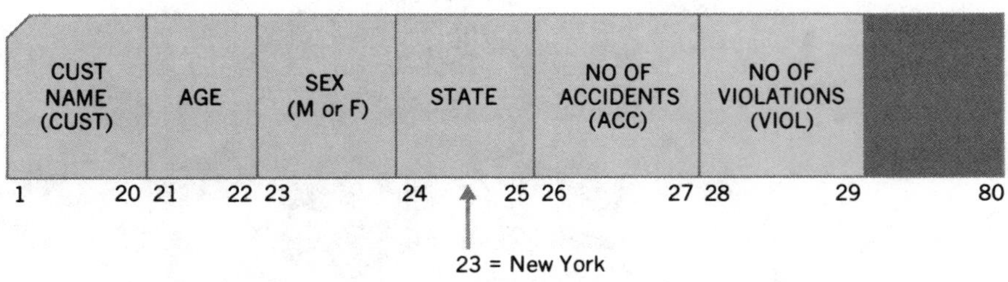

SUMMARY Printer Spacing Chart

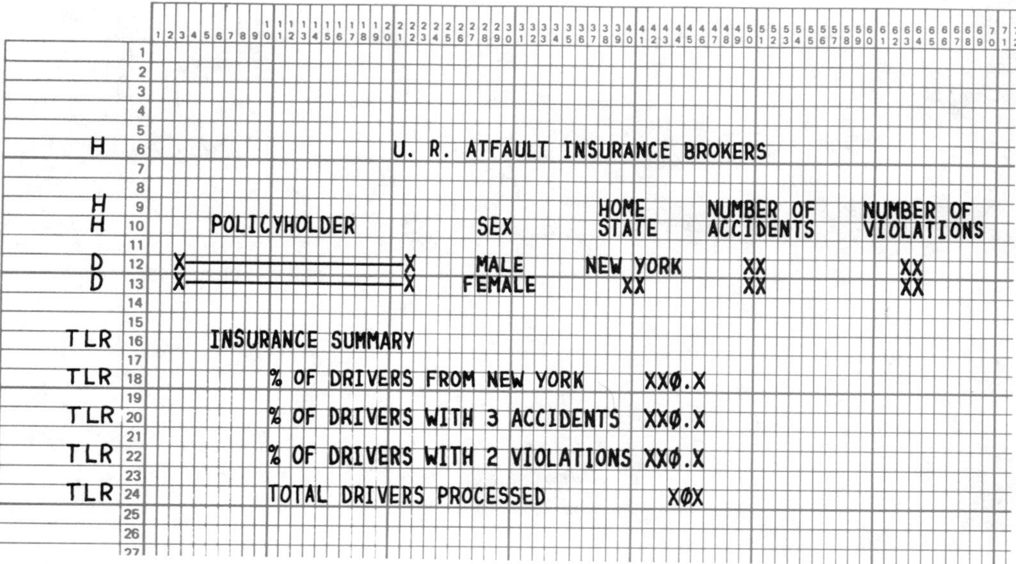

5. Code an RPG program to identify items in an inventory file that are below or equal to the reorder point (sometimes referred to as a minimum) or greater than the maximum number that should be on hand. The problem definition is shown here.

Systems Flowchart

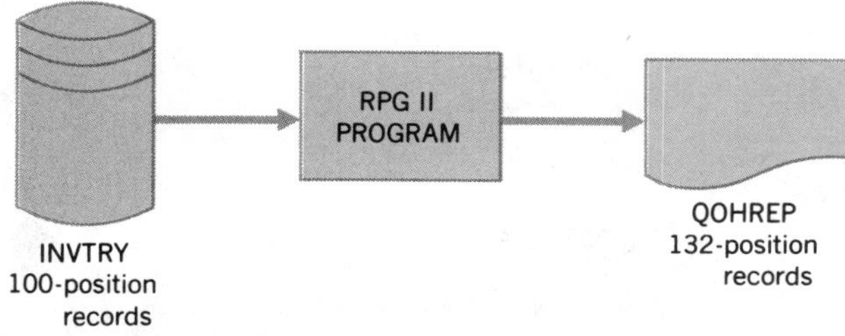

INVTRY Record Layout

ITEM	MIN	MAX	QOH (QUANTITY ON HAND)	
1–5	6–10	11–15	16–20	21–100

QOHREP Printer Spacing Chart

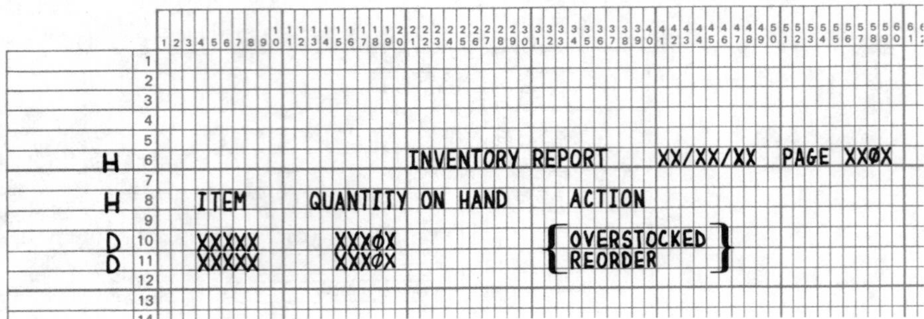

For each item, print quantity on hand (QOH). *If* QOH *is greater than the maximum to be stocked, print* "OVERSTOCKED". *If* QOH *is less than the minimum to be stocked, print* "REORDER".

6. Using the following problem definition, code an RPG program to produce the required output. Print the name and description for each blue-eyed blonde over 6 feet tall and weighing more than 18Ø pounds.

Systems Flowchart

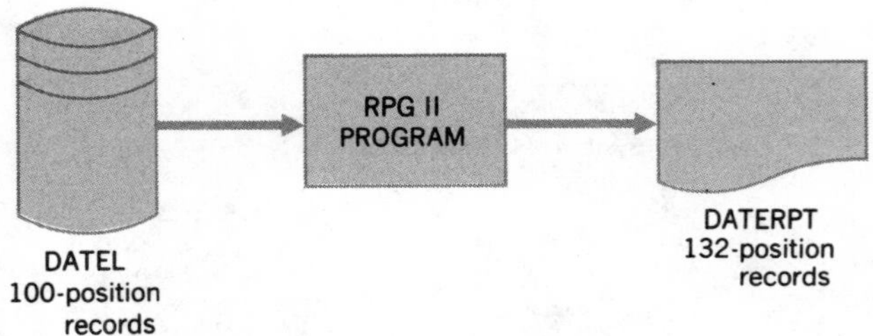

DATEL Record Layout

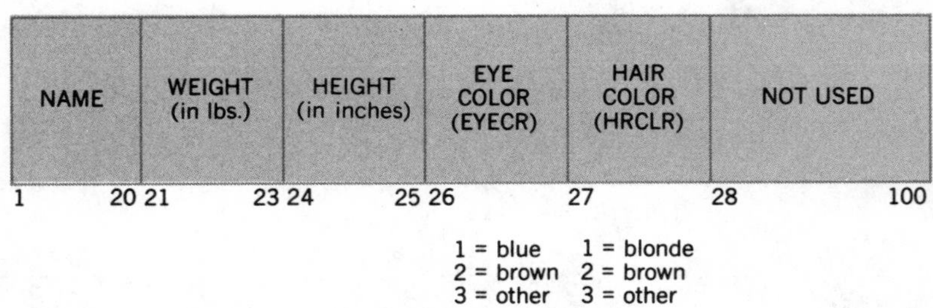

DATERPT Printer Spacing Chart

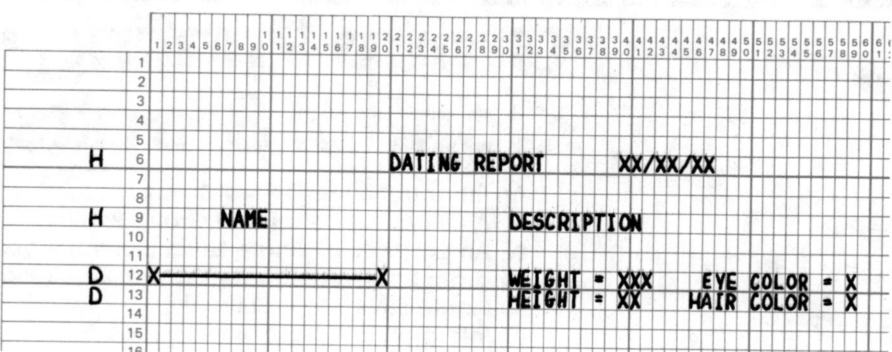

CHAPTER 5

Group Printing Using Control Breaks

Objectives

To provide an understanding of

- What a control break is and how it is used in printing.
- Programming requirements for single, double, and triple level control break printing.
- How data can be printed as a group-indicated field.
- How to handle the test for a page overflow condition.

I.

An Introduction to Control Break Processing

A. A Review of Detail and Group Printing

Thus far, we have focused on the printing of an individual line for each input record read. This is called **detail printing**. Sometimes, however, we wish to print total or summary lines for a group of records. This is called **group printing**. Group printing can be performed either in place of or in addition to detail printing. Thus far, we have considered group printing only for purposes of printing a final total. You will recall that we may accumulate a total field by adding to it each time a record is read. We print the T or total line that will contain the final total when the LR (last record) indicator is turned on. For a comparison of detail printing and group printing, see Figure 5.1.

This chapter considers group printing in far more depth, focusing on a specific type of group printing that uses **control fields** to indicate when totals are to print.

Figure 5.1
Comparison of detail printing and group printing

(*a*) Detail Report

SALES REPORT
BY ITEM NUMBER

Ø8/Ø4/85

PAGE 2

ITEM NO.	ITEM DESCRIPTION	SALES AMOUNT
587	WIDGETS	142.38
587	WIDGETS	382.27
763	WAXED PAPER	872.53
763	WAXED PAPER	821.33
763	WAXED PAPER	168.38
923	BALLOONS	858.21
923	BALLOONS	923.73
923	BALLOONS	15.82
923	BALLOONS	77.93

(*b*) Group Report

SUMMARY SALES REPORT
BY ITEM NUMBER

Ø8/Ø4/85

PAGE 2

ITEM NO.	ITEM DESCRIPTION	SALES AMOUNT
587	WIDGETS	524.65*
763	WAXED PAPER	1862.24*
923	BALLOONS	1875.69*

B. An Example of Single Level Control Break Processing

Consider the problem definition in Figure 5.2. The output requires the processing of three input fields: DEPT, SLSNAM, and AMT. Each input record consists of the salesperson's department number, the salesperson's name, and the amount

Figure 5.2 Problem definition for single level control break program.

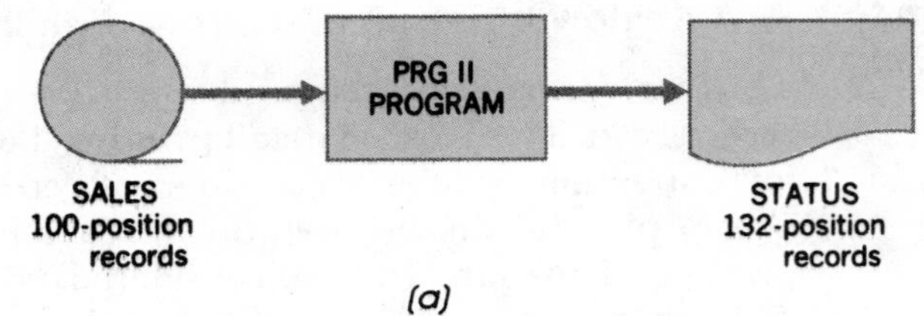

(a)

SALES Record Layout

S	DEPT	SLSNAM	AMT XXX.XX	UNUSED
1	2 3	4 15	16 21	22 100

(b)

STATUS Printer Spacing Chart

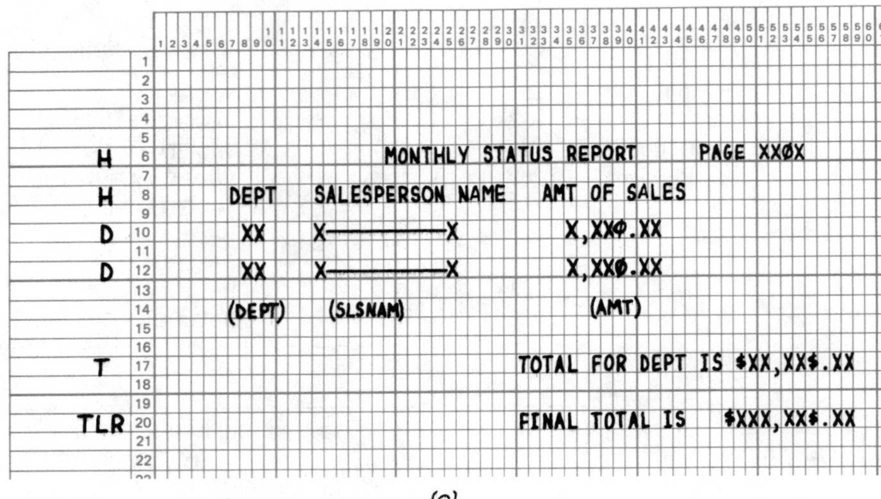

(c)

of sales that he or she accrued for the week. There may be numerous salesperson records for DEPT Ø1, Ø2, and so on. Thus each department will contain records for several different salespersons.

For this problem, detail printing is required; that is, each input record is to be printed, as in previous examples. In addition to this detail printing, summary lines indicating department totals must also print. Thus group printing is required where a group or total line is written for each department.

In summary, after all records for DEPT Ø1 have been read and printed, a total for DEPT Ø1 will print. Similarly, after all records for DEPT Ø2 have been read and printed, a total for DEPT Ø2 will print. This type of processing requires all DEPT Ø1 records to be entered first followed by the next DEPT's records, and so on. That is, the file of input records must be in sequence by department number.

Detail lines print in the usual way after each input record is read and processed. In addition to detail printing after each input record is read, the amount of sales is then added to a DEPT total. Department totals will print whenever a change in DEPT occurs. DEPT, then, is called the control field.

Thus all salesperson records for DEPT Ø1 will be read and printed, and a DEPT total will be accumulated. This processing continues until a salesperson record is read that contains a *different* DEPT. When this record with a different DEPT is read, the totals for DEPT Ø1 will print. Since totals are printed after a change occurs in DEPT, the control field, this type of group processing is called **control break** processing.

In order for the department totals to print correctly, one for each department, the input records must be sorted into DEPT sequence. That is, all salesperson records for DEPT Ø1 must be read first, followed by salesperson records for DEPT Ø2, and so on. See Figure 5.3 for an illustration of the output that this type of control break processing produces.

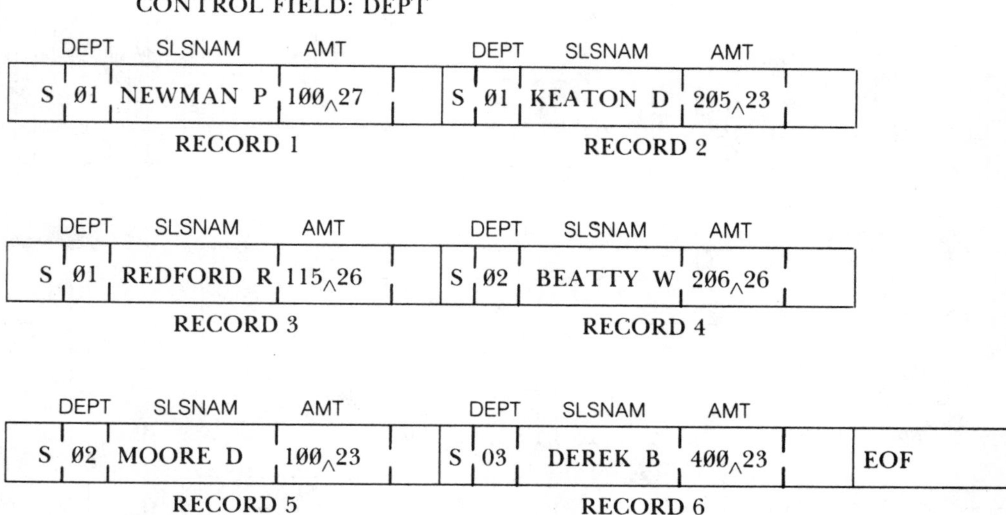

MONTHLY STATUS REPORT PAGE 2

DEPT	SALESPERSON NAME	AMT OF SALES
Ø1	NEWMAN P	1ØØ.27
Ø1	KEATON D	2Ø5.23
Ø1	REDFORD R	115.26
		TOTAL FOR DEPT IS $42Ø.76
Ø2	BEATTY W	2Ø6.26
Ø2	MOORE D	1ØØ.23
		TOTAL FOR DEPT IS $3Ø6.49
Ø3	DEREK B	4ØØ.23
		TOTAL FOR DEPT IS $4ØØ.23
		FINAL TOTAL IS $1,127.48

Figure 5.3
Example of input and output for a control break procedure.

II. Program Requirements for Control Break Processing

A. Single Level Control Breaks

For each input record read, a detail line will be printed. In addition, the AMT field will be added to a department total, which we will call DTOTAL.

All DEPT Ø1 records, then, will be read, and the DTOTAL will be accumulated. The total line, "TOTAL FOR DEPT IS $XX,XXX.XX" will print only *after* a record with the next DEPT is read.

The File Description Specifications are similar to those in previous programs.

RPG CONTROL AND FILE DESCRIPTION SPECIFICATIONS

Program | Keying Instruction | Graphic | Key | Card Electro Number | Page (1 2) of | Program Identification (75 76 77 78 79 80)
Programmer | Date

Control Specifications

For the valid entries for a system, refer to the RPG reference manual for that system.

H — Line (3–5) | Form Type (6) | Size to Compile (7–9) | Object Output (10) | Listing Options (11) | Size to Execute (12–14) | Debug (15) | Reserved (16–17) | Currency Symbol (18) | Date Format (19) | Date Edit (20) | Inverted Print (21) | Reserved (22) | Number of Print Positions (23–25) | Alternate Collating Sequence (26) | Reserved (27–36) | Inquiry (37) | Reserved (38–39) | Sign Handling (40) | 1 P Forms Position (41) | Indicator Setting (42) | File Translation (43) | Punch MFCU Zeros (44) | Nonprint Characters (45) | Reserved (46) | Table Load Halt (47) | Shared I/O (48) | Field Print (49) | Formatted Dump (50) | RPG to RPG II Conversion (51) | Number of Formats (52–53) | S/3 Conversion (54) | Subprogram (55) | CICS/DL/I (56) | Transparent Literal (57) | 58–74

```
0 1   H
```

File Description Specifications

For the valid entries for a system, refer to the RPG reference manual for that system.

F — Line (3–5) | Form Type (6) | Filename (7–14) | File Type: I/O/U/C/D (15) | File Designation: P/S/C/R/T/D/F (16) | End of File: E (17) | Sequence: A/D (18) | File Format: F/V/S/M/D/E (19) | Block Length (20–23) | Record Length (24–27) | Mode of Processing: L/R (28) | Length of Key Field or of Record Address Field (29–30) | Record Address Type: A/P/I/K (31) | Type of File Organization or Additional Area: I/X/D/T/R/ or 2 (32) | Overflow Indicator (33–34) | Key Field Starting Location (35–38) | External Record Name (19–28) | Extension Code E/L (39) | Device (40–46) | Symbolic Device (47–52) | Labels S/N/E/M (53) | Name of Label Exit (54–59) | Extent Exit for DAM | Storage Index (60–65) | Continuation Lines: K, Option, Entry | A/U (66) | File Addition/Unordered; Number of Tracks for Cylinder Overflow (67–68); Number of Extents (69); Tape Rewind: R/U/N (70); File Condition U1–U8, UC (71–72) | 73–74

```
0 2 Ø F SALES   IP  F     1ØØ             TAPE
0 3 Ø F STATUS  O   F     132      OF     PRINTER
0 4   F
0 5   F
```

The specific input field to be used for the control field is assigned the **level indicator** L1 (level one control field). Thus, to indicate that control break processing will occur, we specify the control field on the Input Specifications form by coding L1 in the Control Level Positions (columns 59–6Ø) of the appropriate input field. Note that one and only one field may be designated as the L1 field.

RPG INPUT SPECIFICATIONS

Line	Form Type	Filename or Record Name	Sequence	Record Identifying Indicator	Position	Not (N)	C/Z/D	Character	From	To	Decimal Positions	RPG Field Name	Control Level (L1–L9)
01	I	SALES	NS	Ø4	1		C	S					
02	I								2	3		DEPT	L1
03	I								4	15		SLSNAM	
04	I								16	21	2	AMT	
05	I			99	1	N	C	S					
06	I												
07	I												

Indicator 01 is turned on when there is an S in column 1

Designates DEPT as control field

*In case column 1 does not have an S—indicator 99 goes on

L1 designates DEPT as a "level one" control field. Level one is used when there is a **single level control break** field to be processed. Multiple level control breaks will be considered later in this chapter.

In the problem just presented, there are two calculations to be performed, one that is performed at **detail time**, after a detail record is read, and one that is performed at "control break" or **total time**, when there is a change in the L1 or DEPT field.

Detail time occurs when the record identifying indicator Ø4 is on. When a record with an "S" in the first position is read, AMT is to be added to a department total, (DTOTAL).

Control break or total time occurs when there is a change in the control field. When a record with a different DEPT is read, DTOTAL is to be added to a final total (FTOTAL).

The following describes the calculations performed at detail time and at total time.

RPG CALCULATION SPECIFICATIONS

Line	Form Type	Control Level (L0–L9, LR, SR, AN/OR)	Indicators	Factor 1	Operation	Factor 2	Result Field Name	Length	Decimal Positions
01	C		Ø4	AMT	ADD	DTOTAL	DTOTAL	7	2
02	C	L1		DTOTAL	ADD	FTOTAL	FTOTAL	8	2
03	C								
04	C								

Once again, it is important to be aware of the RPG II Logic Cycle so that you can become familiar with the sequence of operations performed by the computer. After a record is read, the computer tests for end of file. If there are still records to process, the next operation the computer performs is a test for a change in the control field. If there is a change, the computer performs L1 calculations. It then prints total-line output, which uses L1 specifications. Both the L1 calculations and total-line printing are performed *prior* to processing the new detail record. In this way, a record with a change in DEPT will first cause the previous DEPT total (DTOTAL) to print, prior to any detail calculations or printing for the next DEPT.

The output specifications for a control break problem would include coding for

H records for printing Headings.

D records for printing Detail lines.

T records for printing Control Totals.

The T or Total line will print when the L1 indicator is on. We also wish to print a final total when the LR indicator is on. But after the last record has been processed it is necessary to first print the last control total before printing this final total. This is handled automatically by RPG II. When the LR indicator is turned on, all control level indicators are automatically turned on as well. Thus, when the LR indicator is turned on, the L1 indicator will be turned on too. The computer will print the last DEPT total (DTOTAL) and then the final total (FTOTAL).

The Output Specifications for our control break procedure would be as follows.

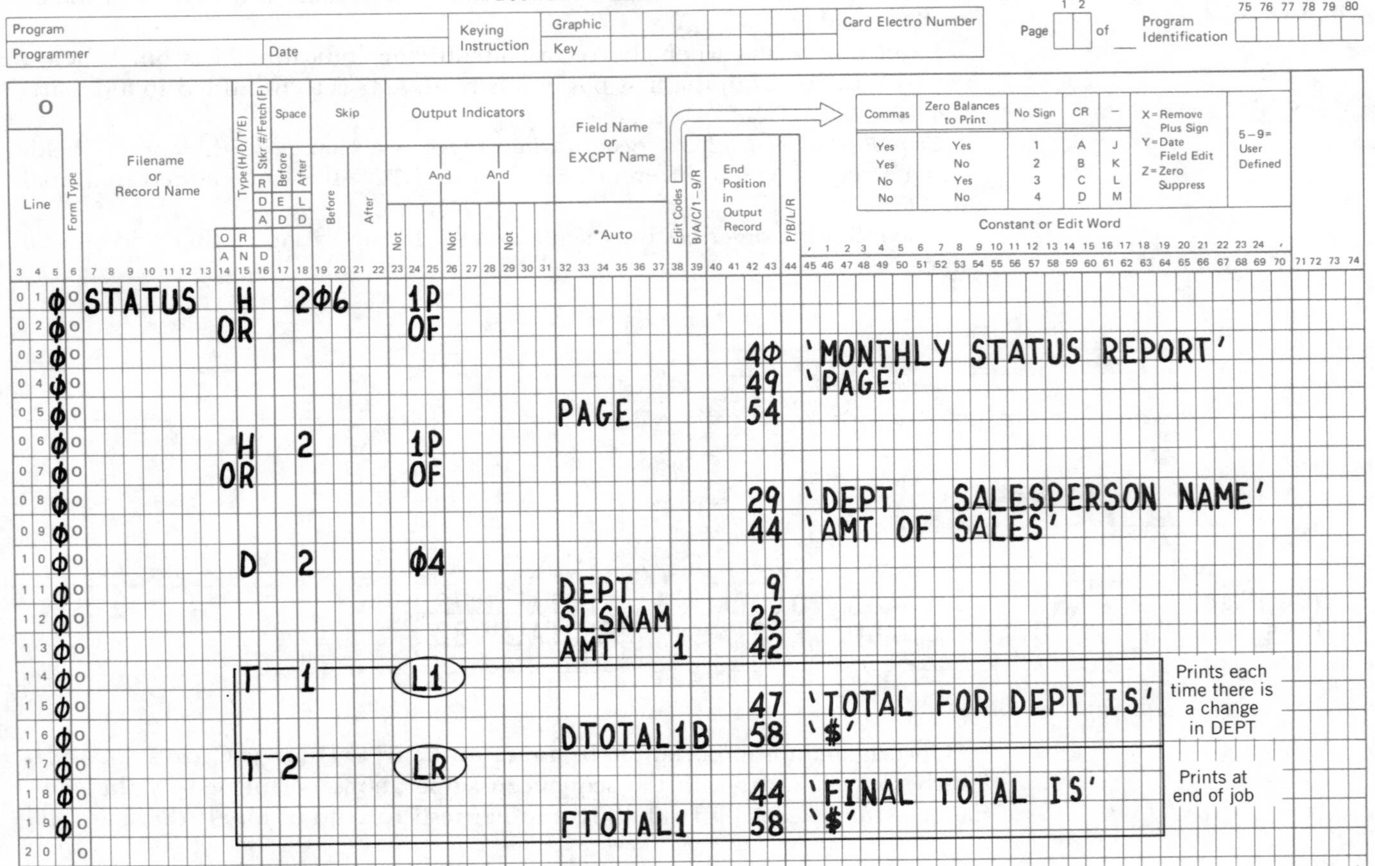
RPG OUTPUT SPECIFICATIONS

Line	Form Type	Filename or Record Name	Type	Space Before	Space After	Skip Before	Skip After	Output Indicators	Field Name or EXCPT Name	Edit Codes	End Position in Output Record	Constant or Edit Word
01	O	STATUS	H	2		06		1P				
02	O		OR					OF				
03	O										40	'MONTHLY STATUS REPORT'
04	O										49	'PAGE'
05	O								PAGE		54	
06	O		H		2			1P				
07	O		OR					OF				
08	O										29	'DEPT SALESPERSON NAME'
09	O										44	'AMT OF SALES'
10	O		D		2			04				
11	O								DEPT		9	
12	O								SLSNAM		25	
13	O								AMT	1	42	
14	O		T		1			L1				
15	O										47	'TOTAL FOR DEPT IS'
16	O								DTOTAL	1B	58	'$'
17	O		T		2			LR				
18	O										44	'FINAL TOTAL IS'
19	O								FTOTAL	1	58	'$'
20	O											

Generally, we have

H lines print on 1P or OF indicators.
D lines print on record or resulting indicators.
T lines print on L indicators.

The B in column 39 of the DTOTAL line means that the contents of DTOTAL will be reset to zero after printing. DTOTAL will thus be re-initialized before the AMTs are accumulated for the next DEPT.

B. Interpreting Control Break Procedures

Suppose the following data is read in.

	CODE	DEPT	SLSNAM	AMT
1.	S	Ø1	BROWN S	$1158_{\wedge}22$
2.	S	Ø1	ADAMS T	$1873_{\wedge}22$
3.	S	Ø2	SMITH J	$Ø922_{\wedge}11$
4.	S	Ø2	JONES R	$Ø123_{\wedge}47$
5.	S	Ø2	FIELD F	$3217_{\wedge}23$

1. The computer reads the first record. There is no need for a control break test on a first record, so the control is bypassed. (This is due to the fact that total calculations and total output are *not* performed in the first cycle.) The AMT is accumulated, and a detail line is printed.
2. The second record is read. Since it is not an end-of-file record, the computer checks to see if the DEPT is the same as the previous DEPT. Since it is the same, the AMT is accumulated and a record is printed.
3. The third record is not an end-of-file record, but it has Ø2 in DEPT which means there is a change in DEPT. L1 Calculations, if any, would then be processed, and T printing, which uses L1 coding, occurs. In this instance, the L1 calculation specifications add the department total, DTOTAL, to a final total, called FTOTAL. Then the total line that contains the sum for DEPT Ø1, the previous group, will print.

This department total, DTOTAL, must be reset to zero before processing the current record. To do this, we code a B in the BLANK AFTER field of DTOTAL on the Output form.

RPG OUTPUT SPECIFICATIONS

Program		Keying Instruction	Graphic		Card Electro Number	Page 1 2 of	Program Identification 75 76 77 78 79 80
Programmer	Date		Key				

Form columns: Line (3–5); Form Type (6) O; Filename or Record Name (7–14); Type (H/D/T/E) (15); Stkr #/Fetch (F) (16); Space Before/After (17–18); Skip Before/After (19–22); Output Indicators: Not, And, Not, And, Not (23–31); Field Name or EXCPT Name / *Auto (32–37); Edit Codes (38); B/A/C/1–9/R (39); End Position in Output Record (40–43); P/B/L/R (44); Constant or Edit Word 1–24 (45–70); (71–74). OR / AND; ADD / DEL.

Edit codes: Commas / Zero Balances to Print / No Sign / CR / –: Yes Yes 1 A J; Yes No 2 B K; No Yes 3 C L; No No 4 D M. X = Remove Plus Sign; Y = Date Field Edit; Z = Zero Suppress; 5–9 = User Defined.

Line	Form Type	Field Name	B/A/C/1–9/R	End Position	Constant or Edit Word
01	O	•			
02	O	•			
03	O	•			
04	O	•			
05	O	DTOTAL1	(B)	58	'$'
06	O				
07	O				
08	O				

By coding the B in BLANK AFTER, DTOTAL will be set to zero *after* the total line is printed. Then the new AMT for DEPT Ø2 can be accumulated and the first detail line for DEPT Ø2 can be printed.

At the end of the file, it is important to print the total that has accumulated for the last DEPT. Recall that the last record or LR indicator in RPG II is turned on at the end of the file; this indicator automatically turns on all level indicators as well. This means that the control level calculations and the total line will print for the last department group without the need for additional coding. All other programming languages require the programmer to "force" the last control break at the end of the job in order to have the computer print the last group of totals. This additional coding is not necessary in RPG, because it is a language uniquely designed to handle these specific types of applications.

Figure 5.4 provides a program flowchart excerpt that depicts the sequence of operations in the RPG II cycle that have just been described. Study the flowchart carefully so that you understand the sequence in which operations are performed.

C. Group Indicate Procedure

If DEPT Ø1 had numerous salespeople, the output would print as follows.

DEPT	SALESPERSON NAME		AMT OF SALES
Ø1	JONES	J	4,826.33
Ø1	DAVIS	T	3,872.17
Ø1	STERN	N	1,173.23
Ø1	ROBERTS	S	6,322.43
.	.		.
.	.		.
.	.		.

TOTAL FOR DEPT IS $44,326.22

Figure 5.4
RPG II Logic Cycle depicting single level control break processing.

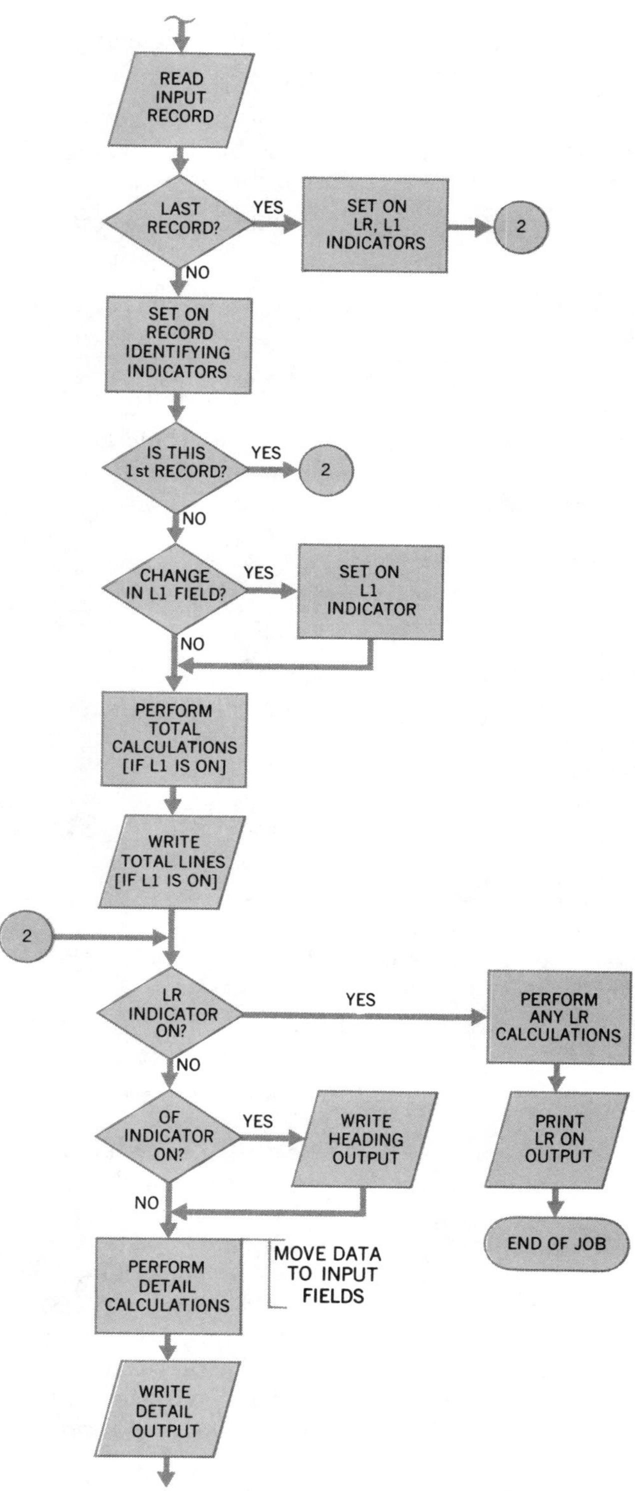

It is unnecessary to print Ø1 for DEPT *each* time, since it will always be the same until a break occurs. We may instruct the computer to print the department number only *once* at the beginning of each control break. In this way, DEPT Ø1 is assumed for all subsequent records in that group and redundant information is suppressed. The next group is highlighted by having its DEPT print only once at the beginning of the group.

DEPT	SALESPERSON NAME		AMT OF SALES
Ø1	JONES	J	4,826.33
	DAVIS	T	3,872.17
	STERN	N	1,173.23
	.		.
	.		.

The output DEPT field, then, would be referred to as a **group indicate** field. Only one change would be required in the detail printing to accomplish group indicate printing.

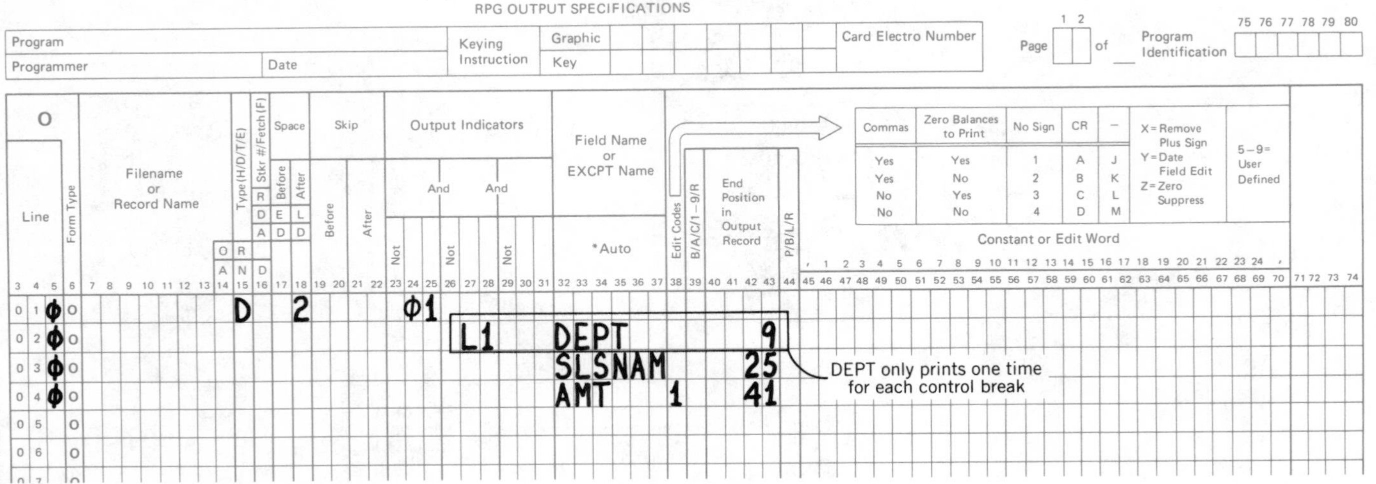

If a change in the L1 field has not yet occurred, the DEPT will not print.

The L1 indicator can be used for detail printing as well as total printing to control which fields will print. Because control level indicators remain on until after detail printing has been completed, an L1 indicator can be used for D or Detail lines as well as for T or Total lines. A change in DEPT will first cause the T line to print, which would write the previous DEPT's total. L1 is coded on the same line as the DEPT field; this means we print the department number only when the L1 indicator is on. For Detail level processing, L1 would only be on for the first record of each group; hence the DEPT prints only once for each group. See Figure 5.5 for a summary of control level indicators as they are used in RPG II.

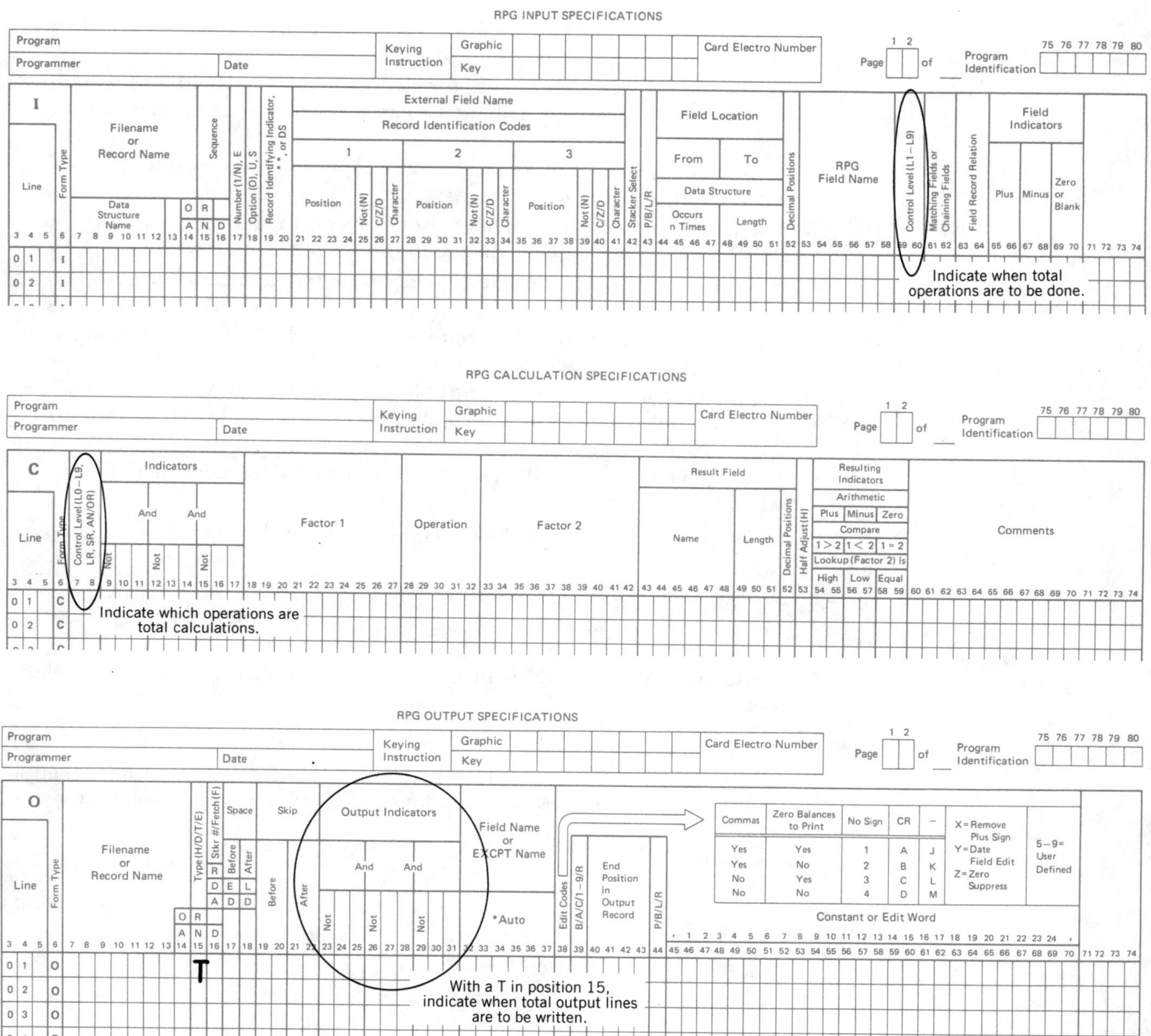

Figure 5.5
Summary of control level indicators.

Self-Evaluating Quiz

1. When a line of output is generated for each input record, this is called ________ printing.
2. When a total or summary line is printed for a group of input records, this is called ________ printing.
3. Suppose a file is entered in ACCTNO sequence where all records for a given ACCTNO appear together, followed by records for another ACCTNO, and so

on. If output is to include totals for each ACCTNO, a ________ procedure is required.

4. In question 3, ACCTNO would be called a(n) ________ field and would be defined on the input form along with an entry in the ________ columns of the form.
5. (T or F) Control break problems require input to be sorted into the correct sequence by control field.
6. Using L1 to control a calculation would mean that the calculation would only be performed when a change in the ________ occurred.
7. After a control break is detected by the computer, ________ are performed, followed by ________ .
8. (T or F) When an end-of-file condition occurs, the LR indicator along with all control level indicators are turned on.
9. Suppose the last group in a control break problem has ACCTNO 999. Once the end-of-file indicator is turned on, the computer will perform two operations. Name them.
10. (T or F) The computer does not perform total calculations or total output when the first record is read.
11. Code an RPG program using the specifications in Figure 5.6.

    Note
    *Extended cost (*EXTCST*) is equal to* QTY × PRICE.

    Compute daily totals. Records are in sequence by DATE, *which is the control field.*

12. Code an RPG program to produce the output specified in the problem definition in Figure 5.7.

    Notes
    a. The input records are in sequence by item number (ITEMNO), which is the control field. There will be several records for each ITEMNO. (Continued on next page.)

Systems Flowchart

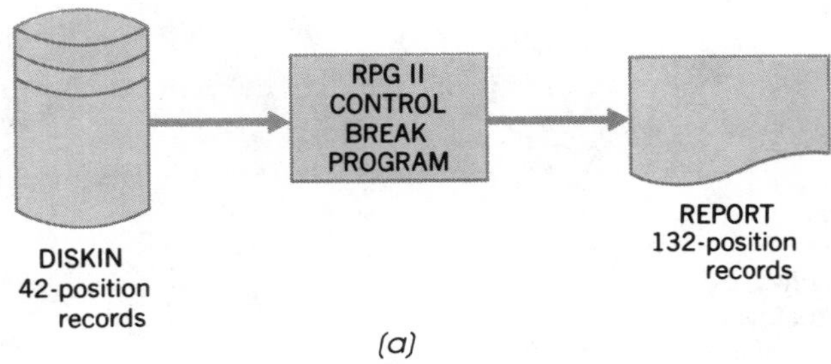

(a)

DISKIN Record Layout

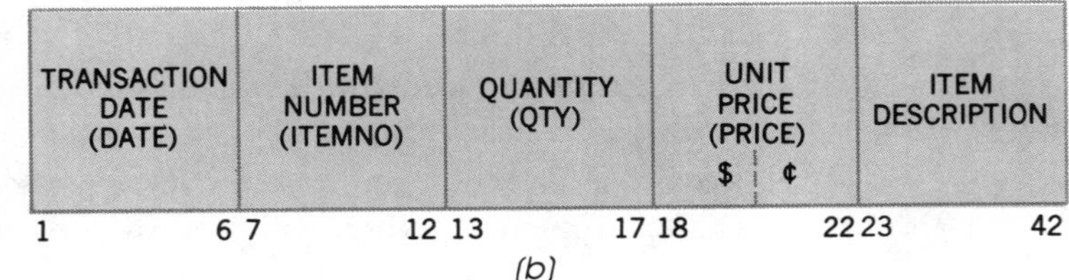

(b)

Figure 5.6
Problem definition for question 11.
(Continued on next page.)

Figure 5.6 *(continued)*

REPORT Printer Spacing Chart

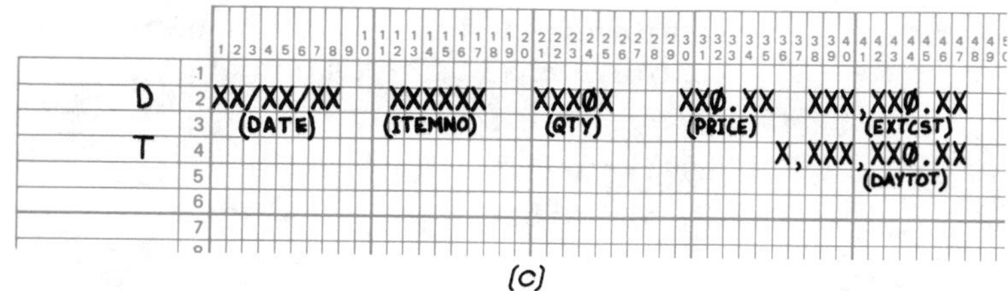

(c)

Figure 5.7 Problem definition for question 12.

Systems Flowchart

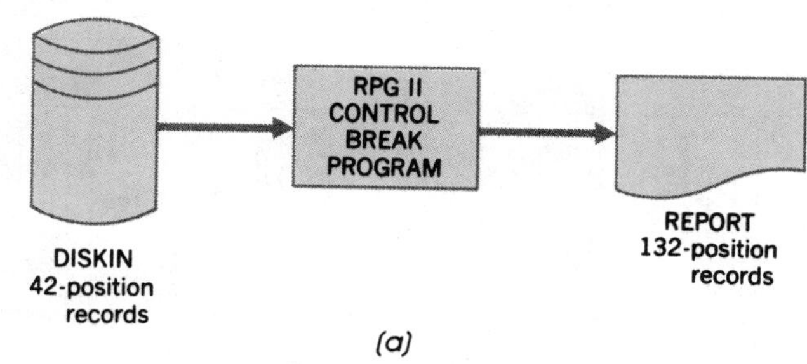

(a)

DISKIN Record Layout

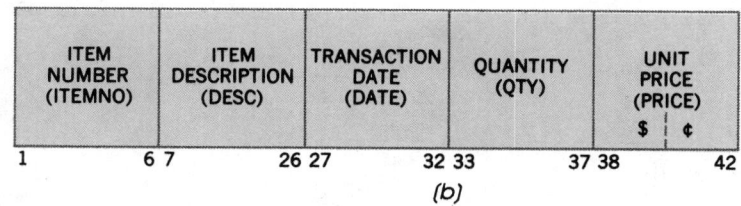

ITEM NUMBER (ITEMNO)	ITEM DESCRIPTION (DESC)	TRANSACTION DATE (DATE)	QUANTITY (QTY)	UNIT PRICE (PRICE) $ ¢
1 – 6	7 – 26	27 – 32	33 – 37	38 – 42

(b)

REPORT Printer Spacing Chart

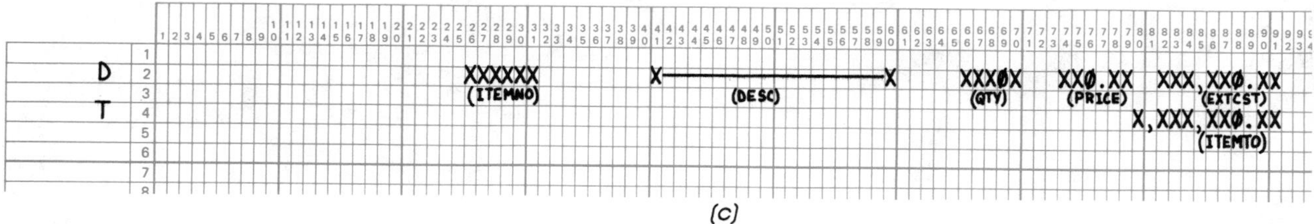

(c)

b. ITEMNO and DESC are group indicated.
c. ITEMTO is the total to be computed for each item. It is the total of all the extended costs for each item.
d. Each extended cost is equal to QTY times PRICE.

Solutions

1. detail
2. group
3. control break
4. control
   control level (59–6Ø)
5. T
6. control field
7. L1 calculations
   total-line printing

8. T
9. control level and LR total calculations
   control level and LR total output
1Ø. T
11. See Figure 5.8.
12. See Figure 5.9 on pages 25Ø and 251.

Figure 5.8
Solution for question 11.

RPG CONTROL AND FILE DESCRIPTION SPECIFICATIONS

Program | Programmer | Date | Keying Instruction | Graphic | Key | Card Electro Number | Page of | Program Identification

Control Specifications

For the valid entries for a system, refer to the RPG reference manual for that system.

Line	Form Type
01	H

File Description Specifications

For the valid entries for a system, refer to the RPG reference manual for that system.

Line	Form Type	Filename	File Type	File Designation	File Format	Record Length	Device
02Ø	F	DISKIN	I	P	F	42	DISK
03Ø	F	REPORT	O		F	132	PRINTER
04	F						
05	F						

RPG INPUT SPECIFICATIONS

Program | Programmer | Date | Keying Instruction | Graphic | Key | Card Electro Number | Page of | Program Identification

Line	Form Type	Filename or Record Name	Sequence	Record Identifying Indicator	Field Location From	Field Location To	Decimal Positions	RPG Field Name	Control Level (L1–L9)
01Ø	I	DISKIN	NS	Ø1					
02Ø	I				1	6	Ø	DATE	L1
03Ø	I				7	12		ITEMNO	
04Ø	I				13	17	Ø	QTY	
05Ø	I				18	22	2	PRICE	
06	I								
07	I								

RPG CALCULATION SPECIFICATIONS

Line	Form Type	Control Level	Indicators	Factor 1	Operation	Factor 2	Result Field Name	Length	Decimal Positions	Half Adjust (H)	Resulting Indicators	Comments
01	C		01	QTY	MULT	PRICE	EXTCST	8	2	H		
02	C		01	EXTCST	ADD	DAYTOT	DAYTOT	9	2			
03	C											
04	C											

RPG OUTPUT SPECIFICATIONS

Line	Form Type	Filename or Record Name	Type (H/D/T/E)	Space Before	Space After	Skip Before	Skip After	Output Indicators	Field Name	Edit Codes	B/A/C/1–9/R	End Position in Output Record	Constant or Edit Word
01	O	REPORT	D		1			01					
02	O								DATE	Y		8	
03	O								ITEMNO			17	
04	O								QTY	Z		25	
05	O								PRICE	1		35	
06	O								EXTCST	1		47	
07	O		T	1	2			L1					
08	O								DAYTOT	1	B	47	
09	O												
10	O												

Figure 5.8 *(continued)*

III. Multiple Level Control Breaks

A. Defining the Problem

It is often useful to have different levels of control fields determine when printing is to occur. The RPG specifications permit **multiple level control breaks**, up to *nine* levels of control, with the use of level indicators L1-L9. We will consider double level controls in this section and end with an illustration of a triple level control break procedure.

Examine the report in Figure 5.1Ø. It uses control break procedures that produce summary data on lines 13, 19, 21, 25, 29, 31, and 33. It also prints detail data from each input record as indicated on lines 9, 11, 15, 17, 23, and 27.

Every time a customer charges a purchase, an input record is created that consists of the customer name, amount of purchase, territory in which purchase was made, and department in which purchase was made. Control fields are usually placed in the left-most positions of an input record because they are

Figure 5.9
Solution for question 12.

RPG CONTROL AND FILE DESCRIPTION SPECIFICATIONS

Program | Programmer | Date | Keying Instruction | Graphic | Key | Card Electro Number | Page of | Program Identification

Control Specifications

For the valid entries for a system, refer to the RPG reference manual for that system.

```
  01 H
```

File Description Specifications

For the valid entries for a system, refer to the RPG reference manual for that system.

```
  02ΦFDISKIN  IP  F      42            DISK
  03ΦFREPORT  O   F     132            PRINTER
  04 F
  05 F
```

RPG INPUT SPECIFICATIONS

Program | Programmer | Date | Keying Instruction | Graphic | Key | Card Electro Number | Page of | Program Identification

```
  01ΦIDISKIN  NS  Φ1
  02ΦI                                        1   6 ITEMNOL1
  03ΦI                                        7  26 DESC
  04ΦI                                       33  37ΦQTY
  05ΦI                                       38  422PRICE
  06 I
  07 I
```

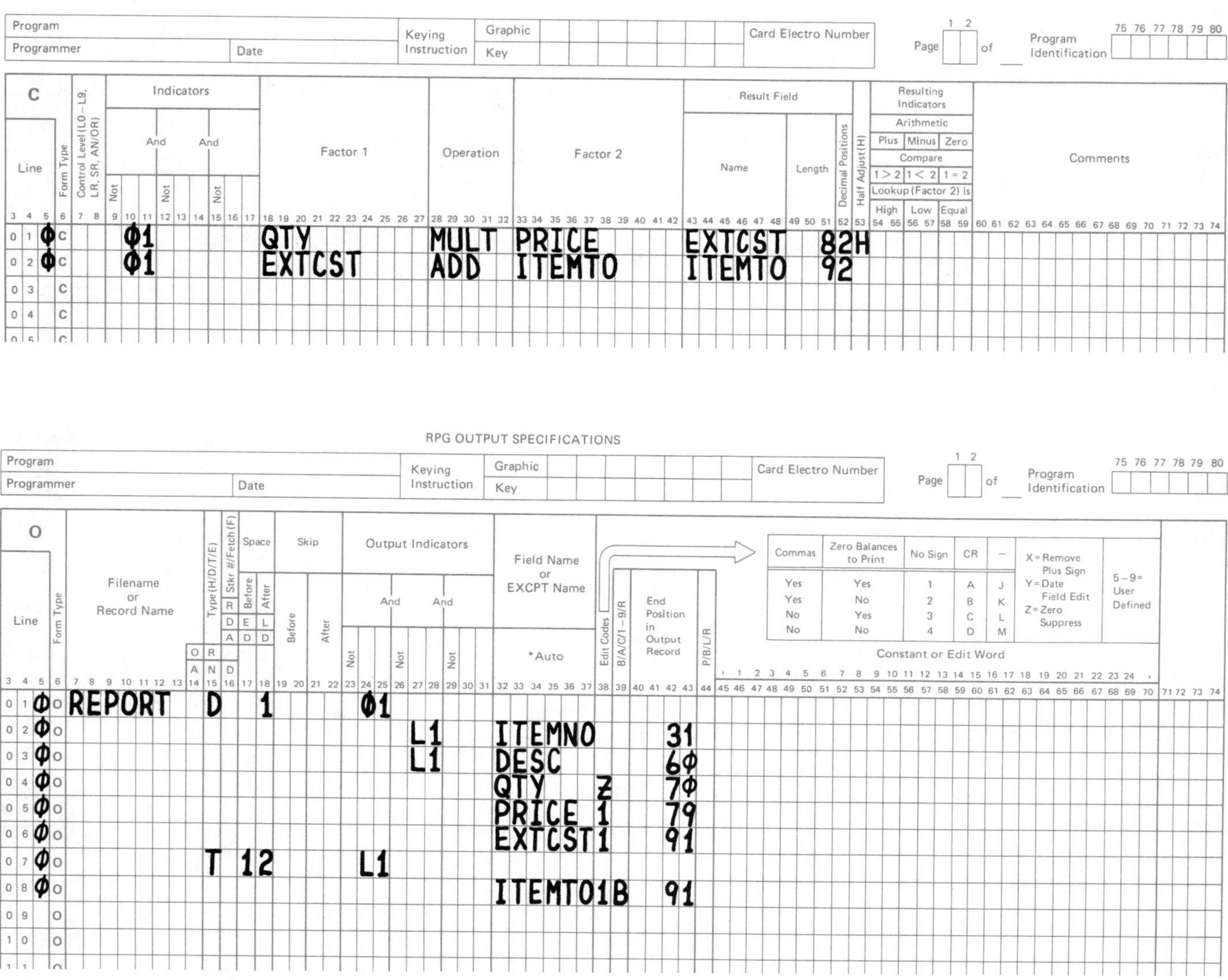

RPG CALCULATION SPECIFICATIONS

Line	Form Type	Indicators	Factor 1	Operation	Factor 2	Result Field Name	Length	Decimal Positions	Half Adjust (H)
01	C	Φ1	QTY	MULT	PRICE	EXTCST	8	2	H
02	C	Φ1	EXTCST	ADD	ITEMTO	ITEMTO	9	2	
03	C								
04	C								

RPG OUTPUT SPECIFICATIONS

Line	Form Type	Filename or Record Name	Type (H/D/T/E)	Space After	Output Indicators	Field Name or EXCPT Name	Edit Codes	B/A/C/1–9/R	End Position in Output Record
01	O	REPORT	D	1	Φ1				
02	O				L1	ITEMNO			31
03	O				L1	DESC			6Φ
04	O					QTY	Z		7Φ
05	O					PRICE	1		79
06	O					EXTCST	1		91
07	O		T	12	L1				
08	O					ITEMTO	1	B	91
09	O								
10	O								

Figure 5.9 *(continued)*

used for control and sorting purposes. Since territory and department are control fields in this instance, they would be coded first on the input record.

Detail printing is required as well as group printing of department totals and territory totals. Since departments exist within each territory, department is a *minor control field* and territory is a *major control field.* Major control fields have higher control level numbers than do minor control fields. Hence we could code department as an L1 control field and territory as an L2 (or L3, L4, etc.) control field.

Territory is considered the major control field, so it is first on the input record. Department, within territory, is a minor control field, so it is placed next on the input record. If there were intermediate control fields, they would typically be placed between TERR and DEPT, although this is not mandatory.

Each input record is printed, and a department total is accumulated. When there is a control break or a change in department, the following occur.

Type	Line							
H	6			CUSTOMER REPORT			PAGE 1	
H	7	TERRITORY	DEPARTMENT	CUSTOMER NAME	AMT OF PURCHASE			
D	9	01	01	PAUL NEWMAN	$100.50			
D	11	01	01	JOHN WAYNE	$250.00			
TL1	13					TOTAL DEPT 01 $350.50*		
D	15	01	02	ROBERT REDFORD	$5,250.40			
D	17	01	02	RICHARD BURTON	$525.10			
TL1	19					TOTAL DEPT 02 $5,775.50*		
TL2	21						TOTAL TERR 01	$6,126.00**
D	23	02	01	WOODY ALLEN	$200.50			
TL1	25					TOTAL DEPT 01 $200.50*		
D	27	02	02	JACK NICHOLSON	$425.30			
TL1	29					TOTAL DEPT 02 $425.30*		
TL2	31						TOTAL TERR 02	$625.80**
TLR	33						FINAL TOTAL	$6,751.80***

Figure 5.10
Printer Spacing Chart illustrating multiple level control breaks.

1. Calculations: The department total is added to the territory total.
2. Printing: The total for the previous department is printed.

The territory total keeps accumulating for each department within the specific territory. This processing continues until there is a major break in territory. A major control break performs the following.

1. Accumulates a final total.
2. Forces the previous department total to print.
3. Prints the territory total.

The final total is printed at the end of the job, when the LR indicator is on. This LR indicator first turns on indicators L1-L9, causing a minor and major control break before printing final totals.

A change in department, the minor level control break, causes a department total to print and that total to be added to the territory total. Minor level controls are the lowest level indicated. We use L1 to denote a department break and we use an asterisk (*) to designate the department total as a control total.

A change in the major level control field, territory, results in the *printing* of

1. The last department total in the previous territory.
2. The previous territory total.

Major level control fields must have a level number higher than minor level ones. We use L2 to denote the major control field, territory, and we use two asterisks (**) to designate the territory total as a major control total. Keep in mind, however, that we could have used any level L2-L9 for denoting the territory as a major control field, although L2 is usually used.

When a control level indicator is turned on because there is a change in the control field, all lower level indicators are automatically set on as well. Hence, if an L2 territory break occurs, this will automatically turn on the L1 indicator, which will cause the last department total for the territory to print.

If five control levels, L1-L5, were used, a break in the L5 control field would automatically turn on indicators L1-L4 (and L5) forcing lower level breaks. Printing and calculations occur from low to high (L1→L5). This is a reasonable procedure because we would always want to print the last department total for a specific territory before we printed the territory total.

Records must be entered in sequence by department within territory. Thus all DEPT Ø1 records for TERR Ø1 would be entered first, followed by DEPT Ø2 records (if any) for TERR Ø1, and so on, until all DEPTs in TERR Ø1 were read and processed; then records for the first DEPT in TERR Ø2 would be read, and so on. Suppose a group of records were processed as shown in Figure 5.11.

TERRITORY	DEPT	CUSTOMER NAME	AMT OF PURCHASE
Ø1	Ø1	X————X	X————X
Ø1	Ø1	X————X	X————X
		TOTAL DEPT Ø1 $————	
Ø1	Ø3	X————X	X————X
Ø1	Ø3	X————X	X————X
		TOTAL DEPT Ø3 $————	
		TOTAL TERR Ø1 $————	
Ø2	Ø3	(Note that this DEPT Ø3 relates to a different TERRITORY.)	

Figure 5.11
Sample output illustration for multiple level control breaks.

Each time there is a change in DEPT a department total prints. When there is a change in TERR the total for the previous department prints followed by the TERR total.

In this example, there is one instance where a change in territory occurs but the DEPT number remains the same. We would still want to print DEPT Ø3 and TERR Ø1 totals before processing the new TERR. In this instance, it might appear as if the L2 indicator is turned on but not the L1 indicator. The processing proceeds properly, however, because the L2 indicator automatically turns on the L1 indicator. Thus the DEPT Ø3 break is "forced" when there is a change in TERR even if it happens that the first DEPT in the next TERR is also Ø3. This guarantees that the processing will be correct.

At the end of the job, three totals print:

1. Department total (*).
2. Territory total (**).
3. Final total (***).

The asterisks (*) are frequently used to designate the level of the total field printing.

The LR indicator automatically turns on all level indicators L1-L9, which will cause all accumulated totals to print.

At total time, the computer prints L1 totals first, followed by L2 totals, and so on. The last total line to print is the LR total line. *You should code L1 totals first, followed by L2 totals, and so on, and end with LR totals.*

B. RPG Coding for Multiple Control Breaks

Recall that Figure 5.1Ø provides the sample output for a double-level control-break problem in which DEPT is the minor control field and TERR is the major control field. Figure 5.12 illustrates the RPG coding.

RPG CONTROL AND FILE DESCRIPTION SPECIFICATIONS

Control Specifications

```
01 H
```

File Description Specifications

```
02ØFINFILE  IP  F 1ØØ 1ØØ            DISK
03ØFPRINTOUTO   F     132     OF     PRINTER
04 F
05 F
```

RPG INPUT SPECIFICATIONS

```
01ØIINFILE  NS  Ø1   1 CP
02ØI                                        2   3 TERR  L2
03ØI                                        4   5 DEPT  L1
04ØI                                        6  19 NAME
05ØI                                       2Ø  242AMT
06 I
07 I
```

Figure 5.12
Coding for a double-level control-break problem.

RPG CALCULATION SPECIFICATIONS

Program		Keying Instruction	Graphic	Card Electro Number	Page	of	Program Identification
Programmer	Date		Key				

Line	Form Type	Control Level (L0–L9, LR, SR, AN/OR)	Indicators	Factor 1	Operation	Factor 2	Result Field Name	Length	Decimal Positions	Half Adjust (H)	Resulting Indicators	Comments
0 1 Ø	C		Ø1	AMT	ADD	TDEPT	TDEPT	6	2			
0 2 Ø	C	L1		TDEPT	ADD	TOTERR	TOTERR	7	2			
0 3 Ø	C	L2		TOTERR	ADD	FINTOT	FINTOT	8	2			
0 4	C											
0 5	C											
0 6	C											

RPG OUTPUT SPECIFICATIONS

Program		Keying Instruction	Graphic	Card Electro Number	Page	of	Program Identification
Programmer	Date		Key				

Line	Form Type	Filename or Record Name	Type (H/D/T/E)	Space Before	Space After	Skip Before	Skip After	Output Indicators	Field Name or EXCPT Name	Edit Codes	B/A/C/1–9/R	End Position in Output Record	Constant or Edit Word
0 1 Ø	O	PRINTOUT	H		1	Ø6		1P					
0 2 Ø	O		OR					OF					
0 3 Ø	O											65	'CUSTOMER REPORT'
0 4 Ø	O											94	'PAGE'
0 5 Ø	O								PAGE	Z		1ØØ	
0 6 Ø	O		H		2			1P					
0 7 Ø	O		OR					OF					
0 8 Ø	O											15	'TERRITORY'
0 9 Ø	O											3Ø	'DEPARTMENT'
1 0 Ø	O											5Ø	'CUSTOMER NAME'
1 1 Ø	O											71	'AMT OF PURCHASE'
1 2 Ø	O		D		2			Ø1					
1 3 Ø	O								TERR			12	
1 4 Ø	O								DEPT			26	
1 5 Ø	O								NAME			51	
1 6 Ø	O								AMT	1		72	'$'
1 7 Ø	O		T		2			L1					
1 8 Ø	O											82	'TOTAL DEPT'
1 9 Ø	O								DEPT			85	
2 0 Ø	O								TDEPT	1	B	95	'$'
21Ø	O											96	'*'
	O												
	O												

Figure 5.12 *(continued)*

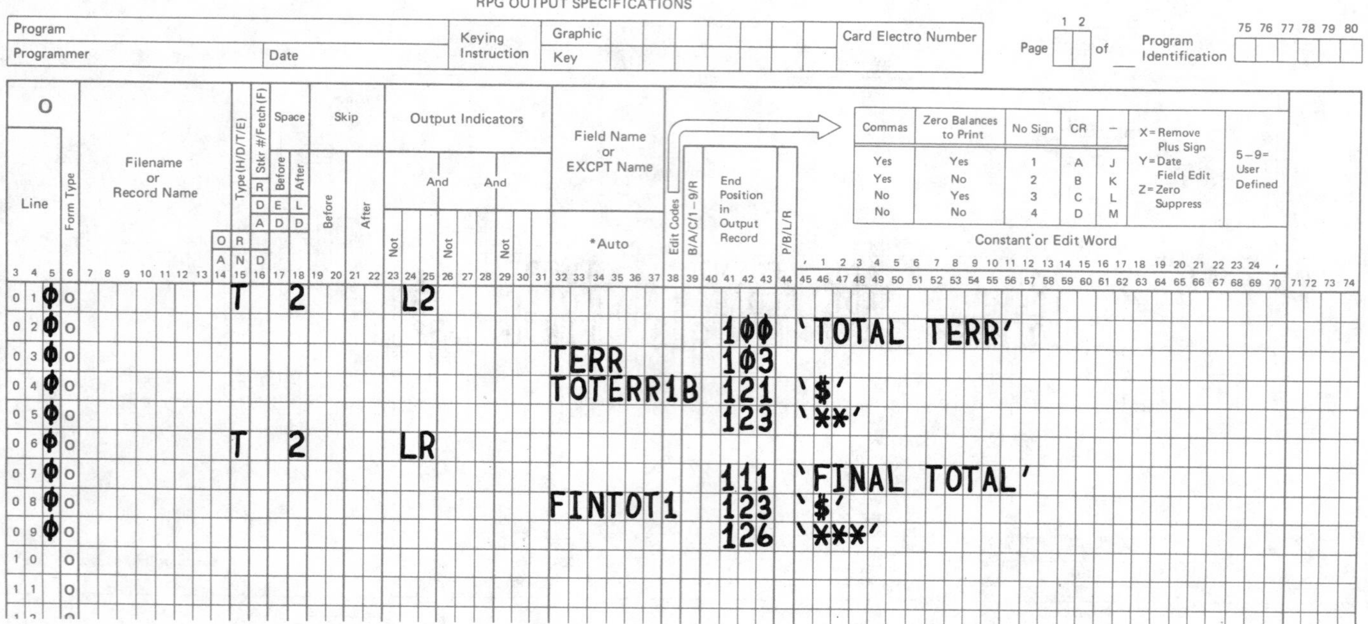

RPG OUTPUT SPECIFICATIONS

Line	Form Type	Filename or Record Name	Type (H/D/T/E)	Space After	Output Indicators	Field Name or EXCPT Name	End Position in Output Record	Constant or Edit Word
01Φ	O		T	2	L2			
02Φ	O						1ΦΦ	'TOTAL TERR'
03Φ	O					TERR	1Φ3	
04Φ	O					TOTERR1B	121	'$'
05Φ	O						123	'**'
06Φ	O		T	2	LR			
07Φ	O						111	'FINAL TOTAL'
08Φ	O					FINTOT1	123	'$'
09Φ	O						126	'***'
10	O							
11	O							

Figure 5.12 *(continued)*

It is important to understand the sequence in which the computer performs control processing. Suppose we are using level indicators L1, L2, L3.

1. A record is read.
2. Level testing is performed in the following sequence.
   a. LR test: If an end-of-file condition exists, L1-L3 indicators are turned on (whichever levels are used by program), as well as LR.
   b. L3 test: If an L3 control break exists, L3, L2, L1 indicators are turned on.
   c. L2 test: If an L2 control break exists, L2, L1 indicators are turned on.
   d. L1 test: If an L1 control break exists, L1 indicator is turned on.

See Figure 5.13 for an illustration of the sequence in which RPG tests the level control indicators.

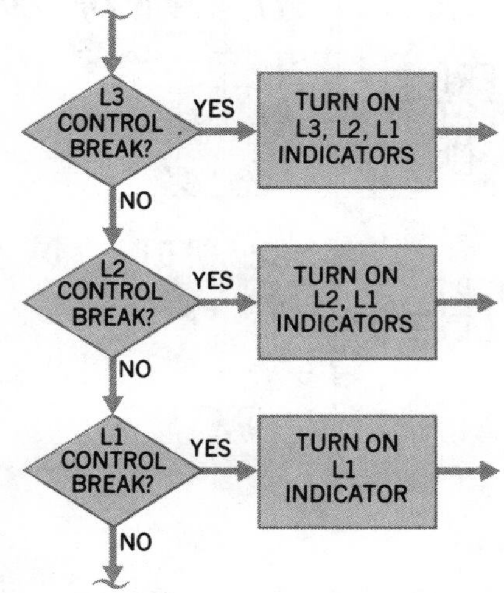

Figure 5.13
The sequence in which RPG tests the level control indicators.

3. Control level calculations are performed in sequence: L1, L2, L3, . . . LR. The calculations must be coded in that sequence as well.
4. Control level totals are printed in sequence: L1, L2, L3, . . . LR. The output specifications should be coded in that sequence as well.
5. If LR is off, detail calculations and printing are performed.
6. If LR is off, all level indicators are turned off and another record is read.

The following is a summary of the steps involved.

Indicator On	*Calculation Performed*	*Field that is Printed*
Ø1	ADD AMT TO TDEPT	AMT
L1	ADD TDEPT TO TOTERR	TDEPT
L2	ADD TOTERR TO FINTOT	TOTERR
LR	None	FINTOT

The flowchart for this facet of the RPG II Logic Cycle appears in Figure 5.14 on page 259.

Self-Evaluating Quiz *Consider the following problem definition, which is continued on the next page.*

Systems Flowchart

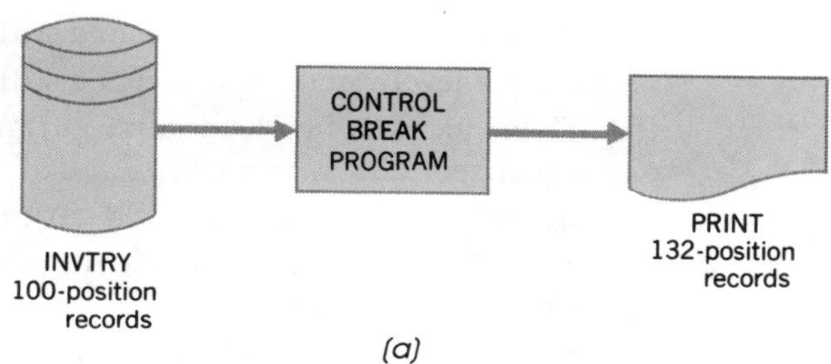

(a)

INVTRY Record Layout

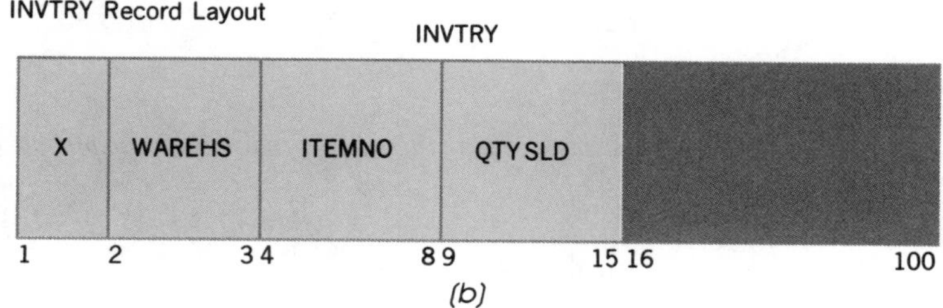

(b)

PRINT Printer Spacing Chart

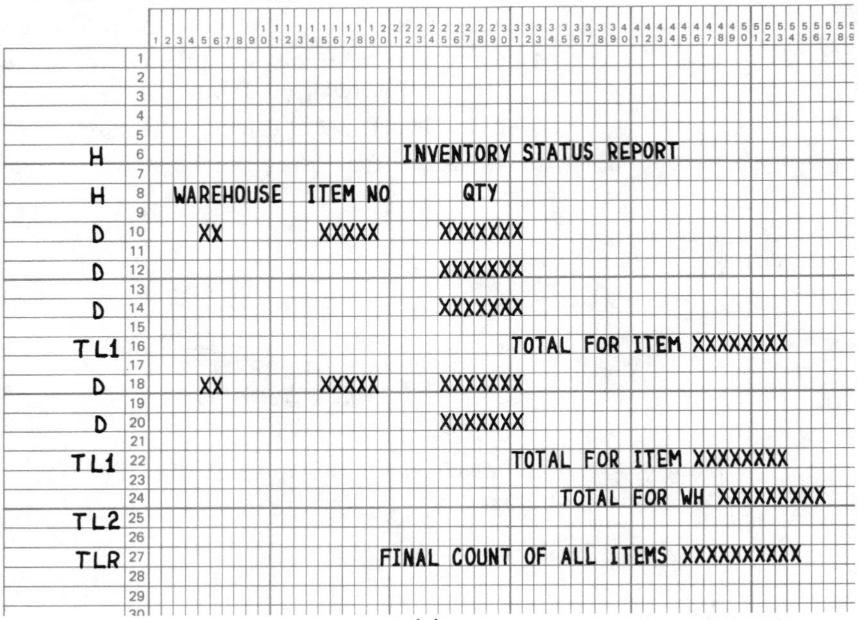

Indicator	Line	Content
H	6	INVENTORY STATUS REPORT
H	8	WAREHOUSE ITEM NO QTY
D	10	XX XXXXX XXXXXXX
D	12	XXXXXXX
D	14	XXXXXXX
TL1	16	TOTAL FOR ITEM XXXXXXXX
D	18	XX XXXXX XXXXXXX
D	20	XXXXXXX
TL1	22	TOTAL FOR ITEM XXXXXXXX
	24	TOTAL FOR WH XXXXXXXXX
TL2	25	
TLR	27	FINAL COUNT OF ALL ITEMS XXXXXXXXXX

(c)

Part 1

1. This would be considered a(n) ________ control break problem.
2. The major control field would be ________, and the minor control field would be ________.
3. The L1 level would be associated with ________.
4. The L2 level would be associated with ________.
5. When an L2 break occurs, (no.) totals print in the following sequence: ________ and ________.
6. An end-of-job condition would turn on which indicators?
7. (T or F) For double-level control problems, the input need not be in any particular sequence.
8. In this problem definition, L1 calculations would include ________.
9. In this problem definition, L2 calculations would include ________.
10. In this problem definition, the LR indicator would cause the printing of ________.

Part 2

Code the program required to produce the output specified in Part 1.

Solutions *Part 1*

1. double-level
2. WAREHS
   ITEMNO
3. ITEMNO
4. WAREHS
5. two
   ITEMNO total
   WAREHS total

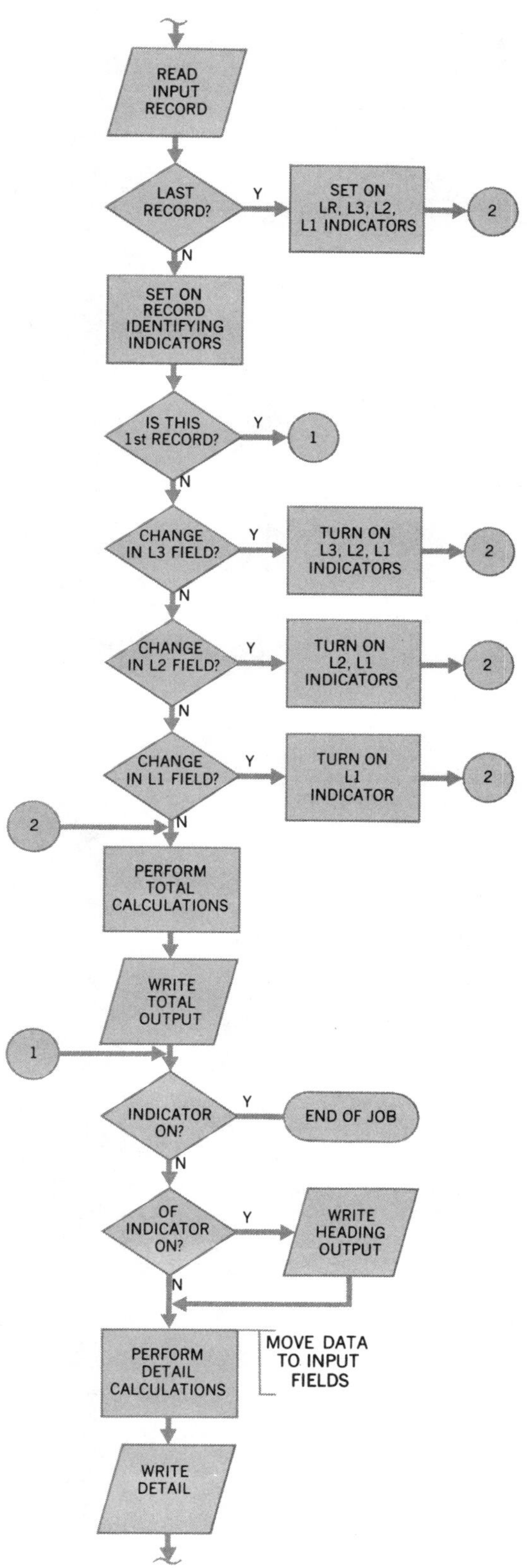

Figure 5.14
RPG II Logic Cycle depicting triple-level control-break processing.

6. LR
   L2
   L1
7. F—It must be in ITEMNO sequence within WAREHS.
8. adding ITEMTO to WHTOT
9. adding WHTOT to FINTOT
1Ø. the final total

Part 2

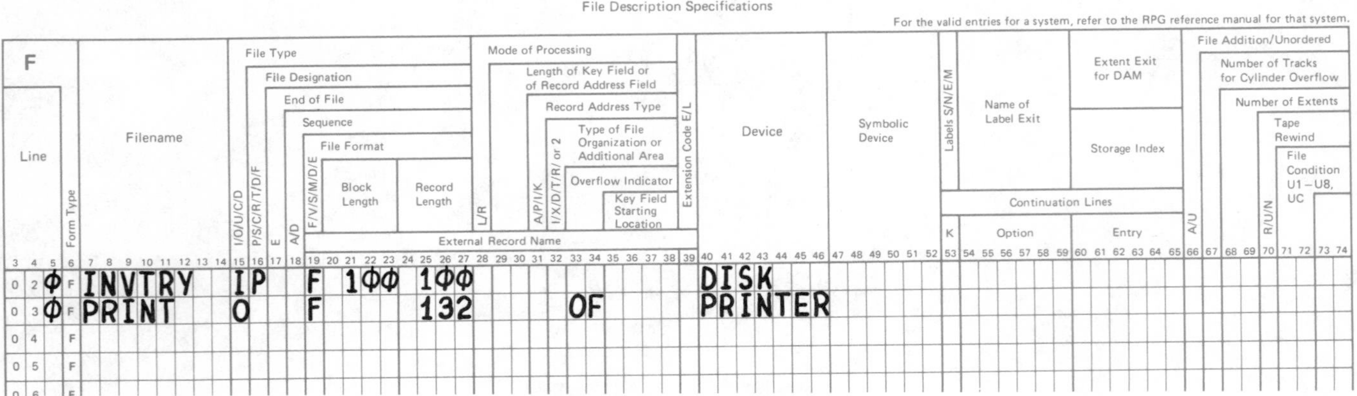
File Description Specifications

For the valid entries for a system, refer to the RPG reference manual for that system.

Line	Form Type	Filename	File Type	File Designation	File Format	Block Length	Record Length	Overflow Indicator	Device
Ø2	F	INVTRY	I	P	F	1ØØ	1ØØ		DISK
Ø3	F	PRINT	O		F		132	OF	PRINTER
Ø4	F								
Ø5	F								

RPG INPUT SPECIFICATIONS

Line	Form Type	Filename or Record Name	Sequence	Record Identifying Indicator	Position	C/Z/D	Character	Field Location From	Field Location To	Decimal Positions	RPG Field Name	Control Level (L1–L9)
Ø1	I	INVTRY	NS	Ø1	1	C	X					
Ø2	I							2	3		WAREHS	L2
Ø3	I							4	8		ITEMNO	L1
Ø4	I							9	15	Ø	QTYSLD	
Ø5	I											
Ø6	I											

RPG CALCULATION SPECIFICATIONS

Line	Form Type	Control Level	Indicators	Factor 1	Operation	Factor 2	Result Field Name	Length	Decimal Positions
01Φ	C		Φ1	QTYSLD	ADD	ITEMTO	ITEMTO	8	Φ
02Φ	C	L1		ITEMTO	ADD	WHTOT	WHTOT	9	Φ
03Φ	C	L2		WHTOT	ADD	FINTOT	FINTOT	1Φ	Φ
04	C								
05	C								

RPG OUTPUT SPECIFICATIONS

Line	Form Type	Filename or Record Name	Type	Space Before	Space After	Skip Before	Output Indicators	Output Indicators (And)	Field Name	Blank After (B)	End Position in Output Record	Constant or Edit Word
01Φ	O	PRINT	H		2	Φ6	1P					
02Φ	O		OR				OF					
03Φ	O										37	'INVENTORY STATUS'
04Φ	O										44	'REPORT'
05Φ	O		H		2		1P					
06Φ	O		OR				OF					
07Φ	O										11	'WAREHOUSE'
08Φ	O										2Φ	'ITEM NO'
09Φ	O										29	'QTY'
10Φ	O		D		2		Φ1					
11Φ	O							L2	WAREHS		6	
12Φ	O							L1	ITEMNO		19	
13Φ	O								QTYSLD		31	
14Φ	O		T		2			L1				
15Φ	O										44	'TOTAL FOR ITEM'
16Φ	O								ITEMTO	B	53	
17Φ	O		T		2			L2				
18Φ	O										46	'TOTAL FOR WH'
19Φ	O								WHTOT	B	56	
20Φ	O		T	1				LR				
21Φ	O										3Φ	'FINAL COUNT'
22Φ	O										43	'OF ALL ITEMS'
23Φ	O								FINTOT		55	

C. Control Break Printing with No Detail Output

Sometimes the user does not need detail output at all, but requires a summary report consisting of totals by specific categories. In this instance, control break processing can be performed without the need for any D or detail output. Figure 5.15 provides the problem definition for such a program, and Figure 5.16 illustrates the RPG program.

Systems Flowchart

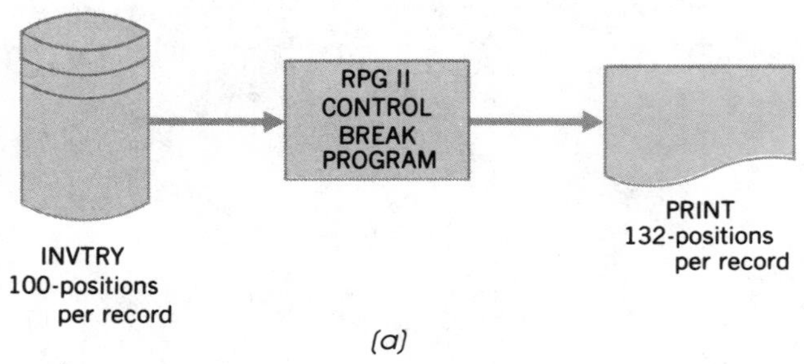

(a)

INVTRY Record Layout

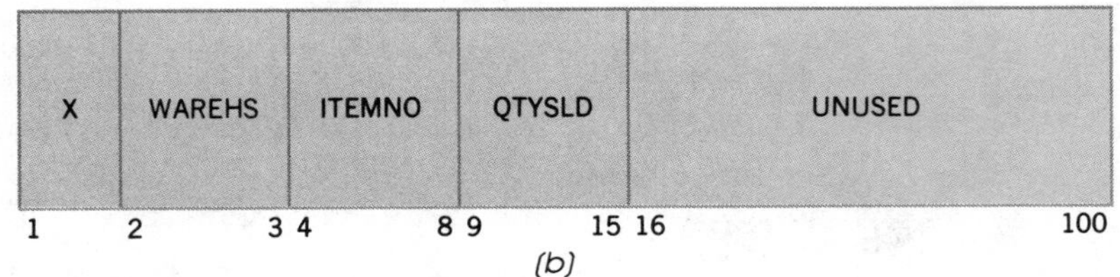

(b)

PRINT Printer Spacing Chart

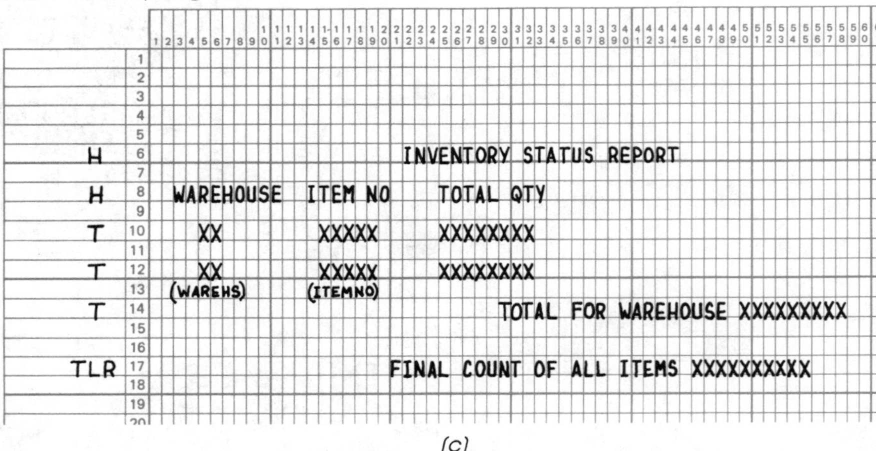

(c)

Figure 5.15
Problem definition for control break procedure with no detail print.

D. Handling Page Overflow Conditions for Group Printing

1. Review of Overflow (OF) Indicator

Detail reports typically contain one output line for each input record read. If no overflow or OF indicator is used, then output will continue to print from one sheet on a continuous form to another, with no attention being given to top and bottom page margins or to perforations separating each sheet. See Figure 5.17

RPG CONTROL AND FILE DESCRIPTION SPECIFICATIONS

Program		Keying Instruction	Graphic	Card Electro Number	Page 1 2 of	Program Identification 75 76 77 78 79 80
Programmer	Date		Key			

Control Specifications

For the valid entries for a system, refer to the RPG reference manual for that system.

Line (3 4 5)	Form Type (6)	Size to Compile (7–9)	Object Output (10)	Listing Options (11)	Size to Execute (12–14)	Debug (15)	Reserved (16–17)	Currency Symbol (18)	Date Format (19)	Date Edit (20)	Inverted Print (21)	Reserved (22)	Number of Print Positions (23–25)	Alternate Collating Sequence (26)	Reserved (27–36)	Inquiry (37)	Reserved (38–39)	Sign Handling (40)	1 P Forms Position (41)	Indicator Setting (42)	File Translation (43)	Punch MFCU Zeros (44)	Nonprint Characters (45)	Reserved (46)	Table Load Halt (47)	Shared I/O (48)	Field Print (49)	Formatted Dump (50)	RPG to RPG II Conversion (51)	Number of Formats (52–53)	S/3 Conversion (54)	Subprogram (55)	CICS/DL/I (56)	Transparent Literal (57)	58–74
0 1	H																																		

File Description Specifications

For the valid entries for a system, refer to the RPG reference manual for that system.

Line (3–5)	Form Type (6)	Filename (7–14)	File Type I/O/U/C/D (15)	File Designation P/S/C/R/T/D/F (16)	End of File E (17)	Sequence A/D (18)	File Format F/V/S/M/D/E (19)	Block Length (20–23)	Record Length (24–27)	Mode of Processing L/R (28)	Length of Key Field or of Record Address Field (29–30)	Record Address Type A/P/I/K (31)	Type of File Organization or Additional Area I/X/D/T/R/ or 2 (32)	Overflow Indicator (33–34)	Key Field Starting Location (35–38)	Extension Code E/L (39)	Device (40–46)	Symbolic Device (47–52)	Labels S/N/E/M (53)	Name of Label Exit (54–59)	Extent Exit for DAM / Storage Index (60–65)	A/U (66)	File Addition/Unordered, Number of Tracks for Cylinder Overflow, Number of Extents (67–69)	Tape Rewind R/U/N (70)	File Condition U1–U8, UC (71–72)
0 2 Ø	F	INVTRY	I	P			F		1ØØ								DISK								
0 3 Ø	F	PRINT	O				F		132					OF			PRINTER								
0 4	F																								
0 5	F																								
0 6	F																								

RPG INPUT SPECIFICATIONS

Program		Keying Instruction	Graphic	Card Electro Number	Page 1 2 of	Program Identification 75 76 77 78 79 80
Programmer	Date		Key			

Line (3–5)	Form Type (6)	Filename or Record Name / Data Structure Name (7–14)	Sequence (15–16)	Number (1/N), E (17)	Option (O), U, S (18)	Record Identifying Indicator, or DS (19–20)	Record Identification Codes 1: Position (21–24)	Not (N) (25)	C/Z/D (26)	Character (27)	2: Position (28–31)	Not (N) (32)	C/Z/D (33)	Character (34)	3: Position (35–38)	Not (N) (39)	C/Z/D (40)	Character (41)	Stacker Select (42)	P/B/L/R (43)	Field Location From (44–47)	To (48–51)	Decimal Positions (52)	RPG Field Name (53–58)	Control Level (L1–L9) (59–60)	Matching Fields or Chaining Fields (61–62)	Field Record Relation (63–64)	Field Indicators Plus (65–66)	Minus (67–68)	Zero or Blank (69–70)	71–74
0 1 Ø	I	INVTRY	NS			Ø1	1		C	X																					
0 2 Ø	I																				2	3		WAREHS	L2						
0 3 Ø	I																				4	8		ITEMNO	L1						
0 4 Ø	I																				9	15	Ø	QTYSLD							
0 5	I																														
0 6	I																														
0 7	I																														

Figure 5.16
Coding for control break procedure with no detail print.
(Continued on next page.)

RPG CALCULATION SPECIFICATIONS

Program		Keying Instruction	Graphic	Card Electro Number	Page 1 2 of	Program Identification 75 76 77 78 79 80
Programmer	Date		Key			

Line (3–5)	Form Type (6)	Control Level (L0–L9, LR, SR, AN/OR) (7–8)	Indicators (9–17)	Factor 1 (18–27)	Operation (28–32)	Factor 2 (33–42)	Result Field Name (43–48)	Length (49–51)	Decimal Positions (52)	Half Adjust (H) (53)	Resulting Indicators (54–59)	Comments (60–74)
01Ø	C		Ø1	QTYSLD	ADD	ITEMTO	ITEMTO	8	Ø			
02Ø	C	L1		ITEMTO	ADD	WHTOT	WHTOT	9	Ø			
03Ø	C	L2		WHTOT	ADD	FINTOT	FINTOT	1Ø	Ø			
04	C											
05	C											

RPG OUTPUT SPECIFICATIONS

Program		Keying Instruction	Graphic	Card Electro Number	Page 1 2 of	Program Identification 75 76 77 78 79 80
Programmer	Date		Key			

Line (3–5)	Form Type (6)	Filename or Record Name (7–14)	Type (H/D/T/E) (15)	Space Before (17)	Space After (18)	Skip Before (19–20)	Skip After (21–22)	Output Indicators (23–31)	Field Name or EXCPT Name (32–37)	Edit Codes (38)	B/A/C/1–9/R (39)	End Position in Output Record (40–43)	P/B/L/R (44)	Constant or Edit Word (45–70)
01Ø	O	PRINT	H		2	Ø6		1P						
02Ø	O		OR					OF						
03Ø	O											37		'INVENTORY STATUS'
04Ø	O											44		'REPORT'
05Ø	O		H		2			1P						
06Ø	O		OR					OF						
07Ø	O											11		'WAREHOUSE'
08Ø	O											2Ø		'ITEM NO'
09Ø	O											33		'TOTAL QTY'
10Ø	O		T		2			L1						
11Ø	O								WAREHS			6		
12Ø	O								ITEMNO			19		
13Ø	O								ITEMTO		B	32		
14Ø	O		T		2			L2						
15Ø	O											38		'TOTAL FOR'
16Ø	O											48		'WAREHOUSE'
17Ø	O								WHTOT		B	58		
18Ø	O		T	1				LR						
19Ø	O											31		'FINAL COUNT'
20Ø	O											44		'OF ALL ITEMS'
21Ø	O								FINTOT			55		

Figure 5.16 *(continued)*

Figure 5.17
Example of a poorly designed output report.

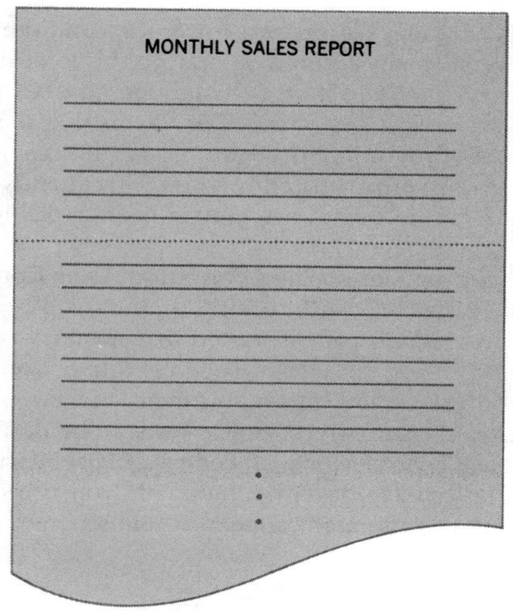

Poor Design of Output

1. Printing occurs over perforation.
2. Heading appears only on the first page.
3. Page numbers are not used.

for an illustration of a poorly designed report that might be printed when no attention is given to page overflow.

Usually, we want the computer to print a heading on each page of a report. The following coding on the Output Specifications form will result in the printing of headings when the first page (1P) or overflow (OF) indicator is on.

RPG OUTPUT SPECIFICATIONS

Line (3–5)	Form Type (6)	Filename or Record Name (7–14)	Type (H/D/T/E) (15)	Space Before (17)	Space After (18)	Skip Before (19–20)	Skip After (21–22)	Output Indicators (23–31)
01Φ	O	LINEOUT	H	2		Φ6		1P
02Φ	O	OR						OF
03	O							
04	O							
05	O							

When an end of page is sensed, the computer will skip to the top of the next page and print the heading.

This type of OF or **page overflow** processing is usually sufficient for printing detail reports. Group printing, however, sometimes requires special page-handling routines. For example, you may wish to

1. Begin a new page after every major control break occurs.
2. Print a final total on a page by itself.
3. Change the sequence in which a test for OF occurs.

That is, you may wish to test for an OF condition at total time when such a test does not normally occur. You may do this to ensure that control totals will print on a new page even if an OF condition occurs while totals are printing.

These are just three typical problems that may arise when printing a group report. As programmers begin to code increasingly complex control break and other group print procedures, they frequently find the need to use the OF indicator in ways that have not yet been explained.

2. Forcing an End-of-Page Condition After Control Totals Have Printed
As noted, you may wish to force an end-of-page condition so that after control totals print, a new page is started that specifies a heading followed by new detail lines. To "force" an end-of-page condition, you must code an instruction that turns on the OF indicator. This instruction would be executed when a control level break has occurred. Since this is to be done after all control level calculations have been performed, code a SETON instruction on the Calculation form as the last control level operation. If you use only one control level, L1, the Calculation form might appear as follows.

RPG CALCULATION SPECIFICATIONS

Program		Keying Instruction	Graphic		Card Electro Number	Page 1 2 of ___	Program Identification 75 76 77 78 79 80
Programmer	Date		Key				

Line (3–5)	Form Type (6)	Control Level (L0–L9, LR, SR, AN/OR) (7–8)	Indicators (9–17)	Factor 1 (18–27)	Operation (28–32)	Factor 2 (33–42)	Result Field Name (43–48)	Length (49–51)	Decimal Positions (52)	Half Adjust (H) (53)	Resulting Indicators: Plus / High / 1>2 (54–55)	Minus / Low / 1<2 (56–57)	Zero / Equal / 1=2 (58–59)	Comments (60–74)
01Φ	C		1Φ	DTOTAL	ADD	AMT	DTOTAL	7	2					
02Φ	C	L1		FTOTAL	ADD	DTOTAL	FTOTAL	8	2					
03Φ	C	L1			SETON						OF			
04	C													
05	C													

For each input record, add AMT to DTOTAL. For each L1 break, add this DTOTAL to a final total called FTOTAL. The FTOTAL will print at the end of the run.

In addition, you may wish to set on the OF indicator when an L1 break occurs.

RPG CALCULATION SPECIFICATIONS

Program		Keying Instruction	Graphic		Card Electro Number	Page 1 2 of ___	Program Identification 75 76 77 78 79 80
Programmer	Date		Key				

Line (3–5)	Form Type (6)	Control Level (L0–L9, LR, SR, AN/OR) (7–8)	Indicators (9–17)	Factor 1 (18–27)	Operation (28–32)	Factor 2 (33–42)	Result Field Name (43–48)	Length (49–51)	Decimal Positions (52)	Half Adjust (H) (53)	Resulting Indicators: Plus / High / 1>2 (54–55)	Minus / Low / 1<2 (56–57)	Zero / Equal / 1=2 (58–59)	Comments (60–74)
01Φ	C	L1			SETON						OF			
02	C													
03	C													

The SETON command is used for turning on one, two, or three indicators using columns 54–55, 56–57, 58–59, respectively, to specify the indicators. As noted in Chapter 4, resulting indicators set on by the programmer remain on until the program turns them off. The OF indicator remains, however, under the control of the RPG II cycle and will "turn off" after there is a skip to a new page.

The instruction to SETON the overflow indicator is executed after a change in DEPT, the L1 field, occurs. This instruction will be executed after the DTOTAL is added to the FTOTAL because it is coded after the ADD. Recall that if there are numerous calculations that are performed when a specific indicator is on, they are executed in the sequence in which they are coded.

After all the L1 calculations are performed, the total lines that specify the L1 indicator will print. It is important to note that the computer does *not* automatically check for an overflow condition at total time. This means that these totals will print on the same page as the previous detail data, even if the detail data caused an overflow condition to occur. After the total lines print, and before new detail data is written, the computer will test for an overflow condition.

Note that the OF indicator will always be on at T or total time because the programmer sets it on, using the Calculation form. Thus, prior to printing a detail line that will contain a new control field, the computer will check for page overflow; since the page overflow indicator will be on, the headings will print on a new page followed by this first detail line for the new control group.

Figure 5.18 provides an illustration of the RPG II Logic Cycle as it relates to overflow processing. Figure 5.19 provides an illustration of how this RPG II cycle can be used to cause headings to print after each control break.

3. Changing the Sequence Normally Used to Test for an Overflow Condition
If no changes are made to the sequence in which steps are performed in RPG

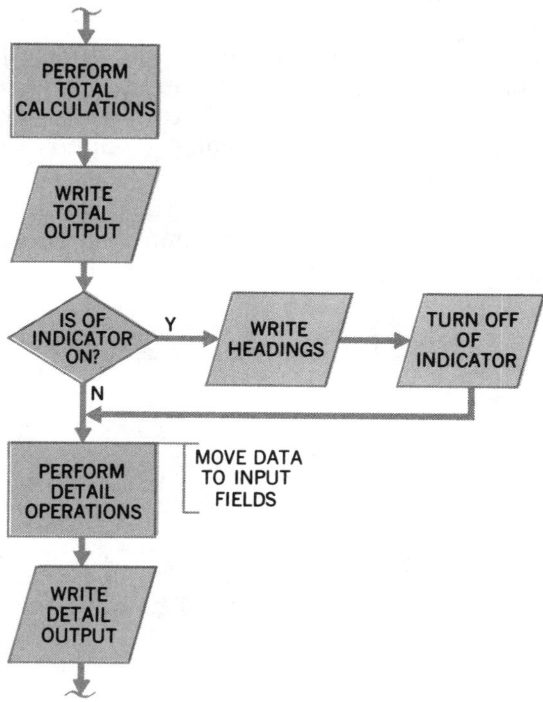

Figure 5.18
RPG II Logic Cycle excerpt indicating how OF processing occurs.

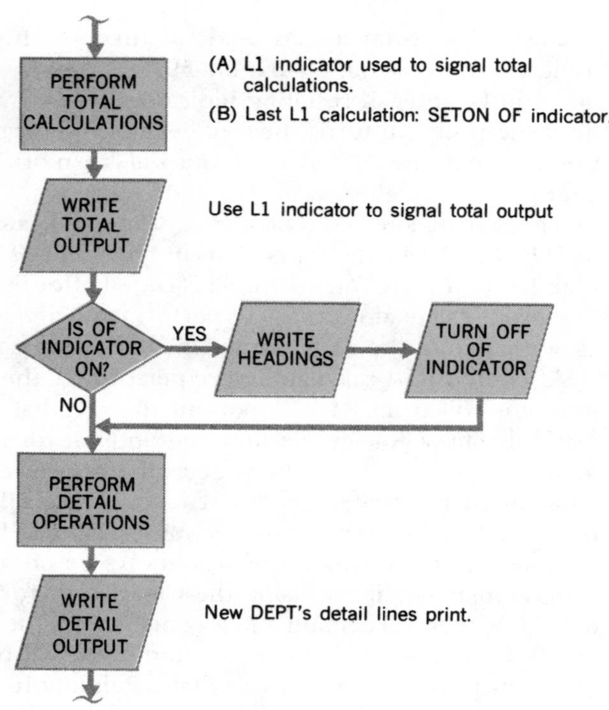

Figure 5.19
Using the RPG II Logic Cycle to cause headings to print after each control break.

II, total output will always appear on the same page as detail data since the OF test is not made until just before the new detail data is to be printed. This has the potential for causing a serious problem.

If there is just one control total line to print, then the possibility exists that there might be one extra print line on some output reports. That is, if the last detail line for a control group turned on the overflow indicator, this indicator would not be tested again until the *next* detail line is to print. If several totals are to print before the next detail line, they will print *on the same page* as the previous detail, with no attention to the page overflow condition.

Since bottom margins usually consist of several lines, this is not of major concern where just one total line is required. But suppose there are five levels of controls to print, each requiring two lines of output. The overflow indicator may turn on after the first line prints. But since OF is not tested again until detail time, the subsequent nine control lines will continue printing on the same page, over the perforation and onto the next page.

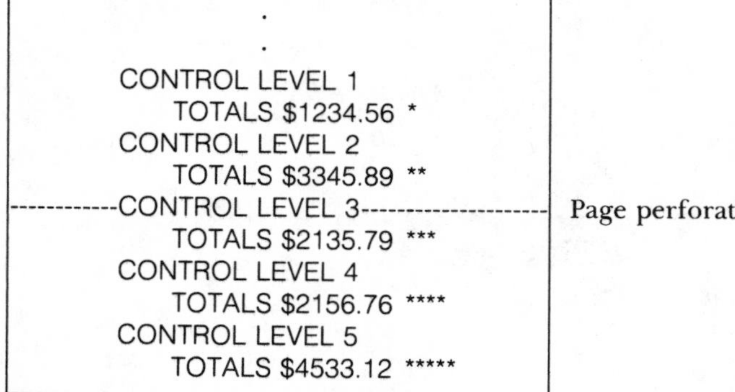

Because OF is not tested at total time, you run the risk of having totals print over perforations producing a decidedly unprofessional-looking output report. To avoid this possibility, you can *force* an overflow test at total time by using the FETCH OVERFLOW option on the Output Specifications form.

Column 16 on the Output form is called the **fetch overflow** position. It may be coded on the Output form with an 'F' on the same line that defines a total line. This will cause the computer to test for overflow before printing the total line. If you wish to test for overflow before several total lines are printed simply use the 'F' in column 16 for each total output line defined. Note that the fetch overflow does not force an overflow condition; it merely tests to see if the OF indicator is on.

Thus the following control total output specifications will avoid the possibility of missing an overflow condition and printing over the perforations of a continuous form.

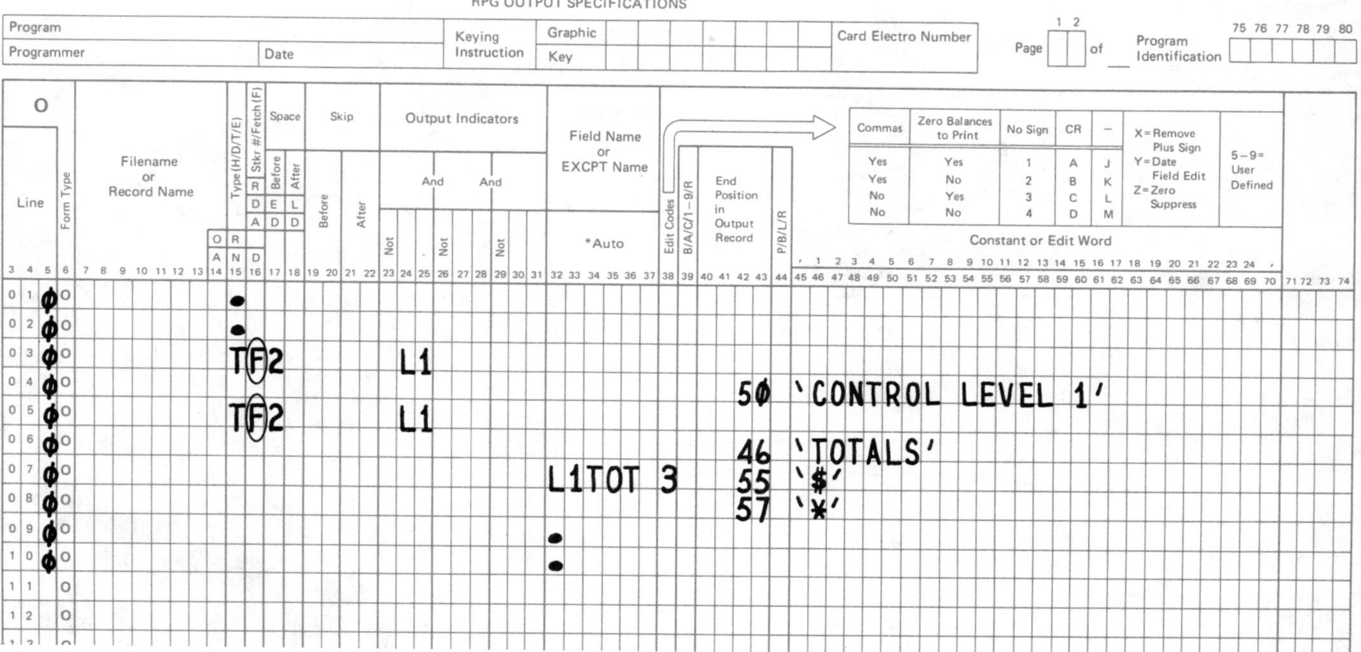

RPG OUTPUT SPECIFICATIONS

```
01 O  .
02 O  .
03 O        TF2      L1
04 O                                  50 'CONTROL LEVEL 1'
05 O        TF2      L1
06 O                                  46 'TOTALS'
07 O                         L1TOT 3  55 '$'
08 O                                  57 '*'
09 O                         .
10 O                         .
```

Note that the F in the FETCH OVERFLOW field causes an overflow test to be performed before the specific output line prints. Note, too, that it is unnecessary to use FETCH OVERFLOW for any output lines other than total lines. Since detail lines are always printed *after* an overflow test, FETCH OVERFLOW is usually unnecessary on D or detail lines.

Using an F in FETCH OVERFLOW, the RPG II Logic Cycle excerpt for overflow processing is amended as indicated in Figure 5.2Ø.

4. An Alternative Method for Beginning Control Totals on a New Page

Thus far, we have begun a new page for each control group by setting on the overflow indicator whenever a major control break occurs. In our example, a major break is denoted by the L2 indicator.

Consider Example 1, which, on first glance, may seem to perform the same function more easily: the printing of a heading each time there is a control break. There is, however, a major flaw in Example 1.

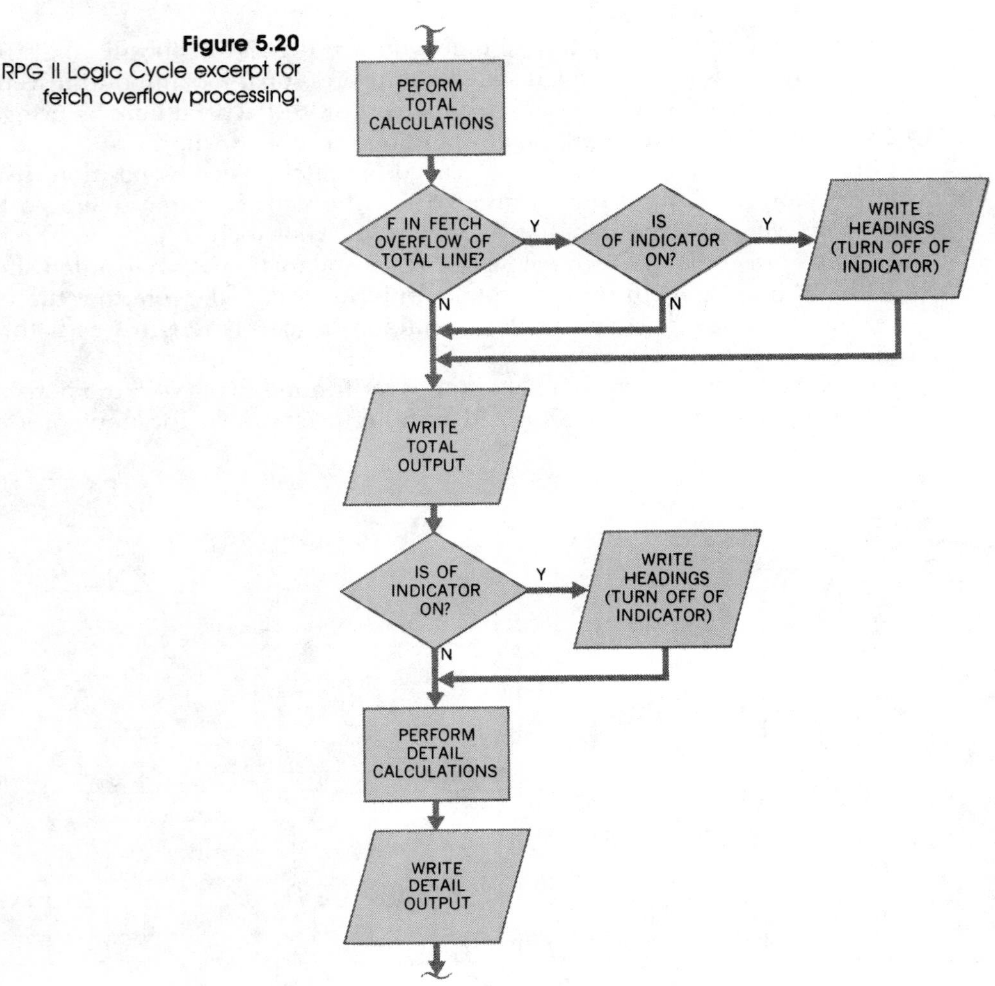

Figure 5.20
RPG II Logic Cycle excerpt for fetch overflow processing.

Example 1

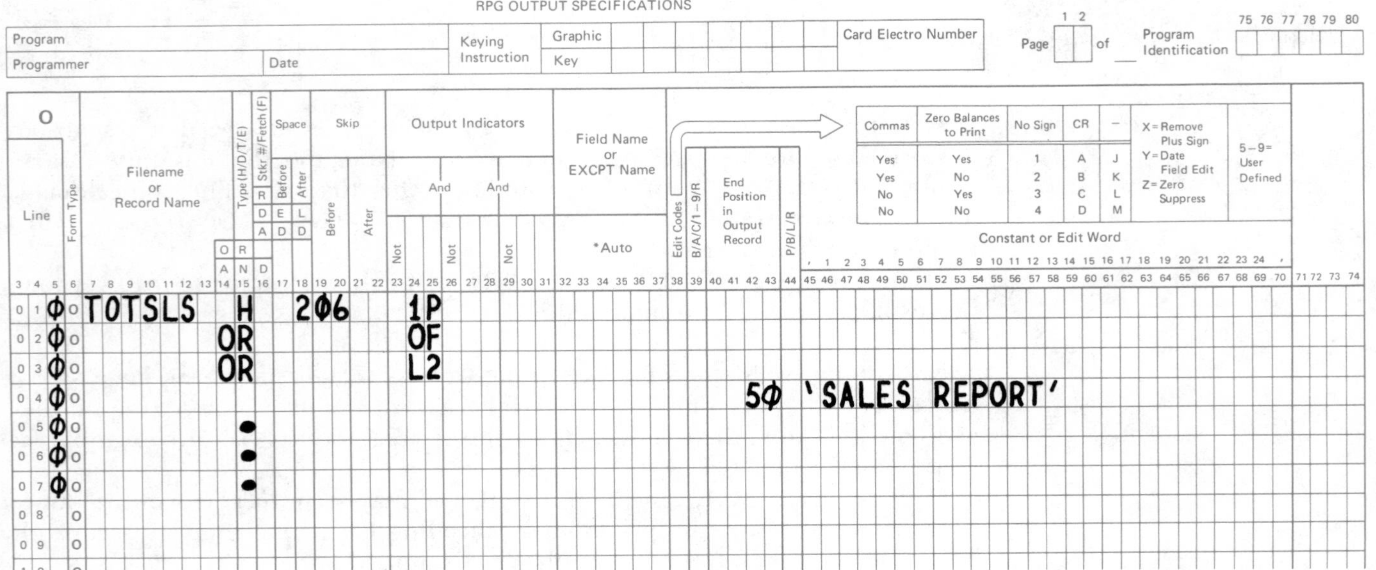

Note that the heading will print if either the 1P, OF, or L2 indicator is on. There is an initial problem, however. You may recall that the RPG II Logic Cycle *turns on* all level indicators when the first input record of a control group is read. This means that after the first input record is read, 1P *and* L2 are on. Since each indicator is tested separately, the heading would print *twice* on two separate pages before the first detail record is printed.

Thus, the logic in Example 1 is fine *except* for the initial heading, which prints twice. Since all level indicators are automatically turned on prior to any processing of the first record, you may use the L2 indicator to force a heading to print *in place of* the 1P indicator. See Example 2. This would certainly seem to alleviate this problem. Thus a heading prints if there is an overflow condition *or* an L2 break. This works fine for all normal processing and for the first record as well, which forces an L2 break.

Example 2

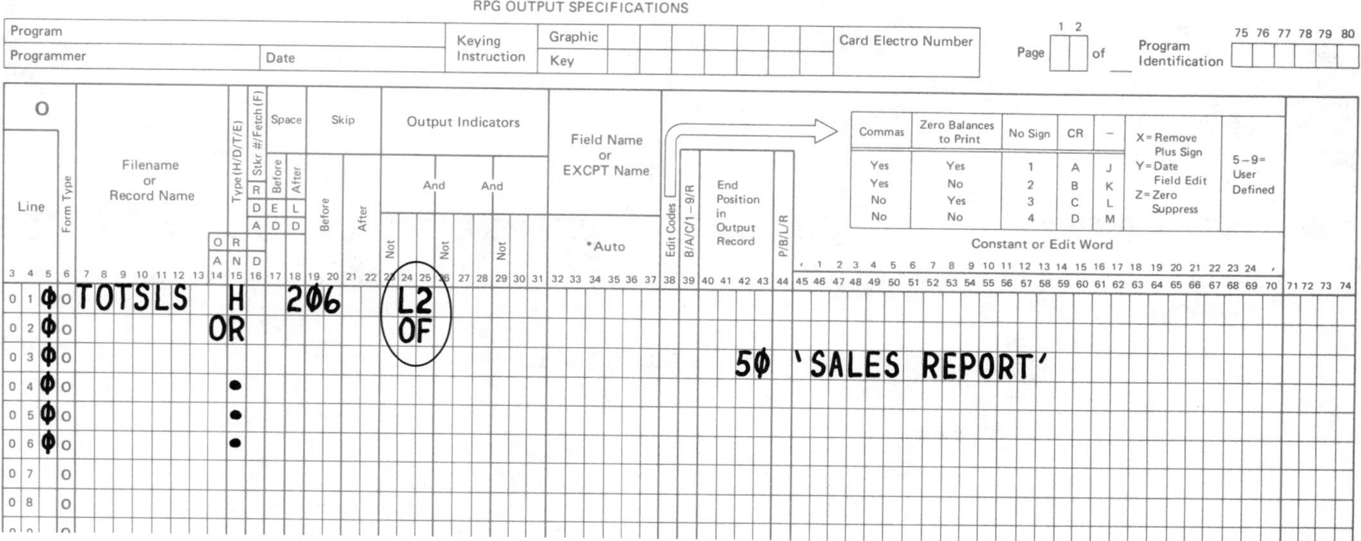

RPG OUTPUT SPECIFICATIONS

Line	Form Type	Filename or Record Name	Type (H/D/T/E)	Space After	Skip Before	Output Indicators	End Position in Output Record	Constant or Edit Word
01	O	TOTSLS	H	2	06	L2		
02	O		OR			OF		
03	O						50	'SALES REPORT'

There is *still* a potential error. If an overflow condition occurs when there is an L2 break, then once again *two* headings will print on two separate pages. To alleviate this problem, print a heading if

1. The L2 indicator is on; or
2. The OF indicator is on *and* the L2 indicator is off.

See Example 3, which can be used to force a page overflow whenever there is a major control break. This eliminates the need for setting on the OF indicator and using a fetch overflow. This represents the best solution to the problem.

Example 3

RPG OUTPUT SPECIFICATIONS

```
0 1 ΦO TOTSLS   H  2Φ6  L2
0 2 ΦO          OR      OFNL2
0 3 ΦO                                      5Φ 'SALES REPORT'
0 4 ΦO           .
0 5 ΦO           .
0 6 ΦO           .
0 7  O
0 8  O
```

IV. Advanced Concepts Relating to Control Breaks

Suppose you have a master disk file with the following format for each record.

PAYROLL RECORD

EMPNO	NAME	DEPT	SALARY	...

Suppose, further, that the records are in sequence by EMPNO and you wish to print a report with the following information.

PAYROLL SUMMARY REPORT

DEPT	TOTAL SALARIES
1	XXX,XXX.XX
.	.
.	.
.	.

If the input file were in sequence by DEPT, this problem would require a single-level control break. But since the file is *not* in the sequence desired, the programmer along with the systems analyst must decide the best course of action. They have three choices.

> ***When File is not in Sequence and Control Totals are Required***
>
> 1. Read each record and add salaries to the corresponding DEPT totals that are set up in storage; print DEPT totals at the end of job.
> 2. Read each record and add salaries to a table or array of totals; print the totals at the end of job.
> 3. Sort the file into the required sequence using a utility package, and then program a control break procedure.

Let us consider each of these alternatives in detail.

1. Read Each Record and Add Salaries to Corresponding DEPT Totals

On the Calculation Specifications form, you could compare each DEPT read to Ø1, Ø2, . . . Ø5 and add to the appropriate TOTAL. This would require five comparisons and five separate additions.

RPG CALCULATION SPECIFICATIONS

Program | Programmer | Date | Keying Instruction | Graphic | Key | Card Electro Number | Page of | Program Identification

Line	Form Type	Control Level (L0–L9, LR, SR, AN/OR)	Indicators	Factor 1	Operation	Factor 2	Result Field Name	Length	Decimal Positions	Half Adjust (H)	Resulting Indicators High (1>2)	Low (1<2)	Equal (1=2)	Comments
01Ø	C		Ø1	DEPT	COMP	1							99	
02Ø	C		Ø1 99	TOTAL1	ADD	SALARY	TOTAL1	8	2					
03Ø	C		Ø1	DEPT	COMP	2							88	
04Ø	C		Ø1 88	TOTAL2	ADD	SALARY	TOTAL2	8	2					
05Ø	C		Ø1	DEPT	COMP	3							77	
06Ø	C		Ø1 77	TOTAL3	ADD	SALARY	TOTAL3	8	2					
07Ø	C		Ø1	DEPT	COMP	4							66	
08Ø	C		Ø1 66	TOTAL4	ADD	SALARY	TOTAL4	8	2					
09Ø	C		Ø1	DEPT	COMP	5							55	
10Ø	C		Ø1 55	TOTAL5	ADD	SALARY	TOTAL5	8	2					
11	C													
12	C													
13	C													

After the last record has been processed and the LR indicator is on, at T or total time, the five totals would be printed.

You will note that the calculations for this are somewhat tedious. Moreover, if there were many more departments, for example DEPT Ø1–99, then such calculations would prove even more tedious, since 99 comparisons and 99 additions would be required!

Note, too, that reading and storing as in this example uses a significant amount of storage. The data must be collected in numerous total areas during the course of processing. Thus if there are a large number of control fields, this method of processing would be extremely inefficient.

2. Use a Table or Array

It would be possible to store a table or array as follows.

Table Entries

DEPT Ø1	
DEPT Ø2	
.	
.	
.	
.	

You would add to the appropriate table entry and then at the end of the job print all the totals.

This procedure enables the programmer to add a total to the appropriate table entry without having to make individual comparisons. That is, to add to DEPT Ø5 when a salary record containing DEPT 5 is read, simply instruct the computer to add to the fifth table entry.

It is not our intention in this chapter to teach the fundamentals of **table handling**, but simply to indicate that the use of tables is an alternative to control break procedures, particularly when the input file is not in sequence. For a full discussion of table-handling procedures, see Chapter 1Ø.

In summary, there is one major alternative to control break processing if there are numerous control field values: store the control totals in a table and then print them out after all records have been read and processed. This method has the major advantage of not requiring data to be in sequence by the control field. It does, however, require significantly more internal storage for storing the tables, which is a decided disadvantage of this type of processing. In the end, the programmer and the systems analyst must weigh the advantages and disadvantages.

3. Sort the File and Then Use a Control Break Procedure

Control break procedures are frequently far more efficient to code and run than are programs that require control totals to be stored. But control break programs require the input to be in the specific format required for output, in this instance, DEPT number sequence.

If the problem requires a small number of control fields (for example, DEPT varies from 1 to 3), you could use simple comparisons and additions rather than a control break procedure. Where there are more numerous entries, it is frequently best to sort the input into the required sequence and then perform the control break procedure.

A sort can be performed by an external utility package available on most systems. The user simply indicates the size of the record and the location of the sort field; the sort utility performs the required operations.

Summary

1. There are nine control level indicators: L1-L9.
2. A control level indicator is assigned on the Input form. It is used to identify an input field as a control field. Fields may be located within the record in any sequence, but, if feasible, it is good practice to specify control fields on the Input form beginning with the minor field (L1) and continuing in ascending sequence to the major field.

3. When an input record is read, the computer determines if there is a change in the control field; if there is,

   Total calculations using the specified level indicator are performed in the sequence specified on the Calculation form.

   Total output that specifies the same level indicator is printed.

4. After a control field is tested and total processing is performed when a change in the control field occurs, then,

   Detail calculations are performed in the sequence in which they appear on the Calculation form.

   Detail output is produced.

   Note *The record that caused a control break is not printed until the previous totals have been computed and printed.*

5. Control level arithmetic operations are entered on the Calculation form and follow the detail calculations. These entries are also in L1, L2, L3, etc. sequence. Remember, these instructions are executed during total calculation time only if the level indicators are coded in columns 7–8 of the Calculation form.
6. When a level indicator is coded in columns 9–17, and columns 7–8 contain blanks, the indicator is turned on only for the *first* record of each group. The programmer could use this to advantage by setting a counter to zero when the first record of a new group is processed. The number of detail records within each group could then be counted by the program. It should again be emphasized that control level indicators entered in columns 9–17 are processed during detail calculation time.
7. Control level entries on the Output form require a T in column 15 as well as level indicator entries in columns 23–31. Again, these entries follow the detail output coding on the form in ascending level (L1, L2, L3, etc.) sequence. These instructions are executed during total output time and print the *previous group's* totals.
8. Control level indicators L1-L9 are automatically turned off at the end of the RPG II Logic Cycle.
9. Despite the fact that control break totals are calculated and printed before detail data, output should be coded in the following sequence.

   H
   D
   T

   Moreover, total output should be coded with the lowest level (L1) followed by subsequent levels if used.

10. Calculations should be specified with detail calculations coded before total calculations. Total calculations should also be in sequence, with L1 calculations preceding L2, L3, . . . LR.
11. Level indicators are normally used to condition total lines but may condition fields on detail lines as well, specifically for group indicate purposes.
12. Any fields used for summing or accumulating group totals must be reset to zero once they have been printed. Coding a B in column 39, the Blank After position of the Output form, provides this capability.

Figure 5.21 provides the problem definition for a triple level control break problem. The RPG II coding required to produce the output indicated is in Figure 5.22.

Systems Flowchart

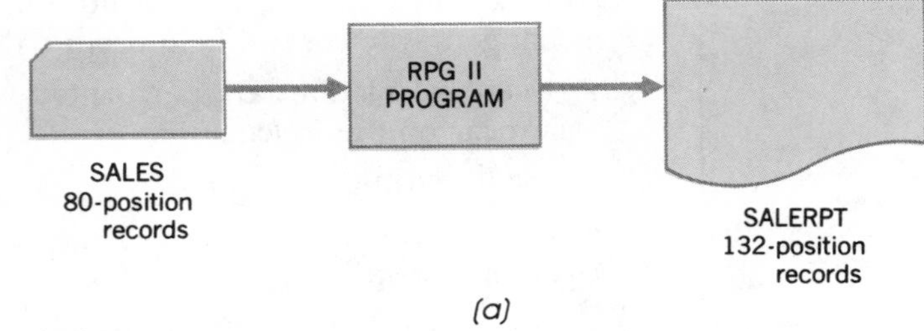

(a)

SALES Record Layout

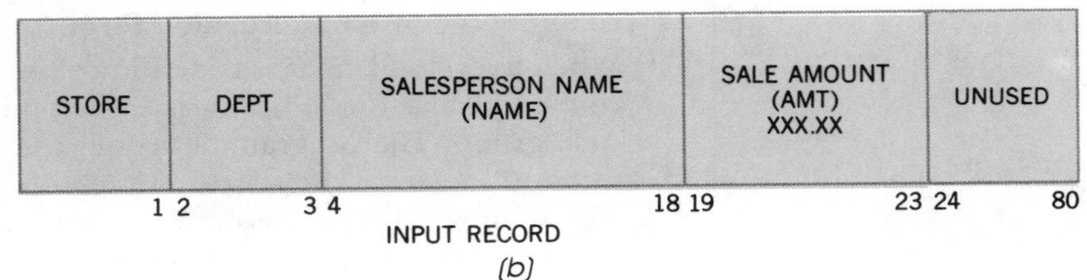

(b)

SALERPT Printer Spacing Chart

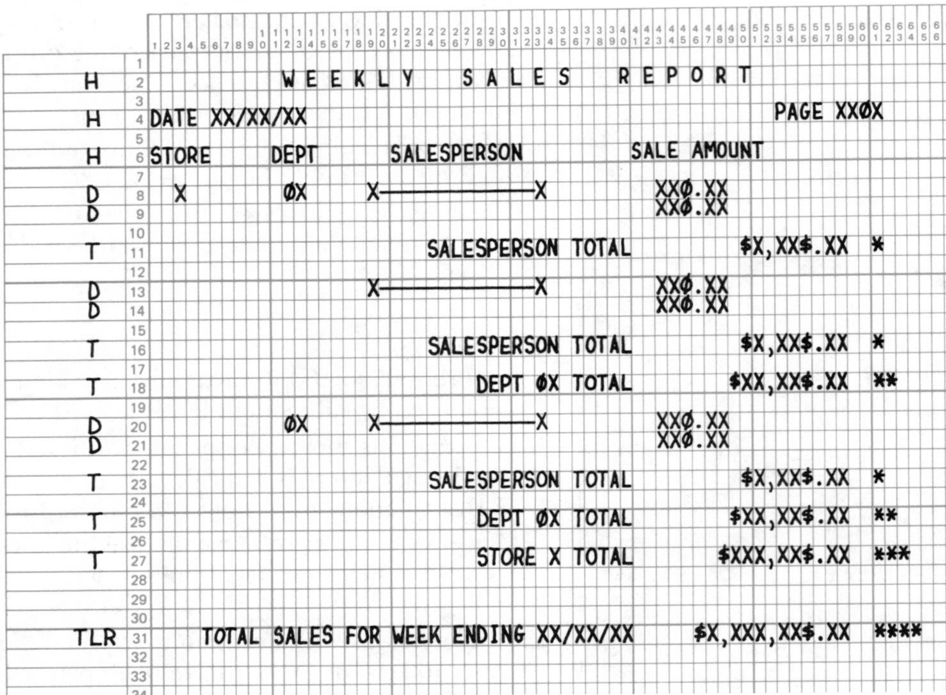

(c)

Figure 5.21
Problem definition for a triple-level control-break program.

Figure 5.22
Triple-level control break program with output.
(Continued on next page.)

```
        01-010  F******************************************************************SSS05A
        01-020  F*    THIS PROGRAM UTILIZES TRIPLE LEVEL CONTROL BREAK TO PRODUCE     *SSS05A
        01-030  F*   GROUP INDICATED WEEKLY SALES REPORT CALCULATING SALESPERSON      *SSS05A
        01-040  F*   TOTALS,DEPT TOTALS,STORE TOTALS,AND FINAL TOTAL FOR ALL STORES.*SSS05A
        01-050  F******************************************************************SSS05A
        01-060  F*                                                                 SSS05A
0001    01-070  FSALES   IP  F      80            READ01 SYSIPT                    SSS05A
0002    01-080  FSALERPT O   F     132     OF     PRINTERSYSLST                    SSS05A
        01-090  F*                                                                 SSS05A
        02-010  I************************** INPUT RECORD **************************SSS05A
        02-020  I*                                                                 SSS05A
0003    02-030  ISALES   NS  10                                                    SSS05A
0004    02-040  I                                           1   10STORE L3         SSS05A
0005    02-050  I                                           2   30DEPT  L2         SSS05A
0006    02-060  I                                           4  18 NAME  L1         SSS05A
0007    02-070  I                                          19  232AMT              SSS05A
        02-080  I*                                                                 SSS05A
        03-010  C************************** CALCULATIONS **************************SSS05A
        03-020  C*                                                                 SSS05A
0008    03-030  C   10       AMT       ADD  TSALE     TSALE   62                   SSS05A
0009    03-040  CL1          TSALE     ADD  TDEPT     TDEPT   72                   SSS05A
0010    03-050  CL2          TDEPT     ADD  TSTORE    TSTORE  82                   SSS05A
0011    03-060  CL3          TSTORE    ADD  FTOTAL    FTOTAL  92                   SSS05A
        03-070  C*                                                                 SSS05A
        04-010  O************************** HEADING LINES *************************SSS05A
        04-020  O*                                                                 SSS05A
0012    04-030  OSALERPT H  201    1P                                              SSS05A
0013    04-040  O       OR         OF                                              SSS05A
0014    04-050  O                                   35 'W E E K L Y   S A L E S'   SSS05A
0015    04-060  O                                   50 'R E P O R T'               SSS05A
0016    04-070  O        H  2      1P                                              SSS05A
0017    04-080  O       OR         OF                                              SSS05A
0018    04-090  O                                    4 'DATE'                      SSS05A
0019    04-100  O                         UDATE Y   13                             SSS05A
0020    04-110  O                                   56 'PAGE'                      SSS05A
0021    04-120  O                         PAGE      61                             SSS05A
0022    04-130  O        H  2      1P                                              SSS05A
0023    04-140  O       OR         OF                                              SSS05A
0024    04-150  O                                    5 'STORE'                     SSS05A
0025    04-160  O                                   14 'DEPT'                      SSS05A
0026    04-170  O                                   31 'SALESPERSON'               SSS05A
0027    04-180  O                                   51 'SALE AMOUNT'               SSS05A
        04-190  O*                                                                 SSS05A
        04-200  O************************** DETAIL LINE ***************************SSS05A
        04-210  O*                                                                 SSS05A
0028    04-220  O        D  1      10                                              SSS05A
0029    04-230  O                    L3   STORE      3                             SSS05A
0030    04-240  O                    L2   DEPT  Z   13                             SSS05A
0031    04-250  O                    L1   NAME      33                             SSS05A
0032    04-260  O                         AMT   1   48                             SSS05A
        04-270  O*                                                                 SSS05A
        05-010  O************************** TOTAL LINES ***************************SSS05A
        05-020  O*                                                                 SSS05A
0033    05-030  O        T 12      L1                                              SSS05A
0034    05-040  O                                   40 'SALESPERSON TOTAL'         SSS05A
0035    05-050  O                         TSALE 1B  58 '$'                         SSS05A
0036    05-060  O                                   61 '*'                         SSS05A
0037    05-070  O        T  2      L2                                              SSS05A
0038    05-080  O                                   31 'DEPT'                      SSS05A
0039    05-090  O                         DEPT  Z   34                             SSS05A
0040    05-100  O                                   40 'TOTAL'                     SSS05A
0041    05-110  O                         TDEPT 1B  58 '$'                         SSS05A
0042    05-120  O                                   62 '**'                        SSS05A
0043    05-130  O        T  3      L3                                              SSS05A
0044    05-140  O                                   32 'STORE'                     SSS05A
0045    05-150  O                         STORE     34                             SSS05A
0046    05-160  O                                   40 'TOTAL'                     SSS05A
0047    05-170  O                         TSTORE1B  58 '$'                         SSS05A
0048    05-180  O                                   63 '***'                       SSS05A
0049    05-190  O        T 1       LR                                              SSS05A
0050    05-200  O                                   15 'TOTAL SALES'               SSS05A
0051    05-210  O                                   31 'FOR WEEK ENDING'           SSS05A
0052    05-220  O                         UDATE Y   40                             SSS05A
0053    05-230  O                         FTOTAL1   58 '$'                         SSS05A
0054    05-240  O                                   64 '****'                      SSS05A
        05-250  O*                                   .                             SSS05A
        05-260  O******************************************************************SSS05A
```

```
              W E E K L Y   S A L E S   R E P O R T

DATE 11/29/82                                          PAGE    1

STORE      DEPT      SALESPERSON          SALE AMOUNT

  1          2      CHARLIE SMITH            29.95
                                             37.63

                           SALESPERSON TOTAL           $67.58  *
```

Figure 5.22
(continued)

```
                  SHIRLEY GREENE             101.01
                       SALESPERSON TOTAL                $101.01  *
                           DEPT  2 TOTAL                $168.59  **
            5     JOE THOMPSON                68.57
                       SALESPERSON TOTAL                 $68.57  *
                           DEPT  5 TOTAL                 $68.57  **
           10     DANIEL MURPHY               87.65
                                               9.97
                       SALESPERSON TOTAL                 $97.62  *
                           DEPT 10 TOTAL                 $97.62  **
                           STORE 1 TOTAL                $334.78  ***

   2        1     ALLAN DARRONE               52.34
                       SALESPERSON TOTAL                 $52.34  *
                  MIKE WILLIAMS              298.50
                       SALESPERSON TOTAL                $298.50  *
                           DEPT  1 TOTAL                $350.84  **
            5     JOANNA LITTLE               49.98
                       SALESPERSON TOTAL                 $49.98  *
                           DEPT  5 TOTAL                 $49.98  **
                           STORE 2 TOTAL                $400.82  ***

   3        5     BOB ALBERTSON               99.99
                       SALESPERSON TOTAL                 $99.99  *
                           DEPT  5 TOTAL                 $99.99  **


            W E E K L Y    S A L E S    R E P O R T
DATE 11/29/82                                           PAGE    2
STORE      DEPT      SALESPERSON           SALE AMOUNT
            7     ELAINE RICHARDS             62.73
                                               4.89
                       SALESPERSON TOTAL                 $67.62  *
                  JOHN JOHNSON               112.34
                                              24.98
                       SALESPERSON TOTAL                $137.32  *
                  HARRY HIGGINS               79.98
                       SALESPERSON TOTAL                 $79.98  *
                           DEPT  7 TOTAL                $284.92  **
           12     FRANK JONES                  9.95
                       SALESPERSON TOTAL                  $9.95  *
                  MARY CUMMINGS               34.48
                                              47.89
                                              27.45
                       SALESPERSON TOTAL                $109.82  *
                  JIM ANDERSON               100.00
                       SALESPERSON TOTAL                $100.00  *
                           DEPT 12 TOTAL                $219.77  **
                           STORE 3 TOTAL                $604.68  ***


     TOTAL SALES FOR WEEK ENDING 11/29/82             $1,340.28  ****
```

Key Terms

Control break
Control field
Detail printing
Detail time
Fetch overflow
Group indicate
Group printing
Level indicator
Multiple level control break
Page overflow
Single level control break
Table handling
Total time

Self-Evaluating Quiz

1. When summary totals for each DEPT are required and the input is in sequence by department number, then the type of processing to be performed is called ________ .
2. In question 1, DEPT is referred to as the ________ field.
3. Suppose that detail printing was required in question 1 as well. If the DEPT field is only printed on the *first* detail line of each group, then it is referred to as a(n) ________ field.
4. (T or F) Using control break processing, detail records must be printed.
5. (T or F) Using control break processing, control totals must be accumulated if a final total is required.
6. (T or F) If a final total is required in a control break procedure, then it can be accumulated at detail time or at L1 time.
7. If three control breaks are needed and L1-L3 are used to define them, then the ________ level is considered the major level.
8. Suppose you are using L1-L3. A change in the input field associated with the L2 level will automatically force (*no.*) breaks.
9. (T or F) When the last record has been processed, L1-L9 indicators, when used, are turned on along with the LR indicator.
10. (T or F) In a control break procedure. the last record at the end of the job will not be accumulated properly unless the programmer makes specific changes to the normal flow of logic.
11. When a L1 control break occurs, (calculation, detail output, total output) operations that use L1 indicators are executed, followed by (calculation, detail output, total output) operations that use L1 indicators.
12. When an L1 control break occurs, L1 operations (precede, follow) detail operations. Explain your answer.
13. When performing a multiple-level control-break operation, the computer checks for a change in the (highest, lowest) level of control first.
14. Using the following input, how would you tell the computer that branch offices are arranged within regions and that control totals will be necessary for branch offices within regions and for regions as well?

RPG INPUT SPECIFICATIONS

Program | Keying Instruction | Graphic | Key | Card Electro Number | Page 1 2 of | Program Identification 75 76 77 78 79 80
Programmer | Date

Line (3–5)	Form Type (6)	Filename or Record Name / Data Structure Name (7–14)	Sequence (15–16)	Number (1/N), E (17)	Option (O), U, S (18)	Record Identifying Indicator, **, or DS (19–20)	Record Identification Codes 1: Position (21–24)	Not (N) (25)	C/Z/D (26)	Character (27)	Record Identification Codes 2 (28–34)	Record Identification Codes 3 (35–41)	Stacker Select (42)	P/B/L/R (43)	Field Location From (44–47)	Field Location To (48–51)	Decimal Positions (52)	RPG Field Name (53–58)	Control Level (L1–L9) (59–60)	Matching Fields or Chaining Fields (61–62)	Field Record Relation (63–64)	Field Indicators Plus (65–66)	Minus (67–68)	Zero or Blank (69–70)	(71–74)
0 1 Ø	I	SALES	NS			Ø1	1		C	S															
0 2 Ø	I														2	5		SLSNO							
0 3 Ø	I														6	1Ø	2	AMT							
0 4 Ø	I														11	12	Ø	BRANCH							
0 5 Ø	I														13	14	Ø	REGION							
0 6	I																								
0 7	I																								
0 8	I																								

15. Using the input specifications for question 14, code the calculations for producing double level control breaks for the AMT field, with branch totals and region totals printing.

RPG CALCULATION SPECIFICATIONS

Program | Keying Instruction | Graphic | Key | Card Electro Number | Page 1 2 of | Program Identification 75 76 77 78 79 80
Programmer | Date

Line (3–5)	Form Type (6)	Control Level (L0–L9, LR, SR, AN/OR) (7–8)	Indicators: Not (9)	(10–11)	And: Not (12)	(13–14)	And: Not (15)	(16–17)	Factor 1 (18–27)	Operation (28–32)	Factor 2 (33–42)	Result Field: Name (43–48)	Length (49–51)	Decimal Positions (52)	Half Adjust (H) (53)	Resulting Indicators: Arithmetic Plus / Compare 1 > 2 / Lookup (Factor 2) is High (54–55)	Minus / 1 < 2 / Low (56–57)	Zero / 1 = 2 / Equal (58–59)	Comments (60–74)
0 1	C																		
0 2	C																		
0 3	C																		
0 4	C																		
0 5	C																		

16. Could the following coding be used to produce correct branch and region totals? Explain your answer.

RPG CALCULATION SPECIFICATIONS

Line	Form Type	Control Level	Indicators	Factor 1	Operation	Factor 2	Result Field Name
01Ø	C		Ø1	BRTOT	ADD	REGTOT	REGTOT
02Ø	C	L1		REGTOT	ADD	FINTOT	FINTOT
03	C						
04	C						

17. Code the Output form for question 16, printing only branch totals and region totals when control breaks occur.

RPG OUTPUT SPECIFICATIONS

18. (T or F) After each control break, clearing the region total field after printing is entirely optional.
19. (T of F) The programmer must turn off all level indicators prior to processing each record.
2Ø. (T or F) If data is not in sequence by the control field, then control break processing cannot be used.

Solutions

1. control break processing
2. control
3. group indicate
4. F—It is feasible to produce just summary data from detail input using control break processing.
5. T
6. T—It is, however, more efficient to accumulate a final total when there is a control break. Suppose, for example, that there are 1Ø,ØØØ input records but only 5 control fields, such as DEPT Ø1-DEPT Ø5. If final totals were accumulated at detail time, there would be 1Ø,ØØØ additions necessary; if final totals were accumulated whenever there was a change in DEPT, there would only be 5 additions necessary.
7. L3
8. two (L2 and L1)
9. T
1Ø. F—The LR indicator as well as all level indicators are turned on at the end of the job. This forces appropriate control breaks when there is no more data.
11. calculation
    total output
12. precede
    This enables a control total that has been accumulated to print *prior to* the new control field.
13. highest
14.

RPG INPUT SPECIFICATIONS

Program		Keying Instruction	Graphic		Card Electro Number	Page 1 2 of	Program Identification 75 76 77 78 79 80
Programmer	Date		Key				

Line (3-5)	Form Type (6)	Filename or Record Name (7-14)	Sequence (15-16)	Record Identifying Indicator (19-20)	Record Identification Codes 1: Position (21-24)	C/Z/D (26)	Character (27)	Field Location From (44-47)	To (48-51)	Decimal Positions (52)	RPG Field Name (53-58)	Control Level (L1-L9) (59-60)
01Ø	I	SALES	NS	Ø1	1	C	S					
02Ø	I							2	5		SLSNO	
03Ø	I							6	1Ø	2	AMT	
04Ø	I							11	12	Ø	BRANCH	L1
05Ø	I							13	14	Ø	REGION	L2
06	I											
07	I											

15.

RPG CALCULATION SPECIFICATIONS

Line	Form Type	Control Level	Indicators	Factor 1	Operation	Factor 2	Result Field Name	Length	Decimal Positions
01	C		01	AMT	ADD	BRTOT	BRTOT	7	2
02	C	L1		BRTOT	ADD	REGTOT	REGTOT	8	2
03	C	L2		REGTOT	ADD	FINTOT	FINTOT	9	2
04	C								
05	C								

Note: This line is coded only if final total is required

16. No.

RPG CALCULATION SPECIFICATIONS

Line	Form Type	Control Level	Indicators	Factor 1	Operation	Factor 2	Result Field Name	Length	Decimal Positions
01	C		01	BRTOT	ADD	REGTOT	REGTOT		
02	C								
03	C								

Not defined

On 01 level should be adding amt to BRTOT

Must be defined

17.

RPG OUTPUT SPECIFICATIONS

Line	Form Type	Filename or Record Name	Type (H/D/T/E)	Space Before	Space After	Skip Before	Skip After	Output Indicators	Output Indicators (And)	Field Name or EXCPT Name	Edit Codes	End Position in Output Record	Constant or Edit Word
01Φ	O	TOTSLS	H		2	Φ6		1P					
02Φ	O		OR					OF					
03Φ	O											5Φ	'SALES REPORT'
04Φ	O									UDATE	Y	6Φ	
05Φ	O		D		2			Φ1					
06Φ	O								L1	BRANCH		5	
07Φ	O									SLSNO		1Φ	
08Φ	O									AMT	3	2Φ	'$'
09Φ	O		T		2			L1					
10Φ	O											6Φ	'TOTAL FOR BRANCH'
11Φ	O									BRTOT	1	75	'$'
12Φ	O		T		2			L2					
13Φ	O											8Φ	'TOTAL FOR REGION'
14Φ	O									REGTOT	1	95	'$'
15Φ	O		T		2			LR					
16Φ	O											1ΦΦ	'FINAL TOTAL'
17Φ	O									FINTOT	1	115	'$'
18	O												
19	O												

18. F—Failing to clear it will result in incorrect processing of region totals.
19. F—These are automatically turned off.
2Ø. T

Review Questions

Define the meaning of the following (1–3).

1. Control break
2. Group indicate field
3. Fetch overflow
4. Indicate how a triple level control break is performed. Specify the RPG II Logic Cycle for this procedure.
5. Provide a sample listing for a program that has double level control breaks, a group indicate field, and detail printing.

Debugging Exercise 1

The problem definition for this exercise is shown in Figure 5.23. The program coding sheets in Figure 5.24 contain syntax errors. Identify them and illustrate the corrections you would make to the program.

Figure 5.25 shows the listing produced by running the program as coded. Note that the syntax errors in this case do not cause diagnostic messages to print. Note, also, that the output is erroneous. The syntax corrections are circled on the computer listing shown in Figure 5.26. There are, however, logic errors in the program. Your assignment is to desk check this program carefully, find the logic errors, and make the necessary corrections.

Figure 5.23 Problem definition for Debugging Exercise 1.

Systems Flowchart

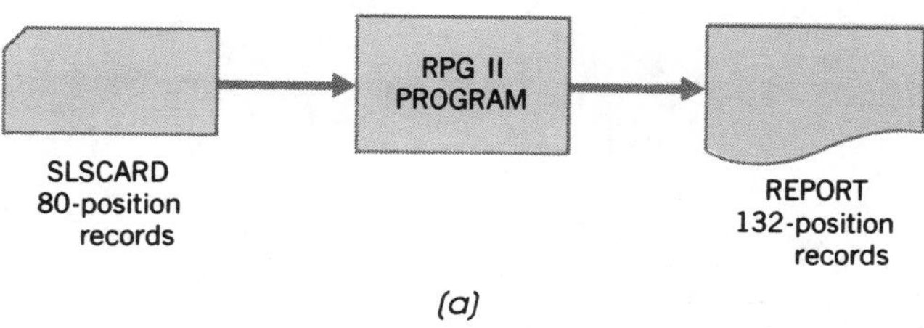

(a)

SLSCARD Record Layout

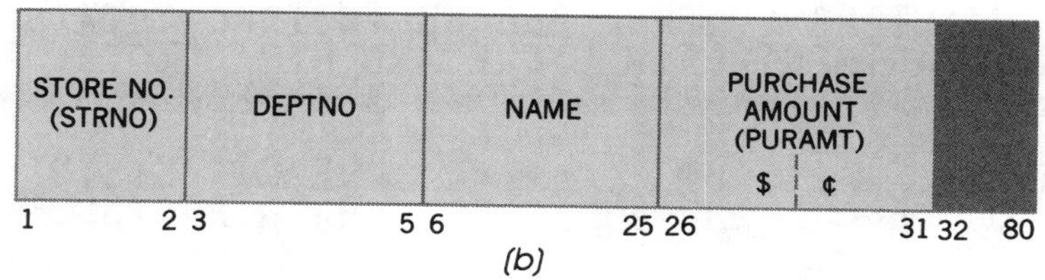

(b)

REPORT Printer Spacing Chart

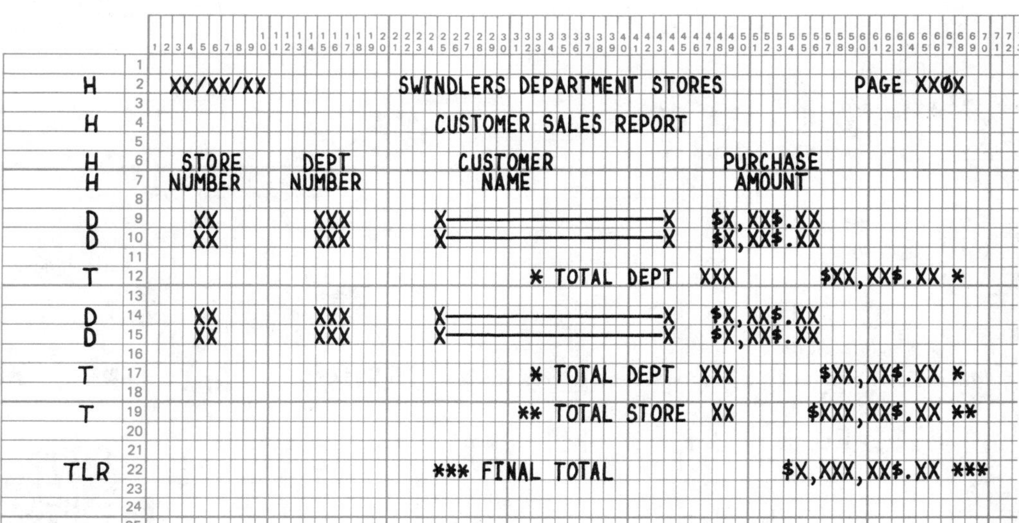

(c)

Figure 5.24
Coding sheets for Debugging
Exercise 1.

RPG CONTROL AND FILE DESCRIPTION SPECIFICATIONS

Program: CUSTOMER SALES — Programmer: N. JOHNKE — Date: 6/11/-- — Keying Instruction: Graphic Ø 1 2, Key ZERO ONE TWO — Card Electro Number — Page Ø1 of 5 — Program Identification (75–80): SSSØ5

Control Specifications

For the valid entries for a system, refer to the RPG reference manual for that system.

```
01Ø H
```

File Description Specifications

For the valid entries for a system, refer to the RPG reference manual for that system.

```
02Ø F*********************************************************************
03Ø F*           THIS PROGRAM CREATES A CUSTOMER SALES REPORT WHICH      *
04Ø F*           UTILIZES CONTROL BREAKS TO TAKE TOTALS FOR EACH         *
05Ø F*           DEPARTMENT,EACH STORE AND FINAL TOTAL FOR ALL STORES    *
06Ø F*********************************************************************
07Ø F*
08Ø FSLSCARD IP  F      8Ø                READØ1 SYSIPT
09Ø FREPORT  O   F     132      OF        PRINTERSYSLST
10Ø F*
    F
    F
```

RPG INPUT SPECIFICATIONS

Program: CUSTOMER SALES — Programmer: N. JOHNKE — Date: 6/11/-- — Keying Instruction: Graphic Ø 1 2, Key ZERO ONE TWO — Card Electro Number — Page Ø2 of 5 — Program Identification (75–80): SSSØ5

```
01Ø I************************ INPUT RECORD ****************************
02Ø I*
03Ø ISLSCARD NS   19
04Ø I                                          1   2ØSTRNO L2
05Ø I                                          3   5ØDEPTNOL1
06Ø I                                          6  25 NAME
07Ø I                                         26  312PURAMT
08Ø I*
09  I
10  I
```

Figure 5.24 *(continued)*

RPG CALCULATION SPECIFICATIONS

Program: CUSTOMER SALES — Programmer: N. JOHNKE — Date: 6/11/-- — Graphic: Ø 1 2 — Key: ZERO ONE TWO — Page: Ø3 of 5 — Program Identification: SSSØ5

Line	Form Type	Control Level	Indicators	Factor 1	Operation	Factor 2	Result Field Name	Length	Decimal Positions	Comments
Ø1Ø	C	******************** CALCULATION ROUTINE ********************								
Ø2Ø	C	*								
Ø3Ø	C		L1	PURAMT	ADD	TOTDPT	TOTDPT	7	2	DEPT TOTAL
Ø4Ø	C		L2	TOTDPT	ADD	TOTSTR	TOTSTR	8	2	STORE TOTAL
Ø5Ø	C		LR	FINTOT	ADD	TOTSTR	FINTOT	9	2	FINAL TOTAL
Ø6Ø	C	*								
07	C									
08	C									

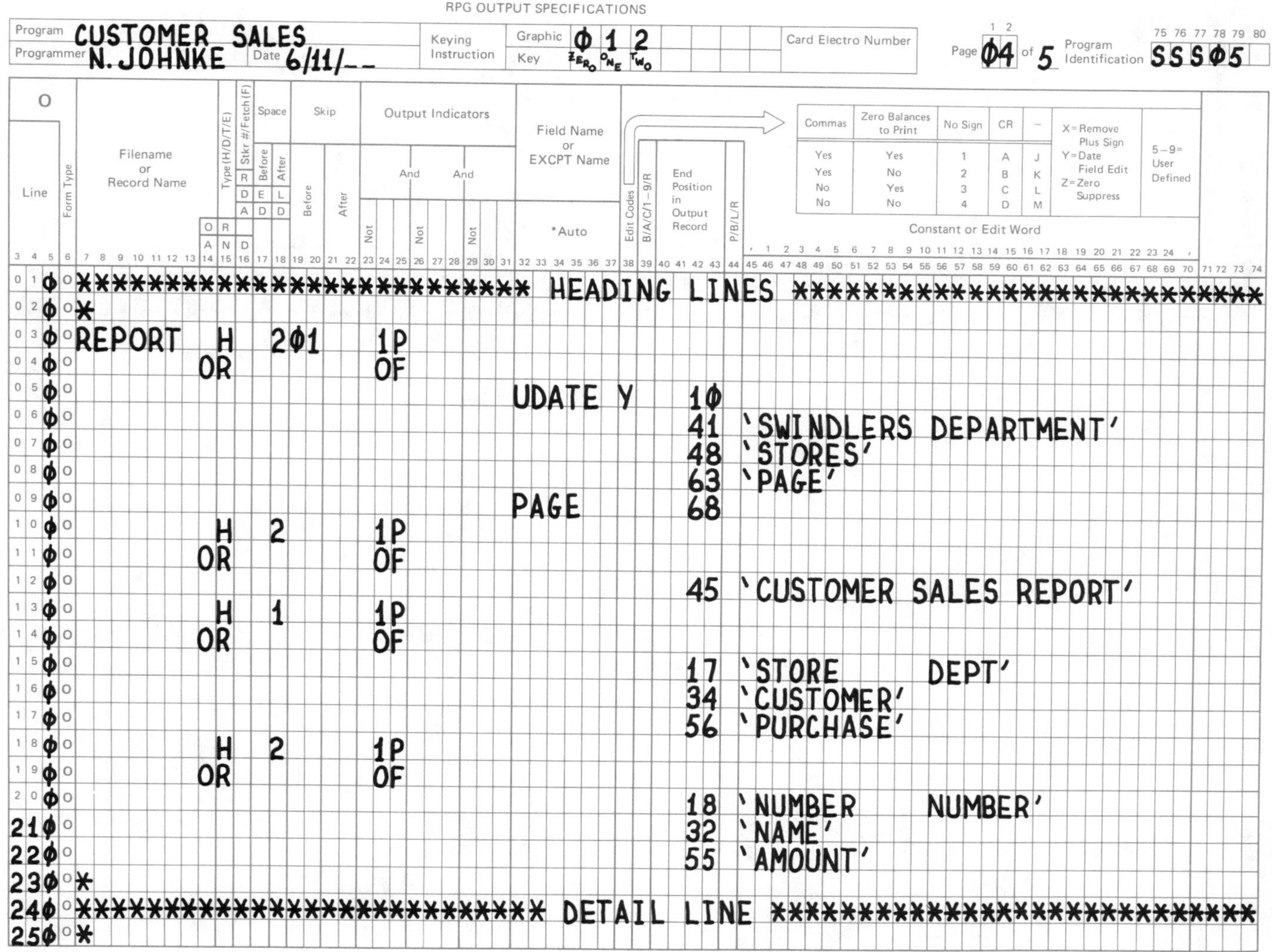

RPG OUTPUT SPECIFICATIONS

Program: CUSTOMER SALES — Programmer: N. JOHNKE — Date: 6/11/-- — Graphic: Ø 1 2 — Key: ZERO ONE TWO — Page: Ø4 of 5 — Program Identification: SSSØ5

Line	Form Type	Filename or Record Name	Type	Space/Skip	Output Indicators	Field Name	Edit Codes	End Position	Constant or Edit Word
Ø1Ø	O	******************** HEADING LINES ********************							
Ø2Ø	O	*							
Ø3Ø	O	REPORT	H	2Ø1	1P				
Ø4Ø	O		OR		OF				
Ø5Ø	O					UDATE	Y	1Ø	
Ø6Ø	O							41	'SWINDLERS DEPARTMENT'
Ø7Ø	O							48	'STORES'
Ø8Ø	O							63	'PAGE'
Ø9Ø	O					PAGE		68	
1ØØ	O		H	2	1P				
11Ø	O		OR		OF				
12Ø	O							45	'CUSTOMER SALES REPORT'
13Ø	O		H	1	1P				
14Ø	O		OR		OF				
15Ø	O							17	'STORE DEPT'
16Ø	O							34	'CUSTOMER'
17Ø	O							56	'PURCHASE'
18Ø	O		H	2	1P				
19Ø	O		OR		OF				
2ØØ	O							18	'NUMBER NUMBER'
21Ø	O							32	'NAME'
22Ø	O							55	'AMOUNT'
23Ø	O	*							
24Ø	O	******************** DETAIL LINE ********************							
25Ø	O	*							

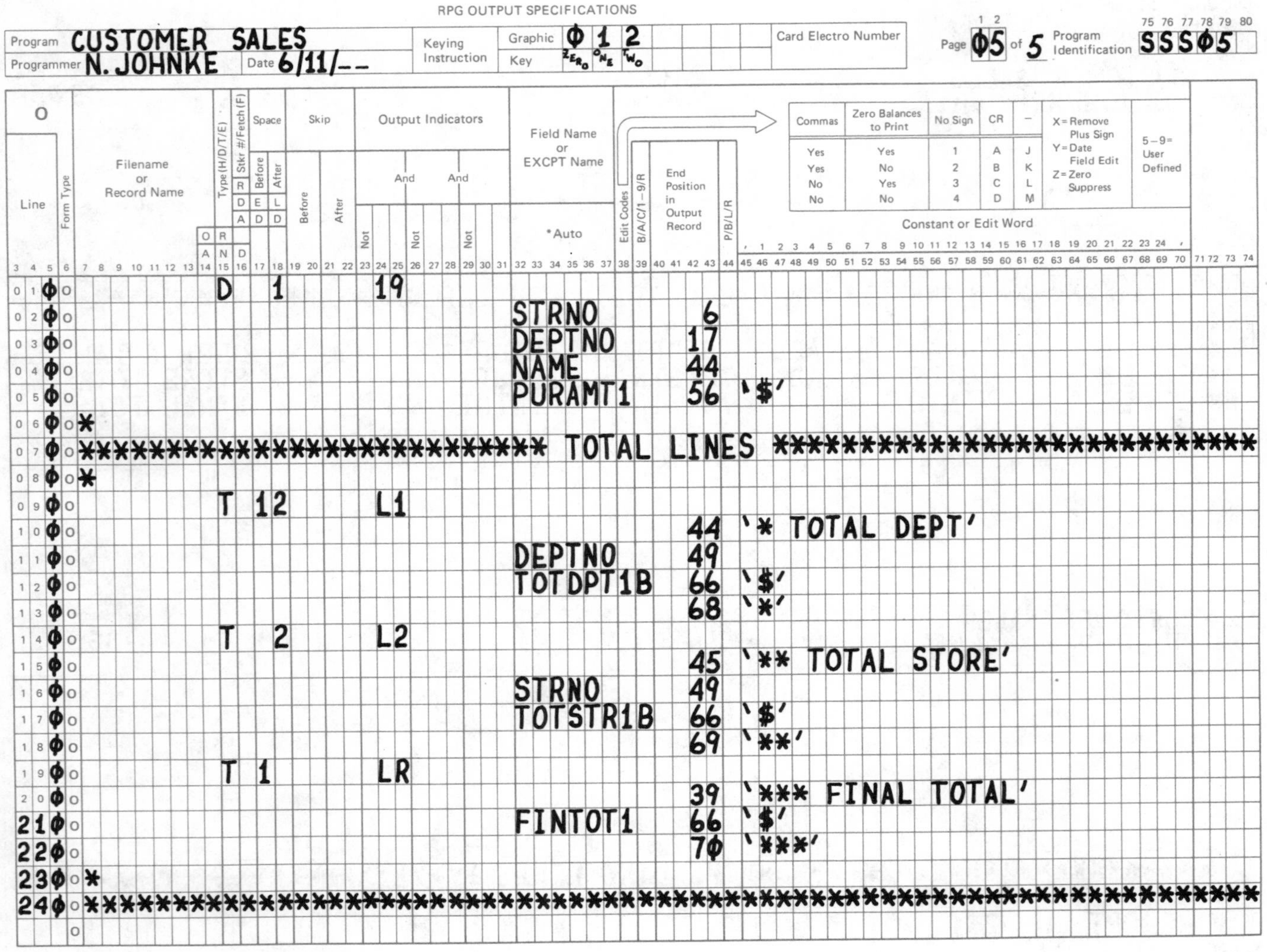

RPG OUTPUT SPECIFICATIONS

Program: CUSTOMER SALES — Programmer: N. JOHNKE — Date: 6/11/-- — Keying Instruction: Graphic Ø 1 2, Key ZERO ONE TWO — Page Ø5 of 5 — Program Identification: SSSØ5

Line	Form Type	Filename or Record Name	Type	Space Before	Space After	Output Indicators	Field Name	Edit Codes	B/A/C/1–9/R	End Position in Output Record	Constant or Edit Word
01Ø	O		D		1	19					
02Ø	O						STRNO			6	
03Ø	O						DEPTNO			17	
04Ø	O						NAME			44	
05Ø	O						PURAMT	1		56	'$'
06Ø	O	*									
07Ø	O	****************************** TOTAL LINES *****************************									
08Ø	O	*									
09Ø	O		T	1	2	L1					
10Ø	O									44	'* TOTAL DEPT'
11Ø	O						DEPTNO			49	
12Ø	O						TOTDPT	1	B	66	'$'
13Ø	O									68	'*'
14Ø	O		T		2	L2					
15Ø	O									45	'** TOTAL STORE'
16Ø	O						STRNO			49	
17Ø	O						TOTSTR	1	B	66	'$'
18Ø	O									69	'**'
19Ø	O		T	1		LR					
20Ø	O									39	'*** FINAL TOTAL'
21Ø	O						FINTOT	1		66	'$'
22Ø	O									7Ø	'***'
23Ø	O	*									
24Ø	O	**									

Figure 5.24
(continued)

Figure 5.25
First program listing produced for Debugging Exercise 1.
(Continued on next page.)

```
F*************************************************************************SSS05
F*        THIS PROGRAM CREATES A CUSTCMER SALES REPORT WHICH             *SSS05
F*        UTILIZES CCNTRCL BREAKS TO TAKE TOTALS FOR EACH                *SSS05
F*        DEPARTMENT,EACH STCRE AND FINAL TOTAL FOR ALL STORES           *SSS05
F*************************************************************************SSS05
F*                                                                        SSS05
FSLSCARD IP  F      80               READ01 SYSIPT                        SSS05
FREPORT  O   F     132     CF        PRINTERSYSLST                        SSS05
F*                                                                        SSS05
I**************************** INPUT RECCRD *******************************SSS05
I*                                                                        SSS05
ISLSCARD NS  19                                                           SSS05
I                                                 1   20STRNO L2          SSS05
I                                                 3   50DEPTNOL1          SSS05
I                                                 6  25 NAME              SSS05
I                                                26  312PURAMT            SSS05
I*                                                                        SSS05
C************************ CALCULATION ROUTINE ****************************SSS05
C*                                                                        SSS05
C   L1      PURAMT    ADD  TCTDPT     TCTDPT  72          DEPT TOTAL      SSS05
C   L2      TOTDPT    ADD  TOTSTR     TCTSTR  82          STCRE TOTAL     SSS05
C   LR      FINTOT    ACC  TOTSTR     FINTOT  92          FINAL TOTAL     SSS05
C*                                                                        SSS05
O*************************** HEADING LINES *******************************SSS05
C*                                                                        SSS05
OREPCRT  H  201    1P                                                     SSS05
O       CR         OF                                                     SSS05
C                              UDATE Y   10                               SSS05
C                                        41 'SWINDLERS DEPARTMENT'        SSS05
O                                        48 'STORES'                      SSS05
C                                        63 'PAGE'                        SSS05
O                              PAGE      68                               SSS05
C        H  2      1P                                                     SSS05
C       CR         OF                                                     SSS05
O                                        45 'CUSTOMER SALES REPCRT'       SSS05
C        H  1      1P                                                     SSS05
O       CR         OF                                                     SSS05
O                                        17 'STORE      DEPT'             SSS05
O                                        34 'CUSTCMER'                    SSS05
C                                        56 'PURCHASE'                    SSS05
C        H  2      1P                                                     SSS05
O       CR         CF                                                     SSS05
C                                        18 'NUMBER     NUMBER'           SSS05
C                                        32 'NAME'                        SSS05
C                                        55 'AMCUNT'                      SSS05
C*                                                                        SSS05
O**************************** DETAIL LINE *******************************SSS05
C*                                                                        SSS05
C        D  1      19                                                     SSS05
C                              STRNO      6                               SSS05
O                              DEPTNC    17                               SSS05
O                              NAME      44                               SSS05
C                              PURAMT1   56 '$'                           SSS05
O*                                                                        SSS05
O**************************** TOTAL LINES *******************************SSS05
C*                                                                        SSS05
C        T 12      L1                                                     SSS05
C                                        44 '* TCTAL DEPT'                SSS05
O                              DEPTNO    49                               SSS05
O                              TCTDPT1B  66 '$'                           SSS05
O                                        68 '*'                           SSS05
C        T  2      L2                                                     SSS05
C                                        45 '** TOTAL STORE'              SSS05
C                              STRNC     49                               SSS05
O                              TOTSTR1B  66 '$'                           SSS05
O                                        69 '**'                          SSS05
C        T 1       LR                                                     SSS05
O                                        39 '*** FINAL TOTAL'             SSS05
C                              FINTOT1   66 '$'                           SSS05
O                                        70 '***'                         SSS05
C*                                                                        SSS05
O*************************************************************************SSS05

E N D  O F  S C U R C E
```

Figure 5.25
(continued)

```
7/29/82            SWINDLERS DEPARTMENT STORES          PAGE    1
                        CUSTOMER SALES REPORT

 STORE      DEPT          CUSTOMER              PURCHASE
NUMBER     NUMBER           NAME                 AMOUNT

  01        101        STEELE,C.A.                $97.89
  01        101        MARK,E.Z.                 $234.56

                          * TOTAL DEPT  101                  $97.89 *

  01        102        RICH,M.I.               $1,842.03

                          * TOTAL DEPT  102               $1,842.03 *

                         ** TOTAL STORE  01                  $97.89 **

  02        102        WALLITT,M.T.              $101.00

                          * TOTAL DEPT  102                 $101.00 *

  02        105        BACKE,I.B.                  $9.98
  02        105        SALES,N.E.                 $57.35

                          * TOTAL DEPT  105                   $9.98 *

                         ** TOTAL STORE  02                 $101.00 **

  03        102        BROQUE,I.M.                $85.42
  03        102        OWEN,R.U.                 $625.70

                          * TOTAL DEPT  102                  $85.42 *

                         ** TOTAL STORE  03                  $85.42 **

                       *** FINAL TOTAL                         $.00 ***
```

Figure 5.26
Second program listing produced for Debugging Exercise 1.
(Continued on next page.)

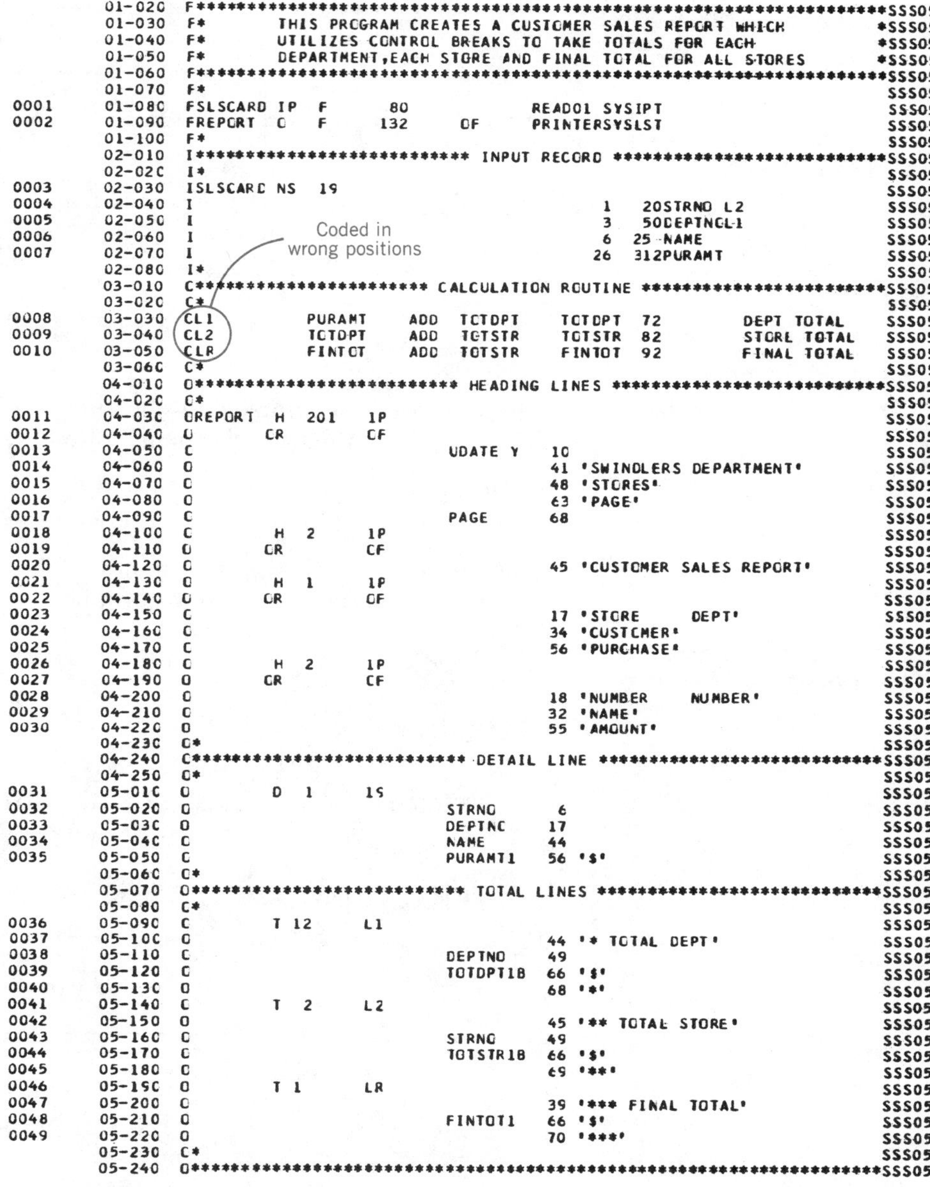


```
          01-020 F*********************************************************************SSS05
          01-030 F*         THIS PROGRAM CREATES A CUSTOMER SALES REPORT WHICH          *SSS05
          01-040 F*         UTILIZES CONTROL BREAKS TO TAKE TOTALS FOR EACH             *SSS05
          01-050 F*         DEPARTMENT,EACH STORE AND FINAL TOTAL FOR ALL STORES        *SSS05
          01-060 F*********************************************************************SSS05
          01-070 F*                                                                     SSS05
0001      01-080 FSLSCARD IP  F      80              READ01 SYSIPT                       SSS05
0002      01-090 FREPORT  O   F     132      OF      PRINTERSYSLST                       SSS05
          01-100 F*                                                                     SSS05
          02-010 I*************************** INPUT RECORD ****************************SSS05
          02-020 I*                                                                     SSS05
0003      02-030 ISLSCARD NS  19                                                        SSS05
0004      02-040 I                                        1   20STRNO L2                SSS05
0005      02-050 I                                        3   50DEPTNOL1                SSS05
0006      02-060 I                                        6  25 NAME                    SSS05
0007      02-070 I                                       26  312PURAMT                  SSS05
          02-080 I*                                                                     SSS05
          03-010 C*********************** CALCULATION ROUTINE ************************SSS05
          03-020 C*                                                                     SSS05
0008      03-030 CL1        PURAMT    ADD  TOTDPT    TOTDPT  72         DEPT TOTAL      SSS05
0009      03-040 CL2        TOTDPT    ADD  TOTSTR    TOTSTR  82         STORE TOTAL     SSS05
0010      03-050 CLR        FINTOT    ADD  TOTSTR    FINTOT  92         FINAL TOTAL     SSS05
          03-060 C*                                                                     SSS05
          04-010 O************************** HEADING LINES ****************************SSS05
          04-020 O*                                                                     SSS05
0011      04-030 OREPORT  H  201    1P                                                  SSS05
0012      04-040 O        OR        OF                                                  SSS05
0013      04-050 O                           UDATE Y   10                               SSS05
0014      04-060 O                                     41 'SWINDLERS DEPARTMENT'        SSS05
0015      04-070 O                                     48 'STORES'                      SSS05
0016      04-080 O                                     63 'PAGE'                        SSS05
0017      04-090 O                           PAGE      68                               SSS05
0018      04-100 O        H  2      1P                                                  SSS05
0019      04-110 O        OR        OF                                                  SSS05
0020      04-120 O                                     45 'CUSTOMER SALES REPORT'       SSS05
0021      04-130 O        H  1      1P                                                  SSS05
0022      04-140 O        OR        OF                                                  SSS05
0023      04-150 O                                     17 'STORE      DEPT'             SSS05
0024      04-160 O                                     34 'CUSTOMER'                    SSS05
0025      04-170 O                                     56 'PURCHASE'                    SSS05
0026      04-180 O        H  2      1P                                                  SSS05
0027      04-190 O        OR        OF                                                  SSS05
0028      04-200 O                                     18 'NUMBER     NUMBER'           SSS05
0029      04-210 O                                     32 'NAME'                        SSS05
0030      04-220 O                                     55 'AMOUNT'                      SSS05
          04-230 O*                                                                     SSS05
          04-240 O*************************** DETAIL LINE *****************************SSS05
          04-250 O*                                                                     SSS05
0031      05-010 O        D  1      1S                                                  SSS05
0032      05-020 O                           STRNO      6                               SSS05
0033      05-030 O                           DEPTNO    17                               SSS05
0034      05-040 O                           NAME      44                               SSS05
0035      05-050 O                           PURAMT1   56 '$'                           SSS05
          05-060 O*                                                                     SSS05
          05-070 O************************** TOTAL LINES ******************************SSS05
          05-080 O*                                                                     SSS05
0036      05-090 O        T 12      L1                                                  SSS05
0037      05-100 O                                     44 '* TOTAL DEPT'                SSS05
0038      05-110 O                           DEPTNO    49                               SSS05
0039      05-120 O                           TOTDPT1B  66 '$'                           SSS05
0040      05-130 O                                     68 '*'                           SSS05
0041      05-140 O        T  2      L2                                                  SSS05
0042      05-150 O                                     45 '** TOTAL STORE'              SSS05
0043      05-160 O                           STRNO     49                               SSS05
0044      05-170 O                           TOTSTR1B  66 '$'                           SSS05
0045      05-180 O                                     69 '**'                          SSS05
0046      05-190 O        T 1       LR                                                  SSS05
0047      05-200 O                                     39 '*** FINAL TOTAL'             SSS05
0048      05-210 O                           FINTOT1   66 '$'                           SSS05
0049      05-220 O                                     70 '***'                         SSS05
          05-230 O*                                                                     SSS05
          05-240 O*********************************************************************SSS05

    E N D  O F  S O U R C E
```

```
7/29/82           SWINDLERS DEPARTMENT STORES           PAGE    1

                     CUSTOMER SALES REPORT

 STORE      DEPT          CUSTOMER              PURCHASE
 NUMBER    NUMBER           NAME                 AMOUNT

  01        101       STEELE,C.A.                $97.89
  01        101       MARK,E.Z.                 $234.56

                        * TOTAL DEPT  101                 $234.56 *

  01        102       RICH,M.I.               $1,842.03

                        * TOTAL DEPT  102               $1,842.03 *

                       ** TOTAL STORE  01               $1,842.03 **
```

Incorrect: should be 332.45 (TOTAL DEPT 101)

Incorrect: should be 2,174.48 (TOTAL STORE 01)

Figure 5.26 *(continued)*

```
02      102      WALLITT,M.T.            $101.00
                      * TOTAL DEPT  102               $101.00 *

02      105      BACKE,I.B.                $9.98
02      105      SALES,N.E.               $57.35
                      * TOTAL DEPT  105                $57.35 *     Incorrect: should be 67.33

                     ** TOTAL STORE  02                $57.35 **    Incorrect: should be 168.33

03      102      BROQUE,I.M.              $85.42
03      102      OWEN,R.U.               $625.70
                      * TOTAL DEPT  102               $625.70 *     Incorrect: should be 711.12

                     ** TOTAL STORE  03               $625.70 **

                 *** FINAL TOTAL                      $625.70 ***   Incorrect: should be 3,053.93
```

Debugging Exercise 2

You have successfully completed Debugging Exercise 1 and your new supervisor has changed the output requirements as follows.

1. Group indication is to be provided
2. Final totals are to appear on a separate page.

The Printer Spacing Chart is shown in Figure 5.27. Identify the changes required to modify the program to produce the output specified.

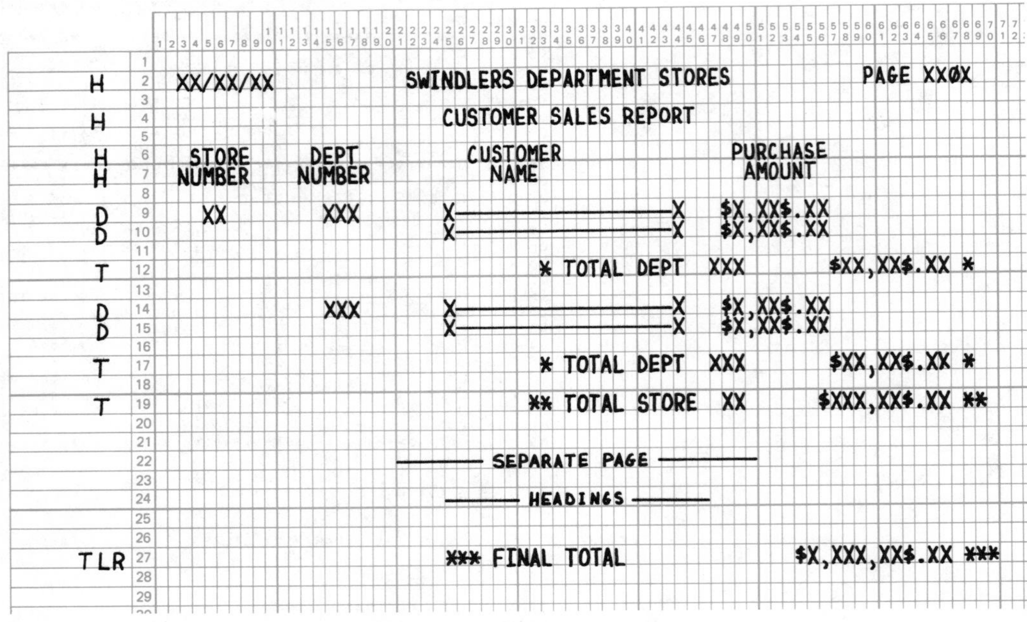

Figure 5.27
Printer Spacing Chart for Debugging Exercise 2.

Practice Problems

1. Using the problem definition shown in Figure 5.28, code an RPG program to produce the required results.

   Notes

   a. There will be one input record for each purchase made by a customer.
   b. Input is in sequence by CUSTNO.

2. Using the problem definition shown in Figure 5.29, code an RPG program to produce the required results.

Figure 5.28 Problem definition for Practice Problem 1.

Systems Flowchart

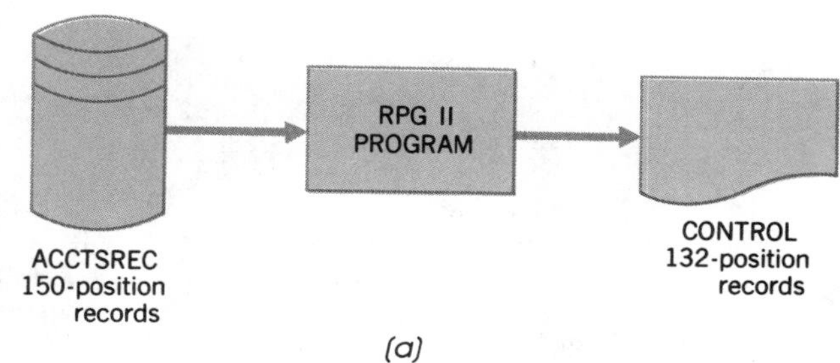

(a)

ACCTSREC Record Layout

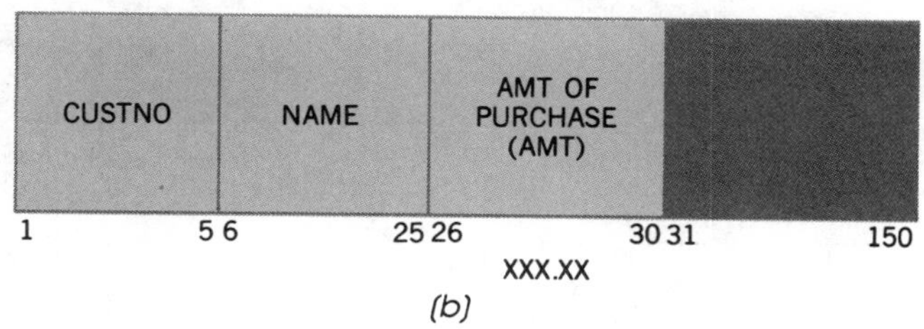

(b)

CONTROL Printer Spacing Chart

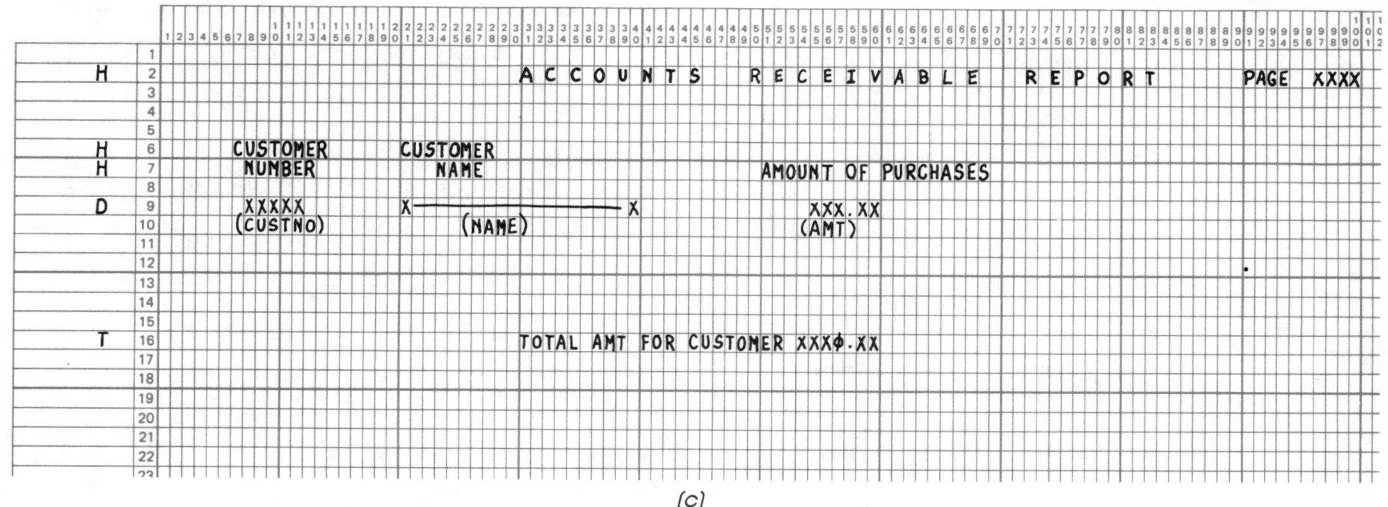

(c)

Notes

a. Input records are in sequence by DEPT.
b. DEPT is a group indicate field.

3. Using the problem definition shown in Figure 5.3Ø, code an RPG program to produce the required results.

Notes

a. Input records are in sequence by salesperson number within department. Each sales made by a salesperson is recorded in a separate record; hence, there may be numerous input records for each salesperson.
b. This is a double level control problem with no detail printing. Only *totals* for each salesperson are to print followed by a department total. DEPT is a group indicate field.

Figure 5.29 Problem definition for Practice Problem 2.

Systems Flowchart

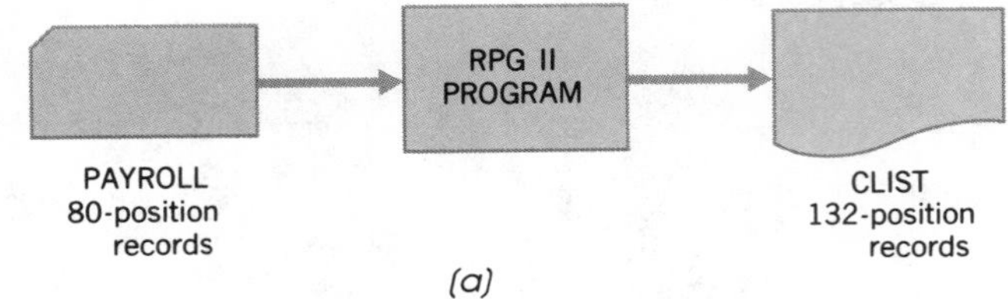

(a)

PAYROLL Record Layout

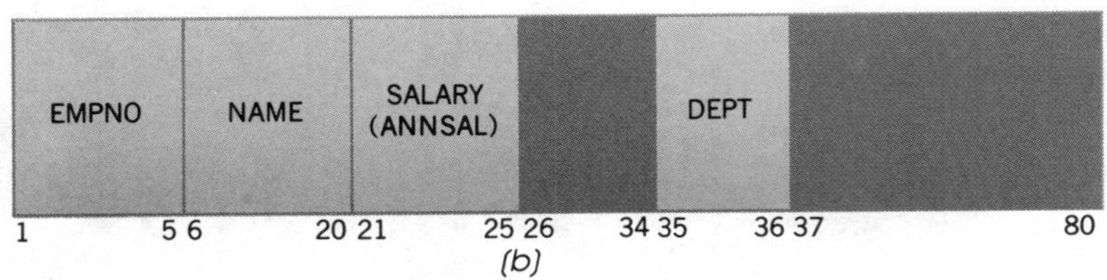

(b)

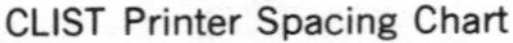

CLIST Printer Spacing Chart

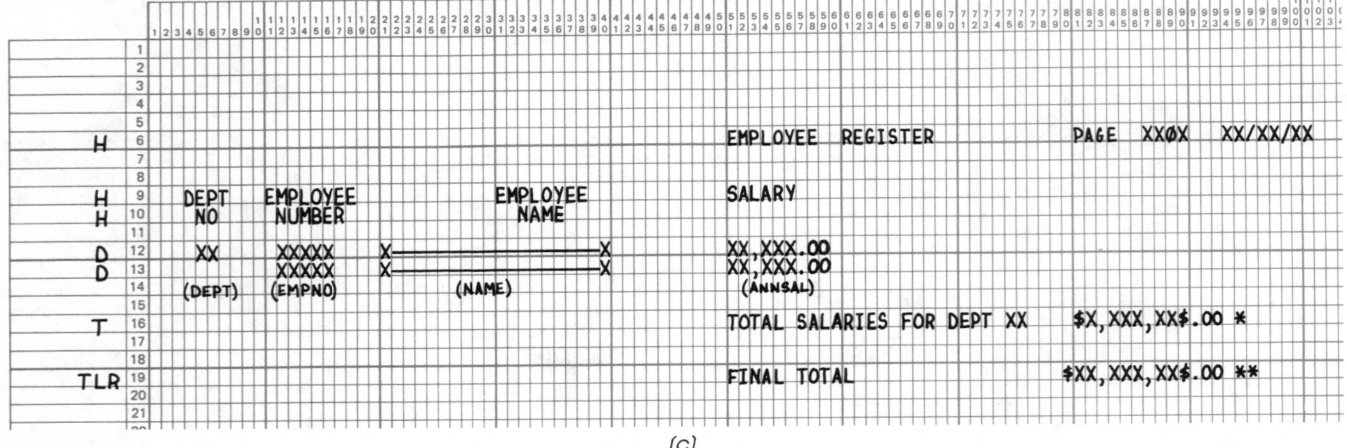

(c)

Figure 5.30 Problem definition for Practice Problem 3.

(Continued on next page.)

Systems Flowchart

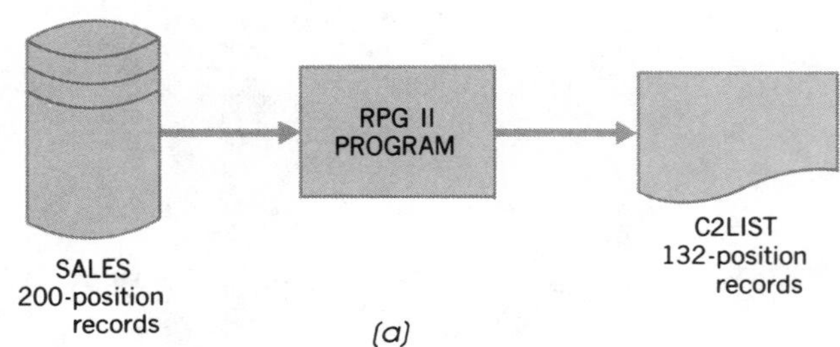

(a)

SALES Record Layout

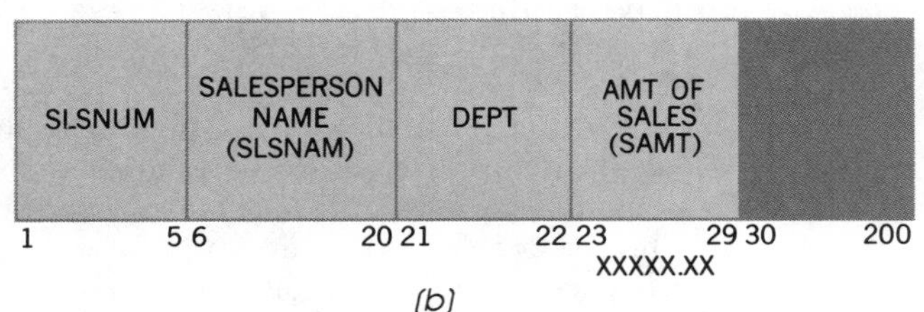

(b)

C2LIST Printer Spacing Chart

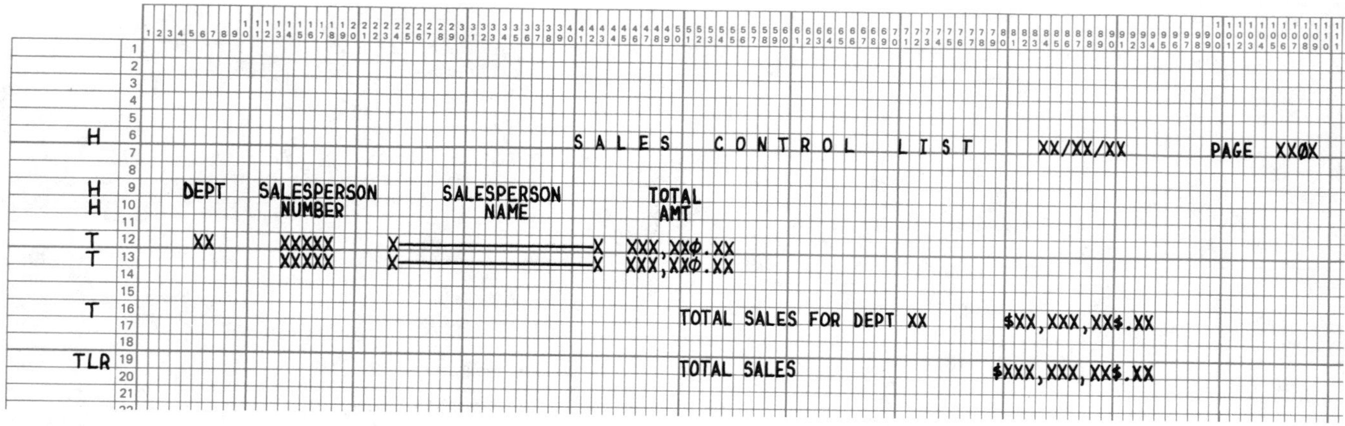

Figure 5.30
(continued)

(c)

4. Using the problem definition shown in Figure 5.31, code an RPG program to produce the required results.

Notes

a. There is one input record for each employee. Records are in sequence by level within department within branch office.
b. Add 1 to the total fields for each input record to accumulate proper sums. Individual records do not print.

Systems Flowchart

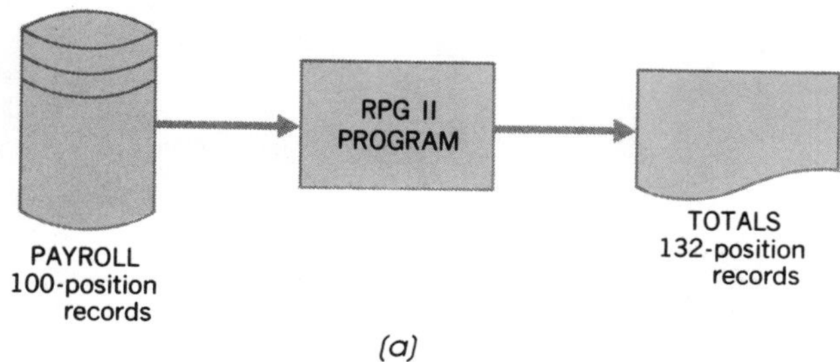

(a)

PAYROLL Record Layout

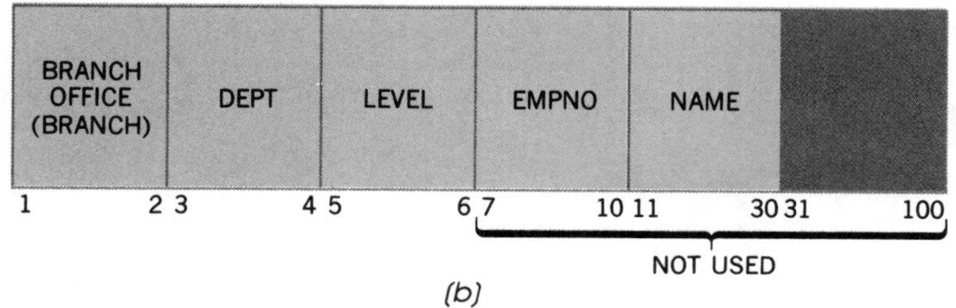

(b)

Figure 5.31
Problem definition for Practice Problem 4.
(Continued on next page.)

TOTALS Printer Spacing Chart

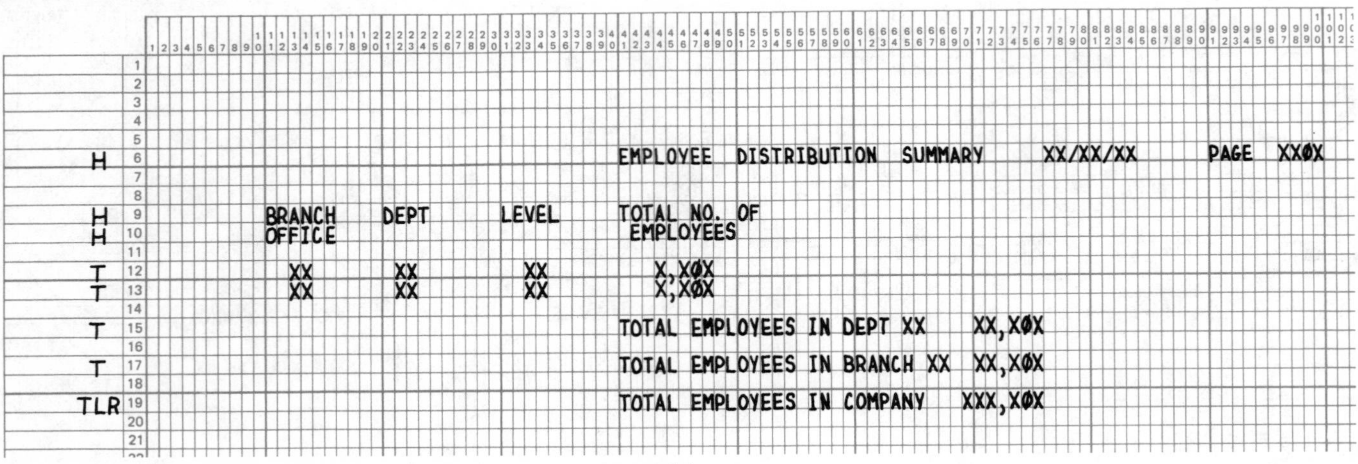

(c)

Figure 5.31
(continued)

CHAPTER 6

Branching, Looping, and Exception Reporting

Objectives

- To develop an understanding of the concepts used in looping.
- To identify the differences between conditional and unconditional branches.
- To code the GOTO and TAG commands correctly.
- To use exception reporting in RPG programs.
- To understand the use of the fetch overflow in conjunction with exception output.
- To identify the need for test data and the DEBUG option in locating program errors.
- To correctly code the various options available with the DEBUG instruction.

I.

Introduction to Looping Concepts

In programming business applications, there are many instances where a series of instructions are to be executed a fixed number of times. This repetition of a group of instructions, called a **loop**, is an important programming concept. Loops are used for a wide variety of programming applications and may be accomplished in two ways: with a conditional branch and/or an unconditional branch.

The **conditional branch** requires that a comparison be made. Figure 6.1 provides an illustration. In RPG, if the condition specified is true, then a resulting indicator is set "on." The resulting indicator may then be used to condition a GOTO instruction that will cause the computer to leave one point in the calculations of a program and begin executing instructions at some other point. If, however, the condition tested is not satisfied, the resulting indicator would not be set and the next instruction in the top-down sequence would then be carried out. That is, if the condition tested is not met, the GOTO instruction, which transfers control to some other point in the program, is not executed and the next sequential instruction is performed.

In the illustration in Figure 6.1, the Z-ADD (zero-and-add) instruction would be executed *only if* the condition tested were not met. Thus, the sequence of instructions denoted with the arrows will be continually executed as long as a specific condition (low) was met. (The sequence of instructions denoted by the arrows is called a *loop*.) Once the condition is no longer met, then the computer will terminate the loop and proceed with the Z-ADD. Thus, when CTR is greater than or equal to 5, the loop is terminated.

Let us consider the conditional branch in the RPG program excerpt in Figure 6.1 more carefully. Note that CTR is compared to the numeric literal 5. Resulting

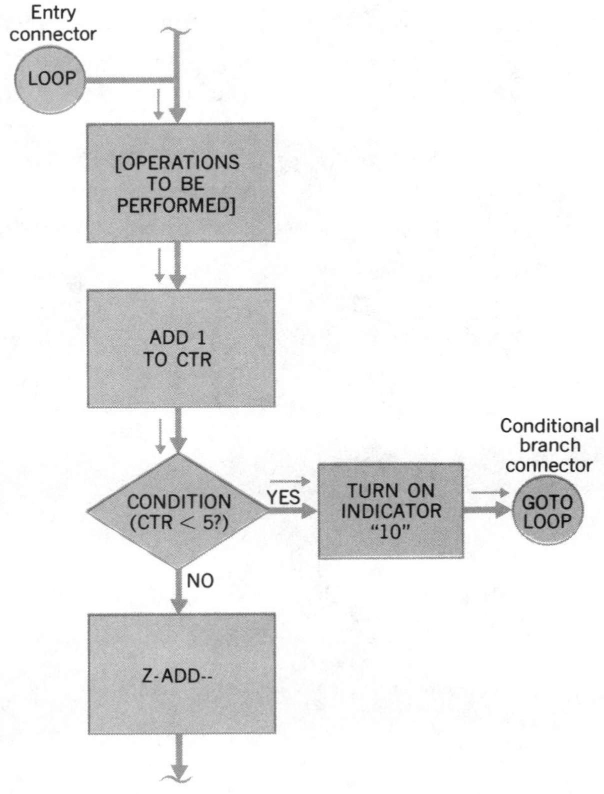

Figure 6.1
Use of a conditional branch in a loop.
(Continued on next page.)

RPG CALCULATION SPECIFICATIONS

Line	Form Type	Indicators	Factor 1	Operation	Factor 2	Result Field Name	Length	Resulting Indicators (High / Low / Equal)	Comments
01Ø	C			•					
02Ø	C		LOOP	TAG					
03Ø	C			•					
04Ø	C		CTR	ADD	1	CTR	2Ø		
05Ø	C			•					
06Ø	C			•					
07Ø	C		CTR	COMP	5			Low: 1Ø	
08Ø	C	1Ø		GOTO	LOOP				
09Ø	C			Z-ADD	TOTAL1	TOTAL2			
10	C								
11	C								

Entry connector

Conditional branch connector

10 "ON" then branch to loop

Figure 6.1
(continued)

indicator 1Ø is always turned "on" when the *compare* yields a low result, that is, as long as CTR is less than 5. If indicator 1Ø is "on," the program branches to line Ø2Ø, the TAG specification bearing the name LOOP. A **TAG** operation provides a name to which the program can branch. The name is specified in Factor 1, and the operation code, TAG, is specified in columns 28–32 of the Calculation form. It represents an **entry point** of a routine to be branched to.

Let us consider Figure 6.1 again. The decision symbol specifies a branch or transfer point using a conditional branch connector. This branch connector, with the notation GOTO LOOP, must correspond to an entry connector (TAG) indicating where the LOOP begins. Thus every branch connector must be matched to an entry connector as illustrated in Figure 6.2. Note that the name specified

Figure 6.2
Every branch connector must be matched to an entry connector.

RPG CALCULATION SPECIFICATIONS

Line	Form Type	Indicators	Factor 1	Operation	Factor 2	Result Field Name	Length	Resulting Indicators	Comments
01Ø	C			•					
02Ø	C		LOOP	TAG					
03Ø	C			•					
04Ø	C			•					
05Ø	C			•					
06Ø	C			•					
07Ø	C			•					
08Ø	C	1Ø		GOTO	LOOP				
09	C								
10	C								

Entry connector

Conditional branch connector

in Factor 1 of the TAG instruction is the name referenced in Factor 2 of the GOTO. Each TAG statement in the program must be assigned a unique name in Factor 1. Once this name is assigned to the TAG instruction, it *cannot* be used with another TAG. It can only be used again in a GOTO instruction to indicate where to send control. Hence, TAG statements are used to identify entry points in the program. These entry points are the targets for the GOTO commands. They are similar to statement numbers in BASIC and paragraph names in COBOL. Refer to the following example and note that if an equal condition occurs, the GOTO is used to skip forward.

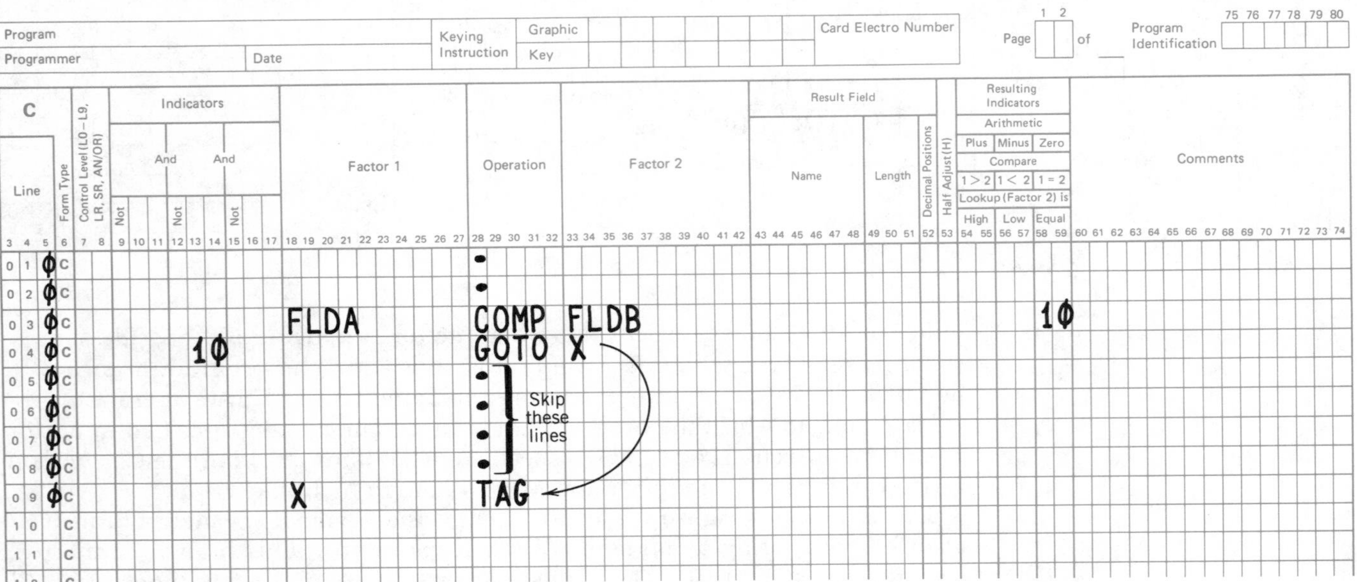

Once again, referring to Figure 6.1, when a low condition results from the *compare* operation, the GOTO instruction will be executed and the program will branch to the entry point called LOOP. However, when an equal or high condition occurs, indicator 10 will be turned "off," the GOTO will *not* be conditioned, and the next instruction in the sequence after the conditional branch will be carried out.

Recalling the counter concepts previously discussed in Chapter 4, note that with each pass through the loop, 1 is added to the counter. As a result, the loop coded in Figure 6.1 would be repeated *five* times. If, instead, you were required to perform the loop 12 times, the numeric literal in the *compare* instruction would simply be changed from 5 to 12 as illustrated here.

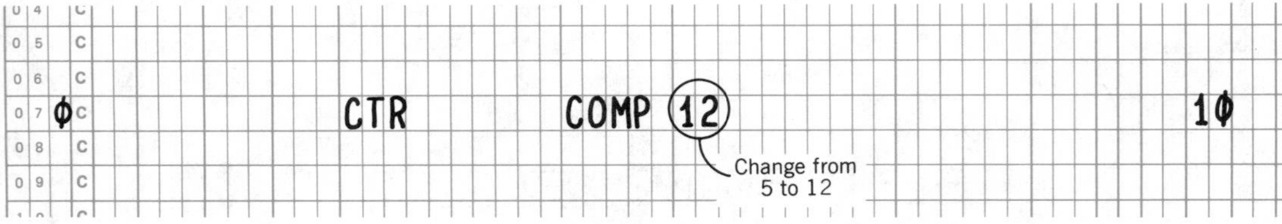

During the twelfth pass through the loop, CTR would contain the value 12; an equal condition would result, and indicator 1Ø would be set "off." With indicator 1Ø in the "off" state, the looping process would terminate. That is, the GOTO conditioned by indicator 1Ø would *not* be executed and the program would continue with the next sequential step.

A. Programming Loops

Several fundamental steps are involved in developing a loop. One way to control the number of times the loop or set of desired instructions is to be executed is to use a counter. With each pass through the loop, the counter is increased or incremented by one. The value of the counter is tested in order to determine if the loop should be repeated or not. Thus, if the counter is less than a fixed number (for example, 12), the loop will be repeated. Once the counter is equal to or exceeds that number, the program continues with the next instruction rather than branching. In this way, the procedure called LOOP would be executed 12 times, assuming that the counter was set to zero prior to entering the loop. The process is summarized in Figure 6.3.

Figure 6.3
Steps involved with a loop.
(Continued on next page.)

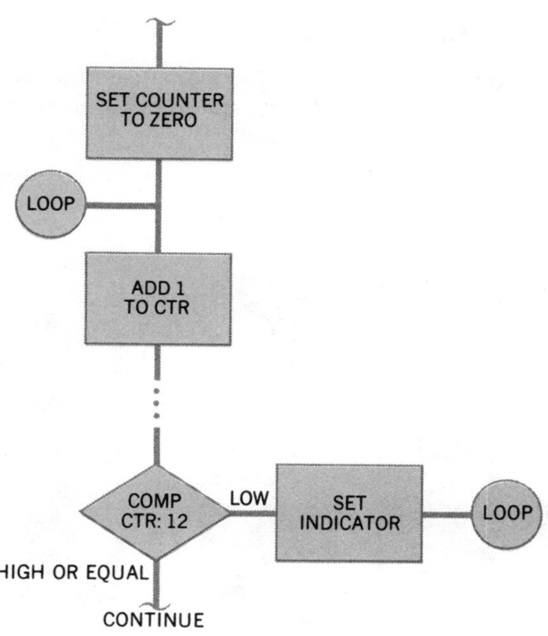

1. Initialize a counter (CTR) to zero before entering the loop.
2. Increment the counter with each pass through the loop.
3. Compare the counter with the number of times the loop is to be executed.
4. If condition is met, execute a branch to the entry point LOOP.

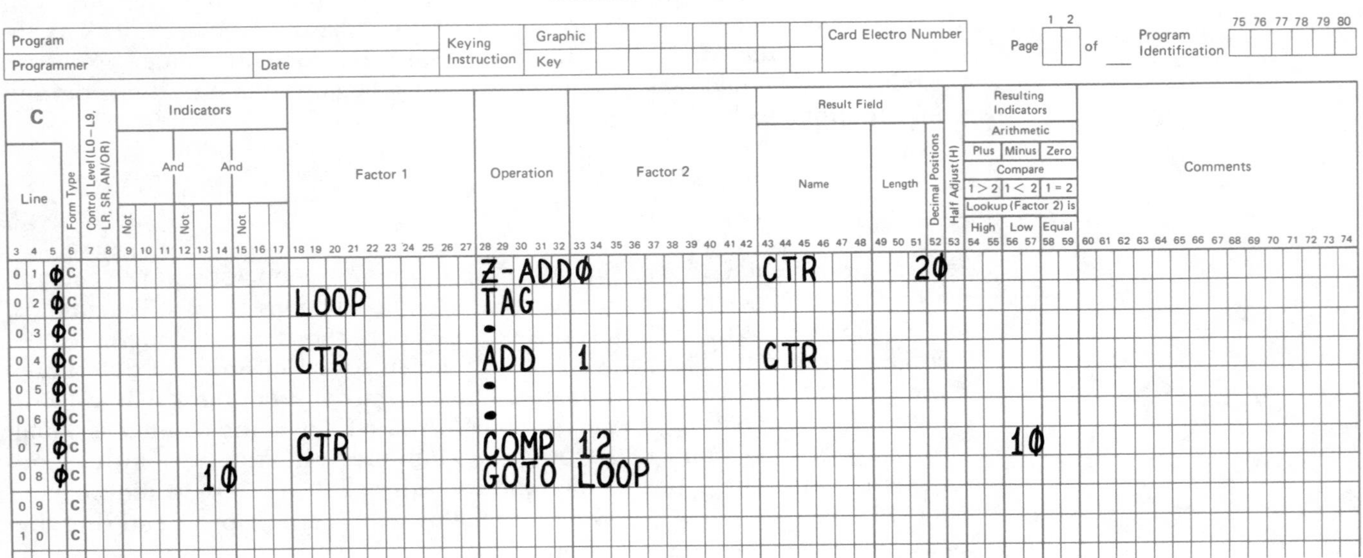
RPG CALCULATION SPECIFICATIONS

Line	Form Type	Control Level	Indicators	Factor 1	Operation	Factor 2	Result Field Name	Length	Decimal Positions	Resulting Indicators (High / Low / Equal)
01	C				Z-ADD	0	CTR	2	0	
02	C			LOOP	TAG					
03	C				.					
04	C			CTR	ADD	1	CTR			
05	C				.					
06	C				.					
07	C			CTR	COMP	12				Low: 10
08	C		10		GOTO	LOOP				
09	C									
10	C									

Figure 6.3
(continued)

B. Unconditional Branch

A loop procedure could also make use of an **unconditional branch**. An unconditional branch is a GOTO statement that when executed causes a branch *regardless* of any conditions.

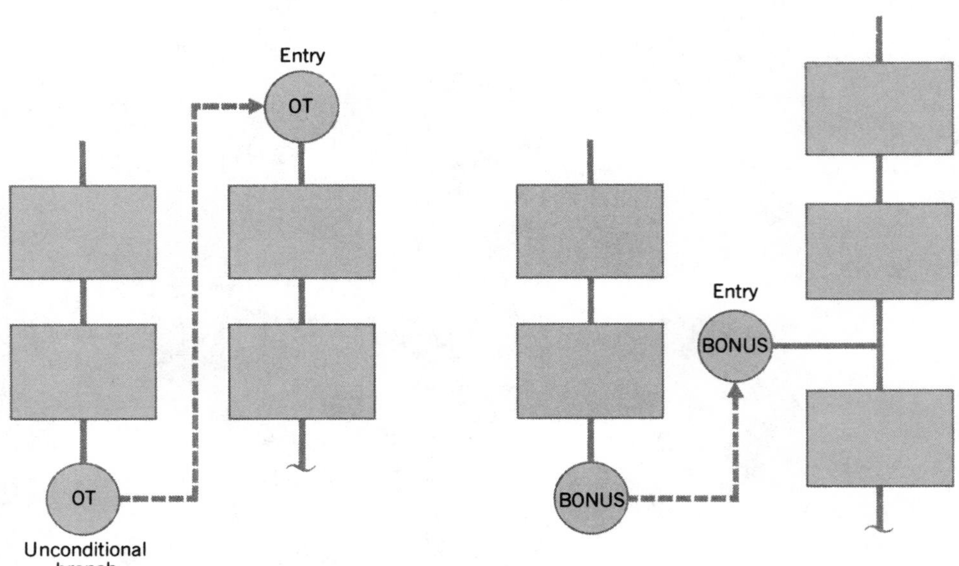

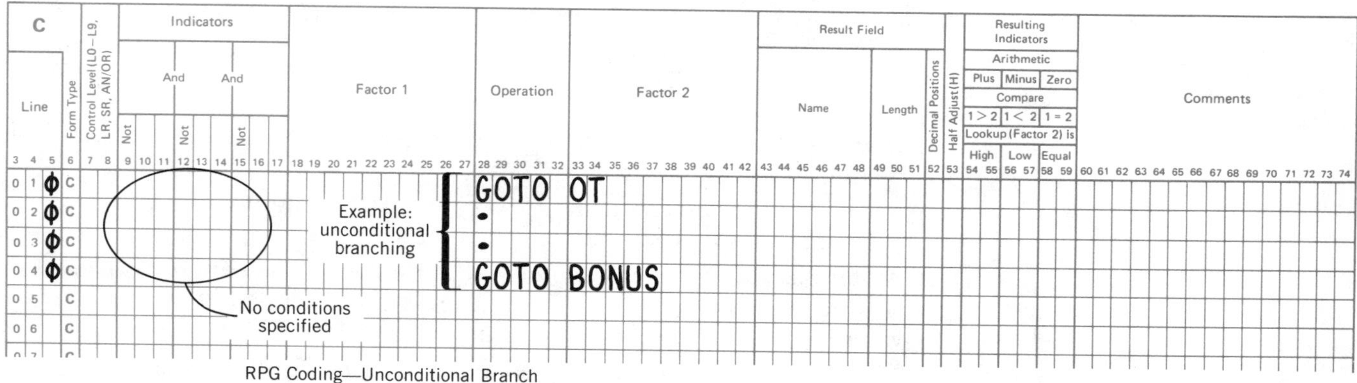

RPG Coding—Unconditional Branch

In this illustration the branch always occurs because the instruction is *not* conditioned by an indicator. That is, when the instruction is encountered, it always causes a branch. Another example of the unconditional branch is as follows.

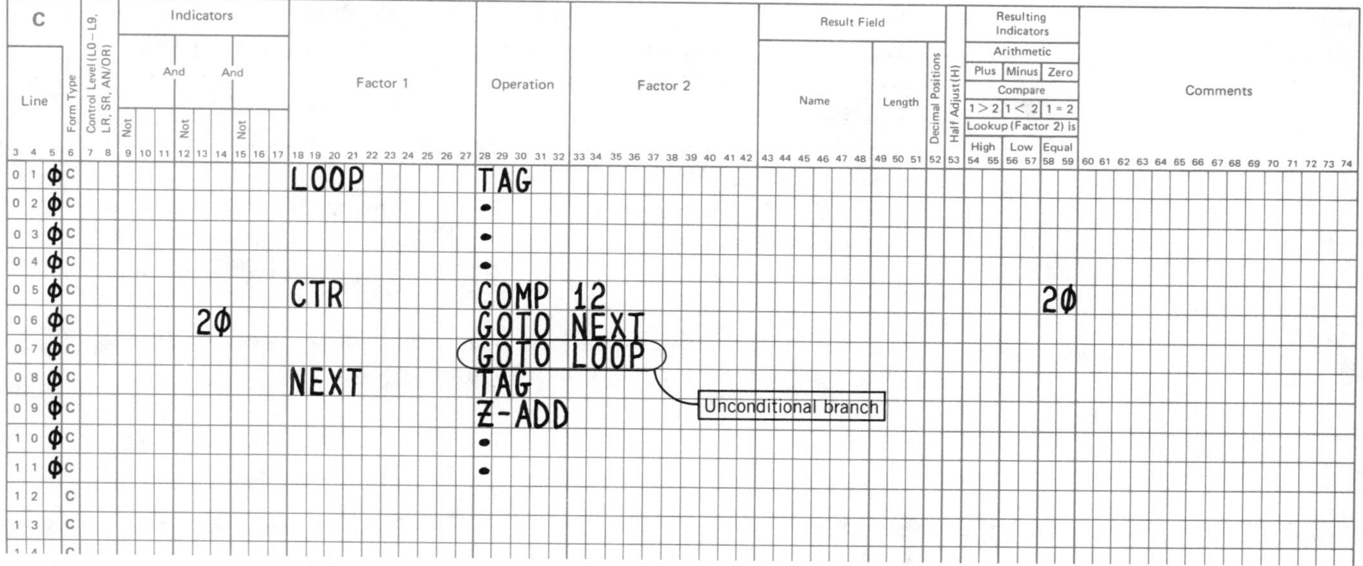

If the counter, CTR, is less than 12, indicator 2Ø is *not* conditioned and the GOTO LOOP instruction is executed. However, on the twelfth pass through the loop, the *compare* will be equal and indicator 2Ø will be set "on." In this instance, the unconditional branch, GOTO NEXT will terminate the looping procedure. Again, an unconditional branch is simply the GOTO instruction without conditioning indicators, meaning that a branch will *always* take place when the instruction is executed.

It must be emphasized that excessive use of unconditional GOTO's makes debugging difficult. The use of this instruction should be minimized.

Structured programming is a concept that is designed to maximize efficient coding. As will be seen in Chapter 11, structured programming favors a top-down approach to coding that avoids the indiscriminate use of GOTO instructions. Subroutines and related techniques are used extensively in structured programming.

C. Summary of Conditional and Unconditional Branching

Looping

1. Initialize the counter to zero *before* entering the loop. The Z-ADD can be used for this purpose.
2. Recall that the variable name for a counter must always appear as either Factor 1 or Factor 2.
3. A literal is added to the counter within the loop. The counter is usually incremented by 1 in a loop, but could be incremented by any value, depending on the application.
4. The counter is tested for loop control purposes with a compare instruction. Indicators are set according to the desired objectives of the looping procedure.

GOTO/TAG ***Operation Codes***

1. The GOTO instruction can be used to branch around certain calculations or to loop back and repeat certain operations.
2. When looping procedures are used, be sure there is a provision within the loop to branch to some point outside the loop when the procedure has been executed the required number of times.
3. For each GOTO statement indicating a branch point, there must be a corresponding TAG or entry point.
4. Many GOTOs can branch to the same TAG instruction, but the entry point named in the TAG, as specified in Factor 1, must be unique.
5. A conditional branch is simply a GOTO that is executed if the specific indicators are on.
6. An unconditional branch always branches regardless of conditions and does not use any conditioning indicators.

D. Applications of Looping Procedures

Application 1

Problem Definition. Sum all the even numbers between Ø and 1ØØ and accumulate the result in a field named TOTAL.

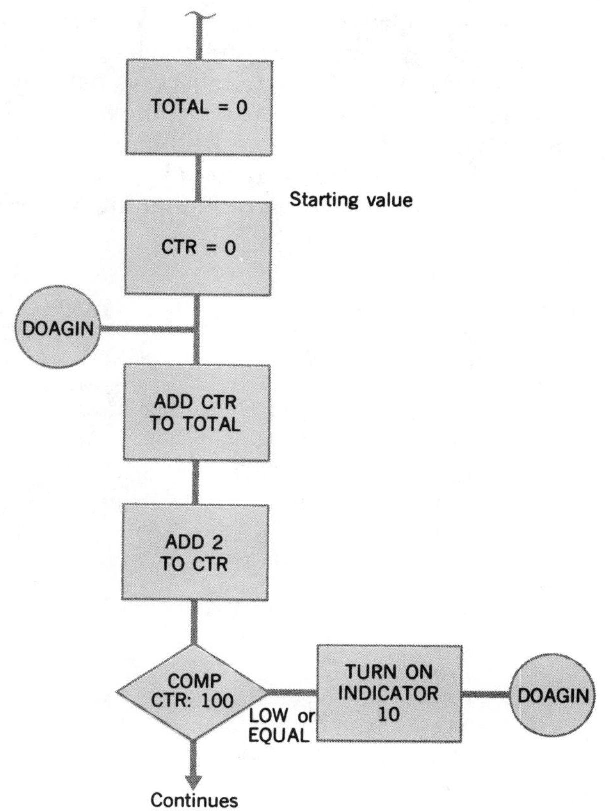

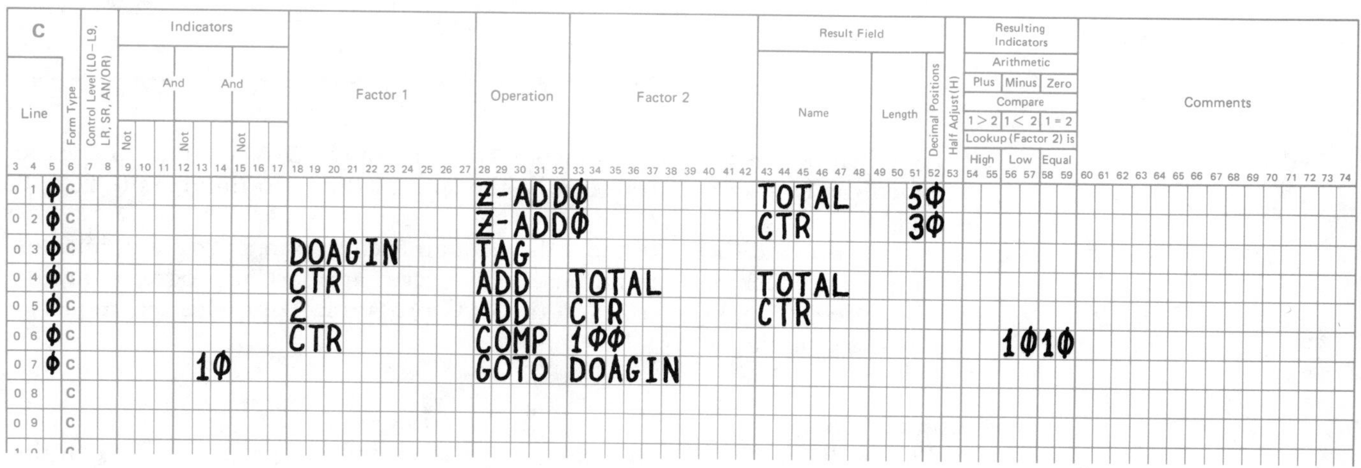

Line	Form Type	Control Level	Indicators (9–11)	Indicators (12–14)	Indicators (15–17)	Factor 1	Operation	Factor 2	Result Field Name	Length	Decimal Positions	Half Adjust	Resulting Indicators High (54–55)	Low (56–57)	Equal (58–59)	Comments
01Ø	C						Z-ADD	Ø	TOTAL	5	Ø					
02Ø	C						Z-ADD	Ø	CTR	3	Ø					
03Ø	C					DOAGIN	TAG									
04Ø	C					CTR	ADD	TOTAL	TOTAL							
05Ø	C					2	ADD	CTR	CTR							
06Ø	C					CTR	COMP	1ØØ						1Ø	1Ø	
07Ø	C			1Ø			GOTO	DOAGIN								
08	C															
09	C															
10	C															

Study the Calculation form to reinforce your understanding of looping. Walk through the problem, substituting values to see if the program will operate as intended. Try this for even numbers from Ø to 6. It is not necessary to manually test until CTR reaches 1ØØ; that is, if the logic performs correctly from Ø–6, then presumably it will work from Ø–1ØØ. The only difference is that we think of Factor 2 of the *compare* instruction having a value of 6 rather than of 1ØØ. The table that follows illustrates the summing of the even numbers from Ø to 6.

TAG	*Line*	*Instruction*	*Total*	CTR	*Result of Compare*	GOTO
	Ø1Ø	Zero total	Ø			
	Ø2Ø	Zero CTR	Ø	Ø		
X	Ø3Ø	Entry point				
	Ø4Ø	Add CTR to total	Ø	Ø		
	Ø5Ø	Add 2 to CTR		2		
	Ø6Ø	Compare CTR:6			LOW	
	Ø7Ø					DOAGIN
X	Ø3Ø	Entry point				
	Ø4Ø	Add CTR to total	2			
	Ø5Ø	Add 2 to CTR		4		
	Ø6Ø	Compare CTR:6			LOW	
	Ø7Ø					DOAGIN
X	Ø3Ø	Entry point				
	Ø4Ø	Add CTR to total	6			
	Ø5Ø	Add 2 to CTR		6		
	Ø6Ø	Compare CTR:6			EQUAL	
	Ø7Ø					DOAGIN
X	Ø3Ø	Entry point				
	Ø4Ø	Add CTR to total	12			
	Ø5Ø	Add 2 to CTR		8		
	Ø6Ø	Compare CTR:6				
	Ø7Ø				HIGH	
	—— Loop terminates ——					

Note that the program does function correctly since TOTAL contains the value 12 when the loop terminates. Clearly, the sum of the even numbers Ø, 2, 4, 6 is equal to 12.

It may seem a difficult task to walk through each step in a program, but this form of **desk checking** is an important and necessary part of programming. It will help detect any logic errors in the RPG program. Apply this technique to the following applications.

Application 2

Problem Definition. A value named N is read into the program. Sum all the integers from 1 to N. Walk through the problem using an N of 3 and determine if the SUM ends up with a value of 6, the summation of the integers 1, 2, and 3.

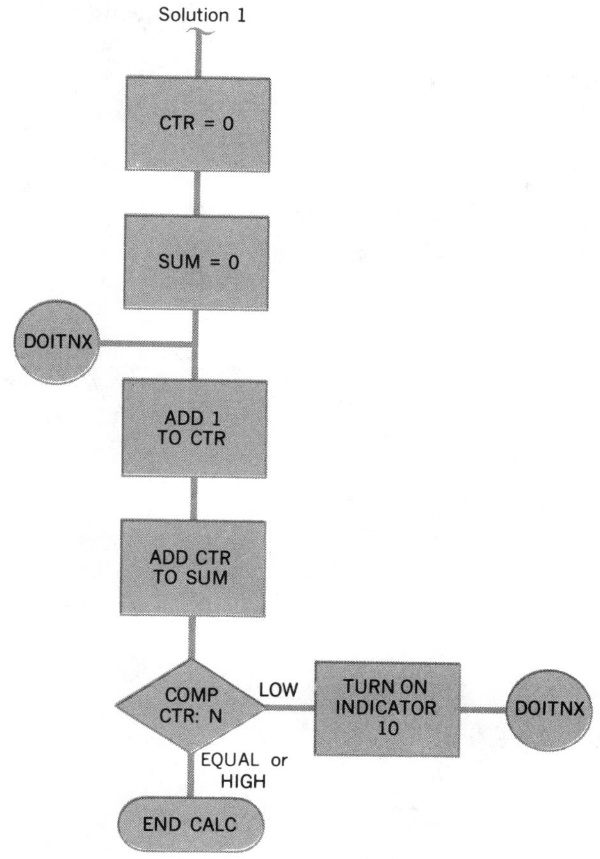

Line	Form Type	Control Level (L0–L9, LR, SR, AN/OR)	Indicators	Factor 1	Operation	Factor 2	Result Field Name	Length	Decimal Positions	Half Adjust (H)	Resulting Indicators High (1 > 2)	Low (1 < 2)	Equal (1 = 2)	Comments
01Ø	C				Z-ADDØ		CTR	4	Ø					
02Ø	C				Z-ADDØ		SUM	7	Ø					
03Ø	C			DOITNX	TAG									
04Ø	C			CTR	ADD	1	CTR							
05Ø	C			CTR	ADD	SUM	SUM							
06Ø	C			CTR	COMP	N						1Ø		
07Ø	C		1Ø		GOTO	DOITNX								
08	C													
09	C													
10	C													

Validate the correctness of the following alternate solution by again walking through the steps.

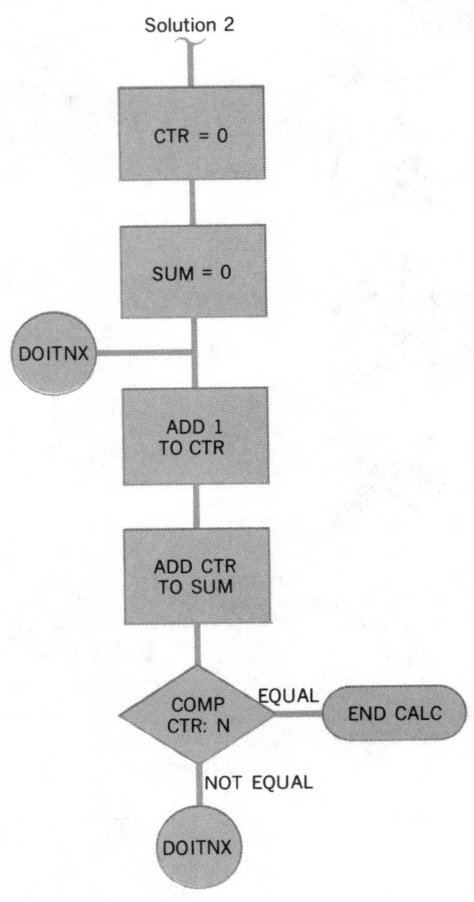

Line	Form Type	Control Level (L0–L9, LR, SR, AN/OR)	Indicators	Factor 1	Operation	Factor 2	Result Field Name	Length	Decimal Positions	Half Adjust (H)	Resulting Indicators High (1>2, Plus)	Resulting Indicators Low (1<2, Minus)	Resulting Indicators Equal (1=2, Zero)	Comments
01Ø	C				Z-ADD	Ø	CTR	4	Ø					
02Ø	C				Z-ADD	Ø	SUM	7	Ø					
03Ø	C			DOITNX	TAG									
04Ø	C			CTR	ADD	1	CTR							
05Ø	C			CTR	ADD	SUM	SUM							
06Ø	C			CTR	COMP	N							2Ø	
07Ø	C		2Ø		GOTO	ENDCAL								
08Ø	C				GOTO	DOITNX								
09Ø	C			ENDCAL	TAG									
10	C													
11	C													
12	C													

Application 3

Problem Definition. A value, M, is read into the program. Calculate M factorial, which is M times (M – 1) times (M – 2) . . . times (1) = FACT. M factorial is usually specified as M!.

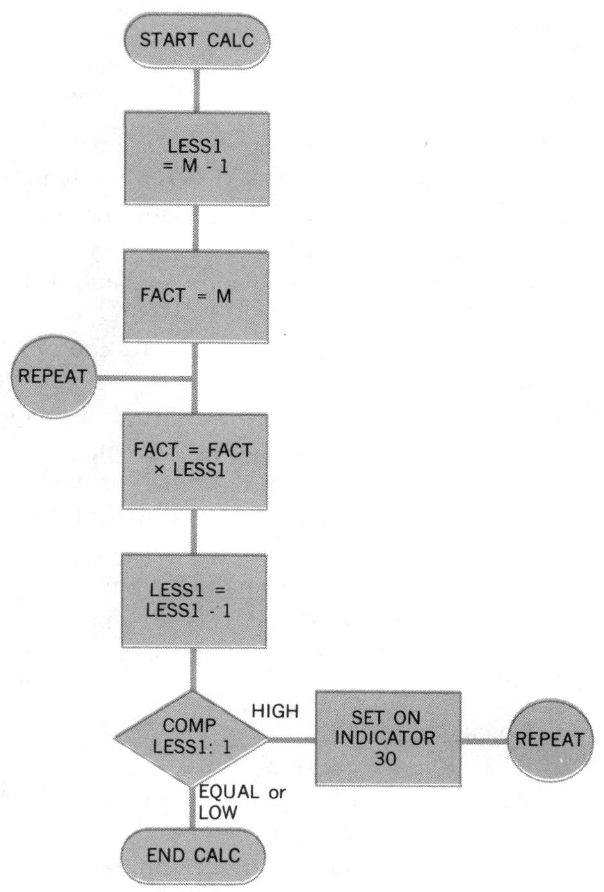

Line	Form Type	Control Level (L0–L9, LR, SR, AN/OR)	Indicators	Factor 1	Operation	Factor 2	Result Field Name	Length	Decimal Positions	Half Adjust (H)	Resulting Indicators High (1>2)	Resulting Indicators Low (1<2)	Resulting Indicators Equal (1=2)	Comments
01Ø	C			M	SUB	1	LESS1	2	Ø					
02Ø	C				Z-ADD	M	FACT	8	Ø					
03Ø	C			REPEAT	TAG									
04Ø	C			FACT	MULT	LESS1	FACT							
05Ø	C			LESS1	SUB	1	LESS1							
06Ø	C			LESS1	COMP	1					3Ø			
07Ø	C		3Ø		GOTO	REPEAT								
08	C													
09	C													
10	C													

If M was equal to 4, for example, M factorial (FACT) would be 4 × 3 × 2 × 1 or 24. The result of your walkthrough should produce the value of 24 in the field called FACT. If the result of a walkthrough does not produce the correct answer, check your own manual procedure first. If the walkthrough was performed properly and the answer is still wrong, then the program logic must be revised.

Self-Evaluating Quiz

1. The GOTO and TAG operations are coded on the ________ form.
2. (T or F) Several GOTO instructions may branch to the same TAG.
3. When the GOTO instruction is conditioned with an indicator, it is considered a(n) ________ branch.
4. (T or F) TAG names may be repeated if the logic of the program requires it.
5. (T or F) The unconditional GOTO can only be used to branch forward in order to skip instructions.
6. Looping is best achieved with the (conditional/unconditional) branch.
7. (T or F) For each GOTO instruction, an entry point or tag must exist in order for the program to branch properly.
8. (T or F) With a looping procedure, it is best to initialize the counter to zero inside the loop.
9. We usually add (number) to a counter with each pass through the loop.
10. (T or F) The GOTO and TAG commands are entered in the operation field of the Calculation form and are left-justified.

Solutions

1. Calculation
2. T
3. conditional branch—The instruction is only executed when the indicator is "on."
4. F—Duplicate TAGs are not permitted.
5. F—It can be used to branch backward to instructions prior to the GOTO as well as forward to instructions after the GOTO.
6. conditional—A means of ending the loop must exist.
7. T
8. F—Always initialize the counter *before* entering the loop.
9. 1
10. T

II. Looping with the EXCPT Instruction

A. Summary of the EXCPT Instruction

If a programmer had to perform a loop five times, the following instructions could be used to control the looping process.

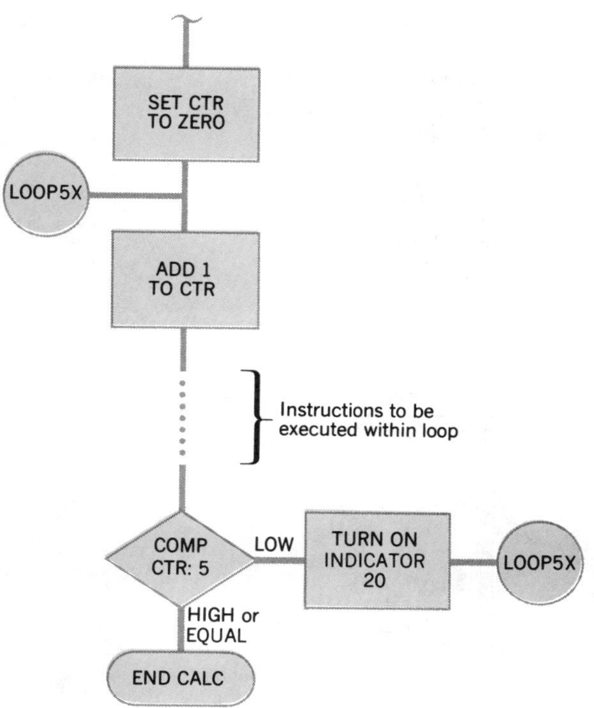

The instructions used are part of the fundamental operations of all looping procedures. That is,

Looping Procedures

1. Initialize a counter (CTR) to zero before entering the loop.
2. Increment or add 1 to the counter with each pass through the loop.
3. Execute instructions within the loop.
4. Test the counter to determine if the loop should be continued.

Therefore, any instructions inserted in the looping procedure just shown would be executed five times.

We will now consider the use of looping in conjunction with specific print routines. The basic RPG Logic Cycle usually causes *each* input record to print *one* detail line on an output report. The sequence of operations in the RPG Logic Cycle includes the following steps.

1. A record is read.
2. Input data may then be referenced by the field names specified on the Input form.
3. Detail calculations are performed.
4. A detail line is printed.

Frequently, however, certain business applications require several lines of output for each input record read by the program. For example, an input record may contain a customer's name and address, and the program may be required to print five identical mailing labels for each customer. By using a looping procedure in the detail calculations, this multiple line printing could be accomplished as illustrated in Figure 6.4.

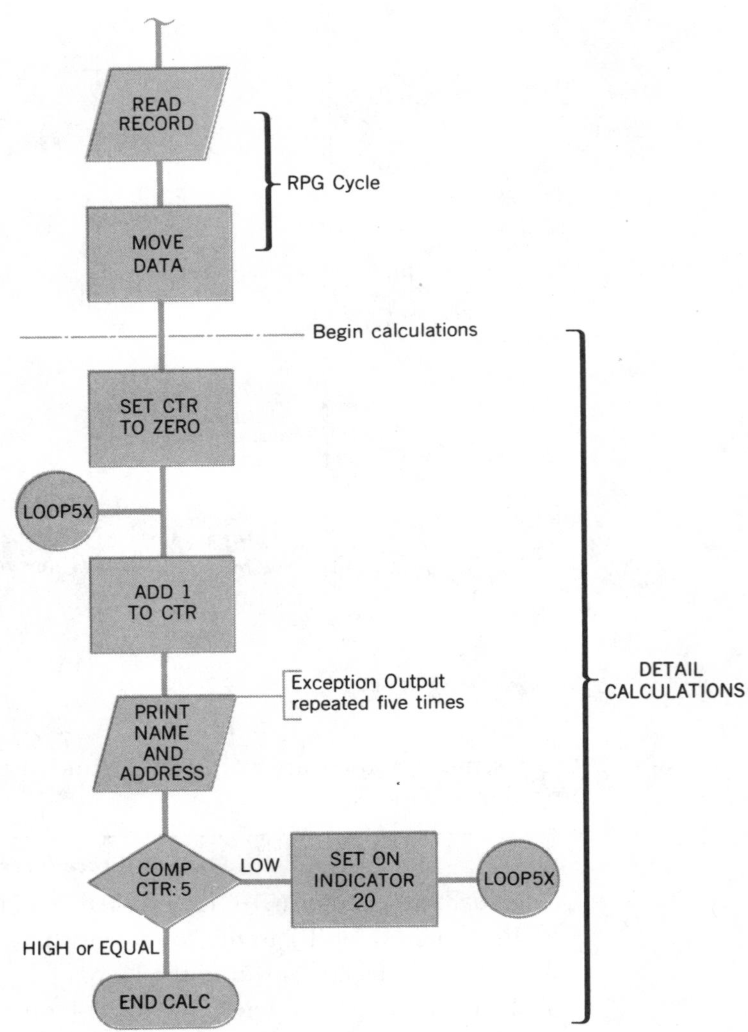

Figure 6.4
Logic for multiple line printing.

Because of the looping procedure, the output instruction would be executed a total of five times, producing five copies of the printed output. The detail line or group of lines would be repeated, thereby producing five labels for each customer. The EXCPT operation allows records to be written at the time calculations are being performed, which is *not* the usual time for such printing using the standard RPG cycle. This type of operation, which is called **exception output**, is used primarily when you wish to have a number of similar or identical records written during one program cycle. EXCPT output is not to be confused with an *exception report* discussed in Chapter 2, which prints output that represents an exception to a pre-established rule. EXCPT output is usually employed in conjunction with looping. That is, the number of output records printed for each input record is controlled by using a looping procedure.

Practical applications of exception output include

1. The printing of any number of identical mailing labels.
2. The printing of payment books. Each payment book consists of individual bills indicating the amount due for each payment period.

3. Developing and printing a schedule of payments for each customer based on interest rates, principal borrowed, and the duration of the loan.
4. Printing of tables that require a looping procedure to solve the problem. These include interest tables and depreciation tables, in which the same formula may be used repeatedly.

Remember, when several copies of a record are desired, the programmer may use exception output combined with looping to provide printing during *calculation* time, prior to standard detail printing. We will now review the exception output (EXCPT) instruction.

Example Code the RPG II program to list a 12-month payment book for each customer. The customer records are contained in the input file named CUST. The Record Layout and the Printer Spacing Chart depicting the output requirements are illustrated here.

Systems Flowchart

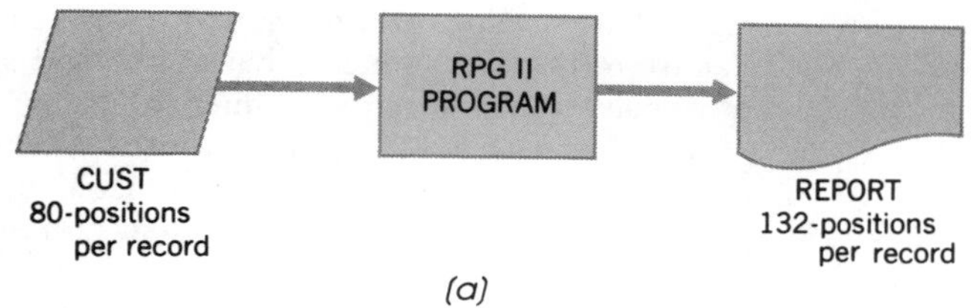

(a)

CUST Record Layout

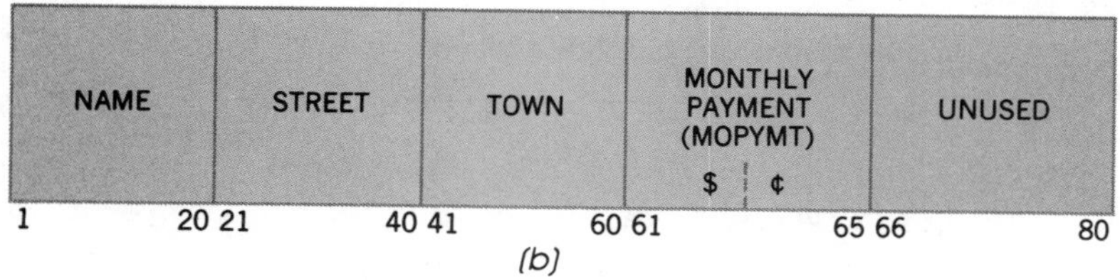

(b)

REPORT Printer Spacing Chart

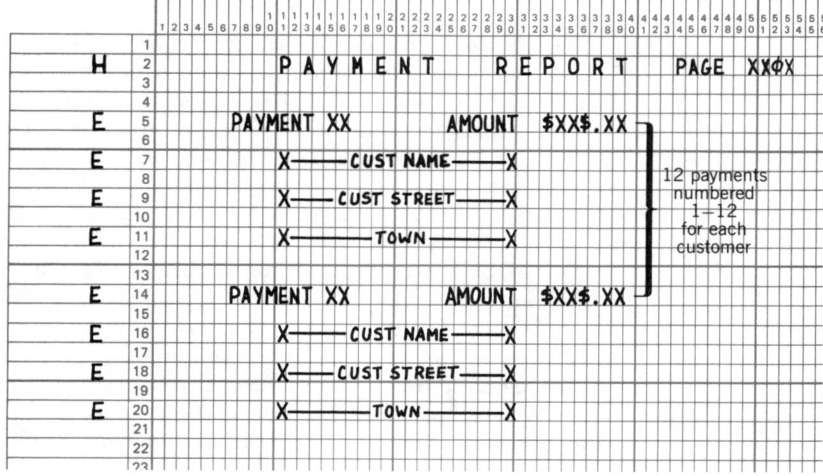

(c)

The RPG program appears in Figure 6.5. The objective of the sample program is to list 12 copies of each customer record and to number each payment, starting with one and continuing until the twelfth copy is printed.

In order to create 12 copies of each input record, a loop will be necessary. With each pass through the loop, a counter (CTR) will be used in the looping process. This CTR can also be used to indicate the number of the payment. The first time through, CTR is 1, the second time it is 2, and so on.

The flowchart depicted in Figure 6.6 illustrates the logic used on the Calculation form of the program. Note that the EXCPT operation is thought of as a print instruction in the flowchart. Its effect is precisely the same as an output instruction; however, it is executed during calculation time when the EXCPT instruction is encountered. As with any output instruction, the data may be written on the printer, disk, tape, and so on. In this instance, we are using the printer.

Referring to line Ø1Ø of the Calculation form, we find the counter (CTR) is initialized to zero using the Z-ADD instruction. Each time a new record is to be processed, the counter is reset to zero before the looping procedure is executed. Had this step been omitted, the looping procedure would have executed properly for the first input record only. All subsequent records would only pass through the loop once since the counter would have a value of 12 or more. Be sure to initialize counters prior to entering a loop. Failure to do so may mean that the second attempt to execute the loop will produce erroneous results since the counter would not contain the proper initial value.

The next instruction on the Calculation form, line Ø2Ø, is the TAG instruction, which specifies an entry point that is referenced by the GOTO operation. In the sample program, the TAG serves as the first instruction of the loop. The counter is updated at line Ø3Ø as previously discussed. On the first pass through the loop, note that the counter will have a value of one. Recall from the Printer Spacing Chart that the counter is used to number each payment as well as count the number of passes through the loop. Hence, the first payment will be listed as Ø1, the second as Ø2, and so on until the last payment, 12, is finally printed. The exception output using the EXCPT instruction serves to print the desired output. Usually, output is described on the Output form and may be summarized as follows.

Output Form Summary

Column 15	*Type of Record*
H	Heading record
D	Detail record
T	Total record
E	Exception record

Referring to the sample program, note how the EXCPT instruction on the Calculation form references the output specified with an "E" in column 15 of the Output form. Hence, each time the EXCPT is executed, and indicator Ø1 is conditioned "on," the customer payment, name, address, and so on will be listed on the output device.

Referring to Figure 6.7, we find that EXCPT operations may be conditioned with indicators in a way similar to that used on detail and total lines. After printing, the counter (CTR) is compared to the value 12 with each pass through the loop. Although the value of the counter ranges from 1 to 11, a low condition will turn on indicator 1Ø. The GOTO is executed each time indicator 1Ø is "on"; the program then branches to the TAG entry called DO12X and the loop is repeated. After the printing of the twelfth copy of the output, the *compare* instruction will yield an equal condition, setting indicator 1Ø "off." The GOTO is no longer conditioned and therefore is not executed. This will terminate the processing in the calculation section.

As each input record is read, 12 copies of the input data will be printed and numbered as required by the output specifications contained in the Printer Spacing Chart.

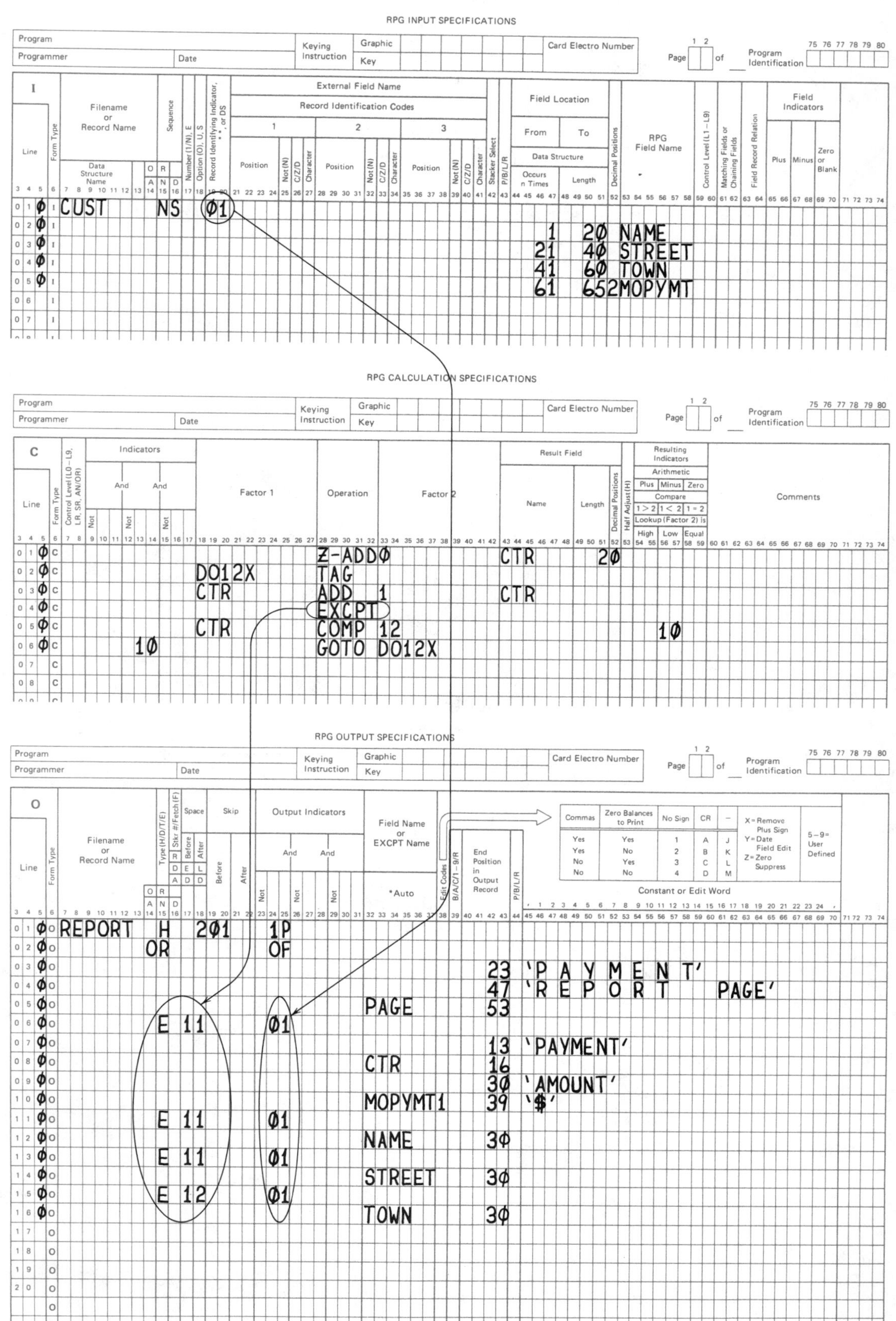

RPG INPUT SPECIFICATIONS

```
01Ø I CUST          NS  Ø1
02Ø I                                              1  2Ø NAME
03Ø I                                             21  4Ø STREET
04Ø I                                             41  6Ø TOWN
05Ø I                                             61  652MOPYMT
```

RPG CALCULATION SPECIFICATIONS

```
01Ø C                       Z-ADDØ         CTR     2Ø
02Ø C           DO12X       TAG
03Ø C           CTR         ADD  1         CTR
04Ø C                       EXCPT
05Ø C           CTR         COMP 12                    1Ø
06Ø C        1Ø             GOTO DO12X
```

RPG OUTPUT SPECIFICATIONS

```
01Ø O REPORT  H  2Ø1    1P
02Ø O       OR          OF
03Ø O                                  23 'P A Y M E N T'
04Ø O                                  47 'R E P O R T     PAGE'
05Ø O                       PAGE       53
06Ø O         E  11     Ø1
07Ø O                                  13 'PAYMENT'
08Ø O                       CTR        16
09Ø O                                  3Ø 'AMOUNT'
10Ø O                       MOPYMT1    39 '$'
11Ø O         E  11     Ø1
12Ø O                       NAME       3Ø
13Ø O         E  11     Ø1
14Ø O                       STREET     3Ø
15Ø O         E  12     Ø1
16Ø O                       TOWN       3Ø
```

Figure 6.5 Program to print a 12-month payment book for each customer.

Figure 6.6
Logic on Calculation form for Figure 6.5

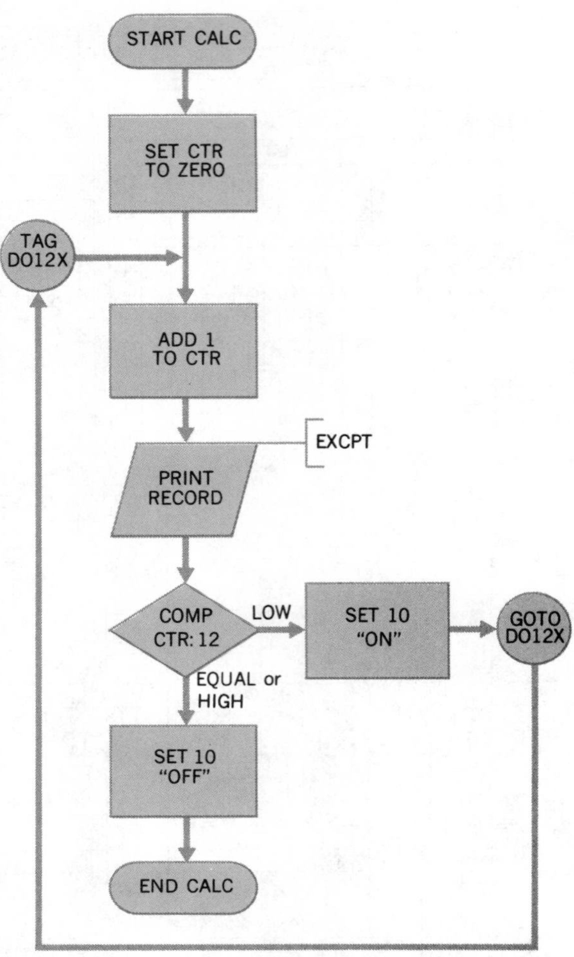

1. Set counter (CTR) to zero.
2. Add 1 or increment counter with each pass through the loop.
3. Print exception output.
4. Compare counter with the number of times the loop is to be executed.

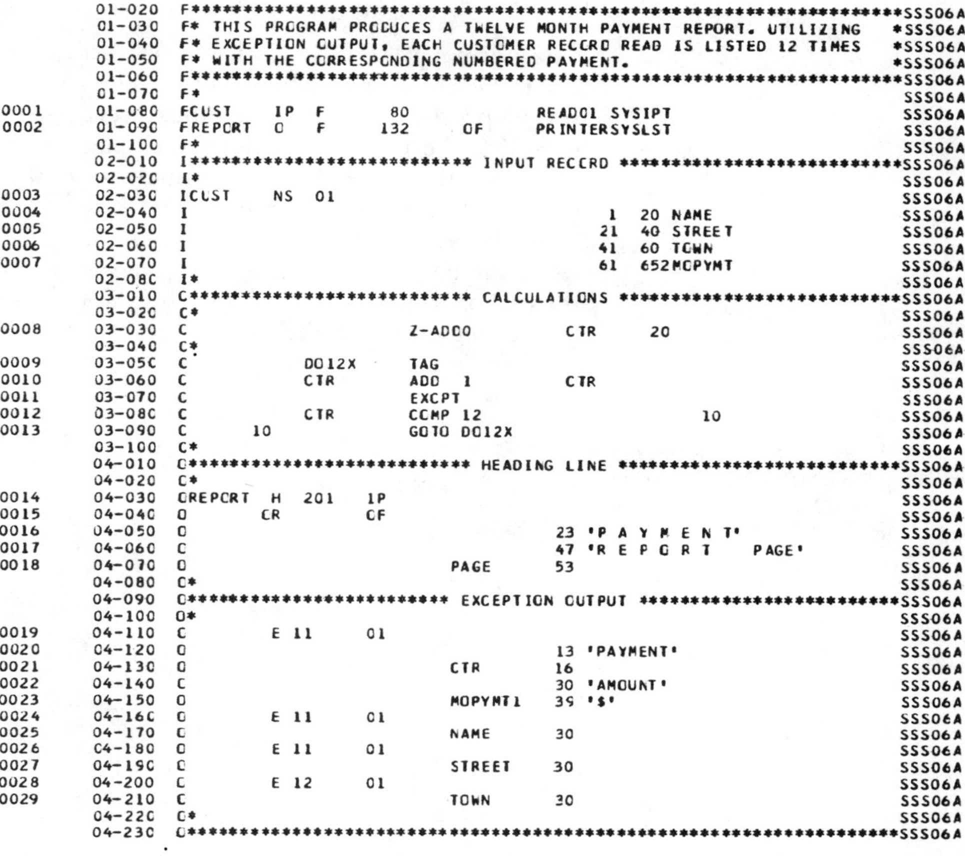

```
          01-020  F**********************************************************************SSS06A
          01-030  F* THIS PRCGRAM PRCCUCES A TWELVE MONTH PAYMENT REPORT. UTILIZING   *SSS06A
          01-040  F* EXCEPTION CUTPUT, EACH CUSTOMER RECCRD READ IS LISTED 12 TIMES   *SSS06A
          01-050  F* WITH THE CORRESPCNDING NUMBERED PAYMENT.                          *SSS06A
          01-060  F**********************************************************************SSS06A
          01-070  F*                                                                    SSS06A
0001      01-080  FCUST    IP  F      80              READ01 SYSIPT                     SSS06A
0002      01-090  FREPCRT  C   F     132     OF       PRINTERSYSLST                     SSS06A
          01-100  F*                                                                    SSS06A
          02-010  I************************* INPUT RECCRD ****************************SSS06A
          02-020  I*                                                                    SSS06A
0003      02-030  ICUST    NS  01                                                       SSS06A
0004      02-040  I                                        1  20 NAME                   SSS06A
0005      02-050  I                                       21  40 STREET                 SSS06A
0006      02-060  I                                       41  60 TCWN                   SSS06A
0007      02-070  I                                       61  652MCPYMT                 SSS06A
          02-08C  I*                                                                    SSS06A
          03-010  C************************* CALCULATIONS ****************************SSS06A
          03-02C  C*                                                                    SSS06A
0008      03-030  C                    Z-ADD0         CTR     20                        SSS06A
          03-040  C*                                                                    SSS06A
0009      03-05C  C           DO12X    TAG                                              SSS06A
0010      03-060  C           CTR      ADD  1         CTR                               SSS06A
0011      03-070  C                    EXCPT                                            SSS06A
0012      03-08C  C           CTR      CCMP 12                    10                    SSS06A
0013      03-090  C      10            GOTO DO12X                                       SSS06A
          03-100  C*                                                                    SSS06A
          04-010  O************************* HEADING LINE ****************************SSS06A
          04-020  C*                                                                    SSS06A
0014      04-030  OREPCRT  H  201   1P                                                  SSS06A
0015      04-040  O       CR        CF                                                  SSS06A
0016      04-050  O                                    23 'P A Y M E N T'               SSS06A
0017      04-060  C                                    47 'R E P O R T    PAGE'         SSS06A
0018      04-070  O                           PAGE     53                               SSS06A
          04-080  C*                                                                    SSS06A
          04-090  O*********************** EXCEPTION OUTPUT *************************SSS06A
          04-100  O*                                                                    SSS06A
0019      04-110  C       E 11      01                                                  SSS06A
0020      04-120  O                                    13 'PAYMENT'                     SSS06A
0021      04-130  O                           CTR      16                               SSS06A
0022      04-140  C                                    30 'AMOUNT'                      SSS06A
0023      04-150  O                           MOPYMT1  39 '$'                           SSS06A
0024      04-16C  O       E 11      01                                                  SSS06A
0025      04-170  C                           NAME     30                               SSS06A
0026      C4-180  O       E 11      01                                                  SSS06A
0027      04-19C  C                           STREET   30                               SSS06A
0028      04-200  C       E 12      01                                                  SSS06A
0029      04-210  C                           TOWN     30                               SSS06A
          04-22C  C*                                                                    SSS06A
          04-23C  O**********************************************************************SSS06A

   E N D  O F  S C U R C E
```

Figure 6.7
Program with EXCPT operation.

Summary

Instruction:	EXCPT
Meaning:	Exception output is produced during calculation time. That is, the EXCPT instruction may be included in detail calculations and/or total calculations.
Calculation form:	EXCPT is entered in columns 28–32. Conditioning indicators may be specified in columns 7–17. All other columns must be blank. EXCPT may be incorporated within a looping procedure in order to produce multiple copies of similar records.
Output form:	E is entered in column 15.

B. Page Overflow Considerations Using EXCPT

The normal RPG II Logic Cycle will *not* automatically control page overflow when the EXCPT instruction is used. The reason for this is clear when we again review precisely how RPG handles overflow. In the illustration in Figure 6.8, note that the test for overflow takes place *after* the total output is completed. However, the EXCPT instruction may be used *during* detail calculation time as illustrated in the flowchart in Figure 6.8.

In the sample program presented earlier, overflow would not be detected while the loop is printing the 12 copies of the payment records. Therefore, if the end of page was reached, printing would continue from the end of the page to the beginning of the next, over the perforation *without* execution of the

Figure 6.8
Use of the EXCPT instruction during detail calculation time.

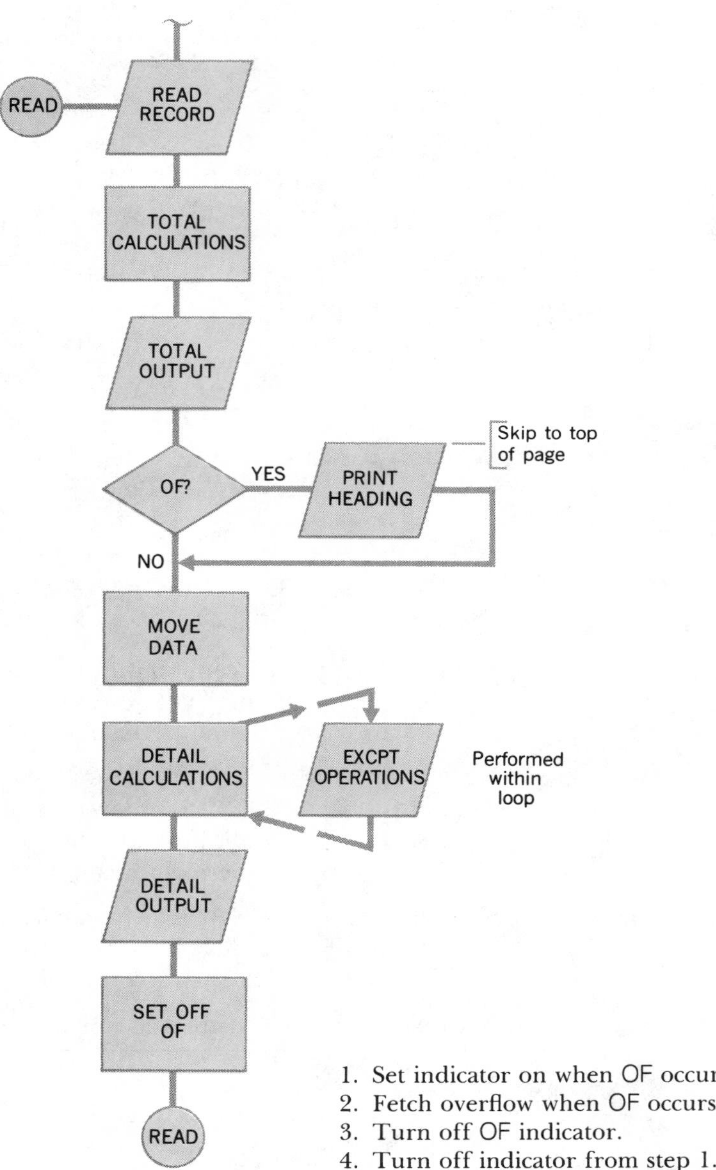

1. Set indicator on when OF occurs.
2. Fetch overflow when OF occurs.
3. Turn off OF indicator.
4. Turn off indicator from step 1.

necessary overflow procedure. The overflow indicator may be set "on" when an exception line is printed; however, RPG does not automatically test for overflow during *detail calculation time*.

Study the flowchart in Figure 6.8 before continuing and note that the overflow will not be checked by the RPG Logic Cycle until the next record is read. **Fetch overflow** can be used to cause exception lines to be printed if the overflow indicator is on. (Fetch overflow was discussed in the previous chapter; it will be reviewed here.) By using fetch overflow, the programmer can force the skipping to a new page and the printing of headings. However, once the overflow routine is executed, the programmer must *turn off* the overflow indicator to ensure that it does not affect subsequent printing. This can be accomplished as shown in Figure 6.9.

Figure 6.9
Illustration of fetched overflow.

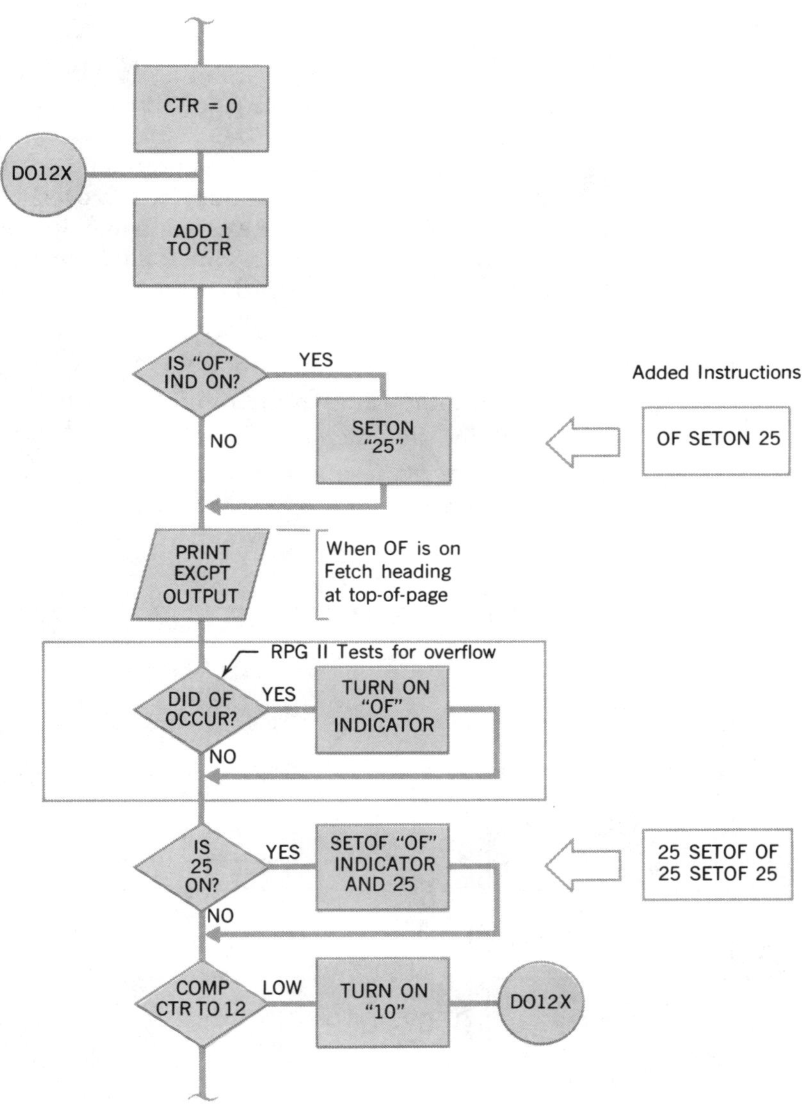

C. Fetch Overflow: Exception Output Summary

> ***Summary***
>
> 1. When overflow occurs, set "on" an indicator using the SETON instruction. Let us use indicator 25 for this example.
> 2. By entering an "F" in column 16 of the Output form, headings will print at the top of the next page if an overflow condition has occurred. When the overflow indicator is "on," headings will first be printed at the top of the page followed by the exception output.
> 3. Test to see if indicator 25 is "on" after printing. If it is, turn off indicator 25.

The coding in the calculations section is revised to include the SETON and SETOF instructions. See Figure 6.1Ø and note that the only changes necessary are the SETON and SETOF. The Output form must be revised to include the fetched output by coding "F" in column 16 to skip to a new page if an overflow condition has occurred.

Reviewing the coding, we will assume that we are on pass 7 through the loop when overflow occurs. As a result, the overflow indicator is turned "on" and the program branches to the TAG instruction. Since the overflow indicator, OF, is "on," the SETON instruction is conditioned to turn "on" indicator 25. Exception output is fetched, again because of the overflow. Headings print at the top of a new page followed by the exception line. Recall that indicator 25 is "on." Hence the SETOF instruction is executed which turns off the overflow indicators and indicator 25. Remember, when fetch overflow is to be used with exception reporting, the programmer must

1. Set on an indicator (indicator 25 in the example).
2. Fetch headings at the top of a new page.
3. Print the exception line(s) with the EXCPT instruction.
4. Turn off the OF indicator and the indicator set "on" when overflow occurred.

Figure 6.10
Use of the SETON and SETOF instruction.
(Continued on next page.)

Line	Form Type	Indicators	Factor 1	Operation	Factor 2	Result Field Name	Length	Decimal Positions	Resulting Indicators High (1>2)	Resulting Indicators Low (1<2)	Resulting Indicators Equal (1=2)	Comments
01Ø	C			Z-ADD	Ø	CTR	2	Ø				
02Ø	C		DO12X	TAG								
03Ø	C		CTR	ADD	1	CTR						
04Ø	C	OF		SETON					25			
05Ø	C			EXCPT								
06Ø	C	25		SETOF					OF			
07Ø	C	25		SETOF					25			
08Ø	C		CTR	COMP	12					1Ø		
09Ø	C	1Ø		GOTO	DO12X							
10	C											
11	C											
12	C											

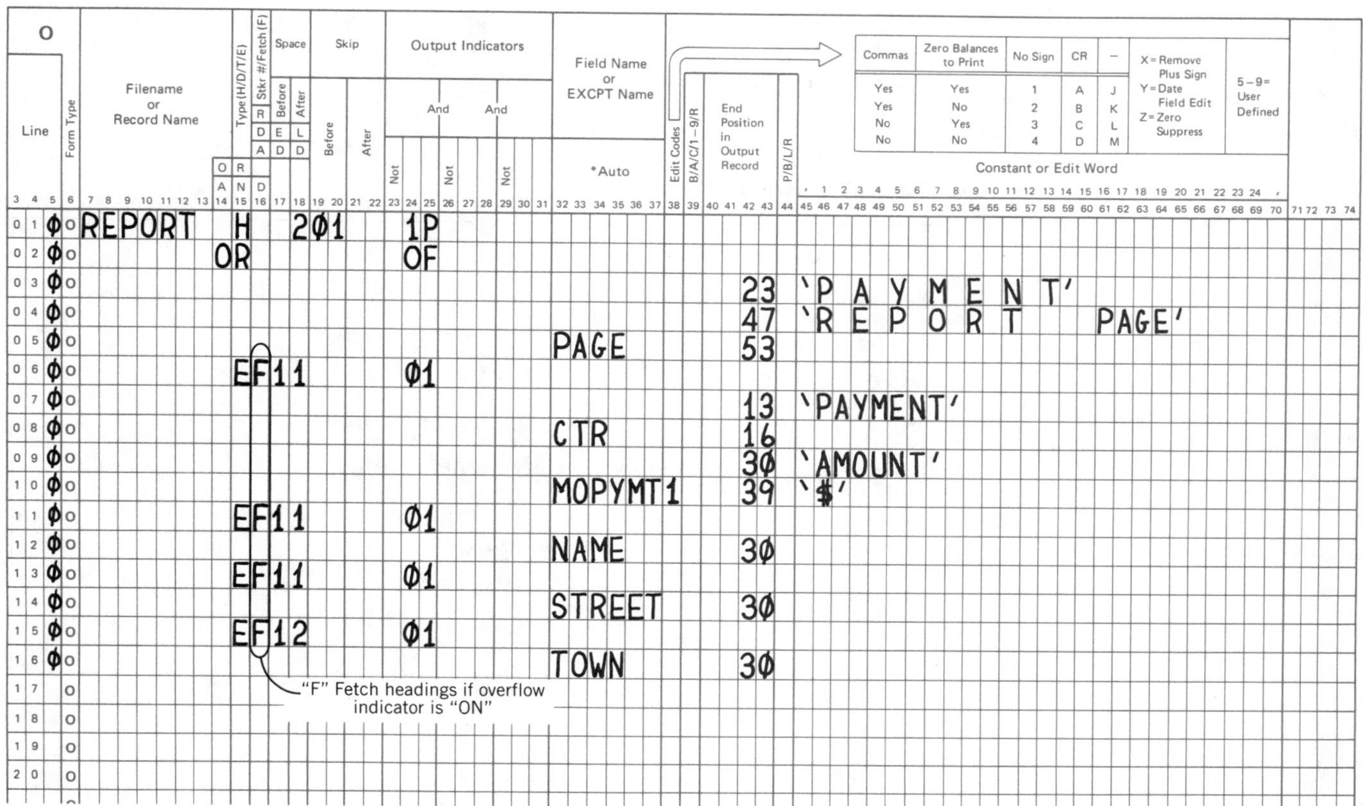

Line	Form Type	Filename or Record Name	Type (H/D/T/E)	Fetch (F)	Space Before	Space After	Skip Before	Output Indicators	Field Name or EXCPT Name	End Position in Output Record	Constant or Edit Word
Ø1	O	REPORT	H			2	Ø1	1P			
Ø2	O	OR						OF			
Ø3	O									23	'P A Y M E N T'
Ø4	O									47	'R E P O R T PAGE'
Ø5	O								PAGE	53	
Ø6	O		E	F	1	1		Ø1			
Ø7	O									13	'PAYMENT'
Ø8	O								CTR	16	
Ø9	O									3Ø	'AMOUNT'
1Ø	O								MOPYMT1	39	'$'
11	O		E	F	1	1		Ø1			
12	O								NAME	3Ø	
13	O		E	F	1	1		Ø1			
14	O								STREET	3Ø	
15	O		E	F	1	2		Ø1			
16	O								TOWN	3Ø	
17	O										
18	O										
19	O										
20	O										

Figure 6.10 *(continued)*

III. MOVE Operations

In writing RPG programs, it is frequently necessary to move data from one storage location to another. Sometimes only a single character is moved, but most often groups of characters or fields are moved. Whereas the Z-ADD instruction is used to move numeric fields, the **MOVE** operation is used with either alphanumeric or numeric data. However, it is strongly recommended that the MOVE instruction be limited to *moving alphanumeric data.*

When moving numeric fields, the programmer should use the Z-ADD rather than the MOVE instruction. The problem with using MOVE instructions to move numeric data fields is that *decimal positions are ignored.* Hence, if numeric fields are not the same size and do not contain the same number of decimal positions, the value of the data may be changed as a result of the MOVE. For example, if the data $1_\wedge ØØ$ is moved into a 3-position numeric field with one decimal position, the result is $1Ø_\wedge Ø$. It should be clear, therefore, that the programmer should avoid using the MOVE instruction when numeric data is to be moved. Instead, use the Z-ADD, since alignment of decimal points is automatic with the zero-and-add instruction.

When moving integers or whole numbers to numeric fields of the same size, the chances for error are reduced; but, again, the Z-ADD is strongly recommended. It is also important for the programmer to recognize that although a field may contain numbers, it is not necessarily always numeric. Numeric fields are those data fields used in calculations. However, data fields such as employee number, social security number, and edited dates containing slashes are not treated as numeric fields in programming. These can be transmitted to other areas of storage using the MOVE instruction. With this in mind, we will now summarize the MOVE instruction.

A. The MOVE Instruction

Instruction:	MOVE
Meaning:	Move or copy characters from one field to another starting with the *right*-most position.
Factor 1:	Not used.
Factor 2:	Sending field, remains unchanged.
Result Field:	Receiving field, contents change.
Limitations:	Half-adjusting and resulting indicators are not used with this instruction.
Comment:	Avoid using the MOVE instruction when *numeric* data is to be moved. Use the Z-ADD for proper decimal alignment of numeric fields.

Example 1

RPG CALCULATION SPECIFICATIONS

Program		Keying Instruction	Graphic	Card Electro Number	Page 1 2 of	Program Identification 75 76 77 78 79 80
Programmer	Date		Key			

Line (3–5)	Form Type (6)	Control Level (L0–L9, LR, SR, AN/OR) (7–8)	Indicators (9–17)	Factor 1 (18–27)	Operation (28–32)	Factor 2 (33–42)	Result Field Name (43–48)	Length (49–51)	Decimal Positions (52)	Half Adjust (H) (53)	Resulting Indicators: Plus / Minus / Zero; Compare 1>2 / 1<2 / 1=2; Lookup (Factor 2) is High / Low / Equal (54–59)	Comments (60–74)
01Φ	C				MOVE	EMPNO	EMPOUT					
02	C											
03	C											
04	C											

The data in Factor 2 replaces the previous contents of the result field. After execution, the result field contains an exact copy of Factor 2 when the fields are of the same size. Movement of the characters is from *right to left,* one character at a time. The move operation ends whenever all characters in the sending field are moved or the receiving field is filled. This proves critical when the result field is longer than the sending field, since there will be data remaining from the result field's previous contents. An example will clarify this point.

Example 2 *Receiving Field Longer than Sending Field*

RPG CALCULATION SPECIFICATIONS

Line	Form Type	Factor 1	Operation	Factor 2	Result Field Name
01	C		MOVE	NAMEIN	NAMEO
02	C				
03	C				

NAMEIN

Before MOVE: P O R T

After MOVE: P O R T

Contents unchanged

NAMEO

Before MOVE: R E M A K E

After MOVE: R E P O R T

Contents unchanged (R E) — Contents change (P O R T)

Note the results in NAMEO after the move. Since NAMEO, the receiving field, contains 6 characters and only 4 characters are moved, the *left-most* 2 *characters remain unchanged.* There are applications where such a move may prove desirable. In the illustration that follows, for example, we are able to change the year in the date field without disturbing the month and day data.

RPG CALCULATION SPECIFICATIONS

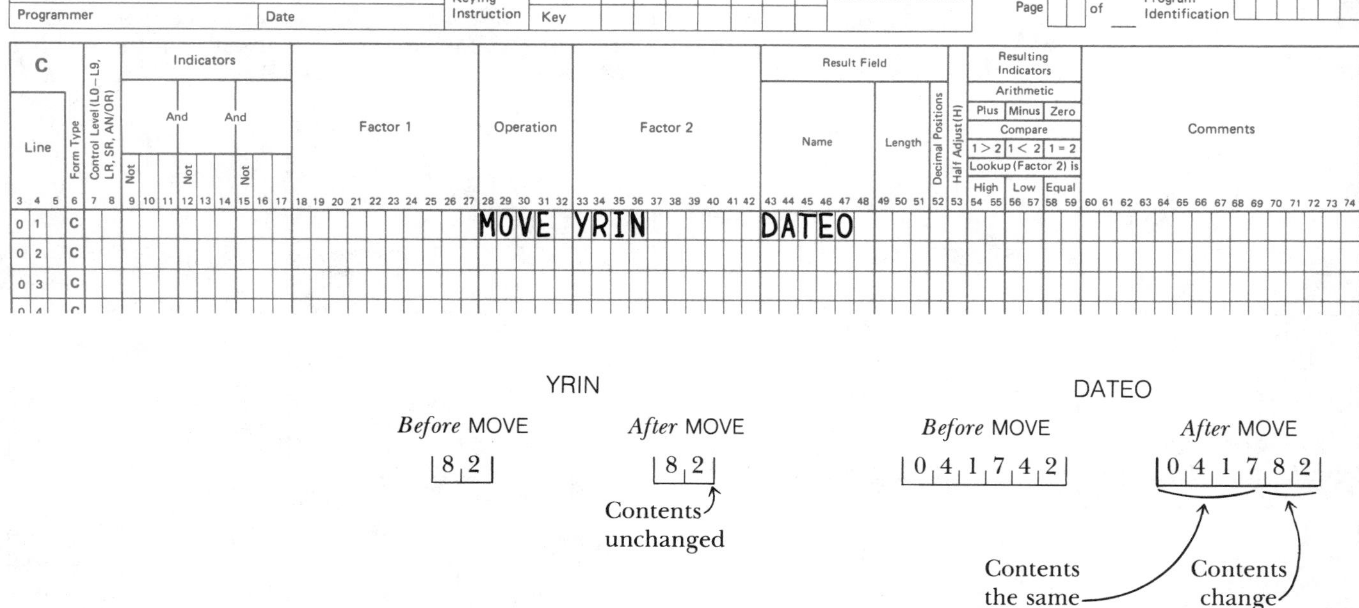

With business applications, this use of the MOVE instruction is a desired feature when *properly* used.

In the following example, the receiving field (result field) is shorter than the sending field contained in Factor 2.

Example 3 *Receiving Field Shorter than Sending Field*

RPG CALCULATION SPECIFICATIONS

Line	Form Type	Control Level	Indicators	Factor 1	Operation	Factor 2	Result Field Name	Length	Decimal Positions	Half Adjust	Resulting Indicators	Comments
01ϕ	C				MOVE	LONGFD	SHORT					
02	C											
03	C											

	LONGFD		SHORT	
	Before MOVE	*After* MOVE	*Before* MOVE	*After* MOVE
	B I C Y C L E	B I C Y C L E	A B C D E	C Y C L E
		Contents unchanged		Contents change

Note: BI of bicycle not moved.

The results obtained in the receiving field, SHORT, are important in understanding the MOVE instruction. Since the receiving or result field is 5 characters in length and the sending field contains 7 characters, two characters will be lost or *truncated* as a result of this operation. Since the MOVE instruction begins on the right and progresses one character at a time, there is not any room left in the receiving field for the two left-most characters. Consequently, the BI of "BICYCLE" are lost. Also recall that the sending field is not altered; hence "BICYCLE" is still available in LONGFD.

Literals may also be moved with the MOVE instruction. For example,

RPG CALCULATION SPECIFICATIONS

Line	Form Type	Control Level	Indicators	Factor 1	Operation	Factor 2	Result Field Name	Length	Decimal Positions	Half Adjust	Resulting Indicators	Comments
01ϕ	C				MOVE	'A'	CODE	1				
02ϕ	C*											
03ϕ	C				MOVE	'ERROR'	MSSG	5				
04	C											
05	C											

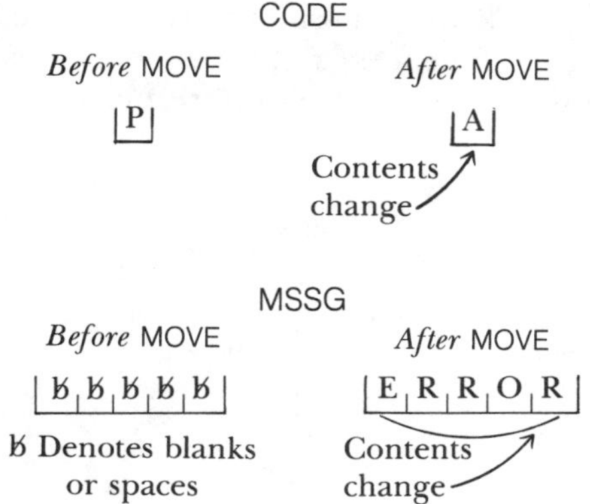

Based on certain indicator conditions, the programmer may want to move a unique code or message into a field. (Note that alphanumeric literals are enclosed in quotes.)

The MOVE instruction is subject to several limitations. Recall that Factor 1 is not used in this instruction. No resulting indicators or half-adjusting is permitted. Numeric fields may be changed to alphameric fields by simply moving the data to a field defined as alphameric.

To change an alphameric field to a numeric field, move the data to a numeric result field, one that is defined by using an integer in the Decimal Positions field. Clearly, the *format* of the result field establishes the format of the contents. Most other programming languages *do not* allow this unique capability of changing data from alphameric to numeric and vice versa. The potential problems arising from manipulating data in this manner are enormous, particularly with respect to decimal alignment of numeric fields. Therefore, it is strongly recommended that this practice *be avoided*.

B. The MOVELeft Instruction

Instruction:	MOVEL
Meaning:	Move or copy characters from one field to another, starting with the *left-most* character and moving from left to right.
Factor 1:	Not used.
Factor 2:	Sending field, remains unchanged.
Result Field:	Receiving field, contents change.
Limitations:	Half-adjust and resulting indicators are not used. If the receiving field is shorter than the sending field, right-most positions are truncated. If the receiving field is longer than the sending field, the extra positions in the receiving field remain unchanged.

The MOVEL operation is similar to the MOVE instruction, but the movement of the data begins from the *left* instead of from the right. As with the MOVE instruction, if the sending field contained in Factor 2 is longer than the receiving or result field, the extra positions are truncated. However, the positions truncated would be the excess right-most positions in this case. For example, the following instruction produces the results indicated.

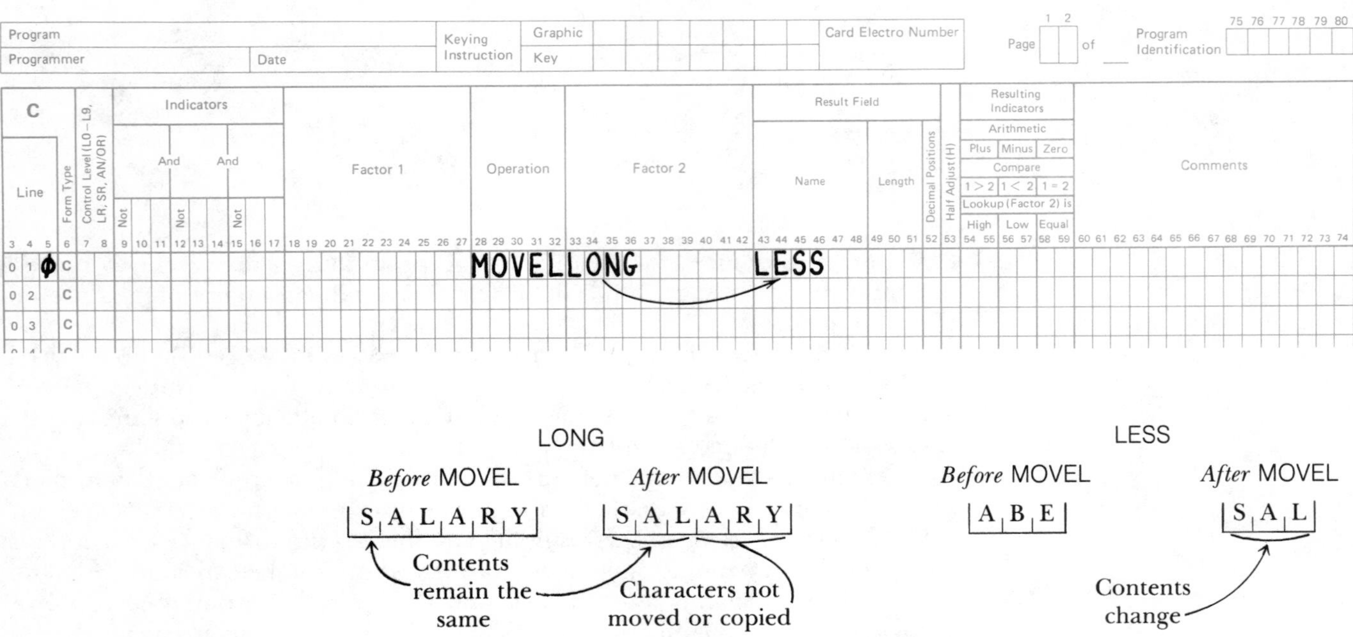

This operation would result in copying only 3 of the 6 characters contained in the sending field. Since the MOVEL instruction begins the movement of data from the left, only the left-most three characters contained in LONG would be moved or copied into the receiving field called LESS.

If, however, the sending field is smaller than the receiving field, the extra *right-most* positions of the receiving field remain unchanged. For example,

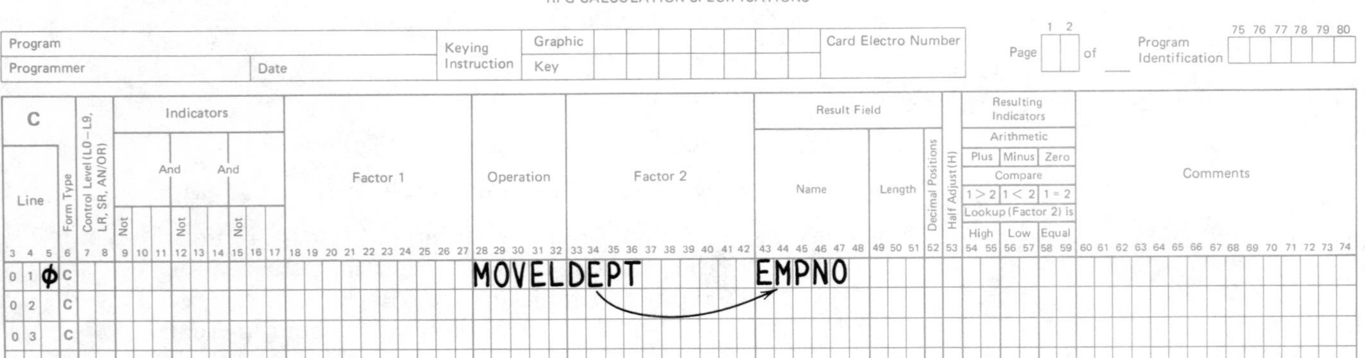

	DEPT		EMPNO
Before MOVEL	*After* MOVEL	*Before* MOVEL	*After* MOVEL
3 2	3 2	7 7 7 7 7	3 2 7 7 7
	Contents unchanged		Contents change

Again, the MOVEL instruction, in effect, left-justifies the field being copied into the receiving field. Additional positions that occur from unequal field lengths are *always the right-most positions*. If the receiving field is the shorter field, the excess positions to the right are truncated or lost. If, however, the receiving field is the longer field, the receiving field's extra positions to the right remain unchanged. To ensure correct results, it is best to use fields of the same length in a MOVEL instruction.

Literals may be used in either MOVE or MOVEL instructions. They are enclosed in quotes and entered in Factor 2 of the coding form. However, the data moved will be left-justified in the result field in a MOVEL instruction. For example,

RPG CALCULATION SPECIFICATIONS

Line	Form Type	Control Level	Indicators	Factor 1	Operation	Factor 2	Result Field Name	Length	Decimal Positions	Half Adjust	Resulting Indicators	Comments
01Ø	C				MOVEL	'MY T'	ITEMO					
02	C											
03	C											

ITEMO	
Before MOVEL	*After* MOVEL
F I N E	M Y T F I N E

Recall, however, that the maximum length of an alphameric literal is eight characters.

Key Terms

Conditional branch	Loop
Entry point	MOVE instruction
Exception output	MOVEL instruction
EXCPT instruction	Structured programming
Fetch overflow	TAG
GOTO instruction	Unconditional branch

Self-Evaluating Quiz

1. Determine the contents of the Result Field used in the following MOVE instructions. The contents of each field before the MOVE is as follows.

   FLDA = 'AB56'
   LONG = 'XXXZZZ'
   SHORT = 'YY'

   a. MOVE FLDA LONG
   b. MOVEL FLDA SHORT
   c. MOVEL FLDA LONG
   d. MOVE FLDA SHORT
   e. MOVEL SHORT LONG
   f. MOVE LONG SHORT
   g. MOVEL LONG SHORT
   h. MOVE SHORT LONG
   i. MOVEL 'M' SHORT
   j. MOVEL 'L' LONG
   k. MOVEL '12' FLDA
   l. MOVE 'HI' FLDA
2. When output is required during calculation time, the ________ instruction is used.
3. Looping instructions may be entered on the ________ form.
4. When multiple copies of labels are needed, the EXCPT statement is contained within a(n) ________ .
5. (T or F) When EXCPT output is used, overflow is handled automatically by RPG II.
6. List the following steps in the sequence in which they occur in the RPG cycle. Begin with the Read instruction.
   a. Test for overflow
   b. Total calculations
   c. Read record
   d. Detail calculations
   e. Detail output
   f. Move data to fields
   g. Total output
7. An unconditional branch requires the word(s) ________ in the operation field.
8. A conditional branch requires that ________ be used in conjunction with the GOTO instruction.
9. Entry points in the program are identified by ________ instructions.
10. (T or F) The MOVEL instruction is used to right-justify data transmitted to the receiving field.
11. When exception output is used, the Type field (column 15) on the Output form is coded with a(n) ________ .
12. (T or F) The most efficient way to move numeric data is with the MOVE instruction.

Solutions

1. a. XXAB56
   b. AB
   c. AB56ZZ
   d. 56
   e. YYXZZZ
   f. ZZ

g. XX
h. XXXZYY
i. MY
j. LXXZZZ
k. 1256
l. ABHI

2. EXCPT
3. Calculation
4. loop
5. F—EXCPT output occurs during calculation time, and the RPG cycle is not able to check or test for overflow until the calculation section is completed.
6. c b g a f d e
7. GOTO
8. indicators
9. TAG
10. F—The MOVE is used for this purpose.
11. E
12. F—Always use the Z-ADD.

Review Questions

1. Using the Calculation form, code the RPG II instruction to test if CTR > 17. If CTR > 17, then branch to NOGO routine; otherwise, branch to OK.
2. Using the Calculation form, code the RPG II instructions to unconditionally branch to a routine called READ.
3. Using the flowchart excerpt shown below at left, code the program segment.
4. Using the Calculation form, code the excerpt illustrated below at right in RPG II.

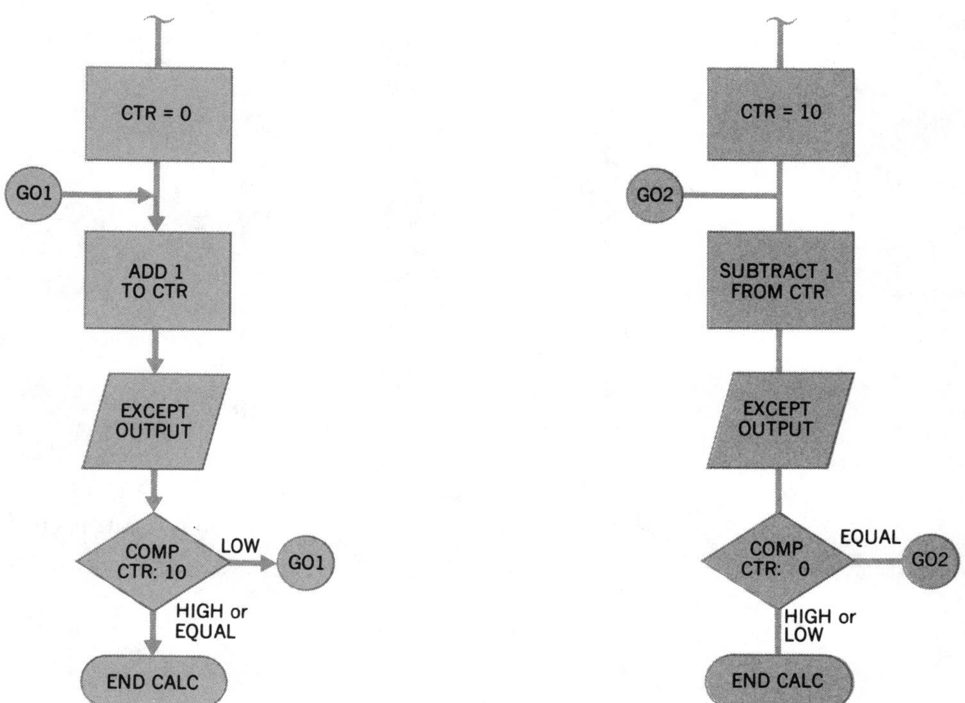

5. Referring to the flowchart here, code the Calculation form to accomplish the sequence of steps shown.

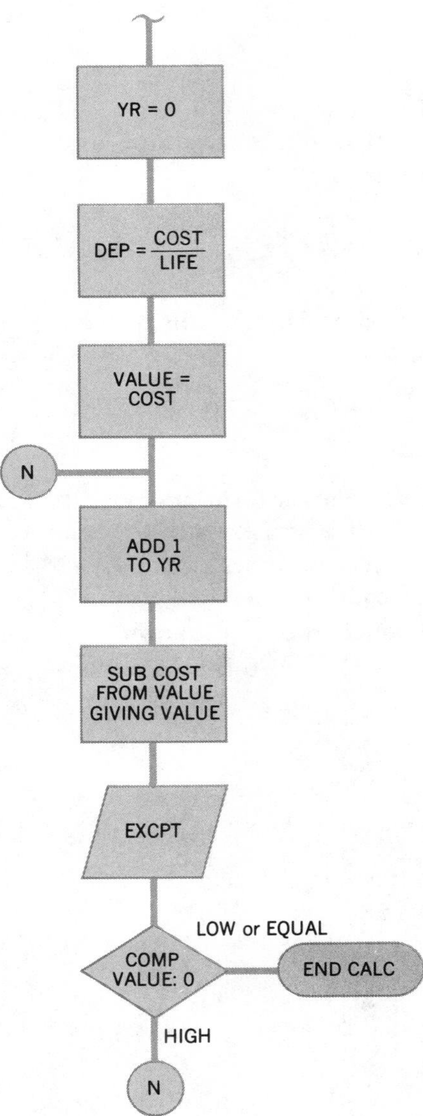

6. Suppose a programmer wishes to use the fetch overflow option when overflow occurs during exception output. Identify what is logically incorrect with the following loop.

RPG CALCULATION SPECIFICATIONS

Program		Keying Instruction	Graphic		Card Electro Number	Page 1 2 of	Program Identification 75 76 77 78 79 80
Programmer	Date		Key				

Line (3–5)	Form Type (6)	Control Level (L0–L9, LR, SR, AN/OR) (7–8)	Indicators: Not / And Not / And Not (9–17)	Factor 1 (18–27)	Operation (28–32)	Factor 2 (33–42)	Result Field Name (43–48)	Length (49–51)	Decimal Positions (52)	Half Adjust (H) (53)	Resulting Indicators: Plus / 1>2 / High (54–55)	Minus / 1<2 / Low (56–57)	Zero / 1=2 / Equal (58–59)	Comments (60–74)
01Ø	C			BEGIN	TAG									
02Ø	C				●									
03Ø	C		OF		SETOF						OF			
04Ø	C				EXCPT									
05Ø	C			CTR	COMP	1Ø						2Ø		
06Ø	C		2Ø		GOTO	BEGIN								
07	C													
08	C													
09	C													

7. Code the following flowchart excerpt.

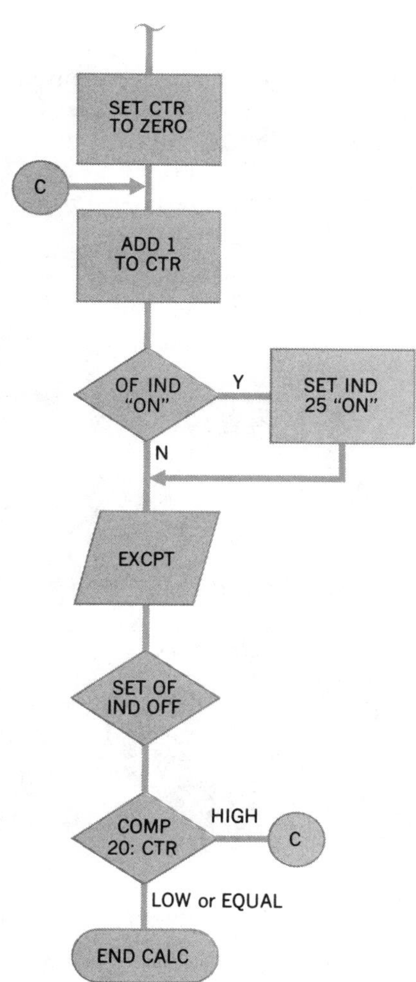

Debugging Exercises

The following program contains the formula used to calculate annual depreciation of capital equipment.

$$\text{Annual depreciation} = \frac{\text{COST} - \text{SCRAP}}{\text{LIFE}}$$

At the end of the anticipated life, the value of the equipment should depreciate to the scrap value. Note, however, that rounding of the annual depreciation frequently occurs and the last year's depreciation must be increased or decreased a few cents in order for the exact scrap value to be attained. For example, to depreciate an item costing \$78,ØØØ over a 14-year period having a scrap value of \$14,ØØØ, you would calculate

$$\text{Annual depreciation} = \frac{\text{COST} - \text{SCRAP}}{\text{LIFE}} = \frac{\$78{,}000 - \$14{,}000}{14}$$
$$= \frac{\$64{,}000}{14} = \$4{,}571.43 \text{ per year}$$

If you used this figure for a 14-year period, however, you would depreciate the equipment by \$64,ØØØ.Ø2 and not the \$64,ØØØ.ØØ we had intended. Thus you have an error of 2 cents. The program, however, recalculates the annual depreciation during the last pass through the loop, thus avoiding this problem.

The problem definition for this program is shown in Figure 6.11. The coding sheets contained in Figure 6.12, however, contain errors in syntax and execution errors. The listing in Figure 6.13 includes the error diagnostics produced by running the program as shown. The syntax corrections are circled on the computer listing shown in Figure 6.14. There are, however, logic errors. Your assignment is to desk check this program carefully, find the logic errors, and make the necessary corrections.

Figure 6.11
Problem definition for the debugging exercise.
(Continued on next page.)

Systems Flowchart

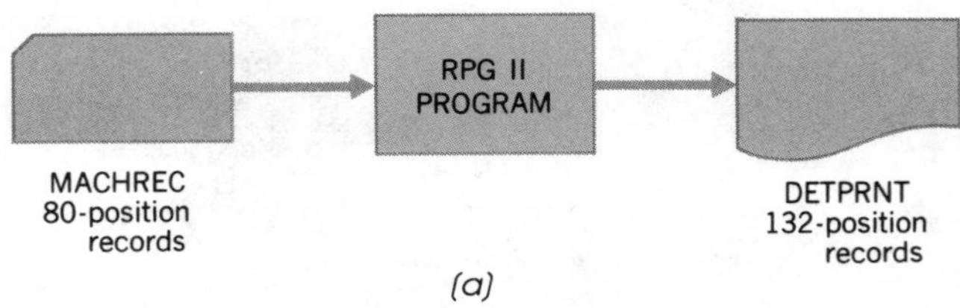

(a)

MACHREC Record Layout

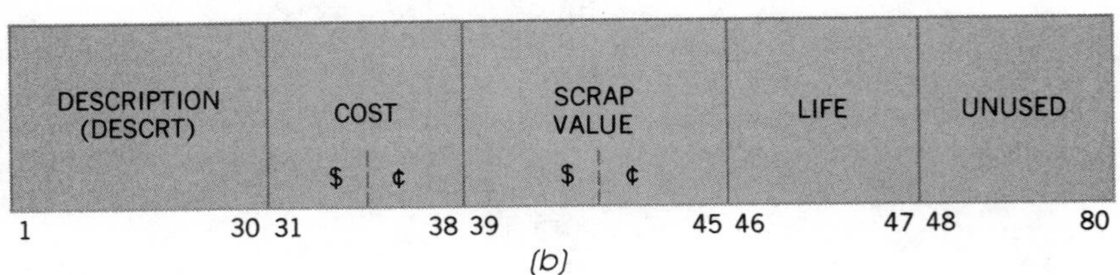

(b)

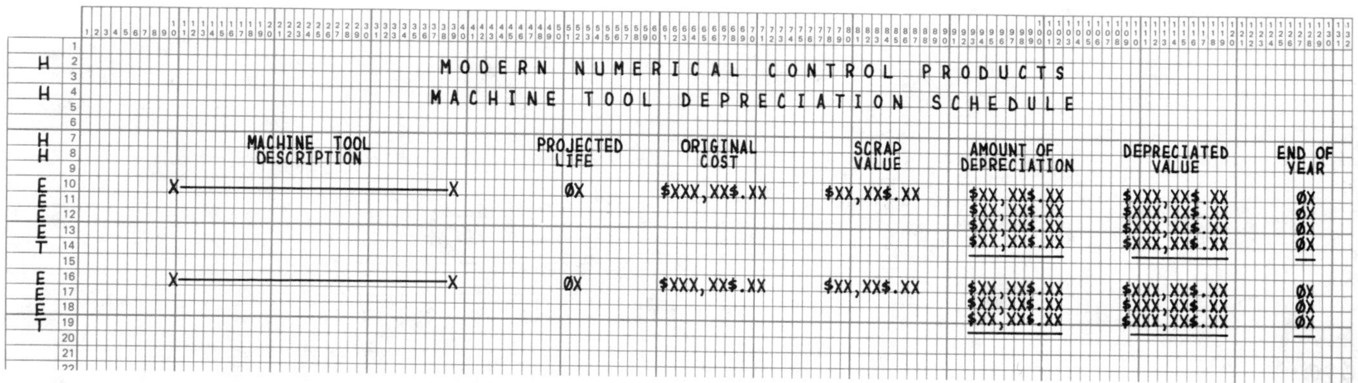

Figure 6.11 *(continued)* (c)

Figure 6.12
Coding sheets for the debugging exercise.

RPG CONTROL AND FILE DESCRIPTION SPECIFICATIONS

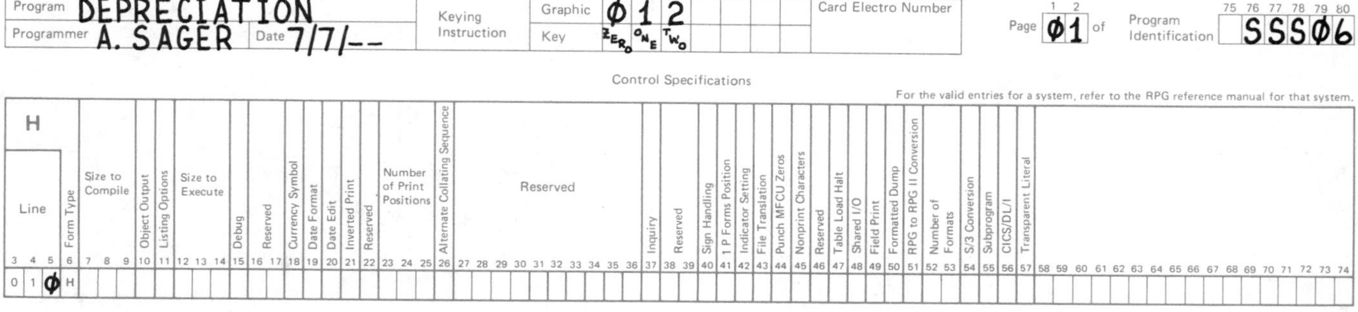

File Description Specifications

```
02Ø F*****************************************************************
03Ø F* THIS PROGRAM GENERATES A STRAIGHT LINE DEPRECIATION TABLE     *
04Ø F* USED TO WRITE OFF COSTS OVER THE USEFUL LIFE OF THE ASSET.    *
05Ø F* AT THE END OF THE USEFUL LIFE, THE ASSET WILL HAVE BEEN       *
06Ø F* REDUCED TO A SCRAP OR SALVAGE VALUE.  THE DEPRECIATION IS     *
07Ø F* THE COST MINUS THE SCRAP VALUE.  THE ANNUAL DEPRECIATION      *
08Ø F* IS CALCULATED BY DIVIDING THE TOTAL DEPR. BY THE USEFUL       *
09Ø F* LIFE.                                                         *
10Ø F*****************************************************************
Ø1Ø FMACHREC IP  F      8Ø            READØ1 SYSIPT
Ø2Ø FDETPRNT O   F     132     OF     PRINTERSYSLST
```

Figure 6.12
(continued)

RPG INPUT SPECIFICATIONS

```
Ø3ØI*
Ø4ØI**************************** INPUT RECORD *****************************
Ø5ØI*
Ø6ØIMACHREC NS  Ø1
Ø7ØI                                                1  3Ø DESCRT
Ø8ØI                                               31  382COST
Ø9ØI                                               39  452SCRAP
1ØØI                                               46  47ØLIFE
```

RPG CALCULATION SPECIFICATIONS

```
Ø1ØC                     Z-ADDØ         YEAR    2Ø
Ø2ØC                     Z-ADDCOST      DEPVAL  82
Ø3ØC*
Ø4ØC************************************************************
Ø5ØC* CALCULATE ANNUAL DEPRECIATION                            *
Ø6ØC************************************************************
Ø7ØC*
Ø8ØC           COST      SUB  SCRAP     TOTDEP
Ø9ØC           TOTDEP    DIV  LIFE      ANLDEP  72H
1ØØC*
11ØC************************************************************
12ØC* PERFORM LOOP IN ORDER TO PRINT THE ANNUAL DEPRECIATION.  *
13ØC* GROUP INDICATION ACCOMPLISHED BY THE Ø1 INDICATOR.  WHEN *
14ØC* OVERFLOW OCCURS, INDICATORS Ø1 AND 5Ø ARE SET ON. HEADINGS*
15ØC* WILL BE FETCHED AND INDICATORS Ø1, 5Ø AND OF WILL THEN BE *
16ØC* SET OFF.  WHEN THE LOOP IS COMPLETED Ø1 IS RESET TO ON   *
17ØC* IN ORDER TO CONDITION THE TOTAL-TIME OUTPUT & SPACING.    *
18ØC************************************************************
19ØC*
2ØØC           TAG       DOLIFE
21ØC           YEAR      ADD  1         YEAR
22ØC           YEAR      COMP LIFE                  15  15
23ØC*
```

RPG CALCULATION SPECIFICATIONS

```
24Ø C*****************************************************************
25Ø C* ADJUST ANNUAL DEPR. FOR ROUNDING ON THE LAST PASS.             *
26Ø C*****************************************************************
27Ø C*
28Ø C   15     DEPVAL    SUB  SCRAP     ANLDEP
29Ø C          DEPVAL    SUB  ANLDEP    DEPVAL
30Ø C   OF               SETON                     5Ø  Ø1
31Ø C                    EXCPT
32Ø C   5Ø               SETOF                     5Ø  OF
33Ø C                    SETOF                     Ø1
34Ø C  N15               GOTO DOLIFE
35Ø C                    SETON                     Ø1
```

RPG OUTPUT SPECIFICATIONS

```
01Ø O*
02Ø O************************** HEADING LINES *************************
03Ø O*
04Ø ODETPRNT H  2Ø1   1P
05Ø O       OR        OF
06Ø O                                  48 'M O D E R N'
07Ø O                                  68 'N U M E R I C A L'
08Ø O                                  84 'C O N T R O L'
09Ø O                                 1Ø2 'P R O D U C T S'
10Ø O        H  3     1P
11Ø O       OR        OF
12Ø O                                  59 'M A C H I N E   T O O L'
13Ø O                                  85 'D E P R E C I A T I O N'
14Ø O                                 1Ø3 'S C H E D U L E'
15Ø O        H  1     1P
16Ø O       OR        OF
17Ø O                                  3Ø 'MACHINE  TOOL'
18Ø O                                  56 'PROJECTED'
19Ø O                                  7Ø 'ORIGINAL'
20Ø O                                  85 'SCRAP'
21Ø O                                 1Ø1 'AMOUNT OF'
22Ø O                                 119 'DEPRECIATED'
23Ø O                                 13Ø 'END OF'
24Ø O        H  2     1P
25Ø O       OR        OF
```

RPG OUTPUT SPECIFICATIONS

```
O                                   29 'DESCRIPTION'
O                                   53 'LIFE'
O                                   68 'COST'
O                                   85 'VALUE'
O                                  103 'DEPRECIATION'
O                                  116 'VALUE'
O                                  129 'YEAR'
O*
O************************* TOTAL LINE ***********************************
O*
O        T  03     01
O                                  103 '-----------'
O                                  119 '-----------'
O                                  128 '--'
O*
O************************* EXCEPTION OUTPUT *********************
O*
O        E  1
O                       01DESCRT    39
O                       01LIFE  Z   52
O                       01COST  1   71 '$'
O                       01SCRAP 1   87 '$'
O                         ANLDEP1B 102 '$'
O                         DEPVAL1B 119 '$'
O                         YEAR  Z  128
O**********     END OF PROGRAM    **************************************
```

Figure 6.12
(continued)

Figure 6.13
Program listing with error diagnostics for the debugging exercise.
(Continued on next page.)

```
                 F*
                 F*         D E P R E C I A T I O N
       01-020    F*************************************************************    SSS06
       01-030    F* THIS PROGRAM GENERATES A STRAIGHT LINE DEPRECIATION TABLE *    SSS06
       01-040    F* USED TO WRITE OFF COSTS OVER THE USEFUL LIFE OF THE ASSET.*    SSS06
       01-050    F* AT THE END CF THE USEFUL LIFE, THE ASSET WILL HAVE BEEN   *    SSS06
       01-060    F* REDUCED TO A SCRAP OR SALVAGE VALUE.  THE DEPRECIATION IS *    SSS06
       01-070    F* THE COST MINUS THE SCRAP VALUE.  THE ANNUAL DEPRECIATION  *    SSS06
       01-080    F* IS CALCULATED BY DIVIDING THE TCTAL DEPR. BY THE USEFUL   *    SSS06
       01-090    F* LIFE.                                                     *    SSS06
       01-100    F*************************************************************    SSS06
0001   02-010    FMACHREC IP  F       80              READ01 SYSIPT                SSS06
0002   02-020    FDETPRNT O   F      132      OF      PRINTERSYSLST                SSS06
       02-030    I*                                                                SSS06
       02-040    I************************** INPUT RECCRD **************************** SSS06
       02-050    I*                                                                SSS06
0003   02-060    IMACHREC NS  01                                                   SSS06
0004   02-070    I                                          1  30 DESCRT           SSS06
0005   02-080    I                                         31  382COST             SSS06
0006   02-090    I                                         39  452SCRAP            SSS06
0007   02-100    I                                         46  470LIFE             SSS06
0008   03-010    C                         Z-ADDO         YEAR    20               SSS06
0009   03-020    C                         Z-ADDCCST      DEPVAL  82               SSS06
       03-030    C*                                                                SSS06
       03-040    C*************************************************************    SSS06
       03-050    C* CALCULATE ANNUAL DEPRECIATION                             *    SSS06
       03-060    C*************************************************************    SSS06
       03-070    C*                                                                SSS06
0010   03-080    C           COST      SUB  SCRAP     TCTDEP                       SSS06
0011   03-090    C           TCTDEP    DIV  LIFE      ANLDEP  72H                  SSS06
       03-100    C*                                                                SSS06
       03-110    C*************************************************************    SSS06
       03-120    C* PERFORM LCCP IN ORDER TO PRINT THE ANNUAL DEPRECIATION.   *    SSS06
       03-130    C* GROUP INDICATICN ACCCMPLISHED BY THE 01 INDICATCR.  WHEN  *    SSS06
       03-140    C* OVERFLOW CCCURS, INDICATORS 01 AND 50 ARE SET ON. HEADINGS*    SSS06
       03-150    C* WILL BE FETCHED AND INDICATORS 01, 50 AND OF WILL THEN BE *    SSS06
       03-160    C* SET CFF.  WHEN THE LCCP IS CCMPLETED 01 IS RESET TC ON    *    SSS06
       03-170    C* IN ORDER TO CONDITION THE TOTAL-TIME OUTPUT & SPACING.    *    SSS06
       03-180    C*************************************************************    SSS06
       03-190    C*                                                                SSS06
0012   03-200    C           TAG       DCLIFE                                      SSS06
                                       $
0013   03-210    C           YEAR      ADD  1         YEAR                         SSS06
0014   03-220    C           YEAR      COMP LIFE                    15  15         SSS06
       03-230    C*                                                                SSS06
       03-240    C*************************************************************    SSS06
       03-250    C* ADJUST ANNUAL DEPR. FCR RCUNDING CN THE LAST PASS.        *    SSS06
       03-260    C*************************************************************    SSS06
       03-270    C*                                                                SSS06
0015   03-280    C   15      DEPVAL    SUB  SCRAP     ANLDEP                       SSS06
0016   03-290    C           DEPVAL    SUB  ANLDEP    DEPVAL                       SSS06
0017   03-300    C   OF                SETCN                        50  01         SSS06
0018   03-310    C                     EXCPT                                       SSS06
0019   03-320    C   50                SETCF                        50  OF         SSS06
0020   03-330    C                     SETCF                        01             SSS06
0021   03-340    C  N15                GCTC DCLIFE                                 SSS06
0022   03-350    C                     SETCN                        01             SSS06
       04-010    C*                                                                SSS06
       04-020    O************************** HEADING LINES ************************** SSS06
       04-030    O*                                                                SSS06
0023   04-040    ODETPRNT H  201    1P                                             SSS06
0024   04-050    O        CR        OF                                             SSS06
0025   04-060    O                                     48 'M C D E R N'            SSS06
0026   04-070    O                                     68 'N U M E R I C A L'      SSS06
0027   04-080    O                                     84 'C O N T R O L'          SSS06
0028   04-090    O                                    102 'P R C D U C T S'        SSS06
0029   04-100    O          H  3    1P                                             SSS06
0030   04-110    O        CR        OF                                             SSS06
0031   04-120    O                                     59 'M A C H I N E  T O O L' SSS06
0032   04-130    O                                     85 'D E P R E C I A T I O N' SSS06
0033   04-140    O                                    103 'S C H E D U L E'        SSS06
0034   04-150    O          H  1    1P                                             SSS06
0035   04-160    O        CR        OF                                             SSS06
0036   04-170    O                                     30 'MACHINE  TOOL'          SSS06
0037   04-180    O                                     56 'PRCJECTED'              SSS06
0038   04-190    O                                     70 'ORIGINAL'               SSS06
0039   04-200    O                                     85 'SCRAP'                  SSS06
0040   04-210    O                                    101 'AMCUNT OF'              SSS06
0041   04-220    O                                    119 'DEPRECIATED'            SSS06
0042   04-230    O                                    130 'END OF'                 SSS06
0043   04-240    O          H  2    1P                                             SSS06
0044   04-250    O        CR        OF                                             SSS06
0045   04-260    O                                     29 'DESCRIPTION'            SSS06
0046   04-270    O                                     53 'LIFE'                   SSS06
0047   04-280    O                                     68 'CCST'                   SSS06
0048   04-290    O                                     85 'VALUE'                  SSS06
0049   04-300    O                                    103 'DEPRECIATION'           SSS06
0050   04-310    O                                    116 'VALUE'                  SSS06
0051   04-320    O                                    129 'YEAR'                   SSS06
       04-330    C*                                                                SSS06
       04-340    O************************** TCTAL LINE ***************************** SSS06
       04-350    O*                                                                SSS06
0052   04-360    O          T 03    01                                             SSS06
0053   04-370    O                                    103 '----------'             SSS06
```

Figure 6.13 *(continued)*

```
0054      04-380  C                                     119 '-----------'                  SSS06
0055      04-390  C                                     128 '--'                           SSS06
          04-400  C*                                                                       SSS06
          04-410  C**************************** EXCEPTION OUTPUT ************************ SSS06
          04-420  C*                                                                       SSS06
0056      04-430  C          E  1                                                          SSS06
0057      04-440  C                         01DESCRT     39                                SSS06
0058      04-450  O                         01LIFE  Z    52                                SSS06
0059      04-460  O                         01COST  1    71 '$'                            SSS06
0060      04-470  C                         01SCRAP 1    87 '$'                            SSS06
0061      04-480  O                           ANLDEP1B 102 '$'                             SSS06
0062      04-490  O                           DEPVAL1B 119 '$'                             SSS06
0063      04-500  O                           YEAR  Z  128                                 SSS06
          04-510  O**********  END OF PROGRAM  ****************************************SSS06

      E N D   O F   S O U R C E


      C O M P I L E R   D I A G N O S T I C S   S U M M A R Y


ILN141   INVALID OPERATION. SPEC IS DROPPED.

     D  0012     03-200      DCLIF

ILN398   FIELD NAME UNDEFINED. SPEC IS DROPPED.

     C  0010     03-080      TOTDEP
     D  0011     03-090      TOTDEP
     C  0012     03-200      E
     C  0012     03-200      TAG
     D  0021     03-340      DCLIFE
```

Figure 6.14
Program listing that contains logic errors for the debugging exercise.
(Continued on next page.)

```
        F*
        F*       D E P R E C I A T I O N
01-020  F****************************************************************    SSS06
01-030  F* THIS PROGRAM GENERATES A STRAIGHT LINE DEPRECIATION TABLE *    SSS06
01-040  F* USED TO WRITE OFF COSTS OVER THE USEFUL LIFE OF THE ASSET.*    SSS06
01-050  F* AT THE END OF THE USEFUL LIFE, THE ASSET WILL HAVE BEEN    *    SSS06
01-060  F* REDUCED TO A SCRAP OR SALVAGE VALUE.  THE DEPRECIATION IS *    SSS06
01-070  F* THE COST MINUS THE SCRAP VALUE.  THE ANNUAL DEPRECIATION  *    SSS06
01-080  F* IS CALCULATED BY DIVIDING THE TOTAL DEPR. BY THE USEFUL   *    SSS06
01-090  F* LIFE.                                                      *    SSS06
01-100  F****************************************************************    SSS06
02-010  FMACHREC IP  F      80             READ01 SYSIPT                       SSS06
02-020  FDETPRNT O   F     132    OF       PRINTERSYSLST                       SSS06
02-030  I*                                                                     SSS06
02-040  I*************************** INPUT RECORD ************************** SSS06
02-050  I*                                                                     SSS06
02-060  IMACHREC NS  01                                                        SSS06
02-070  I                                         1  30 DESCRT                 SSS06
02-080  I                                        31  382COST                   SSS06
02-090  I                                        39  452SCRAP                  SSS06
02-100  I                                        46  470LIFE                   SSS06
03-010  C                    Z-ADDO         YEAR    20                         SSS06
03-020  C                    Z-ADDCOST      DEPVAL  82                         SSS06
03-030  C*                                                                     SSS06
03-040  C****************************************************************    SSS06
03-050  C* CALCULATE ANNUAL DEPRECIATION                                 *    SSS06
03-060  C****************************************************************    SSS06
03-070  C*                                                                     SSS06
03-080  C           COST      SUB  SCRAP     TOTDEP  82                        SSS06
03-090  C           TOTDEP    DIV  LIFE      ANLDEP  72H                       SSS06
03-100  C*                                                                     SSS06
03-110  C****************************************************************    SSS06
03-120  C* PERFORM LOOP IN ORDER TO PRINT THE ANNUAL DEPRECIATION.     *    SSS06
03-130  C* GROUP INDICATION ACCOMPLISHED BY THE 01 INDICATOR.  WHEN    *    SSS06
03-140  C* OVERFLOW OCCURS, INDICATORS 01 AND 50 ARE SET ON. HEADINGS*    SSS06
03-150  C* WILL BE FETCHED AND INDICATORS 01, 50 AND OF WILL THEN BE *    SSS06
03-160  C* SET OFF.  WHEN THE LOOP IS COMPLETED 01 IS RESET TO ON     *    SSS06
03-170  C* IN ORDER TO CONDITION THE TOTAL-TIME OUTPUT & SPACING.     *    SSS06
03-180  C****************************************************************    SSS06
03-190  C*                                                                     SSS06
03-200  C           DOLIFE    TAG                                              SSS06
03-210  C           YEAR      ADD  1         YEAR                              SSS06
03-220  C           YEAR      COMP LIFE                      15  15            SSS06
03-230  C*                                                                     SSS06
03-240  C****************************************************************    SSS06
03-250  C* ADJUST ANNUAL DEPR. FOR ROUNDING ON THE LAST PASS.           *    SSS06
03-260  C****************************************************************    SSS06
03-270  C*                                                                     SSS06
03-280  C  15       DEPVAL    SUB  SCRAP     ANLDEP                            SSS06
03-290  C           DEPVAL    SUB  ANLDEP    DEPVAL                            SSS06
03-300  C   OF                SETON                      50  01                SSS06
03-310  C                     EXCPT                                            SSS06
03-320  C   50                SETOF                      50  OF                SSS06
03-330  C                     SETOF                      01                    SSS06
03-340  C  N15                GOTO DOLIFE                                      SSS06
03-350  C                     SETON                      01                    SSS06
04-010  C*                                                                     SSS06
04-020  O*************************** HEADING LINES ************************* SSS06
04-030  C*                                                                     SSS06
04-040  ODETPRNT H  201   1P                                                   SSS06
04-050  O        OR       OF                                                   SSS06
04-060  O                                   48 'M O D E R N'                   SSS06
04-070  O                                   68 'N U M E R I C A L'             SSS06
04-080  O                                   84 'C O N T R O L'                 SSS06
04-090  O                                  102 'P R O D U C T S'               SSS06
04-100  O         H  3    1P                                                   SSS06
04-110  O        OR       OF                                                   SSS06
04-120  O                                   59 'M A C H I N E   T O O L'       SSS06
04-130  O                                   85 'D E P R E C I A T I O N'       SSS06
04-140  O                                  103 'S C H E D U L E'               SSS06
04-150  O         H  1    1P                                                   SSS06
04-160  O        OR       OF                                                   SSS06
04-170  O                                   30 'MACHINE  TOOL'                 SSS06
04-180  O                                   56 'PROJECTED'                     SSS06
04-190  O                                   70 'ORIGINAL'                      SSS06
04-200  O                                   85 'SCRAP'                         SSS06
04-210  O                                  101 'AMOUNT OF'                     SSS06
04-220  O                                  119 'DEPRECIATED'                   SSS06
04-230  O                                  130 'END OF'                        SSS06
04-240  O         H  2    1P                                                   SSS06
04-250  O        OR       OF                                                   SSS06
04-260  O                                   29 'DESCRIPTION'                   SSS06
04-270  O                                   53 'LIFE'                          SSS06
04-280  O                                   68 'COST'                          SSS06
04-290  O                                   85 'VALUE'                         SSS06
04-300  O                                  103 'DEPRECIATION'                  SSS06
04-310  O                                  116 'VALUE'                         SSS06
04-320  O                                  129 'YEAR'                          SSS06
04-330  C*                                                                     SSS06
04-340  O*************************** TOTAL LINE **************************** SSS06
04-350  C*                                                                     SSS06
04-360  O         T 03    01                                                   SSS06
04-370  O                                  103 '----------'                    SSS06
04-380  O                                  119 '----------'                    SSS06
```

Figure 6.14
(continued)

```
0055      04-390  C                                    128 '--'                 SSS06
          04-400  C*                                                            SSS06
          04-410  C************************** EXCEPTION OUTPUT ******************** SSS06
          04-420  C*                                                            SSS06
0056      04-430  C            E  1                                             SSS06
0057      04-440  C                          01DESCRT     39                    SSS06
0058      04-450  O                          01LIFE   Z   52                    SSS06
0059      04-460  C                          01COST   1   71 '$'                SSS06
0060      04-470  C                          01SCRAP  1   87 '$'                SSS06
0061      04-480  C                            ANLDEP1B 102 '$'                 SSS06
0062      04-490  C                            DEPVAL1B 119 '$'                 SSS06
0063      04-500  O                            YEAR   Z 128                     SSS06
          04-510  O**********  END OF PROGRAM *******************************SSS06

E N D   O F   S O U R C E
```

M O D E R N   N U M E R I C A L   C O N T R O L   P R O D U C T S

M A C H I N E   T O O L   D E P R E C I A T I O N   S C H E D U L E

MACHINE TOOL DESCRIPTION	PROJECTED LIFE	ORIGINAL COST	SCRAP VALUE	AMOUNT OF DEPRECIATION	DEPRECIATED VALUE	END OF YEAR
G & L TURRET LATHE	17	$58,000.00	$12,000.00	$2,705.88	$55,294.12	1
				$.00	$.00	2
				$.00	$.00	3
				$.00	$.00	4
				$.00	$.00	5
				$.00	$.00	6
				$.00	$.00	7
				$.00	$.00	8
			"0" values? →	$.00	$.00	9
				$.00	$.00	10
				$.00	$.00	11
				$.00	$.00	12
				$.00	$.00	13
				$.00	$.00	14
				$.00	$.00	15
				$.00	$.00	16
				$12,000.00	$12,000.00	17
				----------	----------	--
CINCINNATI NC SKIN MILL	29	$650,000.00	$50,000.00	$20,689.66	$629,310.34	1
				$.00	$.00	2
				$.00	$.00	3
				$.00	$.00	4
				$.00	$.00	5
				$.00	$.00	6
				$.00	$.00	7
				$.00	$.00	8
				$.00	$.00	9
				$.00	$.00	10
				$.00	$.00	11
				$.00	$.00	12
				$.00	$.00	13
				$.00	$.00	14
				$.00	$.00	15
				$.00	$.00	16
				$.00	$.00	17
				$.00	$.00	18
				$.00	$.00	19
				$.00	$.00	20
				$.00	$.00	21
				$.00	$.00	22
				$.00	$.00	23
				$.00	$.00	24
				$.00	$.00	25
				$.00	$.00	26
				$.00	$.00	27
				$.00	$.00	28
				$50,000.00	$50,000.00	29
				----------	----------	--

Practice Problems

1. Consider the following problem definition and code the RPG II program to produce three address labels for each input record.

Systems Flowchart

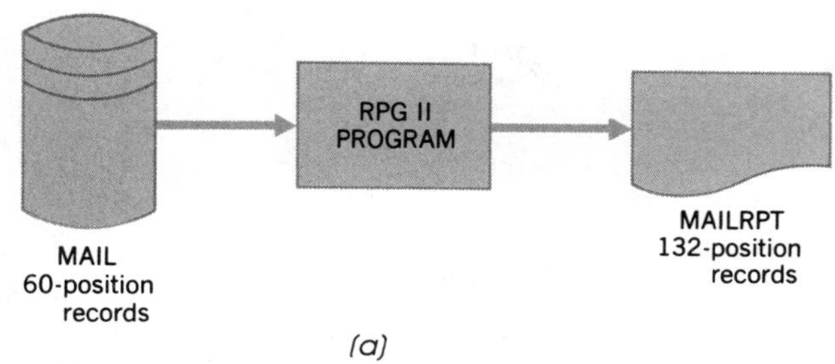

(a)

MAIL Record Layout

NAME	STREET ADDRESS (STREET)	CITY	STATE	ZIP	UNUSED
1 – 20	21 – 40	41 – 50	51 – 52	53 – 57	58 – 60

(b)

MAILRPT Printer Spacing Chart

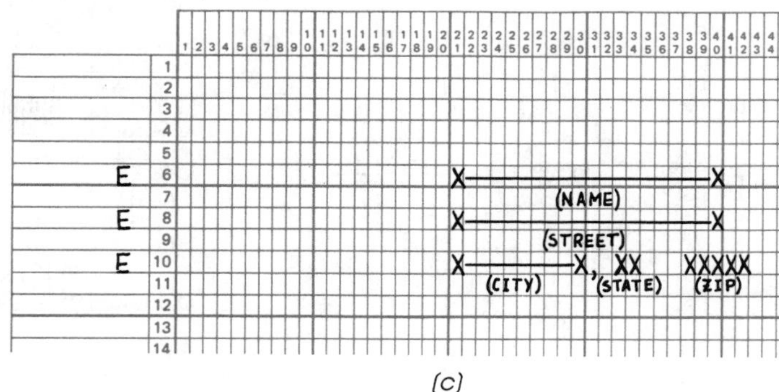

(c)

2. Consider the following problem definition and code the RPG II program to produce the desired results. The monthly payment is calculated using these formulas.

Number of payments (N) = 12 × number of loan years
Monthly payment = (Loan amount × 1.005^N)/N

Systems Flowchart

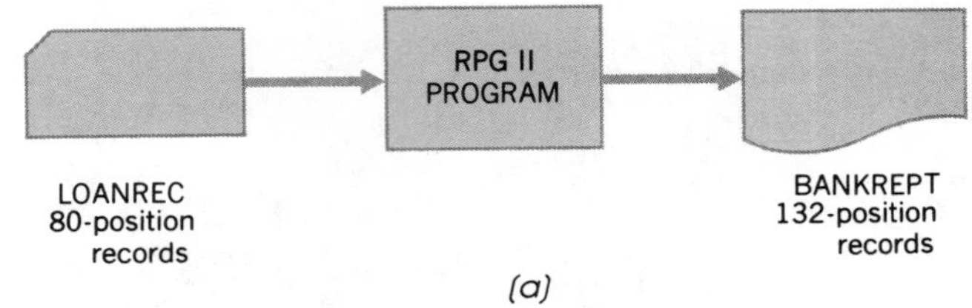

(a)

LOANREC Record Layout

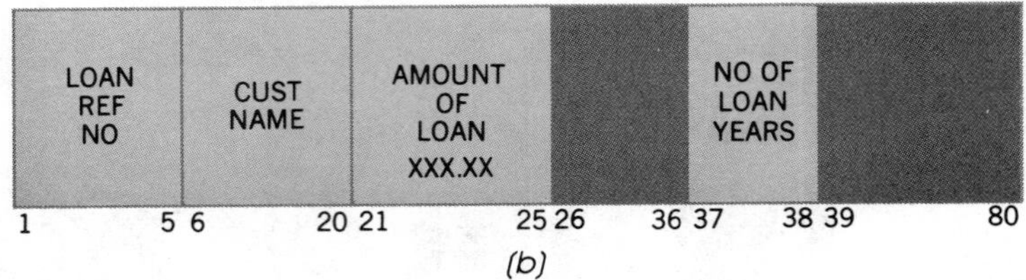

(b)

BANKREPT Printer Spacing Chart

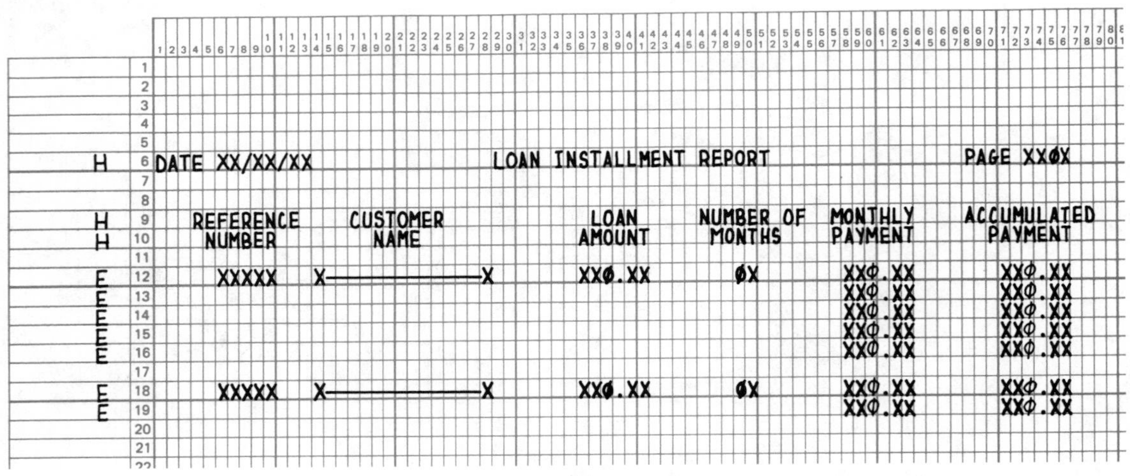

(c)

3. Consider the following problem definition and code the RPG II program to produce the desired results.

Systems Flowchart

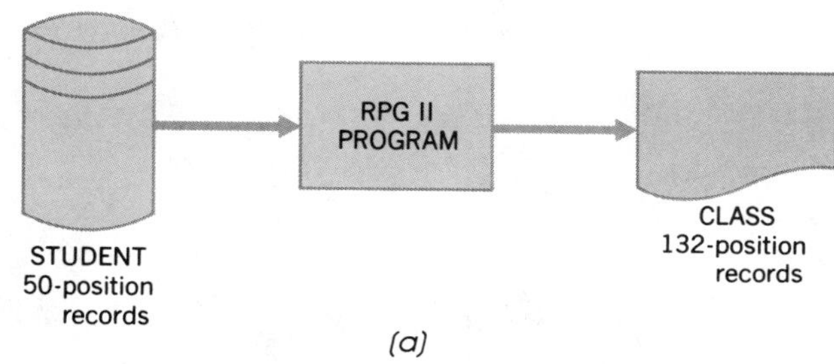

(a)

STUDENT Record Layout

STUDENT NAME (NAME)	FINAL GRADE (GRADE)	UNUSED
1 – 20	21 – 23	24 – 50

(b)

CLASS Printer Spacing Chart

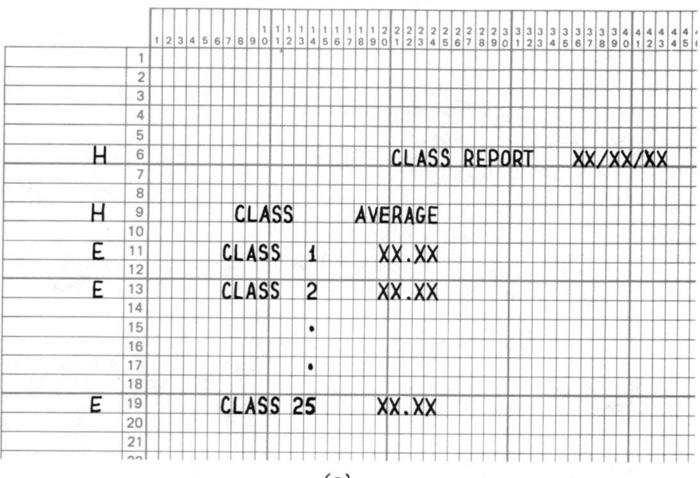

(c)

Notes

1. Each class has exactly 2Ø students.
2. The grade for each student is in each record and ranges from 000 to 100. We do not need the student name for this problem.
3. Thus, the first 2Ø records are for the students in class 1, the second 2Ø records are for students in class 2, and so on. There are exactly 25 classes.
4. Print a report with the class average for each class.

4. Consider the following problem definition. A depreciation table is to be printed using the double-declining balance method. The following formulas are used.

   Annual depreciation rate (AR) = 2/LIFE
   Annual depreciation = AR × current value
   New current value = Current value − depreciation

   Note: *The final current value must be equal to the scrap value.*

Systems Flowchart

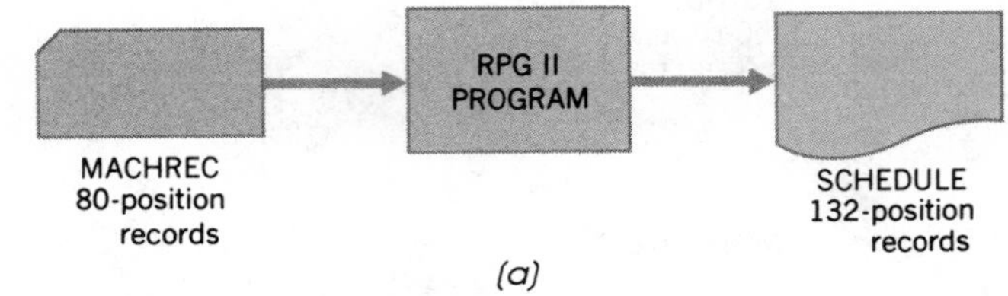

(a)

MACHREC Record Layout

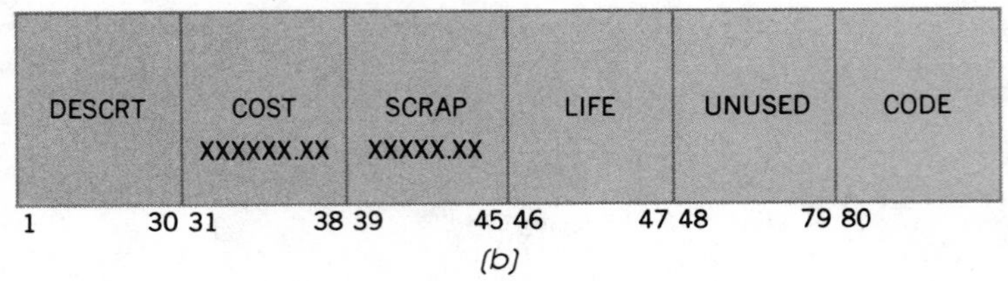

(b)

SCHEDULE Printer Spacing Chart

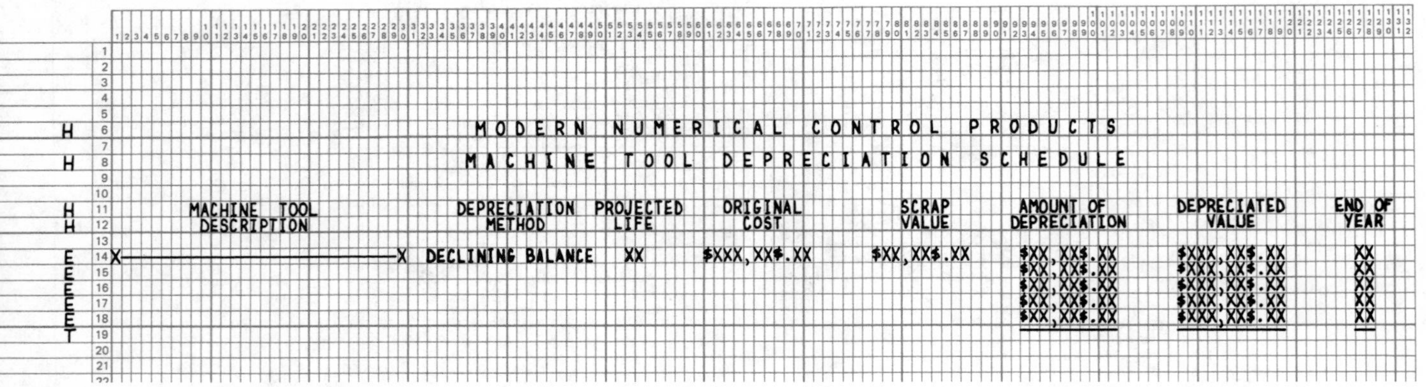

(c)

SPECIAL SECTION:

A Guide to Debugging

I.

The RPG Debugging Template

Computer programs seldom execute correctly on the first run. Program errors frequently occur in several ways. These include syntax errors and errors in logic that are discovered with the use of test data.

The **RPG Debugging Template** is a most useful tool designed to assist the programmer in finding and correcting syntax errors as well as providing a ready reference to the RPG logic cycle. See Figure S.1 for an illustration of the various segments of this template.

As we have learned, the position of each line of coding is especially critical in RPG due to the strict format of the language specifications. When syntax errors are detected, error messages are printed on the source listing. The template includes exact images of the RPG specification forms, making it easy to check each line of the source listing to ensure that the line was coded properly. By aligning column 6 of the RPG Debugging Template with the corresponding position of a line on the source program listing, the coding of each instruction can be checked. In this way, many syntax errors can be easily detected and corrected by comparing each entry against the template to validate that it is properly positioned.

In Figure S.2 the Debugging Template is aligned with the 'O' specification in column 6 on the source listing. By comparing the template image of the Output Specifications form to the source listing code, we see that the character 'H' for the heading line is in the wrong column. The entry is incorrectly placed in column 14, when it was intended to be coded in column 15. This resulted in a syntax error since the RPG compiler interpreted the 'H' entry as part of the filename. With the aid of the Debugging Template, errors of this nature are easily found.

Changes or program modifications are also facilitated by using the Debugging Template. When only a few instructions are to be coded, the template provides a ready reference to all of the various specification forms used by RPG. The locations of fields and acceptable codes that may be entered are clearly specified on the template. If the programmer was required to code a calculation instruction, he/she would simply refer to the 'C' specification form and key the required entries.

On-line processing of RPG programs has one major advantage over batch processing; the formats of each specification form is stored within the system. These may be referenced at any time and displayed on a CRT screen, enabling a programmer to check each entry as it is entered. If on-line facilities are not available, however, the Debugging Template will prove an invaluable aid and reference in coding and debugging RPG instructions.

Logic errors present yet another set of problems for the programmer; these, too, can be more easily detected with the use of the Debugging Template. In order to determine if errors in logic exist, the programmer must create test data to test the program during execution time. The programmer must manually calculate the results that should be obtained with this input test data against the computer-produced results.

The test data must be designed so that it tests all the possible conditions that may occur during the execution of the program. After generating test results by running the program, the programmer should compare the actual test results with those manually calculated. If they are the same, the program is functioning as intended. If not, further investigation and debugging is necessary.

Logic errors may result from performing calculations in the wrong sequence,

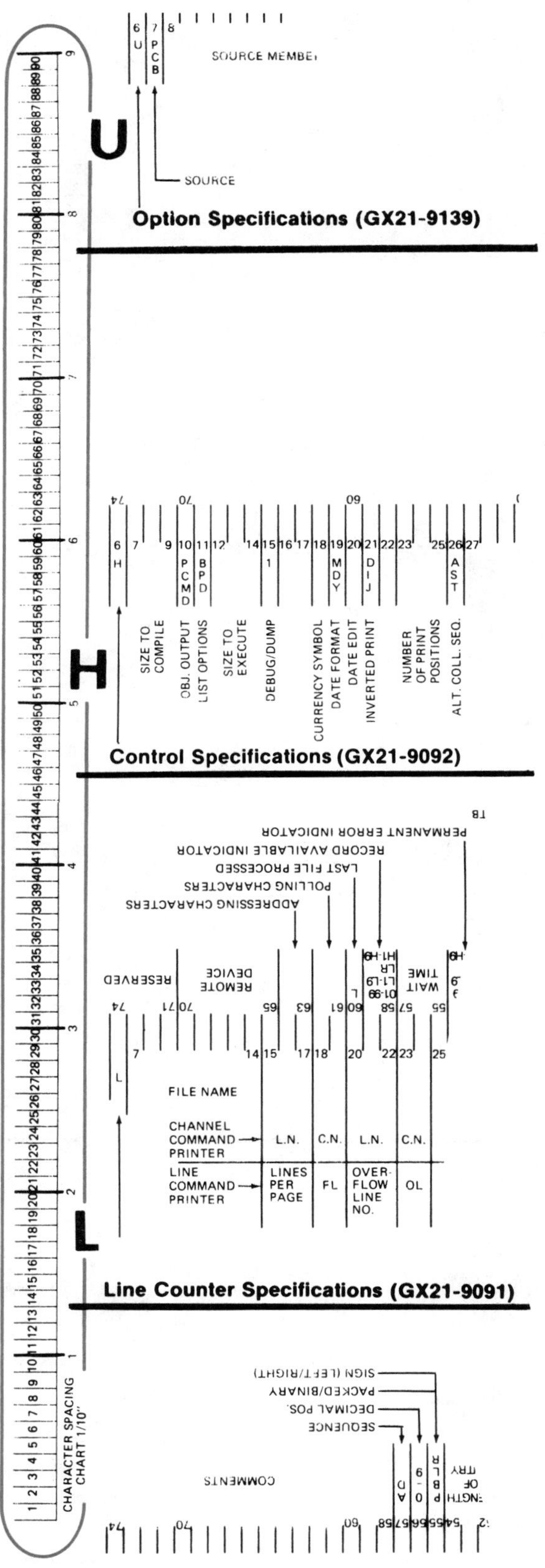

Figure S.1
RPG Debugging Template.
(Continued on next page.)

Figure S.1 *(continued)*

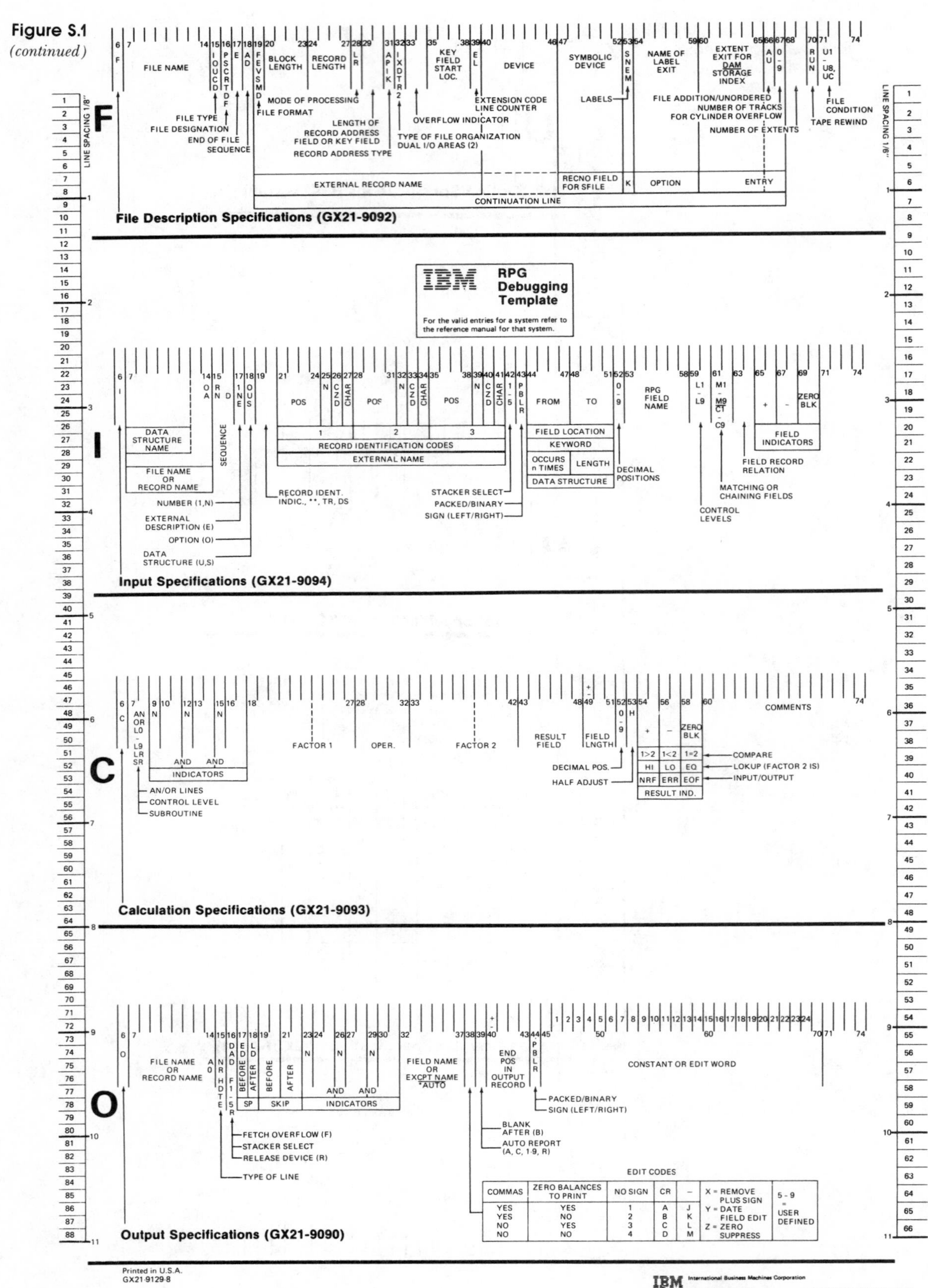

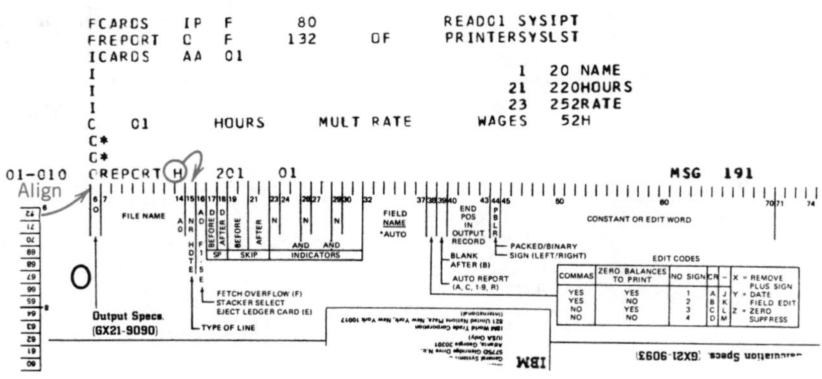

Figure S.2
Use of the Debugging Template.

interpreting RPG instructions incorrectly, or from misunderstanding the RPG Logic Cycle.

The Debugging Template includes an overview of the RPG Logic Cycle, which serves as an aid in detecting logic errors. Figure S.3 illustrates the section of the Debugging Template that incorporates this logic cycle.

It is essential that the programmer clearly understand the sequence of events taking place in the program. The flowchart presented in Figure S.3 that is part of the template makes readily available to the programmer the RPG Logic Cycle, which is fundamental to debugging programs.

The Debugging Template also provides the programmer with a means of checking the output listing. The output listing should be compared with the Printer Spacing Chart to verify that data is correctly positioned in the output. This can be facilitated by using the Character Spacing Chart of the Debugging Template, which includes images of print positions. As illustrated in Figure S.4, the Character Spacing Chart provides a reference to the positions that should include printed output.

In addition, line spacing can be validated and checked against the Printer Spacing Chart Specifications using the Debugging Template. This is accomplished by referencing the line spacing of 6 lines per inch (1/6″ spacing) or 8 lines per inch (1/8″ spacing) according to the printer equipment used. Figure S.5 illustrates that segment of the Debugging Template that provides examples of 6 inches per line and 8 inches per line of printing.

We therefore see the importance and many uses of the Debugging Template. The programmer will find this reference an invaluable aid in debugging programs.

II. Printing Tape and Disk Files for Validation Purposes

Another important facet of debugging is to ensure the correct creation of both tape and disk files. Always verify that these media have been correctly created by coding a program to simply display the records produced or by using job control specifications to print the file. If incorrect results are generated by a program, irrevocable damage may result and an entire system's integrity may be jeopardized. Therefore, Murphy's law, one adage with which professional programmers are familiar, should always be kept in mind: if it is possible for something to go wrong, eventually it will go wrong. Prevent the creation of invalid or erroneous files by coding a simple program to display the records created or use job control to print out tape or disk files. Again, the positions of the fields within the records should be checked with the template. The program illustrated in Figure S.6 is used to validate the contents of a disk file.

Figure S.3
Overview of the RPG Logic Cycle on the Debugging Template.

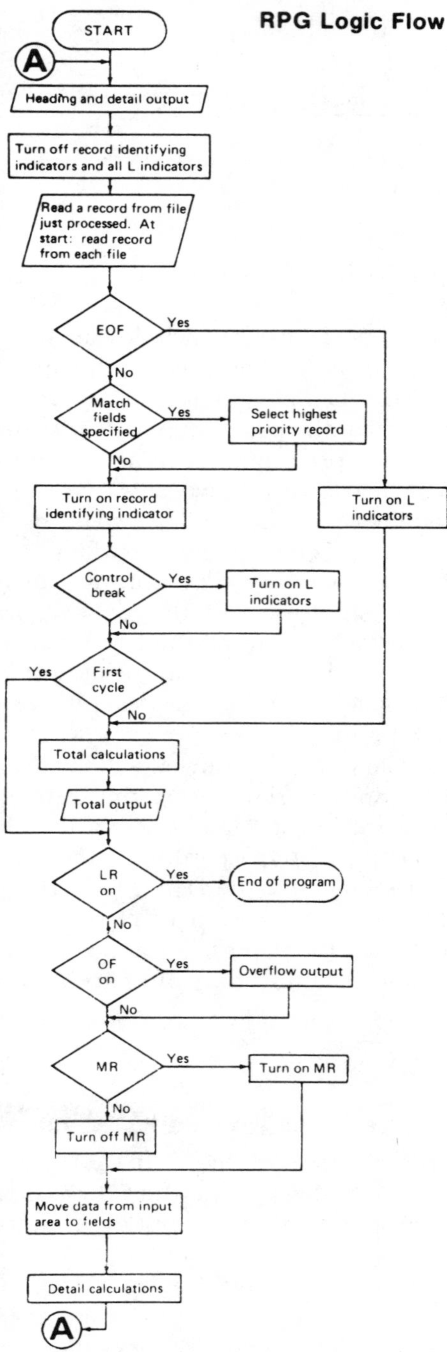

Figure S.4
Character Spacing Chart.

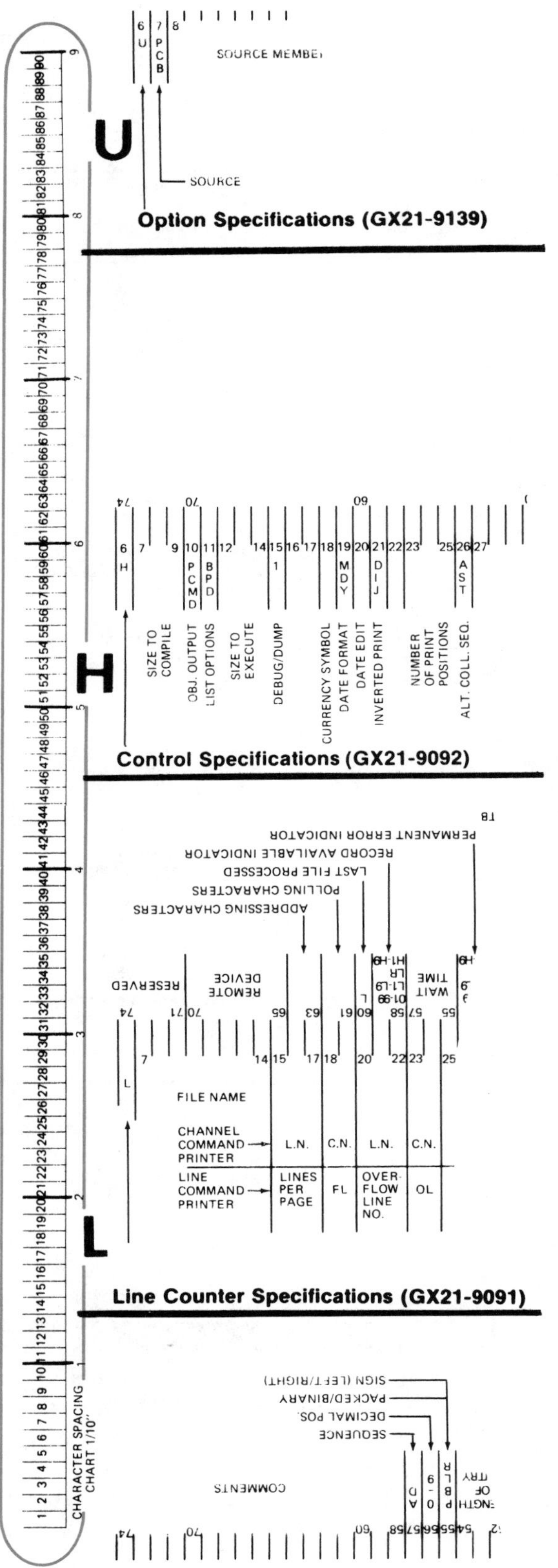

Figure S.5
Line spacing of reports.

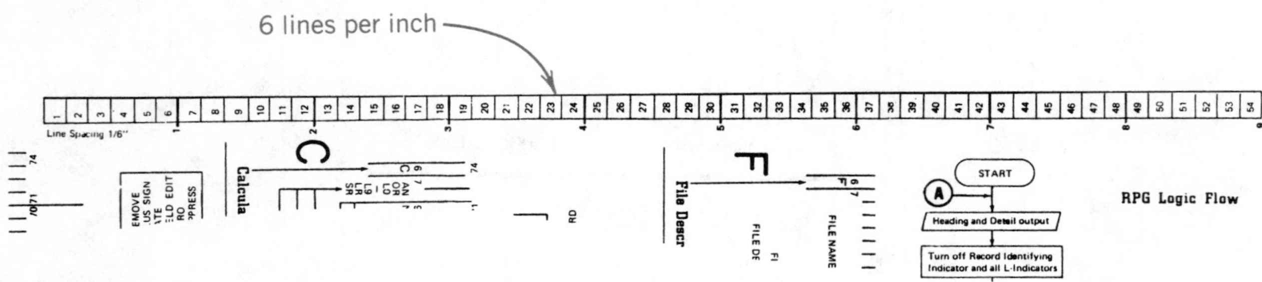

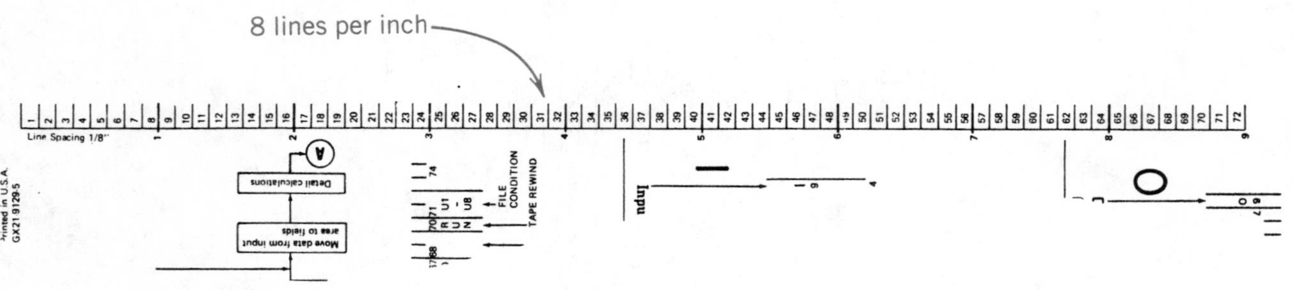

Figure S.6
Program to validate the contents of a disk file.

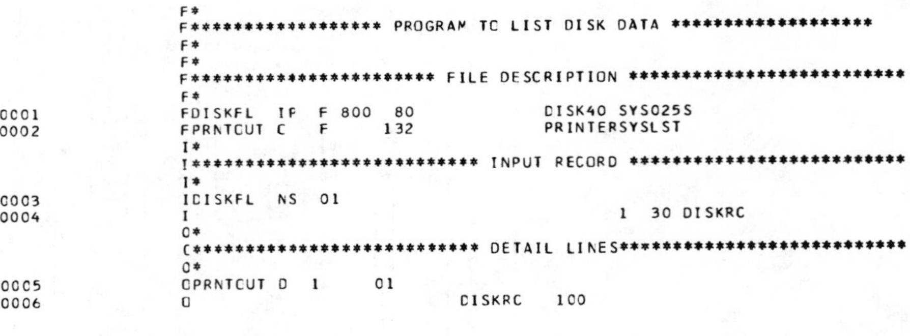

```
F*
F****************** PROGRAM TO LIST DISK DATA *******************
F*
F*
F*********************** FILE DESCRIPTION *************************
F*
FDISKFL  IF  F 800  80              DISK40 SYS025S
FPRNTCUT C   F      132             PRINTERSYSLST
I*
I*************************** INPUT RECORD *************************
I*
IDISKFL  NS  01
I                                         1  30 DISKRC
O*
O*************************** DETAIL LINES**************************
O*
OPRNTCUT D  1       01
O                             DISKRC    100

          E N D  O F  S O U R C E
```

III.

The DEBUG **Option**

After a translation phase has been successfully completed so that no diagnostics are generated, the program's ability to execute properly must be tested. Although the program contains no syntax errors, it may contain errors in logic that will cause inaccurate or incomplete processing. The execution of the program is used to "debug" or eliminate errors that may exist in it. Often logic errors are very difficult to locate.

We run or execute a program with test or sample data. The programmer uses this sample data to test if the program is executing properly. First, the expected results are computed manually by the programmer. Then the program is executed and the output obtained is compared against the manually produced results. If they match, then the program is executing properly. If they do not match, then the cause of the error must be determined.

To assist the programmer in finding logic errors in an RPG program, the DEBUG instruction can be used. This instruction can be entered in one or several places on the RPG Calculation form. The DEBUG statement is a *temporary instruction* included in the program during testing. Once the program is operational, the DEBUG instruction is omitted.

When the DEBUG instruction is executed, a line is printed listing all the indicators that are "on" at that specific time in the calculation phase. Since the RPG language is indicator-oriented, the logic of the program depends on indicators being correctly set "on" and "off." Use of the DEBUG instruction aids the programmer in determining whether the indicators are functioning as the programmer intended. After the program has been tested, the DEBUG command is no longer needed.

Another use of the DEBUG operation is to display or print the contents of various fields. That is, whenever calculations are made and the programmer wants to display the results of the calculation for checking purposes, he or she may use the DEBUG instruction. By examining the contents of specific fields at key points in the calculation section, the programmer is better able to determine if any particular instruction is causing a problem. The results calculated manually can then be compared to the results calculated by the program.

Hence, each calculation can be checked for accuracy by displaying the contents of the data fields with the DEBUG instruction. This method permits the printing of intermediate results, which proves so useful in debugging programs in other languages. A step-by-step evaluation of the calculations may then be made until all program errors are found and corrected.

The DEBUG instruction may produce either one or two lines of output. When the DEBUG instruction is executed, it will

1. Always list all the indicators that are "on" when the DEBUG operation was encountered.
2. Display the contents of a result field if it has been specified. This line will only be printed when the DEBUG entry specifies a result field. Note that decimal points are not printed and negative numbers print as the letters J-R on many computers, representing the negative numbers 1 through 9, respectively.

A. Coding the DEBUG Option

The RPG Control Specifications or H form requires the entry 1 in column 15. If this entry is omitted, the DEBUG specification will be ignored by the computer.

RPG CONTROL AND FILE DESCRIPTION SPECIFICATIONS

Program | Keying Instruction | Graphic | Key | Card Electro Number | Page of | Program Identification
Programmer | Date

Control Specifications

For the valid entries for a system, refer to the RPG reference manual for that system.

H | Line | Form Type | Size to Compile | Object Output | Listing Options | Size to Execute | Debug | Reserved | Currency Symbol | Date Format | Date Edit | Inverted Print | Reserved | Number of Print Positions | Alternate Collating Sequence | Reserved | Inquiry | Reserved | Sign Handling | 1 P Forms Position | Indicator Setting | File Translation | Punch MFCU Zeros | Nonprint Characters | Reserved | Table Load Halt | Shared I/O | Field Print | Formatted Dump | RPG to RPG II Conversion | Number of Formats | S/3 Conversion | Subprogram | CICS/DL/I | Transparent Literal

0 1 H ... 1 (column 15, Debug)

Must be coded or DEBUG operations are ignored

Entries on the Calculation form always include

1. DEBUG in the operation field in columns 28–32.
2. The output file, usually assigned to the printer, specified in Factor 2, beginning in column 33.

These entries will cause a line to be printed listing all the indicators that are "on" when the DEBUG instruction was executed. See Figure S.7. However, when the contents of fields are to be displayed, the following additional entries may be used.

1. Any valid indicator may be specified in columns 9 through 17.
2. Factor 1 is optional and may contain an entry to identify the DEBUG instruction. From 1 to 6 characters may be used to label specific DEBUG commands when several such commands are used in the calculation section. Usually the programmer numbers the instructions as 1ØØ, 2ØØ, and so on in order to associate the output results correctly with the particular

RPG CALCULATION SPECIFICATIONS

Program | Keying Instruction | Graphic | Key | Card Electro Number | Page of | Program Identification
Programmer | Date

C | Line | Form Type | Control Level (L0–L9, LR, SR, AN/OR) | Indicators (Not, And, Not, And, Not) | Factor 1 | Operation | Factor 2 | Result Field (Name, Length) | Decimal Positions | Half Adjust (H) | Resulting Indicators (Arithmetic: Plus, Minus, Zero; Compare: 1 > 2, 1 < 2, 1 = 2; Lookup (Factor 2) is: High, Low, Equal) | Comments

```
01ØC        .
02ØC        .
03ØC        DEBUGREPORT
04 C
05 C
```

All indicators in the "ON" state will be listed.

File name of printer used for output.

Figure S.7
Coding required to print the indicators that are "on" when DEBUG is executed.

DEBUG instruction being executed. That is, if more than one DEBUG is used, it is useful to be able to identify which one is being displayed at a given time.

3. The field or variable to be displayed is entered in the Result Field in columns 43–48.
4. Columns 49–59 *must* contain blanks.

The DEBUG instruction will always provide a listing of the indicators that are "on" when the instruction is executed. Typical coding and the output generated by the DEBUG operation are illustrated in Figure S.8.

Referring to Figure S.8, note that the first line to be printed when a DEBUG instruction is executed displays the indicators that are "on" and the second line contains the contents of the field specified in the Result Field, if any. Thus, the contents of YRMORG are displayed when the second DEBUG is executed and the contents of YRTAX are displayed when the third DEBUG is executed. These fields print after all indicators that are "on" are displayed.

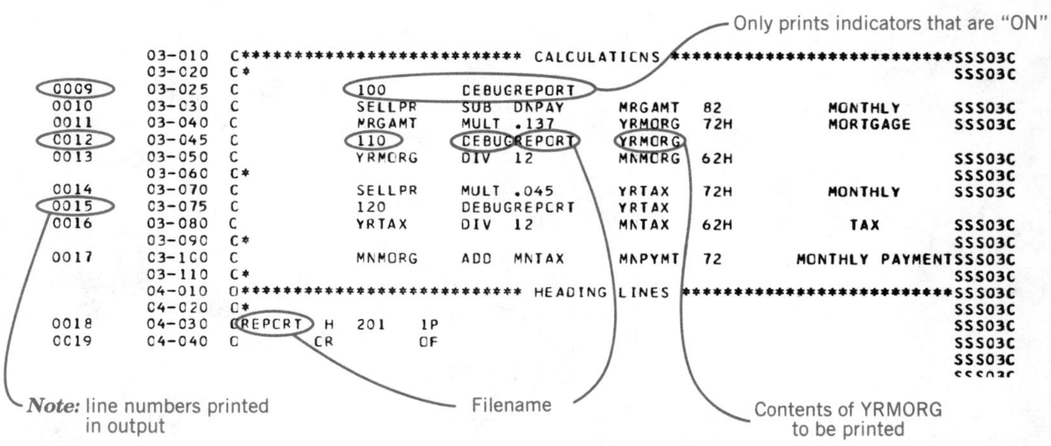

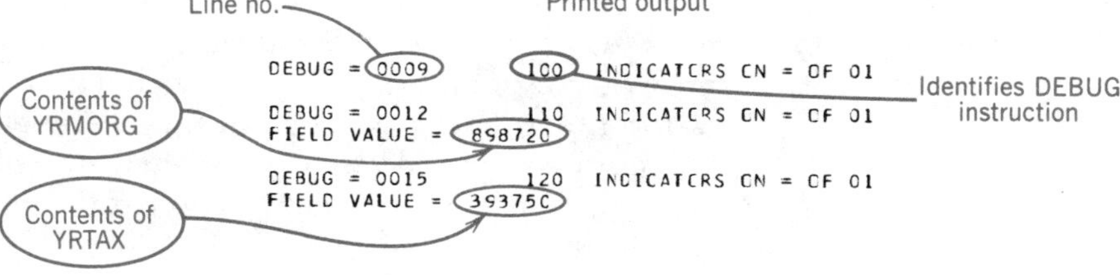

Figure S.8
Typical coding and the output generated by the DEBUG operation.

B. Summary of the DEBUG Option

Consider the following.

RPG CALCULATION SPECIFICATIONS

Line	Form Type	Control Level	Indicators	Factor 1	Operation	Factor 2	Result Field Name	Length	Decimal Positions	Half Adjust (H)	Resulting Indicators	Comments
01	C											
02	C											
03	C											
04	C											
05	C		01	100	DEBUG	REPORT	CTR					
06	C											
07	C											

Annotations on the form:
- Indicators (01): Any valid indicator (optional)
- Factor 1 (100): Identifies particular DEBUG instruction (optional)
- Operation (DEBUG) and Factor 2 (REPORT): Required entries
- Factor 2 (REPORT): Output file (usually printer)
- Result Field Name (CTR): Field to be printed* (optional)
- Length through Resulting Indicators (columns 49–59): Must be *blank*

*May be whole array or array element or table element as discussed in chapter 10

Note that the entries identified as required will produce a listing of the indicators that are "on." If the contents of a field is to be printed, the Name entry of the Result Field *must* be coded. Optional entries may be used as desired. The program in Figure S.9 illustrates how logic errors can be detected with use of the DEBUG option.

IV

The Display (DSPLY) Instruction

The DSPLY instruction allows the programmer to display the contents of data fields for the purpose of debugging. Data fields can be displayed on a printer, typewriter terminal, or CRT terminal. The field to be displayed is entered as Factor 1, and DSPLY is coded in the operation field beginning in column 28. The output device desired is specified in Factor 2 beginning in column 33. Indicators can be specified in positions 7 through 17; positions 49–59, however, must be blank.

Figure S.9
Detecting logic errors with use of the DEBUG option.
(Continued on next page.)

```
        01-010  F****************************************************************************SSSDBG
        01-020  F* THIS PRCGRAM PRCDUCES A PAYRCLL REPCRT, CALCULATING WAGES EARNED *SSSDBG
        01-030  F* BY MULTIPLYING TCTAL NUMBER OF HOURS WORKED BY THE RATE OF PAY    *SSSDBG
        01-040  F* FOR EACH EMPLOYEE.  THE TCTAL HCURS AND TOTAL WAGES ARE ALSO      *SSSDBG
        C1-050  F* ACCUMULATED AND PRINTEC AFTER THE LAST RECORD IS PRCCESSED.       *SSSDBG
        01-060  F****************************************************************************SSSDBG
        01-070  F*                                                                    SSSDBG
0001    C1-080  FCARDS   IP  F       80           READ01 SYSIPT                       SSSDBG
0002    01-090  FREPORT  C   F      132     OF    PRINTERSYSLST                       SSSDBG
        01-10C  F*                                                                    SSSDBG
        02-010  I**************************** INPUT RECCRD ***************************SSSDBG
        02-C2C  I*                                                                    SSSDBG
0003    C2-030  ICARDS    AA  01                                                      SSSDBG
0004    C2-C40  I                                           1  20 NAME                SSSDBG
0005    C2-C5C  I                                          21  220HOURS               SSSDBG
0C06    02-060  I                                          23  252RATE                SSSDBG
        02-C7C  I*                                                                    SSSDBG
        03-010  C**************************** CALCULATIONS ***************************SSSDBG
        03-02C  C*                                                                    SSSDBG
0007    03-030  C    01       TWAGES    ADD  WAGES      TWAGES  72                    SSSDBG
0008    03-040  C    01       HCURS     MULT RATE       WAGES   52H                   SSSDBG
0009    03-050  C    01       THCURS    ADD  HCURS      THOURS  72                    SSSDBG
0010    03-060  C    01       100       CEBUGREPCRT     TWAGES                        SSSDBG
0011    03-070  C    01       200       DEBUGREPCRT     THCURS                        SSSDBG
        03-080  C*                                                                    SSSDBG
        04-010  O**************************** HEADING LINE ***************************SSSDBG
        C4-C2C  C*                                                                    SSSDBG
0012    C4-030  OREPORT  H  201    1P                                                 SSSDBG
0013    C4-040  C      CR          CF                                                 SSSDBG
0014    04-050  C                                     73 'PAYRCLL REPORT'             SSSDBG
        04-06C  C*                                                                    SSSDBG
        04-070  O**************************** DETAIL LINE ****************************SSSDBG
        C4-080  C*                                                                    SSSDBG
0015    C4-090  C        D  1      01                                                 SSSDBG
0016    04-1C0  C                            NAME       40                            SSSDBG
0017    04-110  O                            HOURS Z    60                            SSSDBG
0018    04-12C  C                            RATE  1    80                            SSSDBG
0C19    04-13C  O                            WAGES 1   100                            SSSDBG
        05-01C  C*                                                                    SSSDBG
        05-020  O**************************** TOTAL LINES ***************************** SSSDBG
        C5-C3C  C*                                                                    SSSDBG
0020    C5-C4C  C        T 3       LR                                                 SSSDBG
0021    05-050  C                                     48 'TOTAL WAGES ***'            SSSDBG
0022    05-060  C                            TWAGES1    60 '$'                        SSSDBG
0023    C5-070  O                                     88 'TOTAL HOURS ***'            SSSDBG
0024    C5-08C  O                            THCURS1   1C0 '$'                        SSSDBG
        C5-09C  C*                                                                    SSSDBG
        05-100  O************************ END CF SOURCE ******************************SSSDBG
        05-110  C*                                                                    SSSDBG

          E N D   C F   S C U R C E
```

```
                                                   PAYRCLL REPCRT

CEBUG = 001C        1C0   INCICATCRS CN = 01
FIELC VALUE =      (C)
                                -TWAGES is zero—check program logic—should be
CEBUG = 0011        2CC   INCICATCRS CN = 01
FIELD VALUE =      (40CC)  -THOURS is correct
                    ABLE,AARCN                       40           7.50          300.00

DEBUG = 001C        1C0   INCICATCRS CN = 01
FIELD VALUE =      3C00C

CEBUG = 0011        2C0   INDICATCRS CN = C1
FIELD VALUE =       7700
                    BROWN,BETTY                      37           6.35          234.95

CEBUG = 0010        1C0   INCICATCRS CN = 01
FIELC VALUE =      53495

DEBUG = 0011        2C0   INDICATCRS ON = 01
FIELC VALUE =      1120C
                    CAVIS,DCNALD                     35           5.00          175.00

CEBUG = 0010        10C   INCICATCRS CN = C1
FIELD VALUE =      70995

DEBUG = 0011        2C0   INDICATCRS CN = C1
FIELD VALUE =      152CC
                    MCRRIS,MARY                      4C           6.75          270.00

CEBUG = 0010        1C0   INDICATCRS CN = C1
FIELC VALUE =      97995

DEBUG = 0011        2C0   INDICATCRS CN = 01
```

```
FIELD VALUE =   17700
                    SMITH,SAM                          25              5.50             137.50

DEBUG = 0010        100  INDICATORS ON = 01
FIELD VALUE =  111745

DEBUG = 0011        200  INDICATORS ON = 01
FIELD VALUE =   19200
                    THOMAS,TONY                        15              7.00             105.00

DEBUG = 0010        100  INDICATORS ON = 01
FIELD VALUE =  122245

DEBUG = 0011        200  INDICATORS ON = 01
FIELD VALUE =   22900
                    WILSON,WESLEY.                     37              5.85             216.45


                               TOTAL WAGES ***  $1,222.45        TOTAL HOURS ***     $229.00
```

Figure S.9 *(continued)*

UNIT III

MASTER FILE PROCESSING

CHAPTER 7

Magnetic Tape and Disk Concepts

Objectives

- To provide an analysis of the hierarchy of data as it relates to tape and disk.
- To study the features of tape and disk.
- To study the features of tape and disk drives.
- To study the characteristics of processing tape and disk files.
- To provide an explanation of how and why fields are packed on tape and disk.

I. The Hierarchy of Data

We have learned how **fields** are used to indicate individual units of data on computer media. A collection of related fields is referred to as a **record**. In Figure 7.1, each card represents a record, since it consists of fields related to a particular individual—NAME, POSITION, SOCIAL SECURITY NUMBER, and so on. If we take all the cards as a group, we have a **file** of records. Thus, the collection of cards for all employees would constitute a file. Figure 7.1 illustrates this hierarchy of data.

Although punched cards are still used in some computer systems for input and output, they are not usually used to store a file of data. This chapter shows that other types of media, such as magnetic tape and magnetic disk, are better suited for file processing.

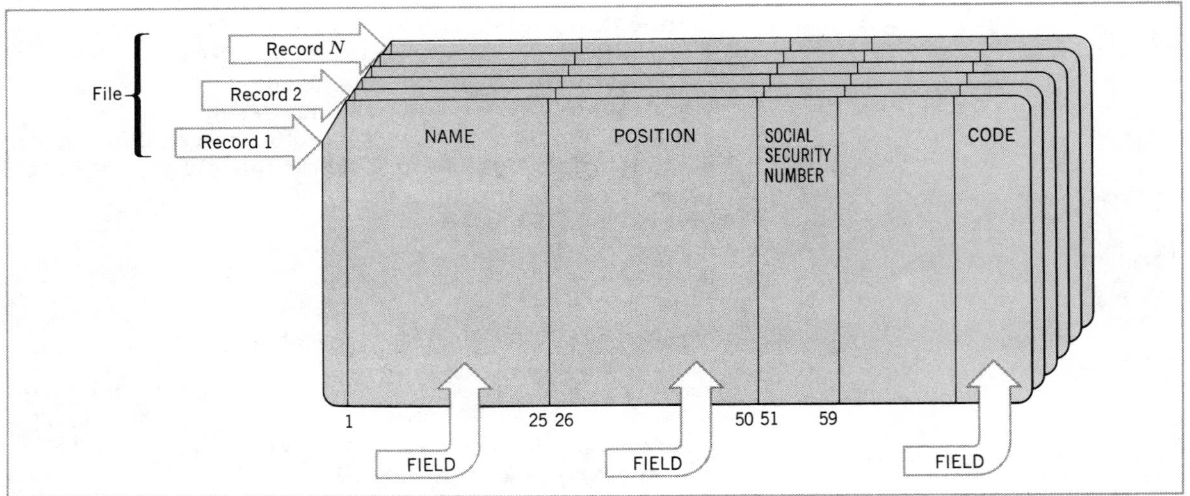

Figure 7.1
The hierarchy of data.

II. Significance of Tape and Disk Processing

Numerous devices can be linked to a CPU. Each can read data into or write information from a CPU; in fact, some can do both.

In this chapter, tape and disk drives are considered as the most common high-speed input/output devices. Before discussing each in depth, let us consider several features of both tape and disk processing that make these media very useful. (If you are familiar with tape and disk concepts and handling procedures, you may skip this chapter.)

Features of Tape and Disk Processing

1. I/O capability of tape and disk drives. A tape or disk drive can serve as *both* an input and an output device. One can read from or write onto tapes using a **tape drive**; similarly, one can read from or write onto disks using a **disk drive**.
2. High-speed processing.

3. Ability to store hundreds of thousands of records on one reel of magnetic tape or on one disk pack.
4. Ability to process any size record.

Because of these features of tapes and disks, they are ideal media for storing master files or other high-volume data. A **master file** is the main collection of records for a specific application. Businesses have master payroll files, master accounts receivable files, master inventory files, and so on, usually stored on tape or disk. Some small systems still use punched card master files, but these are becoming obsolete.

Tapes are best used if master file processing is performed in a batch mode; that is, records are processed in groups or batches, usually at fixed intervals. This is referred to as **batch processing**. Disks are best used if master file processing is performed on-line, that is, with records processed immediately as the data is transacted. **On-line processing** uses devices such as terminals that are directly under the control of the CPU. Thus, if a terminal is to access information from a master airline reservation file, that master file would usually be stored on disk.

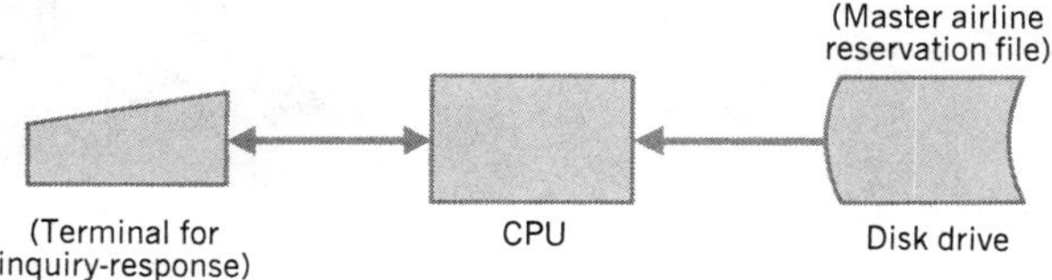

III. Magnetic Tape Files and Tape Drives

A. Features of Magnetic Tape Media

A magnetic tape drive is a high-speed device that, like a home tape recorder, can read data from a magnetic tape and can also record data onto a tape.

The tape itself, then, is a file type that can serve as input to a computer or as output from a computer. It is one of the most common file types for storing high-volume data that is typically processed in a batch mode (see Figure 7.2.)

1. Physical Characteristics

A typical magnetic tape is generally 24ØØ feet long, but larger and smaller sizes are available. Most tapes are ½-inch wide. The tape is made of plastic with an iron oxide coating that can be magnetized to represent data. Since the magnetized spots or **bits** are extremely small and not visible to the human eye, large volumes of data can be condensed into a relatively small area of tape. Data that can be punched into an 8Ø-column card, for example, can typically be stored in 1/10 of an inch of magnetic tape, or less. The average tape, which costs approximately $2Ø, can store more than 2Ø million characters. After a tape file has been processed and is no longer needed, the same tape may be reused repeatedly to store other information.

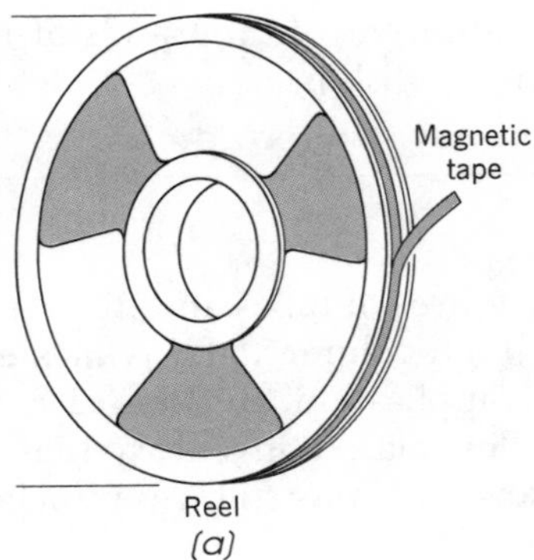

Figure 7.2
(*a*) Magnetic tape reel.
(*b*) Magnetic tape drive (Courtesy Burroughs).

2. Representation of Data on a Magnetic Tape

a. Nine-track Representation Data is represented on **nine-track tape** in a manner very similar to the computer's internal code. There are nine longitudinal tracks or recording surfaces on a tape, each capable of storing one magnetized bit.

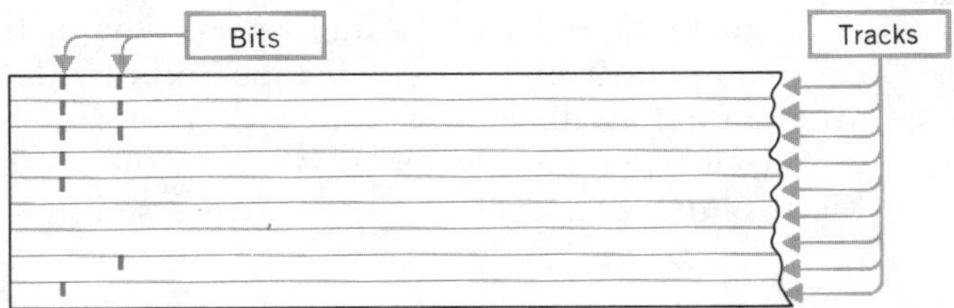

The computer's internal code, called **EBCDIC** on IBM and IBM-compatible computers, also uses nine bits for the representation of data within a computer. The nine bits are specified as follows.

4 zone bits.

4 digit bits.

1 parity bit.

The **parity bit** is a check bit that is used to minimize the risk of undetected transmission errors. On **even parity** computers, there must always be an even number of bits in one storage position at any time. The parity bit is turned on if, without it, there would be an odd number of bits on; otherwise, the parity bit is off. In this way, the loss or gain of a single bit in transmission would be easily detected since such a transmission error would result in an odd number of bits on. There are **odd parity** computers as well, which require an odd number of bits in each storage position.

The nine-bit EBCDIC code, including the parity bit, is illustrated in Figure 7.3.

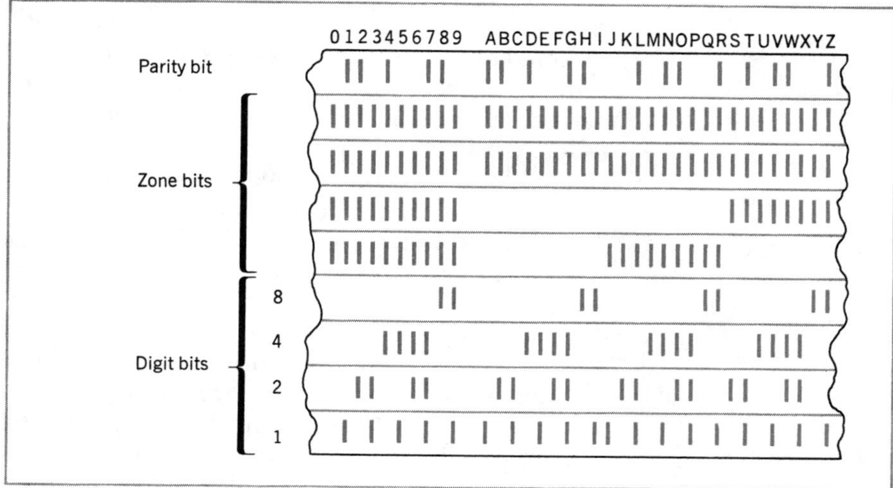

Figure 7.3 Representation of characters on nine-track, even-parity tape.

The representation of the number 173 on a nine-track tape, using even parity, would directly conform to the EBCDIC representation.

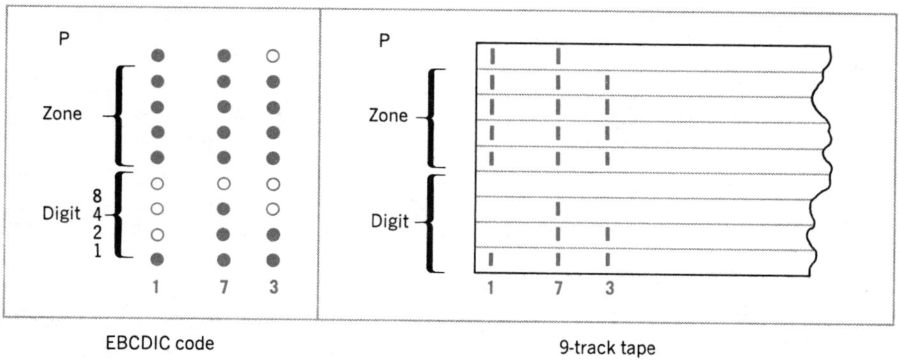

See Figure 7.4 for the representation of some other characters.

Two main advantages of tape processing derive from the fact that data is represented on tape as magnetized bits.

1. Tapes can be written onto or read from at very high speeds.
2. Large volumes of data can be stored on a single tape.

b. Tape Density Millions of characters can be recorded as magnetized bits on a single magnetic tape. The primary reason for this storage capacity is the fact that bits are exceedingly small, so that hundreds of them can be placed on

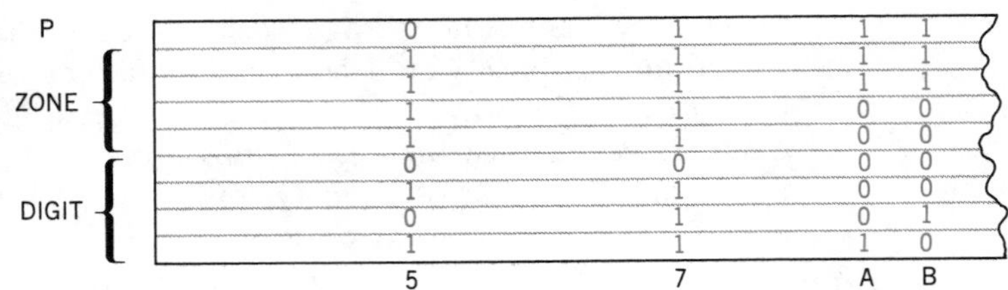

Figure 7.4 Representation of the characters 5, 7, A, and B on nine-track tape.

a very small area of tape. The actual number of characters that can be represented in an inch of tape is called tape **density**. Since each character is represented by a series of bits in a specific position on the tape, densities are measured in terms of bits per inch (bpi). The term bytes per inch, however, would be more appropriate since the density indicates the number of characters per inch. The most common tape densities are 8ØØ bpi, 16ØØ bpi, or 325Ø bpi, but some tapes have densities of 65ØØ or more characters per inch. Thus, on most tapes, 8ØØ to 16ØØ characters of data or the equivalent of 1Ø to 2Ø cards of data can be represented in a single inch of tape. This storage capacity is one reason why magnetic tapes are so frequently used at computer installations.

c. Specifying Tape Records

(1) Size of Records. As previously noted, a tape can have any record size; it is not restricted, like cards, to an 8Ø-column format. Moreover, all tape records within a given file need not have the same length. That is, tapes can store (1) **fixed-length records**, where all records are the same size, or (2) **variable-length records**, where the lengths differ. We focus on fixed-length tape records because they are most frequently used and are easier to process.

(2) Interblock Gap. Between physical tape records the computer automatically reserves a fraction of an inch of blank tape called an **interblock gap (IBG)**. Thus, when a tape is produced as computer output, it is created as indicated in Figure 7.5.

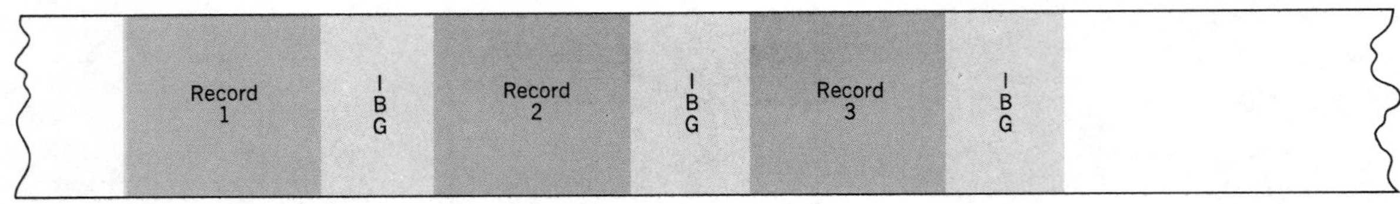

Figure 7.5 Physical tape records separated by interblock gaps (IBGs).

The purpose of this interblock gap relates to the high-speed processing capability of tapes. When a tape record is read at high speeds, it takes a fraction of a second for the drive to physically stop when it senses the end of the record. This delay is analogous to that of applying the brakes on a car: it takes several feet before the automobile physically comes to a halt. The interblock gap (IBG) is created so that, when a record is read, the mechanism will not pass over data from the next record in the time it takes to come to a halt.

This interblock gap is usually a fraction of an inch, being as large as 3/4 or 3/5 of an inch, depending on the computer. Thus, if small record sizes are established for a given file, there will be a significant amount of unused tape between each record (see Figure 7.6).

(3) Blocking Records to Minimize Wasted Space. To minimize wasted space, tape

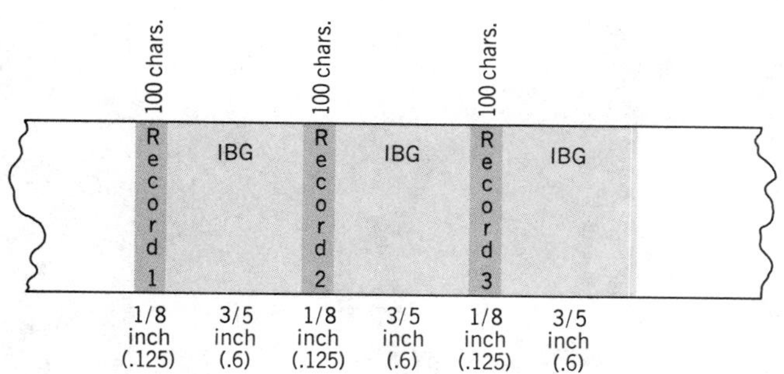

Figure 7.6
Representation of data showing unused tape (IBGs).

records are frequently blocked so that several actual or logical tape records are grouped together in a block (see Figure 7.7). **Blocking** of logical records maximizes the efficient use of the tape.

Each record established as an independent collection of data by the programmer is called a **logical record**. Each block is identified as a **physical record**, or group of logical records.

In many programming languages, it is relatively simple to instruct the computer that there are, for example, 1ØØ-character logical records that are blocked 2Ø. In that case, the computer will read in a block of 2ØØØ characters (1ØØ × 2Ø), processing each logical record within the block in sequence. In short, blocking makes more efficient use of the tape. The processing of blocked tape files is relatively easy in programming languages such as RPG.

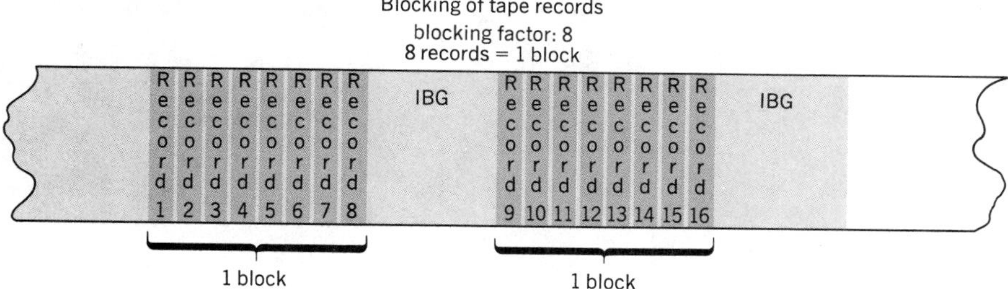

Figure 7.7
Blocking of tape records.

d. Recording Data on a Magnetic Tape Two methods are used for recording data on a tape.

(1) Magnetic Tape Drive. A program can be written to read data from some input medium such as cards or a terminal and to produce, as output, a magnetic tape.

(2) Key-to-Tape Encoder. A key-to-tape encoder or converter (Figure 7.8) is a device similar to a keypunch machine. An operator codes data from a source document to a magnetic tape using a typewriter-like keyboard. The operator depresses a key for a specific character, and the device converts it to the appropriate magnetized coding. Tapes encoded in this manner may be verified by the same device to ensure the accuracy of the data that is entered.

B. Characteristics of Magnetic Tape Drives

1. A Tape Drive is Like a Tape Recorder

Magnetic tape drives function like home tape or cassette recorders.

Figure 7.8
Key-to-tape encoder (Courtesy Honeywell).

- Data can be recorded or written onto a tape and stored for future processing.
- Data can be read from the same tape at any time to produce output reports or other data.
- When data is written on a tape, all previous information is written over or destroyed. For this reason, precautions must be taken to prevent the inadvertent destruction of important tape files.

A tape drive has a **read/write head** (Figure 7.9), which is programmed to either read data or write data, depending on the job requirements.

2. Tapes Drives Have High-Speed Capability
Because tape drives read data electronically by sensing magnetized areas and write data electronically by magnetizing areas, tapes may be processed at very high speeds. Data can be read or written at speeds of from 100,000 to 300,000 characters per second on the average, that is, approximately 200 inches of tape per second.

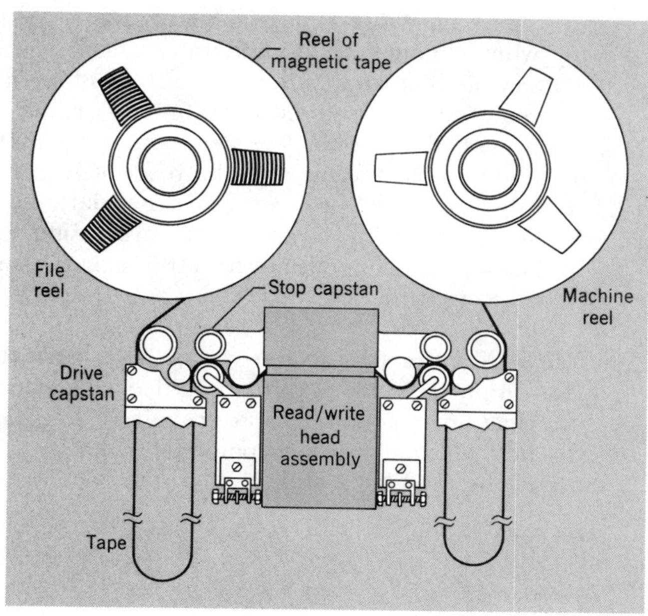

Figure 7.9
Read/write head on tape drive (Courtesy IBM).

C. Characteristics of Magnetic Tape Processing

1. Tapes are Used for High-Volume Files

Because magnetic tapes can be processed very quickly and can store large amounts of data, they are frequently used for high-volume master files.

2. Tapes are Used for Sequential Processing

To access a record with TRANSACTION NUMBER 254 from a tape file that is maintained in TRANSACTION NUMBER sequence, for example, you must read past the first 253 records. You would instruct the computer to read a record, test if it contains TRANSACTION NUMBER 254, and, if it does not, read the next record. Thus, 254 records are read. There is no convenient method to instruct the tape drive to skip the first few inches of tape or to go directly to the middle of the tape. Tapes must be processed *sequentially*.

This sequential feature of tape processing makes it ideally suited for batch processing. That is, if a master file is stored on magnetic tape, the input records used to update or make the file current can be processed in a batch mode.

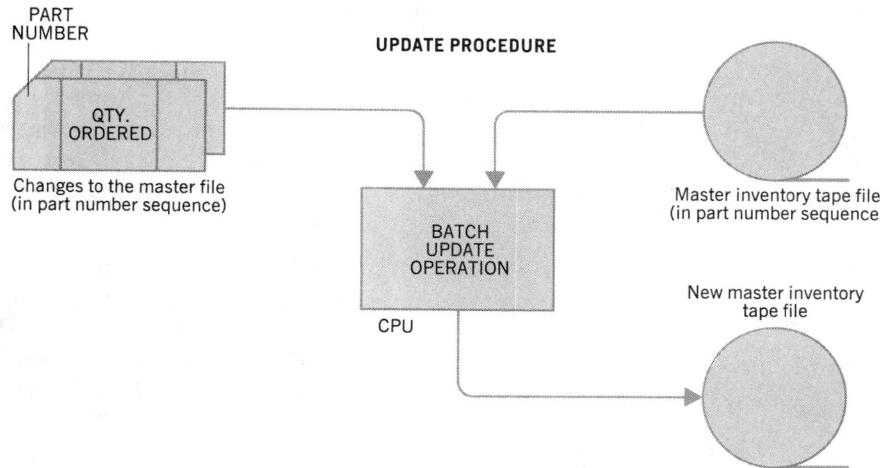

As a result of this sequential feature, tapes are rarely used for on-line processing where immediate or random accessing of files is a requirement. If an inventory file is created on tape with 100,000 records and only a handful of these are required to be printed in an on-line or immediate mode, then tapes would not provide the best file type. Processing time and, thus, cost would be excessive, because most of the file must be read even to process only a small number of records. Sequential processing is beneficial only when most records in a high-volume file are required for normal processing. In short, tapes are ideally suited for batch processing but not for on-line processing or for storing files that need to be accessed randomly.

3. It is Not Practical to Rewrite or Alter Records Directly on a Tape
If an input tape file is to be modified or altered so that it includes additional information, two tape files are required: one for the original file and one for the new file that will incorporate the changes. That is, the same tape cannot usually be read from and then written on. Consider the following schematic.

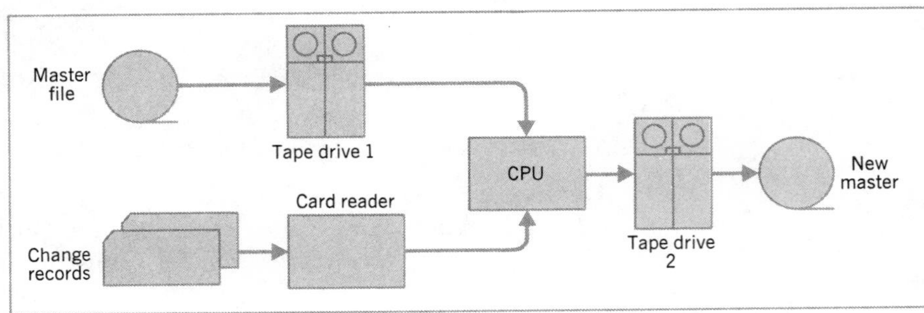

A procedure to make changes to a tape requires three files: the original tape, the file of changes, and a *new* tape that will incorporate the original tape data along with the changes. One advantage to this procedure is that an automatic backup tape exists. That is, the tape that served as input can be used for backup in case the new tape is damaged or inadvertently erased. Note that many installations have numerous tape drives to accommodate the batch processing needs of the organization.

4. The Need for Controls to Maintain the Integrity of Tape Files
Most medium- and large-scale computer installations have hundreds or even thousands of magnetic tapes, each used for a specific application. Because data recorded on these tapes is not "readable" or visible to the naked eye, it is often difficult to maintain control. If a master accounts receivable tape is inadvertently "written over," or used as output for some other job, for example, the result could be an expensive re-creation process, since the writing of output would destroy the existing information. Several steps have been implemented at most installations to prevent such occurrences, or to reduce the extent of damage, should a disaster or system failure occur.

a. External Tape Labels External gummed labels are placed on the surface of each tape (see Figure 7.10), identifying it and indicating its **retention cycle**, or how long it should be maintained. These labels are clearly visible to anyone, so that chances of inadvertent misuse of a valuable tape are reduced. The problem with gummed labels, however, is that they sometimes become unglued. Their effectiveness is also directly related to the effort and training of the computer staff. If operators are negligent, then the labels are sometimes ignored.

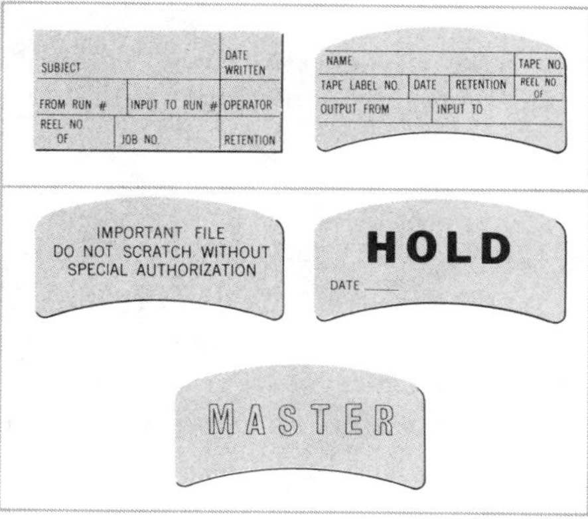

Figure 7.10
External tape labels.

b. Tape Librarian Most medium- and large-scale companies have numerous tapes that must be filed or stored and released for reuse when no longer required. Such companies employ a tape librarian to maintain the tape files. If he or she performs the job properly, there will be less misuse or misplacing of tapes (see Figure 7.11).

c. Programmed Tape Labels To make the identification of tapes more reliable, most programs include a built-in routine that, for output tapes, creates a **programmed label record**. The label is the *first* record on the tape. When the tape is used as input, at some later date, then this first label record, called a **header label**, is checked as part of the program, to ascertain that the correct tape is being used.

Thus, header labels are created on output tapes and later checked on input tapes. This label creation for output and label checking for input is a standard procedure in most programs. Since it uses the computer to verify that the correct tapes are being used, there is less danger of errors resulting from carelessness. In RPG, a single coded entry is all that is necessary to create labels on output tapes or to check labels on input tapes.

Figure 7.11
Tape library and librarian (Courtesy IBM).

d. File Protection Ring Those available tapes that may be written on, or used as output, have a **file protection ring** inserted in the back (see Figure 7.12). The tape drive is electronically sensitized so that it will *not* create an output record unless this ring is in its proper place. For those tapes that are to be maintained and not "written over" the ring has been removed. Thus, if an operator erroneously uses such a tape for an output operation, the computer prints a message that states, in effect, "NO RING—NO WRITE." If the operator is cautious, he or she will examine the external label and realize that the wrong tape is being used. Sometimes, however, an operator will merely place a ring on the tape (any file protection ring fits all tapes) and restart the job. Thus this method, alone, deters the misuse of tapes but does not totally alleviate the problem.

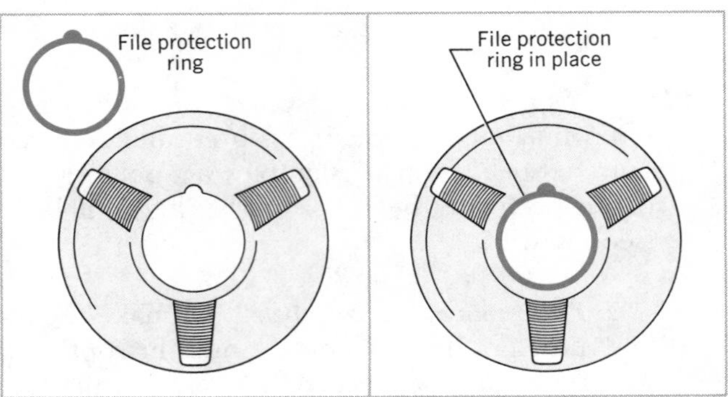

Figure 7.12 File protection ring.

e. Backup Tapes as a Control Since tapes can sometimes be written over or even become physically damaged, it is necessary to maintain backup tapes so that the re-creation process, should it become necessary, is not enormously costly and cumbersome.

Suppose a new master tape is created each month. After processing, users find it best to store the old master tape and update transactions *along with* the new master tape. In this way, if some mishap should befall the new master tape, it is a simple task to re-create it. Normally, operators maintain *two* previous tapes as backup in addition to the present one, in order to prevent any serious problem.

D. Other Types of Tapes

It is generally not practical to have large tape drives with micro- or minicomputer systems. Instead, these systems use tape cassettes or tape cartridges along with the corresponding devices (see Figure 7.13). Tape cassette and cartridge devices are miniature versions of the larger drives.

Self-Evaluating Quiz

1. Data is recorded on magnetic tape on a thin film of ________ .
2. Most computer centers use (no.) -track tapes.
3. ________ is the term used to represent the technique of ensuring that an even number of bits is always on for each character.
4. The number of characters per inch of tape is called ________ .

Figure 7.13 Example of a tape cassette and a tape cartridge (Courtesy Verbatim).

5. To make maximum use of the tape area so that less tape is wasted, logical records are often grouped or ________ .
6. When records on a single tape file have different sizes, depending on the format of each record, then the file uses ________ records.
7. Between tape records the computer automatically reserves a fraction of an inch of blank tape called a(n) ________ .
8. (T or F) A magnetic tape can serve as either input to or output from a computer system.
9. A magnetic tape drive resembles, in concept, a home ________ .
10. (T or F) After a tape has been processed and is no longer needed, the same tape may be reused to store other data.
11. The three major advantages of tape processing as compared to card processing are: ________ , ________ , and ________ .
12. Two methods of recording data onto a magnetic tape are with the use of a(n) and a(n) ________ .
13. Because of a tape's capacity to handle large volumes of data in a relatively short time, it is ideally suited for ________ processing.
14. A disadvantage of tapes is that they can only be processed ________ .
15. The sequential method of processing tape records is ideal when ________ .
16. Because of the vast numbers of magnetic tapes in many installations, ________ often becomes a problem.
17. The creation of programmed ________ on an output tape is used for checking purposes when the tape is read as input.
18. In addition to using labels, most computer installations employ ________ to ensure proper handling of tapes.
19. Minicomputer systems sometimes use ________ instead of tape drives.
20. (T or F) Updating a master tape file requires the creation of a new master tape file.

Solutions

1. iron oxide coating
2. nine
3. even parity

4. the tape density (or bpi)
5. blocked
6. variable-length
7. interblock gap (IBG)
8. T
9. tape or cassette recorder
10. T
11. speed
    ability to store large volumes of records
    ability to store any size record
12. key-to-tape encoder
    tape drive
13. master file or batch
14. sequentially
15. most of the records are required for processing, in sequence
16. control or identification
17. labels
18. a tape librarian
19. tape cassette or cartridge drives
20. T

IV. Features of Magnetic Disk Media

A. Introduction

Magnetic disks are the most widely used media for storing master files. In this unit, we will see that disks have many of the same features and advantages of tapes, and, in addition, can provide for random processing, which makes them even more versatile than tapes.

B. Types of Disks

A **hard disk** is a standard disk used with most large and medium-sized computer systems and some minis as well. It is accessed by a *magnetic disk drive* (see Figure 7.14). Smaller disks can store 6 to 1Ø million characters, but some hard disks can store hundreds of millions or even billions of characters.

A **floppy disk** is a "soft" or flexible disk that is a smaller version of a hard disk used with most mini- and microcomputer systems. Floppy disks are accessed by floppy disk drives.

The two most popular types of floppy disks are the 8 inch and 5¼ inch, although several 3-inch versions and other sizes are available (see Figure 7.15). The 8-inch version can store up to 1.2 million characters, and the 5¼-inch floppy can store up to 32ØK.

Despite the differences in size and capacity among hard disks, 8-inch floppies and 5 ¼-inch floppies, the concepts used for processing disk files are very similar.

We will briefly consider the physical characteristics of hard disks and floppy disks before discussing file processing techniques.

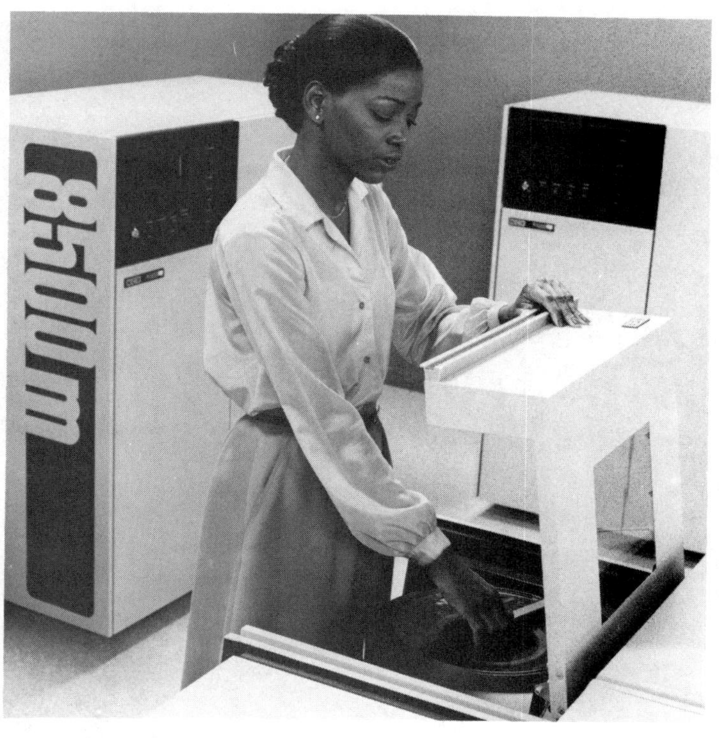

(a)

(b)

Figure 7.14
(a) Magnetic disk drive (Courtesy NCR). (b) Magnetic disk pack (Courtesy Burroughs).

C. Physical Characteristics of Hard Disks

1. The Disk Surface

Like magnetic tape, a disk has an iron oxide or nickel coating that is used to store hundreds or even thousands of characters in less than 1 inch of disk space.

2. Defining a Disk Pack

A hard disk is really a **disk pack**, which consists of a series of platters or disks arranged in a vertical stack and connected by a central shaft. The concept is similar to a group of phonograph records stacked on a spindle. The actual number of disks in a disk pack varies with the unit, but many have 11 disks as in Figure 7.16.

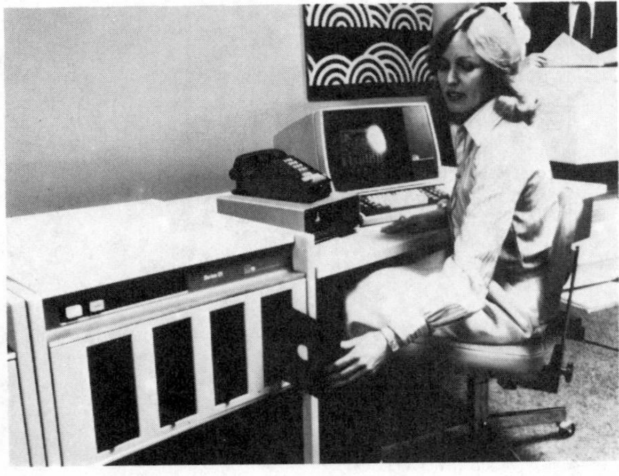
(a)

(b)

Figure 7.15
(*a*) Floppy disk drive (Courtesy Mohawk Data Sciences). (*b*) Example of an 8-inch floppy disk (Courtesy BASF).

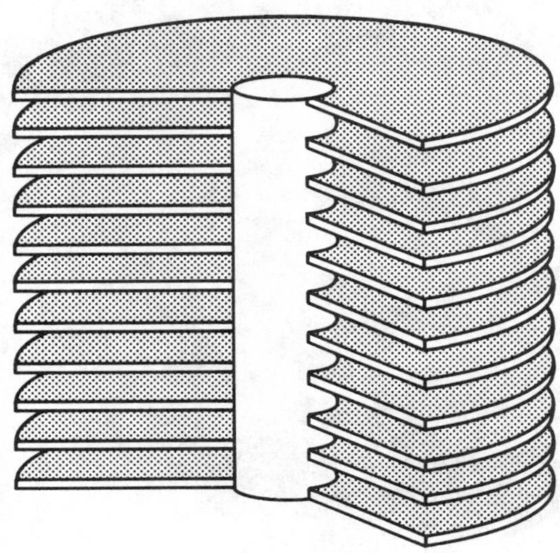

Figure 7.16
Cross-sectional view of a typical disk pack.

3. Recording Data on a Disk

Data may be recorded on both sides of a platter. There are, however, only 2Ø recording surfaces for an 11-disk unit, because the top surface of the uppermost disk and the bottom surface of the lowest disk do not contain data. These two surfaces tend to collect dust and hence are not viable for data storage.

4. Access Mechanism on a Disk Drive

A magnetic disk drive that accesses an 11-disk pack with 2Ø recording surfaces would have 1Ø **access arms**, each with two read/write heads for reading and writing data on two adjacent surfaces (see Figure 7.17). Since the drive has 1Ø access arms, the speed of access is clearly much faster than that of a tape drive, which has only one read/write mechanism.

Each disk surface records data as magnetized bits in one of 2ØØ or more concentric circles called **tracks** (see Figure 7.18). The number of tracks per

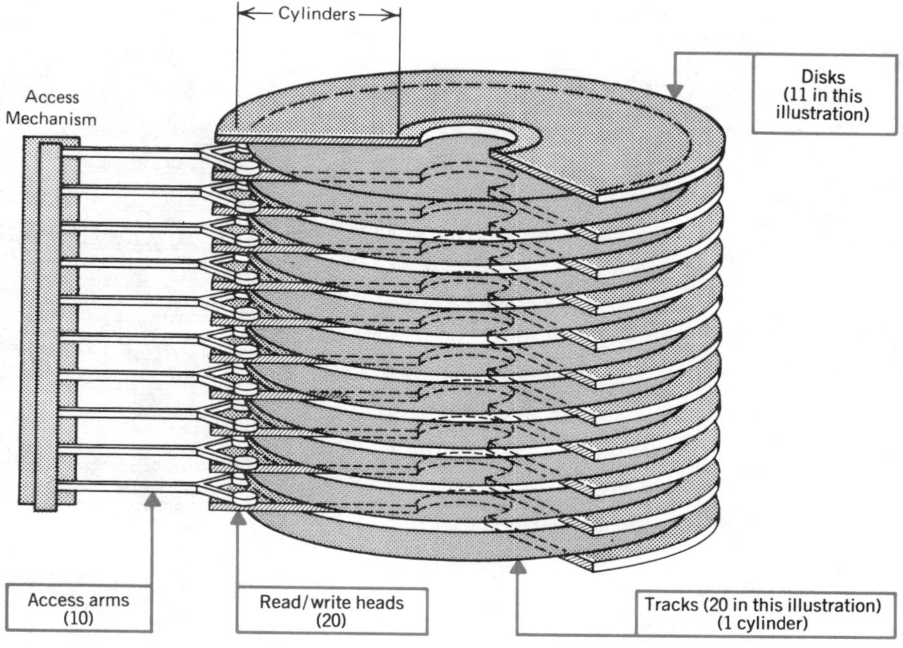

Figure 7.17 How data is accessed from a disk pack. Each read/write head accesses a specific surface. The read/write heads move in and out together as a function of the access mechanism.

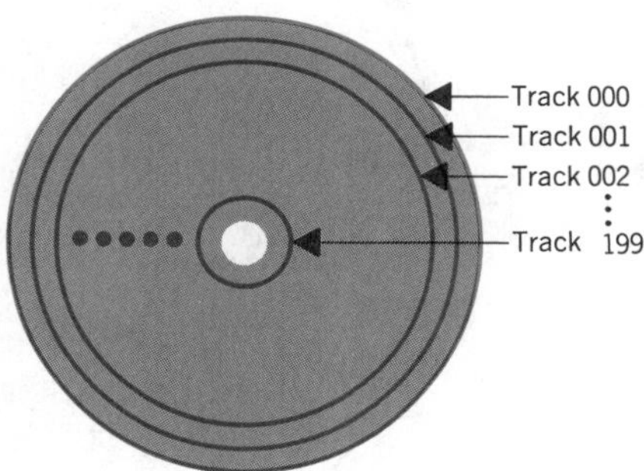

Figure 7.18 Tracks on a disk surface.

surface depends on the particular model of disk pack being used. Each track can store thousands of characters of data. The capacity of each track is exactly the same even though the innermost tracks have less surface space than the outermost ones. As with phonograph records, the *density* or number of characters stored on the innermost tracks is considerably greater than for outermost tracks.

5. Addressing Disk Records

Disks vary in storage capacity and format, but most can be addressed by the following terms, which are illustrated in Figure 7.19.

1. Surface number (Ø to 19 in Figure 7.19*a*).
2. Track number (Ø to 199 in Figure 7.19*b*). Data on track Ø5Ø for *all* surfaces would constitute a **cylinder** (see Figure 7.19*a*).
3. Sector number: On some disks, particularly floppy disks, each track may be further subdivided into a series of sectors, as shown in Figure 7.19*b*.

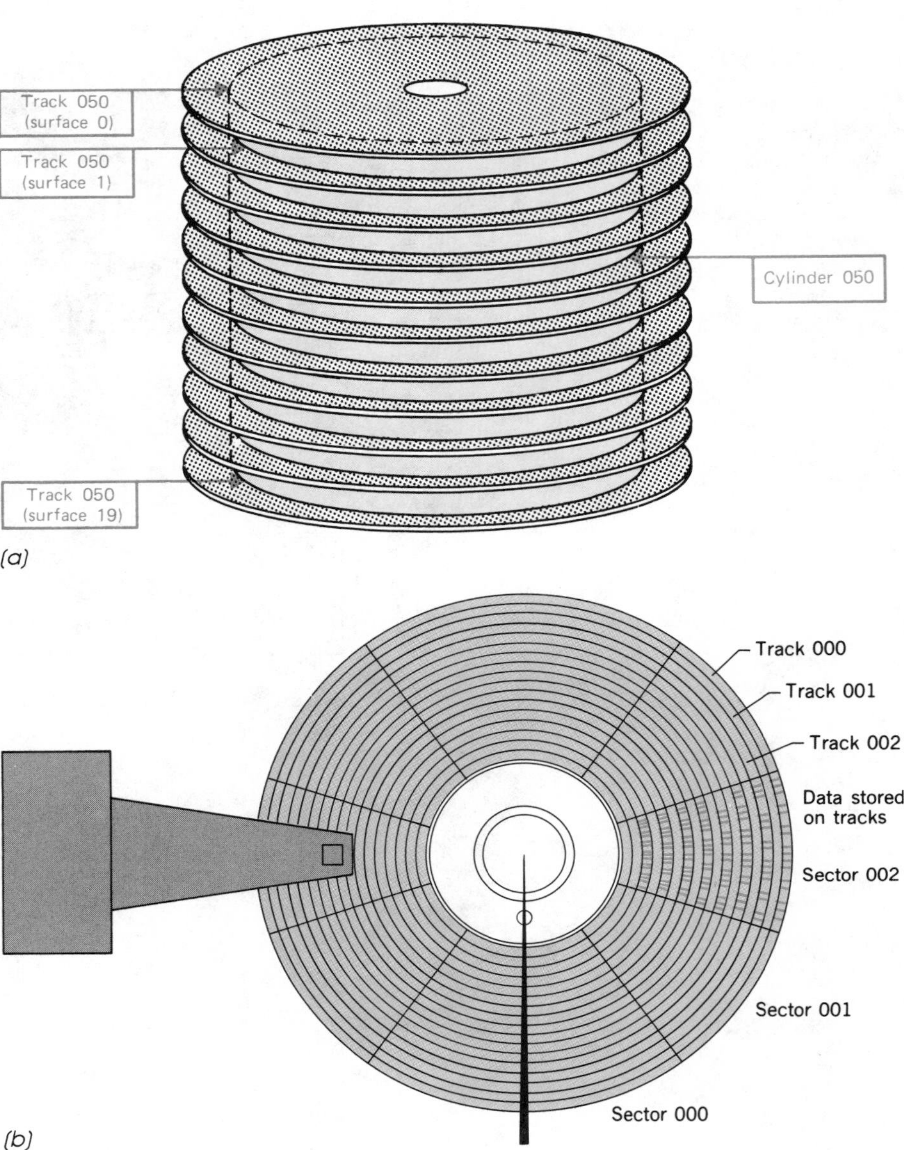

Figure 7.19
(*a*) The cylinder concept on a magnetic disk. (*b*) The sector concept on a magnetic disk.

6. Accessing Disk Records

The access time of a disk varies considerably, depending on the device used. Factors affecting access time include the following.

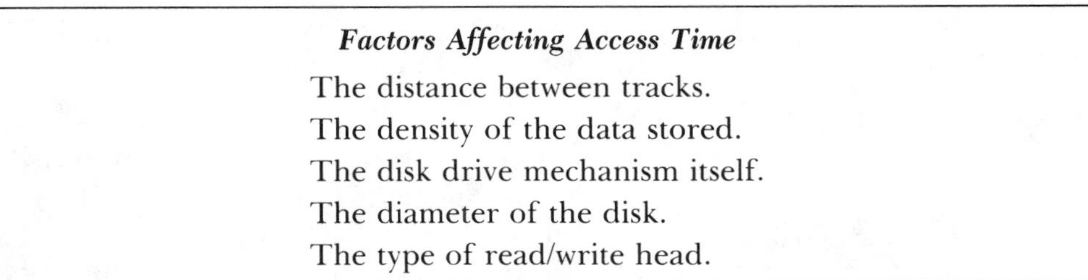

Factors Affecting Access Time

The distance between tracks.
The density of the data stored.
The disk drive mechanism itself.
The diameter of the disk.
The type of read/write head.

To access a given disk record, the computer determines its surface, track, and sector number, if used. Then the disk drive

1. Moves the read/write heads to the cylinder desired.
2. Activates the proper head (depending on the surface number).
3. Waits for the specific record to spin past the head.

At that point, the program can read or write data from the disk.

The total time it takes to read a disk record into storage or write a disk record from storage is called the **access time** of the disk. Typical access times range from 20 to 75 milliseconds, which, although fast, is slower than the access time of internal memory.

7. Removable Disks versus Fixed Disks

Some disk drives enable the user to utilize different disk packs with the drive. The disks, then, are referred to as **removable disks**. In some instances, the disk pack is permanently encased in the drive. This is referred to as a **fixed disk**.

8. Moving-Head Disks versus Fixed-Head Disks

In a **moving-head disk** system, all the read/write heads are attached to a single movable access mechanism. Thus the access mechanism moves directly to a specific disk location, as indicated by the computer.

Because all the read/write heads move together to locate a record, this type of mechanism has a relatively slow access rate as compared to other disks. The access time, however, is still considerably faster than that for tape. Since disks are generally used for high-speed access of records from a file (for example, an airline reservation file), any method that can reduce access time would result in a substantial benefit. For this reason, **fixed-head disks** were developed. These devices do not have a movable access arm. Instead, each track has its own read/write mechanism that accesses a record as it rotates past the arm. The disks in this device are not removable and the capacity of each disk is somewhat less, but the access time is significantly reduced.

Still other disk devices combine the technologies of both moving- and fixed-head mechanisms to produce a high-capacity, rapid access device.

9. Representing Data on a Disk

Data is stored on a disk in the form of magnetized bits. The nine-bit EBCDIC code or the eight-bit ASCII code may be used for representing data, depending on the computer used.

As with tapes, records can be blocked on a disk to maximize the efficient use of storage space. When using a tape, the blocking factor can be any size, but it is limited by the physical memory space available in primary storage. With a disk, greater care must be taken in determining the blocking factor.

Full blocks are usually stored on each surface. Thus if a surface had a storage capacity of 3000 bytes, for example, a block size of 1200 bytes (200 characters per record blocked six) would not be as efficient as a block size of 1400 bytes (200 characters per record blocked seven). In the first instance, the computer would store two blocks and leave blank space on the disk equivalent to 600 bytes ($3000 - 2 \times 1200$). In the second instance, the computer would also store two blocks but leave space equivalent to only 200 bytes ($3000 - 2 \times 1400$). If the 200 character records were blocked eight, however, only *one* block of 1600 characters would be written and space equivalent to 1400 characters would be left blank. In summary, determining the blocking factor for disk records can be a complex task.

As with tapes, identification of disks is difficult; thus standard magnetic labels or identifiers are usually written on an output disk and checked on an input disk to minimize the risk of executing a program with the wrong file.

Data on disk, as on tape, can be stored in traditional display or zoned-decimal format. Or, numeric data can be packed to maximize the efficient use of the disk. (We will discuss packing of data later in this chapter.) Similarly, disk records can be any length, and both fixed- and variable-length records are permitted.

D. Physical Characteristics of Floppy Disks

As noted, floppy disks are used with most micro- and some minicomputer systems. The standard 8-inch floppy was originally developed by IBM as part of its IBM 374Ø key-to-disk data entry system. This disk has 77 concentric tracks, each track consisting of 26 sectors. For most floppies, each sector can store 128 characters, but other versions do exist.

Thus the standard 8-inch floppy disk with 128 bytes or characters per sector would hold approximately 256K characters (77 tracks × 26 sectors × 128 bytes).

Advances in technology have resulted in drives that can format disks to have 15Ø tracks instead of the standard 77. This technique produces *double-density* floppy disks that have twice the storage capacity of standard single-density floppy disks.

Another advance permits reading and writing on both sides of a floppy disk. The disk drive would then have *two* read/write heads. These disks are referred to as *double-sided* floppy disks and have twice the capacity of single-sided disks.

Thus a double-sided, double-density floppy has a storage capacity in excess of one million bytes (actually the number is closer to 1.2 million bytes).

A 5¼-inch floppy or *minifloppy* can store approximately 8Ø,ØØØ characters in single-density format. Double-sided, double-density minifloppies can store 32ØK. Numerous versions of 3-inch floppies are also available.

Because of all these variations, floppies are not standardized, which means it is likely that one system would not be able to read a disk created by another system. The single-density 8-inch disks, however, referred to as IBM 374Ø-compatible disks, do share some features in common and can typically be used on more than one type of system.

In general, hard disk units are both more expensive and more versatile than floppy disk drives. Hard disks have a faster transfer rate between CPU and disk and greater capacity and faster access speed than 8-inch floppies. 8-inch floppies, in turn, are more expensive and more versatile than 5¼-inch floppies.

V. Disks Used for Master File Processing

A. Advantages of Disks over Tape

With ever increasing frequency, disks are being used to store **master files**. A master file is the major collection of records for a given application. A payroll master file, for example, contains payroll information for all employees within a company.

Disks have some major advantages over tape for storing master files.

Advantages of Disk

1. Disks can be processed randomly as well as sequentially.
2. It is possible to update and add to a disk record directly without having to re-create the entire file.

3. Changes to a master disk file can be made immediately as the changes occur, in an on-line environment.
4. Inquiries on the status of records can be made in an on-line environment, with responses available within seconds.

B. Disk File Organization

1. Sequential Access Method
Disks can be created and accessed sequentially just like tapes. Thus far, in all our programs that used disk as input or output, we have used the disk in sequential access mode, just like we would a tape or card. This means that when reading from a disk, we began with the first record, proceeded to the next disk record, and so on.

2. Types of File Organization That Allow for Random Access
Disks can, however, be accessed directly as well. When disks need to be accessed in some manner other than sequential, there are three methods of file organization that can be used.

Methods of Disk File Organization That Allow for Random Access

1. Indexed file organization.
2. Relative file organization.
3. Direct file organization.

a. Indexed File Organization When an **indexed file** is created, each record is placed on the disk in ascending sequence. But, at the same time, the computer establishes an index on the disk that keeps track of where each record is physically located. If, at some later time, you wish to access any record, the computer "looks up" the address on the index and goes directly to that location to find the record. The index, then, operates exactly like a book index. To locate data, "look up" the address in the index.

When creating an indexed file, the programmer must designate a field on the record as a **key field**, or control field which uniquely identifies the record to the computer. For a payroll file, the key field may be Social Security number; for an inventory file, the key field may be part number; for an accounts receivable file, the key field may be customer number. The computer stores in the index the key field and the actual address where the corresponding record is located. The actual address is typically specified in terms of surface number and track or cylinder number. Although there may be numerous records with the same surface and track number, this address certainly narrows down the search for the record. Sector number may also be a component of the address for some disks, particularly floppy disks.

In summary, indexed files are created sequentially with each record placed on the file as it is read in, at the same time that an index is created associating actual addresses to each key field. After the indexed file has been created, it may be accessed or updated randomly or sequentially, as the need arises.

Chapter 9 discusses the two major types of indexed files that can be created.

1. ISAM (Indexed Sequential Access Method) files.
2. VSAM (Virtual Storage Access Method) files.

b. Relative File Organization **Relative files** use key fields for directly determining the location of each record. In this way, an index is not needed, and a look-up of the index is not required to access a record.

In the simplest instance, the key field is used to designate a physical location on the file. Thus, an inventory record with PARTNO 127 would actually be the 127th record on the disk. The records could be accessed directly by using the key field PARTNO. If no record existed for PARTNO Ø2, there would be a blank space on the disk.

PARTNO		PARTNO	PARTNO		PARTNO	
001		003	004		006	...

This organization method results in extremely fast access rates. That is, to access a record with PARTNO 887, the computer simply goes to the 887th record on the disk. There is no need even for a look-up on an index. A major disadvantage of this method, however, is that numerous gaps or unused portions of disk may result. This can lead to an inefficient use of disk space.

c. Direct File Organization Frequently, files cannot use relative keys to determine record locations but require some conversion process whereby the key field can be reduced to a physical location. It would not be possible, for example, to use a nine-digit Social Security number key field to place records on a relative file. For one thing, there would be more gaps than records; for another, disks do not have capacities of 999,999,999 locations, a potential Social Security number!

To use **direct file organization** in this instance, you would need a formula or algorithm for converting a Social Security number into a physical location. You could arbitrarily divide the number by 85 and subtract 23,115 to yield a cylinder number, add 27 and divide by 498 to obtain a track number, and so on. There are, however, standard algorithms available that are frequently used for determining physical addresses of records on a disk file. These algorithms minimize duplication and attempt to maximize the efficient use of the disk.

Even if a conversion is necessary to reduce a key field to its actual address, the access time is still faster than for indexed files. But indexed files have one major advantage that makes them very popular; they are easier for the programmer to process. In most programming languages, the programmer need only specify the key field and the computer will create an indexed file or access one automatically, as the need arises.

Thus, unless access speed is the most critical factor, indexed files are most likely to be used by organizations that require random access capability. Chapter 9 will focus on indexed files.

Summary: Physical Characteristics of Magnetic Disk

A. Hard disk
   1. This is the standard used with large and medium-sized systems.
   2. Can store millions of characters.
   3. Consists of a series of disks arranged in a disk pack; each surface can store data and can be accessed as necessary.

B. Floppy disk
   1. Used with minis and micros.
   2. Three primary sizes, although others exist.
      a. 8 inch, can store from 256K to 1.2 million bytes.
      b. 5¼ inch, can store from 8Ø to 32ØK bytes.
      c. 3-inch versions.
   3. Floppies can be double- or single-sided, with double or single density.

C. Comparison of hard disk and floppy disk: hard disks have greater storage capacity and are faster.

Summary: Master File Storage Media

A. Advantages of disk over tape
   1. Disks can be accessed randomly.
   2. Disk records can be updated directly.
   3. Disks can be processed in an on-line mode.

B. Types of disk file organization
   1. Sequential: disk is processed just like tape.
   2. Random access modes
      a. Indexed: a key field is used to establish an index that contains the location of each record.
      b. Relative: a key field indicates the actual location of a record; for example, a record with CUSTNO 125 is the 125th record in the disk file.
      c. Direct: a key field is used to calculate the actual location of a record.

Self-Evaluating Quiz

1. A ________ is a standard disk used with most large- and medium-sized computer systems.
2. The device used to write on a standard disk is called a ________ .
3. A ________ is a flexible disk used with most micros which is a smaller version of the hard disk.
4. The three primary sizes of floppies are ________ , ________ , and ______ .
5. A disk has a(n) ________ coating that can be used to store characters.
6. A series of platters or disks arranged in a vertical stack is referred to as a(n) ________ .
7. (T or F) The actual number of disks in a disk pack is the same for all systems.
8. (T or F) The topmost and bottommost surfaces of a disk pack are not used for storing data since they have a tendency to collect dust.
9. (T or F) Most disk drives have numerous read/write heads.

10. The two components typically used to address a disk record are ________ and ________ .
11. Data is stored on disk in the form of ________ bits.
12. A floppy disk that can be formatted to have 15Ø tracks instead of the standard 77 is called a(n) ________ .
13. If a floppy disk can contain data on both sides, it is called a(n) ________ .
14. (T or F) It is not possible for two different micros to read one floppy disk.
15. (T or F) 5¼-inch floppies have a greater transfer rate, in general, than 8-inch floppies.

Solutions

1. hard disk
2. magnetic disk drive
3. floppy disk
4. 8 inch
   5¼ inch
   3-inch versions
5. iron oxide or nickel
6. disk pack
7. F—It varies.
8. T
9. T
10. surface number
   track or cylinder number
   (sector number may also be a component for some disks)
11. magnetized
12. double-density floppy
13. double-sided floppy
14. F—Some are compatible (i.e., single-sided, single-density 8-inch floppies).
15. F

VI.

Packing Numeric Data Fields on Tape and Disk

The Hollerith code is used to represent data on punched cards. The EBCDIC code is used by many computers as an internal machine code for representing data. Hexadecimal code is the way in which the EBCDIC code can be displayed by the computer.

The following chart shows the EBCDIC, Hollerith, and hexadecimal codes for letters and numbers. You need not learn or memorize this chart, but you should be familiar with the methods used for representing data.

Character	EBCDIC Zone	EBCDIC Digit	Hollerith	Hexadecimal
A	1100	0001	12-1	C1
B	1100	0010	12-2	C2
C	1100	0011	12-3	C3
D	1100	0100	12-4	C4
E	1100	0101	12-5	C5
F	1100	0110	12-6	C6
G	1100	0111	12-7	C7
H	1100	1000	12-8	C8
I	1100	1001	12-9	C9
J	1101	0001	11-1	D1
K	1101	0010	11-2	D2
L	1101	0011	11-3	D3
M	1101	0100	11-4	D4
N	1101	0101	11-5	D5
O	1101	0110	11-6	D6
P	1101	0111	11-7	D7
Q	1101	1000	11-8	D8
R	1101	1001	11-9	D9
S	1110	0010	0-2	E2
T	1110	0011	0-3	E3
U	1110	0100	0-4	E4
V	1110	0101	0-5	E5
W	1110	0110	0-6	E6
X	1110	0111	0-7	E7
Y	1110	1000	0-8	E8
Z	1110	1001	0-9	E9
0	1111	0000	0	F0
1	1111	0001	1	F1
2	1111	0010	2	F2
3	1111	0011	3	F3
4	1111	0100	4	F4
5	1111	0101	5	F5
6	1111	0110	6	F6
7	1111	0111	7	F7
8	1111	1000	8	F8
9	1111	1001	9	F9

Packed Format

Thus far, we have seen how data may be represented in **zoned decimal format** using one byte or position of storage for each character. For numeric items, we have seen how a byte can store one digit, where the zone portion is equivalent to all bits on, a hexadecimal F, and the digit portion is the binary equivalent of the decimal numbers 0 to 9.

Consider the number 68254. Using zoned decimal format, it would take five bytes to represent this number in storage, one for each digit. The zone portion of each byte would indicate all bits on, as shown below.

It really is unnecessary to represent a zone for each digit within the number. That is, one zone for the entire field to indicate that the number is in fact positive would suffice. There is a method that can be employed so that the computer eliminates or strips the zone of all digits except one to indicate the sign. In this way, the zone portion of each byte can be employed to represent *another digit*. Thus, *two* digits can be represented by a single byte. This technique is called *packing*. **Packed data** is obtained as follows.

1. The zone and digit portions of the *low-order* or right-most byte are switched. This designates the field as a packed field.
2. All other zones are stripped, and two digits are *packed* into a single byte.

Example 1 Zoned Decimal Representation of the Number 68254 (5 Bytes)

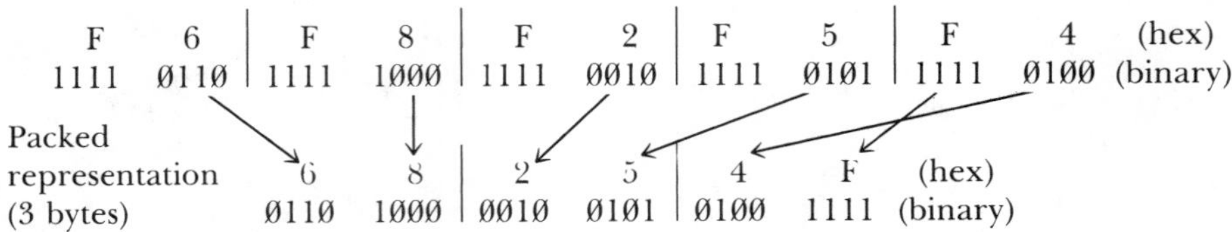

Example 2 Representation of 835674 in Zoned Decimal Format (6 Bytes)

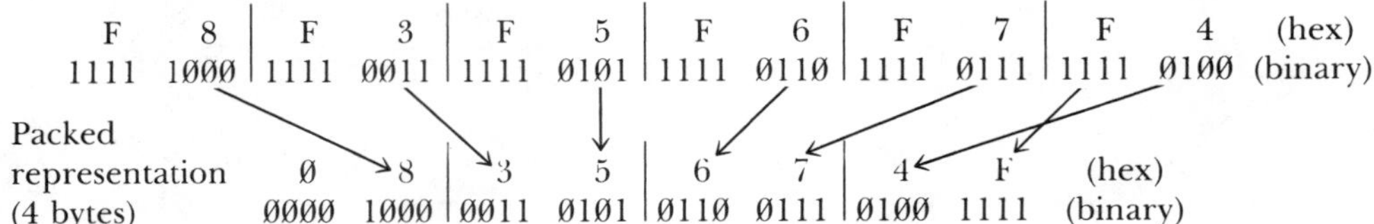

Thus all 1's or a hexadecimal F in the low-order four bits of a byte indicate that the byte contains a packed number. (Because all 1's could not be used to represent any single digit, the computer assumes this to be a packed field.)

Note in Example 1 that the number in zoned decimal format uses five bytes whereas in packed format it uses only three bytes. A major advantage of packing numbers is to conserve storage.

In Example 2, in order to complete or "fill up" the high-order byte, the computer adds four zero-bits at the beginning of the field.

Thus, for numeric fields, you can save considerable storage space by using the packed format. In addition, the computer *requires* numeric fields to be packed in order to perform arithmetic operations on them. To print out or display numeric fields, however, they must be in zoned decimal format. Thus, if data is entered in zoned decimal format and you code an ADD instruction, the computer must first pack the field, perform the ADD, and then unpack the field again. This is all performed automatically in high-level programming languages such as RPG.

To conserve space on tape and disk, we frequently *pack* numeric fields. Since the data on tape and disk need not be readable, packing numeric data on these media is very efficient. It eliminates the need for the computer to pack each field before performing arithmetic operations and then unpacking the field after they have been completed.

Packing numeric fields in RPG is a very simple matter. Simply code a P in column 44 of the Output Specifications form for each field you want the computer to pack.

RPG OUTPUT SPECIFICATIONS

Program | Keying Instruction | Graphic | Key | Card Electro Number | Page 1 2 of | Program Identification 75 76 77 78 79 80
Programmer | Date

O — Line (3–5) | Form Type (6) | Filename or Record Name (7–14) | Type (H/D/T/E) | Stkr #/Fetch (F) | OR / AND | ADD / DEL | Space Before / After | Skip Before / After | Output Indicators: Not, And, Not, And, Not (23–31) | Field Name or EXCPT Name (32–37), *Auto | Edit Codes (38) | B/A/C/1–9/R (39) | End Position in Output Record (40–43) | P/B/L/R (44) | Constant or Edit Word (45–70) | 71–74

Commas / Zero Balances to Print / No Sign / CR / –: Yes Yes 1 A J; Yes No 2 B K; No Yes 3 C L; No No 4 D M
X = Remove Plus Sign; Y = Date Field Edit; Z = Zero Suppress; 5–9 = User Defined

0 1 O
0 2 O AMT 4ØP
0 3 O
0 4 O

Designates a numeric field as packed

Self-Evaluating Quiz *Consult the chart on page 385 to answer these questions.*

1. In the hexadecimal numbering system, *(number)* binary digits are grouped to represent a single hexadecimal digit.
2. A single storage position consisting of *(number)* bits is called a(n) ________ .
3. Each byte is divided into a ________ portion and a ________ portion, each of which consists of *(number)* bits.
4. The letter C is represented in a byte as ________ .
5. The letter M is represented in a byte as ________ .
6. The number 8 is represented in a byte as ________ .
7. Zero is represented in a byte as ________ .
8. Four 1's in the zone portion of a byte are used to denote ________ .
9. How would the letter D appear in a hexadecimal printout?
10. How would the unsigned number 7 (in one byte) appear in a hexadecimal printout?
11. Using zoned decimal format, how many bytes are required to store the unsigned number 118753?
12. In packed format, the number in question 11 would require *(number)* bytes.
13. (T or F) Numeric fields must be packed in order to perform arithmetic operations.

Solutions

1. four
2. eight (Technically, it is nine if you include the parity bit.)
   byte
3. zone
   digit
   four
4. 11ØØ (zone) ØØ11 (digit) or C3 in hex
5. 11Ø1 (zone) Ø1ØØ (digit) or D4 in hex

6. 1111 (zone) 1ØØØ (digit) or F8 in hex
7. 1111 (zone) ØØØØ (digit) or FØ in hex
8. an unsigned number that is assumed to be positive
9. Binary 1100 0100; Hexadecimal C 4

Binary	11ØØ	Ø1ØØ
Hexadecimal	C	4

10.

Binary	1111	Ø111
Hexadecimal	F	7

11. Six (one for each digit)
12. Four (Ø1 18 75 3F)
13. T

Key Terms

Access arm
Access time
Batch processing
Bit
Blocking
Cylinder
Density
Direct file
Disk drive
Disk pack
EBCDIC
Even parity
Field
File
File protection ring
Fixed disk
Fixed-head disk
Fixed-length record
Floppy disk
Hard disk
Header label
IBG (interblock gap)
Indexed file
Key field
Logical record
Master file
Moving-head disk
Nine-track tape
Odd parity
On-line processing
Packed data
Parity bit
Physical record
Programmed label record
Read/write head
Record
Relative file
Removable disk
Retention cycle
Tape drive
Track
Variable-length record
Zoned decimal format

Review Questions

I. True or False

1. (T or F) Major files in most data processing installations are stored on cards.
2. (T or F) A tape file is generally used when most records from a large master file are required for sequential processing during each run.
3. (T or F) Punched cards are a high-speed medium that can serve as input to, or output from, a computer.

4. (T or F) Relative files use key fields for determining directly the location of each record.
5. (T or F) Some devices are equipped to process records directly whereas others can only process them sequentially.
6. (T or F) Batch processing refers to the accumulation of data prior to its entry into the computer flow.
7. (T or F) Batch processing is most often used with direct-access files.
8. (T or F) To conserve space, alphanumeric data may be stored in packed format.
9. (T or F) A record on a tape may be read by a computer system and additional information may then be added to that record.
10. (T or F) If a tape is used as output (that is, "written over"), then information that was originally recorded on it will be destroyed.
11. (T or F) A file protection ring is used to ensure that a tape is not inadvertently destroyed.
12. (T or F) Information can be more densely stored on a magnetic tape than on a punched card.

II. Fill in the Blanks

1. The basic advantages of card processing are ________ and ________ .
2. A record on a tape may be any ________ , as long as it is physically consistent with the size of primary storage.
3. A(n) ________ is a device that requires an operator to code data from a source document onto a magnetic tape via a typewriter-like keyboard.
4. When most records are required for processing in a specified sequence, then ________ is considered the most suitable file type.
5. Two disadvantages of tape processing are ________ and ________ .
6. The creation of a header label record on a tape is required because ________ .
7. A tape librarian is employed by many companies because ________ .
8. A disk index is used to ________ .
9. Two advantages of disk processing are ________ and ________ .
10. The direct method of file organization on a disk requires a key field to be converted to a(n) ________ .

CHAPTER 8

Sequential File Processing and File Maintenance Routines

Objectives

- To provide an understanding of sequential file processing concepts.
- To provide an understanding of sequential file maintenance routines.
- To develop an ability to code basic edit and update procedures.
- To develop an ability to understand matching record concepts and to code programs based on these concepts.

I. An Introduction to File Maintenance Processing

A. Review of Sequential File Processing Concepts

You will recall that a **file** is a collection of data records for a given application. The following are illustrations of file processing procedures frequently used in many RPG applications.

> ***Illustrative File Processing Procedures***
>
> 1. Edit a file—check for accuracy.
> 2. Update a file—incorporate changes to make it current by
>   a. Posting transactions or changes.
>   b. Adding records.
>   c. Deleting records.
> 3. Print a report.
> 4. Answer inquiries.

Two methods can be used to process a file.

> ***File Processing Methods***
>
> 1. Sequential access.
> 2. Random access.

Sequential access means that the file is processed in sequence, starting with the record that is physically located at the beginning of the file and proceeding sequentially through the file until the last record is processed. Thus, to access the 55,ØØØth record in a file sequentially, for example, the computer first reads past 54,999 records in sequence. If a file is only accessible sequentially, then there is no convenient shortcut method of moving directly to the middle of the file or to some point near the end of the file.

Card files and magnetic tape files can only be accessed sequentially. Disk files can be accessed either sequentially or randomly depending on the method of file organization specified by the programmer. Thus far, all our programs—even those that have used disk—have processed data sequentially.

In general, a large file that is to be processed sequentially would be stored on either magnetic tape or magnetic disk. However, one major advantage of magnetic disk processing over magnetic tape is that disks have higher transfer rates for transmitting data. This is one factor that has contributed to the popularity of disk processing with today's computer systems. Thus, very large files that need to be processed sequentially and accessed by several programs would usually be stored on disk. In business, many files are processed sequentially; for these applications, either magnetic disk or magnetic tape is ideal. A payroll file, for example, that is updated with payroll change records and used for printing checks and reports would typically be stored on either disk or tape.

Note, however, that files that are to be accessed randomly for inquiry or updating purposes would not be stored on tape since access time would be too slow. For example, an airline reservation file designed to maintain records of flight reservations would *not* use tape, since access to the file would be based on randomly entered customer inquiries, which means the access is not in any particular sequence.

Recall from Chapter 7 that the following features of magnetic tape and magnetic disk make them ideal for storing large business data files.

Features of Tape and Disk Processing

1. I/O capability of tape and disk. A tape or disk drive can serve as *both* an input and an output device. One can read from or write onto tapes using a tape drive; similarly, one can read from or write onto disks using a disk drive.
2. High-speed capability.
3. Storage capacity. Tapes and disks can store several hundred thousand records.
4. Records can be any reasonable size.

For most sequential processing routines, tape and disk could be processed in exactly the same way. For example, suppose an accounts receivable file is arranged in customer number sequence. If you wish to print the file alphabetically in customer name sequence, you would first sort the file into alphabetic sequence, and then print it sequentially.

When using randomly entered changes to update a file on a disk, records may be read from the master file in any sequence, changed, and rewritten in place. As illustrated below, direct access or random programming procedures are necessary to support this type of file update.

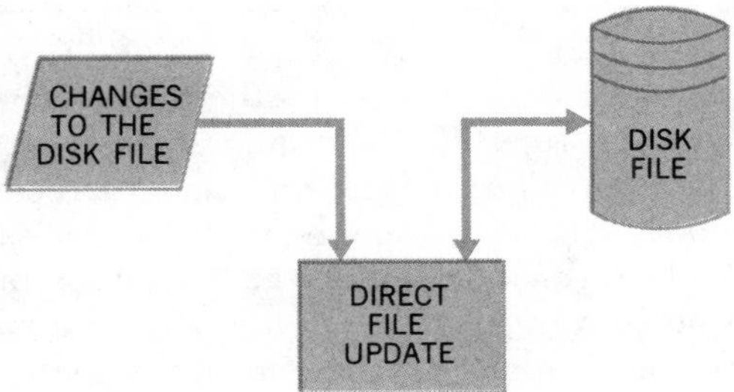

Magnetic tape is a sequential medium that cannot be used for applications requiring direct access capability. With sequential processing, we will use a procedure where both the existing master file and the file of change records are read, and a new updated sequential file is created as output. The following illustration uses a magnetic tape as the master file; as we have already learned, however, a disk file may also be processed sequentially in the same way.

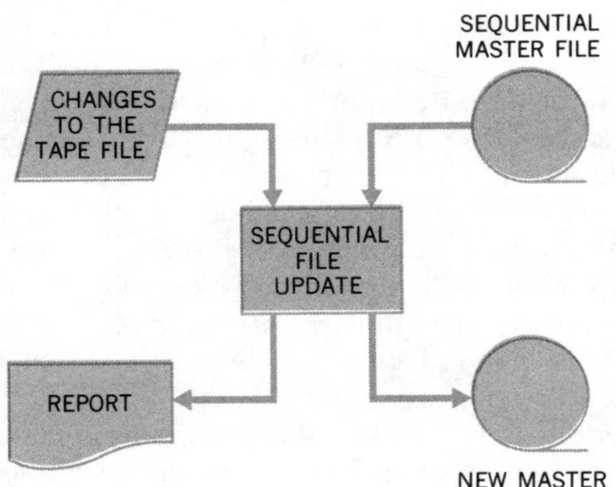

Note that with this type of sequential processing, *all the records* in the master file are rewritten onto the new master, not simply the records that change. We will see later that sequential disk records can be updated in place but for now when we update a master tape or disk we will create a new output master file. This new file will contain existing records along with all changes.

At first, this procedure of rewriting all records onto the new master may appear to be wasteful and inefficient; there are, however, applications for which this updating procedure is ideally suited. When file activity is high, that is, when a large percentage of the records in the master file are to be updated, sequential processing is very efficient. For high activity files, most records will need to be altered; hence, re-creating the entire file in a sequential procedure would not be wasteful.

Before a sequential file update procedure can be executed, both the master file and the change file *must* be sorted into the same sequence. A key field or control field is used to establish the master file sequence. For example, in a payroll system the control field on a master payroll file would usually be the individual's Social Security or employee number. The payroll change records would also be on a file that includes this **key field** (or **control field**). Thus both the master file and the file of change records would be sorted in the same sequence. Typically, files are sorted into ascending sequence.

It is possible in RPG II to check to make certain that both files contain records in the appropriate sequence. The RPG II logic cycle would set on the halt (HØ) indicator if a record was out of sequence and immediately terminate processing. The programming of this halt condition will be discussed in detail later in the chapter.

Although the direct or random method of processing has certain advantages, sequential file updating has one implicit advantage: the sequential update procedure results in automatic backup. That is, at the end of the file update procedure, there are two master files: a new master and an old one. If the new master file becomes unusable for some reason, it is easy to re-create it.

With random update procedures on disk, changes are made directly to the existing disk. If this disk becomes unusable, it would be exceedingly difficult to re-create it. Thus backup files must be produced after each disk update just in case a problem arises on the new disk file. This requirement is not necessary with sequential files because the old master and the new master files are both available after an update procedure.

This chapter will focus on sequential processing of both disk and tape. Note, however, that RPG II and RPG III programs most frequently use disk in their applications. Note, too, that the same fundamental rules can be applied to both tape and disk processing of sequential files. Later on, we will demonstrate an alternative method of updating disks. The next chapter considers the random access features of disk files.

Summary

Sequential File Processing	*Direct File Processing*
1. Records must be arranged in sequence (sorted) by a key or control field.	1. Transaction records need not be in sequence.
2. Update procedures require all the records to be written on a new master file.	2. Only those records that change are rewritten.

3. The original master is unaltered; therefore, backup is automatically provided.	3. Records are changed in place and therefore measures must be taken to provide backup.
4. Efficient only when file has high activity.	4. Efficient for on-line processing.
5. Not to be used for random applications.	5. Supports random inquiry.

Self-Evaluating Quiz

1. (T or F) Sequential files are usually arranged in a predetermined sequence established by a control or key field.
2. (T or F) Tape files may be accessed randomly if the programmer provides the correct system commands.
3. (T or F) When files are processed using sequential update procedures, backup is automatic.
4. (T or F) With sequential processing, only the records that are altered are rewritten when the file is updated.
5. (T or F) The key field or control field always occupies the same position(s) within a record for a given file.
6. (T or F) A file that has low activity is ideally suited for sequential disk processing.
7. (T or F) The popularity of magnetic tape is apparent, since magnetic disk is being slowly replaced by magnetic tape because of the higher transfer rate of tape.
8. (T or F) Random or direct access methods are always the fastest and most efficient means of processing data files.
9. (T or F) An inquiry system requiring immediate access to student records at a college or university would be ideally suited for magnetic disk processing using direct-access methods of retrieval.
10. (T or F) With sequential file processing, the old master file, the newly created master file, and the change file must all be in the same sequence.

Solutions

1. T
2. F—Only sequential processing is permitted.
3. T
4. F—A new master is created.
5. T—A basic data processing principle is that *all* fields within a given record are fixed with regard to position.
6. F—Only when high activity prevails.
7. F
8. F—When file activity is high, sequential processing is usually faster and more efficient.
9. T
10. T

B. Creating Sequential Files

A **master file** is the major collection of records for a given application. For example, payroll applications require a payroll master file that contains all the employees' payroll information. When an application is computerized, a master file must be initially created. Careful attention must be given to creating this master file to ensure that it is as error free as possible. Thus, error control routines would be included and a control listing would be provided so that users could make certain that the master file is accurate.

1. Creating a Sequential Master File

The illustration that we will use here creates a sequential master file on disk. The procedures employed are exactly the same as for tape processing. The only difference is the device specifications on the File Description form.

The input for this procedure could be a card file, tape cassette, floppy disk, or records entered on a terminal. All input is in sequence by a control field or key field. In the example shown, the CUSTNO will serve as the control field.

Figure 8.1 illustrates the problem definition for creating the sequential master file. Error control procedures should be incorporated to eliminate records containing

1. A blank or zero customer number field.
2. A blank name field.
3. A blank or zero balance due field.

Editing is defined as the process of verifying that data entered into the computer is relatively error-free.

As always, the file specifications are derived from the systems flowchart. The Printer Spacing Chart reflects the error messages to be provided as well as other program output requirements.

Figure 8.1
Problem definition for creating a sequential master file.
(Continued on next page.)

Systems Flowchart

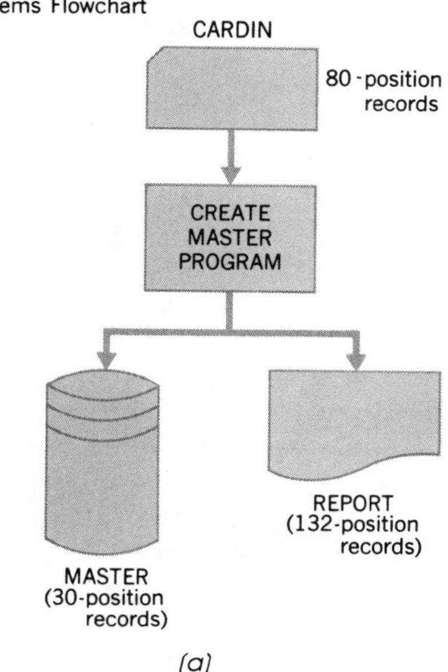

(a)

CARDIN Record Layout

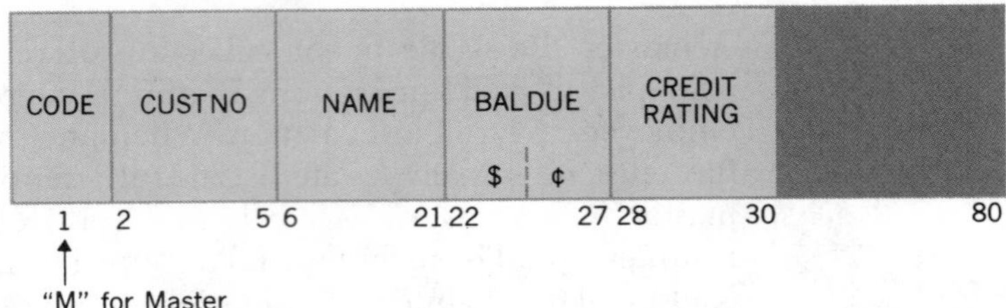

Note: CREDIT RATING does not have to be defined on the Input form since it is not used in creating the control listing.

(b)

REPORT Printer Spacing Chart

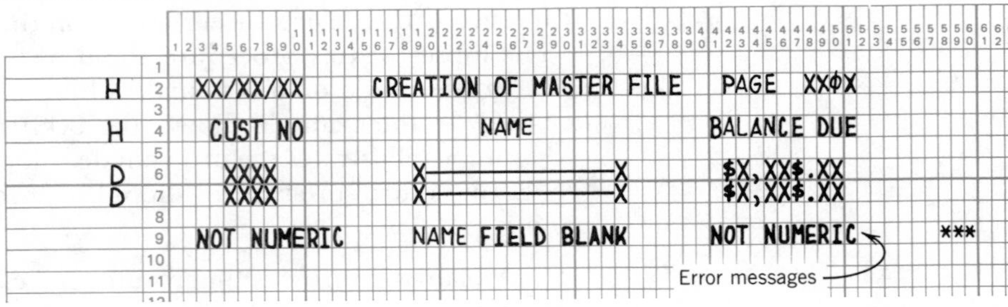

Figure 8.1 *(continued)*

(c)

The RPG program necessary to create the master file is illustrated in Figure 8.2. The systems analyst has established a blocking factor of six records per block; hence each block contains 180 characters (6 × 30) as well as standard labels specified by an "S" in column 53 of the File Description form.

Recall that when a numeric field contains a blank or zero, the indicator specified in columns 69-70 of the Input form will be set on. In this example, we are using indicators 10 and 12 to test the CUSTNO and BALDUE fields for blanks or zeros. Similarly when the NAME field contains only blanks, indicator 11 will also be set on.

A listing of all records written on the master file is also required. Records that were not placed on the master because of specific errors (as noted by indicators 10, 11, and 12) have been flagged on the control listing (REPORT) with an error message.

Notice that this file creation routine uses techniques and procedures outlined in previous chapters. No new concepts have been employed.

2. Creating the File of Changes to the Master

The master file is created only once when a system is implemented. After the initial creation, it is kept current using an **update procedure**.

A file of change records called a **transaction file** is created on a regular basis and is used to update the master file. For a payroll application, this transaction file may consist of payroll changes, new hires, separations from the company, name changes, and so on. The transaction file is created using a procedure similar to master file creation. Transaction records are *edited* or checked for reasonableness and then used to update the master file. A control listing is produced for users to check, indicating totals of records processed, error conditions, and a listing of records, if appropriate.

Figure 8.2 Program to create a master disk file.

```
01-010  F*********************************************************************** SSS08A
C1-020  F* THIS PROGRAM CREATES A MASTER SEQUENTIAL FILE ON DISK AND TESTS     SSS08A
01-030  F*THE INPUT FIELDS FOR BLANKS OR ZEROS.  WHEN BLANK FIELDS ARE         SSS08A
C1-040  F* FOUND AN ERROR MESSAGE IS PRINTED.                                  SSS08A
01-050  F************************************************************************SSS08A
01-060  FCARDIN  IP  F      80            READC1 SYSIPT                        SSS08A
01-070  FMASTER  O   F 180  30            DISK40 SYS025S                       SSS08A
01-C80  FREPORT  O   F     132     CF     PRINTERSYSLST                        SSS08A
C2-010  I*                                                                     SSS08A
02-020  I*************************** INPUT RECORDS ******************************SSS08A
02-030  I*                                                                     SSS08A
02-040  ICARDIN  NS  01   1 CM                                                 SSS08A
02-050  I                                           2   50CUSTNO       10      SSS08A
02-060  I                                           6  21 NAME         11      SSS08A
02-070  I                                          22  272BALDUE       12      SSS08A
02-C80  I                                           1  30 CRDREC               SSS08A
02-C90  I*                                                                     SSS08A
02-100  U*********************** CREATE MASTER ******************************** SSS08A
C2-110  I*                                                                     SSS08A
C3-010  OMASTER  D       N10N11N12                                             SSS08A
03-020  C        AND     01                                                    SSS08A
03-030  O                           CRDREC    30                               SSS08A
03-040  O*                                                                     SSS08A
03-050  C**************************** HEADING LINES ****************************SSS08A
03-060  O*                                                                     SSS08A
C3-070  CREPORT  H  201   1P                                                   SSS08A
C3-C80  C        CR       CF                                                   SSS08A
03-090  O                           UDATE Y   10                               SSS08A
C3-100  O                                     38 'CREATION OF MASTER FILE'     SSS08A
03-110  C                                     46 'PAGE'                        SSS08A
03-120  O                           PAGE      51                               SSS08A
C3-130  O         H 22    1P                                                   SSS08A
03-140  O        CR       OF                                                   SSS08A
03-150  O                                     10 'CUST. NO'                    SSS08A
03-16C  O                                     27 'NAME'                        SSS08A
C3-170  O                                     52 'BALANCE DUE'                 SSS08A
03-180  C*                                                                     SSS08A
03-190  O*************************** DETAIL LINES *****************************SSS08A
C3-200  C*                                                                     SSS08A
C3-210  C        D 11     01                                                   SSS08A
C3-220  O                        N10CUSTNOZ    8                               SSS08A
C3-230  O                        N11NAME      34                               SSS08A
C3-240  C                         10          13 'NOT NUMERIC'                 SSS08A
C3-250  O                         10          60 '****'                        SSS08A
C3-260  O                         11          34 'NAME FIELD BLANK'            SSS08A
03-270  O                         11          60 '****'                        SSS08A
03-280  C                         12          51 'NOT NUMERIC'                 SSS08A
C3-290  C                        N12BALDUE    50                               SSS08A
C3-300  O                         12          60 '****'                        SSS08A

E N C  O F  S C U R C E
```

Figure 8.3 illustrates the problem definition for creating the transaction file and producing a control listing.

Note, again, that the file medium is of no consequence in this application. The transaction file could be created on cards, tape, disk, or any storage medium. The processing would be the same for each type of file. Since the transaction file is used to update the *sequential* master file, it must be created *in the same sequence* as the master file. In this instance, the transaction file is in customer number sequence, the same sequence as the master file. If the transaction file was not created in the same sequence as the master file, it would need to be sorted before a sequential update could be performed.

The program in this illustration must perform the following validation procedures.

1. The CODE field should contain one of the following.

   A Denotes a record to be added to the master file.

   C Denotes a record to be changed on the master file.

   D Denotes a record to be deleted from the master file.

   The code is checked for an "A" (addition of a record), "C" (change or update of a record), or "D" (deletion of a record). Any other code is un-

Figure 8.3 Problem definition for creating a transaction file.

Systems Flowchart

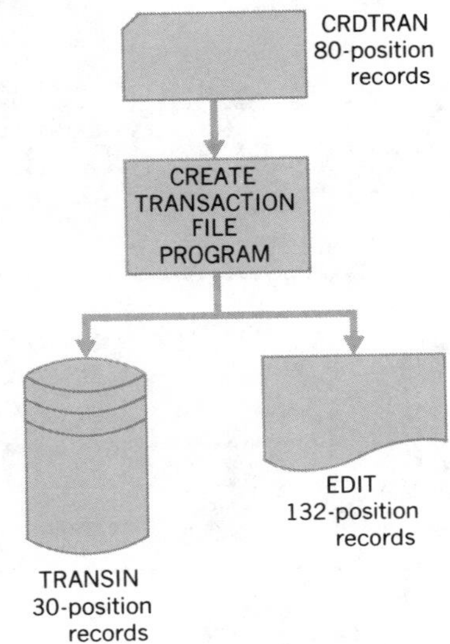

CRDTRAN Record Layout - For Changes and Deletions

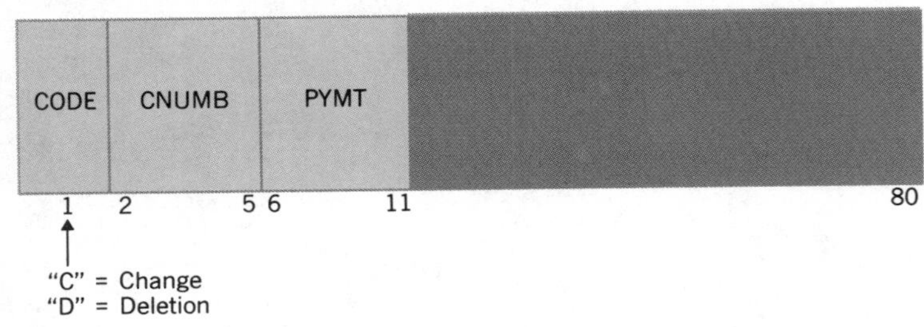

CRDTRAN Record Layout - For Additions

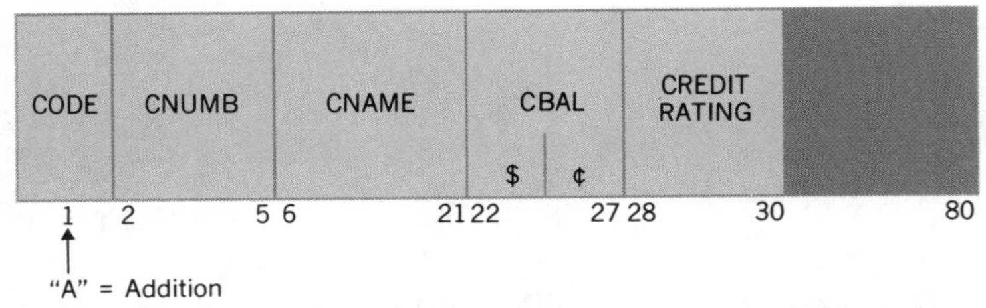

Note: CREDIT RATING does not have to be defined on the Input form since it is not used in creating the control listing.

EDIT Printer Spacing Chart

Type	Line	Content
	1	
H	2	PAGE XXØX T R A N S A C T I O N E D I T R E P O R T XX/XX/XX
	3	
H	4	CUSTOMER NO PAYMENT ERROR MESSAGES ***DATA FOR NEW ACCOUNTS ***
	5	
D	6	XXXX X,XX.XX INCORRECT CODE
D	7	XXXX X,XX.XX CUST.# NOT NUMERIC
D	8	XXXX X,XX.XX PAYMENT NOT NUMERIC
D	9	X——NEW RECORD——X
D	10	XXXX **SEQUENCE ERROR**
	11	
	12	
TLR	13	NUMBER OF RECORDS PROCESSED XXX,XØX
	14	
TLR	15	TOTAL PAYMENTS XX,XX.XX
	16	
TLR	17	NUMBER OF RECORDS ADDED X,XØX
	18	
TLR	19	NUMBER OF RECORDS DELETED X,XØX
	20	
	21	
	22	

acceptable and will be flagged by the program as an error, as illustrated. The following Input form provides for the appropriate codes.

RPG INPUT SPECIFICATIONS

Line	Form Type	Filename or Record Name	AND/OR	Sequence	Number (1/N), E	Option (O), U, S	Record Identifying Indicator, **, or DS	1 Position	1 Not (N)	1 C/Z/D	1 Character	2 Position	2 Not (N)	2 C/Z/D	2 Character	3 Position	3 Not (N)	3 C/Z/D	3 Character
01Ø	I	CRDTRAN		NS			Ø1	1		C	A								
02Ø	I		OR				Ø2	1		C	C								
03Ø	I		OR				Ø3	1		C	D								
04Ø	I		OR				Ø4	1	N	C	A	1	N	C	C	1	N	C	D
05	I																		
06	I																		
07	I																		

2. CNUMB, the customer number field, and PYMT, the payment field, are tested to ensure that they only contain numeric data. Recall that the TESTN instruction tests a field defined as *alphanumeric* (i.e., Decimal Positions is blank) for the presence of numeric data. As a result of the test, the resulting indicator specified in columns 54-55 will be set on when the field is numeric. Following validation, the data must be moved to a numeric field if arithmetic or editing operations are to be performed. In this example, indicator Ø8 is set on if the PYMT field is numeric. The PYMT data is then moved to NUMFD, a numeric field, for subsequent addition to TOTAL.

RPG CALCULATION SPECIFICATIONS

Line	Form Type	Indicators	And	And	Factor 1	Operation	Factor 2	Result Field Name	Length	Decimal Positions	Resulting Indicators High (54-55)	Low (56-57)	Equal (58-59)
01Ø	C					TESTN		CNUMB			Ø9		
02Ø	C	Ø2				TESTN		PYMT			Ø8		
03Ø	C	Ø8	Ø2			MOVE	PYMT	NUMFD	6	2			
04Ø	C	Ø8	Ø2		TOTAL	ADD	NUMFD	TOTAL	7	2			
05	C												
06	C												
07	C												

3. The key field or control field is checked to verify that the records are in ascending sequence, which would be the same order as the master file. This is done on the Calculation form. The procedure used is flowcharted on the next page.

CNUMB > PREVNO?
NO
SET ERROR INDICATOR 12
YES
MOVE CNUMB TO PREVNO

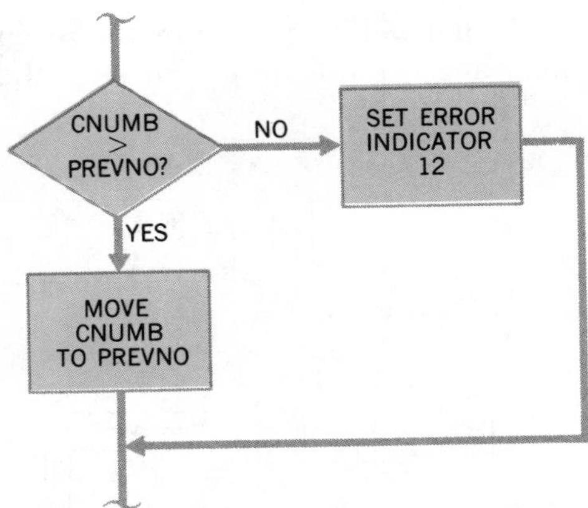

As long as each customer number is greater than the previous customer number, we know the file is in sequence. However, if the CNUMB is less than or equal to the previous record's CNUMB, indicator 12 is set on in order to condition an appropriate error message as illustrated.

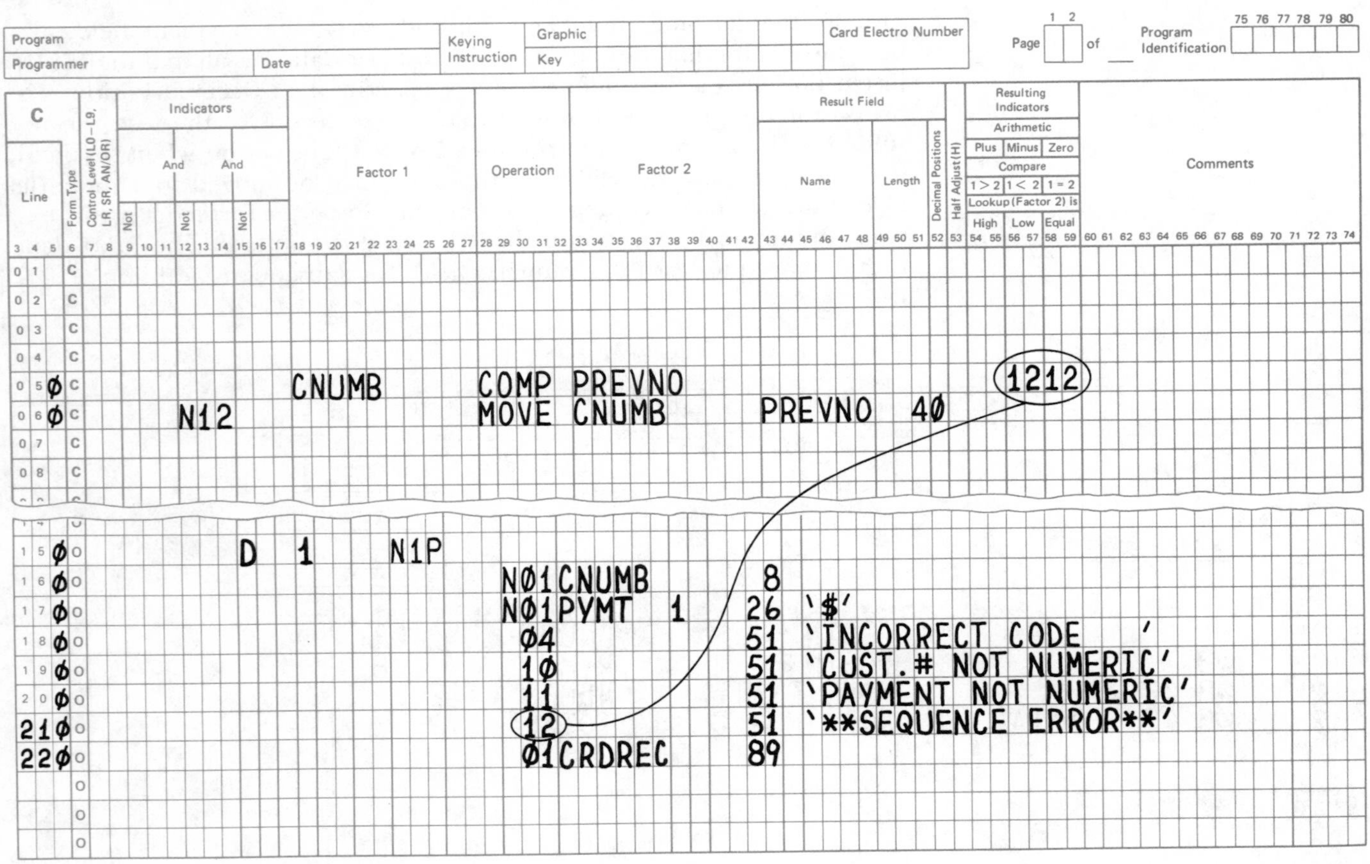

RPG CALCULATION SPECIFICATIONS
05Ø C CNUMB COMP PREVNO 1212
06Ø C N12 MOVE CNUMB PREVNO 4Ø
15Ø O D 1 N1P
16Ø O NØ1CNUMB 8
17Ø O NØ1PYMT 1 26 '$'
18Ø O Ø4 51 'INCORRECT CODE '
19Ø O 1Ø 51 'CUST.# NOT NUMERIC'
20Ø O 11 51 'PAYMENT NOT NUMERIC'
21Ø O 12 51 '**SEQUENCE ERROR**'
22Ø O Ø1CRDREC 89

4. All the records processed are counted (NORCDS) as shown here.

RPG CALCULATION SPECIFICATIONS

Line	Form Type	Control Level	Indicators			Factor 1	Operation	Factor 2	Result Field Name	Length	Decimal Positions	Half Adjust	Resulting Indicators	Comments
01Ø	C		Ø8	Ø2		NORCDS	ADD	1	NORCDS	6	Ø			
02Ø	C		Ø8	Ø2		TOTAL	ADD	NUMFD	TOTAL	7	2			
03Ø	C			Ø1		NOADD	ADD	1	NOADD	4	Ø			
04Ø	C			Ø3		NODLTE	ADD	1	NODLTE	4	Ø			
05	C													
06	C													
07	C													

5. A running total of all payments (TOTAL) is accumulated. For verification purposes, this total would typically be compared by a clerk to a manually prepared total of all monies received.
6. The number of new accounts (NOADD) is listed.
7. The number of records deleted (NODLTE) is also printed at the end of the "Transaction Edit Report." See the Printer Spacing Chart in Figure 8.3.

The complete program for creating the transaction file is shown in Figure 8.4. Again, the validation of transaction data is of paramount importance in developing an effective system. Notice that columns 63-64 (Field Record Relation) of the Input form have been coded with Ø1 for CNAME and Ø1 for CBAL in the record layout for additions. As a result, when indicator Ø1 is turned on because a code of "A" is found in position 1 of a transaction record, the program will know that CNAME and CBAL are included in the record just read.

It is important to ensure **system integrity**; this means that errors must be minimized by validating the transaction data prior to updating the master file. Although these procedures demand additional programming, this effort provides a system of controls that will produce a transaction file which is relatively free of errors. In this way, the risk of updating a master file with inaccurate data can be minimized.

When errors are detected by the program, the transaction record is *not* used to update the master file. Only when the transaction file is free from errors and all totals prove correct can the updating procedure begin.

3. Sequential File Updates: Disk and Tape Concepts Using Matching Records

Three files are required for the sequential update procedure.

Figure 8.4
Program to create a transaction file.

```
01-010  F*********************************************************************SSS088
01-020  F*                                                                    SSS088
01-030  F* THIS PROGRAM EDITS TRANSACTION RECORDS AND CHECKS THE INPUT FOR    SSS088
01-040  F* THE FOLLOWING ERROR CONDITIONS.                                    SSS088
01-050  F*      INCORRECT RECORD TYPE                   INDICATOR 04 ON       SSS088
01-060  F*      PAYMENT FIELD NOT NUMERIC               INDICATOR 08 OFF      SSS088
01-070  F*      CUSTOMER NUMBER NOT NUMERIC             INDICATOR 09 OFF      SSS088
01-080  F*      RECORDS OUT OF SEQUENCE                 INDICATOR 12 ON       SSS088
01-090  F* A COUNT OF THE ADDITIONS, DELETIONS, AND TOTAL NUMBER OF RECORDS   SSS088
01-100  F* PROCESSED ARE ALSO ACCUMULATED                                     SSS088
01-110  F*                                                                    SSS088
01-120  F*********************************************************************SSS088
01-130  FCRDTRAN IP  F     80           READ01 SYSIPT                         SSS088
01-140  FTRANSIN O   F 180  30          DISK40 SYS025S                        SSS088
01-150  FEDIT    O   F     132     OF   PRINTERSYSLST                         SSS088
01-160  I*                                                                    SSS088
01-170  I*************************** INPUT RECORDS ***************************SSS088
01-180  F*                                                                    SSS088
02-010  ICRDTRAN NS  01   1 CA                                                SSS088
02-020  I        OR  02   1 CC                                                SSS088
02-030  I        OR  03   1 CD                                                SSS088
02-040  I        OR  04   1NCA   1NCC   1NCD                                  SSS088
02-050  I                                          1   1 CODE                 SSS088
02-060  I                                          2   5 CNUMB                SSS088
02-070  I                                          6  11 PYMT                 SSS088
02-080  I*                                                                    SSS088
02-090  *******************************************************               SSS088
02-100  I*     RECORD LAYOUT FOR   A D D I T I O N S          *               SSS088
02-110  I******************************************************               SSS088
02-120  I*                                                                    SSS088
02-130  I                                          6  21 CNAME     01         SSS088
02-140  I                                         22  272CBAL      01         SSS088
02-150  I                                          1  30 CRDREC               SSS088
02-160  C*                                                                    SSS088
02-170  C******************************************************               SSS088
02-180  C*      TEST FIELDS FOR NUMERIC DATA                  *               SSS088
02-190  C*     IF PAYMENT IS NUMERIC MOVE TO NUMFD            *               SSS088
02-200  C*      IN ORDER TO PERFORM CALCULATIONS              *               SSS088
02-210  C******************************************************               SSS088
02-220  C*                                                                    SSS088
03-010  C                    TESTN          CNUMB       09                    SSS088
03-020  C   02               TESTN          PYMT        08                    SSS088
03-030  C   08 02            MOVE PYMT      NUMFD   62                        SSS088
03-040  C   08 02   TOTAL    ADD  NUMFD     TOTAL   72                        SSS088
03-050  C*                                                                    SSS088
03-060  C******************************************************               SSS088
03-070  C*      COUNT THE NUMBER OF ADDITIONS (NOADD),        *               SSS088
03-080  C*      THE NO OF DELETIONS (NODLTE)                  *               SSS088
03-090  C*      AND THE NUMBER OF CARDS PROCESSED (NOCRDS)    *               SSS088
03-100  C******************************************************               SSS088
03-110  C*                                                                    SSS088
03-120  C       01   NOADD     ADD  1         NOADD   30                      SSS088
03-130  C       03   NODLTE    ADD  1         NODLTE  40                      SSS088
03-140  C            NOCRDS    ADD  1         NOCRDS  40                      SSS088
03-150  C*                                                                    SSS088
03-160  C******************************************************               SSS088
03-170  C*      PERFORM THE SEQUENCE CHECK OPERATION          *               SSS088
03-180  C******************************************************               SSS088
03-190  C*                                                                    SSS088
03-200  C            CNUMB     COMP PREVNO               141212               SSS088
03-210  C   14                 MOVE CNUMB     PREVNO  4                       SSS088
03-220  O*                                                                    SSS088
03-230  O*************************** HEADING LINES ***************************SSS088
03-240  O*                                                                    SSS088
04-010  OEDIT    H  201   1P                                                  SSS088
04-020  O      OR         CF                                                  SSS088
04-030  O                                      5 'PAGE'                       SSS088
04-040  O                          PAGE       10                              SSS088
04-050  O                                     41 'T R A N S A C T I O N'      SSS088
04-060  O                                     69 'E D I T     R E P O R T'    SSS088
04-070  O                          UDATE Y    89                              SSS088
04-080  O        H 22     1P                                                  SSS088
04-090  O      OR         OF                                                  SSS088
04-100  O                                     14 'CUSTOMER NO'                SSS088
04-110  O                                     27 'PAYMENT'                    SSS088
04-120  O                                     50 'PROGRAM MESSAGES'           SSS088
04-130  O                                     84 '***DATA FOR NEW ACCOUNTS'   SSS088
04-140  O                                     88 '****'                       SSS088
04-150  O*                                                                    SSS088
04-160  O**************************** DETAIL LINES ***************************SSS088
04-170  O*                                                                    SSS088
04-180  O        D  1     N1P                                                 SSS088
04-190  O                          CNUMB       8                              SSS088
04-200  O                   02   08NUMFD 1    26 '$'                          SSS088
04-210  O                   02  N08PYMT       26                              SSS088
04-220  O                   03                26 '******'                     SSS088
04-230  O                   01                26 '******'                     SSS088
04-240  O                       03            48 'RECORD DELETED'             SSS088
04-250  O                       04            53 'INCORRECT CODE-CONTAINS'    SSS088
04-260  O                       04CODE        55                              SSS088
04-270  O                     N09 02          51 'CUST.# NOT NUMERIC'         SSS088
04-280  O                     N08 02          51 'PAYMENT NOT NUMERIC'        SSS088
04-290  O                      01             47 'NEW ACCOUNT'                SSS088
04-300  O                      01             68 'NAME:'                      SSS088
04-310  O                      01   CNAME     90                              SSS088
```

Figure 8.4 *(continued)*

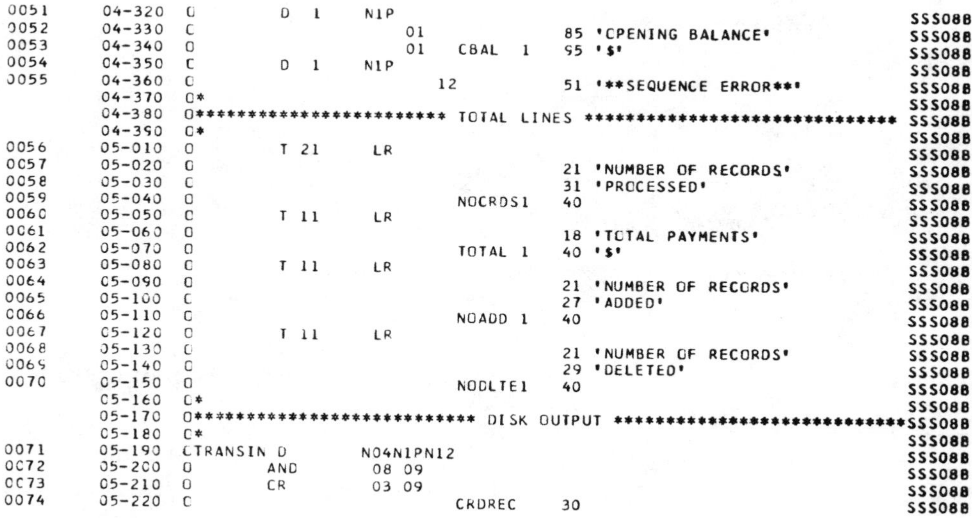

```
0051   04-320  O         D  1   N1P                                              SSS08B
0052   04-330  O                       01             85 'OPENING BALANCE'       SSS08B
0053   04-340  O                       01    CBAL   1 95 '$'                     SSS08B
0054   04-350  O         D  1   N1P                                              SSS08B
0055   04-360  O                          12          51 '**SEQUENCE ERROR**'    SSS08B
       04-370  O*                                                                SSS08B
       04-380  O************************ TOTAL LINES ****************************** SSS08B
       04-390  O*                                                                SSS08B
0056   05-010  O         T 21     LR                                             SSS08B
0057   05-020  O                                      21 'NUMBER OF RECORDS'     SSS08B
0058   05-030  O                                      31 'PROCESSED'             SSS08B
0059   05-040  O                             NOCRDS1  40                         SSS08B
0060   05-050  O         T 11     LR                                             SSS08B
0061   05-060  O                                      18 'TOTAL PAYMENTS'        SSS08B
0062   05-070  O                             TOTAL 1  40 '$'                     SSS08B
0063   05-080  O         T 11     LR                                             SSS08B
0064   05-090  O                                      21 'NUMBER OF RECORDS'     SSS08B
0065   05-100  O                                      27 'ADDED'                 SSS08B
0066   05-110  O                             NOADD 1  40                         SSS08B
0067   05-120  O         T 11     LR                                             SSS08B
0068   05-130  O                                      21 'NUMBER OF RECORDS'     SSS08B
0069   05-140  O                                      29 'DELETED'               SSS08B
0070   05-150  O                             NODLTE1  40                         SSS08B
       05-160  O*                                                                SSS08B
       05-170  O*************************** DISK OUTPUT *****************************SSS08B
       05-180  O*                                                                SSS08B
0071   05-190  OTRANSIN D       N04N1PN12                                        SSS08B
0072   05-200  O        AND      08 09                                           SSS08B
0073   05-210  O        OR       03 09                                           SSS08B
0074   05-220  O                             CRDREC   30                         SSS08B

    E N D   O F   S O U R C E
```

Files Required for a Sequential Update	
Input Master File	Contains all the data except that which is most current. That is, it contains master information only up to the previous update cycle. This file is in sequence by a key or control field.
Input Transaction File	Contains changes that occurred since the previous updating cycle. This file is in sequence by the same key or control field as used in the master file.
Output Master File	Incorporates the current transaction data and the previous master information. That is, the output master file will combine data from the old master and the input transaction file.

The input and output *master* files are typically on disk or tape. For purposes of illustration, the *transaction* data in this example will be stored on disk. A control listing may also be produced if desired. The systems flowchart in Figure 8.5 indicates the operations to be performed.

To update sequential files, data must be read into the computer in a specific sequence. Since we wish to update a master record with a transaction record, both files must always be in the same sequence.

Consider the following example. The master accounts receivable file is in ascending sequence by customer number (CUSTNO).

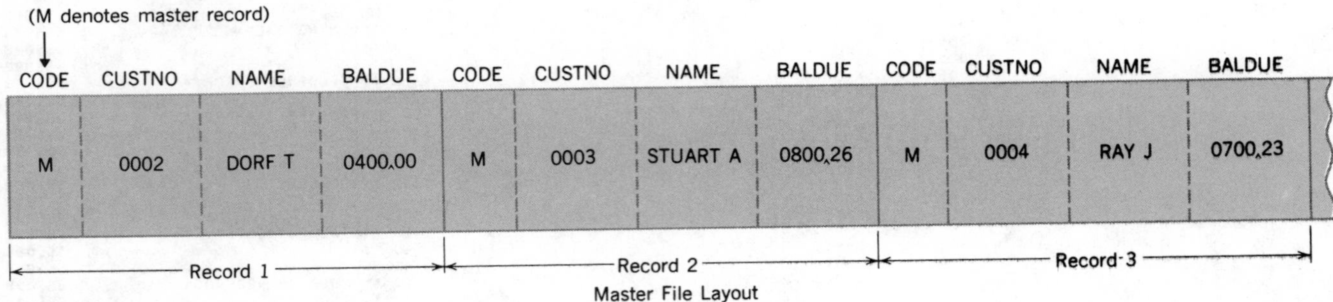

Master File Layout

The transaction records are in ascending sequence by CUSTNO. The transaction codes are as follows.

- A Add new account to the master file.
- C Change or update an existing master record.
- D Delete a record from the master file.

Transaction File Layout

CODE	CUSTNO	NAME	BALDUE	CODE	CUSTNO	PAYMENT	CODE	CUSTNO	UNUSED	CODE	CUSTNO	PAYMENT
A	0001	WHITE F	0123.45	C	0002	075.00	D	0004		C	0005	0150.00
Denotes ADD record				Denotes CHANGE or UPDATE record			Denotes DELETE record			Denotes CHANGE or UPDATE record		

OLD MASTER FILE
TRANS-ACTION FILE
SEQUENTIAL UPDATE PROGRAM
CONTROL LISTING
NEW MASTER FILE

Figure 8.5
Systems flowchart for a sequential file update.

The first transaction record is a new account as noted by the "A" in the code field. Therefore, there should *not* be a corresponding master record for customer ØØØ1, since that would indicate an error. If the new transaction record does not have a corresponding master, then the transaction record should be written on the new master. Once processed, the new master should contain customer ØØØ1, reflecting the information obtained from the transaction file as shown.

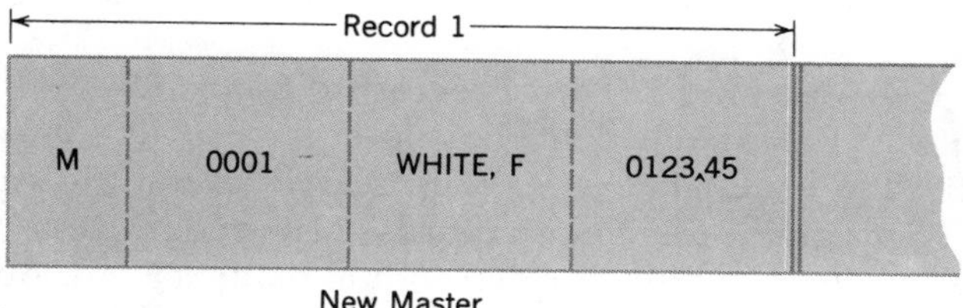

New Master

Transaction record 2 is a change record as noted by the "C" in the code field. There should be a corresponding master record for customer ØØØ2, and we find that there is. The master record (ØØØ2) contains the name DORF, with an outstanding balance of $4ØØ.ØØ. However, DORF made a payment of $75.ØØ as noted in the transaction record. The new balance due for customer ØØØ2 should be the previous balance due (4ØØ.ØØ) less the payment (75.ØØ), or $325.ØØ. The updated record should be written on the new master resulting in a new balance of $325.ØØ for DORF.

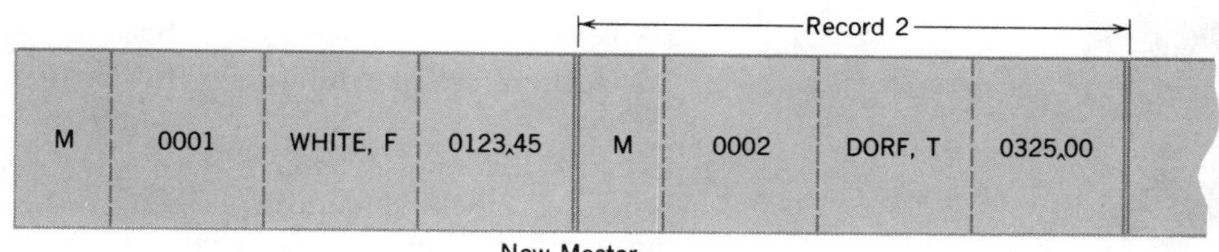

New Master

We see that the master record ØØØ3 does not have a current payment to post against the balance due of $8ØØ.26, because no transaction record exists. When a matching transaction record is not present, the master record should be recreated or copied to the new master as is. The new master now contains the following records.

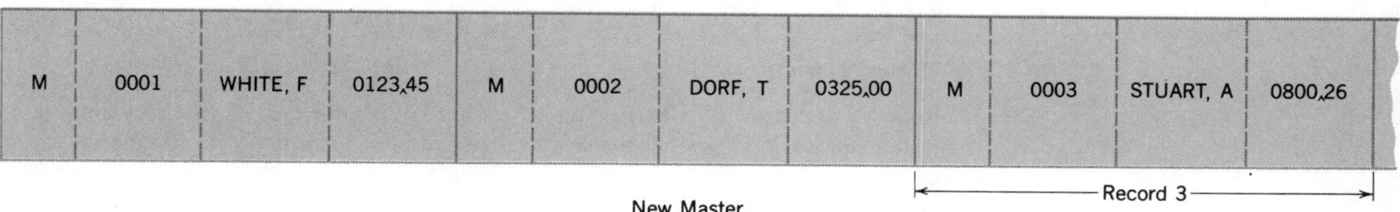

New Master

The transaction record for customer number ØØØ4 contains a delete code. It should match an existing master record. The new master file should not, however, contain customer number ØØØ4, since it is being deleted from the master file. With some system designs, the record may contain a code indicating the record is either active ("A") or inactive ("I"). When the analyst selects this approach, the record would be written to the new master, but the status of the record would change from "A" meaning active to "I" indicating inactive. However, in this example, we have decided not to include deleted records on the new master. Thus, rather than re-creating master records with a delete code of "I", we simply do not rewrite them on the new master at all. In this way, they are physically deleted from the file.

Using the master and transaction files created earlier, we will begin our update procedure, which is based on the matching record concept.

4. Matching Record Processing Concepts

As indicated earlier, the master file usually contains the major collection of data and is designated as the primary file; thus, it will control the processing of the program. Matching records (MR) require that all input files be arranged in either ascending or descending sequence. For our examples, we will always use ascending sequence. The matching fields (M1-M9) entered on the Input form will determine which file will supply the record to be processed next. The net effect is to merge the two files together into a new master file. The order of processing is in accordance with the following rules.

Rules for Processing Input Files

1. Records that have no matching fields are processed before records that have matching fields.
2. When two records contain unmatched fields, the lower numbered record will be processed first (if both are in ascending sequence).
3. When there are matching records, the record from the primary file *will always be processed before the record from the secondary file.*
4. If more than one secondary file is specified, the secondary files will be processed in the sequence specified on the Input form. Note that the input specifications for each file must correspond with the sequence specified on the File Description form.

To illustrate this point, examine Figure 8.6 and note the sequence in which the records are processed. The rules presented provide guidelines to determine the order in which records will be processed.

Master (Primary)			*Transaction (Secondary)*		
Control Field	*Record Identifier*	*Processing Sequence*	*Control Field*	*Record Identifier*	*Processing Sequence*
ØØ2	Ø1	2	ØØ1	Ø2	1
ØØ3	Ø1	6	ØØ2	Ø2	3
ØØ4	Ø1	7	ØØ2	Ø2	4
ØØ5	Ø1	9	ØØ2	Ø2	5
ØØ6	Ø1	12	ØØ4	Ø2	8
ØØ7	Ø1	13	ØØ5	Ø2	10
ØØ8	Ø1	14	ØØ5	Ø2	11

Figure 8.6
Example of processing sequence.

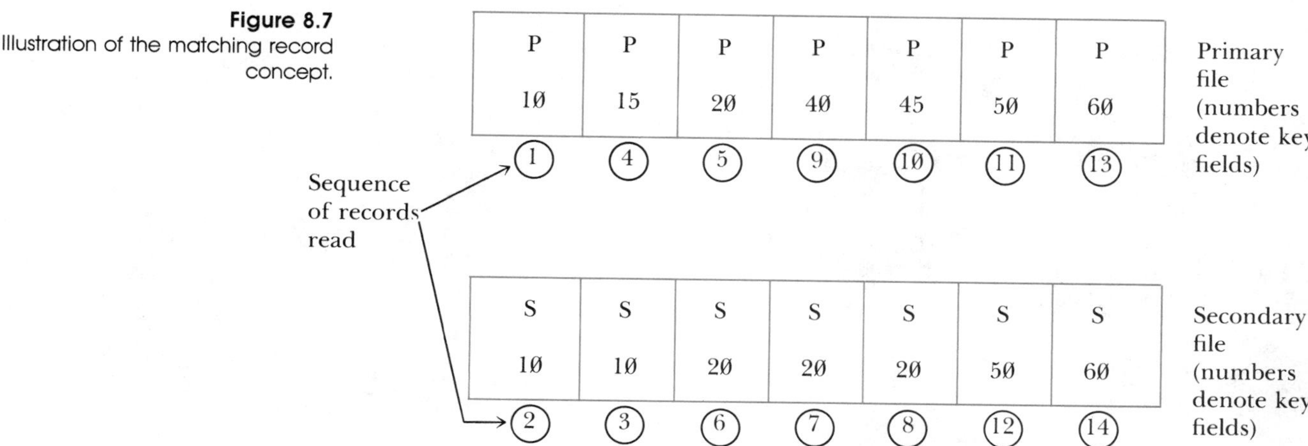

Figure 8.7
Illustration of the matching record concept.

Initially, the master record (ØØ2) is compared to the transaction record (ØØ1). Rule 2 applies since the records do not match; that is, record ØØ1 would be processed first from the transaction file. After processing, another record from the transaction file is read. Since both the master and transaction records now contain matching fields (ØØ2), the primary is processed first, followed by the secondary. Hence rule 3 applies. Records from each file are read next. (See Figure 8.7 for another illustration of the matching record concept.)

The processing of both the master and transaction files has the effect of merging the data from the old master and transaction file in order to create the new master file. The logic for matching record file processing is as shown in Figure 8.8.

The **MR** (matching record) **indicator** is always turned on when the secondary record matches the record in the primary file. Since the primary is always read first, the record identifying indicator will always be set "on" by the matching secondary record since it is read after the primary. RPG sets the MR indicator "off" when all total calculations and printing required for this record are complete.

Assigning Matching Fields (M1-M9)
Matching record fields may be specified as either numeric, meaning an entry has been made in the decimal positions field, or alphameric, where the decimal positions field is blank. There can be up to nine matching field entries specified for each record (M1-M9). When there is more than one type of record within a file, RPG II permits the field locations for the different record types to occupy different positions. The illustration on top of page 409 shows the use of an M1 indicator on the Input Specifications form.

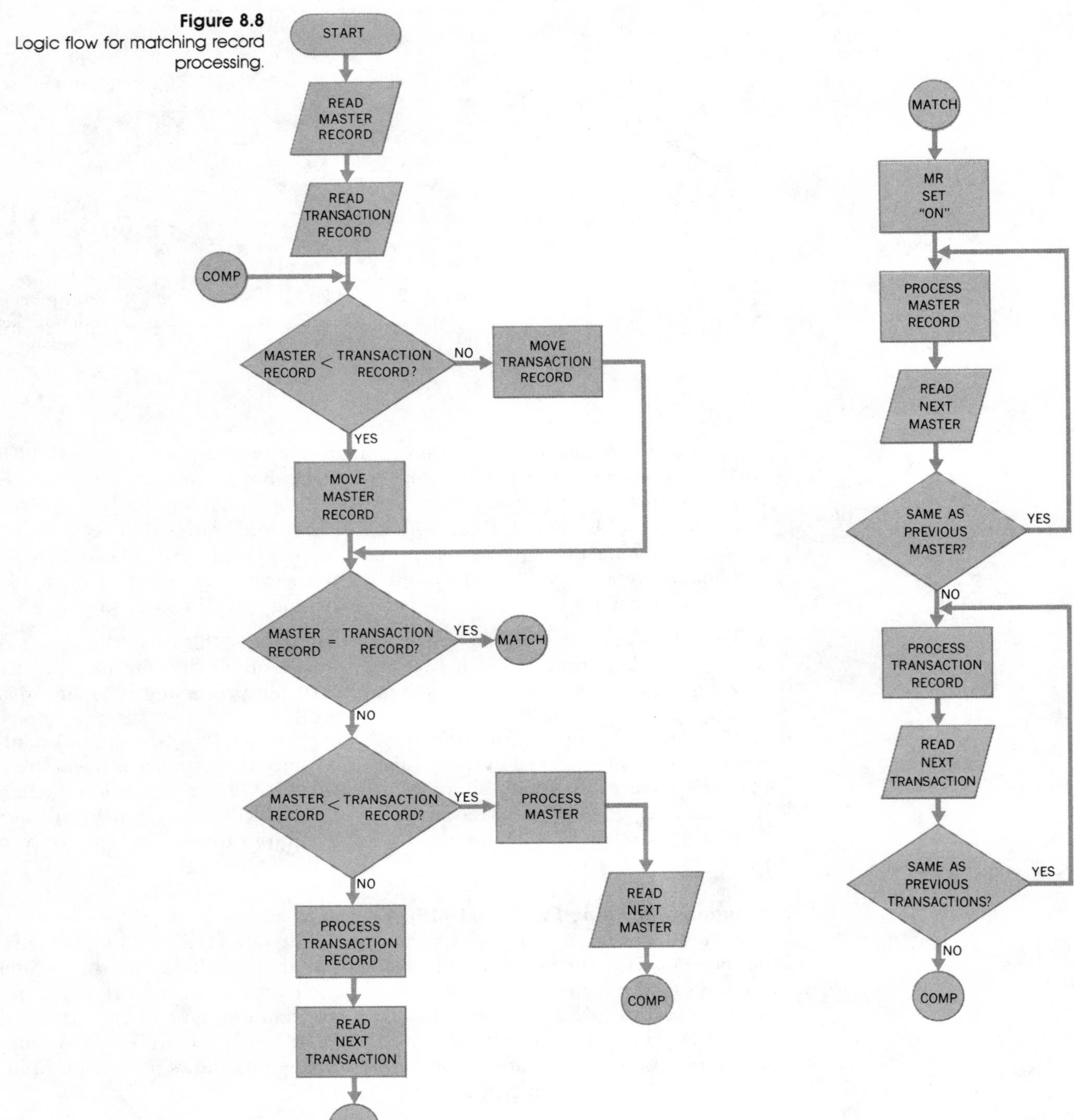

Figure 8.8
Logic flow for matching record processing.

RPG INPUT SPECIFICATIONS

Line	Form Type	Filename or Record Name	Sequence	Record Identifying Indicator	Position	C/Z/D	Character	From	To	Decimal Positions	RPG Field Name	Matching Fields
Ø1	I	MASTER	AA	Ø1	8Ø	C	M					
Ø2	I							1	5	Ø	PARTNO	M1
Ø3	I							21	26	2	UNITP	
Ø4	I							31	35	Ø	QTYOH	
Ø5	I							41	6Ø		DESC	
Ø6	I	DETAIL	BB	Ø2	8Ø	C	D					
Ø7	I							1	3	Ø	DIVSN	
Ø8	I							4	6	Ø	PLANT	
Ø9	I							11	18	Ø	EMPNO	
1Ø	I							21	23	Ø	QTY	
11	I							26	3Ø	Ø	DETPRT	M1
12	I											
13	I											

Matching fields in different positions

Matching field is numeric

In addition, all the record types contained in a primary file need not have matching fields on the secondary file. In fact, if an entire file is specified without there being any matching fields, the primary file will be read and processed first. This feature could prove useful if a table, report, or related stream of input data were to be read and we wanted it processed prior to using a secondary file.

Whenever matching fields are coded for the primary file, the same matching indicators must be specified in the corresponding fields of the secondary file. Incorrect results can be expected if the same matching indicators are not specified for corresponding fields.

The assignment of major, intermediate, and minor fields is referred to as **split matching fields** and would be coded as shown on the next page.

		Example 1	*Example 2*
Major field	M3	Division	State
Intermediate	M2	Plant	County
Minor	M1	Department	Town

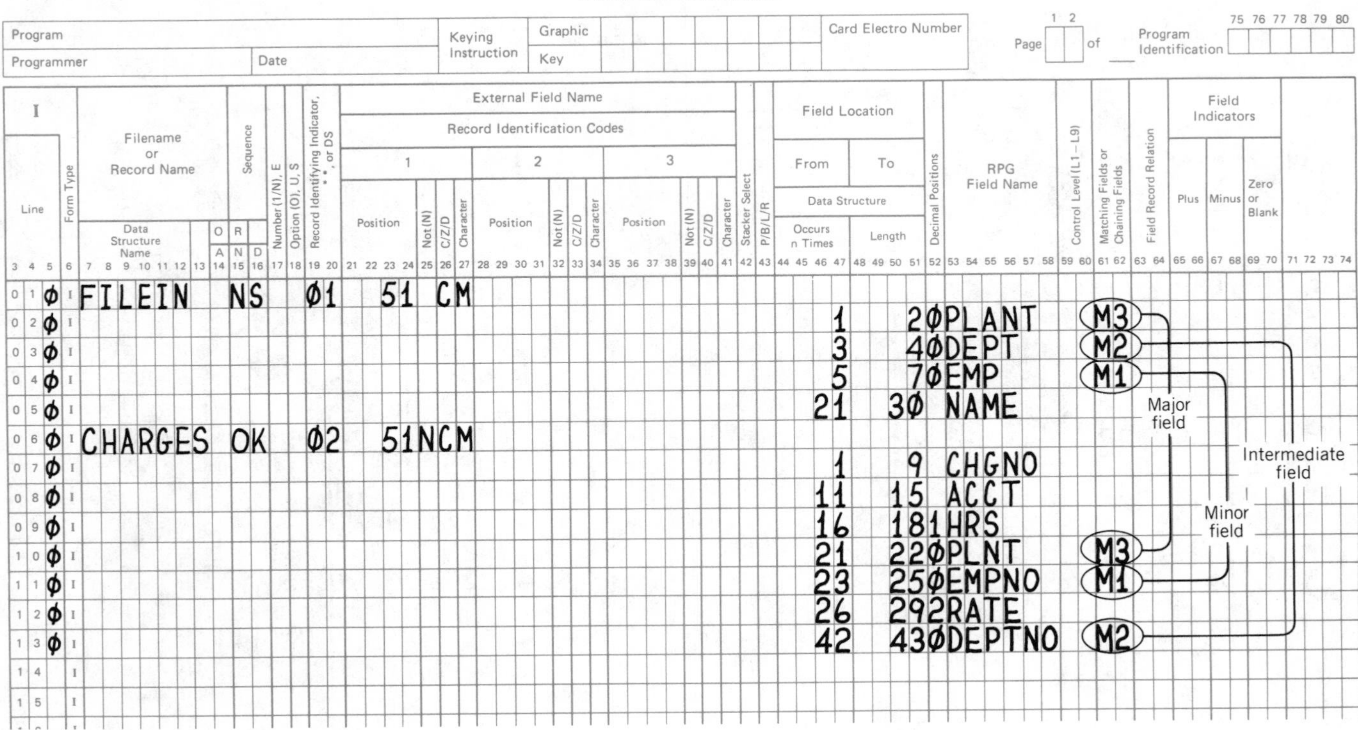

Again, the position of the fields within the record is of no consequence for matching procedures. Only when the contents of *all* the split matching fields are identical will the matching record indicator (MR) be turned on.

We are now prepared to develop the sample program for matching records.

C. Matching Record Sample Program

The following program uses the concepts learned in this chapter. Figure 8.9 illustrates the systems flowchart for this problem along with the Printer Spacing Chart for the report that is to be produced.

File Specifications

The procedure used for performing a sequential update relies on *matching records.* On the File Description form, the input master file is designated as the *primary* file. This means it is read first and will be used to match against the transaction file. The transaction file would be designated as the *secondary* file. Figure 8.1Ø illustrates the File Description Specifications.

The entries are essentially the same as in the previous program with the following exceptions.

Column 16	"P"	Denotes the master file as the primary file.
Column 16	"S"	Establishes the transaction file as the secondary file.
Column 18	"A"	Indicates that the file is arranged in ascending sequence. The letter "D" would be used to denote descending sequence.

Columns 2Ø–23	The block length is always a multiple of the record length. The specifications for both the input master and output master must be identical; that is, if the block size of the input master is 25Ø characters, then the output master must also contain the same specification (25Ø).
Columns 4Ø–46	The device entry determines if the files are to be stored on magnetic tape or magnetic disk.
Column 53	S is used to denote standard labels, whereas N is used to indicate nonstandard labels. Only experienced programmers should specify nonstandard labels for purposes of file protection and file security.

Figure 8.9 (*a*) Systems flowchart for sample program. (*b*) Printer Spacing Chart for sample program.

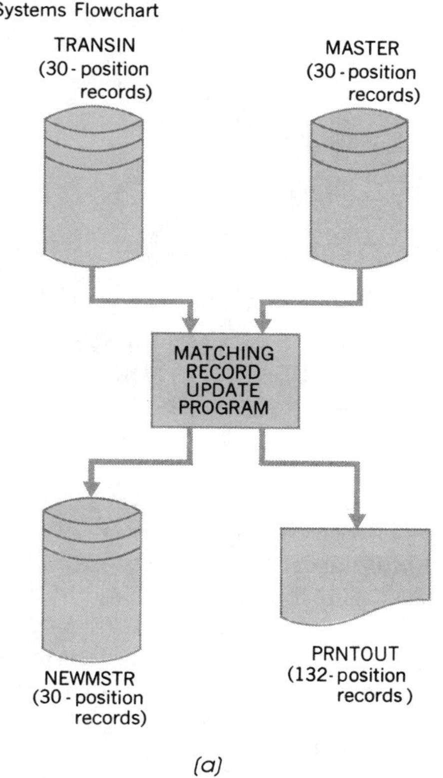

(*a*)

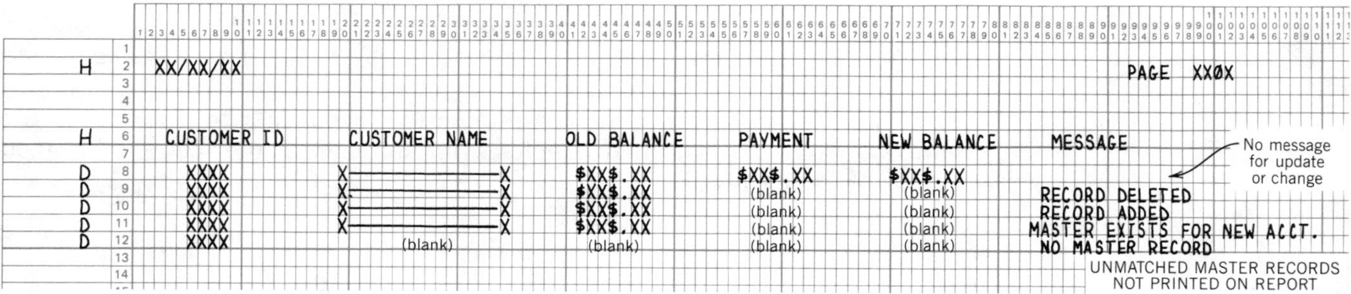

(*b*)

RPG CONTROL AND FILE DESCRIPTION SPECIFICATIONS

Program | Keying Instruction | Graphic | Key | Card Electro Number | Page 1 2 of | Program Identification 75 76 77 78 79 80

Programmer | Date

Control Specifications

For the valid entries for a system, refer to the RPG reference manual for that system.

H — Line | Form Type | Size to Compile | Object Output | Listing Options | Size to Execute | Debug | Reserved | Currency Symbol | Date Format | Date Edit | Inverted Print | Reserved | Number of Print Positions | Alternate Collating Sequence | Reserved | Inquiry | Reserved | Sign Handling | 1 P Forms Position | Indicator Setting | File Translation | Punch MFCU Zeros | Nonprint Characters | Reserved | Table Load Halt | Shared I/O | Field Print | Formatted Dump | RPG to RPG II Conversion | Number of Formats | S/3 Conversion | Subprogram | CICS/DL/I | Transparent Literal

```
01 H
```

File Description Specifications

For the valid entries for a system, refer to the RPG reference manual for that system.

F — Line | Form Type | Filename | File Type (I/O/U/C/D) | File Designation (P/S/C/R/T/D/F) | End of File (E) | Sequence (A/D) | File Format (F/V/S/M/D/E) | Block Length | Record Length | Mode of Processing (L/R) | Length of Key Field or of Record Address Field | Record Address Type (A/P/I/K) | Type of File Organization or Additional Area (I/X/D/T/R/ or 2) | Overflow Indicator | Key Field Starting Location | Extension Code E/L | Device | Symbolic Device | Labels S/N/E/M | Name of Label Exit | Extent Exit for DAM | Storage Index | Continuation Lines: K, Option, Entry | A/U | File Addition/Unordered | Number of Tracks for Cylinder Overflow | Number of Extents | Tape Rewind | File Condition U1–U8, UC | R/U/N | External Record Name

```
02ØFMASTER  IP AF 18Ø  3Ø            DISK4Ø  SYSØ25S
03ØFTRANSIN IS AF 18Ø  3Ø            DISK4Ø  SYSØ25S
04ØFNEWMSTR O    F 18Ø  3Ø            DISK4Ø  SYSØ25S
05ØFPRNTOUT O    F     132      OF    PRINTERSYSLST
06 F
07 F
```

Primary file; Secondary file; Ascending sequence; 6 records per block; Device; Standard labels

Figure 8.10
File Description Specifications for sample program.

The fields in the master record would be designated as shown in Figure 8.11, which illustrates the rest of the program. Notice that columns 63-64 (Field Record Relation) of the transaction input record indicate that if indicator Ø2 is on, then the record just read contains NAME and NEWBAL. If indicator Ø4 is on, then the record just read contains a payment (PYMNT) field.

The transaction record is also specified in Figure 8.11. Note that when a new account is added, the transaction record (TRNREC) is referenced as a separate entity; in this way it is not necessary to move each individual field.

To indicate that we wish to process records by matching customer numbers on the two files, we code M1 in columns 61-62 of the Input form for CUSTNO in both input records.

A record from the primary file, which is the input master file, is read first followed by a record from the secondary or transaction file. If the customer number on each of these files is the same, then the MR indicator will be turned on as well as the corresponding record identifying indicator. The MR indicator is used in conjunction with the record identifying indicator to determine what processing is to be performed. The following summarizes the action to be taken when specific events occur.

Event	*Indicators*	*Action to be Taken*
A new record is to be added from the transaction file.	NMR, Ø2	Write a new master record from transaction data.

(Continued on page 414)

Figure 8.11
Entire sample program.

```
        01-010  F*********************************************************************** SSS08C
        01-020  F* THIS PROGRAM UPDATES A SEQUENTIAL DISK FILE BY MATCHING TRANSACT-  SSS08C
        01-030  F* ION RECORDS WITH A MASTER FILE AND CREATING A NEW MASTER FILE      SSS08C
        01-040  F* THE NEW MASTER CONTAINS ADDITIONS, DELETIONS AND CHANGES.          SSS08C
        01-050  F*********************************************************************** SSS08C
        01-060  F*                                                                      SSS08C
0001    01-070  FMASTER  IP AF 180  30             DISK40 SYS025S                       SSS08C
0002    01-080  FTRANSIN IS AF 180  30             DISK40 SYS025S                       SSS08C
0003    01-090  FNEWMSTR O    F 180  30             DISK40 SYS025S                       SSS08C
0004    01-100  FPRNTOUT O    F      132      OF    PRINTERSYSLST                       SSS08C
        02-010  I*                                                                      SSS08C
        02-020  I* MASTER  INPUT RECORD                                          *      SSS08C
        02-030  I*                                                                      SSS08C
0005    02-040  IMASTER  AA  01    1 CM                                                 SSS08C
0006    02-050  I                                             1  30 MSTREC              SSS08C
0007    02-060  I                                             2   50CUSTNO  M1          SSS08C
0008    02-070  I                                             6  21 NAME                SSS08C
0009    02-080  I                                            22  272BALDUE              SSS08C
        02-090  I*                                                                      SSS08C
        02-100  I* TRANSACTION INPUT RECORD                                             SSS08C
        02-110  I*                                                                      SSS08C
0010    02-120  ITRANSIN BB  02    1 CA                                                 SSS08C
0011    02-130  I        OR  03    1 CD                                                 SSS08C
0012    02-140  I        OR  04    1 CC                                                 SSS08C
0013    02-150  I                                             2  30 TRNREC              SSS08C
0014    02-160  I                                             2   50CUSTNO  M1          SSS08C
0015    02-170  I                                             6  21 NAME       02       SSS08C
0016    02-180  I                                            22  272NEWBAL     02       SSS08C
0017    02-190  I                                             6  112PYMNT      04       SSS08C
        03-010  C*                                                                      SSS08C
        03-020  C********************** CALCULATIONS ***********************************SSS08C
        03-030  C*                                                                      SSS08C
0018    03-040  C   04 MR   BALDUE     SUB  PYMNT     NEWBAL                            SSS08C
0019    03-050  C   02NMR              Z-ADDO         BALDUE                            SSS08C
        04-010  C*                                                                      SSS08C
        04-020  O************************HEADING LINES *********************************SSS08C
        04-030  C*                                                                      SSS08C
0020    04-040  OPRNTOUT H  201    1P                                                   SSS08C
0021    04-050  C        OR        OF                                                   SSS08C
0022    04-060  O                            UDATE Y    10                              SSS08C
0023    04-070  O                                       96 'PAGE'                       SSS08C
0024    04-080  O                            PAGE      102                              SSS08C
0025    04-090  C          H 22    1P                                                   SSS08C
0026    04-100  O        CR        OF                                                   SSS08C
0027    04-110  C                                       14 'CUSTOMER ID'                SSS08C
0028    04-120  C                                       33 'CUSTOMER NAME'              SSS08C
0029    04-130  O                                       51 'OLD BALANCE'                SSS08C
0030    04-140  C                                       63 'PAYMENT'                    SSS08C
0031    04-150  C                                       80 'NEW BALANCE'                SSS08C
0032    04-160  O                                       92 'MESSAGE'                    SSS08C
        04-170  O*                                                                      SSS08C
        05-010  O********************** DETAIL LINES ***********************************SSS08C
        05-020  C*                                                                      SSS08C
0033    05-030  O          D  1     MR 04                                               SSS08C
0034    05-040  O        CR         MR 03                                               SSS08C
0035    05-050  O        CR            02                                               SSS08C
0036    05-060  O                            CUSTNO      9                              SSS08C
0037    05-070  C                            NAME       35                              SSS08C
0038    05-080  O                            BALDUE1    48 '$'                          SSS08C
0039    05-090  C                         04 PYMNT 1    63 '$'                          SSS08C
0040    05-100  O                         04 NEWBAL1    77 '$'                          SSS08C
0041    05-110  O                       MR 03           98 'RECORD DELETED'             SSS08C
0042    05-120  O                      NMR 02           96 'RECORD ADDED'               SSS08C
0043    05-130  O                      NMR 02NEWBAL1    77 '$'                          SSS08C
0044    05-140  O                       MR 02          100 'MASTER EXISTS FOR'          SSS08C
0045    05-150  C                       MR 02          110 'NEW ACCT.'                  SSS08C
0046    05-160  O          D  1    NMR 03                                               SSS08C
0047    05-170  C        CR        NMR 04                                               SSS08C
0048    05-180  C                            CUSTNO      9                              SSS08C
0049    05-190  O                                      100 'NO MASTER RECORD'           SSS08C
        05-200  C*                                                                      SSS08C
        06-010  O*                                                                      SSS08C
        06-020  O************************* WRITE NEW MASTER FILE ******************** SSS08C
        06-030  O*                                                                      SSS08C
0050    06-040  ONEWMSTR D          MR 04                                               SSS08C
0051    06-050  C                                        1 'M'                          SSS08C
0052    06-060  O                            CUSTNO      5                              SSS08C
0053    06-070  O                            NAME       21                              SSS08C
0054    06-080  O                            NEWBAL     27                              SSS08C
0055    06-090  C                                       30 '    '                       SSS08C
0056    06-100  O          D       NMR 01                                               SSS08C
0057    06-110  O        CR         MR 02                                               SSS08C
0058    06-120  O                            MSTREC     30                              SSS08C
0059    06-130  O          D       NMR 02                                               SSS08C
0060    06-140  C                                        1 'M'                          SSS08C
0061    06-150  C                            TRNREC     30                              SSS08C

E N D   O F   S O U R C E
```

Event	*Indicators*	*Action to be Taken*
A master record is to be changed by a transaction record.	MR, Ø4	Subtract amount of payment from balance due on master and create a new master record.
A master record exists, but there is no corresponding transaction record.	NMR, Ø1	A master record is to be copied on new master as is—no change to the record is necessary.
A record is to be deleted from the master file.	MR, Ø3	No record is written to the new master.

The following indicates the action to be taken when various error conditions occur.

Error Condition	*Indicators*	*Action*
A transaction record with a code of "C" indicates that a change exists, but there is no corresponding master record.	NMR, Ø4	Print error message "NO MASTER RECORD"
A transaction record exists with a code of "D" meaning deletion, but there is no matching master record.	NMR, Ø3	Print error message "NO MASTER RECORD"
A transaction record with a code of "A" denoting addition matches an existing master.	MR, Ø2	Print error message "MASTER EXISTS FOR NEW ACCT."

A summary of these conditions is presented in Figure 8.12. This summary will assist you in understanding what action is necessary for the various conditions that may exist in the program.

Figure 8.12
Summary of actions to be taken in sample program.

Activity	*Change*	*(No Change) Copy*	*Add Record*	*Delete Record*	*Error Conditions*		
Indicators	MR Ø4	NMR Ø1	NMR Ø2	MR Ø3	NMR Ø4	NMR Ø3	MR Ø2
Print Report Line	YES	NO	YES	YES	YES	YES	YES
Message to Print	—	—	"RECORD ADDED"	"RECORD DELETED"	"NO MASTER RECORD" (FOR UPDATE)	"NO MASTER RECORD" (TO DELETE)	"MASTER EXISTS FOR NEW ACCOUNT"
Write New Master	WRITE UPDATED MASTER RECORD	WRITE MASTER RECORD (NO CHANGE)	WRITE TRANS-ACTION RECORD	NO	NO	NO	WRITE MASTER RECORD

Sequence Checking

By assigning a matching indicator (M1-M9) to a field, a file may be checked to ensure that it is in sequential order. If, during the program run, any record is found out of sequence, RPG II will set on a **halt indicator (HØ)** and the program will terminate. Frequently, the programmer only needs an error message printed while bypassing the writing of the record to the new master. In this case, the program is not to terminate when a record is out of sequence. This can be accomplished as shown in Figure 8.13.

RPG CALCULATION SPECIFICATIONS

Program | Programmer | Date | Keying Instruction: Graphic / Key | Card Electro Number | Page 1 2 of | Program Identification 75 76 77 78 79 80

Line (3-5)	Form Type (6)	Control Level (LO–L9, LR, SR, AN/OR) (7-8)	Indicators (9-17)	Factor 1 (18-27)	Operation (28-32)	Factor 2 (33-42)	Result Field Name (43-48)	Length (49-51)	Decimal Positions (52)	Half Adjust (H) (53)	Resulting Indicators: Plus / High 1>2 (54-55)	Minus / Low 1<2 (56-57)	Zero / Equal 1=2 (58-59)	Comments (60-74)
0 1 Ø	C		HØ		SETON						25			May be used to condition error message
0 2 Ø	C		HØ		SETOF						HØ			
0 3	C													
0 4	C													

Figure 8.13
Use of halt indicator to condition an error message.

As indicated earlier, sequence checking can also be performed in the calculation section of the program. The programmer may elect to code the sequence checking routine or to use the matching record sequence technique. If the programmer wishes to terminate the program when an out-of-sequence condition is found, this can be accomplished by turning on the last record indicator (LR) with a **SETON instruction**. Whenever possible, the programmer should provide error messages in order that the user be made aware of the reason why a program terminates.

II. Processing Multiple-Transaction Records with the Same Key Field

In many applications, there may exist more than one transaction record for a given master. Suppose the master file consists of accounts receivable records that include the fields customer number (CUSTNO) and balance due (BALDUE). Each time the customer makes a purchase, a transaction record is created that includes CUSTNO and amount of purchase (AMTPUR), which could be negative for a credit. AMTPUR, then, must be added to BALDUE for the customer.

It is possible that there will be more than one transaction record for the master since a customer can conceivably purchase more than one item during the update period. Consider the following.

MASTER MCUSTNO	TRANSACTION TCUSTNO
	ØØØ4
ØØØ4	
	ØØØ4
ØØØ5	ØØØ5

To simply use MR indicators in this example would produce incorrect results, since the second transaction record with the same CUSTNO would create a duplicate master record.

When there may be multiple-transaction records for a given master record, use the same matching record concept but also include a *control break* on the key field to indicate when the output master record is to be produced. That is, the output master record is not created until a control break on the key field has occurred. Also use the master file as the primary and the transaction file as the secondary.

The M1 indicator is still used on the Input Specifications form to signal matching records, but L1 is also coded for control break processing.

Consider a master file with the following fields.

```
 2–5  CUSTNO
 6–21 NAME
22–26 BALDUE
```

A transaction record exists for every purchase made by the customer.

```
2–5  CNUMB
6–11 AMTPUR
```

The File Description Specifications form is shown here.

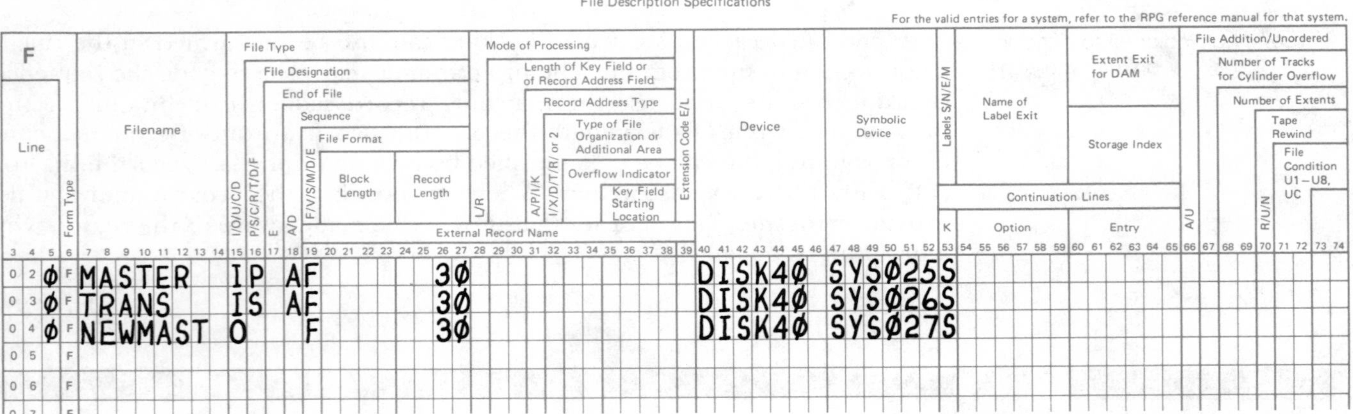

File Description Specifications

For the valid entries for a system, refer to the RPG reference manual for that system.

Line	Form Type	Filename	File Type	File Designation	End of File	Sequence	File Format	Block Length	Record Length	Device	Symbolic Device	Labels S/N/E/M
02∅	F	MASTER	I	P		A	F		3∅	DISK4∅	SYS∅25	S
03∅	F	TRANS	I	S		A	F		3∅	DISK4∅	SYS∅26	S
04∅	F	NEWMAST	O				F		3∅	DISK4∅	SYS∅27	S
05	F											
06	F											

Both the master and the transaction files are in sequence by customer number. There may be numerous transactions for each master record. The Input Specifications includes M1 *along with* an L1 indicator for CNUMB.

Assume that record identifying indicator Ø1 has been assigned to the primary file, which is the master in this instance. Indicator Ø2 is used with the secondary file, which is the transaction file.

RPG INPUT SPECIFICATIONS

Line	Form Type	Filename or Record Name	Sequence	Record Identifying Indicator	Position	C/Z/D	Character	From	To	Decimal Positions	RPG Field Name	Control Level (L1–L9)	Matching Fields or Chaining Fields
01	I	MASTER	AA	Ø1	1	C	M						
02	I							1	3Ø		MSTREC		
03	I							2	5	Ø	CNUMB	L1	M1
04	I							6	21		NAME		
05	I							22	26	2	BALDUE		
06	I	TRANS	BB	Ø2	1	C	C						
07	I							2	3Ø		TRNREC		
08	I							2	5	Ø	CUSTNO		M1
09	I							6	11	2	AMTPUR		
10	I												
11	I												
12	I												

If a master record is read and no match is found, the indicators L1, Ø1, and NMR will be turned on. Thus L1, Ø1, and NMR are used to condition the copying of the master record because no updating is required. When a master record is read and there are transactions to be posted, the matching record indicators, MR and Ø1, would both be automatically set on. When the transaction records are read, both the MR and Ø2 indicators are on. Therefore, indicators MR and Ø2 can be used to perform typical update calculations directly on the master record as follows.

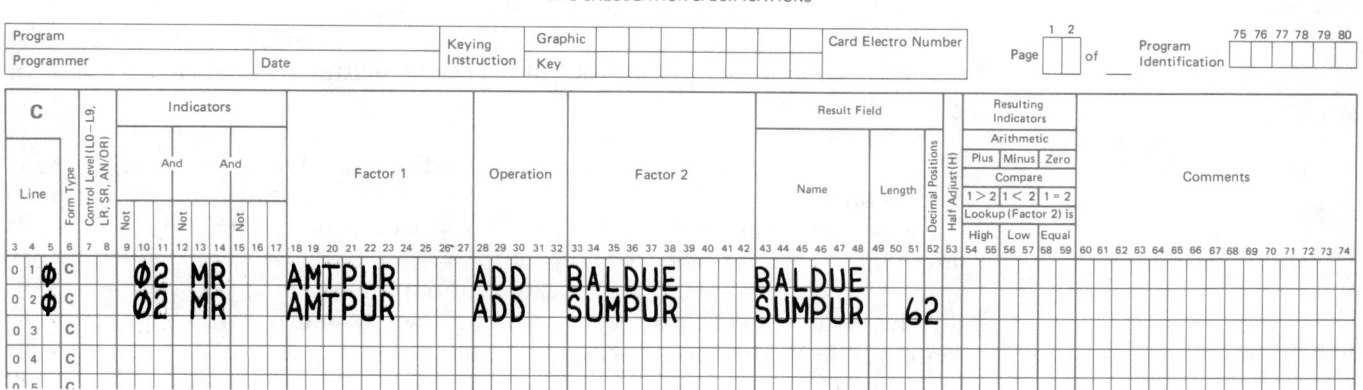

RPG CALCULATION SPECIFICATIONS

Line	Form Type	Indicators		Factor 1	Operation	Factor 2	Result Field Name	Length	Decimal Positions
01	C	Ø2	MR	AMTPUR	ADD	BALDUE	BALDUE		
02	C	Ø2	MR	AMTPUR	ADD	SUMPUR	SUMPUR	6	2
03	C								
04	C								
05	C								

Figure 8.14
Condition of indicators as sample data is processed.

Indicators L1	Ø1	Ø2	MR	*Master File*	*Trans File*	*Action Required*
L1	Ø1		NMR	ADAMS		COPY (DETAIL OUTPUT)
L1	Ø1		MR	BROWN		
		Ø2	MR		BROWN	
		Ø2	MR		BROWN	
L1	Ø1		MR	CHASE		UPDATE BROWN (TOTAL OUTPUT)
		Ø2	MR		CHASE	
L1	Ø1		NMR	DAVIS		UPDATE CHASE (TOTAL OUTPUT) COPY DAVIS (DETAIL OUTPUT)
L1	Ø1		MR	EDWARDS		
		Ø2	MR		EDWARDS	
		Ø2	MR		EDWARDS	
		Ø2	MR		EDWARDS	
L1	Ø1		NMR	FLEMING		UPDATE EDWARDS (TOTAL OUTPUT) COPY FLEMING (DETAIL OUTPUT)

RPG will continue to read the secondary file of transaction records as long as they match the master. When there is no longer a match, a new record from the primary or master file will be read and indicators L1, Ø1, and NMR will be turned on. At that point, we have not as yet written the updated record to disk. Figure 8.14 illustrates the condition of the indicators as we process the files with sample data.

On reading the new master, the L1, Ø1, and NMR indicators will be set on. Using a T or total time output operation, conditioned by an L1 break, we would then create the new output record, which has the accumulated BALDUE.

We then use the L1 indicator to condition writing the updated record during total output time. Recalling the RPG cycle, during total output time, the previous record (that is, the record that was updated), is available for processing. See Figure 8.15 for a summary of the RPG Logic Cycle.

Thus each time the L1 indicator is on, a master record is created. This master record is written using data from the previous master record and includes the transaction changes.

Refer again to Figure 8.14. Note that when BROWN's transaction records are all processed, the master will contain a new BALDUE. Where there are no more transactions for this master record, the record for CHASE is read; at that point L1 is on as well as Ø1. Since the CHASE record has not yet been moved to the input fields, we are able to write out BROWN's updated record during total output using the L1 control break to condition the output.

The BALDUE field must be specified on the Output Specifications form. To simply code MSTREC would create a duplicate of the old MSTREC. To indicate that the BALDUE of the old master record may have been changed as a result of transaction processing, you must code the following.

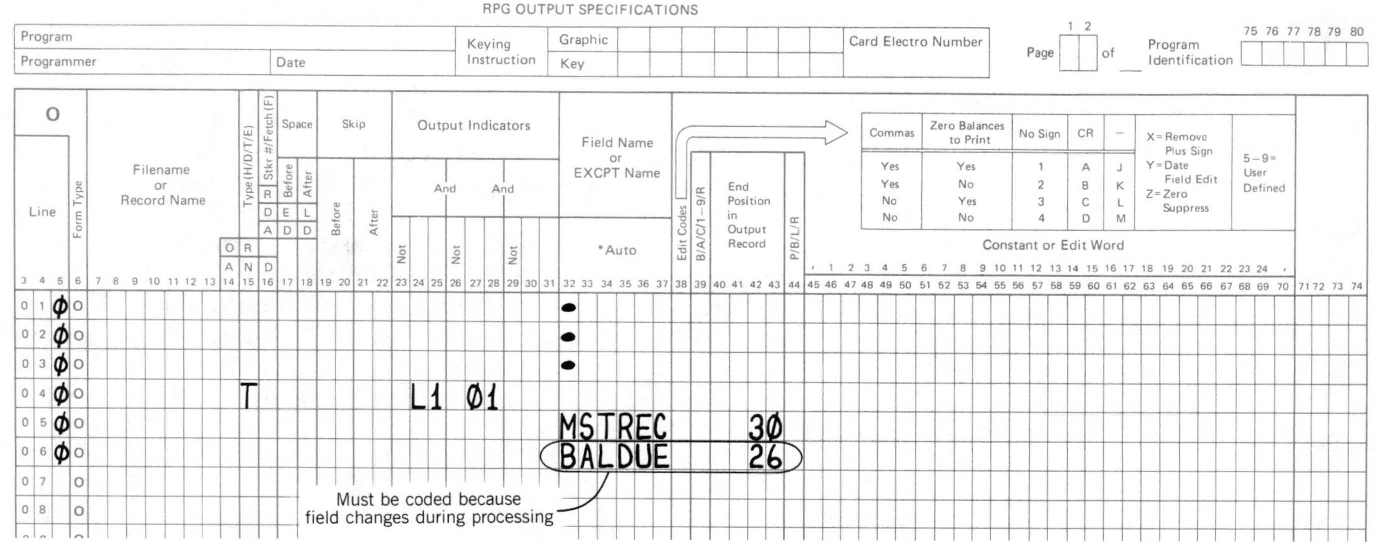

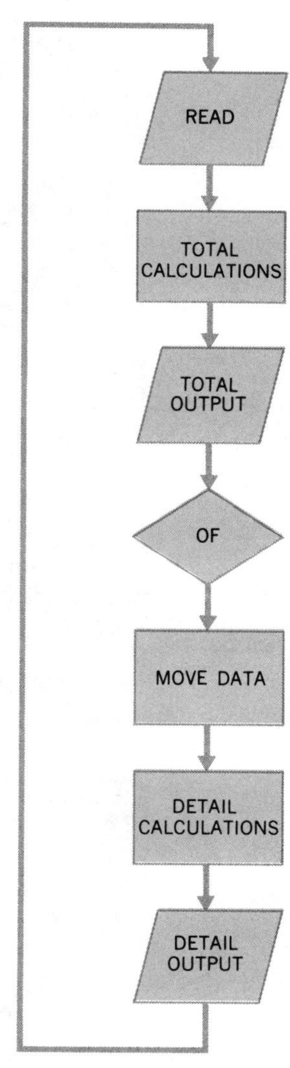

Figure 8.15
Summary of RPG Logic Cycle.

III.

Updating Sequential Disk Records in Place

Updating a master tape always means re-creating the master onto a new tape that incorporates old master information along with the transaction data. We may update a sequential master disk in exactly the same way, as we saw in the previous section. Or we may update a disk record in place. That is, we access the disk record that requires changes, make the changes and write the record back into its original location.

To do this we do *not* need a master output disk. The master input disk becomes a file specified with a U in column 15 on the File Description form designating it as an input/output file to be updated. The output specifications would include the name of this master disk so that it is associated with detail-time output.

The transaction file is used as the primary file and the master disk is used as the secondary:

RPG CONTROL AND FILE DESCRIPTION SPECIFICATIONS

Control Specifications

```
01H
```

File Description Specifications

```
  02ØFMASTER  US AF       3Ø           DISK4Ø SYSØ25S
  03ØFTRANS   IP AF       3Ø           DISK4Ø SYSØ26S
  04 F
  05 F
  06 F
```

All other processing, including matching record indicators, would be the same as above.

IV.

Coding a Program to Only Add Records to a File

The coding just presented is adequate if changes are to be made. If, however, you only wish to add records directly to a master file, slightly different processing is required. If records are added to the end of a sequential file, it would then be necessary to sort the file for it to be in proper sequence by key field.

It is not feasible to add records in sequence to a sequential file. You cannot "squeeze" them between existing records. Thus records to be added will be placed at the end of the file. As noted, after processing the additions, a sort procedure will be required to reorder the file into the correct sequence.

The coding in Figure 8.16 would be used to add records to a master file, without re-creating the file onto a new device.

Note that this add procedure is not available to IBM users who have the operating system referred to as DOS (Disk Operating System).

V.

Coding a Program to Physically Delete Records from a File

To delete records using a standard update procedure requires maintaining a master file where each record has an activity or delete code field. Active records are specified with one value in the code field; inactive records to be deleted have a different value. When a record is to be deleted, you cannot "erase" it from the disk, so you include a delete code that designates the record as inactive.

At some point, an additional program would be required to read from the master disk and write a new master disk that eliminates the records designated as inactive. This is referred to as a **file clean-up procedure**.

If a master record has a status of "A" for active, you would re-create it on a new, "clean" master file. If a master record has a status of "I" for inactive, you would not write it on the new "clean" master. At the end of this file clean-up procedure, you would have a master file with all active records.

Figure 8.16
Coding to add records to a master file.
(Continued on next page.)

RPG CONTROL AND FILE DESCRIPTION SPECIFICATIONS

Program | Keying Instruction | Graphic | Card Electro Number | Page 1 2 of | Program Identification 75 76 77 78 79 80
Programmer | Date | Key

Control Specifications

For the valid entries for a system, refer to the RPG reference manual for that system.

Line (3–5)	Form Type (6)
01	H

File Description Specifications

For the valid entries for a system, refer to the RPG reference manual for that system.

Line (3–5)	Form Type (6)	Filename (7–14)	File Type (15)	File Designation (16)	Mode/Format (19)	Block Length (20–23)	Record Length (24–27)	Device (40–46)	Symbolic Device (47–52)	Labels S/N/E/M (53)	A/U (66)
020	F	TRANSIN	I	P	F	180	30	DISK40	SYS025	S	
030	F	MASTER	O		F	180	30	DISK40	SYS025	S	A
04	F										
05	F										

Ⓐ To indicate that records will be added to the file

RPG INPUT SPECIFICATIONS

```
     I Filename/   Seq  Rec.Id  Record Identification Codes   Field Location        RPG
Line   Record Name      Ind.    Position  C/Z/D  Character    From   To  Dec.  Field Name
0 1 ØI TRANSIN     AA   Ø1          1       C      A
0 2 ØI                                                           2    5  Ø     CUSTNO
0 3 ØI                                                           6   21        NAME
0 4 ØI                                                          22   27  2     BALDUE
0 5  I
0 6  I
0 7  I
0 8  I
```

RPG OUTPUT SPECIFICATIONS

```
     O Filename/   Type  Output       Field Name/   End
Line   Record Name       Indicators   EXCPT Name    Position
0 1 ØO MASTER      DADD  Ø1
0 2 ØO                                CNUMB           5
0 3 ØO                                NAME           21
0 4 ØO                                BALDUE         27
0 5  O
0 6  O
```

Add record to master file

Figure 8.16
(continued)

Key Terms

- Control field
- Editing
- File
- Halt indicator (HØ)
- Key field
- Master file
- MR (matching record) indicator
- Primary file
- Record
- Secondary file
- Sequential access
- Sequential file
- SETON instruction
- Split matching fields
- System integrity
- Transaction file
- Update procedure

Self-Evaluating Quiz

1. During a processing run, when matching records have been processed, the (primary/secondary) file will be read next.
2. Which form specifies whether the data is in ascending or descending order?
3. Which form specifies the fields to be used for determining matching records?
4. (T or F) The matching field in the primary file must be located in the same positions as those in the secondary.
5. When assigning split matching records, would the major field be designated as M1, M2, or M3 if a major, intermediate, and minor field were used?
6. Determine the order in which the following records will be processed.

Master Records	*Transaction Records*
ØØ1	ØØ1
ØØ2	ØØ1
ØØ3	ØØ1
ØØ4	ØØ2
ØØ5	ØØ2
ØØ6	ØØ3

7. Matching record indicators may be used to condition both ________ and ________ processing.
8. Identify the errors in the following coding.

File Description Specifications

For the valid entries for a system, refer to the RPG reference manual for that system.

```
02ØFMASTER  IP AF 288  96
03ØFTRANS   IS AF      60
04ØFNEWMSTR O       96  96
05 F
06 F
07 F
```

9. Complete the Input Specification for matching the EMPNO fields that follow. The primary file (EMP) contains EMPNO (1-5), NAME (11-3Ø), RATE (32-35), with two decimal positions. The secondary file (HRSWKD) contains EMPNO (1-5), REG (7-1Ø), for regular hours, with two decimal positions, and OTHS (11-14), for overtime hours, also with two decimal positions.
10. The ________ indicator is turned on when matching records are found out of sequence.
11. The letter "A" coded in column 18 of the File Description form indicates ________ .
12. When split fields are used, the major field is assigned the *(higher/lower)* numbered matching indicator?

Solutions

1. primary
2. Column 18 (SEQUENCE ENTRY) of the File Description form.
3. Columns 61-62 (MATCHING FIELD ENTRY) of the Input form.
4. F
5. major field M3
   intermediate field M2
   minor field M1
6.

Master Records		*Transaction Records*	
Reference	*Sequence*	*Reference*	*Sequence*
ØØ1	1	ØØ1	2
ØØ2	5	ØØ1	3
ØØ3	8	ØØ1	4
ØØ4	1Ø	ØØ2	6
ØØ5	11	ØØ2	7
ØØ6	12	ØØ3	9

7. calculations output
8.

File Description Specifications

For the valid entries for a system, refer to the RPG reference manual for that system.

Line (3–5)	Form Type (6)	Filename (7–14)	File Type (15)	File Designation (16)	End of File (17)	Sequence (18)	File Format (19)	Block Length (20–23)	Record Length (24–27)
02φ	F	MASTER	I	P		A	F	288	96
03φ	F	TRAN	I	S		A	F		6φ
04φ	F	NEWMSTR	O					288	96
05	F								
06	F								

Must match old master (288)

9.

RPG INPUT SPECIFICATIONS

Line	Form Type	Filename or Record Name	Sequence	Number (1/N), E	Option (O), U, S	Record Identifying Indicator, **, or DS	From	To	Decimal Positions	RPG Field Name	Control Level (L1–L9)	Matching Fields or Chaining Fields
01Ø	I	EMP	AA			Ø1						
02Ø	I						1	5	Ø	EMPNO		M1
03Ø	I						11	3Ø		NAME		
04Ø	I						32	35	2	RATE		
05Ø	I	HRSWKD	BB			Ø2						
06Ø	I						1	5	Ø	EMPNO		M1
07Ø	I						7	1Ø	2	REG		
08Ø	I						11	14	2	OTHRS		
09	I											
10	I											
11	I											

10. HØ halt indicator
11. ascending sequence
12. higher

Review Questions

1. (T or F) Tape updating is the process of making a tape file current.
2. (T or F) Exactly two files are necessary for sequential file updating.
3. (T or F) Records on a tape or disk can be any length.
4. (T or F) Tapes may be processed randomly or sequentially.
5. (T or F) A transaction record with no corresponding master record always means an error.
6. Provide program flowcharts for the following routines.
   a. Sequential update
   b. Sequence check
   c. Merge
   d. Matching records—print only those records that do not match

Debugging Exercises

The following matching record program uses a card transaction file to update a master disk file containing a salesperson number, name, year-to-date sales, and status. If the salesperson is currently active, then the status field contains the letter "A." Inactive records contain an "I" denoting, in effect, that the record has been deactivated; it will be treated as if it had been deleted from the active file. Typically, the transaction records contain a type code of "C" for changes, "A" for additions, and "D" for deletions. A summary of the indicators and their related activities is contained in Figure 8.17. Figure 8.18 shows the problem definition for this program.

Condition	*Change Record*	*Delete Record*	*Add Record*	*No Transaction for Master*	*Error Condition*	*Error Condition*	*Error Condition*
Indicators	MR, Ø1	MR, Ø4	NMR, Ø3	NMR, Ø2	MR, Ø3	NMR, Ø1	NMR, Ø4
Message	None	"Master record deleted"	"Record added to Master"	None	"Record exists on Master"	"No Master to update"	"No master to delete"
Print Report Detail Line	No	Yes	Yes	No	Yes	Yes	Yes
Write New Master	Write updated record	Move 'I' to status and write Master	Write transaction record with "M" in position 8Ø	Copy Master	Copy Master	No	No

Notes: 1. Master record has an M in column 8Ø.
2. Transaction record has a code in column 80, where
C denotes change or update matching master record.
A denotes addition of a new salesperson.
D denotes the deletion of the record from the file by changing the *status* from "A" to "I".

Figure 8.17
Summary of the indicators and their related functions for the Debugging Exercise.

The listing in Figure 8.19 contains syntax errors. Identify them and indicate the corrections you would make to the program. The syntax corrections are circled on the computer listing shown in Figure 8.2Ø. There is, however, a logic error in the output specifications. Your assignment is to desk check the program carefully, find the logic error, and make the necessary corrections.

Figure 8.18
Problem definition for the Debugging Exercise.
(Continued on next page.)

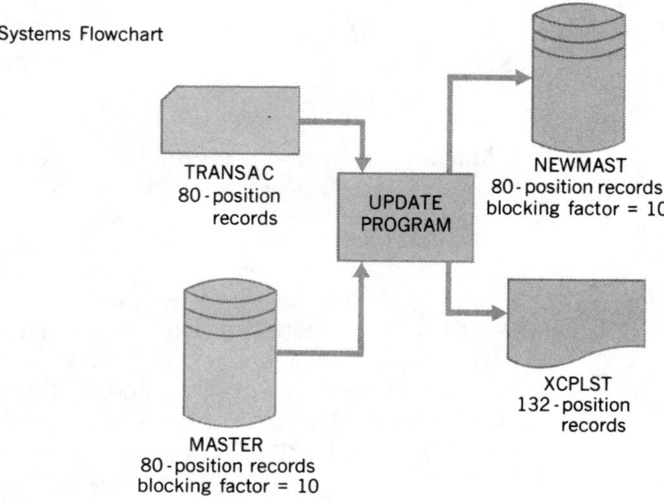

(a)

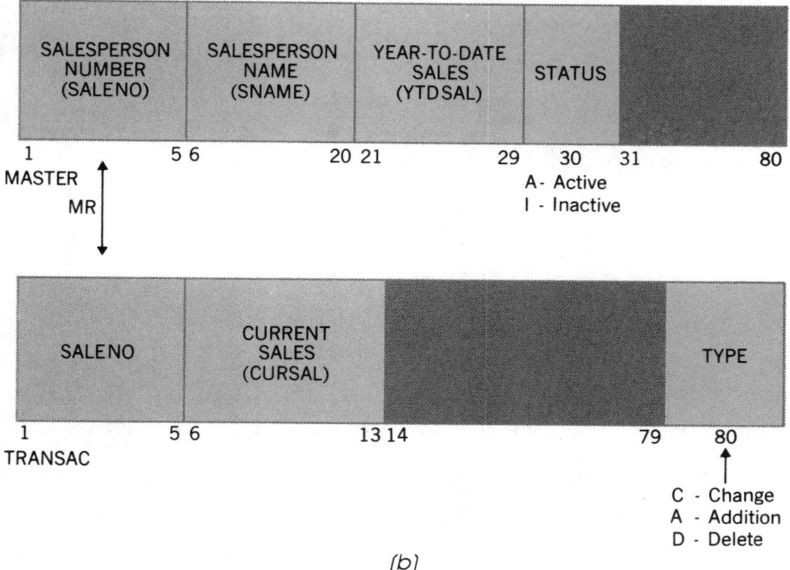

(b)

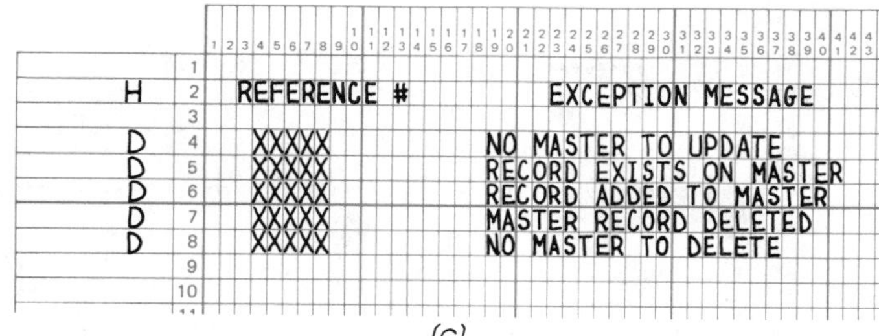

(c)

Figure 8.18 *(continued)*

Helpful Hint

Whenever a file is created by a program, always list the contents of the file with a simple list program and manually check the results. It is critical that files produced by programs be 1ØØ% accurate!

It is also advisable to use the DEBUG instruction in the preliminary runs to note the conditioning of the program indicators. This will allow the programmer to detect logic errors at an early point in program development. Since the halt indicator is set on when the records are out of sequence, or not of the type specifically handled by the program, a resulting indicator should be set on in order to print an error message. Once the resulting indicator has been set, the halt indicator must then be set off as shown in Figure 8.21.

Practice Problems

1. Using the problem definition shown in Figure 8.22, code an RPG program to produce the required results. The RPG II program should match the professor and course files in order to produce the output depicted on the Printer Spacing Chart.

Figure 8.19
Listing with syntax errors for the Debugging Exercise.

```
        01-010  F***********************************************************           SSS08
        01-020  F* THIS PRCGRAM UTILIZES A CARD TRANSACTION FILE TO UPDATE   *           SSS08
        01-030  F* A MASTER DISK FILE USIING MATCHING RECORDS TECHNIQUES     *           SSS08
        01-040  F***********************************************************           SSS08
0001    01-050  FMASTER  IP  F 800  80             DISK40 SYS025S                      SSS08
0002    01-060  FTRANSAC IS  F  80  80             READ01 SYSIPT                       SSS08
0003    01-070  FNEWMAST O   F 800  80             DISK40 SYS025S                      SSS08
0004    01-080  FXCPLST  O   F 132 132             PRINTERSYSLST                       SSS08
        02-010  I*                                                                     SSS08
        02-020  I******************** INPUT RECORDS ********************************SSS08
        02-030  I*                                                                     SSS08
0005    02-040  IMASTER  AA  02  80 CM                                                 SSS08
0006    02-050  I                                           1  80 MSTREC               SSS08
0007    02-060  I                                           1   5 SALENO  MR           SSS08
                                                                          $                      MSG  119
0008    02-070  I                                           6  20 SNAME                SSS08
0009    02-080  I                                          21  292YTDSAL               SSS08
0010    02-090  I                                          30  30 STATUS               SSS08
0011    02-100  ITRANSAC BB  01  80 CC                                                 SSS08
0012    02-110  I        OR  03  80 CA                                                 SSS08
0013    02-120  I        OR  04  80 CD                                                 SSS08
0014    02-130  I                                           1  80 TRNREC               SSS08
0015    02-140  I                                           1   5 SALENO  MR           SSS08
                                                                          $                      MSG  119
0016    02-150  I                                           6  132CURSAL               SSS08
0017    02-160  I                                          80  80 TYPE                 SSS08
        03-010  C************************************************************          SSS08
        03-020  C* UPDATE THE YEAR-TC-DATE SALES WITH THE CURRENT SALES      *          SSS08
        03-030  C************************************************************          SSS08
0018    03-040  C   MR 01   YTDSAL    ADD  CURSAL    CURSAL  92                        SSS08
        04-010  C*                                                                     SSS08
        04-020  O********************** WRITE OUTPUT FILE *************************SSS08
        C4-030  C*                                                                     SSS08
0019    04-040  ONEWMAST D        NMR 02                                               SSS08
0020    04-050  O        OR        MR 03                                               SSS08
0021    04-060  O                           MSTREC     80                              SSS08
0022    04-070  O          D      NMR 03                                               SSS08
0023    04-080  O                           TRNREC     80                              SSS08
0024    04-090  C                                      80 'M'                          SSS08
0025    04-100  O          D       MR 01                                               SSS08
0026    04-110  C                           MSTREC     80                              SSS08
0027    04-120  C                           YTDSAL     29                              SSS08
0028    04-130  O          D       MR 04                                               SSS08
0029    04-140  C                           MSTREC     80                              SSS08
0030    04-150  C                                      30 'I'                          SSS08
        05-010  O*                                                                     SSS08
        05-020  O****************** HEADINGS FOR EXCEPTION REPORT ******************SSS08
        05-030  O*                                                                     SSS08
0031    05-040  OXCPLST  H  201   1P                                                   SSS08
0032    05-050  C                                      13 'REFERENCE #'                SSS08
0033    05-060  O                                      39 'EXCEPTION MESSAGE'          SSS08
        05-070  O*                                                                     SSS08
        05-080  O********************** DETAIL LINES *******************************SSS08
        05-090  O*                                                                     SSS08
0034    05-100  C          D  1   NMR 01                                               SSS08
0035    05-110  O        OR       NMR 03                                               SSS08
0036    05-120  O        OR       NMR 04                                               SSS08
0037    05-130  C                           SALENO      8                              SSS08
        05-140  C*                                                                     SSS08
        05-150  O****************** MESSAGES TC BE PRINTED *************************SSS08
        05-160  O*                                                                     SSS08
0038    05-170  O                 NMR 01               37 'NO MASTER TO UPDATE'        SSS08
0039    05-180  O                  MR 03               41 'RECORD EXISTS ON MASTER'    SSS08
0040    05-190  O                 NMR 03               40 'RECORD ADDED TO MASTER'     SSS08
0041    05-200  O                  MR 04               39 'MASTER RECORD DELETED'      SSS08
0042    05-210  O                 NMR 04               37 'NO MASTER TO DELETE'        SSS08

     E N D  O F  S C U R C E


     C O M P I L E R   D I A G N O S T I C S   S U M M A R Y


ILN119   MATCH/CHAIN ENTRY IN PCSITIONS 61-62 IS INVALID. ASSUME M FOR 61, 1 FOR 62.

          0007    02-060     SALENO
          0015    02-140     SALENO

ILN393   RESULT FIELD DEFINED WITH DIFFERENT ATTRIBUTES. FIRST DEFINITION IS USED.

          0018    03-040     CURSAL

ILN397   DUPLICATE NAME DEFINED WITH INCOMPATIBLE ATTRIBUTES. FIRST DEFINITION IS USED.

          0016    02-150     CURSAL
          0018    03-040     CURSAL
          0018    03-040     CURSAL

ILN399   STRUCTURE, SUBFIELD, OR FIELD NAME UNREFERENCED. WARNING.

                             0008                  SNAME                                 MSG  399
                             0010                  STATUS                                MSG  399
                             0017                  TYPE                                  MSG  399
```

Figure 8.20
Listing with logic errors for the Debugging Exercise.

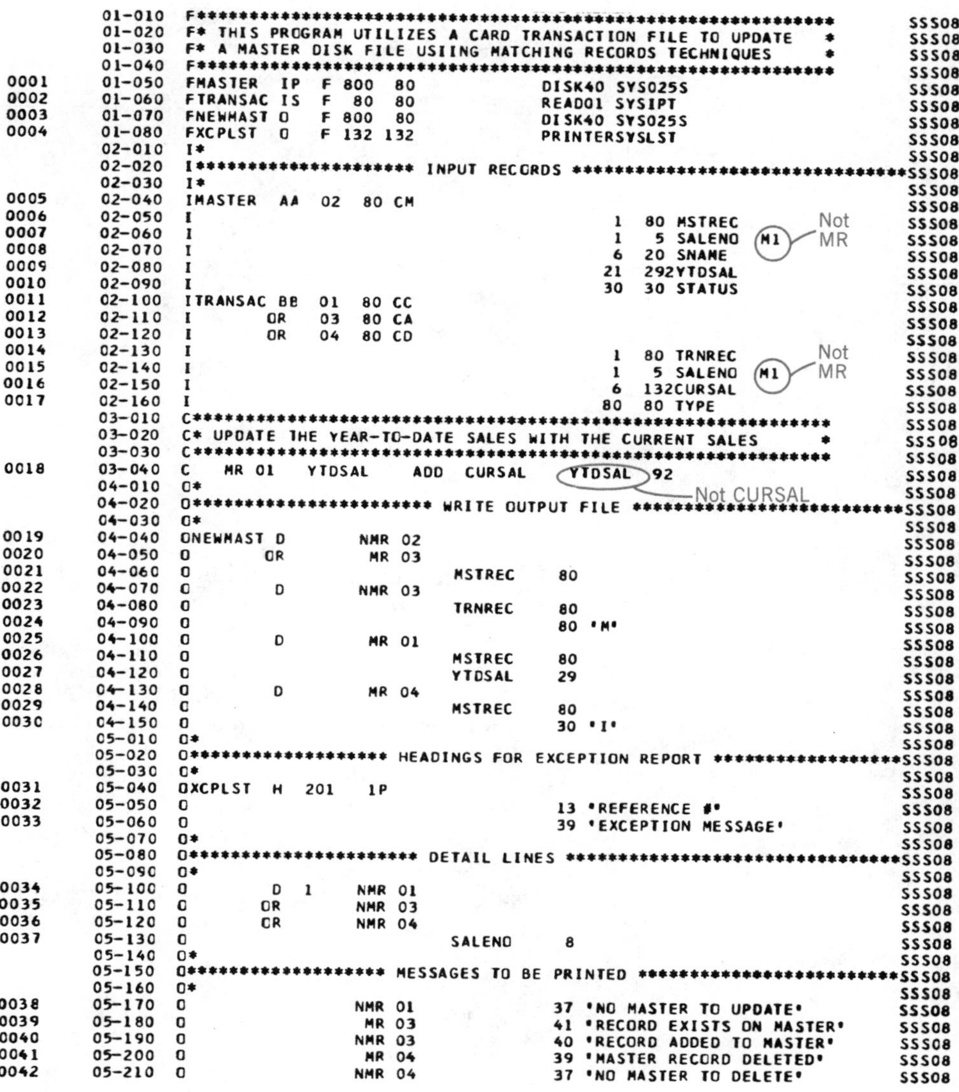

```
          01-010  F***************************************************************        SSS08
          01-020  F* THIS PROGRAM UTILIZES A CARD TRANSACTION FILE TO UPDATE       *        SSS08
          01-030  F* A MASTER DISK FILE USIING MATCHING RECORDS TECHNIQUES         *        SSS08
          01-040  F***************************************************************        SSS08
0001      01-050  FMASTER  IP  F 800  80             DISK40 SYS025S                        SSS08
0002      01-060  FTRANSAC IS  F  80  80             READ01 SYSIPT                         SSS08
0003      01-070  FNEWMAST O   F 800  80             DISK40 SYS025S                        SSS08
0004      01-080  FXCPLST  O   F 132 132             PRINTERSYSLST                         SSS08
          02-010  I*                                                                      SSS08
          02-020  I********************** INPUT RECORDS ******************************SSS08
          02-030  I*                                                                      SSS08
0005      02-040  IMASTER  AA  02  80 CM                                                  SSS08
0006      02-050  I                                        1  80 MSTREC                   SSS08
0007      02-060  I                                        1   5 SALENO  M1               SSS08
0008      02-070  I                                        6  20 SNAME                    SSS08
0009      02-080  I                                       21  292YTDSAL                   SSS08
0010      02-090  I                                       30  30 STATUS                   SSS08
0011      02-100  ITRANSAC BB  01  80 CC                                                  SSS08
0012      02-110  I        OR  03  80 CA                                                  SSS08
0013      02-120  I        OR  04  80 CD                                                  SSS08
0014      02-130  I                                        1  80 TRNREC                   SSS08
0015      02-140  I                                        1   5 SALENO  M1               SSS08
0016      02-150  I                                        6  132CURSAL                   SSS08
0017      02-160  I                                       80  80 TYPE                     SSS08
          03-010  C***************************************************************        SSS08
          03-020  C* UPDATE THE YEAR-TO-DATE SALES WITH THE CURRENT SALES          *        SSS08
          03-030  C***************************************************************        SSS08
0018      03-040  C   MR 01   YTDSAL    ADD  CURSAL    YTDSAL  92                          SSS08
          04-010  O*                                                                      SSS08
          04-020  O************************ WRITE OUTPUT FILE ************************SSS08
          04-030  O*                                                                      SSS08
0019      04-040  ONEWMAST D        NMR 02                                                SSS08
0020      04-050  O        OR        MR 03                                                SSS08
0021      04-060  O                           MSTREC    80                                SSS08
0022      04-070  O         D       NMR 03                                                SSS08
0023      04-080  O                           TRNREC    80                                SSS08
0024      04-090  O                                     80 'M'                            SSS08
0025      04-100  O         D        MR 01                                                SSS08
0026      04-110  O                           MSTREC    80                                SSS08
0027      04-120  O                           YTDSAL    29                                SSS08
0028      04-130  O         D        MR 04                                                SSS08
0029      04-140  O                           MSTREC    80                                SSS08
0030      04-150  O                                     30 'I'                            SSS08
          05-010  O*                                                                      SSS08
          05-020  O******************* HEADINGS FOR EXCEPTION REPORT ******************SSS08
          05-030  O*                                                                      SSS08
0031      05-040  OXCPLST  H  201   1P                                                    SSS08
0032      05-050  O                                     13 'REFERENCE #'                  SSS08
0033      05-060  O                                     39 'EXCEPTION MESSAGE'            SSS08
          05-070  O*                                                                      SSS08
          05-080  O*********************** DETAIL LINES **************************SSS08
          05-090  O*                                                                      SSS08
0034      05-100  O         D  1    NMR 01                                                SSS08
0035      05-110  O        OR       NMR 03                                                SSS08
0036      05-120  O        OR       NMR 04                                                SSS08
0037      05-130  O                           SALENO     8                                SSS08
          05-140  O*                                                                      SSS08
          05-150  O******************* MESSAGES TO BE PRINTED ************************SSS08
          05-160  O*                                                                      SSS08
0038      05-170  O                 NMR 01              37 'NO MASTER TO UPDATE'          SSS08
0039      05-180  O                  MR 03              41 'RECORD EXISTS ON MASTER'      SSS08
0040      05-190  O                 NMR 03              40 'RECORD ADDED TO MASTER'       SSS08
0041      05-200  O                  MR 04              39 'MASTER RECORD DELETED'        SSS08
0042      05-210  O                 NMR 04              37 'NO MASTER TO DELETE'          SSS08

     E N D  O F  S O U R C E
```



```
REFERENCE #          EXCEPTION MESSAGE

 00450           NO MASTER TO DELETE
 00550           NO MASTER TO UPDATE
 00850           RECORD ADDED TO MASTER
```

The following messages are missing:
← Record exists on master
Master record deleted

RPG CALCULATION SPECIFICATIONS

Line	Form Type	Control Level	Indicators	Factor 1	Operation	Factor 2	Result Field	Resulting Indicators (High)
01Ø	C		HØ		SETON			25
02Ø	C		HØ		SETOF			HØ
03	C							
04	C							
05	C							

Figure 8.21
Setting off the halt indicator in the Debugging Exercise.

2. Using the problem definition shown in Figure 8.23, code an RPG program to produce the required results.

   Notes

   1. For every transaction (PAYROLL) record, update the annual salary on the master with the newly assigned annual salary on the transaction.
   2. If a record exists on the transaction file, PAYROLL, but does not exist on the master, print the name and an error message.
   3. At the end of the job, print the total number of transaction and master records processed.

3. Using the problem definition shown in Figure 8.24, code an RPG program to produce the required results.

   Notes

   1. Each record from the TRANS file must match a record on the MASTER file. If not, print an error message.
   2. There may be more than one TRANS record for a given MASTER.
   3. The output BALDUE is equal to the sum of all purchases minus the sum of all credits.
   4. Each file is in sequence by ACCTNO.

4. Using the problem definition shown in Figure 8.25, code an RPG program to produce the required results.

   Notes

   1. Both input files are in sequence by transaction number.
   2. Output is to combine both input files into one file in transaction number sequence.
   3. Transaction numbers for each file must be unique; if a record exists on one input file with the same TRANNO as the other, this is an error.

Figure 8.22 Problem definition for Practice Problem 1.

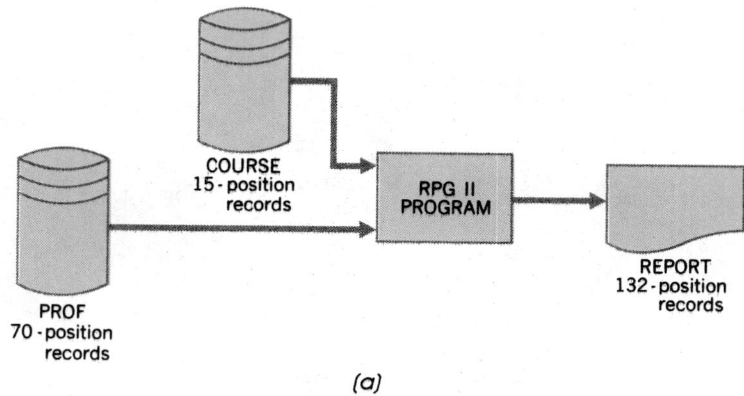

(a)

PROF Record Layout

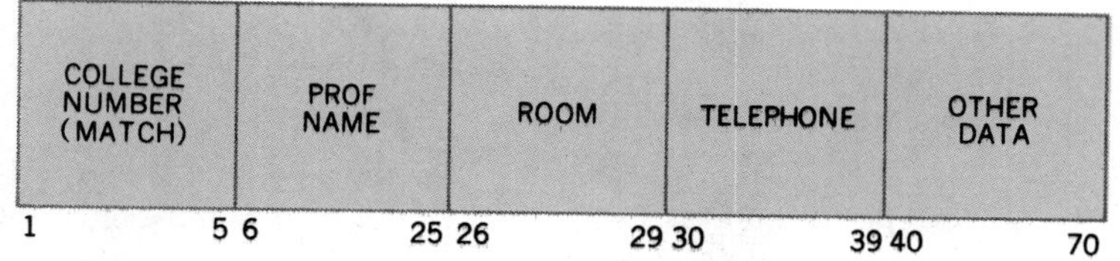

COURSE Record Layout

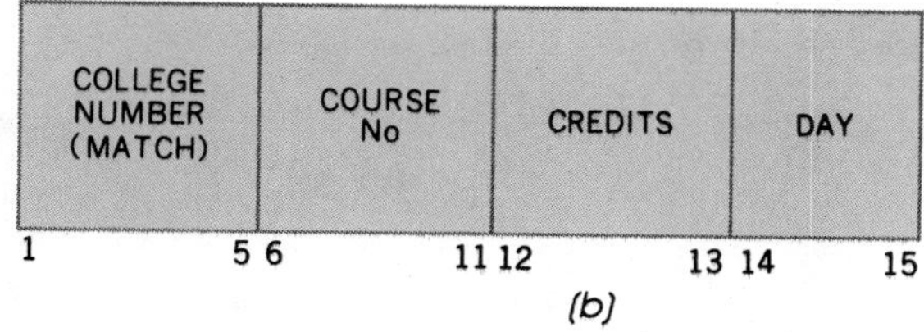

(b)

REPORT Printer Spacing Chart

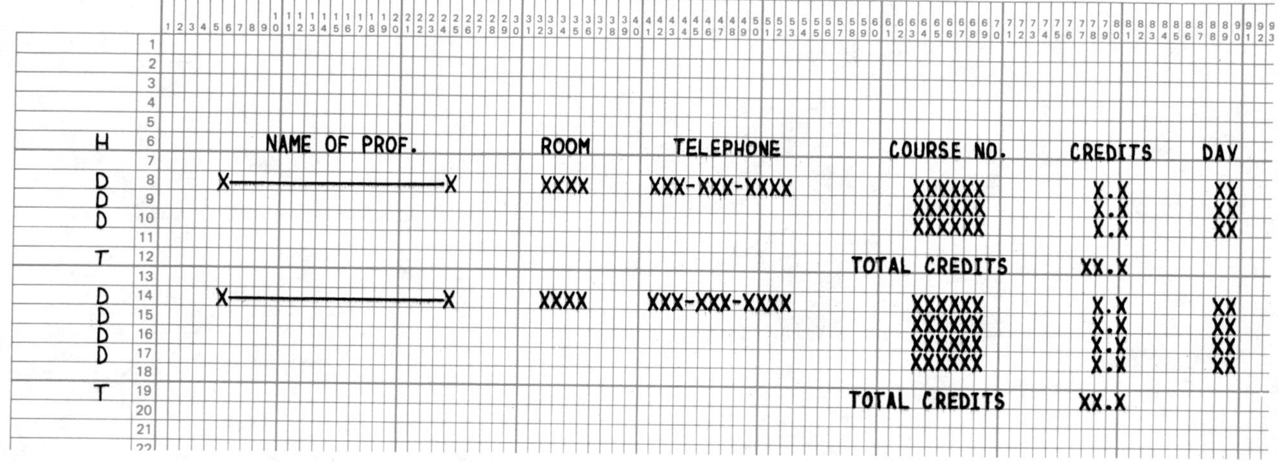

(c)

Figure 8.23 Problem definition for Practice Problem 2.

Systems Flowchart

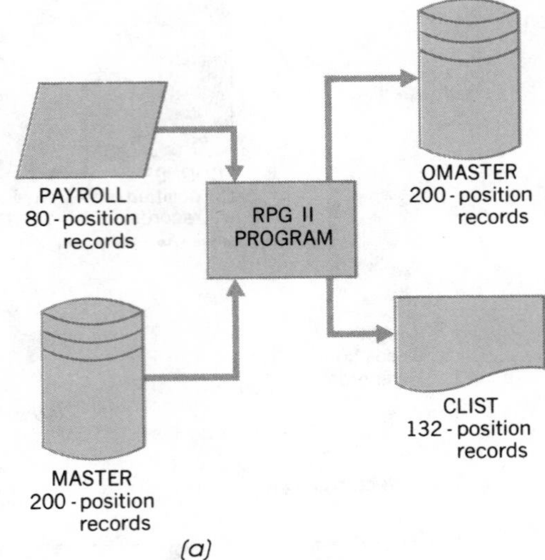

(a)

Payroll Record Layout

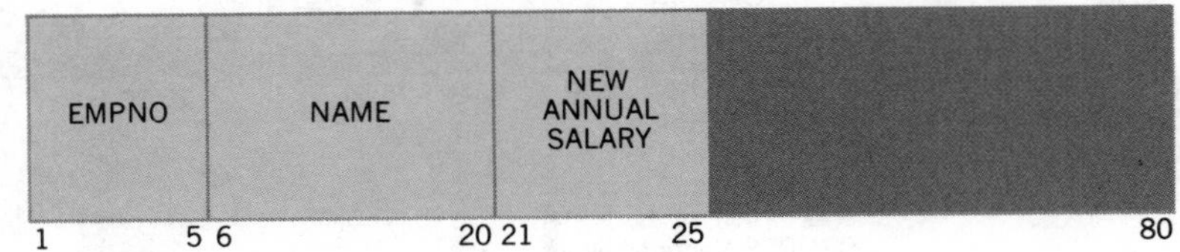

MASTER and OMASTER have the same format

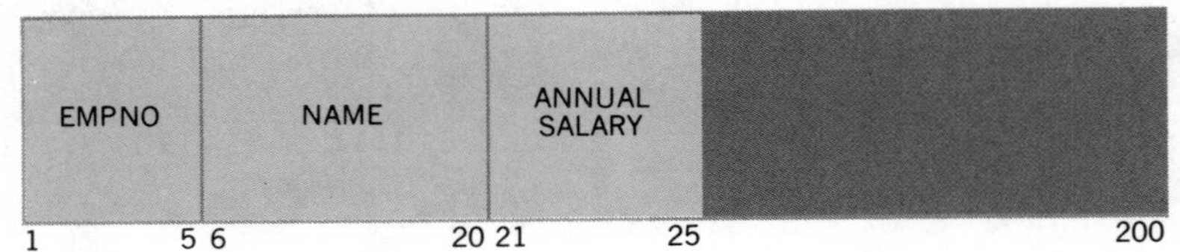

Records are blocked 20 with standard labels

(b)

CLIST Printer Spacing Chart

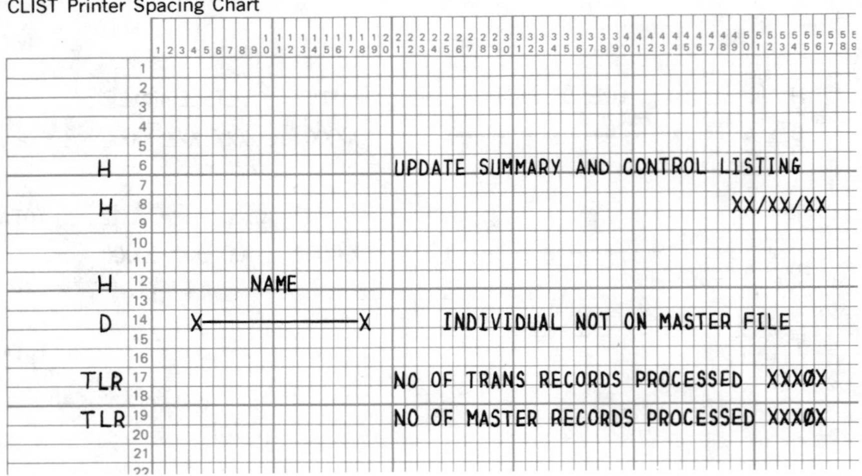

(c)

Figure 8.24 Problem definition for Practice Problem 3.

Systems Flowchart

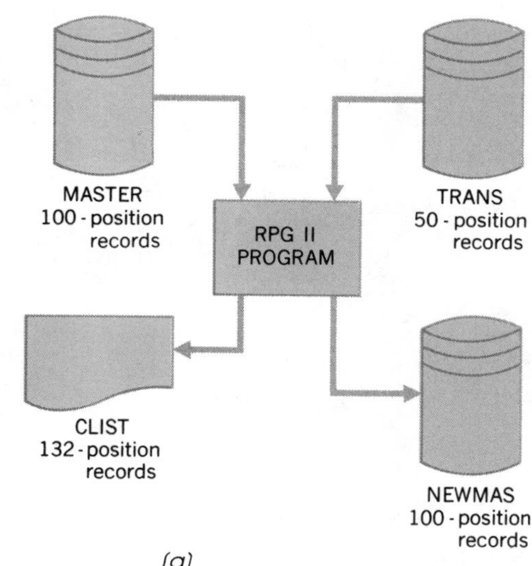

(a)

MASTER (and NEWMAS) Record Layout

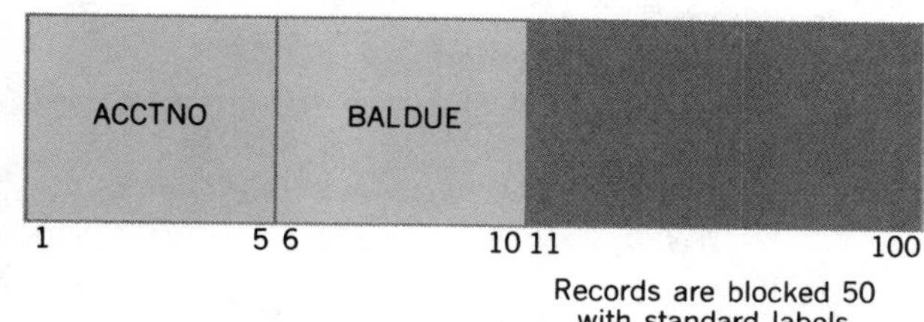

Records are blocked 50 with standard labels

TRANS Record Layout

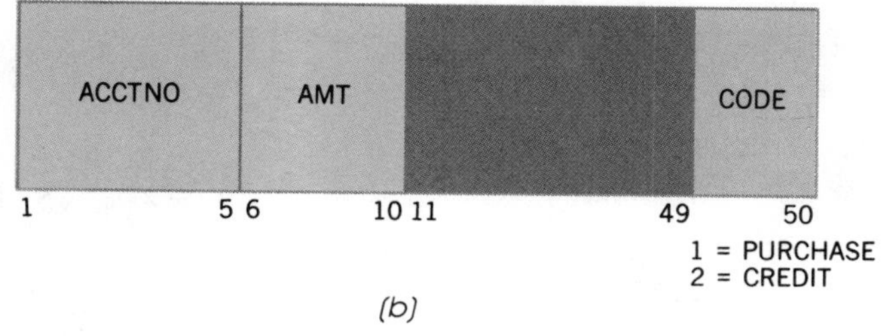

(b)

CLIST Printer Spacing Chart

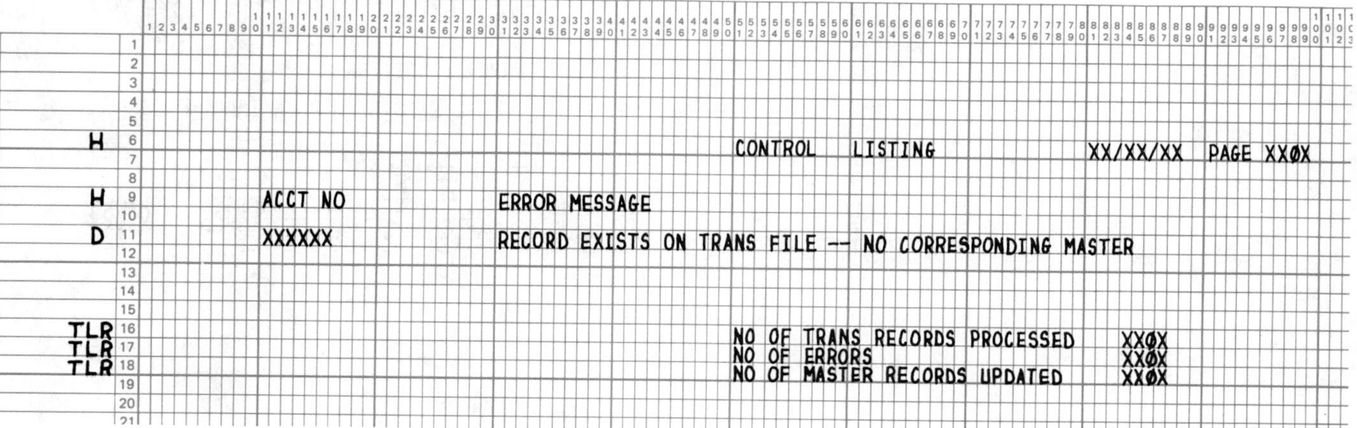

(c)

Figure 8.25 Problem definition for Practice Problem 4.

Systems Flowchart

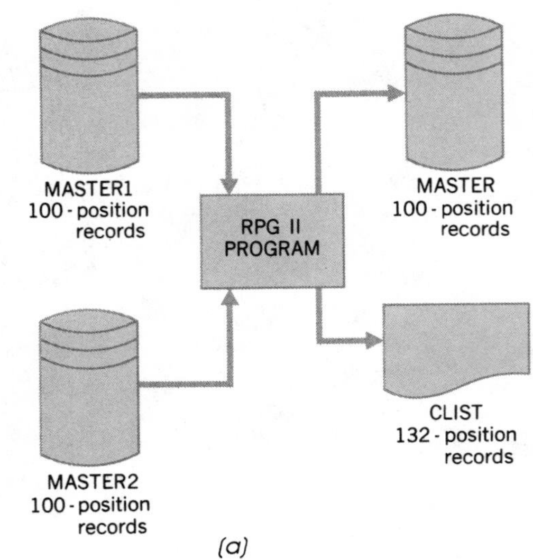

(a)

Record Layouts

All files have the same format

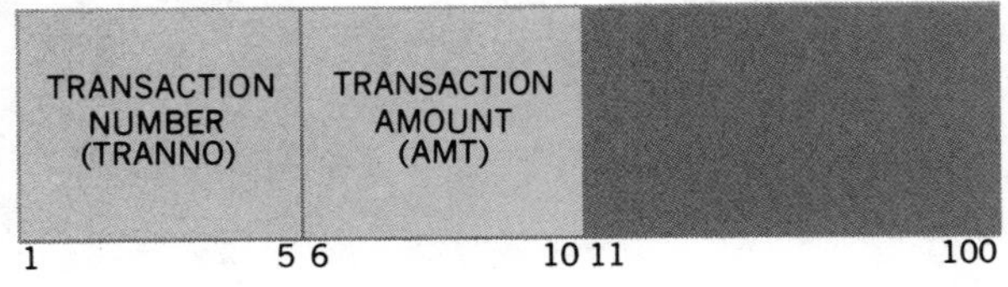

All files are blocked 50 with standard labels

(b)

CLIST Printer Spacing Chart

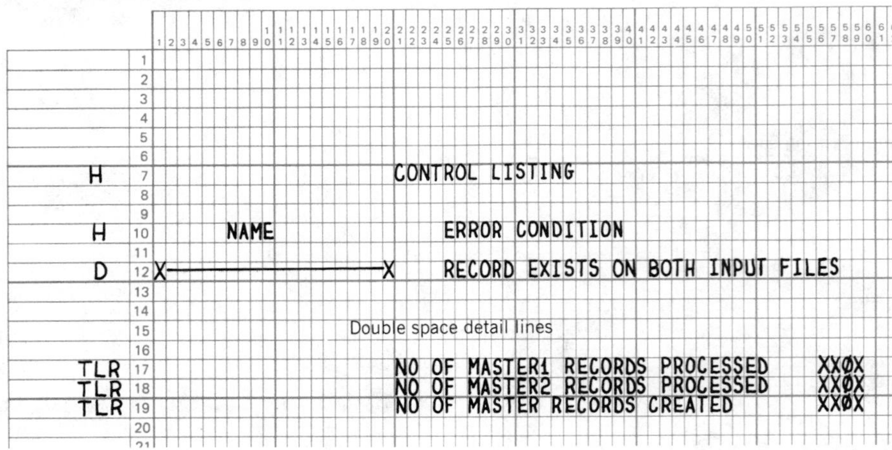

(c)

CHAPTER 9

Indexed Files: ISAM and VSAM Processing

Objectives

To consider

- RPG coding for creating indexed sequential master files.
- RPG coding for editing a transaction file and using it to chain to the master file.
- RPG coding for updating an ISAM file.
- VSAM files and how they are processed.

I.

An Introduction to ISAM Processing in RPG

Thus far, many of our programs have used disk as a high-speed medium that can serve as input to or output from a computer system. We have used disk sequentially in much the same way we would use magnetic tape or even cards. In this chapter, we focus on disks that are organized using either the indexed sequential access method (ISAM) or the virtual storage access method (VSAM). We will thus be able to perform random as well as sequential processing.

A. A Review of Indexed File Processing

As we saw in Chapter 7, when an **indexed file** is created, each record is placed on the disk in ascending sequence. But, at the same time, the computer establishes an index on the disk which keeps track of where each record is physically located. If, at some later time, you wish to access any record randomly, the computer "looks up" the address on the index and goes directly to that location to find the record. The index, then, operates exactly like a book index. To locate data, you "look up" the address in the index.

When creating an indexed file, the programmer must designate a field on the record as a **key field** that uniquely identifies the record to the computer. For a payroll file, the key field may be Social Security number; for an inventory file, the key field may be part number; for an accounts receivable file, the key field may be customer number. The computer stores in the index the key field and the actual address where the corresponding record is located. The actual address may be specified in terms of surface number, sector number, and track number. Although there may be several records with the same surface, sector, and track number, this address narrows down the search for a particular record.

In summary, indexed files are created sequentially with each record placed on the file as it is read in, at the same time that an index is created associating actual addresses to each record's key field. After the indexed file has been created, it may be accessed or updated randomly or sequentially, as the need arises.

Two major types of indexed files can be created.

1. **ISAM** (Indexed Sequential Access Method) files.
2. **VSAM** (Virtual Storage Access Method) files.

After a discussion of general procedures required for master file processing, this chapter will present ISAM processing in detail. Then it will discuss VSAM processing.

B. A Review of Master File Procedures

A **master file** is the major collection of records for a given application. Regardless of whether the master file is stored on tape or disk, there are a series of general procedures required for master file processing in a business environment.

First, a master file for a specific application must be created with the use of a **create program**. This is an initial procedure required when the system is first implemented. At that point, the indexed file will be in sequential order by the key field.

After it is created, the master file must be made current or **updated** on a regular basis. This update requires the creation of a file of records that includes all changes to the master file. This second file is called a **transaction file**. For a payroll procedure, for example, a transaction file could consist of new hires, salary changes, name changes, and so on.

Before updating the master file with change or transaction records, the transaction file must be **edited** or checked for errors to minimize the risk of making erroneous changes to the master file.

Once edited, the transaction file is used to update or make the master file current on a periodic basis. Even then, errors may occur, but we can at least minimize the risk.

The master file is also used for reporting purposes. Reports can be produced on a scheduled basis, or reporting can occur whenever there is an inquiry into the status of the master file.

In summary, then, there are four general procedures associated with master file processing regardless of what type of device is used for storing the master file.

Master File Processing Procedures

1. Creating the Master File
   A master file is created initially when the system is implemented.
2. Editing the Transaction File
   The transaction file contains the changes to the master. It must be edited to minimize obvious errors before it is used to alter the master.
3. Updating the Master File
   An **update procedure** is the process of making a master file current using transaction records to indicate the changes.
4. Master File Reporting
   Reports produced may be scheduled, or on-demand, where output can consist of responses to inquiries. The master file may also be used for reference purposes.

Self-Evaluating Quiz

1. The major collection of records for a given application is referred to as a(n) ________ .
2. Disks can be processed ________ as well as sequentially.
3. The process of making a master file current is called ________ .
4. If on-line updating of a master file is preferred, then the master file must be stored on ________ .
5. When an indexed file is created, the computer establishes a(n) ________ on the disk which keeps track of where each record is physically located.
6. (T or F) Indexed files can be accessed randomly.
7. When creating an indexed file, the programmer must designate a field as a(n) ________ that uniquely identifies the record to the computer.
8. A typical key field for a master payroll file would be ________ .
9. The file used for updating a master file is called the ________ .
10. Before updating a master file, all change records must be ________ to minimize errors.
11. Editing a file is the process of ________ .
12. Disk files can be used for creating reports on a regularly ________ basis or a(n) ________ basis whenever they are needed.

13. VSAM is an abbreviation for ________ .
14. ISAM is an abbreviation for ________ .

Solutions

1. master file
2. randomly
3. updating
4. disk
5. index
6. T
7. key field
8. Social Security number or employee number
9. transaction file
10. edited
11. minimizing input errors by checking input data before using it to update a master file
12. scheduled
    on-demand (inquiry-response)
13. virtual storage access method
14. indexed sequential access method

C. Creating an ISAM Master File in RPG

Once a systems analyst decides what data is required in the master file and what organization is required, a programmer is assigned the task of writing the master file creation procedure. This program will be functionally operational only once. Subsequently, the master file is updated or kept current using a different program.

Once an ISAM master file is created, it becomes the main source of data on the system as a whole. Ensuring the integrity, reliability, and validity of this master file must be the primary objective of the programmer. Files could be inadvertently tampered with or unscrupulously altered if care is not taken when creating them. Every control procedure that is reasonable must be incorporated in the program to minimize the risk of errors on a master file.

The input used to produce the ISAM master file is created from source documents or originating information for the system. Source documents for an accounts receivable file, for example, might be customer account records such as bills or charge slips. The ISAM master file can also be created from a sequential tape or disk file.

The source documents are used by data entry operators to create cassette tapes, floppy disks, or standard tapes or disks containing the master data. These media might then be merged into one master file. Or the master file may simply be entered from a terminal. In any case, the input file consisting of source document entries must be thoroughly validated by the create program, which then produces:

1. The master ISAM file.
2. An error control listing.

The master ISAM file would consist of all records that the program recognized as valid. The program would also establish an index using a field on the

ISAM file as the key field. Typically, the key field is a unique field on the record that identifies that record to the system. Once the programmer designates the key field and indicates that the output file is an ISAM file, the RPG program will *automatically* create the index.

The error control listing is for the user or operating staff. It contains all data that is placed on the ISAM file so that the data can be checked for accuracy. It consists of a list of all incoming records flagged as errors. It also contains control totals indicating the number of records processed, the number of errors flagged, and so on.

Figure 9.1 is an example of a systems flowchart indicating the processing required for creating a master ISAM file.

The File Description Specifications for SALESIN and CLIST would be identical to other programs. If SALESIN is to be entered using a terminal, the specific device name will depend on the installation. The following are some common device names for terminals.

Common Device Names for Terminals	
WORKSTN	an abbreviation for 'WORKSTATION'
CONSOLE	
KEYBOARD	
BSCA	an abbreviation for binary synchronous communications terminal
TERMINL	
SPECIAL	

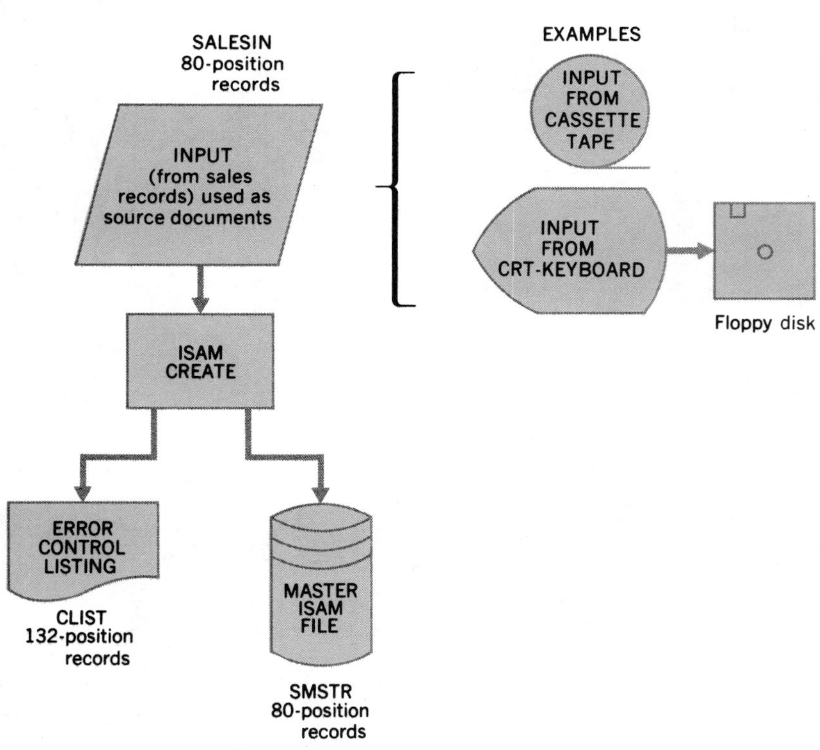

Figure 9.1
Processing required for creating a master ISAM file.

Check your specifications manual or ask someone at your computer installation for the device names used. We will use CONSOLE to designate a terminal. Thus the input file that is keyed in on a terminal and the output list file that is printed would have the following two File Description entries.

File Description Specifications

For the valid entries for a system, refer to the RPG reference manual for that system.

```
Line Form  Filename  File   File  End   Seq  File    Block   Record  Mode  ...  Device   Symbolic
     Type            Type   Desig of File    Format  Length  Length                  Device
0 2 ΦF  SALESIN   I      P                F               8Φ                  CONSOLE  SYSΦΦ1
0 3 ΦF  CLIST     O                       F              132          OF      PRINTER  SYSLST
0 4  F
0 5  F
```

The ISAM master file to be created requires all the entries just shown plus the following, which specifically relate to indexed sequential disk files.

RPG CONTROL AND FILE DESCRIPTION SPECIFICATIONS

Program | Programmer | Date | Keying Instruction | Graphic | Key | Card Electro Number | Page of | Program Identification

Control Specifications

For the valid entries for a system, refer to the RPG reference manual for that system.

```
0 1 H
```

File Description Specifications

For the valid entries for a system, refer to the RPG reference manual for that system.

```
0 2 ΦF SMSTR   O        F  8ΦΦ   8Φ  Φ5AI       2 DISK    SYSΦΦ8S           U
0 3  F
0 4  F
0 5  F
0 6  F
0 7  F
0 8  F
```

where in the record the key field begins
Indicates the number of bytes in the key field
I for indexed
A is used to denote that the record key is in alphanumeric format
S for standard labels
Indicates that input is to create a master file

File Description Entries for ISAM Files

Length of Key Field (columns 29–3Ø)
Specify the number of bytes in the key field.

Record Address Type (column 31)
For creating an ISAM file, the specification could be
A—For an alphanumeric or zoned decimal key field.
P—For a packed key field.

Type of File Organization (column 32)
For ISAM processing, enter I.

Key Field Starting Location (columns 35 to 38)
Enter the high-order or left-most byte in the disk record where the key field is to begin. Right-justify this number in columns 35 to 38.

File Addition/Unordered (column 66)
Column 66 is used for ISAM files as follows.
A—Used to add records to the file.
U—Used to load or create the file. For efficiency, the computer will sort the index into key field sequence after the program has been executed. Each time records are added, the index is resequenced. Note that many systems require ISAM files to be ordered. In these cases, column 66 would be blank.

Number of Tracks for Cylinder Overflow (column 67)
Column 67 is used for indicating the number of tracks for cylinder overflow. Some systems require a Ø in this position if none are used.

Other fields on the File Description Specifications form may be coded as needed. For indicating label records, for example, column 53 may be used. An S in column 53 would denote standard labels. A **standard label** is one that is created automatically based on identifying information provided by the program and job control procedures. If S is used for an input file, then the label is checked for a standard format. Coding an N for nonstandard labels or a U for user labels would require additional coding in columns 54-59. If column 53 is left blank, the computer assumes that no label is used for identifying the disk file.

Suppose the input from the console has the following format.

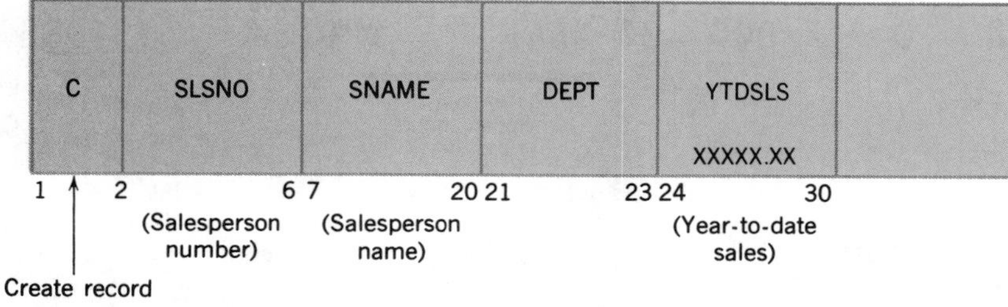

The record identifying code of C would typically be included in most forms of input to verify that this is a create record. With input from the terminal, however, the coding of C may be deemed unnecessary for some applications.

The master file will have the following format.

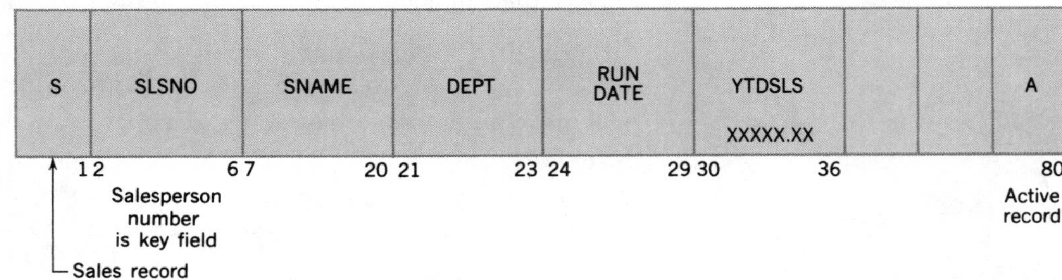

The full File Description specification is as follows.

RPG CONTROL AND FILE DESCRIPTION SPECIFICATIONS

Program | Keying Instruction | Graphic | Key | Card Electro Number | Page 1 2 of | Program Identification 75 76 77 78 79 80
Programmer | Date

Control Specifications

For the valid entries for a system, refer to the RPG reference manual for that system.

Line 01 H

File Description Specifications

For the valid entries for a system, refer to the RPG reference manual for that system.

```
02Ø F SALESIN IP   F         8Ø            CONSOLESYSØØ1
03Ø F CLIST   O    F        132      OF    PRINTERSYSLST
04Ø F SMSTR   O    F  8ØØ   8Ø ØSAI      2 DISK    SYSØØ8S             U
```

This is an indexed file.

Key field is alphanumeric in positions 2-6

Labels are standard

The file is to be created from unordered input

The types of tests performed on input data vary with the application. One common test is to determine if a specific field is within pre-established limits. Suppose, for example, that DEPT must be between ØØ1 and 823. Before putting the input data onto the master disk, the programmer should ensure that DEPT falls within the required limits.

The following coding would be used on the Calculation form.

RPG CALCULATION SPECIFICATIONS

Line	Form Type	Control Level	Indicators	Factor 1	Operation	Factor 2	Result Field Name	Length	Decimal Positions	Half Adjust	High (54–55)	Low (56–57)	Equal (58–59)	Comments
01Ø	C		Ø1	DEPT	COMP	ØØ1						15		
02Ø	C		Ø1N15	DEPT	COMP	823					25			
03	C													
04	C													

If indicator 15 or indicator 25 was turned on, then the programmer would code the Output form to print an error message. Thus the Output form would print a "DEPT ERROR" message if 15 or 25 was on.

Such limit tests serve to *minimize* input errors. Note that no program can ensure input accuracy altogether. If a DEPT was erroneously entered as 915, this procedure would flag it as an error; but if the DEPT was coded as 623 when it should have been 263, no error message would be generated. Because input errors are so difficult to pinpoint, many systems have two different data entry operators enter the *same data* and have the system compare these inputs before the data is processed. If the two versions are not identical, an input error is flagged even before it is processed by the create program. This method of dual data entry is called **data verification**.

Limit tests and other validity checks are typically incorporated in procedures that create master files, as well as those that create transaction files. These edit procedures will be reviewed later on in this chapter.

Creating the ISAM file from the input and printing the error control listing would include the same type of processing as in previous illustrations (see Figure 9.2).

Figure 9.2
Sample input and output specifications for a program that creates an ISAM file.
(Continued on next page.)

RPG INPUT SPECIFICATIONS

Line	Form Type	Filename or Record Name	Sequence	Record Identifying Indicator	Position (1)	Not (N)	C/Z/D	Character	Field Location From	To	Decimal Positions	RPG Field Name
01Ø	I	SALESIN	NS	Ø1	1		C	C				
02Ø	I								2	6	Ø	SLSNO
03Ø	I								7	2Ø		SNAME
04Ø	I								21	23	Ø	DEPT
05Ø	I								24	3Ø	2	YTDSLS
06Ø	I			Ø2	1	N	C	C				
07	I											
08	I											

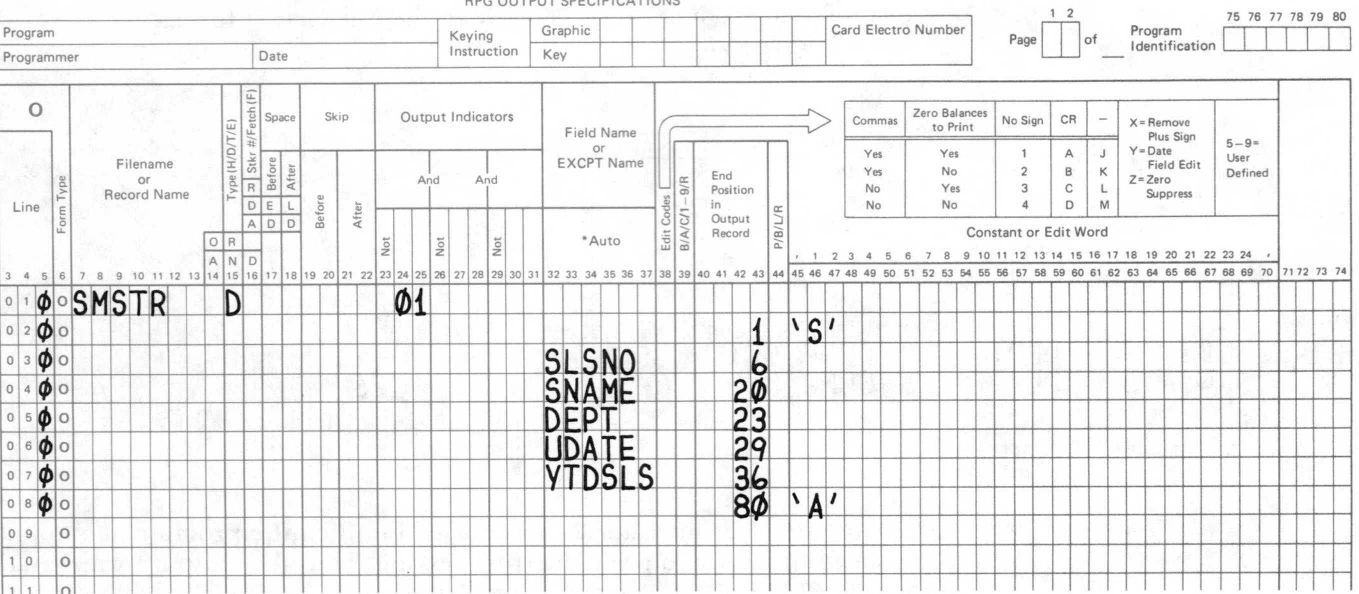

RPG OUTPUT SPECIFICATIONS

Line	Form Type	Filename or Record Name	Type (H/D/T/E)	Output Indicators	Field Name or EXCPT Name	End Position in Output Record	Constant or Edit Word
01	O	SMSTR	D	01			
02	O					1	'S'
03	O				SLSNO	6	
04	O				SNAME	20	
05	O				DEPT	23	
06	O				UDATE	29	
07	O				YTDSLS	36	
08	O					80	'A'
09	O						
10	O						
11	O						

Figure 9.2
(continued)

CLIST should include a listing of the following.

1. Errors
   Each error that becomes evident in the input data should be listed along with a message indicating the type of error. All erroneous data will have to be corrected by the user and re-entered as input.
2. Input processed
   All input data that is used to create a master file should be listed. This can be used by the operating staff or the user for checking purposes.
3. Totals
   Any totals that could be used to minimize the risk of data being lost should be included. Most frequently, the programmer would include the following totals.
   a. A count of records processed
      The operating staff can manually count the records to be created *before* processing begins. The computer-produced total should match the manually prepared one. If not, the discrepancy must be found and corrected. Or, if an input tape or disk file is used to create an ISAM file, the program should provide for the counting of input records.
   b. A control total
      A **control total** is a total of an amount field within the record. Typically, the operating staff is interested in obtaining total amount data for control purposes and for informational purposes as well. In this instance, we might maintain a running total of all year-to-date sales (YTDSLS).
   c. A hash total
      A **hash total** is a total of a field that is not usually used in an arithmetic operation. One would typically use a key or control field for this purpose. The user would manually calculate a hash total on SLSNO, for example. The computer-produced hash total should match the manually produced one. If there is a discrepancy, it might mean that one

or more input records were not processed or were incorrectly processed. Suppose the manually produced hash total is 12387 and the computer-produced hash total is 12153. It may be that the record with SLSNO 234 (12387 − 12153) was lost or not processed.

In our illustration, the input data should be checked to make certain that

1. Key fields are not blank or zero.
2. Specified fields are within pre-established limits or ranges; for example, DEPT should be any number from ØØ1 to 823 and YTDSLS (year-to-date sales) should be greater than zero.

If there is any error in input, the programmer would be instructed by the systems analyst to either write the record onto the file anyway or "flag" it as an error on the listing and not create the record. We will assume that all records with erroneous fields are *not* to be placed on the disk.

Thus far, we have coded an ISAM create program for producing a master disk from data keyed onto a terminal. Figure 9.3 illustrates the Printer Spacing Chart for the error control listing, CLIST. Figure 9.4 illustrates the complete program, including totals and error checks.

D. Editing a Transaction File

Once a master file has been created, it will need to be updated periodically to keep it current. Changes to the master file are stored in a transaction file. The transaction file should be edited or checked for errors before it is used to update the master. This will minimize the risk of errors. Failure to ensure the integrity of the transaction file adequately will mean that the master file might be updated with erroneous data.

A transaction file is created in a manner similar to a master file. It can be keyed into a terminal using source documents to create a tape or disk or it can be keypunched into cards.

```
H    4              ERROR CONTROL LISTING      XX/XX/XX  PAGE XXØX
H    6      SALESMAN NUMBER      NAME        DEPT      YTD SALES
D    8           XXXXX       X-----------X  XXX       $XX,XX$.XX
     9          (SLSNO)         (SNAME)     (DEPT)     (YTDSLS)
D   10            ***
    13                      (***beneath entry designates error)
TLR 15                TOTAL RECORDS PROCESSED               XXØX
TLR 18                HASH TOTAL ON SALESMAN NUMBER XXXXXXØX
TLR 21                TOTAL YEAR-TO-DATE SALES $X,XXX,XX$.XX
```

Figure 9.3
Printer Spacing Chart for an error control listing.

Figure 9.4
Complete program to create an ISAM file.

File Description Specifications

For the valid entries for a system, refer to the RPG reference manual for that system.

```
02ØFSALESIN IP  F      8Ø            CONSOLESYSØØ1
03ØFCLIST   O   F     132     OF     PRINTERSYSLST
04ØFSMSTR   O   F 8ØØ  8ØØ5AI      2 DISK   SYSØØ8S            U
```

RPG INPUT SPECIFICATIONS

```
01ØISALESIN NS  Ø1   1 CC
02ØI                                        2   6ØSLSNO           1Ø
03ØI                                        7  2Ø SNAME
04ØI                                       21  23ØDEPT
05ØI                                       24  3Ø2YTDSLS          2Ø
```

Figure 9.4 *(continued)*

RPG CALCULATION SPECIFICATIONS

Line	Form Type	Control Level	Indicators	Factor 1	Operation	Factor 2	Result Field Name	Length	Decimal Positions	Half Adjust	High	Low	Equal	Comments
01Ø	C		Ø1	1	ADD	COUNT	COUNT	4	Ø					
02Ø	C		Ø1N2Ø	YTDSLS	ADD	TOTAL	TOTAL	9	2					
03Ø	C		Ø1N1Ø	SLSNO	ADD	HASH	HASH	8	Ø					
04Ø	C		Ø1	DEPT	COMP	ØØ1						15		DETERMINES IF
05Ø	C		Ø1N15	DEPT	COMP	823					25			DEPT IS BETWEEN
06Ø	C	*												ØØ1 AND 823
07	C	*												
08	C	*												
09	C	*												
10	C													
11	C													
12	C													
13	C													

NOTE: For protection it would be useful to set off all resulting indicators after processing each record

RPG OUTPUT SPECIFICATIONS

Line	Form Type	Filename or Record Name	Type (H/D/T/E)	Space Before	Space After	Skip Before	Skip After	Output Indicators	Field Name or EXCPT Name	Edit Codes	End Position in Output Record	Constant or Edit Word
01Ø	O	CLIST	H		2	Ø4		1P				
02Ø	O		OR					OF				
03Ø	O										38	'ERROR CONTROL LISTING'
04Ø	O								UDATE	Y	51	
05Ø	O										57	'PAGE'
06Ø	O								PAGE		62	
07Ø	O		H		2			1P				
08Ø	O		OR					OF				
09Ø	O										2Ø	'SALESMAN NUMBER'
10Ø	O										29	'NAME'
11Ø	O										53	'DEPT YTD SALES'
12Ø	O		D		2			Ø1				
13Ø	O								SLSNO		14	
14Ø	O								SNAME		35	
15Ø	O								DEPT		39	
16Ø	O								YTDSLS	1	53	'$'
17Ø	O		D		2			Ø1				
18Ø	O							15			39	'***'
19Ø	O							25			39	'***'
20Ø	O							1Ø			13	'***'
21Ø	O							2Ø			5Ø	'***'

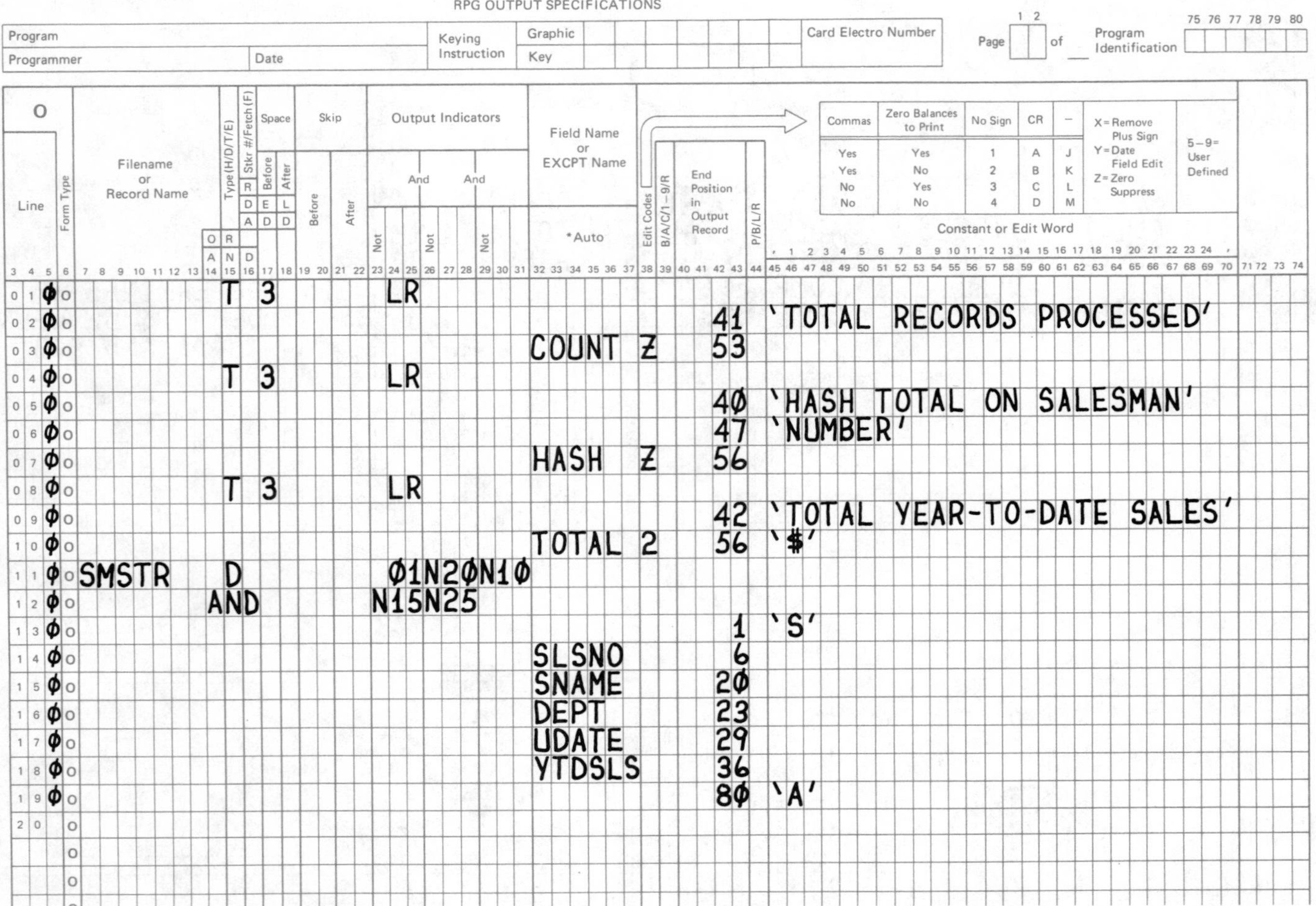

RPG OUTPUT SPECIFICATIONS

Line	Form Type	Filename or Record Name	Type (H/D/T/E) / AND	Space Before	Output Indicators	Field Name or EXCPT Name	Edit Codes	End Position in Output Record	Constant or Edit Word
Ø1	O		T	3	LR				
Ø2	O							41	'TOTAL RECORDS PROCESSED'
Ø3	O					COUNT	Z	53	
Ø4	O		T	3	LR				
Ø5	O							4Ø	'HASH TOTAL ON SALESMAN'
Ø6	O							47	'NUMBER'
Ø7	O					HASH	Z	56	
Ø8	O		T	3	LR				
Ø9	O							42	'TOTAL YEAR-TO-DATE SALES'
1Ø	O					TOTAL	2	56	'$'
11	O	SMSTR	D		Ø1N2ØN1Ø				
12	O		AND		N15N25				
13	O							1	'S'
14	O					SLSNO		6	
15	O					SNAME		2Ø	
16	O					DEPT		23	
17	O					UDATE		29	
18	O					YTDSLS		36	
19	O							8Ø	'A'

Figure 9.4
(continued)

A transaction file will contain data used to keep the master file current. A payroll transaction file, for example, may contain the following data.

> ***Sample Payroll Transaction Data***
>
> 1. Promotions.
> 2. Salary changes.
> 3. Name and address changes.
> 4. Changes in the number of dependents.
> 5. Records to be deleted, for example, if an employee resigns, is fired, or retires.

1. Typical Edit Procedures
The following are typical procedures used in editing a transaction file.

> ***Typical Checks Performed on Transaction Data***
>
> 1. Validate record identifying codes, if used.

2. Test for reasonableness. For example, is input data within appropriate limits? Is a code in one field compatible with another? For example, is the salary consistent with the job title?
3. Test for completeness. Is input data complete?
4. Check totals. Were all records in the original batch actually processed? Do record counts check? In addition, control totals including year-to-date totals and hash totals should be maintained.

Validating Record Identifying Codes Suppose incoming transaction records are to have a 'P' in column or position 1. Thus far, we have been coding input specifications so that only records with the appropriate record identifying codes were processed.

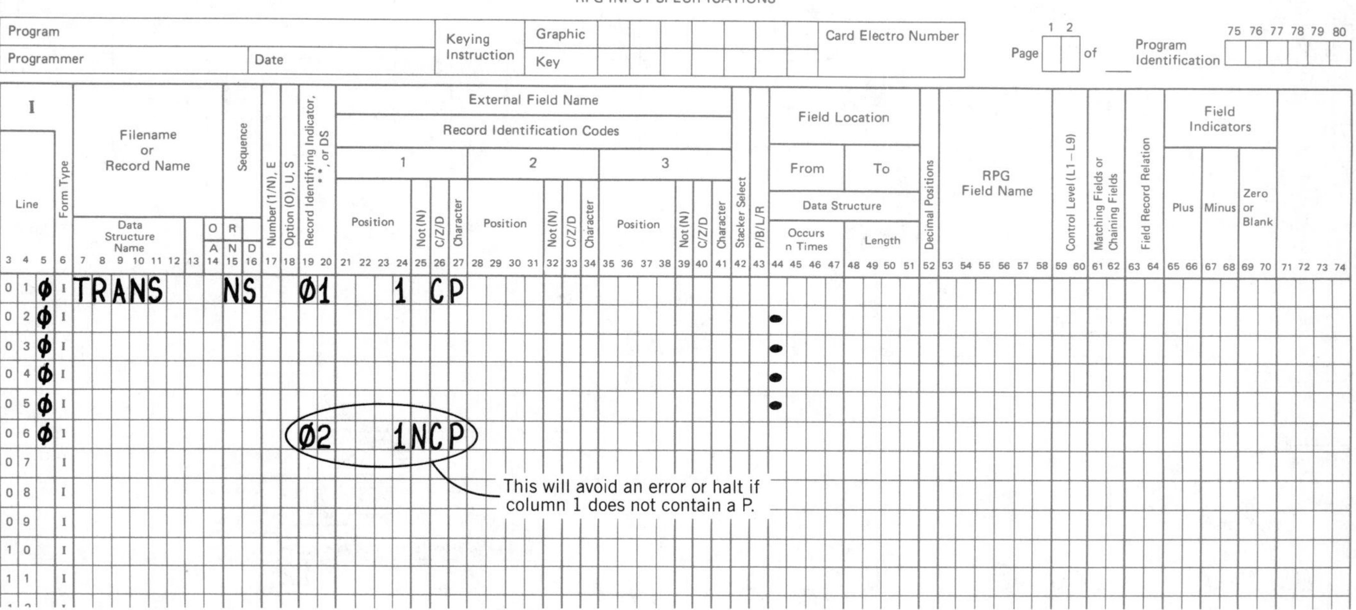

Indicator Ø1 is turned on for all records with a 'P' in column 1. If a record is entered that does not have a P in column 1, then the Ø1 indicator is not turned on and the record is not processed at all.

A more appropriate technique for using record identifying indicators is to turn on another indicator, for example Ø2, for all records without a P in column 1. If we do not use a second indicator, the halt indicator will be turned on when a record is read that does not have a P in column 1; this will abort the run. Coding NØ1 or Ø2 in the detail line will allow us to print an error message and continue processing when a record without a P in position 1 is read.

Although the above technique produces the correct processing, there are alternatives that allow us to flag, as an error, an incoming record that does *not* have a 'P' in column 1. To either print errors or accumulate a total of such errors, we can specifically *test* for a 'P' in column 1. To do this, establish the first character *not* as a record identifying code but as an input field that we will compare against, using the Input Specifications shown here.

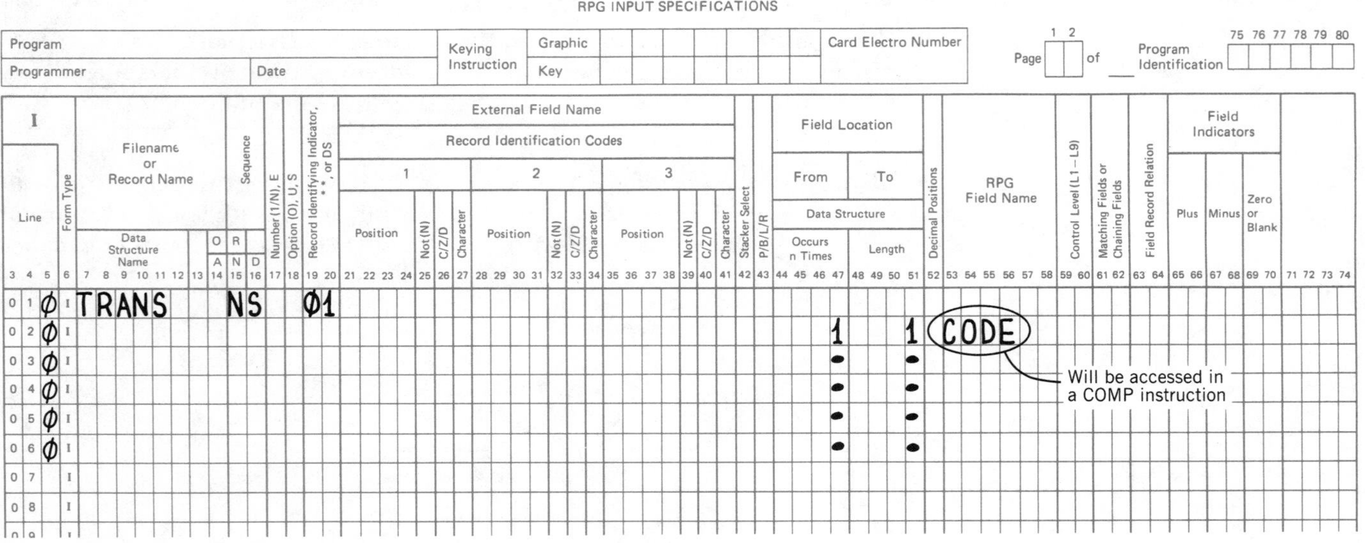

RPG INPUT SPECIFICATIONS

Line	Form Type	Filename or Record Name	Sequence	Record Identifying Indicator	Field Location From	Field Location To	RPG Field Name
01Ø	I	TRANS	NS	Ø1			
02Ø	I				1	1	CODE
03Ø	I						
04Ø	I						
05Ø	I						
06Ø	I						
07	I						
08	I						

The Calculation Specifications would be coded as follows.

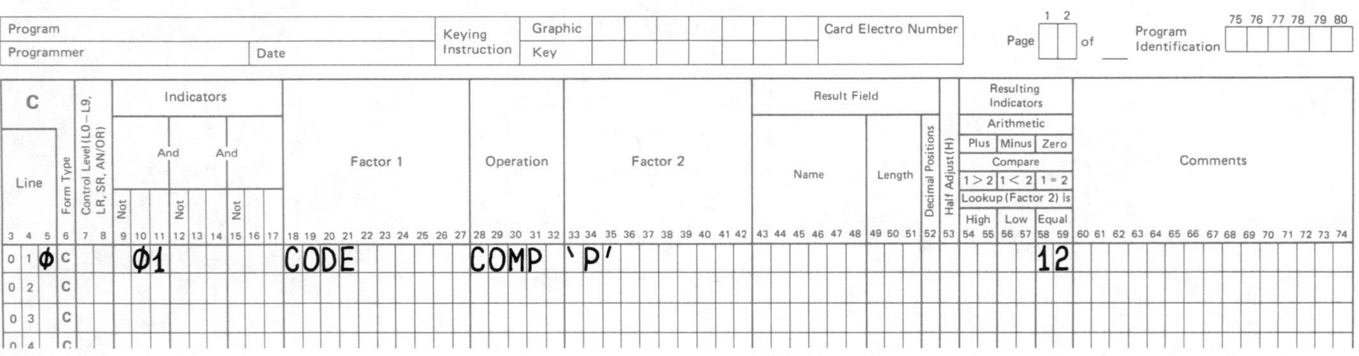

RPG CALCULATION SPECIFICATIONS

Line	Form Type	Indicators	Factor 1	Operation	Factor 2	Resulting Indicators (Equal)
01Ø	C	Ø1	CODE	COMP	'P'	12
02	C					
03	C					

If indicator 12 is turned on, then the transaction record has the appropriate code. If not, we can print an error message 'INVALID CODE IN COL 1' when identifier 12 is not on. This can be accomplished by testing for N12. Or we can add 1 to a TOT when N12 is designated. This will accumulate the total number of such errors.

The tests for reasonableness and completeness are similar to those performed for creating a master file. Critical fields must be tested to determine if they are filled and if they are within established limits. The control totals and record counts produced during the editing of a transaction file are similar as well and will be determined by the user's needs.

Depending on the application, then, it may be necessary to use all the edit procedures described or only some of them. On the other hand, some applications may require even more rigorous editing.

2. Chaining: Editing the Transaction File by Comparing It Against the Master File

The edit steps just described can be performed using only the transaction file as input. If a procedure is required to check that each transaction record is actually associated with an active master record, however, then the master file would also be required as input. That is, the transaction record would be checked to see that it corresponds to an existing, active master record.

Checking the transaction record against the master may be performed as part of the edit procedure or it may be part of the update procedure itself. Usually, however, it is part of updating. To facilitate our discussion of updating later on, however, we will include a check against the master as part of our edit program. To do this, we must use the CHAIN operation.

The* CHAIN *Operation Each time a change is to be made to a master file, a transaction record is created. Thus our transaction file will consist of records that are to alter an existing master file. The edit procedure reads a transaction record, performs the error control procedures just described, and determines if the record corresponds, as it should, to an active master record.

To perform this procedure, the key field of each record on the transaction file is used to "look up" the corresponding record on the master file. If CUSTNO is the key field on a master ISAM file, then the CUSTNO field in each input transaction record is used to find the corresponding master disk record. Thus, we need two input files for verifying that a transaction record corresponds to an active master record.

1. *Transaction file.* This is the *primary* file for this application. A 'P' in column 16 of the File Description Specifications form designates the transaction file as a primary file.
2. *Master file.* This file is accessed using the transaction file to determine which record is required. This procedure is referred to as **chaining**. A 'C' in column 16 of the File Description Specifications form designates the master as the file to be chained.

Chaining, then, is the process of "looking up" a master disk record using the transaction file to signal the look-up. The transaction record serves as a "pointer" to the corresponding ISAM record using the key field as the source (see Figure 9.5).

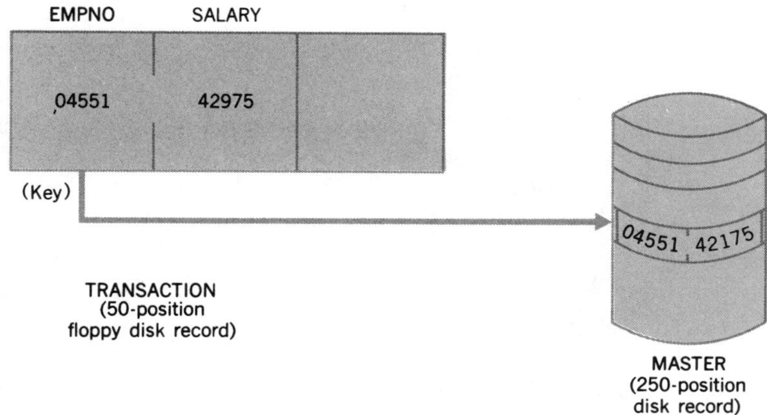

Figure 9.5
Example of chaining.

The key field on the transaction file is defined on the Calculation Specifications form along with the CHAIN command. The precise location, length, and specification of the master key field must be defined on the File Description form.

The following File Description Specifications form may be used for a program in which a transaction floppy disk consisting of 5Ø-position records is edited. The transaction file will be compared against the master, which consists of 25Ø-position disk records. An edit listing is produced. If a transaction record is not associated with a corresponding active master record, an error message will print.

RPG CONTROL AND FILE DESCRIPTION SPECIFICATIONS

Program | Keying Instruction | Graphic | Key | Card Electro Number | Page 1 2 of | Program Identification 75 76 77 78 79 80

Programmer | Date

Control Specifications

For the valid entries for a system, refer to the RPG reference manual for that system.

```
01 H
```

File Description Specifications

For the valid entries for a system, refer to the RPG reference manual for that system.

```
02ØFTRANS   IP  F      5Ø            DISK   SYSØØ5S
03ØFMASTER  IC  F     25ØRØ5AI     2 DISK   SYSØØ6S
04ØFEDITOUT O   F     132     OF     PRINTERSYSLST
05 F
06 F
07 F
08 F
09 F
```

(Arrow at the R in position 28 of line 03:) Records will be accessed randomly

The file description entries for the TRANS and EDITOUT files are self-explanatory and follow other programs that have been illustrated. The file description entries for the MASTER file, however, may require some explanation.

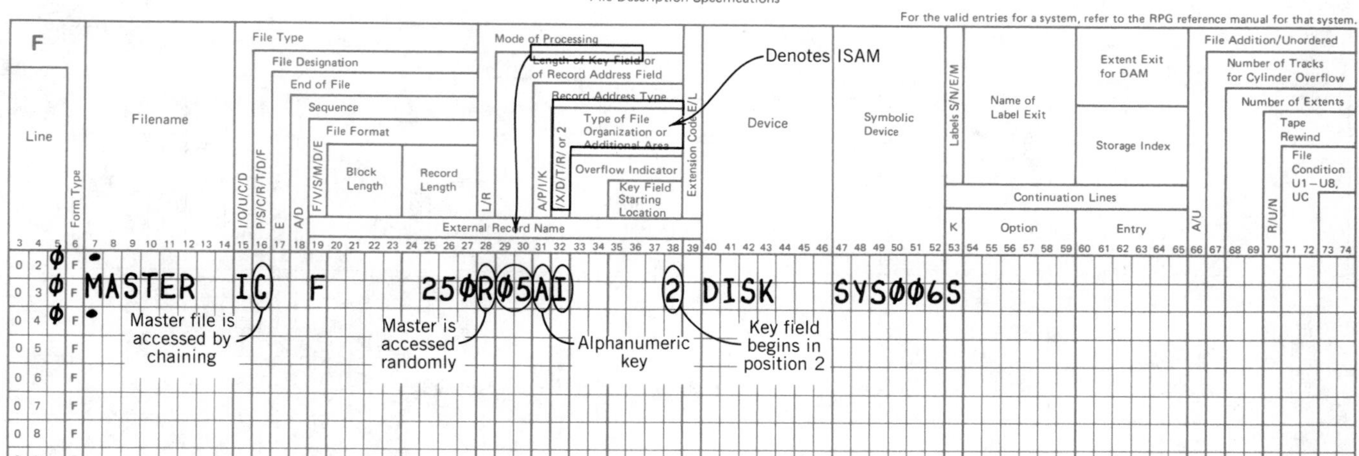

The file description entries for MASTER indicate the following:

1. MASTER is an indexed sequential file.
2. The key field is alphanumeric.
3. The key field begins in position 2 and is five positions long; that is, it appears in positions 2 to 6 of each master record.
4. The master file is accessed randomly by chaining, using the transaction file as the primary file.

The input specifications for the TRANS file would include all fields used for edit purposes.

If the master file is simply used to determine that a master record exists for each corresponding transaction record, then only those fields necessary for the comparison are specified. Note that the key field of the master file does not need to be indicated on the Input Specifications form since we already included its specification on the File Description form. Typically, each master record includes a coded field that indicates if it is an active record or if it has been deactivated. For a master payroll file, deactivated records may pertain to employees who have left the company or died. They are retained on the master for some reporting purposes, but they should not be updated by transaction data. That is, a transaction record corresponding to an inactive master should be printed as an error.

Let us assume that the last character in the master record will designate STATUS: 'A' for active and 'I' for inactive. Our input specifications may be as follows.

RPG INPUT SPECIFICATIONS

Line	Form Type	Filename or Record Name	Sequence	Record Identifying Indicator	Field Location From	Field Location To	Decimal Positions	RPG Field Name
01	I	TRANS	NS	01				
02	I				1	1		CODE
03	I				2	6		EMPNO
04	I				7	10	2	REGHR
05	I				11	14	2	OTHRS
06	I				15	16		DEPT
07	I				17	17		PAYCOD
08	I	MASTER	NT	02				
09	I				250	250		STATUS

On the Calculation Specifications form, we determine if a master record exists for a given transaction record by using a CHAIN command. This command specifies the following.

1. The key field on the transaction file (EMPNO).
2. The file to chain against (MASTER).
3. The indicator to be turned on if the record on the master with that key does not exist. This must be coded in columns 54 and 55 only.

The following coding will illustrate the chaining operation.

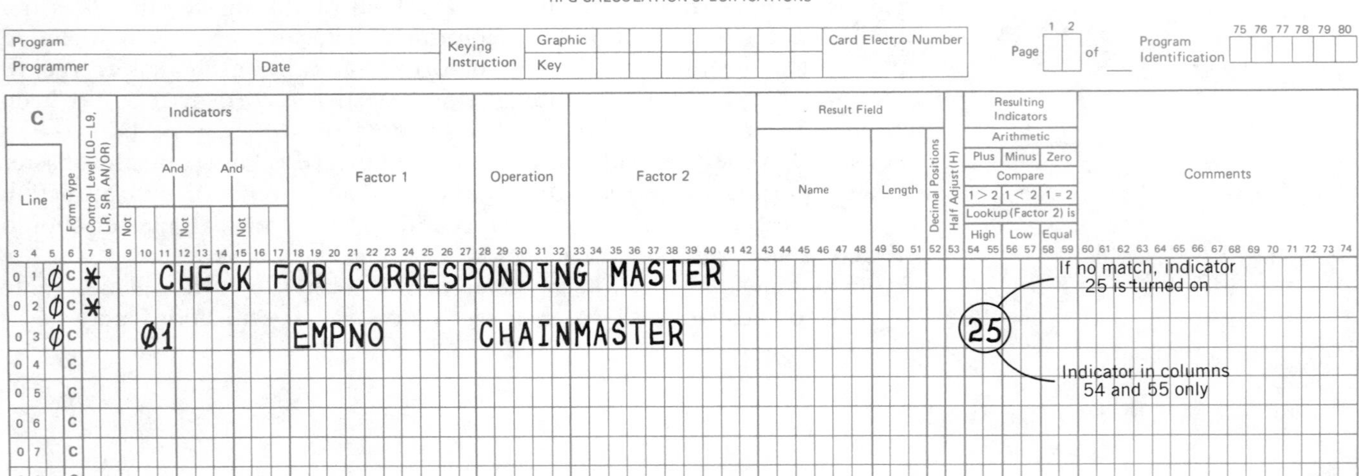

RPG CALCULATION SPECIFICATIONS

Line	Form Type	Indicators	Factor 1	Operation	Factor 2	Resulting Indicators (cols 54–55)
01	C	* CHECK FOR CORRESPONDING MASTER				
02	C	*				
03	C	01	EMPNO	CHAIN	MASTER	25

If no match, indicator 25 is turned on
Indicator in columns 54 and 55 only

EMPNO is the key field on the TRANS file. The CHAIN operation is performed for each transaction record, that is, when the Ø1 indicator is on. This chain operation compares the EMPNO on the transaction file against the five-byte key field in positions 2 to 6 of each master record. If no match is found, then indicator 25 is turned on. When indicator 25 is off, then a match has occurred; that is, there is a corresponding master record for the transaction record.

If there is a match, we must determine if the status in the master record is 'A' for active; if it is not, then the transaction record corresponds to an inactive master. This would be an error because transaction data should not be used to update inactive records.

The following coding will be used to print *two* types of errors.

1. When indicator 25 is on, we print the error message 'NO CORRESPONDING MASTER RECORD'.
2. When indicator 35 is on, we print the error message 'CORRESPONDING MASTER RECORD IS INACTIVE'.

RPG CALCULATION SPECIFICATIONS

Line	Form Type	Control Level	Indicators	Factor 1	Operation	Factor 2	Result Field Name	Length	Decimal Positions	Half Adjust	Resulting Indicators High (Plus, 1>2)	Low (Minus, 1<2)	Equal (Zero, 1=2)	Comments
01	C		Ø1	EMPNO	CHAIN	MASTER					25			
02	C		Ø1 N25	STATUS	COMP	'A'					35	35		
03	C													
04	C													

The COMP instruction is performed to make certain that when a match occurs, the master record is active. If it is not, indicator 35 is turned on and the above message prints. Note that the indicators used to cause the COMP instruction to execute are Ø1 and N25. This occurs when a record from the TRANS file has been read that chains properly to MASTER. A proper chain would also cause the Ø2 indicator to be turned on. Recall that the Ø2 indicator on the Input form indicates that a master record has been read. Thus, we could have used Ø1 and Ø2, instead of Ø1 and N25, to trigger the COMP. The Output Specifications used to print these messages would be as follows.

RPG OUTPUT SPECIFICATIONS

Line	Form Type	Filename or Record Name	Type (H/D/T/E)	Space / Skip	Output Indicators	Field Name or EXCPT Name	End Position in Output Record	Constant or Edit Word
01Ø	O		•					
02Ø	O		•					
03Ø	O		•					
04Ø	O		D		Ø1			
05Ø	O					•		
06Ø	O					•		
07Ø	O				25		75	'NO CORRESPONDING'
08Ø	O				25		89	'MASTER RECORD'
09Ø	O				N25 35		72	'CORRESPONDING'
10Ø	O				N25 35		86	'MASTER RECORD'
11Ø	O				N25 35		98	'IS INACTIVE'
12	O							
13	O							
14	O							

Consider Figure 9.6, which provides a full problem definition for an edit procedure. We want to produce an edit listing of the transactions in the file STRANS. The edit checks and controls include the following.

1. The record code for the transaction records must be an 'S'.
2. Each sales number in the transaction file must chain properly to an active master record in the SMSTR file. If there is no corresponding master record, that is an error. If it is there and inactive, that is also an error.
3. The district where the sale was made must match the salesperson's territory (DISTR = TERR).
4. The commission percentage must be between Ø.Ø5 and Ø.1Ø.
5. Control totals are required for total sales and a hash total on the sales number.

The output report should appear as shown in the Printer Spacing Chart in Figure 9.6.

1. If there is an active master record, print the SNAME; if there is not, print 'NOT ON FILE' in place of the name.
2. If there is a master record but it is inactive, print the SNAME, but print 'INACTIVE' below it.
3. *ERROR* prints if there is *any* error; the *** print directly below whatever field(s) are wrong.

Systems Flowchart

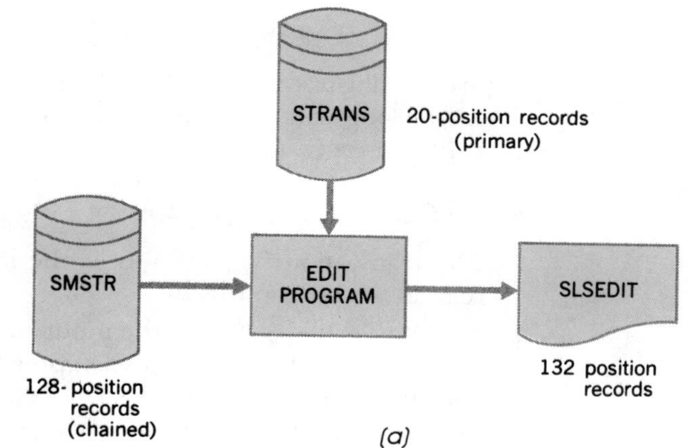

(a)

STRANS Record Layout

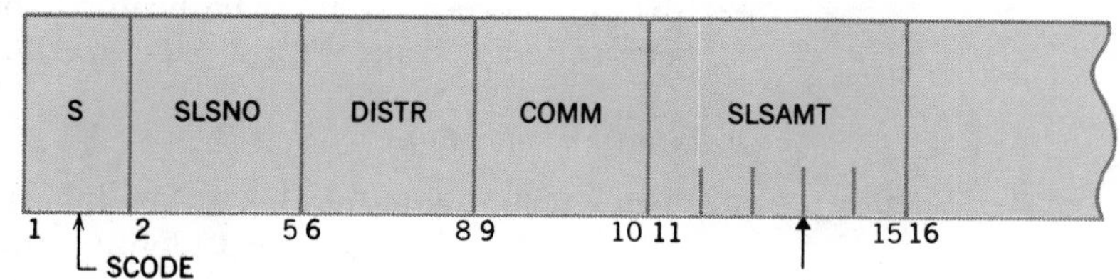

SMSTR Record Layout

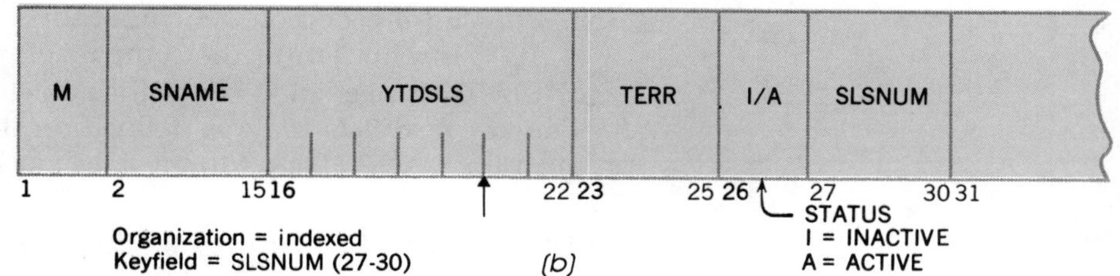

(b)

SLSEDIT Printer Spacing Chart

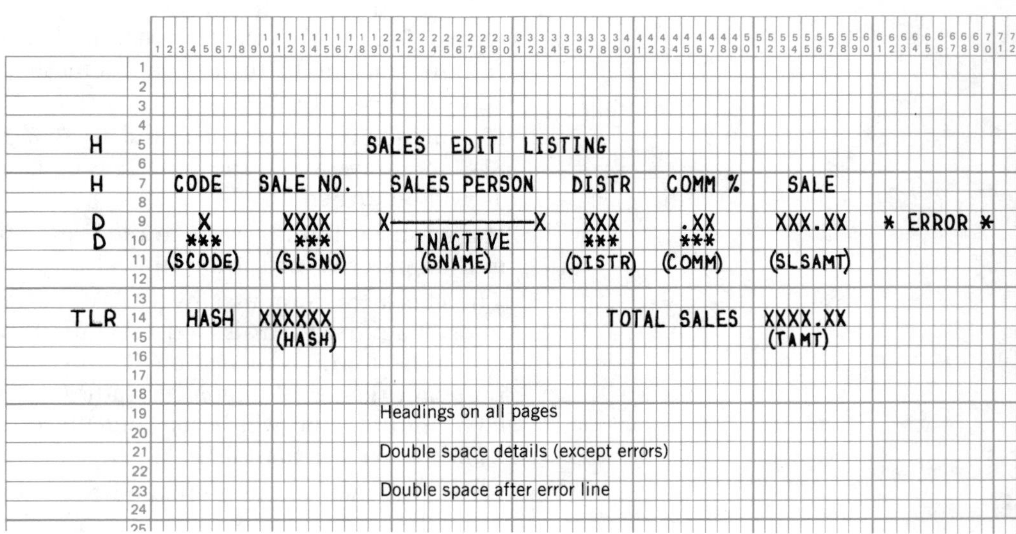

(c)

Figure 9.6
Problem definition for an edit procedure.

Figure 9.7 illustrates the RPG coding that will perform the required editing.

The following comments for each segment of the program will clarify the coding that has been used.

a. File Description Specifications

1. The transaction file, STRANS, is the input primary file since we want to read all records in this file.
2. The master file, SMSTR, is the input chained file to be processed randomly. We only want to access those master records that have a corresponding sales transaction record. The key field (SLSNUM—positions 27 to 3Ø) and the file organization (I = indexed) must be defined on the File Description Specifications form to help RPG correctly process the records.
3. The print file will contain the edit listing of the transactions in the file STRANS. Since there must be headings on all pages, the OF indicator has been coded to control for a page overflow condition.

b. Input Specifications

1. Each of the fields for the STRANS file has been defined. We have used indicator Ø1 with no record identification code. The field SCODE will be checked on the Calculation Specifications form to ensure that it is valid.
2. The only fields defined for the SMSTR file are those required for the edit checks or the output.
   a. SNAME is needed on the edit report.
   b. TERR is required for the comparison to DISTR.
   c. STATUS is needed to check for an active master.
3. The key field SLSNUM was defined on the File Description Specifications form for SMSTR. Therefore, it does not have to be described here.

c. Calculation Specifications The following edit checks have been coded.

1. SCODE is compared to the alphabetic literal 'S' and indicator 22 will be turned on if the comparison is unequal (high or low).
2. A CHAIN to the master file is made to check for the presence of a master record. SLSNO from the transaction file is used to CHAIN to the SMSTR file. Indicator 33 will be turned on if a master record with a key field equal to SLSNO is *not* found.
3. If a master record is *not* found (NOT 33), a check is made to see if the STATUS is inactive. If the STATUS is equal to I, for inactive, then indicator 44 will be turned on.
4. If a master is found, DISTR in the transaction record is compared to TERR in the master record. Indicator 55 is turned on if they are unequal.
5. The check for commissions (COMM) between Ø.Ø5 and Ø.1Ø requires two steps. The first check is to determine if COMM is less than Ø.Ø5, in which case indicator 66 is turned on. The second check is to determine if COMM is greater than Ø.1Ø, but *only* if indicator 66 is *not* on. If COMM is less than Ø.Ø5, indicator 66 will be on and there is no point in checking to see if COMM is greater than Ø.1Ø.
6. HASH and TAMT are accumulated control totals as discussed previously.

Figure 9.7 Program to perform an edit procedure. *(Continued on next page.)*

RPG CONTROL AND FILE DESCRIPTION SPECIFICATIONS

Control Specifications

```
01 H
```

File Description Specifications

```
02ØFSTRANS  IP  F      20           DISK   SYSØØ8S
03ØFSMSTR   IC  F     128R04AI    27 DISK   SYSØØ9S
04ØFSLSEDIT O   F     132      OF    PRINTERSYSLST
05 F
06 F
```

RPG INPUT SPECIFICATIONS

```
01ØISTRANS  NS  Ø1
02ØI                                        1   1 SCODE
03ØI                                        2   5ØSLSNO
04ØI                                        6   8 DISTR
05ØI                                        9  1Ø2COMM
06ØI                                       11  152SLSAMT
07ØISMSTR   NT  Ø2   1 CM
08ØI                                        2  15 SNAME
09ØI                                       23  25 TERR
10ØI                                       26  26 STATUS
11 I
```

RPG CALCULATION SPECIFICATIONS

Line	Form Type	Control Level	Indicators	Factor 1	Operation	Factor 2	Result Field Name	Length	Decimal Positions	Resulting Indicators High (1>2)	Low (1<2)	Equal (1=2)	Comments
01Ø	C				SETOF					77	44	55	
02Ø	C		Ø1	SCODE	COMP	'S'				22	22		
03Ø	C		Ø1	SLSNO	CHAIN	SMSTR				33			
04Ø	C		N33 Ø1	STATUS	COMP	'I'						44	
05Ø	C		N33 Ø1	DISTR	COMP	TERR				55	55		
06Ø	C		Ø1	COMM	COMP	.Ø5					66		
07Ø	C		N66 Ø1	COMM	COMP	.1Ø				66			
08Ø	C		Ø1	SLSNO	ADD	HASH	HASH	6	Ø				
09Ø	C		Ø1	SLSAMT	ADD	TAMT	TAMT	6	2				
10Ø	C		22										
11Ø	C	OR	33										
12Ø	C	OR	44										
13Ø	C	OR	55										
14Ø	C	OR	66		SETON						77		
15	C												
16	C												

RPG OUTPUT SPECIFICATIONS

Line	Form Type	Filename or Record Name	Type (H/D/T/E)	Space Before	Space After	Skip Before	Skip After	Output Indicators	Field Name or EXCPT Name	Edit Codes	End Position in Output Record	Constant or Edit Word
01Ø	O	SLSEDIT	H		2	Ø5		1P				
02Ø	O		OR					OF				
03Ø	O										29	'SALES EDIT'
04Ø	O										38	'LISTING'
05Ø	O		H		2			1P				
06Ø	O		OR					OF				
07Ø	O										6	'CODE'
08Ø	O										18	'SALES NO.'
09Ø	O										32	'SALES PERSON'
10Ø	O										49	'DISTR COMM %'
11Ø	O										57	'SALE'
12Ø	O		D		2			Ø1N77				
13Ø	O		OR		1			Ø1 77				
14Ø	O								SCODE		5	
15Ø	O								SLSNO		15	
16Ø	O							N33	SNAME		33	
17Ø	O							33			33	'NOT ON FILE'
18Ø	O								DISTR		39	
19Ø	O								COMM	3	47	
20Ø	O								SLSAMT	3	58	
21Ø	O							77			7Ø	'* ERROR *'

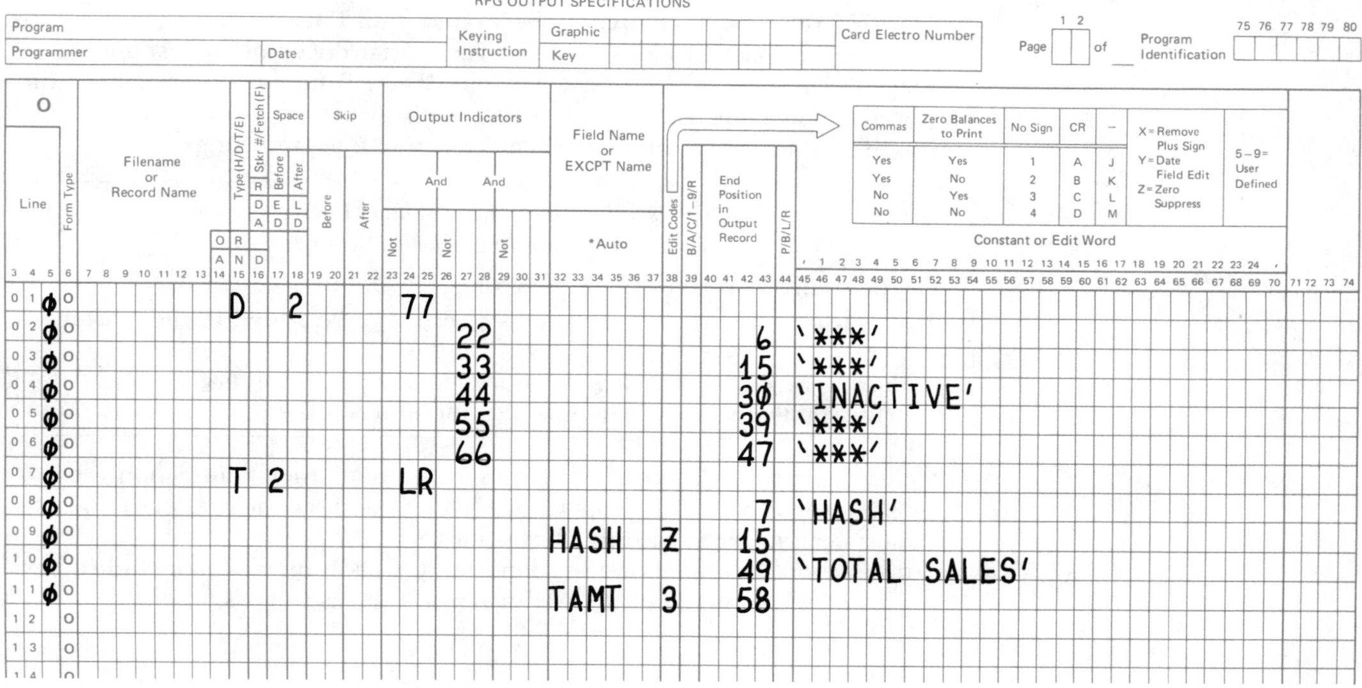

RPG OUTPUT SPECIFICATIONS

Line	Form Type	Filename or Record Name	Type (H/D/T/E)	Space Before	Space After	Output Indicators	Output Indicators (And)	Field Name or EXCPT Name	Edit Codes	End Position in Output Record	Constant or Edit Word
01Ø	O		D		2	77					
02Ø	O						22			6	'***'
03Ø	O						33			15	'***'
04Ø	O						44			3Ø	'INACTIVE'
05Ø	O						55			39	'***'
06Ø	O						66			47	'***'
07Ø	O		T	2		LR					
08Ø	O									7	'HASH'
09Ø	O							HASH	Z	15	
10Ø	O									49	'TOTAL SALES'
11Ø	O							TAMT	3	58	
12	O										
13	O										
14	O										

Figure 9.7
(continued)

7. Indicator 77 will represent any of the other error situations. If any of the indicators 22, 33, 44, 55, or 66 is on, then SETON 77.
8. The SETOF turns off three indicators at the beginning of calculations: 77, 44, and 55. SETOF is used for the following reasons.
   a. If indicator 77 is turned on during one cycle, it will remain on until it is turned off. Therefore, it must be turned off at the beginning of the calculations and set back on if necessary.
   b. It is necessary to turn off indicators 44 and 55 because of the following possibility. Suppose a transaction record is found to correspond to an inactive master or to have a wrong territory. Either indicator 44 or indicator 55 will be turned on, depending on which error has been detected. Suppose that the next transaction record is one without a master record, in which case indicator 33 will be turned on. Comparisons of the STATUS to 'I' and the DISTR to TERR cannot be made, since these comparisons are only made when indicator 33 is off. However, indicator 44 or indicator 55 will still be on from the previous transaction that was checked, which will incorrectly trigger a specific error condition. It is thus necessary to set off indicators 44 and 55 at the beginning of the calculations. Note that it is not necessary to set off indicators 22 and 33, since they will be reset each time the corresponding operations are performed for every record.

d. Output Specifications The Output Specifications produce the report shown in the Printer Spacing Chart in Figure 9.6.

3. Checking for New Accounts on the Transaction File

Suppose the transaction file contains a record that does not correspond to an existing master record. That is, when the CHAIN command is executed, the indicator specified in columns 54–55 on the Calculation form is turned on. Depending on the application, this could mean one of two things.

> ***Transaction Record for Which There is no Corresponding Master Record***
>
> 1. The transaction record has an erroneously entered key field.
> 2. The transaction record represents a record to be added to the master file.
>   (For a payroll file, this may be a new employee; for an accounts receivable file, this may be a new account, and so on.)

If new records are *not* entered as transaction data, then transaction records that do not correspond to master records would be designated as errors just as they have been in the preceding illustrations.

If transaction data can, however, denote a new account, we can include a new record code in column 8Ø of the transaction record as follows.

RPG INPUT SPECIFICATIONS

Line (3–5)	Form Type (6)	Filename or Record Name (7–14)	Sequence (15–16)	Record Identifying Indicator (19–20)	Field Location From (44–47)	Field Location To (48–51)	RPG Field Name (53–58)
01Ø	I	TRANS	NS	Ø1			
02Ø	I						•
03Ø	I						•
04Ø	I						•
05Ø	I				8Ø	8Ø	NEWCDE
06	I						
07	I						

Using the Calculation Specifications form, a high condition on CHAIN could mean a new account on the transaction file. Thus the CHAIN command would then be followed by a test to see if there was an 'N' in NEWCDE for records with no corresponding master. An 'N' in NEWCDE would mean that the transaction record represents a new account.

RPG CALCULATION SPECIFICATIONS

Program		Keying Instruction	Graphic	Card Electro Number	Page 1 2 of	Program Identification 75 76 77 78 79 80
Programmer	Date		Key			

Line	Form Type	Control Level (L0–L9, LR, SR, AN/OR)	Indicators (Not, And Not, And Not)	Factor 1	Operation	Factor 2	Result Field Name	Length	Decimal Positions	Half Adjust (H)	Resulting Indicators High (Plus, 1>2)	Low (Minus, 1<2)	Equal (Zero, 1=2)	Comments
Ø1	C		Ø1	EMPNO	CHAIN	MASTER					25			
Ø2	C		Ø1 N25	STATUS	COMP	'A'					35	35		
Ø3	C		Ø1 25	NEWCDE	COMP	'N'							5Ø	
04	C													
05	C													

The following will thus be known if indicator 5Ø is turned on.

1. The transaction record did not match any master record.
2. The transaction record has an 'N' in column 8Ø, designating it as a new account.

Self-Evaluating Quiz

1. A ________ is a major collection of data for a particular application.
2. The process of keeping a master file current is called ________ .
3. The file of change records used to update the master file is called the ________ file.
4. The first program to be executed when a system is implemented is usually one that ________ the master file.
5. Before a master file is updated with transaction data, the transaction file should be ________ to minimize the risk of errors.
6. Typical procedures used to find errors in transaction data include ________ and ________ .
7. Control ________ are also produced in most creation, editing, and updating procedures to ensure that all records have been processed.
8. The output from a master file creation program would typically be a(n) ________ and a(n) ________ .
9. The output from a program that edits a transaction file would typically be a(n) ________ and a(n) ________ .
10. The output from an update program would typically be a(n) ________ and a(n) ________ .
11. In most procedures, as in the above instances, a ________ listing is created.
12. If an edit program is to include a procedure that checks to see that each transaction record corresponds to an active master record, then a(n) ________ operation is required.
13. In a chaining operation, the specifications for the key field on the master file are denoted on the ________ Specifications form.
14. In a chaining operation, the transaction field used for looking up the corresponding master record is specified on the ________ Specifications form along with the ________ .

Solutions

1. master file
2. updating
3. transaction
4. creates
5. edited
6. tests for reasonableness
   tests for completeness
7. totals
8. master file
   control listing
9. edited transaction file including only valid records
   control listing
10. updated or current master file
    control listing
11. control
12. chaining
13. File Description. These include (a) the starting position of the key field, (b) the length of the key field, and (c) the format of the key field.
14. Calculation
    name of the file to be "looked up," that is, the master file

II. ISAM Update Procedures

The last section focused on routines necessary for ensuring that a master file update will proceed properly. These routines include the following.

Procedure	*Secondary Output*	*Primary Consideration*
Creating a master file	Error control listing	Data used to create the master must be carefully edited to ensure accuracy.
Creating a transaction file	Error control listing	Data used to create the transaction file must be carefully edited to ensure accuracy.
Chaining from a transaction file to the master file	Error control listing	Checks must be performed to make sure that transaction records designated as new accounts are not already on the master and that transaction records designated as change records have corresponding master records.

We will discuss ISAM file updating in general and then consider a specific illustration.

A. Files Used

In this section, we will assume the existence of a master disk file with indexed sequential organization and an edited transaction file. The procedure used to make the master file current by incorporating transaction change data is called

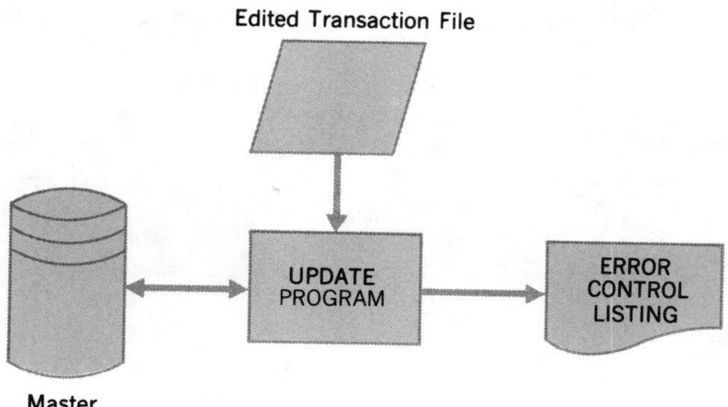

Figure 9.8
Update procedure.

the **update procedure** (see Figure 9.8). The edited transaction file will contain all changes that have occurred during an update cycle.

Changes to an ISAM file are made directly to the disk itself. Thus the master file serves as both input and output. This is in contrast to tape update procedures that use the input master file and a transaction file to create an entirely new master tape as output. A "U" in column 15 on the File Description form designates the ISAM file as an input/output file to be updated. An "A" in position 66 of the File Description form for this ISAM file indicates that records may be added.

B. Updating Records

The edited transaction file is chained to the master. If the transaction record is a change record, one which is to revise a master record, then the chaining procedure should cause the corresponding master record to be read into storage. If the transaction record does not have a corresponding master record, then an error has occurred and a message should be printed on the error control listing.

Transaction records that denote changes are the most common types of update records. For an accounts receivable master file, transaction change records would include sales, or purchases, and credits. If an update procedure is performed daily, the transaction file would include all sales and credits that occurred during the preceding day.

Transaction records used to update a payroll master file might include changes to salary, level, job description, name, address, number of dependents, and job location.

The transaction record would include a code to indicate the type of change.

For example, a payroll transaction record may include the following.

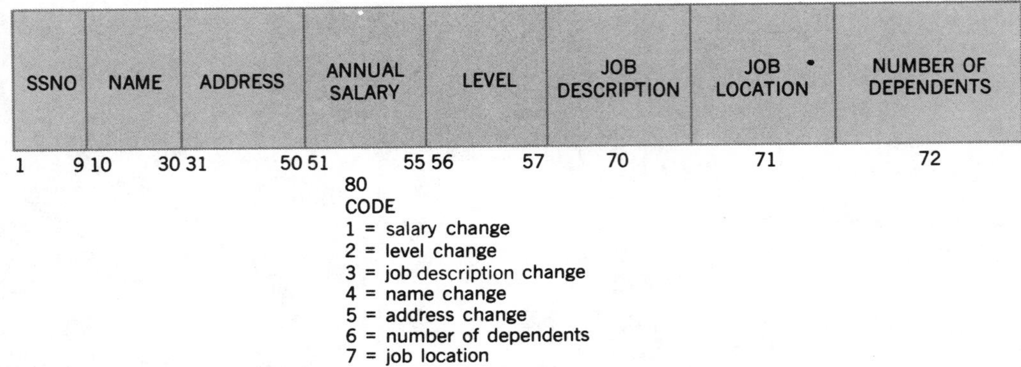

For an accounts receivable transaction file, we might have

1–5 ACCTNO
6–1Ø AMT
15 CODE (1 = Purchase; 2 = Credit)

The RPG programmer would turn on an indicator depending on the code in the transaction record. Then the corresponding changes would be made to update the master record. The programming excerpt for the accounts receivable procedure is as follows.

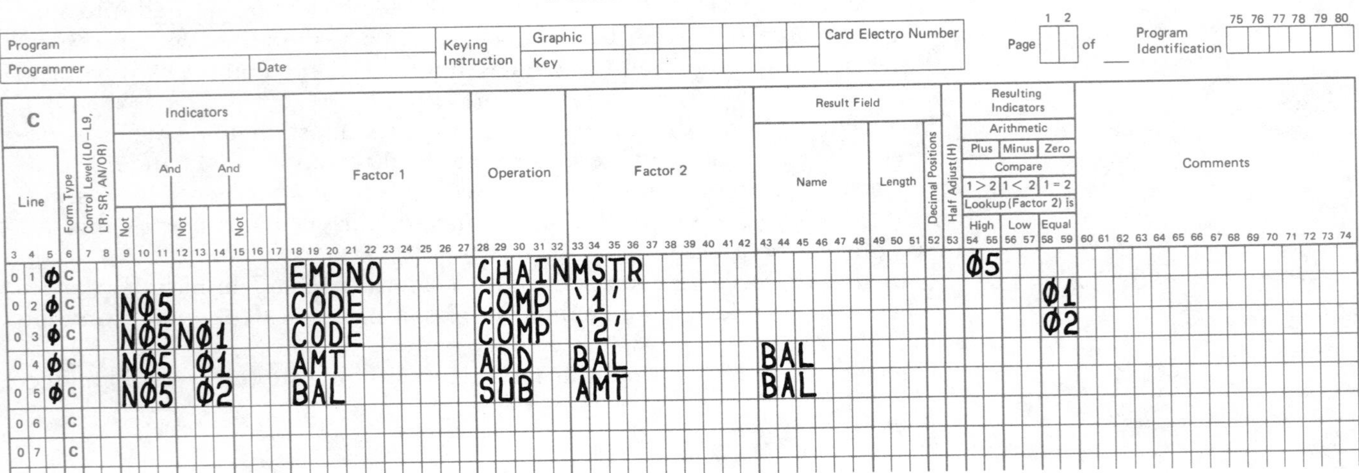

RPG CALCULATION SPECIFICATIONS

Line	Form Type	Indicators	Factor 1	Operation	Factor 2	Result Field Name	Resulting Indicators
01Ø	C		EMPNO	CHAIN	MSTR		Ø5 (High)
02Ø	C	NØ5	CODE	COMP	'1'		Ø1 (Equal)
03Ø	C	NØ5NØ1	CODE	COMP	'2'		Ø2 (Equal)
04Ø	C	NØ5 Ø1	AMT	ADD	BAL	BAL	
05Ø	C	NØ5 Ø2	BAL	SUB	AMT	BAL	
06	C						
07	C						
08	C						

RPG OUTPUT SPECIFICATIONS

Line	Form Type	Filename or Record Name	Output Indicators	Field Name or EXCPT Name	End Position in Output Record	Constant or Edit Word
01Ø	O		-			
02Ø	O		-			
03Ø	O		-			
04Ø	O		Ø1			'AMT OF PURCHASE'
05Ø	O		Ø2			'AMT OF CREDIT'
06	O					
07	O					

C. Changing the Status of Master Records

Recall that a master disk file includes active records, which are those that are currently part of the file, as well as inactive records, which are those that are retained for legal, control, or historical purposes but are no longer used for common updating or reporting. An inactive master payroll record, for example, might pertain to an employee who has retired, resigned, or been fired. An inactive master accounts receivable record might pertain to a customer who no longer has an active charge account.

Transaction records are sometimes created to change the status of master records from active to inactive. That is, a transaction record might specify a master record to be deactivated. Consider the following transaction accounts receivable record.

```
 1-5  ACCTNO
6-1Ø  AMT
  25  CODE      (1 = Purchase; 2 = Credit; 3 = Deactivate the account)
```

In this instance, as in the previous cases, a CHAIN operation should result in the reading of a corresponding master record with the same ACCTNO. If no corresponding master record exists, this would be an error and an error message should be printed.

Assuming that a valid master record exists with the same ACCTNO as the transaction record, then the CODE is checked. If CODE = 3, 'I' (for inactive) is moved to the STATUS field of the master record and the record is rewritten.

RPG CALCULATION SPECIFICATIONS

Line	Form Type	Control Level	Indicators	Factor 1	Operation	Factor 2	Result Field Name	Length	Decimal Positions	Half Adjust	Resulting Indicators High	Low	Equal	Comments
0 1 Ø	C			EMPNO	CHAIN	MSTR					Ø5			
0 2 Ø	C		NØ5	CODE	COMP	'3'							Ø3	CHANGE TO INACT
0 3	C													
0 4	C													

RPG OUTPUT SPECIFICATIONS

Line	Form Type	Filename or Record Name	Type	Space Before	Space After	Skip Before	Skip After	Output Indicators	Field Name or EXCPT Name	Edit Codes	B/A/C/1–9/R	End Position in Output Record	P/B/L/R	Constant or Edit Word
0 1 Ø	O								•					
0 2 Ø	O								•					
0 3 Ø	O								•					
0 4 Ø	O							Ø3	STATUS					'I'
0 5 Ø	O							NØ3	STATUS					'A'
0 6	O													
0 7	O													

D. Adding New Records to a Master File

As noted, transaction records are sometimes used to designate a new account that must be *added to* the master file. In this instance, a CHAIN command should be executed to ensure that a corresponding master record does *not* already exist. That is, if ACCTNO 12345 is designated as a new account on the transaction file, the programmer must make certain that ACCTNO 12345 does not already exist on the master.

Thus, if the CHAIN operation produces a 'HIGH' indicator, then check to see if the transaction record specifies a new account. If it does, add the new record to the master file. Later in this chapter, we will see in detail the procedure that is used to add records to an ISAM file. Basically, we use the appropriate output indicators to write an output record and code "ADD" in columns 16–18 of the Output Specifications form.

If, however, the transaction record specifies an update, then the CHAIN command resulted in an error since a corresponding master record should have been found. When an error condition occurs, an error message should print indicating that a record was not found.

All updating procedures should produce error control listings indicating the following.

1. All changes made.
2. The number of records processed, added, and deleted.
3. The number of occurrences of each type of error and a listing of each error record.

In many instances, there might be more than one transaction record for a specific master record. For a transaction accounts receivable file, for example, a given ACCTNO may have several purchases or transactions that need to be chained to the master. Similarly, a transaction payroll file may include two change records for the same employee. Suppose a female employee marries; typically, a name change record and an address change record might be required.

If, in fact, there is more than one transaction for a given master record, each is chained as per our illustration and each is processed individually. The fact that there may be numerous changes for a given master record just means that the indexed master record will be retrieved and rewritten more than once.

Before considering a specific illustration of an ISAM update procedure, the following will serve as a general review of concepts.

Summary of Update Procedures

Changes

1. For each transaction record, CHAIN to the master file to make certain that an active master record exists.
2. If an active master record exists, make the appropriate changes. Z-ADD can be used on the Calculation form for changing numeric fields; MOVE can be used for changing nonnumeric fields.
3. Rewrite the master record by indicating on the Output form all the fields to be changed.
4. For control purposes, add 1 to the count of records updated.
5. As an extra edit check, you may want to determine if the field to be changed is, in fact, different from the field currently in the master record.

Deletions

1. CHAIN to the master file to bring the master record corresponding to the transaction record into storage.
2. Move 'I' to the status field of the master record to indicate 'Inactive.'
3. For control purposes, add 1 to the count of records deleted.
4. As an extra edit check, make sure the record was active before deactivating it.
5. Rewrite the inactive record on the disk.

Additions

1. CHAIN to the master file to make sure that a record with the same key field does not already exist in the master file.
2. Add the new record to the master file.
3. Add 1 to the count of new records.

III. Illustrating an ISAM Update Procedure in Its Entirety

The following is the format for a master sales file called SMSTR.

SMSTR 128-position records

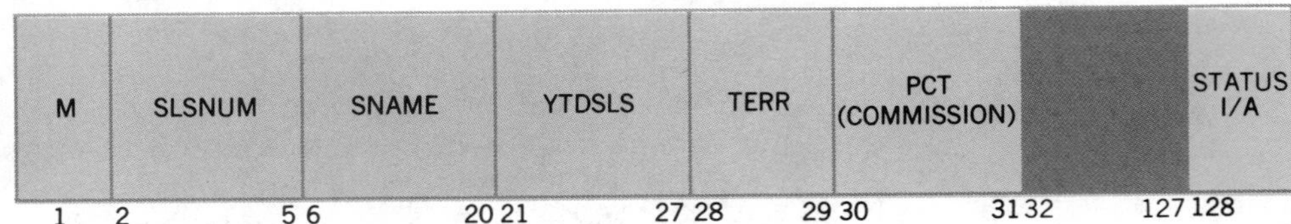

SMSTR is an indexed sequential master file with SLSNUM (salesperson number) as the key field. It will be accessed randomly, so that only master records with corresponding transaction records need to be read into storage to be updated. SNAME is the salesperson's name, YTDSLS is the year-to-date sales credited to the salesperson, TERR is the person's territory, PCT is the commission percent, STATUS is 'A' for active records and 'I' for inactive records.

SMSTR is an indexed input/output file. We read from it to access master records that correspond to the transaction file, and we write to it with changes, additions, and deletions. It is accessed randomly. Its file type is 'U' for 'UPDATE'.

The transaction file called MAINT contains the changes that will update SMSTR. Position 1 of each transaction record will always contain a 'C'. TSLSNO must always be coded to indicate the key field, and CODE must be included to indicate the type of transaction. The format for MAINT is as follows.

MAINT 64-position records

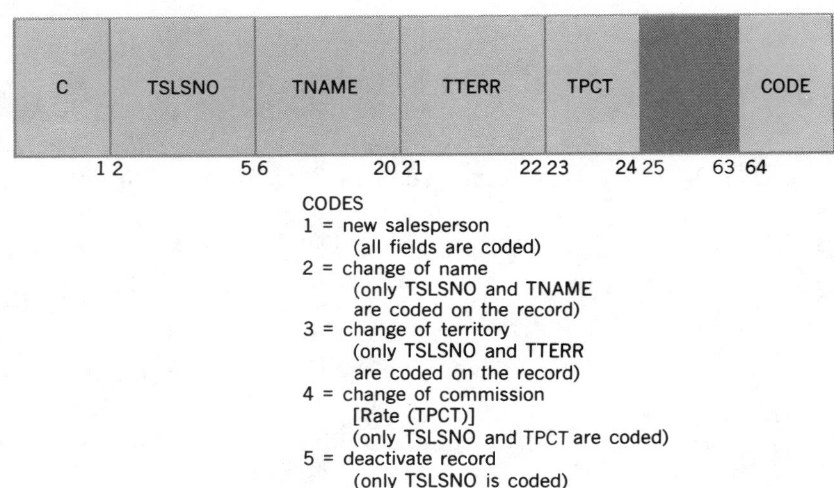

Note that in using these codes, only *one* record format is required for MAINT. All records—updates, additions, and deletions—use this same format.

The error control listing, called SLSMAINT, has the following format.

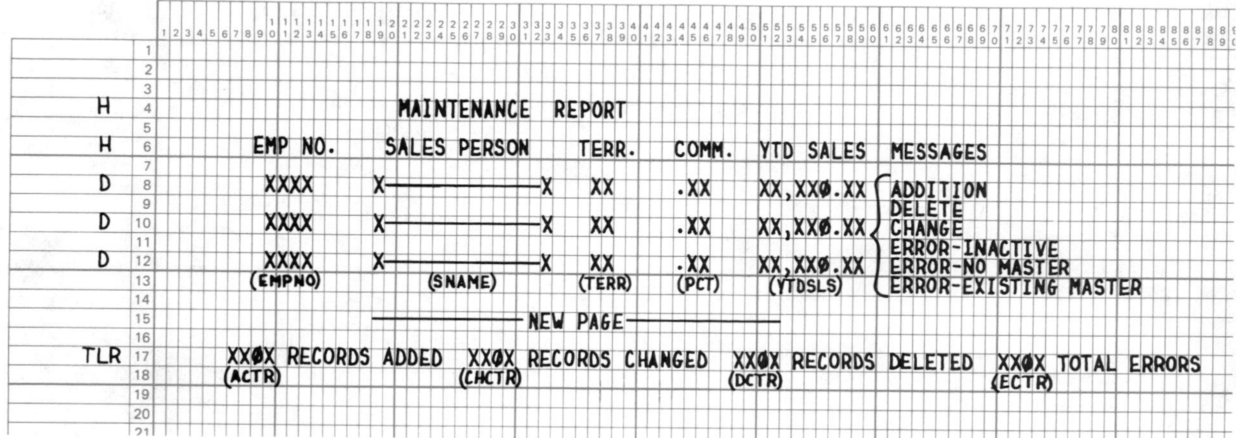

	Line	Printer spacing chart content
H	4	MAINTENANCE REPORT
H	6	EMP NO. SALES PERSON TERR. COMM. YTD SALES MESSAGES
D	8	XXXX X————X XX .XX XX,XXØ.XX { ADDITION
	9	DELETE
D	10	XXXX X————X XX .XX XX,XXØ.XX { CHANGE
	11	ERROR-INACTIVE
D	12	XXXX X————X XX .XX XX,XXØ.XX { ERROR-NO MASTER
	13	(EMPNO) (SNAME) (TERR) (PCT) (YTDSLS) ERROR-EXISTING MASTER
	15	———— NEW PAGE ————
TLR	17	XXØX RECORDS ADDED XXØX RECORDS CHANGED XXØX RECORDS DELETED XXØX TOTAL ERRORS
	18	(ACTR) (CHCTR) (DCTR) (ECTR)

The File Description Specifications form for this update procedure is as follows.

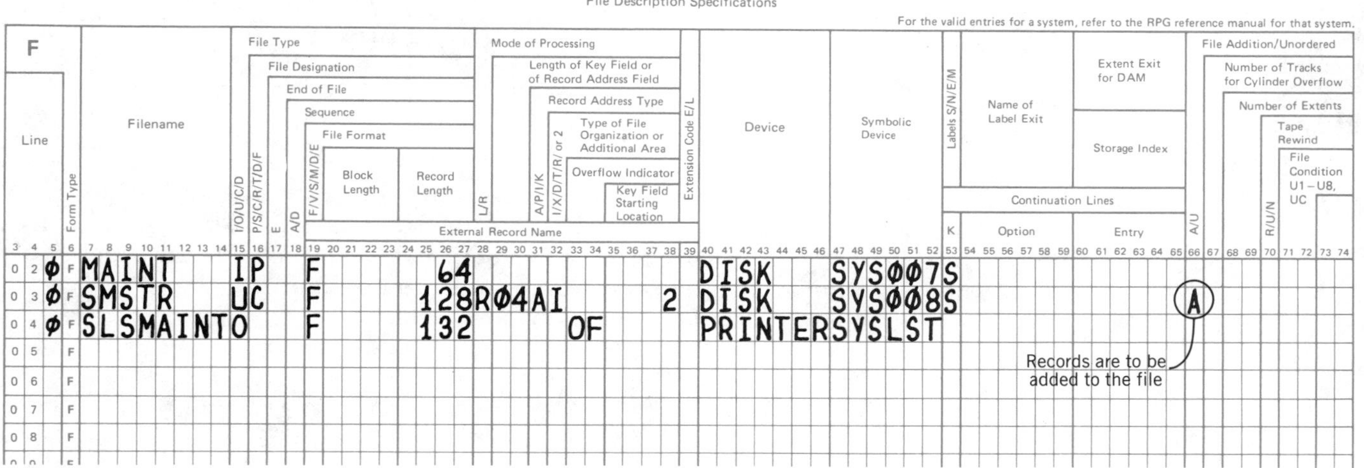

File Description Specifications

Line	Form Type	Filename	File Type	File Designation	File Format	Record Length	Mode of Processing	Length of Key Field	Record Address Type	Type of File Organization	Overflow Indicator	Key Field Starting Location	Device	Symbolic Device	Labels	File Addition
02Ø	F	MAINT	I	P	F	64							DISK	SYSØØ7	S	
03Ø	F	SMSTR	U	C	F	128	R	Ø4	A	I		2	DISK	SYSØØ8	S	A
04Ø	F	SLSMAINT	O		F	132					OF		PRINTER	SYSLST		

The transaction file called MAINT is considered to be the primary input file. That is, each record from MAINT is read first and then chained to find the corresponding master record, if one exists.

SMSTR is an *U*pdate, *C*hained file that is to be processed randomly. A file designated with a file type of 'U' is treated as both an input and output file. When mode of processing is designated with 'R' for random processing, the following entries are required.

1. Key field length: Ø4 in this illustration.
2. Starting location of the key field: 2 in this illustration. (The key field, SLSNUM, starts in column 2.)
3. File organization: I for indexed in this illustration.

Since we will also be adding records to the ISAM file, we code A for 'Additions' in column 66 of the File Description Specifications. Adding records to an ISAM file places records in the overflow areas of the disk; the index, however, is in sequence so that, even if a record is added, it can be accessed correctly later on. That is, the index is resequenced after each update procedure if records have been added to the master file.

The Input Specifications for SMSTR are as follows.

RPG INPUT SPECIFICATIONS

Line	Form Type	Filename or Record Name	Sequence	Record Identifying Indicator	Position	C/Z/D	Character	Field Location From	To	Decimal Positions	RPG Field Name
01Φ	I	SMSTR	AA	Φ4	1	C	M				
02Φ	I							2	5		SLSNUM
03Φ	I							6	2Φ		SNAME
04Φ	I							21	27	2	YTDSLS
05Φ	I							28	29		TERR
06Φ	I							3Φ	31	2	PCT
07Φ	I							128	128		STATUS
08	I										
09	I										

All input fields on SMSTR that are necessary for processing are included on the Input Specifications form. STATUS is the field that will include 'A' for active records and 'I' for inactive records. Numeric fields must include the number of decimal positions in the field by coding a digit in column 52.

The Input Specifications for MAINT are as follows.

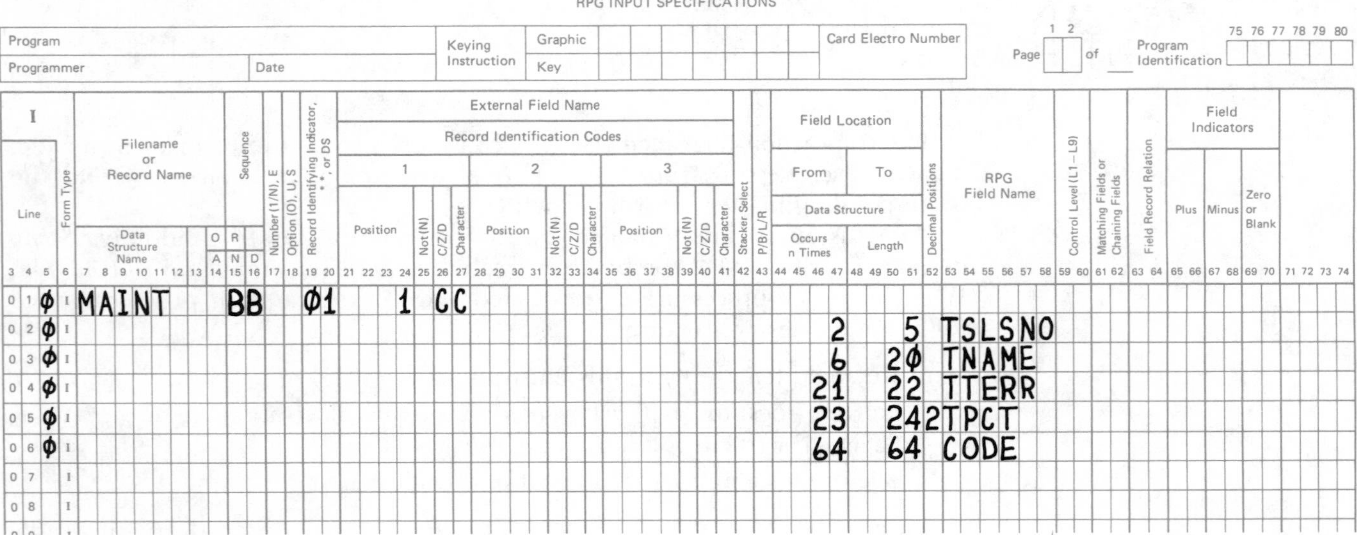

RPG INPUT SPECIFICATIONS

Line	Form Type	Filename or Record Name	Sequence	Record Identifying Indicator	Position	C/Z/D	Character	Field Location From	To	Decimal Positions	RPG Field Name
01Φ	I	MAINT	BB	Φ1	1	C	C				
02Φ	I							2	5		TSLSNO
03Φ	I							6	2Φ		TNAME
04Φ	I							21	22		TTERR
05Φ	I							23	24	2	TPCT
06Φ	I							64	64		CODE
07	I										
08	I										

TSLSNO will be used for chaining to the master file, SMSTR.

Calculation Specifications for Updating Existing Master Records

The transaction field TSLSNO is chained to SMSTR file when indicator Ø1 is on. That is, TSLSNO is compared to SLSNUM on SMSTR. The CHAIN operation compares the field specified in Factor 1 to the key field that is designated for SMSTR on the File Description form.

If the corresponding master record is found, then the programmer should make certain that the transaction code field does not equal 1, which would indicate a new salesperson. For update transaction records, the CHAIN command *should* result in a corresponding master being read in, but for new accounts, the CHAIN command should result in a 'HIGH' indicator.

If the CHAIN command results in a 'HIGH' indicator and the transaction record is *not* a new account, this would be an error. It would mean that the transaction file contains a record to be used to update the master, but that no record exists. An error message should be printed in this instance.

If the CHAIN command results in an equal condition, make certain that the status of the master record is 'A' for active. If not, this too would be an error.

The Calculation Specifications form for this series of steps is as follows.

RPG CALCULATION SPECIFICATIONS

```
01ØC***        CHAIN TO MASTER AND MAKE CERTAIN THAT PROPER    ***
02ØC***              CORRESPONDENCE EXISTS                     ***
03ØC*
04ØC   Ø1      TSLSNO    CHAINSMSTR                22
05ØC   Ø1      CODE      COMP '1'                      1Ø
06ØC   Ø1N22   STATUS    COMP 'I'                      33
07ØC   Ø1N22N33
08ØCANN1Ø      1         ADD  CHCTR     CHCTR     4Ø
09ØC   Ø1 22N1Ø
10ØCOR Ø1N22 33
11ØCOR Ø1N22 1Ø1         ADD  ECTR      ECTR      4Ø
12ØC*
13ØC***   CHCTR = COUNT OF RECORDS CHANGED OR UPDATED          ***
14ØC***   ECTR  = COUNT OF TRANS CHANGE RECORDS WITH NO        ***
15ØC***                  CORRESPONDING MASTER, OR              ***
16ØC***                  AN INACTIVE MASTER, OR                ***
17ØC***                  EXISTING MASTER WHEN CODE = ADDITION  ***
18 C
19 C
20 C
```

The following indicators, then, denote a valid change or update condition.

Indicators On	*Meaning*
Ø1	A transaction record exists.
N22	Found a master record with the same salesperson number as the transaction record. Ø4 could be used in place of N22 because when a master record is read, indicator Ø4 is turned on.
N33	The status of the master record is not 'I'—assume it is 'A' for active.

If N22, Ø1, and N33 are on, then the type of change record must be determined by testing the CODE field. Recall that a code of 2 is a NAME change, 3 is TERR change, 4 is PCT change, and 5 is a record to be deactivated. The RPG coding necessary for designating the appropriate change is as follows.

RPG CALCULATION SPECIFICATIONS

```
01ΦC***        CHANGE THE MASTER RECORD                        ***
02ΦC*
03ΦC   Φ1N22N33CODE      COMP '2'                        4Φ
04ΦC   Φ1N22N33
05ΦCAN 4Φ                MOVE TNAME     SNAME
06ΦC   Φ1N22N33CODE      COMP '3'                        5Φ
07ΦC   Φ1N22N33
08ΦCAN 5Φ                MOVE TTERR     TERR
09ΦC   Φ1N22N33CODE      COMP '4'                        6Φ
10ΦC   Φ1N22N33
11ΦCAN 6Φ                Z-ADDTPCT      PCT
12ΦC   Φ1N22N33CODE      COMP '5'                        7Φ
13ΦC   Φ1N22N33
14ΦCAN 7Φ                MOVE 'I'       STATUS
15ΦC   Φ1N22N33
16ΦCAN 7Φ       1        ADD  DCTR      DCTR   4Φ
17 C
18 C
19 C
```

Z-ADD is used to copy a numeric field such as PCT. MOVE is used to transfer fields not designated as numeric.

For transaction records that designate new accounts, we would have the following indicators set.

Indicators On	*Meaning*
Ø1	A transaction record exists.
22	No master record exists for the transaction record.
1Ø	The CODE on the transaction record is equal to 1, denoting a new account.

For new accounts, all transaction fields would be moved to the master area and the status should be set to 'A' for active.

The following calculations are used to add a record to the master file.

RPG CALCULATION SPECIFICATIONS

Line	Form Type	Control Level	Indicators	Factor 1	Operation	Factor 2	Result Field Name	Length	Decimal Positions	Comments
01Ø	C	***		ADD NEW MASTER RECORD TO FILE						***
02Ø	C	*								
03Ø	C		Ø1 22 1Ø		MOVE	TSLSNO	SLSNUM			
04Ø	C		Ø1 22 1Ø		MOVE	TNAME	SNAME			
05Ø	C		Ø1 22 1Ø		MOVE	TTERR	TERR			
06Ø	C		Ø1 22 1Ø		Z-ADD	Ø	YTDSLS			
07Ø	C		Ø1 22 1Ø		Z-ADD	TPCT	PCT			
08Ø	C		Ø1 22 1Ø		MOVE	'A'	STATUS			
09Ø	C		Ø1 22 1Ø	1	ADD	ACTR	ACTR	4	Ø	
10	C									
11	C									

There are two types of output in this program: disk output, which will be the updated ISAM master file; and printed output, indicating errors and control totals.

Disk Output

In most of our previous problems that used disk output, each output field was defined on the Output Specifications form. This is required if each output record is created anew from an input record.

In the update procedure defined in this chapter, an SMSTR record already exists—in the input area—for transaction records in which a successful CHAIN operation was performed. Thus, for records to be changed, only the fields that require changing need be defined. You will recall that the following indicators denote a successful CHAIN, where an active master record exists.

Ø1 A transaction record exists.
N22 A chain to the master file results in a corresponding record.
N33 The master record is active.

In this instance, the changes to the master are defined by the following indicators, which would be turned on during calculations.

Indicator	*Meaning*
4Ø	SNAME change
5Ø	STERR change
6Ø	PCT change
7Ø	STATUS change (record is to be deactivated)

The following Output Specifications coding would result in the appropriate changes to the master.

RPG OUTPUT SPECIFICATIONS

```
OSMSTR    D        Ø1N22N33
O                            4ØSNAME    2Ø
O                            5ØTERR     29
O                            6ØPCT      31
O                            7ØSTATUS  128
```

For transaction records that denote new accounts, all SMSTR fields must be specified in the output area since a new record is to be created. You will recall that the following indicators are used to designate a new account.

Ø1 A transaction record exists.

22 A corresponding master record does not exist.

1Ø The transaction code field indicates a new account.

For these transaction records, a new SMSTR record must be created. ADD is coded on the detail line in columns 16–18 to indicate that an entirely new record is to be added to the disk file. The fields to serve as output must also be specified:

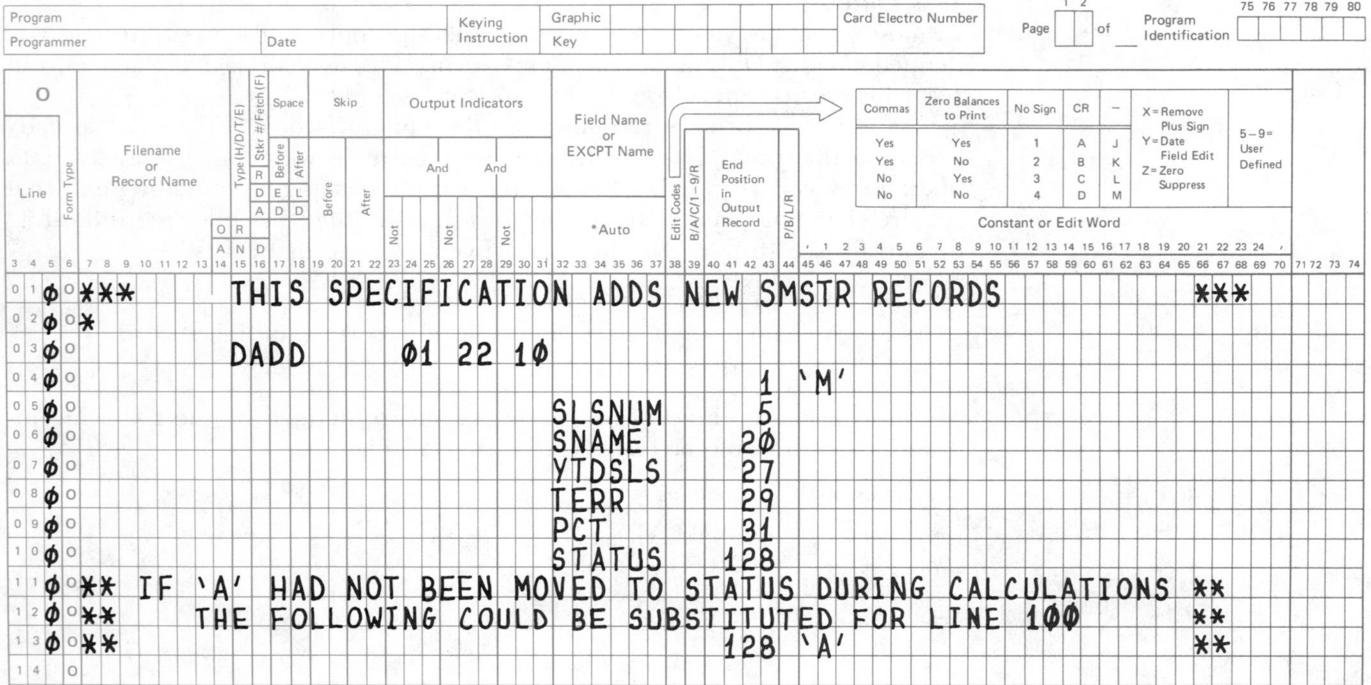

RPG OUTPUT SPECIFICATIONS

```
01Ø O***      THIS SPECIFICATION ADDS NEW SMSTR RECORDS        ***
02Ø O*
03Ø O         DADD      Ø1 22 1Ø
04Ø O                                          1 'M'
05Ø O                               SLSNUM     5
06Ø O                               SNAME     2Ø
07Ø O                               YTDSLS    27
08Ø O                               TERR      29
09Ø O                               PCT       31
10Ø O                               STATUS   128
11Ø O** IF 'A' HAD NOT BEEN MOVED TO STATUS DURING CALCULATIONS **
12Ø O**     THE FOLLOWING COULD BE SUBSTITUTED FOR LINE 1ØØ     **
13Ø O**                                      128 'A'            **
```

Printed Output

The following Output Specifications will produce the printed results specified on the Printer Spacing Chart. (The Output Specifications are continued on the next page.)

RPG OUTPUT SPECIFICATIONS

Line	Form Type	Filename or Record Name	Type (H/D/T/E)	Space Before	Space After	Skip Before	Output Indicators	Field Name or EXCPT Name	Edit Codes	End Position in Output Record	Constant or Edit Word
01ϕ	O	SLSMAINT	H		2	ϕ4	1P				
02ϕ	O		OR				OF				
03ϕ	O									39	'MAINTENANCE REPORT'
04ϕ	O		H		2		1P				
05ϕ	O		OR				OF				
06ϕ	O									15	'EMP NO.'
07ϕ	O									31	'SALES PERSON'
08ϕ	O									48	'TERR. COMM.'
09ϕ	O									69	'YTD SALES MESSAGES'
10ϕ	O		D		2		ϕ1				
11ϕ	O						N22	EMPNO		13	
12ϕ	O						N22	SNAME		33	
13ϕ	O						N22	TERR		39	
14ϕ	O						N22	PCT	3	46	
15ϕ	O						N22	YTDSLS	1	59	
16ϕ	O						22	TSLSNO		13	
17ϕ	O						22	TNAME		33	
18ϕ	O						22	TTERR		39	
19ϕ	O						22	TPCT		46	
20ϕ	O						N22N33			67	'CHANGE'
21ϕ	O						N22 33 7ϕ			67	'DELETE'
22ϕ	O						22 1ϕ			69	'ADDITION'
23ϕ	O						N22 33			75	'ERROR-INACTIVE'
24ϕ	O						22N1ϕ			76	'ERROR-NO MASTER'
25ϕ	O						N22 1ϕ			82	'ERROR-EXISTING MASTER'

RPG OUTPUT SPECIFICATIONS

Line	Form Type	Filename or Record Name	Type (H/D/T/E)	Skip Before	Output Indicators	Field Name or EXCPT Name	Edit Codes	End Position in Output Record	Constant or Edit Word
01	O		T	04	LR				
02	O					ACTR	Z	10	
03	O							24	'RECORDS ADDED'
04	O					CHCTR	Z	30	
05	O							46	'RECORDS CHANGED'
06	O					DCTR	Z	52	
07	O							68	'RECORDS DELETED'
08	O					ECTR	Z	74	
09	O							87	'TOTAL ERRORS'
10	O								
11	O								
12	O								

Note that this printed output is used for correcting errors and for providing control totals. In general, the more information provided on an error control listing, the better.

Summary of Disk Updating

You may have noticed that it is possible to update both sequential and indexed sequential disks in similar ways. By using the file type of U (column 15) on the File Description Specifications form, you may designate a disk as an existing file to be updated. If we want to add records to that file as well as change existing records, we code 'A' in column 66 on the File Description Specifications form.

Disk files can have the following specifications.

File Description Specifications	*Meaning*
F or V in column 16	Fixed (F) or variable length (V) records.
Block length must be a multiple of the record length.	Disk records are usually blocked for efficiency.

For ISAM files we code,

ISAM File Description Entries	
Mode of processing (column 28)	For records to be processed randomly (R).
Type of file organization (column 32)	I for indexed.
Length of key field (columns 29–3Ø)	Numeric entry, right-justified.

Key field starting position (columns 33-38)	Numeric entry, right-justified.
Record address type (column 31)	A for alphanumeric. P for packed.
File additions/unordered	A for adding records, U if creating an ISAM file in no specific sequence.

To access the disk file that has been designated with a 'U', use the following, depending on the disk file organization.

Disk Organization	*Method of Access*
Sequential file organization	Matching transaction records.
Indexed	CHAIN command on Calculation form.

To add records to a file designated as an update file, code ADD in columns 16–18 of the D line of the Output Specifications form. This will add records to the end of the file. When using sequential file organization, the file will need to be sorted after updating so that it will again be in correct sequence.

For ISAM files, it is not necessary to sort the file since the index is automatically sorted into the correct key field sequence after each update. That is, the physical location of the records is not important since the index can direct us to the appropriate record on a random access basis.

Making Inquiries Into an ISAM File

Thus far, we have seen one benefit of ISAM files—you can CHAIN to the master with transaction records in no specific sequence and update the file as necessary. A second major advantage of ISAM files is that you can inquire into the status of any record. Only those records to be changed are accessed.

Updating a Master Disk File

1. The file to be updated is treated as both an input and output file.
2. The update file is described on the following forms.
   File Description
   Input
   Output
3. Only the fields to be changed need be described on the Input Specifications form.
4. Records to be changed must already exist on the master.
5. Records to be added should not have the same key field as one already on the master.

IV. VSAM Processing

VSAM (virtual storage access method) is another access method developed by IBM for processing indexed files. It may be used for direct and/or sequential processing of fixed and variable-length records on direct-access storage devices that have established indexes for records.

The following capabilities make VSAM more flexible than ISAM.

1. Creating records with multiple keys is permitted so that the records can be accessed in different ways.
2. Performance is more efficient.
3. Provides better data integrity and improved data organization.
4. Permits processing of variable-length records.
5. Allows the specification of alternate keys with duplicates and thus facilitates data base processing. For example, it is possible to access all records directly with DEPT = Ø2, where DEPT is one key field. In this case, DEPT would not be a unique field since several records could have the same DEPT.
6. Records can be processed *both* sequentially and randomly (called *dynamically*) in a single run.

ISAM files may be converted to VSAM files by using the method described in the following IBM manuals.

G32Ø–6Ø29 *VSAM Tuning and ISAM to VSAM Conversion Guide*
G32Ø–5774 *VSAM Primer and Reference*

The records in a VSAM file are usually arranged in logical sequence by a key field. Like an ISAM file, the VSAM file has an index that allows records to be processed either sequentially or randomly. The key field uniquely identifies each record in the file. The key may be located anywhere within the record and may vary in length from one byte to a maximum of 255 bytes. In addition, the key may be numeric or alphanumeric but must be arranged in ascending sequence. As with an ISAM file, duplicate keys are never permitted as the primary key sequence in VSAM files but numerous keys are permitted. That is, duplicate keys are allowed as alternate key fields.

A major advantage of VSAM is that alternate keys may be specified for a simple data file. Therefore, you do not need multiple copies of the same information organized for different applications. If a VSAM file has been created with two keys (for example, EMPNO and NAME), it is possible to access a record directly from that file if the user has either the EMPNO or the NAME. This is *not* the case with ISAM processing. Since only one key is used with ISAM, it would not be possible to access a record directly without knowing the specific key.

A. Data Organization

When a key sequence VSAM file is created, certain segments of the disk can be left empty. This means that free space is distributed throughout the file. The free space may be distributed equally as a percentage of the space used by the file or allocated in accordance to the job requirements. This free space is used by the system when inserting new records or lengthening existing records. Free space eliminates the need for overflow chaining, which decreases the efficiency of ISAM files. Therefore, VSAM files are more efficient, since access time is not adversely affected by the addition of records to the file. Remember, ISAM files require the system to chain to overflow areas when records are added to the file. Hence, access time increases, resulting in a corresponding loss of performance. In addition, VSAM files do not require reorganization as frequently

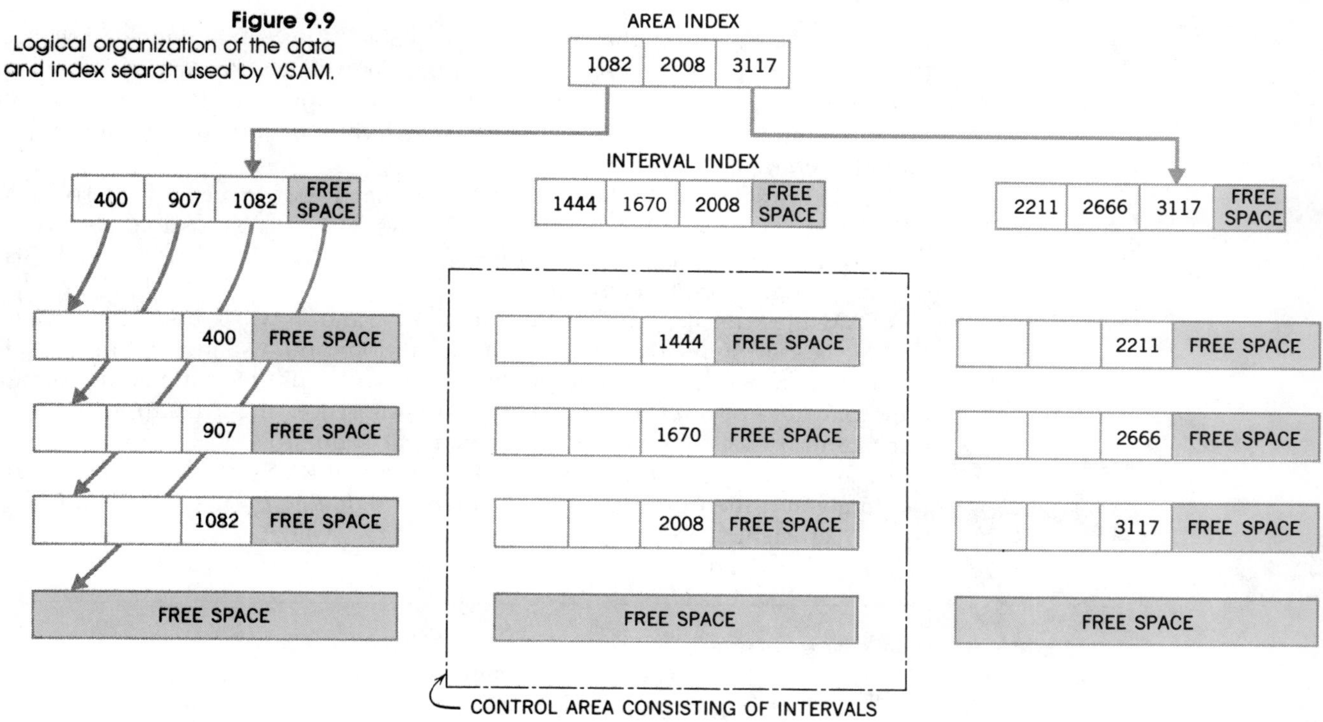

Figure 9.9
Logical organization of the data and index search used by VSAM.

*NOTE MASTER INDEX NOT SHOWN.

as do ISAM files, since additions to a VSAM file can use free space that is available. VSAM also *reclaims* space when a record is deleted or shortened; this space becomes additional free space.

Figure 9.9 illustrates the logical organization of the data and index search used by VSAM. Data is grouped into control areas that are further subdivided into control intervals. Note that the control areas contain free space as illustrated.

The logic used in processing records is very similar to that of ISAM in that the *highest* keys for the data areas are stored in the area index. The highest key for each interval is similarly stored in the interval index. To access a record, the index is searched (see Figure 9.10).

If the key to be found is *less than* or equal to the index key, then control is transferred to the next lower subdivision. Finally the control interval is searched sequentially until the record is found.

If a record is to be added, it is inserted in the control interval where it logically

Search	*Activity*
Master Index	Find high record for control area containing record and branch to control area index.
Control Area Index	Find high record for control interval containing record and branch to control interval index.
Control Interval Index	Search sequentially for record.

Figure 9.10
Searching the index to access a record.

belongs, making use of the free space available. This movement of records is done in primary storage before any writing takes place. Record movement for insertions, deletions, and updating takes place in primary storage before any actual input/output operations are performed, thereby improving data integrity and efficiency.

Another significant feature of VSAM is that files can be moved from one DOS/VS system to another or to an OS/VS system. This is possible because the data formats of the files are identical. Note that VSAM is most widely used under DOS and OS systems.

VSAM files can be processed sequentially, randomly, or both. Processing a VSAM file during a single run as both a random and a sequential file is called **dynamic processing**. Dynamic processing provides the most flexibility because the capabilities of both sequential and random processing are supported at the same time. Processing can be switched from sequential to random and vice-versa, as many times as is necessary. For example, if a VSAM file is to be updated randomly and then printed out in sequence, dynamic processing would be extremely efficient.

The primary advantages of VSAM files may be summarized as follows.

Summary

1. Improved performance for additions to the file.
2. Reorganization requirements are less frequent.
3. Multiple keys eliminate the need for duplicate files.
4. Cross system compatibility (OS/DOS).
5. Better system integrity.

B. RPG Coding for VSAM Applications

VSAM files can be processed sequentially, sequentially within limits, randomly, or dynamically (i.e., both sequentially and randomly). The processing of VSAM files is essentially the same as the processing of ISAM files; the File Description Specifications form includes most of the differences. The mode of processing is specified by an entry in position 28 of the File Description Specifications form.

1. An R indicates random processing.
2. An L indicates sequential processing between limits.
3. A blank indicates sequential processing or dynamic processing. A READ or SETLL that follows a CHAIN changes the mode from random to sequential. A CHAIN following a READ or SETLL *automatically* changes the mode from sequential to random.

Key Terms

Chaining
Control total
Create program
Data verification
Dynamic processing
Editing
Hash total
Indexed file
ISAM
Key field
Master file
Standard label
Transaction file
Update procedure
VSAM

Self-Evaluating Quiz

1. A(n) ________ procedure is the process of making a master file current.
2. (T or F) An indexed sequential disk file can be used as both input and output during an update procedure.
3. The ________ file contains the changes to be made to the master file.
4. When the key field on a transaction file is used to look up a record with the same key field on a master disk file, this is called ________ .
5. In general, there are three types of transaction records: ________ , ________ , and ________ .
6. To delete a master record from an ISAM file, we generally ________ .
7. The two forms of output in an update procedure are the ________ and an ________ .
8. To add new records to a master ISAM file, code ________ on the D line of the Output form.
9. When records are to be added to a master ISAM file, a CHAIN procedure should be used to ensure that ________ .
10. When a CHAIN procedure results in a high condition, this means that ________ .

Solutions

1. update
2. T
3. transaction
4. chaining
5. changes to the master file
   additions to the master file
   deletions from the master file
6. deactivate the record or change the STATUS from 'A' (active) to 'I' (inactive)
7. updated master
   error control listing
8. ADD
9. a record with the same key field does not already exist on the master
10. there is no master record with a key field corresponding to the key field on the transaction file

Review Questions

1. When an ISAM disk file is created, the computer establishes a(n) ________ on the disk that keeps track of where each record is physically located.
2. When creating an ISAM file, the programmer must designate a field on the record as a(n) ________ that uniquely identifies the record to the computer.
3. When an ISAM file is created, it is created in ________ sequence.
4. After it is created, the master file must be made current or ________ on a regular basis.
5. The file that contains changes to the master file is called the ________ .
6. Before updating the master file with change records, the transaction file must be ________ or checked for errors.
7. The four general procedures used for master file processing are: ________ , ________ , ________ , and ________ .
8. The output from a program that creates a master file is ________ and ________ .

9. The ________ consists of a list of all incoming records flagged as errors during the file creation routine.
10. For ISAM files, the fields required on the File Description form to designate the key field are ________ , ________ , and ________ .
11. The type of file organization (column 32 of the File Description form) for an ISAM file is ________ .
12. A ________ is a total of a field that is not usually used in an arithmetic operation.
13. If a procedure is required to check that each transaction record is actually associated with an active master record, the ________ procedure is used.
14. For chaining operations, the transaction file is the (primary/secondary) file.
15. (T or F) A key field used in a chaining operation may be alphanumeric.

Debugging Exercises

The problem definition for this exercise is shown in Figure 9.11. The coding sheets in Figure 9.12 contain a syntax error. Identify the error and illustrate the correction you would make to the program.

Figure 9.11 Problem definition for the Debugging Exercise.

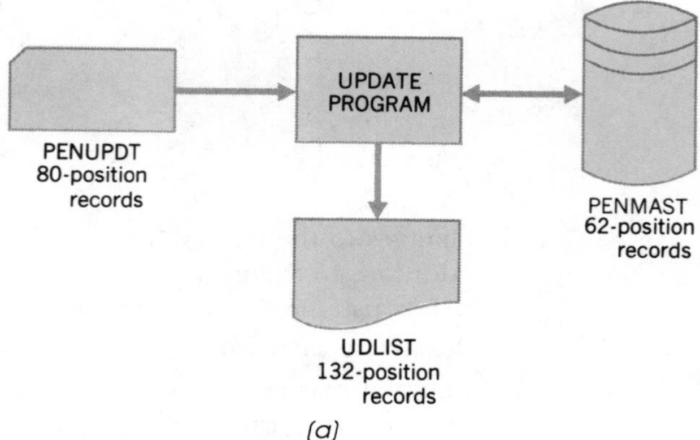

(a)

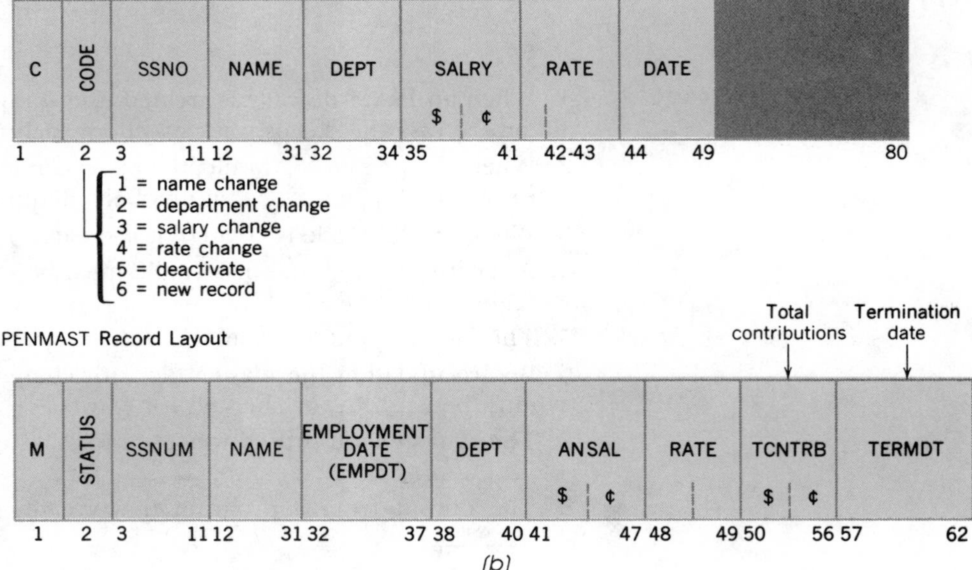

(b)

Figure 9.11 *(continued)*

UDLIST Printer Spacing Chart

```
H    2              PENSION FUND MASTER FILE UPDATE
H    3                          XX/XX/XX
     4
H    5  SOC. SEC.                                   ANNUAL     RATE OF
H    6   NUMBER            NAME             DEPT    SALARY    CONTRIBUTION
     7
D    8  X-------X  X----------------------X  XXX  $XX,XX$.XX     ØX%
D    9             ***************           ***  **********     ***     (only fields that change are marked)
D   10  X-------X  X----------------------X  XXX  $XX,XX$.XX     ØX%     ** NEW RECORD EFFECTIVE XX/XX/XX
    11
D   12  X-------X  X----------------------X  XXX  $XX,XX$.XX     ØX%     ** DEACTIVATED EFFECTIVE XX/XX/XX
    13
D   14  X-------X  X----------------------X  XXX  $XX,XX$.XX     ØX%     ** ERROR - EXISTING RECORD
    15
    16
TLR 17       *** NUMBER OF RECORDS ADDED ØX
    18
TLR 19       *** NUMBER OF RECORDS DEACTIVATED ØX
    20
TLR 21       *** TOTAL NUMBER OF RECORDS PROCESSED XØX
    22
    23
```

(c)

Figure 9.12 Coding sheets for the Debugging Exercise. *(Continued on next page.)*

RPG CONTROL AND FILE DESCRIPTION SPECIFICATIONS

Program: ISAM UPDATE
Programmer: N. JOHNKE Date: 9/27/--
Graphic: Ø 1 2 Key: ZERO ONE TWO
Page Ø1 of 9 Program Identification: SSSØ9

Control Specifications

```
01Φ H
```

File Description Specifications

```
02Φ F*************************************************************************
03Φ F*   THIS PROGRAM UPDATES A PENSION FUND MASTER ISAM FILE USING A          *
04Φ F* TRANSACTION CARD FILE TO RECORD CHANGES IN NAME,DEPARTMENT              *
05Φ F* NUMBER,ANNUAL SALARY,AND RATE OF CONTRIBUTION,AS WELL AS ADDING         *
06Φ F* NEW RECORDS AND DEACTIVATING TERMINATED RECORDS.                        *
07Φ F*************************************************************************
08Φ F*
09Φ FPENUPDT IP  F    8Φ                 READØ1 SYSIPT
10Φ FPENMAST UC  F 62Φ   62RØ9AI         DISK4Ø SYSØ25S            AØ
11Φ FUDLIST  O   F    132      OF        PRINTERSYSLST
12Φ F*
```

RPG INPUT SPECIFICATIONS

Program: ISAM UPDATE   Programmer: N. JOHNKE   Date: 9/27/--
Keying Instruction: Graphic Ø 1 2 — Key ZERO ONE TWO
Page Ø2 of 9   Program Identification: SSSØ9

```
I*****************************  INPUT  RECORDS  ************************
I*
I************************************
I* TRANSACTION FILE                  *
I************************************
I*
IPENUPDT AA  Ø1   1 CC
I                                        2   2ØCODE
I                                        3  11ØSSNO
I                                       12  31 CNAME
I                                       32  34ØCDEPT
I                                       35  412CSALRY
I                                       42  432CRATE
I                                       44  49ØCDATE
I*
I************************************
I* MASTER FILE                       *
I************************************
I*
IPENMAST BB  Ø2   1 CM
I                                        2   2 STATUS
I                                        3  11ØSSNUM
I                                       12  31 NAME
I                                       32  37ØEMPDT
I                                       38  4ØØDEPT
```

RPG INPUT SPECIFICATIONS

Program: ISAM UPDATE   Programmer: N. JOHNKE   Date: 9/27/--
Keying Instruction: Graphic Ø 1 2 — Key ZERO ONE TWO
Page Ø3 of 9   Program Identification: SSSØ9

```
I                                       41  472ANSAL
I                                       48  492RATE
I                                       5Ø  562TCNTRB
I                                       57  62ØTERMDT
I*
```

RPG CALCULATION SPECIFICATIONS

Program	ISAM UPDATE	Keying Instruction	Graphic	Ø	1	2	Card Electro Number	Page	Ø4 of 9	Program Identification	SSSØ9
Programmer	N. JOHNKE, Date 9/27/--		Key	ZERO	ONE	TWO					

Line	Form Type	Control Level (L0–L9, LR, SR, AN/OR)	Indicators	Factor 1	Operation	Factor 2	Result Field Name	Length	Decimal Positions	Half Adjust (H)	Resulting Indicators High (1>2)	Low (1<2)	Equal (1=2)	Comments
01Ø	C	*************************** CALCULATIONS **************************												
02Ø	C	*												
03Ø	C		Ø1	TOTCTR	ADD	1	TOTCTR	3	Ø					
04Ø	C		Ø1	SSNO	CHAIN	PENMAST					12			
05Ø	C		Ø1N12	STATUS	COMP	'A'							25	-ACTIVE RECORD
06Ø	C	*												
07Ø	C	***												
08Ø	C	* UPDATE ACTIVE RECORD *												
09Ø	C	***												
10Ø	C	*												
11Ø	C		Ø1N12 25	CODE	COMP	1							1Ø	-NAME CHANGE
12Ø	C		Ø1N12 25											
13Ø	C	AN	1Ø		MOVE	CNAME	NAME							
14Ø	C	*												
15Ø	C		Ø1N12 25	CODE	COMP	2							2Ø	-DEPT CHANGE
16Ø	C		Ø1N12 25											
17Ø	C	AN	2Ø		Z-ADD	CDEPT	DEPT							
18Ø	C	*												
19Ø	C		Ø1N12 25	CODE	COMP	3							3Ø	-SALARY CHANGE
20Ø	C		Ø1N12 25											
21Ø	C	AN	3Ø		Z-ADD	CSALRY	ANSAL							
22Ø	C	*												
23Ø	C		Ø1N12 25	CODE	COMP	4							4Ø	-RATE CHANGE
24Ø	C		Ø1N12 25											
25Ø	C	AN	4Ø		Z-ADD	CRATE	RATE							

Figure 9.12
(continued)

RPG CALCULATION SPECIFICATIONS

Program	ISAM UPDATE	Keying Instruction	Graphic	Ø	1	2	Card Electro Number	Page	Ø5 of 9	Program Identification	SSSØ9
Programmer	N. JOHNKE, Date 9/27/--		Key	ZERO	ONE	TWO					

Line	Form Type	Control Level	Indicators	Factor 1	Operation	Factor 2	Result Field Name	Length	Decimal Positions	Resulting Indicators (Equal)	Comments
01Ø	C	*									
02Ø	C		Ø1N12 25	CODE	COMP	5				5Ø	-DEACTIVATE
03Ø	C		Ø1N12 25								
04Ø	C	AN	5Ø		MOVE	'I'	STATUS				
05Ø	C		Ø1N12 25								
06Ø	C	AN	5Ø		Z-ADD	CDATE	TERMDT				
07Ø	C		Ø1N12 25								
08Ø	C	AN	5Ø	DELCTR	ADD	1	DELCTR	2	Ø		
09Ø	C	*									
10Ø	C	**********************************									
11Ø	C	* ADD NEW RECORD *									
12Ø	C	**********************************									
13Ø	C	*									
14Ø	C		Ø1	CODE	COMP	6				6Ø	-NEW RECORD
15Ø	C		Ø1 12 6Ø		MOVE	'A'	STATUS				
16Ø	C		Ø1 12 6Ø		Z-ADD	SSNO	SSNUM				
17Ø	C		Ø1 12 6Ø		MOVE	CNAME	NAME				
18Ø	C		Ø1 12 6Ø		Z-ADD	CDEPT	DEPT				
19Ø	C		Ø1 12 6Ø		Z-ADD	CSALRY	ANSAL				
20Ø	C		Ø1 12 6Ø		Z-ADD	CRATE	RATE				
21Ø	C		Ø1 12 6Ø		Z-ADD	CDATE	EMPDT				
22Ø	C		Ø1 12 6Ø		Z-ADD	Ø	TCNTRB				
23Ø	C		Ø1 12 6Ø		Z-ADD	Ø	TERMDT				
24Ø	C		Ø1 12 6Ø	ADDCTR	ADD	1	ADDCTR	2	Ø		
25Ø	C	*									

Figure 9.12
(continued)

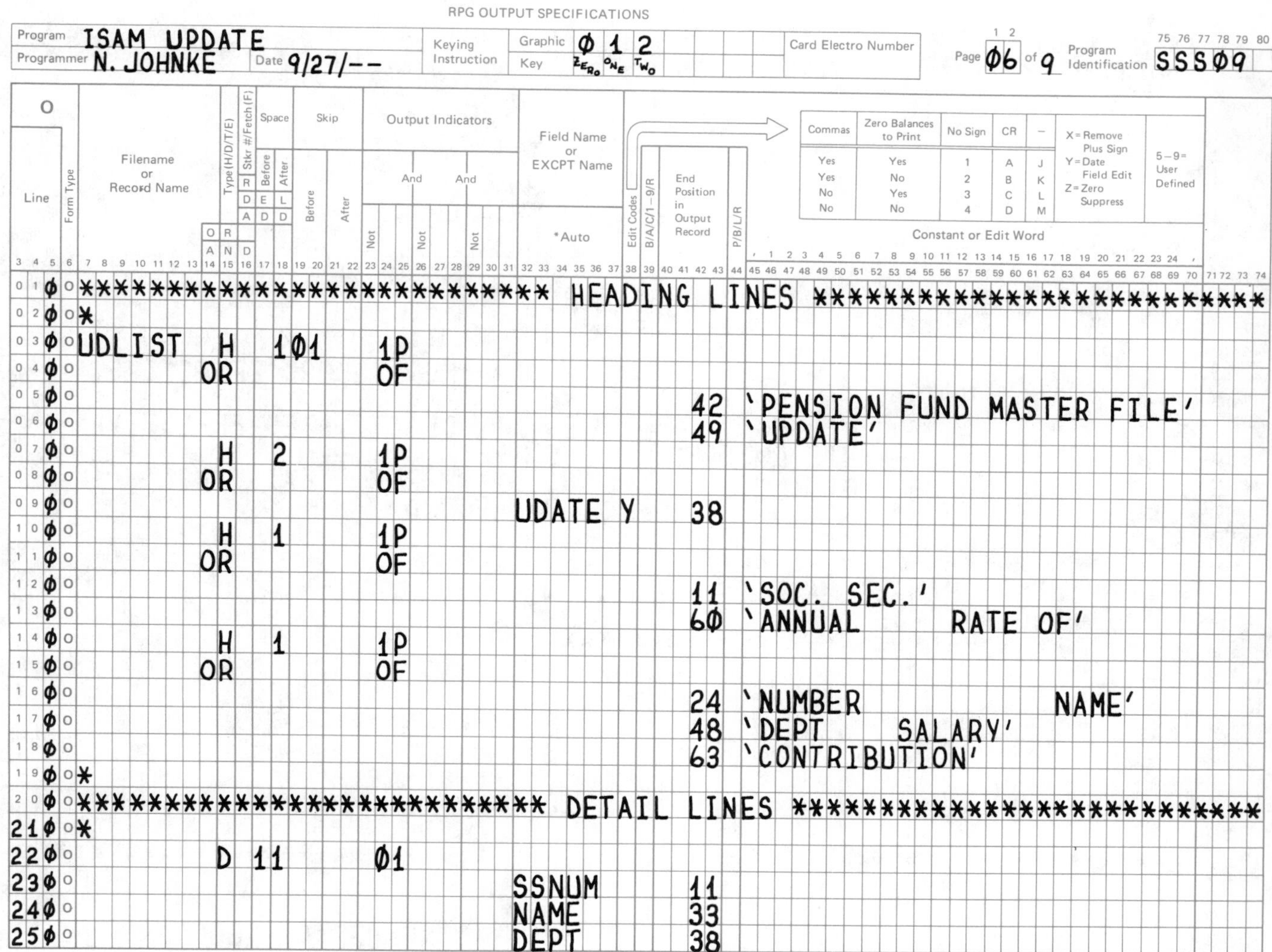

RPG OUTPUT SPECIFICATIONS

Program: ISAM UPDATE — Programmer: N. JOHNKE — Date: 9/27/-- — Keying Instruction: Graphic Ø 1 2, Key ZERO ONE TWO — Card Electro Number — Page Ø6 of 9 — Program Identification SSSØ9

```
01Ø O*************************** HEADING LINES **************************
02Ø O*
03Ø OUDLIST  H  1Ø1   1P
04Ø O      OR         OF
05Ø O
06Ø O                                  42 'PENSION FUND MASTER FILE'
07Ø O        H  2     1P               49 'UPDATE'
08Ø O      OR         OF
09Ø O                        UDATE Y   38
10Ø O        H  1     1P
11Ø O      OR         OF
12Ø O                                  11 'SOC. SEC.'
13Ø O                                  6Ø 'ANNUAL      RATE OF'
14Ø O        H  1     1P
15Ø O      OR         OF
16Ø O                                  24 'NUMBER              NAME'
17Ø O                                  48 'DEPT      SALARY'
18Ø O                                  63 'CONTRIBUTION'
19Ø O*
20Ø O************************** DETAIL LINES ***************************
21Ø O*
22Ø O        D 11     Ø1
23Ø O                        SSNUM     11
24Ø O                        NAME      33
25Ø O                        DEPT      38
```

Figure 9.12
(continued)

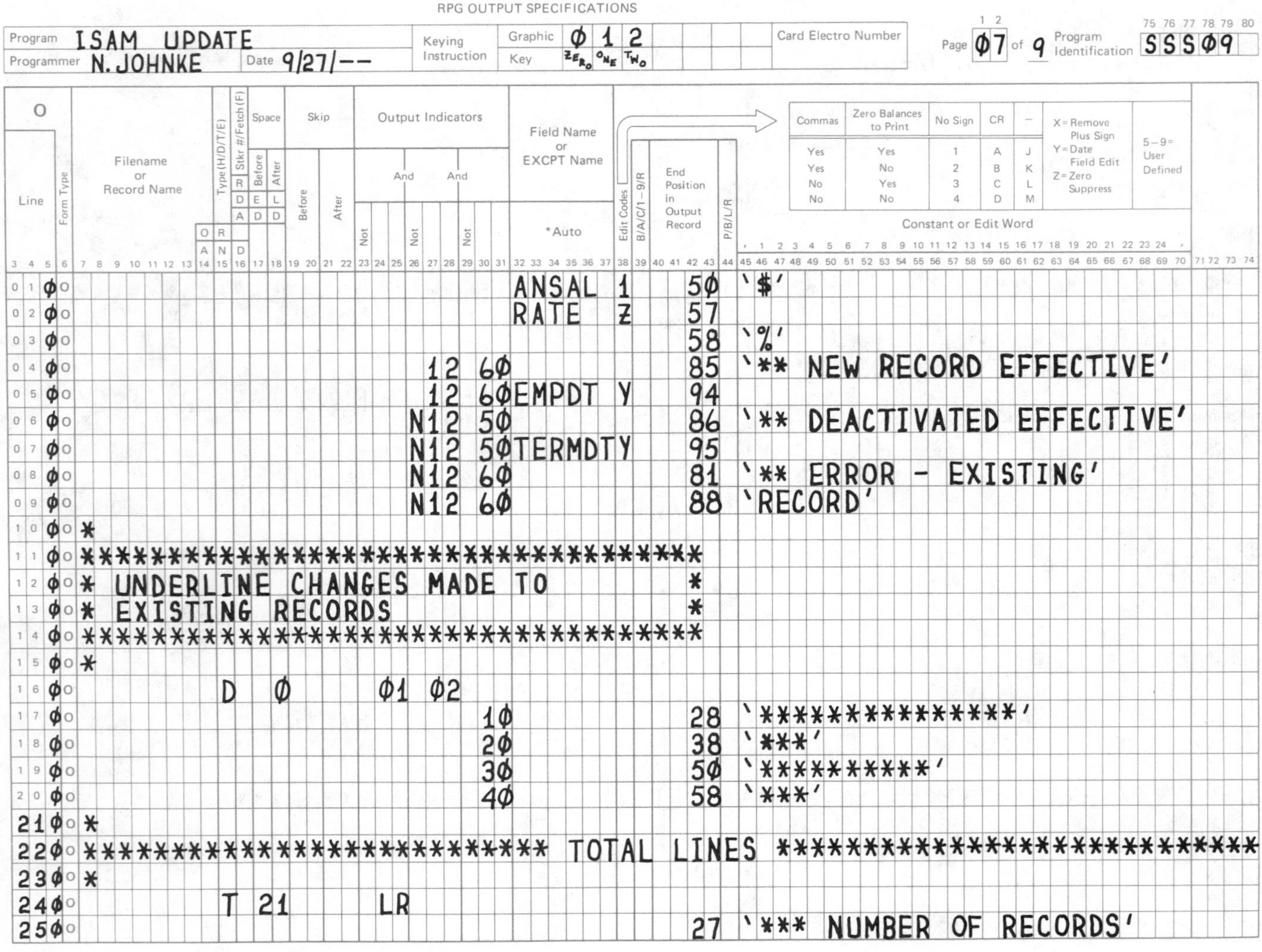

RPG OUTPUT SPECIFICATIONS

Program: ISAM UPDATE | Programmer: N.JOHNKE | Date: 9/27/-- | Keying Instruction: Graphic Ø 1 2, Key ZERO ONE TWO | Card Electro Number | Page Ø7 of 9 | Program Identification SSSØ9

```
01ØO                         ANSAL 1   5Ø '$'
02ØO                         RATE  Z   57
03ØO                                   58 '%'
04ØO                    12 6Ø          85 '** NEW RECORD EFFECTIVE'
05ØO                    12 6ØEMPDT Y   94
06ØO                   N12 5Ø          86 '** DEACTIVATED EFFECTIVE'
07ØO                   N12 5ØTERMDTY   95
08ØO                   N12 6Ø          81 '** ERROR - EXISTING'
09ØO                   N12 6Ø          88 'RECORD'
10ØO*
11ØO************************************
12ØO* UNDERLINE CHANGES MADE TO        *
13ØO* EXISTING RECORDS                 *
14ØO************************************
15ØO*
16ØO        D  Ø     Ø1 Ø2
17ØO                       1Ø          28 '**************'
18ØO                       2Ø          38 '***'
19ØO                       3Ø          5Ø '**********'
20ØO                       4Ø          58 '***'
21ØO*
22ØO*************************** TOTAL LINES ****************************
23ØO*
24ØO        T  21    LR
25ØO                                   27 '*** NUMBER OF RECORDS'
```

Figure 9.12
(continued)

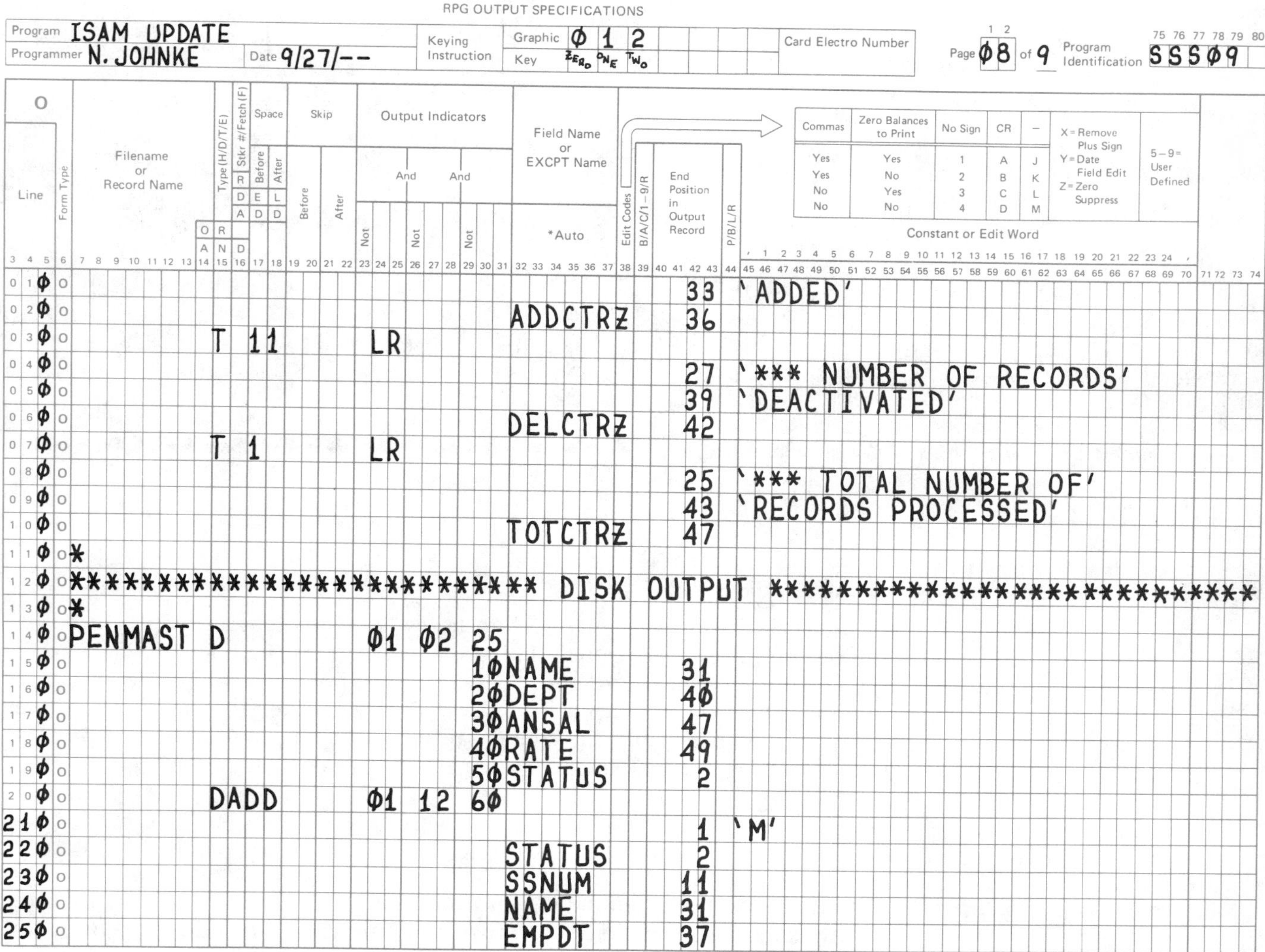

RPG OUTPUT SPECIFICATIONS

Program	ISAM UPDATE	Keying Instruction	Graphic	Ø 1 2	Card Electro Number	Page	Ø8 of 9	Program Identification	SSSØ9
Programmer	N. JOHNKE Date 9/27/--		Key	ZERO ONE TWO					

```
01Ø O                                       33 'ADDED'
02Ø O                             ADDCTRZ   36
03Ø O        T 11      LR
04Ø O                                       27 '*** NUMBER OF RECORDS'
05Ø O                                       39 'DEACTIVATED'
06Ø O                             DELCTRZ   42
07Ø O        T 1       LR
08Ø O                                       25 '*** TOTAL NUMBER OF'
09Ø O                                       43 'RECORDS PROCESSED'
10Ø O                             TOTCTRZ   47
11Ø O*
12Ø O************************** DISK OUTPUT **************************
13Ø O*
14Ø OPENMAST D         Ø1 Ø2 25
15Ø O                           1ØNAME      31
16Ø O                           2ØDEPT      4Ø
17Ø O                           3ØANSAL     47
18Ø O                           4ØRATE      49
19Ø O                           5ØSTATUS     2
20Ø O        DADD      Ø1 12 6Ø
21Ø O                                        1 'M'
22Ø O                             STATUS     2
23Ø O                             SSNUM     11
24Ø O                             NAME      31
25Ø O                             EMPDT     37
```

Figure 9.12
(continued)

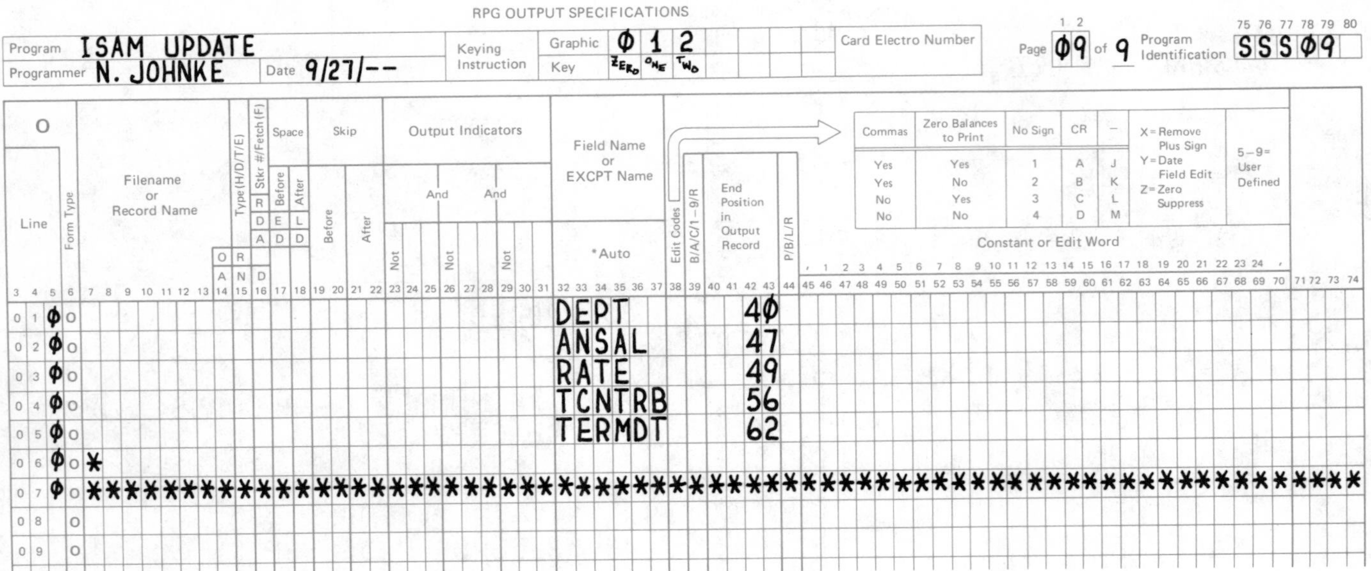
RPG OUTPUT SPECIFICATIONS

Program ISAM UPDATE — Programmer N. JOHNKE — Date 9/27/--

Keying Instruction: Graphic Ø 1 2 — Key ZERO ONE TWO

Page Ø9 of 9 — Program Identification SSSØ9

Line	Form Type	Filename or Record Name	Field Name or EXCPT Name	End Position in Output Record
01Ø	O		DEPT	4Ø
02Ø	O		ANSAL	47
03Ø	O		RATE	49
04Ø	O		TCNTRB	56
05Ø	O		TERMDT	62
06Ø	O	*		
07Ø	O	**		
08	O			
09	O			

Figure 9.12
(continued)

The partial listing in Figure 9.13 includes the error diagnostic produced by running the program as coded. The syntax correction is circled on the partial computer listing shown in Figure 9.14. There is, however, a logic error in the program. The printed output is correct. However, after the update, inactive records in the master disk file contain an incorrect termination date. Your assignment is to desk check the program carefully, find the logic error, and make the necessary corrections.

Practice Problems

1. Using the problem definition shown in Figure 9.15, write an RPG program to update, add, and delete records randomly from an indexed sequential master file, depending on the activity code in each transaction record. Print the error control listing shown.
2. Using the problem definition shown in Figure 9.16, write an RPG program to update a master payroll file with salary changes. Print the error control listing shown.
3. Using the problem definition shown in Figure 9.17, write an RPG program to update an indexed sequential disk file. Print the error control listing shown.
4. Using the problem definition shown in Figure 9.18, write an RPG program to create an indexed sequential disk file as shown.

```
         01-020  F**************************************************************************SSS09
         01-030  F*  THIS PROGRAM UPDATES A PENSION FUND MASTER ISAM FILE USING A       *SSS09
         01-040  F* TRANSACTICN CARD FILE TC RECORD CHANGES IN NAME,DEPARTMENT          *SSS09
         01-050  F* NUMBER,ANNUAL SALARY,AND RATE OF CONTIBUTION,AS WELL AS ADDING      *SSS09
         01-060  F* NEW RECORDS AND DEACTIVATING TERMINATED RECORDS.                    *SSS09
         01-070  F**************************************************************************SSS09
         01-080  F*                                                                      SSS09
0001     01-090  FPENUPDT IP  F      80             READ01 SYSIPT                        SSS09
0002     01-1C0  FPENMAST UC  F 620  62R09AI        DISK40 SYS025S           A0          SSS09
                                                                                                  MSG  036
0003     01-110  FUDLIST  C   F      132     CF     PRINTERSYSLST                        SSS09
         01-120  F*                                                                      SSS09
         02-010  I************************** INPUT RECORDS ****************************SSS09
         02-020  I*                                                                      SSS09
         02-030  I*************************************                                  SSS09
         02-040  I* TRANSACTION FILE                  *                                  SSS09
         02-050  I*************************************                                  SSS09
         02-060  I*                                                                      SSS09
0004     C2-070  IPENUPDT AA  01   1 CC                                                  SSS09
0005     02-080  I                                         2   20CODE                    SSS09
0006     02-090  I                                         3  110SSNO                    SSS09
0007     02-100  I                                        12  31 CNAME                   SSS09
0008     02-110  I                                        32  340CDEPT                   SSS09
0009     02-120  I                                        35  412CSALRY                  SSS09
001C     02-130  I                                        42  432CRATE                   SSS09
0011     C2-140  I                                        44  490CDATE                   SSS09
         02-150  I*                                                                      SSS09
         02-160  I*************************************                                  SSS09
         C2-170  I* MASTER FILE                       *                                  SSS09
         02-180  I*************************************                                  SSS09
         02-190  I*                                                                      SSS09
0012     02-200  IPENMAST BB  02   1 CM                                                  SSS09
0013     02-210  I                                         2   2 STATUS                  SSS09
0014     02-220  I                                         3  110SSNUM                   SSS09
0015     02-230  I                                        12  31 NAME                    SSS09
0016     02-240  I                                        32  370EMPDT                   SSS09
0017     02-250  I                                        38  400DEPT                    SSS09
0018     03-010  I                                        41  472ANSAL                   SSS09
0019     03-020  I                                        48  492RATE                    SSS09
002C     03-030  I                                        50  562TCNTRB                  SSS09
0021     03-040  I                                        57  620TERMDT                  SSS09
         03-050  I*                                                                      SSS09
         04-010  C************************** CALCULATIONS ****************************SSS09
         04-020  C*                                                                      SSS09
0022     04-030  C   01       TOTCTR    ADD  1          TCTCTR  30                       SSS09
0023     04-040  C   01       SSNO      CHAINPENMAST              12                     SSS09
0024     04-050  C   01N12    STATUS    CCMP 'A'                        25-ACTIVE RECORD SSS09
         04-060  C*                                                                      SSS09
         04-070  C*************************************                                  SSS09
         04-080  C* UPDATE ACTIVE RECCRD              *                                  SSS09
         04-090  C*************************************                                  SSS09
         04-10C  C*                                                                      SSS09
0025     04-110  C   01N12 25CODE       CCMP 1                          10-NAME CHANGE   SSS09
0026     04-120  C   01N12 25                                                            SSS09
0027     04-130  CAN 10                 MOVE CNAME      NAME                             SSS09
         04-140  C*                                                                      SSS09
0028     04-150  C   01N12 25CODE       CCMP 2                          20-DEPT CHANGE   SSS09


         C O M P I L E R   D I A G N O S T I C S   S U M M A R Y


ILN036   KEY FIELC STARTING LOCATION IS INVALID. ASSUME 1.

         00C2    01-100     PENMAST
```

Figure 9.13
Program listing with a syntax error for the Debugging Exercise.

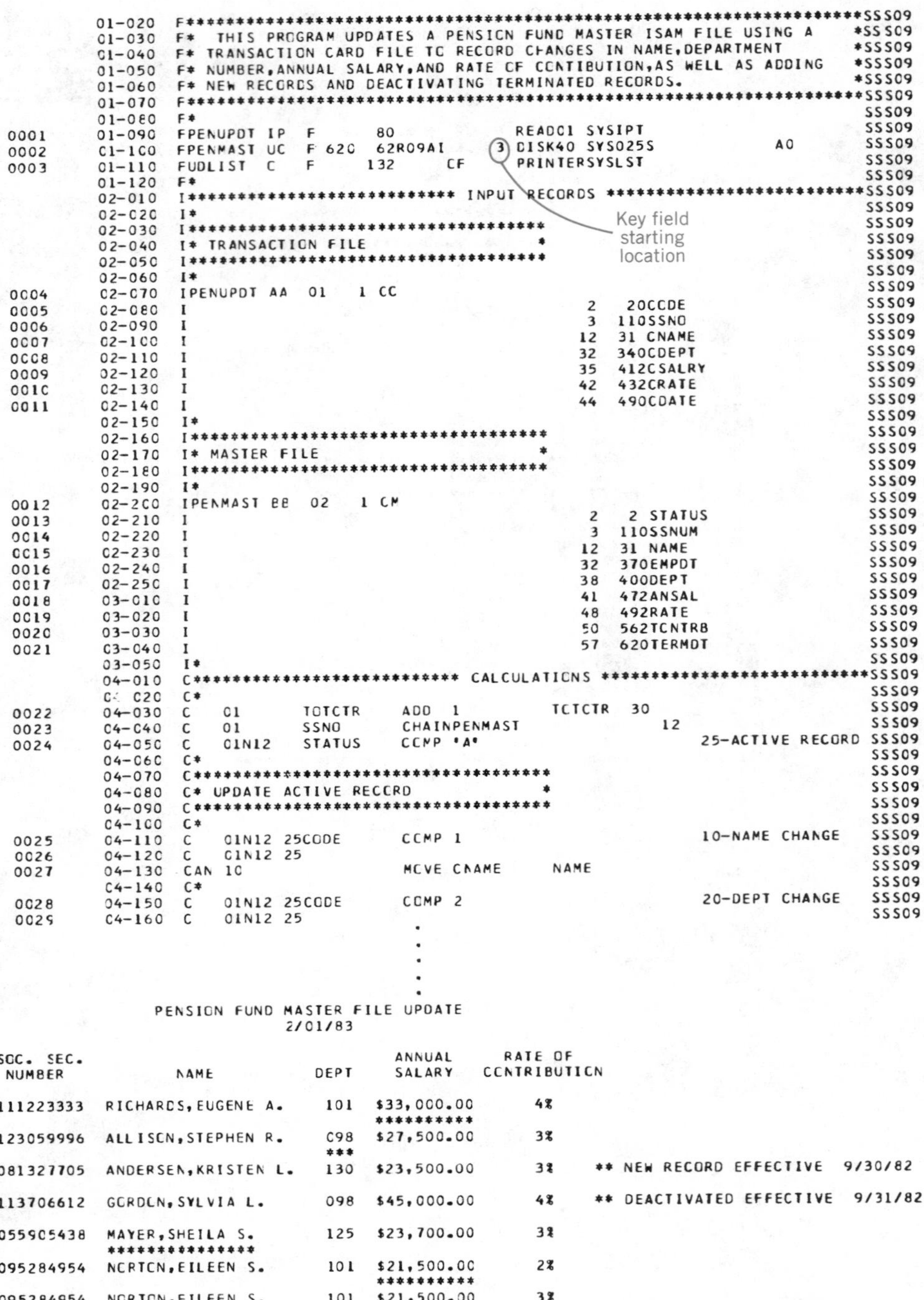


```
                01-020  F*************************************************************************SSS09
                01-030  F*  THIS PROGRAM UPDATES A PENSION FUND MASTER ISAM FILE USING A     *SSS09
                01-040  F* TRANSACTION CARD FILE TO RECORD CHANGES IN NAME,DEPARTMENT        *SSS09
                01-050  F* NUMBER,ANNUAL SALARY,AND RATE OF CONTIBUTION,AS WELL AS ADDING    *SSS09
                01-060  F* NEW RECORDS AND DEACTIVATING TERMINATED RECORDS.                  *SSS09
                01-070  F*************************************************************************SSS09
                01-080  F*                                                                   SSS09
0001            01-090  FPENUPDT IP  F      80              READ01 SYSIPT                    SSS09
0002            01-100  FPENMAST UC  F 620  62R09AI       3 DISK40 SYS025S            A0     SSS09
0003            01-110  FUDLIST  C   F     132      CF        PRINTERSYSLST                  SSS09
                01-120  F*                                                                   SSS09
                02-010  I**************************** INPUT RECORDS ****************************SSS09
                02-020  I*                                                                   SSS09
                02-030  I*************************************                               SSS09
                02-040  I* TRANSACTION FILE                  *                               SSS09
                02-050  I*************************************                               SSS09
                02-060  I*                                                                   SSS09
0004            02-070  IPENUPDT AA  01   1 CC                                               SSS09
0005            02-080  I                                          2   20CCDE                SSS09
0006            02-090  I                                          3  110SSNO                SSS09
0007            02-100  I                                         12  31 CNAME               SSS09
0008            02-110  I                                         32  340CDEPT               SSS09
0009            02-120  I                                         35  412CSALRY              SSS09
0010            02-130  I                                         42  432CRATE               SSS09
0011            02-140  I                                         44  490CDATE               SSS09
                02-150  I*                                                                   SSS09
                02-160  I*************************************                               SSS09
                02-170  I* MASTER FILE                       *                               SSS09
                02-180  I*************************************                               SSS09
                02-190  I*                                                                   SSS09
0012            02-200  IPENMAST BB  02   1 CM                                               SSS09
0013            02-210  I                                          2   2 STATUS              SSS09
0014            02-220  I                                          3  110SSNUM               SSS09
0015            02-230  I                                         12  31 NAME                SSS09
0016            02-240  I                                         32  370EMPDT               SSS09
0017            02-250  I                                         38  400DEPT                SSS09
0018            03-010  I                                         41  472ANSAL               SSS09
0019            03-020  I                                         48  492RATE                SSS09
0020            03-030  I                                         50  562TCNTRB              SSS09
0021            03-040  I                                         57  620TERMDT              SSS09
                03-050  I*                                                                   SSS09
                04-010  C**************************** CALCULATIONS *****************************SSS09
                04-020  C*                                                                   SSS09
0022            04-030  C    01        TOTCTR    ADD  1         TOTCTR  30                   SSS09
0023            04-040  C    01        SSNO      CHAINPENMAST              12                SSS09
0024            04-050  C    01N12     STATUS    COMP 'A'                        25-ACTIVE RECORD SSS09
                04-060  C*                                                                   SSS09
                04-070  C*************************************                               SSS09
                04-080  C* UPDATE ACTIVE RECORD              *                               SSS09
                04-090  C*************************************                               SSS09
                04-100  C*                                                                   SSS09
0025            04-110  C    01N12 25CODE        COMP 1                      10-NAME CHANGE  SSS09
0026            04-120  C    01N12 25                                                        SSS09
0027            04-130  CAN 10                   MOVE CNAME      NAME                        SSS09
                04-140  C*                                                                   SSS09
0028            04-150  C    01N12 25CODE        COMP 2                      20-DEPT CHANGE  SSS09
0029            04-160  C    01N12 25                                                        SSS09
                                           .
                                           .
                                           .
                                           .
                                           .
```

```
                  PENSION FUND MASTER FILE UPDATE
                              2/01/83

SOC. SEC.                                   ANNUAL     RATE OF
 NUMBER            NAME             DEPT    SALARY   CONTRIBUTION

111223333  RICHARDS,EUGENE A.        101  $33,000.00      4%
                                          **********
123059996  ALLISON,STEPHEN R.        098  $27,500.00      3%
                                     ***
081327705  ANDERSEN,KRISTEN L.       130  $23,500.00      3%     ** NEW RECORD EFFECTIVE  9/30/82

113706612  GORDON,SYLVIA L.          098  $45,000.00      4%     ** DEACTIVATED EFFECTIVE  9/31/82

055905438  MAYER,SHEILA S.           125  $23,700.00      3%
           ***************
095284954  NORTON,EILEEN S.          101  $21,500.00      2%
                                          **********
095284954  NORTON,EILEEN S.          101  $21,500.00      3%
                                                         ***
115049123  MURPHY,DANIEL J.          080  $24,000.00      3%     ** ERROR - EXISTING RECORD

009574225  O'REILLY,SEAN M.          080  $52,000.00      4%     ** DEACTIVATED EFFECTIVE  9/01/82

111006789  THOMPSON,PHILLIP M.       080  $41,000.00      4%     ** NEW RECORD EFFECTIVE  9/15/82

     *** NUMBER OF RECORDS ADDED  2

     *** NUMBER OF RECORDS DEACTIVATED  2

     *** TOTAL NUMBER OF RECORDS PROCESSED  10
```

Figure 9.14
Program listing with logic errors for the Debugging Exercise.

Figure 9.14
(continued)

```
                    MASTER DISK FILE
MI0095742250'REILLY,SEAN M.    0601520805200000046240000000000
MI032177294PENNIMAN,ALPHONSE T.120155071495000004495000120180
MA055905438MAYER,SHEILA S.     0623771252370000030373275000000
MA062193854WILLIAMS,MICHAEL J. 0517780712010000030271350000000
MA081327705ANDERSEN,KRISTEN L. 0930821302350000030000000000000
MA095284954NORTON,EILEEN S.    1115811012150000030039900000000
MA106061738JOHNSON,ROBERT Q.   1201691303960000042019600000000
MA111006789THOMPSON,PHILLIP M. 0915820804100000400000000000000
MA111223333RICHARDS,EUGENE A.  0917691013300000041408000000000
MI113706612GORDON,SYLVIA L.    0701630984500000043510000000000
MA115049123MURPHY,DANIEL J.    0519800802400000030162000000000
MA123059996ALLISON,STEPHEN R.  0130790982750000030309375000000
```

Termination date is incorrect (first record); Incorrect (GORDON record)

Figure 9.15
Problem definition for Practice Problem 1.
(Continued on next page.)

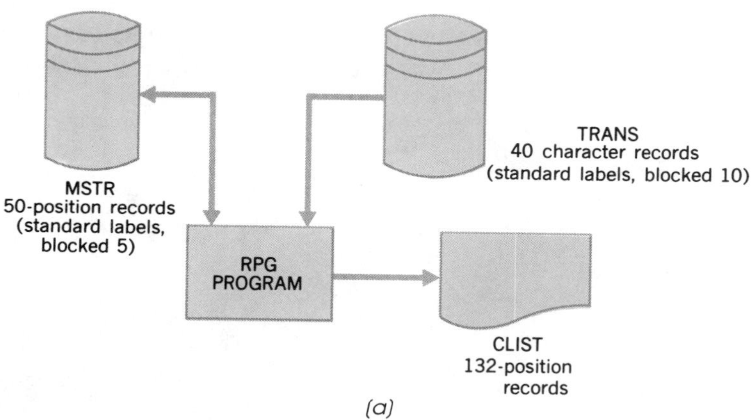

(a)

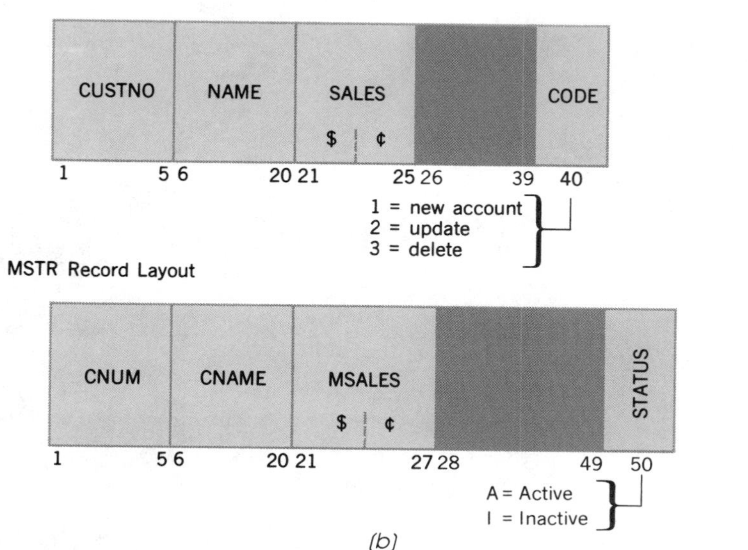

(b)

Figure 9.15 *(continued)*

CLIST Printer Spacing Chart

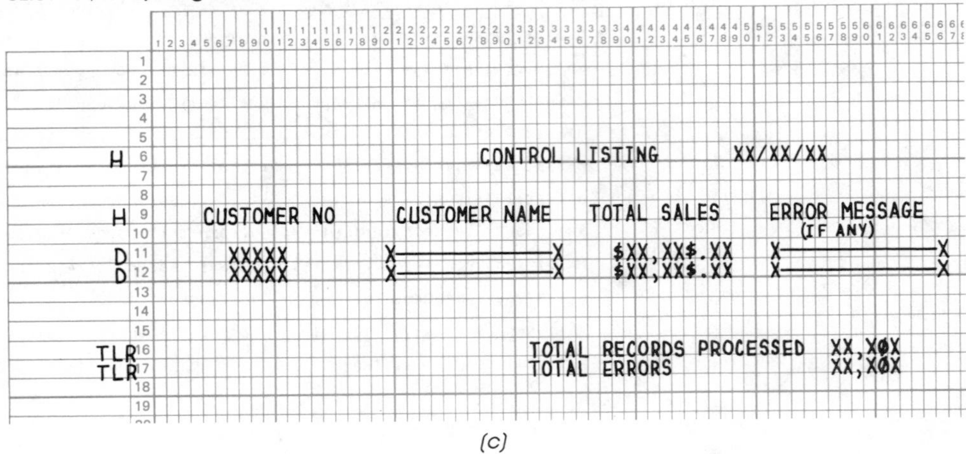

(c)

Notes

1. Customer number is the key field.
2. For a transaction record with a corresponding master record, add the amount of sales (SALES) in the transaction record to MSALES in the master record.
3. For a new account transaction record, add the record to the master file.
4. For a delete record, deactivate the corresponding master record.

Figure 9.16 Problem definition for Practice Problem 2.

Systems Flowchart

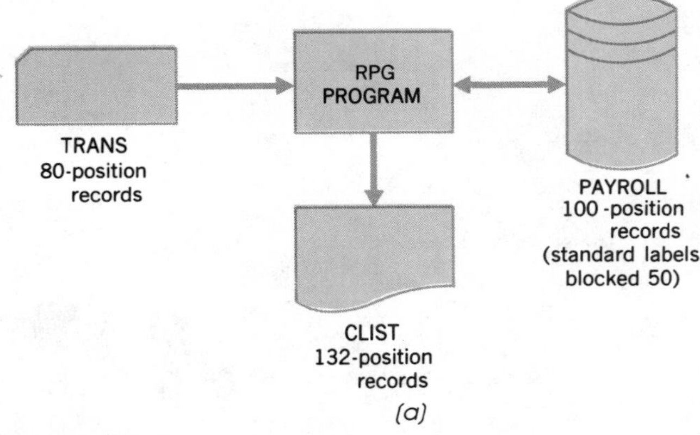

(a)

TRANS Record Layout

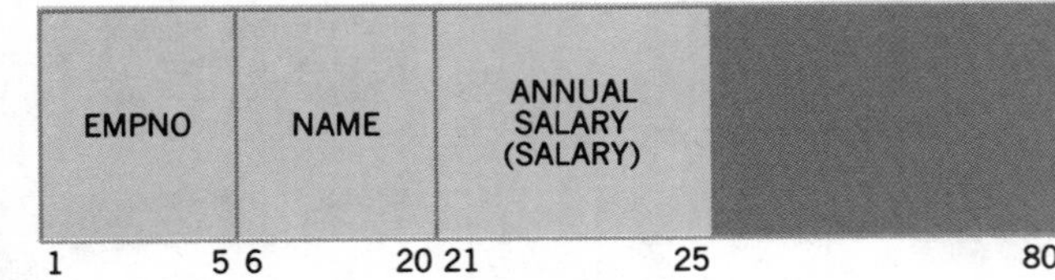

PAYROLL Record Layout

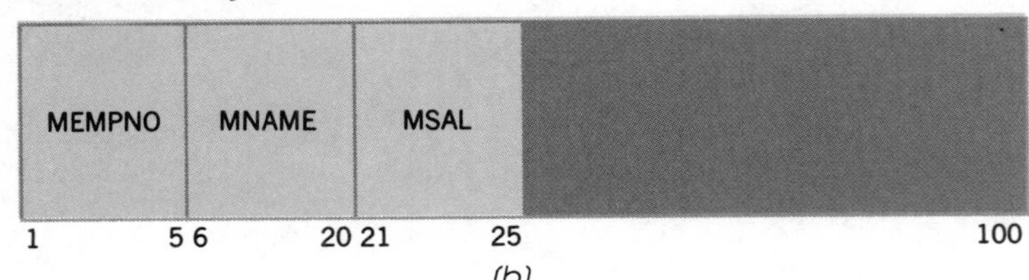

(b)

Figure 9.16 *(continued)*

CLIST Printer Spacing Chart

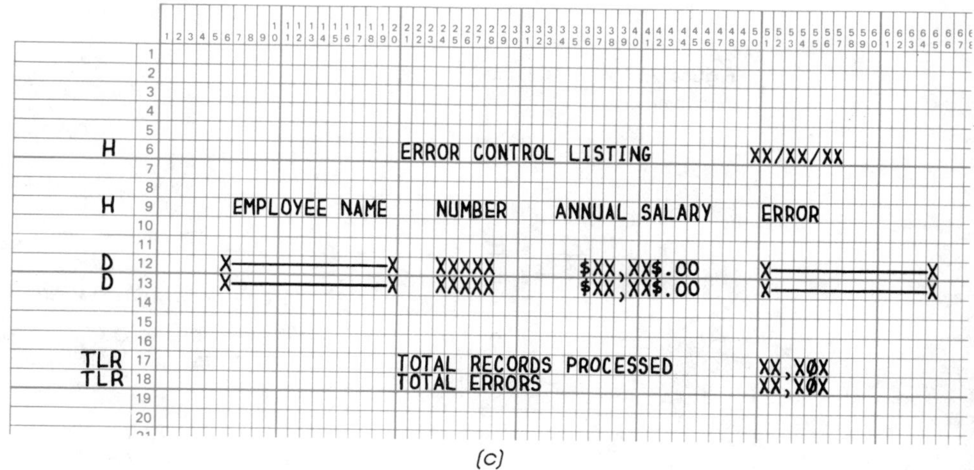

(c)

Notes

1. All records in the transaction file should be in the master file. If any transaction record does not have a corresponding master record, there is an error.
2. Employee number is the key field.
3. Z-ADD SALARY to MSAL.

Figure 9.17 Problem definition for Practice Problem 3. *(Continued on next page)*

Systems Flowchart

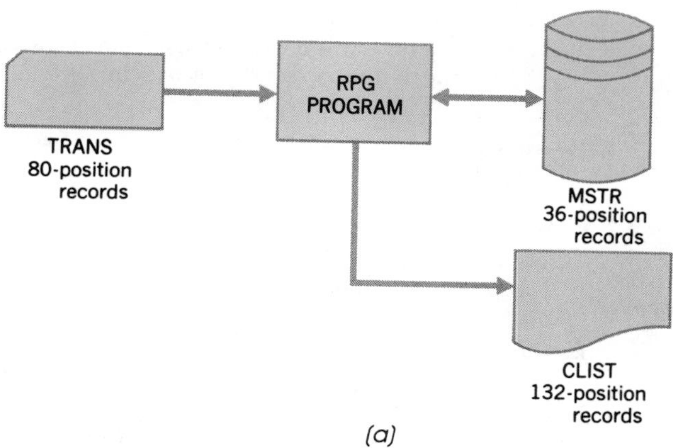

(a)

TRANS Record Layout

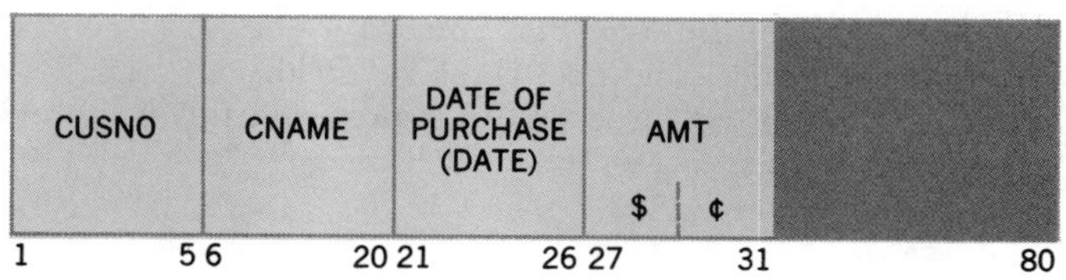

MSTR Record Layout

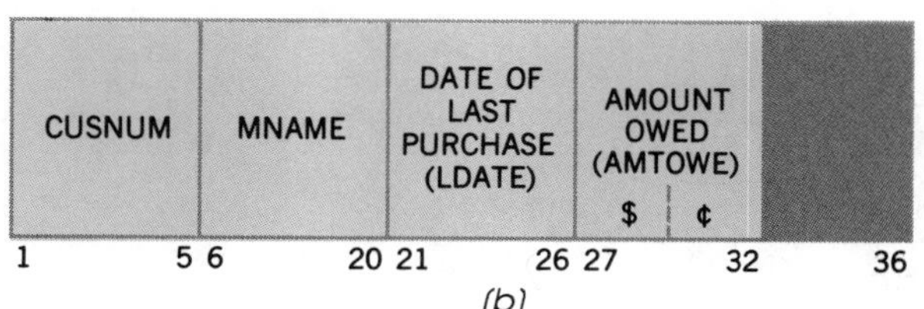

(b)

Figure 9.17 *(continued)* CLIST Printer Spacing Chart

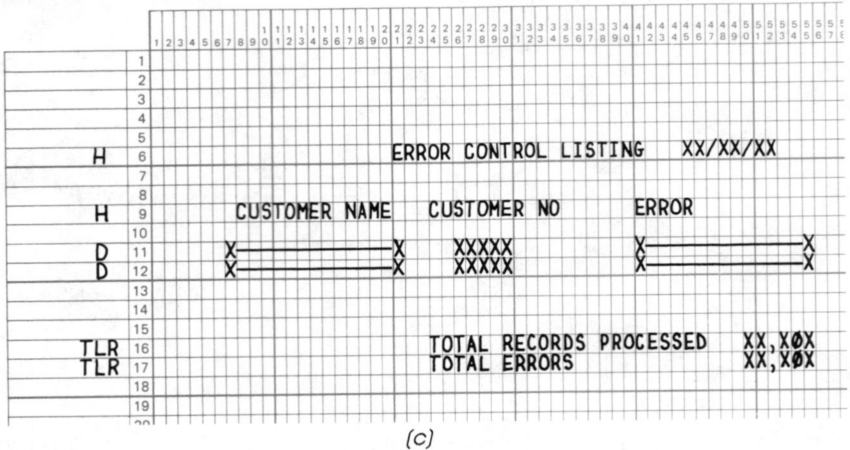

(c)

Notes

1. Customer number is the key field.
2. Create a disk record for any transaction record that does not have a corresponding master record.
3. For a transaction record with a corresponding master record, (*a*) add the amount of purchase from the transaction record to the amount owed in the master record, and (*b*) update the date of last purchase.
4. There does not have to be a transaction record for each master record.
5. The transaction records are not in sequence.

Figure 9.18
Problem definition for Practice Problem 4.
(Continued on next page.)

Notes

1. DISK1 is an input file that has the unit price for each product number. There are 15Ø product numbers with individual unit prices in this indexed sequential disk file.
2. DISK2 is an input indexed sequential file that indicates the product number and the quantity purchased by each customer.
3. DISK3 is an indexed sequential disk file that is to be created by taking each DISK2 record and calculating the amount owed.

   $$\text{Amount Owed} = \text{Quantity} \times \text{Unit Price}$$

   The appropriate unit price is obtained from DISK1 by using the product number that is in the DISK2 record.
4. Product number is the key field.
5. An edit procedure has preceded this program. Thus, an error listing is not required.

Figure 9.18 *(continued)* Systems Flowchart

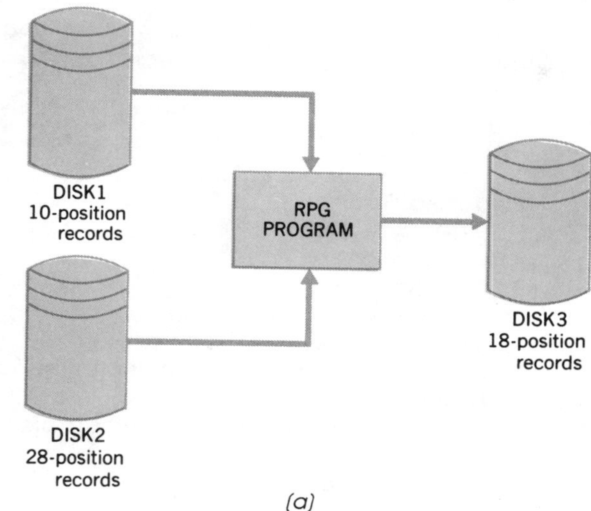

(a)

DISK1 Record Layout

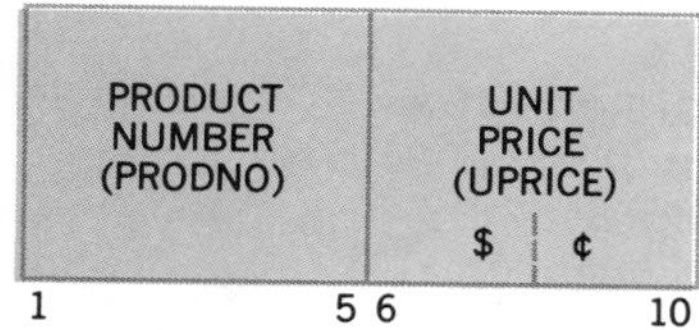

DISK2 Record Layout

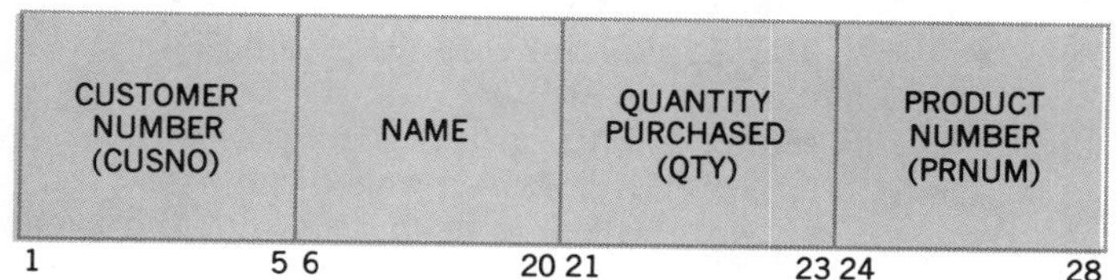

DISK3 Record Layout

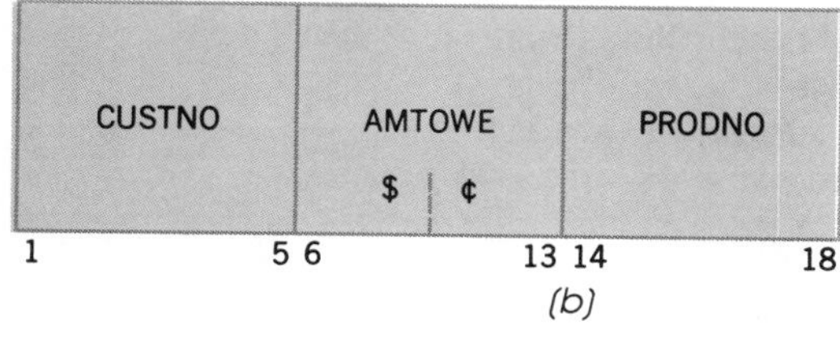

(b)

CHAPTER 10

Table Handling and Array Processing

Objectives

- To enable you to determine why, when, and how tables should be used in an RPG program.
- To help you understand the advantages and disadvantages of compile time tables and pre-execution time tables.
- To provide an understanding of how tables are established and used in a LOKUP procedure.
- To enable you to process single-entry and related tables in RPG.
- To perform array processing.

I. Purpose of Tables

A **table** provides a list of related data items contained in main storage that may be accessed or referenced by an RPG program. The table consists of a list of entries not part of the actual program that are stored in consecutive locations within main storage as illustrated in Figure 10.1. Since tables are used by the program and occupy main storage, the computer system must be made aware of the following.

1. The name to be assigned to the table.
2. The maximum number of entries in the table.
3. The length of each entry in the table.

This information is necessary in order to allocate storage for the tables in the RPG program and is handled by the coding of the Extension Specifications form.

Tables are typically used when processing or calculations are based on information that varies from one run to another. Examples of tables include:

1. A discount table based on the quantity of items ordered.
2. A table of accounts that are no longer valid.
3. A tax table indicating federal tax based on each employee's gross pay.
4. A table of shipping charges based on the weight of items mailed.

Without a table, the discounts shown in Figure 10.1 that are given for quantity orders would require the programmer to code a number of compare instructions using the input quantity field to determine the discount percentage. We avoid entering the actual discounts on the Calculation form since they may change over time. Changes are easily made to table entries but changes to constants established in a program can result in errors.

Another alternative to maintaining a table would be to build a disk file and access the data directly from the disk. However, there is usually not enough data to justify the use of a disk for looking up values such as discount percentages, tax percentages, or shipping charges.

The function of the table is to organize the data systematically so that it can

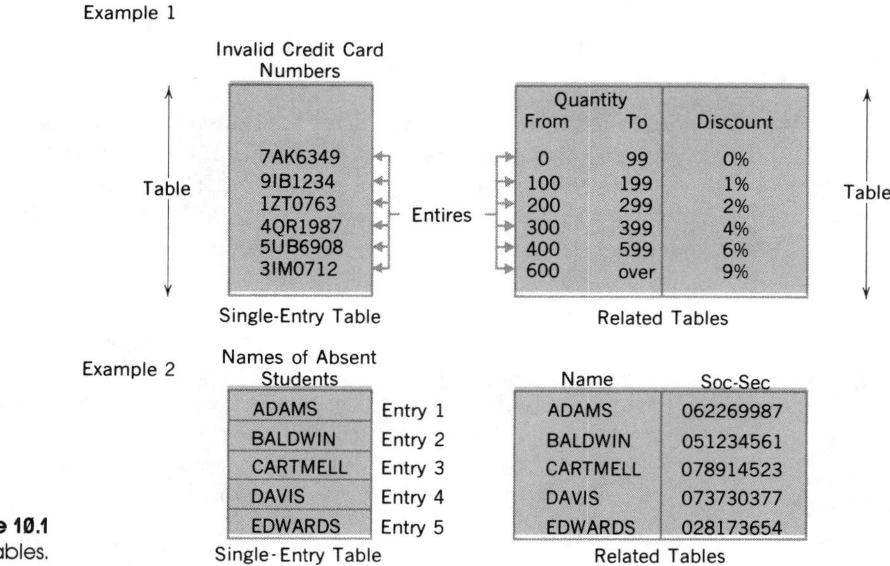

Figure 10.1
Examples of tables.

be readily referenced within the program. The table serves as a small file, which provides the programmer with access to any of the entries. Based on an input field, you can look up a corresponding value from the table.

The two general categories of tables are single-entry tables and related tables. A **single-entry table** simply consists of a series of entries. Examples of single-entry tables include a table of out-of-stock part numbers and a table of account numbers that are in arrears. **Related tables** are two or more tables that have related entries, such as discount percentages corresponding to each quantity ordered, or credit ratings corresponding to each customer number. This chapter will present sample programs illustrating the use of both single-entry and related tables.

II. Single-Entry Tables

A. Applications

A single-entry table is simply a list of single entries or items such as a table of overdrawn checking account numbers (see Figure 1Ø.2).

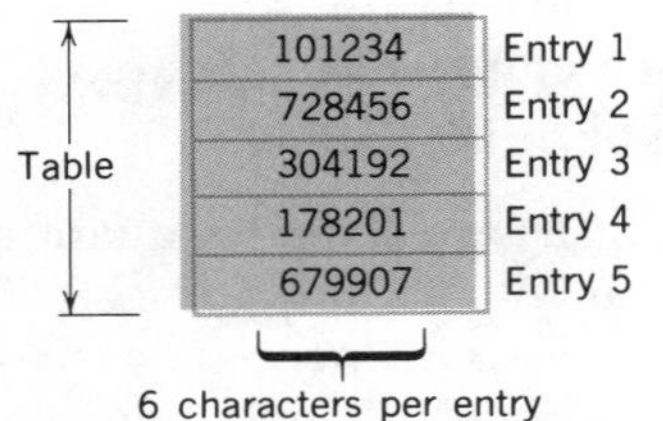

Figure 1Ø.2
Example of a single-entry table.

Single-entry tables are frequently used for checking purposes. Before processing a personal check, a bank teller should enter the account number via a computer terminal or other device, checking to determine if the account is overdrawn. If the account number is listed in the table that contains all overdrawn accounts, a message would be issued instructing the teller not to cash the check. This is a typical application using a single-table lookup. The processing required to accomplish this would be as follows.

1. A teller enters the account number as input.
2. A lookup or search is performed to determine if the account entered is equal to any of the table entries.
3. If an equal condition is found, an indicator will be set on.
4. The indicator would then be used to condition printing a message to reject the transaction.
5. If the account number is not in the table, the indicator would not be set and the transaction would be processed in the normal way.

B. Size Considerations

Single-entry tables may consist of either numeric or alphanumeric entries that are arranged in ascending order, descending order, or in no specific sequence at all. A most important consideration concerning tables is that all entries in the table must be exactly the same length. The table in Figure 1Ø.3, for example, lists the months of the year. The month of September, with nine letters, is the longest entry in the table. Because the length of all entries must be the same, blanks are padded to the right of the other month names to make each of them nine characters in length.

In other words, one table entry cannot be three positions long (MAY) and another nine positions long (SEPTEMBER). All the entries must be nine positions, which is the length of the *longest* table entry. The shorter month names contain right-justified spaces so that all are the same length.

When numeric table entries are employed, again the same rule applies and the largest entry is used for determining the size requirement. Since numeric

Figure 10.3
Table of months.

```
JANUARYbb
FEBRUARYb
MARCHbbbb
APRILbbbb
MAYbbbbbb
JUNEbbbbb
JULYbbbbb
AUGUSTbbb
SEPTEMBER
OCTOBERbb
NOVEMBERb
DECEMBERb
```

TABMO

All entries must have the same length. Those items that are not as long as the longest item must be padded with blanks (b).

fields are right-justified, high-order zeros are placed in the unfilled left-most positions of entries with fewer digits than the longest entry. Decimal points are not included in tables but are, however, specified on the Extension Specification form using a decimal position field. Thus the decimal point is implied.

A single-entry table is used when it is necessary to determine if a certain name or account number in a table matches an input or a result field used in the program. If, however, the program requires data to be retrieved from the table, then *related tables* should be used for those applications. That is, if a match between an input NAME and a table NAME is used to print the corresponding Social Security number from the table specified in Figure 10.1, then the table is called a related table. If, however, the input name is used simply to determine if a match exists in the table, a simple table is sufficient.

III. Processing Single-Entry Tables

A. Creating Table Input Records

The table data must be entered in a form that is readable by the program. Depending on the system devices available, the table records could be on cards, diskette, disk, or other medium. Regardless of the device used, the following rules will always apply.

Rule Summary

1. Begin the table entries in position 1 of the record regardless of whether the medium is card, diskette, or disk.
2. One or more entries may be recorded on each input record; however, entries may not be split or continued from one record to another. Suppose for example that each table entry entered from cards is 10 characters long. Each card could contain a single table entry or each card could contain up to eight table entries.
3. Place one entry per record or as many complete entries as will fit on each record. Whatever number you choose per record will be the same for all records except the last, which may contain a complete entry or only the remaining characters necessary to complete the table.
4. The maximum number of table names permitted in a program is 60.

In Figure 1Ø.2, we have five table entries each consisting of a six-character checking account number. The checking account entries in Figure 1Ø.2 could be entered by five records as in Figure 1Ø.4, where each record is six positions long. Or, the checking accounts in Figure 1Ø.2 could be entered on two records, with each record containing 18 positions (three checking-account entries in record 1 and two in record 2 as in Figure 1Ø.5). Note that record 2 in Figure 1Ø.5 contains only the two remaining entries that are necessary to complete the table.

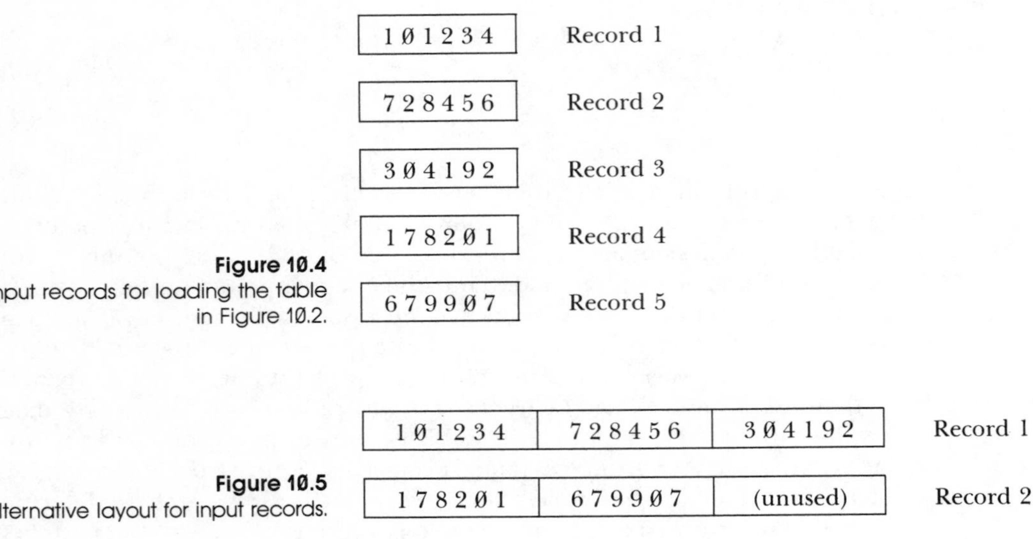

Figure 1Ø.4 Input records for loading the table in Figure 1Ø.2.

Figure 1Ø.5 Alternative layout for input records.

B. Compile Time and Pre-Execution Time Tables

Several methods are available to the programmer for entering table data into the computer. However, the two most popular methods are the following.

1. **Compile time table**. The table records are read in along with the program during compilation.
2. **Pre-execution time table**. The table records are read in just before the program is executed.

C. Loading Compile Time Tables

Compile time tables are entered along with the RPG program using the sequence specified in Figure 1Ø.6. The Extension Specifications form directly follows the File Description Specifications form. The record following the Output Specifications form contains a double asterisk (**) to indicate that table data follows. Table data, then, is part of the program and is not treated as input.

The advantage of compile time tables is that the table is always an integral part of the program itself. The disadvantage is that when the table changes, the entire RPG program must be recompiled. If a table does not change or changes infrequently, the compile time table is usually used. The student will find the compile time table to be the most popular and the most frequently used type, especially with IBM System 34 or 38 users. These systems do not use punched

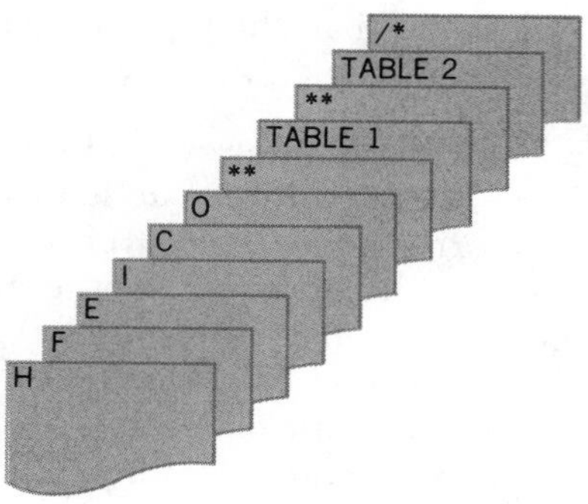

Figure 10.6
Placing compile time tables with a source program.

cards and would thus store a table on a magnetic medium such as disk along with the RPG program.

Pre-execution time tables are *not* compiled with the program, but rather, the table records are stored on cards, diskette, or disks. They are entered just prior to standard input. Thus, once the program is loaded, but immediately before the RPG cycle begins, the pre-execution table(s) are read into the program as shown in Figure 10.7.

Pre-execution time tables are used when entries change with some frequency. With a pre-execution time table, changes do not necessitate a recompilation since the table is stored on an external device. Thus, once the table data is read in, it is exactly the same as if it had been originally included as part of the program.

D. LOKUP Instruction for Single-Entry Tables

As noted earlier, a table may be searched for a high, low, and/or equal condition. That is, an input or result field may be compared against table entries until

1. An equal condition exists.

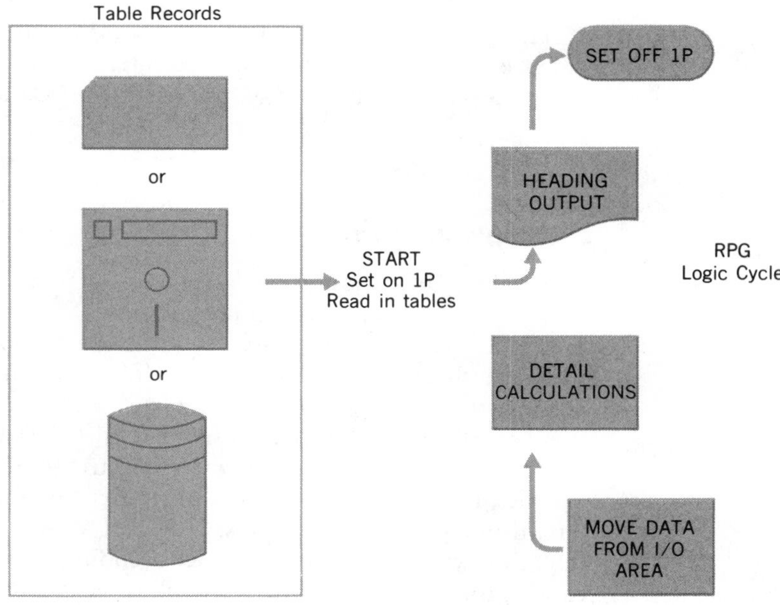

Figure 10.7
Reading in pre-execution tables.

2. The table entry is lower than the input or result field.
3. The table entry is greater than the input or result field.

When simple tables are used, however, always specify the equal condition in a look-up procedure. The **LOKUP instruction** causes a comparison to be made between Factor 1, referred to as the **search argument**, and each entry of the table, coded as Factor 2. If an equal condition is found, that is, the search argument equals one of the table entries, then the indicator is set on and is used to condition further processing or output. With the LOKUP instruction, Factor 2 always contains the name of the table. In the example that follows, an account number (ACCTNO) has been entered as input and the table containing invalid account numbers (TABACC) is to be searched. If the input account number is found in the table, indicator 1Ø will be set on. That is, if the input ACCTNO field matches a table entry, indicator 1Ø is set. The coding for this search is illustrated here.

RPG CALCULATION SPECIFICATIONS

Program | Keying Instruction | Graphic | Key | Card Electro Number | Page of | Program Identification
Programmer | Date

Line	Form Type	Control Level	Indicators	Factor 1	Operation	Factor 2	Result Field Name	Length	Decimal Positions	Half Adjust (H)	Resulting Indicators High	Low	Equal	Comments
01Ø	C			ACCTNO	LOKUP	TABACC							1Ø	
02	C													
03	C													
04	C													
05	C													

*Search word or search argument

Table to be searched– the search argument

Indicator is set on if search is successful

*Usually defined on the Input Specifications Form.

This illustrates a LOKUP with a *single table*. The use of the LOKUP with related tables is discussed and summarized later in this chapter. We are now prepared to develop a full sample program using the LOKUP instruction with single-entry tables.

E. Sample Program 1

1. Problem Definition

A table is to be created containing a list of out-of-stock part numbers. We will establish a compile time table for this illustration. When parts are requested, they are checked against the table file to see if they are out of stock. If the requested item is found in the table, the part number and requesting department are listed on a report entitled "OUT OF STOCK ITEMS." The problem definition for this program is shown in Figure 1Ø.8.

The file specifications for the program are familiar and no different than for any of our previous programs. However, since we will be using a compile time table, we will use an additional RPG coding sheet called the Extension Specifications form. This form directly follows the File Specifications form.

Figure 10.8
Problem definition for Sample Program 1.

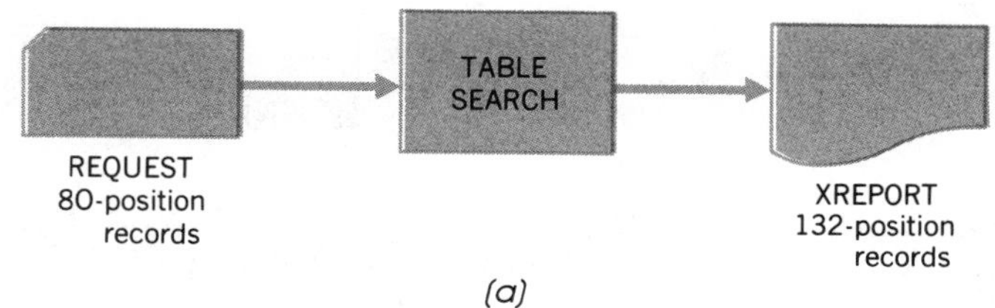

(a)

REQUEST Record Layout

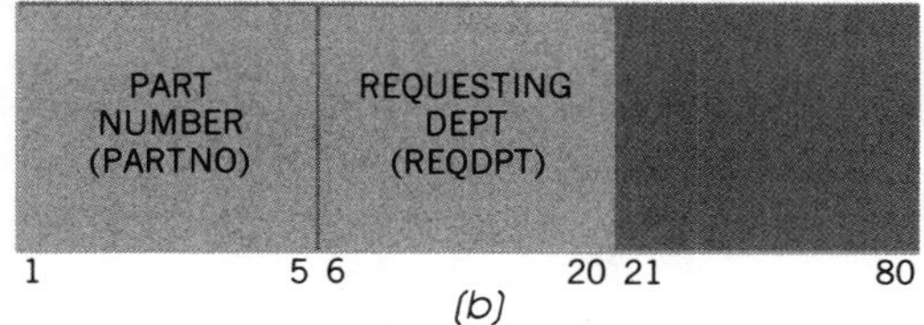

(b)

XREPORT Printer Spacing Chart

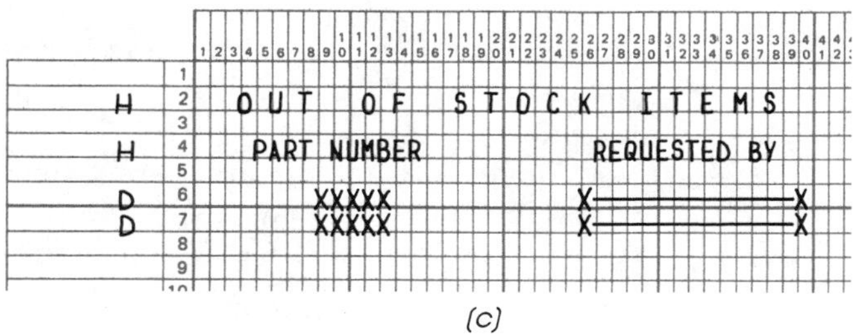

(c)

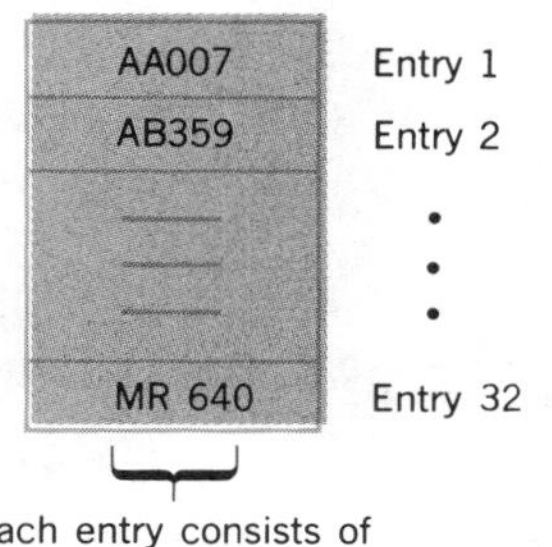

Figure 10.9
Table for Sample Program 1.

2. Extension Specifications
The Extension Specifications are used to

1. Identify the name of the table.
2. Allocate storage for the table in the program.

In this example, each part number consists of five characters, and the table is to contain 32 part-number entries. Hence the table will be 160 positions long (see Figure 10.9).

The table will be created from input records punched on 80-column cards. Each input record is to contain 16 five-column part number fields. Since the table is to contain 32 entries, only two cards will be necessary to provide the table data. The Extension Specifications are indicated in Figure 10.10. The entries have the following meanings.

1. ***Table or Array Name***
   The name of the table must begin with TAB in columns 27–29 of the Extension Specifications form. We chose the name TABOSI to denote out-of-stock items. However, any name is acceptable, providing it begins with TAB.
2. ***Number of Entries per Record***
   Each table input record contains 16 table entries. Thus 16 is coded in columns 34–35 of the Extension Specifications form.

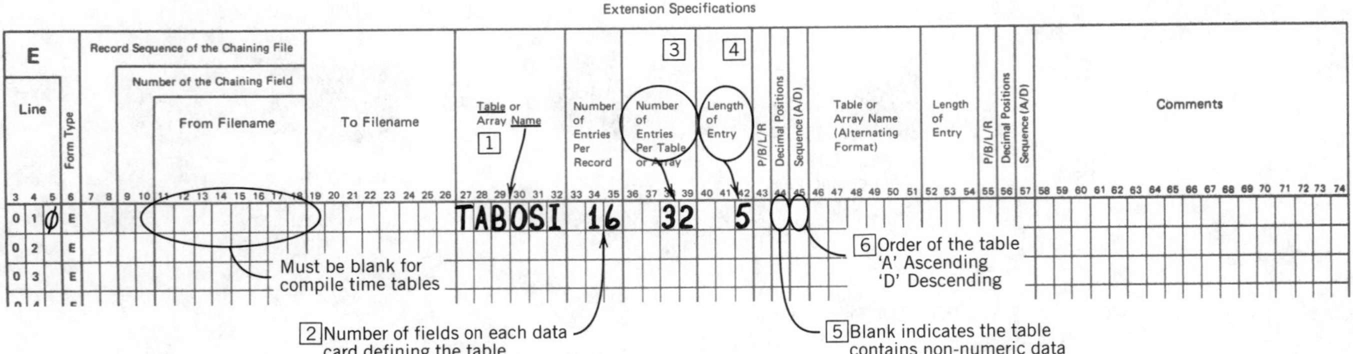

Figure 10.10
Extension Specifications form for Sample Program 1.

3. ***Number of Entries per Table or Array***
   The entire table is to contain 32 entries. Thus 32 is coded in columns 38–39.
4. ***Length of Entry***
   Each entry is five characters in length. Thus 5 is coded in column 42.
5. ***Decimal Positions***
   The Decimal Positions field (column 44) is blank when the table fields are *not* numeric. The decimal position will contain a digit for numeric table entries.
6. ***Sequence***
   With single-entry tables, no order need be specified. However, with related tables, the table data may be organized in ascending (A) or descending (D) sequence by specifying A or D in column 45.

The rest of the Extension Specifications are left blank for compile time tables.

Thus the entries just listed represent all the coding necessary to describe the TABOSI table to the program. The programmer should prepare the 16Ø-character table data on two punched cards (16 entries of five positions each per card). The source program should be organized as previously noted in Figure 1Ø.6. Remember that the compile time table data always follows the double asterisk (**) card in the source program.

Also note that the table entries will be listed on the Table MAPs, as illustrated in Figure 1Ø.11. During debugging, the MAP listing should be carefully reviewed

Figure 1Ø.11
Listing of the table entries.

```
                              T A B L E S   AND   M A P S

RESULTING INDICATOR TABLE

  OFFSET  RI      OFFSET  RI      OFFSET  RI      OFFSET  RI      OFFSET  RI      OFFSET  RI      OFFSET  RI

   0503   OA       0525   LR       0526   HO       0531   1P       0534   01       0535   50

OFFSETS OF VARIABLE NAMES AND CONSTANT NAMES

  OFFSET   NAME        OFFSET   NAME        OFFSET   NAME        OFFSET   NAME        OFFSET   NAME

  0638 TLF TABOSI      03C9     *ERROR      064D     PARTNO      0652     REQDPT

TABLE/ARRAY   TABOSI     000698

    AA007AB359AB913AR375AS009AT332AX198BB142BC963BE111BG653BT301BZ193CA165CB338CC654
    CD328CT123DD001DR610DT387DX921GE199GS333GU610JR017JX910LE370LG989LX328MM321MR640
```

Table data. Every 5 characters represent a new entry.

by the programmer to validate the accuracy of the table. Inaccuracies in the table could cause extensive debugging effort. Always validate the contents of programming tables before checking the logic of the program.

3. Coding the Program

The program is shown in Figure 10.12. Figure 10.13 shows sample output produced by the program. The only new instruction introduced is the LOKUP, which is used to search the TABOSI table. Using the LOKUP command, the search argument, PARTNO, is compared to the table entries; indicator 50 is set on when the input PARTNO is equal to a table entry. Indicator 50 is then used to condition the printing of the detail lines in the exception report. All the other instructions in this program should already be familiar to you.

Remember, any time an application requires a check to determine if a specific name, number, or item is present, a single-entry table may be used. An input or result field is simply compared to the table and an indicator set if the LOKUP produces a match or equal condition. If, however, additional data stored in the table is to be *retrieved,* then *related* or *multiple tables* are necessary. That is, if a match exists between an input field and a table entry in a related table, then a corresponding table entry is accessed.

Figure 10.12
Sample Program 1.

```
        01-010  F*                                                                   SSS10A
        01-020  F************************ FILE DESCRIPTION ************************** SSS10A
        01-030  F*                                                                   SSS10A
0001    01-040  FREQUEST IP  F      80                READ01 SYSIPT                  SSS10A
0002    01-050  FXREPORT O   F     132                PRINTERSYSLST                  SSS10A
        02-010  E*                                                                   SSS10A
        02-020  E****************** EXTENSION SPECIFICATIONS************************ SSS10A
        02-030  E*                                                                   SSS10A
0003    02-040  E                   TABOSI 16  32  5                                 SSS10A
        03-010  I*                                                                   SSS10A
        03-020  I************************** INPUT RECORD *************************** SSS10A
        03-030  I*                                                                   SSS10A
0004    03-040  IREQUEST NS  01                                                      SSS10A
0005    03-050  I                                           1   5 PARTNO             SSS10A
0006    03-060  I                                           6  20 REQDPT             SSS10A
        04-010  C*                                                                   SSS10A
        04-020  C******************** PERFORM TABLE SEARCH ************************* SSS10A
        04-030  C*                                                                   SSS10A
0007    04-040  C   01       PARTNO    LOKUPTABOSI                      50           SSS10A
        05-010  O*                                                                   SSS10A
        05-020  O*************************** HEADING LINES ************************* SSS10A
        05-030  O*                                                                   SSS10A
        05-040  O*                                                                   SSS10A
0008    05-050  OXREPORT H  201    1P                                                SSS10A
0009    05-060  O                                      26 'O U T   O F   S T O C K'  SSS10A
0010    05-070  O                                      38 'I T E M S'                SSS10A
0011    05-080  O          H  1    1P                                                SSS10A
0012    05-090  O                                      15 'PART NUMBER'              SSS10A
0013    05-100  O                                      38 'REQUESTED BY'             SSS10A
        05-110  O*                                                                   SSS10A
        05-120  O*************************** DETAIL LINES*************************** SSS10A
        05-130  O*                                                                   SSS10A
0014    05-140  O          D  1    50 01                                             SSS10A
0015    05-150  O                         PARTNO    13                               SSS10A
0016    05-160  O                         REQDPT    40                               SSS10A
        05-170  O*********************** END OF SOURCE **************************** SSS10A

    E N D  O F  S O U R C E
```

```
O U T   O F   S T O C K   I T E M S

PART NUMBER        REQUESTED BY
     MR64C        MACHINE PARTS
     JX910        SPINNING DEPT
     AA007        WELDING DEPT
     LG989        WELDING DEPT
     BE111        DIE CASTING
     AS005        TOOL & DIE SHOP
     JR017        CARPENTER SHOP
     CB338        ELECTRICAL ASSY
```

Figure 10.13
Sample output produced by Program 1.

IV. Related Tables

A. Applications

Related tables are two or more tables that are related to one another. For an entry in one table, there is a corresponding entry in another table. See Figure 1Ø.14 for an illustration.

A typical application using the table illustrated would be to calculate the cost of shipping items of different weights. The processing of the related tables would include the following steps.

1. Input a transaction record that contains the weight of the item to be shipped.
2. Look up in the table the exact weight; if it is not there, find the entry that is closest to the input item weight, but greater than it. For example, if the weight was 38 pounds, the charge would be 24.95 for an item more than 25 pounds but not greater than 5Ø pounds.
3. Once the correct argument has been found, use the corresponding charge from the function table.
4. The charge retrieved from the function table is used in any required program calculations. Again, note that with related tables, we search the argument table in order to find an entry, then return with the corresponding field from the function table.

The *argument* is used to compare against an input or result field. If a match is found, the corresponding *function* of the table is used to calculate a total price. Thus the weight of an input item is compared to the weight indicated in the table. When the input weight is less than the argument weight, the corresponding freight charge, or function, is added to the total price.

Figure 1Ø.14
Example of related tables.

	Weight*	Charge
Entry 1	Up to 1Ø	Ø5.95
Entry 2	Up to 25	12.5Ø
Entry 3	Up to 5Ø	24.95
Entry 4	Up to 1ØØ	48.ØØ
	Argument table	Function table

Related tables

**Note:* No item over 1ØØ lbs. will be shipped.

B. Loading Related Tables

If you were required to enter the related tables illustrated in Figure 1Ø.14, you would define them separately as shown in Example 1 of Figure 1Ø.15.

The Extension Specifications form for Example 1 is illustrated in Figure 1Ø.16.

In Example 1, the related tables were coded as two individual tables. However, when the look-up operation is performed in the weight table, the corresponding entry in the charge table can be referenced and used by the program.

Figure 10.15 Alternative ways of entering related tables.

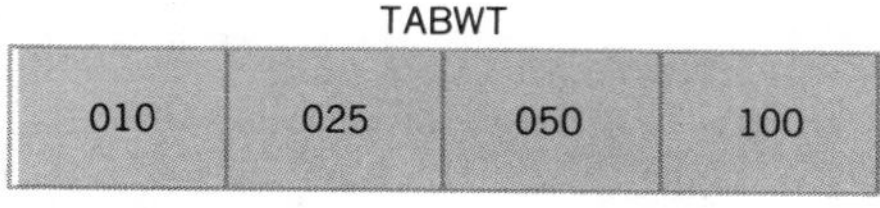

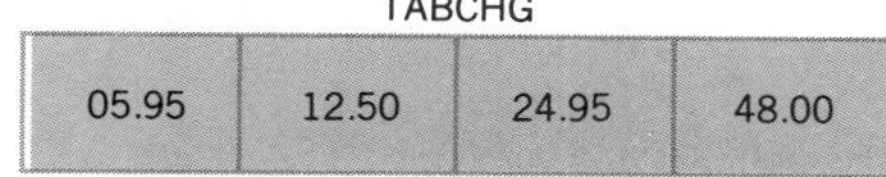

Two Single-Entry Tables

Example 2

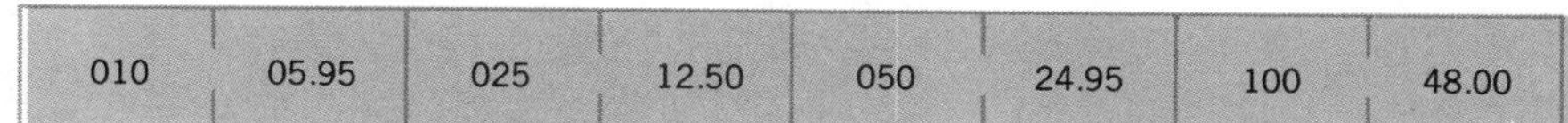

010
05.95
025
12.50
050
24.95
100
48.00

Related Tables with Alternating Format

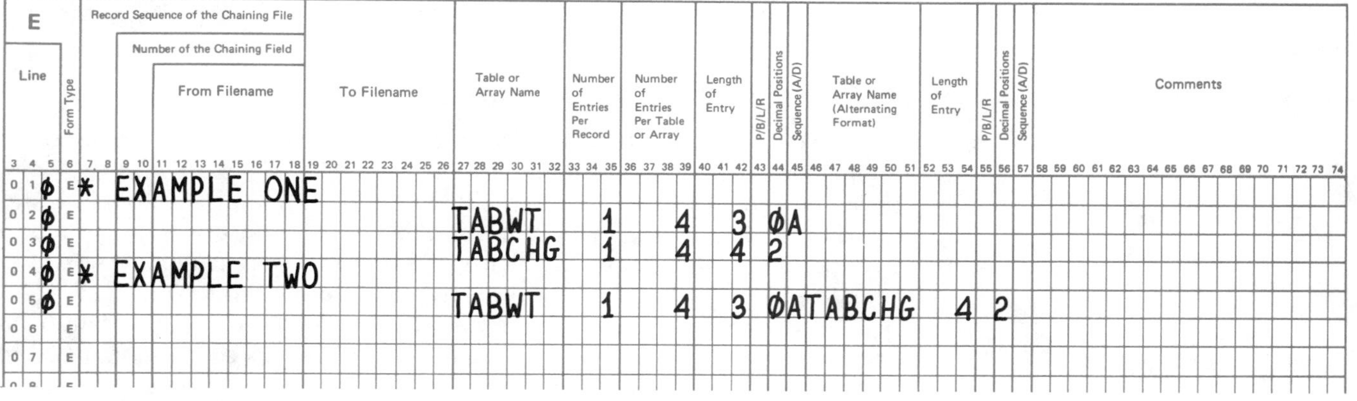

Extension Specifications

Line (3–5)	Form Type (6)	(7–10) / From Filename (11–18)	To Filename (19–26)	Table or Array Name (27–32)	Number of Entries Per Record (33–35)	Number of Entries Per Table or Array (36–39)	Length of Entry (40–42)	P/B/L/R (43)	Decimal Positions (44)	Sequence (A/D) (45)	Table or Array Name (Alternating Format) (46–51)	Length of Entry (52–54)	P/B/L/R (55)	Decimal Positions (56)	Sequence (A/D) (57)	Comments (58–74)
01Ø	E	* EXAMPLE ONE														
02Ø	E			TABWT	1	4	3		Ø	A						
03Ø	E			TABCHG	1	4	4		2							
04Ø	E	* EXAMPLE TWO														
05Ø	E			TABWT	1	4	3		Ø	A	TABCHG	4		2		
06	E															
07	E															

Figure 10.16 Extension Specifications form for Figure 10.15.

Note the following in the Extension Specifications form for Example 1.

1. The table names always begin with TAB.
2. Each table entry is contained on a single record. Because the table contains four entries, the weight table would be defined on four records. Similarly, the charge table would also be defined on four records.

The sequence of the table data must follow the same order as coded on the Extension Specifications form. Again refer to Figure 10.6 for the organization of the source program.

The Extension Specifications form also indicates the following.

1. The length of each weight entry is three; the length of the charge field is four with two decimal places. These definitions are identical to those previously used in the Input or Calculation Specifications.
2. An "A" is coded in column 45, denoting that the weight table is in ascending sequence. If the search argument is not equal to the weight, the programmer must specify the sequence of the table data in order for the program to select the correct corresponding entry based on a high/low condition.

Example 2 contains the coding for related tables in an alternating format. All the entries in the two examples contain the same specifications. However, the input records are formatted as indicated in Figure 1Ø.17.

In Example 2 of Figure 1Ø.16, note that the input records contain the data for both tables. Again, only four input records will be used to define the tables, as shown in Figure 1Ø.17.

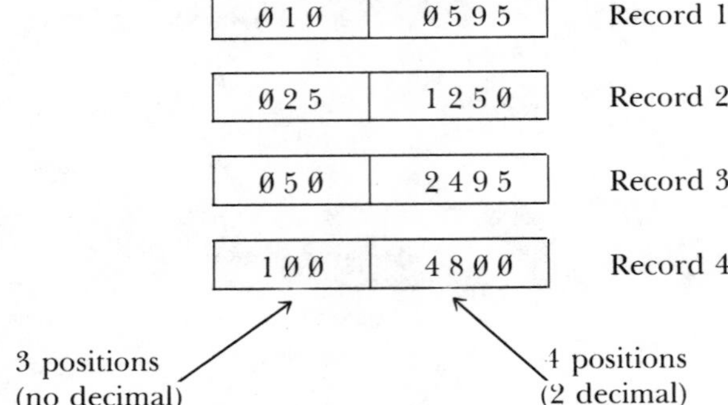

Figure 1Ø.17
Format of input records for Example 2.

C. LOKUP Instruction for Related Tables

With single-entry tables, the LOKUP instruction always searches for an equal condition. With related tables, RPG uses the same LOKUP instruction to search one table and return with the corresponding entry from another table in order to perform calculations and/or output operations. This concept is illustrated in the example in Figure 1Ø.18, in which we search the weight table (TABWT) to determine the appropriate amount due from the charge table (TABCHG).

The LOKUP instruction is used to search TABWT and return with the data from TABCHG. The search word or search argument, WEIGHT, is a field contained in the input record and is coded as Factor 1. The table to be searched, the argument table, is coded as Factor 2. The related function table, TABCHG, is entered as the Result field. Note that the specifications for the resulting indicators are set for high and equal.

The coding causes the computer to search and find the exact weight on the

Figure 1Ø.18
LOKUP instruction.

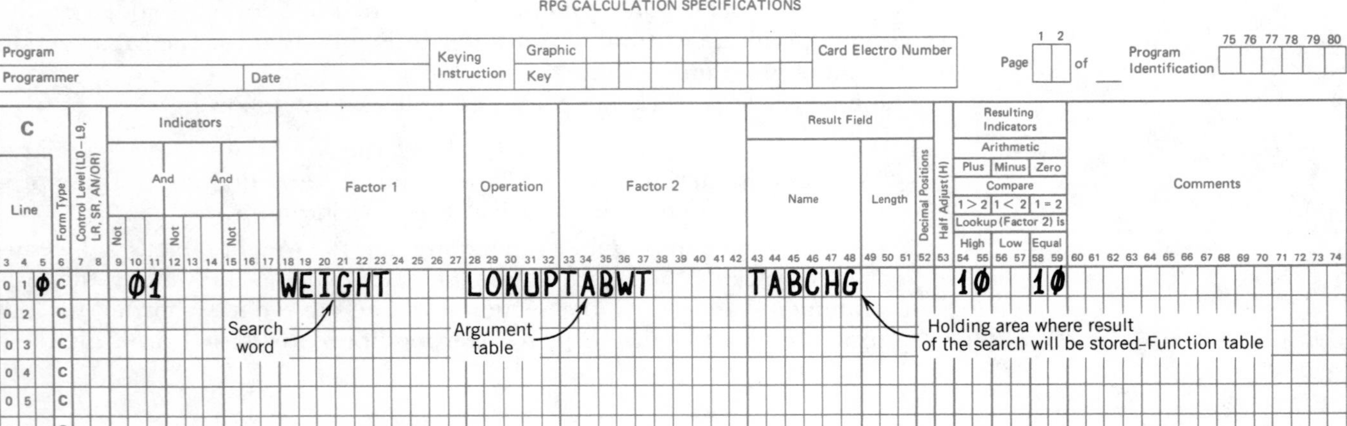

table equal to the input field; or the table argument closest to the weight but *higher* than the input field is to be found. For example, an item weighing 38 pounds has a shipping charge of 24.95. If the search is successful, indicator 1Ø is set on and the field TOTAL is calculated using the resulting field called TABCHG (see Figure 1Ø.19).

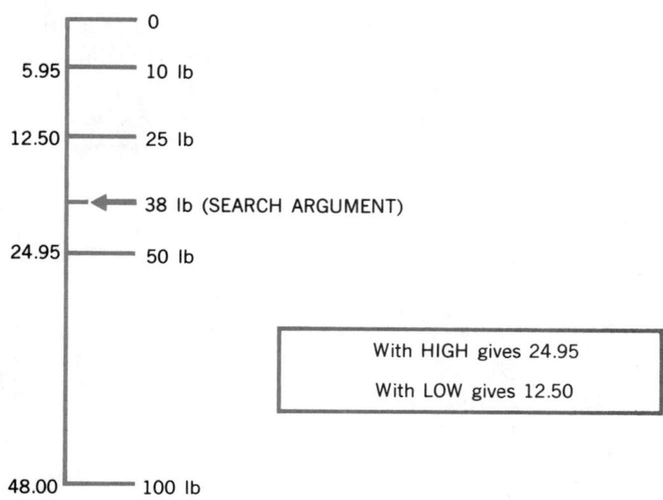

Figure 1Ø.19
Example of search.

When the search is successful, the name of the table TABCHG is used to reference the corresponding table entry that is needed for calculations.

The LOKUP instruction may be summarized as follows.

Instruction:	LOKUP
Meaning:	Search a table for the conditions specified by the resulting indicators.
Factor 1:	Specifies the search word containing the data for the search. Usually defined on the Input Specifications form or the Calculation Specifications form. The length of the search word must always be the same as the length of the entry in the argument table. If the argument table contains numeric data, then the search word must also be defined as numeric.
Factor 2:	The name of the table to be searched is coded as Factor 2. The argument table is always defined on the Extension Specifications form.
Result Field:	When related tables are used, the function table name is coded in the Result field. If the search is successful, the data from the corresponding function table is copied and moved to a special holding area that is referenced by the function table name.
Limitations:	Related tables must be in ascending or descending order if a condition other than equal is specified. Hence, A or D is entered in column 45 of the Extension Specifications form when either a high or low resulting indicator is specified.

D. Sample Program 2

1. Problem Definition

A compile time table is to be established containing a list of item weights and a corresponding list of delivery charges that depend on item weight. When an item is to be shipped, the weight table is searched to determine the shipping charges. The shipping charges are added to the selling price to obtain a total amount due. The data is then printed in accordance with specifications provided in the Printer Spacing Chart. In addition, when the weight of an item exceeds 100 pounds, the program sets the resulting indicator off, which conditions the printing of the message '*** WEIGHT EXCEEDS 100 POUNDS ***'. The systems flowchart, record layout, and Printer Spacing Chart for this program are shown in Figure 10.20.

Figure 10.20 Problem definition for Sample Program 2.

Systems Flowchart

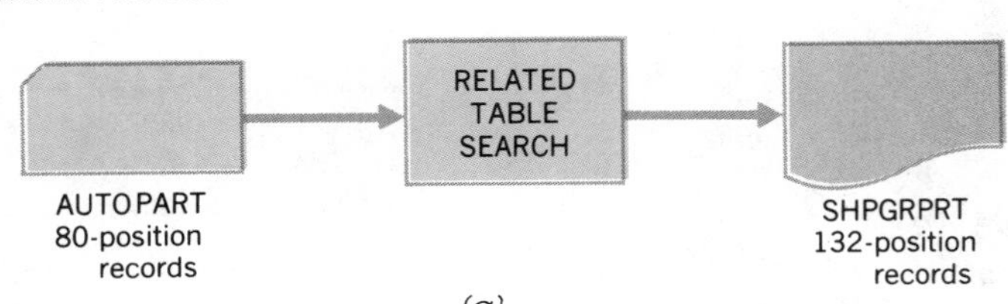

(a)

AUTOPART Record Layout

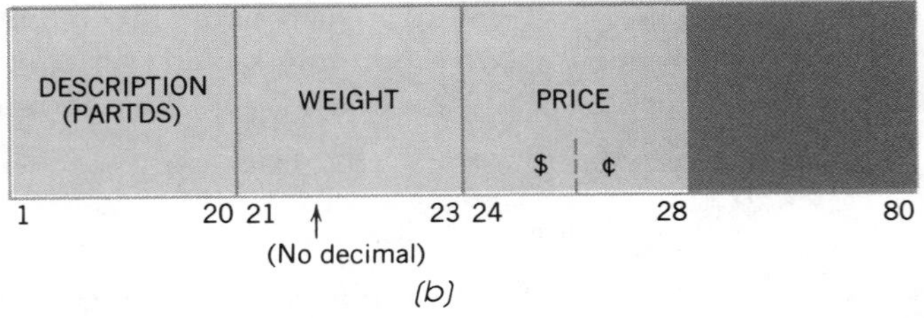

(b)

SHPGRPRT Printer Spacing Chart

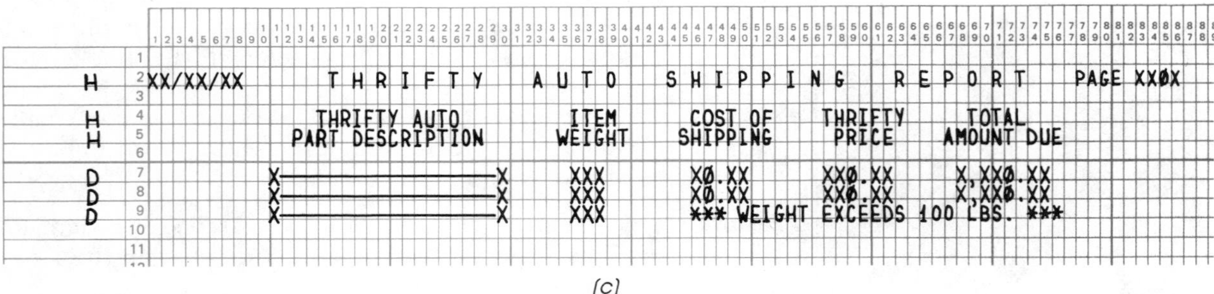

(c)

2. Coding the Program

Again, the Extension Specifications are used to allocate storage within the program for the tables. The Extension Specifications form in this Sample Program is coded as previously illustrated in Example 2 of Figure 10.16. The specifications provide the following.

- The name of the table.

- The number of entries coded on each input record.
- The maximum number of entries required for the table.
- The length of each entry and the decimal positions required (for numeric fields).
- The order of the table (ascending or descending) when a resulting indicator other than equal is specified in the LOKUP instruction.

If you do not recall these specifications, review Figures 10.17 and 10.18 to ensure your understanding of this material. The LOKUP instruction is used to compare the WEIGHT of the input field with the argument table (TABWT) in order to determine the shipping charges that are found in the function table TABCHG. If the search is successful, the corresponding charges are placed in a field called TABCHG in order that they can be used in calculations. Also note that the field TABCHG is used with the Output Specifications in printing the detail lines. The coding for this program is illustrated in Figure 10.21.

```
        01-010  F*                                                                        SSS10B
        01-020  F************************* FILE DESCRIPTION ***************************** SSS10B
        01-030  F*                                                                        SSS10B
0001    01-040  FAUTOPARTIP  F      80              READ01 SYSIPT                         SSS10B
0002    01-050  FSHPGRPRTO   F     132      OF      PRINTERSYSLST                         SSS10B
        02-010  E*                                                                        SSS10B
        02-020  E****************** EXTENSION SPECIFICATIONS************************* SSS10B
        02-030  E*                                                                        SSS10B
0003    02-040  E                    TABWT    1   4   3 0ATABCHG   4 2                    SSS10B
        03-010  I*                                                                        SSS10B
        03-020  I**************************** INPUT RECORD *************************** SSS10B
        03-030  I*                                                                        SSS10B
0004    03-040  IAUTOPARTNS  01                                                           SSS10B
0005    03-050  I                                              1  20 PARTDS               SSS10B
0006    03-060  I                                             21  232WEIGHT               SSS10B
0007    03-070  I                                             24  282PRICE                SSS10B
        04-010  C*                                                                        SSS10B
        04-020  C**************************** CALCULATIONS *************************** SSS10B
        04-030  C*                                                                        SSS10B
0008    04-040  C   01        WEIGHT    LOKUPTABWT      TABCHG      10  10                SSS10B
0009    04-050  C   01 10     PRICE     ADD  TABCHG     TOTAL   62                        SSS10B
        05-010  O*                                                                        SSS10B
        05-020  O**************************** HEADING LINES ************************** SSS10B
        05-030  O*                                                                        SSS10B
0010    05-040  OSHPGRPRTH  201    1P                                                     SSS10B
0011    05-050  O        CR        OF                                                     SSS10B
0012    05-060  O                              UDATE Y     8                              SSS10B
0013    05-070  O                                         39 'T H R I F T Y   A U T O'    SSS10B
0014    05-080  O                                         58 'S H I P P I N G'            SSS10B
0015    05-090  O                                         73 'R E P O R T'                SSS10B
0016    05-100  O                                         81 'PAGE'                       SSS10B
0017    05-110  O                              PAGE       86                              SSS10B
0018    05-120  O        H  1      1P                                                     SSS10B
0019    05-130  O        CR        OF                                                     SSS10B
0020    05-140  O                                         26 'THRIFTY AUTO'               SSS10B
0021    05-150  O                                         39 'ITEM'                       SSS10B
0022    05-160  O                                         52 'COST OF'                    SSS10B
0023    05-170  O                                         63 'THRIFTY'                    SSS10B
0024    05-180  O                                         73 'TOTAL'                      SSS10B
0025    06-010  O        H  2      1P                                                     SSS10B
0026    06-020  O        OR        OF                                                     SSS10B
0027    06-030  O                                         28 'PART DESCRIPTION'           SSS10B
0028    06-040  O                                         40 'WEIGHT'                     SSS10B
0029    06-050  O                                         52 'SHIPPING'                   SSS10B
0030    06-060  O                                         62 'PRICE'                      SSS10B
0031    06-070  O                                         76 'AMOUNT DUE'                 SSS10B
        06-080  O*                                                                        SSS10B
        06-090  O**************************** DETAIL LINES**************************** SSS10B
        06-100  O*                                                                        SSS10B
0032    06-110  O        D  1      01 10                                                  SSS10B
0033    06-120  O                              PARTDS     30                              SSS10B
0034    06-130  O                              WEIGHT     38                              SSS10B
0035    06-140  O                              TABCHG1    50                              SSS10B
0036    06-150  O                              PRICE 1    62                              SSS10B
0037    06-160  O                              TOTAL 1    75                              SSS10B
        07-010  O*                                                                        SSS10B
        07-020  O**************************** ERROR MESSAGE ************************** SSS10B
        07-030  O*                                                                        SSS10B
0038    07-040  O        D  1      01N10                                                  SSS10B
0039    07-050  O                              PARTDS     30                              SSS10B
0040    07-060  O                              WEIGHT     38                              SSS10B
0041    07-070  O                                         63 '*** WEIGHT EXCEEDS'         SSS10B
0042    07-080  O                                         76 '100 LBS. ***'               SSS10B
        07-090  O************************** END OF SOURCE **************************** SSS10B
```

Figure 10.21
Sample Program 2.

Also recall that the table should be checked for accuracy by referring to the Table Map before attempting to debug the program. See Figure 10.22 for an illustration of the Table Map.

The output generated by this program conforms to the Printer Spacing Chart as established in the problem definition (see Figure 10.23).

Figure 10.22 Illustration of a Table Map.

```
                                     T A B L E S   AND   M A P S

RESULTING INDICATCR TABLE
  OFFSET  RI       OFFSET  RI       OFFSET  RI       OFFSET  RI       OFFSET  RI       OFFSET  RI       CFFSET  RI
   0508   OF        0525   LR        0526   HO        0531   1P        0534   01        0535   10

OFFSETS OF VARIABLE NAMES AND CONSTANT NAMES
  OFFSET    NAME         CFFSET    NAME         CFFSET    NAME         OFFSET    NAME         OFFSET    NAME
  0638 TLF TABWT         0648 TLF TABCHG        03C9      *ERROR       065D      PARTDS       0671      WEIGHT
  0673     PRICE         0676     TCTAL         0400      UDATE        067E      PAGE

TABLE/ARRAY - TABWT          00073F
TABLE/ARRAY - TABCHG         000747

           0100595
           0251250
           0502495
           1004800
```

Figure 10.23 Sample output produced by Program 2.

```
1/28/83      T H R I F T Y    A U T O    S H I P P I N G    R E P O R T    PAGE     1

              THRIFTY AUTO          ITEM      CCST CF     THRIFTY      TOTAL
            PART DESCRIPTION       WEIGHT     SHIPPING     PRICE     AMOUNT DUE

          CARBURETCR ASSEMBLY       017        12.50      128.50       141.00
          FUEL PUMP #12835          025        12.50       73.20        85.70
          CAMSHAFT  #37085          088        48.00      311.00       359.00
          ELECTRICAL BCX ASSY       003         5.95       17.85        23.80
          TRANSMISSION #12812       245        *** WEIGHT EXCEEDS 100 LBS. ***
          VALVE CCVER PLATE         061        48.00       79.95       127.95
          T-RCOF INSERT RIGHT       034        24.95      183.95       208.90
          ELECTRONIC DISTRIB.       003         5.95       89.95        95.90
          POWER BRAKE CYL ASSY      100        48.00      362.85       410.85
          DISK BRAKE CALIPERS       026        24.95       70.90        95.85
```

V. Pre-execution Time Tables

Thus far, all the tables used have been compile time tables. Pre-execution tables may also be used in RPG programs.

A. Single-entry Tables

Pre-execution tables are *not* compiled with the program but instead are maintained on an external medium such as disk, diskette, cards or tape. After the program is compiled but before the RPG cycle begins, the program will read the table data from an external medium into the program. Once the table is read and stored in the program, it is used in the same way as if it had been originally defined within the program. In order to read the table from an external medium, an additional File Specification entry is required. This is because the table is, in actuality, a separate file stored on an external medium. The File Specification form serves to link the device with the table area of the program. Since pre-execution tables are entered as a file, they must be assigned a file name in the same manner as names are given to input and output files. Assume the table data for the out-of-stock items was stored on disk. The File and Extension Specifications forms would be as shown in Figure 10.24.

We are already familiar with most of the entries on the File Specifications form. However, the following additional details should be noted.

- Columns 15 and 16 indicate that the file OSITABLE is an input table file.
- Since each of the disk records is five characters long, the record length is five.
- To link the file description with the area in the program set aside for the table, an E is specified in column 39. RPG will then refer to the Extension Specifications for more detailed information required to store the table. The entries on the Extension Specification remain the same except for the

Figure 10.24
Defining a pre-execution, single-entry table.

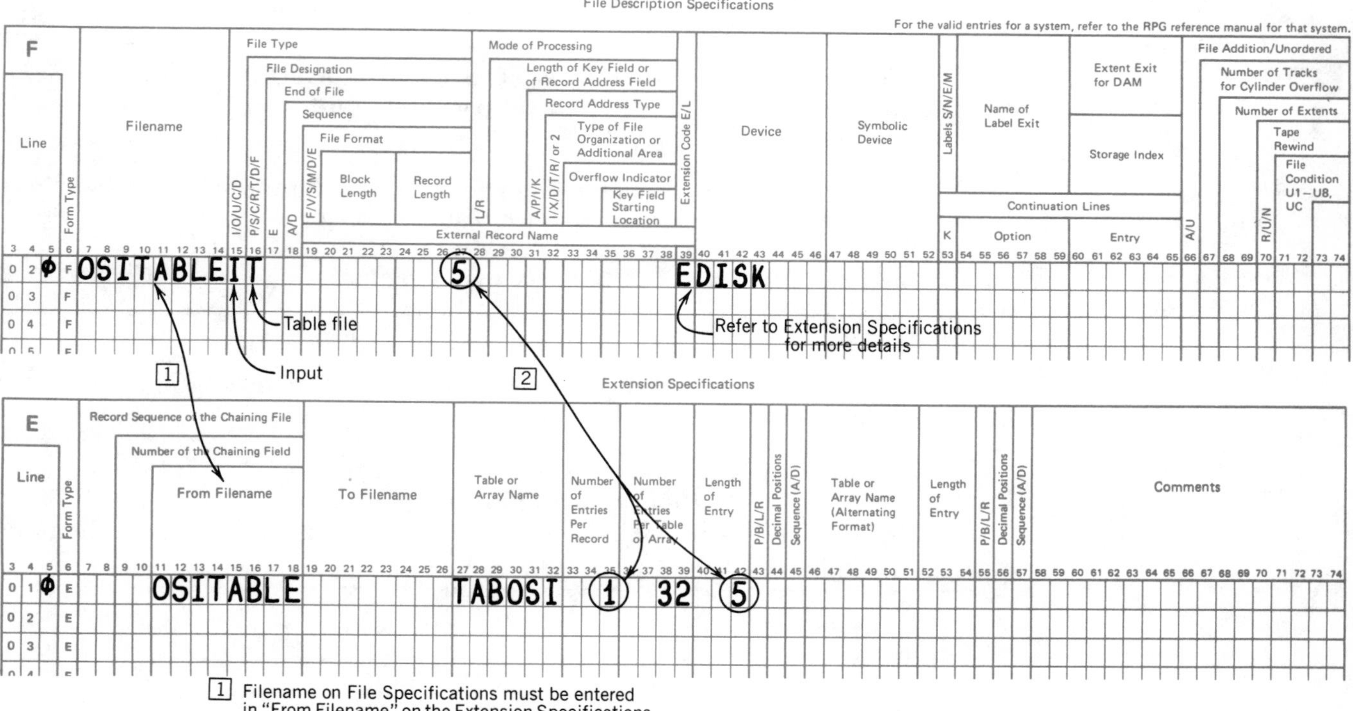

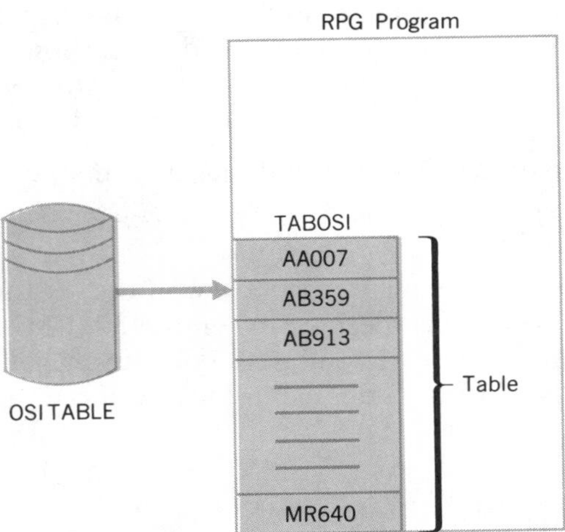

Figure 1Ø.25
Defining a pre-execution, single-entry table of out-of-stock items.

addition of the filename entry. This entry informs the computer system that the named file is to be read before the program begins (see Figure 1Ø.25).

Again, the File Specification identifies the device from which the table file is to be read, whereas the Extension Specifications provide the detailed description of the storage area needed for the table.

The following features of pre-execution tables should be kept in mind.

> ***Advantage of Pre-execution Tables***
>
> The advantage of this type of table is that a production program does not have to be recompiled whenever the table changes.

> ***Disadvantage of Pre-execution Tables***
>
> The device or media containing the table must always be available whenever the program is run.

Thus, when table data changes with great frequency, pre-execution tables are usually used; otherwise, the tendency is to use compile time tables.

B. Pre-execution Related Tables

Related tables are described in much the same manner as single-entry tables. The only difference occurs on the Extension Specifications form. Recalling the weight/charge tables presented earlier, the coding in Figure 1Ø.26 would be used to create these tables from a disk file using the pre-execution method.

A desk check of your program is recommended to be sure that the length of the table entries specified on the Extension Specifications form in columns 4Ø–42 for the first table and columns 52–54 of the second table add up to the record length specified on the File Specifications form in columns 24–27. Your program will not execute properly if the table lengths are defined incorrectly. In the example given, the length of the table entries (3 + 4) equals the record length of 7 specified on the File Specifications form.

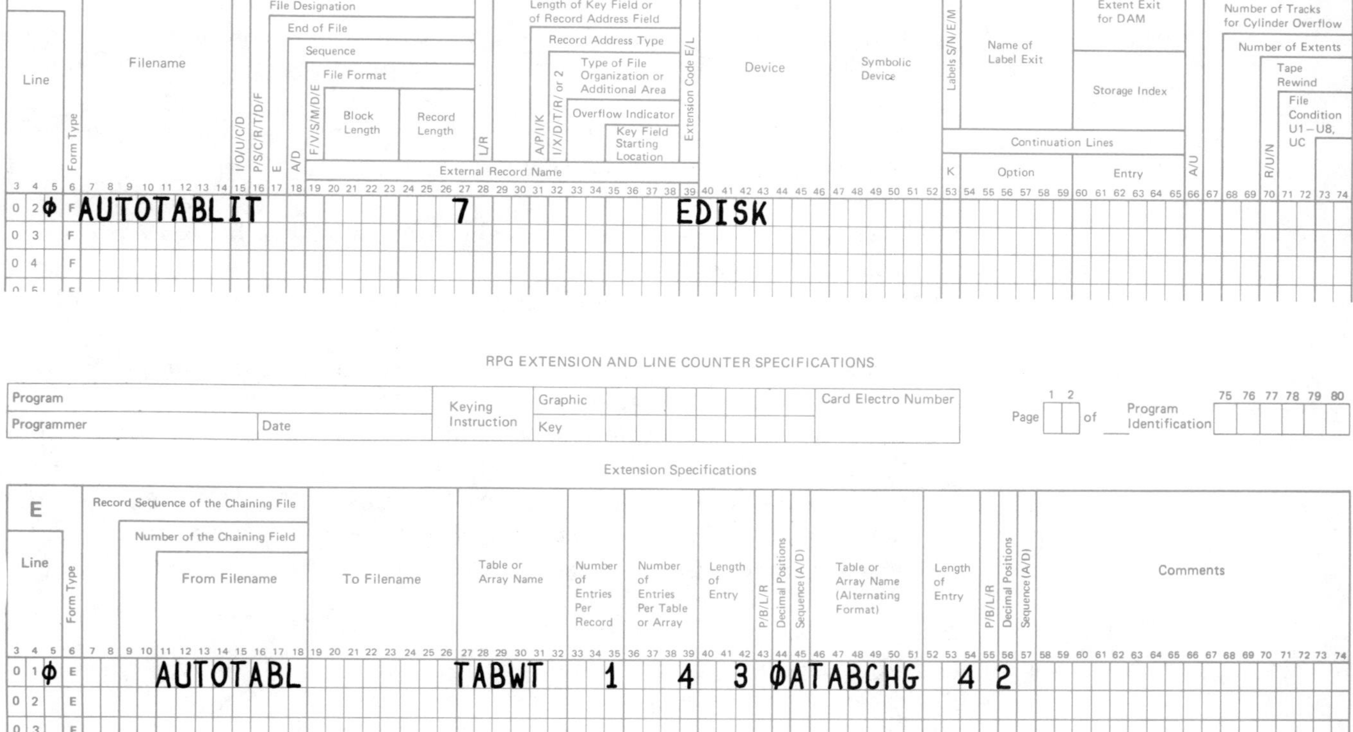

Figure 10.26
Defining pre-execution related tables.

Self-Evaluating Quiz

1. (T or F) If a search is not successful, the resulting indicator(s) specified in the LOKUP are set off.
2. When the LOKUP is used with a simple table, the table to be searched is entered as (<u>Factor 1/Factor 2/Result Field</u>) of the Calculation form.
3. The search argument is usually defined on the (<u>Output Specifications, Input Specifications, Extension Specifications</u>) form.
4. (T or F) When tables do not change or change infrequently, compile time tables are a good choice.
5. When compile time tables change, the programmer must ________ the program.
6. Code the Extension Specifications form to define the related tables shown here. Each record contains data for both tables; therefore, five input records would be used to create the table.

TABNO	TABMSG		
Ø1	PARCEL POST	Ø4	UNITED PARCEL SERVICE
Ø2	S & S TRUCKING	Ø5	MESSENGER SERVICE
Ø3	AIR MAIL		

7. For the tables defined in Question 6, assume the search argument is a field called CODE. Complete the Calculation Specifications form to search the TABNO table and set on indicator 77.
8. If the search in Question 7 is successful, what field will be referenced in the Output Specifications in order to print the messages 'AIR MAIL', and so forth?
9. Would CODE in Question 7 be defined as a numeric or nonnumeric field?
10. In creating table input records, can more than two entries be placed on each input record?
11. What coding on the File Specifications form tells RPG that a pre-execution table is to be read in before the RPG Logic Cycle begins?
12. What entry on the Extension Specifications form informs RPG as to where the table data is coming from?
13. (T or F) When the equal condition is specified for the resulting indicators, when performing a LOKUP the table must be in ascending order.
14. When a LOKUP indicator assigned to HIGH is on, what is the relationship between the search argument and the table argument entered as Factor 2?
15. Differentiate between the NUMBER OF TABLE ENTRIES PER TABLE and the NUMBER OF TABLE ENTRIES PER RECORD on the Extension form.
16. The RPG form used to allocate or reserve storage in the program for tables is the ______ Specifications form.

Solutions

1. T
2. Factor 2
3. Input Specifications
4. T
5. recompile
6.

Extension Specifications

Line (3–5)	Form Type (6)	Record Sequence of the Chaining File (7–8)	Number of the Chaining Field (9–10)	From Filename (11–18)	To Filename (19–26)	Table or Array Name (27–32)	Number of Entries Per Record (33–35)	Number of Entries Per Table or Array (36–39)	Length of Entry (40–42)	P/B/L/R (43)	Decimal Positions (44)	Sequence (A/D) (45)	Table or Array Name (Alternating Format) (46–51)	Length of Entry (52–54)	P/B/L/R (55)	Decimal Positions (56)	Sequence (A/D) (57)	Comments (58–74)
01Ø	E					TABNO	1	5	2		Ø		TABMSG	21				
02	E																	
03	E																	
04	E																	

7.

RPG CALCULATION SPECIFICATIONS

Line	Form Type	Factor 1	Operation	Factor 2	Result Field Name	Resulting Indicators (Equal)
01Ø	C	CODE	LOKUP	TABNO	TABMSG	77
02	C					
03	C					
04	C					
05	C					

Search word or argument — Table to be searched — Result field to be referenced — Indicator set on when search is successful

8. TABMSG. Remember, when the search is successful the data from the corresponding related table is placed in a special holding area assigned to the name of the array.
9. CODE must be numeric if TABNO entries are numeric. If TABNO entries are not numeric, then CODE would not be numeric. This is checked by referring to the Extension Specifications form. If column 44 is blank, TABNO is not numeric. However, if a zero was entered, then the field is numeric.
10. Yes. You may use as many table entries on a record as will fit completely. Remember, table entry records cannot be split.
11. The filename is entered on the File Specifications form. Column 16 contains the letter "T" denoting that a table file is used, and column 39 contains the letter "E" meaning that additional information is provided on the Extension Specifications form.
12. The From filename entry in columns 11-18 of the Extension Form.
13. F. When the equal condition is specified, the organization of the table data is of no consequence. However, items having a high activity are placed near the top of the table to reduce the amount of time used in performing the search. This will improve the efficiency of the table LOKUP operation.
14. The table argument selected will be the one just higher than the search argument. Therefore, Factor 1, the search argument, is less than Factor 2, the table argument.
15. NUMBER OF TABLE ENTRIES PER TABLE denotes the length or the total number of entries for that table. A table of states, for example, would consist of 5Ø entries.

    NUMBER OF ENTRIES PER RECORD designates the number of entries contained on each input record used to create the table.
16. Extension

VI.

Why Tables are Entered Externally

Tables are entered as variable data and are not defined as constants within a program. Suppose you had a table of discount rates for each item sold by a company. You would *not* define the table containing discount rates for each product as a *constant*. The reason that tables are not defined as constants is that table entries change from time to time. If the table were actually coded as part of the program, then each change would require a modification of the program coding. One rule of programming is that you code procedures so that changes or subsequent modifications are minimized. Since each program change increases the risk of error, we do not include as constant data any item that is apt to change. Note that compile time tables are not considered constants within the program, but are handled as separate input records.

Thus table data that changes frequently is always entered as *variable* input along with the specific input to be processed. In this way, if a table entry is to be changed, you simply alter the entry and do not need to modify the program. Thus all pre-execution table programs are processed as follows.

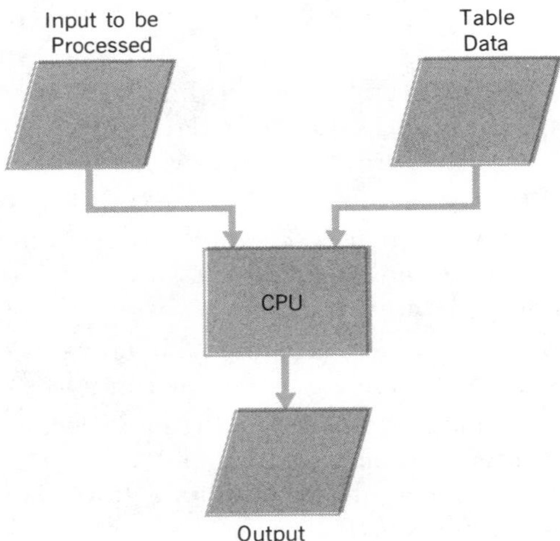

VII. Purpose of Arrays

Once the table is entered as input, it is used exclusively for look-up purposes. That is, you compare an input field search argument against the entries in the table to find the condition specified by the indicators. In our table, for example, along with the corresponding product number, we would enter our discount rate. For each customer purchase order, we would compare the product number purchased to the product number in the table to find the corresponding discount rate. When we find a match, the discount associated with the product number as part of the related table would be used for computing the customer's bill.

Tables, then, remain constant or unchanged during the execution of a program. They are used exclusively for look up; if a table entry requires modification, it would be changed prior to execution. User programs, then, generally use tables for read-only purposes.

There are, however, instances in which you would want to establish areas in storage that contain repeated occurrences of a specific entry that you will alter as the program is executed or that will be used for storing totals or amounts. For example, you may wish to establish a series of 12 total fields, one for each month of the year. We will add to a specific total field, depending on the contents of each input record. This series of total fields would be called an array. An **array** consists of a series of elements with similar characteristics that are stored as one unit. Each element of an array, like a table, has similar characteristics. The contents of an array, however, usually change during program execution. Array processing greatly extends the ability of RPG programs to calculate results for specific applications. The following provides a comparison of arrays and tables.

Comparison of Arrays and Tables

1. Similarities
   Elements within an array or table have similar characteristics: the same field lengths, the same type of data, the same number of decimal positions (if numeric).
2. Differences
   A table generally contains data that will be used for look-up purposes. An array is generally used for accumulating results or storing totals or amounts.

VIII. Manipulating Arrays

A. Referencing Elements of an Array

Once an array has been established, each element may be referenced directly by specifying its relative position within the array. An **index** is used to indicate which element in an array you wish to access. Suppose you have an array called WKTEMP (for weekly temperatures), which contains seven temperature figures, one for each day of the week. To access the temperature for the third day of the week, you would use WKTEMP,3. This reference uses the array name and the index separated by a comma (see Figure 1Ø.27). Note that the array name is limited to a maximum of four characters on the Output Specifications form if individual elements are to be printed.

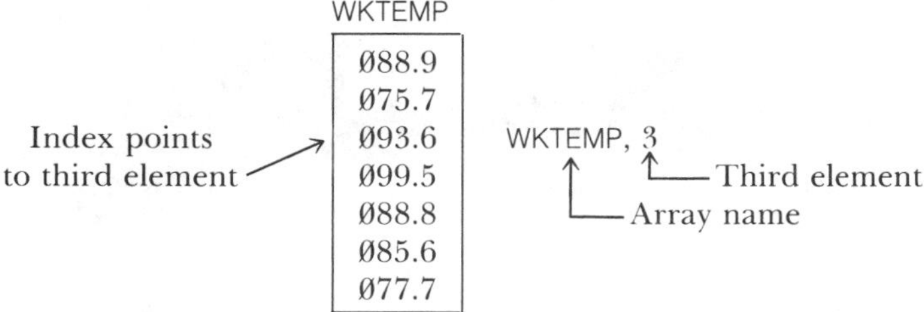

Figure 1Ø.27
Accessing an array.

The index serves as a pointer to identify the particular element of the array that is to be accessed. Since the array name is the same for each element, the index is used to identify the specific element to be used in calculations or output operations.

Accessing an array called EXAM that has 1Ø elements is performed in exactly the same way. EXAM,3 refers to the third element or exam in the array (see Figure 1Ø.28).

Figure 10.28
Accessing an array called EXAM.

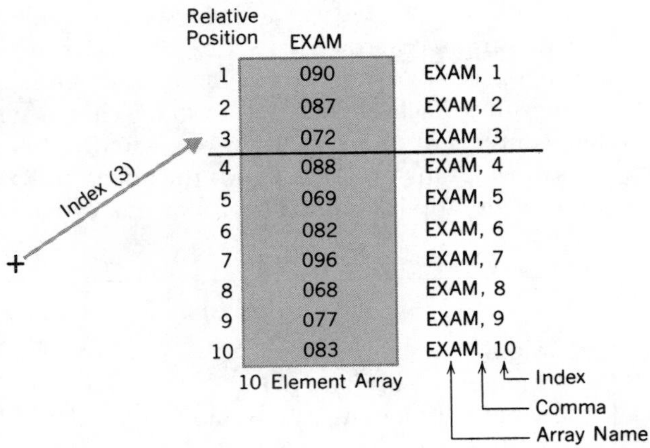

Consider the following array.

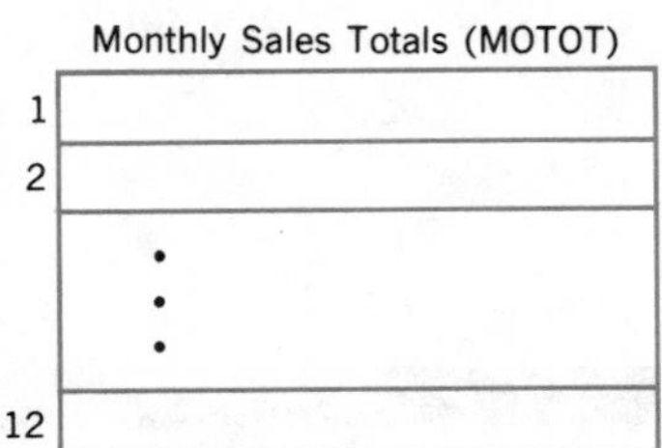

To add to a specific monthly total, specify the array name and the index that indicates the element to be changed. To add to the monthly total for February, for example, add to MOTOT,2. The array name is separated from the index by a comma. To add to the MOTOT depending on the contents of the Month field on the input, see Figure 10.29.

Input

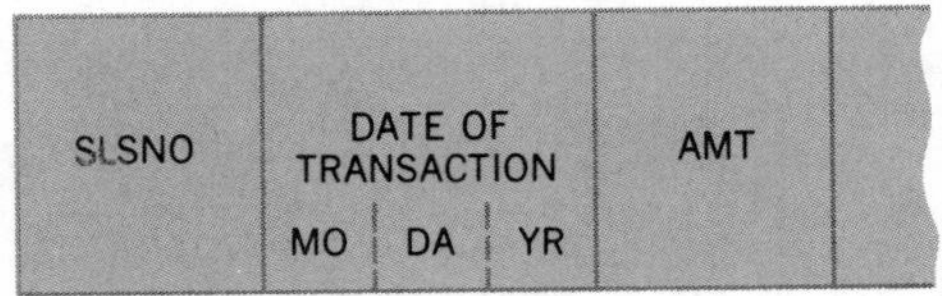

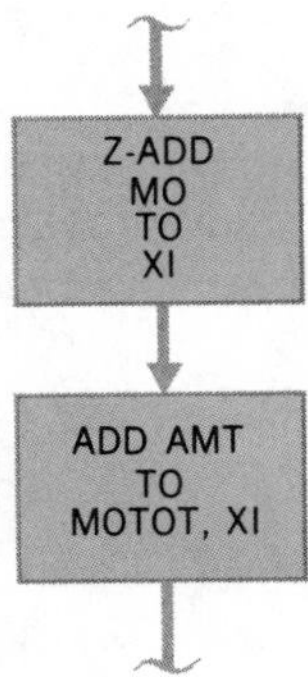

Figure 10.29
Adding to the appropriate element of an array.

To print the contents of an array after all the calculations have been performed on the elements, use a *loop*. One main advantage to looping is that the index changes with each pass through the loop. Typically, the index begins with a value of one and is incremented each time you step through the routine that accesses the array. You continue with this procedure until the entire array has been processed, at which point you no longer remain in the loop (see Figure 10.30).

Figure 10.30
Printing monthly totals after all records have been processed.

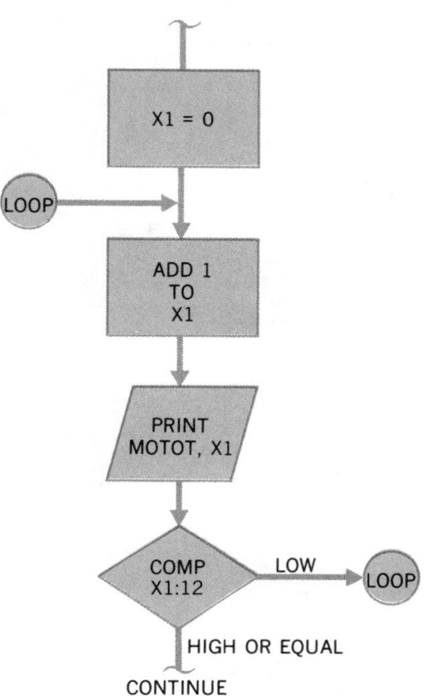

B. Adding Elements in an Array: The XFOOT Instruction

Suppose you have 10 exam grades for a student, which you wish to average. If the 10 exam grades were entered as individual entries, 10 instructions would be necessary to obtain a sum that you would then divide by 10 to obtain an average. If a student took 20 or 50 exams, then obtaining an average would require even more instructions and prove exceedingly cumbersome. The use of an array minimizes the coding of a procedure to operate on 10, 20, or 50 similar items.

Consider an array that contains 10 exam scores for a student. To obtain the average of these 10 scores, you could use the coding shown in Figure 10.31.

Array processing can be simplified even further. An instruction called "crossfoot" and coded as XFOOT can be used to sum all the elements in an array. Thus, the elementary loop summing the 10 elements of the array just presented could be simplified even further as shown in Figure 10.32.

To obtain an average, then, simply code the instruction shown in Figure 10.33.

Regardless of the number of entries in the array, XFOOT can be used to sum all the elements. The array to be summed is entered in Factor 2, and the field to serve as the sum is entered in the Result field. When required, the programmer may use Half Adjust for rounding.

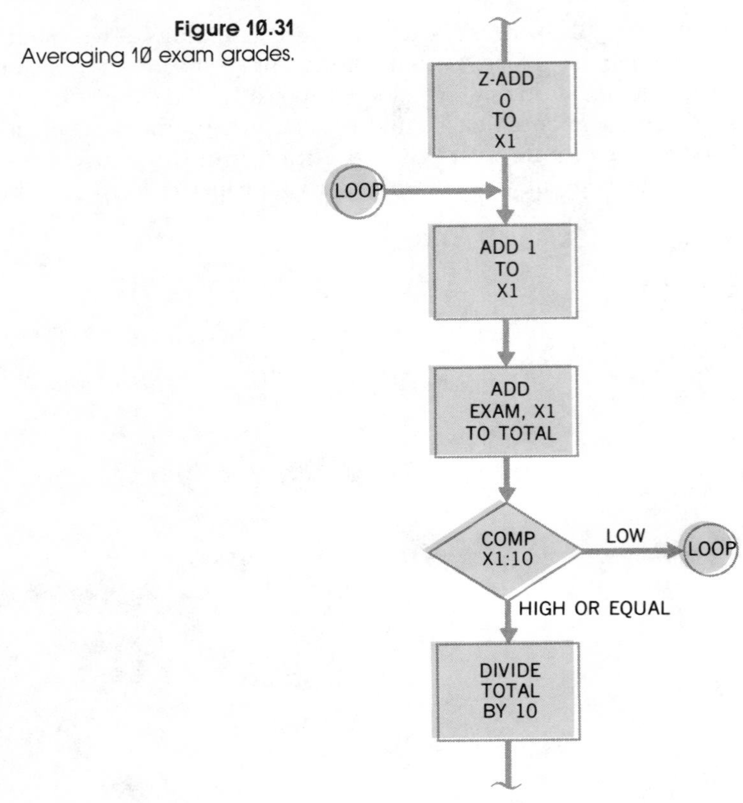

Figure 10.31
Averaging 10 exam grades.

RPG CALCULATION SPECIFICATIONS

Program		Keying Instruction	Graphic	Card Electro Number	Page	of	Program Identification
Programmer	Date		Key				

Line	Form Type	Control Level (L0–L9, LR, SR, AN/OR)	Indicators	And	And	Factor 1	Operation	Factor 2	Result Field Name	Length	Decimal Positions	Half Adjust (H)	Resulting Indicators High (1>2)	Low (1<2)	Equal (1=2)	Comments
01Ø	C						Z-ADDØ		X1	2	Ø					
02Ø	C					LOOP	TAG									
03Ø	C					1	ADD	X1	X1							
04Ø	C					EXAM,X1	ADD	TOTAL	TOTAL	4	Ø					
05Ø	C					X1	COMP	1Ø						15		
06Ø	C		15				GOTO	LOOP								
07Ø	C		N15			TOTAL	DIV	1Ø	AVG	5	2					
08	C															
09	C															

C. Determining the Largest Element in an Array

A common programming requirement is to examine the contents of an array to determine the largest element. This is best accomplished with the use of a program loop.

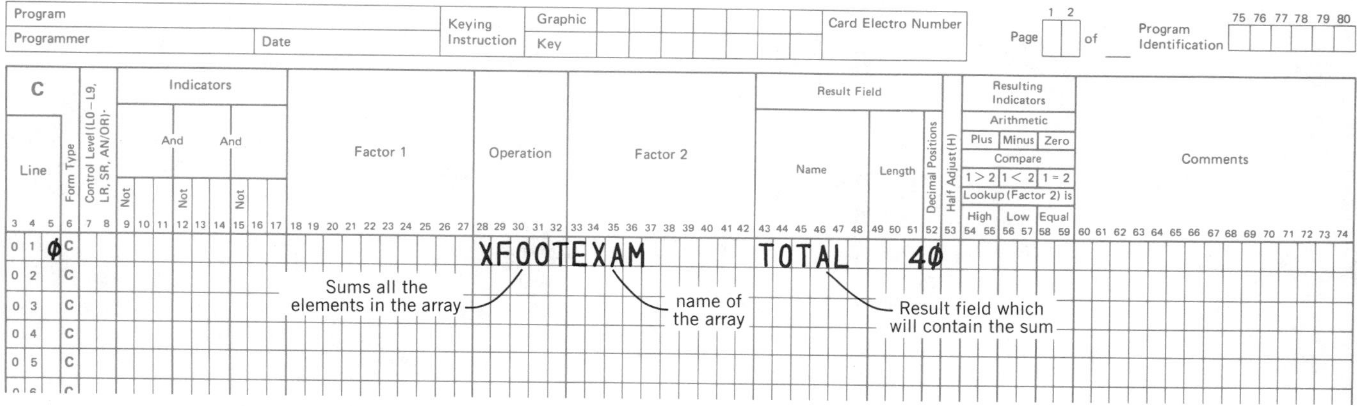

Figure 10.32
The XFOOT instruction.

RPG CALCULATION SPECIFICATIONS

Line	Form Type	Factor 1	Operation	Factor 2	Result Field Name	Length	Decimal Positions
01Ø	C		XFOOT	EXAM	TOTAL	4	Ø
02Ø	C	TOTAL	DIV	1Ø	AVG	5	2
03	C						
04	C						
05	C						

Figure 10.33
A simplified way of finding an average.

Suppose you have 1Ø exams and you wish to select the highest grade (see Figure 1Ø.34). Establish an index and call it SUB. SUB varies from 1 to n, where n is the number of elements in the array. In this instance, there are 1Ø exams, so SUB varies from 1 to 1Ø.

For each value of SUB from 1 to 1Ø, compare the element in the array called EXAM to a field we will call BIGEX. If the element referenced as EXAM,SUB is smaller than or equal to BIGEX, do not process that element but simply increment the index, SUB, and test the next element. If the element referenced by EXAM,SUB is larger than BIGEX, move it into BIGEX with the use of a Z-ADD instruction. In this way, 1Ø passes through the loop will produce in the field called BIGEX, the largest value in the array. See Figure 1Ø.35 for the program coding.

Hence, each element is compared during the looping procedure and the largest exam is selected by the program and stored in BIGEX. The variable BIGEX may therefore be referenced in the Output Specifications and printed as necessary.

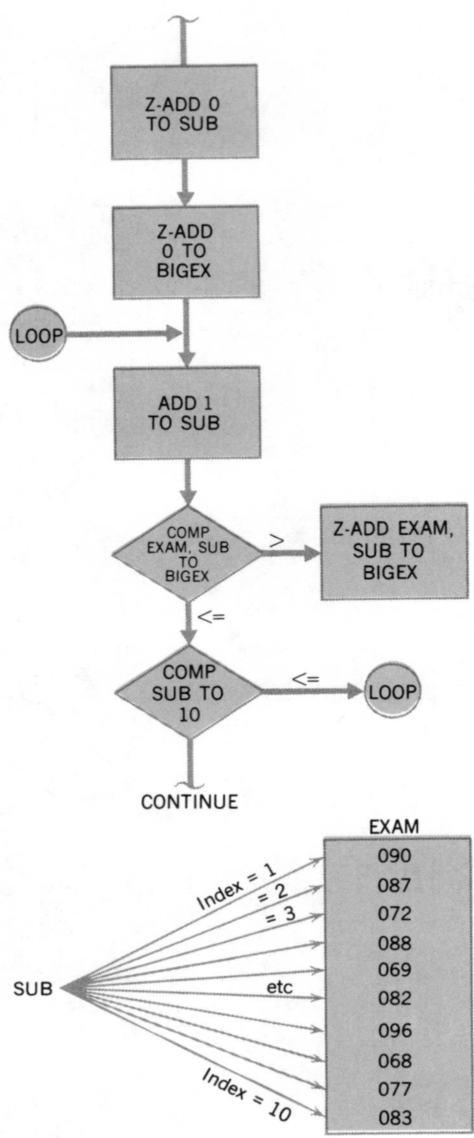

Figure 10.34
Finding the largest element in an array.

D. Counting Elements Greater Than the Average

Now consider an array of final grades called GRADE. We wish to determine the number of grades that exceed the average grade.

Relative Position	GRADE
1	Ø88.Ø
2	Ø77.Ø
3	Ø91.Ø
4	Ø82.Ø
5	Ø66.Ø

RPG CALCULATION SPECIFICATIONS

Line	Form Type	Indicators (9–17)	Factor 1 (18–27)	Operation (28–32)	Factor 2 (33–42)	Result Field Name (43–48)	Length (49–51)	Decimal Positions (52)	Half Adjust (53)	Resulting Indicators High (54–55)	Low (56–57)	Equal (58–59)	Comments
01Ø	C			Z-ADD	Ø	SUB	2	Ø					
02Ø	C			Z-ADD	Ø	BIGEX	3	Ø					
03Ø	C		LOOP	TAG									
04Ø	C		SUB	ADD	1	SUB							
05Ø	C		EXAM,SUB	COMP	BIGEX					15			
06Ø	C	15		Z-ADD	EXAM,SUB	BIGEX							
07Ø	C		SUB	COMP	1Ø						25		
08Ø	C	25		GOTO	LOOP								
09	C												
10	C												
11	C												

Figure 1Ø.35
Coding to find the largest value in an array.

The average of 8Ø.8 is calculated by using the XFOOT operation to sum the elements of the GRADE array, which is then divided by the number of grades (five). A loop is needed to compare each element of the GRADE array to the calculated average. If the value contained in an element of the GRADE array is greater than the class average, an indicator is set on. One is added to a count field when the indicator is on. We will turn indicator 35 on if a grade exceeds the average.

By adding one to a counter each time a value larger than the average is found, a count of the grades greater than the average is obtained. See Figure 1Ø.36 for an illustration of this procedure.

Figure 1Ø.36
Counting grades greater than the average.

RPG CALCULATION SPECIFICATIONS

Line	Form Type	Indicators (9–17)	Factor 1 (18–27)	Operation (28–32)	Factor 2 (33–42)	Result Field Name (43–48)	Length (49–51)	Decimal Positions (52)	Half Adjust (53)	Resulting Indicators High (54–55)	Low (56–57)	Equal (58–59)	Comments
01Ø	C			XFOOT	GRADE	SUM	4	1					
02Ø	C		SUM	DIV	5	AVG	4	1					
03Ø	C			Z-ADD	Ø	OVER	2	Ø					
04Ø	C			Z-ADD	Ø	PTR	2	Ø					
05Ø	C		DO5X	TAG									
06Ø	C		PTR	ADD	1	PTR							
07Ø	C		GRADE,PTR	COMP	AVG					35			
08Ø	C	35	OVER	ADD	1	OVER							
09Ø	C		PTR	COMP	5						4Ø		
10Ø	C	4Ø		GOTO	DO5X								
11	C												
12	C												
13	C												

E. Referencing an Entire Array

To reference an entire array, use the array name *without* an index. The following arithmetic operations may be used with an array name: Z-ADD, ADD, and SUB.

Z-ADD Instruction

The Z-ADD instruction may be used to move data from one array to another. If it is necessary to move data to an array that is to be used in a subroutine, for example, it can be accomplished with a single instruction. However, the more common problem of swapping or interchanging arrays requires that a third temporary array be used. If the data in ARRAY1 and ARRAY2 are to be interchanged, the coding in Figure 10.37 would be used.

Figure 10.37
Use of the Z-ADD to move data from one array to another.

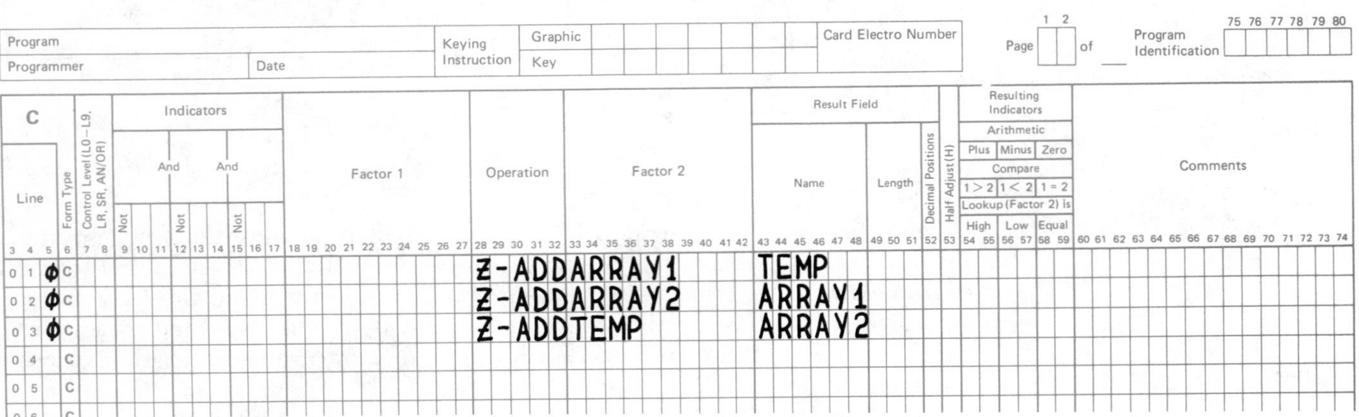

RPG CALCULATION SPECIFICATIONS

```
01ØC                      Z-ADDARRAY1         TEMP
02ØC                      Z-ADDARRAY2         ARRAY1
03ØC                      Z-ADDTEMP           ARRAY2
```

Similarly, an entire array may be initialized with a single instruction. For example, if it was necessary in a program to reinitialize an entire array to zero, the instruction in Figure 10.38 would accomplish this objective.

Figure 10.38
Initializing an array to zero.

RPG CALCULATION SPECIFICATIONS

```
01ØC                      .
02ØC                      .
03ØC                      Z-ADDØ              ARRAY3
04ØC                      .
05ØC                      .
```

ADDing Arrays

A programmer may frequently find the need to add arrays together. For example, a business may require a total of the sales for each of ten departments for January, February, and March in order to create a first quarter total. In other words, the corresponding ten elements of the arrays SJAN, SFEB, and SMARCH are to be accumulated in a first quarter TOTAL array.

Dept.	SJAN *Jan Sales*		SFEB *Feb Sales*		SMARCH *March Sales*		TOTAL *1st Quarter*
Ø1	2,5ØØ.ØØ	+	6,1ØØ.ØØ	+	7,8ØØ.ØØ	→	16,4ØØ
Ø2	8ØØ.ØØ		79Ø.ØØ		839.ØØ		2,429
.	.		.				
.	.		.				
.	.		.				
1Ø	1,3ØØ.ØØ		2,5ØØ.ØØ		1,8ØØ.ØØ		5,6ØØ

Each element of TOTAL is calculated by adding SJAN + SFEB + SMARCH

In the illustration that follows the elements are added individually to the total. Since the factors and the result field are all arrays with the same number of elements, the operation is performed using the first element from each array, then the second, and so on until all the elements in the arrays are processed. However, if the arrays do not have the same number of elements, the operations terminates when the last element of the shortest array is processed. The following coding provides for the addition of the SJAN, SFEB, and SMARCH arrays.

RPG CALCULATION SPECIFICATIONS

Line	Form Type	Factor 1	Operation	Factor 2	Result Field Name	Length
0Ø	C	SJAN	ADD	TOTAL	TOTAL	72
0Ø	C	SFEB	ADD	TOTAL	TOTAL	
0Ø	C	SMARCH	ADD	TOTAL	TOTAL	
04	C					
05	C					
06	C					

F. Developing Totals for Control Breaks

A frequent problem in the coding of RPG control break programs is the difficulty in determining when to accumulate the various control fields. Arrays may be used to eliminate this confusion. Examine the coding in Figure 1Ø.39 and note that sales totals are being accumulated as follows.

- Sales are accumulated into a salesperson total.

RPG CALCULATION SPECIFICATIONS

Program		Keying Instruction	Graphic	Card Electro Number	Page	of	Program Identification
Programmer	Date		Key				

Line	Form Type	Control Level (L0–L9, LR, SR, AN/OR)	Indicators	Factor 1	Operation	Factor 2	Result Field Name	Length	Decimal Positions	Half Adjust (H)	Resulting Indicators (Plus/Minus/Zero)	Comments
01Φ	C		Φ1	SAMT	ADD	SPER	SPER	6	2			
02Φ	C	L1		SPER	ADD	DEPTOT	DEPTOT	6	2			
03Φ	C	L2		DEPTOT	ADD	STRTOT	STRTOT	7	2			
04Φ	C	L3		STRTOT	ADD	FINTOT	FINTOT	8	2			
05	C											
06	C											
07	C											
08	C											
09	C											

Figure 10.39
Use of arrays in a control break program.

- Salesperson totals are accumulated by department.
- Department totals are summed into store totals.
- Store totals are added to a final total.

Figure 10.40 can perform the same operation with a single instruction.

TARRAY consists of four elements, where TARRAY,1 represents the salesperson (SPER) total, TARRAY,2 denotes the department total (DEPTOT), TARRAY,3 corresponds to the store total (STRTOT), and TARRAY,4 is the final total.

The ADD instruction adds the sales amount (SAMT) to all four elements of the total array (TARRAY).

All that is necessary is to reset the totals to zero once they are printed using the Output Specifications form. Therefore, when an L1 break occurs, the accrued salesperson field *must* be reset to zero once the total output has been completed. Similarly, the department total is reset to zero for an L2 control break. The store total (STRTOT) is reset to zero after printing as a result of the L3 level indicator.

Figure 10.40
Using only one array in a control break program.

RPG CALCULATION SPECIFICATIONS

Program		Keying Instruction	Graphic	Card Electro Number	Page	of	Program Identification
Programmer	Date		Key				

Line	Form Type	Control Level (L0–L9, LR, SR, AN/OR)	Indicators	Factor 1	Operation	Factor 2	Result Field Name	Length	Decimal Positions	Half Adjust (H)	Resulting Indicators (Plus/Minus/Zero)	Comments
01Φ	C		Φ1	SAMT	ADD	TARRAY	TARRAY					
02	C											
03	C											
04	C											

Key Terms

Array	Related tables
Compile time array or table	Search argument
Index	Single-entry table
LOKUP instruction	Table
Pre-execution time array or table	XFOOT instruction

Self-Evaluating Quiz

1. A group of related items that is used for look-up purposes is called a(n) ________ .
2. A group of related items that is used for storing totals is called a(n) _____.
3. (T or F) If a table consists of only 1Ø items, it is best to define them as constants within the program rather than read them in as variable data.
4. (T or F) Typically, tables remain unchanged during the execution of a program, whereas arrays may change.

For Questions 5 to 8, consider the following array of population figures for a specific state.

	POPUL
District 1	12387
District 2	24282
•	•
•	•
•	•
•	•
District 25	4362

5. To access the population for district 5, you would use ________ .
6. The simplest way to obtain the total state population is to use the _______ operation.
7. Write a routine to find the district with the smallest population.
8. Write a routine to find the total number of districts with population figures less than 5ØØØ.
9. Suppose you had three population tables just like the one here called POP1, POP2, and POP3. Write a routine to determine the total population for the three states.
10. (T or F) Using ADD and XFOOT with an array produces the identical results.

Solutions

1. table
2. array
3. F—Always define tables as variable data to be entered as input.
4. T
5. POPUL,5
6. XFOOT

7.

RPG CALCULATION SPECIFICATIONS

Line	Form Type	Control Level	Indicators	Factor 1	Operation	Factor 2	Result Name	Length	Decimal Positions	Half Adjust	High	Low	Equal	Comments
01Ø	C				Z-ADD	Ø	X1	2	Ø					
02Ø	C				Z-ADD	9999999	SMALL	7	Ø					
03Ø	C				Z-ADD	Ø	DSML	2	Ø					
04Ø	C			LOOP	TAG									
05Ø	C			X1	ADD	1	X1							
06Ø	C			POPUL,X1	COMP	SMALL						2Ø		
07Ø	C		2Ø		Z-ADD	POPUL,X1	SMALL							
08Ø	C		2Ø		Z-ADD	X1	DSML							
09Ø	C			X1	COMP	25						25		
10Ø	C		25		GOTO	LOOP								
11	C													
12	C													

8.

RPG CALCULATION SPECIFICATIONS

Line	Form Type	Control Level	Indicators	Factor 1	Operation	Factor 2	Result Name	Length	Decimal Positions	Half Adjust	High	Low	Equal	Comments
01Ø	C				Z-ADD	Ø	X1	2	Ø					
02Ø	C				Z-ADD	Ø	COUNT	2	Ø					
03Ø	C			LOOP	TAG									
04Ø	C			X1	ADD	1	X1							
05Ø	C			POPUL,X1	COMP	5ØØØ						5Ø		
06Ø	C		5Ø	COUNT	ADD	1	COUNT							
07Ø	C			X1	COMP	25						25		
08Ø	C		25		GOTO	LOOP								
09	C													
10	C													

9.

RPG CALCULATION SPECIFICATIONS

Program		Keying Instruction	Graphic	Card Electro Number	Page 1 2 of	Program Identification 75 76 77 78 79 80
Programmer	Date		Key			

Line (3–5)	Form Type (6)	Control Level (L0–L9, LR, SR, AN/OR) (7–8)	Indicators: Not, And Not, And Not (9–17)	Factor 1 (18–27)	Operation (28–32)	Factor 2 (33–42)	Result Field Name (43–48)	Length (49–51)	Decimal Positions (52)	Half Adjust (H) (53)	Resulting Indicators: Arithmetic Plus Minus Zero / Compare 1>2 1<2 1=2 / Lookup (Factor 2) is High Low Equal (54–59)	Comments (60–74)
01Ø	C			POP1	ADD	POP2	POP2					
02Ø	C			POP2	ADD	POP3	POP3					
03Ø	C				XFOOT	POP3	TOTAL3	9	Ø			
04Ø	C	*										
05Ø	C	*		———	OR	———						
06Ø	C	*										
07Ø	C				XFOOT	POP1	TOT1	9	Ø			
08Ø	C				XFOOT	POP2	TOT2	9	Ø			
09Ø	C				XFOOT	POP3	TOT3	9	Ø			
10Ø	C			TOT1	ADD	TOTAL3	TOTAL3	9	Ø			
11Ø	C			TOT2	ADD	TOTAL3	TOTAL					
12Ø	C			TOT3	ADD	TOTAL3	TOTAL					
13	C											
14	C											
15	C											

10. F—The ADD instruction adds each element in an array to a corresponding element in a second array; the XFOOT instruction sums all the elements in an array.

Review Questions

1. State the differences between an array and a table.
2. State the differences between a single-entry table and a related table.
3. What is a table lookup? How is it used in a program?
4. Indicate how the XFOOT operation is used in RPG.
5. Give examples of procedures that might require the use of the ADD instruction to add arrays.

Debugging Exercises

The problem definition for the Debugging exercise is shown in Figure 1Ø.41. The coding sheets in Figure 1Ø.42 contain syntax errors. Identify the errors and make the necessary corrections. The listing in Figure 1Ø.43 includes the error diagnostics produced by running the program as coded. The syntax corrections are circled on the computer listing shown in Figure 1Ø.44. There are, however, logic errors in the program. Your assignment is to desk check the program carefully, find the logic errors, and make the necessary corrections.

Figure 10.41 Problem definition for the Debugging Exercise.

Systems Flowchart

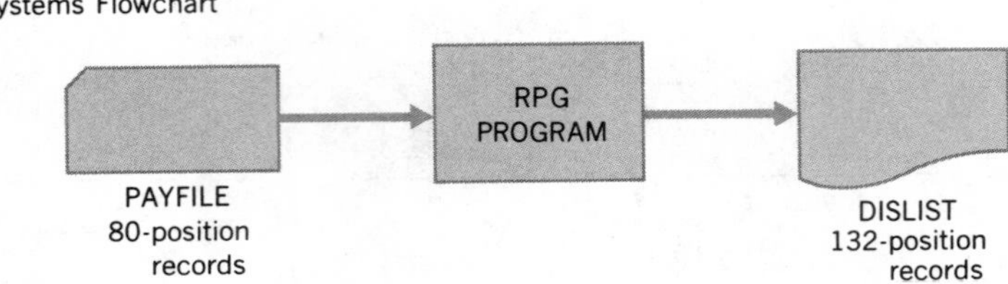

(a)

PAYFILE Record Layout

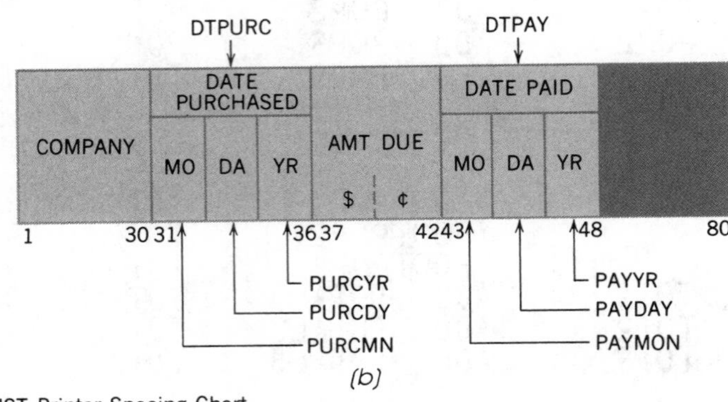

(b)

DISLIST Printer Spacing Chart

```
H  2 XX/XX/XX                                            R E D T A P E   O F F I C E   S U P P L I E S, I N C.                   PAGE XXØX
H  4                                                                  PAYMENT DISCOUNTS LISTING
H  7                   PURCHASER                             TOTAL        DATE OF      DATE OF     NO. OF    DISCOUNT        NET
H  8                                                      AMOUNT DUE     PURCHASE      PAYMENT      DAYS      TAKEN        PAYMENT
D 10    X------------------------------X                   X,XXØ.XX      XX/XX/XX     XX/XX/XX      XØX       XXØ.XX       X,XXØ.XX
D 11    X------------------------------X                   X,XXØ.XX      XX/XX/XX     XX/XX/XX      XØX       XXØ.XX       X,XXØ.XX
```

(c)

Notice that this program uses a Julian date format to determine if customer payments have been made within a 15-day discount period. Using the Julian date format basically means that we will convert month and day to a day number that will vary from 1 to 365. (Assume that the date is not in a leap year.) For example, February 10th would have a day number equal to 041 (31 days in January and 10 days in February).

Practice Problems

1. Using the problem definition shown in Figure 10.45, on page 544, code an RPG program to list the table and print an error report.
2. Using the problem definition in Figure 10.46, on page 545, code an RPG program to print the total amount of sales for each salesperson.
3. Using the problem definition shown in Figure 10.47, on page 546, code an RPG program to print the monthly take-home pay for each employee.

(Practice Problems are continued on page 547.)

Figure 10.42
Coding sheets for the Debugging Exercise.

RPG CONTROL AND FILE DESCRIPTION SPECIFICATIONS

Program DISCOUNTS LISTING
Programmer N. JOHNKE Date 1/10/--
Keying Instruction: Graphic Ø 1 2 / Key ZERO ONE TWO
Card Electro Number
Page Ø1 of 7 Program Identification SSS1Ø

Control Specifications

For the valid entries for a system, refer to the RPG reference manual for that system.

```
01ØH
```

File Description Specifications

For the valid entries for a system, refer to the RPG reference manual for that system.

```
02ØF*********************************************************************
03ØF*    THIS PROGRAM CREATES A DISCOUNT REPORT LISTING ALL CUSTOMER    *
04ØF* PAYMENTS MADE WITHIN A 15 DAY DISCOUNT PERIOD, TOTAL AMOUNT OF    *
05ØF* SALE, AMOUNT OF DISCOUNT TAKEN (AT 2%) AND NET PAYMENT RECEIVED.  *
06ØF*********************************************************************
07ØF*
08ØFPAYFILE IP  F      8Ø            READØ1 SYSIPT
09ØFDISLIST O   F     132      OF    PRINTERSYSLST
10ØF*
```

RPG EXTENSION AND LINE COUNTER SPECIFICATIONS

Program DISCOUNTS LISTING
Programmer N. JOHNKE Date 1/10/--
Keying Instruction: Graphic Ø 1 2 / Key ZERO ONE TWO
Card Electro Number
Page Ø2 of 7 Program Identification SSS1Ø

Extension Specifications

```
01ØE******************** EXTENSION SPECIFICATIONS ********************
02ØE*
03ØE                    TABMON  12  12   2 ØATABDAY   3 Ø
04ØE*
05 E
06 E
```

RPG INPUT SPECIFICATIONS

Program: DISCOUNTS LISTING — Programmer: N.JOHNKE — Date: 1/1Ø/-- — Keying Instruction: Graphic Ø 1 2, Key ZERO ONE TWO — Page Ø3 of 7 — Program Identification SSS1Ø

```
01Ø I*************************** INPUT RECORD ***************************
02Ø I*
03Ø IPAYFILE NS    Ø1
04Ø I                                                     1  3Ø COMPNY
05Ø I                                                    31  36ØDTPURC
06Ø I                                                    31  32ØPURCMN
07Ø I                                                    33  34ØPURCDY
08Ø I                                                    35  36ØPURCYR
09Ø I                                                    37  422AMTDUE
10Ø I                                                    43  48ØDTPAY
11Ø I                                                    43  44ØPAYMON
12Ø I                                                    45  46ØPAYDAY
13Ø I                                                    47  48ØPAYYR
14Ø I*
```

RPG CALCULATION SPECIFICATIONS

Program: DISCOUNTS LISTING — Programmer: N.JOHNKE — Date: 1/1Ø/-- — Keying Instruction: Graphic Ø 1 2, Key ZERO ONE TWO — Page Ø4 of 7 — Program Identification SSS1Ø

```
01Ø C************************** CALCULATIONS ***************************
02Ø C*
03Ø C****************************************
04Ø C* CONVERT DATE OF PURCHASE TO JULIAN     *
05Ø C****************************************
06Ø C*
07Ø C   Ø1       PURCMN    LKUP TABMON    TABDAY          12
08Ø C   Ø1 12    PURCDY    ADD  TABDAY    PURDT   3Ø
09Ø C*
10Ø C****************************************
11Ø C* CONVERT DATE PAID TO JULIAN            *
12Ø C****************************************
13Ø C*
14Ø C   Ø1       PAYMON    LKUP TABMON    TABDAY          13
15Ø C   Ø1 13    PAYDAY    ADD  TABDAY    PAYDT   3Ø
16Ø C*
17Ø C****************************************
18Ø C* IF YEAR OF PAYMENT IS GREATER THAN     *
19Ø C* YEAR OF PURCHASE, NODAYS IS COMPUTED   *
20Ø C* WITH FOLLOWING FORMULA :               *
21Ø C*     NODAYS = (365 - PURDT) + PAYDT     *
22Ø C****************************************
23Ø C*
```

RPG CALCULATION SPECIFICATIONS

Program: DISCOUNTS LISTING — Programmer: N.JOHNKE — Date: 1/1Ø/-- — Keying Instruction: Graphic Ø 1 2, Key ZERO ONE TWO — Page Ø5 of 7 — Program Identification SSS1Ø

Line	Form Type	Control Level	Indicators	Factor 1	Operation	Factor 2	Result Name	Length	Decimal Positions	Half Adjust	High (1>2)	Low (1<2)	Equal (1=2)	Comments
Ø1	C		Ø1	PAYYR	COMP	PURCYR					15			
Ø2	C		Ø1 15	365	SUB	PURDT	XDAYS	3	Ø					
Ø3	C		Ø1 15	XDAYS	ADD	PAYDT	NODAYS	3	Ø					
Ø4	C		Ø1 N15	PAYDT	SUB	PURDT	NODAYS							
Ø5	C		Ø1	NODAYS	COMP	15					2Ø	2Ø	2Ø	
Ø6	C		Ø1 2Ø	AMTDUE	MULT	.Ø2	DISCNT	5	2	H				
Ø7	C		Ø1 2Ø	AMTDUE	SUB	DISCNT	AMTDUE	6	2					
Ø8	C	*												
09	C													
10	C													

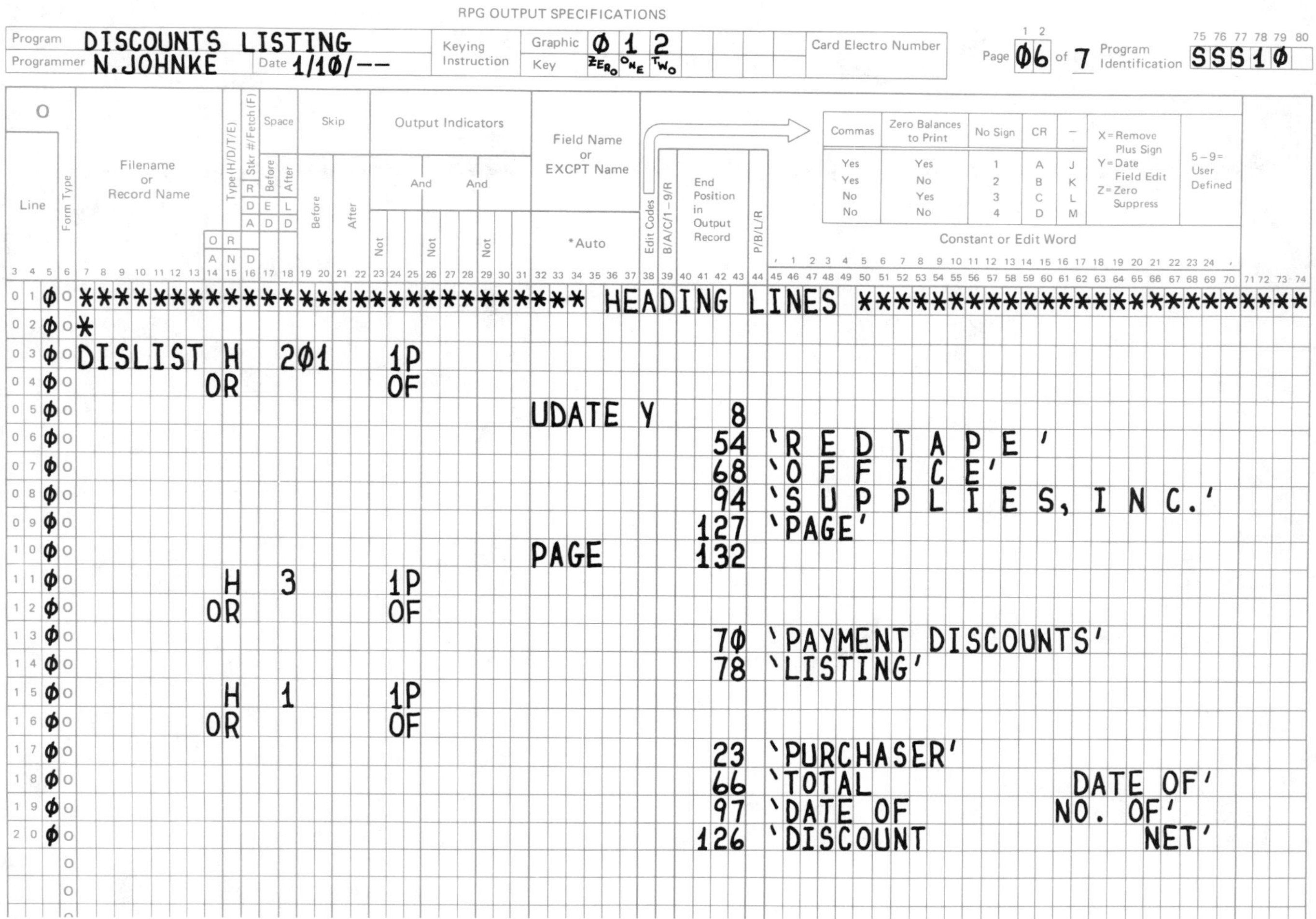

RPG OUTPUT SPECIFICATIONS

Program: DISCOUNTS LISTING — Programmer: N.JOHNKE — Date: 1/1Ø/-- — Keying Instruction: Graphic Ø 1 2, Key ZERO ONE TWO — Page Ø6 of 7 — Program Identification SSS1Ø

Line	Form Type	Filename or Record Name	Type	Space Before	Space After	Skip Before	Skip After	Output Indicators	Field Name or EXCPT Name	Edit Codes	B/A/C/1-9/R	End Position in Output Record	Constant or Edit Word
Ø1	O	************************** HEADING LINES ************************											
Ø2	O	*											
Ø3	O	DISLIST	H	2		Ø1		1P					
Ø4	O		OR					OF					
Ø5	O								UDATE	Y		8	
Ø6	O											54	'R E D T A P E '
Ø7	O											68	'O F F I C E'
Ø8	O											94	'S U P P L I E S, I N C.'
Ø9	O											127	'PAGE'
1Ø	O								PAGE			132	
11	O		H		3			1P					
12	O		OR					OF					
13	O											7Ø	'PAYMENT DISCOUNTS'
14	O											78	'LISTING'
15	O		H		1			1P					
16	O		OR					OF					
17	O											23	'PURCHASER'
18	O											66	'TOTAL DATE OF'
19	O											97	'DATE OF NO. OF'
2Ø	O											126	'DISCOUNT NET'

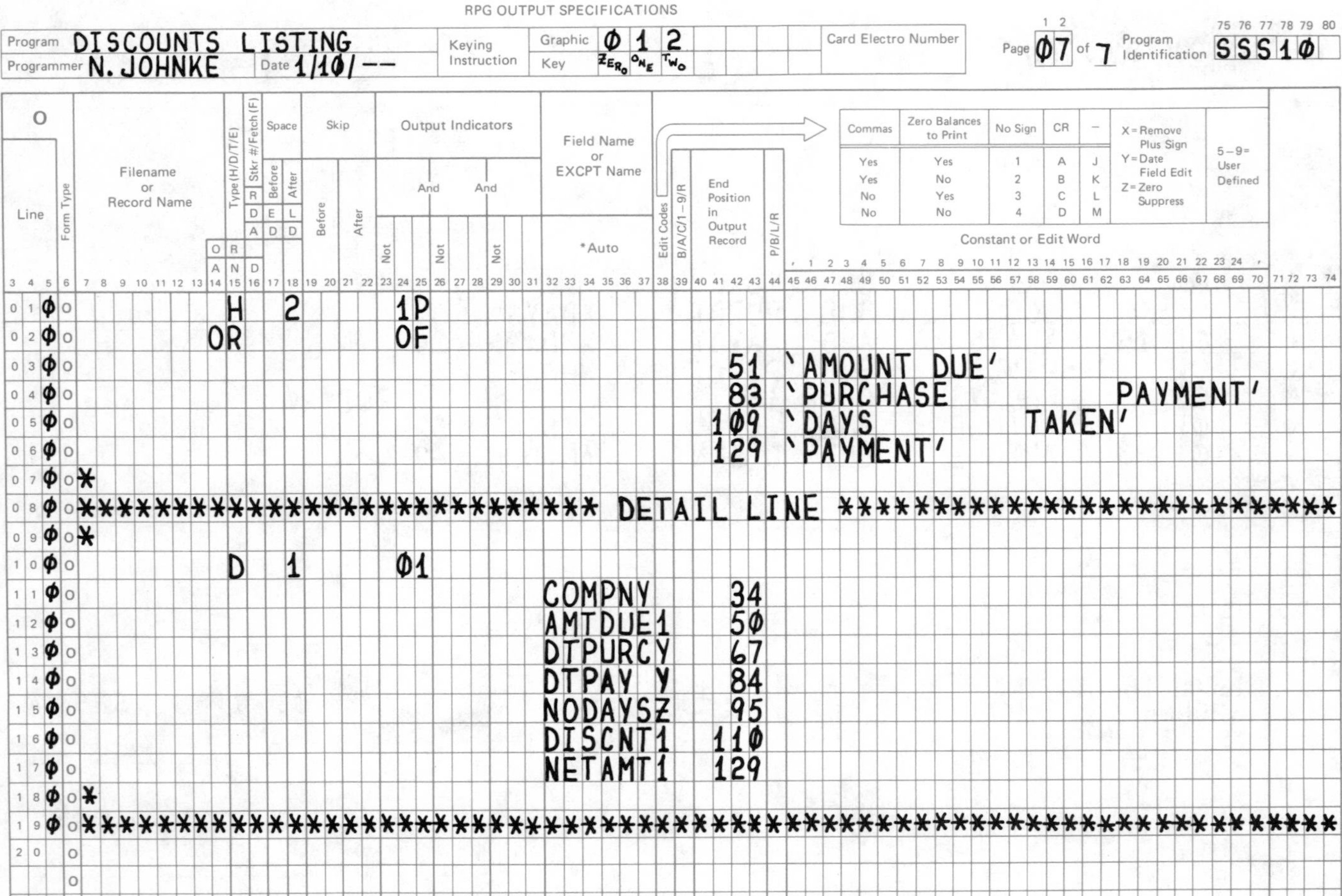

RPG OUTPUT SPECIFICATIONS

Program: DISCOUNTS LISTING | Programmer: N. JOHNKE | Date: 1/1Ø/-- | Keying Instruction: Graphic Ø 1 2, Key ZERO ONE TWO | Page Ø7 of 7 | Program Identification: SSS1Ø

Line	Form Type	Filename or Record Name	Type (H/D/T/E)	Space Before	Space After	Output Indicators	Field Name or EXCPT Name	Edit Codes	End Position in Output Record	Constant or Edit Word
Ø1Ø	O		H		2	1P				
Ø2Ø	O	OR				OF				
Ø3Ø	O								51	'AMOUNT DUE'
Ø4Ø	O								83	'PURCHASE PAYMENT'
Ø5Ø	O								1Ø9	'DAYS TAKEN'
Ø6Ø	O								129	'PAYMENT'
Ø7Ø	O*									
Ø8Ø	O************************ DETAIL LINE ************************									
Ø9Ø	O*									
1ØØ	O		D		1	Ø1				
11Ø	O						COMPNY		34	
12Ø	O						AMTDUE	1	5Ø	
13Ø	O						DTPURC	Y	67	
14Ø	O						DTPAY	Y	84	
15Ø	O						NODAYS	Z	95	
16Ø	O						DISCNT	1	11Ø	
17Ø	O						NETAMT	1	129	
18Ø	O*									
19Ø	O**									

Figure 1Ø.42
(continued)

Figure 10.43 Program listing with syntax errors for the Debugging Exercise.
(Continued on next page.)

```
        01-020  F********************************************************************SSS10
        01-030  F*  THIS PROGRAM CREATES A DISCOUNT REPORT LISTING ALL CUSTOMER     *SSS10
        01-040  F* PAYMENTS MADE WITHIN A 15 DAY DISCOUNT PERIOD, TOTAL AMOUNT OF   *SSS10
        01-050  F* SALE, AMOUNT OF DISCOUNT TAKEN (AT 2%) AND NET PAYMENT RECEIVED. *SSS10
        01-060  F********************************************************************SSS10
        01-070  F*                                                                   SSS10
0001    01-080  FPAYFILE IP  F      80             READ01 SYSIPT                     SSS10
0002    01-090  FDISLIST O   F     132      CF     PRINTERSYSLST                     SSS10
        01-100  F*                                                                   SSS10
        02-010  E******************** EXTENSION SPECIFICATIONS **********************SSS10
        02-020  E*                                                                   SSS10
0003    02-030  E                  TABMON 12  12  2 0ATABDAY  3 0                    SSS10
        02-040  E*                                                                   SSS10
        03-010  I************************** INPUT RECORD ***************************SSS10
        03-020  I*                                                                   SSS10
0004    03-030  IPAYFILE NS  01                                                      SSS10
0005    03-040  I                                         1  30 COMPNY               SSS10
0006    03-050  I                                        31  360DTPURC               SSS10
0007    03-060  I                                        31  320PURCMN               SSS10
0008    03-070  I                                        33  340PURCDY               SSS10
0009    03-080  I                                        35  360PURCYR               SSS10
0010    03-090  I                                        37  422AMTDUE               SSS10
0011    03-100  I                                        43  480DTPAY                SSS10
0012    03-110  I                                        43  440PAYMON               SSS10
0013    03-120  I                                        45  460PAYDAY               SSS10
0014    03-130  I                                        47  480PAYYR                SSS10
        03-140  I*                                                                   SSS10
        04-010  C************************** CALCULATIONS ***************************SSS10
        04-020  C*                                                                   SSS10
        04-030  C****************************************                            SSS10
        04-040  C* CONVERT DATE OF PURCHASE TO JULIAN    *                           SSS10
        04-050  C****************************************                            SSS10
        04-060  C*                                                                   SSS10
0015    04-070  C   01       PURCMN    LKUP TABMON    TABDAY          12             SSS10
                                       $                                                        MSG  141
0016    04-080  C   01 12    PURCDY    ADD  TABDAY    PURDT   30                     SSS10
        04-090  C*                                                                   SSS10
        04-100  C****************************************                            SSS10
        04-110  C* CONVERT DATE PAID TO JULIAN           *                           SSS10
        04-120  C****************************************                            SSS10
        04-130  C*                                                                   SSS10
0017    04-140  C   01       PAYMON    LKUP TABMON    TABDAY          13             SSS10
                                       $                                                        MSG  141
0018    04-150  C   01 13    PAYDAY    ADD  TABDAY    PAYDT   30                     SSS10
        04-160  C*                                                                   SSS10
        04-170  C****************************************                            SSS10
        04-180  C* IF YEAR OF PAYMENT IS GREATER THAN    *                           SSS10
        04-190  C* YEAR OF PURCHASE, NODAYS IS COMPUTED  *                           SSS10
        04-200  C* WITH FOLLOWING FORMULA :              *                           SSS10
        04-210  C*    NODAYS = (365 - PURDT) + PAYDT     *                           SSS10
        04-220  C****************************************                            SSS10
        04-230  C*                                                                   SSS10
0019    05-010  C   01       PAYYR     COMP PURCYR                15                 SSS10
0020    05-020  C   01 15    365       SUB  PURDT     XDAYS   30                     SSS10
0021    05-030  C   01 15    XDAYS     ADD  PAYDT     NODAYS  30                     SSS10
0022    05-040  C   01    N15PAYDT     SUB  PURDT     NODAYS                         SSS10
0023    05-050  C   01       NODAYS    COMP 15                    202020             SSS10
0024    05-060  C   01 20    AMTDUE    MULT .02       DISCNT  52H                    SSS10
0025    05-070  C   01 20    AMTDUE    SUB  DISCNT    AMTDUE  62                     SSS10
        05-080  C*                                                                   SSS10
        06-010  O************************** HEADING LINES **************************SSS10
        06-020  C*                                                                   SSS10
0026    06-030  ODISLIST H  201    1P                                                SSS10
0027    06-040  O       OR         OF                                                SSS10
0028    06-050  O                            UDATE Y    8                            SSS10
0029    C6-060  O                                      54 'R E D T A P E '           SSS10
0030    06-070  O                                      68 'O F F I C E'              SSS10
0031    06-080  O                                      94 'S U P P L I E S, I N C.'  SSS10
0032    06-090  O                                     127 'PAGE'                     SSS10
0033    06-100  C                            PAGE     132                            SSS10
0034    06-110  O        H  3      1P                                                SSS10
0035    06-120  O       OR         OF                                                SSS10
0036    06-130  O                                      70 'PAYMENT DISCOUNTS'        SSS10
0037    06-140  O                                      78 'LISTING'                  SSS10
0038    06-150  O        H  1      1P                                                SSS10
0039    06-160  O       OR         OF                                                SSS10
0040    06-170  O                                      23 'PURCHASER'                SSS10
0041    06-180  O                                      66 'TOTAL          DATE OF'   SSS10
0042    06-190  O                                      97 'DATE OF       NO. OF'     SSS10
0043    06-200  O                                     126 'DISCOUNT            NET'  SSS10
0044    07-010  O        H  2      1P                                                SSS10
0045    07-020  O       OR         OF                                                SSS10
0046    07-030  O                                      51 'AMOUNT DUE'               SSS10
0047    07-040  O                                      83 'PURCHASE          PAYMENT' SSS10
0048    07-050  O                                     109 'DAYS         TAKEN'       SSS10
0049    07-060  O                                     129 'PAYMENT'                  SSS10
        07-070  O*                                                                   SSS10
        07-080  O*************************** DETAIL LINE ***************************SSS10
        07-090  O*                                                                   SSS10
0050    07-100  O        D  1      01                                                SSS10
0051    07-110  O                            COMPNY    34                            SSS10
0052    07-120  O                            AMTDUE1   50                            SSS10
0053    07-130  O                            DTPURCY   67                            SSS10
0054    07-140  O                            DTPAY Y   84                            SSS10
0055    07-150  C                            NODAYSZ   95                            SSS10
0056    07-160  O                            DISCNT1  110                            SSS10
0057    07-170  O                            NETAMT1  129                            SSS10
        07-180  O*                                                                   SSS10
        07-190  O********************************************************************SSS10


    E N D   O F   S C U R C E
```

Figure 10.43 *(continued)*

T A B L E S AND M A P S

RESULTING INDICATOR TABLE

OFFSET	RI	OFFSET	RI	OFFSET	RI	OFFSET	RI	OFFSET	RI	OFFSET	RI	OFFSET	RI
0508	OF	0525	LR	0526	HO	0531	1P	0534	01	0535	12	0536	13
0537	15	0538	20										

OFFSETS OF VARIABLE NAMES AND CONSTANT NAMES

OFFSET	NAME	OFFSET	NAME	OFFSET	NAME	OFFSET	NAME	OFFSET	NAME
063C TLF	TABMON	064C TLF	TABDAY	03C9	*ERROR	0660	COMPNY	067E	DTPURC
0682	PURCMN	0684	PURCDY	0686	PURCYR	0688	AMTDUE	068C	DTPAY
069C	PAYMON	0692	PAYDAY	0694	PAYYR	0696	PURDT	0698	PAYDT
069A	XDAYS	069C	NODAYS	069E	DISCNT	0400	UDATE	06A5	PAGE

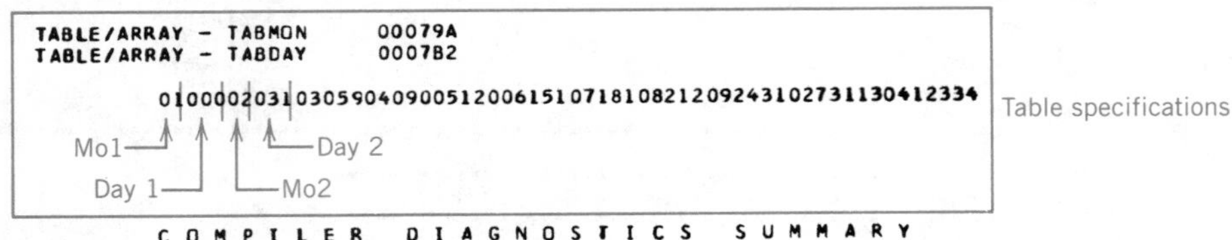
TABLE/ARRAY - TABMON 00079A
TABLE/ARRAY - TABDAY 0007B2

010000203103059040900512006151071810821209243102731130412334

C O M P I L E R D I A G N O S T I C S S U M M A R Y

```
ILN141   INVALID OPERATION. SPEC IS DROPPED.

      D  0015     04-070     LKUP
      D  0017     04-140     LKUP

ILN398   FIELD NAME UNDEFINED. SPEC IS DROPPED.

      C  0057     07-170     NETAMT
```

Figure 10.44
Program listing with logic errors for the Debugging Exercise.
(Continued on next page.)

```
      01-020  F*************************************************************************SSS10
      01-030  F*  THIS PROGRAM CREATES A DISCOUNT REPORT LISTING ALL CUSTOMER          *SSS10
      01-040  F* PAYMENTS MADE WITHIN A 15 DAY DISCOUNT PERIOD, TOTAL AMOUNT OF      *SSS10
      01-050  F* SALE, AMOUNT OF DISCOUNT TAKEN (AT 2%) AND NET PAYMENT RECEIVED.  *SSS10
      01-060  F*************************************************************************SSS10
      01-070  F*                                                                       SSS10
0001  01-080  FPAYFILE IP  F      80            READ01 SYSIPT                          SSS10
0002  01-090  FDISLIST O   F     132     OF     PRINTERSYSLST                          SSS10
      01-100  F*                                                                       SSS10
      02-010  E********************* EXTENSION SPECIFICATIONS **********************SSS10
      02-020  E*                                                                       SSS10
0003  02-030  E                    TABMON 12  12  2 0ATABDAY  3 0                      SSS10
      02-040  E*                                                                       SSS10
      03-010  I**************************** INPUT RECORD ****************************SSS10
      03-020  I*                                                                       SSS10
0004  03-030  IPAYFILE NS  01                                                          SSS10
0005  03-040  I                                             1  30 COMPNY               SSS10
0006  03-050  I                                            31  360DTPURC               SSS10
0007  03-060  I                                            31  320PURCMN               SSS10
0008  03-070  I                                            33  340PURCDY               SSS10
0009  03-080  I                                            35  360PURCYR               SSS10
0010  03-090  I                                            37  422AMTDUE               SSS10
0011  03-100  I                                            43  480DTPAY                SSS10
0012  03-110  I                                            43  440PAYMON               SSS10
0013  03-120  I                                            45  460PAYDAY               SSS10
0014  03-130  I                                            47  480PAYYR                SSS10
      03-140  I*                                                                       SSS10
      04-010  C***************************** CALCULATIONS ****************************SSS10
      04-020  C*                                                                       SSS10
      04-030  C*******************************************                            SSS10
      04-040  C* CONVERT DATE OF PURCHASE TO JULIAN      *                            SSS10
      04-050  C*******************************************                            SSS10
      04-060  C*                        Not LKUP                                       SSS10
0015  04-070  C   01      PURCMN    LOKUPTABMON     TABDAY            12               SSS10
0016  04-080  C   01 12   PURCDY    ADD  TABDAY     PURDT   30                         SSS10
      04-090  C*                                                                       SSS10
      04-100  C*******************************************                            SSS10
      04-110  C* CONVERT DATE PAID TO JULIAN             *                            SSS10
      04-120  C*******************************************                            SSS10
      04-130  C*                        Not LKUP                                       SSS10
0017  04-140  C   01      PAYMON    LOKUPTABMON     TABDAY            13               SSS10
0018  04-150  C   01 13   PAYDAY    ADD  TABDAY     PAYDT   30                         SSS10
      04-160  C*                                                                       SSS10
      04-170  C*******************************************                            SSS10
      04-180  C* IF YEAR OF PAYMENT IS GREATER THAN      *                            SSS10
      04-190  C* YEAR OF PURCHASE, NODAYS IS COMPUTED    *                            SSS10
      04-200  C* WITH FOLLOWING FORMULA :                *                            SSS10
      04-210  C*      NODAYS = (365 - PURDT) + PAYDT     *                            SSS10
      04-220  C*******************************************                            SSS10
      04-230  C*                                                                       SSS10
0019  05-010  C   01      PAYYR     COMP PURCYR                   15                   SSS10
0020  05-020  C   01 15   365       SUB  PURDT      XDAYS   30                         SSS10
0021  05-030  C   01 15   XDAYS     ADD  PAYDT      NODAYS  30                         SSS10
0022  05-040  C   01   N15PAYDT     SUB  PURDT      NODAYS                             SSS10
0023  05-050  C   01      NODAYS    COMP 15                     202020                 SSS10
0024  05-060  C   01 20   AMTDUE    MULT .02        DISCNT  52H                        SSS10
0025  05-070  C   01 20   AMTDUE    SUB  DISCNT     NETAMT  62   Not AMTDUE            SSS10
      05-080  C*                                                                       SSS10
      06-010  O**************************** HEADING LINES ***************************SSS10
      06-020  O*                                                                       SSS10
0026  06-030  ODISLIST H  201    1P                                                    SSS10
0027  06-040  O        OR        OF                                                    SSS10
0028  06-050  O                          UDATE Y    8                                  SSS10
0029  06-060  O                                    54 'R E D T A P E '                 SSS10
0030  06-070  O                                    68 'O F F I C E'                    SSS10
0031  06-080  O                                    94 'S U P P L I E S, I N C.'        SSS10
0032  06-090  O                                   127 'PAGE'                           SSS10
0033  06-100  O                          PAGE     132                                  SSS10
0034  06-110  O          H  3    1P                                                    SSS10
0035  06-120  O        OR        OF                                                    SSS10
0036  06-130  O                                    70 'PAYMENT DISCOUNTS'              SSS10
0037  06-140  O                                    78 'LISTING'                        SSS10
0038  06-150  O          H  1    1P                                                    SSS10
0039  06-160  O        OR        OF                                                    SSS10
0040  06-170  O                                    23 'PURCHASER'                      SSS10
0041  06-180  O                                    66 'TOTAL              DATE OF'     SSS10
0042  06-190  O                                    97 'DATE OF          NO. OF'        SSS10
0043  06-200  O                                   126 'DISCOUNT              NET'      SSS10
0044  07-010  O          H  2    1P                                                    SSS10
0045  07-020  O        OR        OF                                                    SSS10
0046  07-030  O                                    51 'AMOUNT DUE'                     SSS10
0047  07-040  O                                    83 'PURCHASE           PAYMENT'     SSS10
0048  07-050  O                                   109 'DAYS          TAKEN'            SSS10
0049  07-060  O                                   129 'PAYMENT'                        SSS10
      07-070  O*                                                                       SSS10
      07-080  O**************************** DETAIL LINE *****************************SSS10
      07-090  O*                                                                       SSS10
0050  07-100  O          D  1    01                                                    SSS10
0051  07-110  O                          COMPNY    34                                  SSS10
0052  07-120  O                          AMTDUE1   50                                  SSS10
0053  07-130  O                          DTPURCY   67                                  SSS10
0054  07-140  O                          DTPAY Y   84                                  SSS10
0055  07-150  O                          NODAYSZ   95                                  SSS10
0056  07-160  O                          DISCNT1  110                                  SSS10
0057  07-170  O                          NETAMT1  129                                  SSS10
      07-180  O*                                                                       SSS10
      07-190  O*************************************************************************SSS10

E N D   O F   S C U R C E
```

Figure 10.44
(continued)

1/28/83 REDTAPE OFFICE SUPPLIES, INC. PAGE 1

PAYMENT DISCOUNTS LISTING

PURCHASER	TOTAL AMOUNT DUE	DATE OF PURCHASE	DATE OF PAYMENT	NO. OF DAYS	DISCOUNT TAKEN	NET PAYMENT
YOUR FAULT INSURANCE CORP.	1,125.50	10/15/82	10/30/82	15	22.51	1,102.99
WIDGET PRODUCTS	767.67	10/29/82	11/05/82	7	15.35	752.32
MISGIVEN REALTORS	583.25	10/30/82	11/30/82	31	11.67	571.58
SWINDLERS DEPARTMENT STORES	1,000.00	11/03/82	11/15/82	12	20.00	980.00
ALDEN RESEARCH & DESIGN	99.75	11/25/82	12/06/82	11	2.00	97.75
ABC PUBLISHING COMPANY	829.35	11/29/82	12/15/82	16	16.59	812.76
LEMON AUTOMOTIVE DISTRIBUTORS	329.65	12/28/82	1/06/83	9	6.59	323.06
MEAGER SAVINGS & LOAN ASSOC.	1,234.50	1/03/83	1/13/83	10	24.69	1,209.81
GOODTIME CHARLIE CATERERS	499.00	1/05/83	1/17/83	12	9.98	489.02

Over 15 days should not appear on listing

Figure 10.45
Problem definition for Practice Problem 1.

Systems Flowchart

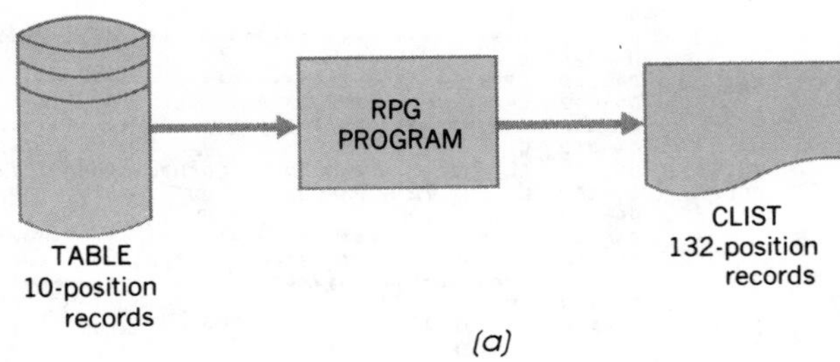

(a)

TABLE Record Layout

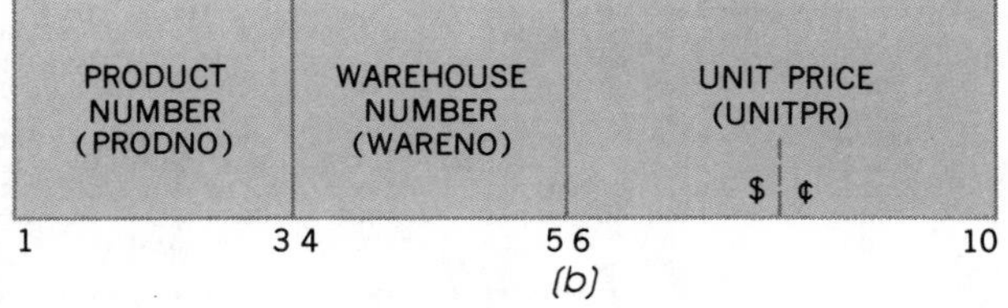

(b)

CLIST Printer Spacing Chart

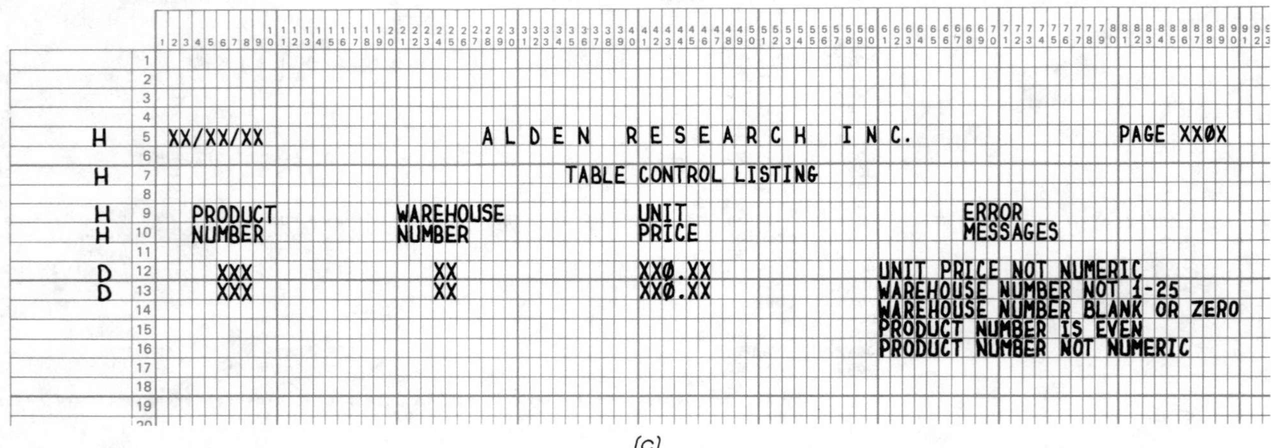

(c)

Notes

1. Errors include the following.
   a. A warehouse number not between 1 and 25.
   b. A product number that is blank or even. (All product numbers should be odd.)
   c. The unit price field does not contain numeric data.
2. The table contains 25 entries.

Figure 10.46 Problem definition for Practice Problem 2.

Systems Flowchart

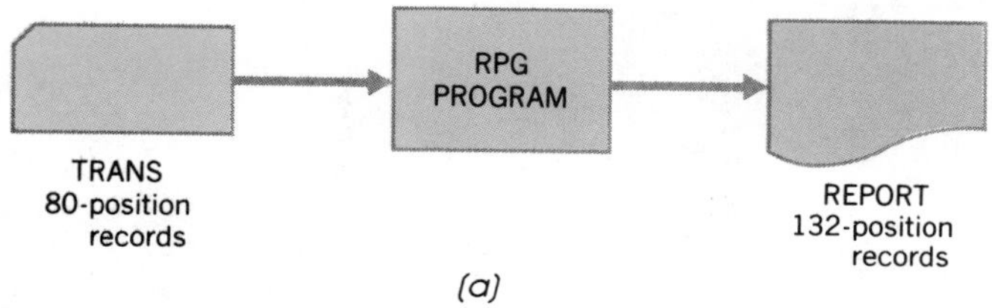

(a)

TRANS Record Layout

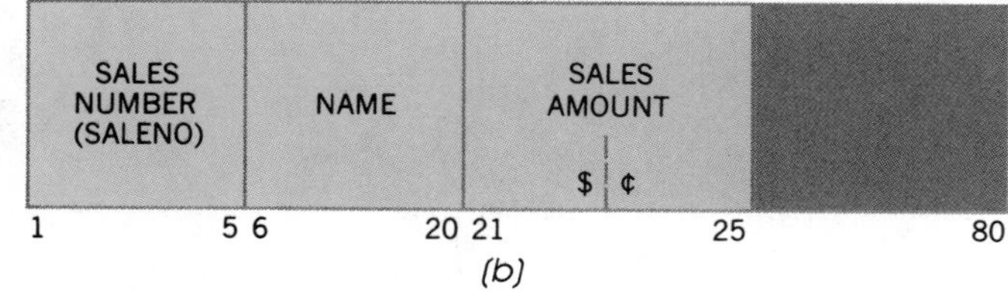

(b)

REPORT Printer Spacing Chart

```
H    6                 TOTAL AMOUNT OF SALES BY SALESPERSON    XX/XX/XX
H    8           SALESPERSON               TOTAL AMOUNT
TLR 10                1                    $XX,XX$.XX
TLR 12                2                    $XX,XX$.XX
    14                •                        •
    15                •                        •
    16                •                        •
    17                •                        •
    18                •                        •
TLR 20               20                    $XX,XX$.XX
```

(c)

Notes

1. There are 2Ø salespeople, with sales numbers ranging from 1 to 2Ø.
2. Each sale made by a salesperson appears in a separate input record.
3. The number of input records for each salesperson is unknown.
4. Do not assume that the input records are in sequence.

Figure 10.47 Problem definition for Practice Problem 3.

Systems Flowchart

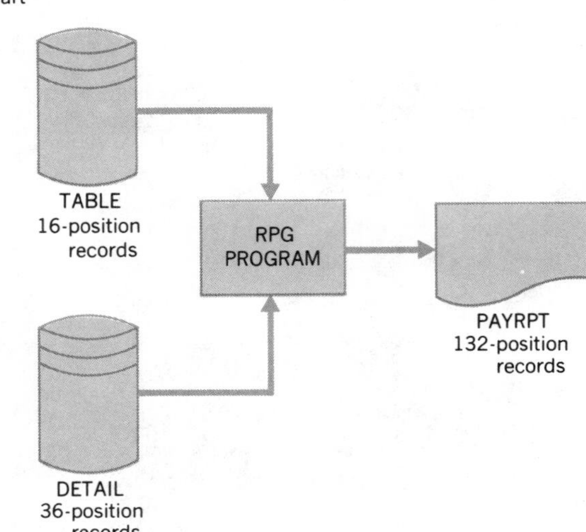

(a)

TABLE Record Layout

LOW BOUND SALARY (LOWBND)	HIGH BOUND SALARY (HIBND)	STATE TAX % (STAX)	FED. TAX % (FTAX)
1–5	6–10	11–13	14–16

Note: Salary figures are in dollars (no cents).

DETAIL Record Layout

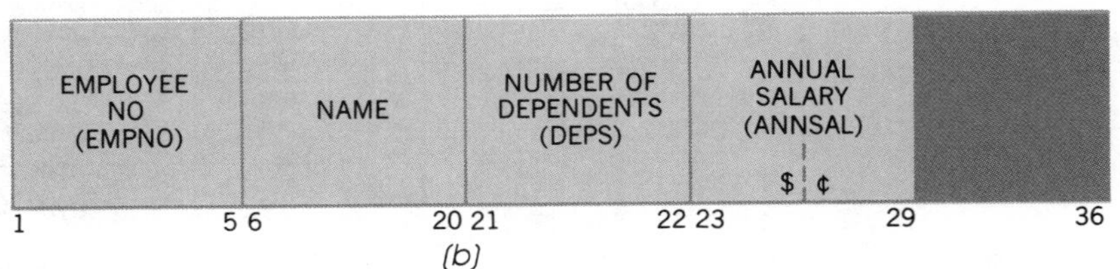

(b)

PAYRPT Printer Spacing Chart

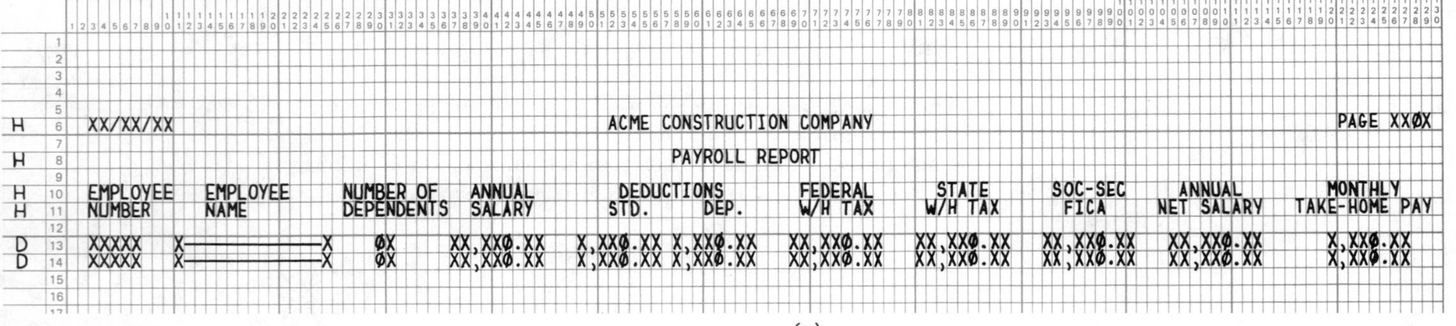

(c)

Notes

1. There are 2Ø input table records.
2. The Low Bound Salary and High Bound Salary fields in each input table record indicate the salary range for which the state tax percentage and federal tax per-

Figure 1Ø.47 *(continued)*

centage figures are provided. Implied decimal points are used for the percentages. A value of 1Ø5 in positions 14 to 16, for example, is to be interpreted as Ø.1Ø5 (1Ø.5%).

3. Monthly take-home pay is computed as follows.
   a. Standard deduction = 1Ø% of the first $1Ø,ØØØ of annual salary.
   b. Dependent deduction = $1ØØØ times the number of dependents.
   c. FICA (Social Security tax) = 6.7% of the first $35,7ØØ of annual salary.
   d. Taxable income = annual salary − standard deduction − dependent deduction.
   e. The tax on taxable income is found in the tax table.
   f. Annual take-home pay = annual salary − (state tax % × taxable income) − (federal tax % × taxable income) − FICA.
   g. Monthly take-home pay = annual take-home pay ÷ 12.

---

4. Using the problem definition shown in Figure 1Ø.48, code an RPG program to print the desired report.

   Notes

   1. An unknown number of records will serve as input for each salesperson.
   2. The input records are in SALENO (salesperson number) sequence only. Totals must be accumulated for each salesperson for each day of the week. In addition, accumulate a weekly sales total for each salesperson and a daily total of all sales in the company.

5. Using the problem definition shown in Figure 1Ø.49, code an RPG program to print the desired report. Use the table from Problem 1. Assume it is valid. The transaction records are in customer name sequence.
6. Using the problem definition shown in Figure 1Ø.5Ø, code an RPG program to produce the desired report. To calculate the elapsed days, you must convert the dates to Julian form.

   Elapsed days (N) = Paid date (Julian) − Loan date (Julian)
   Daily interest (I) = Annual interest ÷ 365
   Amount due = Loan amount × $(1 + I)^N$

   The Debugging Exercise in this chapter will serve as a guide to demonstrate how a date can be converted to a day number from ØØ1 to 365, which is then in Julian form. (Assume that the date is not in a leap year.)

Figure 10.48 Problem definition for Practice Problem 4.

Systems Flowchart

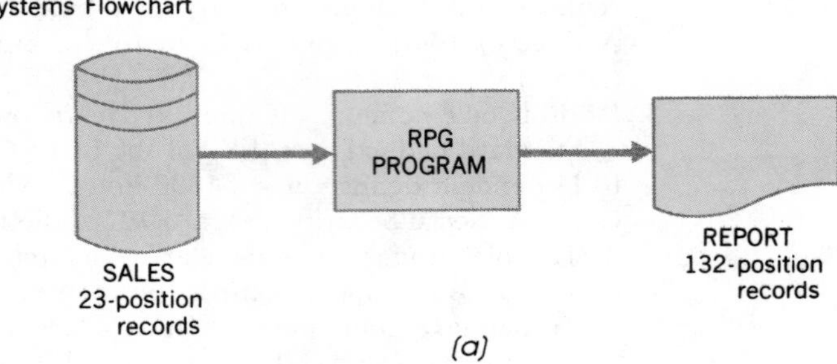

(a)

SALES Record Layout

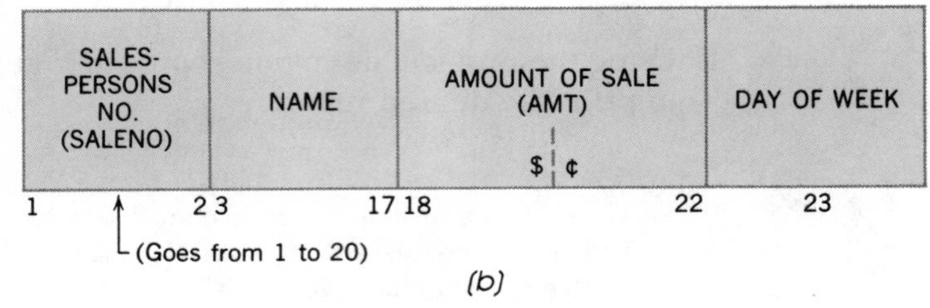

(b)

REPORT Printer Spacing Chart

Type	Line	Content
H	6	XX/XX/XX H O N E S T J O H N S A L E S, I N C. PAGE XXØX
H	8	WEEKLY SALES REPORT
H	10	SALESPERSON SALESPERSON D A I L Y S A L E S WEEKLY
H	11	NUMBER NAME DAY 1 DAY 2 DAY 3 DAY 4 DAY 5 SALES
D	13	XX X————————X XXØ.XX XXØ.XX XXØ.XX XXØ.XX XXØ.XX X,XXØ.XX
D	14	XX X————————X XXØ.XX XXØ.XX XXØ.XX XXØ.XX XXØ.XX X,XXØ.XX
TLR	18	W E E K L Y T O T A L S XX,XX.XX XX,XX.XX XX,XX.XX XX,XX.XX XX,XX.XX XXX,XX.XX

(c)

Figure 10.49 Problem definition for Practice Problem 5.
(Continued on next page.)

Systems Flowchart

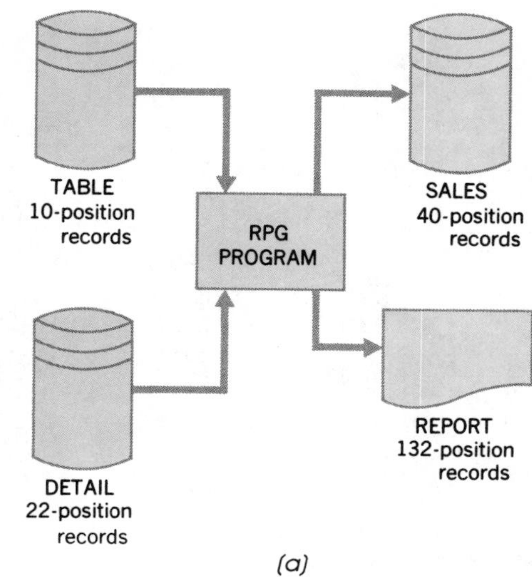

(a)

TABLE Record Layout

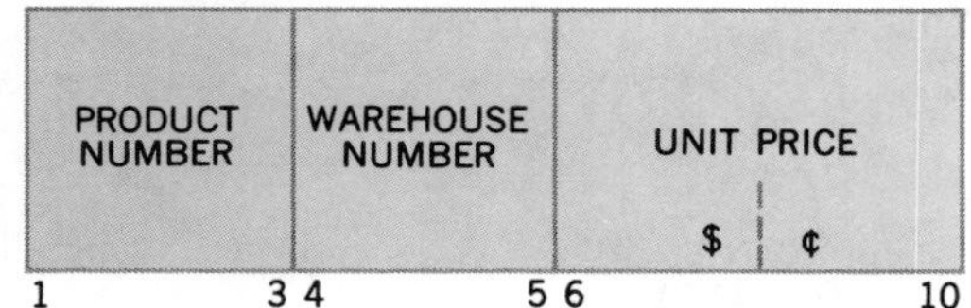

DETAIL Record Layout

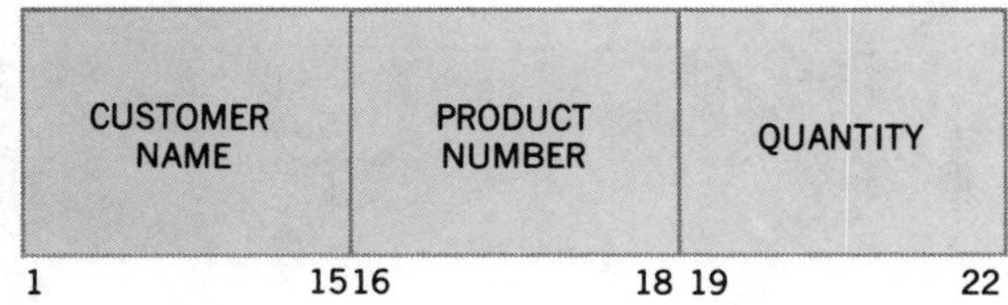

SALES Record Layout

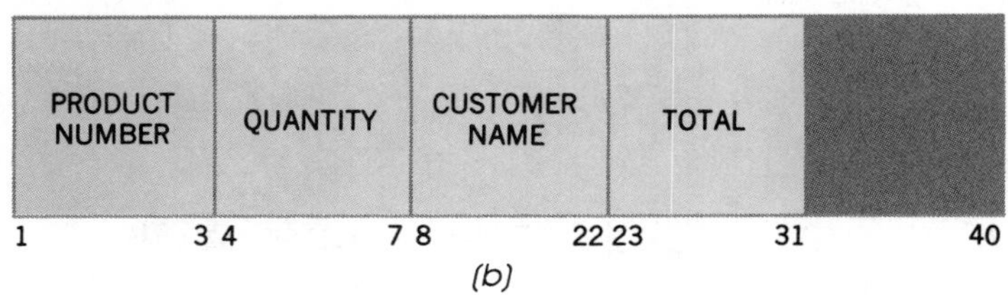

(b)

Figure 10.49
(continued)

REPORT Printer Spacing Chart

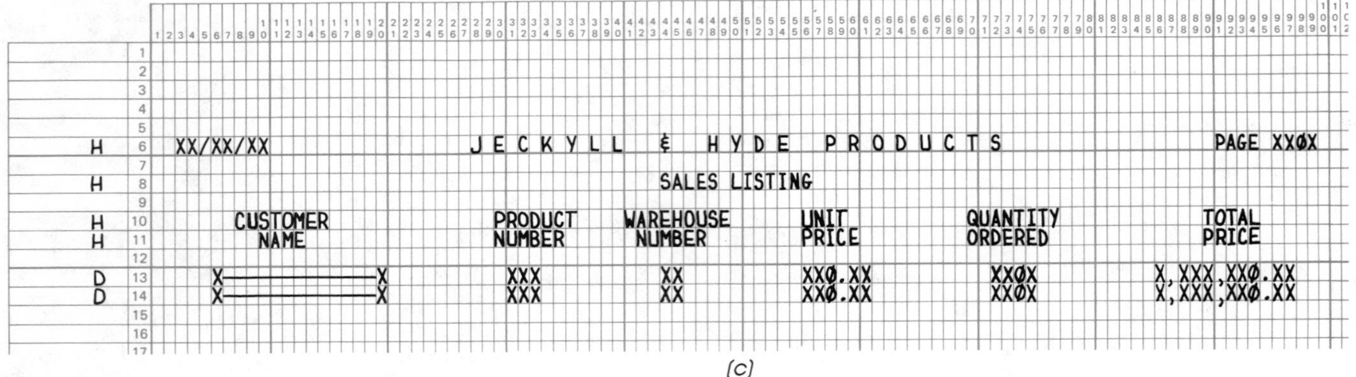

(c)

Figure 10.50 Problem definition for Practice Problem 6.

Systems Flowchart

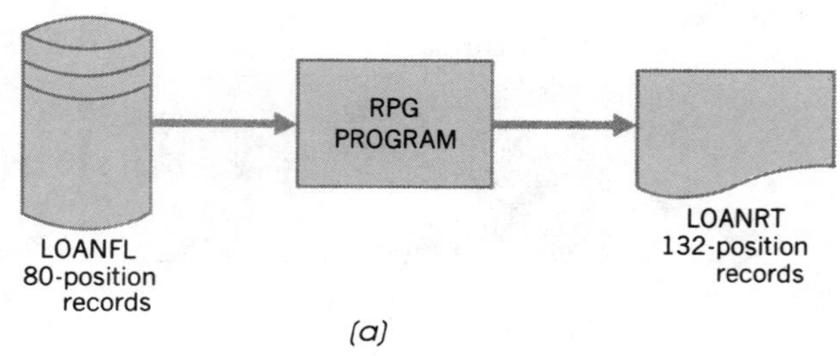

(a)

LOANFL Record Layout

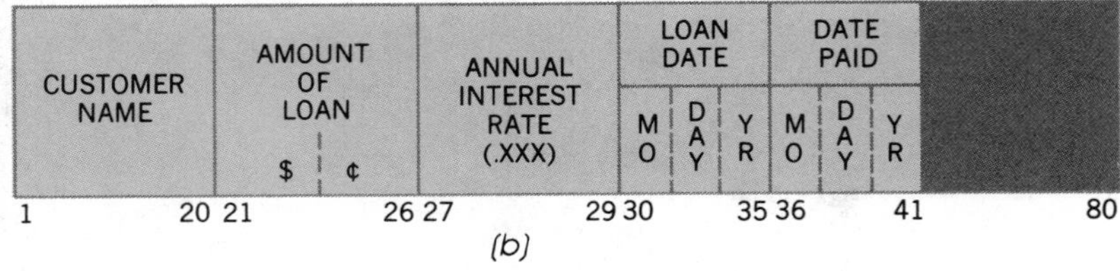

(b)

LOANRT Printer Spacing Chart

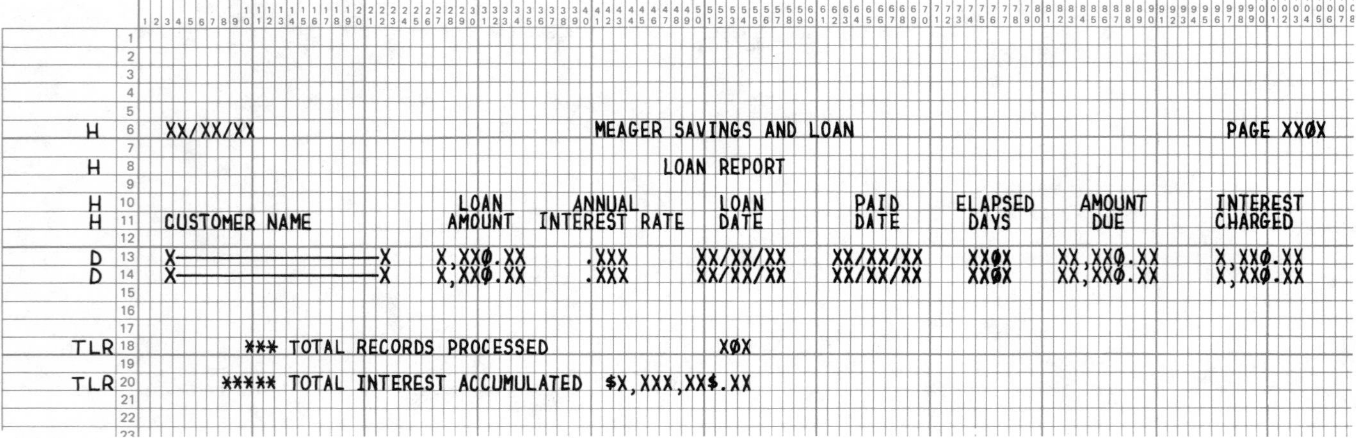

(c)

CHAPTER 11

Structured Programming in RPG II and RPG III

Objectives

- To examine the advantages of structured programming.
- To consider the top-down approach, modular programming concepts, and the various program structures used in structured programming.
- To focus on the programming techniques employed in structured programming.
- To compare a few of the different methodologies used in writing structured programs.
- To code internal and external subroutines in RPG II.
- To explore the use of DO groups for structured programming in RPG III.

I. Structured Concepts

A. Introduction

One main reason why computerized systems sometimes fail to produce the most effective results possible is because there are very few meaningful standards to help in designing or assessing systems or programs.

Until recently, each program was viewed by programmers, their managers, and users as a unique, individual creation. This perspective made it very difficult to assess the competence of programmers, to evaluate their work, or to make modifications to existing programs. As a result, many leaders in the field have been arguing for a less individualized or "ego-oriented" approach to programming, one that would not rely on the creativity of each programmer but on a standardized instruction format.

Structured programming is one method designed to standardize and improve programs so that they are easier to write, evaluate, debug, and modify. The technique consists of modularizing or segmenting each program into distinct blocks. A **module** is a self-contained procedure that is executed from the main routine of a program. These modules or blocks

1. Can be written in a standardized way.
2. Enable one program to be written and debugged by a team of programmers.
3. Are used in discussion groups where a team of programmers evaluates the program. Structured programming also facilitates the use of structured walkthroughs where each module is manually checked by a programming team to make certain it is correct even before it is run on a computer.
4. Can be used or copied in several programs.

To enable each module to function as a stand-alone entity, branches or "GO TO" instructions are to be avoided in a structured program. Thus, structured programming is sometimes referred to as **GO TO-less programming**. The branch or GO TO is replaced by subroutines in RPG II, DO groups in RPG III, DO statements in FORTRAN or PL/1, or PERFORM . . . UNTIL in COBOL. Where DO groups are not feasible, a main module executes a series of subroutines that can function as independent modules.

Another technique used to standardize programs is the coding of modules in decreasing order of importance. The first module is referred to as the main module, and this is followed by subordinate blocks or modules in decreasing order of significance. This technique is referred to as the **top-down approach**. It is often used along with structured programming to standardize program design.

Summary

1. *Structured programming*
   Used to standardize programs and to improve their reliability.
2. *Advantages*
   a. Makes it easier to evaluate programs.
   b. Makes it easier to debug programs.
   c. Makes it easier to modify existing programs.
   d. Enables teams of programmers to work together.

3. *Features*
   a. Modules
      Each program consists of independent modules, blocks, or segments.
   b. GO TO-less
      GO TO or branch instructions are avoided. Instead, we use
      (1) Subroutines in RPG II.
      (2) DO groups in RPG III, FORTRAN, or PL/1; PERFORM . . . UNTIL statements in COBOL.
   c. Top-down approach
      The main module is coded first. This is followed by subordinate modules in decreasing order of importance. All modules are executed from the main module.

B. Program Structures

1. Sequential Top-Down Structure
The following indicates the modular approach to program coding.

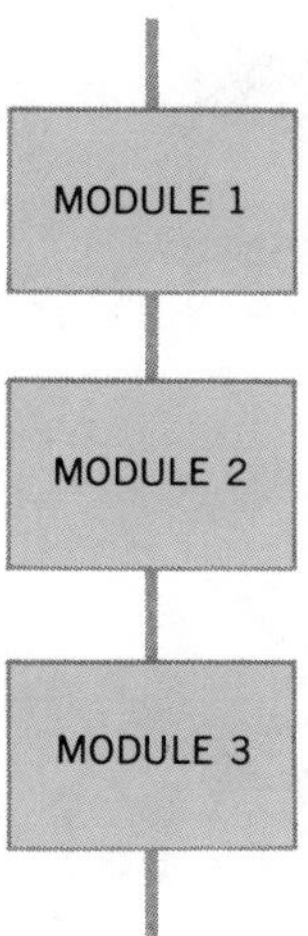

A program should be segmented into modules where each module performs a specific function. The sequence control structure means that one module calls in another; when the second module is executed, control returns to the main or **calling module** (see Figure 11.1). Since each module has only one entry and one exit point, program execution takes place in an ordered, top-down sequence. However, each module may call or perform other subroutines or modules. The only restriction is that after the **called module** has been executed, the computer returns to the calling module. In Figure 11.1, when RTNA is completed, the next instruction, CALL RTNB, in the main module would be executed.

In RPG II, RTNA, RTNB, and RTNC may be **internal subroutines**, that is, part of the user program, or **external subroutines**, called in from a library of program modules. These will be discussed in detail later.

2. IF-THEN-ELSE Structure
The second control structure in a program is one with which we are already familiar, namely the conditional branch or **IF-THEN-ELSE structure**. Figure 11.2 reviews the flowchart excerpt for the IF-THEN-ELSE sequence.

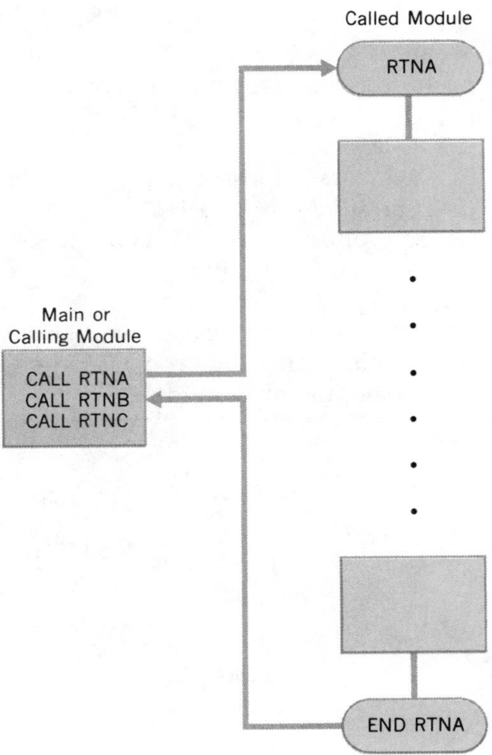

Figure 11.1
Modules in a structured program.

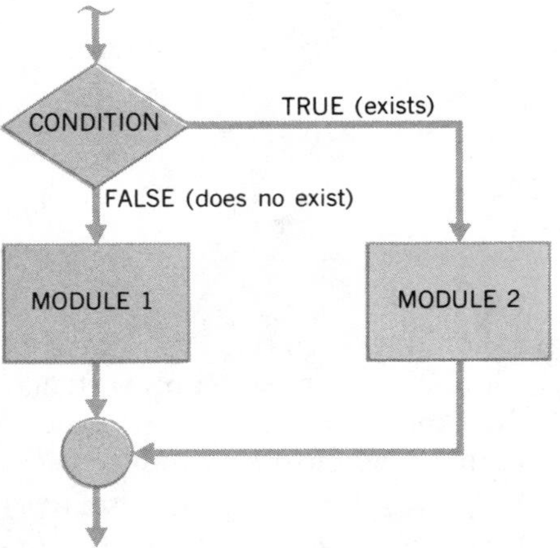

Figure 11.2
Flowchart excerpt for the IF-THEN-ELSE sequence.

If the condition specified is satisfied, module 2 will be executed. Otherwise, the program will execute module 1. One of the two modules will *always* be executed, depending on the result of the conditional test.

The following structures common to many programming languages are an integral part of RPG III but are not currently available in RPG II.

a. Do . . . While or Perform . . . While Structure The Do . . . While or Perform . . . While structure is used to execute a program module when a given condition is true. *While* the condition is true, the looping procedure will continue to execute module 1, as indicated in Figure 11.3.

When the condition changes to false, the module in the illustration, module

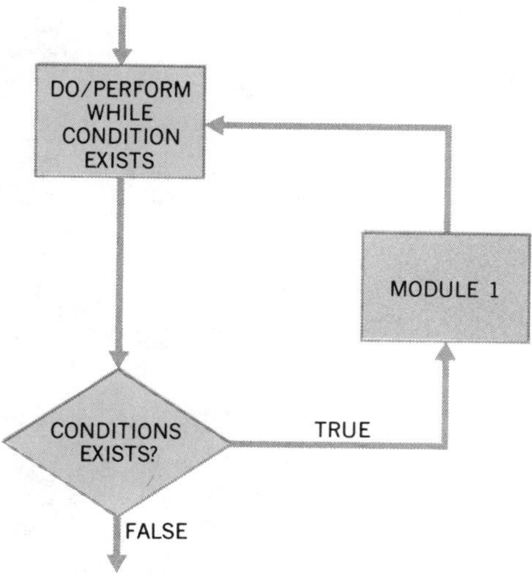

Figure 11.3
Flowchart excerpt for the DO/PERFORM WHILE sequence.

1, will no longer be executed. Note that the condition is always checked *before* the module is executed. It is important to realize that as soon as a false condition results, the loop is immediately terminated.

b. Do . . . Until or Perform . . . Until A similar structure to the Do . . . While or Perform . . . While in many languages is the Perform . . . Until. However, the difference between the two depends on whether the condition being tested is true or false. When employing the Perform or Do . . . Until structure, the loop continues *as long as* the condition is not met or is false (see Figure 11.4).

When comparing the While and the Until structures, it should be emphasized that

1. The Perform . . . While sequence continues to loop when a *true* condition prevails.
2. The Perform . . . Until sequence continues to loop when the *false* condition prevails.

Although these structures may appear to have limited capabilities, in actual practice they can be combined in various ways to solve any programming prob-

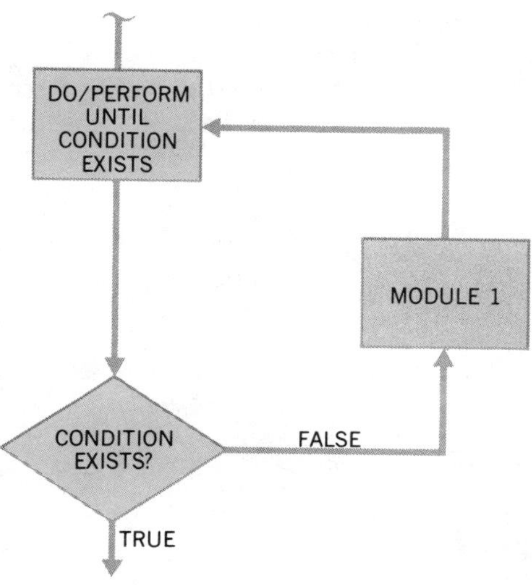

Figure 11.4
Flowchart excerpt for DO/PERFORM UNTIL sequence.

Figure 11.5
The last record test is an integral part of the READ sequence.

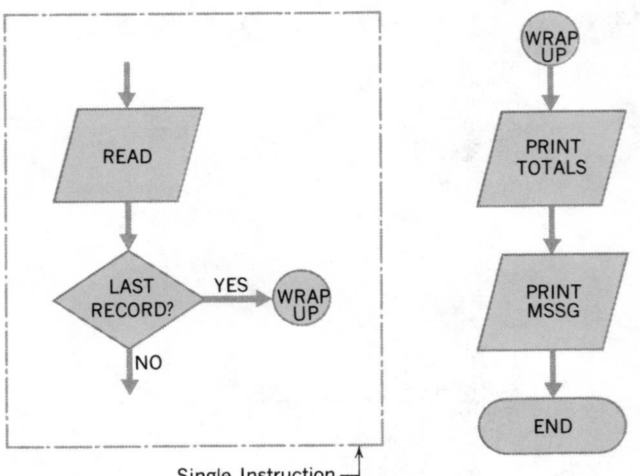

lem. An important result of using these standard structures is the minimizing of the GO TO statements and the standardizing of programs.

There has been a debate for the last several years whether or not the GO TO can or should be completely eliminated. If the GO TO instruction can most efficiently satisfy a programming requirement, then it should be used; if it can be avoided and proper program structure maintained, then every effort should be made to code GO TO-less programs.

3. End-of-File Considerations

When using most high-level programming languages, the last record (LR) is checked automatically by the computer. In fact, the last record is an integral part of the READ instruction and should be flowcharted as shown in Figure 11.5. This is true even in RPG, where last record indicators are handled automatically.

Note, however, that the LR indicator in RPG is automatically turned on by the computer when an end-of-file condition is sensed. End-of-file conditions are usually indicated by a /* or other job control record. In RPG, the LR indicator forces T time operations to be performed and bypasses all detail operations. This is automatic and is difficult to override.

An alternative method for processing end-of-file conditions, one that provides the programmer with greater flexibility, is using a programmed end-of-file or trailer record, similar to those used in BASIC. That is, establish a trailer record, for example, with all nines in some field such as ACCTNO. No actual data record will have all nines in this field. ACCTNO will only be equal to all nines at the end of job; at that point, the RPG programmer can provide for D time calculations as well as T calculations if desired. The logic for this is as follows.

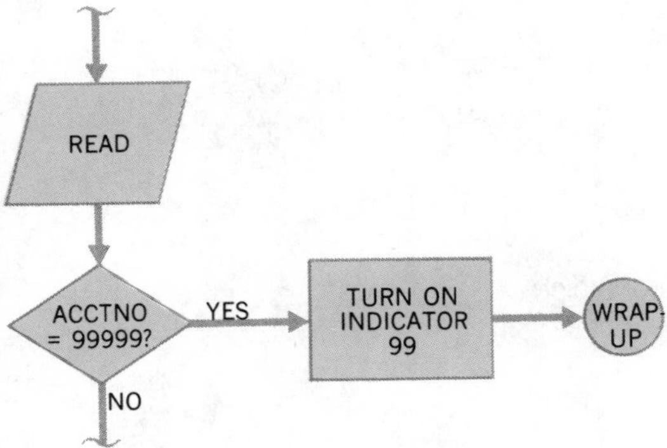

In structured programs, the use of this trailer record and the setting of a specific indicator is recommended.

When employing the principles of structured programming, the READ instruction is usually found in a routine using the Perform Until or DO Until structure. The Perform Until structure would continue to READ records *until a specified condition is met.* The condition could simply be the setting of an indicator, such as indicator 99, when all records have been processed. That is, when indicator 99 is on, this means that all the records have been read and the loop being performed should be terminated (see Figure 11.6).

In Figure 11.6, the last record is used to set on indicator 99. Once the indicator is set, the Until condition of the perform is satisfied, thereby terminating the loop. In structured RPG, we would SETON indicator 99 when ACCTNO = 99999.

4. Structured Programs

There are several ways to structure a program. In the most simplistic form, a general structured program should appear as follows. Note that this structure applies to all programming languages, including RPG.

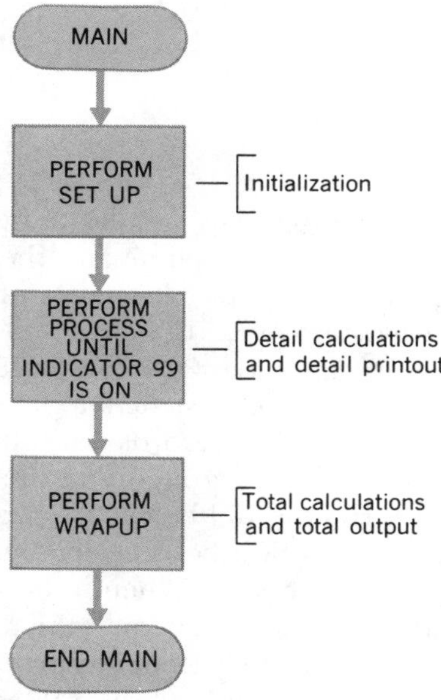

Let us return to a payroll program. The PROCESS module of this program should calculate and print the gross pay for each employee record. The PROCESS module is executed UNTIL indicator 99 is turned on, that is, until there is no more data. Review the flowchart in Figure 11.7.

Indicator 99 is initially set off in the SETUP module. The PROCESS module is then executed until indicator 99 is on, indicating the last record has already been processed. Once the test condition for the UNTIL structure in PROCESS is satisfied, the computer returns to the calling module, whereby the next sequential step is executed. This would be the step after PERFORM PROCESS. In Figure 11.7, the WRAPUP routine would typically serve to print any totals or end-of-job messages.

The structured flowchart in Figure 11.7 has an initial READ in PROCESS and then tests for the end-of-file; if the file has been completely processed, a branch

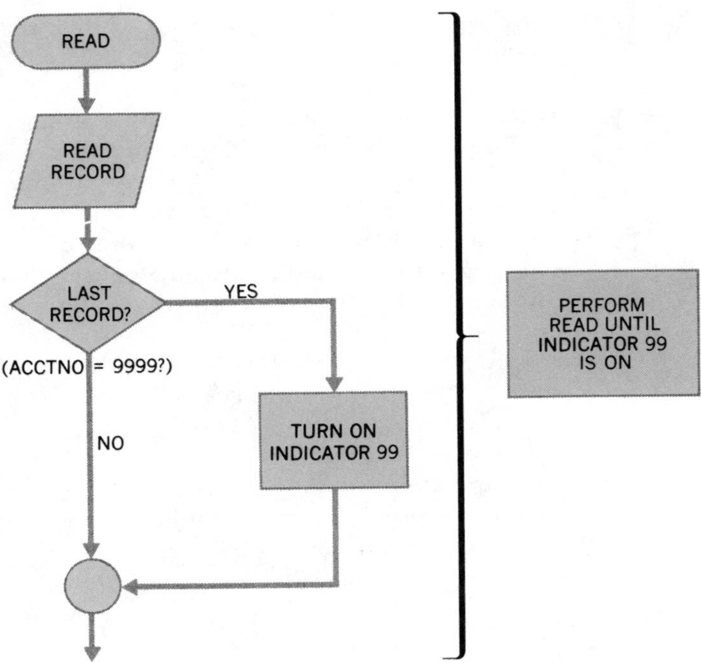

Figure 11.6
Example of the PERFORM UNTIL structure.

or GO TO alters the sequence. This violates the technique of avoiding GO TOs. Another structured approach that eliminates the need for a GO TO instruction is shown in Figure 11.8. Note the placement of the initial READ in the main module, following execution of SETUP.

The main module has an initial READ. PROCESS, which operates on the first record, is then executed.The last instruction in PROCESS reads another record. PROCESS continues operating on records until there is no more data. Note that the initial READ could also be integrated into the SETUP module if so desired.

Thus, the PROCESS routine will be executed continuously until indicator 99 is on. The PROCESS routine will be repeated each time a record is read until the last record has been processed. When indicator 99 is on, the Perform loop is terminated. Again, remember that the initial READ takes place in the main module or the SETUP module. The looping procedure must continue until the last record has been processed and indicator 99 is turned on. Once indicator 99 is on, the PROCESS routine terminates and the WRAPUP module is executed. No GO TO is needed.

The next module to be performed, WRAPUP, will print any totals or counters required at the end of the program. Study Figure 11.8 and observe the following.

1. An initial read is included in the main module.
2. PROCESS operates on this first record and ends by reading another record.
3. The PROCESS routine operates on all data until the last record has been processed.
4. The loop is terminated by setting indicator 99 on when the end of the file has been reached.

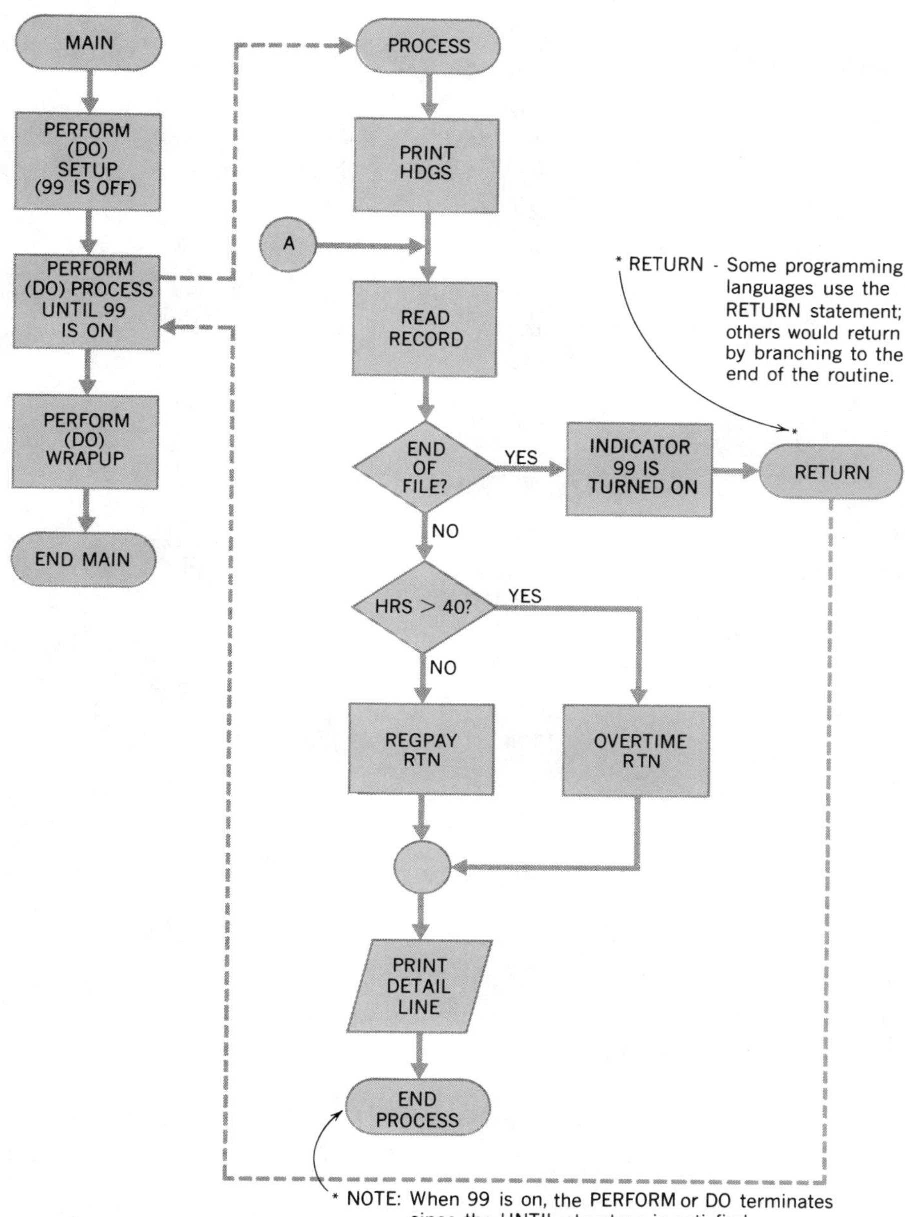

Figure 11.7 Flowchart of a structured payroll program.

This technique of having the initial READ in the main module is generally used for structured programs.

Another form of structuring the sample program is shown in Figure 11.9. The design of this program is quite different from that of Figure 11.8, but either of these forms is acceptable.

Referring to the READ routine in the flowchart, notice the READ instruction at the beginning. Many programmers prefer the location of the READ at the

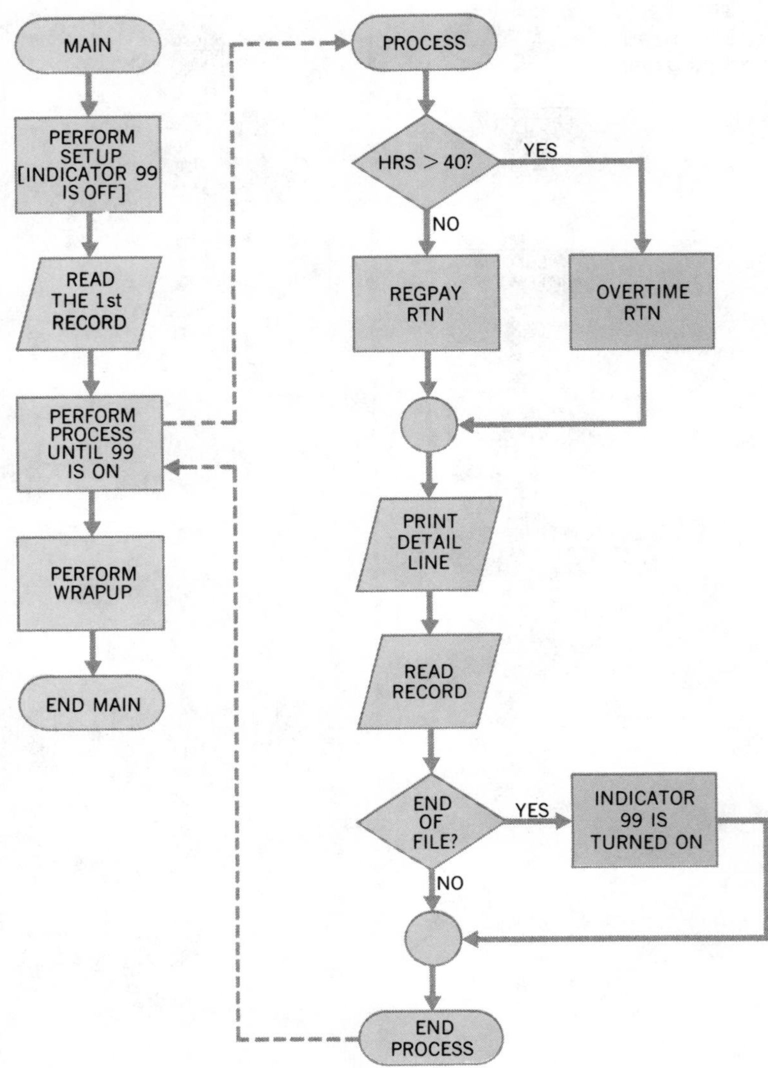

Figure 11.8 Structured logic for the payroll program without GO TO instructions.

beginning; that is, it closely resembles the typical input-process-output structure with which programmers are familiar.

As before, the main module performs the READ routine until indicator 99 is turned on. However, the READ routine performs a PROCESS routine as long as indicator 99 is off. Once the last record is processed, indicator 99 is turned on and the conditional branch that follows returns the program to the main module. The mechanics of the RETURN step may vary from one programming language to another. In many instances, the RETURN simply denotes the end of the routine. Recall that each time the performed routine is completed, a test is made to determine if the UNTIL condition has been satisfied. If the condition has been satisfied, then the Perform is completed and control returns to the calling routine (the main module).

This presentation of structured programming is detailed, but by no means complete. Entire books are written on the topic. Every attempt has been made to present the concepts independent of any programming language. Again, the material presented is concept-oriented and should provide you with a basic understanding of the various aspects and methodologies of structured programming. Structuring a program in RPG is sometimes cumbersome because the

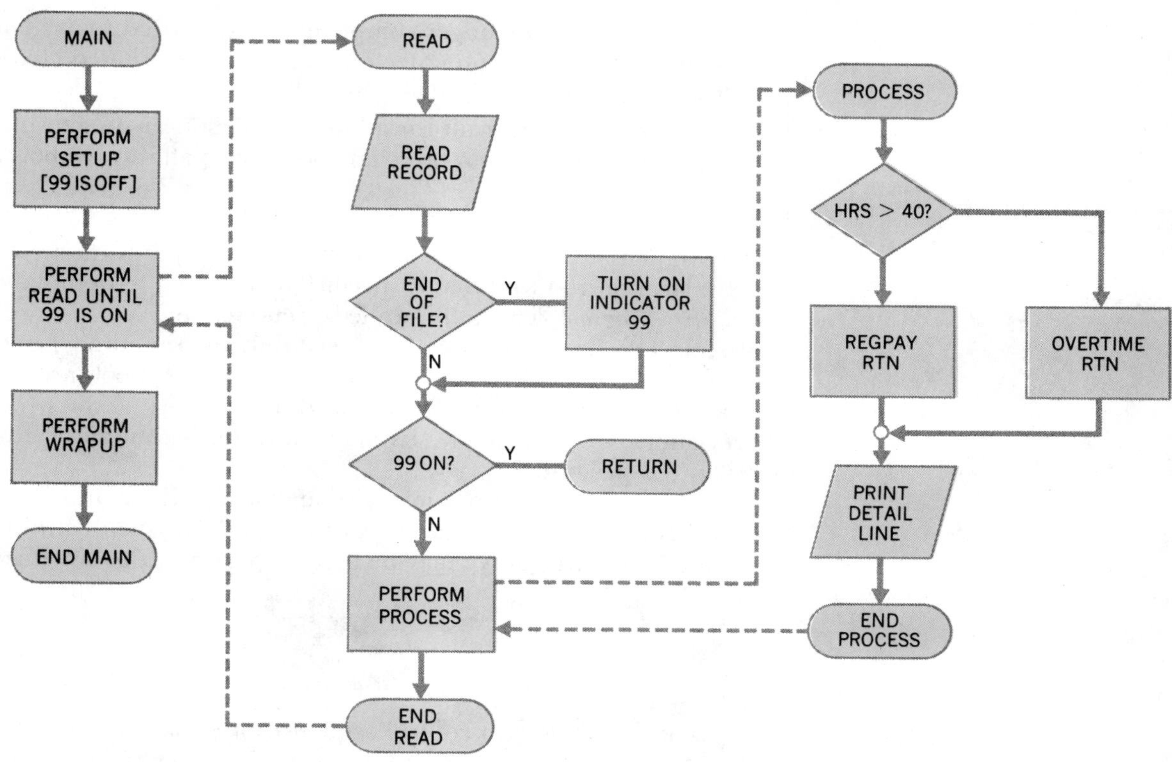

Figure 11.9
Alternative flowchart for the structured payroll program.

computer performs various tasks at specific intervals and these are not always under the control of the programmer.

C. Pseudocode: A Tool for Depicting Structured Programming Concepts

As has been indicated, a program flowchart is the primary tool used to depict the logic flow in a program. The flowchart serves two main purposes.

Advantages of Flowcharts

1. Before coding begins, the flowchart assists the programmer in determining the type of logical control to be used in a program.
2. The flowchart is a pictorial representation that may be useful to the business person or user who wishes to examine some facet of the logic used in the program.

Despite these advantages, program flowcharts have been the subject of considerable controversy in recent years, for the following reasons.

Limitations of Flowcharts

1. Program flowcharts are cumbersome for the programmer to draw. As a result, many programmers do not draw the chart until *after* the program has been completed, which, of course, defeats one of its main purposes, that of organizing the logic in a program.

2. Flowcharts are no longer completely standardized tools. The newer structured programming techniques have necessitated changes in the traditional format of a flowchart.
3. It is sometimes difficult for a business person or user to understand the logic depicted in a flowchart because of all the symbols and connecting flowlines.

To compensate for some of the shortcomings of program flowcharting, a new tool has been introduced that is specifically designed to depict the logic flow of a *structured program*. This tool is called **pseudocode**.

Pseudocode has been designed specifically as a method for facilitating the representation of logic in a structured program. No symbols are used, just words. As with flowcharts, the pseudocode need not indicate *all* the processing details; abbreviations are permissible. Its main function is to indicate the logic flow in a structured program.

Using a flowchart it is possible, although somewhat cumbersome, to indicate a logical control sequence that is executed until a given condition exists. The following flowchart symbol may be used to perform a routine until a condition is met.

PERFORM
. . . UNTIL

In pseudocode, logical control sequences are placed under the control of a PERFORM . . . UNTIL, a DO . . . group, or an IF-THEN-ELSE structure. All instructions under the control of these statements are indented in pseudocode. Each sequence is written in pseudocode as follows.

1. PERFORM . . . UNTIL
   .
   .
   .
   ENDPERFORM

2. DO . . . WHILE
   .
   .
   .
   ENDDO

3. IFTHENELSE
   .
   .
   .
   ENDIF

You have seen that a flowchart indicating the logical flow of a structured program is somewhat different from the flowcharts thus far illustrated. Figure 11.1Ø illustrates the flowchart for a structured program. We will review the logic depicted in this flowchart before considering the corresponding pseudocode. Note that the flowchart performs the following actions.

1. Files are opened or prepared for processing.
2. Indicator 99 is turned off. 99 is a special end-of-file indicator that is

initially off and turned on only *after* the last input record has been read and processed. Thus, indicator 99 is off throughout the entire sequence except when ACCTNO = 99999.

3. A record is read. If ACCTNO = 99999, an AT END condition is denoted, and indicator 99 is turned on.
4. A separate routine called CALC-RTN is executed repeatedly until indicator 99 is on; that is, until there are no more records.
5. CALC-RTN will be executed until all input records have been processed; then the files are deactivated by closing them. CALC-RTN may be considered a subroutine or module.
6. The job is terminated by a STOP RUN or HALT command.

Figure 11.10
Flowchart for a structured program.

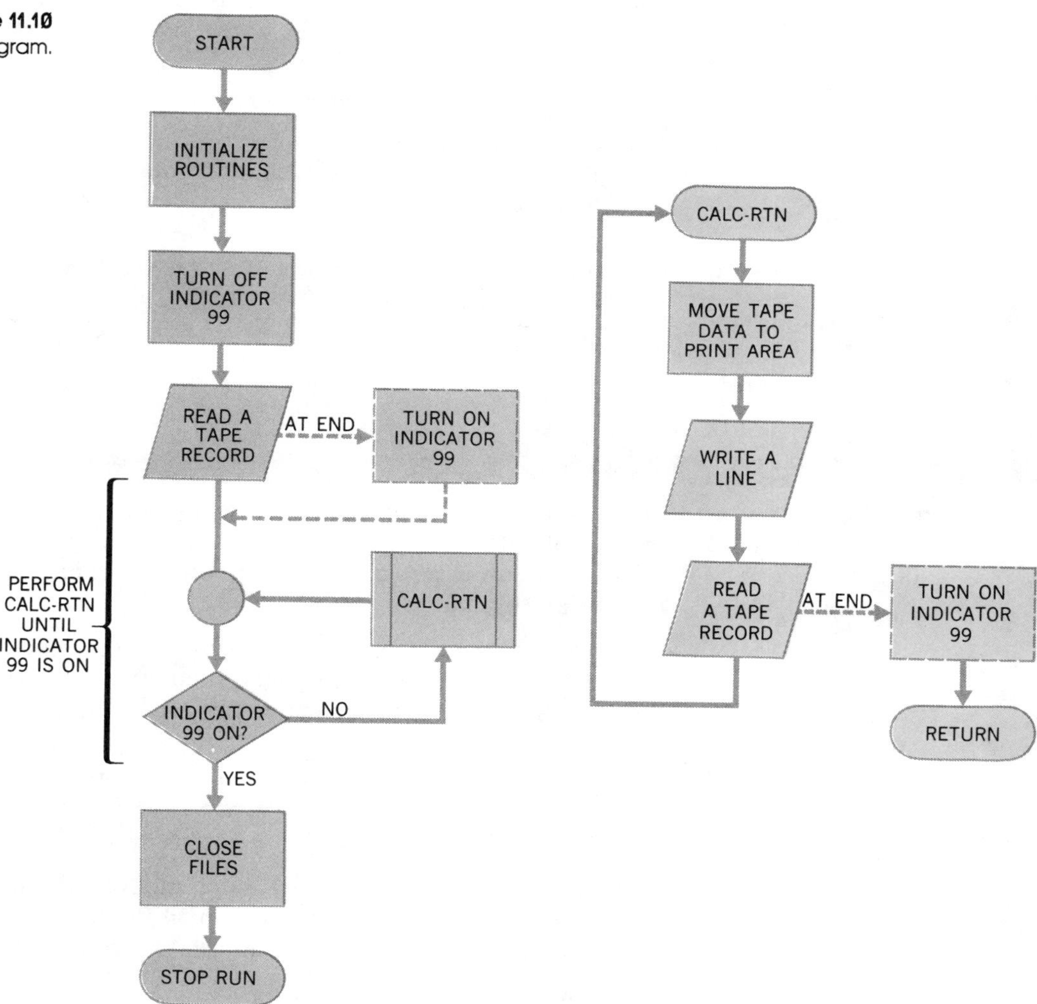

The pseudocode for this flowchart is as follows.

Pseudocode for Flowchart 11.10

Initialize Operations

Read a Tape Record; At End Move 1 to EOF

```
PERFORM . . . UNTIL indicator 99 is on
              Move Tape Data to Print Area
              Write a Line
              Read a Tape Record; When ACCTNO = 99999 (At End)
                 turn on indicator 99
ENDPERFORM
End-of-Job Functions
Stop Run
```

Let us consider another illustration. From sales records on tape, we wish to determine the amount to be paid to each salesperson. If sales are greater than $100, commission is equal to 10% of sales; otherwise, commission is 5% of sales. The flowchart for this problem is illustrated in Figure 11.11. The pseudocode for this structured procedure is shown in Figure 11.12.

Summary of Structured Concepts

A. *Structured programming*
Structured concepts have been developed to facilitate debugging, to modularize programs, and to reduce program maintenance costs.

B. *Pseudocode*
Structured program logic can be expressed in pseudocode, which is a top-down, English-like description of the modules used in a program.

II. Structured Programming in RPG II

One way to code structured programs in RPG II, as in other languages, is with the use of subroutines. A **subroutine** is a series of steps that can be executed from anywhere in a program. There are two main reasons for coding subroutines in a program.

1. Using a top-down, structured approach, a main module will call in subroutines as they need to be executed. This avoids GO TO instructions which transfer control to other parts of a program, making it difficult to follow the logic.
2. If the same series of operations is to be performed from more than one point in a program, this series is coded as a subroutine that is called in for execution as needed.

A subroutine is called in by the main module of a program as needed. After it is executed, control returns to the main module.

A subroutine may be either an internal subroutine or an external subroutine.

1. An **internal subroutine** is one that is part of the actual program (called here the user program).
2. An **external subroutine** is one that is independent of the user program but is called in as needed from a library. External subroutines are available for use in many programs. A sequence check routine, error procedure, and control total routine are examples of external subroutines that may be called into different programs as needed.

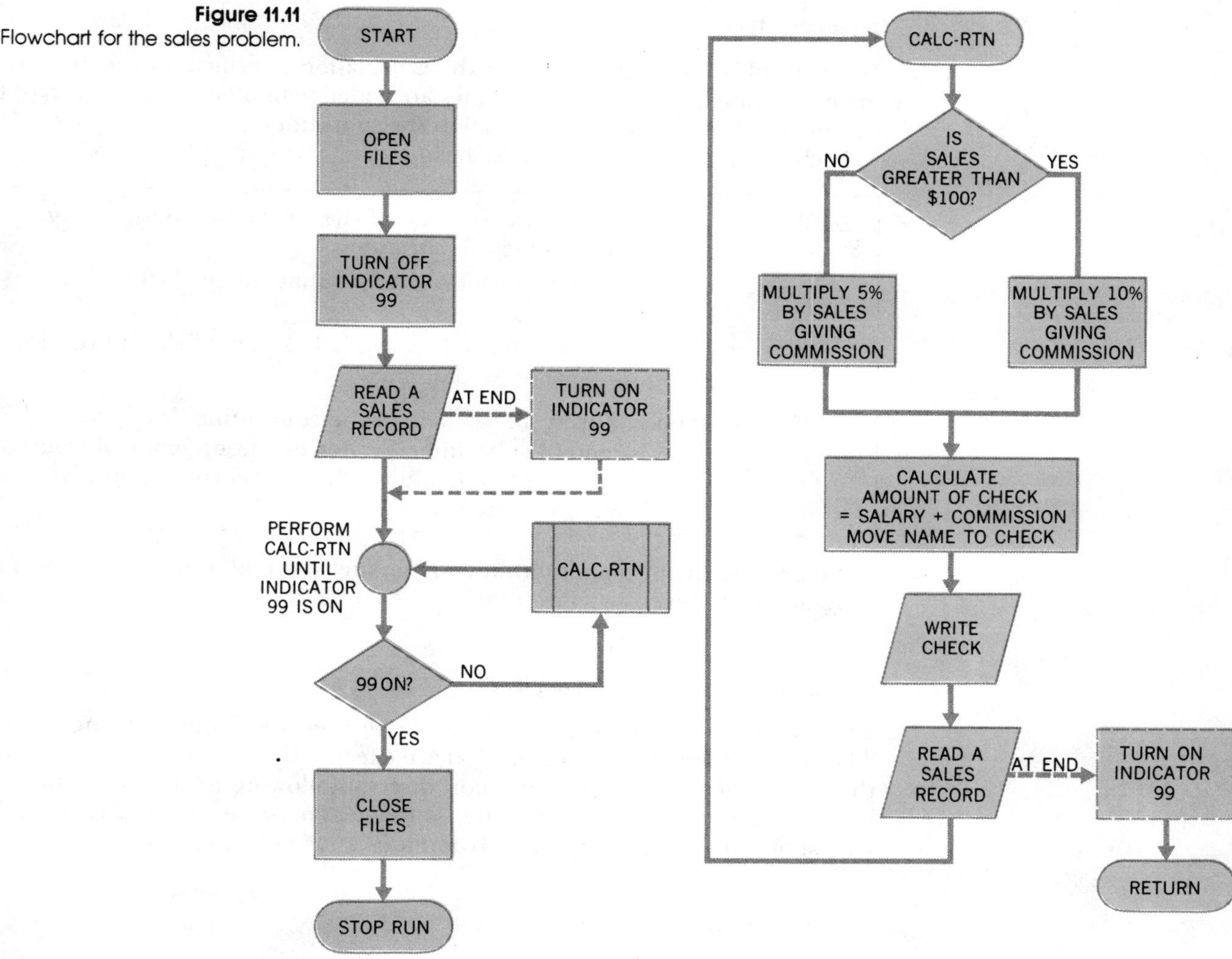

Figure 11.11
Flowchart for the sales problem.

```
  Open files
  Turn off indicator 99
  Read a sales record; at end turn on indicator 99
PERFORM CALC-RTN UNTIL INDICATOR 99 IS ON
  IF sales greater than 100.00
  THEN
    Multiply 10% (0.10) by sales giving commission
  ELSE
    Multiply 5% (0.05) by sales giving commission
  ENDIF
  Calculate amount of check = salary + commission
  Move name to check
  Write check
  Read a sales record; When sales no = 99999 turn on indicator 99
ENDPERFORM
Close files
Stop run
```

Figure 11.12
The pseudocode for Figure 11.11.

A. Internal Subroutines

Internal subroutines are coded on the Calculation Specifications form *after* all main program operations. Subroutines are coded with SR in columns 7–8 of the Calculation form. SR is an abbreviation for subroutine.

Each subroutine includes the following.

BEGSR operation	This is the first line of the subroutine designating "beginning of subroutine." Factor 1 includes a subroutine name (1–8 characters). Instructions to be included as part of the subroutine follow the BEGSR line.
ENDSR operation	This is the last line of the subroutine designating "end of subroutine." After execution, control returns to the calling module. The ENDSR corresponds to a RETURN statement.

To execute the internal subroutine from anywhere in a main module of the program, code "execute subroutine" as

Operation	*Factor 2*
EXSR	(Subroutine name)

This instruction causes the subroutine to be executed from a calling module. The steps between BEGSR and ENDSR are executed and then control returns to the calling module, to the instruction directly following EXSR. The subroutine name in Factor 2 of EXSR and Factor 1 of BEGSR must be exactly the same. The *same* subroutine may be executed from numerous points in a program.

RPG CALCULATION SPECIFICATIONS

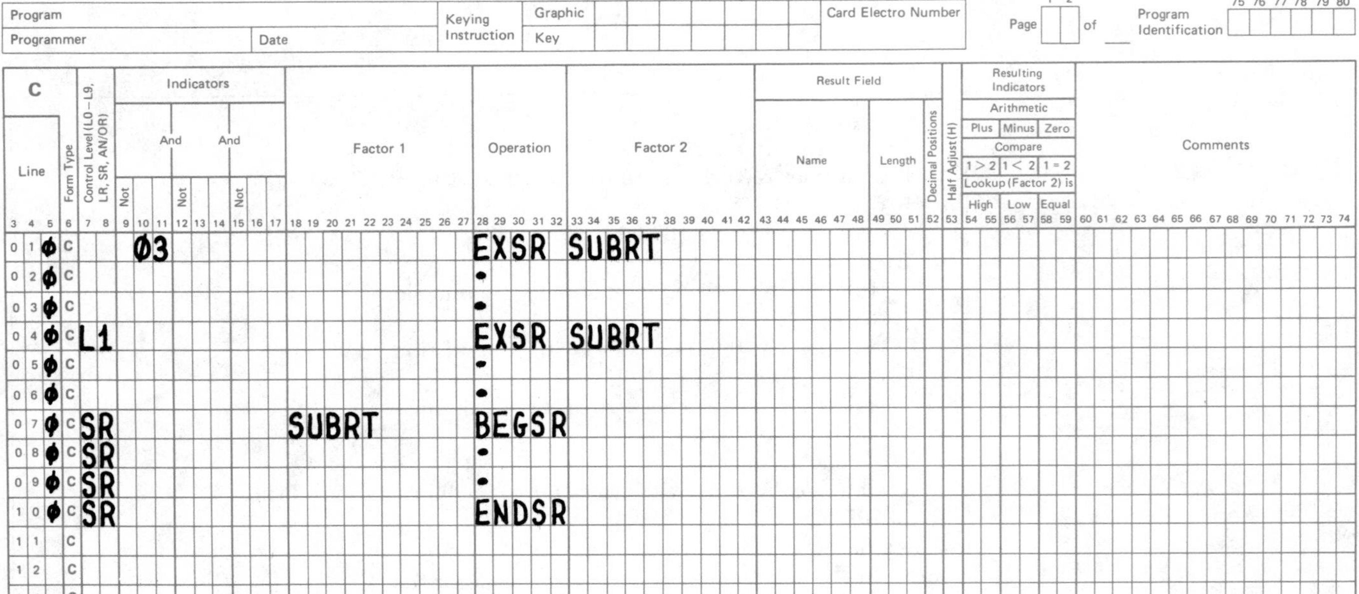

Line	Form Type	Control Level	Indicators	Factor 1	Operation	Factor 2
01ϕ	C		ϕ3		EXSR	SUBRT
02ϕ	C				•	
03ϕ	C				•	
04ϕ	C	L1			EXSR	SUBRT
05ϕ	C				•	
06ϕ	C				•	
07ϕ	C	SR		SUBRT	BEGSR	
08ϕ	C	SR			•	
09ϕ	C	SR			•	
10ϕ	C	SR			ENDSR	
11	C					
12	C					
13	C					

In this example, SUBRT is executed at two different points in the program. After each execution, control returns to the statement directly following EXSR.

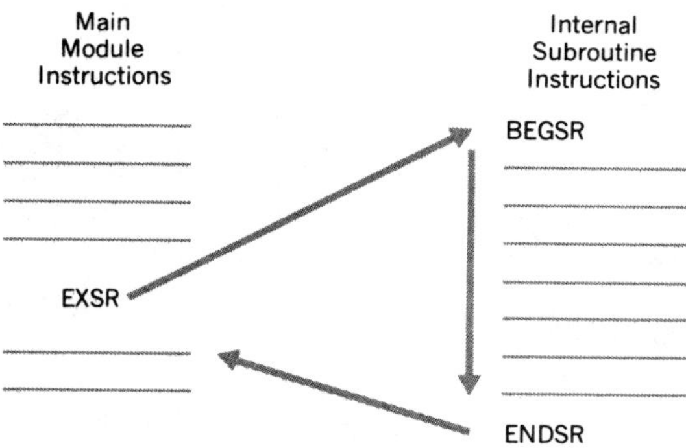

Each subroutine should be viewed as an independent entity. Thus, if a GO TO cannot be avoided in a subroutine, it should cause a branch to another point *within* the subroutine and not cause a branch external to the subroutine. To branch to a point outside the subroutine can cause logic errors.

With the use of internal subroutines, the modular approach to programming can be realized. That is, if a program is to perform edit functions, tally control totals, and check for errors, the calculations can be coded in the main or calling module as follows.

RPG CALCULATION SPECIFICATIONS

Program		Keying Instruction	Graphic	Card Electro Number	Page 1 2 of	Program Identification 75 76 77 78 79 80
Programmer	Date		Key			

Line (3–5)	Form Type (6)	Control Level (L0–L9, LR, SR, AN/OR) (7–8)	Indicators (9–17)	Factor 1 (18–27)	Operation (28–32)	Factor 2 (33–42)	Result Field Name (43–48)	Length (49–51)	Decimal Positions (52)	Half Adjust (H) (53)	Resulting Indicators (54–59)	Comments (60–74)
01Ø	C		Ø1NØ2		EXSR	SETUP	Execute on 1st record					
02Ø	C		Ø1 Ø2N99		EXSR	PROCESS	Execute on all but 1st record					
03Ø	C		99		EXSR	WRAPUP	Execute at end of job					
04	C											
05	C											

The RPG II program is executed via these three modules. At SETUP, indicator Ø2 will be turned on, which means that SETUP will only be executed *once* at the beginning. After indicator Ø2 is on, the PROCESS module performs all calculations.

RPG CALCULATION SPECIFICATIONS

```
01ØC*         PERFORM ALL INITIALIZING
02ØC*
03ØCSR        SETUP     BEGSR
04ØCSR                  .
05ØCSR                  .
06ØCSR                  .
07ØCSR                  SETON                     Ø2
08ØCSR                  ENDSR
09 C
10 C
```

WRAPUP performs all end-of-job functions.

RPG CALCULATION SPECIFICATIONS

```
01ØCSR        WRAPUP    BEGSR
02ØCSR                  .
03ØCSR                  .
04ØCSR                  .
05ØCSR                  ENDSR
06 C
07 C
```

PROCESS is executed from the main module for all records with indicator Ø1 on. Ø2 will remain on for the entire run. Thus PROCESS is executed for each record read. At PROCESS, indicator 99 is turned on when the last record has been processed and the trailer record has been read.

RPG CALCULATION SPECIFICATIONS

Line	Form Type	Control Level (L0–L9, LR, SR, AN/OR)	Indicators	Factor 1	Operation	Factor 2	Result Field Name	Length	Decimal Positions	Half Adjust (H)	Resulting Indicators High	Low	Equal	Comments
01Ø	C	SR		PROCESS	BEGSR									
02Ø	C	SR			.									
03Ø	C	SR			.									
04Ø	C	SR			.									
05Ø	C	SR		ACCTNO	COMP	99999							99	
06Ø	C	SR			ENDSR									
07	C													
08	C													
09	C													

At the end-of-job, when 99 has been turned on, WRAPUP is executed.

To code this entire procedure under the control of a main module, we would have the following.

RPG CALCULATION SPECIFICATIONS

Line	Form Type	Control Level (L0–L9, LR, SR, AN/OR)	Indicators	Factor 1	Operation	Factor 2	Result Field Name	Length	Decimal Positions	Half Adjust (H)	Resulting Indicators High	Low	Equal	Comments
01Ø	C		Ø1		EXSR	MAIN								
02Ø	C	*												
03Ø	C	SR		MAIN	BEGSR									
04Ø	C	SR	Ø1NØ2		EXSR	SETUP								
05Ø	C	SR	Ø1 Ø2N99		EXSR	PROCESS								
06Ø	C	SR	Ø1 99		EXSR	WRAPUP								
07Ø	C	SR			ENDSR									
08	C													
09	C													

Thus the main sequence of steps will themselves be under the control of a module called MAIN.

Separate programmers can be called on to code and debug each of these subroutines independently. Moreover, if a modification is required to one subroutine, it will not affect the logic of other modules. In this way, subroutines can be *tested* independently.

The modular approach to programming, using internal subroutines, helps to standardize the programming activity and makes it easier to code, debug, and modify programs. It also makes it easier for managers to assess individual programs and to evaluate the programming proficiency of their staff.

Figure 11.13 illustrates the use of an internal subroutine to create a compound-interest table.

Figure 11.13
Use of an internal subroutine to create a compound-interest table.

```
01-010  F********************************************************************SSS11A
01-020  F*  THIS PROGRAM CREATES A COMPOUND INTEREST TABLE LISTING THE     *SSS11A
01-030  F* PRINCIPAL AND COMPOUNDED INTEREST RATE FOR EACH YEAR INVESTED   *SSS11A
01-040  F********************************************************************SSS11A
01-050  F*                                                                   SSS11A
01-060  FINVFILE IP  F      80            READ01 SYSIPT                      SSS11A
01-070  FINTABLE O  F     132     OF     PRINTERSYSLST                       SSS11A
01-080  F*                                                                   SSS11A
02-010  I*************************** INPUT RECORD ***************************SSS11A
02-020  I*                                                                   SSS11A
02-030  IINVFILE NS  01                                                      SSS11A
02-040  I                                        1   82PRIN  L1              SSS11A
02-050  I                                        9  102RATE                  SSS11A
02-060  I                                       11  120YEARS                 SSS11A
02-070  I*                                                                   SSS11A
03-010  C*************************** CALCULATIONS ***************************SSS11A
03-020  C*                                                                   SSS11A
03-030  C                     Z-ADD0         CRATE   42                      SSS11A
03-040  C                     MOVELRATE      CRATE                           SSS11A
03-050  C                     Z-ADD0         CTR     20                      SSS11A
03-060  C*                                                                   SSS11A
03-070  C           LOOP      TAG                                            SSS11A
03-080  C   OF                SETON                     25                   SSS11A
03-090  C                     EXCPT                                          SSS11A
03-100  C   25                SETOF                     250F                 SSS11A
03-110  C                     EXSR INCALC                                    SSS11A
03-120  C           CTR       ADD  1         CTR                             SSS11A
03-130  C           CTR       COMP YEARS                 40                  SSS11A
03-140  C   N40               GOTO LOOP                                      SSS11A
03-150  C*                                                                   SSS11A
03-160  C************************************************                    SSS11A
03-170  C* THIS SUBROUTINE CALCULATES THE PRINCIPAL     *                    SSS11A
03-180  C* AND THE COMPOUNDED INTEREST RATE             *                    SSS11A
03-190  C************************************************                    SSS11A
03-200  C*                                                                   SSS11A
04-010  CSR         INCALC    BEGSR                                          SSS11A
04-020  CSR         PRIN      MULT RATE      INT     72H                     SSS11A
04-030  CSR         PRIN      ADD  INT       PRIN    82                      SSS11A
04-040  CSR         CRATE     MULT RATE      RATEX   32H                     SSS11A
04-050  CSR         CRATE     ADD  RATEX     CRATE                           SSS11A
04-060  CSR                   ENDSR                                          SSS11A
04-070  C*                                                                   SSS11A
05-010  O*************************** HEADING LINES **************************SSS11A
05-020  O*                                                                   SSS11A
05-030  OINTABLE H  201   1P                                                 SSS11A
05-040  O       OR        OF                                                 SSS11A
05-050  O                                   31 'COMPOUND INTEREST TABLE'     SSS11A
05-060  O                                   40 'PAGE'                        SSS11A
05-070  O                         PAGE      45                               SSS11A
05-080  O        H  1     1P                                                 SSS11A
05-090  O       OR        OF                                                 SSS11A
05-100  O                                   11 'PRINCIPAL'                   SSS11A
05-110  O                                   27 'COMPOUNDED'                  SSS11A
05-120  O                                   38 'YEARS'                       SSS11A
05-130  O        H  2     1P                                                 SSS11A
05-140  O       OR        OF                                                 SSS11A
05-150  O                                   28 'INTEREST RATE'               SSS11A
05-160  O                                   39 'INVESTED'                    SSS11A
06-010  O*                                                                   SSS11A
06-020  O*************************** TOTAL LINE *****************************SSS11A
06-030  O*                                                                   SSS11A
06-040  O        T  2     L1                                                 SSS11A
06-050  O                                   12 '______________'              SSS11A
06-060  O                                   23 '______'                      SSS11A
06-070  O                                   36 '__'                          SSS11A
06-080  O*                                                                   SSS11A
06-090  O*************************** EXCEPTION OUTPUT ***********************SSS11A
06-100  O*                                                                   SSS11A
06-110  O        EF 1     01                                                 SSS11A
06-120  O                         PRIN  1   12 '$'                           SSS11A
06-130  O                         CRATE 1   23                               SSS11A
06-140  O                                   25 '%'                           SSS11A
06-150  O                         CTR   1   36                               SSS11A
06-160  O*                                                                   SSS11A
06-170  O********************************************************************SSS11A

E N D  O F  S O U R C E
```

B. External Subroutines

An external subroutine is a module that will be included in several programs and is separate from any one RPG program that will use it. Because these external subroutines are standard modules used in numerous programs, they help standardize the programming activity and make individual programs easier to code, debug, and modify. Specific functions, then, would not need to be coded over and over again but only once and could be called in to programs as needed. These would include summary routines, edit checks, and sequence checking.

The following operations are used on the Calculation Specifications form of the user program to execute external subroutines defined in a library.

1. EXIT (*External subroutine name*)
   Used in the main program to cause the external subroutine to be executed at this point, the EXIT statement causes the program to branch to the external subroutine specified and to execute it. The subroutine is stored in a library of functions, usually on a disk. When the subroutine is completed, control returns to the next sequential operation after the EXIT (not including ULABL and RLABL operations to be discussed).
2. RLABL (*Result field name*)
   The RLABL operation allows the external subroutine to reference a field, table, array, or indicator *defined in the user program.* Thus the external subroutine can manipulate areas described in the user program. The name of the user program's field, table, or array to be referenced is specified in columns 43 to 48, the result field. Numerous RLABL operations can be included after the EXIT statement as needed.
3. ULABL (*Result field name*)
   The ULABL operation allows the user program to reference a field described *within the external subroutine.* Thus a field defined in the external program can be referenced and used in the user program. Field specifications, including field length and decimal positions must be included in the ULABL operation. This is the way a field manipulated in the external subroutine can become a part of the user program. Numerous ULABL operations can be included after the EXIT statement as needed.

Example Execute an external edit subroutine called EDITSR. AMT, NAME, and ACCTNO are fields within the user program that need to be accessed by the external subroutine. TALLY is a count field generated within the external subroutine that needs to be accessed in the user program.

RPG CALCULATION SPECIFICATIONS

Program		Keying Instruction	Graphic		Card Electro Number	Page 1 2 of	Program Identification 75 76 77 78 79 80
Programmer	Date		Key				

Line (3–5)	Form Type (6)	Control Level (L0–L9, LR, SR, AN/OR) (7–8)	Indicators (9–17)	Factor 1 (18–27)	Operation (28–32)	Factor 2 (33–42)	Result Field Name (43–48)	Length (49–51)	Decimal Positions (52)	Half Adjust (H) (53)	Resulting Indicators (54–59)	Comments (60–74)
01ø	C				EXIT	EDITSR						
02ø	C				ULABL		TALLY	4	ø			
03ø	C				RLABL		AMT					
04ø	C				RLABL		NAME					
05ø	C				RLABL		ACCTNO					
06ø	C				•							
07ø	C				•							
08	C											
09	C											
10	C											

EDITSR is *not* part of your program but is an external subroutine that has been standardized so that it can be used by numerous programs.

III. Structured Programming in RPG III

RPG III is a programming language that currently runs on only a few IBM computers, most specifically the IBM s/38. But because of its structured programming features and other advances, it is likely to be used on a wide variety of computers in the near future. This chapter will consider the structured programming features of RPG III. These specifically use the DO statements explained in the beginning of the chapter.

A. DO . . . Groups in RPG III

A **DO group** permits execution of a series of instructions a fixed number of times. In its simplest form, it is coded on the Calculation Specifications form as follows.

RPG CALCULATION SPECIFICATIONS

Line	Form Type	Control Level	Indicators	Factor 1	Operation	Factor 2	Result Field Name	Length	Decimal Positions	Half Adjust	Resulting Indicators	Comments
01ϕ	C	*										
02ϕ	C			Starting value	DO	Ending value	Name of field	Specs				
03ϕ	C				•							
04ϕ	C				•							
05ϕ	C				•							
06ϕ	C				END	Incrementing value						
07	C											
08	C											

When it is encountered, the computer will execute the DO loop as follows.

1. Set field name to starting value (Factor 1).
2. Test to see if field name = ending value (Factor 2). If it does, execution of the DO loop is terminated and control returns to the statement following END.
3. If field name is not equal to the ending value, the DO loop is executed.
4. At END, field name is increased by the incrementing value.
5. Control returns to STEP 2 above.

Example Determine the sum of odd numbers from 1 to 1ϕ1.

RPG CALCULATION SPECIFICATIONS

Line	Form Type	Control Level	Indicators	Factor 1	Operation	Factor 2	Result Field Name	Length	Decimal Positions	Half Adjust	Resulting Indicators	Comments
01ϕ	C			1	DO	1ϕ1	INDEX	3	ϕ			
02ϕ	C			INDEX	ADD	TOTAL	TOTAL	5	ϕ			
03ϕ	C				END	2						
04ϕ	C				•							
05ϕ	C				•							
06ϕ	C				•							
07	C											
08	C											

1. INDEX is set equal to 1. (INDEX is a three-digit, integer field.)
2. A test is made to determine if INDEX is equal to 1Ø1.
   If yes, the statement after END is executed.
3. If INDEX is not equal to 1Ø1, ADD INDEX (1, 3, 5, . . .) TO TOTAL.
4. Increment INDEX by 2.
5. Go to Step 2 above.

The flowchart for a DO . . . group is illustrated in Figure 11.14. If the field name indicated is *initially* equal to the final value even before execution, then the statements in the DO loop do not get executed *even once*. Note that if the starting value is not specified, it is assumed to be 1. If the incrementing value is not specified, it, too, is assumed to be 1.

B. Other Options of the DO . . . Group

The computer can be instructed to execute a series of instructions based on the following conditions.

Operation	*Meaning*
DOW	DO . . . WHILE a condition exists
DOU	DO . . . UNTIL a condition exists

The conditions that can be tested include

LT (Factor 1 < Factor 2)

GT (Factor 1 > Factor 2)

EQ (Factor 1 = Factor 2)

LE (Factor 1 ≤ Factor 2)

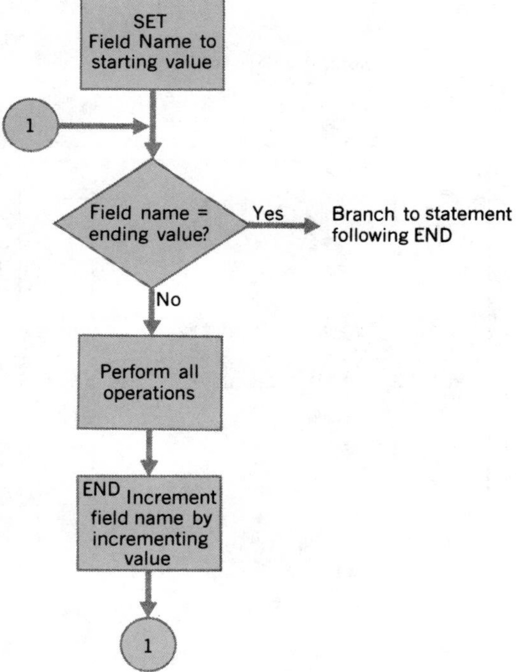

Figure 11.14
Flowchart for a DO . . . group.

GE (Factor 1 ≥ Factor 2)

NE (Factor 1 ≠ Factor 2)

In all cases, the DO . . . group must end with an END statement. DO . . . UNTIL coding is usually specified as DOUxx where xx can be LT, GT, EQ, and so on as listed. Similarly DO . . . WHILE coding is usually specified as DOWxx.

Example 1 Execute a series of steps until AMT1 < AMT2.

RPG CALCULATION SPECIFICATIONS

Line (3–5)	Form Type (6)	Control Level (7–8)	Indicators (9–17)	Factor 1 (18–27)	Operation (28–32)	Factor 2 (33–42)	Result Field Name (43–48)	Length (49–51)	Decimal Positions (52)	Half Adjust (53)	Resulting Indicators (54–59)	Comments (60–74)
01ϕ	C			AMT1	DOULT	AMT2						
02ϕ	C				•							
03ϕ	C				•							
04ϕ	C				•							
05ϕ	C				END							
06	C											
07	C											
08	C											

To be effective, the steps within the DO . . . group would alter AMT1 and/or AMT2 so that at some point AMT1 is, in fact, less than AMT2; otherwise, the program would be in an infinite loop.

Example 2 Execute a series of steps for as long as AMT3 = AMT4.

RPG CALCULATION SPECIFICATIONS

Line (3–5)	Form Type (6)	Control Level (7–8)	Indicators (9–17)	Factor 1 (18–27)	Operation (28–32)	Factor 2 (33–42)	Result Field Name (43–48)	Length (49–51)	Decimal Positions (52)	Half Adjust (53)	Resulting Indicators (54–59)	Comments (60–74)
01ϕ	C			AMT3	DOWEQ	AMT4						
02ϕ	C				•							
03ϕ	C				•							
04ϕ	C				•							
05ϕ	C				END							
06	C											
07	C											
08	C											

Let us code the routine to sum the odd numbers from 1 to 1Ø1 in several different ways.

1.

RPG CALCULATION SPECIFICATIONS

Program		Keying Instruction	Graphic	Card Electro Number	Page 1 2 of	Program Identification 75 76 77 78 79 80
Programmer	Date		Key			

Line (3–5)	Form Type (6)	Control Level (LO–L9, LR, SR, AN/OR) (7–8)	Indicators (9–17)	Factor 1 (18–27)	Operation (28–32)	Factor 2 (33–42)	Result Field Name (43–48)	Length (49–51)	Decimal Positions (52)	Half Adjust (H) (53)	Resulting Indicators (54–59)	Comments (60–74)
01Ø	C				Z-ADD	1	INDEX	3	Ø			
02Ø	C			INDEX	DOUEQ	1Ø3						
03Ø	C			INDEX	ADD	TOTAL	TOTAL	5	Ø			
04Ø	C			2	ADD	INDEX	INDEX					
05Ø	C				END							
06	C											
07	C											
08	C											

2.

RPG CALCULATION SPECIFICATIONS

Program		Keying Instruction	Graphic	Card Electro Number	Page 1 2 of	Program Identification 75 76 77 78 79 80
Programmer	Date		Key			

Line (3–5)	Form Type (6)	Control Level (LO–L9, LR, SR, AN/OR) (7–8)	Indicators (9–17)	Factor 1 (18–27)	Operation (28–32)	Factor 2 (33–42)	Result Field Name (43–48)	Length (49–51)	Decimal Positions (52)	Half Adjust (H) (53)	Resulting Indicators (54–59)	Comments (60–74)
01Ø	C				Z-ADD	1	INDEX	3	Ø			
02Ø	C			INDEX	DOWLT	1Ø3						
03Ø	C			INDEX	ADD	TOTAL	TOTAL	5	Ø			
04Ø	C			2	ADD	INDEX	INDEX					
05Ø	C				END							
06	C											
07	C											
08	C											

3.

RPG CALCULATION SPECIFICATIONS

Program		Keying Instruction	Graphic		Card Electro Number	Page 1 2 of	Program Identification 75 76 77 78 79 80
Programmer	Date		Key				

Line (3–5)	Form Type (6)	Control Level (L0–L9, LR, SR, AN/OR) (7–8)	Indicators (9–17)	Factor 1 (18–27)	Operation (28–32)	Factor 2 (33–42)	Result Field Name (43–48)	Length (49–51)	Decimal Positions (52)	Half Adjust (H) (53)	Resulting Indicators (54–59)	Comments (60–74)
01Ø	C				Z-ADD	1	INDEX	3	Ø			
02Ø	C			1Ø1	DOWGE	INDEX						
03Ø	C			INDEX	ADD	TOTAL	TOTAL	5	Ø			
04Ø	C			2	ADD	INDEX	INDEX					
05Ø	C				END							
06	C											
07	C											
08	C											

Example 3 A value for N is read. Find N! called "N Factorial" = N × (N − 1) × (N − 2) × . . . × 1. For example, 5! = 5 × 4 × 3 × 2 × 1 = 12Ø, 3! = 3 × 2 × 1. We will code this problem in three ways.

1.

RPG CALCULATION SPECIFICATIONS

Program		Keying Instruction	Graphic		Card Electro Number	Page 1 2 of	Program Identification 75 76 77 78 79 80
Programmer	Date		Key				

Line (3–5)	Form Type (6)	Control Level (L0–L9, LR, SR, AN/OR) (7–8)	Indicators (9–17)	Factor 1 (18–27)	Operation (28–32)	Factor 2 (33–42)	Result Field Name (43–48)	Length (49–51)	Decimal Positions (52)	Half Adjust (H) (53)	Resulting Indicators (54–59)	Comments (60–74)
01Ø	C				Z-ADD	1	TOTAL	7	Ø			
02Ø	C			2	DO	N	M	5	Ø			
03Ø	C			M	MULT	TOTAL	TOTAL					
04Ø	C				END							
05	C											
06	C											
07	C											

2.

RPG CALCULATION SPECIFICATIONS

Line	Form Type	Factor 1	Operation	Factor 2	Result Field Name	Length	Decimal Positions
01 ϕ	C		Z-ADD	1	TOTAL	7	ϕ
02 ϕ	C	N	DOWGT	1			
03 ϕ	C	N	MULT	TOTAL	TOTAL		
04 ϕ	C	N	SUB	1	N		
05 ϕ	C		END				
06	C						
07	C						

3.

RPG CALCULATION SPECIFICATIONS

Line	Form Type	Factor 1	Operation	Factor 2	Result Field Name	Length	Decimal Positions
01 ϕ	C		Z-ADD	1	TOTAL	7	ϕ
02 ϕ	C	N	DOULE	1			
03 ϕ	C	N	MULT	TOTAL	TOTAL		
04 ϕ	C	N	SUB	1	N		
05 ϕ	C		END				
06	C						
07	C						

Using the DO . . . groups, it becomes totally unnecessary to code GO TO statements. That is, with DO . . . group processing there is no need to transfer control from one segment of a program to another. Thus control remains in the main module and programs are easier to code, debug, modify, and even evaluate.

C. IF-THEN-ELSE

You will recall that structured programs make use of logical control procedures such as IF-THEN-ELSE specifications as well as DO . . . groups. Pseudocode has ample provision for both these control mechanisms. RPG III can handle IF-THEN-ELSE logic as well as DO . . . groups.

RPG CALCULATION SPECIFICATIONS

Program | Programmer | Date | Keying Instruction | Graphic | Key | Card Electro Number | Page of | Program Identification

Line	Form Type	Control Level (L0–L9, LR, SR, AN/OR)	Indicators	Factor 1	Operation	Factor 2	Result Field Name	Length	Decimal Positions	Half Adjust (H)	Resulting Indicators	Comments
01Ø	C				IFXX							
02Ø	C				•							
03Ø	C				•							
04Ø	C				•							
05Ø	C				ELSE							
06Ø	C				•							
07Ø	C				•							
08Ø	C				•							
09Ø	C				END							
10	C											
11	C											
12	C											

xx as in DO groups can be

- LT Less than
- GT Greater than
- EQ Equal to
- NE Not equal to
- LE Less than or equal to
- GE Greater than or equal to

IF-THEN-ELSE specifications also end with an END statement.

Example Multiply A by B giving C if AMT = Ø. ADD D to E giving F if AMT ≠ Ø.

RPG CALCULATION SPECIFICATIONS

Program | Programmer | Date | Keying Instruction | Graphic | Key | Card Electro Number | Page of | Program Identification

Line	Form Type	Control Level (L0–L9, LR, SR, AN/OR)	Indicators	Factor 1	Operation	Factor 2	Result Field Name	Length	Decimal Positions	Half Adjust (H)	Resulting Indicators	Comments
01Ø	C			AMT	IFEQ	Ø						
02Ø	C			A	MULT	B	C	5	Ø			
03Ø	C				ELSE							
04Ø	C			D	ADD	E	F	5	Ø			
05Ø	C				END							
06	C											
07	C											
08	C											

Note that an ELSE statement is optional when using an IF. Without it, control would pass to the END statement if the condition were not met.

Thus the IFxx operation allows a group of calculations to be performed if the relationship specified by xx (GT, LT, EQ, NE, LE, GE) exists between Factor 1 and Factor 2. If the relationship between Factor 1 and Factor 2 does not exist, then control passes to either (1) the ELSE statement, if one exists, or (2) the END statement, if no ELSE is specified.

An END statement is required to close an IFxx group. If an IFxx statement is followed by an ELSE, *one* END statement is added *after* the ELSE; if there is no ELSE, the END follows the IFxx specifications.

Key Terms

Called module
Calling module
DO ... group
External subroutine
GO TO-less programming
IF-THEN-ELSE structure
Internal subroutine
Module
Pseudocode
Structured programming
Subroutine
Top-down approach

Self-Evaluating Quiz

1. ________, sometimes called GO TO-less programming, is one method designed to standardize and improve programs so that they are easier to write.
2. The technique referred to in Question 1 segments each program into distinct blocks called ________ .
3. (T or F) Structured programming enables one program to be written and debugged by a team of programmers.
4. To evaluate a structured program, a team of programmers can desk check the results of a series of modules. This is known as a(n) ________ .
5. To enable each module in a structured program to function as a standalone entity, branches or ________ instructions are to be avoided.
6. (T or F) Structured programming frequently uses an initial read in the main module.
7. Programming in which the main module is coded first followed by subordinate modules is referred to as the ________ approach.
8. Flowcharts are no longer completely standardized tools because ________ in programming have necessitated changes in the traditional format of a flowchart.
9. The tool specifically designed to depict the logic flow in a structured program is called ________ .
10. Two logical control procedures used in pseudocode are called ________ and ________ .
11. The last statement in either logical control procedure in Question 1Ø is a(n) ________ statement.
12. A ________ is a module to be performed from a specific point in a program.
13. The two types of subroutines that can be coded in RPG are called ________ and ________ .
14. A(n) ________ subroutine is one that is part of the user program.

15. A(n) ________ subroutine is one that is independent of the user program but is called in as needed from a library.
16. A sequence check routine used by several RPG programs would be coded as a(n) ________ subroutine.
17. A subroutine that begins with a BEGSR operation and ends with an ENDSR operation is called a(n) ________ subroutine.
18. To execute an internal subroutine from anywhere in the program, code ________ .
19. After an internal subroutine is executed, control returns to ________ .
20. The EXIT statement is used to execute a(n) ________ .
21. To use a field generated with an external subroutine, use the ________ operation.
22. To use a field defined within the user program in an external subroutine, use the ________ operation.
23. One main advantage of RPG III is that it enables the programmer to ________ .
24. RPG III uses ________ to execute a series of instructions a fixed number of times.
25. X DOWGT Y means ________ .

Solutions

1. Structured programming
2. modules
3. T
4. structured walkthrough
5. GO TO
6. T
7. top-down
8. structured techniques
9. pseudocode
10. DO . . . WHILE
    PERFORM . . . UNTIL
11. END
12. subroutine
13. internal subroutines
    external subroutines
14. internal
15. external
16. external
17. internal
18. EXSR (subroutine name)
19. the statement following the EXSR
20. external subroutine
21. ULABL (result field name)
22. RLABL (result field name)
23. efficiently code structured programming routines
24. DO groups
25. execute the following group of instructions while X is greater than Y

Review Questions

1. Indicate the main advantages and disadvantages of structured programming.
2. How is structured programming performed in RPG II and RPG III?
3. Indicate the differences between pseudocode and flowcharts.
4. Explain how the DO . . . group is used in RPG III.
5. Explain how internal and external subroutines are used in RPG.

Debugging Exercise

The problem definition for this exercise is shown in Figure 11.15. The coding sheets in Figure 11.16 contain syntax errors. The listing in Figure 11.17 includes the diagnostics produced by running the program as coded. The syntax corrections are circled on the computer listing shown in Figure 11.18. There is, however, a logic error in the program. The second line of the subheading (DESCRIPTION, METHOD, and so forth) is missing on the second page. Your assignment is to desk check the program carefully, find the logic error, and make the necessary corrections.

Figure 11.15 Problem definition for the Debugging Exercise.

Systems Flowchart

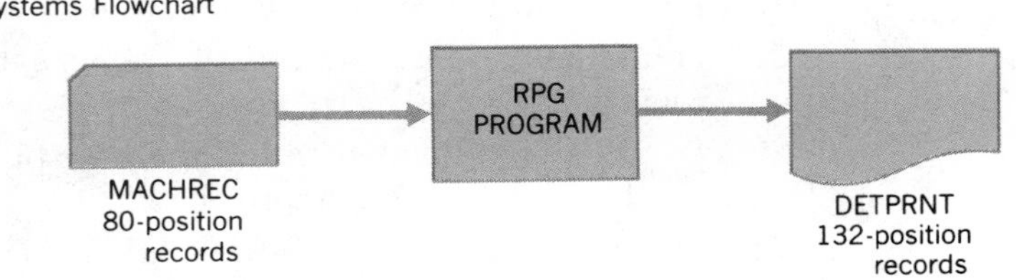

MACHREC Record Layout

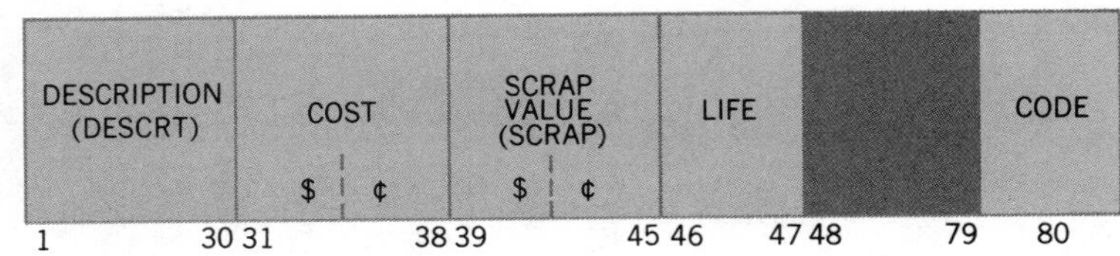

DETPRNT Printer Spacing Chart

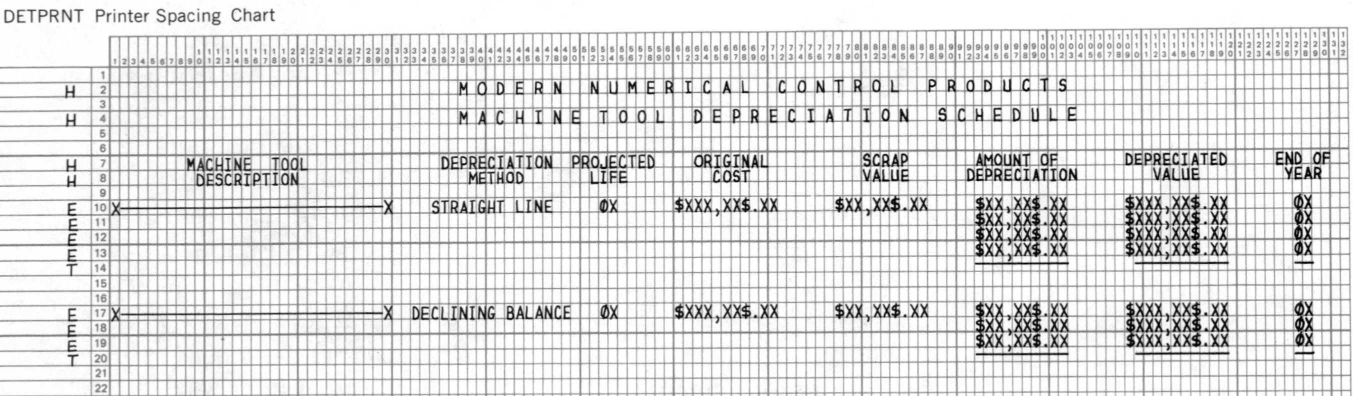

RPG CONTROL AND FILE DESCRIPTION SPECIFICATIONS

Program: DEPRECIATION TABLE
Programmer: N. JOHNKE   Date: 2/5/--
Keying Instruction — Graphic: Ø 1 2 — Key: ZERO ONE TWO
Card Electro Number
Page Ø1 of 8   Program Identification (75–80): SSS11

Control Specifications

For the valid entries for a system, refer to the RPG reference manual for that system.

```
01ØH
```

File Description Specifications

For the valid entries for a system, refer to the RPG reference manual for that system.

```
02ØF*******************************************************************
03ØF*   THIS PROGRAM GENERATES A DEPRECIATION TABLE,USING ONE OF TWO    *
04ØF* METHODS (STRAIGHT LINE OR DOUBLE DECLINING BALANCE),TO CALCULATE  *
05ØF* THE DEPRECIATION USED TO WRITE OFF COSTS OVER THE USEFUL LIFE     *
06ØF* OF THE ASSET.                                                     *
07ØF*******************************************************************
08ØF*
09ØFMACHREC IP  F      8Ø            READØ1 SYSIPT
10ØFDETPRNT O   F     132            PRINTERSYSLST
11ØF*
   F
```

RPG INPUT SPECIFICATIONS

Program: DEPRECIATION TABLE
Programmer: N. JOHNKE   Date: 2/5/--
Keying Instruction — Graphic: Ø 1 2 — Key: ZERO ONE TWO
Card Electro Number
Page Ø2 of 8   Program Identification (75–80): SSS11

```
01ØI*************** ************ INPUT RECORD **************************
02ØI*
03ØIMACHREC NS  Ø1
04ØI                                           1  3Ø DESCRT
05ØI                                          31  382COST
06ØI                                          39  452SCRAP
07ØI                                          46  47ØLIFE
08ØI                                          8Ø  8Ø CODE
09 I
10 I
```

Figure 11.16
Coding sheets for the Debugging Exercise.
(Continued on next page.)

RPG CALCULATION SPECIFICATIONS

Program: DEPRECIATION TABLE — Programmer: N. JOHNKE — Date: 2/5/--

Keying Instruction: Graphic Φ 1 2 — Key ZERO ONE TWO

Page Φ3 of 8 — Program Identification SSS11

```
01ΦC*
02ΦC************************** CALCULATIONS ***************************
03ΦC*
04ΦC                     Z-ADDΦ         YEAR    2Φ
05ΦC                     Z-ADDCOST      DEPVAL  82
06ΦC           CODE      COMP S                    2Φ2Φ1Φ
07ΦC*
08ΦC**************************************************************
09ΦC* CALCULATE ANNUAL DEPRECIATION - STRAIGHT LINE METHOD *
10ΦC**************************************************************
11ΦC*
12ΦC   1Φ      COST      SUB  SCRAP     TOTDEP  82
13ΦC   1Φ      TOTDEP    DIV  LIFE      ANDEP   72H
14ΦC*
15ΦC**************************************************************
16ΦC* CALCULATE ANNUAL DEPRECIATION - DOUBLE                      *
17ΦC* DECLINING BALANCE METHOD                                    *
18ΦC**************************************************************
19ΦC*
20ΦC   2Φ      1.ΦΦ      DIV  LIFE      DRX     22H
21ΦC   2Φ      DRX       MULT 2         DRATE   22H
22ΦC*
23ΦC**************************************************************
24ΦC* LOOP TO PRINT THE ANNUAL DEPRECIATION. GROUP INDICA-        *
25ΦC* TION ACCOMPLISHED BY Φ1 INDICATOR. WHEN OVERFLOW            *
```

Figure 11.16
(continued)

RPG CALCULATION SPECIFICATIONS

Program: DEPRECIATION TABLE
Programmer: N. JOHNKE Date: 2/5/--
Keying Instruction — Graphic: Ø 1 2; Key: ZERO ONE TWO
Card Electro Number
Page Ø4 of 8 Program Identification SSS11

```
Ø1ØC* OCCURS,INDICATORS Ø1 AND 5Ø ARE SET ON,HEADINGS ARE      *
Ø2ØC* FETCHED AND INDICATORS Ø1,5Ø,AND OF ARE THEN SET OFF.*
Ø3ØC* WHEN LOOP IS COMPLETED Ø1 IS RESET TO ON TO CONDITION*
Ø4ØC* THE TOTAL-TIME OUTPUT AND SPACING.                    *
Ø5ØC********************************************************
Ø6ØC*
Ø7ØC           DOLIFE    TAG
Ø8ØC   1Ø                EXSR STLINE
Ø9ØC   2Ø                EXSR DBLDCL
1ØØC   OF                SETON                     5Ø  Ø1
11ØC                     EXCPT
12ØC   5Ø                SETOF                     5Ø  OF
13ØC                     SETOF                     Ø1
15ØC  N15                GOTO DOLIFE
16ØC                     SETON                     Ø1
17ØC*
18ØC********************************************************
19ØC* SUBROUTINE TO CALCULATE DEPRECIATION BY                *
2ØØC* STRAIGHT LINE METHOD                                   *
21ØC********************************************************
22ØC*
23ØCSR         STLINE    BEGSR
24ØCSR         YEAR      ADD  1         YEAR
25ØCSR         YEAR      COMP LIFE                 15  15
   C
```

RPG CALCULATION SPECIFICATIONS

Program	DEPRECIATION TABLE	Keying Instruction	Graphic	Ø 1 2	Card Electro Number	Page Ø5 of 8	Program Identification	SSS11
Programmer	N. JOHNKE Date 2/5/--		Key	ZERO ONE TWO				

Line	Form Type	Control Level (L0–L9, LR, SR, AN/OR)	Indicators	Factor 1	Operation	Factor 2	Result Field Name	Length	Decimal Positions	Half Adjust (H)	High (1>2, Plus, Lookup)	Low (1<2, Minus, Lookup)	Equal (1=2, Zero, Lookup)	Comments
01	ØC		15	DEPVAL	SUB	SCRAP	ANLDEP							
02	ØC	SR		DEPVAL	SUB	ANLDEP	DEPVAL							
03	ØC	SR			ENDSR									
04	ØC	*												
05	ØC	**												
06	ØC	* SUBROUTINE TO CALCULATE DEPRECIATION BY *												
07	ØC	* DOUBLE DECLINING BALANCE METHOD *												
08	ØC	**												
09	ØC	*												
10	ØC	SR		DBLDCL	BEGSR									
11	ØC	SR		YEAR	ADD	1	YEAR							
12	ØC	SR		DEPVAL	MULT	DRATE	ANLDEP			H				
13	ØC	SR		DEPVAL	SUB	ANLDEP	DEPVAL							
14	ØC	SR		DEPVAL	COMP	SCRAP						15		
15	ØC	SR	15	DEPVAL	SUB	SCRAP	DEPVAL							
16	ØC	SR	15		Z-ADD	DEPVAL	ANLDEP							
17	ØC	SR	15	DEPVAL	SUB	ANLDEP	DEPVAL							
18	ØC	SR			ENDSR									
19	ØC	*												
20	C													

Figure 11.16
(continued)

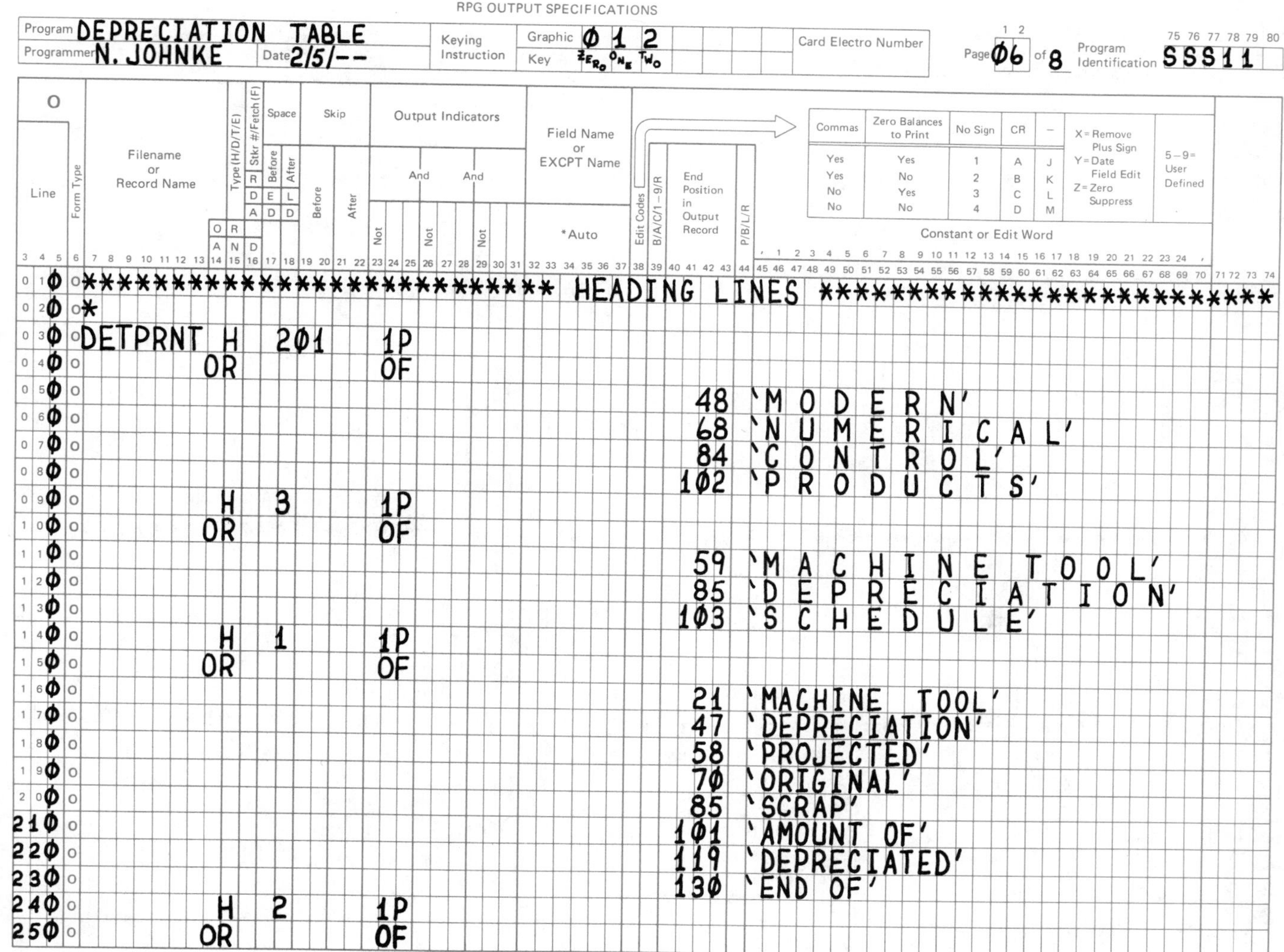
RPG OUTPUT SPECIFICATIONS

Program DEPRECIATION TABLE
Programmer N. JOHNKE Date 2/5/--
Keying Instruction — Graphic: Ø 1 2; Key: ZERO ONE TWO
Card Electro Number
Page Ø6 of 8
Program Identification SSS11

Line	Form Type	Filename or Record Name	Type (H/D/T/E)	Space / Skip	Output Indicators	Field Name or EXCPT Name	End Position in Output Record	Constant or Edit Word
Ø1Ø	O	******************************* HEADING LINES ************************						
Ø2Ø	O	*						
Ø3Ø	O	DETPRNT	H	2Ø1	1P			
Ø4Ø	O	OR			OF			
Ø5Ø	O						48	'M O D E R N'
Ø6Ø	O						68	'N U M E R I C A L'
Ø7Ø	O						84	'C O N T R O L'
Ø8Ø	O						1Ø2	'P R O D U C T S'
Ø9Ø	O		H	3	1P			
1ØØ	O	OR			OF			
11Ø	O						59	'M A C H I N E T O O L'
12Ø	O						85	'D E P R E C I A T I O N'
13Ø	O						1Ø3	'S C H E D U L E'
14Ø	O		H	1	1P			
15Ø	O	OR			OF			
16Ø	O						21	'MACHINE TOOL'
17Ø	O						47	'DEPRECIATION'
18Ø	O						58	'PROJECTED'
19Ø	O						7Ø	'ORIGINAL'
2ØØ	O						85	'SCRAP'
21Ø	O						1Ø1	'AMOUNT OF'
22Ø	O						119	'DEPRECIATED'
23Ø	O						13Ø	'END OF'
24Ø	O		H	2	1P			
25Ø	O	OR			OF			

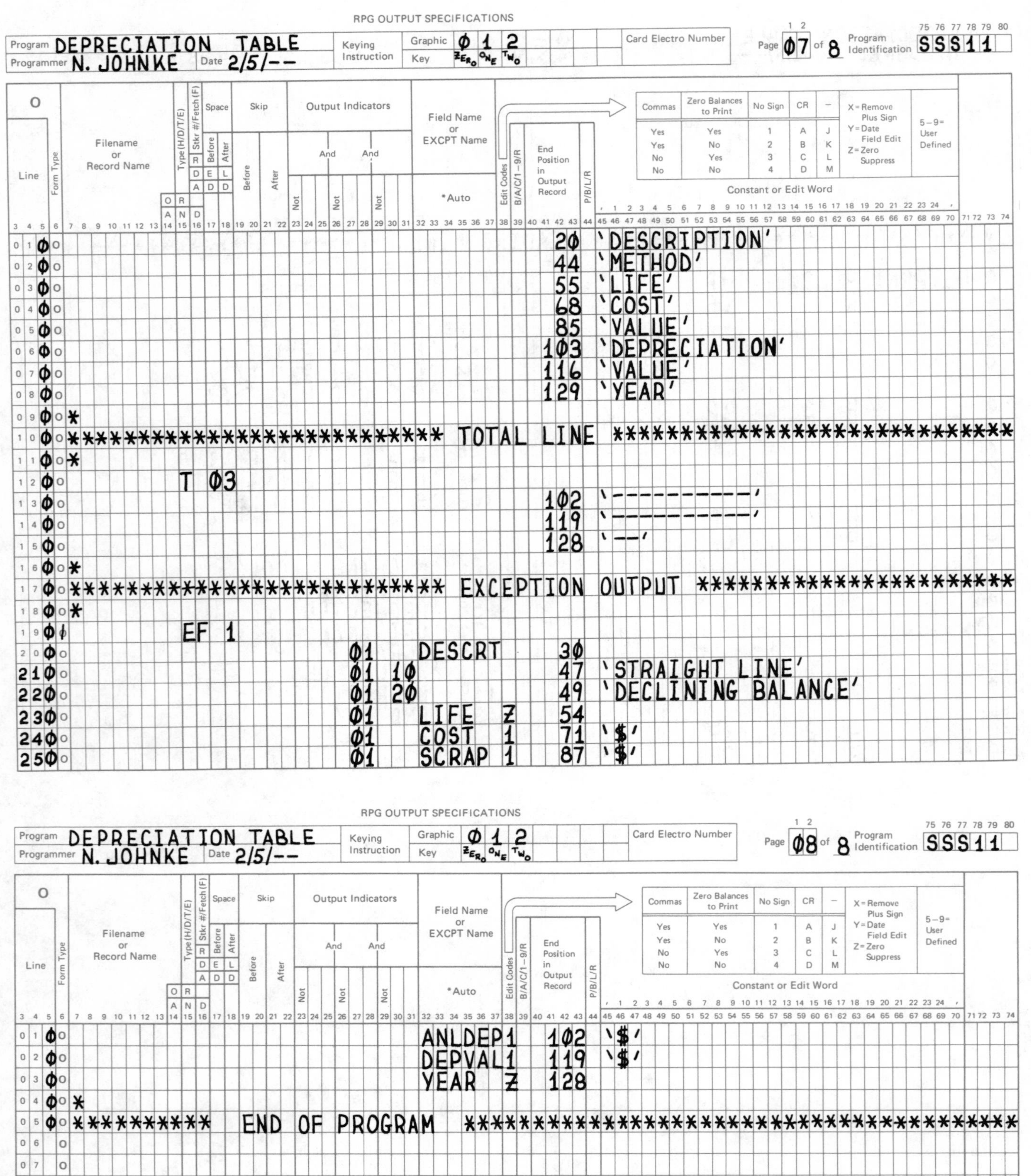

RPG OUTPUT SPECIFICATIONS

Program: DEPRECIATION TABLE — Programmer: N. JOHNKE — Date: 2/5/-- — Graphic: Ø 1 2 — Key: ZERO ONE TWO — Page Ø7 of 8 — Program Identification: SSS11

```
01Ø O                                      2Ø  'DESCRIPTION'
02Ø O                                      44  'METHOD'
03Ø O                                      55  'LIFE'
04Ø O                                      68  'COST'
05Ø O                                      85  'VALUE'
06Ø O                                     1Ø3  'DEPRECIATION'
07Ø O                                     116  'VALUE'
08Ø O                                     129  'YEAR'
09Ø O*
10Ø O*************************** TOTAL LINE ***************************
11Ø O*
12Ø O        T Ø3
13Ø O                                     1Ø2  '----------'
14Ø O                                     119  '-----------'
15Ø O                                     128  '--'
16Ø O*
17Ø O*************************** EXCEPTION OUTPUT ************************
18Ø O*
19Ø O        EF 1
20Ø O                  Ø1    DESCRT        3Ø
21Ø O                  Ø1 1Ø               47  'STRAIGHT LINE'
22Ø O                  Ø1 2Ø               49  'DECLINING BALANCE'
23Ø O                  Ø1    LIFE  Z       54
24Ø O                  Ø1    COST  1       71  '$'
25Ø O                  Ø1    SCRAP 1       87  '$'
```

RPG OUTPUT SPECIFICATIONS

Program: DEPRECIATION TABLE — Programmer: N. JOHNKE — Date: 2/5/-- — Graphic: Ø 1 2 — Key: ZERO ONE TWO — Page Ø8 of 8 — Program Identification: SSS11

```
01Ø O                        ANLDEP1      1Ø2  '$'
02Ø O                        DEPVAL1      119  '$'
03Ø O                        YEAR  Z      128
04Ø O*
05Ø O**********   END OF PROGRAM   *****************************************
06  O
07  O
```

Figure 11.16
(continued)

Figure 11.17
Program listing with syntax errors for the Debugging Exercise.
(Continued on next page.)

```
01-020 F*********************************************************************SSS11
01-030 F*  THIS PROGRAM GENERATES A DEPRECIATION TABLE,USING ONE OF TWO       *SSS11
01-040 F* METHODS (STRAIGHT LINE OR DOUBLE DECLINING BALANCE),TO CALCULATE   *SSS11
01-050 F* THE DEPRECIATION USED TO WRITE OFF COSTS OVER THE USEFUL LIFE      *SSS11
01-060 F* OF THE ASSET.                                                      *SSS11
01-070 F*********************************************************************SSS11
01-080 F*                                                                     SSS11
01-090 FMACHREC IP  F      80            READ01 SYSIPT                        SSS11
01-100 FDETPRNT O   F     132            PRINTERSYSLST                        SSS11
01-110 F*                                                                     SSS11
02-010 I*************************** INPUT RECORD ****************************SSS11
02-020 I*                                                                     SSS11
02-030 IMACHREC NS  01                                                        SSS11
02-040 I                                        1  30 DESCRT                  SSS11
02-050 I                                       31  382COST                    SSS11
02-060 I                                       39  452SCRAP                   SSS11
02-070 I                                       46  470LIFE                    SSS11
02-080 I                                       80  80 CODE                    SSS11
03-010 C*                                                                     SSS11
03-020 C*************************** CALCULATIONS ****************************SSS11
03-030 C*                                                                     SSS11
03-040 C                           Z-ADD0         YEAR    20                  SSS11
03-050 C                           Z-ADDCOST      DEPVAL  82                  SSS11
03-060 C                 CODE      COMP S                     202010          SSS11
03-070 C*                                                                     SSS11
03-080 C********************************************************              SSS11
03-090 C* CALCULATE ANNUAL DEPRECIATION - STRAIGHT LINE METHOD *              SSS11
03-100 C********************************************************              SSS11
03-110 C*                                                                     SSS11
03-120 C   10            COST      SUB  SCRAP     TOTDEP  82                  SSS11
03-130 C   10            TOTDEP    DIV  LIFE      ANDEP   72H                 SSS11
03-140 C*                                                                     SSS11
03-150 C********************************************************              SSS11
03-160 C* CALCULATE ANNUAL DEPRECIATION RATE - DOUBLE          *              SSS11
03-170 C* DECLINING BALANCE METHOD                             *              SSS11
03-180 C********************************************************              SSS11
03-190 C*                                                                     SSS11
03-200 C   20            1.00      DIV  LIFE      DRX     22H                 SSS11
03-210 C   20            DRX       MULT 2         DRATE   22H                 SSS11
03-220 C*                                                                     SSS11
03-230 C********************************************************              SSS11
03-240 C* LOOP TO PRINT THE ANNUAL DEPRECIATION. GROUP INDICA- *              SSS11
03-250 C* TION ACCOMPLISHED BY 01 INDICATOR. WHEN OVERFLOW     *              SSS11
04-010 C* OCCURS,INDICATORS 01 AND 50 ARE SET ON,HEADINGS ARE  *              SSS11
04-020 C* FETCHED AND INDICATORS 01,50,AND OF ARE THEN SET OFF.*              SSS11
04-030 C* WHEN LOOP IS COMPLETED 01 IS RESET TO ON TO CONDITION*              SSS11
04-040 C* THE TOTAL-TIME OUTPUT AND SPACING.                   *              SSS11
04-050 C********************************************************              SSS11
04-060 C*                                                                     SSS11
04-070 C                 DOLIFE    TAG                                        SSS11
04-080 C   10                      EXSR STLINE                                SSS11
04-090 C   20                      EXSR DBLDCL                                SSS11
04-100 C   OF                      SETON                      50  01          SSS11
                                                                                        MSG  353
04-110 C                           EXCPT                                      SSS11
04-120 C   50                      SETOF                      50  OF          SSS11
04-130 C                           SETOF                      01              SSS11
04-150 C   N15                     GOTO DOLIFE                                SSS11
04-160 C                           SETON                      01              SSS11
04-170 C*                                                                     SSS11
04-180 C********************************************************              SSS11
04-190 C* SUBROUTINE TO CALCULATE DEPRECIATION BY              *              SSS11
04-200 C* STRAIGHT LINE METHOD                                 *              SSS11
04-210 C********************************************************              SSS11
04-220 C*                                                                     SSS11
04-230 CSR               STLINE    BEGSR                                      SSS11
04-240 CSR               YEAR      ADD  1         YEAR                        SSS11
04-250 CSR               YEAR      COMP LIFE                  15  15          SSS11
05-010 C   15            DEPVAL    SUB  SCRAP     ANLDEP                      SSS11
         $                                                                              MSG  136
05-020 CSR               DEPVAL    SUB  ANLDEP    DEPVAL                      SSS11
05-030 CSR                         ENDSR                                      SSS11
05-040 C*                                                                     SSS11
05-050 C********************************************************              SSS11
05-060 C* SUBROUTINE TO CALCULATE DEPRECIATION BY              *              SSS11
05-070 C* DOUBLE DECLINING BALANCE METHOD                      *              SSS11
05-080 C********************************************************              SSS11
05-090 C*                                                                     SSS11
05-100 CSR               DBLDCL    BEGSR                                      SSS11
05-110 CSR               YEAR      ADD  1         YEAR                        SSS11
05-120 CSR               DEPVAL    MULT DRATE     ANLDEP    H                 SSS11
05-130 CSR               DEPVAL    SUB  ANLDEP    DEPVAL                      SSS11
05-140 CSR               DEPVAL    COMP SCRAP                     15          SSS11
05-150 CSR 15            DEPVAL    SUB  SCRAP     DEPVAL                      SSS11
05-160 CSR 15                      Z-ADDDEPVAL    ANLDEP                      SSS11
05-170 CSR 15            DEPVAL    SUB  ANLDEP    DEPVAL                      SSS11
05-180 CSR                         ENDSR                                      SSS11
05-190 C*                                                                     SSS11
06-010 O************************** HEADING LINES ***************************SSS11
06-020 O*                                                                     SSS11
06-030 ODETPRNT H  201   1P                                                   SSS11
06-040 O        OR       OF                                                   SSS11
                         $                                                              MSG  202
06-050 O                                  48 'M O D E R N'                    SSS11
06-060 O                                  68 'N U M E R I C A L'              SSS11
06-070 O                                  84 'C O N T R O L'                  SSS11
06-080 O                                 102 'P R O D U C T S'                SSS11
06-090 O          H  3   1P                                                   SSS11
06-100 O        OR       OF                                                   SSS11
```

Figure 11.17 *(continued)*

```
                                $                                                                    MSG  202
0048      06-110  O                                   59 'M A C H I N E  T O O L'       SSS11
0049      06-120  O                                   85 'D E P R E C I A T I O N'      SSS11
0050      06-130  O                                  103 'S C H E D U L E'              SSS11
0051      06-140  O         H  1        1P                                              SSS11
0052      06-150  O        OR           OF                                              SSS11
                                $                                                                    MSG  202
0053      06-160  O                                   21 'MACHINE  TOOL'                SSS11
0054      06-170  O                                   47 'DEPRECIATION'                 SSS11
0055      06-180  O                                   58 'PROJECTED'                    SSS11
0056      06-190  O                                   70 'ORIGINAL'                     SSS11
0057      06-200  O                                   85 'SCRAP'                        SSS11
0058      06-210  O                                  101 'AMOUNT OF'                    SSS11
0059      06-220  O                                  119 'DEPRECIATED'                  SSS11
0060      06-230  O                                  130 'END OF'                       SSS11
0061      06-240  O         H  2        1P                                              SSS11
0062      06-250  O        OR           OF                                              SSS11
                                $                                                                    MSG  202
0063      07-010  O                                   20 'DESCRIPTION'                  SSS11
0064      07-020  O                                   44 'METHOD'                       SSS11
0065      07-030  O                                   55 'LIFE'                         SSS11
0066      07-040  O                                   68 'COST'                         SSS11
0067      07-050  O                                   85 'VALUE'                        SSS11
0068      07-060  O                                  103 'DEPRECIATION'                 SSS11
0069      07-070  O                                  116 'VALUE'                        SSS11
0070      07-080  O                                  129 'YEAR'                         SSS11
          07-090  O*                                                                    SSS11
          07-100  O**************************** TOTAL LINE *****************************SSS11
          07-110  O*                                                                    SSS11
0071      07-120  O         T 03                                                        SSS11
0072      07-130  O                                  102 '----------'                   SSS11
0073      07-140  O                                  119 '----------'                   SSS11
0074      07-150  O                                  128 '--'                           SSS11
          07-160  O*                                                                    SSS11
          07-170  O**************************** EXCEPTION OUTPUT ***********************SSS11
          07-180  O*                                                                    SSS11
0075      07-190  O         EF 1                                                        SSS11
                  $                                                                                  MSG  186
0076      07-200  O                       01   DESCRT     30                            SSS11
0077      07-210  O                       01 10           47 'STRAIGHT LINE'            SSS11
0078      07-220  O                       01 20           49 'DECLINING BALANCE'        SSS11
0079      07-230  O                       01   LIFE  Z    54                            SSS11
0080      07-240  O                       01   COST  1    71 '$'                        SSS11
0081      07-250  O                       01   SCRAP 1    87 '$'                        SSS11
0082      08-010  O                            ANLDEP1   102 '$'                        SSS11
0083      08-020  O                            DEPVAL1   119 '$'                        SSS11
0084      08-030  O                            YEAR  Z   128                            SSS11
          08-040  O*                                                                    SSS11
          08-050  O**********  END OF PROGRAM  *****************************************SSS11
```

```
       E N D  O F  S O U R C E

       C O M P I L E R   D I A G N O S T I C S   S U M M A R Y


ILN136    NON-SR (SUBROUTINE) SPEC FOLLOWS AN SR SPEC. ASSUME SR IN POSITIONS 7-8.

            0028     05-010      SUB

ILN186    SPEC TYPE IS NOT O. SPEC IS DROPPED.

          C 0075     07-190

ILN202    INDICATOR IS INVALID OR UNDEFINED. DROP ENTRY.

            0041     06-040
            0047     06-100
            0052     06-150
            0062     06-250

ILN353    OVERFLOW INDICATOR USED INCORRECTLY. DROP INDICATOR.

            0019     04-100      SETON
            0021     04-120      SETOF

ILN398    FIELD NAME UNDEFINED. SPEC IS DROPPED.

          D 0011     03-060      S
          D 0028     05-010      ANLDEP
          D 0029     05-020      ANLDEP
          D 0033     05-120      ANLDEP
          D 0034     05-130      ANLDEP
          D 0037     05-160      ANLDEP
          D 0038     05-170      ANLDEP
          C 0082     08-010      ANLDEP

ILN399    STRUCTURE, SUBFIELD, OR FIELD NAME UNREFERENCED. WARNING.

ILN479    EXCPT OPERATION USED BUT NO EXCEPTION LINES IN PROGRAM. SPEC IS DROPPED.

          C 0020     04-110
```

Figure 11.18
Program listing with a logic error for the Debugging Exercise.
(Continued on next page.)

```
F***********************************************************************SSS11
F*  THIS PROGRAM GENERATES A DEPRECIATION TABLE,USING ONE OF TWO       *SSS11
F* METHODS (STRAIGHT LINE OR DOUBLE DECLINING BALANCE),TO CALCULATE   *SSS11
F* THE DEPRECIATION USED TO WRITE OFF COSTS OVER THE USEFUL LIFE       *SSS11
F* OF THE ASSET.                                                       *SSS11
F***********************************************************************SSS11
F*                                                                      SSS11
FMACHREC IP  F      80                READ01 SYSIPT                     SSS11
FDETPRNT O   F     132      OF        PRINTERSYSLST                     SSS11
F*                                                                      SSS11
I*************************** INPUT RECORD *****************************SSS11
I*                                                                      SSS11
IMACHREC NS  01                                                         SSS11
I                                              1  30 DESCRT             SSS11
I                                             31  382COST               SSS11
I                                             39  452SCRAP              SSS11
I                                             46  470LIFE               SSS11
I                                             80  80 CODE               SSS11
C*                                                                      SSS11
C*************************** CALCULATIONS *****************************SSS11
C*                                                                      SSS11
C                          Z-ADD0         YEAR    20                    SSS11
C                          Z-ADDCOST      DEPVAL  82                    SSS11
C           CODE           COMP 'S'                 202010              SSS11
C*                                                                      SSS11
C*************************************************************          SSS11
C* CALCULATE ANNUAL DEPRECIATION - STRAIGHT LINE METHOD *               SSS11
C*************************************************************          SSS11
C*                                                                      SSS11
C   10      COST           SUB  SCRAP     TOTDEP  82                    SSS11
C   10      TOTDEP         DIV  LIFE      ANLDEP  72H                   SSS11
C*                                                                      SSS11
C*************************************************************          SSS11
C* CALCULATE ANNUAL DEPRECIATION RATE - DOUBLE               *          SSS11
C* DECLINING BALANCE METHOD                                  *          SSS11
C*************************************************************          SSS11
C*                                                                      SSS11
C   20      1.00           DIV  LIFE      DRX     22H                   SSS11
C   20      DRX            MULT 2         DRATE   22H                   SSS11
C*                                                                      SSS11
C*************************************************************          SSS11
C* LOOP TO PRINT THE ANNUAL DEPRECIATION. GROUP INDICA-      *          SSS11
C* TION ACCOMPLISHED BY 01 INDICATOR. WHEN OVERFLOW          *          SSS11
C* OCCURS,INDICATORS 01 AND 50 ARE SET ON,HEADINGS ARE       *          SSS11
C* FETCHED AND INDICATORS 01,50,AND OF ARE THEN SET OFF.     *          SSS11
C* WHEN LOOP IS COMPLETED 01 IS RESET TO ON TO CONDITION     *          SSS11
C* THE TOTAL-TIME OUTPUT AND SPACING.                        *          SSS11
C*************************************************************          SSS11
C*                                                                      SSS11
C           DOLIFE         TAG                                          SSS11
C   10                     EXSR STLINE                                  SSS11
C   20                     EXSR DBLDCL                                  SSS11
C   OF                     SETON                     50  01             SSS11
C                          EXCPT                                        SSS11
C   50                     SETOF                     50  OF             SSS11
C                          SETOF                     01                 SSS11
C  N15                     GOTO DOLIFE                                  SSS11
C                          SETON                     01                 SSS11
C*                                                                      SSS11
C*************************************************************          SSS11
C* SUBROUTINE TO CALCULATE DEPRECIATION BY                   *          SSS11
C* STRAIGHT LINE METHOD                                      *          SSS11
C*************************************************************          SSS11
C*                                                                      SSS11
CSR         STLINE         BEGSR                                        SSS11
CSR         YEAR           ADD  1         YEAR                          SSS11
CSR         YEAR           COMP LIFE                 15  15             SSS11
CSR 15      DEPVAL         SUB  SCRAP     ANLDEP                        SSS11
CSR         DEPVAL         SUB  ANLDEP    DEPVAL                        SSS11
CSR                        ENDSR                                        SSS11
C*                                                                      SSS11
C*************************************************************          SSS11
C* SUBROUTINE TO CALCULATE DEPRECIATION BY                   *          SSS11
C* DOUBLE DECLINING BALANCE METHOD                           *          SSS11
C*************************************************************          SSS11
C*                                                                      SSS11
CSR         DBLDCL         BEGSR                                        SSS11
CSR         YEAR           ADD  1         YEAR                          SSS11
CSR         DEPVAL         MULT DRATE     ANLDEP    H                   SSS11
CSR         DEPVAL         SUB  ANLDEP    DEPVAL                        SSS11
CSR         DEPVAL         COMP SCRAP                    15             SSS11
CSR 15      DEPVAL         SUB  SCRAP     DEPVAL                        SSS11
CSR 15                     Z-ADDDEPVAL    ANLDEP                        SSS11
CSR 15      DEPVAL         SUB  ANLDEP    DEPVAL                        SSS11
CSR                        ENDSR                                        SSS11
C*                                                                      SSS11
O*************************** HEADING LINES ****************************SSS11
O*                                                                      SSS11
ODETPRNT H  201   1P                                                    SSS11
O        OR       OF                                                    SSS11
O                                     48 'M O D E R N'                  SSS11
O                                     68 'N U M E R I C A L'            SSS11
O                                     84 'C O N T R O L'                SSS11
O                                    102 'P R O D U C T S'              SSS11
O        H  3     1P                                                    SSS11
O        OR       OF                                                    SSS11
O                                     59 'M A C H I N E   T O O L'      SSS11
O                                     85 'D E P R E C I A T I O N'      SSS11
O                                    103 'S C H E D U L E'              SSS11
O        H  1     1P                                                    SSS11
```

Annotations: OF — Required; 'S' — Quotes needed; CSR — Needed

```
06-150 O        OR        OF                                    SSS11
06-160 O                                   21 'MACHINE  TOOL'    SSS11
06-170 O                                   47 'DEPRECIATION'     SSS11
06-180 O                                   58 'PROJECTED'        SSS11
06-190 O                                   70 'ORIGINAL'         SSS11
06-200 O                                   85 'SCRAP'            SSS11
06-210 O                                  101 'AMOUNT OF'        SSS11
06-220 O                                  119 'DEPRECIATED'      SSS11
06-230 O                                  130 'END OF'           SSS11
06-240 O        H  2     1P                                      SSS11
06-250 O                                   20 'DESCRIPTION'      SSS11
07-010 O                                   44 'METHOD'           SSS11
07-020 O                                   55 'LIFE'             SSS11
07-030 O                                   68 'COST'             SSS11
07-040 O                                   85 'VALUE'            SSS11
07-050 O                                  103 'DEPRECIATION'     SSS11
07-060 O                                  116 'VALUE'            SSS11
07-070 O                                  129 'YEAR'             SSS11
07-080 O*                                                        SSS11
07-090 O************************** TOTAL LINE *******************SSS11
07-100 O*                                                        SSS11
07-110 O        T 03                                             SSS11
07-120 O                                  102 '----------'       SSS11
07-130 O                                  119 '----------'       SSS11
07-140 O                                  128 '--'               SSS11
07-150 O*                                                        SSS11
07-160 O************************** EXCEPTION OUTPUT *************SSS11
07-170 O*                                                        SSS11
07-180 O        EF 1                                             SSS11
07-190 O                  01    DESCRT    30                     SSS11
07-200 O                  01 10           47 'STRAIGHT LINE'     SSS11
07-210 O                  01 20           49 'DECLINING BALANCE' SSS11
07-220 O                  01    LIFE  Z   54                     SSS11
07-230 O                  01    COST  1   71 '$'                 SSS11
07-240 O                  01    SCRAP 1   87 '$'                 SSS11
07-250 O                        ANLDEP1  102 '$'                 SSS11
08-010 O                        DEPVAL1  119 '$'                 SSS11
08-020 O                        YEAR  Z  128                     SSS11
08-030 O*                                                        SSS11
08-040 O**********  END OF PROGRAM  *****************************SSS11
```

E N D   O F   S O U R C E

M O D E R N   N U M E R I C A L   C O N T R O L   P R O D U C T S

M A C H I N E   T O O L   D E P R E C I A T I O N   S C H E D U L E

MACHINE TOOL DESCRIPTION	DEPRECIATION METHOD	PROJECTED LIFE	ORIGINAL COST	SCRAP VALUE	AMOUNT OF DEPRECIATION	DEPRECIATED VALUE	END OF YEAR
G & L TURRET LATHE	STRAIGHT LINE	17	$58,000.00	$12,000.00	$2,705.88	$55,294.12	1
					$2,705.88	$52,588.24	2
					$2,705.88	$49,882.36	3
					$2,705.88	$47,176.48	4
					$2,705.88	$44,470.60	5
					$2,705.88	$41,764.72	6
					$2,705.88	$39,058.84	7
					$2,705.88	$36,352.96	8
					$2,705.88	$33,647.08	9
					$2,705.88	$30,941.20	10
					$2,705.88	$28,235.32	11
					$2,705.88	$25,529.44	12
					$2,705.88	$22,823.56	13
					$2,705.88	$20,117.68	14
					$2,705.88	$17,411.80	15
					$2,705.88	$14,705.92	16
					$2,705.92	$12,000.00	17
					----------	----------	--
CINCINNATI NC SKIN MILL	DECLINING BALANCE	25	$650,000.00	$50,000.00	$52,000.00	$598,000.00	1
					$47,840.00	$550,160.00	2
					$44,012.80	$506,147.20	3
					$40,491.78	$465,655.42	4
					$37,252.43	$428,402.99	5
					$34,272.24	$394,130.75	6
					$31,530.46	$362,600.29	7
					$29,008.02	$333,592.27	8
					$26,687.38	$306,904.89	9
					$24,552.39	$282,352.50	10
					$22,588.20	$259,764.30	11
					$20,781.14	$238,983.16	12
					$19,118.65	$219,864.51	13
					$17,589.16	$202,275.35	14
					$16,182.03	$186,093.32	15
					$14,887.47	$171,205.85	16
					$13,696.47	$157,509.38	17
					$12,600.75	$144,908.63	18
					$11,592.69	$133,315.94	19
					$10,665.28	$122,650.66	20
					$9,812.05	$112,838.61	21
					$9,027.09	$103,811.52	22
					$8,304.92	$95,506.60	23
					$7,640.53	$87,866.07	24
					$7,029.29	$80,836.78	25
					$6,466.94	$74,369.84	26
					$5,949.59	$68,420.25	27
					$5,473.62	$62,946.63	28
					$5,035.73	$57,910.90	29

Figure 11.18
(continued)

```
                    M O D E R N   N U M E R I C A L   C O N T R O L   P R O D U C T S

                    M A C H I N E  T O O L   D E P R E C I A T I O N   S C H E D U L E

     MACHINE  TOOL                DEPRECIATION  PROJECTED    ORIGINAL         SCRAP       AMOUNT OF      DEPRECIATED    END OF
CINCINNATI NC SKIN MILL          DECLINING BALANCE  25     $650,000.00     $50,000.00     $4,632.87      $53,278.03       30
                                                                                            $984.21            $.00       31
                                                                                         ----------      ----------       --

MILWAUKEMATIC TOOL CHANGER       DECLINING BALANCE  15     $250,000.00     $30,000.00    $35,000.00     $215,000.00        1
                                                                                         $30,100.00     $184,900.00        2
                                                                                         $25,886.00     $159,014.00        3
                                                                                         $22,261.96     $136,752.04        4
                                                                                         $19,145.29     $117,606.75        5
                                                                                         $16,464.95     $101,141.80        6
                                                                                         $14,159.85      $86,981.95        7
                                                                                         $12,177.47      $74,804.48        8
                                                                                         $10,472.63      $64,331.85        9
                                                                                          $9,006.46      $55,325.39       10
                                                                                          $7,745.55      $47,579.84       11
                                                                                          $6,661.18      $40,918.66       12
                                                                                          $5,728.61      $35,190.05       13
                                                                                          $4,926.61      $30,263.44       14
                                                                                          $3,973.44            $.00       15
                                                                                         ----------      ----------       --

B & S AUTCMATIC SCREW MCH.         STRAIGHT LINE    14      $78,000.00     $17,000.00     $4,357.14      $73,642.86        1
                                                                                          $4,357.14      $69,285.72        2
                                                                                          $4,357.14      $64,928.58        3
                                                                                          $4,357.14      $60,571.44        4
                                                                                          $4,357.14      $56,214.30        5
                                                                                          $4,357.14      $51,857.16        6
                                                                                          $4,357.14      $47,500.02        7
                                                                                          $4,357.14      $43,142.88        8
                                                                                          $4,357.14      $38,785.74        9
                                                                                          $4,357.14      $34,428.60       10
                                                                                          $4,357.14      $30,071.46       11
                                                                                          $4,357.14      $25,714.32       12
                                                                                          $4,357.14      $21,357.18       13
                                                                                          $4,357.18      $17,000.00       14
                                                                                         ----------      ----------       --

K & T 5-AXIS NC HOR. MILLER      DECLINING BALANCE  16     $375,000.00     $42,000.00    $45,000.00     $330,000.00        1
                                                                                         $39,600.00     $290,400.00        2
                                                                                         $34,848.00     $255,552.00        3
                                                                                         $30,666.24     $224,885.76        4
                                                                                         $26,986.29     $197,899.47        5
                                                                                         $23,747.94     $174,151.53        6
                                                                                         $20,898.18     $153,253.35        7
                                                                                         $18,390.40     $134,862.95        8
                                                                                         $16,183.55     $118,679.40        9
                                                                                         $14,241.53     $104,437.87       10
                                                                                         $12,532.54      $91,905.33       11
```

Practice Problems

1. Code a program to compute the sum of all integers from 1ØØ1 to 5ØØØ using
   a. DO
   b. DOW
   c. DOU
   d. IF
2. Suppose you read in two numbers A and B. A is in positions 49–5Ø; B is in positions 51–52. Code a routine using a DO group to compute the product using successive additions rather than the MULT instruction.
3. Code a program to compute the sum of all even integers from 2 to 2ØØØ using:
   a. DOWGT
   b. DOULT
   c. DOUEQ
   d. DOWLE

Figure 11.19 Problem definition for Practice Problem 4.

Systems Flowchart

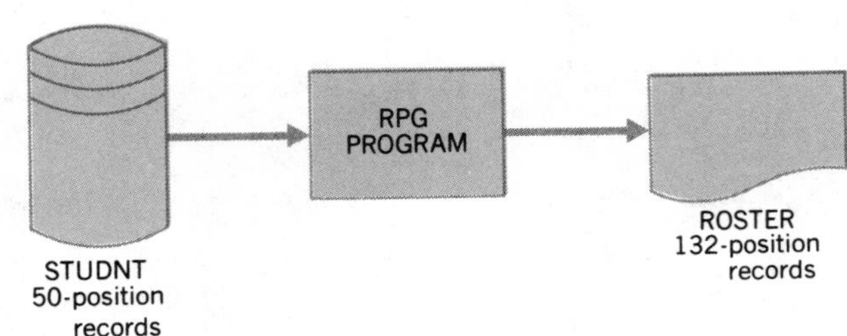

STUDNT Record Layout

COURSE I.D.	STUDENT NAME	NUMBER OF TESTS	TEST 1	TEST 2	TEST 3	TEST 4	TEST 5	
1–6	7–30	31	32–34	35–37	38–40	41–43	44–46	50

ROSTER Printer Spacing Chart

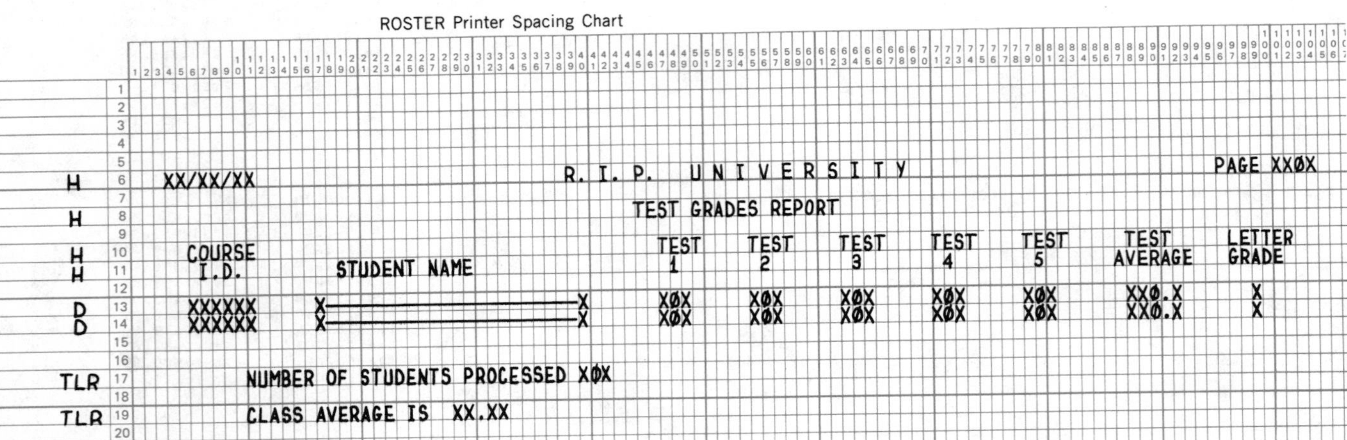

Note A record may contain from one to five test scores.

---

4. Using the problem definition shown in Figure 11.19, code a subroutine to compute an average of student test grades. It is also necessary to determine the letter grade as follows.

Test Average	*Letter Grade*
9Ø–1ØØ	A
8Ø–89	B
7Ø–79	C
6Ø–69	D
Ø–59	F

Each student's average is determined by dividing the sum of all test grades by the number of tests taken.

CHAPTER 12

A Summary of RPG III Programming

Objectives

- To provide an overview of RPG III programming enhancements
- To indicate how a data base and externally described data are best used in a system
- To specify how RPG III can process inquiries from an interactive workstation

Thus far, we have considered the commands in RPG III that make it highly suitable for structured programming. The following provides a brief description of other advances and enhancements available with RPG III.

I. Externally Described Data

One major innovation in information processing in recent years is the design of a single, integrated, centralized **data base** for all data stored, manipulated, or used by an organization. Traditionally, each unit or department within an organization had its own unique file. Using an integrated data base, however, requires a *single* storage medium containing data accessible by *all* subsystems. In this way, data does not need to be redefined or duplicated by each system or program that requires it. It can be stored on a single device and accessed as needed.

RPG III enables the programmer to use record descriptions for a file or data base that is stored external to the RPG program. This is referred to as **externally described data**. In this way, data to be used by a system is described only once to the control program facility; it need not be described by each user program that accesses the file. A **control program facility** is the system support program that provides many functions that are fully integrated in the system. These functions include data base management, message handling, and job control.

A control program facility makes it easier for a programmer to code the program. It helps to standardize the system by using a *single* set of data descriptors that are used by all programmers. It also makes it easier to modify a file or data base; the changes required are indicated *only once*, to the control program facility. Thus, if the format of the file changes, the data description changes are given to the control program facility, and the RPG code need not be changed at all.

A. The Data Description Specifications Form

To define an externally described file to the control program facility, the RPG III programmer uses a new specification form called Data Description Specifications. See Figure 12.1 for an illustration. The description of the records in an externally described file is called a **record format**. (In the following discussion, the numbers in brackets ([ ]) refer to specific locations in Figure 12.1.) The record format is identified by a unique name and by an R in position 17 [1]. The PFILE keyword identifies the physical file CUSMSTP that contains the data to be used by this file [2]. The record format contains the field names [3], the field lengths [4], and other field attributes (such as an indication of whether the field is alphameric or numeric). An entry in the decimal positions [5] indicates a numeric field. As in RPG II, if these positions are blank, the field is assumed to be alphameric. The TEXT keyword and the description in positions 45 through 79 [6] identify the contents of the field.

B. Using Externally Described Data

Figure 12.2 is a schematic of how processing is performed using externally described files. The programmer enters the data description specifications into the system and uses control language commands provided by the control program facility to create and name the file. After the file is created, data is entered into the system and stored in the file; that data can then be accessed by the program that uses the file. The file and its description are stored in the system's

DATA DESCRIPTION SPECIFICATIONS

File		Keying Instruction	Graphic	Description	Page of
Programmer	Date		Key		

Form Type	Conditioning	Name Type	Name	Length	Data Type	Decimal Positions	Functions
A*	CUSTOMER MASTER FILE -- CUSMSTL						
A	[1]	R	CUSREC				PFILE(CUSMSTP) [2]
A			CUST	5			TEXT('Customer Number')
A			NAME	2Ø			TEXT('Customer Name')
A			ADDR	2Ø			TEXT('Customer Address')
A	[3]		CITY	2Ø			TEXT('Customer City')
A			STATE	2			TEXT('State Abbreviation')
A			ZIP	5		Ø	TEXT('Zip Code')
A			CRDCHK	1			TEXT('Credit Check')
A			SRHCOD	3			TEXT('Customer Name Search Code')
A			CUSTYP	1			TEXT('Customer Type')
A			ARBAL	1Ø		2	TEXT('Accounts Receivable Balance')
A		K	CUST				TEXT('Key Field')
A				[4]		[5]	[6]

Figure 12.1
The Data Description Specifications form.

data base, external to any application program. The file and its description can then be used by application programs (see Figure 12.2*a*). The RPG program references the externally described file by the name that is specified on the File Description Specifications form. When the RPG program is compiled, the external description of the file is retrieved from the system and included in the compiled RPG program. Because the fields are defined to the control program facility, input and/or output specifications are not required in the RPG program to further define the file. However, input and/or output specifications can be used to add RPG functions to the external description (see Figure 12.2*b*).

Sample Program

The purpose of this program is to print a list of the records read from an externally described file called DETORDL (detail orders). The output file, which is a program described file, is named QPRINT. No calculations are performed on the data in the input records. Only the fields QTYORD, ITEM, DESCRP, and EXTENS are to be printed in the detail output record.

To write the specifications for this program, you need to

- Refer to the description of the externally described file DETORDL so you can use the correct field names and field lengths in describing the output file.
- Refer to the format of the printed report specified by a Printer Spacing Chart (see Figure 12.3).
- Code the File Description Specifications form.

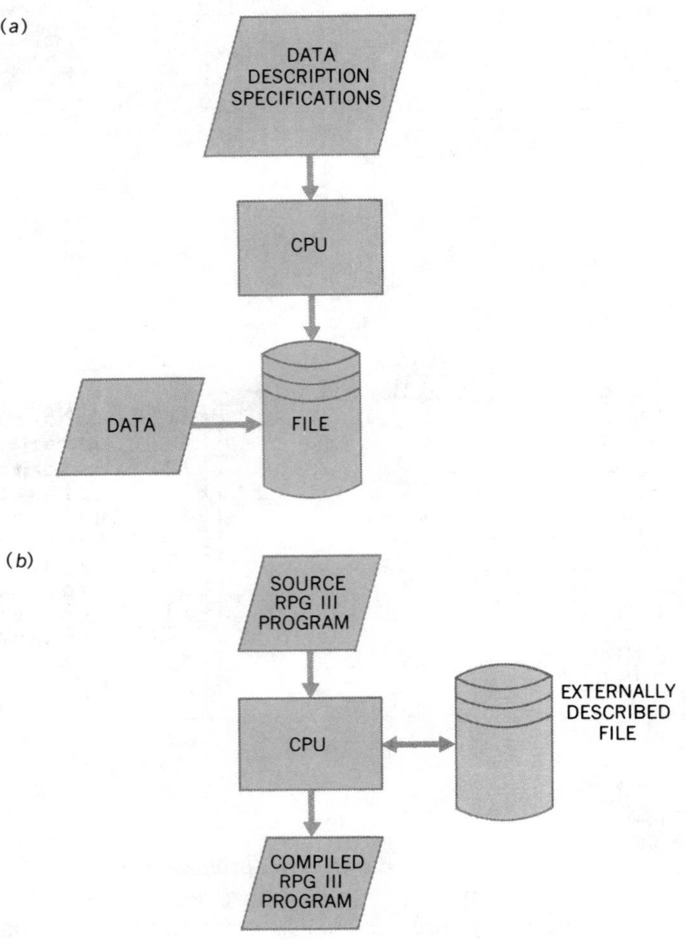

Figure 12.2 Schematic of how externally described files can be (*a*) created and (*b*) referenced.

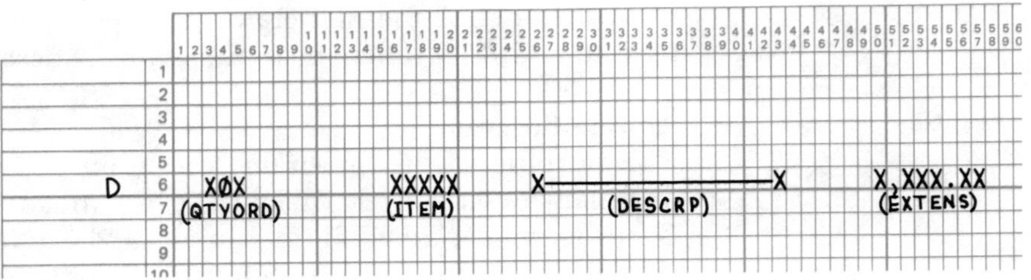

Figure 12.3 Printer Spacing Chart for Sample Program.

a. Externally Described File The description of the externally described file (DETORDL), which was created by data description specifications and control program facility commands, is stored in the system independently of any program. The data description specifications that were used to define the DETORDL file are shown in Figure 12.4. The external description of the DETORDL file includes [1] the record format name (which is identified by the **R** in position 17), [2] the name of each field in the record, [3] the length of each field, and

DATA DESCRIPTION SPECIFICATIONS

File		Keying Instruction	Graphic	Description	Page of
Programmer	Date		Key		

Form Type (6)	And/Or/Comment (7)	Conditioning (8–16)	Name Type (17)	Name (19–28)	Length (30–34)	Decimal Positions (36–37)	Functions (45–80)
A	*	DETAIL ORDER FILE -- DETORDL					
A		[1]	R	ORDDTL			PFILE(DETORDP)
A				CUST	5		TEXT('Customer Number')
A				ORDER	5	Ø	TEXT('Order Number')
A				LINNUM	3	Ø	TEXT('Line Number on Invoice')
A				ITEM	5		TEXT('Item Number')
A		[2]		QTYORD	3	Ø	TEXT('Quantity Ordered')
A				DESCRP	18		TEXT('Item Description')
A				PRICE	5	2	TEXT('Price per Unit')
A				EXTENS	6	2	TEXT('Extension of QTYORD x PRICE')
A				WHSLOC	3		TEXT('Warehouse Location')
A				ORDDAT	6	Ø	TEXT('Order Date')
A				CUSTYP	1		TEXT('Customer Type')
A				STATE	2		TEXT('State Abbreviation')
A					[3]	[4]	

Figure 12.4
Data Description Specifications for Sample Program.

[4] the number of decimal positions in a numeric field. If no entry is made for decimal positions, the field is assumed to be alphameric. The text descriptions in positions 45 through 79 further describe the fields. The PFILE keyword identifies the file DETORDP that contains the data to be used by this file. When the RPG III program is compiled, the compiler retrieves this description of the DETORDL file and includes it in the program.

b. Control and File Description Specifications In this sample program, there is one input file (DETORDL) and one output file (QPRINT). The File Description Specifications form is shown in Figure 12.5.

The specifications on line Ø2 describe the input file DETORDL. Positions 7 through 14 contain the name of the file. The I in position 15 identifies the file as an input file, and the P in position 16 identifies it as a primary file. The device associated with the file is DISK (positions 4Ø through 46). Because the file is an externally described file, position 19 contains an E, which tells the compiler to retrieve the description of the file from the system.

The specifications on line Ø3 describe the output file QPRINT. Positions 7 through 14 contain the name of the file. The O in position 15 identifies the file as an output file. The device associated with the file is PRINTER (positions 4Ø through 46). Because the file is a program-described file, position 19 contains an F, which tells the compiler that the file's records are described within the program. For a program-described file, the record length must be specified in positions 24 through 27, and the entry must be right-justified. The record length

RPG CONTROL AND FILE DESCRIPTION SPECIFICATIONS

Program | Keying Instruction | Graphic | Key | Card Electro Number | Page 01 of 2 | Program Identification PROG1

Programmer | Date

Control Specifications

For the valid entries for a system, refer to the RPG reference manual for that system.

H — Line; Form Type; Size to Compile; Object Output; Listing Options; Size to Execute; Debug; Reserved; Currency Symbol; Date Format; Date Edit; Inverted Print; Reserved; Number of Print Positions; Alternate Collating Sequence; Reserved; Inquiry; Reserved; Sign Handling; 1 P Forms Position; Indicator Setting; File Translation; Punch MFCU Zeros; Nonprint Characters; Reserved; Table Load Halt; Shared I/O; Field Print; Formatted Dump; RPG to RPG II Conversion; Number of Formats; S/3 Conversion; Subprogram; CICS/DL/I; Transparent Literal

```
01 H
```

File Description Specifications

For the valid entries for a system, refer to the RPG reference manual for that system.

F — Line; Form Type; Filename; File Type; File Designation; End of File; Sequence; File Format; Block Length; Record Length; Mode of Processing; Length of Key Field or of Record Address Field; Record Address Type; Type of File Organization or Additional Area; Overflow Indicator; Key Field Starting Location; Extension Code E/L; External Record Name; Device; Symbolic Device; Labels S/N/E/M; Name of Label Exit; Extent Exit for DAM; Storage Index; Continuation Lines (K, Option, Entry); A/U; File Addition/Unordered; Number of Tracks for Cylinder Overflow; Number of Extents; Tape Rewind; File Condition U1–U8, UC; R/U/N

```
02F DETORDL IP   E                        DISK
03F QPRINT  O    F       132              PRINTER
04F
05F
06F
```

Figure 12.5
File Description Specifications for Sample Program.

specified for a printer file can be the actual length of the output record (which is 57 in this program), or it can be the length of the print line (which is 132). The length of the print line is used in this example.

C. Output Specifications

The Output Specifications form for this program is shown in Figure 12.6. Line Ø1 (called a record specification line) contains the name of the output file (QPRINT) in positions 7 through 14, and it identifies the line to be printed as a detail line, which is indicated by a D in position 15. The fields are defined on lines Ø2 through Ø5.

Note that the 1 in position 18 causes the printer to space one line after it prints a line. The N1P entry in positions 23 through 25 conditions the line so it is not printed on the first program cycle, and the Z and 2 entries in position 38 edit the QTYORD and EXTENS fields.

II. Simplified Calculations

In RPG II, all calculations require Factor 1, Factor 2, and the Result field to be coded. In RPG III, Factor 1 may be omitted for ease of coding. For arithmetic operations in RPG III, if Factor 1 is omitted, the computer assumes it to be the same as the Result field.

RPG OUTPUT SPECIFICATIONS

Program | Programmer | Date | Keying Instruction | Graphic | Key | Card Electro Number | Page ϕ2 of | Program Identification PROG1

Line	Form Type	Filename or Record Name	Type (H/D/T/E)	Space After	Output Indicators	Field Name or EXCPT Name	Edit Codes	End Position in Output Record
01ϕ	O	QPRINT	D	1	N1P			
02ϕ	O					QTYORD	Z	5
03ϕ	O					ITEM		2ϕ
04ϕ	O					DESCRP		43
05ϕ	O					EXTENS	2	57
06	O							
07	O							

Figure 12.6
Output Specifications for Sample Program.

To add AMT to TOTAL in RPG II, you have

RPG CALCULATION SPECIFICATIONS

Line	Form Type	Factor 1	Operation	Factor 2	Result Field Name
01ϕ	C	TOTAL	ADD	AMT	TOTAL
02	C				
03	C				

In RPG III, you can simplify this as follows.

RPG CALCULATION SPECIFICATIONS

Line	Form Type	Factor 1	Operation	Factor 2	Result Field Name
01ϕ	C		ADD	AMT	TOTAL
02	C				
03	C				

In an ADD operation, then, if Factor 1 is omitted, RPG III assumes Factor 1 to be the same as the Result field.

In a SUB operation, once again if Factor 1 is omitted it is assumed to be the same as the Result field. Thus the following two lines would produce the same results.

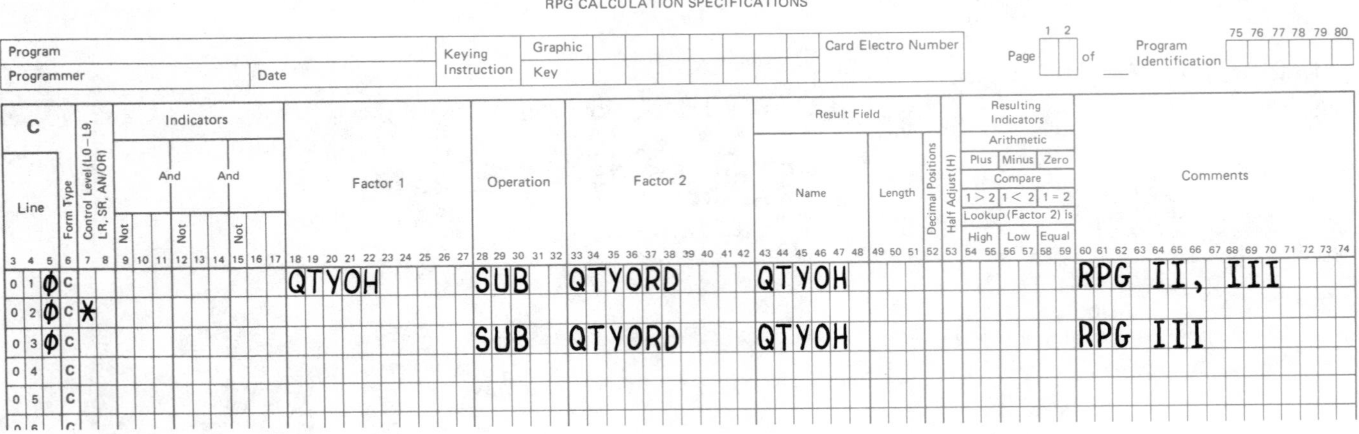

RPG CALCULATION SPECIFICATIONS

Line	Form Type	Control Level	Factor 1	Operation	Factor 2	Result Field Name	Comments
01φ	C		QTYOH	SUB	QTYORD	QTYOH	RPG II, III
02φ	C	*					
03φ	C			SUB	QTYORD	QTYOH	RPG III
04	C						
05	C						

Similarly, MULT and DIV operations do not require the coding of Factor 1. The following two MULT instructions produce the same results in RPG III.

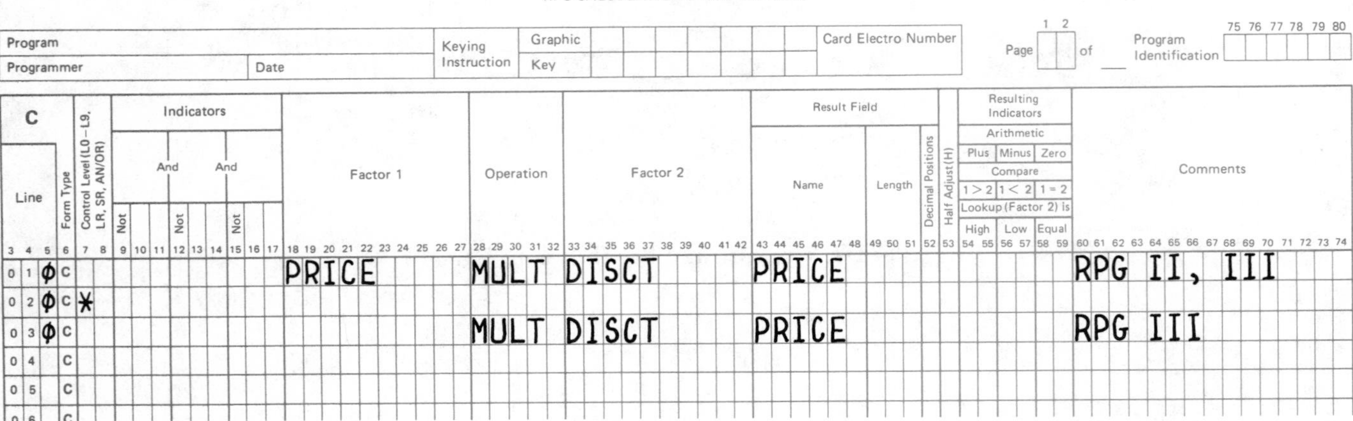

RPG CALCULATION SPECIFICATIONS

Line	Form Type	Control Level	Factor 1	Operation	Factor 2	Result Field Name	Comments
01φ	C		PRICE	MULT	DISCT	PRICE	RPG II, III
02φ	C	*					
03φ	C			MULT	DISCT	PRICE	RPG III
04	C						
05	C						

The following two division operations also produce the same results in RPG III.

RPG CALCULATION SPECIFICATIONS

Line	Form Type	Control Level	Factor 1	Operation	Factor 2	Result Field Name	Comments
01ϕ	C		DOZEN	DIV	12	DOZEN	RPG II, III
02ϕ	C	*					
03ϕ	C			DIV	12	DOZEN	RPG III
04	C						
05	C						

Of course, if you wish to perform an arithmetic operation on two fields and place the results in an independent third field, you will need to use both Factors 1 and 2 as well as the Result field in both RPG III and RPG II.

III. Processing Inquiries or Data from an Interactive Workstation

Any typewriter terminal or CRT-keyboard can be used as a workstation. With these devices, the user communicates with the computer in an interactive mode. The program displays a **prompt**, which is a message requesting the user to enter some data. The user must then respond to the prompt. Subsequent processing by the program depends on the user's response. The following display shows two prompts.

```
ENTER CUSTOMER NUMBER ____________
ENTER ZL TO TERMINATE THIS RUN
```

If the user enters a customer number the program proceeds. If, instead, the user enters ZL, the program will terminate.

In RPG III, data description specifications and control program facility commands are used to create the external descriptions to a workstation file (defined as WORKSTN). To retrieve the description of the WORKSTN file that has already been defined to the control program, use the coding that follows.

RPG CONTROL AND FILE DESCRIPTION SPECIFICATIONS

Control Specifications

Line	Form Type
01	H

File Description Specifications

Line	Form Type	File Designation	Device
02	F	E	WORKSTN
03	F		
04	F		

WORKSTN entries, then, may be used to

1. Inquire about the status of records in a file.
2. Update records on a file.

The format for the WORKSTN entries can be defined on a Data Description Specifications form external to the program. See Figure 12.7 for entries that would be used in an update procedure.

The Data Description Specifications form for this display file, which is named CUSUPD (customer update), includes the following information.

[1] The name of each record format in the file.

[2] Association of CF1 with indicator 15. When the user presses CF1, indicator 15 is set on in the RPG program.

[3] For each record format, constants are defined that are to appear on the screen as prompts for the user and as informational messages. The constant 'CUSTOMER MASTER UPDATE' identifies the purpose of this display. The constant 'Customer Number' is the prompt for the user to enter a customer number. The constant 'USE CF1 TO END THIS PROGRAM' tells the user how to end the program.

[4] CUST is the name of the input field into which the user enters a customer number in response to the prompt 'CUSTOMER NUMBER'. The input field is five characters long and is identified as an input field by the I in position 38. If a field is identified as an input field, the user can enter information into that field.

DATA DESCRIPTION SPECIFICATIONS

File		Keying Instruction	Graphic	Description	Page of
Programmer	Date		Key		

```
     A*CUSTOMER MASTER UPDATE FILE -- CUSUPD
     A      [1] R CUSRQST                   TEXT('Customer Number Request')
     A                                      CAØ1(15 'End of Program') [2]
     A                                    1  3'Customer Master Update' [3]
     A                                    3  3'Customer Number'
     A      [4]   CUST           5   I  3 2Ø
     A99                                 [5]ERRMSG('Customer Number Not Found: +
     A                                      Press Reset, then enter Valid numbe+
     A                                      r' 99)
     A                                    5  3'Use CF1 to end this program'
     A      [1] R CUSMAIN
     A                                      OVERLAY[6]
     A                                    7  3'Name'
     A            NAME          2Ø   B  7 11
     A                                    8  3'Address'
     A            ADDR          2Ø   B  8 11
     A      [8]                           9  3'City'        [7]
     A            CITY          2Ø   B  9 11
     A                                   1Ø  3'State'
     A            STATE          2   B 1Ø 11
     A                                   1Ø 21'Zip Code'
     A            ZIP            5  ØB 1Ø 31
```

Figure 12.7
WORKSTN entries for an update procedure.

[5] The ERRMSG keyword identifies an error message. This message appears on the display only if indicator 99 is set on in the RPG III program.

[6] The OVERLAY keyword indicates that the CUSMAIN record overlays the CUSRQST record. Because of the OVERLAY keyword, both records appear on the display at the same time. If OVERLAY is not specified, the CUSRQST record is erased when the CUSMAIN record is written to the display.

[7] These constants identify the fields that are written to the display when the CUSMAIN record is displayed. The user cannot change these constants when the program is executing.

[8] These fields are written to the display from the program. The lengths of the fields are specified in positions 3Ø through 34. The B in position 38 identifies each field as both an input field and an output field (an input/output field). Data is written to the display from the program, and the user can change this data before the fields are read back into the program.

The CUSRQST record format defines the following display, which is the first record written to the display by the program. This record prompts the user to enter a customer number. The message 'CUSTOMER NUMBER NOT FOUND' is written to the display only if indicator 99 is set on by the program.

CUSTOMER MASTER UPDATE
CUSTOMER NUMBER ____________
USE CF1 TO END THIS PROGRAM

CUSTOMER NUMBER NOT FOUND: PRESS RESET, THEN ENTER VALID NUMBER

The CUSMAIN record format defines the following display. Because the OVERLAY keyword is specified for the CUSMAIN record, the CUSRQST record remains on the display. The NAME, ADDR, CITY, and STATE fields are defined as output/input fields, which means that data is written to these fields from the program and that data can be changed by the user before it is read back into the program.

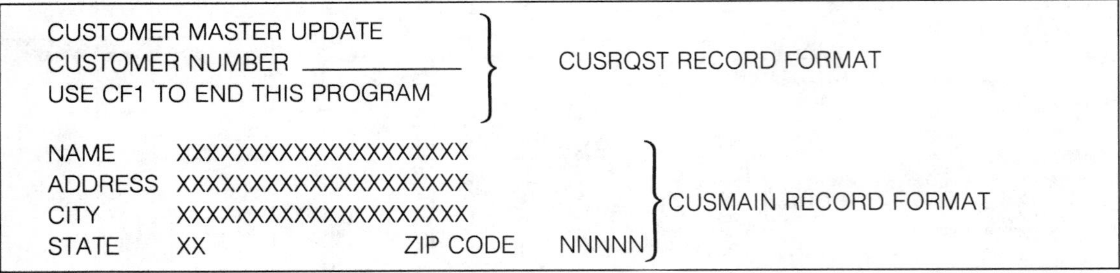
CUSTOMER MASTER UPDATE
CUSTOMER NUMBER ____________ } CUSRQST RECORD FORMAT
USE CF1 TO END THIS PROGRAM

NAME XXXXXXXXXXXXXXXXXXXX
ADDRESS XXXXXXXXXXXXXXXXXXXX
CITY XXXXXXXXXXXXXXXXXXXX } CUSMAIN RECORD FORMAT
STATE XX ZIP CODE NNNNN

The operation code used to write records to and read records from a WORKSTN file is EXFMT (execute format). The EXFMT operation performs two functions.

1. It writes a prompt to the display.
2. When the user responds to the prompt displayed on the screen, the EXFMT returns the record to the program.

The prompt in our illustration is defined as CUSRQST. To execute it, code

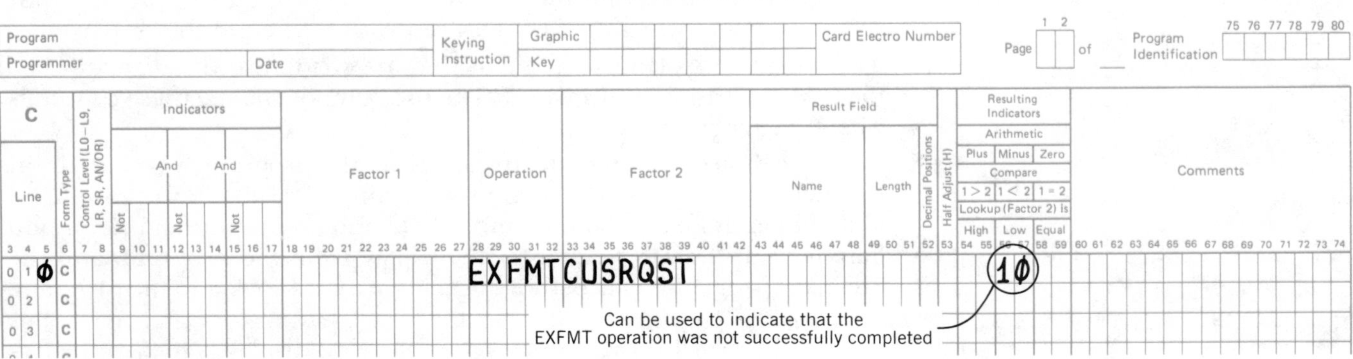
RPG CALCULATION SPECIFICATIONS

Line	Form Type	Operation	Factor 2	Resulting Indicators (Low)
01Ø	C	EXFMT	CUSRQST	1Ø
02	C			
03	C			

Can be used to indicate that the EXFMT operation was not successfully completed

To modify existing records in our file, we use the UPDAT operation code. After EXFMT has been executed successfully, a CUST number will be read. We chain to our CUSTREC file. We then display the existing record using the format specified under CUSMAIN. CUSMAIN enables the user to make any changes necessary to CUSREC. After the user presses enter, the UPDAT operation is executed, which automatically changes all entries indicated by the user. Figure 12.8 shows the Calculation Specifications form for the procedure described thus far.

To execute these instructions repeatedly, we use a GOTO statement. To terminate the job, we will SETON the LR indicator when indicator 15 is on. You will recall that indicator 15 is turned on when the user depresses CF1 to indicate the end of the job. Figure 12.9 shows the entire procedure on the Calculation Specifications form. Note that *no* input specifications are required for this pro-

Figure 12.8
Calculation Specifications for processing from an interactive workstation.

RPG CALCULATION SPECIFICATIONS

```
010C********************************************************************
020C***        TO RETRIEVE FIRST PROMPT AND READ IN CUST             ***
030C********************************************************************
040C*
050C                     EXFMTCUSRQST
060C*
070C********************************************************************
080C***        TO OBTAIN DISK RECORD THAT CORRESPONDS TO CUST        ***
090C***        NOTE: INDICATOR 15 IS TURNED ON IF CF1 IS DEPRESSED   ***
100C********************************************************************
110C*
120C  N15      CUST      CHAINCUSREC               99
130C*
140C********************************************************************
150C***        IF THERE IS NO CORRESPONDING RECORD, 99 IS TURNED ON  ***
160C***        IF N99, DISPLAY 2ND MESSAGE LISTING CUSREC INFO       ***
170C***                          AND                                 ***
180C***        WITH A PROMPT -- ASKING FOR CHANGES                   ***
190C********************************************************************
200C*
210C  N15N99             EXFMTCUSMAIN
220C*
230C********************************************************************
240C***        USER HAS UPDATED FIELDS TO BE CHANGED                 ***
250C***        UPDAT OPERATION MAKES THE CORRESPONDING CHANGES       ***
260C***                  TO THE DISK FILE                            ***
270C********************************************************************
280C*
290C  N15N99             UPDATCUSREC
300C*
```

RPG CALCULATION SPECIFICATIONS

Line	Form Type	Indicators	Factor 1	Operation	Factor 2	Resulting Indicators
01Ø	C		START	TAG		
02Ø	C			EXFMT	CUSRQT	
03Ø	C	N15	CUST	CHAIN	CUSREC	99
04Ø	C	N15N99		EXFMT	CUSMAIN	
05Ø	C	N15N99		UPDAT	CUSREC	
06Ø	C	N15		GOTO	START	
07Ø	C	15		SETON		LR

Figure 12.9
Entire Calculation Specifications for Sample Program.

gram since the data description specifications includes all entries needed. No output specifications are needed since the UPDAT operation will write to the disk. The File Description Specifications are shown in Figure 12.1Ø.

Figure 12.1Ø
File Description Specifications for Sample Program.

RPG CONTROL AND FILE DESCRIPTION SPECIFICATIONS

Control Specifications

Line	Form Type
01	H

File Description Specifications

Line	Form Type	Filename	File Type	File Designation	File Format	Record Address Type	Device
02Ø	F	CUSUPD	C	F	E		WORKSTN
03Ø	F	CUSMSTL	U	F	E	K	DISK

Both files are defined externally

Indicates that there is a key field on the DISK file

Designates that all I/O is controlled by procedures in calculations

Key Terms

Control program facility	Interactive workstation
Data base	Prompt
Externally described data	Record format

Self-Evaluating Quiz

1. (T or F) There are commands available in RPG III that make it ideally suited for structured programming.
2. (T or F) RPG III is currently as widely available as RPG II.
3. Using an integrated ________ , a single-storage medium can contain all the data used by the organization as a whole.
4. Using ________ , RPG III enables the record descriptions to be standardized for the organization as a whole.
5. (T or F) Using externally described data, each time a record changes, the RPG III programmer must alter the input specifications form.
6. Using externally described data, the data description is provided only once to the ________ .
7. (T or F) In RPG III, the following two commands produce the same results.

RPG CALCULATION SPECIFICATIONS

Program		Keying Instruction	Graphic	Card Electro Number	Page 1 2 of	Program Identification 75 76 77 78 79 80
Programmer	Date		Key			

Line (3–5)	Form Type (6)	Control Level (L0–L9, LR, SR, AN/OR) (7–8)	Indicators (9–17)	Factor 1 (18–27)	Operation (28–32)	Factor 2 (33–42)	Result Field Name (43–48)	Length (49–51)	Decimal Positions (52)	Half Adjust (H) (53)	Resulting Indicators (54–59)	Comments (60–74)
01Ø	C			AMT2	ADD	AMT3	AMT2					
02Ø	C	*										
03Ø	C				ADD	AMT2	AMT3					
04	C											
05	C											
06	C											

8. (T or F) Using RPG III, it is possible to process inquiries directly from an interactive workstation.
9. The operation code used to write records to and read records from a workstation file is ________ .
10. A workstation file is typically defined in RPG III as ________ .

Solutions

1. T
2. F—It is currently used on only a small number of IBM computers.
3. data base
4. externally described data
5. F
6. control program facility
7. F—ADD AMT3 AMT2 would produce the same result as the first instruction.

8. T
9. EXFMT
10. WORKSTN

Review Questions

1. Indicate in your own words the major enhancements of RPG III as compared to RPG II.
2. When would externally described data be advantageous in a system? Give specific examples.
3. When would inquiries from an interactive terminal be used in a system? Give specific examples.
4. How is a "prompt" used in a system? Give specific examples.
5. Indicate the meaning of the following terms.
   a. Data base
   b. Control program facility
   c. EXFMT
   d. WORKSTN

APPENDIX A

Line Counter Specifications

A. Nonstandard Forms

When the RPG programmer codes OF in columns 33–34 of the File Description Specifications form on the lines associated with the print file, the computer will automatically

1. Turn on the OF indicator when the end of a printed page is reached.
2. Enable the programmer to print headings on a new page when the OF indicator is on.

The assumption made by the computer is that the continuous forms used for printing are standard sized—that is, 66 lines. The OF indicator is automatically turned on when line 6Ø has been reached, that is, six lines from the bottom.

If a specific application requires a different sized form or the overflow indicator to be turned on at some point other than line 6Ø, a new specifications form is required—the Line Counter Specifications form, which directly follows the File Description form (see Figure A.1).

> ***Rules for Using Line Counter Specifications***
>
> 1. The form is only required if the length of the continuous form is not standard or the overflow line is not to be line 6Ø.
> 2. The File Description Specifications form is coded with an L in column 39 on the line associated with the print file. The L indicates that the Line Counter Specifications form will be used. OF must also be included in columns 33–34 of the form.
> 3. The filename on the Line Counter Specifications form must be the same as the print filename on the File Description Specifications form.
> 4. The line number field of the Line Counter Specifications form (columns 15–17) indicates the length of the form. Columns 18–19 are coded with FL to denote form length.
> 5. Columns 2Ø–22 indicate the overflow line number, and columns 23–24 are coded with OL to denote overflow line.

Figure A.1
Line Counter Specifications form.

Line Counter Specifications

L			1		2		3		4		5		6		7		8		9		10		11		12	
Line	Form Type	Filename	Line Number	FL or Channel Number	Line Number	OL or Channel Number	Line Number	Channel Number	Line Number	Channel Number	Line Number	Channel Number	Line Number	Channel Number	Line Number	Channel Number	Line Number	Channel Number	Line Number	Channel Number	Line Number	Channel Number	Line Number	Channel Number	Line Number	Channel Number
3 4 5	6	7 8 9 10 11 12 13 14	15 16 17	18 19	20 21 22	23 24	25 26 27	28 29	30 31 32	33 34	35 36 37	38 39	40 41 42	43 44	45 46 47	48 49	50 51 52	53 54	55 56 57	58 59	60 61 62	63 64	65 66 67	68 69	70 71 72	73 74
1 1	L																									
1 2	L																									
	L																									

Other entries may be included for more sophisticated page control printing. Figure A.2 illustrates a File Description form for a print file. The corresponding Line Counter Specification in Figure A.3 indicates that

1. The form length is 44 lines.
2. The overflow line is line 38.

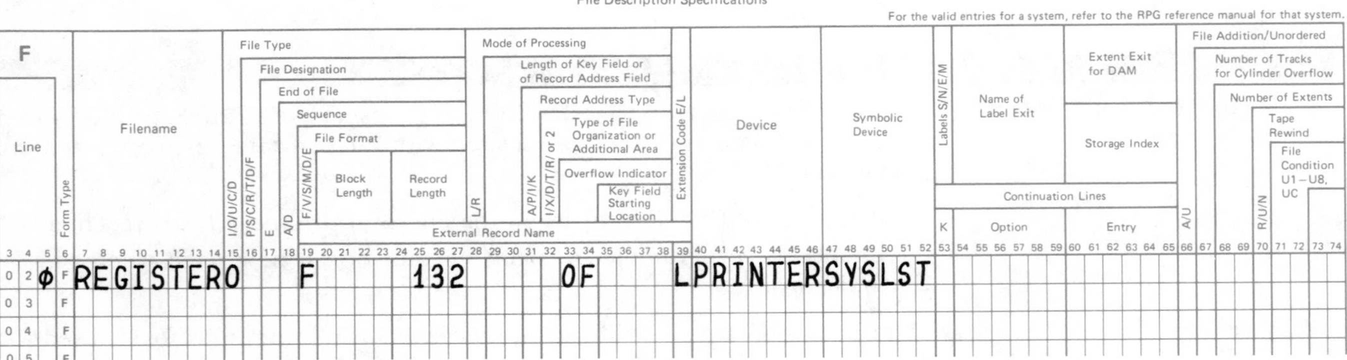
File Description Specifications

For the valid entries for a system, refer to the RPG reference manual for that system.

F | Line | Form Type | Filename | File Type | File Designation | End of File | Sequence | File Format | Block Length | Record Length | Mode of Processing | Length of Key Field or of Record Address Field | Record Address Type | Type of File Organization or Additional Area | Overflow Indicator | Key Field Starting Location | Extension Code E/L | Device | Symbolic Device | Labels S/N/E/M | Name of Label Exit | Extent Exit for DAM | Storage Index | Continuation Lines | K | Option | Entry | A/U | File Addition/Unordered | Number of Tracks for Cylinder Overflow | Number of Extents | Tape Rewind | File Condition U1–U8, UC

```
0 2 Φ F REGISTERO    F       132       OF     LPRINTERSYSLST
0 3   F
0 4   F
0 5   F
```

Figure A.2
File Description form for a print file.

Line Counter Specifications

L | Line | Form Type | Filename | 1–12: Line Number | FL or Channel Number / OL or Channel Number / Channel Number

```
1 1 Φ L REGISTERΦ44FLΦ38OL
1 2   L
      L
```

Figure A.3
The corresponding Line Counter Specifications for Figure A.2.

B. Spooling

The slowest operations performed by a computer are input/output functions. These operations can significantly increase the overall processing time if the output is to be printed because printers are in general very slow devices.

One technique used to minimize this problem is to first store output to be printed on a fast-access intermediate device such as a tape or disk drive. In this way, report output can be generated rapidly without slowing down the computer. Many reports can be accumulated and then printed using the printer in an off-line mode with a tape-to-print or disk-to-print utility program.

This use of an intermediate high-speed secondary storage medium is called **spooling** and is very successful in off-loading computer use. It does, however, mean that special techniques must be used that would not otherwise be required if the printed output was produced directly.

A **carriage control tape** attached to the printer is the mechanism used for detecting the end of a page or form overflow condition. Since a tape-to-print or disk-to-print utility does not make use of the carriage control tape, some other technique is necessary for indicating when an end of page is reached.

The Line Counter Specifications form is used to correlate specific lines of the printed page of a report to corresponding punches in the carriage control tape. Typically, a 12 punch in a carriage control tape corresponds to the last line to be printed, usually line 6Ø. When this 12 punch is sensed, a form overflow condition occurs. Similarly, the instruction to skip to channel 1 means to begin on the first line of printing, which is usually line 6. When output is printed directly, the carriage control tape that has been properly punched will produce the desired results. When output is spooled, a Line Counter Specifications form must be used to achieve the desired result.

Consider the following File Description form.

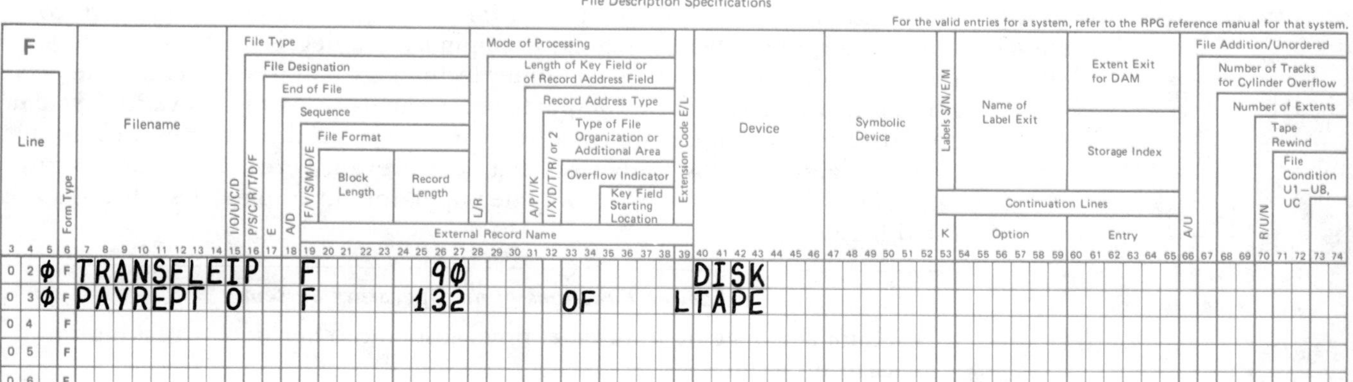

File Description Specifications

Line	Form Type	Filename	File Type	File Designation	File Format	Record Length	Overflow Indicator	Extension Code E/L	Device
02Ø	F	TRANSFLE	I	P	F	9Ø			DISK
03Ø	F	PAYREPT	O		F	132	OF	L	TAPE
04	F								
05	F								
06	F								

In this illustration, the output will be spooled onto a tape and printed at some later point. Hence, the input device is a DISK and the output device is a TAPE, even though the output data will ultimately be printed.

Note that column 39 includes an L to indicate that a Line Counter Specifications form will be used. This form would have the following coding.

Line Counter Specifications

Line	Form Type	Filename	1 Line Number	1 FL or Channel Number	2 Line Number	2 OL or Channel Number	3–12
11Ø	L	PAYREPT	ØØ6	Ø1	Ø6Ø	12	
12	L						
	L						

The Line Counter form should directly follow the File Description form.

The entries on the Line Counter form simulate the channel punches in the carriage control tape. When a program is executed, with a Line Counter Specifications form, an internal line count is automatically maintained. When line 6Ø has printed, the overflow indicator (OF) is turned on and can condition printing as if a 12 punch in the carriage control tape was sensed.

Similarly, an instruction to skip to channel 1 of a new page will begin printing on line 6.

APPENDIX B

Communicating with the Operating System Using Job Control Language

What Is an Operating System?

Since computers can operate on data far more quickly than people can, computer systems have been designed to minimize the degree of human intervention. A major development in computer technology that has decreased the need for operator intervention in computer processing is called the **operating system.** An operating system is a sophisticated control system that enables a computer to handle automatically many tasks that have previously required time-consuming manual intervention by a computer operator. Examples of such tasks are listed here.

Sample Functions of an Operating System

1. Automatic logging in of date, time, cost, and other details relating to each program.
   Savings: Operator not needed to maintain this information for each program.
2. Automatic maintenance and easy access of compilers, assemblers, and other special programs usually supplied by the manufacturer.
   Savings: Less operation time needed to load programs from off-line devices.
3. Automatic procedures for terminating jobs even if errors have occurred; automatic restart procedures that can read new jobs so that they can be batched.
   Savings: Operator not needed to watch for programming errors or input errors that may cause the computer to halt; operator not needed to clear out malfunctioning program or to load in each program as needed.
4. Automatic communication of requirements from computer to operator and from operator to computer via a console.
   Savings: Operator can determine the status and requirements of each program easily and efficiently.
5. Automatic operations permitting terminal, real-time, and time-sharing functions that would otherwise be impossible.

How Operating System Interfaces with Computer

A major program providing the operating system with much of its capability and flexibility is the **supervisor.** The supervisor, sometimes called a **monitor,** controls the functions of the operating system, which is typically stored on a high-speed, direct-access medium such as magnetic disk. The supervisor must be *loaded* into storage each day prior to any processing, unless the computer operates on a 24-hour basis, in which case it permanently resides in storage. This control program calls in each user program for execution and extracts items, routines, or programs, as needed, from the system.

Example of Supervisory Functions Called for by Programmer

A programmer who writes a program in RPG must, for example, instruct the supervisor to

1. Call in the RPG compiler program from the operating system.
2. Release control to the compiler for translation.
3. Call in the appropriate subroutines that will supply a source listing, diagnostic messages, storage maps, and any other features deemed appropriate.
4. Abort the run if major errors have occurred.
5. Load the object program into main storage for execution.
6. Release control to the object program for execution.
7. At the end of the job, read in a new program.

Programmers communicate their job requirements to the supervisor in a special instruction format called **job control language.** Job control languages are dependent on the type of operating system on which one is running.

Types of Operating Systems

The type of operating system employed with a computer depends on its size and processing requirements. The three most common types of operating systems are the following.

Types of IBM Operating Systems

DOS	Disk Operating System
OS	(Full) Operating System
VS	Virtual Storage Operating System

These operating systems reside on direct-access devices such as disk and are called in, as needed, by the supervisor. A DOS system is somewhat less comprehensive and sophisticated than an OS or VS system. (It should be noted that with a virtual storage computer, it is possible to have a DOS/VS system or an OS/VS system.) The job control language, that is, the method of communicating with the supervisor, differs somewhat depending on which operating system is used.

Job Control Language (JCL)

Main Purpose of Job Control Language

1. To communicate the programmer's needs to the supervisor.
2. To access features of the operating system required by the programmer.

Every programmer must become familiar with job control specifications. We would like to supply them in their entirety as part of this text but, unfortunately, there are numerous options and entries to be coded that are dependent on the requirements of each computer installation. Hence, the JCL used at one data processing center will differ, if only slightly, from that used at another center. We will consider JCL for several IBM and UNIVAC systems. Before providing specific rules for each of these systems, let us consider some generalizations. The actual sequence of JCL commands discussed is considered in the next section.

Coding Rules Coding rules must be followed *precisely*. If a command requires // JOB in positions 1–6, for example, with a blank in position 3, then *no* variations are permitted.

1. JOB Command—IBM or LOGON Command—UNIVAC

A JOB or LOGON command indicates to the supervisor that a new job is being entered. Such a command normally specifies identifying information such as programmer name, job name, and date. Sometimes JOB commands are also required to have codes or passwords that are only known to authorized users.

> JOB name—usually 1 to 8 alphanumeric characters, with the first being alphabetic.

2. OPTION or PARAM Command

An OPTION or PARAM command is that part of JCL that specifies the options or parameters required for the specific run. There are numerous options that may be called for in a program. See Figures B.1 and B.5 for a listing of the more common ones.

Each computer system sets up its operating system to supply some of these options automatically, without even the need to call for them with a JCL command. In such cases, the JCL OPTION or PARAM command can be used to *suppress* the option.

> ***Summary of* OPTION *or* PARAM *Command***
>
> 1. Determine which options are provided as a standard.
> 2. Use the OPTION or PARAM command to call for additional options not automatically provided.
> 3. Use the OPTION or PARAM command to suppress options not needed.

3. EXEC Command

This JCL command specifies the program or routine to be executed. Since RPG programs require translation, linkage, and execution, usually three EXEC commands are included in a run.

Figure B-1
Sample options.

PARAM *or* OPTION *Coded*	*Meaning*
LOG	Log control statements on SYSLST (printer) are desired.
NOLOG	Suppress LOG option.
DUMP	DUMP registers and storage if an interrupt occurs.
NODUMP	Suppress DUMP option.
LINK	Write the output of the language translator.
NOLINK	Suppress LINK.
LIST	Produce output listing of source statements on SYSLST.
NOLIST	Suppress LIST.
LISTX	Produce output listing of object program on SYSLST (usually printer).
NOLISTX	Suppress LISTX.
XREF	Produce symbolic cross-reference list on SYSLST.
NOXREF	Suppress XREF.
ERRS	Produce listing of errors in source program on SYSLST.
NOERRS	Suppress ERRS

Note: The order indicated here is usually the one required. Hence if LIST, XREF, and ERRS are required, they must be coded in that sequence. Remember to check the defaults of your system to see which options are automatically provided.

a. Translation of Program
The first EXEC command calls for execution of the compiler—using your program as input and creating an object program as output. This object program may then be executed.

b. EXEC LNKEDT
Prior to the execution of an object program, that program must be loaded into an appropriate area of main storage and prepared for the run. These processes are placed under control of the linkage editor and must be executed *before* the object program can be run.

c. Execution of Program
The third EXEC command calls for execution of the object program.

4. Data Definition Commands (ASSGN or DD)

For every device used in a program, a device specification command is required, indicating the device classification, unit number, features of the file type, and so on. Since a terminal is frequently designated as the system's input device and a printer as the system's output device, these devices sometimes do not require data definition commands. For all other file types, however, such as tape and disk, data definition commands are required.

5. /* Command

This JCL command is used to denote the end of a file. It is the *last* JCL command of a *source program,* signaling the compiler that there are no more instructions to be compiled. It is also used sometimes as an end-of-file record. A /* command is automatically interpreted to mean there are no more records to be processed.

6. // (IBM) or /LOGOFF (UNIVAC)

This JCL command indicates the end of the run. It returns control to the supervisor, which automatically loads in the next job.

Job Control: IBM DOS

Figure B.2 illustrates JCL coding for RPG programs run on some IBM systems.

```
1.  // JOB job name
2.  // OPTION option1,option2,...
3.  // ASSGN SYSnnn,X'cuu'(optional specifications may also be included)
4.  // EXEC RPG
     (source program inserted at this point)
5.  /*
6.  // EXEC LNKEDT
7.  // EXEC
     (test data, if on cards, is entered here)
8.  /*
9.  /&
```

Figure B.2
JCL for RPG programs run on some IBM DOS systems.

> *Note:*
>
> Uppercase letters—required entries.
> Lowercase letters—programmer supplied.
> Phrases in parentheses are optional or system dependent.
> Required entries must be coded in the precise positions indicated.

Summary of Functions of JCL for IBM/DOS

1. JOB command
   JOB name
   - Programmer supplied.
   - Name by which computer will refer to program.
   - 1 to 8 alphanumeric characters.

   Other identifying information such as programmer name and password may be required at specific installations.
2. OPTION
   See Figure B.1 for an illustration of possible entries. Each system establishes its own defaults—options that are automatically supplied. The programmer, then, need only include options that are different from defaults.
3. ASSGN

   SYSnnn is the symbolic name for the device(s) used in the program.

   SYSnnn may be any number SYSØØØ–244. Sometimes SYSØØ1–SYSØØ4 are reserved.

   SYSIPT—system input device.

   SYSRDR—system's input device for reading control messages.

   SYSLST—system's main output device, usually printer.

   SYSPCH—card punch.

   SYSLOG—console typewriter.

   SYSRES—system resident disk unit.

   SYSLNK—disk unit used by linkage editor.

   The symbolic device assignment is made by each individual computer installation.

   Note. *An assign statement is only required for each device used by the program.*

   X'cuu'—address of physical unit used only for tapes or disk
   - c—channel number
   - uu—device number

   Check installation for exact specification.
4. // EXEC RPG
   RPG compiler called in—must be followed by source program.
5. /*
   Signals the end of source program.
6. // EXEC LNKEDT
   Links object module in preparation for execution.
7. // EXEC
   Executes the object program—followed by test data.
8. /*
   Signals the end of test data (only included if test data is on cards).
9. /&
   Signals the end of the run.

Job Control—IBM OS or OS/VS

Figure B.3 includes the job control used with RPG programs on some IBM OS systems.

```
1. //jobname JOB (password),programmer name
2. // EXEC RPGCLG
3. // RPG.SYSIN DD *
   (source program follows)
4. /*
5. //GO.SYSPRINT DD SYSOUT=A
6. //GO.SYSIN    DD *
   (test data entered here)
7. /*
8. //
```

Figure B.3
JCL for RPG programs run on some IBM OS systems.

> *Note:*
>
> Uppercase letters—required entries.
> Lowercase letters—programmer supplied.
> Phrases in parentheses are optional or system dependent.
> Required entries must be coded in the precise positions indicated or directly following programmer-supplied entry.

1. JOB command
   JOB name—1 to 8 characters placed directly after //.
   Other identifying data following JOB may be required by your specific system.
2. // EXEC RPGCLG. This is followed by the source program. RPGCLG is the name of the procedure for compiling, linkage editing, and executing the program. Note the name of the RPG compiler may be different for your installation. Check your specifications manual.
3. // RPG.SYSIN DD*
   Notifies the compiler that the source program is on punched cards.
4. /*
   Signals the end of the source program.
5. // GO.SYSPRINT DD SYSOUT = A
   Indicates that all output from execution of program will be on printer.
6. // GO.SYSIN DD*—followed by test data
   Indicates that test data for execution of the program is on cards.
7. /*
   Indicates the end of test data.

8. //
   Indicates end of run.

To change an option, we use the PARM parameter with the EXEC command in OS.

```
// EXEC RPGCLG, PARM.RPG = option 1, option 2, . . .
```

Job Control—UNIVAC

See Figure B.4.

```
1. /LOGON user id.,A (account no.)
2. /OPTION DUMP=YES
                    YES                 YES
3. /PARAM option1=NO,    option2=NO,  ......
4. /EXEC RPG
    (source program entered here)
5. /*
6. /EXEC LNKEDT
7. /EXEC
    (test data entered here)
8. /*
9. /LOGOFF
```

Figure B.4
JCL for RPG programs run on some UNIVAC systems.

> *Note:*
>
> Uppercase letters—required entries.
>
> Lowercase letters—programmer supplied (phrases in parentheses are optional).
>
> Required entries must be coded in the precise positions indicated.

Review of UNIVAC JCL

1. LOGON
   Identifies the program to the system.
2. /OPTION
   If a dump is required when a program is aborted, then /OPTION DUMP = YES must be coded.
3. /PARAM
   Specifies the options that may be included.
   Figure B.5 specifies some UNIVAC options.

4. /EXEC RPG is followed by the source program.
   This statement calls in the compiler, which will translate the source program into an object program.
5. /*
   Indicates the end of the source program.
6. /EXEC LNKEDT
   Indicates that the object module is to be linked in preparation for execution.
7. /EXEC—followed by test data—executes the object program.
8. /*
   Indicates the end of the test data.
9. /LOGOFF
   Indicates the end of the run.

Figure B.5
Some PARAM statement parameters for UNIVAC.

Parameter	*Meaning*
LIST { = YES, = NO* }	Indicates if a source program listing is to be included.
MAP { = YES*, = NO }	Indicates if the program's object summary and storage maps are to be printed.
DISC { = YES*, = NO }	Indicates if an object module is to be generated.
DEBUG { = YES, = NO* }	Indicates that object time diagnostics from the debug routine contain source statement line numbers generated by the compiler.

*Denotes the default that is automatically included.

Operating Command Language for IBM System 3, System 34, and System 38

RPG II is commonly run on IBM System/3 and IBM System 34. RPG II and RPG III are commonly run on IBM System 38. Hence we will include job control commands for these systems as well as the IBM System/3. Note that JCL is called OCL (operating command language).

System/3

Compile and Execute

```
// CALL RPG, (program name)
// RUN
   (Source program here)
/*
/&
// LOAD*
// FILE NAME (name of file)
// RUN
```

```
/*
   (Card or line data goes here if used)
/*
/&
```

System 34

1. To enter (key) a program named "PROG1" into a library named "LIBRARYS", use the following.

   SEU PROG1,R,,,LIBRARYS

   The R option prompts the user in the image of the RPG specification forms and also does some syntax checking.
2. To compile a program "PROG1" in a library named "LIBRARYS":

   // COMPILE SOURCE-PROG1,INLIB-LIBRARYS,OUTLIB-LIBRARYS

3. To list the source module "PROG1" in "LIBRARYS":

   LISTLIBR PROG1,SOURCE,LIBRARYS

4. To establish a procedure (PROC) to execute "PROG1" in "LIBRARYS":

   ```
   // LOAD PROG1
   // FILE NAME-MASTER
   // RUN
   ```

   Use SEU to place this PROC in "LIBRARYS." To execute the program, just key "PROG1".

Note. *The* HELP *key provides prompts for all the system utility formats.*

System 38

Entering the Source Program into the System

After you have written your RPG program on the specification forms, you must enter the source into source files in the system. The normal ways of entering source are as follows.

- You can enter it interactively by using the Source Entry Utility (SEU) of the Interactive Data Base Utilities Licensed Program (IDU).

When you have identified your source as RPG, you can enter the CRTSRC (Create Source) command to call SEU.

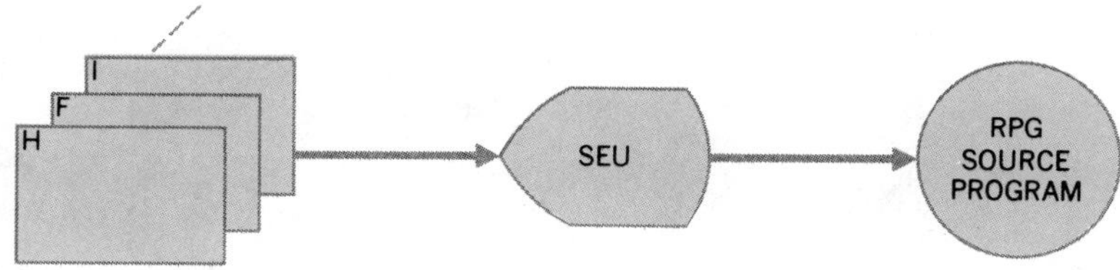

- You can enter your source program in a batch manner (that is, from cards or diskettes) by using either the copy or spooling functions of the control program.

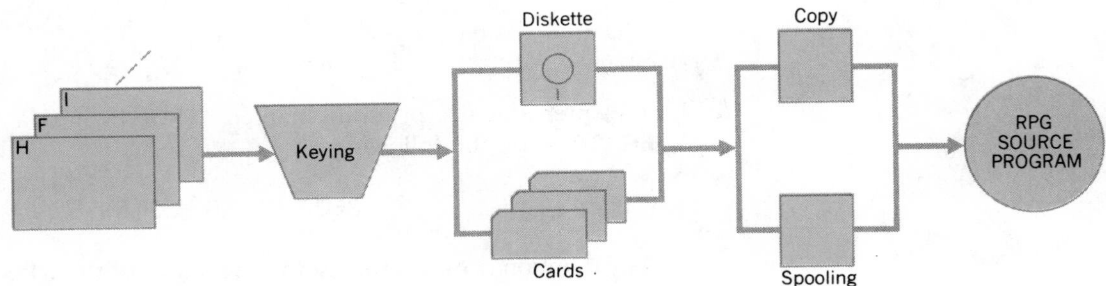

SEU has special display screen formats supplied by RPG that correspond to the RPG specification forms to help you enter your RPG source program specifications. You can enter specifications position-by-position or you can enter a specification field-by-field. Figure B.6 shows a display screen format, the relationship between the headings on the specifications form and the labels on the display screen, and where you can enter specifications on the display screen.

If you specify the APP (QSEURPG) parameter on the CRTSRC command, SEU invokes an RPG syntax checker that checks each specification line as you enter it for errors. The RPG syntax checker checks each position of the specification line for valid entries; it checks that all field, indicator, and operation code names are valid; it checks that the proper fields are specified for each operation code (for example, the arithmetic operations must have a result field entry); and it checks that literals are specified correctly. If a position contains an invalid entry, an error message is displayed that allows you to correct the error. The syntax checker cannot detect logic or relational errors between two or more statements (for example, no TAG exists for a GOTO operation). These errors are detected by the RPG compiler when you compile your program. The RPG syntax checker also skips fields that are designated as skip fields and enters predefined constants (for example, C on the display screen format for calculation specifications).

Compiling the Source Program

After you have entered the source program into the system, you need to compile the source program. This process of compilation is done by the RPG compiler, which is part of the RPG III Licensed Program. If externally described files are used by the program, CPF provides information about the files to the compiled program. The compiler is invoked to create an executable RPG program and a listing.

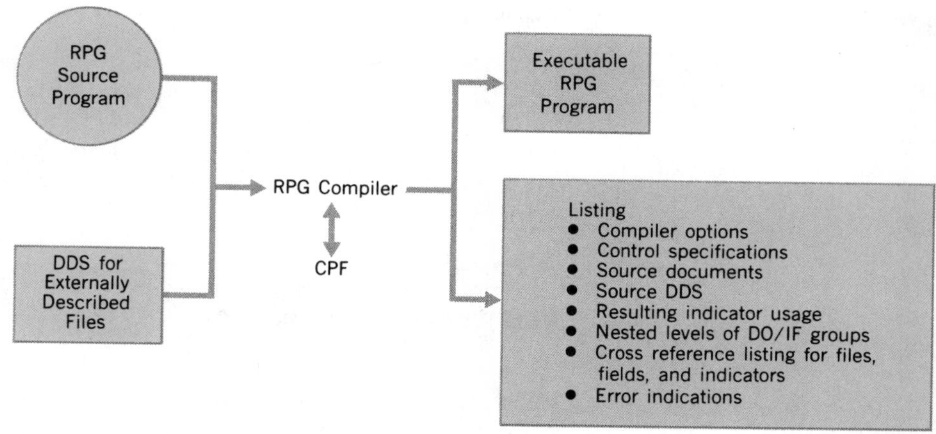

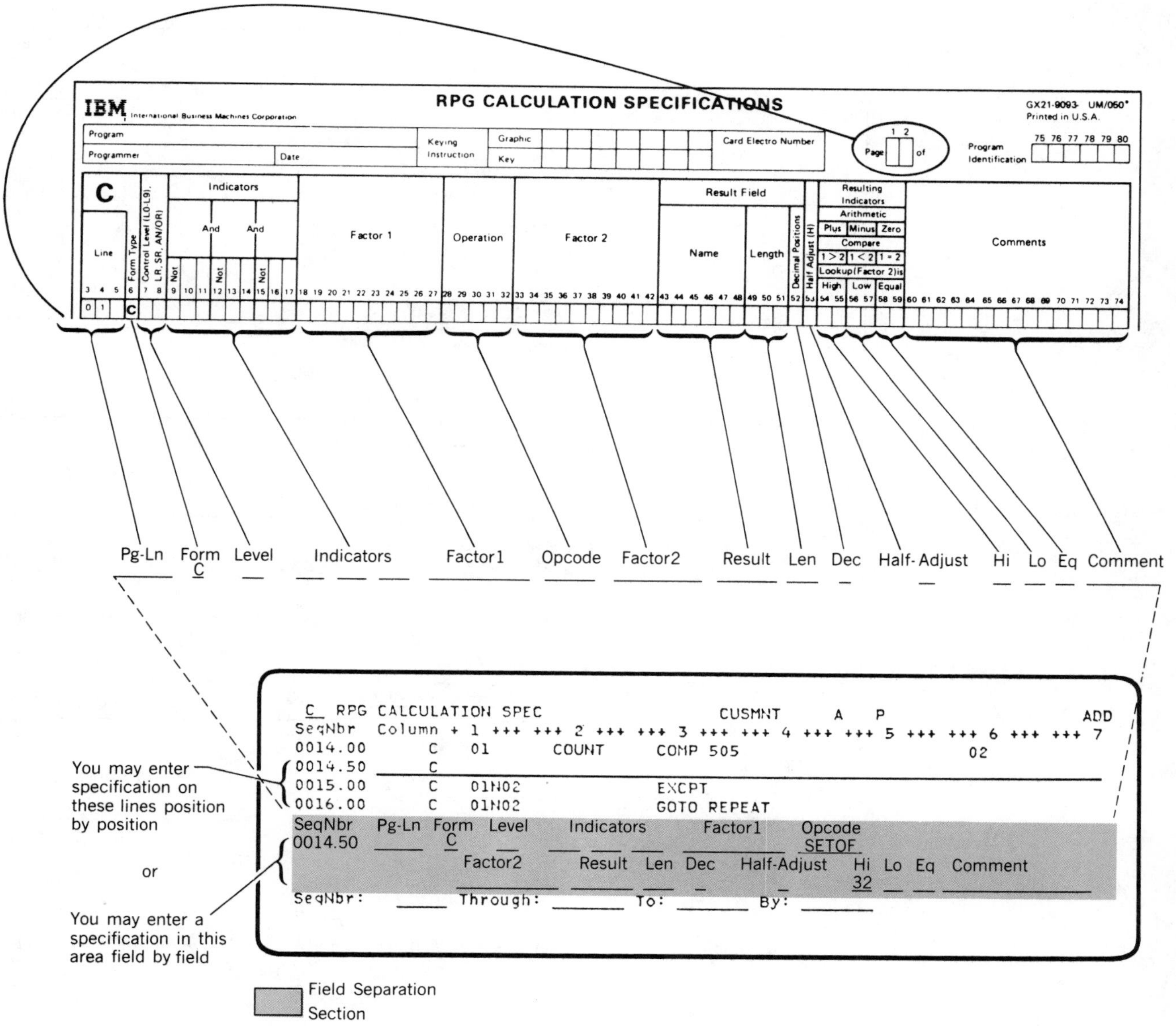

IBM International Business Machines Corporation

RPG CALCULATION SPECIFICATIONS

GX21-9093- UM/050* Printed in U.S.A.

Program | Programmer | Date | Keying Instruction | Graphic | Key | Card Electro Number | Page of | Program Identification

C | Line | Form Type | Control Level (L0-L9, LR, SR, AN/OR) | Indicators (Not, And, Not, And, Not) | Factor 1 | Operation | Factor 2 | Result Field (Name, Length) | Decimal Positions | Half Adjust (H) | Resulting Indicators: Arithmetic (Plus, Minus, Zero), Compare (1>2, 1<2, 1=2), Lookup (Factor 2) is (High, Low, Equal) | Comments

Pg-Ln Form C Level Indicators Factor1 Opcode Factor2 Result Len Dec Half-Adjust Hi Lo Eq Comment

```
 C  RPG CALCULATION SPEC                    CUSMNT      A    P                    ADD
SeqNbr  Column + 1 +++ +++ 2 +++ +++ 3 +++ +++ 4 +++ +++ 5 +++ +++ 6 +++ +++ 7
0014.00       C    01       COUNT      COMP 505                      02
0014.50       C
0015.00       C    01N02               EXCPT
0016.00       C    01N02               GOTO REPEAT
SeqNbr  Pg-Ln  Form  Level   Indicators      Factor1      Opcode
0014.50 ____    C    __    __ __ __       __________    SETOF
                 Factor2         Result  Len  Dec  Half-Adjust  Hi  Lo  Eq  Comment
                 __________    ______   __   _       _         32  __  __  ________
SeqNbr:   _____  Through: _______  To: _______  By: _______
```

You may enter specification on these lines position by position

or

You may enter a specification in this area field by field

Field Separation Section

Figure B.6
Relationship between Calculation Specifications and display screen format.

The compiler syntax checks the RPG source program line-by-line and the interrelationships between the lines. For example, it checks that all field names are defined and, if a field is multiply defined, that each definition has the same attributes.

RPG Command Statement

To compile an RPG source program into an executable program, you must enter the CRTRPGPGM (Create RPG Program) command that invokes the RPG compiler. The command is valid in batch and interactive jobs, and in CL programs. The command syntax is as follows (the defaults are underlined).

```
                                                                  Optional
                                              QGPL (default)
CRTRPGPGM ---- PGM program-name --<                          >---------->
                                              library-name

             QRPGSRC (default)
>-- SRCFILE --<                        *LIBL (default)        >---------->
             source-file-name --<                       >
                                       library-name

             *PGM (default)
>-- SRCMBR --<                                >------------------------->
             source-file-member-name

             *SOURCE (default)       *XREF (default)
>-- OPTION --<                  >--<                  >----------------->
             *NOSOURCE               *NOXREF

             *GEN (default)          *NODUMP (default)
           >--<               >--<                    >----------------->
             *NOGEN                  *DUMP

             *NOLIST (default)       *NOXREF (default)
>-- GENOPT --<                  >--<                  >----------------->
             *LIST                   *XREF

             *NOPATCH (default)      *NODUMP (default)
           --<                  >--<                  >----------------->
             *PATCH                  *DUMP

             *QSYSPRT (default)
>-- PRTFILE --<                   *LIBL (default)     >----------------->
             file-name --<                       >
                                  library-name

             *USER (default)                     *NORMAL (default)
>-- USRPRF --<               >------- PUBAUT --<  *ALL            >------>
             *OWNER                              *NONE

             *BLANK (default)
>-- TEXT --<                  >------
             'text'
```

The description of the parameters follows. The defaults are explained first and are underlined.

PGM parameter. Specifies the qualified name by which the compiled RPG program can be known and the library in which the compiled program is to be located. The program name can also be specified in positions 75 through 8Ø of the control specification. However, a program name specified on the PGM parameter overrides an entry in positions 75 through 8Ø of the control specification. If a program name is not provided on the PGM parameter or in positions 75 through 8Ø of the control specification, the default name is RPGOBJ.

QGPL: Name of the temporary library in which the created program is stored if no library name is specified.

library name: Specifies the name of the library in which the created program is stored.

SRCFILE ***parameter.*** Specifies the name of the source file that contains the RPG source to be compiled.

QRPGSRC: Specifies that the IBM-supplied source file, QRPGSRC, contains the RPG source to be compiled.

qualified-source-file-name: Enter the qualified name of the source file that contains the RPG source to be compiled. If no library qualifier is given, *LIBL is used to find the file.

SRCMBR parameter. Specifies the name of the member of the source file that contains the RPG source to be compiled. This parameter is specified only when SRCFILE is a data base file.

*PGM: The RPG source to be compiled is in the member of the source file that has the same name as that specified for the compiled program in the PGM parameter.

source-file-member-name: Enter the name of the member that contains the RPG source.

OPTION parameter. Specifies whether the following options are to be written on the compiler listing when the RPG source is compiled.

*SOURCE: Source input and diagnostic listings are written.

*NOSOURCE: No source input or diagnostic listings are written.

*XREF: A cross-reference listing is written for variable data item references in the source data.

*NOXREF: No cross-reference listing is written for variable data item references in the source data.

*GEN: An executable program is generated after compilation time.

*NOGEN: No executable program is generated after compilation time.

*NODUMP: The compiler does not dump all data areas.

*DUMP: The compiler dumps all data areas.

GENOPT ***parameter.*** Specifies whether the following options are to be in effect during program creation.

*NOLIST: No source input and generated output (along with any messages) are written.

*LIST: The source input and generated output (along with any messages) are written.

*NOXREF: No cross-reference listing is written for all objects defined in the source input.

*XREF: A cross-reference listing is written for all objects defined in the source input.

*NOPATCH: No space is to be reserved in the compiled program for a program patch area.

*PATCH: Space is to be reserved in the compiled program for a program patch area. The size of the patch area is based on the size of the generated program.

*NODUMP: The compiler does not dump all data areas.

*DUMP: The compiler dumps all data areas.

PRTFILE ***parameter.*** Specifies the file name that the program uses to refer to the printer file.

*QSYSPRT: Specifies that the IBM-supplied file, QSYSPRT, receives printer output.

qualified-file-name: Specifies the file name to receive printer output.

USRPRF ***parameter.*** Specifies under which user security profile the compiled RPG program is to execute. The user profile of either the program owner or the program user determines what storage resources, scheduling priority, and operational rights are used to execute the program.

*USER: The compiled RPG program executes under the program user's security profile.

*OWNER: The compiled RPG program executes under the program owner's user security profile.

PUBAUT ***parameter.*** Specifies what authority the public users (all users not specifically authorized by name) have for the program and its description. The different levels of authority are described in the *CPF Programmer's Guide.*

*NORMAL: The public has only operational authority for the program. Any user can execute the program, but cannot change or debug it.

*ALL: The public has all levels of authority for the program.

*NONE: No user, other than the program owner, can use the program, unless the owner authorizes specific levels of authority to users by name in the GRTOBJAUT (Grant Object Authority) command. (For information on the GRTOBJAUT command, see the *CPF Reference Manual—Control Language.*)

TEXT ***parameter.*** Lets the user enter text that briefly describes the program and its function. For example, the DSPOBJD (Display Object Description) command can be used to display text. (For information on the DSPOBJD command and other ways to enter text see the *CPF Reference Manual—Control Language.*)

*BLANK: No text is specified.

'text': The text that briefly describes the program and its function can be a maximum of 50 characters in length and must be enclosed in apostrophes. The apostrophes are not part of the 50-character string.

APPENDIX C

Basic Elements of Flowcharting

A useful tool for analyzing the logic necessary in a program is called a **flowchart.** A flowchart is a diagram, or pictorial representation, of the logic flow of a program; it is drawn *before* the problem is coded. It is like the blueprint an architect prepares before a house is built. Through the use of a flowchart, programmers can organize and verify the logic they must employ.

This section is designed to illustrate the *elements* of program flowcharting. It does not presume to teach the beginner how to *write* such diagrams. It will, however, indicate the method used to *read* flowcharts, since they have been employed throughout the text to denote program logic. It is hoped that the ability to write flowcharts will come with constant exposure to their use.

Consider the program flowchart indicated in Figure C.1. This flowchart depicts the logic flow used to print salary checks for all salespeople in a company. If a salesperson has made $1ØØ or more in sales, the commission is 1Ø% of sales, which is added to his or her salary. Similarly, if a salesperson has made $5Ø or more (but not more than $1ØØ), the commission is 5% of sales, which is added to his or her salary. The unfortunate salesperson who has made less than $5Ø receives a salary with no commission.

The logic flow, as denoted in a flowchart, is fairly easy to read. In addition, we will see later that it is relatively simple to code the program from a flowchart.

Several important points may be noted from this illustration.

1. A logic flow is read from top to bottom unless a specific condition alters the path.
2. Different symbols are used to denote different functions.
3. All symbols have explanatory notes indicating the specific operations.

Since a symbol denotes a major class of function such as input-output or processing, a note is required within the symbol to describe the specific operation to be performed. The following symbols are the ones most frequently used in program flowcharts.

Symbol	Name	Use
	Input/Output	Used for all I/O operations. For example, the reading of a record, the writing of a line, and the writing of a magnetic tape are considered I/O functions.
	Processing	Used for all arithmetic and data transfer operations. For example, moving of data from one area of storage (input) to another area (output), and multiplying percentage by total sales are processing functions.

Symbol	Name	Use
	Decision	Used to test all conditions. For example, testing whether one field is larger than another, and testing whether a given field has specific contents (zeros, blanks) are considered decision functions.
	Connector	Used to change the normal path of a flowchart. There are two kinds of branches.

1. Unconditional branch connector:

When an unconditional branch connector is indicated, control is transferred to another point. For example, BEGIN When this symbol is reached, a transfer to BEGIN *always* occurs.

2. Conditional branch connector:

denotes that *if* a specific condition exists, then a transfer or branch will occur. Conditional branches are always the result of a decision.

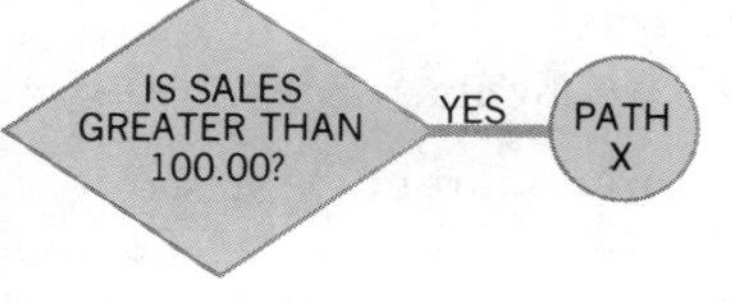

If sales exceed $100 a conditional branch to PATH-X occurs.

The symbol

or

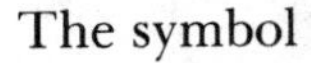

is called an *entry connector* and denotes entry points into the logic flow.

Observe that the flowchart illustrated in Figure C.1 reads sales records as input. Note, however, that there is no indication of when the job is terminated. All flowcharts must indicate under what conditions a job is considered to be completed. Unless this is done, the flowchart seems to indicate an **infinite loop;** that is, it appears as if the program will read records indefinitely and the flow will never end.

Thus we must modify the flowchart to indicate an end of job, EOJ. The logical ending of the flowchart in Figure C.1 is reached when there are no more records to be read. Figure C.2 illustrates the completed program.

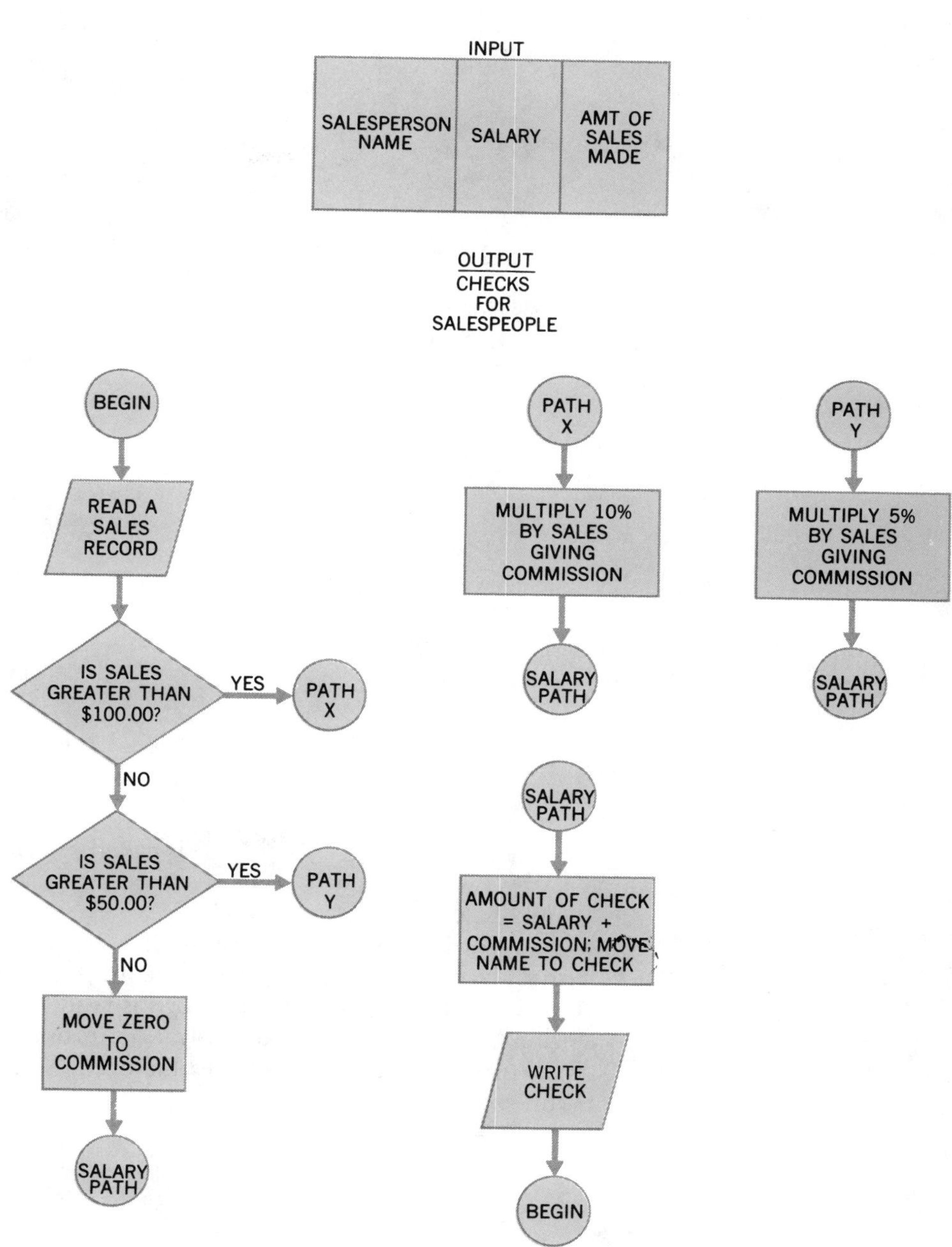

Figure C.1
Sample program flowchart.

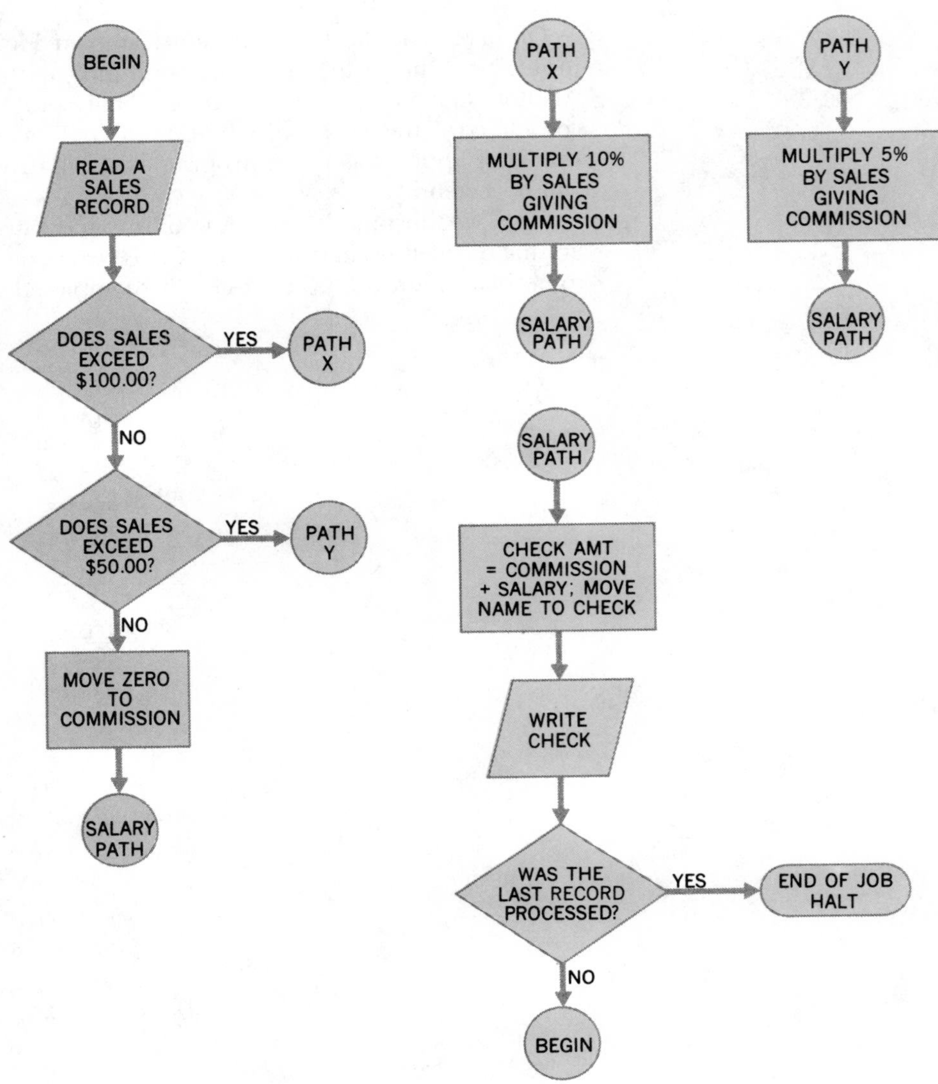

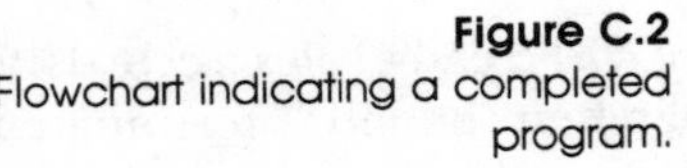
Figure C.2 Flowchart indicating a completed program.

The symbol (END OF JOB HALT) is called a **terminal** symbol and is used to denote a halt.

A record is tested to determine if it is an end-of-file or trailer record. The usual place for testing for the last record is after a READ command, as in Figure C.3. If an EOF or end-of-file record is read, the job is terminated.

Let us consider a second illustration. From the following record format, we wish to print the names of all blue-eyed, blonde males and all brown-eyed, brunette females.

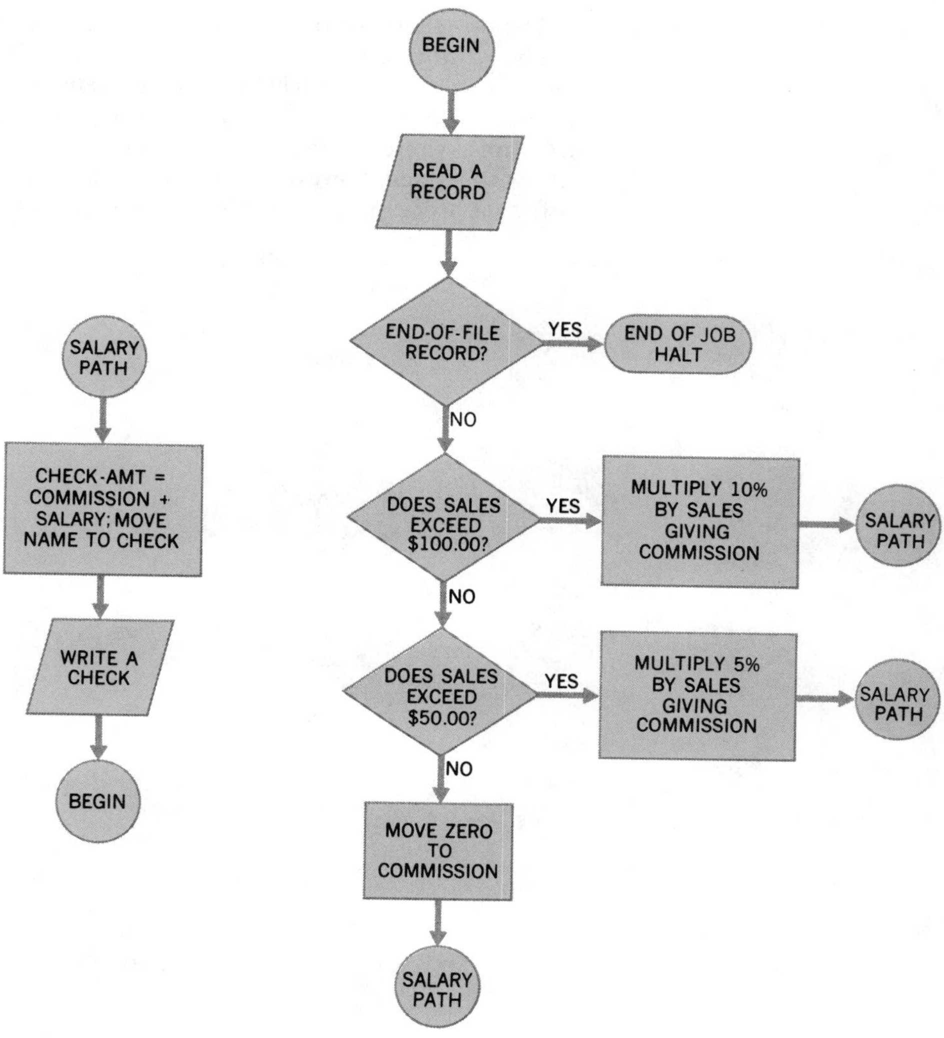

Figure C.3
The usual place for testing for the last record.

Record Format

Positions:

1-2Ø	NAME
21	SEX (M-male, F-female)
22	COLOR OF EYES (1-Blue, 2-Brown, 3-Other)
23	COLOR OF HAIR (1-Brown, 2-Blonde, 3-Other)
24-8Ø	Not used

The flowchart for this problem is illustrated in Figure C.4.

The writing of flowcharts is a difficult task for the beginner in data processing. One advantage of RPG is that the elementary level programs are relatively simple to code and a flowchart is therefore unnecessary. For intermediate level programs, where the logic flow is often complex, a flowchart can be quite helpful. At this stage, however, it is hoped that the student will be familiar enough with data processing to be able to write adequate flowcharts.

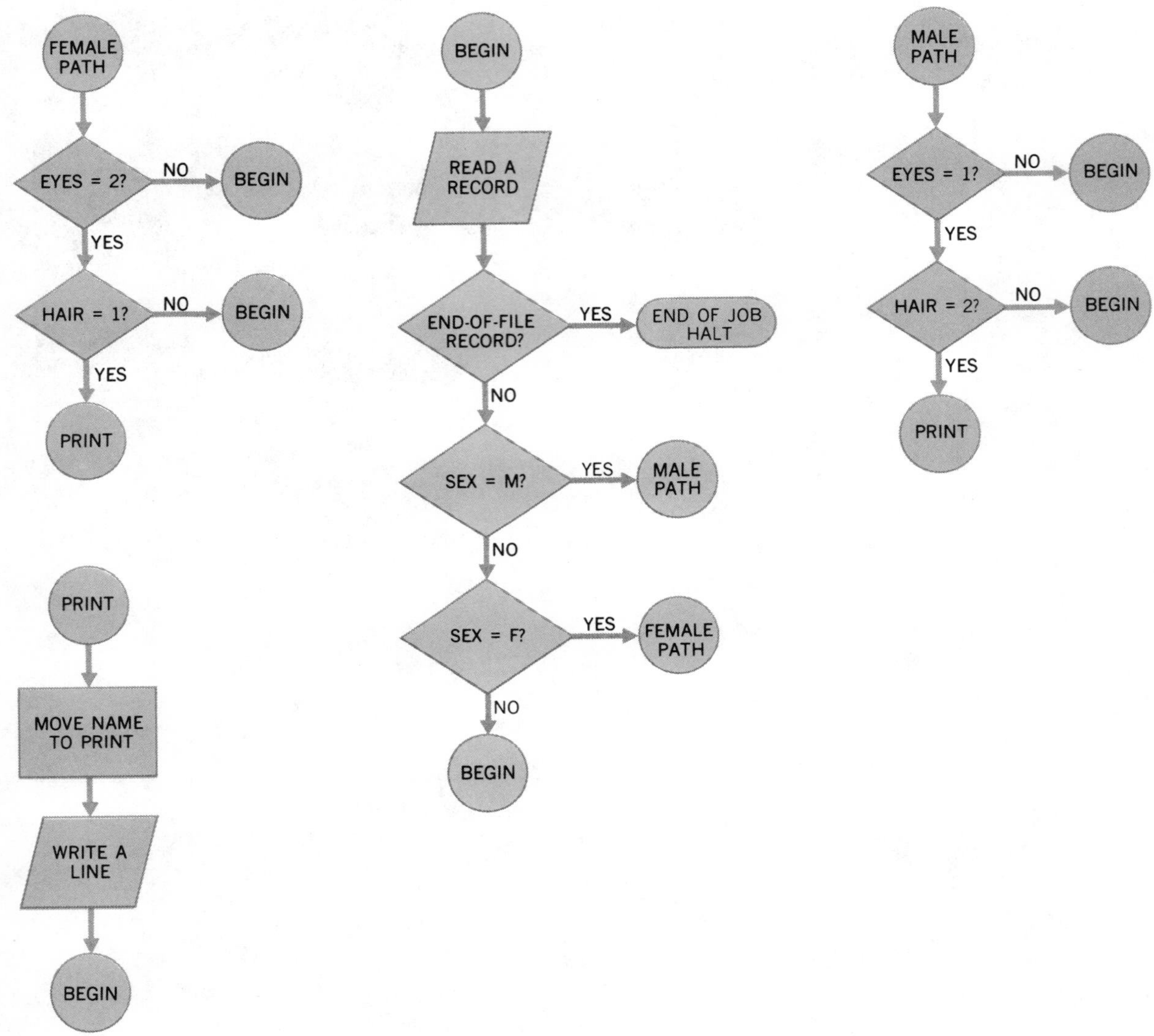

Figure C.4
Sample program flowchart.

Self-Evaluating Quiz

1. A flowchart is used for analyzing the ________ necessary in a program.
   logic
2. A flowchart is drawn (before/after) the problem is coded.
   before
3. A program flowchart is read from ________ to ________ .
   top
   bottom
4. Different ________ are used to denote different functions.
   symbols
5. The input-output symbol is coded as ________ .

6. A processing symbol is coded as ________ .

7.  is called a ________ symbol.

   decision
8. The three kinds of connector symbols are ________ , ________ , and ________ .
   unconditional branch connector
   conditional branch connector
   entry connector
9. A conditional branch connector always accompanies a ________ symbol.
   decision
10. All symbols have ________ indicating the specific operations.
    explanatory notes
11. A last record test usually ________ the READ command.
    directly follows

Review Questions

1. Give four examples of input-output functions.
2. Give four examples of processing functions.
3. Give two examples of decision functions.
4. (T or F) A program flowchart is required before any programs are written.
5. What is the purpose of a last record test?

Practice Problems

1. Consider the flowchart in Figure C.5. With the following input records, what will be the contents of TOTAL at the end of all operations?

Record No.	*Contents of Position 18*	*Contents of Position 19*
1	1	2
2	1	3
3	1	2
4	1	Ø
5	(Blank)	(Blank)
6	(Blank)	1
7	1	(Blank)
8	1	2
9	1	2
1Ø	(Blank)	2

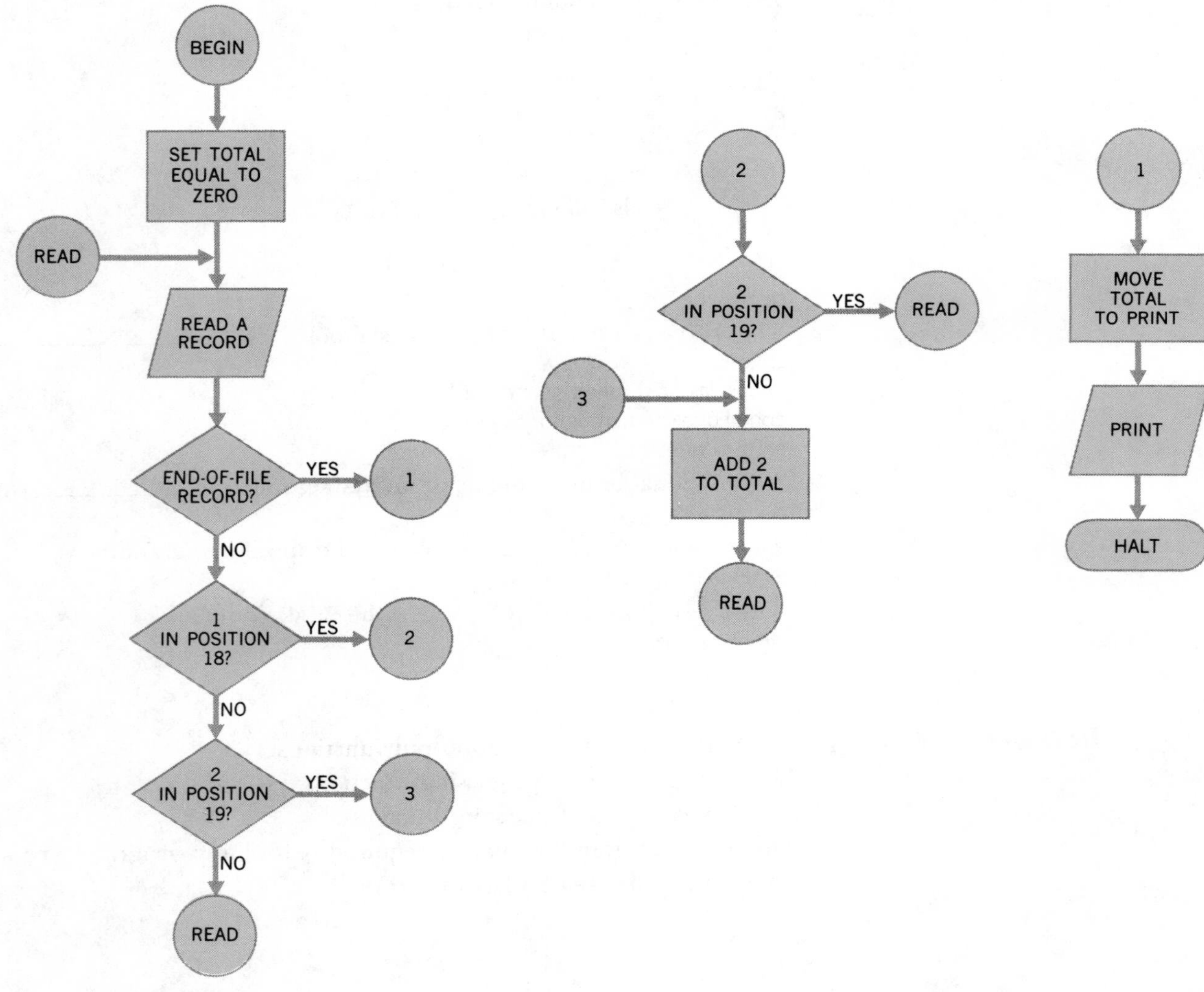

Figure C.5
Flowchart for Practice Problem 1.

2. Consider the flowchart in Figure C.6.
   a. A record is punched after reading how many records? Explain.
   b. The system is printing a record after reading how many records? Explain.
   c. The system is writing on tape after reading how many records? Explain.
3. Questions a-d refer to the flowchart in Figure C.7. Codes in 15 records are: 1, 2, 3, 2, 1, 1, 2, 2, 3, 3, 1, 2, 3, 1, 2.
   a. How many records will be read?
   b. What is the value of switch when a branch to EOJ occurs?
   c. What is the value of ACCUM when a branch to EOJ occurs?
   d. How many records would have been read if ACCUM were originally set to 1 instead of Ø?

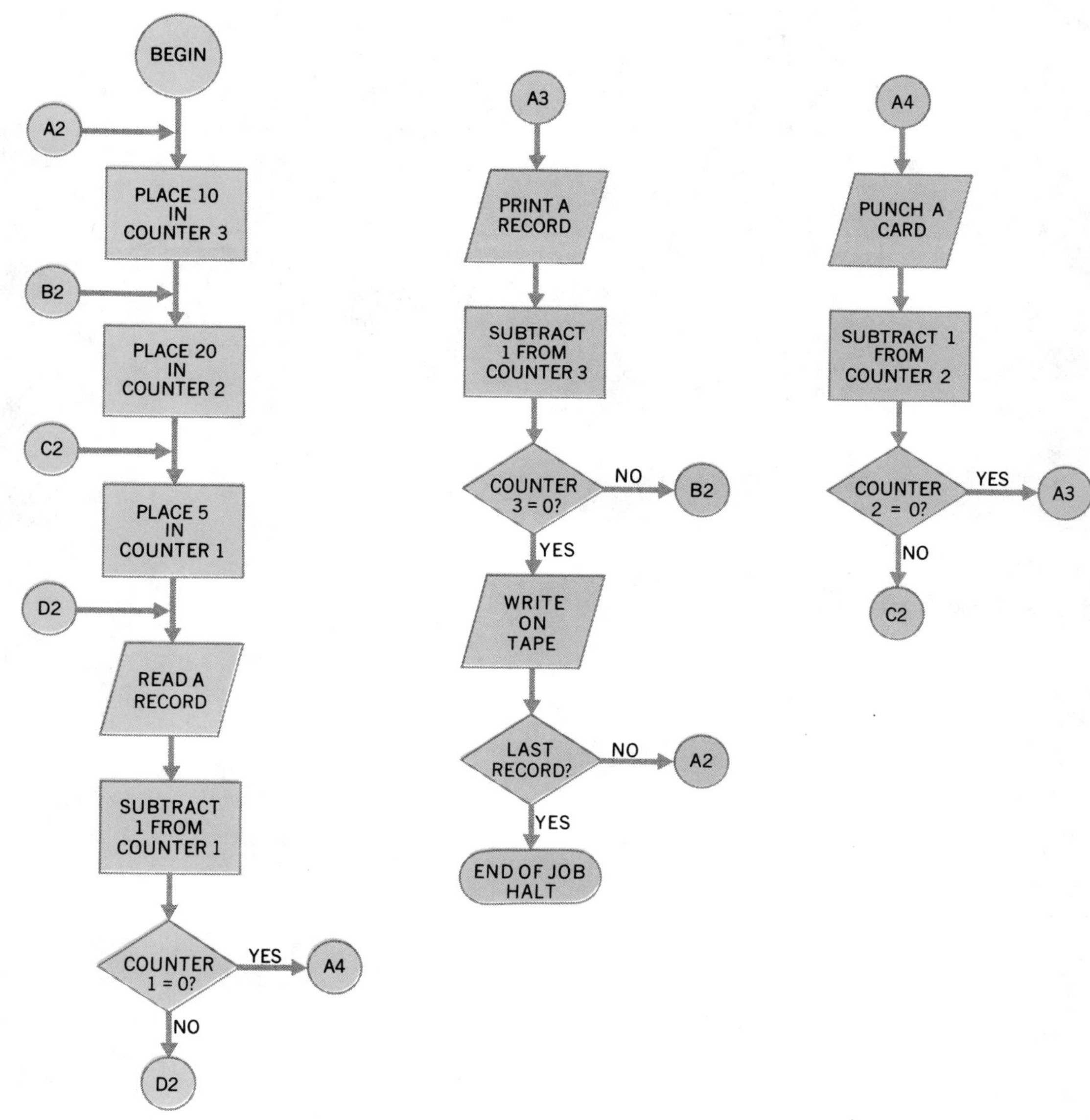

Figure C.6
Flowchart for Practice Problem 2.

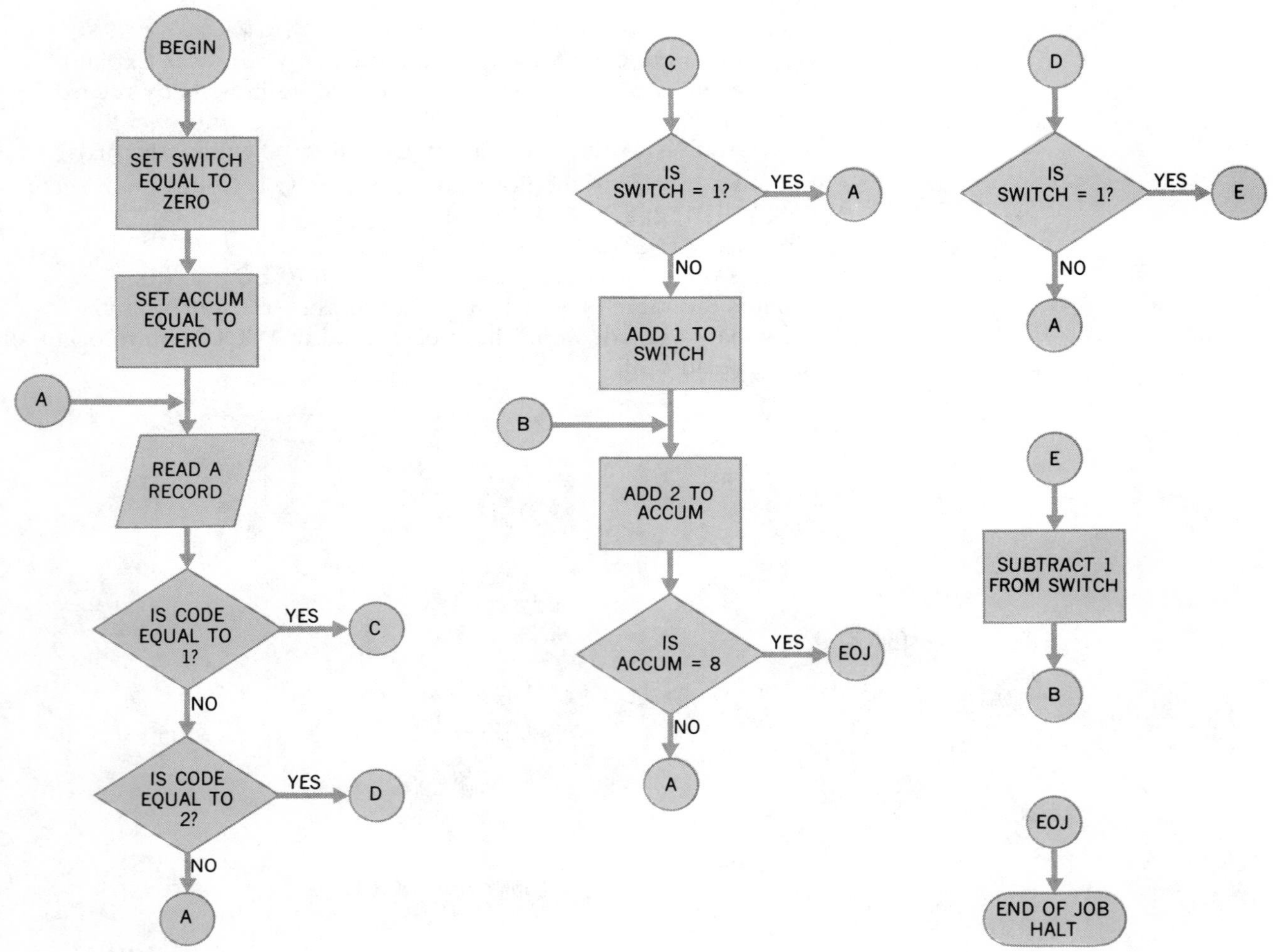

Figure C.7
Flowchart for Practice Problem 3.

APPENDIX D

Elements of Punched Cards

Consider the blank card in Figure D.1. Notice that at the very bottom of the card there are small digits numbered 1 to 8Ø. Note also that below the first horizontal group of numbers (zero) there are the same 8Ø numbers. Each number corresponds to a card column. Hence, the standard punched card has **8Ø columns,** numbered 1 to 8Ø. The card in Figure D.1 has a shaded portion in columns 34 to 56 for illustrative purposes.

Each column or position holds one character of data, where a **character** is a letter, digit, or special symbol such as a +, $, %. Thus, the standard 8Ø-column card can hold 8Ø characters of data, that is, 8Ø letters, digits, and special symbols.

Cards may be used in RPG for (1) a source program or (2) data. Data on a card will be identified by the columns in which it is located and by the characters actually punched in the columns. Characters, represented by holes punched in the cards, are then sensed by special card reader devices that are part of a computer system. We see later in this section that data is typically recorded on punched cards with the use of a keypunch machine, which is similar to a typewriter.

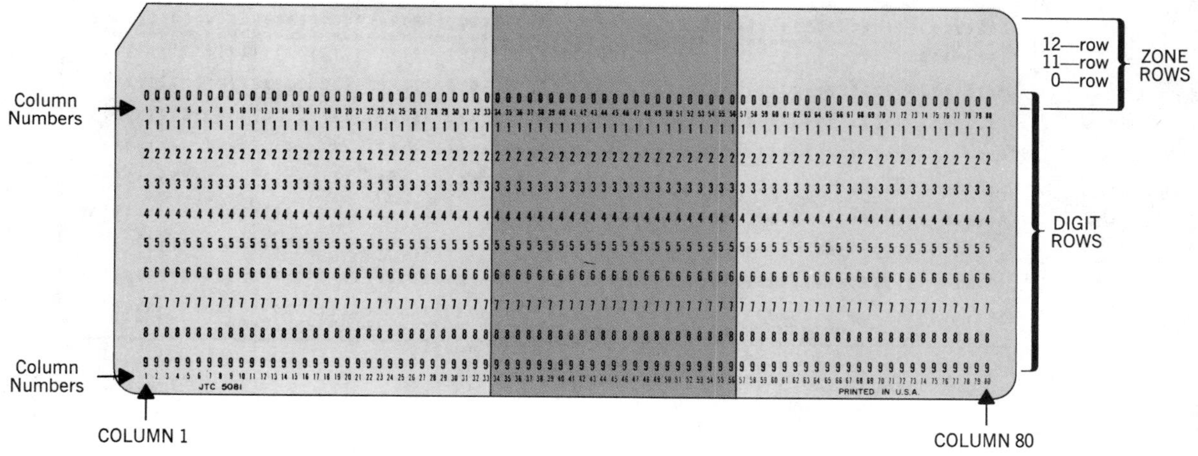

Figure D.1
(*a*) Standard punched card (columns 34 to 56 shaded). (*b*) Illustration of zone and digits rows.

I. The Hollerith Code

The holes in punched cards are punched according to a code devised by Herman Hollerith, called the **Hollerith code.**

Look again at the punched card illustrated in Figure D.1. Notice that the numbers Ø to 9 are printed in every single column of the card along with the specific column number. These numbers Ø to 9 are called the Ø to 9 **rows,** respectively.

A. Representing Digits with the Hollerith Code

To code a digit or number in a particular column, a hole is punched in the corresponding row of that column.

Figure D.2 illustrates a series of cards in an RPG source program. In the first card of Figure D.2, column 45 contains a "4" because it has a punch in the 4-row. In the same figure, columns 1 and 2 contain a "Ø1" because there is a punch in the Ø-row of column 1 and a punch in the 1-row of column 2. Hence, using the Hollerith code, numbers are represented by a corresponding hole in the digit row of the column desired.

Figure D.2
Sample cards used in an RPG source program.

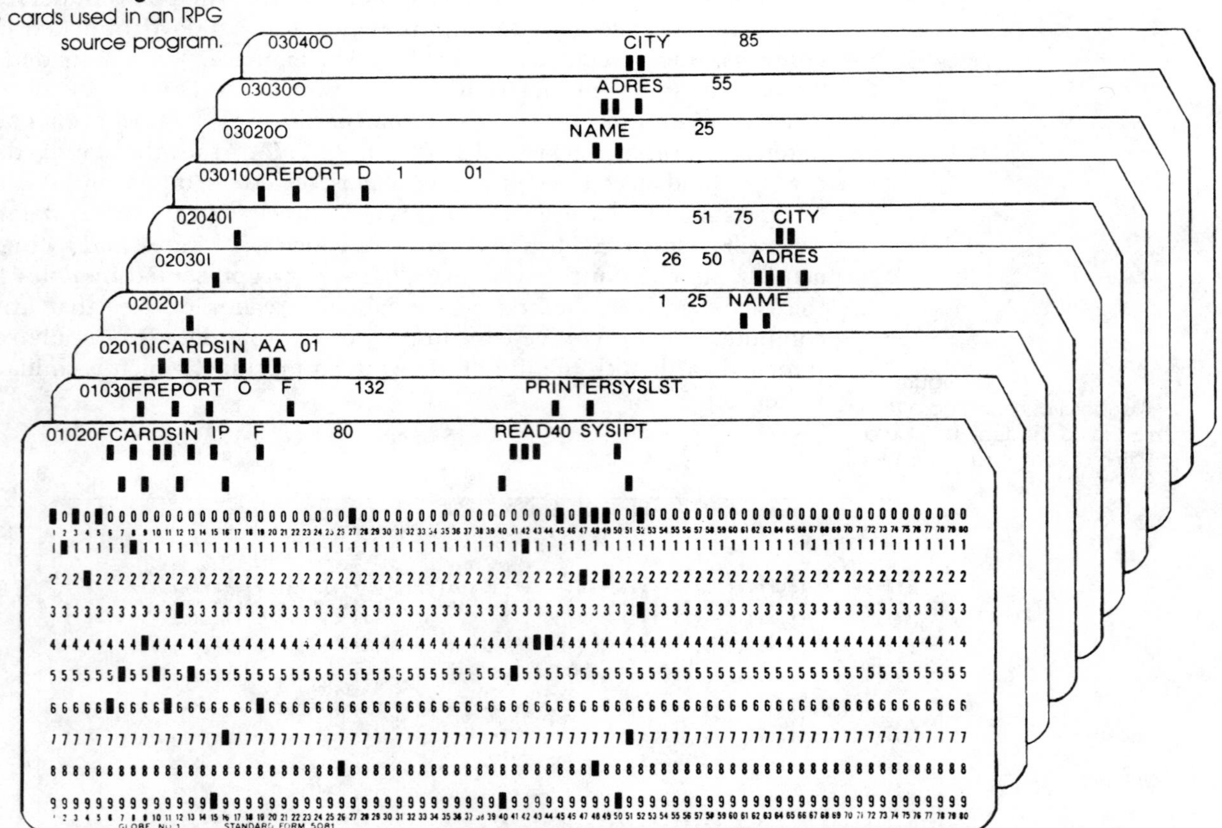

Self-Evaluating Quiz

1. The number of characters that can be represented on a standard punched card is ________ .
2. Each character is contained in one ________ of the card.
3. A character can be a number or a ________ .
4. The term *punched card* means that data is represented on cards in the form of ________ .
5. The code for punching characters on an 8Ø-column card is called the ________ code.
6. (a) Show how the following card would look if it had a "3" in column 6.
   (b) Show how the card would look if it had a "5" in column 4Ø.
   (c) Show how the card would look if it had a "56" in columns 23–24.

(d) Indicate what area of the card has been shaded.

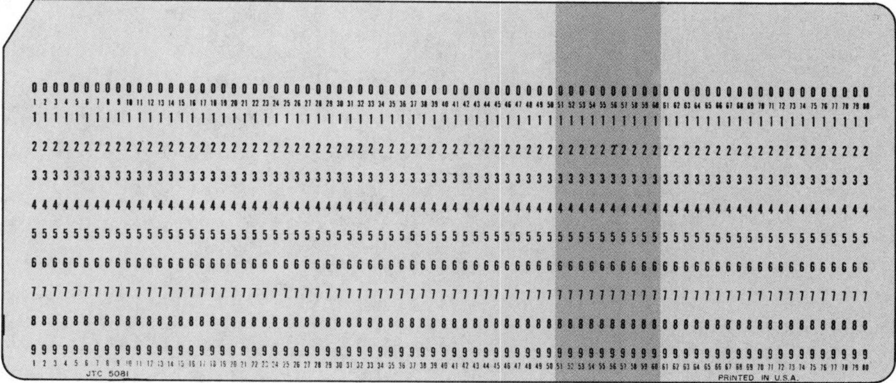

7. How are punched cards "read" by data processing equipment?

Solutions

1. 8Ø
2. column or position—These words mean the same thing, but "column" is normally used when referring to cards.
3. letter or special symbol such as +, $, %
4. punched holes
5. Hollerith
6. (a), (b), (c) follow; (d) 51 to 6Ø.

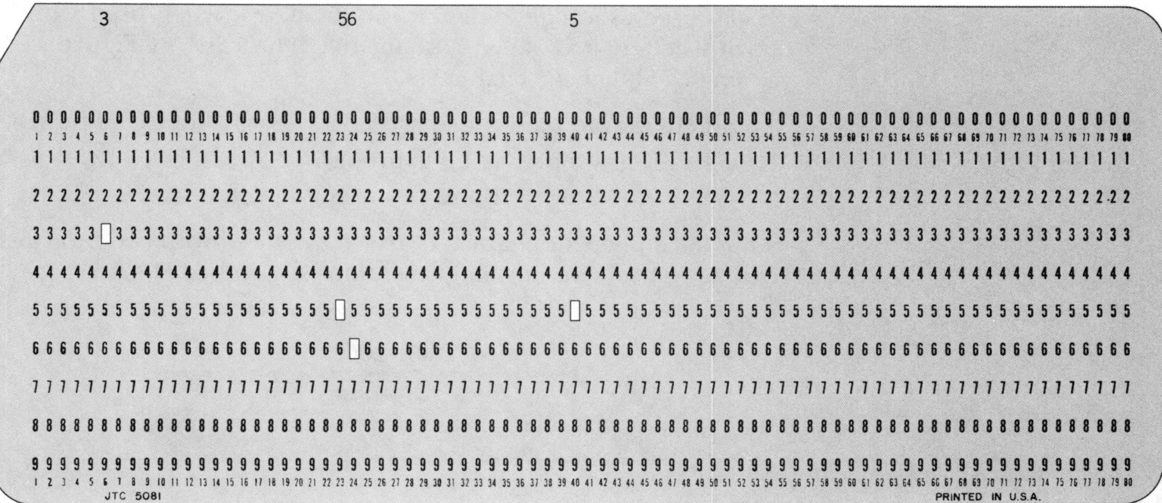

7. The holes punched in the cards are sensed by a card reader device.

B. Representing Alphabetic Data with the Hollerith Code

The representation of letters and special symbols with the Hollerith Code is somewhat more complicated than the representation of numbers because you generally need to use more than one punch in a single column.

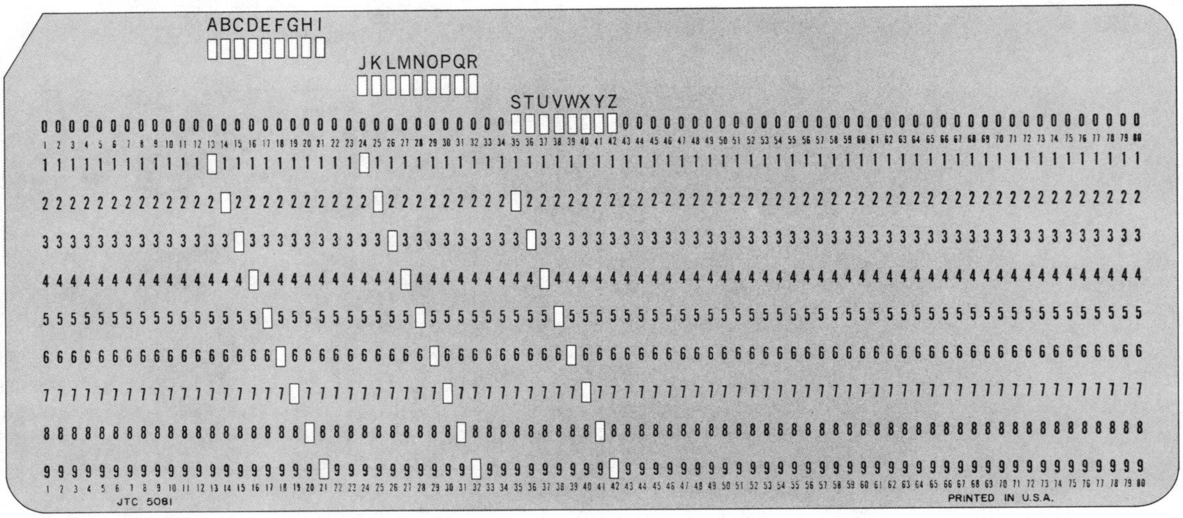

Figure D.3
Card showing Hollerith code for letters.

To represent alphabetic data, you must use a digit punch in conjunction with another punch. Consider again the card illustrated in Figure D.1. There are, you will note, 1Ø numbered rows (Ø to 9) and two without printing, called the 11- and 12-rows. You use the Ø-, 11-, and 12-rows in conjunction with a digit punch, in a *single* column, to represent the letters of the alphabet. Thus, the Ø-, 11-, 12-rows are referred to as the **zone** rows and the Ø to 9 as the **digit** rows. For convenience, the Ø-row is considered both a zone and a digit row. When used as a digit, alone, it is a digit row; when used with another digit to form a letter, it is called a zone row. The card in Figure D.3 illustrates the coding of alphabetic characters.

- Letters A to I are coded as 12-1, 12-2, through 12-9 punches, respectively.
- J to R are coded as 11-1 through 11-9, respectively.
- S to Z are coded as Ø-2 through Ø-9, respectively.

Thus, all alphabetic characters are represented with two punches, a zone punch and a digit punch, in a single column (see Figure D.4).

HOLLERITH CODE

ZONE PUNCHES	DIGIT PUNCHES								
	1	2	3	4	5	6	7	8	9
12	A	B	C	D	E	F	G	H	I
11	J	K	L	M	N	O	P	Q	R
0	/	S	T	U	V	W	X	Y	Z

Figure D.4
Hollerith code for letters.

II. Features of a Punched Card

Figure D.5 illustrates significant facts about the punched card. The top of the card is called the **12-edge,** since the 12-row is located there. Similarly, the bottom of the card is called the **9-edge,** since the 9-row is at the bottom.

Notice that punched cards typically have one of the corners at the top cut. This is simply to facilitate proper alignment of the cards when they are being handled by a computer operator.

The special characters that can be represented on a card are indicated in columns 51 to 76 of Figure D.5. Use one, two, or three punches in a single column. An asterisk, *, for example, (column 6Ø) is represented by the 11-4-8 punches.

It is not necessary to memorize the Hollerith code for letters and symbols, since machines, not people, do the actual punching. But it is useful to be familiar with the code for several reasons. First, it is possible for a card to be punched with data but to have no printing on the top. To identify the data, you might need to translate the punches into characters. Second, the Hollerith code corresponds, to some extent, to the machine code used in many computers and thus is useful to know.

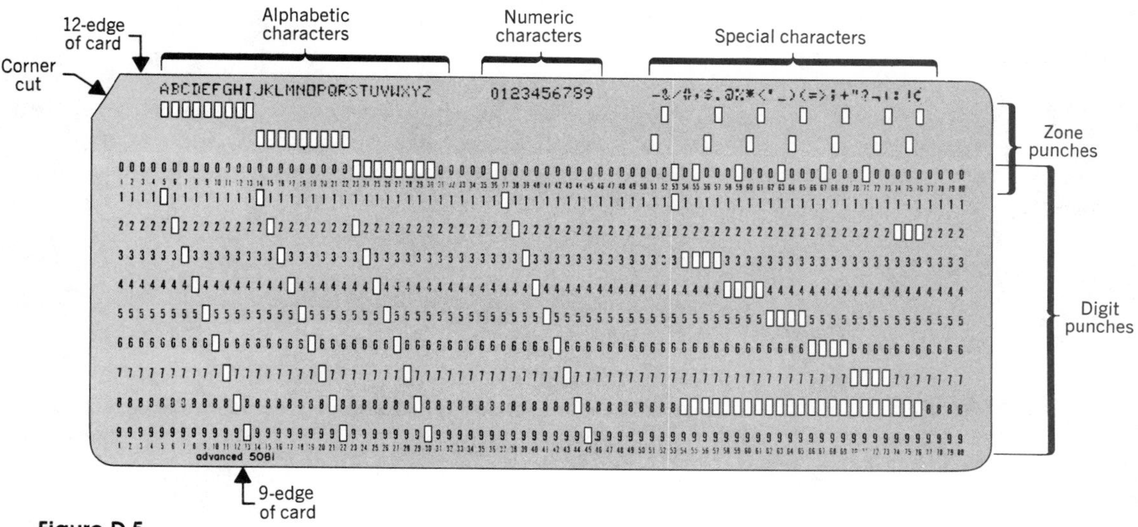

Figure D.5
Features of a punched card.

A set of adjacent positions used to represent a unit of data is called a **field.** Fields can be numeric, alphabetic, or *alphanumeric,* where they can contain any combination of letters, digits, and special symbols. An ADDRESS field, for example, is an alphanumeric field.

Examine the punched card in Figure D.6. Notice that in this case the LAST NAME, FIRST NAME, and MIDDLE INITIAL fields are completely filled with data and appear to run together. The computer will, however, be able to distinguish the LAST NAME from the other fields since it will be instructed that columns 1 through 1Ø contain *only* the LAST NAME, 11 through 18 the FIRST NAME, and so on.

Although the data appears on the card in the order shown, it can be printed out in any order that is desired (see Figure D.6).

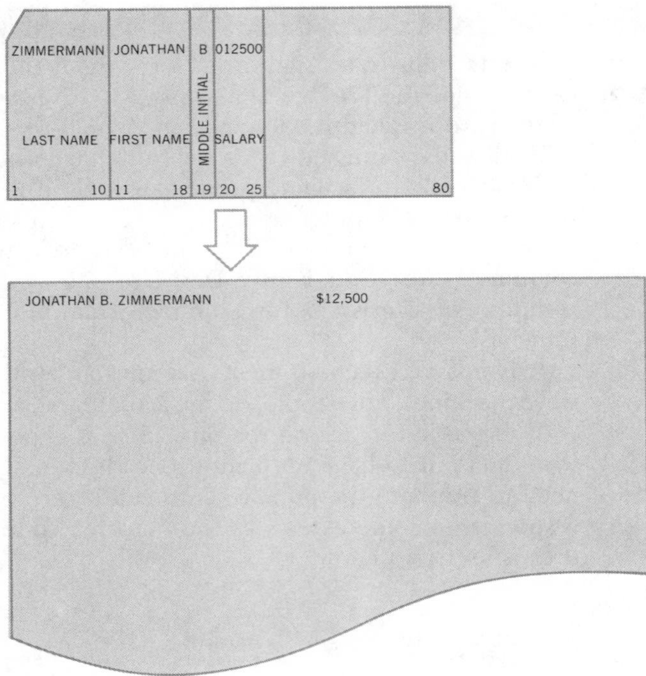

Figure D.6 Printing information from a punched card.

As you can see, the computer can be instructed not only to rearrange the fields for output, but to add punctuation, such as a period after the middle initial and a dollar sign and comma with the dollar amount. Thus there is no need to include edit symbols on a punched card. In fact, data is represented very concisely on a card for several reasons.

Why Data on a Card Is Concise

1. It is a waste of space on a card to allow room for punctuation, which can easily be inserted in the output by means of a program. Keep in mind that since the punched card has a limited number of columns—either 8Ø or 96—it is necessary to conserve space so that as many fields as possible can be included in a given card. To save additional space on a card, fields are frequently coded. For example, an ACCOUNT NUMBER of three digits can be used to replace a CUSTOMER NAME field, which would require far more than three characters.
2. It takes additional time to key unnecessary characters into cards.
3. The more characters that are included on input data cards, the greater the likelihood of keypunch errors.

Self-Evaluating Quiz

1. (T or F) Data is recorded on most cards in the form of round punched holes used to represent a code.
2. (T or F) There are machines that can mechanically sense holes on a punched card and then sort, merge, or compile the data.
3. (T or F) Characters of data on a punched card are represented by punched holes.

4. (T or F) There are 12 columns on a punched card.
5. (T or F) Each row of a card can store a character of data.
6. (T or F) Most punched cards can store 8Ø characters of data.
7. (T or F) The rows on a card are numbered Ø to 9.
8. (T or F) To represent alphabetic data on a card, you must use a digit punch in conjunction with another punch in the same column.
9. Data is the combination of ________ consisting of letters, digits, and symbols that results in meaningful information.
10. A vertical section of a card is called a ________ , of which there are (no.) ________ for most cards.

Use Figure D.5 to answer questions 11 to 15.

11. The Hollerith code representation for the letter V is ________ .
12. The Hollerith code representation for the letter Q is ________ .
13. The Hollerith code representation for the letter D is ________ .
14. The Hollerith code representation for the letter G is ________ .
15. The Hollerith code representation for the number 6 is ________ .
16. The top of the card is generally referred to as the (no.) ________ -edge and the bottom of the card is generally referred to as the (no.) ________ -edge.

Solutions

1. F—Holes are rectangular.
2. T
3. T
4. F—There are 12 rows.
5. F—Each column can store a character.
6. T
7. T—But there are two more—11 and 12.
8. T
9. characters
10. column
    8Ø
11. Ø-5
12. 11-8
13. 12-4
14. 12-7
15. 6
16. 12
    9

III. Other Forms of Punched Cards

A. The 96-Column Card

In addition to the standard 8Ø-column card, there is a 96-column card (Figure D.7), which is used by some systems. It is a very useful variation for punched card users because it can contain 2Ø% additional data. It can, however, be used only with certain computer systems such as the IBM System/3.

The 96-column card is smaller than the standard 8Ø-column card and is subdivided into three separate **tiers** or punching areas, each capable of storing 32 characters of information. The code used with this card is a variation of the Hollerith Code called BCD or *B*inary *C*oded *D*ecimal. Note that holes punched on a 96-column card are round, not rectangular.

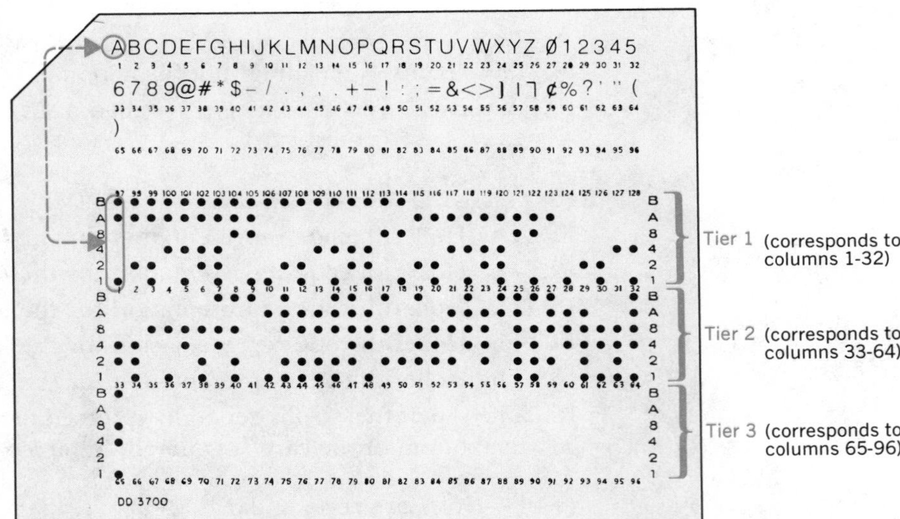

Figure D.7
Sample 96-column card.

APPENDIX E

The following chart consists of a sample data set that can be used with Practice Problem number 2 of each chapter.

```
ØØØØ1ADAMSON        15ØØØ124579283Ø1Ø125ØØØ61ØØØ1ØØ5
ØØØØ2BAKER          225ØØØ36441ØØØØ1Ø3175ØØ5ØØØØØ815
ØØØØ3CARTNELL       185ØØØ143Ø4ØØ1Ø1Ø318ØØØ425ØØ15Ø7
ØØØØ4DORSEY         255ØØ11Ø114Ø23Ø1Ø3225ØØ65ØØØØ8Ø8
ØØØØ5HAMMOND        12ØØØØ65342Ø1ØØ2Ø319ØØØ58ØØØ1911
ØØØØ6NOLTE          18ØØØØØ7326Ø1ØØ2Ø1225ØØ4ØØØØØ515
ØØØØ7REDFORD        6ØØØØØØ134836ØØ2Ø325ØØØ375ØØ12Ø7
ØØØØ8JOHNKE         2Ø5ØØØØ1371ØØØØ2Ø218ØØØ4ØØØØ18Ø5
ØØØØ9WHITE          75ØØØ1182Ø3Ø21Ø3Ø219ØØØ65ØØØØ9Ø9
ØØØ1ØMARSHALL       225ØØØ8531ØØ3ØØ3Ø325ØØØ5ØØØØØ8Ø9
ØØØ11EISEN          25ØØØØ9Ø324Ø15Ø3Ø125ØØØ45ØØØ12Ø8
ØØØ12SAGER          265ØØ123Ø23478Ø3Ø2185ØØ55ØØØØ611
ØØØ13STERN          265ØØ113311 2Ø5Ø3Ø219ØØØ425ØØ12Ø4
ØØØ14SUMMERS        85ØØØ718651Ø15Ø4Ø12ØØØØ525ØØ19Ø9
ØØØ15JONES          195ØØ4Ø222ØØ13Ø4Ø317ØØØ6ØØØØØ913
ØØØ16JOHNSON        9ØØØØ9197ØØ8Ø5Ø4Ø32ØØØØ5ØØØØØ811
ØØØ17NOLAN          22ØØØ183733ØØ43Ø5Ø118ØØØ525ØØ14Ø7
ØØØ18CANTWELL       6ØØØØ2131ØØ765Ø5Ø219ØØØ65ØØØ12Ø3
ØØØ19SMITH          5ØØØØ434ØØ1759Ø5Ø1195ØØ425ØØØ813
ØØØ2ØNEWMAN         75ØØØ6837Ø1115Ø5Ø1225ØØ4ØØØØ19Ø6
```

Appendix F

Complete RPG II Logic Cycle

Figure F.1 represents the complete RPG II Logic Cycle.

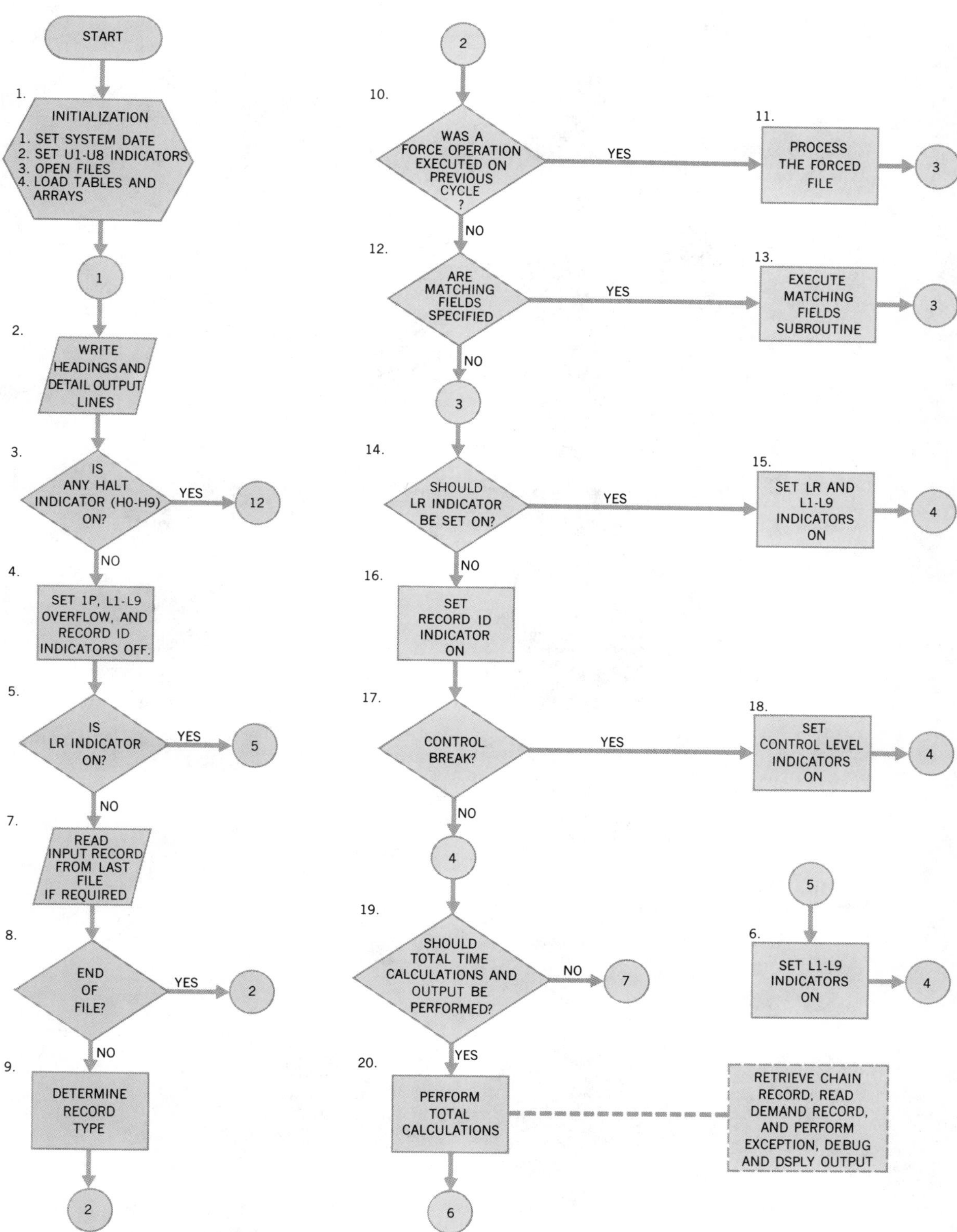

Figure F.1 Overall RPG II Logic Cycle. *(continued on next page)*

Figure F.1
(continued)

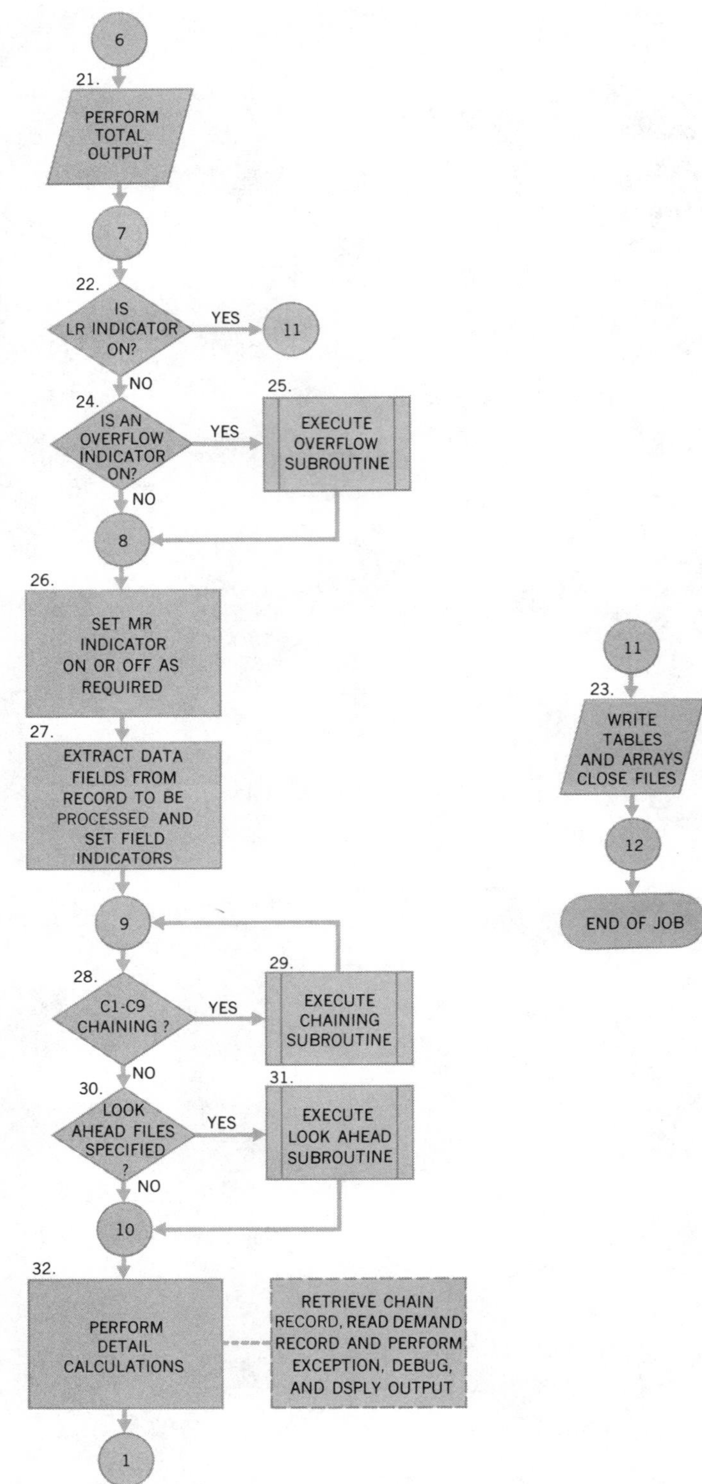

Glossary

Access arm. The mechanism used in a disk drive for retrieving or transmitting data. The access arm holds one or more read/write heads.

Access time. The time it takes to read a disk record into storage or write a disk record from storage.

ADDition operation. An RPG instruction that adds data to a result field.

Alphabetic field. A data field that can only contain letters and/or blanks.

Alphameric field. See **alphanumeric field**.

Alphanumeric field. A data field that can contain any combination of letters, digits, or special characters.

Array. A series of elements with similar characteristics that are stored as one unit. Each element can be accessed with the use of an index.

Batch processing. The processing of records in groups or batches, usually at fixed intervals.

Binary number. A series of 1s and Øs that represent a number in base 2.

Bit. A contraction for *b*inary dig*it*. The term refers to the representation of data in binary form, as a series of on-off or 1-Ø digits.

Blank after. An output specification that initializes a numeric field with zeros or an alphanumeric field with blanks after that field has been used for output.

Blocking. Combining several logical records into one physical record to conserve space on a magnetic tape or disk.

Blocking factor. The number of logical records in each physical block of data on a tape or disk. See **blocking**.

Bpi (bits per inch). An abbreviation for bits per inch. Tape densities are measured in bits per inch (bpi), where a density of 8ØØ bpi, for example, actually means 8ØØ characters per inch.

Buffer. An alternate input/output area designed to permit overlapped processing by the CPU. Buffers help to maximize the efficiency of the computer.

Byte. The representation of a character by eight bits. Each byte of storage can generally hold one character. See **packed data** for the exception.

Calculation Specifications form. An RPG coding form used to indicate the type of processing to be performed.

Called module. When a subroutine is accessed by the main procedure in an RPG II program, the subroutine is referred to as the called module.

Calling module. When a procedure accesses a subroutine, that procedure is referred to as the calling module.

Chaining (CHAIN). The process of looking up a record in a master file by using the key field of a record in a transaction file.

Character. A letter, digit, or special symbol representing the smallest unit of data.

Check bit. See **parity bit**.

Clearing storage (Z-ADD). An RPG instruction that zeros out a field of storage.

Collating sequence. The hierarchy of characters. For EBCDIC computers, for example, the collating sequence is b̸ABC . . . ZØ123 . . . 9, going from low to high.

Comment. A word or statement in a program that serves as documentation rather than as instructions to the compiler.

Compare (COMP). Testing to determine if one field is less than, equal to, or greater than another field.

Compile time array or table. An array or table in which the data is compiled with the source program and becomes a permanent part of the object program. Contrast with **pre-execution time array or table.**

Compiler. The special program that translates a source program into an object program.

Condition code. Set equal to high, low, or equal when a comparison is made.

Conditional branch. A branch, or transfer, that occurs in a program or flowchart only when a particular condition is met.

Conditioning. The use of indicators to control when calculations or output operations are to be performed.

Constant. A fixed value that is part of a program; this value does not change during the execution of the program. Same as **literal**.

Continuous form. The output form generally produced by a computer printer. Although a continuous form can be separated into individual sheets, it is fed through the printer in one continuous sheet to increase speed and facilitate processing.

Control and File Description Specifications form. An RPG coding form that indicates the system requirements and describes the files used in the program.

Control break. When data is processed such that the contents of a key field controls the calculations and printing to be performed, this is referred to as control break processing. Typically, a change in the contents of a key field causes output to be produced and a new control group to be accumulated.

Control field. A key field used to control the processing of data. Typically, when the contents of the control field change from one record to another, output is generated and new totals are accumulated.

Control program facility (RPG III). The system support program that provides many functions that are fully integrated in the system. These functions include data base management, message handling, and job control.

Control total. A total of an amount field is accumulated for all records with the same control field.

Counter. A field used to count the number of occurrences of a specific event.

Create program. A program designed to create a master file; when a new system is implemented, primary attention is given to data validation and edit routines in the create program.

Cylinder. A series of vertical tracks on a magnetic disk pack that is used for storing data. In addressing a disk record, the computer typically uses the track, surface, and cylinder or sector number.

Data base. When a company maintains one single, common set of data that can be accessed by individual departments, this is referred to as a data base. One data base is much more efficient than having each department maintain its own files, which would result in frequent duplication of effort and lack of proper control and integration.

Data verification. The editing of input data to detect errors before the data is processed.

Date field. See **UDATE**.

Debug. To correct errors in a program.

DEBUG. An RPG operation that helps the programmer find errors in a program that is not working properly.

Default. An assumption made by the computer in the absence of specific coding.

Demand file. A file that serves as either an input, update, or special file and that is read sequentially.

Density. The number of characters that can be represented in an inch of magnetic tape or on a disk track; often expressed as bpi (bits per inch).

Desk check. To correct errors in a program by manually verifying coding, even before the program is compiled.

Detail calculation (RPG Cycle). A calculation that is performed each time an input record is read.

Detail output. Output that is printed or produced for each input record read.

Detail printing. The printing of an output record from each input record.

Detail report. A report that generates one or more lines of output for each input record read; it requires more computer time than other reports and tends to be the most costly type of output. Contrast with **exception report** and **summary report**.

Detail time. An operation in the RPG program cycle in which calculation and output operations are performed for each record read.

Diagnostic. A compile-time message that identifies RPG specification errors. All rule violations will be listed as diagnostics.

Direct access. The method of processing data independent of the actual location of that data. This method can be used with magnetic disk, drum, and data cell, all of which are classified as direct-access devices. Contrast with **sequential access**. The term **random access** is sometimes used in place of direct access.

Direct file. A file that uses the direct method of file organization on a disk; the key field in each record of the disk file can be directly converted to an actual disk location or address.

Direct method of file organization. Disk records are accessed by converting a key field, through some arithmetic calculation, to an actual address that typically identifies the surface and track or cylinder number.

Disk drive. A direct-access device designed to minimize the access time required to locate specific records; disk drives are frequently used for on-line processing.

Disk pack. A storage medium that consists of a series of platters or disks arranged in a vertical stack and connected by a central shaft.

DIV**ide operation**. An RPG instruction that divides Factor 1 by Factor 2 and places the quotient in the Result Field.

DO **. . . group (RPG III)**. A series of operations that are executed one or more times depending on the parameters specified. A DO operation and an END operation are the delimiters for a DO group. See **looping**.

Documentation. The set of records used to explain in detail how the program operates and what it is intended to accomplish.

Dynamic processing. Processing a VSAM file during a single run as both a direct and a sequential file.

EBCDIC. See **Extended Binary Coded Decimal Interchange Code**.

Edit and validation program. A program designed to minimize the risk of generating errors on output.

Edit code. A number or letter used on the Output form to indicate the type of editing that should be performed. Types of editing include zero suppression and printing of dollar signs.

Editing. The process of verifying that data entered into the computer is relatively error-free. Editing operations minimize computer-produced errors.

Elementary item. A data field that is not further subdivided.

END **(RPG III).** The last statement in a DO . . . group.

End of file (EOF). The condition reached when there are no more input records to be read.

Entry point. The beginning point of a routine to be branched to from other points in the program; specified by use of the TAG operation.

Even parity. See **parity bit.**

Exception output. The writing of a number of similar or identical records at the time calculations are being performed.

Exception report. The printing of only that output that does not fall within established guidelines.

EXCPT **operation.** Allows records to be written at the time calculations are being performed, which is not the usual time for printing using the standard RPG cycle.

Execution. The running of a program with data.

EXSR. The instruction code in RPG that calls in an internal subroutine.

Extended Binary Coded Decimal Interchange Code (EBCDIC). A computer code used to represent characters; most frequently used on many third- and fourth-generation computers and nine-track tapes.

Extension and Line Counter Specifications form. An RPG coding form used to provide information about (1) arrays and tables used in a program and (2) the number of lines to be printed on forms.

External subroutine. A subroutine not part of a program that is called in from a library of functions or routines.

Externally described data (RPG III). A file from which the fields in the records are described to the control program facility. The programmer uses a standard data description specification, which is established when the file is created. The field descriptions can be used by the program when the file is processed.

Factor 1. The first value specified on an RPG Calculation form in positions 18 to 27.

Factor 2. The second value specified on an RPG Calculation form in positions 33 to 42.

Fetch overflow. A routine that allows the user to alter the standard RPG Logic Cycle so that printing can begin on a new page whenever the programmer deems it necessary.

Field. A group of adjacent positions used to represent a unit of data such as NAME or SALARY. A group of consecutive storage positions used to represent an item of data.

File. A collection of individual records that are treated as one unit. A payroll file, for example, refers to a company's complete collection of employee records.

File Description Specifications form. The RPG coding form that defines and describes the files used in the program.

File update. The process of making a file current.

First page (1P) indicator. Used to print headings; the 1P indicator is automatically turned on at the beginning of the program cycle and then turned off after the heading lines print.

Fixed disk. A disk pack that is permanently encased in a disk drive.

Fixed-head disk. This disk device does not have a movable access arm; each track has its own read/write mechanism that accesses a record as it rotates past the arm.

Fixed-length record. Used to describe a file in which all records are the same length.

Floating dollar sign. A dollar sign that prints directly to the left of the first significant digit; the dollar sign is said to "float" with the field.

Floppy disk. A "soft" or flexible disk that is a smaller version of a hard disk used with most mini- and microcomputer systems.

Flowchart. A pictorial representation of the logic to be used in a program or a system.

GOTO. An unconditional branch instruction; when the instruction is encountered, the program will automatically transfer control to some other point in the program.

GO TO**-less programming.** Another term for **structured programming.** Such programming enables each module to function as a stand-alone entity and avoids branches or GO TO instructions.

Group indicate. The printing of control information for only the first record of a group of records containing identical control information.

Group item. A data field that is further subdivided; a major field consisting of minor fields.

Group report (printing). Reports that print totals that can sometimes provide the user with enough information so that detail reports are not necessary.

Half adjust. A method of rounding off a number by determining whether the low-order digit is less than five.

If it is less than five, then the last digit is truncated; if the low-order digit is five or more, then one is added to the next position. Thus, 12.75, for example, half adjusted to one decimal place becomes 12.8.

Halt indicator (HØ). An indicator that will terminate a program if a record is found out of sequence during a sequential file update.

Halt indicator (H1-H9). An indicator that will terminate a program if set on; H1-H9 indicators either are automatically set by the computer or can be turned on by the programmer when a certain unacceptable condition occurs.

Hard disk. A standard disk used with most large and medium-sized computer systems and some minis as well.

Hash total. A control total consisting of the sum of numbers in a field such as ACCTNO that would not otherwise be summed.

Header label. The first record in a tape or disk file that is used to identify the file.

Heading. A constant printed on the top of each page of a report identifying the information on the page.

High-level language. A symbolic programming language that requires compilation; it is easier to code than a low-level language but is more difficult to translate since it is English-like and not machinelike.

High-order position. The left-most, or most significant, character in a field.

High-order truncation. When a receiving field does not have enough integer positions to hold a result, the high-order or most significant digit is truncated or lost. This is referred to as high-order truncation and should be avoided.

IBG. See **interblock gap**.

IF-THEN-ELSE **structure**. This is a technique used to represent a test for a specific condition; it is a pseudocode representation for depicting logical control procedures.

Implied decimal point. When a decimal point does not actually appear in a numeric field but the number is assumed to have a decimal point, we say that the decimal point is implied.

Index (for an array). Used to indicate which element in an array is to be accessed.

Index (for an ISAM file). Used to indicate where each record is physically located.

Indexed file. A file with an index that indicates where each record is physically located.

Indexed sequential access method (ISAM). A method of organizing data on a disk so that on-line processing is facilitated. The disk uses an index to access records.

Indicator. A two digit or two character entry used to indicate when specific operations are to be performed. Indicators include control level indicator, field indicator, first page indicator, last record indicator, overflow indicator, record identifying indicator, resulting indicator.

Input Specifications form. An RPG coding form that describes the records and fields to be processed as input.

Interactive workstation. A terminal used for inquiry-response purposes.

Interblock gap (IBG). An area of a tape or disk between physical records. The computer requires an IBG between physical records because a fixed amount of tape or disk area will be bypassed between the time an end of record is reached and the time it takes for the drive to physically stop transmitting data.

Internal subroutine. A series of instructions within a program that is executed by a calling module. An internal subroutine may be executed from several different points in a program.

ISAM. See **indexed sequential access method.**

Key field. A field that uniquely defines a record within a file. A key field on a payroll file, for example, may be Social Security number.

Last Record (LR) indicator. An indicator that is turned on after the last record has been processed. This indicator is commonly used to condition calculation and output operations to be performed at the end of a job.

Level indicator (L1-L9). An indicator that is turned on when there is a change in a control field; commonly used to condition group indicators for group or summary printing.

Line Counter Specifications form. An RPG coding form used to indicate or override the system defaults regarding length of printed forms and the number of lines to be printed.

Literal. A constant that is used by a program but that remains unchanged during processing. Same as **constant**.

Logic error. A logic error occurs when a sequence of programming steps is not executed properly; it is caused by incorrect sequencing of program instructions or misunderstanding of the problem or the logic flow.

Logical record. A tape or disk record that is to be processed as an individual unit; logical records are commonly grouped into physical records or blocks to maximize the efficient use of the tape or disk.

LOKUP **instruction**. An RPG instruction that causes a search to be made for a specific element in a table or array.

Look ahead field. A field that allows the program to look at information in the corresponding field on the *next* record that will become available for processing.

Loop. A series of programming steps that are executed a fixed number of times; when a specific condition occurs, control is transferred outside the loop.

Low-order position. The right-most or least significant position in a field.

Low-order truncation. When a receiving field does not have enough decimal positions to accommodate a result, the least significant or low-order decimal position is truncated.

LR indicator. See **Last Record indicator**.

Machine language. The machine's own code; a program written in machine language requires no translation process.

Magnetic disk (drive). See **disk drive**.

Magnetic tape (drive). See **tape drive**.

Master file. A major classification of data, containing records for a given application. Companies typically have payroll files, accounts receivable files, inventory files, and so forth. Contrast with **data base**.

Matching Record (MR) indicator. An indicator used in calculation or output specifications to specify operations to be performed when the key fields of records in a primary and secondary file match.

Module. A series of instructions treated as a unit by the program. It is considered good programming form to include a series of modules in a program that makes it easier to debug and understand the logic.

MOVE. An RPG instruction that transmits data from one area of storage to another. Data is moved from right to left.

MOVEL. An RPG instruction that moves data from one area of storage to another; transmission begins from the left-most position and proceeds to the right-most position.

Moving-head disk. All the read/write heads on a disk are attached to a single movable access mechanism. These read/write heads move together to locate a specific record.

Multiple-level control break. A series of control fields (minor, intermediate, and major) determine what calculations are to be performed and what output is to be produced.

MULT**iply operation**. An RPG instruction that multiplies Factor 1 by Factor 2 and places the product in the Result field.

Nine-track tape. A form of tape that has nine longitudinal tracks, each capable of storing magnetized bits. A character is stored in a vertical section of tape by using a coded combination of nine bits.

Nonnumeric field. A field that contains alphanumeric data.

Not (N) entry. An entry used to specify that the absence of an indicator is to signal an operation.

Numeric field. A field consisting of digits Ø–9 with decimal alignment specified; a field that is typically used in an arithmetic operation.

Numeric literal. A constant consisting of digits Ø–9, a decimal point, and a + or − sign.

Object program. A machine-language equivalent of a source program. Object programs are the only ones that can be executed without being translated first.

Odd parity. See **parity bit.**

On-line processing. The processing of data with devices such as terminals that are directly under the control of the main CPU.

Output indicator. An indicator used to define the conditions under which an output operation is to be performed.

Output Specifications form. An RPG coding form used to describe the format of fields in an output record and to indicate when a record is to be produced.

Overflow (OF) indicator. An indicator used to determine when the end of a page has been reached; used to print headings on the top of a new page.

Packed data. Each byte within a field contains two numeric digits rather than one. The right-most byte, however, includes a sign and thus contains only one digit. Thus +123 in packed form would be represented in *two* bytes as | 12 | 3 + |. Contrast with **zoned decimal format.**

Page. A reserved word used to instruct the computer to print page numbers on printed output.

Page overflow. See **overflow (OF) indicator**.

Parity bit. A check bit used to minimize the risk of undetected computer transmission errors. An extra bit is used to ensure that an odd number of bits are always on (for odd parity machines) or that an even number of bits are on (for even parity machines).

PERFORM. A logical control procedure that enables a program to execute a series of steps and return to the original module. PERFORM statements are an essential element of structured programs. In RPG III, DO . . . groups are used to perform sequences of instructions.

Physical record. A block of one or more logical records read from or written onto an input/output device at one time; logical records are grouped or blocked into physical records to maximize the efficient use of a tape or disk. Contrast with **logical record**.

Pre-execution time array or table. An array or table that is loaded at the same time as the source program, that is, before actual execution of the program begins. Contrast with **compile time or array table.**

Preprinted form. A form that can contain computer-produced output but that enters a computer system with heading and identifying information already imprinted.

Primary file. The main file from which a program first reads records.

Program. A series of instructions that enables a computer to read input data, process it, and convert it to output.

Program flowchart. The pictorial representation of the logic in a program.

Program walkthrough. A technique used to follow the logic in a program by stepping through each sequence of steps manually before actually running the program. This technique saves computer time and helps to minimize logic errors.

Programmed label record. To make the identification of tape and disk files more reliable, most programs include a built-in routine that creates a label record at the beginning of the file that specifies the contents of the tape or disk.

Prompt. A request for information or response from a user. A prompt is typically displayed on a CRT. In order for the program to proceed, the user must respond to the prompt by keying in the appropriate characters.

Pseudocode. This tool specifically depicts the logic flow of a structured program. It is a planning tool that uses a code similar to a program code for depicting logic. It is used for applications that have complex logical control procedures where a structured approach is most useful.

Random access. See **direct access**.

Read/write head. The part of a magnetic tape or magnetic disk drive that enables the device to read magnetic data or to record magnetic data, depending on the application.

Record. A set of related fields treated as a unit. A payroll record on magnetic disk, for example, contains fields relating to a particular employee such as Social Security number, name, salary, and address.

Record format. The description of the records in an externally described RPG III file.

Record identifying code. Characters placed in a record to identify it to the system are designated with the use of a record identifying code.

Record identifying indicator. An indicator that identifies the type of record being processed during the current program cycle.

Related tables. Two or more tables that are related to one another. For an entry in one table, there is a corresponding entry in another table.

Relative file. A file that uses a key field in each record for directly determining the location of each record.

Removable disk. A disk pack that is not permanently encased in a disk drive.

Report heading. A line of output that provides identifying information such as a report name, page number, and date that defines the report to the user.

Result field. A field specified on the Calculation form that will contain the outcome or result of an arithmetic operation.

Resulting indicator. An indicator that signals the result of a calculation, such as whether the result is plus, minus, or zero; a resulting indicator can also be used for determining whether a given field is greater than, less than, or equal to another field.

Rounding numeric fields. See **Half adjust**.

Routine. A series of instructions that performs a specific operation or procedure.

RPG. A high-level program generator; an acronym for *Re*port *P*rogram *G*enerator; most suited for printing reports and producing output files.

RPG coding sheet. One of several specification forms used in RPG; each has space for 8Ø columns of information per line.

RPG II Logic Cycle. The precise sequence in which RPG performs all operations; not directly under the programmer's control.

Running total. A field that keeps track of a total as it is being accumulated.

Search argument. Factor 1 in a LOKUP instruction.

Secondary file. Any file other than the primary file used when multiple input files are required.

Sequence checking. An RPG function that checks the sequence of records in a file.

Sequential access. A method of processing records in a file in sequence, starting with the record that is physically located at the beginning of the file and proceeding sequentially through the file.

Sequential file. A file in which records are processed in sequence as they appear on the file; to access a record in ACCTNO sequence on a sequential file, for example, begin with the first ACCTNO, proceed to the next, and so on.

SETOF operation. An RPG instruction used to turn off indicators.

SETON operation. An RPG instruction used to turn on indicators.

Single-entry table. A table that simply consists of a series of entries such as a table of out-of-stock part numbers.

Single-level control break. When one control field is used to condition calculation and printing operations.

Sizing fields. Determining the number of integer and dec-

imal digits required in a field that will be used for storing the result of an arithmetic operation.

Skipping. Advancing the continuous form or paper to a specific line.

Source program. A program written in a symbolic programming language; source programs must be translated into machine language before they can be executed.

Spacing. Advancing the continuous form or paper a fixed number of lines.

Specification form. RPG coding form.

Split matching fields. The assignment of major, intermediate, and minor fields for a matching procedure.

Standard label. See **programmed label record**.

Structured programming. An efficient programming technique that can facilitate the processing of programs in all languages; referred to as GO TO-less or modular programming.

Subroutine. A series of steps that can be executed from anywhere in a program. See **external subroutine** and **internal subroutine**.

SUB**tract operation**. An RPG instruction that subtracts data from a field.

Summary printing. See **group report**.

Symbolic device. The device specification defined on the File Description form indicating the specific name assigned to the device at the computer center.

Symbolic programming language. The writing of a program in an English-like language. Symbolic programs must be translated into machine language before they can be executed.

Syntax error. Any programming rules that have been violated will cause the computer to print an error message during the program translation phase. See **diagnostic**.

System integrity. Maintaining the reliability of a system by validating transaction data before it is used to update a master file.

Table. A list of related data items not part of a program that is stored in consecutive locations within main storage and may be accessed or referenced by an RPG program. See **related tables** and **single-entry table**.

TAG. Provides a name to which the program can branch; that is, it represents an entry point of a routine to be branched to.

Tape drive. A high-speed device that can read data from a magnetic tape and can also record data onto a tape.

Test data. Data created by a programmer to test the logic in a program; test data should include every condition that is to be processed by the program.

TESTN **operation**. An RPG instruction that tests to determine if a field is numeric.

Top-down approach. An approach to programming where each module is written in sequence, with the first being the most significant module.

Total operation. A calculation or output operation that is performed only after a control group of records has been processed or at the end of the program.

Total time. The part of the RPG program cycle in which calculations or output specified for a group of records is performed. Total time operations are conditioned by control level indicators L1-L9.

Track. A recording surface on a magnetic tape or magnetic disk.

Transaction file. A file that contains changes to be incorporated in a master file. A master file is updated with transaction records.

Truncation. See **high-order truncation** and **low-order truncation**.

UDATE. The RPG specification for obtaining the date of the run specified as mm/dd/yr.

Unconditional branch. A branch, or transfer, in a program or flowchart that occurs regardless of any existing condition.

Update procedure. The process of making a file of data current.

User-friendly. A form of processing designed to facilitate processing by a noncomputer person or user. Instructions and output are clear and easy to read and interpret.

Variable data. Data that is unknown when the program is written and changes during every run.

Variable-length record. The term used to describe a file in which records are of different sizes.

Virtual storage access method (VSAM). An efficient method of organizing data on a disk so that on-line processing is facilitated, multiple keys may be used, and variable-length records can be processed.

VSAM. See **virtual storage access method**.

Walkthrough. See **program walkthrough**.

XFOOT **instruction**. An RPG instruction that is used for summing elements in an array.

Z-ADD **operation**. An RPG instruction used for initializing a result field with zeros and then adding the contents of another field to it.

Zero suppression. The elimination of leading zeros in a report. For example, ØØ26 becomes 26 when zero suppressed.

Zoned decimal format. Representation of data so that one byte contains a character consisting of both a zone and digit portion.

Index

RPG CONTROL AND FILE DESCRIPTION SPECIFICATIONS

Program		Keying Instruction	Graphic	Card Electro Number
Programmer	Date		Key	

Page (1 2) of — Program Identification (75 76 77 78 79 80)

Control Specifications

For the valid entries for a system, refer to the RPG reference manual for that system.

H

Line (3–5)	Form Type (6)	Size to Compile (7–9)	Object Output (10)	Listing Options (11)	Size to Execute (12–14)	Debug (15)	Reserved (16–17)	Currency Symbol (18)	Date Format (19)	Date Edit (20)	Inverted Print (21)	Reserved (22)	Number of Print Positions (23–25)	Alternate Collating Sequence (26)	Reserved (27–36)	Inquiry (37)	Reserved (38–39)	Sign Handling (40)	1 P Forms Position (41)	Indicator Setting (42)	File Translation (43)	Punch MFCU Zeros (44)	Nonprint Characters (45)	Reserved (46)	Table Load Halt (47)	Shared I/O (48)	Field Print (49)	Formatted Dump (50)	RPG to RPG II Conversion (51)	Number of Formats (52–53)	S/3 Conversion (54)	Subprogram (55)	CICS/DL/I (56)	Transparent Literal (57)	58–74
0 1	H																																		

File Description Specifications

For the valid entries for a system, refer to the RPG reference manual for that system.

F

Line (3–5)	Form Type (6)	Filename (7–14)	File Type: I/O/U/C/D (15)	File Designation: P/S/C/R/T/D/F (16)	End of File: E (17)	Sequence: A/D (18)	File Format: F/V/S/M/D/E (19)	Block Length (20–23)	Record Length (24–27)	Mode of Processing: L/R (28)	Length of Key Field or of Record Address Field (29–30)	Record Address Type: A/P/I/K (31)	Type of File Organization or Additional Area: I/X/D/T/R/ or 2 (32)	Overflow Indicator (33–34)	Key Field Starting Location (35–38)	Extension Code E/L (39)	Device (40–46)	Symbolic Device (47–52)	Labels S/N/E/M (53)	Name of Label Exit (54–59)	Extent Exit for DAM / Storage Index (60–65)	A/U (66)	File Addition/Unordered (66)	Number of Tracks for Cylinder Overflow (67)	Number of Extents (68–69)	Tape Rewind: R/U/N (70)	File Condition U1–U8, UC (71–72)	73–74
0 2	F																											
0 3	F																											
0 4	F																											
0 5	F																											
0 6	F																											
0 7	F																											
0 8	F																											
0 9	F																											
1 0	F																											
	F																											
	F																											

External Record Name (19–38). Continuation Lines: K (53), Option (54–59), Entry (60–65).

RPG INPUT SPECIFICATIONS

Program		Keying Instruction	Graphic	Card Electro Number
Programmer	Date		Key	

Page (1 2) of ___ Program Identification (75 76 77 78 79 80)

Line (3 4 5)	Form Type (6)	Filename or Record Name (7–14); Data Structure Name (7–12)	Sequence (15–16); OR / AND (14–16)	Number (1/N), E (17)	Option (O), U, S (18)	Record Identifying Indicator, **, or DS (19 20)	External Field Name / Record Identification Codes 1: Position (21–24), Not (N) (25), C/Z/D (26), Character (27)	2: Position (28–31), Not (N) (32), C/Z/D (33), Character (34)	3: Position (35–38), Not (N) (39), C/Z/D (40), Character (41)	Stacker Select (42)	P/B/L/R (43)	Field Location From (44–47) / Data Structure Occurs n Times	To (48–51) / Length	Decimal Positions (52)	RPG Field Name (53–58)	Control Level (L1–L9) (59 60)	Matching Fields or Chaining Fields (61 62)	Field Record Relation (63 64)	Field Indicators Plus (65 66)	Minus (67 68)	Zero or Blank (69 70)	(71 72 73 74)
0 1	I																					
0 2	I																					
0 3	I																					
0 4	I																					
0 5	I																					
0 6	I																					
0 7	I																					
0 8	I																					
0 9	I																					
1 0	I																					
1 1	I																					
1 2	I																					
1 3	I																					
1 4	I																					
1 5	I																					
1 6	I																					
1 7	I																					
1 8	I																					
1 9	I																					
2 0	I																					
	I																					
	I																					
	I																					
	I																					
	I																					

RPG CALCULATION SPECIFICATIONS

Program		Keying Instruction	Graphic	Card Electro Number	Page (1 2) of ___	Program Identification (75 76 77 78 79 80)
Programmer	Date		Key			

Line (3 4 5)	Form Type (6)	Control Level (L0–L9, LR, SR, AN/OR) (7 8)	Indicators: Not (9 10 11)	And: Not (12 13 14)	And: Not (15 16 17)	Factor 1 (18–27)	Operation (28–32)	Factor 2 (33–42)	Result Field: Name (43–48)	Result Field: Length (49 50 51)	Decimal Positions (52)	Half Adjust (H) (53)	Resulting Indicators: Arithmetic Plus / Compare 1 > 2 / Lookup (Factor 2) is High (54 55)	Minus / 1 < 2 / Low (56 57)	Zero / 1 = 2 / Equal (58 59)	Comments (60–74)
0 1	C															
0 2	C															
0 3	C															
0 4	C															
0 5	C															
0 6	C															
0 7	C															
0 8	C															
0 9	C															
1 0	C															
1 1	C															
1 2	C															
1 3	C															
1 4	C															
1 5	C															
1 6	C															
1 7	C															
1 8	C															
1 9	C															
2 0	C															
	C															
	C															
	C															
	C															
	C															

RPG OUTPUT SPECIFICATIONS

Program | Keying Instruction | Graphic | Key | Card Electro Number | Page 1 2 of | Program Identification 75 76 77 78 79 80

Programmer | Date

Commas	Zero Balances to Print	No Sign	CR	–	X = Remove Plus Sign; Y = Date Field Edit; Z = Zero Suppress	5–9 = User Defined
Yes	Yes	1	A	J		
Yes	No	2	B	K		
No	Yes	3	C	L		
No	No	4	D	M		

Line (3–5)	Form Type (6)	Filename or Record Name (7–14)	Type (H/D/T/E) (15)	Stkr #/Fetch (F) (16)	Space Before (17)	Space After (18)	Skip Before (19–20)	Skip After (21–22)	Output Indicators: Not (23)	(24–25)	And Not (26)	(27–28)	And Not (29)	(30–31)	Field Name or EXCPT Name / *Auto (32–37)	Edit Codes (38)	B/A/C/1–9/R (39)	End Position in Output Record (40–43)	P/B/L/R (44)	Constant or Edit Word (45–70)	(71–74)
01	O																				
02	O																				
03	O																				
04	O																				
05	O																				
06	O																				
07	O																				
08	O																				
09	O																				
10	O																				
11	O																				
12	O																				
13	O																				
14	O																				
15	O																				
16	O																				
17	O																				
18	O																				
19	O																				
20	O																				
	O																				
	O																				
	O																				
	O																				
	O																				

1 2 3 4 5 6 7 8 9 10 11 12 13 14 15 16 17 18 19 20 21 22 23 24 25 26 27 28 29 30 31 32 33 34 35 36 37 38 39 40 41 42 43 44 45 46 47 48 49 50

1 2 3 4 5 6 7 8 9 10 11 12 13 14 15 16 17 18 19 20 21 22 23 24 25 26 27 28 29 30 31 32 33 34 35 36 37 38 39 40 41 42 43 44 45 46 47 48 49 50 51 52 53 54 55 56 57 58 59 60 61 62 63 64 65 66 67 68 69 70 71 72 73 74 75 76 77 78 79 80 81 82 83 84 85 86 87 88 89 90 91 92 93 94 95 96 97 98 99 100 101 102 103 104 105 106 107 108 109 110 111 112 113 114 115 116 117 118 119 120 121 122 123 124 125 126 127 128 129 130 131 132

1 2 3 4 5 6 7 8 9 10 11 12 13 14 15 16 17 18 19 20 21 22 23 24 25 26 27 28 29 30 31 32 33 34 35 36 37 38 39 40 41 42 43 44 45 46 47 48 49 50 51 52 53 54 55 56 57 58 59 60 61 62 63 64 65 66 67 68 69 70 71 72 73 74 75 76 77 78 79 80 81 82 83 84 85 86 87 88 89 90 91 92 93 94 95 96 97 98 99 100 101 102 103 104 105 106 107 108 109 110 111 112 113 114 115 116 117 118 119 120 121 122 123 124 125 126 127 128 129 130 131 132

1 2 3 4 5 6 7 8 9 10 11 12 13 14 15 16 17 18 19 20 21 22 23 24 25 26 27 28 29 30 31 32 33 34 35 36 37 38 39 40 41 42 43 44 45 46 47 48 49 50

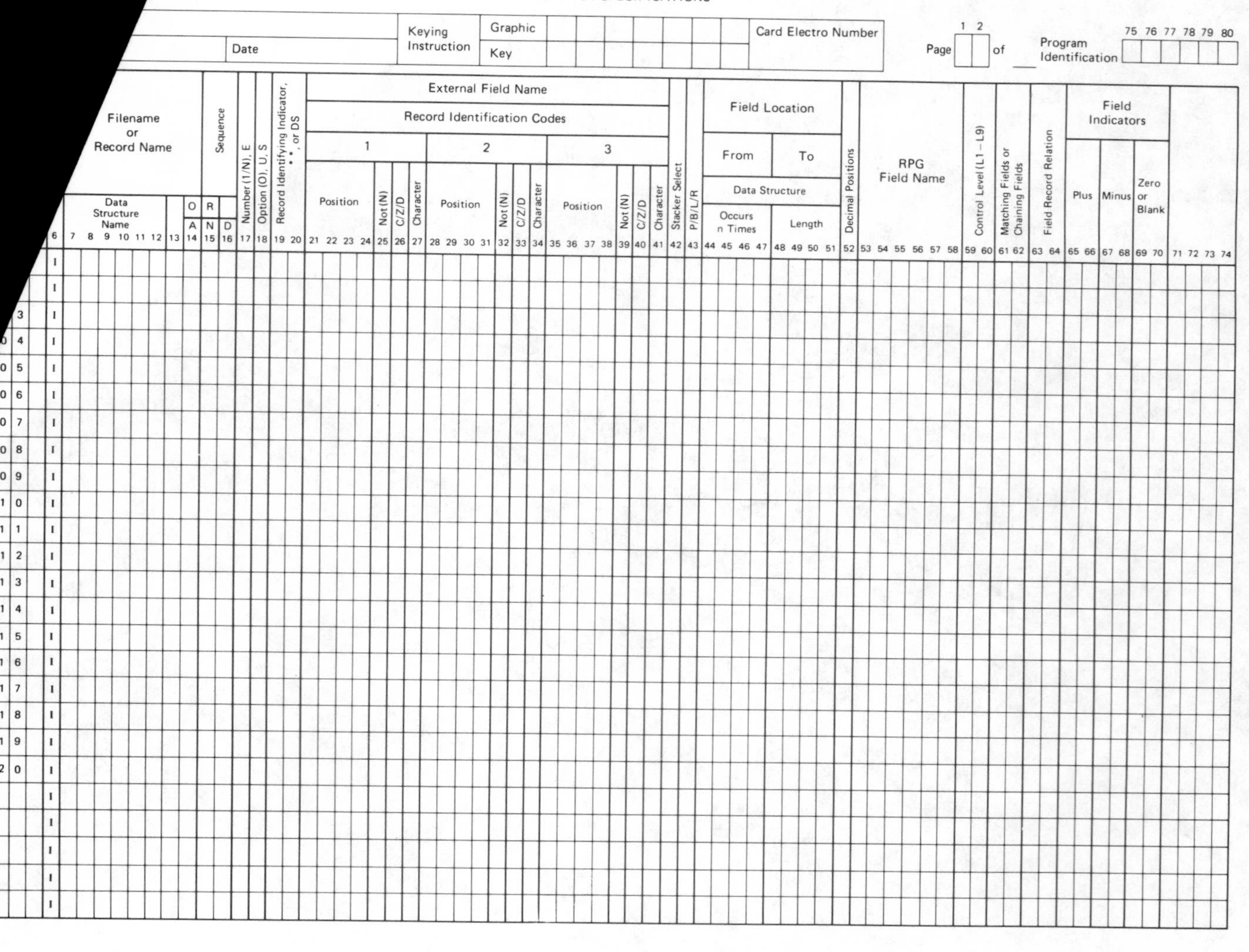

RPG INPUT SPECIFICATIONS

Date		Keying Instruction	Graphic	Card Electro Number	Page (1 2) of ___	Program Identification (75 76 77 78 79 80)
			Key			

6	Filename or Record Name — Data Structure Name (7 8 9 10 11 12 13)	Sequence — OR / AND (14 15 16)	Number (1/N), E (17)	Option (O), U, S (18)	Record Identifying Indicator, **, or DS (19 20)	External Field Name / Record Identification Codes — 1: Position (21 22 23 24), Not (N) (25), C/Z/D (26), Character (27)	2: Position (28 29 30 31), Not (N) (32), C/Z/D (33), Character (34)	3: Position (35 36 37 38), Not (N) (39), C/Z/D (40), Character (41)	Stacker Select (42)	P/B/L/R (43)	Field Location — From / Data Structure Occurs n Times (44 45 46 47)	To / Length (48 49 50 51)	Decimal Positions (52)	RPG Field Name (53 54 55 56 57 58)	Control Level (L1 – L9) (59 60)	Matching Fields or Chaining Fields (61 62)	Field Record Relation (63 64)	Field Indicators — Plus (65 66)	Minus (67 68)	Zero or Blank (69 70)	71 72 73 74
I																					
I																					
3 I																					
4 I																					
0 5 I																					
0 6 I																					
0 7 I																					
0 8 I																					
0 9 I																					
1 0 I																					
1 1 I																					
1 2 I																					
1 3 I																					
1 4 I																					
1 5 I																					
1 6 I																					
1 7 I																					
1 8 I																					
1 9 I																					
2 0 I																					
I																					
I																					
I																					
I																					
I																					

RPG CONTROL AND FILE DESCRIPTION SPECIFICATIONS

Program		Keying Instruction	Graphic	Card Electro Number
Programmer	Date		Key	

Page (1 2) of — Program Identification (75 76 77 78 79 80)

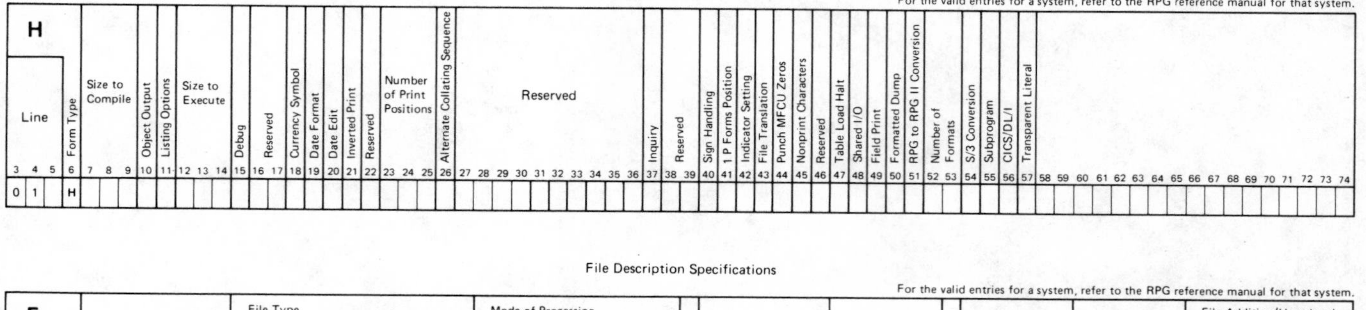

Control Specifications

For the valid entries for a system, refer to the RPG reference manual for that system.

H

- Line (3–5)
- Form Type (6)
- Size to Compile (7–9)
- Object Output (10)
- Listing Options (11)
- Size to Execute (12–14)
- Debug (15)
- Reserved (16–17)
- Currency Symbol (18)
- Date Format (19)
- Date Edit (20)
- Inverted Print (21)
- Reserved (22)
- Number of Print Positions (23–25)
- Alternate Collating Sequence (26)
- Reserved (27–36)
- Inquiry (37)
- Reserved (38–39)
- Sign Handling (40)
- 1 P Forms Position (41)
- Indicator Setting (42)
- File Translation (43)
- Punch MFCU Zeros (44)
- Nonprint Characters (45)
- Reserved (46)
- Table Load Halt (47)
- Shared I/O (48)
- Field Print (49)
- Formatted Dump (50)
- RPG to RPG II Conversion (51)
- Number of Formats (52–53)
- S/3 Conversion (54)
- Subprogram (55)
- CICS/DL/I (56)
- Transparent Literal (57)
- 58–74

Line 0 1, Form Type H

File Description Specifications

For the valid entries for a system, refer to the RPG reference manual for that system.

F

- Line (3–5)
- Form Type (6)
- Filename (7–14)
- File Type: I/O/U/C/D (15)
- File Designation: P/S/C/R/T/D/F (16)
- End of File: E (17)
- Sequence: A/D (18)
- File Format: F/V/S/M/D/E (19)
- Block Length (20–23)
- Record Length (24–27)
- Mode of Processing: L/R (28)
- Length of Key Field or of Record Address Field (29–30)
- Record Address Type: A/P/I/K (31)
- Type of File Organization or Additional Area: I/X/D/T/R/ or 2 (32)
- Overflow Indicator (33–34)
- Key Field Starting Location (35–38)
- External Record Name (19–38)
- Extension Code E/L (39)
- Device (40–46)
- Symbolic Device (47–52)
- Labels S/N/E/M (53)
- Name of Label Exit (54–59)
- Extent Exit for DAM (60–65)
- Storage Index (60–65)
- Continuation Lines: K (53), Option (54–59), Entry (60–65)
- A/U (66)
- File Addition/Unordered (66)
- Number of Tracks for Cylinder Overflow (67–68)
- Number of Extents (69)
- Tape Rewind: R/U/N (70)
- File Condition U1–U8, UC (71–72)
- 73–74

Lines 0 2, 0 3, 0 4, 0 5, 0 6, 0 7, 0 8, 0 9, 1 0, (blank), (blank) — Form Type F

RPG CALCULATION SPECIFICATIONS

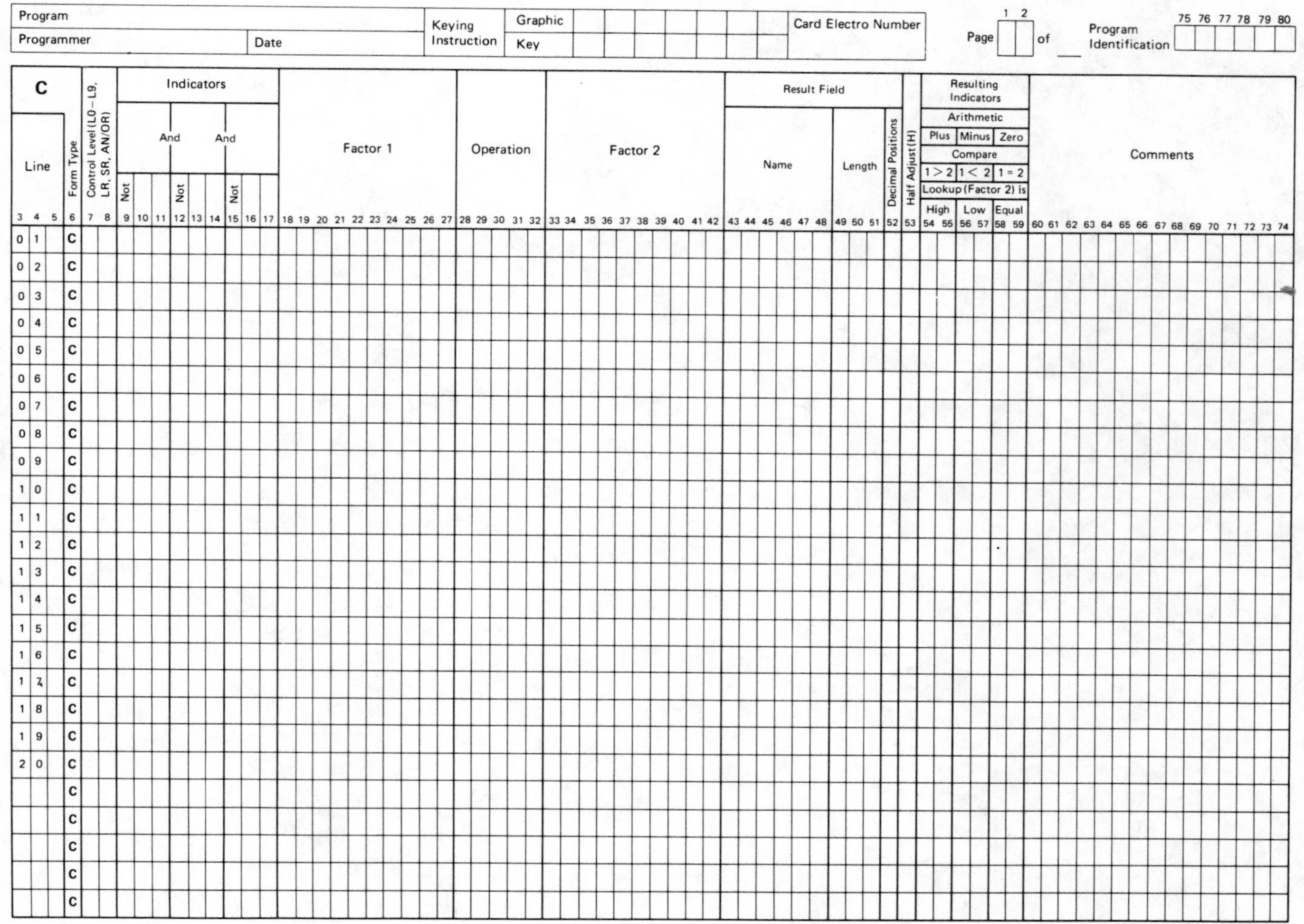

Program		Keying Instruction	Graphic	Card Electro Number	Page 1 2 of ___	Program Identification 75 76 77 78 79 80
Programmer	Date		Key			

Line (3 4 5)	Form Type (6)	Control Level (L0–L9, LR, SR, AN/OR) (7 8)	Indicators: Not (9 10 11)	Indicators: And, Not (12 13 14)	Indicators: And, Not (15 16 17)	Factor 1 (18–27)	Operation (28–32)	Factor 2 (33–42)	Result Field: Name (43–48)	Result Field: Length (49 50 51)	Decimal Positions (52)	Half Adjust (H) (53)	Resulting Indicators — Arithmetic: Plus / Compare: 1 > 2 / Lookup (Factor 2) is: High (54 55)	Arithmetic: Minus / Compare: 1 < 2 / Lookup: Low (56 57)	Arithmetic: Zero / Compare: 1 = 2 / Lookup: Equal (58 59)	Comments (60–74)
0 1	C															
0 2	C															
0 3	C															
0 4	C															
0 5	C															
0 6	C															
0 7	C															
0 8	C															
0 9	C															
1 0	C															
1 1	C															
1 2	C															
1 3	C															
1 4	C															
1 5	C															
1 6	C															
1 7	C															
1 8	C															
1 9	C															
2 0	C															
	C															
	C															
	C															
	C															
	C															

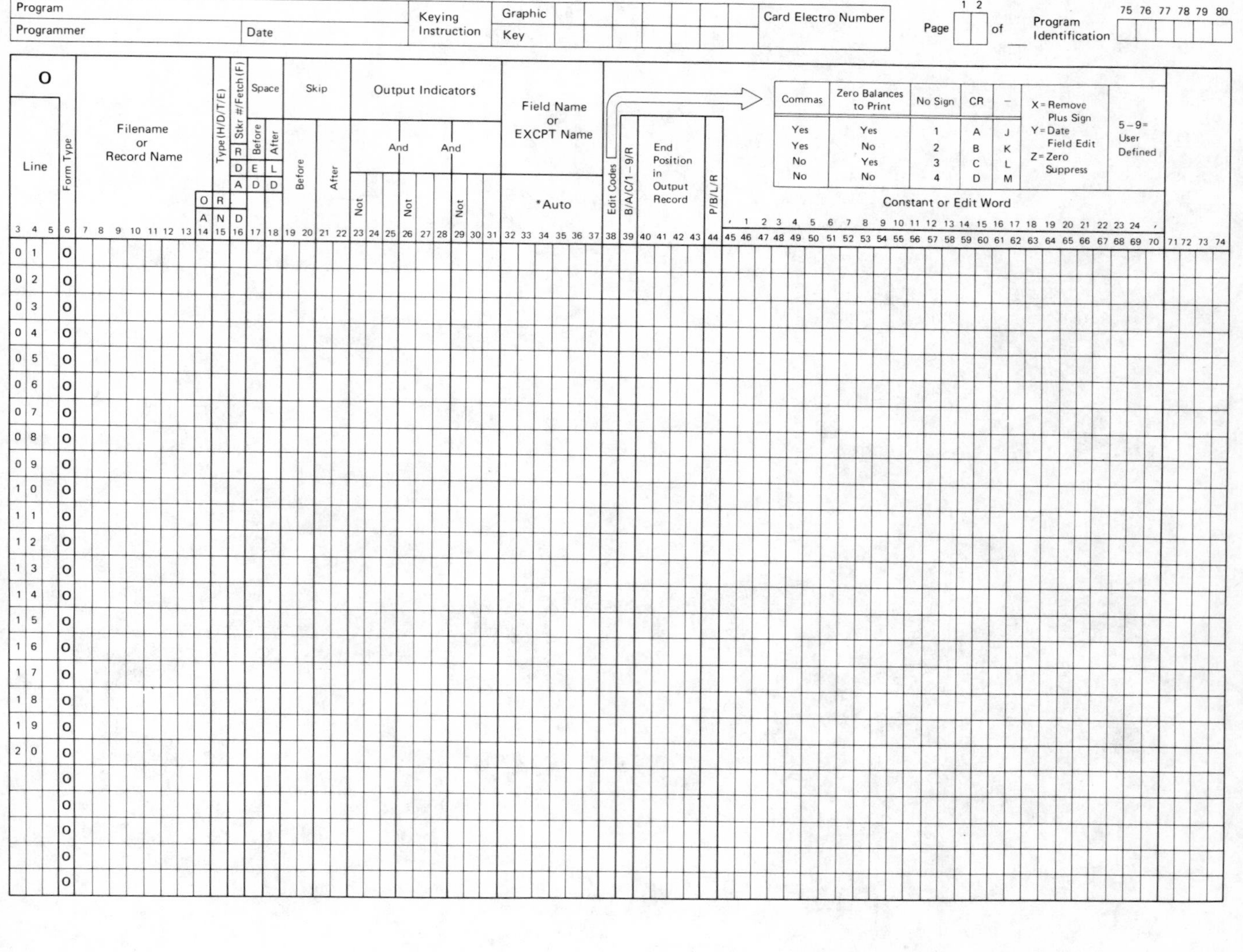

RPG OUTPUT SPECIFICATIONS

Program		Keying Instruction	Graphic	Card Electro Number
Programmer	Date		Key	

Page (1 2) of ___ Program Identification (75 76 77 78 79 80)

Line (3–5)	Form Type (6)	Filename or Record Name (7–14)	Type (H/D/T/E) (15)	Stkr #/Fetch (F) (16)	Space Before (17)	Space After (18)	Skip Before (19–20)	Skip After (21–22)	Output Indicators: Not (23)	(24–25)	And Not (26)	(27–28)	And Not (29)	(30–31)	Field Name or EXCPT Name (32–37)	Edit Codes (38)	B/A/C/1–9/R (39)	End Position in Output Record (40–43)	P/B/L/R (44)	Constant or Edit Word (45–70)	(71–74)
0 1	O																				
0 2	O																				
0 3	O																				
0 4	O																				
0 5	O																				
0 6	O																				
0 7	O																				
0 8	O																				
0 9	O																				
1 0	O																				
1 1	O																				
1 2	O																				
1 3	O																				
1 4	O																				
1 5	O																				
1 6	O																				
1 7	O																				
1 8	O																				
1 9	O																				
2 0	O																				
	O																				
	O																				
	O																				
	O																				
	O																				

Column 14–16 alternatives: OR / AND; Stkr #/Fetch (F) and Space alternatives: R, DEL, ADD.

Commas	Zero Balances to Print	No Sign	CR	–
Yes	Yes	1	A	J
Yes	No	2	B	K
No	Yes	3	C	L
No	No	4	D	M

X = Remove Plus Sign
Y = Date Field Edit
Z = Zero Suppress
5–9 = User Defined

1 2 3 4 5 6 7 8 9 10 11 12 13 14 15 16 17 18 19 20 21 22 23 24 25 26 27 28 29 30 31 32 33 34 35 36 37 38 39 40 41 42 43 44 45 46 47 48 49 50 51 52 53 54 55 56 57 58 59 60 61 62 63 64 65 66 67 68 69 70 71 72 73 74 75 76 77 78 79 80 81 82 83 84 85 86 87 88 89 90 91 92 93 94 95 96 97 98 99 100 101 102 103 104 105 106 107 108 109 110 111 112 113 114 115 116 117 118 119 120 121 122 123 124 125 126 127 128 129 130 131 132

1
2
3
4
5
6
7
8
9
10
11
12
13
14
15
16
17
18
19
20
21
22
23
24
25
26
27
28
29
30
31
32
33
34
35
36
37
38
39
40
41
42
43
44
45
46
47
48
49
50